For Personal and friendly advice and service;
Consult the experts.

D0525983

AIR SUPPLY
— YEADON —

83B HIGH STREET, YEADON, LEEDS, LS19 7TA

NEW OPENING HOURS FROM 1 JANUARY 1996: 10AM TO 5PM TUESDAY TO SATURDAY, CLOSED SUNDAY AND MONDAY

THE NORTH'S LEADING SUPPLIER TO AVIATION ENTHUSIASTS AND LISTENERS

STOCKISTS OF SCANNERS, SHORT WAVE
RADIOS, AND QUALITY ACCESSORIES

2nd Edition Catalogue now out

Send £1:50 refundable on purchase
Phone : Ken Cothliff
on 0113 250 9581
Faximilie: 0113 250 0119

THE AVIATION HOBBY CENTRE

VISITORS CENTRE - MAIN TERMINAL

BIRMINGHAM INTERNATIONAL AIRPORT B26 3QJ

Tel: 0121 782 2112 or Fax: 0121 782 6423

Why not come and pay us a visit at our prime site in the Visitors Centre here at Birmingham International Airport (50p Admission Fee is refundable from us) and see the planes at the same time. Or telephone/send your name and address for our FREE latest catalogue full of aviation goodies. Our mail order service is second to none - we despatch the same day order is received if items are in stock. As well as offering good advice, we stock Airband Radios, Scanners, Accessories, Antennas, over 700 Aviation Book Titles! Plus a large selection of Aviation Videos. From Intelligent TV & Video, Avion, Just Planes, Ikon to name a few. We accept Visa, Access, Amex, Diners, Switch, Cheques, Postal Orders and we are open 7 days a week 8am 'till 7pm. We hope to see or hear from you soon.

Always available for immediate delivery:

The Pocket UK VHF/UHF

Airband Frequency Guide . . . .£4.45 post paid

Fully updated and includes 4 letter Airfield Codes and 2&3 Letter Airline Codings.

The Airband Jargon Book . . . .£6.95 post free

Explains simply though thoroughly everything you hear on your Airband Radio. Will appeal to everyone interested in aviation from beginner to advanced. You will be amazed at the information gained from just this one book - you'll be hooked!

On The Flightdeck Volume One - Video . . . .£15.95 post paid

5 varied flights giving nearly 2 hours of aviation video with full ATC chit-chat.

abc CIVIL AIRCRAFT MARKINGS 1996

Alan J. Wright

IAN ALLAN
Publishing

Contents

This forty-seventh edition published 1996

ISBN 0 7110 2424 3

All rights reserved. No part of this book may be
reproduced or transmitted in any form or by any
means, electronic or mechanical, including photocopying,
recording or by any information storage and
retrieval system, without permission from the
Publisher in writing.

© Ian Allan Ltd 1996

Published by Ian Allan Publishing

an imprint of Ian Allan Ltd,
Terminal House, Station Approach,
Shepperton, Surrey TW17 8AS.
Printed by Ian Allan Printing Ltd,
Coombelands House, Coomelands Lane,
Addlestone, Surrey KT15 1HY.

Front cover: Airbus A.320-231. *John Dibbs*

Back cover: Boeing 757-225.
All photographs by Alan J. Wright unless otherwise indicated.

Introduction

The 'G' prefixed four letter registration system was adopted in 1919 after a short-lived spell of about three months with serial numbers beginning at K-100. Until July 1928 the UK allocations were in the G-Exxx range, but as a result of further International agreements, this series was ended at G-EBZZ, the replacement being G-Axxx. From this point the registrations were issued in a reasonably orderly manner through to G-AZZZ, reached in July 1972. There were two exceptions. To avoid possible confusion with signal codes, the G-AQxx sequence was omitted, while G-AUxx was reserved for Australian use originally. In recent years however, an individual request for a mark in the latter range has been granted by the Authorities.

Although the next logical sequence was started at G-Bxxx, it was not long before the strictly applied rules relating to aircraft registration began to be relaxed. Permission was readily given for personalised marks to be issued incorporating virtually any four letter combination, while re-registration has also become a common feature, a practice almost unheard of in the past. In this book, where this has taken place at some time, the previous UK civil identity appears in parenthesis after the owner's/operator's name. An example of this is One-Eleven G-BBMG which originally carried G-AWEJ.

Some aircraft have also been allowed to wear military markings without displaying their civil identity. In this case the serial number actually carried is shown in parenthesis after the type's name. For example Mosquito G-ASKH flies as RR299 in RAF colours. As an aid to the identification of these machines, a military conversion list is provided.

Other factors caused a sudden acceleration in the number of registrations allocated by the Civil Aviation Authority in the early 1980s. The first surge came with the discovery that it was possible to register plastic bags and other items even less likely to fly, on payment of the standard fee. This erosion of the main register was checked in early 1982 by the issue of a special sequence for such devices commencing at G-FYAA. Powered hang-gliders provided the second glut of allocations as a result of the decision that these types should be officially registered. Although a few of the early examples penetrated the normal in-sequence register, the vast majority were given marks in other special ranges, this time G-MBxx, G-MGxx, G-MJxx, G-MMxx, G-MNxx, G-MTxx, G-MVxx, G-MWxx, G-MYxx and G-MZxx. At first it was common practice for microlights to ignore the requirement to carry their official identity. However the vast majority now display their registration somewhere on the structure, the size and position depending on the dimensions of the component to which it is applied.

Throughout the UK section of this book, there are many instances where the probable base of the aircraft has been included. This is positioned at the end of the owner/operator details preceded by an oblique stroke. It must of course be borne in mind that changes do take place and that no attempt has been made to record the residents at the many private strips. The base of airline equipment has been given as the company's headquarter's airport, although frequently aircraft are outstationed for long periods.

Non-airworthy preserved aircraft are shown with a star after the type.

The three-letter codes used by airlines to prefix flight numbers are included for those carriers appearing in the book. Radio frequencies for the larger airfields/airports are also listed.

The air transport scene has changed considerably through the years with many airlines now leasing aircraft as required. It has therefore become increasingly difficult to record all of the frequent changes, especially since the companies often do not finalise their plans until the early months of the year. However, every effort is made to produce an accurate source of reference, but it must be borne in mind that it is inevitable that discrepancies will occur.

Acknowledgements
Once again thanks are extended to the Registration Department of the Civil Aviation Authority for its assistance and allowing access to its files. The comments and amendments flowing from the indefatigable Wal Gandy have as always proved of considerable value, while Richard Cawsey, Bob Elliot and Kenneth Nimbley also contributed useful facts. The help given by numerous airlines or their information agencies has been much appreciated. Both A. S. Wright and C. P. Wright provided valuable assistance during the update of this edition which enabled the multitude of facts to be assembled to meet the press deadline.   **AJW**

International Civil Aircraft Markings

A2-	Botswana	LN-	Norway
A3-	Tonga	LV-	Argentine Republic
A4O-	Oman	LX-	Luxembourg
A5-	Bhutan	LY-	Lithuania
A6-	United Arab Emirates	LZ-	Bulgaria
A7-	Qatar	MT-	Mongolia
A9C-	Bahrain	N-	United States of America
AP-	Pakistan	OB-	Peru
B-	China/Taiwan	OD-	Lebanon
C-F, C-G	Canada	OE-	Austria
C2-	Nauru	OH-	Finland
C3	Andora	OK-	Czechia
C5-	Gambia	OM-	Slovakia
C6-	Bahamas	OO-	Belgium
C9-	Mozambique	OY-	Denmark
CC-	Chile	P-	Korea (North)
CN-	Morocco	P2-	Papua New Guinea
CP-	Bolivia	P4-	Aruba
CS-	Portugal	PH-	Netherlands
CU-	Cuba	PJ-	Netherlands Antilles
CX-	Uruguay	PK-	Indonesia and West Irian
D-	Germany	PP-, PT-	Brazil
D2-	Angola	PZ-	Surinam
D4-	Cape Verde Islands	RA-	Russia
D6-	Comores Islands	RDPL-	Laos
C9-	Mozambique	RP-	Philippine Republic
CC-	Chile	S2-	Bangladesh
CN-	Morocco	S5-	Slovenia
CP-	Bolivia	S7-	Seychelles
CS-	Portugal	S9-	São Tomé
CU-	Cuba	SE-	Sweden
CX-	Uruguay	SP-	Poland
D-	Germany	ST-	Sudan
D2-	Angola	SU-	Egypt
D4-	Cape Verde Islands	SX-	Greece
D6-	Comores Islands	T2-	Tuvalu
DQ-	Fiji	T3-	Kiribati
E3-	Eritrea	T7-	San Marino
EC-	Spain	T9-	Bosnia-Hercegovina
EI-	Republic of Ireland	TC-	Turkey
EK-	Armenia	TF-	Iceland
EL-	Liberia	TG-	Guatemala
EP-	Iran	TI-	Costa Rica
ER-	Moldova	T.I-	United Republic of Cameroon
ES-	Estonia	TL-	Central African Republic
ET-	Ethiopia	TN-	Republic of Congo (Brazzaville)
EW-	Belarus	TR-	Gabon
EX-	Kyrgyzstan	TS-	Tunisia
EY-	Tajikistan	TT-	Chad
EZ-	Turkmenistan	TU-	Ivory Coast
F-	France, Colonies and Protectorates	TY-	Benin
G-	United Kingdom	TZ-	Mali
GR-	Georgia	UK-	Uzbekistan
H4-	Solomon Islands	UN-	Kazakhstan
HA-	Hungary	UR-	Ukraine
HB-	Switzerland and Liechtenstein	V2-	Antigua
HC-	Ecuador	V3-	Belize
HH-	Haiti	V4	St Kitts & Nevis
HI-	Dominican Republic	V5-	Namibia
HK-	Colombia	V6	Micronesia
HL-	Korea (South)	V7-	Marshall Islands
HP-	Panama	V8-	Brunei
HR-	Honduras	VH-	Australia
HS-	Thailand	VN-	Vietnam
HV-	The Vatican	VP-F	Falkland Islands
HZ-	Saudi Arabia	VP-LA	Anguilla
I-	Italy	VP-LM	Montserrat
J2-	Djibouti	VP-LV	Virgin Islands
J3-	Grenada	VQ-T	Turks & Caicos Islands
J5-	Guinea Bissau	VR-B	Bermuda
J6-	St Lucia	VR-C	Cayman Islands
J7-	Dominica	VR-G	Gibraltar
J8-	St Vincent	VR-H	Hong Kong
JA-	Japan	VT-	India
JY-	Jordan	XA-, XB-, XC-	Mexico

XT-	Burkina Faso
XU-	Cambodia
XY-	Myanmar
YA-	Afghanistan
YI-	Iraq
YJ-	Vanuatu
YK-	Syria
YL-	Latvia
YN-	Nicaragua
YR-	Romania
YS-	El Salvador
YU-	Yugoslavia
YV-	Venezuela
Z-	Zimbabwe
Z3-	Macedonia
ZA-	Albania
ZK-	New Zealand
ZP-	Paraguay
ZS-	South Africa
3A-	Monaco
3B-	Mauritius
3C-	Equatorial Guinea
3D-	Swaziland
3X-	Guinea
4K-	Azerbaijan
4L-	Georgia
4R-	Sri Lanka
4U-	United Nations Organisation
4X-	Israel
5A-	Libya
5B-	Cyprus
5H-	Tanzania
5N-	Nigeria
5R-	Malagasy Republic (Madagascar)
5T-	Mauritania
5U-	Niger
5V-	Togo
5W-	Western Samoa (Polynesia)
5X-	Uganda
5Y-	Kenya
6O-	Somalia
6V-	Senegal
6Y-	Jamaica
7O-	Yemen
7P-	Lesotho
7Q-	Malawi
7T-	Algeria
8P-	Barbados
8Q-	Maldives
8R-	Guyana
9A-	Croatia
9G-	Ghana
9H-	Malta
9J-	Zambia
9K-	Kuwait
9L-	Sierra Leone
9M-	Malaysia
9N-	Nepal
9Q-	Zaire
9U-	Burundi
9V-	Singapore
9XR-	Rwanda
9Y-	Trinidad and Tobago

Aircraft Type Designations & Abbreviations

(eg PA-28 Piper Type 28)

A.	Beagle, Auster
AA-	American Aviation, Grumman American
AB	Agusta-Bell
AG	American General
AS	Aérospatiale
A.S.	Airspeed
ATI	Aero Trasporti Italiani
A.W.	Armstrong Whitworth
B.	Blackburn, Bristol, Boeing, Beagle
BAC	British Aircraft Corporation
BAe	British Aerospace
BAT	British Aerial Transport
B.K.	British Klemm
BN	Britten-Norman
Bo	Bolkow
Bu	Bucker
CAARP	Co-operative des Ateliers Aer de la Région Parisienne
CCF	Canadian Car & Foundry Co
C.H.	Chrislea
CHABA	Cambridge Hot-Air Ballooning Association
CLA	Comper
CP.	Piel
Cycl	Cyclone
D.	Druine
DC-	Douglas Commercial
D.H.	de Havilland
D.H.C.	de Havilland Canada
DR.	Jodel (Robin-built)
EMB	Embraer
EoN	Elliotts of Newbury
EP	Edgar Percival
F.	Fairchild, Fokker
FFA	Flug und Fahrzeugwerke AG
FH	Fairchild-Hiller
G.	Grumman
GA	Gulfstream American
G.A.L.	General Aircraft
G.C.	Globe
GY	Gardan
H	Helio
HM.	Henri Mignet
HP.	Handley Page
HR.	Robin
H.S.	Hawker Siddeley
IL	Ilyushin
IMCO	Intermountain Manufacturing Co
J.	Auster
L.	Lockheed
L.A.	Luton
M.	Miles, Mooney
MBB	Messerschmitt-Bölkow-Blohm
MJ	Jurca
M.S.	Morane-Saulnier
NA	North American
P.	Hunting (formerly Percival), Piaggio
PA-	Piper
PC.	Pilatus
QAC	Quickie Aircraft Co
R.	Rockwell
RAFGSA	Royal Air Force Gliding & Soaring Association
S.	Short, Sikorsky
SA., SE, SO.	Sud-Aviation, Aérospatiale, Scottish Aviation
SC	Short
SCD	Side Cargo Door
Soc	Society
S.R.	Saunders-Roe, Stinson
ST	SOCATA
SW	Solar Wings
T.	Tipsy
TB	SOCATA
Tu	Tupolev
UH.	United Helicopters (Hiller)
UTA	Union de Transports Aérien
V.	Vickers-Armstrongs, BAC
V.S.	Vickers-Supermarine
WAR	War Aircraft Replicas
W.S.	Westland
Z.	Zlin

NOW YOU HAVE PURCHASED CIVIL AIRCRAFT MARKINGS WHY NOT EXPAND YOUR KNOWLEDGE WITH THE 'TAHS' RANGE OF SPECIALIST BOOKS FOR THE ENTHUSIAST, HISTORIAN OR SPOTTER?

AIRBAND RADIOS
We specialise in top quality airband radios. Usually available from stock are the YUPITERU range of radios, io the VT125-11, VT-225, MVT7000 and the MVT-7100.

AIRLINES '96
The 14th edition available late March is the established spotters favourite for coverage of the world's airline fleet listing. Every airline in the world where aircraft from light twin to wide bodies are operated. 170 countries, 1,700 airlines, over 25,000 registrations. Each aircraft is listed with registration, type, c/n, p/i, and where applicable line and fleet number and name. Available as Comb Bound (ie metal lay flat binding at just £9.95 or in a loose leaf binder at £13.95.

AIRPORT MOVEMENTS
is a monthly magazine published and distributed by THE AVIATION HOBBY SHOP. AIRPORT MOVEMENTS gives airport movements on a regular basis for the following airports: Heathrow, Gatwick, Stanstead, Luton, Birmingham, Shannon, Bournemouth, Bristol, Cardiff, East Midlands, Jersey, Northolt, Southampton, Southend as well as foreign airport reports on a space available basis. Average monthly page content is around 28. AIRPORT MOVEMENTS is available around the 15th to the 20th of the month from a number of different outlets in the South of England, the Midlands and the Manchester area at a price of 75p per copy. However, should you wish to have a regular standing order for this publication to be dispatched hot from the press we will be more than happy to place your name on our regular mailing list. To have your own copy of AIRPORT MOVEMENTS sent to you each month costs £1 per copy and this includes first-class mail delivery in the UK. You can subscribe for three, six or 12 months. To recieve a free sample copy of your choice send a stamped 9in x 6in envelope.

TURBO PROP AIRLINER PRODUCTION LIST
Now available the second edition of Turbo Prop Airliners Production List gives full production and service histories of EVERY WESTERN - BUILT TURBOPROP AIRLINER to enter service since 1948. Each aircraft is listed by manufacturer and type in construction number sequence. Each individual entry then lists line number (where applicable), sub-type, and first flight date where known. The entry then goes on to list every registration carried by the airframe, owners and delivery dates, leases, crash or withdrawal from service dates and any other relevant information. There is a complete cross reference of registration to c/n for every type covered. This publication is available in two formats:- Soft-back in card covers with sewn binding at £10.95 or in a loose-leaf binder at £13.95.

WORLD AIRLINE FLEET NEWS
Published monthly, World Airline Fleet News is dedicated to the ever changing and exciting world of airlines and airliners-reporting new airlines, new and used airliner transactions, livery changes and much more. Unrivalled photographic coverage on a worldwide basis is complimented by the generous use of colour. Each issue contains approximately 50 illustrations with around 30 in colour. World Airline Fleet News is produced on quality gloss art paper for the best photographic reproduction. Sample issue £3.25.

MILITARY AIRCRAFT SERIALS OF EUROPE
The eagerly awaited third edition of MILITARY AIRCRAFT SERIALS OF EUROPE is now available. MILITARY AIRCRAFT SERIALS OF EUROPE covers thirty five European countries. Each county is listed in alphabeticalorder, with in most cases a brief synopsis of their serial systems and units. Each countries aircraft are then covered in details by typs, each line showing serial number, sub-type, unit allocation and date last noted as such. Where known or applicable fates are also shown, including write-off dates etc. COUNTRIES COVERED INCLUDE:- Albania, Austria, Belguim, Bosnia, Bulgaria, Croatia, Cyprus, Czech Republic, Denmark, Estonia, Finland, France, Germany, Greece, hungary, Iceland, Ireland, Italy, Latvia, Lithuania, Malta, NATO/Luxembourg, The Netherlands, Norway, Poland, Portugal, Romania, Slovak Republic, Slovenia, Spain, Sweden, Switzerland, Turkey, United Kingdom and Yugoslavia. The book comes with full colour front and rear covers and the nearly 350 pages includes a selection of black & white photographs and the individual serial number content is in excess of 25,000.

MILITARY AIRCRAFT SERIALS OF EUROPE is available in a handy A5 size and is available in a choice of finish (1) comb bound lay-flat price **£9.95**; (2) Square bound with duty metal stitching price **£9.95**: (3) Refill pages for those already have a loose-leaf binder price **£9.95**: (4) Loose-leaf Binder edition price **£13.95**.

JET AIRLINER PRODUCTION LIST - Volume 1 - BOEING
NOW AVAILABLE Jet Airliner Production List - Volume 1 - BOEING is completely revised and updated. Jet Airliner Production List gives full production and service histories of EVERY BOEING - BUILT JET AIRLINER that has entered service since the start of the Jet age. Each aircraft is listed by manufacturer and type in contruction number sequence. Each individual entry then lists line number (where applicable), sub-type, and first flight date where known. The entry then goes on to list every registration carried by the airframe, owners and delivery dates, leases, crash or withdrawal from service dates and any other relevant information. There is a complete cross reference of registration to c/n for every type covered. This publication will be available in three formats:- (1) Soft-back in card covers with sewn binding at price **£9.95**. (2) Comb bound-lay flat at price **£9.95**: (3) or in a ripid blue loose-leaf binder at price **£13.95**.

JET AIRLINER PRODUCTION LIST - Volume 2
Published in December 1995 Jet Airliner Production List - Volume 2 - is completely revised and updated. Jet Airliner Production List gives full production and service histories of every JET AIRLINER (not covered in Volume one) that has entered service since the start of the Jet age. The types covered in Volume 2 include:- Airbus A.300, Airbus A.310, Airbus A.319/320/321, Airbus A.330/340, British Aerospace 146, British Aircraft Corporation/Aerospatiale Concorde, British Aircraft Corporation 1-11, Canadair Regional Jet, Convair 880, Convair 990, Dassault Mercure, DH.106 Comet 1-4, Douglas DC-8, Douglas DC-9, Douglas DC-10, Fokker F.28, Fokker 100, HS.121 Trident, Lockheed 1011 Tri-Star, McDonnell-Douglas MD-11, ROMBAC 1-11, Sud Aviation SE.210 Caravelle, VFW/Fokker 614 & Vickers VC-10. Each aircraft is listed by manufacturer and type in construction number sequence. Each individual entry then lists line number (where applicable), sub-type, and first flight date where known. The entry then goes on to list every registration carried by the airframe, owners and delivery dates, leases, crash or withdrawal from service dates and any other relevant information. There is a complete cross reference of registration to c/n for every type covered. Over 370 pages. This publication will be available in three formats:- (1) Soft-back in card covers with sewn binding at price **£10.95**: (2) Comb bound-lay flat at price **£10.95**: (3) or in a loose-leaf binder at price **£14.95**.

AIRLINES TO EUROPE 1996
Following the excellent response to the 1st edition of Airlines to Europe, the 1996 edition is now available. As with the first edition we have taken the main date base and stripped out any airlines of aircraft not likely to be seen in Europe. Airlines to Europe only lists 1) Aircraft registration, 2) Aircraft type and 3) Constructors number and line number if applicable. Colour cover and nearly one hundred pages. Price **£3.99**.

96 JET & PROP JET - NEW LAY-FLAT EDITION
The only standard reference for the total world-wide corporate fleet identification. Available again by popular demand - in one pocket-sized book. More than 7,700 Jets and 8,600 Propjets listed with registration marks, construction numbers and owner identification. Over 250 different models and model derivatives and 43 manufacturers from 143 countries. **Available now £11.95**

FREE CATALOGUES
All our goods are listed in our two free catalogues. Catalogue 1 books, colour prints and airband radios. Catalogue 2: plastic kits, decals and modelling accessories. Write, ring or fax for your free copy today.

We are just 10 minutes drive from Heathrow Airport, just off the M4/M25 motorways. Bus U3 operates between Heathrow Central and West Drayton BR station, two minutes walk from the shop. All major credit cards accepted. 24hr 'Ansaphone' service.

The Aviation Hobby Shop

(Dept CAM), 4 HORTON PARADE, HORTON ROAD, WEST DRAYTON, MIDDLESEX UB7 8EA
Tel: 01895 442123 Fax: 01895 421412

British Civil Aircraft Registrations

Reg.	Type (†False registration)	Owner or Operator	Notes
G-EAGA	Sopwith Dove (replica)	R. H. Reeves	
G-EASD	Avro 504L	AJD Engineering Ltd	
G-EASQ†	Bristol Babe (replica) (BAPC87) ★	(stored) Bristol Aero Collection	
G-EAVX	Sopwith Pup (B1807)	K. A. M. Baker	
G-EBHX	D.H.53 Humming Bird	Shuttleworth Collection/O. Warden	
G-EBIA	RAF SE-5A (F904)	Shuttleworth Collection/O. Warden	
G-EBIB	RAF SE-5A ★	Science Museum/S. Kensington	
G-EBIC	RAF SE-5A (F938) ★	RAF Museum	
G-EBIR	D.H.51	Shuttleworth Collection/O. Warden	
G-EBJE	Avro 504K (E449) ★	RAF Museum	
G-EBJG	Parnall Pixie III ★	Midland Aircraft Preservation Soc	
G-EBJO	ANEC II ★	Shuttleworth Collection/O. Warden	
G-EBKY	Sopwith Pup (N6181)	Shuttleworth Collection/O. Warden	
G-EBLV	D.H.60 Cirrus Moth	British Aerospace PLC/Woodford	
G-EBMB	Hawker Cygnet I ★	RAF Museum	
G-EBNV	English Electric Wren	Shuttleworth Collection/O. Warden	
G-EBQP	D.H.53 Humming Bird (J7326) ★	Russavia Collection	
G-EBWD	D.H.60X Hermes Moth	Shuttleworth Collection/O. Warden	
G-EBXU	D.H.60X Moth Seaplane	D. E. Cooper-Maguire	
G-EBZM	Avro 594 Avian IIIA ★	Manchester Museum of Science & Industry	
G-EBZN	D.H.60X Moth	J. Hodgkinson (G-UAAP)	
G-AAAH†	D.H.60G Moth (replica) (BAPC 168) ★	Hilton Hotel/Gatwick	
G-AAAH	D.H.60G Moth Jason ★	Science Museum/S. Kensington	
G-AACA†	Avro 504K (BAPC 177)	Brooklands Museum of Aviation/ Weybridge	
G-AACN	H.P.39 Gugnunc ★	Science Museum/Wroughton	
G-AADR	D.H.60GM Moth	H. F. Moffatt	
G-AAEG	D.H.60G Moth	J. Dixon	
G-AAHI	D.H.60G Moth	N. J. W. Reid	
G-AAHY	D.H.60M Moth	M. E. Vaisey	
G-AAIN	Parnall Elf II	Shuttleworth Collection/O. Warden	
G-AAMX	D.H.60GM Moth	M. P. Parkhouse	
G-AAMY	D.H.60GMW Moth	H. M. Brooks	
G-AAMZ	D.H.60G Moth	C. C. & J. M. Lovell	
G-AANG	Blériot XI	Shuttleworth Collection/O. Warden	
G-AANH	Deperdussin Monoplane	Shuttleworth Collection/O. Warden	
G-AANI	Blackburn Monoplane	Shuttleworth Collection/O. Warden	
G-AANJ	L.V.G.-C VI (7198/18)	Shuttleworth Collection/O. Warden	
G-AANL	D.H.60M Moth	P. L. Allwork	
G-AANM	Bristol 96A F.2B (D7889)	Aero Vintage Ltd	
G-AANO	D.H.60GMW Moth	A. W. & M. E. Jenkins	
G-AANV	D.H.60G Moth	R. I. Souch	
G-AAOK	Curtiss Wright Travel Air 12Q	Shipping & Airlines Ltd/Biggin Hill	
G-AAOR	D.H.60G Moth (EM-01)	J. A. Pothecary/Shoreham	
G-AAPZ	Desoutter I (mod.)	Shuttleworth Collection/O. Warden	
G-AAUP	Klemm L.25-1A	J. I. Cooper	
G-AAWO	D.H.60G Moth	N. J. W. Reid & L. A. Fenwick	
G-AAXK	Klemm L.25-1A ★	C. C. Russell-Vick (stored)	
G-AAYX	Southern Martlet	Shuttleworth Collection/O. Warden	
G-AAZP	D.H.80A Puss Moth	R. P. Williams	
G-ABAA	Avro 504K ★	Manchester Museum of Science & Industry	
G-ABAG	D.H.60G Moth	Shuttleworth Collection/O. Warden	
G-ABDA	D.H.60G-III Moth Major	I. M. Castle	
G-ABDW	D.H.80A Puss Moth (VH-UQB) ★	Museum of Flight/E. Fortune	
G-ABDX	D.H.60G Moth	M. D. Souch	
G-ABEV	D.H.60G Moth	Wessex Aviation & Transport Ltd	
G-ABLM	Cierva C.24 ★	Mosquito Aircraft Museum	
G-ABLS	D.H.80A Puss Moth	R. C. F. Bailey	
G-ABMR	Hart 2 (J9941) ★	RAF Museum	
G-ABNT	Civilian C.A.C.1 Coupe	Shipping & Airlines Ltd/Biggin Hill	
G-ABNX	Redwing 2	J. A. Pothecary (stored)	
G-ABOI	Wheeler Slymph ★	Midland Air Museum	
G-ABOX	Sopwith Pup (N5195)	Museum of Army Flying/Middle Wallop	

Notes	Reg.	Type	Owner or Operator
	G-ABSD	D.H.60G Moth	M. E. Vaisey
	G-ABTC	CLA.7 Swift	P. Channon (stored)
	G-ABUL†	D.H.82A Tiger Moth ★	F.A.A. Museum (G-AOXG)/Yeovilton
	G-ABUS	CLA.7 Swift	R. C. F. Bailey
	G-ABUU	CLA.7 Swift	H. F. Moffatt
	G-ABVE	Arrow Active 2	J. D. Penrose
	G-ABWP	Spartan Arrow	R. E. Blain/Barton
	G-ABXL	Granger Archaeopteryx ★	Shuttleworth Collection/O. Warden
	G-ABYN	Spartan Three Seater II	J. D. Souch
	G-ABZB	D.H.60G-III Moth Major	R. E. & B. A. Ogden
	G-ACAA	Bristol 96A F.2B (D8084†)	Patina Ltd/Duxford
	G-ACBH	Blackburn B.2 ★	R. Coles
	G-ACCB	D.H.83 Fox Moth	E. A. Gautrey
	G-ACDA	D.H.82A Tiger Moth	R. J. Biddle
	G-ACDC	D.H.82A Tiger Moth	Tiger Club Ltd/Headcorn
	G-ACDD	D.H.83 Fox Moth	—
	G-ACDI	D.H.82A Tiger Moth	J. A. Pothecary/Shoreham
	G-ACDJ	D.H.82A Tiger Moth	P. Henley & J. K. Moorhouse
	G-ACEJ	D.H.83 Fox Moth	J. I. Cooper
	G-ACET	D.H.84 Dragon	M. D. Souch
	G-ACGT	Avro 594 Avian IIIA ★	Yorkshire Light Aircraft Ltd/Leeds
	G-ACIT	D.H.84 Dragon ★	Science Museum/Wroughton
	G-ACLL	D.H.85 Leopard Moth	D. C. M. & V. M. Stiles
	G-ACMA	D.H.85 Leopard Moth	S. J. Filhol/Sherburn
	G-ACMD	D.H.82A Tiger Moth	J. A. Pothecary/Shoreham
	G-ACMN	D.H.85 Leopard Moth	H. D. Labouchere
	G-ACOJ	D.H.85 Leopard Moth	M. Gibbs
	G-ACOL	D.H.85 Leopard Moth	M. J. Abbott
	G-ACSP	D.H.88 Comet	Saltair Ltd/Staverton
	G-ACSS	D.H.88 Comet ★	Shuttleworth Collection Grosvenor House/ O. Warden
	G-ACTF	CLA.7 Swift ★	Brooklands Museum of Aviation/ Weybridge
	G-ACUS	D.H.85 Leopard Moth	T. P. A. Norman/Panshanger
	G-ACUU	Cierva C.30A (HM580) ★	G. S. Baker/Duxford
	G-ACUX	S.16 Scion (VH-UUP) ★	Ulster Folk & Transport Museum
	G-ACVA	Kay GyroplaneH	Glasgow Museum of Transport
	G-ACWM	Cierva C.30A (AP506) ★	International Helicopter Museum/ Weston-s-Mare
	G-ACWP	Cierva C.30A (AP507) ★	Science Museum/S. Kensington
	G-ACXB	D.H.60G-III Moth Major	D. F. Hodgkinson
	G-ACXE	B.K.L-25C Swallow	J. C. Wakeford
	G-ACYK	Spartan Cruiser III ★	Museum of Flight (front fuselage)/ E. Fortune
	G-ACZE	D.H.89A Dragon Rapide	Wessex Aviation & Transport Ltd (G-AJGS)/Henstridge
	G-ADAH	D.H.89A Dragon Rapide ★	Manchester Museum of Science & Industry Pioneer
	G-ADEV	Avro 504K (H5199)	Shuttleworth Collection (G-ACNB)/ O. Warden
	G-ADFO	Blackburn B-2 ★	R. Cole
	G-ADFV	Blackburn B-2 ★	Lincolnshire Aviation Heritage Centre/ E. Kirkby
	G-ADGP	M.2L Hawk Speed Six	R. I. Souch
	G-ADGT	D.H.82A Tiger Moth	D. R. & Mrs M. Wood
	G-ADGV	D.H.82A Tiger Moth	K. J. Whitehead
	G-ADHA	D.H.83 Fox Moth	Wessex Aviation & Transport Ltd
	G-ADHD	D.H.60G-III Moth Major	M. E. Vaisey
	G-ADIA	D.H.82A Tiger Moth	F. A. de Munck
	G-ADJJ	D.H.82A Tiger Moth	J. M. Preston
	G-ADKC	D.H.87B Hornet Moth	L. E. Day/Carlisle
	G-ADKK	D.H.87B Hornet Moth	C. P. B. Horsley & R. G. Anniss
	G-ADKL	D.H.87B Hornet Moth	A. de Cadenet
	G-ADKM	D.H.87B Hornet Moth	L. V. Mayhead
	G-ADLY	D.H.87B Hornet Moth	Glidegold Ltd/Booker
	G-ADMT	D.H.87B Hornet Moth	P. A. de Courcy Swaffer
	G-ADMW	M.2H Hawk Major (DG590) ★	Museum of Army Flying/Middle Wallop
	G-ADND	D.H.87B Hornet Moth (W9385)	Shuttleworth Collection/O. Warden
	G-ADNE	D.H.87B Hornet Moth	G-ADNE Ltd
	G-ADNL	M.5 Sparrowhawk	K. D. Dunkerley
	G-ADNZ	D.H.82A Tiger Moth	D. C. Wall

Reg.	Type	Owner or Operator	Notes
G-ADOT	D.H.87B Hornet Moth ★	Mosquito Aircraft Museum	
G-ADPC	D.H.82A Tiger Moth	N. J. Baker & J. Beattie	
G-ADPJ	B.A.C. Drone ★	N. H. Ponsford/Breighton	
G-ADPS	B.A. Swallow 2	Wessex Aviation & Transport Ltd	
G-ADRA	Pietenpol Air Camper	A. J. Mason	
G-ADRG†	Mignet HM.14 (replica) (BAPC77) ★	Stratford Aircraft Collection	
G-ADRR	Aeronca C.3	S. J. Rudkin	
G-ADRY†	Mignet HM.14 (replica) (BAPC29) ★	Brooklands Museum of Aviation/ Weybridge	
G-ADSK	D.H.87B Hornet Moth	R. G. Grocott	
G-ADUR	D.H.87B Hornet Moth	Wessex Aviation & Transport Ltd	
G-ADWJ	D.H.82A Tiger Moth	C. R. Hardiman	
G-ADWO	D.H.82A Tiger Moth (BB807)	Wessex Aviation Soc	
G-ADXS	Mignet HM.14 ★	Thameside Aviation Museum/E. Tilbury	
G-ADXT	D.H. 82A Tiger Moth	R. G. Hanauer/Goodwood	
G-ADYS	Aeronca C.3	B. C. Cooper	
G-AEBB	Mignet HM.14 ★	Shuttleworth Collection/O. Warden	
G-AEBJ	Blackburn B-2	British Aerospace (Operations) Ltd/Warton	
G-AEDB	B.A.C. Drone 2	M. C. Russell	
G-AEDT	D.H.90 Dragonfly	Wessex Aviation & Transport Ltd	
G-AEDU	D.H.90 Dragonfly	T. P. A. Norman	
G-AEEG	M.3A Falcon	Skysport Engineering Ltd	
G-AEEH	Mignet HM.14 ★	Aerospace Museum/Cosford	
G-AEFG	Mignet HM.14 (BAPC75) ★	N. H. Ponsford/Breighton	
G-AEFT	Aeronca C.3	G-AEFT Group/Yeovil	
G-AEGV	Mignet HM.14 ★	Midland Air Museum/Coventry	
G-AEHM	Mignet HM.14 ★	Science Museum/Wroughton	
G-AEJZ	Mignet HM.14 (BAPC120) ★	Bomber County Museum/Hemswell	
G-AEKR	Mignet HM.14 (BAPC121) ★	S. Yorks Aviation Soc/Breighton	
G-AEKV	Kronfeld Drone ★	Brooklands Museum of Aviation/ Weybridge	
G-AELO	D.H.87B Hornet Moth	D. E. Wells	
G-AEML	D.H.89 Dragon Rapide	Amanda Investments Ltd	
G-AENP	Hawker Hind (K5414) (BAPC78)	Shuttleworth Collection/O. Warden	
G-AEOA	D.H.80A Puss Moth	P. & A. Wood/O. Warden	
G-AEOF†	Mignet HM.14 (BAPC22) ★	Aviodome/Schiphol, Holland	
G-AEOF	Rearwin 8500	Shipping & Airlines Ltd/Biggin Hill	
G-AEOH	Mignet HM.14 ★	Midland Air Museum	
G-AEPH	Bristol F.2B (D8096)	Shuttleworth Collection/O. Warden	
G-AERV	M.11A Whitney Straight ★	Ulster Folk & Transport Museum	
G-AESB	Aeronca C.3	D. S. & I. M. Morgan	
G-AESE	D.H.87B Hornet Moth	J. G. Green/Redhill	
G-AESZ	Chilton D.W.1	R. E. Nerou	
G-AETA	Caudron G.3 (3066) ★	RAF Museum/Hendon	
G-AEUJ	M.11A Whitney Straight	R. E. Mitchell	
G-AEVS	Aeronca 100	A. M. Lindsay & N. H. Ponsford/Breighton	
G-AEVZ	B. A. Swallow 2	J. R. H. Ealand	
G-AEXD	Aeronca 100	Mrs M. A. & R. W. Mills	
G-AEXF	P.6 Mew Gull	J. D. Penrose/Old Warden	
G-AEXT	Dart Kitten II	A. J. Hartfield	
G-AEXZ	Piper J-2 Cub	Mrs M. & J. R. Dowson/Leicester	
G-AEYY	Martin Monoplane ★	Martin Monoplane Syndicate	
G-AEZF	S.16 Scion 2 ★	Acebell Aviation/Redhill	
G-AEZJ	P.10 Vega Gull	R. A. J. Spurrell/White Waltham	
G-AEZX	Bucker Bu133C Jungmeister (LG+03)	A. J. E. Ditheridge	
G-AFAP†	C.A.S.A. C.352L ★	Aerospace Museum/Cosford	
G-AFAX	B. A. Eagle 2	J. G. Green	
G-AFBS	M.14A Hawk Trainer 3 ★	G. D. Durbridge-Freeman (G-AKKU)/ Duxford	
G-AFCL	B. A. Swallow 2	A. M. Dowson/O. Warden	
G-AFDO	Piper J-3F-60 Cub	R. Wald	
G-AFDX	Hanriot HD.1 (75) ★	RAF Museum/Hendon	
G-AFEL	Monocoupe 90A	M. Rieser	
G-AFFD	Percival Q-6 ★	B. D. Greenwood	
G-AFFH	Piper J-2 Cub	M. J. Honeychurch	
G-AFFI	Mignet HM.14 (replica) (BAPC76) ★	Yorkshire Air Museum/Elvington	
G-AFGC	B. A. Swallow 2	G. E. Arden	
G-AFGD	B. A. Swallow 2	A. T. Williams & ptnrs/Shobdon	

Notes	Reg.	Type	Owner or Operator
	G-AFGE	B. A. Swallow 2	G. R. French
	G-AFGH	Chilton D.W.1.	M. L. & G. L. Joseph
	G-AFGI	Chilton D.W.1.	J. E. McDonald
	G-AFGM	Piper J-4A Cub Coupé	A. J. P. Marshall/Carlisle
	G-AFGZ	D.H.82A Tiger Moth	M. R. Paul & P. A. Shaw (G-AMHI)
	G-AFHA	Mosscraft M.A.1. ★	C. V. Butler
	G-AFIN	Chrislea Airguard ★	Aeroplane Collection Ltd
	G-AFIR	Luton LA-4 Minor	A. J. Mason
	G-AFIU	Parker C.A.4 Parasol (LA-3 Minor) ★	Aeroplane Collection Ltd
	G-AFJA	Watkinson Dingbat ★	K. Woolley
	G-AFJB	Foster-Wikner G.M.1. Wicko (DR613) ★	K. Woolley
	G-AFJR	Tipsy Trainer 1	M. E. Vaisey (stored)
	G-AFJU	M.17 Monarch ★	Museum of Flight/E. Fortune
	G-AFJV	Mosscraft MA.2	C. V. Butler
	G-AFLW	M.17 Monarch	N. I. Dalziel/Biggin Hill
	G-AFNG	D.H.94 Moth Minor	M. A. Hales
	G-AFNI	D.H.94 Moth Minor	B. N. C. & C. M. Mogg
	G-AFOB	D.H.94 Moth Minor	Wessex Aviation & Transport Ltd
	G-AFOJ	D.H.94 Moth Minor	Mosquito Aircraft Museum
	G-AFPN	D.H.94 Moth Minor	J. W. & A. R. Davy/Carlisle
	G-AFPR	D.H.94 Moth Minor	M. D. Souch
	G-AFRZ	M.17 Monarch	R. E. Mitchell (G-AIDE)
	G-AFSC	Tipsy Trainer 1	R. V. & M. H. Smith
	G-AFSV	Chilton D.W.1A	R. E. Nerou
	G-AFSW	Chilton D.W.2 ★	R. I. Souch
	G-AFTA	Hawker Tomtit (K1786)	Shuttleworth Collection/O. Warden
	G-AFTN	Taylorcraft Plus C2	Leicestershire County Council Museums
	G-AFUP	Luscombe 8A Silvaire	Trust Me Airtours
	G-AFVE	D.H.82 Tiger Moth (T7230)	P. A. Shaw & M. R. Paul
	G-AFVN	Tipsy Trainer 1	D. F. Lingard
	G-AFWH	Piper J-4A Cub Coupé	J. R. Edwards & D. D. Smith
	G-AFWI	D.H.82A Tiger Moth	E. Newbigin
	G-AFWT	Tipsy Trainer 1	J. S. Barker/Redhill
	G-AFYD	Luscombe 8F Silvaire	J. D. Iliffe
	G-AFYO	Stinson H.W.75	R. N. Wright
	G-AFZA	Piper J-4A Cub Coupé	J. R. Joiner & M. L. Ryan
	G-AFZE	Heath Parasol	K. C. D. St Cyrien
	G-AFZK	Luscombe 8A Silvaire	M. G. Byrnes
	G-AFZL	Porterfield CP.50	P. G. Lucas & S. H. Sharpe/ White Waltham
	G-AFZN	Luscombe 8A Silvaire	A. L. Young/Henstridge
	G-AGAT	Piper J-3F-50 Cub	G. S. Williams
	G-AGBN	G.A.L.42 Cygnet 2 ★	Museum of Flight/E. Fortune
	G-AGEG	D.H.82A Tiger Moth	T. P. A. Norman
	G-AGFT	Avia FL.3	P. A. Smith
	G-AGHY	D.H.82A Tiger Moth	P. Groves
	G-AGIV	Piper J-3C-65 Cub	P. C. & F. M. Gill
	G-AGJG	D.H.89A Dragon Rapide	M. J. & D. J. T. Miller/Duxford
	G-AGLK	Auster 5D	Goldhawk Print Services Ltd/Biggin Hill
	G-AGMI	Luscombe 8A Silvaire	P. R. Bush
	G-AGNJ	D.H.82A Tiger Moth	B. P. Borsberry & Ptnrs
	G-AGNV	Avro 685 York 1 (TS798) ★	Aerospace Museum/Cosford
	G-AGOH	J/1 Autocrat*	Newark Air Museum
	G-AGOS	R.S.4 Desford Trainer (VZ728)	Museum of Flight/E. Fortune
	G-AGOY	M.48 Messenger 3 (U-0247)	P. A. Brook
	G-AGPG	Avro 19 Srs 2 ★	Brenzett Aviation Museum
	G-AGPK	D.H.82A Tiger Moth	P. D. Castle
	G-AGRU	V.498 Viking 1A ★	Brooklands Museum of Aviation/Weybridge
	G-AGSH	D.H.89A Dragon Rapide 6	Venom Jet Promotions Ltd/Bournemouth
	G-AGTM	D.H.89A Dragon Rapide 6	Aviation Heritage Ltd
	G-AGTO	J/1 Autocrat	M. J. Barnett & D. J. T. Miller/Duxford
	G-AGTT	J/1 Autocrat	R. Farrer
	G-AGVG	J/1 Autocrat	S. J. Riddington/Leicester
	G-AGVN	J/1 Autocrat	G. H. Farrar
	G-AGVV	Piper J-3C-65 Cub	M. Molina-Ruano/Spain
	G-AGXN	J/1N Alpha	R. J. Fray & J. Evans
	G-AGXT	J/1N Alpha ★	Nene Valley Aircraft Museum
	G-AGXU	J/1N Alpha	G. T. Fisher/Sibson
	G-AGXV	J/1 Autocrat	B. S. Dowsett

Reg.	Type	Owner or Operator	Notes
G-AGYD	J/1N Alpha	P. D. Hodson	
G-AGYH	J/1N Alpha	W. R. V. Marklew	
G-AGYK	J/1 Autocrat	Autocrat Syndicate	
G-AGYL	J/1 Autocrat ★	Military Vehicle Conservation Group	
G-AGYT	J/1N Alpha	P. J. Barrett	
G-AGYU	DH.82A Tiger Moth (DE208)	A. Grimshaw	
G-AGYY	Ryan ST.3KR (27)	G-AGYY Group/Sandown	
G-AGZZ	D.H.82A Tiger Moth	G. C. P. Shea-Simonds/Netheravon	
G-AHAL	J/1N Alpha	Wickenby Flying Club Ltd	
G-AHAM	J/1 Autocrat	A. J. Twemlow	
G-AHAN	D.H.82A Tiger Moth	Interflight (Air Charters) Ltd/Redhill	
G-AHAP	J/1 Autocrat	V. H. Bellamy	
G-AHAV	J/1 Autocrat	C. J. Freeman/Headcorn	
G-AHBL	D.H.87B Hornet Moth	Dr Ursula H. Hamilton	
G-AHBM	D.H.87B Hornet Moth	P. A. & E. P. Gliddon	
G-AHCK	J/1N Alpha	Skegness Air Taxi Service Ltd	
G-AHCL	J/1N Alpha	Electronic Precision Ltd (G-OJVC)	
G-AHCR	Gould-Taylorcraft Plus D Special	D. E. H. Balmford & D. R. Shepherd/Dunkeswell	
G-AHEC	Luscombe 8A Silvaire	S. P. Parsons	
G-AHED	D.H.89A Dragon Rapide (RL962) ★	RAF Museum Storage & Restoration Centre/Cardington	
G-AHGD	D.H.89A Dragon Rapide	R. Jones	
G-AHGW	Taylorcraft Plus D (LB375)	C. V. Butler/Coventry	
G-AHGZ	Taylorcraft Plus D	M. Pocock	
G-AHHH	J/1 Autocrat	H. A. Jones/Norwich	
G-AHHP	J/1N Alpha	D. J. Hutcheson (G-SIME)	
G-AHHT	J/1N Alpha	A. C. Barber & N. J. Hudson	
G-AHHU	J/1N Alpha ★	L. A. Groves & I. R. F. Hammond	
G-AHIP	Piper J-3C-65 Cub	R. T. & D. H. Tanner	
G-AHIZ	D.H.82A Tiger Moth	C.F.G. Flying Ltd/Cambridge	
G-AHKX	Avro 19 Srs 2	British Aerospace PLC/Woodford	
G-AHKY	Miles M.18 Series 2 ★	Museum of Flight/E. Fortune	
G-AHLI	Auster 3	G. A. Leathers	
G-AHLK	Auster 3	E. T. Brackenbury/Leicester	
G-AHLT	D.H.82A Tiger Moth	R. C. F. Bailey	
G-AHMJ	Cierva C.30A (K4235)	Shuttleworth Collection/O. Warden	
G-AHMN	D.H.82A Tiger Moth (N6985)	Museum of Army Flying/Middle Wallop	
G-AHNR	Taylorcraft BC-12D	P. E. Hinkley/Redhill	
G-AHOO	D.H.82A Tiger Moth	G. W. Bisshopp	
G-AHRI	D.H.104 Dove 1 ★	Newark Air Museum	
G-AHRO	Cessna 140	R. H. Screen/Kidlington	
G-AHSA	Avro 621 Tutor (K3215)	Shuttleworth Collection/O. Warden	
G-AHSD	Taylorcraft Plus D	A. Tucker	
G-AHSO	J/1N Alpha	W. P. Miller	
G-AHSP	J/1 Autocrat	N. J. Hudson & A. C. Barber	
G-AHSS	J/1N Alpha	Felthorpe Auster Group	
G-AHST	J/1N Alpha	M. J. Bonnick	
G-AHTE	P.44 Proctor V	D. K. Tregilgas	
G-AHTW	A.S.40 Oxford (V3388) ★	Skyfame Collection/Duxford	
G-AHUF	D.H.82A Tiger Moth	D. S. & I. M. Morgan	
G-AHUG	Taylorcraft Plus D	D. Nieman	
G-AHUI	M.38 Messenger 2A ★	Museum of Berkshire Aviation/Woodley	
G-AHUJ	M.14A Hawk Trainer 3 (R1914)	—	
G-AHUN	Globe GC-1B Swift	R. J. Hamlett	
G-AHUV	D.H.82A Tiger Moth	W. G. Gordon	
G-AHVU	D.H.82A Tiger Moth (T6313)	Foley Farm Flying Group	
G-AHVV	D.H.82A Tiger Moth	R. Jones	
G-AHWJ	Taylorcraft Plus D (LB294)	Museum of Army Flying/Middle Wallop	
G-AHXE	Taylorcraft Plus D (HH982)	J. M. C. Pothecary/Shoreham	
G-AIBE	Fulmar II (N1854) ★	F.A.A. Museum/Yeovilton	
G-AIBH	J/1N Alpha	M. J. Bonnick	
G-AIBM	J/1 Autocrat	D. G. Greatrex	
G-AIBR	J/1 Autocrat	A. A. Marshall	
G-AIBW	J/1N Alpha	W. E. Bateson/Blackpool	
G-AIBX	J/1 Autocrat	Wasp Flying Group	
G-AIBY	J/1 Autocrat	D. Morris/Sherburn	
G-AICX	Luscombe 8A Silvaire	R. V. Smith/Henstridge	
G-AIDL	D.H.89A Dragon Rapide 6	Atlantic Air Transport Ltd/Caernarfon	
G-AIDS	D.H.82A Tiger Moth	K. D. Pogmore & T. Dann	
G-AIEK	M.38 Messenger 2A (RG333)	J. Buckingham	

13

Notes	Reg.	Type	Owner or Operator
	G-AIFZ	J/1N Alpha	M. D. Ansley & P. V. Flack
	G-AIGD	J/1 Autocrat	C. J. Harrison
	G-AIGF	J/1N Alpha	A. R. C. Mathie
	G-AIGT	J/1N Alpha	P. R. & J. S. Johnson
	G-AIGU	J/1N Alpha	N. K. Geddes
	G-AIIH	Piper J-3C-65 Cub	J. A. de Salis
	G-AIJI	J/1N Alpha ★	C. J. Baker
	G-AIJM	Auster J/4	N. Huxtable
	G-AIJR	Auster J/4	R. J. Bentley
	G-AIJS	Auster J/4 ★	stored
	G-AIJT	Auster J/4 Srs 100	Aberdeen Auster Flying Group
	G-AIJZ	J/1 Autocrat	stored
	G-AIKE	Auster 5	C. J. Baker
	G-AIPR	Auster J/4	MPM Flying Group/Booker
	G-AIPV	J/1 Autocrat	W. P. Miller
	G-AIRC	J/1 Autocrat	R. C. Tebbett
	G-AIRI	D.H.82A Tiger Moth	E. R. Goodwin (stored)
	G-AIRK	D.H.82A Tiger Moth	R. C. Teverson & ptnrs
	G-AISA	Tipsy B Srs 1	G. A. Cull
	G-AISC	Tipsy B Srs 1	Wagtail Flying Group
	G-AISS	Piper J-3C-65 Cub	K. W. Wood & F. Watson
	G-AIST	V.S.300 Spitfire 1A (AR213)	Proteus Holdings Ltd/Goodwood
	G-AISX	Piper J-3C-65 Cub	V. Luck
	G-AISY	D.H.82A Tiger Moth	R. H. & J. A. Cooper
	G-AITB	A.S.10 Oxford (MP425) ★	RAF Museum Store/Cardington
	G-AIUA	M.14A Hawk Trainer 3	P. A. Brook
	G-AIUL	D.H.89A Dragon Rapide 6	I. Jones
	G-AIXA	Taylorcraft Plus D	A. A. & M. J. Copse
	G-AIXJ	D.H.82A Tiger Moth	D. Green
	G-AIXN	Benes-Mraz M.1c Sokol	P. Knott
	G-AIYG	SNCAN Stampe SV-4B	D. E. A. J. Cabooter
	G-AIYR	D.H.89A Dragon Rapide	Clacton Aero Club (1988) Ltd/Duxford
	G-AIYS	D.H.85 Leopard Moth	Wessex Aviation & Transport Ltd
	G-AIZE	F.24W Argus 2 ★	RAF Museum/Henlow
	G-AIZF	D.H.82A Tiger Moth ★	stored
	G-AIZG	V.S. Walrus 1 (L2301) ★	F.A.A. Museum/Yeovilton
	G-AIZU	J/1 Autocrat	C. J. & J. G. B. Morley
	G-AJAC	J/1N Alpha	N. J. Mortimore & H. A. Bridgman
	G-AJAD	Piper J-3C-65 Cub	R. A. D. Wilson & D. J. Morris
	G-AJAE	J/1N Alpha	M. G. Stops
	G-AJAJ	J/1N Alpha	R. B. Lawrence
	G-AJAM	J/2 Arrow	D. A. Porter
	G-AJAO	Piper J-3C-65 Cub	G. M. Perfect & M. Stow
	G-AJAP	Luscombe 8A Silvaire	R. J. Thomas
	G-AJAS	J/1N Alpha	C. J. Baker
	G-AJCP	D.31 Turbulent	B. R. Pearson
	G-AJDW	J/1 Autocrat	D. R. Hunt
	G-AJDY	J/1 Autocrat	Truck Panels Ltd
	G-AJEB	J/1N Alpha ★	Manchester Museum of Science & Industry
	G-AJEE	J/1 Autocrat	A. R. C. De Albanoz/Bournemouth
	G-AJEH	J/1N Alpha	J. T. Powell-Tuck
	G-AJEI	J/1N Alpha	W. P. Miller
	G-AJEM	J/1 Autocrat	K. A. Jones
	G-AJES	Piper J-3C-65 Cub (330485)	P. A. Crawford
	G-AJGJ	Auster 5 (RT486)	British Classic Aircraft Restoration Flying Group
	G-AJHJ	Auster 5	stored
	G-AJHS	D.H.82A Tiger Moth	J. M. Voeten & H. van der Paauw/Holland
	G-AJHU	D.H.82A Tiger Moth (T7471)	G. Valentini
	G-AJIH	J/1 Autocrat	A. H. Diver
	G-AJIS	J/1N Alpha	Husthwaite Auster Group
	G-AJIT	J/1 Kingsland Autocrat	A. J. Kay
	G-AJIU	J/1 Autocrat	M. D. Greenhalgh/Netherthorpe
	G-AJIW	J/1N Alpha	Millair Services Ltd
	G-AJJP	Jet Gyrodyne (XJ389) ★	Aerospace Museum/Cosford
	G-AJJS	Cessna 120	Robhurst Flying Group
	G-AJJT	Cessna 120	J. S. Robson
	G-AJJU	Luscombe 8E Silvaire	L. C. Moon
	G-AJKB	Luscombe 8E Silvaire	A. F. Hall & P. S. Hatwell/Ipswich
	G-AJOA	D.H.82A Tiger Moth (T5424)	F. P. Le Coyte
	G-AJOC	M.38 Messenger 2A ★	Ulster Folk & Transport Museum

Reg.	Type	Owner or Operator	Notes
G-AJOE	M.38 Messenger 2A	Cotswold Aircraft Restoration Group	
G-AJON	Aeronca 7AC Champion	A. Biggs & J. L. Broad/Booker	
G-AJOV†	Sikorsky S-51 ★	Aerospace Museum/Cosford	
G-AJOZ	F.24W Argus 2 ★	Thorpe Camp Preservation Group	
G-AJPI	F.24R-41a Argus 3 (314887)	T. H. Bishop	
G-AJPZ	J/1 Autocrat ★	Wessex Aviation Soc	
G-AJRB	J/1 Autocrat	N. Ravine	
G-AJRC	J/1 Autocrat	A. Foster	
G-AJRE	J/1 Autocrat (Lycoming)	C. W. & A. A. M. Huke	
G-AJRH	J/1N Alpha	Leicestershire Museum of Science & Industry/Coalville	
G-AJRS	M.14A Hawk Trainer 3 (P6382)	Shuttleworth Collection/O. Warden	
G-AJTW	D.H.82A Tiger Moth (N6965)	J. A. Barker/Tibenham	
G-AJUD	J/1 Autocrat	C. L. Sawyer	
G-AJUE	J/1 Autocrat	P. H. B. Cole	
G-AJUL	J/1N Alpha	M. J. Crees	
G-AJVE	D.H.82A Tiger Moth	R. W. J. Foster	
G-AJWB	M.38 Messenger 2A	P. G. Lee	
G-AJXC	Auster 5	J. E. Graves	
G-AJXV	Auster 4 (NJ695)	B. A. Farries/Leicester	
G-AJXY	Auster 4	P. D. Lowdon	
G-AJYB	J/1N Alpha	P. J. Shotbolt	
G-AKAA	Piper J-3C-65 Cub	A. A. Fernandez	
G-AKAZ	Piper J-3C-65 Cub	AKAZ Group	
G-AKBM	M.38 Messenger 2A ★	Bristol Plane Preservation Unit	
G-AKBO	M.38 Messenger 2A	B. du Cros	
G-AKDN	D.H.C. 1A Chipmunk 10	D. S. Backhouse	
G-AKDW	D.H.89A Dragon Rapide	De Havilland Aircraft Museum Trust Ltd	
G-AKEL	M.65 Gemini 1A ★	Ulster Folk & Transport Museum	
G-AKER	M.65 Gemini 1A ★	Berkshire Aviation Group	
G-AKEZ	M.38 Messenger 2A (RG333)	P. G. Lee	
G-AKGD	M.65 Gemini 1A ★	Berkshire Aviation Group	
G-AKGE	M.65 Gemini 3C ★	Ulster Folk & Transport Museum	
G-AKHP	M.65 Gemini 1A	P. G. Lee	
G-AKHZ	M.65 Gemini 7 ★	Museum of Berkshire Aviation/Woodley	
G-AKIB	Piper J-3C-90 Cub (480015)	M. C. Bennett	
G-AKIF	D.H.89A Dragon Rapide	Airborne Taxi Services Ltd/Booker	
G-AKIN	M.38 Messenger 2A	R. Spiller & Sons/Sywell	
G-AKIU	P.44 Proctor V	G. Reddish	
G-AKKB	M.65 Gemini 1A	J. Buckingham	
G-AKKH	M.65 Gemini 1A	M. C. Russell	
G-AKKR	M.14A Magister (T9707) ★	Manchester Museum of Science & Industry	
G-AKKY	M.14A Hawk Trainer 3 (L6906) (BAPC44) ★	Museum of Berkshire Aviation/Woodley	
G-AKLW	SA.6 Sealand 1 ★	Ulster Folk & Transport Museum	
G-AKOE	D.H.89A Dragon Rapide 4	J. E. Pierce/Chirk	
G-AKOT	Auster 5 ★	C. J. Baker	
G-AKOW	Auster 5 (TJ569) ★	Museum of Army Flying/Middle Wallop	
G-AKPF	M.14A Hawk Trainer 3 (V1075)	P. A. Brook/Shoreham	
G-AKPI	Auster 5 (NJ703)	B. H. Hargrave/Doncaster	
G-AKRA	Piper J-3C-65 Cub	W. R. Savin	
G-AKRP	D.H.89A Dragon Rapide ★	Fordaire Ltd/Little Gransden	
G-AKSY	Auster 5	Aerofab Flying Group	
G-AKSZ	Auster 5	A. R. C. Mathie	
G-AKTH	Piper J-3C-65 Cub	A. L. Wickens	
G-AKTI	Luscombe 8A Silvaire	N. C. W. N. Lester	
G-AKTK	Aeronca 11AC Chief	R. W. Marshall & ptnrs	
G-AKTM	Luscombe 8F Silvaire	B. Bayley	
G-AKTN	Luscombe 8A Silvaire	M. G. Rummey	
G-AKTO	Aeronca 7BCM Champion	D. C. Murray	
G-AKTP	PA-17 Vagabond	L. A. Maynard	
G-AKTR	Aeronca 7AC Champion	C. & G. Fielder	
G-AKTS	Cessna 120	J. J. Boon/Popham	
G-AKTT	Luscombe 8A Silvaire	S. J. Charters	
G-AKUE	D.H.82A Tiger Moth	D. F. Hodgkinson	
G-AKUF	Luscombe 8F Silvaire	A. G. Palmer	
G-AKUG	Luscombe 8A Silvaire	P. & L. A. Groves	
G-AKUH	Luscombe 8E Silvaire	I. M. Bower	
G-AKUI	Luscombe 8E Silvaire	J. A. Pothecary	
G-AKUJ	Luscombe 8E Silvaire	P. R. Edwards	
G-AKUK	Luscombe 8A Silvaire	Leckhampstead Flying Group	

Notes	Reg.	Type	Owner or Operator
	G-AKUL	Luscombe 8A Silvaire	E. A. Taylor
	G-AKUM	Luscombe 8F Silvaire	M. J. Willies
	G-AKUN	Piper J-3F-65 Cub	W. A. Savin
	G-AKUO	Aeronca 11AC Chief	KUO Flying Group/White Waltham
	G-AKUP	Luscombe 8E Silvaire	M. J. Willies
	G-AKUR	Cessna 140	J. Greenaway & C. A. Davies/Popham
	G-AKUW	C.H.3 Super Ace	D. R. Bean
	G-AKVF	C.H.3 Super Ace	T. Pate
	G-AKVM	Cessna 120	N. Wise & S. Walker
	G-AKVN	Aeronca 11AC Chief	Breckland Aeronca Group
	G-AKVO	Taylorcraft BC-12D	Albion Flyers
	G-AKVP	Luscombe 8A Silvaire	J. M. Edis
	G-AKVZ	M.38 Messenger 4B	Shipping & Airlines Ltd/Biggin Hill
	G-AKWS	Auster 5A-160	J. E. Homewood
	G-AKWT	Auster 5 ★	Loughborough & Leicester Aircraft Preservation Soc
	G-AKXP	Auster 5	M. Pocock
	G-AKXS	D.H.82A Tiger Moth	P. A. Colman
	G-AKZN	P.34A Proctor 3 (Z7197) ★	RAF Museum/Hendon
	G-ALAH	M.38 Messenger 4A (RH377) ★	RAF Museum/Henlow
	G-ALAX	D.H.89A Dragon Rapide ★	Durney Aeronautical Collection/Andover
	G-ALBJ	Auster 5	P. N. Elkington
	G-ALBK	Auster 5	S. J. Wright & Co (Farmers) Ltd
	G-ALBN	Bristol 173 (XF785) ★	RAF Museum Storage & Restoration Centre/Cardington
	G-ALCK	P.34A Proctor 3 (LZ766) ★	Skyfame Collection/Duxford
	G-ALCS	M.65 Gemini 3C ★	stored
	G-ALCU	D.H.104 Dove 2 ★	Midland Air Museum/Coventry
	G-ALDG	HP.81 Hermes 4 ★	Duxford Aviation Soc (fuselage only)
	G-ALEH	PA-17 Vagabond	A. D. Pearce/White Waltham
	G-ALFA	Auster 5	Golf Alpha Auster Group
	G-ALFM	D.H.104 Devon C.2	C. Charalambous
	G-ALFT	D.H.104 Dove 6 ★	Caernarfon Air World
	G-ALFU	D.H.104 Dove 6 ★	Duxford Aviation Soc
	G-ALGA	PA-15 Vagabond	D. A. Lord
	G-ALIJ	PA-17 Vagabond	Popham Flying Group/Popham
	G-ALIW	D.H.82A Tiger Moth	D. I. M. Geddes & F. Curry/Booker
	G-ALJF	P.34A Proctor 3	J. F. Moore/Biggin Hill
	G-ALJL	D.H.82A Tiger Moth	C. G. Clarke
	G-ALLF	Slingsby T.30A Prefect (ARK)	J. F. Hopkins & K. M. Fresson
	G-ALNA	D.H.82A Tiger Moth	R. J. Doughton
	G-ALND	D.H.82A Tiger Moth (N9191)	J. T. Powell-Tuck
	G-ALNV	Auster 5 ★	C. J. Baker (stored)
	G-ALOD	Cessna 140	J. R. Stainer
	G-ALRH	EoN Type 8 Baby	P. D. Moran/Chipping
	G-ALRI	D.H.82A Tiger Moth (T5672)	Wessex Aviation & Transport Ltd
	G-ALSP	Bristol 171 (WV783) Sycamore ★	R.N Fleetlands Museum
	G-ALSS	Bristol 171 (WA576) Sycamore ★	Dumfries & Galloway Aviation Museum
	G-ALST	Bristol 171 (WA577) Sycamore ★	N.E. Aircraft Museum/Usworth
	G-ALSW	Bristol 171 (WT933) Sycamore ★	Newark Air Museum
	G-ALSX	Bristol 171 (G-48-1) Sycamore ★	International Helicopter Museum/ Weston-s-Mare
	G-ALTO	Cessna 140	J. P. Bell
	G-ALTW	D.H.82A Tiger Moth ★	A. Mangham
	G-ALUC	D.H.82A Tiger Moth	D. R. & M. Wood
	G-ALVP	D.H.82A Tiger Moth ★	V. & R. Wheele (stored)
	G-ALWB	D.H.C.1 Chipmunk 22A	M. L. & J. M. Soper/Perth
	G-ALWF	V.701 Viscount ★	Viscount Preservation Trust RMA Sir John Franklin/Duxford
	G-ALWS	D.H.82A Tiger Moth	A. P. Benyon
	G-ALWW	D.H.82A Tiger Moth	D. E. Findon
	G-ALXT	D.H.89A Dragon Rapide ★	Science Museum/Wroughton
	G-ALXZ	Auster 5-150	M. F. Cuming
	G-ALYB	Auster 5 (RT520) ★	S. Yorks Aircraft Preservation Soc
	G-ALYG	Auster 5D	A. L. Young/Henstridge
	G-ALYW	D.H.106 Comet 1 ★	RAF Exhibition Flight (fuselage converted to Nimrod)
	G-ALZE	BN-1F ★	M. R. Short/Southampton Hall of Aviation
	G-ALZO	A.S.57 Ambassador ★	Duxford Aviation Soc
	G-AMAI	D.H.89A Rapide	J. Koch/Sandown
	G-AMAW	Luton LA-4 Minor	R. H. Coates

Reg.	Type	Owner or Operator	Notes
G-AMBB	D.H.82A Tiger Moth	J. Eagles	
G-AMCA	Douglas C-47B	Air Atlantique Ltd/Coventry	
G-AMCK	D.H.82A Tiger Moth	D. L. Frankel	
G-AMCM	D.H.82A Tiger Moth	B. C. Cooper & ptnrs	
G-AMDA	Avro 652A Anson 1 (N4877) ★	Skyfame Collection/Duxford	
G-AMEN	PA-18 Super Cub 95	A. Lovejoy & W. Cook	
G-AMHF	D.H.82A Tiger Moth	Wavendon Social Housing Ltd	
G-AMHJ	Douglas C-47A	Air Atlantique Ltd/Coventry	
G-AMIU	D.H.82A Tiger Moth	R. & Mrs J. L. Jones	
G-AMKU	J/1B Aiglet	P. G. Lipman	
G-AMLZ	P.50 Prince 6E ★	Caernarfon Air World Museum	
G-AMMS	J/5K Aiglet Trainer	A. J. Large	
G-AMNN	D.H.82A Tiger Moth	M. Thrower/Shoreham	
G-AMOG	V.701 Viscount ★	Aerospace Museum/Cosford	
G-AMPG	PA-12 Super Cruiser	R. Simpson	
G-AMPI	SNCAN Stampe SV-4C	M-A. Newman	
G-AMPO	Douglas C-47B	Air Atlantique Ltd/Coventry	
G-AMPY	Douglas C-47B	Air Atlantique Ltd/Coventry	
G-AMPZ	Douglas C-47B	Air Atlantique Ltd/Coventry	
G-AMRA	Douglas C-47B	Air Atlantique Ltd/Coventry	
G-AMRF	J/5F Aiglet Trainer	A. I.I Topps/E. Midlands	
G-AMRK	G.37 Gladiator I (N2308)	Shuttleworth Collection/O. Warden	
G-AMSG	SIPA 903	S. W. Markham	
G-AMSN	Douglas C-47B	Aces High Ltd/North Weald	
G-AMSV	Douglas C-47B	Air Atlantique Ltd/Coventry	
G-AMTA	J/5F Aiglet Trainer	N. H. T. Cottrell	
G-AMTD	J/5F Aiglet Trainer	Leicestershire Aero Club Ltd	
G-AMTF	D.H.82A Tiger Moth (T7842)	M. W. Zipfell	
G-AMTK	D.H.82A Tiger Moth	S. W. McKay & M. E. Vaisey	
G-AMTM	J/1 Autocrat	R. Stobo & D. Clewley (G-AJUJ)	
G-AMTV	D.H.82A Tiger Moth	Medalbest Ltd	
G-AMUF	D.H.C.1 Chipmunk 21	Redhill Tailwheel Flying Club Ltd	
G-AMUI	J/5F Aiglet Trainer	M. J. & A. A. Copse	
G-AMVD	Auster 5	R. F. Tolhurst	
G-AMVP	Tipsy Junior	A. R. Wershat	
G-AMVS	D.H.82A Tiger Moth	J. T. Powell-Tuck	
G-AMXA	D.H.106 Comet 2 ★	(nose only) Spectators' Terrace/Gatwick	
G-AMXT	D.H.104 Sea Devon C.20	W. Gentle & P. C. Gill	
G-AMYA	Zlin Z.381	D. M. Fenton	
G-AMYD	J/5L Aiglet Trainer	G. H. Maskell	
G-AMYJ	Douglas C-47B	Air Atlantique Ltd/Coventry	
G-AMYI	PA-17 Vagabond	P. J. Penn-Sayers/Shoreham	
G-AMZI	J/5F Aiglet Trainer	J. F. Moore/Biggin Hill	
G-AMZT	J/5F Aiglet Trainer	D. Hyde & J. W. Saull/Cranfield	
G-AMZU	J/5F Aiglet Trainer	J. A. Longworth & ptnrs	
G-ANAF	Douglas C-47B	Air Atlantique Ltd/Coventry	
G-ANAP	D.H.104 Dove 6 ★	Brunel Technical College/Lulsgate	
G-ANCF	B.175 Britannia 308 ★	(stored) Bristol Aero Collection	
G-ANCS	D.H.82A Tiger Moth	M. A. B. Mitchell	
G-ANCX	D.H.82A Tiger Moth	D. R. Wood/Biggin Hill	
G-ANDE	D.H.82A Tiger Moth	Chauffair Ltd	
G-ANDM	D.H.82A Tiger Moth	J. G. Green	
G-ANDP	D.H.82A Tiger Moth	A. H. Diver	
G-ANDX	D.H.104 Devon C.2 (XG496) ★	Solway Aviation Soc/Carlisle	
G-ANEC	D.H.82A Tiger Moth ★	(stored)	
G-ANEF	D.H.82A Tiger Moth (T5493)	RAF College Flying Club Co Ltd/Cranwell	
G-ANEH	D.H.82A Tiger Moth (N6797)	P. L. Gaze	
G-ANEL	D.H.82A Tiger Moth	Chauffair Ltd	
G-ANEM	D.H.82A Tiger Moth	P. J. Benest	
G-ANEN	D.H.82A Tiger Moth	M. D. Souch	
G-ANEW	D.H.82A Tiger Moth	A. L. Young	
G-ANEZ	D.H.82A Tiger Moth	C. D. J. Bland & T. S. Warren/Sandown	
G-ANFC	D.H.82A Tiger Moth	H. J. Jauncey/Rochester	
G-ANFH	Westland S-55 ★	International Helicopter Museum/ Weston-s-Mare	
G-ANFI	D.H.82A Tiger Moth (DE623)	G. P. Graham	
G-ANFL	D.H.82A Tiger Moth	R. P. Whitby & ptnrs	
G-ANFM	D.H.82A Tiger Moth	S. A. Brook & ptnrs/Booker	
G-ANFP	D.H.82A Tiger Moth ★	Mosquito Aircraft Museum	
G-ANFU	Auster 5 (NJ/19) ★	N.E. Aircraft Museum	
G-ANFV	D.H.82A Tiger Moth (DF155)	R. A. L. Falconer	
G-ANFW	D.H.82A Tiger Moth	G. M. Fraser/Denham	

Notes	Reg.	Type	Owner or Operator
	G-ANGK	Cessna 140A	D. W. Munday
	G-ANHK	D.H.82A Tiger Moth	J. D. Iliffe
	G-ANHR	Auster 5	C. G. Winch
	G-ANHS	Auster 4	Tango Uniform Group
	G-ANHU	Auster 4	D. J. Baker *(stored)*
	G-ANHX	Auster 5D	D. J. Baker
	G-ANIE	Auster 5 (TW467)	S. J. Partridge
	G-ANIJ	Auster 5D (TJ672)	M. Pocock & R. Eastmann
	G-ANIS	Auster 5	J. Clarke-Cockburn
	G-ANJA	D.H.82A Tiger Moth (N9389)	J. J. Young
	G-ANJD	D.H.82A Tiger Moth	H. J. Jauncey *(stored)*/Rochester
	G-ANJK	D.H.82A Tiger Moth	A. D. Williams
	G-ANJV	W.S.55 Whirlwind 3 (VR-BET) ★	International Helicopter Museum/ Weston-s-Mare
	G-ANKL	D.H.82A Tiger Moth (T5854)	Halfpenny Green Tiger Group
	G-ANKL	D.H.82A Tiger Moth	M. D. Souch
	G-ANKT	D.H.82A Tiger Moth (T6818)	Shuttleworth Collection/O. Warden
	G-ANKV	D.H.82A Tiger Moth ★	Westmead Business Group/Croydon
	G-ANKZ	D.H.82A Tiger Moth (N6466)	D. W. Graham
	G-ANLD	D.H.82A Tiger Moth	K. Peters
	G-ANLH	D.H.82A Tiger Moth	Wessex Aviation & Transport Ltd
	G-ANLS	D.H.82A Tiger Moth	P. A. Gliddon
	G-ANLU	Auster 5	B. H. Hargrave
	G-ANLW	W.B.1. Widgeon (MD497) ★	—
	G-ANLX	D.H.82A Tiger Moth	B. J. Borsberry & ptnrs
	G-ANMO	D.H.82A Tiger Moth	E. & K. M. Lay
	G-ANMV	D.H.82A Tiger Moth (T7404)	J. W. Davy/Cardiff
	G-ANMY	D.H.82A Tiger Moth (DE470)	R. Earl & B. Morris
	G-ANNB	D.H.82A Tiger Moth	Cormack (Aircraft Services) Ltd
	G-ANNE	D.H.82A Tiger Moth	C. R. Hardiman
	G-ANNG	D.H.82A Tiger Moth	P. F. Walter
	G-ANNI	D.H.82A Tiger Moth	A. R. Brett
	G-ANNK	D.H.82A Tiger Moth	P. J. Wilcox/Cranfield
	G-ANNN	D.H.82A Tiger Moth	T. Pate
	G-ANOA	Hiller UH-12A ★	Redhill Technical College
	G-ANOD	D.H.82A Tiger Moth	P. G. Watson
	G-ANOH	D.H.82A Tiger Moth	N. Parkhouse/White Waltham
	G-ANOK	Saab S.91C Safir ★	A. F. Galt & Co *(stored)*
	G-ANOM	D.H.82A Tiger Moth	P. R. & A. L. Williams
	G-ANON	D.H.82A Tiger Moth (T7909)	A. C. Mercer/Sherburn
	G-ANOO	D.H.82A Tiger Moth	R. K. Packman
	G-ANOR	D.H.82A Tiger Moth (T6991)	C. L. Keith-Lucas & Aero Vintage Ltd
	G-ANOV	D.H.104 Dove 6 ★	Museum of Flight/E. Fortune
	G-ANPE	D.H.82A Tiger Moth	I. E. S. Huddleston (G-IESH)
	G-ANPK	D.H.82A Tiger Moth	The D. & P. Group
	G-ANPP	P.34A Proctor 3	C. P. A. & J. Jeffrey
	G-ANRF	D.H.82A Tiger Moth	C. D. Cyster
	G-ANRM	D.H.82A Tiger Moth	Clacton Aero Club (1988) Ltd & A. B. Cutting
	G-ANRN	D.H.82A Tiger Moth	J. J. V. Elwes
	G-ANRP	Auster 5 (TW439)	A. Brier
	G-ANRS	V.732 Viscount *(fuselage only)* ★	Airport Fire Service/Cardiff
	G-ANRX	D.H.82A Tiger Moth ★	Mosquito Aircraft Museum
	G-ANSM	D.H.82A Tiger Moth	J. L. Bond
	G-ANTE	D.H.82A Tiger Moth	T. I. Sutton & B. J. Champion/Chester
	G-ANTK	Avro 685 York ★	Duxford Aviation Soc
	G-ANTS	D.H.82A Tiger Moth (N6532)	J. G. Green
	G-ANUO	D.H.114 Heron 2D	Avtech Ltd/Biggin Hill
	G-ANUW	D.H.104 Dove 6 ★	Aces High Ltd/North Weald
	G-ANWB	D.H.C.1 Chipmunk 21	G. Briggs/Blackpool
	G-ANWO	M.14A Hawk Trainer 3 ★	P. A. Brook
	G-ANXB	D.H.114 Heron 1B ★	Newark Air Museum
	G-ANXC	J/5R Alpine	C. J. Repek & ptnrs
	G-ANXR	P.31C Proctor 4 (RM221)	L. H. Oakins/Biggin Hill
	G-ANYP	P.31C Proctor 4 (NP184)	R. A. Anderson
	G-ANZJ	P.31C Proctor 4 (NP303) ★	A. Hillyard
	G-ANZT	Thruxton Jackaroo	D. J. Neville & P. A. Dear
	G-ANZU	D.H.82A Tiger Moth	P. A. Jackson
	G-ANZZ	D.H.82A Tiger Moth	D. L. Frankel
	G-AOAA	D.H.82A Tiger Moth	R. C. P. Brookhouse
	G-AOAR	P.31C Proctor 4 (NP181) ★	Historic Aircraft Preservation Soc
	G-AOBG	Somers-Kendall SK.1 ★	*stored*/Breighton

Reg.	Type	Owner or Operator	Notes
G-AOBH	D.H.82A Tiger Moth (NL750)	P. Nutley	
G-AOBJ	D.H.82A Tiger Moth (DE970)	D. H. R. Jenkins	
G-AOBO	D.H.82A Tiger Moth	P. A. Brook	
G-AOBU	P.84 Jet Provost T.1	T. J. Manna/Cranfield	
G-AOBV	J/5P Autocar	P. E. Champney (stored)	
G-AOBX	D.H.82A Tiger Moth	P. G. Watson	
G-AOCP	Auster 5 ★	C. J. Baker (stored)	
G-AOCR	Auster 5D	A. McLeod	
G-AOCU	Auster 5	S. J. Ball/Leicester	
G-AODA	Westland S-55 Srs 3 ★	International Helicopter Museum/ Weston-s-Mare	
G-AODT	D.H.8"2A Tiger Moth	A. H. Warminger	
G-AOEH	Aeronca 7AC Champion	R. A & S. P. Smith	
G-AOEI	D.H.82A Tiger Moth	C.F.G. Flying Ltd/Cambridge	
G-AOEL	D.H.82A Tiger Moth ★	Museum of Flight/E. Fortune	
G-AOES	D.H.82A Tiger Moth	A. Twemlow & G. A. Cordery	
G-AOET	D.H.82A Tiger Moth	Venom Jet Promotions Ltd/Bournemouth	
G-AOEX	Thruxton Jackaroo	A. T. Christian	
G-AOFE	D.H.C.1 Chipmunk 22A (WB702)	E. J. F. McEntee	
G-AOFM	J/5P Autocar	N. P. Beaumont	
G-AOFS	J/5L Aiglet Trainer	P. N. A. Whitehead	
G-AOGA	M.75 Aries ★	Irish Aviation Museum (stored)	
G-AOGE	P.34A Proctor 3	N. I. Dalziel/Biggin Hill	
G-AOGI	D.H.82A Tiger Moth	W. J. Taylor	
G-AOGR	D.H.82A Tiger Moth (T6099)	M. I. Edwards	
G-AOGV	J/5R Alpine	R. E. Heading	
G-AOHL	V.802 Viscount ★	British World Airlines Ltd (Cabin Trainer)/ Southend	
G-AOHM	V.802 Viscount	British World Airlines Ltd Viscount Sir George Edwards/Southend	
G-AOHY	D.H.82A Tiger Moth	C. R. & S. A. Hardiman/Shobdon	
G-AOHZ	J/5P Autocar	A. D. Hodgkinson	
G-AOIL	D.H.82A Tiger Moth	T. C. Lawless	
G-AOIM	D.H.82A Tiger Moth	C. R. Hardiman/Shobdon	
G-AOIR	Thruxton Jackaroo	L. H. Smith & I. M. Oliver	
G-AOIS	D.H.82A Tiger Moth	J. K. Ellwood	
G-AOIY	J/5G Autocar	J. B. Nicholson	
G-AOJC	V.802 Viscount ★	Wales Aircraft Museum/Cardiff	
G-AOJH	D.H.83C Fox Moth	R. M. Brooks	
G-AOJJ	D.H.82A Tiger Moth (DF128)	E. & K. M. Lay	
G-AOJK	D.H.82A Tiger Moth	P. A. de Courcy Swoffer	
G-AOJS	D.H.C.1 Chipmunk 22A	R. H. Cooper	
G-AOJT	D.H.106 Comet 1 (fuselage only) (F-BGNX) ★	Mosquito Aircraft Museum	
G-AOJZ	D.H.C.1 Chipmunk 22	A.S.T. Ltd/Perth	
G-AOKH	P.40 Prentice 1	J. F. Moore/Biggin Hill	
G-AOKL	P.40 Prentice 1 (VS610)	G-AOKL Flying Group	
G-AOKO	P.40 Prentice 1 ★	J. F. Coggins/Coventry	
G-AOKZ	P.40 Prentice 1 (VS623) ★	Midland Air Museum	
G-AOLK	P.40 Prentice 1	Hilton Aviation Ltd/Southend	
G-AOLU	P.40 Prentice 1 (VS356) ★	P. Morris	
G-AORB	Cessna 170B	Eaglescott Parachute Centre	
G-AORG	D.H.114 Heron 2	Duchess of Brittany (Jersey) Ltd	
G-AORW	D.H.C.1 Chipmunk 22A	R. C. McCarthy	
G-AOSF	D.H.C.1 Chipmunk 22 (WB571)	D. Mercer	
G-AOSK	D.H.C.1 Chipmunk 22	E. J. Leigh	
G-AOSO	D.H.C.1 Chipmunk 22	Earl of Suffolk & Berkshire & J. Hoerner	
G-AOSU	D.H.C.1 Chipmunk 22 (Lycoming)	RAFGSA/Bicester	
G-AOSY	D.H.C.1 Chipmunk 22 (WB585)	Franbrave Ltd	
G-AOTD	D.H.C.1 Chipmunk 22 (WB588)	Assigntravel Ltd/Biggin Hill	
G-AOTF	D.H.C.1 Chipmunk 23 (Lycoming)	RAFGSA/Bicester	
G-AOTI	D.H.114 Heron 2D ★	Mosquito Aircraft Museum	
G-AOTK	D.53 Turbi	The T. K. Flying Group	
G-AOTR	D.H.C.1 Chipmunk 22	M. R. Woodgate	
G-AOTY	D.H.C.1 Chipmunk 22A (WG472)	T. E. W. Terrell	
G-AOUJ	Fairey Ultra-Light ★	International Helicopter Museum/ Weston-s-Mare	
G-AOUO	D.H.C.1 Chipmunk 22 (Lycoming)	RAFGSA/Bicester	
G-AOUP	D.H.C.1 Chipmunk 22	A. R. Harding	
G-AOUR	D.H.82A Tiger Moth ★	Ulster Folk & Transport Museum	
G-AOVF	B.175 Britannia 312F ★	Aerospace Museum/Cosford	
G-AOVT	B 175 Britannia 312F ★	Duxford Aviation Soc	
G-AOVW	Auster 5	B. Marriott/Cranwell	

Notes	Reg.	Type	Owner or Operator
	G-AOXN	D.H.82A Tiger Moth	S. L. G. Darch
	G-AOZH	D.H.82A Tiger Moth (K2572)	R. G. & G. J. Wheele/Shoreham
	G-AOZL	J/5Q Alpine	E. A. Taylor/Southend
	G-AOZP	D.H.C.1 Chipmunk 22	M. Darlington
	G-AOZU	D.H.C.1 Chipmunk 22A	R. H. Cooper & R. I. Vaughan
	G-APAA	J/5R Alpine ★	L. A. Groves (stored)
	G-APAF	Auster 5 (TW511)	J. E. Allen (G-CMAL)
	G-APAH	Auster 5	Cumbernauld Cubbers
	G-APAL	D.H.82A Tiger Moth (N6847)	P. S. & R. A. Chapman
	G-APAM	D.H.82A Tiger Moth	R. P. Williams
	G-APAO	D.H.82A Tiger Moth	Clacton Aero Club (1988) Ltd
	G-APAP	D.H.82A Tiger Moth	J. Romain/Duxford
	G-APAS	D.H.106 Comet 1XB ★	Aerospace Museum/Cosford
	G-APBE	Auster 5	C. W. Wilkinson/Panshanger
	G-APBI	D.H.82A Tiger Moth (EM903)	R. Devaney & ptnrs/Audley End
	G-APBO	D.53 Turbi	R. C. Hibberd
	G-APBW	Auster 5	N. Huxtable
	G-APCB	J/5Q Alpine	A. A. Beswick & I. A. Freeman
	G-APCC	D.H.82A Tiger Moth	L. J. Rice/Henstridge
	G-APDB	D.H.106 Comet 4 ★	Duxford Aviation Soc
	G-APEG	V.953C Merchantman ★	Airport Fire Service/E. Midlands
	G-APEP	V.953C Merchantman	Hunting Cargo Airlines Ltd Superb
	G-APES	V.953C Merchantman	Hunting Cargo Airlines Ltd (stored)
	G-APEY	V.806 Viscount	British World Airlines Ltd/Southend
	G-APFA	D.54 Turbi	A. Eastelow & F. J. Keitch/Dunkeswell
	G-APFG	Boeing 707-436 ★	Cabin water spray tests/Cardington
	G-APFJ	Boeing 707-436 ★	Aerospace Museum/Cosford
	G-APFU	D.H.82A Tiger Moth	Mithril Racing Ltd/Goodwood
	G-APGL	D.H.82A Tiger Moth	K. A. Broomfield
	G-APHV	Avro 19 Srs 2 (VM360) ★	Museum of Flight/E. Fortune
	G-APIE	Tipsy Belfair B	J. Jennings & D. Beale
	G-APIH	D.H.82A Tiger Moth	K. Stewering
	G-APIK	J/1N Alpha	N. D. Voce
	G-APIM	V.806 Viscount ★	Brooklands Museum of Aviation/ Weybridge
	G-APIT	P.40 Prentice 1 (VR192) ★	WWII Aircraft Preservation Soc/Lasham
	G-APIU	P.40 Prentice 1 ★	J. F. Coggins/Coventry
	G-APIY	P.40 Prentice 1 (VR249) ★	Newark Air Museum
	G-APIZ	D.31 Turbulent	M. J. Whatley/Booker
	G-APJB	P.40 Prentice 1 (VR259)	Atlaîntic Air Transport Ltd/Coventry
	G-APJJ	Fairey Ultra-light ★	Midland Aircraft Preservation Soc
	G-APJO	D.H.82A Tiger Moth	D. R. & M. Wood
	G-APJZ	J/1N Alpha	P. G. Lipman
	G-APKH	D.H.85 Leopard Moth	R. G. Grocott (G-ACGS)
	G-APKM	J/1N Alpha	D. E. A. Huggins (stored)
	G-APKN	J/1N Alpha	P. R. Hodson Ltd
	G-APKY	Hiller UH-12B	D. A. George (stored)
	G-APLG	J/5L Aiglet Trainer	G. R. W. Brown
	G-APLK	MIles M.100 Student 2	A. S. Topen (G-MIOO)/Cranfield
	G-APLO	D.H.C.1 Chipmunk 22A (WD379)	Lindholme Aircraft Ltd/Jersey
	G-APLU	D.H.82A Tiger Moth	R. A. Bishop & M. E. Vaisey
	G-APMB	D.H.106 Comet 4B ★	Gatwick Handling Ltd (ground trainer)
	G-APMH	J/1U Workmaster	J. L. Thorogood
	G-APML	Douglas C-47B	Air Atlantique Ltd/Coventry
	G-APMX	D.H.82A Tiger Moth	G. A. Broughton
	G-APMY	PA-23 Apache 160 ★	NE Wales Institute of Higher Education (instructional airframe)/Clwyd
	G-APNJ	Cessna 310 ★	Chelsea College/Shoreham
	G-APNS	Garland-Bianchi Linnet	Paul Penn-Sayers Model Services Ltd
	G-APNT	Currie Wot	J. W. Salter
	G-APNZ	D.31 Turbulent	J. Knight
	G-APOD	Tipsy Belfair	L. F. Potts
	G-APOI	Saro Skeeter Srs 8 ★	—
	G-APOL	D.31 Turbulent	A. Gregori & S. Tinker
	G-APPA	D.H.C.1 Chipmunk 22	I. R. Young/Glasgow
	G-APPL	P.40 Prentice 1	S. J. Saggers/Biggin Hill
	G-APPM	D.H.C.1 Chipmunk 22	Freston Aviation Ltd
	G-APRF	Auster 5	J. T. & J. R. Sime
	G-APRJ	Avro 694 Lincoln B.2 ★	Aces High Ltd/North Weald
	G-APRL	AW.650 Argosy 101 ★	Midland Air Museum/Coventry
	G-APRR	Super Aero 45	R. H. Jowett
	G-APRS	SA. Twin Pioneer 3	Bravo Aviation Ltd (G-BCWF)

Reg.	Type	Owner or Operator	Notes
G-APRT	Taylor JT.1 Monoplane	M. J. Snelling	
G-APSA	Douglas DC-6A	Instone Air Line Ltd/Coventry	
G-APSR	J/1U Workmaster	D. & K. Aero Services Ltd/Shobdon	
G-APTP	PA-22 Tri-Pacer 150 (tailwheel)	Contest (Ralph & Susan Chesters) Ltd	
G-APTR	J/1N Alpha	C. J. & D. J. Baker	
G-APTU	Auster 5	G-APTU Flying Group	
G-APTW	W.B.1 Widgeon ★	N.E. Aircraft Museum/Usworth	
G-APTY	Beechñ G.35 Bonanza	G. E. Brennand & ptnrs	
G-APTZ	D.31 Turbulent	F. R. Hutchings	
G-APUD	Bensen B.7M (modified) ★	Manchester Museum of Science & Industry	
G-APUE	L.40 Meta Sokol	S. E. & M. J. Aherne	
G-APUP	Sopwith Pup (replica) (N5182) ★	RAF Museum/Hendon	
G-APUR	PA-22 Tri-Pacer 160	P. J. Hewitt	
G-APUW	J/5V-160 Autocar	Anglia Auster Syndicate	
G-APUY	D.31 Turbulent	C. Jones/Barton	
G-APUZ	PA-24 Comanche 250	P. A. Brook	
G-APVF	Putzer Elster B (97+04)	A. J. Robinson	
G-APVG	J/5L Aiglet Trainer	C. M. Daggett/Cranfield	
G-APVN	D.31 Turbulent	R. Sherwin/Shoreham	
G-APVS	Cessna 170B	N. Simpson	
G-APVU	L.40 Meta Sokol	S. E. & M. J. Aherne	
G-APVZ	D.31 Turbulent	M. J. A. Trudgill	
G-APWA	HPR-7 Herald 101 ★	Museum of Berkshire Aviation/Woodley	
G-APWJ	HPR-7 Herald 201 ★	Duxford Aviation Soc	
G-APWL	EoN 460 Srs 1A	A. J. Langdon & R. A. Munday	
G-APWN	WS-55 Whirlwind 3 ★	Midland Air Museum	
G-APWY	Piaggio P.166 ★	Science Museum/Wroughton	
G-APWZ	EP.9 Prospector	Prospector Flying Group	
G-APXJ	PA-24 Comanche 250	T. Wildsmith/Netherthorpe	
G-APXM	PA-22 Tri-Pacer 160	R. J. Chinn	
G-APXR	PA-22 Tri-Pacer 160	A. Troughton	
G-APXT	PA-22 Tri-Pacer 150 (modified)	J. W. & I. Daniels	
G-APXU	PA-22 Tri-Pacer 125	Medway Aircraft Preservation Soc Ltd	
G-APXW	EP.9 Prospector (XM819) ★	Museum of Army Flying/Middle Wallop	
G-APXX	D.H.A.3 Drover 2 (VH-FDT) ★	WWII Aircraft Preservation Soc/Lasham	
G-APXY	Cessna 150	Merlin Flying Club Ltd/Hucknall	
G-APYB	Tipsy T.66 Nipper 3	B. O. Smith	
G-APYD	D.H.106 Comet 4B ★	Science Museum/Wroughton	
G-APYG	D.H.C.1 Chipmunk 22	E. J. I. Musty & P. A. Colman	
G-APYI	PA-22 Tri-Pacer 135	B. T. & J. Cullen	
G-APYN	PA-22 Tri-Pacer 160	W. D. Stephens	
G-APYT	Champion 7FC Tri-Traveller	B. J. Anning	
G-APZJ	PA-18 Super Cub 150	Southern Sailplanes	
G-APZL	PA-22 Tri-Pacer 160	R. T. Evans	
G-APZR	Cessna 150 ★	*Engine test-bed*/Biggin Hill	
G-APZS	Cessna 175A	G. A. Nash/Booker	
G-APZX	PA-22 Tri-Pacer 150	Applied Signs Ltd	
G-ARAD	Luton LA-5A Major	D. J. Bone & P. L. Jobes	
G-ARAI	PA-22 Tri-Pacer 160	T. Richards & G. C. Winters	
G-ARAM	PA-18 Super Cub 150	Clacton Aero Club (1988) Ltd	
G-ARAN	PA-18 Super Cub 150	A. P. Docherty/Redhill	
G-ARAO	PA-18 Super Cub 95 (607327)	R. G. Manton	
G-ARAS	Champion 7FC Tri-Traveller	Clipgate Flying Group	
G-ARAT	Cessna 180C	S. Peck	
G-ARAW	Cessna 182C Skylane	P. Channon	
G-ARAX	PA-22 Tri-Pacer 150	M. Gardiner	
G-ARAZ	D.H.82A Tiger Moth	S. G. North	
G-ARBE	D.H.104 Dove 8	M. Whale & M. W. A. Lunn	
G-ARBG	Tipsy T.66 Nipper 2	J. Horovitz & J. McLeod	
G-ARBM	J/1B Aiglet	B. V. Nabbs & C. Chaddock	
G-ARBO	PA-24 Comanche 250	D. M. Harbottle & I. S. Graham/Goodwood	
G-ARBP	Tipsy T.66 Nipper 2	F. W. Kirk	
G-ARBS	PA-22 Tri-Pacer 160 (tailwheel)	S. D. Rowell	
G-ARBV	PA-22 Tri-Pacer 160	The Oaksey Pacers	
G-ARBZ	D.31 Turbulent	J. Mickleburgh	
G-ARCC	PA-22 Tri-Pacer 150	Popham Flying Group/Popham	
G-ARCF	PA-22 Tri-Pacer 150	M. M. Mason	
G-ARCH	Cessna 310D ★	*Instructional airframe*/Perth	
G-ARCS	Auster D6/180	E. A. Matty/Shobdon	
G-ARCT	PA-18 Super Cub 95	M. J. Kirk	
G-ARCV	Cessna 175A	R. Francis & C. Campbell	

Notes	Reg.	Type	Owner or Operator
	G-ARCW	PA-23 Apache 160	D. R. C. Reeves
	G-ARCX	AW Meteor 14 ★	Museum of Flight/E. Fortune
	G-ARDB	PA-24 Comanche 250	Delta Bravo Aircraft Associates/Booker
	G-ARDD	CP.301C1 Emeraude	R. M. Shipp
	G-ARDE	D.H.104 Dove 6	R. J. H. Small/North Weald
	G-ARDG	EP.9 Prospector ★	Museum of Army Flying/Middle Wallop
	G-ARDJ	Auster D.6/180	RN Aviation (Leicester Airport) Ltd
	G-ARDO	Jodel D.112	W. R. Prescott
	G-ARDP	PA-22 Tri-Pacer 150	G. M. Jones
	G-ARDS	PA-22 Caribbean 150	A. C. Donaldson & C. I. Lavery
	G-ARDT	PA-22 Tri-Pacer 160	M. Henderson
	G-ARDV	PA-22 Tri-Pacer 160	G. L. Brown
	G-ARDY	Tipsy T.66 Nipper 2	P. R. Teager
	G-ARDZ	Jodel D.140A	M. J. Wright
	G-AREA	D.H.104 Dove 8 ★	Mosquito Aircraft Museum
	G-AREB	Cessna 175B Skylark	R. J. Postlethwaite & ptnrs/Wellesbourne
	G-AREF	PA-23 Aztec 250 ★	Southall College of Technology
	G-AREH	D.H.82A Tiger Moth	N. K. Geddes
	G-AREI	Auster 3 (MT438)	J. A. Vetch
	G-AREL	PA-22 Caribbean 150	H. H. Cousins/Fenland
	G-AREO	PA-18 Super Cub 150	DRA (Farnborough) Gliding Club Ltd
	G-ARET	PA-22 Tri-Pacer 160	I. S. Runnalls
	G-AREV	PA-22 Tri-Pacer 160	Spatrek Ltd/Barton
	G-AREX	Aeronca 15AC Sedan	R. J. Middleton-Turnbull & P. Lowndes
	G-AREZ	D.31 Turbulent	J. St. Clair-Quentin/Shobdon
	G-ARFB	PA-22 Caribbean 150	C. T. Woodward & ptnrs
	G-ARFD	PA-22 Tri-Pacer 160	J. R. Dunnett
	G-ARFG	Cessna 175A Skylark	Foxtrot Golf Group
	G-ARFH	PA-24 Comanche 250	L. M. Walton
	G-ARFI	Cessna 150A	J. H. Fisher
	G-ARFL	Cessna 175B Skylark	D. J. Mason
	G-ARFN	Cessna 150A ★	*Instructional airframe*/Perth
	G-ARFO	Cessna 150A	Tindon Ltd/Little Snoring
	G-ARFT	Jodel DR. 1050	R. Shaw
	G-ARFV	Tipsy T.66 Nipper 2	C. G. Stone/Biggin Hill
	G-ARGB	Auster 6A ★	C. J. Baker *(stored)*
	G-ARGG	D.H.C.1 Chipmunk 22 (WD305)	B. Hook
	G-ARGO	PA-22 Colt 108	B. E. Goodman/Liverpool
	G-ARGV	PA-18 Super Cub 180	Deeside Gliding Club (Aberdeenshire) Ltd/Aboyne
	G-ARGY	PA-22 Tri-Pacer 160	G. K. Hare (G-JEST)
	G-ARGZ	D.31 Turbulent	J. C. Mansell
	G-ARHB	Forney F-1A Aircoupe	A. V. Rash & D. R. Wickes
	G-ARHC	Forney F-1A Aircoupe	A. P. Gardner/Elstree
	G-ARHI	PA-24 Comanche 180	A. H. Entress
	G-ARHL	PA-23 Aztec 250	C. J. Freeman/Headcorn
	G-ARHM	Auster 6A	D. Hollowell & ptnrs/Finmere
	G-ARHN	PAE-22 Caribbean 150	D. B. Furniss & A. Munro/Doncaster
	G-ARHP	PA-22 Tri-Pacer 160	R. N. Morgan
	G-ARHR	PA-22 Caribbean 150	C. C. Wagner
	G-ARHT	PA-22 Caribbean 150 ★	Moston Technical College
	G-ARHU	PA-22 Tri-Pacer 160	B. L. Newbold & H. Streets
	G-ARHW	D.H.104 Dove 8	Pacelink Ltd
	G-ARHX	D.H.104 Dove 8 ★	N.E. Aircraft Museum/Usworth
	G-ARHZ	D.62 Condor	T. J. Goodwin/Andrewsfield
	G-ARID	Cessna 172B	L. M. Edwards
	G-ARIE	PA-24 Comanche 250	Zendair Ltd
	G-ARIF	Ord-Hume O-H.7 Minor Coupé	N. H. Ponsford
	G-ARIH	Auster 6A (TW591)	India Hotel Group
	G-ARIK	PA-22 Caribbean 150	C. J. Berry
	G-ARIL	PA-22 Caribbean 150	K. Knight
	G-ARJB	D.H.104 Dove 8 ★	J. C. Bamford *(stored)*
	G-ARJC	PA-22 Colt 108	F. W. H. Dulles
	G-ARJE	PA-22 Colt 108	Touchdown Aviation Ltd
	G-ARJF	PA-22 Colt 108	M. J. Collins
	G-ARJH	PA-22 Colt 108	G. P. A. Elborough & A. Vine
	G-ARJR	PA-23 Apache 160G ★	*Instructional airframe*/Kidlington
	G-ARJS	PA-23 Apache 160G	Bencray Ltd/Blackpool
	G-ARJT	PA-23 Apache 160G	Hiveland Ltd
	G-ARJU	PA-23 Apache 160G	G. R. Manley
	G-ARJV	PA-23 Apache 160G	Economic Insulations Ltd
	G-ARJW	PA-23 Apache 160G	*stored*/Bristol
	G-ARJZ	D.31 Turbulent	C. J. Tilson

Reg.	Type	Owner or Operator	Notes
G-ARKG	J/5G Autocar	C. M. Milborrow	
G-ARKJ	Beech N35 Bonanza	T. Cust	
G-ARKK	PA-22 Colt 108	Rochford Hundred Flying Group/Southend	
G-ARKM	PA-22 Colt 108	B. V. & E. A. Howes/Earls Colne	
G-ARKN	PA-22 Colt 108	R. A. & N. L. E. Spooner	
G-ARKP	PA-22 Colt 108	C. J. & J. Freeman/Headcorn	
G-ARKR	PA-22 Colt 108	B. J. M. Montegut	
G-ARKS	PA-22 Colt 108	R. A. Nesbitt-Dufort	
G-ARLG	Auster D.4/108	Auster D4 Group	
G-ARLK	PA-24 Comanche 250	M. Walker & C. Robinson	
G-ARLO	A.61 Terrier 1 ★	stored	
G-ARLP	A.61 Terrier 1	Gemini Flying Group	
G-ARLR	A.61 Terrier 2	M. J. Breeze	
G-ARLU	Cessna 172B Skyhawk ★	Instructional airframe/Irish AC	
G-ARLW	Cessna 172B Skyhawk ★	(spares' source)/Barton	
G-ARLX	Jodel D.140B	Shipping & Airlines Ltd/Biggin Hill	
G-ARLZ	D.31A Turbulent	Turb Group	
G-ARMA	PA-23 Apache 160G ★	Instructional airframe/Kidlington	
G-ARMB	D.H.C.1 Chipmunk 22A (WB660)	P. A. Layzell	
G-ARMC	D.H.C.1 Chipmunk 22A (WB703)	John Henderson Children's Trust	
G-ARMD	D.H.C.1 Chipmunk 22A ★	K. & L. Aero Services (stored)	
G-ARMF	D.H.C.1 Chipmunk 22A (WZ868)	Chipmunk G-BCIW Syndicate	
G-ARMG	D.H.C.1 Chipmunk 22A	MG Group/Wellesbourne	
G-ARML	Cessna 175B Skylark	R. W. Boote	
G-ARMN	Cessna 175B Skylark	G. A. Nash	
G-ARMO	Cessna 172B Skyhawk	G. M. Jones	
G-ARMR	Cessna 172B Skyhawk	Sunsaver Ltd/Barton	
G-ARMZ	D.31 Turbulent	J. Mickleburgh	
G-ARNB	J/5G Autocar	R. F. Tolhurst	
G-ARND	PA-22 Colt 108	E. J. Clarke	
G-ARNE	PA-22 Colt 108	T. D. L. Bowden/Shipdham	
G-ARNG	PA-22 Colt 108	S. S. Delwarte/Shoreham	
G-ARNH	PA-22 Colt 108 ★	Fenland Aircraft Preservation Soc	
G-ARNI	PA-22 Colt 108	B. A. Drury	
G-ARNJ	PA-22 Colt 108	M. A. Vincent	
G-ARNK	PA-22 Colt 108 (tailwheel)	G. K. Hare	
G-ARNL	PA-22 Colt 108	J. A. Dodsworth/White Waltham	
G-ARNP	A.109 Airedale	S. W. & M. Isbister	
G-ARNY	Jodel D.117	D. P. Jenkins	
G-ARNZ	D.31 Turbulent	N. J. Mathias	
G-AROA	Cessna 172B Skyhawk	D. F. Partridge	
G-AROE	Aero 145	K. Plaza	
G-AROF	L.40 Meta-Sokol	G. D. H. Crawford	
G-AROJ	A.109 Airedale ★	D. J. Shaw (stored)	
G-AROM	PA-22 Colt 108 (tailwheel)	J. R. Colthurst	
G-ARON	PA-22 Colt 108	K. N. Stephens	
G-AROO	Forney F-1A Aircoupe	W. J. McMeekan/Newtownards	
G-AROW	Jodel D.140B	Cubair Ltd/Redhill	
G-AROY	Boeing Stearman A.75N.1	W. A. Jordan	
G-ARPH	H.S.121 Trident 1C ★	Aerospace Museum, Cosford	
G-ARPK	H.S.121 Trident 1C ★	Manchester Airport Authority	
G-ARPL	H.S.121 Trident 1C ★	BAA Airport Fire Service/Edinburgh	
G-ARPO	H.S.121 Trident 1C ★	CAA Fire School/Teesside	
G-ARPP	H.S.121 Trident 1C ★	BAA Airport Fire Service/Glasgow	
G-ARPW	H.S.121 Trident 1C ★	CAA Fire School/Teesside	
G-ARPX	H.S.121 Trident 1C ★	Air Service Training Ltd/Perth	
G-ARPZ	H.S.121 Trident 1C ★	RFD Ltd/Dunsfold	
G-ARRD	Jodel DR.1050	C. M. Fitton	
G-ARRE	Jodel DR.1050	A. Luty & M. P. Edwards/Barton	
G-ARRF	Cessna 150A	Electrical Engineering Services	
G-ARRL	J/1N Alpha	G. N. Smith & C. Webb	
G-ARRM	Beagle B.206-X ★	(stored) Bristol Aero Collection	
G-ARRS	CP.301A Emeraude	M. J. A. Trudgill	
G-ARRT	Wallis WA-116-1	K. H. Wallis	
G-ARRU	D.31 Turbulent	N. A. Morgan & J. Paget	
G-ARRX	Auster 6A (VF512)	J. E. D. Mackie	
G-ARRY	Jodel D.140B	Fictionview Ltd	
G-ARRZ	D.31 Turbulent	C. I. Jefferson	
G-ARSG	Roe Triplane Type IV replica	Shuttleworth Collection/O. Warden	
G-ARSJ	CP.301-C2 Emeraude	R. J. Lewis	
G-ARSU	PA-22 Colt 108	D. P. Owen	
G-ARSW	PA-22 Colt 108	Sierra Whisky Flying Group/Sibson	
G-ARSX	PA-22 Tri-Pacer 160	S. Hutchinson	

Notes	Reg.	Type	Owner or Operator
	G-ARTD	PA-23 Apache 160	Dr. D. A. Jones/Caernarfon
	G-ARTH	PA-12 Super Cruiser	R. I. Souch & B. J. Dunford
	G-ARTJ	Bensen B.8M ★	Museum of Flight/E. Fortune
	G-ARTL	D.H.82A Tiger Moth (T7281)	P. A. Jackson
	G-ARTT	M.S.880B Rallye Club	R. N. Scott
	G-ARTW	Cessna 150B ★	*Instructional airframe*/Perth
	G-ARTX	Cessna 150B ★	*Instructional airframe*/Perth
	G-ARTY	Cessna 150B ★	*Instructional airframe*/Perth
	G-ARTZ	McCandless M.4 Gyrocopter	W. E. Partridge *(stored)*
	G-ARUG	J/5G Autocar	D. P. H. Hulme/Biggin Hill
	G-ARUH	Jodel DR.1050	PFA Group/Denham
	G-ARUI	A.61 Terrier	A. C. Ladd
	G-ARUL	Cosmic Wind	P. G. Kynsey
	G-ARUO	PA-24 Comanche 180	Uniform Oscar Group/Elstree
	G-ARUV	CP.301A Emeraude	J. F. Sully & L. N. Price
	G-ARUY	J/1N Alpha	Gullwing Aviation Ltd
	G-ARUZ	Cessna 175C Skylark	Cardiff Skylark Group
	G-ARVM	V.1101 VC10 ★	Aerospace Museum/Cosford
	G-ARVO	PA-18 Super Cub 95	Deltair Ltd
	G-ARVS	PA-28 Cherokee 160	Skyscraper Ltd/Stapleford
	G-ARVT	PA-28 Cherokee 160	Red Rose Aviation Ltd/Liverpool
	G-ARVU	PA-28 Cherokee 160	D. J. Hockings/Biggin Hill
	G-ARVV	PA-28 Cherokee 160	G. E. Hopkins
	G-ARVZ	D.62B Condor	P. A. Silcox
	G-ARWB	D.H.C.1 Chipmunk 22 (WK611)	L. J. Willcocks
	G-ARWH	Cessna 172C Skyhawk ★	—
	G-ARWO	Cessna 172C Skyhawk	J. P. Stafford
	G-ARWR	Cessna 172C Skyhawk	The Devanha Flying Group Ltd/Aberdeen
	G-ARWS	Cessna 175C Skylark	E. N. Skinner
	G-ARXD	A.109 Airedale	D. Howden
	G-ARXG	PA-24 Comanche 250	P. & H. Robinson
	G-ARXH	Bell 47G	A. B. Searle
	G-ARXP	Luton LA-4A Minor	E. Evans
	G-ARXT	Jodel DR.1050	CJM Flying Group
	G-ARXU	Auster 6A (VF526)	E. C. Tait & M. Pocock/Middle Wallop
	G-ARXW	M.S.885 Super Rallye	A. F. Danton & A. Kennedy
	G-ARYB	H.S.125 Srs 1 ★	Midland Air Museum/Coventry
	G-ARYC	H.S.125 Srs 1 ★	The Mosquito Aircraft Museum
	G-ARYD	Auster AOP.6 (WJ358) ★	Museum of Army Flying/Middle Wallop
	G-ARYF	PA-23 Aztec 250B	I. J. T. Branson/Biggin Hill
	G-ARYH	PA-22 Tri-Pacer 160	Filtration (Water Treatment Engineers) Ltd
	G-ARYI	Cessna 172C	J. Rhodes
	G-ARYK	Cessna 172C	Thermodata Components
	G-ARYR	PA-28 Cherokee 180	G-ARYR Flying Group
	G-ARYS	Cessna 172C Skyhawk	Guildbrook Associates Ltd
	G-ARYV	PA-24 Comanche 250	Ilford Business Machines Ltd
	G-ARYZ	A.109 Airedale	Rutland Aviation
	G-ARZB	Wallis WA-116 Srs 1	K. H. Wallis
	G-ARZE	Cessna 172C ★	*Parachute jump trainer*/Cockerham
	G-ARZM	D.31 Turbulent	Tiger Club (1990) Ltd/Headcorn
	G-ARZN	Beech N35 Bonanza	D. W. Mickleburgh/Leicester
	G-ARZW	Currie Wot	B. R. Pearson
	G-ARZX	Cessna 150B	Gate Flyers/Manston
	G-ASAA	Luton LA-4A Minor	J. W. Cudby
	G-ASAI	A.109 Airedale	K. R Howden & ptnrs
	G-ASAJ	A.61 Terrier 2 (WE569)	G-ASAJ Flying Group
	G-ASAK	A.61 Terrier 2	J. H. Oakins/Biggin Hill
	G-ASAL	SA Bulldog Srs 120/124	Pioneer Flying Co. Ltd
	G-ASAM	D.31 Turbulent	Tiger Club (1990) Ltd/Headcorn
	G-ASAN	A.61 Terrier 2	J. A. Rees
	G-ASAT	M.S.880B Rallye Club	M. Cutovic
	G-ASAU	M.S.880B Rallye Club	T. C. & R. Edwards
	G-ASAX	A.61 Terrier 2	P. G. & F. M. Morris
	G-ASAZ	Hiller UH-12E4	Pan-Air Ltd
	G-ASBA	Currie Wot	M. A. Kaye
	G-ASBB	Beech 23 Musketeer	Five Musketeers Flying Group
	G-ASBH	A.109 Airedale	D. T. Smollett
	G-ASBY	A.109 Airedale	M. R. H. Wheatley & R. K. Wilson
	G-ASCC	Beagle E.3 AOP Mk 11 (XP254)	K. R. Harris
	G-ASCD	A.61 Terrier 2 (TJ704) ★	Yorkshire Air Museum/Elvington
	G-ASCM	Isaacs Fury II (K2050)	M. M. Ward
	G-ASCU	PA-18A Super Cub 150	Farm Aviation Services Ltd

Reg.	Type	Owner or Operator	Notes
G-ASCZ	CP.301A Emeraude	I. Denham-Brown	
G-ASDF	Edwards Gyrocopter ★	B. King	
G-ASDK	A.61 Terrier 2	M. L. Rose	
G-ASDL	A.61 Terrier 2	C. E. Mason	
G-ASDO	Beech 95-A55 Baron ★	No 2498 Sqn ATC/Jersey	
G-ASDY	Wallis WA-116/F	K. H. Wallis	
G-ASEA	Luton LA-4A Minor	C. R. Greenaway	
G-ASEB	Luton LA-4A Minor	S. R. P. Harper	
G-ASEG	A.61 Terrier (VF548)	Beagle Terrier Group	
G-ASEO	PA-24 Comanche 250	Planetalk Ltd	
G-ASEP	PA-23 Apache 235	Arrowstate Ltd/Denham	
G-ASEU	D.62A Condor	W. M. Grant	
G-ASFA	Cessna 172D	D. Halfpenny	
G-ASFD	L-200A Morava	M. Emery/Bournemouth	
G-ASFK	J/5G Autocar	A. I. Milne/Swanton Morley	
G-ASFL	PA-28 Cherokee 180	P. Stoyle	
G-ASFR	Bo 208A1 Junior	S. T. Dauncey	
G-ASFX	D.31 Turbulent	E. F. Clapham & W. B. S. Dobie	
G-ASGC	V.1151 Super VC10 ★	Duxford Aviation Soc	
G-ASHD	Brantly B-2A ★	International Helicopter Museum/ Weston-s-Mare	
G-ASHS	SNCAN Stampe SV-4C	Three Point Flying Ltd	
G-ASHT	D.31 Turbulent	C. W. N. Huke	
G-ASHU	PA-15 Vagabond	G. J. Romanes & T. J. Ventham/ Henstridge	
G-ASHV	PA-23 Aztec 250B	R. J. Ashley & G. O'Gorman	
G-ASHX	PA-28 Cherokee 180	Powertheme Ltd/Barton	
G-ASIB	Cessna F.172D	G-ASIB Flying Group	
G-ASII	PA-28 Cherokee 180	T. R. Hart & Natocars Ltd	
G-ASIJ	PA-28 Cherokee 180	Precision Products Ltd & A. K. Hulme	
G-ASIL	PA-28 Cherokee 180	J. Dickenson & C. D. Powell	
G-ASIT	Cessna 180	A. & P. A. Wood	
G-ASIY	PA-25 Pawnee 235	RAFGSA/Bicester	
G-ASJL	Beech H.35 Bonanza	C. B. Ranald	
G-ASJM	PA-30 Twin Comanche 160 ★	Via Nova Ltd (stored)	
G-ASJO	Beech B.23 Musketeer	S. Boon/Sandown	
G-ASJV	V.S.361 Spitfire IX (MH434)	Nalfire Aviation Ltd/Duxford	
G-ASJY	GY-80 Horizon 160	A. H Wooffindin	
G-ASJZ	Jodel D.117A	P. J. & M. Edwards	
G-ASKC	D.H.98 Mosquito 35 (TA719) ★	Skyfame Collection/Duxford	
G-ASKH	D.H.98 Mosquito T.3 (RR299)	British Aerospace PLC/Chester	
G-ASKJ	A.61 Terrier 1 (VX926)	N. K. & M. D. Freestone	
G-ASKK	HPR-7 Herald 211 ★	Norwich Aviation Museum	
G-ASKL	Jodel 150	J. M. Graty	
G-ASKP	D.H.82A Tiger Moth	Tiger Club (1990) Ltd/Headcorn	
G-ASKS	Cessna 336 Skymaster	N. Foulds	
G-ASKT	PA-28 Cherokee 180	A. Mattacks	
G-ASKV	PA-25 Pawnee 235	Southdown Gliding Club Ltd	
G-ASLH	Cessna 182F	J. M. Powell & J. A. Horton	
G-ASLK	PA-25 Pawnee 235	Bristol Gliding Club (Pty) Ltd/Nympsfield	
G-ASLL	Cessna 336 ★	(stored)/Bournemouth	
G-ASLR	Agusta-Bell 47J-2	N. M. G. Pearson	
G-ASLV	PA-28 Cherokee 235	Sackville Flying Group	
G-ASLX	CP.301A Emeraude	D. Wallace	
G-ASMA	PA-30 Twin Comanche 160 C/R	B. D. Glynn/Redhill	
G-ASME	Bensen B.8M	R. M. Harris & R. T. Bennett	
G-ASMF	Beech D.95A Travel Air	M. J. A. Hornblower	
G-ASMJ	Cessna F.172E	Mike Juliet Group/Audley End	
G-ASML	Luton LA-4A Minor	Fenland Strut Flying Group	
G-ASMM	D.31 Tubulent	G. E. Arthur	
G-ASMO	PA-23 Apache 160G ★	Aviation Enterprises/Fairoaks	
G-ASMS	Cessna 150A	A. K. Jones	
G-ASMT	Fairtravel Linnet 2	A. F. Cashin	
G-ASMV	CP.1310-C3 Super Emeraude	P. F. D. Waltham/Leicester	
G-ASMW	Cessna 150D	Yorkshire Light Aircraft Ltd/Leeds	
G-ASMY	PA-23 Apache 160H	R. D. & E. Forster	
G-ASMZ	A.61 Terrier 2 (VF516)	R. C. Burden	
G-ASNB	Auster 6A (VX118)	M. J. Miller & G. Hengeveld	
G-ASNC	D.5/180 Husky	Peterborough & Spalding Gliding Club/ Boston	
G-ASND	PA-23 Aztec 250	Sky Leisure Aviation Ltd/Shoreham	
G-ASNF	Ercoupe 415CD	C. R. Weldon	

Notes	Reg.	Type	Owner or Operator
	G-ASNH	PA-23 Aztec 250B	J. Hoerner & The Earl of Suffolk & Berkshire
	G-ASNI	CP.1310-C3 Super Emeraude	D. Chapman
	G-ASNK	Cessna 205	Justgold Ltd
	G-ASNN	Cessna 182F ★	(parachute jump trainer)/Tilstock
	G-ASNW	Cessna F.172E	G-ASNW Group
	G-ASOC	Auster 6A	D. J. Moore
	G-ASOH	Beech 95-B55A Baron	GMD Group
	G-ASOI	A.61 Terrier 2	N. K. & C. M. Geddes
	G-ASOK	Cessna F.172E	Okay Flying Group/Denham
	G-ASOM	A.61 Terrier 2	S. J. Tootell (G-JETS)
	G-ASOX	Cessna 205A	Border Parachute Centre/Newcastle
	G-ASPF	Jodel D.120	T. J. Bates
	G-ASPI	Cessna F.172E	Icarus Flying Group/Rochester
	G-ASPK	PA-28 Cherokee 140	Westward Airways (Lands End) Ltd/St Just
	G-ASPP	Bristol Boxkite (replica)	Shuttleworth Collection/O. Warden
	G-ASPS	Piper J-3C-90 Cub	A. J. Chalkley/Blackbushe
	G-ASPU	D.31 Turbulent	C. R. Steer
	G-ASPV	D.H.82A Tiger Moth	B. S. Charters/Shipdham
	G-ASRB	D.62B Condor	T. J. McRae & H. C. Palmer/Shoreham
	G-ASRC	D.62C Condor	O. R. Pluck
	G-ASRF	Jenny Wren	G. W. Gowland (stored)
	G-ASRH	PA-30 Twin Comanche 160	Island Aviation & Travel Ltd
	G-ASRI	PA-23 Aztec 250B ★	Graham Collins Associates Ltd
	G-ASRK	A.109 Airedale ★	R. K. Wilson & M. R. H. Wheatley
	G-ASRO	PA-30 Twin Comanche 160	D. W. Blake
	G-ASRR	Cessna 182G	J. A. Rees
	G-ASRT	Jodel 150	P. Turton
	G-ASRW	PA-28 Cherokee 180	R. J. Keyte
	G-ASSE	PA-22 Colt 108	S. J. Gane
	G-ASSF	Cessna 182G Skylane	B. W. Wells
	G-ASSM	H.S.125 Srs 1/522 ★	Science Museum/S. Kensington
	G-ASSP	PA-30 Twin Comanche 160	P. H. Tavener
	G-ASSS	Cessna 172E	D. H. N. Squires & P. R. March/Bristol
	G-ASST	Cessna 150D	F. R. H. Parker
	G-ASSU	CP.301A Emeraude	R. W. Millward (stored)/Redhill
	G-ASSV	Kensinger KF	C. I. Jefferson
	G-ASSW	PA-28 Cherokee 140	W. G. R. Wunderlich/Biggin Hill
	G-ASTA	D.31 Turbulent	P. A. Cooke
	G-ASTH	Mooney M.20C ★	E. L. Martin (stored)/Guernsey
	G-ASTI	Auster 6A	Islanders Gliding Club Ltd/Jurby
	G-ASTL	Fairey Firefly I (DK431) ★	Skyfame Collection/Duxford
	G-ASTP	Hiller UH-12C ★	International Helicopter Museum/ Weston-s-Mare
	G-ASTV	Cessna 150D (tailwheel) ★	stored
	G-ASUB	Mooney M.20E Super 21	S. C. Coulbeck
	G-ASUD	PA-28 Cherokee 180	S. J. Rogers & M. N. Petchey
	G-ASUE	Cessna 150D	D. Huckle/Panshanger
	G-ASUG	Beech E18S ★	Museum of Flight/E. Fortune
	G-ASUI	A.61 Terrier 2	K. W. Chigwell & D. R. Lee
	G-ASUL	Cessna 182G Skylane	Blackpool & Fylde Aero Club Ltd
	G-ASUP	Cessna F.172E	GASUP Air/Cardiff
	G-ASUR	Dornier Do 28A-1	Sheffair Ltd
	G-ASUS	Jurca MJ.2B Tempete	D. G. Jones/Coventry
	G-ASVG	CP.301B Emeraude	K. R. Jackson
	G-ASVM	Cessna F.172E	GATRL Flying Group
	G-ASVN	Cessna U.206 Super Skywagon	L. Rawson
	G-ASVO	HPR-7 Herald 214	Channel Express (Air Services) Ltd/ Bournemouth
	G-ASVP	PA-25 Pawnee 235	Aquila Gliding Club Ltd
	G-ASVZ	PA-28 Cherokee 140	J. H. Mitchell & A. W. Parker
	G-ASWB	A.109 Airedale	Lawson Engineering
	G-ASWH	Luton LA-5A Major	J. T. Powell-Tuck
	G-ASWJ	Beagle 206 Srs 1 (8449M) ★	Brunel Technical College/Bristol
	G-ASWL	Cessna F.172F	Bagby Aviation Flying Group
	G-ASWN	Bensen B.8M	D. R. Shepherd
	G-ASWP	Beech A.23 Musketeer	J. Holdon & G. Benet
	G-ASWW	PA-30 Twin Comanche 160	R. J. Motors
	G-ASWX	PA-28 Cherokee 180	A. F. Dadds
	G-ASXC	SIPA 901	M. K. Dartford & M. Cookson
	G-ASXD	Brantly B.2B	Lousada PLC
	G-ASXI	Tipsy T.66 Nipper 3	P. F. J. Wells
	G-ASXJ	Luton LA-4A Minor	M. R. Sallows

Reg.	Type	Owner or Operator	Notes
G-ASXR	Cessna 210	A. Schofield	
G-ASXS	Jodel DR.1050	R. A. Hunter	
G-ASXU	Jodel D.120A	T. C. Bayes	
G-ASXX	Avro 683 Lancaster 7 (NX611) ★	Lincolnshire Aviation Heritage Centre/ E. Kirkby	
G-ASXY	Jodel D.117A	P. A. Davies & ptnrs/Cardiff	
G-ASXZ	Cessna 182G Skylane	P. M. Robertson/Perth	
G-ASYD	BAC One-Eleven 475 ★	Brooklands Museum of Aviation/ Weybridge	
G-ASYG	A.61 Terrier 2	G. Rea	
G-ASYJ	Beech D.95A Travel Air	Crosby Aviation (Jersey) Ltd	
G-ASYK	PA-30 Twin Comanche 160	M. S. Harvell	
G-ASYP	Cessna 150E	Henlow Flying Group	
G-ASYW	Bell 47G-2	Bristow Helicopters Ltd	
G-ASYZ	Victa Airtourer 100	N. C. Grayson	
G-ASZB	Cessna 150E	W. A. Smale/Exeter	
G-ASZD	Bo 208A2 Junior	A. J. Watson & ptnrs/O. Warden	
G-ASZE	A.61 Terrier 2	P. J. Moore	
G-ASZJ	S.C.7 Skyvan 3A-100	GEC Marconi Ltd/Luton	
G-ASZR	Fairtravel Linnet 2	Shoreham Linnet Group	
G-ASZS	GY.80 Horizon 160	J. M. B. Duncan	
G-ASZU	Cessna 150E	T. H. Milburn	
G-ASZV	Tipsy T.66 Nipper 2	R. L. Mitcham/Elstree	
G-ASZX	A.61 Terrier 1	C. A. Bailey	
G-ATAF	Cessna F.172F	M. D. Lenney	
G-ATAG	Jodel DR. 1050	T. M. Dawes-Gamble	
G-ATAS	PA-28 Cherokee 180	E. J. Titterrell	
G-ATAT	Cessna 150E	The Derek Pointon Group (stored)	
G-ATAU	D.62B Condor	M. A. Peare/Redhill	
G-ATAV	D.62C Condor	R. W. H. Watson & K. J. Gallagher	
G-ATBG	Nord 1002 (NJ+C11)	L. M. Walton	
G-ATBH	Aero 145	P. D. Aberbach	
G-ATBI	Beech A.23 Musketeer	R. F. G. Dent/Staverton	
G-ATBJ	Sikorsky S-61N	Brintel Helicopters	
G-ATBL	D.H.60G Moth	J. M. Greenland	
G-ATBP	Fournier RF-3	K. McBride	
G-ATBS	D.31 Turbulent	D. R. Keene & J. A. Lear	
G-ATBU	A.61 Terrier 2	P. R. Anderson	
G-ATBW	Tipsy T.66 Nipper 2	Stapleford Nipper Group	
G-ATBX	PA-20 Pacer 135	G. D. & P. M. Thomson	
G-ATBZ	W.S.58 Wessex 60 ★	International Helicopter Museum/ Weston-s-Mare	
G-ATCC	A.109 Airedale	J. R. Bowden	
G-ATCD	D.5/180 Husky	Oxford Flying & Gliding Group/Enstone	
G-ATCE	Cessna U.206	J. Fletcher & D. Hickling/Langar	
G-ATCJ	Luton LA-4A Minor	D. P. Copse	
G-ATCL	Victa Airtourer 100	A. D. Goodall	
G-ATCN	Luton LA-4A Minor	J. C. Gates & C. Neilson	
G-ATCR	Cessna 310 ★	ITD Aviation Ltd/Denham	
G-ATCU	Cessna 337	University of Cambridge	
G-ATCX	Cessna 182H Skylane	K. J. Fisher/Bodmin	
G-ATDA	PA-28 Cherokee 160	S. A. Vale/Basle	
G-ATDB	Nord 1101 Noralpha	J. W. Hardie	
G-ATDN	A.61 Terrier 2 (TW641)	S. J. Saggers/Biggin Hill	
G-ATDO	Bo 208C1 Junior	H. Swift	
G-ATEF	Cessna 150E	Swans Aviation	
G-ATEM	PA-28 Cherokee 180	Chiltern Valley Aviation Ltd	
G-ATEP	EAA Biplane ★	E. L. Martin (stored)/Guernsey	
G-ATES	PA-32 Cherokee Six 260 ★	Parachute jump trainer/Stirling	
G-ATET	PA-30 Twin Comanche 160	R. Marsden & P. E. T. Price	
G-ATEV	Jodel DR. 1050	R. A. Smith	
G-ATEW	PA-30 Twin Comanche 160	Air Northumbria Group/Newcastle	
G-ATEX	Victa Airtourer 100	Medway Victa Group	
G-ATEZ	PA-28 Cherokee 140	J. A. Burton/E. Midlands	
G-ATFD	Jodel DR. 1050	V. Usher	
G-ATFF	PA-23 Aztec 250C	Neatspin Ltd	
G-ATFG	Brantly B.2B ★	Museum of Flight/E. Fortune	
G-ATFK	PA-30 Twin Comanche 160	D. J. Crinnon/White Waltham	
G-ATFM	Sikorsky S-61N	Brintel Helicopters	
G-ATFR	PA-25 Pawnee 150	Borders (Milfield) Gliding Club Ltd	
G-ATFU	D.H.85 Leopard Moth	A. de Cadenet	
G-ATFV	Agusta-Bell 47J-2A ★	Caernarfon Air World	

Notes	Reg.	Type	Owner or Operator
	G-ATFW	Luton LA-4A Minor	C. W. Uldale
	G-ATFY	Cessna F.172G	H. Cowan
	G-ATGE	Jodel DR.1050	J. R. Roberts
	G-ATGH	Brantly B.2B	Helihire Ltd
	G-ATGN	Thorn Coal Gas balloon	British Balloon Museum
	G ATGO	Cessna F.172G	P. J. Spedding & M. Johnston
	G-ATGP	Jodel DR.1050	Madley Flying Group
	G-ATGY	GY.80 Horizon	P. W. Gibberson/Birmingham
	G-ATGZ	Griffiths GH-4 Gyroplane	R. W. J. Cripps
	G-ATHA	PA-23 Apache 235 ★	Brunel Technical College/Bristol
	G-ATHD	D.H.C.1 Chipmunk 22 (WP971)	Spartan Flying Group Ltd/Denham
	G-ATHF	Cessna 150F ★	Lincolnshire Aviation Heritage Centre/ E. Kirkby
	G-ATHK	Aeronca 7AC Champion	N. S. Chittenden
	G-ATHM	Wallis WA-116 Srs 1	Wallis Autogyros Ltd
	G-ATHN	Nord 1101 Noralpha ★	E. L. Martin (stored)/Guernsey
	G-ATHR	PA-28 Cherokee 180	Britannia Airways Ltd/Luton
	G-ATHT	Victa Airtourer 115	D. A. Breeze
	G-ATHU	A.61 Terrier 1	J. A. L. Irwin
	G-ATHV	Cessna 150F	D. Hutchinson
	G-ATHX	Jodel DR. 100A	Mourne Flying Club
	G-ATHZ	Cessna 150F	E. & R. D. Forster
	G-ATIA	PA-24 Comanche 260	L. A. Brown
	G-ATIC	Jodel DR.1050	R. J. Major
	G-ATID	Cessna 337	M. E. Darlington
	G-ATIE	Cessna 150F ★	Parachute jump trainer/Chetwynd
	G-ATIG	HPR-7 Herald 214	BAC Cargo/Stansted
	G-ATIN	Jodel D.117	G. G. Simpson
	G-ATIR	AIA Stampe SV-4C	N. M. Bloom
	G-ATIS	PA-28 Cherokee 160	R. M. Jenner & J. H. Peploe
	G-ATIZ	Jodel D.117	R. Frith & ptnrs
	G-ATJA	Jodel DR.1050	Bicester Flying Group
	G-ATJC	Victa Airtourer 100	Aviation West Ltd
	G-ATJG	PA-28 Cherokee 140	H. M. Wittman
	G-ATJL	PA-24 Comanche 260	M. J. Berry & T. R. Quinn/Blackbushe
	G-ATJM	Fokker Dr.1 (replica) (152/17)	R. Lamplough/Duxford
	G-ATJN	Jodel D.119	R. F. Bradshaw
	G-ATJR	PA-E23 Aztec 250C	S. Lightbown
	G-ATJT	GY.80 Horizon 160	N. Huxtable
	G-ATJV	PA-32 Cherokee Six 260	SMK Engineers Ltd
	G-ATKF	Cessna 150F	B. V. & L. J. Mayo
	G-ATKH	Luton LA-4A Minor	H. E. Jenner
	G-ATKI	Piper J-3C-65 Cub	J. H. Allistone/Booker
	G-ATKT	Cessna F.172G	P. J. Megson
	G-ATKU	Cessna F.172G	Holdcroft Aviation Services Ltd
	G-ATKX	Jodel D.140C	A. J. White & G. A. Piper/Biggin Hill
	G-ATKZ	Tipsy T.66 Nipper 2	M. W. Knights
	G-ATLA	Cessna 182J Skylane	Shefford Transport Engineers Ltd/Luton
	G-ATLB	Jodel DR.1050/M1	La Petite Oiseau Syndicate/Breighton
	G-ATLC	PA-23 Aztec 250C ★	Alderney Air Charter Ltd (stored)
	G-ATLG	Hiller UH-12B	Bristow Helicopters Ltd
	G-ATLM	Cessna F.172G	Air Fotos Aviation Ltd/Newcastle
	G-ATLP	Bensen B.8M	C. D. Julian
	G-ATLT	Cessna U-206A	Army Parachute Association/Netheravon
	G-ATLV	Jodel D.120	L. S. Thorne
	G-ATLW	PA-28 Cherokee 180	R. D. Masters
	G-ATMC	Cessna F.150F	C. J. & E. J. Leigh
	G-ATMG	M.S.893 Rallye Commodore 180	D. R. Wilkinson & T. Coldwell
	G-ATMH	D.5/180 Husky	Dorset Gliding Club Ltd
	G-ATMI	H.S.748 Srs 2A	Emerald Airways Ltd Old Ben/Liverpool
	G-ATMJ	H.S.748 Srs 2A	Emerald Airways Ltd/Liverpool
	G-ATML	Cessna F.150F	B. A. Pickers
	G-ATMM	Cessna F.150F	C. H. Mitchell & P. Bloomfield
	G-ATMT	PA-30 Twin Comanche 160	D. H. T. Bain/Newcastle
	G-ATMU	PA-23 Apache 160G	P. K. Martin & R. W. Harris
	G-ATMW	PA-28 Cherokee 140	Bencray Ltd/Blackpool
	G-ATMX	Cessna F.150F	N. E. Binner
	G-ATMY	Cessna 150F	C. F. Read/Doncaster
	G-ATNB	PA-28 Cherokee 180	R. F. Hill
	G-ATNE	Cessna F.150F	J. & S. Brew
	G-ATNJ	Cessna F.150F ★	Instructional airframe/Perth
	G-ATNK	Cessna F.150F	Pegasus Aviation Ltd
	G-ATNL	Cessna F.150F	G-ATNL Flying Group/Blackbushe

Reg.	Type	Owner or Operator	Notes
G-ATNV	PA-24 Comanche 260	B. S. Reynolds & P. R. Fortescue/Bourn	
G-ATNX	Cessna F.150F	P. Jenkins	
G-ATOA	PA-23 Apache 160G	S. Concadoro	
G-ATOD	Cessna F.150F	E. Watson & ptnrs/St Just	
G-ATOE	Cessna F.150F	Kesîh Flyers Group	
G-ATOF	Cessna F.150F ★	*Instructional airframe*/Perth	
G-ATOG	Cessna F.150F ★	*Instructional airframe*/Perth	
G-ATOH	D.62B Condor	Avon Flying Group	
G-ATOI	PA-28 Cherokee 140	O. & E. Flying Ltd/Stapleford	
G-ATOJ	PA-28 Cherokee 140	A Flight Aviation Ltd	
G-ATOK	PA-28 Cherokee 140	ILC Flying Group	
G-ATOL	PA-28 Cherokee 140	L. J. Nation & G. Alford	
G-ATOM	PA-28 Cherokee 140	A. Flight Aviation Ltd	
G-ATON	PA-28 Cherokee 140	R. G. Walters	
G-ATOO	PA-28 Cherokee 140	I. Wilson	
G-ATOP	PA-28 Cherokee 140	P. R. Coombs/Blackbushe	
G-ATOR	PA-28 Cherokee 140	D. Palmer & V. G. Whitehead	
G-ATOS	PA-28 Cherokee 140	E. Alexander	
G-ATOT	PA-28 Cherokee 180	Totair Flying Group	
G-ATOU	Mooney M.20E Super 21	M20 Flying Group	
G-ATOY	PA-24 Comanche 260 ★	Museum of Flight/E. Fortune	
G-ATOZ	Bensen B.8M	A. H. Brent	
G-ATPD	H.S.125 Srs 1B	Aeromedicare Ltd/Bournemouth	
G-ATPN	PA-28 Cherokee 140	M. F. Hatt & ptnrs/Southend	
G-ATPT	Cessna 182J Skylane	G. B. Scholes	
G-ATPV	JB.01 Minicab	C. F. O'Neill	
G-ATRA	LET L.13 Blanik	Blanik Syndicate/Husbands Bosworth	
G-ATRB	LET L.13 Blanik	Avon Soaring Centre/Bickmarsh	
G-ATRC	Beech B.95A Travel Air	Multi-Air/Biggin Hill	
G-ATRG	PA-18 Super Cub 150	Lasham Gliding Soc Ltd	
G-ATRI	Bo 208C1 Junior	Chertwood Ltd	
G-ATRK	Cessna F.150F	J. Rees & F. Doncaster	
G-ATRL	Cessna F.150F	A. A. W. Stevens	
G-ATRM	Cessna F.150F	Earthline Ltd/Thruxton	
G-ATRO	PA-28 Cherokee 140	390th Flying Group	
G-ATRR	PA-28 Cherokee 140	Marnham Investments Ltd	
G-ATRW	PA-32 Cherokee Six 260	Pringle Brandon Architects	
G-ATRX	PA-32 Cherokee Six 260	J. W. Stow	
G-ATSI	Bo 208C1 Junior	M. R. Reynolds & B. A. Riseborough	
G-ATSL	Cessna F.172G	L. McMullin	
G-ATSM	Cessna 337A	Landscape & Ground Maintenance	
G-ATSR	Beech M.35 Bonanza	Bonanza International Ltd	
G-ATSX	Bo 208C1 Junior	R. J. C. Campbell & M. H. Goley	
G-ATSY	Wassmer WA41 Super Baladou IV	Baladou Flying Group	
G-ATSZ	PA-30 Twin Comanche 160B	P. A. Brook	
G-ATTB	Wallis WA-116-1 (XR944)	D. A. Wallis	
G-ATTD	Cessna 182J Skylane	K. M. Brennan & ptnrs	
G-ATTF	PA-28 Cherokee 140	D. H. Fear	
G-ATTG	PA-28 Cherokee 140	D. E. Spells	
G-ATTI	PA-28 Cherokee 140	Avon Flying Group	
G-ATTK	PA-28 Cherokee 140	G-ATTK Flying Group/Southend	
G-ATTM	Jodel DR.250-160	R. W. Tomkinson	
G-ATTN	Piccard balloon ★	Science Museum/S. Kensington	
G-ATTR	Bo 208C1 Junior	S. Luck	
G-ATTV	PA-28 Cherokee 140	D. B. & M. E. Meeks	
G-ATTX	PA-28 Cherokee 180	IPAC Aviation Ltd	
G-ATTY	PA-32 Cherokee Six 260	F. J. Wadia	
G-ATUB	PA-28 Cherokee 140	R. H. Partington & M. J. Porter	
G-ATUD	PA-28 Cherokee 140	E. J. Clempson	
G-ATUF	Cessna F.150F	D. P. Williams	
G-ATUG	D.62B Condor	HMW Aviation	
G-ATUH	Tipsy T.66 Nipper 1	D. G. Spruce	
G-ATUI	Bo 208C1 Junior	A. W. Wakefield	
G-ATUL	PA-28 Cherokee 180	H. M. Synge	
G-ATVF	D.H.C.1 Chipmunk 22 (Lycoming)	RAFGSA/Dishforth	
G-ATVK	PA-28 Cherokee 140	JRB Aviation Ltd/Southend	
G-ATVL	PA-28 Cherokee 140	White Waltham Airfield Ltd	
G-ATVO	PA-28 Cherokee 140	L. A. Mills	
G-ATVP	F.B.5 Gunbus (2345) ★	RAF Museum/Hendon	
G-ATVS	PA-28 Cherokee 180	Markel Aviation	
G-ATVW	D.62B Condor	J. P. Coulter & J. Chidley/Panshanger	
G-ATVX	Bo 208C1 Junior	G. & G. E. F. Warren	
G-ATWA	Jodel DR.1050	Jodel Syndicate	

Notes	Reg.	Type	Owner or Operator
	G-ATWB	Jodel D.117	Andrewsfield Whiskey Bravo Group
	G-ATWE	M.S.892A Rallye Commodore	D. I. Murray
	G-ATWJ	Cessna F.172F	C. J. & J. Freeman/Headcorn
	G-ATWR	PA-30 Twin Comanche 160B	Lubair (Transport Services) Ltd/ E. Midlands
	G-ATXA	PA-22 Tri-Pacer 150	R. C. Teverson
	G-ATXD	PA-30 Twin Comanche 160B	Jet Heritage Ltd/Bournemouth
	G-ATXF	GY-80 Horizon 150	D. C. Hyde
	G-ATXJ	H.P.137 Jetstream 300 ★	Museum of Flight/E. Fortune
	G-ATXM	PA-28 Cherokee 180	D. J. Bates
	G-ATXN	Mitchell-Proctor Kittiwake 1	P. A. Dawson
	G-ATXO	SIPA 903	S. A. & D. C. Whitehead
	G-ATXZ	Bo 208C1 Junior	Bradbury & Ptnrs
	G-ATYM	Cessna F.150G	J. F. Perry & Co
	G-ATYN	Cessna F.150G	J. S. Grant
	G-ATYS	PA-28 Cherokee 180	W. J. Waite
	G-ATZA	Bo 208C1 Junior	C. M. Barnes/Popham
	G-ATZG	AFB2 gas balloon	Flt Lt S. Cameron
	G-ATZK	PA-28 Cherokee 180	Austen Associates Partnership
	G-ATZM	Piper J-3C-90 Cub	R. W. Davison
	G-ATZS	Wassmer WA41 Super Baladou IV	G. R. Outwin & D. P. Bennett
	G-ATZY	Cessna F.150G	J. Easson/Edinburgh
	G-AVAA	Cessna F.150G	L. J. Cook
	G-AVAK	M.S.893A Rallye Commodore 180	W. K. Anderson (stored)/Perth
	G-AVAR	Cessna F.150G	J. A. Rees & F. Doncaster
	G-AVAU	PA-30 Twin Comanche 160B	L. Batin/Fairoaks
	G-AVAW	D.62B Condor	Condor Aircraft Group
	G-AVAX	PA-28 Cherokee 180	J. J. Parkes
	G-AVBG	PA-28 Cherokee 180	G-AVBG Flying Group/White Waltham
	G-AVBH	PA-28 Cherokee 180	T. R. Smith (Agricultural Machinery) Ltd
	G-AVBP	PA-28 Cherokee 140	W. B. Ware
	G-AVBS	PA-28 Cherokee 180	Camborne Insurance Brokers Ltd
	G-AVBT	PA-28 Cherokee 180	J. F. Mitchell
	G-AVBZ	Cessna F.172H	M. Byl
	G-AVCE	Cessna F.172H	Aardvark Aviation Ltd
	G-AVCM	PA-24 Comanche 260	F. Smith & Sons Ltd/Stapleford
	G-AVCT	Cessna F.150G	M. L. Biggs/Shobdon
	G-AVCU	Cessna F.150G	M. Hussain
	G-AVCV	Cessna 182J Skylane	University of Manchester Institute of Science & Technology/Woodford
	G-AVCX	PA-30 Twin Comanche 160B	T. Barge
	G-AVDA	Cessna 182K Skylane	F. W. Ellis & M. C. Burnett
	G-AVDF	Beagle Pup 100 ★	Beagle Owners Club
	G-AVDG	Wallis WA-116 Srs 1	K. H. Wallis
	G-AVDT	Aeronca 7AC Champion	D. Cheney & J. G. Woods
	G-AVDV	PA-22 Tri-Pacer 150 (tailwheel)	S. C. Brooks/Slinfold
	G-AVDW	D.62B Condor	Druine Condor G-AVDW Group
	G-AVDY	Luton LA-4A Minor	P. J. Manifold & M. J. Nairn
	G-AVEB	Morane MS 230 (157)	T. M. Leaver/Booker
	G-AVEC	Cessna F.172H	W. H. Ekin (Engineering) Co Ltd
	G-AVEF	Jodel 150	Tiger Club (1990) Ltd/Headcorn
	G-AVEH	SIAI-Marchetti S.205	Bob Crowe Aircraft Sales Ltd
	G-AVEM	Cessna F.150G	G-AVEM Flying Group
	G-AVEN	Cessna F.150G	N. J. Budd/Aberdeen
	G-AVER	Cessna F.150G	E. Atherton
	G-AVEU	Wassmer WA.41 Baladou IV	G. J. Richardson
	G-AVEX	D.62B Condor	R. Marsden/Bicester
	G-AVEY	Currie Super Wot	A. Eastelow/Dunkeswell
	G-AVEZ	HPR-7 Herald 210 ★	Rescue Trainer/Norwich
	G-AVFB	H.S.121 Trident 2E ★	Duxford Aviation Soc
	G-AVFE	H.S.121 Trident 2E ★	Belfast Airport Authority
	G-AVFG	H.S.121 Trident 2E ★	Ground handling trainer/Heathrow
	G-AVFH	H.S.121 Trident 2E ★	Mosquito Aircraft Museum (fuselage only)
	G-AVFK	H.S.121 Trident 2E ★	Metropolitan Police Training Centre/ Hounslow
	G-AVFM	H.S.121 Trident 2E ★	Brunel Technical College/Bristol
	G-AVFP	PA-28 Cherokee 140	R. L. Howells/Barton
	G-AVFR	PA-28 Cherokee 140	VFR Flying Group/Newtownards
	G-AVFS	PA-32 Cherokee Six 300	A. S. Janes
	G-AVFU	PA-32 Cherokee Six 300	Ashley Gardner Flying Club Ltd
	G-AVFX	PA-28 Cherokee 140	Wessex Flyers Group/Thruxton
	G-AVFZ	PA-28 Cherokee 140	G-AVFZ Flying Group

Reg.	Type	Owner or Operator	Notes
G-AVGA	PA-24 Comanche 260	Conram Aviation/Biggin Hill	
G-AVGC	PA-28 Cherokee 140	P. A. Hill	
G-AVGD	PA-28 Cherokee 140	S. & G. W. Jacobs	
G-AVGE	PA-28 Cherokee 140	H. H. T. Wolf	
G-AVGI	PA-28 Cherokee 140	D. G. Smith & C. D. Barden	
G-AVGK	PA-28 Cherokee 180	Golf Kilo Flying Group	
G-AVGP	BAC One-Eleven 408EF	Maersk Air Ltd/British Airways/Birmingham	
G-AVGY	Cessna 182K Skylane	R. M. C. Sears & R. N. Howgego	
G-AVGZ	Jodel DR.1050	D. C. Webb	
G-AVHH	Cessna F.172H	M. J. Mann & J. Hickinbotom	
G-AVHL	Jodel DR.105A	Jodel G-AVHL Flying Group	
G-AVHM	Cessna F.150G	A. G. Wintle & J. Knight/Elstree	
G-AVHT	Auster AOP.9 (WZ711)	M. Somerton-Rayner/Middle Wallop	
G-AVHY	Fournier RF.4D	J. Connelly	
G-AVIA	Cessna F.150G	Cheshire Air Training Services Ltd/Liverpool	
G-AVIB	Cessna F.150G	S. R. Smith & P. Hemingway	
G-AVIC	Cessna F.172H	Pembrokeshire Air Ltd/Haverfordwest	
G-AVID	Cessna 182J	J. Rolston	
G-AVII	AB-206A JetRanger	Bristow Helicopters Ltd	
G-AVIL	Alon A.2 Aircoupe (VX147)	M. J. Close	
G-AVIN	M.S.880B Rallye Club	W. Fairney	
G-AVIP	Brantly B.2B	P. J. Troy-Davies	
G-AVIS	Cessna F.172H	R. T. Jones/Rochester	
G-AVIT	Cessna F.150G	Shropshire Aero Club Ltd/Sleap	
G-AVIZ	Scheibe SF.25A Motorfalke	D. C. Pattison & D. A. Wilson	
G-AVJE	Cessna F.150G	G-AVJE Syndicate	
G-AVJF	Cessna F.172H	J. A. & G. M. Rees	
G-AVJG	Cessna 337B	Alderney Air Charter	
G-AVJI	Cessna F.172H	G-AVJI Group	
G-AVJJ	PA-30 Twin Comanche 160B	A. H. Manser	
G-AVJK	Jodel DR.1050/M1	G. Wylde	
G-AVJO	Fokker E.III (replica) (422-15)	Bianchi Aviation Film Services Ltd/Booker	
G-AVJV	Wallis WA-117 Srs 1	K. H. Wallis (G-ATCV)	
G-AVJW	Wallis WA-118 Srs 2	K. H. Wallis (G-ATPW)	
G-AVKB	MB.50 Pipistrelle	B. H. Pickard	
G-AVKD	Fournier RF-4D	Lasham RF4 Group	
G-AVKE	Gadfly HDW.1 ★	International Helicopter Museum/Weston-s-Mare	
G-AVKG	Cessna F.172H	P. E P. Sheppard	
G-AVKI	Slingsby T.66 Nipper 3	J. Fisher	
G-AVKJ	Slingsby T.66 Nipper 3	L. B. Clark	
G-AVKK	Slingsby T.66 Nipper 3	C. Watson	
G-AVKL	PA-30 Twin Comanche 160B	Channel Islands Travel Service Ltd	
G-AVKN	Cessna 401	Law Leasing Ltd	
G-AVKP	A.109 Airedale	D. R. Williams	
G-AVKR	Bo 208C1 Junior	C. W. Grant	
G-AVLB	PA-28 Cherokee 140	M. Wilson	
G-AVLC	PA-28 Cherokee 140	G. E. & A. Murray	
G-AVLD	PA-28 Cherokee 140	WLS Flying Group/Blackbushe	
G-AVLE	PA-28 Cherokee 140	Video Security Services/Tollerton	
G-AVLF	PA-28 Cherokee 140	G. H. Hughesdon	
G-AVLG	PA-28 Cherokee 140	R. Friedlander & D. C. Raymond	
G-AVLH	PA-28 Cherokee 140	Menai Flying Group/Caernarfon	
G-AVLI	PA-28 Cherokee 140	J. V. White	
G-AVLJ	PA-28 Cherokee 140	Demeter Aviation Ltd	
G-AVLN	B.121 Pup 2	C. A. Thorpe	
G-AVLO	Bo 208C1 Junior	P. J. Swain	
G-AVLR	PA-28 Cherokee 140	Group 140/Panshanger	
G-AVLT	PA-28 Cherokee 140	R. W. Harris & ptnrs/Southend	
G-AVLU	PA-28 Cherokee 140	London Transport Flying Club Ltd/Fairoaks	
G-AVLW	Fournier RF-4D	N. M. Groome	
G-AVLY	Jodel D.120A	N. V. de Candole	
G-AVMA	GY-80 Horizon 180	B. R. Hildick	
G-AVMB	D.62B Condor	J. C. Mansell	
G-AVMD	Cessna 150G	Bagby Aviation Flying Group	
G-AVMF	Cessna F. 150G	J. F. Marsh	
G-AVMH	BAC One-Eleven 510ED	Air Belfast Ltd	
G-AVMI	BAC One-Eleven 510ED	European Aircharter Ltd	
G-AVMJ	BAC One-Eleven 510ED ★	European Aviation Ltd (Cabin trainer)	
G-AVMK	BAC One-Eleven 510ED	European Aircharter Ltd	
G-AVML	BAC One-Eleven 510ED	European Aviation Ltd	

Notes	Reg.	Type	Owner or Operator
	G-AVMM	BAC One-Eleven 510ED	European Aviation Ltd
	G-AVMN	BAC One-Eleven 510ED	Air Belfast Ltd
	G-AVMO	BAC One-Eleven 510ED ★	Aerospace Museum/Cosford
	G-AVMP	BAC One-Eleven 510ED	European Aircharter Ltd
	G-AVMR	BAC One-Eleven 510ED	European Aviation Ltd
	G-AVMS	BAC One-Eleven 510ED	European Aviation Ltd
	G-AVMT	BAC One-Eleven 510ED	Air Bristol/AB Shannon
	G-AVMU	BAC One-Eleven 510ED ★	Duxford Aviation Soc
	G-AVMV	BAC One-Eleven 510ED	European Aviation Ltd
	G-AVMW	BAC One-Eleven 510ED	Air Bristol/Filton
	G-AVMX	BAC One-Eleven 510ED	European Aviation Ltd
	G-AVMY	BAC One-Eleven 510ED	European Aviation Ltd
	G-AVMZ	BAC One-Eleven 510ED	European Aviation Ltd
	G-AVNC	Cessna F.150G	J. Turner
	G-AVNE	W.S.58 Wessex Mk 60 Srs 1 ★	International Helicopter Museum/ Weston-s-Mare
	G-AVNN	PA-28 Cherokee 180	B. Andrews & C. S. Mitchell
	G-AVNO	PA-28 Cherokee 180	Allister Flight Ltd/Stapleford
	G-AVNP	PA-28 Cherokee 180	R. W. Harris & ptnrs
	G-AVNR	PA-28 Cherokee 180	R. R. Livingstone
	G-AVNS	PA-28 Cherokee 180	D. D. Delaney/Earls Colne
	G-AVNU	PA-28 Cherokee 180	O. Durrani
	G-AVNW	PA-28 Cherokee 180	Len Smith's School & Sports Ltd
	G-AVNX	Fournier RF-4D	W. G. Woollard
	G-AVNZ	Fournier RF-4D	V. S. E. Norman
	G-AVOA	Jodel DR.1050	D. A. Willies/Cranwell
	G-AVOH	D.62B Condor	Rankhart Ltd
	G-AVOM	Jodel DR.221	M. A. Mountford/Headcorn
	G-AVOO	PA-18 Super Cub 150	London Gliding Club Ltd/ Dunstable
	G-AVOZ	PA-28 Cherokee 180	J. R. Winning/Booker
	G-AVPC	D.31 Turbulent	S. A. Sharp
	G-AVPD	D.9 Bebe	S. W. McKay *(stored)*
	G-AVPH	Cessna F.150G	W. Lancashire Aero Club/Woodvale
	G-AVPI	Cessna F.172H	R. W. Cope
	G-AVPJ	D.H.82A Tiger Moth	C. C. Silk
	G-AVPK	M.S.892A Rallye Commodore	B. A. Bridgewater/Halfpenny Green
	G-AVPM	Jodel D.117	J. C. Haynes
	G-AVPN	HPR-7 Herald 213	Channel Express (Air Services) Ltd/ Bournemouth
	G-AVPO	Hindustan HAL-26 Pushpak	J. A. Rimell
	G-AVPR	PA-30 Twin Comanche 160B	J. O. Coundley
	G-AVPS	PA-30 Twin Comanche 160B	J. M. Bisco/Staverton
	G-AVPT	PA-18 Super Cub 150	Tiger Club (1990) Ltd/Headcorn
	G-AVPV	PA-28 Cherokee 180	S. Moore
	G-AVRK	PA-28 Cherokee 180	J. Gama
	G-AVRP	PA-28 Cherokee 140	T. Hiscox
	G-AVRS	GY-80 Horizon 180	Air Venturas Ltd
	G-AVRT	PA-28 Cherokee 140	Star Aviation Trust Group/Stapleford
	G-AVRU	PA-28 Cherokee 180	G-AVRU Partnership/Clacton
	G-AVRW	GY-20 Minicab	Kestrel Flying Group/Tollerton
	G-AVRY	PA-28 Cherokee 180	Brigfast Ltd/Blackbushe
	G-AVRZ	PA-28 Cherokee 180	Mantavia Group Ltd
	G-AVSA	PA-28 Cherokee 180	G-AVSA Flying Group
	G-AVSB	PA-28 Cherokee 180	T. H. Lloyd
	G-AVSC	PA-28 Cherokee 180	Medidata Ltd
	G-AVSD	PA-28 Cherokee 180	Landmate Ltd
	G-AVSE	PA-28 Cherokee 180	Yorkshire Aeroplane Club Ltd/Leeds
	G-AVSF	PA-28 Cherokee 180	Monday Club/Blackbushe
	G-AVSI	PA-28 Cherokee 140	CR Aviation Ltd
	G-AVSP	PA-28 Cherokee 180	Devon School of Flying/Dunkeswell
	G-AVSR	D.5/180 Husky	A. L. Young
	G-AVSZ	AB-206B JetRanger	Ivory Burt & Co Ltd
	G-AVTJ	PA-32 Cherokee Six 260	L. P. Marsh/Sandown
	G-AVTK	PA-32 Cherokee Six 260	Aeroclub Montagnana SNC/Italy
	G-AVTP	Cessna F.172H	Tango Papa Group
	G-AVTT	Ercoupe 415D	Wright's Farm Eggs Ltd/Andrewsfield
	G-AVTV	M.S.893A Rallye Commodore	D. B. & M. E. Meeks
	G-AVUD	PA-30 Twin Comanche 160B	F. M. Aviation/Biggin Hill
	G-AVUG	Cessna F.150H	Skyways Flying Group
	G-AVUH	Cessna F.150H	C. M. Chinn
	G-AVUS	PA-28 Cherokee 140	Arrow Air Centre Ltd/Shipdham
	G-AVUT	PA-28 Cherokee 140	Bencray Ltd/Blackpool
	G-AVUU	PA-28 Cherokee 140	A. Jahanfar & ptnrs/Southend

Reg.	Type	Owner or Operator	Notes
G-AVUZ	PA-32 Cherokee Six 300	Ceesix Ltd/Jersey	
G-AVVC	Cessna F.172H	J. S. M. Cattle	
G-AVVE	Cessna F.150H ★	R. Windley (stored)	
G-AVVF	D.H.104 Dove ★	Airport Fire Service/Staverton	
G-AVVI	PA-30 Twin Comanche 160B	H. E. Boulter & D. G. Bligh	
G-AVVJ	M.S.893A Rallye Commodore	C. R. & S. A. Hardiman/Shobdon	
G-AVVL	Cessna F.150H	N. E. Sams/Cranfield	
G-AVVO	Avro 652A Anson 19 (VL348) ★	Newark Air Museum	
G-AVVX	Cessna F.150H	Franklyns Flying Group	
G-AVWA	PA-28 Cherokee 140	M. Jarrett	
G-AVWD	PA-28 Cherokee 140	M. P. Briggs	
G-AVWI	PA-28 Cherokee 140	L. M. Veitch	
G-AVWJ	PA-28 Cherokee 140	M. J. Steer/Biggin Hill	
G-AVWL	PA-28 Cherokee 140	P. J. Pratt/Dunkeswell	
G-AVWM	PA-28 Cherokee 140	P. E. Preston & ptnrs/Southend	
G-AVWN	PA-28R Cherokee Arrow 180	Vawn Air Ltd/Jersey	
G-AVWO	PA-28R Cherokee Arrow 180	W. R. Drury	
G-AVWR	PA-28R Cherokee Arrow 180	S. J. French & ptnrs/Exeter	
G-AVWT	PA-28R Cherokee Arrow 180	Cloud Base Aviation Group	
G-AVWU	PA-28R Cherokee Arrow 180	Arrow Flyers Ltd	
G-AVWV	PA-28R Cherokee Arrow 180	Strathtay Flying Group	
G-AVWY	Fournier RF-4D	B. Houghton	
G-AVXA	PA-25 Pawnee 235	S. Wales Gliding Club Ltd	
G-AVXC	Slingsby T.66 Nipper 3	D. S. T. Eggleton	
G-AVXD	Slingsby T.66 Nipper 3	D. A. Davidson	
G-AVXF	PA-28R Cherokee Arrow 180	JDR Arrow Group	
G-AVXI	H.S.748 Srs 2A	Civil Aviation Authority/Teesside	
G-AVXJ	H.S.748 Srs 2A	Civil Aviation Authority/Teesside	
G-AVXW	D.62B Condor	A. J. Cooper/Rochester	
G-AVXY	Auster AOP.9 (XK417)	Auster Nine Group	
G-AVXZ	PA-28 Cherokee 140 ★	ATC Hayle (instructional airframe)	
G-AVYB	H.S.121 Trident 1E-140 ★	SAS training airframe/Hereford	
G-AVYE	H.S.121 Trident 1E-140 ★	–	
G-AVYK	A.61 Terrier 3	A. R. Wright/Booker	
G-AVYL	PA-28 Cherokee 180	Cherokee G-AVYL Flying Group	
G-AVYM	PA-28 Cherokee 180	Carlisle Aviation (1985) Ltd/Crosby	
G-AVYP	PA-28 Cherokee 140	T. D. Reid (Braids) Ltd/Newtownards	
G-AVYR	PA-28 Cherokee 140	D.R. Flying Club Ltd/Staverton	
G-AVYS	PA-28R Cherokee Arrow 180	D. H. Saunders/Ipswich	
G-AVYT	PA-28R Cherokee Arrow 180	E. J. Booth & B. D. Tipler	
G-AVYV	Jodel D.120	A. J. Sephton	
G-AVZB	Aero Z-37 Cmelak ★	Science Museum/Wroughton	
G-AVZI	Bo 208C1 Junior	C. F. Rogers	
G-AVZM	D.121 Pup 1	ARAZ Group/Elstree	
G-AVZN	B.121 Pup 1	E. M. Lewis & C. A. Homewood	
G-AVZO	B.121 Pup 1 ★	Thamesside Aviation Museum/E. Tilbury	
G-AVZP	B.121 Pup 1	T. A. White	
G-AVZR	PA-28 Cherokee 180	Lincoln Aero Club Ltd/Sturgate	
G-AVZU	Cessna F.150H	R. D. & E. Forster/Swanton Morley	
G-AVZV	Cessna F.172H	E. M. & D. S. Lightbown	
G-AVZW	EAA Biplane Model P	R. G. Maidment & G. R. Edmundson/ Goodwood	
G-AVZX	M.S.880B Rallye Club	A. F. K. Horne	
G-AWAA	M.S.880B Rallye Club	P. A. Cairns/Dunkeswell	
G-AWAC	GY-80 Horizon 180	Gardan Party Ltd	
G-AWAH	Beech 95-D55 Baron	B. J. S. Grey	
G-AWAJ	Beech 95-D55 Baron	Standard Hose Ltd/Leeds	
G-AWAT	D.62B Condor	Tarwood Ltd/Redhill	
G-AWAU	Vickers F.B.27A Vimy (replica) (F8614) ★	Bomber Command Museum/Hendon	
G-AWAW	Cessna F.150F ★	Science Museum/S. Kensington	
G-AWAX	Cessna 150D	H. H. Cousins	
G-AWAZ	PA-28R Cherokee Arrow 180	R. Staniszewski & R. Nevitt	
G-AWBA	PA-28R Cherokee Arrow 180	March Flying Group/Stapleford	
G-AWBB	PA-28R Cherokee Arrow 180	M. D. Parker & J. Lowe	
G-AWBC	PA-28R Cherokee Arrow 180	Anglo Aviation (UK) Ltd	
G-AWBE	PA-28 Cherokee 140	B. E. Boyle	
G-AWBH	PA-28 Cherokee 140	R. C. A. Mackworth	
G-AWBJ	Fournier RF-4D	J. M. Adams	
G-AWBL	BAC One-Eleven 416EK	Maersk Air Ltd/British Airways/Birmingham	
G-AWBM	D.31 Turbulent	A. D. Pratt	
G-AWBN	PA-30 Twin Comanche 160B	Stourfield Investments Ltd/Jersey	

Notes	Reg.	Type	Owner or Operator
	G-AWBS	PA-28 Cherokee 140	M. A. English & T. M. Brown
	G-AWBT	PA-30 Twin Comanche 160B ★	*Instructional airframe*/Cranfield
	G-AWBU	Morane-Saulnier N (replica) (MS.824)	Personal Plane Services Ltd/ Booker
	G-AWBV	Cessna 182L Skylane	Tindon Ltd
	G-AWBW	Cessna F.172H ★	Brunel Technical College/Bristol
	G-AWBX	Cessna F.150H	M. Gardner
	G-AWCM	Cessna F.150H	Bobbington Air Training School Ltd
	G-AWCN	Cessna FR.172E	Cubair Ltd/Redhill
	G-AWCP	Cessna F.150H (tailwheel)	C. E. Mason/Shobdon
	G-AWDA	Slingsby T.66 Nipper 3	J. A. Cheesebrough
	G-AWDD	Slingsby T.66 Nipper 3	P. F. J. Wells
	G-AWDI	PA-23 Aztec 250C	*(stored)*
	G-AWDO	D.31 Turbulent	R. N. Crosland
	G-AWDP	PA-28 Cherokee 180	B. H. & P. M. Illston/Shipdham
	G-AWDR	Cessna FR.172E	B. A. Wallace
	G-AWDU	Brantly B.2B	G. E. J. Redwood
	G-AWEF	SNCAN Stampe SV-4B	Tiger Club (1990) Ltd/Headcorn
	G-AWEI	D.62B Condor	M. J. Steer
	G-AWEL	Fournier RF-4D	A. B. Clymo/Halfpenny Green
	G-AWEM	Fournier RF-4D	B. J. Griffin/Wickenby
	G-AWEP	Ord-Hume JB-01 Minicab	J. A. Stewart & S. N. Askey
	G-AWER	PA-23 Aztec 250C	H. McC. Clarke/Ronaldsway
	G-AWET	PA-28 Cherokee 180D	Broadland Flying Group Ltd/ Shipdham
	G-AWEV	PA-28 Cherokee 140	Norflight Ltd
	G-AWEX	PA-28 Cherokee 140	R. Badham
	G-AWEZ	PA-28R Cherokee Arrow 180	T. R. Leighton & ptnrs
	G-AWFB	PA-28R Cherokee Arrow 180	Luke Aviation Ltd/Bristol
	G-AWFC	PA-28R Cherokee Arrow 180	K. A. Goodchild/Southend
	G-AWFD	PA-28R Cherokee Arrow 180	D. J. Hill
	G-AWFF	Cessna F.150H	Shobdon Aircraft Maintenance
	G-AWFJ	PA-28R Cherokee Arrow 180	Parplon Ltd
	G-AWFK	PA-28R Cherokee Arrow 180	Steepletone Products Ltd
	G-AWFN	D.62B Condor	R. James
	G-AWFO	D.62B Condor	T. A. Major
	G-AWFP	D.62B Condor	Blackbushe Flying Club
	G-AWFR	D.31 Turbulent	J. R. Froud
	G-AWFT	Jodel D.9 Bebe	W. H. Cole
	G-AWFW	Jodel D.117	F. H. Greenwell
	G-AWFZ	Beech A23 Musketeer	R. Sweet & B. D. Corbett
	G-AWGA	A.109 Airedale ★	*stored*/Sevenoaks
	G-AWGD	Cessna F.172H	D. Whitton & P. Storey
	G-AWGJ	Cessna F.172H	J. & C. J. Freeman/Headcorn
	G-AWGK	Cessna F.150H	L. A. Groves
	G-AWGM	Arkle Kittiwake 2	M. K. Field
	G-AWGN	Fournier RF-4D	R. H. Ashforth/Staverton
	G-AWGR	Cessna F.172H	P. A. Hallam
	G-AWGZ	Taylor JT.1 Monoplane	R. L. Sambell
	G-AWHB	C.A.S.A. 2-111D (6J+PR) ★	Aces High Ltd/North Weald
	G-AWHX	Rollason Beta B.2	S. G. Jones
	G-AWHY	Falconar F.11-3	J. R. Riley-Gale (G-BDPB)
	G-AWIF	Brookland Mosquito 2	—/Husbands Bosworth
	G-AWII	V.S.349 Spitfire VC (AR501)	Shuttleworth Collection/O. Warden
	G-AWIP	Luton LA-4A Minor	J. Houghton
	G-AWIR	Midget Mustang	K. E. Sword/Leicester
	G-AWIT	PA-28 Cherokee 180	Manco Softwares Ltd
	G-AWIV	Airmark TSR.3	D. J. & F. M. Nunn
	G-AWIW	SNCAN Stampe SV-4B	R. E. Mitchell
	G-AWIY	PA-23 Aztec 250C	Keen Leasing Ltd/Ronaldsway
	G-AWJE	Slingsby T.66 Nipper 3	T. Mosedale
	G-AWJV	D.H.98 Mosquito TT Mk 35 (TA634) ★	Mosquito Aircraft Museum
	G-AWJX	Zlin Z.526 Trener Master	Aerobatics International Ltd
	G-AWJY	Zlin Z.526 Trener Master	M. Gainza
	G-AWKB	M.J.5 Sirocco F2/39	G. D. Claxton
	G-AWKD	PA-17 Vagabond	A. T. & M. R. Dowie/ White Waltham
	G-AWKM	B.121 Pup 1	D. M. G. Jenkins/Swansea
	G-AWKO	B.121 Pup 1	Bustard Flying Club Ltd
	G-AWKP	Jodel DR.253	G-AWKP Group
	G-AWKT	M.S.880B Rallye Club	J. Strain/Portadown
	G-AWKX	Beech A65 Queen Air ★	*(Instructional airframe)*/Shoreham
	G-AWLA	Cessna F.150H	J. A. Clegg
	G-AWLE	Cessna F.172H	H. Mendelssohn & H. I. Shott

Reg.	Type	Owner or Operator	Notes
G-AWLF	Cessna F.172H	Gannet Aviation Ltd/Belfast	
G-AWLG	SIPA 903	S. W. Markham	
G-AWLI	PA-22 Tri-Pacer 150	J. S. Lewery/Shoreham	
G-AWLO	Boeing Stearman E.75	N. D. Pickard/Shoreham	
G-AWLP	Mooney M.20F	I. C. Lomax	
G-AWLR	Slingsby T.66 Nipper 3	C. F. O'Neill	
G-AWLS	Slingsby T.66 Nipper 3	G. A. Dunster & B. Gallagher	
G-AWLZ	Fournier RF-4D	Nympsfield RF-4 Group	
G-AWMD	Jodel D.11	G. E. Valler	
G-AWME	PA-18 Super Cub 150 (modified)	Booker Gliding Club Ltd	
G-AWMI	Glos-Airtourer 115	W. G. Jones	
G-AWMK	AB-206B JetRanger	Bristow Helicopters Ltd	
G-AWMM	M.S.893A Rallye Commodore 180	D. P. & S. White	
G-AWMN	Luton LA-4A Minor	C. F. O'Neill	
G-AWMP	Cessna F.172H	R. J. D. Blois	
G-AWMR	D.31 Turbulent	T. Pearce	
G-AWMT	Cessna F.150H	Oilfield Expertise Ltd/Tilstock	
G-AWMZ	Cessna F.172H ★	*Parachute jump trainer*/Cark	
G-AWNA	Boeing 747-136	British Airways *Colliford Lake*	
G-AWNB	Boeing 747-136	British Airways *Llangorse Lake*	
G-AWNC	Boeing 747-136	British Airways *Lake Windermere*	
G-AWNE	Boeing 747-136	British Airways *Derwent Water*	
G-AWNF	Boeing 747-136	British Airways *Blagdon Lake*	
G-AWNG	Boeing 747-136	British Airways *Rutland Water*	
G-AWNH	Boeing 747-136	British Airways *Devoke Water*	
G-AWNJ	Boeing 747-136	British Airways *Bassenthwaite Lake*	
G-AWNL	Boeing 747-136	British Airways *Ennerdale Water*	
G-AWNM	Boeing 747-136	British Airways *Ullswater*	
G-AWNN	Boeing 747-136	British Airways *Loweswater*	
G-AWNO	Boeing 747-136	British Airways *Grafham Water*	
G-AWNP	Boeing 747-136	British Airways *Hanningfield Water*	
G-AWNT	BN-2A Islander	Aerofilms Ltd/Elstree	
G-AWOA	M.S.880B Rallye Club	Oscar Alpha Group/Barton	
G-AWOE	Aero Commander 680E	J. M. Houlder/Elstree	
G-AWOF	PA-15 Vagabond	C. M. Hicks	
G-AWOH	PA-17 Vagabond	The High Flatts Flying Group	
G-AWOT	Cessna F.150H	J. M. Montgomerie & J. Ferguson	
G-AWOU	Cessna 170B	S. Billington/Denham	
G-AWOX	W.S.58 Wessex 60 ★	International Helicopter Museum/ Weston-s-Mare	
G-AWPH	P.56 Provost T.1	J. A. D. Bradshaw	
G-AWPJ	Cessna F.150H	W. J. Greenfield	
G-AWPN	Shield Xyla	M. J. Herlihy	
G-AWPP	Cessna F.150H	Croxley Flying Group/Denham	
G-AWPS	PA-28 Cherokee 140	D. J. Hewitt/Halfpenny Green	
G-AWPU	Cessna F.150J	LAC (Enterprises) Ltd/Barton	
G-AWPW	PA-12 Super Cruiser	AK Leasing (Jersey) Ltd	
G-AWPY	Bensen B.8M	J. Jordan	
G-AWPZ	Andreasson BA-4B	J. M. Vening	
G-AWRK	Cessna F.150J	Systemroute Ltd/Shoreham	
G-AWRP	Cierva Rotorcraft ★	International Helicopter Museum/ Weston-s-Mare	
G-AWRS	Avro 19 Srs. 2 ★	N. E. Aircraft Museum/Usworth	
G-AWRY	P.56 Provost T.1 (XF836)	Slymar Aviation & Services Ltd	
G-AWSA	Avro 652A Anson 19 (VL349) ★	Norfolk & Suffolk Aviation Museum	
G-AWSL	PA-28 Cherokee 180D	Fascia Services Ltd/Southend	
G-AWSM	PA-28 Cherokee 235	S. J. Green	
G-AWSN	D.62B Condor	J. Leader	
G-AWSP	D.62B Condor	R. Q. & A. S. Bond/Wellesbourne	
G-AWSS	D.62A Condor	G. Bruce/Fordoun	
G-AWST	D.62B Condor	P. L. Clements	
G-AWSV	Skeeter 12 (XM553)	Maj. M. Somerton-Rayner/Middle Wallop	
G-AWSW	D.5/180 Husky (XW635)	Windmill Aviation/Spanhoe	
G-AWTA	Cessna E.310N	Heliscott Ltd	
G-AWTJ	Cessna F.150J	D. G. Williams	
G-AWTL	PA-28 Cherokee 180D	E. Alexander	
G-AWTS	Beech A.23 Musketeer	J. Holden & G. Benet	
G-AWTV	Beech A.23 Musketeer	Channel Airways Ltd/Guernsey	
G-AWTX	Cessna F.150J	Norfolk & Norwich Aero Club	
G-AWUB	GY-201 Minicab	H. P. Burrill	
G-AWUE	Jodel DR.1050	S. Bichan	
G-AWUG	Cessna F.150H	J. Easson/Edinburgh	
G-AWUH	Cessna F.150H	H. D. Hounsell	

Notes	Reg.	Type	Owner or Operator
	G-AWUJ	Cessna F.150H	W. Lawton/Doncaster
	G-AWUL	Cessna F.150H	A. M. Blackburn
	G-AWUN	Cessna F.150H	S. Martin
	G-AWUO	Cessna F.150H	SAS Flying Group
	G-AWUT	Cessna F.150J	S. J. Black/Leeds
	G-AWUU	Cessna F.150J	A. L. Grey
	G-AWUX	Cessna F.172H	D. K. Brian & ptrs
	G-AWUZ	Cessna F.172H	G. F. Burling
	G-AWVA	Cessna F.172H	Barton Air Ltd
	G-AWVB	Jodel D.117	H. Davies
	G-AWVC	B.121 Pup 1	J. H. Marshall & J. J. West
	G-AWVE	Jodel DR.1050/M1	E. A. Taylor/Southend
	G-AWVF	P.56 Provost T.1 (XF877)	Hunter Wing Ltd/Bournemouth
	G-AWVG	AESL Airtourer T.2	C. J. Schofield
	G-AWVN	Aeronca 7AC Champion	W. S. & W. A. Bowker/Rush Green
	G-AWVO	AB-206B JetRanger	Bristow Helicopters Ltd
	G-AWVZ	Jodel D.112	D. C. Stokes
	G-AWWE	B.121 Pup 2	J. M. Randle/Coventry
	G-AWWI	Jodel D.117	J. C. Hatton
	G-AWWM	GY-201 Minicab	J. S. Brayshaw
	G-AWWN	Jodel DR.1051	T. W. M. Beck & ptnrs
	G-AWWO	Jodel DR.1050	Whiskey Oscar Group/Barton
	G-AWWP	Aerosport Woody Pusher III	M. S. Bird & R. D. Bird
	G-AWWT	D.31 Turbulent	P. J. Simpson
	G-AWWU	Cessna FR.172F	Westward Airways (Lands End) Ltd
	G-AWWW	Cessna 401	Treble Whisky Aviation Ltd
	G-AWXA	Cessna 182M	G. M. Shine
	G-AWXR	PA-28 Cherokee 180D	R. Farrer
	G-AWXS	PA-28 Cherokee 180D	Rayhenro Flying Group/Shobdon
	G-AWXU	Cessna F.150J	Howe Aviation Group
	G-AWXY	M.S.885 Super Rallye	K. Henderson
	G-AWXZ	SNCAN Stampe SV-4C	Personal Plane Services Ltd/Booker
	G-AWYB	Cessna FR.172F	C. W. Larkin/Southend
	G-AWYJ	B.121 Pup 2	H. C. Taylor
	G-AWYL	Jodel DR.253B	M. J. McRobert
	G-AWYO	B.121 Pup 1	B. R. C. Wild/Popham
	G-AWYR	BAC One-Eleven 501EX	Maersk Air/British Airways/Birmingham
	G-AWYS	BAC One-Eleven 501EX	Maersk Air/British Airways/Birmingham
	G-AWYV	BAC One-Eleven 501EX	European Aviation Ltd
	G-AWYX	M.S.880B Rallye Club	J. M. L. Edwards/Exeter
	G-AWYY	T.57 Camel replica (B6401) ★	F.A.A. Museum/Yeovilton
	G-AWZE	H.S.121 Trident 3B ★	*Instructional airframe*/Heathrow
	G-AWZI	H.S.121 Trident 3B ★	Surrey Fire Brigade *(instructional airframe)*/Reigate
	G-AWZJ	H.S.121 Trident 3B ★	British Airports Authority/Prestwick
	G-AWZK	H.S.121 Trident 3B ★	*Ground trainer*/Heathrow
	G-AWZM	H.S.121 Trident 3B ★	Science Museum/Wroughton
	G-AWZN	H.S.121 Trident 3B ★	Cranfield
	G-AWZO	H.S.121 Trident 3B ★	British Aerospace PLC/Hatfield
	G-AWZP	H.S.121 Trident 3B ★	Manchester Museum of Science & Industry *(nose only)*
	G-AWZR	H.S.121 Trident 3B ★	CAA Fire School/Teesside
	G-AWZU	H.S.121 Trident 3B ★	BAA Airport Fire Service/Stansted
	G-AWZX	H.S.121 Trident 3B ★	BAA Airport Fire Services/Gatwick
	G-AWZZ	H.S.121 Trident 3B ★	Airport Fire Services/Birmingham
	G-AXAB	PA-28 Cherokee 140	Bencray Ltd/Blackpool
	G-AXAK	M.S.880B Rallye Club	R. L. & C. Stewart
	G-AXAN	D.H.82A Tiger Moth (EM720)	M. E. Carrell
	G-AXAS	Wallis WA-116T	K. H. Wallis (G-AVDH)
	G-AXAT	Jodel D.117A	P. S. Wilkinson
	G-AXAU	PA-30 Twin Comanche 160C	Bartcourt Ltd *(derelict)*/Bournemouth
	G-AXAX	PA-23 Aztec 250D	Target Skysports/Leeds
	G-AXBF	D.5/180 Husky	C. H. Barnes
	G-AXBH	Cessna F.172H	D. F. Ranger
	G-AXBJ	Cessna F.172H	Bravo Juliet Group/Leicester
	G-AXBW	D.H.82A Tiger Moth (T5879)	R. Venning
	G-AXBZ	D.H.82A Tiger Moth	D. H. McWhir
	G-AXCA	PA-28R Cherokee Arrow 200	M. D. & J. E. M. Williams
	G-AXCG	Jodel D.117	Charlie Golf Group/Andrewsfield
	G-AXCI	Bensen B.8M ★	N. Martin *(stored)*
	G-AXCL	M.S.880B Rallye Club	P. P. Loucas/Andrewsfield
	G-AXCM	M.S.880B Rallye Club	D. C. Manifold
	G-AXCN	M.S.880B Rallye Club	J. E. Compton

Reg.	Type	Owner or Operator	Notes
G-AXCX	B.121 Pup 2	L. A. Pink	
G-AXCY	Jodel D.117	C. L. Betts & ptnrs/Shoreham	
G-AXDC	PA-23 Aztec 250D	N. J. Lilley/Bodmin	
G-AXDI	Cessna F.172H	M. F. & J. R. Leusby/Conington	
G-AXDK	Jodel DR.315	Delta Kilo Flying Group/Sywell	
G-AXDM	H.S.125 Srs 400B	GEC Ferranti Defence Systems Ltd/ Edinburgh	
G-AXDN	BAC-Sud Concorde 01 ★	Duxford Aviation Soc	
G-AXDU	B.121 Pup 2	J. R. Clegg	
G-AXDV	B.121 Pup 1	T. A. White	
G-AXDW	B.121 Pup 1	Cranfield Delta Whisky Group	
G-AXDY	Falconar F-11	J. Nunn	
G-AXDZ	Cassutt Racer Srs IIIM	A. Chadwick/Little Staughton	
G-AXEB	Cassutt Racer Srs IIIM	G. E. Horder/Redhill	
G-AXED	PA-25 Pawnee 235	Wolds Gliding Club Ltd/Pocklington	
G-AXEH	B.125 Bulldog 1 ★	Museum of Flight/E. Fortune	
G-AXEI	Ward Gnome ★	Lincolnshire Aviation Museum	
G-AXEO	Scheibe SF.25B Falke	R. Cassidy & W. P. Stephen	
G-AXEV	B.121 Pup 2	D. S. Russell	
G-AXFG	Cessna 337D	Cumbria Constabulary/Carlisle	
G-AXFH	D.H.114 Heron 1B/C	(stored)/Southend	
G-AXFN	Jodel D.119	M. C. Lee & A. M. Westley	
G-AXGC	M.S.880B Rallye Club	P. A. Crawford & M. C. Bennett	
G-AXGE	M.S.880B Rallye Club	R. P. Loxton	
G-AXGG	Cessna F.150J	CTC Associates/Cranfield	
G-AXGP	Piper J-3C-65 Cub	W. K. Butler	
G-AXGR	Luton LA-4A Minor	B. Thomas	
G-AXGS	D.62B Condor	B. W. Haston	
G-AXGV	D.62B Condor	R. J. Wrixon	
G-AXGZ	D.62B Condor	J. Evans	
G-AXHA	Cessna 337A	G. Evans	
G-AXHC	SNCAN Stampe SV-4C	D. L. Webley	
G-AXHE	BN-2A Islander ★	Airport Fire Service/Cumbernauld	
G-AXHO	B.121 Pup 2	L. W. Grundy/Stapleford	
G-AXHP	Piper J-3C-65 Cub (480636)	P. J. Acreman	
G-AXHR	Piper J-3C-65 Cub (329601)	G-AXHR Cub Group	
G-AXHS	M.S.880B Rallye Club	B. & A. Swales	
G-AXHT	M.S.880B Rallye Club	D. E. Guck	
G-AXHV	Jodel D.117A	Derwent Flying Group/Hucknall	
G-AXIA	B.121 Pup 1	Cranfield University	
G-AXIE	B.121 Pup 2	G. A. Ponsford/Goodwood	
G-AXIF	B.121 Pup 2	P. Nash	
G-AXIG	B.125 Bulldog 104	George House (Holdings) Ltd	
G-AXIO	PA-28 Cherokee 140B	White Waltham Airfield Ltd	
G-AXIR	PA-28 Cherokee 140B	J. E. T. Lock	
G-AXIT	M.S.893A Rallye Commodore 180	T. J. Price	
G-AXIW	Scheibe SF.25B Falke	M. B. Hill	
G-AXIX	Glos-Airtourer 150	J. C. Wood	
G-AXIY	Bird Gyrocopter ★	–	
G-AXJB	Omega 84 balloon	Southern Balloon Group	
G-AXJH	B.121 Pup 2	J. S. Chillingworth	
G-AXJI	B.121 Pup 2	Cole Aviation Ltd/Southend	
G-AXJJ	B.121 Pup 2	Bumpf Group	
G-AXJO	B.121 Pup 2	J. A. D. Bradshaw	
G-AXJR	Scheibe SF.25B Falke	D. R. Chatterton	
G-AXJV	PA-28 Cherokee 140B	Mona Aviation Ltd	
G-AXJX	PA-28 Cherokee 140B	Patrolwatch Ltd	
G-AX\JY	Cessna U-206D	Falcon Flying Services/Biggin Hill	
G-AXKH	Luton LA-4A Minor	M. E. Vaisey	
G-AXKI	Jodel D.9 Bebe	M. R. M. Welch	
G-AXKJ	Jodel D.9 Bebe	C. C. Gordon & N. Mowbray	
G-AXKO	Westland-Bell 47G-4A	G. P. Hinkley	
G-AXKS	Westland Bell 47G-4A ★	Museum of Army Flying/Middle Wallop	
G-AXKW	Westland-Bell 47G-4A	Eyre Spier Associates Ltd	
G-AXKX	Westland Bell 47G-4A	Copley Farms Ltd	
G-AXKY	Westland Bell 47G-4A	A. M. Parkes	
G-AXLG	Cessna 310K	Smiths (Outdrives) Ltd	
G-AXLI	Slingsby T.66 Nipper 3	R. Bailes-Brown & M. J. D. Probert	
G-AXLL	BAC One-Eleven 523FJ	European Aircharter Ltd	
G-AXLS	Jodel DR.105A	E. Gee/Southampton	
G-AXLZ	PA-18 Super Cub 95	J. C. Quantrell/Shipdham	
G-AXMA	PA-24 Comanche 180	R. E. Leech	
G-AXMD	Omega O-56 balloon ★	British Balloon Museum	

Notes	Reg.	Type	Owner or Operator
	G-AXMN	J/5B Autocar	A. Phillips
	G-AXMP	PA-28 Cherokee 180	T. M. P. Tomsett
	G-AXMS	PA-30 Twin Comanche 160C	G. C. & M. B. Rogers
	G-AXMT	Bücker Bü133 Jungmeister	G. L. Carpenter
	G-AXMW	B.121 Pup 1	DJP Engineering (Knebworth) Ltd
	G-AXMX	B.121 Pup 2	Susan A. Jones/Cannes
	G-AXNJ	Wassmer Jodel D.120	Clive Flying Group/Sleap
	G-AXNL	B.121 Pup 1	Northamptonshire School of Flying Ltd/ Sywell
	G-AXNM	B.121 Pup 1	J. & F. E. Green
	G-AXNN	B.121 Pup 2	Gabrielle Aviation Ltd/Shoreham
	G-AXNP	B.121 Pup 2	J. W. Ellis
	G-AXNR	B.121 Pup 2	P. A. Jackson
	G-AXNS	B.121 Pup 2	Derwent Aero Group/Netherthorpe
	G-AXNW	SNCAN Stampe SV-4C	C. S. Grace
	G-AXNX	Cessna 182M	D. B. Harper
	G-AXNZ	Pitts S.1C Special	W. A. Jordan
	G-AXOG	PA-E23 Aztec 250D	R. W. Diggens/Denham
	G-AXOH	M.S.894 Rallye Minerva	Bristol Cars Ltd/White Waltham
	G-AXOI	Jodel D.9	L. Powell & A. J. Tanner
	G-AXOJ	B.121 Pup 2	Pup Flying Group
	G-AXOR	PA-28 Cherokee 180D	Oscar Romeo Aviation Ltd
	G-AXOS	M.S.894A Rallye Minerva	A. V. A. Hurley
	G-AXOT	M.S.893 Rallye Commodore 180	P. Evans & J. C. Graves
	G-AXOZ	B.121 Pup 1	R. J. Ogborn
	G-AXPB	B.121 Pup 1	M. J. K. Seary & R. T. Austin
	G-AXPC	B.121 Pup 2	T. A. White
	G-AXPF	Cessna F.150K	D. R. Marks/Denham
	G-AXPG	Mignet HM-293	W. H. Cole (stored)
	G-AXPM	B.121 Pup 1	R. G. Hayes/Elstree
	G-AXPN	B.121 Pup 2	D. J. Elborn & ptnrs
	G-AXPZ	Campbell Cricket	W. R. Partridge
	G-AXRC	Campbell Cricket	K. W. Hayr
	G-AXRO	PA-30 Twin Comanche 160C	S. M. Bogdiukiewicz/Staverton
	G-AXRP	SNCAN Stampe SV-4C	C. C. Manning (G-BLOL)
	G-AXRR	Auster AOP.9 (XR241)	The Aircraft Restoration Co/Duxford
	G-AXRT	Cessna FA.150K (tailwheel)	J. K. Horne
	G-AXRU	Cessna FA.150K	Arrival Enterprises Ltd
	G-AXSC	B.121 Pup 1	D. C. Laidlow
	G-AXSD	B.121 Pup 1	A. C. Townend
	G-AXSF	Nash Petrel	Nash Aircraft Ltd/Lasham
	G-AXSG	PA-28 Cherokee 180	J. Montgomery
	G-AXSI	Cessna F.172H	R. I. Chantry & A. J. G. Davis (G-SNIP)
	G-AXSM	Jodel DR.1051	K. D. Doyle
	G-AXSR	Brantly B.2B	S. Lee (G-ROOF)
	G-AXSV	Jodel DR.340	Leonard F. Jollye Ltd
	G-AXSW	Cessna FA.150K	Furness Aviation Ltd/Walney Island
	G-AXSZ	PA-28 Cherokee 140B	The White Wings Flying Group/ White Waltham
	G-AXTA	PA-28 Cherokee 140B	G-AXTA Syndicate
	G-AXTC	PA-28 Cherokee 140B	G-AXTC Group
	G-AXTD	PA-28 Cherokee 140B	K. P. Rossetti
	G-AXTJ	PA-28 Cherokee 140B	A. P. Merrifield/Stapleford
	G-AXTL	PA-28 Cherokee 140B	M. G. Courage
	G-AXTO	PA-24 Comanche 260	J. L. Wright
	G-AXTP	PA-28 Cherokee 180	C. W. R. Moore/Elstree
	G-AXTX	Jodel D.112	T. J. Price
	G-AXTZ	B.121 Pup 1	R. S. & A. D. Kent
	G-AXUA	B.121 Pup 1	F. R. Blennerhassett & ptnrs
	G-AXUB	BN-2A Islander	Headcorn Parachute Club
	G-AXUC	PA-12 Super Cruiser	J. J. Bunton
	G-AXUF	Cessna FA.150K	A. D. McLeod
	G-AXUJ	J/1 Autocrat	J. H. W. Lee & G. L. Brown/Sibson
	G-AXUK	Jodel DR.1050	C. J. Dark & I. T. James
	G-AXUM	H.P.137 Jetstream 1	Cranfield University
	G-AXUW	Cessna FA.150K	Coventry Air Training School
	G-AXVB	Cessna F.172H	J. E. Compton & R. Turner
	G-AXVK	Campbell Cricket	L. W. Harding
	G-AXVM	Campbell Cricket	D. M. Organ
	G-AXVN	McCandless M.4	W. R. Partridge
	G-AXVS	Jodel DR.1050	D. T. J. Harwood
	G-AXVV	Piper J-3C-65 Cub	J. D. MacCarthy
	G-AXVW	Cessna F.150K	General Aircraft Services

Reg.	Type	Owner or Operator	Notes
G-AXWA	Auster AOP.9 (XN437)	M. L. & C. M. Edwards/Biggin Hill	
G-AXWH	BN-2A Islander	Midland Parachute Centre Ltd	
G-AXWT	Jodel D.11	R. C. Owen	
G-AXWV	Jodel DR.253	J. R. D. Bygraves/O. Warden	
G-AXWZ	PA-28R Cherokee Arrow 200	E. J. M. Kroes	
G-AXXV	D.H.82A Tiger Moth (DE992)	C. N. Wookey	
G-AXXW	Jodel D.117	A. Szep/Netherthorpe	
G-AXYK	Taylor JT.1 Monoplane	D. J. Hulks & R. W. Davies	
G-AXYU	Jodel D.9	D. J. Laughlin	
G-AXYY	WHE Airbuggy	R. A. A. Chiles	
G-AXYZ	WHE Airbuggy	W. B. Lumb	
G-AXZA	WHE Airbuggy	C. Verlaan/Holland	
G-AXZB	WHE Airbuggy	D. R. C. Pugh	
G-AXZD	PA-28 Cherokee 180E	A. W. Bottoms	
G-AXZF	PA-28 Cherokee 180E	E. P. C. & W. R. Rabson/Southampton	
G-AXZK	BN-2A-26 Islander	Factultra Ltd	
G-AXZM	Slingsby T.66 Nipper 3	G. R. Harlow	
G-AXZO	Cessna 180	Golf Centres Balloons Ltd	
G-AXZP	PA-E23 Aztec 250D	D. J. Skidmore	
G-AXZT	Jodel D.117	N. Batty	
G-AXZU	Cessna 182N	S. E. Bradney	
G-AYAA	PA-28 Cherokee 180E	Alpha-Alpha Ltd	
G-AYAB	PA-28 Cherokee 180E	Films Ltd	
G-AYAC	PA-28R Cherokee Arrow 200	Fersfield Flying Group	
G-AYAJ	Cameron O-84 balloon	E. T. Hall	
G-AYAL	Omega 56 balloon ★	British Balloon Museum	
G-AYAN	Slingsby Motor Cadet III	N. C. Stone	
G-AYAR	PA-28 Cherokee 180E	D. M. Markscheffel/Stapleford	
G-AYAT	PA-28 Cherokee 180E	AYAT Flying Group	
G-AYAU	PA-28 Cherokee 180E	Tiarco Ltd	
G-AYAV	PA-28 Cherokee 180E	Tee Tee Aviation Ltd/Biggin Hill	
G-AYAW	PA-28 Cherokee 180E	R. C. Pendle & M. J. Rose	
G-AYBD	Cessna F.150K	Cubair Ltd/Redhill	
G-AYBG	Scheibe SF.25B Falke	D. J. Rickman	
G-AYBO	PA-23 Aztec 250D	Twinguard Aviation Ltd/Elstree	
G-AYBP	Jodel D.112	G-AYBP Group	
G-AYBR	Jodel D.112	D. Lamb	
G-AYCC	Campbell Cricket	D. J. M. Charity	
G-AYCE	CP.301C Emeraude	R. A. Austin/Bodmin	
G-AYCF	Cessna FA.150K	E. J. Atkins/Popham	
G-AYCG	SNCAN Stampe SV-4C	N. Bignall/Booker	
G-AYCJ	Cessna TP.206D	H. O. Holm/Bournemouth	
G-AYCK	AIA Stampe SV-4C	J. F. Graham (G-BUNT)	
G-AYCN	Piper J-3C-65 Cub	W. R. & B. M. Young	
G-AYCO	CEA DR.360	G. T. Birks & T. M. Curry/Booker	
G-AYCP	Jodel D.112	D. J. Nunn	
G-AYCT	Cessna F.172H	Haimoss Ltd	
G-AYDG	M.S.894A Rallye Minerva	Earthline Ltd	
G-AYDI	D.H.82A Tiger Moth	R. B. Woods & ptnrs	
G-AYDR	SNCAN Stampe SV-4C	A. J. McLuskie	
G-AYDV	Coates SA.II-1 Swalesong	J. R. Coates	
G-AYDW	A.61 Terrier 2	A. S. Topen	
G-AYDX	A.61 Terrier 2	D. G. Roberts	
G-AYDY	Luton LA-4A Minor	T. Littlefair & N. Clark	
G-AYDZ	Jodel DR.200	L. J. Cudd & C. A. Bailey	
G-AYEB	Jodel D.112	D. A. Porter	
G-AYEC	CP.301A Emeraude	Redwing Flying Group	
G-AYED	PA-24 Comanche 260	J. V. Hutchinson	
G-AYEE	PA-28 Cherokee 180E	D. J. Beale	
G-AYEF	PA-28 Cherokee 180E	T. & D. E. Beanland	
G-AYEG	Falconar F-9	B. E. Trinder	
G-AYEH	Jodel DR.1050	John Scott Jodel Group	
G-AYEJ	Jodel DR.1050	J. M. Newbold	
G-AYEN	Piper J-3C-65 Cub	P. Warde & C. F. Morris	
G-AYET	M.S.892A Rallye Commodore 150	A. T. R. Bingley	
G-AYEV	Jodel DR.1050	L. G. Evans/Headcorn	
G-AYEW	Jodel DR.1051	Taildragger Group/Halfpenny Green	
G-AYEY	Cessna F.150K	W. J. Moyse	
G-AYFA	SA Twin Pioneer 3 ★	Macclesfield Historical Aviation Soc	
G-AYFC	D.62B Condor	A. D. Pearce	
G-AYFD	D.62B Condor	B. G. Manning	
G-AYFE	D.62C Condor	D. I. H. Johnstone & W. T. Barnard	

Notes	Reg.	Type	Owner or Operator
	G-AYFF	D.62B Condor	A. F. S. Caldecourt
	G-AYFG	D.62C Condor	W. A. Braim
	G-AYFJ	M.S.880B Rallye Club	Rallye FJ Group
	G-AYFP	Jodel D.140	F. L. Rivett
	G-AYFT	PA-39 Twin Comanche 160 C/R	G. A. Barber/Blackbushe
	G-AYFV	Crosby BA-4B	A. R. C. Mathie/Norwich
	G-AYFX	AA-1 Yankee	P. A. Ellway & R. M. Bainbridge
	G-AYGA	Jodel D.117	R. L. E. Horrell
	G-AYGB	Cessna 310Q ★	*Instructional airframe*/Perth
	G-AYGC	Cessna F.150K	Alpha Aviation Group/Barton
	G-AYGD	Jodel DR.1051	P. J. Pengilly
	G-AYGE	SNCAN Stampe SV-4C	The Hon A. M. J. Rothschild/Booker
	G-AYGG	Jodel D.120	G-AYGG Group
	G-AYGK	BN-2A-6 Islander	Pathcircle Ltd/Langar
	G-AYGX	Cessna FR.172G	A. Douglas & J. K. Brockley
	G-AYHA	AA-1 Yankee	Elstree Emus Flying Group
	G-AYHI	Campbell Cricket	J. F. MacKay/Inverness
	G-AYHX	Jodel D.117A	L. J. E. Goldfinch
	G-AYHY	Fournier RF-4D	P. M. & S. M. Wells
	G-AYIA	Hughes 369HS ★	G. D. E. Bilton/Sywell
	G-AYIF	PA-28 Cherokee 140C	The Hare Flying Group/Elstree
	G-AYIG	PA-28 Cherokee 140C	Caernarfon Air World
	G-AYII	PA-28R Cherokee Arrow 200	P. W. J. & P. A. S. Gove/Exeter
	G-AYIJ	SNCAN Stampe SV-4B	E. A. Stevenson-Rouse & T. C. Beadle/Headcorn
	G-AYIM	H.S.748 Srs 2A	Emerald Airways Ltd/Liverpool
	G-AYIT	D.H.82A Tiger Moth	Ulster Tiger Group/Newtownards
	G-AYJA	Jodel DR.1050	G. I. Doake
	G-AYJB	SNCAN Stampe SV-4C	F. J. M. & J. P. Esson/Middle Wallop
	G-AYJD	Alpavia-Fournier RF-3	E. Shouler
	G-AYJP	PA-28 Cherokee 140C	RAF Brize Norton Flying Club Ltd
	G-AYJR	PA-28 Cherokee 140C	RAF Brize Norton Flying Club Ltd
	G-AYJW	Cessna FR.172G	S. Walsh & I. J. A. Charleton
	G-AYJY	Isaacs Fury II	M. G. Jeffries/Little Gransden
	G-AYKA	Beech 95-B55A Baron	Walsh Bros (Tunnelling) Ltd/Elstree
	G-AYKD	Jodel DR.1050	S. D. Morris
	G-AYKF	M.S.880B Rallye Club	F. A. Lemon
	G-AYKJ	Jodel D.117A	Juliet Group/Shoreham
	G-AYKK	Jodel D.117	D. M. Whitham
	G-AYKL	Cessna F.150L	M. A. Judge
	G-AYKS	Leopoldoff L-7	W. B. Cooper
	G-AYKT	Jodel D.117	G. Wright/Sherburn
	G-AYKW	PA-28 Cherokee 140C	T. A. Hird
	G-AYKX	PA-28 Cherokee 140C	Robin Flying Group
	G-AYKZ	SAI KZ-8	R. E. Mitchell/Coventry
	G-AYLA	Glos-Airtourer 115	D. S. P. Disney
	G-AYLB	PA-39 Twin Comanche 160 C/R	G. N. Snell
	G-AYLF	Jodel DR.1051	Sicile Group
	G-AYLL	Jodel DR.1050	C. Joly
	G-AYLP	AA-1 Yankee	D. Nairn & E. Y. Hawkins
	G-AYLV	Jodel D.120	M. R. Henham
	G-AYLX	Hughes 269C	M. Johnson
	G-AYLZ	SPP Super Aero 45 Srs 04	M. Emery
	G-AYME	Fournier RF-5	R. D. Goodger/Biggin Hill
	G-AYMG	HPR-7 Herald 213	Jet Heritage Ltd/Bournemouth
	G-AYMK	PA-28 Cherokee 140C	The Piper Flying Group
	G-AYMO	PA-23 Aztec 250C	R. A. Hastings
	G-AYMP	Currie Wot Special	H. F. Moffatt
	G-AYMR	Lederlin 380L Ladybug	J. S. Brayshaw
	G-AYMT	Jodel DR.1050	Merlin Flying Club Ltd/Hucknall
	G-AYMU	Jodel D.112	M. R. Baker
	G-AYMV	Western 20 balloon	G. F. Turnbull
	G-AYMW	Bell 206A JetRanger 2	Dollar Air Services Ltd/Coventry
	G-AYMZ	PA-28 Cherokee 140C	B. E. Walshe
	G-AYNA	Currie Wot	J. Evans
	G-AYND	Cessna 310Q	Source Ltd/Thruxton
	G-AYNF	PA-28 Cherokee 140C	W. S. Bath
	G-AYNJ	PA-28 Cherokee 140C	Southern Flight Training Ltd
	G-AYNN	Cessna 185B Skywagon	Bencray Ltd/Blackpool
	G-AYNP	W.S.55 Whirlwind Srs 3 ★	International Helicopter Museum/Weston-s-Mare
	G-AYOM	Sikorsky S-61N Mk 2	British International Helicopters
	G-AYOP	BAC One-Eleven 530FX	European Aircharter Ltd

Reg.	Type	Owner or Operator	Notes
G-AYOW	Cessna 182N Skylane	A. T. Jay/Sleap	
G-AYOY	Sikorsky S-61N Mk 2	British International Helicopters	
G-AYOZ	Cessna FA.150L	T. K. Day	
G-AYPD	Beech 95-B55A Baron	F. Sherwood & Sons (Transport) Ltd	
G-AYPE	MBB Bo 209 Monsun	Papa Echo Ltd/Biggin Hill	
G-AYPG	Cessna F.177RG	D. Davies	
G-AYPH	Cessna F.177RG	W. J. D. Tollett	
G-AYPI	Cessna F.177RG	Cardinal Aviation Ltd/Guernsey	
G-AYPJ	PA-28 Cherokee 180	Mona Aviation Ltd	
G-AYPM	PA-18 Super Cub 95	G-AYPM Group/Shoreham	
G-AYPO	PA-18 Super Cub 95	A. W. Knowles	
G-AYPR	PA-18 Super Cub 95	D. G. Holman & J. E. Burrell	
G-AYPS	PA-18 Super Cub 95	Tony Dyer Television	
G-AYPT	PA-18 Super Cub 95	B. L. Proctor & T. F. Lyddon	
G-AYPU	PA-28R Cherokee Arrow 200	Alpine Ltd/Jersey	
G-AYPV	PA-28 Cherokee 140D	Ashley Gardner Flying Club Ltd	
G-AYPZ	Campbell Cricket	A. Melody	
G-AYRF	Cessna F.150L	D. T. A. Rees	
G-AYRG	Cessna F.172K	Comed Aviation Ltd	
G-AYRH	M.S.892A Rallye Commodore 150	J. D. Watt	
G-AYRI	PA-28R Cherokee Arrow 200	E. P. Van Mechelen & Delta Motor Co (Windsor) Sales Ltd/White Waltham	
G-AYRO	Cessna FA.150L Aerobat	Flying Services	
G-AYRS	Jodel D.120A	Claybourns Garage Ltd	
G-AYRT	Cessna F.172K	K. W. J. & A. B. L. Hayward	
G-AYRU	BN-2A-6 Islander	Joint Service Parachute Centre/ Netheravon	
G-AYSA	PA-23 Aztec 250C	N. Parkinson & W. Smith	
G-AYSB	PA-30 Twin Comanche 160C	D. L. Davies	
G-AYSD	Slingsby T.61A Falke	P. W. Hextall	
G-AYSH	Taylor JT.1 Monoplane	C. J. Lodge	
G-AYSJ	Bücker Bü133 Jungmeister (LG+01)	Patina Ltd/Duxford	
G-AYSK	Luton LA-4A Minor	Luton Minor Group	
G-AYSX	Cessna F.177RG	C. P. Heptonstall	
G-AYSY	Cessna F.177RG	Horizon Flyers Ltd/Denham	
G-AYTJ	Cessna 207 Super Skywagon	Foxair/Perth	
G-AYTR	CP.301A Emeraude	G. N. Hopcraft	
G-AYTT	Phoenix PM-3 Duet	H. E. Jenner	
G-AYTV	MJ.2A Tempete	D. Perry	
G-AYTY	Bensen B.8	J. H. Wood & J. S. Knight	
G-AYUA	Auster AOP.9 (XK416) ★	A. S. Topen *(stored)*	
G-AYUB	CEA DR.253B	D. J. Brook	
G-AYUH	PA-28 Cherokee 180F	G-AYUH Group	
G-AYUI	PA-28 Cherokee 180	Ansair Aviation Ltd/Andrewsfield	
G-AYUJ	Evans VP-1	T. N. Howard	
G-AYUM	Slingsby T.61A Falke	Hereward Flying Group//Crowland	
G-AYUN	Slingsby T.61A Falke	C. W. Vigar & R. J. Watts	
G-AYUP	Slingsby T.61A Falke	P. R. Williams	
G-AYUR	Slingsby T.61A Falke	R. Hanningan & R. Lingard	
G-AYUS	Taylor JT.1 Monoplane	R. R. McKinnon	
G-AYUT	Jodel DR.1050	R. Norris	
G-AYVO	Wallis WA-120 Srs 1	K. H. Wallis	
G-AYVP	Woody Pusher	J. R. Wraight	
G-AYVT	Brochet MB.84 ★	Dunelm Flying Group *(stored)*	
G-AYWA	Avro 19 Srs 2 ★	N. K. Geddes	
G-AYWD	Cessna 182N	Chartec Ltd	
G-AYWE	PA-28 Cherokee 140	N. Roberson	
G-AYWH	Jodel D.117A	D. Kynaston & J. Deakin	
G-AYWM	Glos-Airtourer Super 150	The Star Flying Group/Staverton	
G-AYWT	AIA Stampe SV-4C	B. K. Lecomber/Denham	
G-AYXP	Jodel D.117A	G. N. Davies	
G-AYXS	SIAI-Marchetti S205-18R	C. J. Fitzgerald	
G-AYXT	W.S. 55 Whirlwind Srs 2 (XK940)	G. P. Hinkley	
G-AYXU	Champion 7KCAB Citabria	Norfolk Gliding Club Ltd/Tibenham	
G-AYXV	Cessna FA.150L	*Wreck*/Popham	
G-AYXW	Evans VP-1	J. S. Penny/Doncaster	
G-AYYK	Slingsby T.61A Falke	Cornish Gliding & Flying Club Ltd/ Perranporth	
G-AYYL	Slingsby T.61A Falke	C. Wood	
G-AYYO	Jodel DR.1050/M1	Bustard Flying Club Ltd/Old Sarum	
G-AYYT	Jodel DR.1050/M1	Echo November Flight	
G-AYYU	Beech C23 Musketeer	Sundowner Aviation	

Notes	Reg.	Type	Owner or Operator
	G-AYYW	BN-2A-2 Islander	RN & R. Marines Sport Parachute Association/Dunkeswell
	G-AYYX	M.S.880B Rallye Club	J. Turnbull & P. W. Robinson
	G-AYYY	M.S.880B Rallye Club	T. W. Heffer/Elstree
	G-AYZE	PA-39 Twin Comanche 160 C/R	J. E. Palmer/Staverton
	G-AY7H	Taylor JT.2 Titch	P. J. G. Goddard
	G-AYZI	SNCAN Stampe SV-4C	W. H. Smout
	G-AYZJ	W.S. 55 Whirlwind Srs 2 (XM685) ★	Newark Air Museum
	G-AYZK	Jodel DR.1050/M1	D. G. Hesketh & D. Lees
	G-AYZS	D.62B Condor	P. E. J. Huntley & M. N. Thrush
	G-AYZU	Slingsby T.61A Falke	The Falcon Gliding Group/Enstone
	G-AYZW	Slingsby T.61A Falke	J. A. Dandie & R. J. M. Clement/Portmoak
	G-AZAB	PA-30 Twin Comanche 160B	T. W. P. Sheffield/Humberside
	G-AZAD	Jodel DR.1050	Cawdor Flying Group/Inverness
	G-AZAJ	PA-28R Cherokee Arrow 200B	J. McHugh & ptnrs/Stapleford
	G-AZAV	Cessna 337F	Orbit Resource Ltd
	G-AZAW	GY-80 Horizon 160	E. P. Sadler
	G-AZAZ	Bensen B.8M ★	F.A.A. Museum/Yeovilton
	G-AZBA	T.66 Nipper 3	C. R. A. Scrope
	G-AZBB	MBB Bo 209 Monsun 160FV	G. N. Richardson/Staverton
	G-AZBC	PA-39 Twin Comanche 160 C/R	H. G. Orchin
	G-AZBE	Glos-Airtourer Super 150	BE Flying Group/Staverton
	G-AZBI	Jodel 150	F. M. Ward
	G-AZBL	Jodel D.9 Bebe	J. Hill
	G-AZBN	AT-16 Harvard IIB (FT391)	Swaygate Ltd/Shoreham
	G-AZBU	Auster AOP.9	Auster Nine Group
	G-AZBY	W.S.58 Wessex 60 Srs 1 ★	International Helicopter Museum/Weston-s-Mare
	G-AZBZ	W.S.58 Wessex 60 Srs 1 ★	International Helicopter Museum/Weston-s-Mare
	G-AZCB	SNCAN Stampe SV-4C	M. L. Martin
	G-AZCK	B.121 Pup 2	D. R. Newell
	G-AZCL	B.121 Pup 2	L. Bax
	G-AZCN	B.121 Pup 2	R. C. Antonini/Biggin Hill
	G-AZCP	B.121 Pup 1	T. J. Watson/Elstree
	G-AZCT	B.121 Pup 1	Northamptonshire School of Flying Ltd
	G-AZCU	B.121 Pup 1	A. A. Harris
	G-AZCV	B.121 Pup 2	N. R. W. Long/Elstree
	G-AZCY	B.121 Pup 2	Europlus Services Ltd
	G-AZCZ	B.121 Pup 2	L. & J. M. Northover
	G-AZDA	B.121 Pup 1	B. D. Deubelbeiss
	G-AZDD	MBB Bo 209 Monsun 150FF	Double Delta Flying Group/Biggin Hill
	G-AZDE	PA-28R Cherokee Arrow 200B	Electro-Motion UK (Export) Ltd/E. Midlands
	G-AZDF	Cameron O-84 balloon	K. L. C. M. Busemeyer
	G-AZDG	B.121 Pup 2	D. J. Sage/J. R. Heaps
	G-AZDK	Beech 95-B55 Baron	C. C. Forrester
	G-AZDX	PA-28 Cherokee 180F	M. Cowan
	G-AZDY	D.H.82A Tiger Moth	J. B. Mills
	G-AZEE	M.S.880B Rallye Club	J. Shelton
	G-AZEF	Jodel D.120	J. R. Legge
	G-AZEG	PA-28 Cherokee 140D	Ashley Gardner Flying Club Ltd
	G-AZEU	B.121 Pup 2	P. Tonkin & R. S. Kinman
	G-AZEV	B.121 Pup 2	G. P. Martin/Shoreham
	G-AZEW	B.121 Pup 2	K. Cameron
	G-AZEY	B.121 Pup 2	R. Hodgson
	G-AZFA	B.121 Pup 2	K. F. Plummer
	G-AZFC	PA-28 Cherokee 140D	M. L. Hannah/Blackbushe
	G-AZFF	Jodel D.112	C. R. Greenaway
	G-AZFI	PA-28R Cherokee Arrow 200B	G-AZFI Ltd/Sherburn
	G-AZFM	PA-28R Cherokee Arrow 200B	T. N. Jenness
	G-AZFP	Cessna F.177RG	Allen Aviation Ltd/Goodwood
	G-AZFR	Cessna 4501B	Westair Flying Services Ltd/Blackpool
	G-AZFZ	Cessna 414	La Pomme Rouge Ltd/Jersey
	G-AZGA	Jodel D.120	D. H. Pattison
	G-AZGC	SNCAN Stampe SV-4C (No 120)	V. Lindsay
	G-AZGE	SNCAN Stampe SV-4A	M. R. L. Astor/Booker
	G-AZGF	B.121 Pup 2	K. Singh
	G-AZGI	M.S.880B Rallye Club	B. McIntyre
	G-AZGJ	M.S.880B Rallye Club	P. Rose
	G-AZGL	M.S.894A Rallye Minerva	The Cambridge Aero Club Ltd

Reg.	Type	Owner or Operator	Notes
G-AZGY	CP.301B Emeraude	J. R. Riley-Gale	
G-AZGZ	D.H.82A Tiger Moth (NM181)	F. R. Manning	
G-AZHB	Robin HR.100-200	C. & P. P. Scarlett/Sywell	
G-AZHC	Jodel D.112	J. A. Summer & A. Burton/Netherthorpe	
G-AZHD	Slingsby T.61A Falke	J. Sentance	
G-AZHE	Slingsby T.61B Falke	M. R. Shelton/Tatenhill	
G-AZHH	SA 102.5 Cavalier	D. W. Buckle	
G-AZHI	Glos-Airtourer Super 150	H. J. Douglas/Biggin Hill	
G-AZHJ	S.A. Twin Pioneer Srs 3	Prestwick Pioneer Preservation Soc Ltd	
G-AZHK	Robin HR.100/200B	Hotel Kilo Flying Group (G-ILEG)	
G-AZHR	Piccard Ax6 balloon	G. Fisher	
G-AZHT	Glos-Airtourer T.3	Aviation West Ltd/Glasgow	
G-AZHU	Luton LA-4A Minor	W. Cawrey/Netherthorpe	
G-AZIB	ST-10 Diplomate	Diplomate Group	
G-AZID	Cessna FA.150L	Exeter Flying Club Ltd	
G-AZII	Jodel D.117A	J. S. Brayshaw	
G-AZIJ	Jodel DR.360	Rob Airway Ltd/Guernsey	
G-AZIK	PA-34-200 Seneca II	Xaxanaka Aviation Ltd	
G-AZIL	Slingsby T.61A Falke	D. W. Savage/Portmoak	
G-AZIO	SNCAN Stampe SV-4C (Lycoming) ★	—/Booker	
G-AZIP	Cameron O-65 balloon	Dante Balloon Group *Dante*	
G-AZJC	Fournier RF-5	W. St. G. V. Stoney/Italy	
G-AZJE	Ord-Hume JB-01 Minicab	J. B. Evans/Sandown	
G-AZJN	Robin DR.300/140	Wright Farm Eggs Ltd	
G-AZJV	Cessna F.172L	J. A. & A. J. Boyd/Cardiff	
G-AZJY	Cessna FRA.150L	G. Firbank	
G-AZJZ	PA-23 Aztec 250E	Gatherton Ltd	
G-AZKC	M.S.880B Rallye Club	L. J. Martin/Redhill	
G-AZKE	M.S.880B Rallye Club	B. S. Rowden & W. L. Rogers	
G-AZKK	Cameron O-56 balloon	Gemini Balloon Group *Gemini*	
G-AZKN	Robin HR.100/200	Wonderful Flying Circus	
G-AZKO	Cessna F.337F	Crispair Aviation Services Ltd	
G-AZKP	Jodel D.117	J. Lowe	
G-AZKR	PA-24 Comanche 180	S. McGovern	
G-AZKS	AA-1A Trainer	M. D. Henson	
G-AZKW	Cessna F.172L	J. C. C. Wright	
G-AZKZ	Cessna F.172L	R. D. & E. Forster/Swanton Morley	
G-AZLE	Boeing N2S-5 Kaydet	Air Farm Flyers	
G-AZLF	Jodel D.120	M. S. C. Ball	
G-AZLH	Cessna F.150L	P. T. W. Sheffield	
G-AZLL	Cessna FRA.150L	Air Service Training Ltd/Perth	
G-AZLN	PA-28 Cherokee 180F	Liteflite Ltd/Kidlington	
G-AZLO	Cessna F.337F	*Stored*/Bourn	
G-AZLV	Cessna 172K	B. L. F. Karthaus	
G-AZLY	Cessna F.150L	Cleveland Flying School Ltd/Teesside	
G-AZLZ	Cessna F.150L	G-AZLZ Group	
G-AZMB	Bell 47G-3B	Helitech (Luton) Ltd	
G-AZMC	Slingsby T.61A Falke	Essex Gliding Club Ltd	
G-AZMD	Slingsby T.61C Falke	R. A. Rice/Wellesbourne	
G-AZMF	BAC One-Eleven 530FX	European Aircharter Ltd	
G-AZMH	Morane-Saulnier M.S.500 (7A+WN)	Old Flying Machine Co/Duxford	
G-AZMJ	AA-5 Traveler	R. T. Love/Bodmin	
G-AZMN	Glos-Airtourer T.5	W. Crozier & I. Young/Glasgow	
G-AZMX	PA-28 Cherokee 140 ★	NE Wales Institute of Higher Education (*Instructional airframe*)/Clwyd	
G-AZMZ	M.S.893A Rallye Commodore 150	P. J. Wilcox/Cranfield	
G-AZNK	SNCAN Stampe SV-4A	P. D. Jackson	
G-AZNL	PA-28R Cherokee Arrow 200D	B. P. Liversidge	
G-AZNO	Cessna 182P	M&D Aviation/Bournemouth	
G-AZOA	MBB Bo 209 Monsun 150FF	M. W. Hurst	
G-AZOB	MBB Bo 209 Monsun 150FF	G. N. Richardson/Staverton	
G-AZOE	Glos-Airtourer 115	G-AZOE 607 Group	
G-AZOF	Glos-Airtourer Super 150	Cirrus Flying Group/Denham	
G-AZOG	PA-28R Cherokee Arrow 200D	J. G. Collins/Cambridge	
G-AZOL	PA-34-200 Seneca II	St Bridgets Aviation Ltd & ptnrs	
G-AZOR	MBB Bo 105D	Bond Helicopters Ltd/Bourn	
G-AZOS	Jurca MJ.5-F1 Sirocco	M. K. Field	
G-AZOT	PA-34-200 Seneca II	M. R. C. Smerald	
G-AZOU	Jodel DR.1050	Horsham Flying Group/Slinfold	
G-AZOZ	Cessna FRA.150L	Seawing Flying Club Ltd/Southend	
G-AZPA	PA-25 Pawnee 235	Black Mountain Gliding Co Ltd	

Notes	Reg.	Type	Owner or Operator
	G-AZPC	Slingsby T.61C Falke	M. F. Cuming
	G-AZPF	Fournier RF-5	R. Pye/Blackpool
	G-AZPH	Craft-Pitts S-1S Special ★	Science Museum/S. Kensington
	G-AZPV	Luton LA-4A Minor	J. R. Faulkner
	G-AZRA	MBB Bo 209 Monsun 150FF	Alpha Flying Ltd/Denham
	G-AZRD	Cessna 401B	Morbaine Ltd
	G-AZRH	PA-28 Cherokee 140D	Joseph Carter & Sons (Jersey) Ltd
	G-AZRK	Fournier RF-5	P. M. Brocklington & J. F. Rogers
	G-AZRL	PA-18 Super Cub 95	B. J. Stead
	G-AZRM	Fournier RF-5	A. R. Dearden & R. Speer/Shoreham
	G-AZRN	Cameron O-84 balloon	C. A. Butter & J. J. T. Cooke
	G-AZRP	Glos-Airtourer 115	B. F. Strawford
	G-AZRR	Cessna 310Q	Routarrow Ltd/Norwich
	G-AZRS	PA-22 Tri-Pacer 150	Sandpiper Group
	G-AZRV	PA-28R Cherokee Arrow 200B	General Airline Ltd
	G-AZRZ	Cessna U.206F	M. E. Bolton
	G-AZSA	Stampe et Renard SV-4B	J. K. Faulkner/Biggin Hill
	G-AZSC	AT-16 Harvard IIB	Machine Music Ltd/Fairoaks
	G-AZSD	Slingsby T.29B Motor Tutor	Essex Aviation
	G-AZSF	PA-28R Cherokee Arrow 200D	Flight Simulation/Coventry
	G-AZSH	PA-28R Cherokee Arrow 180	C. & G. Clarkex
	G-AZSW	B.121 Pup 1	I. T. Dall/Sywell
	G-AZSZ	PA-23 Aztec 250D	Strata Surveys Ltd
	G-AZTA	MBB Bo 209 Monsun 150FF	A. I. D. Rich/Elstree
	G-AZTD	PA-32 Cherokee Six 300D	Presshouse Publications Ltd/Enstone
	G-AZTF	Cessna F.177RG	Air Tabernacle Ltd/Sandown
	G-AZTK	Cessna F.172F	Small World Aviation
	G-AZTR	SNCAN Stampe SV-4C	P. G. Palumbo/Booker
	G-AZTS	Cessna F.172L	C. E. Stringer
	G-AZTV	Stolp SA.500 Starlet	G. R. Rowland
	G-AZTW	Cessna F.177RG	R. M. Clarke/Leicester
	G-AZUM	Cessna F.172L	Fowlmere Fliers
	G-AZUP	Cameron O-65 balloon	R. S. Bailey & A. B. Simpson
	G-AZUT	M.S.893A Rallye Commodore 180	J. Palethorpe
	G-AZUV	Cameron O-65 balloon ★	British Balloon Museum
	G-AZUY	Cessna E.310L	Euromarine Group Ltd
	G-AZUZ	Cessna FRA.150L	D. J. Parker/Netherthorpe
	G-AZVA	MBB Bo 209 Monsun 150FF	J. Nivison
	G-AZVB	MBB Bo 209 Monsun 150FF	P. C. Logsdon/Dunkeswell
	G-AZVE	AA-5 Traveler	R. Peters/Rochester
	G-AZVF	M.S.894A Rallye Minerva	J. B. Ballagh
	G-AZVG	AA-5 Traveler	Grumair Flying Group
	G-AZVH	M.S.894A Rallye Minerva	P. L. Jubb
	G-AZVI	M.S.892A Rallye Commodore	Shobdon Flying Group
	G-AZVJ	PA-34-200 Seneca II	Skyfotos Ltd/Lydd
	G-AZVL	Jodel D.119	Forest Flying Group/Stapleford
	G-AZVM	Hughes 369HS	Diagnostic Reagents Ltd
	G-AZVP	Cessna F.177RG	Cardinal Flyers Ltd
	G-AZWB	PA-28 Cherokee 140	Skyscraper Ltd
	G-AZWD	PA-28 Cherokee 140	BM Aviation (Winchester)
	G-AZWE	PA-28 Cherokee 140	G-AZWE Flying Group
	G-AZWF	SAN Jodel DR.1050	G-AZWF Jodel Syndicate
	G-AZWS	PA-28R Cherokee Arrow 180	Arrow 88 Flying Group
	G-AZWT	Westland Lysander IIIA (V9441)	Strathallan Aircraft Collection
	G-AZWY	PA-24 Comanche 260	Keymer Son & Co Ltd/Biggin Hill
	G-AZXA	Beech 95-C55 Baron	F.R. Aviation Ltd/Bournemouth
	G-AZXB	Cameron O-65 balloon	R. J. Mitchener & P. F.Smart
	G-AZXC	Cessna F.150L	D. C. Bonsall
	G-AZXD	Cessna F.172L	Birdlake Ltd/Wellesbourne
	G-AZXG	PA-23 Aztec 250D	Overdraft Aviation
	G-AZYA	GY-80 Horizon 160	T. Poole & ptnrs/Sywell
	G-AZYB	Bell 47H-1 ★	International Helicopter Museum/Weston-s-Mare
	G-AZYD	M.S.893A Rallye Commodore	Buckminster Gliding Club Ltd/Saltby
	G-AZYM	Cessna E.310Q	Offshore Marine Consultants Ltd
	G-AZYS	CP.301C-1 Emeraude	F. P. L. Clauson
	G-AZYU	PA-23 Aztec 250E	L. J. Martin/Biggin Hill
	G-AZYV	Burns O-77 balloon	B. F. G. Ribbans Contrary Mary
	G-AZYY	Slingsby T.61A Falke	J. A. Towers
	G-AZYZ	WA.51A Pacific	L. M. Palmer/Biggin Hill
	G-AZZG	Cessna 188 Agwagon	N. C. Kensington
	G-AZZH	Practavia Pilot Sprite 115	A. Moore
	G-AZZO	PA-28 Cherokee 140	R. J. Hind/Elstree

Reg.	Type	Owner or Operator	Notes
G-AZZP	Cessna F.172H	Weald Air Services Ltd/Headcorn	
G-AZZR	Cessna F.150L	R. J. Doughton	
G-AZZS	PA-34-200 Seneca II	Robin Cook Aviation/Shoreham	
G-AZZT	PA-28 Cherokee 180 ★	*Ground instruction airframe*/Cranfield	
G-AZZV	Cessna F.172L	Languedoc Aviation Ltd/France	
G-AZZW	Fournier RF-5	R. G. Trute	
G-AZZZ	D.H.82A Tiger Moth	S. W. McKay	
G-BAAD	Evans Super VP-1	R. A. Burn	
G-BAAF	Manning-Flanders MF1 (replica)	Aviation Film Services Ltd/Booker	
G-BAAI	M.S.893A Rallye Commodore	R. D. Taylor/Thruxton	
G-BAAL	Cessna 172A	Rochester Aviation Ltd	
G-BAAP	PA-28R Cherokee Arrow 200	F. T. Cole	
G-BAAT	Cessna 182P Skylane	J. P. Frewer/St. Just	
G-BAAU	Enstrom F-28C-UK	M. Upton	
G-BAAW	Jodel D.119	K. J. Cockrill/Ipswich	
G-BAAZ	PA-28R Cherokee Arrow 200D	A. W. Rix/Guernsey	
G-BABB	Cessna F.150L	Seawing Flying Club Ltd/Southend	
G-BABC	Cessna F.150L	Fordaire Aviation Ltd	
G-BABD	Cessna FRA.150L	C. J. Hopewell	
G-BABE	Taylor JT.2 Titch	P. D. G. Grist/Sibson	
G-BABG	PA-28 Cherokee 180	Mendip Flying Group/Bristol	
G-BABH	Cessna F.150L	Skyviews & General Ltd	
G-BABK	PA-34-200 Seneca II	D. F. J. Flashman/Biggin Hill	
G-BABY	Taylor JT.2 Titch	R. E. Finlay	
G-BACB	PA-34-200 Seneca II	London Flight Centre (Stansted) Ltd	
G-BACC	Cessna FRA.150L	C. M. & J. H. Cooper/Cranfield	
G-BACE	Fournier RF-5	R. W. K. Stead/Perranporth	
G-BACJ	Jodel D.120	Wearside Flying Association/Newcastle	
G-BACL	Jodel 150	M. L. Sargeant/Biggin Hill	
G-BACN	Cessna FRA.150L	Air Service Training Ltd/Perth	
G-BACO	Cessna FRA.150L	M. M. Pepper/Sibson	
G-BACP	Cessna FRA.150L	B. A. Mills	
G-BADH	Slingsby T.61A Falke	Falke Flying Group	
G-BADI	PA-23 Aztec 250D	W. London Aero Services Ltd/ White Waltham	
G-BADJ	PA-E23 Aztec 250E	Bell Aviation	
G-BADL	PA-34-200 Seneca II	K. Smith & M. Corbett	
G-BADM	D.62B Condor	M Harris & J. Taylor	
G-BADO	PA-32 Cherokee Six 300E	M. A. S. Talbot	
G-BADW	Pitts S-2A Special	R. C. Mitchell/Coventry	
G-BADZ	Pitts S-2A Special	A. F. D. Kingdon	
G-BAEB	Robin DR.400/160	P. D. W. King	
G-BAEC	Robin HR.100/210	Robin Travel & Designways (Interior Design) Ltd	
G-BAED	PA-23 Aztec 250C	K. G. Manktelow & N. Brewitt	
G-BAEE	Jodel DR.1050/M1	R. Little	
G-BAEM	Robin DR.400/125	M. A. Webb/Booker	
G-BAEN	Robin DR.400/180	European Soaring Club Ltd	
G-BAEP	Cessna FRA.150L (modified)	A. M. Lynn	
G-BAER	Cosmic Wind	R. S. Voice/Redhill	
G-BAET	Piper J-3C-65 Cub	C. J. Rees	
G-BAEU	Cessna F.150L	Skyviews & General Ltd	
G-BAEV	Cessna FRA.L150L	B. A. Mills	
G-BAEW	Cessna F.172M	Westley Aircraft/Cranfield	
G-BAEY	Cessna F.172M	R. Fursman/Southampton	
G-BAEZ	Cessna FRA.150L	Donair Flying Club Ltd/E. Midlands	
G-BAFA	AA-5 Traveler	C. F. Mackley/Stapleford	
G-BAFD	MBB Bo 105D	Bond Helicopters Ltd/Aberdeen	
G-BAFG	D.H.82A Tiger Moth	J. E. & P. J. Shaw	
G-BAFH	Evans VP-1	C. M. Gibson	
G-BAFI	Cessna F.177RG	Gloucestershire Flying Club	
G-BAFL	Cessna 182P	Farm Aviation Services Ltd	
G-BAFP	Robin DR.400/160	A. S. Langdale & J. Bevis-Lawson	
G-BAFS	PA-18 Super Cub 150	G-BAFS Group/Sandown	
G-BAFT	PA-18 Super Cub 150	T. J. Wilkinson	
G-BAFU	PA-28 Cherokee 140	R. C. Saunders/Gamston	
G-BAFV	PA-18 Super Cub 95	T. F. & S. J. Thorpe	
G-BAFW	PA-28 Cherokee 140	P. H. Marlow & R. W. Ronner-Davies	
G-BAFX	Robin DR.400/140	K. R. Gough	
G BAGB	SIAI-Marchetti SF.260	British Midland Airways Ltd/E. Midlands	
G-BAGC	Robin DR.400/140	Aeroquest Aviation	
G-BAGE	Cessna T.210L ★	Aeroplane Collection Ltd	

Notes	Reg.	Type	Owner or Operator
	G-BAGF	Jodel D.92 Bebe	E. Evans
	G-BAGG	PA-32 Cherokee Six 300E	Hornair Ltd
	G-BAGI	Cameron O-31 balloon	Red Section Balloon Group
	G-BAGL	SA.341G Gazelle Srs 1	Crown Colourprint Ltd
	G-BAGN	Cessna F.177RG	R. W. J. Andrews
	G-BAGO	Cessna 421B	Demolition Services Ltd
	G-BAGR	Robin DR.400/140	F. C. Aris & J. D. Last/Mona
	G-BAGS	Robin DR.400/180 2+2	Headcorn Flying School Ltd
	G-BAGT	Helio H.295 Courier	B. J. C. Woodall Ltd
	G-BAGV	Cessna U.206F	Scottish Parachute Club/Strathallan
	G-BAGX	PA-28 Cherokee 140	Golf X-Ray Group
	G-BAGY	Cameron O-84 balloon	P. G. Dunnington Beatrice
	G-BAHD	Cessna 182P Skylane	G. G. Ferriman
	G-BAHE	PA-28 Cherokee 140	A. H. Evans & A. O. Jones
	G-BAHF	PA-28 Cherokee 140	W. E. Jevons
	G-BAHG	PA-24 Comanche 260	E. & M. Green
	G-BAHH	Wallis WA-121	K. H. Wallis
	G-BAHI	Cessna F.150 ★	A. G. Brindle/Blackpool
	G-BAHJ	PA-24 Comanche 250	K. Cooper
	G-BAHL	Robin DR.400/160	M. A. Newman/Thruxton
	G-BAHO	Beech C.23 Sundowner	T. Durham
	G-BAHP	Volmer VJ.22 Sportsman	Seaplane Group
	G-BAHS	PA-28R Cherokee Arrow 200-II	Border Reivers Flying Group
	G-BAHX	Cessna 182P	PP Dupost Group
	G-BAIB	Enstrom F-28A	Farmax Helicopters
	G-BAIH	PA-28R Cherokee Arrow 200-II	M. G. West & J. A. Havers
	G-BAII	Cessna FRA.150L	Air Service Training Ltd/Perth
	G-BAIK	Cessna F.150L	Wickenby Aviation Ltd
	G-BAIL	Cessna FR.172J	Gloucestershire Flying Club
	G-BAIM	Cessna 310Q	*(Instructional airframe)*/Perth
	G-BAIN	Cessna FRA.150L	Air Service Training Ltd/Perth
	G-BAIP	Cessna F.150L	G. & S. A. Jones
	G-BAIS	Cessna F.177RG	H. B. A. Griffiths
	G-BAIW	Cessna F.172M	W. J. Greenfield/Humberside
	G-BAIX	Cessna F.172M	R. A. Nichols/Elstree
	G-BAIZ	Slingsby T.61A Falke	Falke Syndicate
	G-BAJA	Cessna F.177RG	Don Ward Productions Ltd/Biggin Hill
	G-BAJB	Cessna F.177RG	C. M. Bain
	G-BAJC	Evans VP-1	R. A. Hazelton
	G-BAJE	Cessna 177 Cardinal	N. C. Butcher
	G-BAJN	AA-5 Traveler	Janacrew Flying Group
	G-BAJO	AA-5 Traveler	G-BAJO Group
	G-BAJR	PA-28 Cherokee 180	Chosen Few Flying Group/Newtownards
	G-BAJY	Robin DR.400/180	Rolines Aviation
	G-BAJZ	Robin DR.400/125	Rochester Aviation Ltd
	G-BAKD	PA-34-200 Seneca II	Andrews Professional Colour Laboratories/ Elstree
	G-BAKH	PA-28 Cherokee 140	Marnham Investments Ltd
	G-BAKJ	PA-30 Twin Comanche 160B	M. F. Fisher & W. R. Lawes/Biggin Hill
	G-BAKK	Cessna F.172H ★	*Parachute jump trainer*/Coventry
	G-BAKL	F.27 Friendship Mk 200	*Permanently withdrawn*
	G-BAKM	Robin DR.400/140	MKS Syndicate
	G-BAKN	SNCAN Stampe SV-4C	M. Holloway
	G-BAKR	Jodel D.117	A. B. Bailey/White Waltham
	G-BAKS	AB-206B JetRanger 2	Stephenson Marine Co Ltd
	G-BAKV	PA-18 Super Cub 150	Pounds Marine Shipping Ltd/Goodwood
	G-BAKW	B.121 Pup 2	Oakley Motor Units Ltd & J. P. Baudrier
	G-BAKY	Slingsby T.61C Falke	Buckminster Gliding Club Ltd/Saltby
	G-BALF	Robin DR.400/140	N. A. Smith
	G-BALG	Robin DR.400/180	R. Jones
	G-BALH	Robin DR.400/140B	G-BALH Flying Group
	G-BALI	Robin DR.400 2+2	Robin Flying Group
	G-BALJ	Robin DR.400/180	D. A. Bett & D. de Lacey-Rowe
	G-BALK	SNCAN Stampe SV-4C	L. J. Rice
	G-BALN	Cessna T.310Q	O'Brien Properties Ltd/Shoreham
	G-BALT	Enstrom F-28A	G. F. Morris
	G-BALX	D.H.82A Tiger Moth (N6848)	S. Cranfield & R. T-W. Fiennes
	G-BALZ	Bell 212	Bristow Helicopters Ltd
	G-BAMB	Slingsby T.61C Falke	G-BAMB Syndicate
	G-BAMC	Cessna F.150L	Barry Aviation Ltd
	G-BAMF	MBB Bo 105D	Bond Helicopters Ltd/Bourn
	G-BAMJ	Cessna 182P	A. E. Kedros
	G-BAMK	Cameron D-96 airship	D. W. Liddiard

Reg.	Type	Owner or Operator	Notes
G-BAML	Bell 206B JetRanger 2	Heliscott Ltd	
G-BAMM	PA-28 Cherokee 235	T. A. Astell/Shoreham	
G-BAMR	PA-16 Clipper	H. Royce	
G-BAMS	Robin DR.400/160	G-BAMS Ltd/Headcorn	
G-BAMU	Robin DR.400/160	The Alternative Flying Group	
G-BAMV	Robin DR.400/180	K. Jones & E. A. Anderson/Booker	
G-BAMY	PA-28R Cherokee Arrow 200-II	G-BAMY Group/Birmingham	
G-BANA	Robin DR.221	G. T. Pryor	
G-BANB	Robin DR.400/180	R. Allen & S. G. Hayman	
G-BANC	GY-201 Minicab	J. T. S. Lewis & J. E. Williams	
G-BAND	Cameron O-84 balloon	Mid-Bucks Farmers Balloon Group Clover	
G-BANE	Cessna FRA.150L	Spectrum Flying Group/Newtownards	
G-BANG	Cameron O-84 balloon	R. F. Harrower	
G-BANK	PA-34-200 Seneca II	Cleveland Flying School Ltd/Teesside	
G-BANU	Wassmer Jodel D.120	C. E. McKinney	
G-BANV	Phoenix Currie Wot	K. Knight	
G-BANW	CP.1330 Super Emeraude	P. S. Milner	
G-BANX	Cessna F.172M	J. F. Davis/Badminton	
G-BAOB	Cessna F.172M	V. B. Cheesewright & Rentair Ltd	
G-BAOG	M.S.880B Rallye Club	G. W. Simpson	
G-BAOH	M.S.880B Rallye Club	R. D. Andrews	
G-BAOJ	M.S.880B Rallye Club	BAOJ Ltd	
G-BAOM	M.S.880B Rallye Club	D. H. Tonkin	
G-BAOP	Cessna FRA.150L	C. M. Dixon	
G-BAOS	Cessna F.172M	F. W. Ellis & ptnrs	
G-BAOU	AA-5 Traveler	S. A. Westhorp	
G-BAOW	Cameron O-65 balloon	I. Chadwick	
G-BAPA	Fournier RF-5B Sperber	Nuthampstead G-BAPA Group	
G-BAPB	D.H.C.1 Chipmunk 22	G. V. Bunyan	
G-BAPC	Luton LA-4A Minor ★	Midland Aircraft Preservation Soc	
G-BAPI	Cessna FRA.150L	Industrial Supplies (Peterborough) Ltd/ Sibson	
G-BAPJ	Cessna FRA.150L	M. D. Page/Manston	
G-BAPK	Cessna F.150L	Andrewsfield Flying Club Ltd	
G-BAPL	PA-23 Turbo Aztec 250E	Donington Aviation Ltd/E. Midlands	
G-BAPM	Fuji FA.200-160	Oakfleet Ltd	
G-BAPP	Evans VP-1	V. Mitchell	
G-BAPR	Jodel D.11	J. B. Liber & J. F. M. Bartlett	
G-BAPS	Campbell Cougar ★	International Helicopter Museum/ Weston-s-Mare	
G-BAPV	Robin DR.400/100	J. D. & M. Millne	
G-BAPW	PA-28R Cherokee Arrow 180	I. W. Lindsey & P. S. Ferren/Elstree	
G-BAPX	Robin DR.400/160	M. A. Musselwhite	
G-BAPY	Robin HR.100/210	Gloria Baby Aviation Ltd	
G-BARC	Cessna FR.172J	Severn Valley Aviation Group	
G-BARD	Cessna 337C	D. W. Horton	
G-BARF	Jodel D.112 Club	J. J. Penney	
G-BARG	Cessna E.310Q	Sally Marine Ltd	
G-BARH	Beech C.23 Sundowner	G. A. Davitt	
G-BARJ	Bell 212	Autair International Ltd/Panshanger	
G-BARN	Taylor JT.2 Titch	R. G. W. Newton	
G-BARP	Bell 206B JetRanger 2	S.W. Electricity Board/Bristol	
G-BARS	D.H.C.1 Chipmunk 22	P. Cawte	
G-BARV	Cessna 310Q	Old England Watches Ltd/Elstree	
G-BARZ	Scheibe SF.28A Tandem Falke	K. Kiely	
G-BASG	AA-5 Traveler	ASG Aviation Group/Glenrothes	
G-BASH	AA-5 Traveler	BASH Flying Group	
G-BASJ	PA-28 Cherokee 180	D. J. Skidmore & E. F. Rowland	
G-BASL	PA-28 Cherokee 140	Air Navigation & Trading Ltd/Blackpool	
G-BASM	PA-34-200 Seneca II	Poplar Aviation Group	
G-BASN	Beech C.23 Sundowner	M. F. Fisher	
G-BASO	Lake LA-4 Amphibian	M. J. Willies	
G-BASP	B.121 Pup 1	B. J. Coutts/Sywell	
G-BASX	PA-34-200 Seneca II	RJH Air Services/Fowlmere	
G-BATC	MBB Bo 105D	Bond Helicopters Ltd/Swansea	
G-BATJ	Jodel D.119	E. G. Waite/Shobdon	
G-BATN	PA-23 Aztec 250E	Marshall of Cambridge Ltd	
G-BATR	PA-34-200 Seneca II	Falcon Flying Services/Biggin Hill	
G-BATT	Hughes 269C	Victoria Helicopters	
G-BATV	PA-28 Cherokee 180D	J. N. Rudsdale	
G-BATW	PA-28 Cherokee 140	Tango Whiskey Flying Partnership	
G-BATX	PA-23 Aztec 250E	Tayside Aviation Ltd/Dundee	
G-BAUA	PA-23 Aztec 250D	David Parr & Associates Ltd/Shobdon	

Notes	Reg.	Type	Owner or Operator
	G-BAUC	PA-25 Pawnee 235	Southdown Gliding Club Ltd
	G-BAUE	Cessna 310Q	A. J. Dyer/Elstree
	G-BAUH	Jodel D.112	G. A. & D. Shepherd
	G-BAUJ	PA-23 Aztec 250E	S. J. & C. J. Westley/Cranfield
	G-BAUK	Hughes 269C	Curtis Engineering (Frome) Ltd
	G-RAUN	Bell 206B JetRanger	Bristow Helicopters Ltd
	G-BAUR	F.27 Friendship Mk 200 ★	*Permanently withdrawn*
	G-BAUV	Cessna F.150L	Skyviews & General Ltd
	G-BAUW	PA-23 Aztec 250E	R. E. Myson
	G-BAUY	Cessna FRA.150L	A. L. Hall-Carpenter
	G-BAUZ	SNCAN NC.854S	W. A. Ashley & D. Horne
	G-BAVB	Cessna F.172M	T. J. Nokes & T. V. Phillips
	G-BAVC	Cessna F.150L	Polestar Aviation Ltd
	G-BAVH	D.H.C.1 Chipmunk 22	Portsmouth Naval Gliding Club/ Lee-on-Solent
	G-BAVL	PA-23 Aztec 250E	S. P. & A. V. Chillott
	G-BAVO	Boeing Stearman N2S (26)	Vallingstone Aviation Ltd
	G-BAVR	AA-5 Traveler	E. R. Pyatt
	G-BAVS	AA-5 Traveler	V. J. Peake/Headcorn
	G-BAVU	Cameron A-105 balloon	J. D. Michaelis
	G-BAVZ	PA-23 Aztec 250E	Ravenair/Manchester
	G-BAWG	PA-28R Cherokee Arrow 200-II	Solent Air Ltd
	G-BAWK	PA-28 Cherokee 140	Newcastle-upon-Tyne Aero Club Ltd
	G-BAWN	PA-30 Twin Comanche 160C	R. A. & J. M. Nunn
	G-BAWR	Robin HR.100/210	T. Taylor
	G-BAWU	PA-30 Twin Comanche 160B	CCH Aviation Ltd
	G-BAXD	BN-2A Mk III Trislander	Aurigny Air Services/Guernsey
	G-BAXE	Hughes 269A	Reethorpe Engineering Ltd
	G-BAXJ	PA-32 Cherokee Six 300B	UK Parachute Services/Ipswich
	G-BAXK	Thunder Ax7-77 balloon	A. R. Snook
	G-BAXP	PA-23 Aztec 250E	Ashcombe Ltd
	G-BAXS	Bell 47G-5	LRC Leisure Ltd
	G-BAXT	PA-28R Cherokee Arrow 200-II	P. R. Phealon/Old Sarum
	G-BAXU	Cessna F.150L	W. Lancs Aero Club Ltd/Woodvale
	G-BAXY	Cessna F.172M	A. Rashid
	G-BAXZ	PA-28 Cherokee 140	H. Martin & D. Norris/Halton
	G-BAYO	Cessna 150L	Rainsford Ltd
	G-BAYP	Cessna 150L	Popham Pilots Flying Group
	G-BAYR	Robin HR.100/210	L. A. Christie/Stapleford
	G-BAYV	SNCAN 1101 Noralpha (3) ★	Macclesfield Historical Aviation Soc
	G-BAYZ	Bellanca 7GCBC Citabria	Cambridge University Gliding Trust Ltd/ Gransden Lodge
	G-BAZC	Robin DR.400/160	Southern Sailplanes
	G-BAZJ	HPR-7 Herald 209 ★	Guernsey Airport Fire Services
	G-BAZM	Jodel D.11	Bingley Flying Group/Leeds
	G-BAZS	Cessna F.150L	Sherburn Aero Club Ltd
	G-BAZT	Cessna F.172M	M. Fraser/Exeter
	G-BAZU	PA-28R Cherokee Arrow 200	S. C. Simmons/White Waltham
	G-BBAE	L.1011-385 TriStar 100	Caledonian Airways *Loch Earn*/Gatwick
	G-BBAF	L.1011-385 TriStar 100	Caledonian Airways *Loch Fyne*/Gatwick
	G-BBAH	L.1011-385 TriStar 100	Caledonian Airways *Loch Avon*/Gatwick
	G-BBAI	L.1011-385 TriStar 100	Caledonian Airways *Loch Inver*/Gatwick
	G-BBAJ	L.1011-385 TriStar 100	Caledonian Airways *Loch Rannoch*/ Gatwick
	G-BBAK	M.S.894A Rallye Minerva	R. B. Hemsworth & C. L. Hill/Exeter
	G-BBAW	Robin HR.100/210	J. R. Williams
	G-BBAX	Robin DR.400/140	G. J. Bissex & P. H. Garbutt
	G-BBAY	Robin DR.400/140	Rothwell Group
	G-BBAZ	Hiller UH-12E	Copley Farms Ltd
	G-BBBC	Cessna F.150L	W. J. Greenfield
	G-BBBI	AA-5 Traveler	D. A. de H. Rowntree
	G-BBBK	PA-28 Cherokee 140	Bencray Ltd/Blackpool
	G-BBBM	Bell 206B JetRanger 2	Express Newspapers PLC
	G-BBBN	PA-28 Cherokee 180	Estuary Aviation Ltd
	G-BBBO	SIPA 903	J. S. Hemmings & C. R. Steer
	G-BBBW	FRED Srs 2	C. Briggs
	G-BBBX	Cessna E310L	Atlantic Air Transport Ltd/Coventry
	G-BBBY	PA-28 Cherokee 140	J. L. Yourell/Luton
	G-BBCA	Bell 206B JetRanger 2	Kelly Trucks Ltd
	G-BBCC	PA-23 Aztec 250D	Northamptonshire School of Flying Ltd/ Sywell
	G-BBCH	Robin DR.400/2+2	Headcorn Flying School Ltd

Reg.	Type	Owner or Operator	Notes
G-BBCI	Cessna 150H	L. Jayasekara	
G-BBCN	Robin HR.100/210	K. T. G. Atkins/Teesside	
G-BBCP	Thunder Ax6-56 balloon	J. M. Robinson Jack Frost	
G-BBCS	Robin DR.400/140	C. J. & S. C. Partridge	
G-BBCW	PA-23 Aztec 250E	JDT Holdings Ltd/Sturgate	
G-BBCY	Luton LA-4A Minor	Shoestring Flying Group/Shoreham	
G-BBCZ	AA-5 Traveler	Sky Leisure Aviation Ltd	
G-BBDC	PA-28 Cherokee 140	A. Dunk	
G-BBDD	PA-28 Cherokee 140	Midland Air Training School	
G-BBDE	PA-28R Cherokee Arrow 200-II	R. L. Coleman & A. E. Stevens	
G-BBDG	Concorde 100 ★	British Aerospace PLC/Filton	
G-BBDH	Cessna F.172M	P. S. C. & B. J. Comina	
G-BBDL	AA-5 Traveler	Delta Lima Flying Group	
G-BBDM	AA-5 Traveler	D. J. & P. L. Hazell	
G-BBDO	PA-23 Turbo Aztec 250E	Anstee & Ware Ltd/Bristol	
G-BBDP	Robin DR.400/160	Robin Lance Aviation Associates Ltd	
G-BBDT	Cessna 150H	U. K. Mercer & J. K. Sibbald	
G-BBDV	SIPA S.903	W. McAndrew	
G-BBEA	Luton LA-4A Minor	K. E. Wells	
G-BBEB	PA-28R Cherokee Arrow 200-II	R. D. Rippingale/Thruxton	
G-BBEC	PA-28 Cherokee 180	J. B. Conway	
G-BBED	M.S.894A Rallye Minerva 220	Vista Products	
G-BBEF	PA-28 Cherokee 140	Comed Aviation Ltd/Blackpool	
G-BBEI	PA-31 Turbo Navajo	BKS Surveys Ltd/Exeter	
G-BBEL	PA-28R Cherokee Arrow 180	J. Paulson	
G-BBEN	Bellanca 7GCBC Citabria	C. A. G. Schofield	
G-BBEO	Cessna FRA.150L	Moray Flying Club (1990) Ltd/Kinloss	
G-BBEV	PA-28 Cherokee 140	Comed Aviation Ltd/Blackpool	
G-BBEX	Cessna 185A	V. M.É McCarthy	
G-BBEY	PA-23 Aztec 250E	M. Hall	
G-BBFC	AA-1B Trainer	I. J. Hiatt	
G-BBFD	PA-28R Cherokee Arrow 200-II	CR Aviation Ltd	
G-BBFL	GY-20 Minicab	D. Silsbury	
G-BBFS	Van Den Bemden gas balloon	A. J. F. Smith	
G-BBFV	PA-32 Cherokee Six 260	Airlaunch/Ipswich	
G-BBGB	PA-E23 Aztec 250E	Ravenair/Manchester	
G-BBGC	M.S.893E Rallye 180GT	Golf Charlie Syndicate	
G-BBGH	AA-5 Traveler	L. W. Mitchell & D. Abbiss	
G-BBGI	Fuji FA.200-160	Sunny Sky Aviation (Jersey) Ltd	
G-BBGL	Baby Great Lakes	F. Ball	
G-BBGR	Cameron O-65 balloon	M. L. & I P. Willoughby	
G-BBGX	Cessna 182P Skylane	WOC Hire Ltd/Sleap	
G-RBGZ	CHABA 42 balloon	G. Laslett & ptnrs	
G-BBHD	Enstrom F-28A	M. G. W. Smith & M. L. Rodwell	
G-BBHF	PA-23 Aztec 250E	Birmingham Aerocentre Ltd	
G-BBHG	Cessna E310Q	G. P. Williams	
G-BBHI	Cessna 177RG	T. G. W. Bunce	
G-BBHJ	Piper J-3C-65 Cub	R. V. Miller & J. Stanbridge	
G-BBHK	AT-16 Harvard IIB (FH153)	Bob Warner Aviation/Exeter	
G-BBHL	Sikorsky S-61N Mk II	Bristow Helicopters Ltd Glamis	
G-BBHM	Sikorsky S-61N	Bristow Helicopters Ltd	
G-BBHY	PA-28 Cherokee 180	Air Operations Ltd/Guernsey	
G-BBIA	PA-28R Cherokee Arrow 200-II	A. G. (Commodities) Ltd/Stapleford	
G-BBIF	PA-23 Aztec 250E	Home Doors (GB) Ltd	
G-BBIH	Enstrom F-28A-UK	Pyramid Precision Engineering Ltd	
G-BBII	Fiat G-46-3B (14)	V. S. E. Norman	
G-BBIL	PA-28 Cherokee 140	India Lima Flying Group	
G-BBIN	Enstrom F-28A	Southern Air Ltd/Shoreham	
G-BBIO	Robin HR.100/210	R. A. King/Headcorn	
G-BBIT	Hughes 269B	Contract Development & Projects (Leeds) Ltd *(stored)*	
G-BBIV	Hughes 269C	Biggin Hill Helicopters	
G-BBIX	PA-28 Cherokee 140	Sterling Contract Hire Ltd	
G-BBJB	Thunder Ax7-77 balloon	St Crispin Balloon Group *Dick Darby*	
G-BBJI	Isaacs Spitfire (RN218)	A. N. R. Houghton & ptnrs	
G-BBJU	Robin DR.400/140	J. C. Lister	
G-BBJV	Cessna F.177RG	Pilot Magazine/Biggin Hill	
G-BBJX	Cessna F.150L	Yorkshire Flying Services Ltd/Leeds	
G-BBJY	Cessna F.172M	J. Lucketti/Barton	
G-BBJZ	Cessna F.172M	Burks, Green & ptnrs	
G-BBKA	Cessna F.150I	R. Hall & L. W. Scattergood	
G-BBKB	Cessna F.150L	Justgold Ltd/Blackpool	
G-BBKC	Cessna F.172M	W. F. Hall	

Notes	Reg.	Type	Owner or Operator
	G-BBKE	Cessna F.150L	Wickenby Aviation Ltd
	G-BBKF	Cessna FRA.150L	Compton Abbas Airfield Ltd
	G-BBKG	Cessna FR.172J	H. J. Edwards & Son
	G-BBKI	Cessna F.172M	C. W. & S.A . Burman
	G-BBKL	CP.301A Emeraude	P. J. Griggs
	G-BDKR	Scheibe SF.24A Motorspatz	P. I. Morgans
	G-BBKU	Cessna FHA.150L	Penguin Group
	G-BBKX	PA-28 Cherokee 180	DRA Flying Club Ltd/Farnborough
	G-BBKY	Cessna F.150L	Automicro Ltd/Barton
	G-BBKZ	Cessna 172M	KZ Flying Group/Exeter
	G-BBLA	PA-28 Cherokee 140	Woodvale Aviation Co Ltd/Woodvale
	G-BBLE	Hiller UH-12E	Agricopters Ltd/Chilbolton
	G-BBLH	Piper J-3C-65 Cub	M. J. Dunkerley & P. Greenyer/Biggin Hill
	G-BBLM	SOCATA Rallye 100S	M. J. White & N. S. Porter
	G-BBLP	PA-23 Aztec 250D	Donington Aviation Ltd/E. Midlands
	G-BBLS	AA-5 Traveler	D. A. Reid & G. Graham/Prestwick
	G-BBLU	PA-34-200 Seneca II	Surrey & Kent Flying Club Ltd
	G-BBMB	Robin DR.400/180	J. T. M. Ball/Biggin Hill
	G-BBME	BAC One-Eleven 401AK	Maersk Air/British Airways (G-AZMI)/ Birmingham
	G-BBMG	BAC One-Eleven 408EF	Maersk Air/British Airways (G-AWEJ)/ Birmingham
	G-BBMH	EAA. Sports Biplane Model P.1	K. Dawson
	G-BBMJ	PA-23 Aztec 250E	Microlight Aircraft
	G-BBMN	D.H.C.1 Chipmunk 22	R. Steiner/Panshanger
	G-BBMO	D.H.C.1 Chipmunk 22	Holland Aerobatics Ltd/Lelystad
	G-BBMR	D.H.C.1 Chipmunk 22 (WB763)	A. J. Parkhouse
	G-BBMT	D.H.C.1 Chipmunk 22	V. F. J. Falconer & W. A. Lee/Dunstable
	G-BBMV	D.H.C.1 Chipmunk 22 (WG348)	P. J. Morgan (Aviation) Ltd
	G-BBMW	D.H.C.1 Chipmunk 22 (WK628)	Mike Whisky Group/Shoreham
	G-BBMX	D.H.C.1 Chipmunk 22	A. L. Brown & P. S. Murchison
	G-BBMZ	D.H.C.1 Chipmunk 22	Wycombe Gliding School Syndicate/ Booker
	G-BBNA	D.H.C.1 Chipmunk 22 (Lycoming)	Coventry Gliding Club Ltd/ Husbands Bosworth
	G-BBNC	D.H.C.1 Chipmunk T.10 (WP790) ★	Mosquito Aircraft Museum
	G-BBND	D.H.C.1 Chipmunk 22 (WD286)	A. J. Organ/Bourn
	G-BBNG	Bell 206B JetRanger 2	Helicopter Crop Spraying Ltd
	G-BBNH	PA-34-200 Seneca II	Lawrence Goodwin Machine Tools Ltd/ Coventry
	G-BBNI	PA-34-200 Seneca II	Channel Aviation Holdings Ltd
	G-BBNJ	Cessna F.150L	Sherburn Aero Club Ltd
	G-BBNO	PA-23 Aztec 250E	Falcon Flying Services/Biggin Hill
	G-BBNT	PA-31-350 Navajo Chieftain	Northern Executive Aviation Ltd/ Manchester
	G-BBNV	Fuji FA.200-160	Caseright Ltd
	G-BBNX	Cessna FRA.150L	General Airline Ltd
	G-BBNZ	Cessna F.172M	R. J. Nunn
	G-BBOA	Cessna F.172M	J. W. J. Adkins/Southend
	G-BBOC	Cameron O-77 balloon	J. A. B. Gray
	G-BBOD	Thunder O-45 balloon	B. R. & M. Boyle
	G-BBOE	Robin HR.200/100	Aberdeen Flying Group
	G-BBOH	Pitts S-1S Special	Venom Jet Promotions Ltd/Bournemouth
	G-BBOJ	PA-23 Aztec 250E ★	Instructional airframe/Cranfield
	G-BBOL	PA-18 Super Cub 150	Lakes Gliding Club Ltd
	G-BBOO	Thunder Ax6-56 balloon	K. Meehan Tigerjack
	G-BBOR	Bell 206B JetRanger 2	Stephenson Marine Co Ltd
	G-BBOX	Thunder Ax7-77 balloon	R. C. Weyda Rocinante
	G-BBPK	Evans VP-1	G. D. E. MacDonald
	G-BBPM	Enstrom F-28A	D. Newman
	G-BBPN	Enstrom F-28A	D. S. Chandler
	G-BBPO	Enstrom F-28A	Southern Air Ltd & Jewelhaven Ltd
·	G-BBPS	Jodel D.117	A. Appleby/Redhill
	G-BBPU	Boeing 747-136	British Airways Virginia Water
	G-BBPW	Robin HR.100/210	S. D. Cole
	G-BBPX	PA-34-200 Seneca II	Richel Investments Ltd/Guernsey
	G-BBPY	PA-28 Cherokee 180	Sunsaver Ltd
	G-BBRA	PA-23 Aztec 250D	Novio Magnum Flying Group
	G-BBRB	D.H.82A Tiger Moth (DF198)	R. Barham/Biggin Hill
	G-BBRC	Fuji FA.200-180	BBRC Ltd
	G-BBRH	Bell 47G-5A	Helicopter Supplies & Engineering Ltd
	G-BBRI	Bell 47G-5A	Alan Mann Helicopters Ltd/Fairoaks

Reg.	Type	Owner or Operator	Notes
G-BBRJ	PA-23 Aztec 250E	Duellist Enterprises Ltd	
G-BBRN	Procter Kittiwake 1 (XW784)	J. A. Rees/Haverfordwest	
G-BBRV	D.H.C.1 Chipmunk 22	Liverpool Flying School Ltd	
G-BBRX	SIAI-Marchetti S.205-18F	R. C. & A. K. West	
G-BBRZ	AA-5 Traveler	C. P. Osbourne	
G-BBSA	AA-5 Traveler	Usworth 84 Flying Associates Ltd	
G-BBSB	Beech C23 Sundowner	Sundowner Group/Manchester	
G-BBSC	Beech B24R Sierra	Beechcombers Flying Group	
G-BBSM	PA-32 Cherokee Six 300E	Paul James Knitware Ltd	
G-BBSS	D.H.C.1A Chipmunk 22	Coventry Gliding Club Ltd/ Husbands Bosworth	
G-BBSU	Cessna 421B	Hoe (Office Equipment Ltd)/Luton	
G-BBSW	Pietenpol Air Camper	J. K. S. Wills	
G-BBTB	Cessna FRA.150L	C. M. Vlieland-Boddy/Compton Abbas	
G-BBTG	Cessna F.172M	R. W. & V. P. J. Simpson/Redhill	
G-BBTH	Cessna F.172M	S. Gilmore/Newtownards	
G-BBTJ	PA-23 Aztec 250E	Cooper Aerial Surveys Ltd/Sandtoft	
G-BBTK	Cessna FRA.150L	Air Service Training Ltd/Perth	
G-BBTL	PA-23 Aztec 250C	Air Navigation & Trading Co Ltd/Blackpool	
G-BBTS	Beech V35B Bonanza	P. S. Bubbear & J. M. Glanville	
G-BBTU	ST-10 Diplomate	D. Hayden-Wright	
G-BBTX	Beech C23 Sundowner	K. Harding/Blackbushe	
G-BBTY	Beech C23 Sundowner	A. W. Roderick & W. Price	
G-BBTZ	Cessna F.150L	Marnham Investments Ltd	
G-BBUE	AA-5 Traveler	Hebog (Mon) Cyfyngedig	
G-BBUF	AA-5 Traveler	W. McLaren	
G-BBUG	PA-16 Clipper	J. Dolan	
G-BBUJ	Cessna 421B	Church Green Aviation Ltd	
G-BBUL	Mitchell-Procter Kittiwake 1	R. C. Bull	
G-BBUT	Western O-65 balloon	G. F. Turnbull	
G-BBUU	Piper J-3C-65 Cub	O. J. J. Rogers	
G-BBUW	SA.102.5 Cavalier ★	Aeroplane Collection Ltd	
G-BBVA	Sikorsky S-61N Mk II	Bristow Helicopters Ltd *Vega*	
G-BBVF	SA Twin Pioneer Srs III ★	Museum of Flight/E. Fortune	
G-BBVG	PA-23 Aztec 250C ★	*(stored)*/Little Staughton	
G-BBVI	Enstrom F-28A ★	*Ground trainer*/Kidlington	
G-BBVJ	Beech B24R Sierra	S. K. T. & C. M. Neofytou	
G-BBVO	Isaacs Fury II (S1579)	C. M. Barnes & D. A. Wirdnam	
G-BBVP	Westland-Bell 47G-3B1	CKS Air Ltd/Southend	
G-BBWN	D.H.C.1 Chipmunk 22 (WZ876)	D. C. Budd	
G-BBXB	Cessna FRA 150L	T. J. Lynn/Bourn	
G-BBXH	Cessna FR.172F	D. Ridley	
G-BBXK	PA-34-200 Seneca	Poyston Aviation	
G-BBXO	Enstrom F-28A	Repetek Ltd	
G-BBXS	Piper J-3C-65 Cub	M. J. Butler (G-ALMA)/Langham	
G-BBXU	Beech B24R Sierra	B. M. Russell/Coventry	
G-BBXY	Bellanca 7GCBC Citabria	R. R. L. Windus	
G-BBXZ	Evans VP-1	R. W. Burrows	
G-BBYB	PA-18 Super Cub 95	Tiger Club (1990) Ltd/Headcorn	
G-BBYE	Cessna 195	S. H. C. Whitfield	
G-BBYH	Cessna 182P	Croftmarsh Ltd	
G-BBYK	PA-23 Aztec 250E	Kraken Air/Cardiff	
G-BBYM	H.P.137 Jetstream 200	British Aerospace (Operations) Ltd (G-AYWR)/Warton	
G-BBYP	PA-28 Cherokee 140	Yankee Papa Flying Ltd	
G-BBYS	Cessna 182P Skylane	I. M. Jones	
G-BBZF	PA-28 Cherokee 140	Winchester 95 Associates Ltd	
G-BBZH	PA-28R Cherokee Arrow 200-II	Zulu Hotel Club	
G-BBZI	PA-31-310 Turbo Navajo	Air Care (South West) Ltd	
G-BBZJ	PA-34-200 Seneca II	Sentry Courier Ltd/Blackbushe	
G-BBZN	Fuji FA.200-180	J. Westwood & P. D. Wedd	
G-BBZO	Fuji FA.200-160	G-BBZO Group	
G-BBZS	Enstrom F-28A	Southern Air Ltd/Shoreham	
G-BBZV	PA-28R Cherokee Arrow 200-II	P. B. Mellor/Kidlington	
G-BCAH	D.H.C.1 Chipmunk 22 (WG316)	T. G. & G. J. Wheele/Shoreham	
G-BCAN	Thunder Ax7-77 balloon	D. D. Owen	
G-BCAP	Cameron O-56 balloon	S. R. Seager	
G-BCAR	Thunder Ax7-77 balloon ★	British Balloon Museum/Newbury	
G-BCAZ	PA-12 Super Cruiser	A. D. Williams	
G-BCBH	Fairchild 24R-46A Argus III	Ebork Ltd	
G-BCBJ	PA-25 Pawnee 235	Deeside Gliding Club (Aberdeenshire) Ltd/Aboyne	

Notes	Reg.	Type	Owner or Operator
	G-BCBK	Cessna 421B	Uphill Aviation Ltd
	G-BCBL	Fairchild 24R-46A Argus III (HB751)	F. J. Cox
	G-BCBM	PA-23 Aztec 250C	S. Lightbrown & M. Kavanagh
	G-BCBR	AJEP/Wittman W.8 Tailwind	R. J. Willies
	G-BCBX	Cessna F.150L	J. Kelly/Newtownards
	G-BCBY	Cessna F.150L	Scottish Airways Flyers (Prestwick) Ltd
	G-BCBZ	Cessna 337C	J. J. Zwetsloot
	G-BCCB	Robin HR.200/100	M. J. Ellis
	G-BCCC	Cessna F.150L	Fleeting Moments Ltd
	G-BCCD	Cessna F.172M	Austin Aviation Ltd
	G-BCCE	PA-23 Aztec 250E	Falcon Flying Services/Biggin Hill
	G-BCCF	PA-28 Cherokee 180	J. T. Friskney Ltd/Skegness
	G-BCCG	Thunder Ax7-65 balloon	N. H. Ponsford
	G-BCCJ	AA-5 Traveler	T. Needham/Manchester
	G-BCCK	AA-5 Traveler	Prospect Air Ltd/Barton
	G-BCCR	CP.301A Emeraude (modified)	J. H. & C. J. Waterman
	G-BCCU	BN-2A Mk.III-1 Trislander	Hebridean Air Services Ltd
	G-BCCX	D.H.C.1 Chipmunk 22 (Lycoming)	RAFGSA/Dishforth
	G-BCCY	Robin HR.200/100	Bristol Strut Flying Group
	G-BCDB	PA-34-200 Seneca II	A. & G. Aviation Ltd/Bournemouth
	G-BCDC	PA-18 Super Cub 95	Chris Ebbs Aeroservices
	G-BCDJ	PA-28 Cherokee 140	C. Wren/Southend
	G-BCDK	Partenavia P.68B	G. Fleck
	G-BCDL	Cameron O-42 balloon	D. P. & Mrs B. O. Turner *Chums*
	G-BCDN	F.27 Friendship Mk 200	*Permanently withdrawn*
	G-BCDR	Thunder Ax7-77 balloon	W. G. Johnston & ptnrs
	G-BCDY	Cessna FRA.150L	Air Service Training Ltd/Perth
	G-BCEA	Sikorsky S-61N Mk II	Brintel Helicopters
	G-BCEB	Sikorsky S-61N Mk II	Brintel Helicopters
	G-BCEC	Cessna F.172M	A. R. & S. D. Bamber
	G-BCEE	AA-5 Traveler	Echo Echo Ltd/Bournemouth
	G-BCEF	AA-5 Traveler	Forest Aviation Ltd/Guernsey
	G-BCEN	BN-2A Islander-26	Atlantic Air Transport Ltd/Coventry
	G-BCEO	AA-5 Traveler	N. F. Lyons
	G-BCEP	AA-5 Traveler	P. Curley & A. J. Radford
	G-BCER	GY-201 Minicab	D. Beaumont/Sherburn
	G-BCEU	Cameron O-42 balloon	Entertainment Services Ltd *Harlequin*
	G-BCEX	PA-23 Aztec 250E	E. W. Pinchbeck & Sons/Thruxton
	G-BCEY	D.H.C.1 Chipmunk 22	Gopher Flying Group
	G-BCEZ	Cameron O-84 balloon	Balloon Collection
	G-BCFC	Cameron O-65 balloon	B. H. Mead *Candy Twist*
	G-BCFD	West balloon ★	British Balloon Museum *Hellfire*/Newbury
	G-BCFF	Fuji FA-200-160	G. W. Brown & M. R. Gibbons
	G-BCFO	PA-18 Super Cub 150	Portsmouth Naval Gliding Club/ Lee-on-Solent
	G-BCFR	Cessna FRA.150L	Rentair Ltd
	G-BCFW	Saab 91D Safir	D. R. Williams
	G-BCFY	Luton LA-4A Minor	G. Capes
	G-BCGB	Bensen B.8	A. Melody
	G-BCGC	D.H.C.1 Chipmunk 22 (WP903)	Culdrose Gliding Club
	G-BCGG	Jodel DR.250 Srs 160	C. G. Gray (G-ATZL)
	G-BCGH	SNCAN NC.854S	Nord Flying Group
	G-BCGI	PA-28 Cherokee 140	A. Dodd/Redhill
	G-BCGJ	PA-28 Cherokee 140	T. J. Nolan & ptnrs
	G-BCGL	Jodel D.112	C. L. Betts & ptnrs/Shoreham
	G-BCGM	Jodel D.120	D. N. K. & M. A. Symon
	G-BCGN	PA-28 Cherokee 140	Oxford Flyers Ltd/Kidlington
	G-BCGS	PA-28R Cherokee Arrow 200	Arrow Aviation Group
	G-BCGT	PA-28 Cherokee 140	EFS Flying Group/Earls Colne
	G-BCGW	Jodel D.11	G. H. & M. D. Chittenden
	G-BCGX	Bede BD-5A/B	R. Hodgson
	G-BCHK	Cessna F.172H	E. C. & A. K. Shimmin
	G-BCHL	D.H.C.1 Chipmunk 22A (WP788)	Shropshire Soaring Ltd/Sleap
	G-BCHM	SA.341G Gazelle 1	Westland Helicopters Ltd/Yeovil
	G-BCHP	CP.1310-C3 Super Emeraude	G. Hughes & A. G. Just (G-JOSI)
	G-BCHT	Schleicher ASK.16	Dunstable K16 Group
	G-BCHV	D.H.C.1 Chipmunk 22	N. F. Charles/Sywell
	G-BCHX	SF.23A Sperling	*(stored)*/Rufforth
	G-BCID	PA-34-200 Seneca II	C. J. Freeman/Headcorn
	G-BCIE	PA-28-151 Warrior	Scottish Airways Flyers (Prestwick) Ltd
	G-BCIF	PA-28 Cherokee 140	Fryer-Robins Aviation Ltd/E. Midlands
	G-BCIH	D.H.C.1 Chipmunk 22 (WD363)	J. M. Hosey/Stansted

Reg.	Type	Owner or Operator	Notes
G-BCIJ	AA-5 Traveler	I. J. Boyd & D. J. McCooke	
G-BCIK	AA-5 Traveler	Trent Aviation Ltd	
G-BCIN	Thunder Ax7-77 balloon	P. G & R. A. Vale	
G-BCIR	PA-28-151 Warrior	P. J. Brennan	
G-BCIT	CIT/A1 Srs 1	Cranfield University	
G-BCJH	Mooney M.20F	P. B. Bossard	
G-BCJM	PA-28 Cherokee 140	Top Cat Aviation Ltd	
G-BCJN	PA-28 Cherokee 140	G. D. Connolly	
G-BCJO	PA-28R Cherokee Arrow 200	R. Ross	
G-BCJP	PA-28 Cherokee 140	K. E. Tolliday & ptnrs	
G-BCJS	PA-23 Aztec 250C ★	derelict/Aldergrove	
G-BCKN	D.H.C.1A Chipmunk 22	RAFGSA/Cranwell	
G-BCKP	Luton LA-5A Major	D. & W. H. Gough	
G-BCKS	Fuji FA.200-180	J. T. Hicks/Goodwood	
G-BCKT	Fuji FA.200-180	Littlewick Green Service Station Ltd/Booker	
G-BCKU	Cessna FRA.150L	Air Service Training Ltd/Perth	
G-BCKV	Cessna FRA.150L	Air Service Training Ltd/Perth	
G-BCLC	Sikorsky S-61N	Bristow Helicopters/HM Coastguard	
G-BCLD	Sikorsky S-61N	Bristow Helicopters Ltd	
G-BCLI	AA-5 Traveler	Hoe (Office Equipment) Ltd	
G-BCLJ	AA-5 Traveler	E. A. A. A. Wiltens	
G-BCLL	PA-28 Cherokee 180	K. J. Scamp	
G-BCLS	Cessna 170B	Teesside Flight Centre Ltd	
G-BCLT	M.S.894A Rallye Minerva 220	S. Clough	
G-BCLU	Jodel D.117	N. A. Wallace	
G-BCLW	AA-1B Trainer	E. J. McMillan	
G-BCMC	Bell 212	Bristow Helicopters Ltd	
G-BCMD	PA-18 Super Cub 95	J. G. Brooks/Dunkeswell	
G-BCMJ	SA.102.5 Cavalier (tailwheel)	R. G. Sykes/Shoreham	
G-BCMT	Isaacs Fury II	M. H. Turner	
G-BCNC	GY.201 Minicab	J. R. Wraight	
G-BCNP	Cameron O-77 balloon	P. Spellward	
G-BCNX	Piper J-3C-65 Cub	K. J. Lord/Ipswich	
G-BCNZ	Fuji FA.200-160	J. Bruton & A. Lincoln/Manchester	
G-BCOB	Piper J-3C-65 Cub (329405)	R. W. & Mrs J. W. Marjoram	
G-BCOG	Jodel D.112	A. J. Craven-Howe & ptnrs	
G-BCOI	D.H.C.1 Chipmunk 22	D. S. McGregor	
G-BCOJ	Cameron O-56 balloon	T. J. Knott & M. J. Webber	
G-BCOL	Cessna F.172M	A. H. Creaser	
G-BCOM	Piper J-3C-65 Cub	Dougal Flying Group/Shoreham	
G-BCOO	D.H.C.1 Chipmunk 22	T. G. Fielding & M. S. Morton/Blackpool	
G-BCOP	PA-28R Cherokee Arrow 200-II	E. A. Saunders/Halfpenny Green	
G-BCOR	SOCATA Rallye 100ST	P. R. W. Goslin & ptnrs	
G-BCOU	D.H.C.1 Chipmunk 22 (WK522)	P. J. Loweth	
G-BCOX	Bede BD-5A	H. J. Cox & B. L. Robinson	
G-BCOY	D.H.C.1 Chipmunk 22 (Lycoming)	Coventry Gliding Club Ltd/Husbands Bosworth	
G-BCPB	Howes radio-controlled model free balloon	R. B. & Mrs C. Howes Posbee 1	
G-BCPD	GY-201 Minicab	A. H. K. Denniss/Halfpenny Green	
G-BCPE	Cessna F.150M	B. W. Jones	
G-BCPF	PA-23 Aztec 250D	Launchpart Ltd	
G-BCPG	PA-28R Cherokee Arrow 200-II	Roses Flying Group/Liverpool	
G-BCPH	Piper J-3C-65 Cub (329934)	M. J. Janaway	
G-BCPJ	Piper J-3C-65 Cub	Piper Cub Group	
G-BCPK	Cessna F.172M	Osprey Flying Club/Cranfield	
G-BCPN	AA-5 Traveler	B.W. Agricultural Equipments Ltd	
G-BCPO	Partenavia P.68B	Commander Aviation Group	
G-BCPU	D.H.C.1 Chipmunk T.10	P. Waller/Booker	
G-BCPX	Szep HFC.125	A. Szep/Netherthorpe	
G-BCRB	Cessna F.172M	D. E. Lamb	
G-BCRE	Cameron O-77 balloon	A. R. Langton	
G-BCRH	Alaparma Baldo B.75 ★	A. L. Scadding/(stored)	
G-BCRI	Cameron O-65 balloon	V. J. Thorne Joseph	
G-BCRJ	Taylor JT.1 Monoplane	J. D. Muldowney & S. A. Cooper	
G-BCRK	SA.102.5 Cavalier	S. B. Churchill	
G-BCRL	PA-28-151 Warrior	F. N. Garland/Biggin Hill	
G-BCRN	Cessna FRA.150L	L. D. Johnston	
G-BCRP	PA-E23 Aztec 250E	County Garage (Cheltenham) Ltd	
G-BCRR	AA-5B Tiger	Capulet Flying Group/Elstree	
G-BCRT	Cessna F.150M	Fordaire Aviation Ltd	
G-BCRX	D.H.C.1 Chipmunk 22 (WD292)	Tuplin Ltd/Denham	

Notes	Reg.	Type	Owner or Operator
	G-BCSA	D.H.C.1 Chipmunk 22 (Lycoming)	RAFGSA/Kinloss
	G-BCSB	D.H.C.1 Chipmunk 22 (Lycoming)	RAFGSA/Cosford
	G-BCSL	D.H.C.1 Chipmunk 22	Jalawain Ltd/Barton
	G-BCSM	Bellanca 8GCBC Scout	B. T. Spreckley/Southampton
	G-BCST	M.S.893A Rallye Commodore 180	P. J. Wilcox/Cranfield
	G-BCSX	Thunder Ax7-77 balloon	C. Wolstenholm
	G-BCSY	Taylor JT.2 Titch	I. L. Harding
	G-BCTA	PA-28-151 Warrior	TG Aviation Ltd/Manston
	G-BCTF	PA-28-151 Warrior	The St. George Flying Club/Teesside
	G-BCTI	Schleicher ASK.16	Tango India Syndicate/Cranfield
	G-BCTJ	Cessna 310Q	TJ Flying Group
	G-BCTK	Cessna FR.172J	W. S. Pryke
	G-BCTT	Evans VP-1	B. J. Boughton
	G-BCTU	Cessna FRA.150M	J. H. Fisher & N. D. Hall
	G-BCUB	Piper J-3C-65 Cub	A. L. Brown & G. Attwell/Bourn
	G-BCUF	Cessna F.172M	D. J. Parkinson
	G-BCUH	Cessna F.150M	M. G. Montgomerie
	G-BCUJ	Cessna F.150M	S. Chappell
	G-BCUL	SOCATA Rallye 100ST	C. A. Ussher & Fountain Estates Ltd
	G-BCUS	SA Bulldog Srs 120/122	S. J. & J. J. Oliver
	G-BCUW	Cessna F.177RG	S. J. Westley
	G-BCUY	Cessna FRA.150M	S. R. Cameron
	G-BCVA	Cameron O-65 balloon	J. C. Bass & ptnrs
	G-BCVB	PA-17 Vagabond	A. T. Nowak/Popham
	G-BCVC	SOCATA Rallye 100ST	C. Smith & P. F. Crosby
	G-BCVE	Evans VP-2	D. Masterson & D. B. Winstanley
	G-BCVF	Practavia Pilot Sprite	D. G. Hammersley
	G-BCVG	Cessna FRA.150L	Surrey Flying Services Ltd
	G-BCVH	Cessna FRA.150L	Yorkshire Light Aircraft Ltd/Leeds
	G-BCVI	Cessna FR.172J	Cumbria Aero Club/Carlisle
	G-BCVJ	Cessna F.172M	Rothland Ltd
	G-BCVW	GY-80 Horizon 180	P. M. A. Parrett/Dunkeswell
	G-BCVY	PA-34-200T Seneca II	C.S.E. Aviation Ltd/Kidlington
	G-BCWB	Cessna 182P	Skylane Whisky Bravo Ltd
	G-BCWH	Practavia Pilot Sprite	R. Tasker/Blackpool
	G-BCWK	Alpavia Fournier RF-3	T. J. Hartwell & D. R. Wilkinson
	G-BCWL	Westland Lysander III (V9281)	Wessex Aviation & Transport Ltd
	G-BCXB	SOCATA Rallye 100ST	A. Smails
	G-BCXE	Robin DR.400/2+2	C. J. Freeman
	G-BCXJ	Piper J-3C-65 Cub (480752)	W. F. Stockdale/Compton Abbas
	G-BCXN	D.H.C.1 Chipmunk 22 (WP800)	G. M. Turner/Duxford
	G-BCYH	DAW Privateer Mk. 2	D. B. Limbert
	G-BCYJ	D.H.C.1 Chipmunk 22 (WG307)	R. A. L. Falconer
	G-BCYK	Avro CF.100 Mk 4 Canuck (18393) ★	Imperial War Museum/Duxford
	G-BCYM	D.H.C.1 Chipmunk 22	C. A. Marren
	G-BCYR	Cessna F.172M	Donne Enterprises
	G-BCZH	D.H.C.1 Chipmunk 22 (WK622)	A. C. Byrne/Norwich
	G-BCZI	Thunder Ax7-77 balloon	R. G. Griffin & R. Blackwell
	G-BCZM	Cessna F.172M	Cornwall Flying Club Ltd/Bodmin
	G-BCZN	Cessna F.150M	Mona Aviation Ltd
	G-BCZO	Cameron O-77 balloon	W. O. T. Holmes *Leo*
	G-BDAD	Taylor JT.1 Monoplane	G-BDAD Group
	G-BDAG	Taylor JT-1 Monoplane	R. S. Basinger
	G-BDAH	Evans VP-1	S. B. Robson
	G-BDAI	Cessna FRA.150M	A. Sharma
	G-BDAK	R. Commander 112A	C. Boydon
	G-BDAL	R. 500S Shrike Commander	Quantel Ltd
	G-BDAM	AT-16 Harvard IIB (FE992)	N. A. Lees & E. C. English
	G-BDAO	SIPA S.91	B. F. Arnall
	G-BDAP	AJEP Tailwind	J. Whiting
	G-BDAR	Evans VP-1	R. B. Valler
	G-BDAY	Thunder Ax5-42A balloon	T. M. Donnelly *Meconium*
	G-BDBD	Wittman W.8 Tailwind	Tailwind Taildragger Group
	G-BDBF	FRED Srs 2	I. D. Worthington
	G-BDBH	Bellanca 7GCBC Citabria	Inkpen Gliding Club Ltd/Thruxton
	G-BDBI	Cameron O-77 balloon	C. A. Butter & J. J. Cook
	G-BDBJ	Cessna 182P	H. C. Wilson
	G-BDBP	D.H.C.1 Chipmunk 22 (WP843)	F. A. de Munck
	G-BDBS	Short SD3-30 ★	Ulster Aviation Soc
	G-BDBU	Cessna F.150M	Andrewsfield Flying Club Ltd
	G-BDBV	Jodel D.11A	Seething Jodel Group

Reg.	Type	Owner or Operator	Notes
G-BDBZ	W.S.55 Whirlwind Srs 2 ★	Ground instruction airframe/Kidlington	
G-BDCC	D.H.C.1 Chipmunk 22 (Lycoming)	Coventry Gliding Club Ltd/	
		Husbands Bosworth	
G-BDCD	Piper J-3C-85 Cub (480133)	Suzanne C. Brooks/Slinfold	
G-BDCE	Cessna F.172H	A. T. Booth & G. Owens	
G-BDCI	CP.301A Emeraude	D. L. Sentance	
G-BDCK	AA-5 Traveler	Northfield Garage Ltd	
G-BDCL	AA-5 Traveler	J. Crowe	
G-BDCO	B.121 Pup 1	Shipdham Aviators Flying Group	
G-BDCS	Cessna 421B	British Aerospace (Operations) Ltd/Warton	
G-BDCU	Cameron O-77 balloon	H. P. Carlton	
G-BDDD	D.H.C.1 Chipmunk 22	DRA Aero Club Ltd/Farnborough	
G-BDDF	Jodel D.120	Sywell Skyriders Flying Group	
G-BDDG	Jodel D.112	Wandering Imp Group	
G-BDDS	PA-25 Pawnee 235	Vale of Neath Gliding Club	
G-BDDT	PA-25 Pawnee 235	Boston Aviation Services	
G-BDDX	Whittaker MW.2B Excalibur ★	Cornwall Aero Park/Helston	
G-BDDZ	CP.301A Emeraude	V. W. Smith & E. C. Mort/Barton	
G-BDEC	SOCATA Rallye 100ST	P. White	
G-BDEF	PA-34-200T Seneca II	Haylock Son & Hunter	
G-BDEH	Jodel D.120A	EH Flying Group/Bristol	
G-BDEI	Jodel D.9 Bebe	G. M. Roberts	
G-BDET	D.H.C.1 Chipmunk 22	C. Zoeteman	
G-BDEU	D.H.C.1 Chipmunk 22 (WP808)	A. Taylor	
G-BDEV	Taylor JT.1 Monoplane	D. A. Bass	
G-BDEW	Cessna FRA.150M	C. M. Vlieland-Boddy/Compton Abbas	
G-BDEX	Cessna FRA.150M	C. M. Vlieland-Boddy/Compton Abbas	
G-BDEY	Piper J-3C-65 Cub	Ducksworth Flying Club	
G-BDEZ	Piper J-3C-65 Cub	R. J. M. Turnbull	
G-BDFB	Currie Wot	J. Jennings	
G-BDFC	R. Commander 112A	R. Fletcher	
G-BDFG	Cameron O-65 balloon	N. A. Robertson Golly II	
G-BDFH	Auster AOP.9 (XR240)	R. O. Holden/Booker	
G-BDFJ	Cessna F.150M	T. J. Lynn/Sibson	
G-BDFM	Caudron C.270 Luciole	G. V. Gower	
G-BDFR	Fuji FA.200-160	A. Wright	
G-BDFS	Fuji FA.200-160	B. Sharbati & B. Lawrence	
G-BDFU	Dragonfly MPA Mk 1 ★	Museum of Flight/E. Fortune	
G-BDFW	R. Commander 112A	M. & D. A. Doubleday	
G-BDFX	Auster 5 (TW517)	J. Eagles	
G-BDFY	AA-5 Traveler	Grumman Group	
G-BDFZ	Cessna F.150M	A. T. Wright	
G-BDGA	Bushby-Long Midget Mustang	J. R. Owen	
G-BDGB	GY-20 Minicab	D. G. Burden	
G-BDGH	Thunder Ax7-77 balloon	R. J. Mitchener & P. F. Smart	
G-BDGM	PA-28-151 Warrior	B. Whiting	
G-BDGN	AA-5B Tiger	R. Stone	
G-BDGO	Thunder Ax7-77 balloon	International Distillers & Vintners Ltd	
G-BDGP	Cameron V-65 balloon	A. Mayers & V. Lawton	
G-BDGY	PA-28 Cherokee 140	W. B. Ware	
G-BDHJ	Pazmany PL.1	C. T. Millner	
G-BDHK	Piper J-3C-65 Cub (329417)	A. Liddiard	
G-BDIC	D.H.C.1 Chipmunk 22 (WD388)	Woodvale Aviation Co Ltd	
G-BDIE	R. Commander 112A	T. D. Saveker	
G-BDIG	Cessna 182P	R. J. & J. M. Z. Keel	
G-BDIH	Jodel D.117	N. D. H. Stokes	
G-BDIJ	Sikorsky S-61N	Bristow Helicopters Ltd	
G-BDIM	D.H.C.1 Chipmunk 22	Historic Flying Ltd/Cambridge	
G-BDIX	D.H.106 Comet 4C ★	Museum of Flight/E. Fortune	
G-BDJB	Taylor JT.1 Monoplane	J. F. Barber	
G-BDJC	AJEP W.8 Tailwind	J. H. Medforth	
G-BDJD	Jodel D.112	R. Everitt	
G-BDJF	Bensen B.8MV	R. P. White	
G-BDJG	Luton LA-4A Minor	A. W. Anderson & A. J. Short	
G-BDJN	Robin HR.200/100	Haimoss Ltd/Old Sarum	
G-BDJP	Piper J-3C-90 Cub	J. M. C. Pothecary (stored)/Shoreham	
G-BDJR	SNCAN NC.858	R. F. M. Marson & P. M. Harmer	
G-BDKB	SOCATA Rallye 150ST	N. C. Anderson	
G-BDKC	Cessna A185F	Bridge of Tilt Co Ltd	
G-BDKD	Enstrom F-28A	Normans (Burton-on-Trent) Ltd	
G-BDKH	CP.301A Emeraude	P. N. Marshall	
G-BDKJ	K. & S. SA.102.5 Cavalier	B. D. Battman	
G-BDKK	Bede BD-5B	A. W. Odell (stored)/Headcorn	

Notes	Reg.	Type	Owner or Operator
	G-BDKM	SIPA 903	S. W. Markham
	G-BDKU	Taylor JT.1 Monoplane	C. M. Harding & J. Ball
	G-BDKW	R. Commander 112A	R. W. Denny/Ipswich
	G-BDLO	AA-5A Cheetah	S. & J. Dolan/Denham
	G-BDLR	AA-5B Tiger	MAGEC Aviation Ltd/Luton
	G-BDLS	AA-1B Trainer	Lima Sierra Partnership
	G-BDLT	R. Commander 112A	D. L. Churchward
	G-BDLY	SA.102.5 Cavalier	P. R. Stevens/Southampton
	G-BDMM	Jodel D.11	P. N. Marshall
	G-BDMS	Piper J-3C-65 Cub (FR886)	A. T. H. Martin
	G-BDMW	Jodel DR.100	R. O. F. Harper
	G-BDNC	Taylor JT.1 Monoplane	A. W. Wright & P. Gaskell
	G-BDNG	Taylor JT.1 Monoplane	W. Buchan
	G-BDNO	Taylor JT.1 Monoplane	D. A. Healey
	G-BDNP	BN-2A Islander ★	*Ground parachute trainer*/Headcorn
	G-BDNR	Cessna FRA.150M	Cheshire Air Training School Ltd/Liverpool
	G-BDNT	Jodel D.92	R. F. Morton
	G-BDNU	Cessna F.172M	J. & K. G. McVicar
	G-BDNW	AA-1B Trainer	P. R. Huntley
	G-BDNX	/AA-1B Trainer	R. M. North
	G-BDNZ	Cameron O-77 balloon	I. L. McHale
	G-BDOC	Sikorsky S-61N Mk II	Bristow Helicopters Ltd
	G-BDOD	Cessna F.150M	D. M. Moreau
	G-BDOE	Cessna FR.172J	Rocket Partnership/Sleap
	G-BDOF	Cameron O-56 balloon	The New Holker Estates Co Ltd
	G-BDOG	SA Bulldog Srs 200/2100	D. C. Bonsall/Netherthorpe
	G-BDOL	Piper J-3C-65 Cub	L. R. Balthazor
	G-BDON	Thunder Ax7-77A balloon	J. R. Henderson & ptnrs
	G-BDOT	BN-2A Mk.III-2 Trislander	Hebridean Air Services Ltd
	G-BDOW	Cessna FRA.150M	M. H. Sims & N. A. Stone
	G-BDPA	PA-28-151 Warrior	G-BDPA Flying Group/Staverton
	G-BDPF	Cessna F.172M	Semloh Aviation Services/Andrewsfield
	G-BDPK	Cameron O-56 balloon	Rango Balloon & Kite Co
	G-BDPV	Boeing 747-136	British Airways *Blea Water*
	G-BDRD	Cessna FRA.150M	Air Service Training Ltd/Perth
	G-BDRF	Taylor JT.1 Monoplane	B. R. Ratcliffe
	G-BDRG	Taylor JT.2 Titch	D. R. Gray
	G-BDRJ	D.H.C.1 Chipmunk 22 (WP857)	J. C. Schooling
	G-BDRK	Cameron O-65 balloon	D. L. Smith *Smirk*
	G-BDRL	Stitts SA-3A Playboy	O. C. Bradley
	G-BDSA	FRED Srs 2	W. D. M. Turtle
	G-BDSB	PA-28-181 Archer II	Testair Ltd/Blackbushe
	G-BDSE	Cameron O-77 balloon	British Airways *Concorde*
	G-BDSF	Cameron O-56 balloon	A. R. Greensides & B. H. Osbourne
	G-BDSH	PA-28 Cherokee 140	The Wright Brothers Flying Group
	G-BDSK	Cameron O-65 balloon	Southern Balloon Group *Carousel II*
	G-BDSL	Cessna F.150M	Cleveland Flying School Ltd/Teesside
	G-BDSM	Slingsby T.31B Cadet III	J. A. L. Parton
	G-BDTB	Evans VP-1	W. J. Standard
	G-BDTL	Evans VP-1	A. K. Lang
	G-BDTN	BN-2A Mk III-2 Trislander	Aurigny Air Services Ltd/Guernsey
	G-BDTU	Omega III gas balloon	G. F. Turnbull
	G-BDTV	Mooney M.20F	S. Redfearn
	G-BDTW	Cassutt Racer	B. E. Smith
	G-BDTX	Cessna F.150M	S. L. Lefley & F. W. Ellis
	G-BDUI	Cameron V-56 balloon	D. C. Johnson
	G-BDUL	Evans VP-1	P. M. Beresford
	G-BDUM	Cessna F.150M	SFG Ltd/Shipdham
	G-BDUN	PA-34-200T Seneca II	Air Medical Ltd
	G-BDUO	Cessna F.150M	Sandown Aero Club
	G-BDUX	Slingsby T.31B Cadet III	J. C. Anderson/Cranfield
	G-BDUY	Robin DR.400/140B	J. M. Dean & A. L. Jubb
	G-BDUZ	Cameron V-56 balloon	Zebedee Balloon Service
	G-BDVA	PA-17 Vagabond	I. M. Callier
	G-BDVB	PA-15 (PA-17) Vagabond	B. P. Gardner
	G-BDVC	PA-17 Vagabond	A. R. Caveen
	G-BDVU	Mooney M.20F	Peakmyth Ltd
	G-BDWA	SOCATA Rallye 150ST	J. Thompson-Wilson/Newtownards
	G-BDWE	Flaglor Scooter	M. Stewart
	G-BDWH	SOCATA Rallye 150ST	M. A. Jones
	G-BDWJ	SE-5A (replica) (F8010)	S. M. Smith/Booker
	G-BDWL	PA-25 Pawnee 235	Peterborough & Spalding Gliding Club
	G-BDWM	Mustang scale replica (FB226)	D. C. Bonsall

Reg.	Type	Owner or Operator	Notes
G-BDWO	Howes Ax6 balloon	R. B. & C. Howes Griffin	
G-BDWP	PA-32R Cherokee Lance 300	W. M. Brown & B. J. Wood/Birmingham	
G-BDWV	BN-2A Mk III-2 Trislander	Aurigny Air Services Ltd/Guernsey	
G-BDWX	Jodel D.120A	J. P. Lassey	
G-BDWY	PA-28 Cherokee 140	Comed Aviation Ltd/Blackpool	
G-BDXA	Boeing 747-236B	British Airways *City of Peterborough*	
G-BDXB	Boeing 747-236B	British Airways *City of Liverpool*	
G-BDXC	Boeing 747-236B	British Airways *City of Manchester*	
G-BDXD	Boeing 747-236B	British Airways *City of Plymouth*	
G-BDXE	Boeing 747-236B	British Airways *City of Glasgow*	
G-BDXF	Boeing 747-236B	British Airways *City of York*	
G-BDXG	Boeing 747-236B	British Airways *City of Oxford*	
G-BDXH	Boeing 747-236B	British Airways *City of Elgin*	
G-BDXI	Boeing 747-236B	British Airways *City of Cambridge*	
G-BDXJ	Boeing 747-236B	British Airways *City of Birmingham*	
G-BDXK	Boeing 747-236B	British Airways *City of Canterbury*	
G-BDXL	Boeing 747-236B	British Airways *City of Winchester*	
G-BDXM	Boeing 747-236B (SCD)	British Airways *City of Derby*	
G-BDXN	Boeing 747-236B (SCD)	British Airways *City of Stoke-on-Trent*	
G-BDXO	Boeing 747-236B	British Airways *City of Bath*	
G-BDXP	Boeing 747-236B (SCD)	British Airways *City of Salisbury*	
G-BDXX	SNCAN NC.858S	J. R. Rowell & J. E. Hobbs/Sandown	
G-BDYD	R. Commander 114	L. A. & A. A. Buckley	
G-BDYF	Cessna 421C	Simco 408 Ltd	
G-BDYG	P.56 Provost T.1 (WV493) ★	Museum of Flight/E. Fortune	
G-BDYH	Cameron V-56 balloon	B. J. Godding	
G-BDZA	Scheibe SF.25E Super Falke	Norfolk Gliding Club Ltd/Tibenham	
G-BDZB	Cameron S-31 balloon	Kenning Motor Group Ltd	
G-BDZC	Cessna F.150M	A. M. Lynn	
G-BDZD	Cessna F.172M	Northamptonshire School of Flying Ltd	
G-BDZS	Scheibe SF.25E Super Falke	S. Sagar	
G-BDZU	Cessna 421C	Eagle Flying Group	
G-BDZX	PA-28-151 Warrior	Catalina Seaplanes Ltd	
G-BDZY	Luton LA-4A Minor	P. J. Dalby	
G-BEAB	Jodel DR.1051	C. Fitton	
G-BEAC	PA-28 Cherokee 140	Clipwing Flying Group/Humberside	
G-BEAD	WG.13 Lynx ★	*Instructional airframe*/Middle Wallop	
G-BEAG	PA-34-200T Seneca II	C.S.E. Aviation Ltd/Kidlington	
G-BEAH	J/2 Arrow	W. J. & Mrs M. D. Horle¡	
G-BEAK	L-1011-385 TriStar 50	British Airways *Carmarthen Bay (stored)*	
G-BEAM	L-1011-385 TriStar 50	British Airways *Swansea Bay (stored)*	
G-BEBC	W.S.55 Whirlwind 3 (XP355) ★	Norwich Aviation Museum	
G-BEBE	AA-5A Cheetah	Bills Aviation Ltd	
G-BEBG	WSK-PZL SDZ-45A Ogar	The Ogar Syndicate	
G-BEBI	Cessna F.172M	Hatfield Flying Club	
G-BEBL	Douglas DC-10-30	British Airways *Forest of Dean*/Gatwick	
G-BEBM	Douglas DC-10-30	British Airways *Sherwood Forest*/Gatwick	
G-BEBN	Cessna 177B	A. J. Franchi	
G-BEBO	Turner TSW-2 Wot	The Turner Special Flying Group	
G-BEBR	GY-201 Minicab	A. S. Jones & D. R. Upton	
G-BEBS	Andreasson BA-4B	N. J. W. Reid	
G-BEBT	Andreasson BA-4B	A. Horsfall	
G-BEBU	R. Commander 112A	R. Hodgkinson	
G-BEBZ	PA-28-151 Warrior	Goodwood Terrena Ltd/Goodwood	
G-BECA	SOCATA Rallye 100ST	Bredon Flying Group	
G-BECB	SOCATA Rallye 100ST	A. J. Trible	
G-BECC	SOCATA Rallye 150ST	D. T. Price	
G-BECF	Scheibe SF.25A Falke	D. A. Wilson & ptnrs	
G-BECG	Boeing 737-204 ADV	GB Leisure/easyJet Ltd	
G-BECH	Boeing 737-204 ADV	GB Leisure/easyJet Ltd	
G-BECK	Cameron V-56 balloon	D. W. & P. Allum	
G-BECN	Piper J-3C-65 Cub (480480)	R. C. Partridge & M. Oliver	
G-BECT	C.A.S.A.1.131E Jungmann 2000	Shoreham 131 Group	
G-BECW	C.A.S.A.1.131E Jungmann 2000	N. C. Jensen/Redhill	
G-BECZ	CAARP CAP.10B	Aerobatic Associates Ltd	
G-BEDA	C.A.S.A.1.131E Jungmann 2000	M. G. Kates & D. J. Berry	
G-BEDB	Nord 1203 Norecrin (5) ★	B. F. G. Lister *(stored)*/Chirk	
G-BEDD	Jodel D.117A	A. T. Croy/Kirkwall	
G-BEDF	Boeing B-17G-105 VE (124485)	B-17 Preservation Ltd/Duxford	
G-BEDG	R. Commander 112A	L. E. Blackburn	
G-BEDI	Sikorsky S-61N	British International Helicopters	
G-BEDJ	Piper J-3C-65 Cub (44-80594)	R. Earl	

Notes	Reg.	Type	Owner or Operator
	G-BEDK	Hiller UH-12E	Agricopters Ltd/Chilbolton
	G-BEDL	Cessna T.337D	T. J. Brammer & D. T. Colley
	G-BEDP	BN-2A Mk.III-2 Trislander	Hebridean Air Services Ltd
	G-BEDV	V.668 Varsity T.1 (WJ945) ★	D. S. Selway/Duxford
	G-BEDZ	BN-2A-26 Islander	Loganair Ltd/British Airways
	G-BEEE	Thunder Ax6-56A balloon	I. R. M. Jacobs *Avia*
	G-BEEG	BN-2A-26 Islander	North West Parachute Centre Ltd
	G-BEEH	Cameron V-56 balloon	B. & N. V. Moreton
	G-BEEI	Cameron N-77 balloon	P. S. & G. G. Rankin
	G-BEEP	Thunder Ax5-42 balloon	B. C. Faithfull/Holland
	G-BEER	Isaacs Fury II (K2075)	Baycol Aviation
	G-BEEU	PA-28 Cherokee 140E	Touch & Go Ltd
	G-BEEW	Taylor JT.1 Monoplane	P. A. Boyden
	G-BEFA	PA-28-151 Warrior	Firmbeam Ltd/Booker
	G-BEFC	AA-5B Tiger	J. F. Gosling & N. R. J. Mifflin
	G-BEFO	BN-2A Mk III-2 Trislander	Keen Leasing Ltd
	G-BEFF	PA-28 Cherokee 140	C. Haymes & S. Besoby
	G-BEFV	Evans VP-2	D. A. Cotton
	G-BEGA	Westland-Bell 47G-3B1	Flight 47 Ltd
	G-BEGG	Scheibe SF.25E Super Falke	G-BEGG Flying Group
	G-BEGV	PA-23 Aztec 250F	Widehawk Aviation Ltd/Ipswich
	G-BEHH	PA-32R Cherokee Lance 300	SMK Engineering Ltd/Leeds
	G-BEHS	PA-25 Pawnee 260C	Southern Sailplanes Ltd
	G-BEHU	PA-34-200T Seneca II	ANT Aviation Ltd
	G-BEHV	Cessna F.172N	J. Easson/Edinburgh
	G-BEHX	Evans VP-2	G. S. Adams
	G-BEIA	Cessna FRA.150M	Air Service Training Ltd/Perth
	G-BEIB	Cessna F.172N	J. Shelton
	G-BEIC	Sikorsky S-61N	Brintel Helicopters
	G-BEIF	Cameron O-65 balloon	C. Vening
	G-BEIG	Cessna F.150M	Herefordshire Aero Club Ltd/Shobdon
	G-BEII	PA-25 Pawnee 235D	Burn Gliding Club Ltd
	G-BEIL	SOCATA Rallye 150T	The Rallye Flying Group
	G-BEIP	PA-28-181 Archer II	C. Royale
	G-BEIS	Evans VP-1	P. J. Hunt
	G-BEJB	Thunder Ax6-56A balloon	International Distillers & Vinters Ltd
	G-BEJD	Avro 748 Srs 1	Emerald Airways Ltd *John Case*/Liverpool
	G-BEJE	Avro 748 Srs 1	Emerald Airways Ltd/Liverpool
	G-BEJK	Cameron S-31 balloon	Rango Balloon & Kite Co
	G-BEJL	Sikorsky S-61N	Brintel Helicopters
	G-BEJM	BAC One-Eleven 423ET	Ford Motor Co Ltd/Stansted
	G-BEJV	PA-34-200T Seneca II	C.S.E. Aviation Ltd/Kidlington
	G-BEKM	Evans VP-1	G. J. McDill/Glenrothes
	G-BEKN	Cessna FRA.150M	RFC (Bourn) Ltd
	G-BEKO	Cessna F.182Q	Tyler International
	G-BEKR	Rand KR-2	A. N. Purchase
	G-BELF	BN-2A Islander-26	Activity Aviation Ltd
	G-BELP	PA-28-151 Warrior	Devon School of Flying/Dunkeswell
	G-BELT	Cessna F.150J	Yorkshire Light Aircraft Ltd (G-AWUV)/ Leeds
	G-BELX	Cameron V-56 balloon	V. & A. M. Dyer
	G-BEMB	Cessna F.172M	Stocklaunch Ltd
	G-BEMD	Beech 95-B55 Baron	A. G. Perkins
	G-BEMM	Slingsby T.31B Motor Cadet	M. N. Martin
	G-BEMU	Thunder Ax5-42 balloon	I. J. Liddiard & A. Merritt
	G-BEMW	PA-28-181 Archer II	J. A. Pothecary
	G-BEMY	Cessna FRA.150M	A. C. Roles
	G-BEND	Cameron V-56 balloon	Dante Balloon Group *Le Billet*
	G-BENJ	R. Commander 112B	E. J. Percival/Blackbushe
	G-BENK	Cessna F.172M	Graham Churchill Plant Ltd
	G-BENN	Cameron V-56 balloon	S. H. Budd
	G-BEOD	Cessna 180 ★	Avionics Research Ltd/Cranfield
	G-BEOE	Cessna FRA.150M	W. J. Henderson
	G-BEOH	PA-28R-201T Turbo Arrow III	G-BEOH Group
	G-BEOI	PA-18 Super Cub 150	Southdown Gliding Club Ltd
	G-BEOK	Cessna F.150M	D. C. Bonsall
	G-BEOO	Sikorsky S-61N Mk. II	Brintel Helicopters
	G-BEOX	L-414 Hudson IV (A16-199) ★	RAF Museum/Hendon
	G-BEOY	Cessna FRA.150L	R. W. Denny
	G-BEOZ	A.W.650 Argosy 101 ★	Aeropark/E. Midlands
	G-BEPB	Pereira Osprey II	J. J. & A. J. C. Zwetsloot/Bourn
	G-BEPC	SNCAN Stampe SV-4C	A. J. Foan & J. A. Bridger
	G-BEPF	SNCAN Stampe SV-4A	L. J. Rice

Reg.	Type	Owner or Operator	Notes
G-BEPH	BN-2A Mk III-2 Trislander	Aurigny Air Services Ltd/Guernsey	
G-BEPI	BN-2A Mk III-2 Trislander	Aurigny Air Services Ltd/Guernsey	
G-BEPO	Cameron N-77 balloon	G. Camplin & V. Aitken	
G-BEPS	SC.5 Belfast	HeavyLift Cargo Airlines Ltd/Stansted	
G-BEPV	Fokker S.11-1 Instructor	L. C. MacKnight	
G-BEPY	R. Commander 112B	A. J. Watson	
G-BERA	SOCATA Rallye 150ST	Air Touring Services Ltd/Biggin Hill	
G-BERC	SOCATA Rallye 150ST	Severn Valley Aero Group	
G-BERD	Thunder Ax6-56A balloon	P. M. Gaines	
G-BERI	R. Commander 114	K. B. Harper/Blackbushe	
G-BERN	Saffrey S-330 balloon	B. Martin *Beeze*	
G-BERT	Cameron V-56 balloon	Southern Balloon Group *Bert*	
G-BERW	R. Commander 114	Malvern Holdings Ltd	
G-BERY	AA-1B Trainer	R. H. J. Levi	
G-BETD	Robin HR.200/100	R. A. Parsons/Bourn	
G-BETE	Rollason B.2A Beta	T. M. Jones/Tatenhill	
G-BETF	Cameron 'Champion' SS balloon	British Balloon Museum/Newbury	
G-BETG	Cessna 180K Skywagon	T. P. A. Norman	
G-BETI	Pitts S-1D Special	P. Metcalfe/Teesside	
G-BETL	PA-25 Pawnee 235D	Boston Aviation Services	
G-BETM	PA-25 Pawnee 235D	Yorkshire Gliding Club (Pty) Ltd	
G-BETP	Cameron O-65 balloon	J. R. Rix & Sons Ltd	
G-BETT	ʃPA-34-200 Seneca II	Andrews Professional Colour Laboratories Ltd/Headcorn	
G-BEUA	PA-18 Super Cub 150	London Gliding Club (Pty) Ltd/Dunstable	
G-BEUD	Robin HR.100/285R	E. A. & L. M. C. Payton/Cranfield	
G-BEUI	Piper J-3C-65 Cub	L-4 Players Flying Group	
G-BEUK	Fuji FA.200-160	BM Aviation	
G-BEUL	Beech 95-58 Baron	Foyle Flyers Ltd/Eglinton	
G-BEUM	Taylor JT.1 Monoplane	P. E. Barker	
G-BEUN	Cassutt Racer IIIM	R. McNulty	
G-BEUP	Robin DR.400/180	A. V. Pound & Co Ltd	
G-BEUR	Cessna F.172M	M. E. Moore/Compton Abbas	
G-BEUU	PA-18 Super Cub 95	F. Sharples/Sandown	
G-BEUV	Thunder Ax6-56A balloon	Silhouette Balloon Group	
G-BEUX	Cessna F.172N	ABK Aviation Services Ltd	
G-BEUY	Cameron N-31 balloon	A. C. Beaumont	
G-BEVA	SOCATA Rallye 150ST	The Rallye Group	
G-BEVB	SOCATA Rallye 150ST	N. R. Haines	
G-BEVC	SOCATA Rallye 150ST	B. W. Walpole	
G-BEVG	PA-34-200T-2 Seneca	Aranair Ltd/Bournemouth	
G-BEVO	Sportavia-Pützer RF-5	T. Barlow	
G-BEVP	Evans VP-2	G. Moscrop & R. C. Crowley	
G-BEVS	Taylor JT.1 Monoplane	D. Hunter	
G-BEVT	BN-2A Mk III-2 Trislander	Aurigny Air Services Ltd/Guernsey	
G-BEVW	SOCATA Rallye 150ST	P. C. Goodwin	
G-BEWJ	Westland-Bell 47G-3B1	Ropeleyville Ltd	
G-BEWM	Sikorsky S-61N Mk II	Brintel Helicopters	
G-BEWN	D.H.82A Tiger Moth	H. D. Labouchere	
G-BEWO	Zlin Z.326 Trener Master	Nimrod Group Ltd/Staverton	
G-BEWR	Cessna F.172N	Cheshire Air Training Services Ltd/Liverpool	
G-BEWX	PA-28R-201 Arrow III	A. Vickers	
G-BEWY	Bell 206B JetRanger 3	PLM Dollar Group Ltd (G-CULL)	
G-BEXK	PA-25 Pawnee 235D	Howard Avis (Aviation) Ltd	
G-BEXN	AA-1C Lynx	Lynx Flying Group	
G-BEXO	PA-23 Apache 160	G. R. Manley	
G-BEXR	Mudry/CAARP CAP-10B	R. P. Lewis	
G-BEXW	PA-28-181 Archer II	Motorman Ltd/Elstree	
G-BEXZ	Cameron N-56 balloon	D. C. Eager & G. C. Clark	
G-BEYA	Enstrom 280C	Hovercam Ltd	
G-BEYB	Fairey Flycatcher (replica) (S1287)	John S. Fairey/Duxford	
G-BEYF	HPR-7 Herald 401	Channel Express (Air Services) Ltd/Bournemouth	
G-BEYK	HPR-7 Herald 401	BAC Cargo/Stansted	
G-BEYL	PA-28 Cherokee 180	B. G. & G. Airlines Ltd/Jersey	
G-BEYO	PA-28 Cherokee 140	A. Grant	
G-BEYT	PA-28 Cherokee 140	H. Foulds	
G-BEYV	Cessna T.210M	Ausen Aviation	
G-BEYW	Taylor JT.1 Monoplane	R. A. Abrahams/Barton	
G-BEYZ	Jodel DR.1051/M1	M. L. Balding	
G-BEZA	Zlin Z.226T Trener	L. Bezak	

Notes	Reg.	Type	Owner or Operator
	G-BEZC	AA-5 Traveler	P. N. & S. E. Field
	G-BEZE	Rutan Vari-Eze	H. C. Mackinnon
	G-BEZF	AA-5 Traveler	G. A. Randall/Leeds
	G-BEZG	AA-5 Traveler	M. D. R. Harling & T. W. Cubbin
	G-BEZH	AA-5 Traveler	L. & S. M. Sims
	G-BEZI	AA 5 Traveler	BEZI Flying Group/Cranfield
	G-BEZJ	MBB Bo 105D	Bond Helicopters Ltd/Bourn
	G-BEZK	Cessna F.172H	Zulu Kilo Flying Group
	G-BEZL	PA-31-310 Turbo Navajo C	London Flight Centre (Stansted) Ltd
	G-BEZO	Cessna F.172M	Staverton Flying Services Ltd
	G-BEZP	PA-32 Cherokee Six 300D	Falcon Styles Ltd/Booker
	G-BEZR	Cessna F.172M	Kirmington Aviation Ltd
	G-BEZV	Cessna F.172M	Insch Flying Group
	G-BEZY	Rutan Vari-Eze	R. J. Jones/Cranfield
	G-BEZZ	Jodel D.112	G-BEZZ Jodel Group
	G-BFAA	GY-80 Horizon 160	Mary Poppins Ltd
	G-BFAC	Cessna F.177RG	Global Avionicare Ltd
	G-BFAF	Aeronca 7BCM (7797)	D. C. W. Harper/Finmere
	G-BFAH	Phoenix Currie Wot	R. W. Clarke
	G-BFAI	R. Commander 114	D. S. Innes/Guernsey
	G-BFAK	M.S.892A Rallye Commodore 150	P. G. Wells & J. D. Hensby
	G-BFAM	PA-31P Pressurised Navajo	CMH Management Services
	G-BFAN	H.S.125 Srs 600F	May Ventures Ltd (G-AZHS)
	G-BFAO	PA-20 Pacer 135	E. A. M. Austin
	G-BFAP	SIAI-Marchetti S.205-20R	A. O. Broin
	G-BFAS	Evans VP-1	A. I. Sutherland
	G-BFAW	D.H.C.1 Chipmunk 22	R. V. Bowles
	G-BFAX	D.H.C.1 Chipmunk 22 (WG422)	AJD Engineering Ltd
	G-BFBA	Jodel DR.100A	W. H. Sherlock
	G-BFBB	PA-23 Aztec 250E	Air Training Sevices Ltd
	G-BFBE	Robin HR.200/100	A. C. Pearson
	G-BFBF	PA-28 Cherokee 140	Marnham Investments Ltd
	G-BFBM	Saffery S.330 balloon	B. Martin *Beeze II*
	G-BFBR	PA-28-161 Warrior II	Lowery Holdings Ltd/Fairoaks
	G-BFBU	Partenavia P.68B	Spitfire Aviation Ltd
	G-BFBY	Piper J-3C-65 Cub	L. W. Usherwood
	G-BFCT	Cessna TU.206F	Cecil Aviation Ltd/Cambridge
	G-BFCZ	Sopwith Camel (B7270) ★	Brooklands Museum Trust Ltd/Weybridge
	G-BFDC	D.H.C.1 Chipmunk 22	N. F. O'Neill/Newtownards
	G-BFDE	Sopwith Tabloid (replica) (168) ★	RAF Museum Storage & Restoration Centre/Cardington
	G-BFDF	SOCATA Rallye 235E	J. H. Atkinson/Skegness
	G-BFDG	PA-28R-201T Turbo-Arrow III	Southern Union Trading Ltd
	G-BFDI	PA-28-181 Archer II	Truman Aviation Ltd/Tollerton
	G-BFDK	PA-28-161 Warrior II	Priory Garage
	G-BFDL	Piper J-3C-65 Cub (454537)	S. Beresford & G. S. Claybourn/Sandtoft
	G-BFDM	Jodel D.120	Worcestershire Gliding Ltd
	G-BFDN	PA-31-350 Navajo Chieftain	G. J. Ticton
	G-BFDO	PA-28R-201T Turbo Arrow III	M. I. & D. G. Goss
	G-BFDZ	Taylor JT.1 Monoplane	L. J. Greenhough
	G-BFEB	Jodel 150	S. Russell
	G-BFEE	Beech 95-E55 Baron	Chase Aviation Ltd
	G-BFEF	Agusta-Bell 47G-3B1	R. C. Hields
	G-BFEH	Jodel D.117A	C. V. & S. J. Philpott
	G-BFEK	Cessna F.152	Staverton Flying Services Ltd
	G-BFER	Bell 212	Bristow Helicopters Ltd
	G-BFEV	PA-25 Pawnee 235	Trent Valley Aerotowing Club Ltd
	G-BFEW	PA-25 Pawnee 235	Cornish Gliding & Flying Club Ltd
	G-BFFC	Cessna F.152-II	Yorkshire Flying Services Ltd/Leeds
	G-BFFE	Cessna F.152-II	J. Easson
	G-BFFG	Beech 95-B55 Baron	V. Westley
	G-BFFJ	Sikorsky S-61N Mk II	British International Helicopters
	G-BFFK	Sikorsky S-61N Mk II	British International Helicopters
	G-BFFP	PA-18 Super Cub 150 (modified)	Booker Gliding Club Ltd
	G-BFFT	Cameron V-56 balloon	R. I. M. Kerr & D. C. Boxall
	G-BFFW	Cessna F.152	Tayside Aviation Ltd/Dundee
	G-BFFY	Cessna F.150M	G. & S. A. Jones
	G-BFFZ	Cessna FR.172 Hawk XP	Bravo Aviation Ltd/Caernarfon
	G-BFGD	Cessna F.172N-II	J. T. Armstrong
	G-BFGF	Cessna F.177RG	J. E. Searson
	G-BFGG	Cessna FRA.150M	Plane Talking Ltd/Elstree
	G-BFGH	Cessna F.337G	T. Perkins/Sherburn

Reg.	Type	Owner or Operator	Notes
G-BFGK	Jodel D.117	B. F. J. Hope	
G-BFGL	Cessna FA.152	Yorkshire Flying Services Ltd/Leeds	
G-BFGO	Fuji FA.200-160	Butane Buzzard Aviation Corporation Ltd	
G-BFGS	M.S.893E Rallye 180GT	K. M. & H. Bowen	
G-BFGW	Cessna F.150H	C. E. Stringer	
G-BFGX	Cessna FRA.150M	Air Service Training Ltd/Perth	
G-BFGZ	Cessna FRA.150M	Air Service Training Ltd/Perth	
G-BFHH	D.H.82A Tiger Moth	P. Harrison & M. J. Gambrell/Redhill	
G-BFHI	Piper J-3C-65 Cub	J. McD. Robinson/Bann Foot	
G-BFHP	Champion 7GCAA Citabria	S. Matten	
G-BFHR	Jodel DR.220/2+2	T. W. Greaves	
G-BFHT	Cessna F.152-II	Westward Airways (Lands End) Ltd	
G-BFHU	Cessna F.152-II	Deltair Ltd/Liverpool	
G-BFHV	Cessna F.152-II	Falcon Flying Services/Biggin Hill	
G-BFHX	Evans VP-1	P. Johnson	
G-BFIB	PA-31 Turbo Navajo	Falcon Aviation Ltd	
G-BFID	Taylor JT.2 Titch Mk III	J. C. Lidgard	
G-BFIE	Cessna FRA.150M	B. J. Parker	
G-BFIG	Cessna FR.172K XPII	Tenair Ltd	
G-BFIJ	AA-5A Cheetah	Auto Recovery Services Ltd	
G-BFIN	AA-5A Cheetah	G-BFIN Group	
G-BFIP	Wallbro Monoplane 1909 replica	K. H. Wallis/Swanton Morley	
G-BFIR	Avro 652A Anson 21 (WD413)	G. M. K. Fraser (stored)/Arbroath	
G-BFIT	Thunder Ax6-56Z balloon	J. A. G. Tyson	
G-BFIU	Cessna FR.172K XP	B. M. Jobling	
G-BFIV	Cessna F.177RG	Kingfishair Ltd/Blackbushe	
G-BFIX	Thunder Ax7-77A balloon	R. Owen	
G-BFJJ	Evans VP-1	M. J. Collins	
G-BFJK	PA-23 Aztec 250F	H. G. Keighley	
G-BFJR	Cessna F.337G	Mannix Aviation/E. Midlands	
G-BFJW	AB-206B JetRanger	European Aviation Ltd	
G-BFJZ	Robin DR.400/140B	Rochester Aviation Ltd	
G-BFKC	Cessna F.172N	R. M. Collins	
G-BFKC	Rand KR-2	L. H. S. Stephens & I. S. Hewitt	
G-BFKD	R. Commander 114B	M. D. Faiers	
G-BFKF	Cessna FA.152	Klingair Ltd/Conington	
G-BFKH	Cessna F.152	TG Aviation Ltd/Manston	
G-BFKL	Cameron N-56 balloon	Merrythought Toys Ltd Merrythought	
G-BFKY	PA-34-200 Seneca II	S.L.H. Construction Ltd/Biggin Hill	
G-BFLH	PA-34-200T Seneca II	Air Medical Ltd	
G-BFLI	PA-28R-201T Turbo Arrow III	J. K. Chudzicki	
G-BFLM	Cessna 150M	Cornwall Flying Club Ltd/Bodmin	
G-BFLP	Amethyst Ax6 balloon	K. J. Hendry Amethyst	
G-BFLU	Cessna F.152	Bravo Aviation Ltd	
G-BFLV	Cessna F.172N	A. H. Soper	
G-BFLX	AA-5A Cheetah	Plane Talking Ltd/Elstree	
G-BFLZ	Beech 95-A55 Baron	K. A. Clarke	
G-BFME	Cameron V-56 balloon	Warwick Balloons	
G-BFMF	Cassutt Racer Mk IIIM	P. H. Lewis	
G-BFMG	PA-28-161 Warrior II	Stardial Ltd	
G-BFMH	Cessna 177B	Span Aviation Ltd/Newcastle	
G-BFMK	Cessna FA.152	RAF Halton Aeroplane Club Ltd	
G-BFMM	PA-28-181 Archer II	Bristol & Wessex Aeroplane Club Ltd	
G-BFMR	PA-20 Pacer 125	J. Knight	
G-BFMX	Cessna F.172N	Photair	
G-BFMY	Sikorsky S-61N	Bristow Helicopters Ltd	
G-BFMZ	Payne Ax6 balloon	E. G. Woolnough	
G-BFNG	Jodel D.112	K. M. Moores	
G-BFNI	PA-28-161 Warrior II	P. Elliott/Biggin Hill	
G-BFNJ	PA-28-161 Warrior II	Fleetlands Flying Association	
G-BFNK	PA-28-161 Warrior II	C.S.E. Aviation Ltd/Kidlington	
G-BFOD	Cessna F.182Q	G. N. Clarke	
G-BFOE	Cessna F.152	Plane Talking Ltd/Elstree	
G-BFOF	Cessna F.152	Staverton Flying School Ltd	
G-BFOG	Cessna 150M	P. H. Wilmot-Allistone	
G-BFOJ	AA-1 Yankee	A. J. Morton/Bournemouth	
G-BFOP	Jodel D.120	R. J. Wesley & G. D. Western/Ipswich	
G-BFOS	Thunder Ax6-56A balloon	N. T. Petty	
G-BFOU	Taylor JT.1 Monoplane	G. Bee	
G-BFOV	Cessna F.172N	D. J. Walker	
G-BFPA	Scheibe SF.25B Falke	N. Meiklejohn & J. Steel	
G-BFPB	AA-5B Tiger	Guernsey Aero Club	
G-BFPH	Cessna F.172K	Linc-Air Flying Group	

Notes	Reg.	Type	Owner or Operator
	G-BFPL	Fokker D.VII (replica) (4253/18)	A. E. Hutton/North Weald
	G-BFPM	Cessna F.172M	N. R. Havercroft
	G-BFPO	R. Commander 112B	J. G. Hale Ltd
	G-BFPP	Bell 47J-2	J. F. Kelly
	G-BFPS	PA-25 Pawnee 235D	Kent Gliding Club Ltd/Challock
	G-BFPZ	Cessna F.177RG	A. B. van Eeckhoudt/Belgium
	G-BFRA	R. Commander 114	Ischia Investments Ltd
	G-BFRD	Bowers Fly-Baby 1A	F. R. Donaldson
	G-BFRF	Taylor JT.1 Monoplane	E. R. Bailey
	G-BFRI	Sikorsky S-61N	Bristow Helicopters Ltd *Braerich*
	G-BFRL	Cessna F.152	M. K. Barnes & G. N. Olsen
	G-BFRM	Cessna 550 Citation II	Marshall of Cambridge (Engineering) Ltd
	G-BFRO	Cessna F.150M	Skyviews & General Ltd/Carlisle
	G-BFRR	Cessna FRA.150M	M. Swanborough
	G-BFRS	Cessna F.172N	Poplar Toys Ltd
	G-BFRV	Cessna FA.152	Turnhouse Flying Club
	G-BFRY	PA-25 Pawnee 260	Yorkshire Gliding Club (Pty) Ltd/ Sutton Bank
	G-BFSA	Cessna F.182Q	Clark Masts Ltd/Sandown
	G-BFSB	Cessna F.152	Tatenhill Aviation
	G-BFSC	PA-25 Pawnee 235D	Farm Aviation Services Ltd/Enstone
	G-BFSD	PA-25 Pawnee 235D	Deeside Gliding Club (Aberdeenshire) Ltd/Aboyne
	G-BFSK	PA-23 Apache 160 ★	*Sub-aqua instructional airframe*/Croughton
	G-BFSR	Cessna F.150J	Air Fenland Ltd
	G-BFSS	Cessna FR.172G	Minerva Services
	G-BFSY	PA-28-181 Archer II	Downland Aviation
	G-BFTC	PA-28R-201 Turbo Arrow III	D. Hughes/Sherburn
	G-BFTF	AA-5B Tiger	F. C. Burrow Ltd/Leeds
	G-BFTG	AA-5B Tiger	D. Hepburn & G. R. Montgomery
	G-BFTH	Cessna F.172N	J. Birkett
	G-BFTT	Cessna 421C	P&B Metal Components Ltd/Manston
	G-BFTX	Cessna F.172N	E. Kent Flying Group
	G-BFTY	Cameron V-77 balloon	Regal Motors (Bilston) Ltd Regal Motors
	G-BFUB	PA-32RT-300 Lance II	Jolida Holdings Ltd
	G-BFUD	Scheibe SF.25E Super Falke	S. H. Hart
	G-BFUG	Cameron N-77 balloon	Headland Services Ltd
	G-BFUZ	Cameron V-77 balloon	Skysales Ltd
	G-BFVF	PA-38-112 Tomahawk	Truman Aviation Ltd/Tollerton
	G-BFVG	PA-28-181 Archer II	G-BFVG Flying Group/Blackpool
	G-BFVH	D.H.2 Replica (5894)	Wessex Aviation & Transport Ltd
	G-BFVI	H.S.125 Srs 700B	Albion Aviation Management Ltd
	G-BFVM	Westland-Bell 47G-3B1	K. R. Dossett
	G-BFVP	PA-23 Aztec 250F	Litton Aviation Services Ltd
	G-BFVS	AA-5B Tiger	S. W. Biroth & T. Chapman/Denham
	G-BFVU	Cessna 150L	Flying Services
	G-BFWB	PA-28-161 Warrior II	Ipswich School of Flying Ltd
	G-BFWD	Currie Wot	F. R. Donaldson
	G-BFWE	PA-23 Aztec 250E	Air Navigation & Trading Co Ltd/Blackpool
	G-BFWK	PA-28-161 Warrior II	Marnham Investments Ltd
	G-BFWL	Cessna F.150L	G-BFWL Flying Group/Barton
	G-BFXD	PA-28-161 Warrior II	C.S.E. Aviation Ltd/Kidlington
	G-BFXE	PA-28-161 Warrior II	C.S.E. Aviation Ltd/Kidlington
	G-BFXF	Andreasson BA.4B	A. Brown/Sherburn
	G-BFXH	Cessna F.152	M. Entwistle
	G-BFXK	PA-28 Cherokee 140	G. S. & Mrs M. T. Pritchard/Southend
	G-BFXL	Albatross D.5A (D5397/17)	F.A.A. Museum/Yeovilton
	G-BFXR	Jodel D.112	Jodel Flying Group
	G-BFXS	R. Commander 114	Keats Printing Ltd
	G-BFXW	AA-5B Tiger	Campsol Ltd
	G-BFXX	AA-5B Tiger	M. J. Porter
	G-BFYA	MBB Bo 105DB	Sterling Helicopters Ltd
	G-BFYB	PA-28-161 Warrior II	C.S.E. Aviation Ltd/Kidlington
	G-BFYC	PA-32RT-300 Lance II	A. A. Barnes
	G-BFYE	Robin HR.100/285 ★	stored/Sywell
	G-BFYI	Westland-Bell 47G-3B1	B. Walker & Co (Dursley) Ltd
	G-BFYK	Cameron V-77 balloon	L. E. Jones
	G-BFYL	Evans VP-2	W. C. Brown
	G-BFYM	PA-28-161 Warrior II	C.S.E. Aviation Ltd/Kidlington
	G-BFYO	SPAD XIII (replica) (3398) ★	F.A.A. Museum/Yeovilton
	G-BFZB	Piper J-3C-85 Cub	Zebedee Flying Group/Shoreham
	G-BFZD	Cessna FR.182RG	R. B. Lewis & Co/Sleap

Reg.	Type	Owner or Operator	Notes
G-BFZG	PA-28-161 Warrior II	C.S.E. Aviation Ltd/Kidlington	
G-BFZH	PA-28R Cherokee Arrow 200	W. E. Lowe	
G-BFZL	V.836 Viscount	British World Airlines Ltd/Southend	
G-BFZM	R. Commander 112TC	R. J. Lamplough/North Weald	
G-BFZN	Cessna FA.152	Falcon Flying Services/Biggin Hill	
G-BFZO	AA-5A Cheetah	Giles & Partners Ltd/Liverpool	
G-BFZT	Cessna FA.152	Zulu Tango Ltd/Guernsey	
G-BFZU	Cessna FA.152	Plane Talking Ltd/Elstree	
G-BFZV	Cessna F.172M	R. Thomas	
G-BGAA	Cessna 152 II	PJC Leasing Ltd	
G-BGAB	Cessna F.152 II	TG Aviation Ltd/Manston	
G-BGAD	Cessna F.152 II	Marnham Investments Ltd/Newtownards	
G-BGAE	Cessna F.152 II	Klingair Ltd/Conington	
G-BGAF	Cessna FA.152	M. F. Hatt & ptnrs/Southend	
G-BGAG	Cessna F.172N	Aerohire Ltd/Halfpenny Green	
G-BGAJ	Cessna F.182Q II	Ground Airport Services Ltd/Guernsey	
G-BGAK	Cessna F.182Q II	D. R. Joubert	
G-BGAX	PA-28 Cherokee 140	C. D. Brack	
G-BGAY	Cameron O-77 balloon	S. W. C. & P. C. A. Hall	
G-BGAZ	Cameron V-77 balloon	Cameron Balloons Ltd Silicon Chip	
G-BGBA	Robin R.2100A	D. Faulkner/Redhill	
G-BGBE	Jodel DR.1050	J. A. & B. Mawby	
G-BGBF	D.31A Turbulent	S. P. Wakeham	
G-BGBG	PA-28-181 Archer II	Harlow Printing Ltd/Newcastle	
G-BGBI	Cessna F.150L	Falcon Flying Services/Biggin Hill	
G-BGBK	PA-38-112 Tomahawk	F. Marshall & R. C. Priest/Netherthorpe	
G-BGBN	PA-38-112 Tomahawk	Bonus Aviation Ltd/Cranfield	
G-BGBP	Cessna F.152	Stapleford Flying Club Ltd	
G-BGBR	Cessna F.172N	Falcon Flying Services/Biggin Hill	
G-BGBU	Auster AOP.9 (XN435)	P. Neilson	
G-BGBW	PA-38-112 Tomahawk	Truman Aviation Ltd/Tollerton	
G-BGBY	PA-38-112 Tomahawk	Ravenair/Manchester	
G-BGBZ	R. Commander 114	R. S. Fenwick/Biggin Hill	
G-BGCG	Douglas C-47A	on rebuild	
G-BGCM	AA-5A Cheetah	G. & S. A. Jones	
G-BGCO	PA-44-180 Seminole	J. R. Henderson	
G-BGCX	Taylor JT.1 Monoplane	G. M. R. Walters	
G-BGCY	Taylor JT.1 Monoplane	M. T. Taylor	
G-BGDA	Boeing 737-236	British Airways Manchester *Bridgwater*	
G-BGDB	Boeing 737-236	British Airways	
G-BGDE	Boeing 737-236	British Airways *Pride of Manchester*	
G-BGDF	Boeing 737-236	British Airways *River Thames*	
G-BGDG	Boeing 737-236	British Airways Manchester *Trough of Bowland*	
G-BGDI	Boeing 737-236	British Airways Manchester *Pennine Way*	
G-BGDJ	Boeing 737-236	British Airways Manchester *Delamere Forest*	
G-BGDK	Boeing 737-236	British Airways Manchester *Ribble Valley*	
G-BGDL	Boeing 737-236	British Airways *Vale of Lune*	
G-BGDO	Boeing 737-236	British Airways	
G-BGDP	Boeing 737-236	British Airways *River Taff*	
G-BGDR	Boeing 737-236	British Airways *River Bann*	
G-BGDS	Boeing 737-236	GB Airways Ltd *Mons Calpe*	
G-BGDT	Boeing 737-236	British Airways Manchester *Wirral Peninsula*	
G-BGDU	Boeing 737-236	GB Airways Ltd *Mons Abyla*	
G-BGEA	Cessna F.150M	Agricultural & General Aviation Ltd/Bournemouth	
G-BGED	Cessna U.206F	Chapman Aviation Ltd	
G-BGEE	Evans VP-1	Evans VP-1 G-BGEE Group	
G-BGEF	Jodel D.112	G. G. Johnson & S. J. Davies	
G-BGEH	Monnett Sonerai II	P. C. Dowbor-Musnicki	
G-BGEI	Baby Great Lakes	I. D. Trask	
G-BGEK	PA-38-112 Tomahawk	Ravenair/Manchester	
G-BGEL	PA-38-112 Tomahawk	Ravenair/Manchester	
G-BGEP	Cameron D-38 balloon	Aeronord SAS/Italy	
G-BGEW	SNCAN NC.854S	Tavair Ltd	
G-BGFC	Evans VP-2	S. W. C. Hollins	
G-BGFF	FRED Srs 2	J. T. Taylor	
G-BGFG	AA-5A Cheetah	European Flyers (Blackbushe Airport) Ltd	
G-BGFH	Cessna F.182Q	Comed Aviation Ltd/Blackpool	
G-BGFI	AA-5A Cheetah	I. J. Hay & A. Nayyar/Biggin Hill	

Notes	Reg.	Type	Owner or Operator
	G-BGFJ	Jodel D.9 Bebe	M. D. Mold
	G-BGFK	Evans VP-1	I. N. M. Cameron
	G-BGFT	PA-34-200T Seneca II	C.S.E. Aviation Ltd/Kidlington
	G-BGFX	Cessna F.152	Falcon Flying Services/Biggin Hill
	G-BGGA	Bellanca 7GCBC Citabria	L. A. King
	G-BGGB	Bellanca 7GCBC Citabria	G. H. N. Chamberlain
	G-BGGC	Bellanca 7GCBC Citabria	H. P. Ashfield & J. P. Stone
	G-BGGD	Bellanca 8GCBC Scout	Bristol & Gloucestershire Gliding Club/ Nympsfield
	G-BGGE	PA-38-112 Tomahawk	Truman Aviation Ltd/Tollerton
	G-BGGF	PA-38-112 Tomahawk	Truman Aviation Ltd/Tollerton
	G-BGGG	PA-38-112 Tomahawk	Teesside Flight Centre Ltd
	G-BGGI	PA-38-112 Tomahawk	Truman Aviation Ltd/Tollerton
	G-BGGL	PA-38-112 Tomahawk	Grunwick Processing Laboratories Ltd/ Elstree
	G-BGGM	PA-38-112 Tomahawk	Grunwick Processing Laboratories Ltd/ Elstree
	G-BGGN	PA-38-112 Tomahawk	Domeastral Ltd/Elstree
	G-BGGO	Cessna F.152	E. Midlands Flying School Ltd
	G-BGGP	Cessna F.152	E. Midlands Flying School Ltd
	G-BGGU	Wallis WA-116/RR	K. H. Wallis
	G-BGGW	Wallis WA-112	K. H. Wallis
	G-BGGY	AB-206B Jet Ranger ★	Instructional airframe/Cranfield
	G-BGHE	Convair L-13A	J. M. Davis/Wichita
	G-BGHF	Westland WG.30 ★	International Helicopter Museum/ Weston-s-Mare
	G-BGHI	Cessna F.152	Taxon Ltd/Shoreham
	G-BGHM	Robin R.1180T	H. Price
	G-BGHP	Beech 76 Duchess	Magneta Ltd
	G-BGHS	Cameron N-31 balloon	W. R. Teasdale
	G-BGHT	Falconar F-12	C. R. Coates
	G-BGHU	NA T-6G Texan (115042)	C. E. Bellhouse
	G-BGHV	Cameron V-77 balloon	E. Davies
	G-BGHW	Thunder Ax8-90 balloon	Edinburgh University Balloon Group
	G-BGHY	Taylor JT.1 Monoplane	R. A. Hand
	G-BGHZ	FRED Srs 2	A. Smith
	G-BGIB	Cessna 152 II	Mona Aviation Ltd
	G-BGIC	Cessna 172N	I. P. Birdsall
	G-BGID	Westland-Bell 47G-3B1	M. J. Cuttell
	G-BGIG	PA-38-112 Tomahawk	Hebridean Air Services Ltd
	G-BGII	PA-32 Cherokee Six 300E	D. L. P. Milligan
	G-BGIO	Bensen B.8M	R. M. Savage & F. G. Shepherd
	G-BGIP	Colt 56A balloon	J. G. N. Perfect
	G-BGIU	Cessna F.172H	P. M. Smalley
	G-BGIV	Bell 47G-5	Abraxas Aviation Ltd
	G-BGIX	H.295 Super Courier	C. M. Lee/Andrewsfield
	G-BGIY	Cessna F.172N	Glasgow 172 Group
	G-BGJE	Boeing 737-236	British Airways River Wear/Gatwick
	G-BGJF	Boeing 737-236	British Airways River Axe/Gatwick
	G-BGJH	Boeing 737-236	British Airways River Lyne/Gatwick
	G-BGJI	Boeing 737-236	British Airways River Wey/Gatwick
	G-BGJJ	Boeing 737-236	British Airways River Swale/Gatwick
	G-BGJU	Cameron V-65 Balloon	J. A Folkes
	G-BGJW	GA-7 Cougar	P. G. Lawrence
	G-BGKC	SOCATA Rallye 110ST	J. H. Cranmer & T. A. Timms
	G-BGKD	SOCATA Rallye 110ST	R. G. Evans
	G-BGKJ	MBB Bo 105D ★	Instructional airframe/Bourn
	G-BGKO	GY-20 Minicab	R. B. Webber
	G-BGKS	PA-28-161 Warrior II	Marnham Investments Ltd
	G-BGKT	Auster AOP.9 (XN441)	Auster Nine Group
	G-BGKU	PA-28R-201 Arrow III	Caplane Ltd
	G-BGKV	PA-28R-201 Arrow III	R. Haverson & R. G. Watson
	G-BGKY	PA-38-112 Tomahawk	Prospect Air Ltd
	G-BGKZ	J/5F Aiglet Trainer	M. J. & A. A. Copse
	G-BGLA	PA-38-112 Tomahawk	Norwich School of Flying
	G-BGLB	Bede BD-5B ★	Science Museum/Wroughton
	G-BGLF	Evans VP-1 Srs 2	R. A. Yates
	G-BGLG	Cessna 152	Skyviews & General Ltd/Bourn
	G-BGLI	Cessna 152	Luton Flying Club (stored)
	G-BGLK	Monnett Sonerai II	N. M. Smorthit
	G-BGLN	Cessna FA.152	Bournemouth Flying Club
	G-BGLO	Cessna F.172N	A. H. Slaughter/Southend
	G-BGLS	Oldfield Super Baby Lakes	J. F. Dowe

Reg.	Type	Owner or Operator	Notes
G-BGLW	PA-34-200 Seneca	Stapleford Flying Club Ltd	
G-BGLX	Cameron N-56 balloon	S. L. G. Williams	
G-BGLZ	Stits SA-3A Playboy	B. G. Ell	
G-BGME	SIPA S.903	M. Emery & C. A. Suckling (G-BCML)/ Redhill	
G-BGMJ	GY-201 Minicab	S. L. Wakefield & ptnrs	
G-BGMP	Cessna F.172G	D. Rowe	
G-BGMR	GY-201 Minicab	T. J. D. Hodge & ptnrs	
G-BGMS	Taylor JT.2 Titch	M. A. J. Spice	
G-BGMT	MS.894E Rallye 235GT	J. Murray	
G-BGMU	Westland-Bell 47G-3B1	V. L. J. & V. English	
G-BGMV	Scheibe SF.25B Falke	Mendip Falke Flying Group	
G-BGMX	Enstrom 280C-UK	Stephenson Aviation Ltd (G-SHXX)	
G-BGNB	Short SD3-30 Variant 100	BAC Leasing Ltd	
G-BGND	Cessna F.172N	A. J. M. Freeman	
G-BGNG	Short SD3-30 Variant 100	Gill Airways Ltd/Newcastle	
G-BGNR	Cessna F.172N	Willow Warm Ltd/Southend	
G-BGNT	Cessna F.152	Klingair Ltd/Conington	
G-BGNV	GA-7 Cougar	G. H. Smith & Son	
G-BGOD	Colt 77A balloon	C. Allen & M. D. Steuer	
G-BGOG	PA-28-161 Warrior II	W. D. Moore	
G-BGOI	Cameron O-56 balloon	S. H. Budd	
G-BGOL	PA-28R-201T Turbo Arrow III	Valley Flying Co Ltd	
G-BGON	GA-7 Cougar	Plane Talking Ltd/Elstree	
G-BGOO	Colt 56 SS balloon	British Gas Corporation	
G-BGOP	Dassault Falcon 20F	Nissan (UK) Ltd/Heathrow	
G-BGOR	AT-6D Harvard III (14863)	M. L. Sargeant	
G-BGOX	PA-31-350 Navajo Chieftain	Keen Leasing Ltd	
G-BGPA	Cessna 182Q	Papa Alpha Group	
G-BGPB	CCF T-6J Texan (20385)	J. Romain/Duxford	
G-BGPD	Piper J-3C-65 Cub (479744)	P. D. Whiteman	
G-BGPH	AA-5B Tiger	A. J. Dales	
G-BGPI	Plumb BGP-1	B. G. Plumb	
G-BGPJ	PA-28-161 Warrior II	W. Lancs Warrior Co Ltd	
G-BGPK	AA-5B Tiger	G. A. Platon/Bournemouth	
G-BGPL	PA-28-161 Warrior II	TG Aviation Ltd/Manston	
G-BGPM	Evans VP-2	M. G. Reilly	
G-BGPN	PA-18 Super Cub 150	Clacton Aero Club (1988) Ltd	
G-BGPU	PA-28 Cherokee 140	Air Navigation & Trading Ltd/Blackpool	
G-BGPZ	M.S.890A Rallye Commodore	Popham Flying Group	
G-BGRC	PA-28 Cherokee 140	Arrow Air Centre Ltd/Shipdham	
G-BGRE	Beech A200 Super King Air	Martin-Baker (Engineering) Ltd/Chalgrove	
G-BGRG	Beech 76 Duchess	Motionscope Ltd/Blackpool	
G-BGRH	Robin DR.400/22	Rochester Aviation Ltd	
G-BGRI	Jodel DR.1051	B. Gunn & K. L. Burnett	
G-BGRK	PA-38-112 Tomahawk	Goodwood Terrena Ltd	
G-BGRL	PA-38-112 Tomahawk	Goodwood Terrena Ltd	
,G-BGRM	PA-38-112 Tomahawk	Goodwood Terrena Ltd	
G-BGRN	PA-38-112 Tomahawk	Goodwood Terrena Ltd	
G-BGRO	Cessna F.172M	Northfield Garage Ltd/Prestwick	
G-BGRR	PA-38-112 Tomahawk	Prospect Air Ltd	
G-BGRS	Thunder Ax7-77Z balloon	P. M. Gaines & P. B. Fountain	
G-BGRT	Steen Skybolt	J. H. Kimber & O. Meier	
G-BGRX	PA-38-112 Tomahawk	Bonus Aviation Ltd	
G-BGSA	M.S.892E Rallye 150GT	D. H. Tonkin	
G-BGSG	PA-44-180 Seminole	D. J. McSorley	
G-BGSH	PA-38-112 Tomahawk	Scotia Safari Ltd/Prestwick	
G-BGSI	PA-38-112 Tomahawk	Ravenair/Manchester	
G-BGSJ	Piper J-3C-65 Cub	W. J. Higgins/Dunkeswell	
G-BGST	Thunder Ax7-65 balloon	J. L. Bond	
G-BGSV	Cessna F.172N	Southwell Air Services Ltd	
G-BGSW	Beech F33 Debonair	Marketprior Ltd/Swansea	
G-BGSX	Cessna F.152	Plane Talking Ltd/Elstree	
G-BGSY	GA-7 Cougar	Van Allen Ltd/Guernsey	
G-BGTB	SOCATA TB.10 Tobago ★	D. Pope (stored)	
G-BGTC	Auster AOP.9 (XP282)	P. T. Bolton	
G-BGTF	PA-44-180 Seminole	NG Trustees & Nominees Ltd	
G-BGTG	PA-23 Aztec 250F	R. J. Howard/Sherburn	
G-BGTI	Piper J-3C-65 Cub	A. P. Broad	
G-BGTJ	PA-28 Cherokee 180	Serendipity Aviation/Staverton	
G-BGTP	Robin HR.100/210	J. C. Parker	
G-BGTT	Cessna 310R	Aviation Beauport Ltd/Jersey	
G-BGTX	Jodel D.117	Madley Flying Group/Shobdon	

Notes	Reg.	Type	Owner or Operator
	G-BGUA	PA-38-112 Tomahawk	Rhodair Maintenance Ltd/Cardiff
	G-BGUB	PA-32 Cherokee Six 300E	A. P. Diplock
	G-BGUY	Cameron V-56 balloon	J. L. Guy
	G-BGVB	Robin DR.315	Victor Bravo Group
	G-BGVE	CP.1310-C3 Super Emeraude	Victor Echo Group
	G-BGVH	Beech 76 Duchess	Velco Marketing
	G-BGVK	PA-28-161 Warrlor II	D. S. Wells
	G-BGVN	PA-28RT-201 Arrow IV	H. S. Davies
	G-BGVS	Cessna F.172M	Kirkwall Flying Club
	G-BGVT	Cessna R.182RG	Turnhouse Flying Club
	G-BGVU	PA-28 Cherokee 180	P. E. Toleman
	G-BGVV	AA-5A Cheetah	A. H. McVicar
	G-BGVW	AA-5A Cheetah	Air (BH) Associates Ltd/Biggin Hill
	G-BGVY	AA-5B Tiger	R. J. C. Neal-Smith
	G-BGVZ	PA-28-181 Archer II	Aerohire Ltd/Halfpenny Green
	G-BGWC	Robin DR.400/180	Shepherd Aviation Ltd/Rochester
	G-BGWH	PA-18 Super Cub 150	Clacton Aero Club (1988) Ltd
	G-BGWI	Cameron V-65 balloon	Army Balloon Club/Germany
	G-BGWJ	Sikorsky S-61N	British Executive Air Services Ltd
	G-BGWK	Sikorsky S-61N	Bristow Helicopters Ltd
	G-BGWM	PA-28-181 Archer II	Thames Valley Flying Club Ltd
	G-BGWN	PA-38-112 Tomahawk	Teesside Flight Centre Ltd
	G-BGWO	Jodel D.112	K. McBride
	G-BGWS	Enstrom 280C Shark	Stephenson Aviation Ltd
	G-BGWU	PA-38-112 Tomahawk	J. S. & L. M. Markey
	G-BGWV	Aeronca 7AC Champion	RFC Flying Group/Popham
	G-BGWW	PA-23 Turbo Aztec 250E	R. & M. International Ltd
	G-BGWY	Thunder Ax6-56Z balloon	P. J. Eley
	G-BGWZ	Eclipse Super Eagle ★	F.A.A. Museum/Yeovilton
	G-BGXA	Piper J-3C-65 Cub (329471)	K. Nicholls
	G-BGXB	PA-38-112 Tomahawk	Sightest Ltd/Biggin Hill
	G-BGXC	SOCATA TB.10 Tobago	N. N. Tullah/Cranfield
	G-BGXD	SOCATA TB.10 Tobago	C. C. Brown
	G-BGXJ	Partenavia P.68B	Cecil Aviation Ltd/Cambridge
	G-BGXK	Cessna 310R	Air Service Training Ltd/Perth
	G-BGXL	Bensen B.8MV	B. P. Triefus
	G-BGXN	PA-38-112 Tomahawk	Panshanger School of Flying Ltd
	G-BGXO	PA-38-112 Tomahawk	Goodwood Terrena Ltd
	G-BGXP	Westland-Bell 47G-3B1	Ace Motor Salvage (Norfolk)
	G-BGXR	Robin HR.200/100	E. G. Cleobury
	G-BGXS	PA-28-236 Dakota	Bawtry Road Service Station Ltd
	G-BGXT	SOCATA TB.10 Tobago	D. A. H. Morris
	G-BGYG	PA-28-161 Warrior II	C.S.E. Aviation Ltd/Kidlington
	G-BGYH	PA-28-161 Warrior II	C.S.E. Aviation Ltd/Kidlington
	G-BGYN	PA-18 Super Cub 150	B. J. Dunford
	G-BGYR	H.S.125 Srs 600B	British Aerospace (Operations) Ltd/Warton
	G-BGYT	EMB-110P1 Bandeirante	Air South West Ltd/Exeter
	G-BGZF	PA-38-112 Tomahawk	Cambrian Flying Club/Swansea
	G-BGZJ	PA-38-112 Tomahawk	W. R. C. M. Foyle
	G-BGZK	Westland-Bell 47G-3B1	Pan Air Ltd
	G-BGZL	Eiri PIK-20E	G-BGZL Flying Group/Enstone
	G-BGZN	WMB.2 Windtracker balloon	S. R. Woolfries
	G-BGZW	PA-38-112 Tomahawk	Ravenair/Manchester
	G-BGZY	Jodel D.120	M. Hale
	G-BGZZ	Thunder Ax6-56 balloon	J. M. Robinson
	G-BHAA	Cessna 152 II	Herefordshire Aero Club Ltd/Shobdon
	G-BHAC	Cessna A.152	Herefordshire Aero Club Ltd/Shobdon
	G-BHAD	Cessna A.152	Shropshire Aero Club Ltd/Sleap
	G-BHAF	PA-38-112 Tomahawk	Notelevel Ltd
	G-BHAI	Cessna F.152	J. Easson/Edinburgh
	G-BHAJ	Robin DR.400/160	Rowantask Ltd
	G-BHAL	Rango Saffery S.200 SS	A. M. Lindsay *Anneky Panky*
	G-BHAM	Thunder Ax6-56 balloon	D. Sampson
	G-BHAR	Westland-Bell 47G-3B1	E. A. L. Sturmer
	G-BHAT	Thunder Ax7-77 balloon	C. P. Witter Ltd *Witter*
	G-BHAV	Cessna F.152	Iceni Leasing
	G-BHAW	Cessna F.172N	A. J. Osmond/Biggin Hill
	G-BHAX	Enstrom F-28C-UK-2	PVS (Barnsley) Ltd
	G-BHAY	PA-28RT-201 Arrow IV	Alpha Yankee Group/Newcastle
	G-BHBA	Campbell Cricket	S. M. Irwin
	G-BHBB	Colt 77A balloon	S. D. Bellew
	G-BHBE	Westland-Bell 47G-3B1 (Soloy)	T. R. Smith (Agricultural Machinery) Ltd

Reg.	Type	Owner or Operator	Notes
G-BHBF	Sikorsky S-76A	Bristow Helicopters Ltd	
G-BHBG	PA-32R Cherokee Lance 300	L. T. Halpin	
G-BHBI	Mooney M.20J	M. Smith	
G-BHBT	Marquart MA.5 Charger	R. G. & C. J. Maidment/Shoreham	
G-BHBZ	Partenavia P.68B	Philip Hamer & Co	
G-BHCC	Cessna 172M	Langtry Flying Group Ltd	
G-BHCE	Jodel D.112	D. M. Parsons	
G-BHCM	Cessna F.172H	The English Connection Ltd/Panshanger	
G-BHCP	Cessna F.152	Sherburn Aero Club Ltd	
G-BHCT	PA-23 Aztec 250F	Falcon Flying Services (G-OLBC)/ Biggin Hill	
G-BHCW	PA-22 Tri-Pacer 150	V. F. Kemp	
G-BHCZ	PA-38-112 Tomahawk	J. E. Abbott	
G-BHDD	V.668 Varsity T.1 (WL626) ★	Aeropark/E. Midlands	
G-BHDE	SOCATA TB.10 Tobago	A. E. Allsop	
G-BHDH	Douglas DC-10-30	British Airways/Gatwick	
G-BHDI	Douglas DC-10-30	British Airways *Forest of Ae*/Gatwick	
G-BHDJ	Douglas DC-10-30	British Airways *Glengap Forest*/Gatwick	
G-BHDK	Boeing B-29A-BN (461748) ★	Imperial War Museum/Duxford	
G-BHDM	Cessna F.152 II	Tayside Aviation Ltd/Dundee	
G-BHDP	Cessna F.182Q II	A. K. Denson	
G-BHDR	Cessna F.152 II	Tayside Aviation Ltd/Dundee	
G-BHDS	Cessna F.152 II	Tayside Aviation Ltd/Dundee	
G-BHDT	SOCATA TB.10 Tobago	R. D. Hill	
G-BHDU	Cessna F.152 II	Falcon Flying Services/Biggin Hill	
G-BHDV	Cameron V-77 balloon	P. Glydon	
G-BHDW	Cessna F.152	Tayside Aviation Ltd/Dundee	
G-BHDX	Cessna F.172N	Skyhawk Group	
G-BHDZ	Cessna F.172N	J. B. Roberts	
G-BHEC	Cessna F.152	Stapleford Flying Club Ltd	
G-BHED	Cessna FA.152	TG Aviation Ltd/Manston	
G-BHEG	Jodel 150	D. W. Rouse	
G-BHEH	Cessna 310G	F. J. Shevill	
G-BHEK	CP.1315-C3 Super Emeraude	D. B. Winstanley/Barton	
G-BHEL	Jodel D.117	N. Wright & C. M. Kettlewell	
G-BHEM	Bensen B.8M	A. M. Sands	
G-BHEN	Cessna FA.152	Leicestershire Aero Club Ltd	
G-BHEO	Cessna FR.182RG	J. G. Hogg	
G-BHER	SOCATA TB.10 Tobago	Vale Aviation Ltd	
G-BHET	SOCATA TB.10 Tobago	Claude Hooper Ltd	
G-BHEU	Thunder Ax7-65 balloon	J. E. R. Govett	
G-BHEV	PA-28H Cherokee Arrow 200	E. & G. H. Kelk	
G-BHEX	Colt 56A balloon	A. S. Dear & ptnrs *Super Wasp*	
G-BHEZ	Jodel 150	B. N. Stevens	
G-BHFC	Cessna F.152	TG Aviation Ltd/Manston	
G-BHFE	PA-44-180 Seminole	Grunwick Ltd/Elstree	
G-BHFF	Jodel D.112	D. Silsbury	
G-BHFG	SNCAN Stampe SV-4C (45)	Stormswift Ltd	
G-BHFH	PA-34-200T Seneca II	Hendefern Ltd/Goodwood	
G-BHFI	Cessna F.152	BAe (Warton) Flying Group/Blackpool	
G-BHFJ	PA-28RT-201T Turbo Arrow IV	T. L. P. Delaney	
G-BHFK	PA-28-151 Warrior	Ilkeston Car Sales Ltd	
G-BHFM	Murphy S.200 balloon	M. Murphy	
G-BHFR	Eiri PIK-20E-1	J. T. Morgan	
G-BHFS	Robin DR.400/180	D. S. Chandler	
G-BHGA	PA-31-310 Turbo Navajo	Heltor Ltd	
G-BHGC	PA-18 Super Cub 150	Portsmouth Naval Gliding Club/ Lee-on-Solent	
G-BHGF	Cameron V-56 balloon	P. Smallward	
G-BHGJ	Jodel D.120	Q. M. B. Oswell	
G-BHGK	Sikorsky S-76A	Bond Helicopters Ltd	
G-BHGM	Beech 76 Duchess	Visual Phantom Ltd	
G-BHGO	PA-32 Cherokee Six 260	A. J. Crisp	
G-BHGP	SOCATA TB.10 Tobago	C. Flanagan	
G-BHGX	Colt 56B balloon	M. N. Dixon	
G-BHGY	PA-28R Cherokee Arrow 200	V. Humphries/Gamston	
G-BHHB	Cameron V-77 balloon	R. Powell	
G-BHHE	Jodel DR.1051/M1	P. Bridges	
G-BHHG	Cessna F.152 II	TG Aviation Ltd/Manston	
G-BHHH	Thunder Ax7-65 balloon	C. A. Hendley (Essex) Ltd	
G-BHHK	Cameron N-77 balloon	I. S. Bridge	
G-BHHN	Cameron V-77 balloon	Itchen Valley Balloon Group	
G-BHHU	Short SD3-30 Variant 100	Gill Airways Ltd/Newcastle	

Notes	Reg.	Type	Owner or Operator
	G-BHHX	Jodel D.112	D. I. Walker
	G-BHHZ	Rotorway Scorpion 133	L. W. & O. Usherwood
	G-BHIB	Cessna F.182Q	J. Blackburn & J. J. Feeney/Elstree
	G-BHIC	Cessna F.182Q	General Building Services Ltd/Leeds
	G-BHIG	Colt 31A balloon	P. A. Lindstrand
	G-BI IIH	Cessna F.172N	K. L. Burnett
	G-BHII	Cameron V-77 balloon	R. V. Brown
	G-BHIJ	Eiri PIK-20E-1	I. W. Paterson/Portmoak
	G-BHIK	Adam RA-14 Loisirs	L. Lewis
	G-BHIN	Cessna F.152	P. Skinner/Egginton
	G-BHIR	PA-28R Cherokee Arrow 200	Factorcore Ltd/Barton
	G-BHIS	Thunder Ax7-65 balloon	Hedgehoppers Balloon Group
	G-BHIT	SOCATA TB.9 Tampico	Air Touring Services Ltd/Biggin Hill
	G-BHIY	Cessna F.150K	Westfield Flying Group
	G-BHJA	Cessna A.152	Cornwall Flying Club Ltd/Bodmin
	G-BHJB	Cessna A.152	Sky Pro Ltd
	G-BHJF	SOCATA TB.10 Tobago	D. G. Dedman
	G-BHJI	Mooney M.20J	S. F. Lister
	G-BHJK	Maule M5-235C Lunar Rocket	P. F. Hall & R. L. Sambell
	G-BHJN	Fournier RF-4D	RF-4 Flying Group
	G-BHJO	PA-28-161 Warrior II	The Brackla Flying Group/Inverness
	G-BHJS	Partenavia P.68B	Shepherd Aviation Ltd
	G-BHJU	Robin DR.400/2+2	T. J. Harlow
	G-BHKA	Evans VP-1	M. L. Perry
	G-BHKH	Cameron O-65 balloon	D. G. Body
	G-BHKJ	Cessna 421C	Crosslee PLC
	G-BHKR	Colt 12A balloon ★	British Balloon Museum
	G-BHKT	Jodel D.112	The Evans Flying Group
	G-BHKV	AA-5A Cheetah	Alouette Flying Club Ltd/Biggin Hill
	G-BHKY	Cessna 310R II	Air Service Training Ltd/Perth
	G-BHLE	Robin DR.400/180	L. H. Mayall
	G-BHLH	Robin DR.400/180	W. A. Clark
	G-BHLJ	Saffery-Rigg S.200 balloon	I. A. Rigg
	G-BHLT	D.H.82A Tiger Moth	P. J. & A. J. Borsberry
	G-BHLU	Fournier RF-3	M. C. Roper
	G-BHLW	Cessna 120	R. T. Meston
	G-BHLX	AA-5B Tiger	Tiger Aviation (Jersey) Ltd
	G-BHLY	Sikorsky S-76A	Bristow Helicopters Ltd
	G-BHMA	SIPA 903	H. J. Taggart
	G-BHME	WMB.2 Windtracker balloon	I. R. Bell & ptnrs
	G-BHMG	Cessna FA.152	R. D. Smith
	G-BHMI	Cessna F.172N	W. Lancs Aero Club Ltd (G-WADE)/ Woodvale
	G-BHMJ	Avenger T.200-2112 balloon	R. Light *Lord Anthony 1*
	G-BHMK	Avenger T.200-2112 balloon	P. Kinder *Lord Anthony 2*
	G-BHMM	Avenger T.200-2112 balloon	M. Murphy *Lord Anthony 4*
	G-BHMO	PA-20M Cerpa Special (Pacer)	A. B. Holloway & ptnrs
	G-BHMR	Stinson 108-3	D. G. French/Sandown
	G-BHMT	Evans VP-1	P. E. J. Sturgeon
	G-BHMW	F.27 Friendship Mk 200	*Permanently withdrawn*
	G-BHMY	F.27 Friendship Mk 200	*Permanently withdrawn*
	G-BHNA	Cessna F.152	Sheffield Aero Club Ltd/Netherthorpe
	G-BHNC	Cameron O-65 balloon	D. & C. Bareford
	G-BHND	Cameron N-65 balloon	S. M. Wellband
	G-BHNK	Jodel D.120A	G-BHNK Flying Group
	G-BHNL	Jodel D.112	G. van der Gaag
	G-BHNO	PA-28-181 Archer II	Davison Plant Hire Co/Compton Abbas
	G-BHNP	Eiri PIK-20E-1	D. A. Sutton
	G-BHNU	Cessna F.172N	T. Beliwar
	G-BHNX	Jodel D.117	R. V. Rendall
	G-BHOA	Robin DR.400/160	M. J. Ferguson
	G-BHOF	Sikorsky S-61N	Bristow Helicopters Ltd
	G-BHOG	Sikorsky S-61N	Bristow Helicopters Ltd
	G-BHOH	Sikorsky S-61N	Bristow Helicopters Ltd
	G-BHOL	Jodel DR.1050	D. G. Hart
	G-BHOM	PA-18 Super Cub 95	C. H. A. Bott
	G-BHOO	Thunder Ax7-65 balloon	D. Livesey & J. M. Purves *Scraps*
	G-BHOR	PA-28-161 Warrior II.	Oscar Romeo Flying Group/Biggin Hill
	G-BHOT	Cameron V-65 balloon	Dante Balloon Group
	G-BHOU	Cameron V-65 balloon	F. W. Barnes
	G-BHOZ	SOCATA TB.9 Tampico	M. Brown
	G-BHPK	Piper J-3C-65 Cub (236800)	L-4 Group
	G-BHPL	C.A.S.A. 1.131E Jungmann 1000	M. G. Jeffries

Reg.	Type	Owner or Operator	Notes
G-BHPM	PA-18 Super Cub 95	P. I. Morgans	
G-BHPN	Colt 14A balloon	Lindstrand Balloons Ltd	
G-BHPO	Colt 14A balloon	C. J. Boxall	
G-BHPS	Jodel D.120A	R. A. Morris & R. V. Emerson	
G-BHPT	Piper J-3C-65 Cub	Rolfe Air Services	
G-BHPX	Cessna 152 II	J. A. Pothecary/Shoreham	
G-BHPY	Cessna 152 II	A. T. Hooper & T. E. Evans/Wellesbourne	
G-BHPZ	Cessna 172N	O'Brian Properties Ltd/Redhill	
G-BHRA	R. Commander 114A	P. A. Warner	
G-BHRB	Cessna F.152 II	LAC (Enterprises) Ltd/Barton	
G-BHRC	PA-28-161 Warrior II	Sherwood Flying Club Ltd/Tollerton	
G-BHRD	D.H.C.1 Chipmunk 22 (WP977)	G-BHRD Group/Kidlington	
G-BHRH	Cessna FA.150K	Merlin Flying Club Ltd/Hucknall	
G-BHRI	Saffery S.200 balloon	N. J. & H. L. Dunnington	
G-BHRM	Cessna F.152	Aerohire Ltd/Halfpenny Green	
G-BHRN	Cessna F.152	J. Easson/Edinburgh	
G-BHRO	R. Commander 112A	John Raymond Transport Ltd/Cardiff	
G-BHRP	PA-44-180 Seminole	Merlinrun Ltd/E. Midlands	
G-BHRR	CP.301A Emeraude	T. W. Offen	
G-BHRW	Jodel DR.221	Dauphin Flying Group	
G-BHRY	Colt 56A balloon	A. S. Davidson	
G-BHSA	Cessna 152 II	Skyviews & General Ltd/Sherburn	
G-BHSB	Cessna 172N	Saunders Caravans Ltd	
G-BHSD	Scheibe SF.25E Super Falke	Lasham Gliding Soc Ltd	
G-BHSE	R. Commander 114	604 Sqdn Flying Group Ltd	
G-BHSN	Cameron N-56 balloon	I. Bentley	
G-BHSP	Thunder Ax7-77Z balloon	Out-Of-The-Blue	
G-BHSS	Pitts S-1C Special	Bottoms Up Syndicate	
G-BHSY	Jodel DR.1050	S. R. Orwin & T. R. Allebone	
G-BHTA	PA-28-236 Dakota	Dakota Ltd	
G-BHTC	Jodel DR.1050/M1	G. Clark	
G-BHTD	Cessna T.188C AgHusky	ADS (Aerial) Ltd/Southend	
G-BHTG	Thunder Ax6-56 balloon	F. R. & Mrs S. H. MacDonald	
G-BHTH	NA T-6G Texan (2807)	J. J. Woodhouse	
G-BHTR	Bell 206B JetRanger 3	Huktra (UK) Ltd	
G-BHUB	Douglas C-47A (315509) ★	Imperial War Museum/Duxford	
G-BHUE	Jodel DR.1050	M. J. Harris	
G-BHUG	Cessna 172N	Air Group 6/Gamston	
G-BHUI	Cessna 152	Roylair Services Ltd	
G-BHUJ	Cessna 172N	Northamptonshire School of Flying Ltd	
G-BHUM	D.H.82A Tiger Moth	S. G. Towers	
G-BHUO	Evans VP-2	D. A. Wood	
G-BHUR	Thunder Ax3 balloon	B. F. G. Ribbans	
G-BHUU	PA-25 Pawnee 235	Pawnee Aviation/Boston	
G-BHVB	PA-28-161 Warrior II	Castle Electronics	
G-BHVC	Cessna 172RG Cutlass	I. B. Willis/Panshanger	
G-BHVE	Saffery S.330 balloon	P. M. Randles	
G-BHVF	Jodel 150A	J. D. Walton	
G-BHVN	Cessna 152 II	Three Counties Aero Engineering Ltd/ Lasham	
G-BHVP	Cessna 182Q	Battleflat Group	
G-BHVR	Cessna 172N	Maxhill Ltd	
G-BHVV	Piper J-3C-65 Cub	P. R. Wright/Barton	
G-BHVZ	Cessna 180	R. Moore/Blackpool	
G-BHWA	Cessna F.152	Wickenby Aviation Ltd	
G-BHWB	Cessna F.152	Wickenby Aviation Ltd	
G-BHWG	Mahatma S.200SR balloon	H. W. Gandy *Spectrum*	
G-BHWH	Weedhopper JC-24A	G. A. Clephane	
G-BHWK	M.S.880B Rallye Club	Arrow Flying Group	
G-BHWS	Cessna F.152 II	Turnhouse Flying Club	
G-BHWY	PA-28R Cherokee Arrow 200-II	Kilo Foxtrot Flying Group/Sandown	
G-BHWZ	PA-28-181 Archer II	I. R. McCue	
G-BHXA	SA Bulldog Srs 120/1210	D. A. Williams/Liverpool	
G-BHXB	SA Bulldog Srs 120/1210	D. A. Williams/Liverpool	
G-BHXD	Jodel D.120	P. H. C. Hall	
G-BHXK	PA-28 Cherokee 140	GXK Flying Group	
G-BHXL	Evans VP-2	R. S. Wharton	
G-BHXS	Jodel D.120	I. R. Willis	
G-BHXT	Thunder Ax6-56Z balloon	Ocean Traffic Services Ltd	
G-BHXV	AB-206B JetRanger 3	Dollar Air Services Ltd (G-OWJM)	
G-BHXY	Piper J-3C-65 Cub (44-79609)	F. W. Rogers/Aldergrove	
G-BHYA	Cessna R.182RG II	Stainless Steel Profile Cutters Ltd	
G-BHYC	Cessna 172RG II	Red Rose International Ltd	

Notes	Reg.	Type	Owner or Operator
	G-BHYD	Cessna R.172K XP II	Sylmar Aviation Services Ltd
	G-BHYE	PA-34-200T Seneca II	C.S.E. Aviation Ltd/Kidlington
	G-BHYF	PA-34-200T Seneca II	C.S.E. Aviation Ltd/Kidlington
	G-BHYG	PA-34-200T Seneca II	C.S.E. Aviation Ltd/Kidlington
	G-BHYI	SNCAN Stampe SV-4A	P. A. Irwin
	G-BHYN	Evans VP-2	D. Cromie
	G-BHYP	Cessna F.172M	Avior Ltd/Biggin Hill
	G-BHYR	Cessna F.172M	Alumvale Ltd/Stapleford
	G-BHYV	Evans VP-1	L. Chiappi/Blackpool
	G-BHYX	Cessna 152 II	Stapleford Flying Club Ltd
	G-BHZE	PA-28-181 Archer II	Northfield Garage Ltd
	G-BHZF	Evans VP-2	W. J. Evans
	G-BHZH	Cessna F.152	1013 Ltd/Guernsey
	G-BHZK	AA-5B Tiger	N. K. Margolis/Elstree
	G-BHZO	AA-5A Cheetah	Scotia Safari Ltd/Prestwick
	G-BHZR	SA Bulldog Srs 120/1210	M. A. Elobeid
	G-BHZS	SA Bulldog Srs 120/1210	D. A. Williams/Liverpool
	G-BHZT	SA Bulldog Srs 120/1210	W. M. Bax
	G-BHZU	Piper J-3C-65 Cub	J. K. Tomkinson
	G-BHZV	Jodel D.120A	K. J. Scott
	G-BHZX	Thunder Ax7-65A balloon	R. J. & H. M. Beattie
	G-BIAB	SOCATA TB.9 Tampico	H. W. A. Thirlway
	G-BIAC	SOCATA Rallye 235E	Aerial Group Ltd
	G-BIAH	Jodel D.112	D. Mitchell
	G-BIAI	WMB.2 Windtracker balloon	I. Chadwick
	G-BIAK	SOCATA TB.10 Tobago	Real Life Ltd
	G-BIAL	Rango NA.8 balloon	A. M. Lindsay
	G-BIAO	Evans VP-2	P. J. Hall
	G-BIAP	PA-16 Clipper	P. J. Bish & M. J. Mothershaw
	G-BIAR	Rigg Skyliner II balloon	I. A. Rigg
	G-BIAU	Sopwith Pup (replica) (N6452)	F.A.A. Museum/Yeovilton
	G-BIAX	Taylor JT.2 Titch	J. T. Everest
	G-BIAY	AA-5 Traveler	M. D. Dupay & ptnrs
	G-BIBA	SOCATA TB.9 Tampico	TB Aviation Ltd
	G-BIBB	Mooney M.20C	B. Walker & Sons (Dursley) Ltd
	G-BIBC	Cessna 310R	Air Service Training Ltd/Perth
	G-BIBG	Sikorksy S-76A	Bristow Helicopters Ltd
	G-BIBJ	Enstrom 280C-UK-2	Tindon Ltd/Little Snoring
	G-BIBK	Taylor JT.2 Titch	J. G. McTaggart
	G-BIBN	Cessna FA.150K	G. A. Eaton & C. G. Wilson
	G-BIBO	Cameron V-65 balloon	I. Harris
	G-BIBP	AA-5A Cheetah	Scotia Safari Ltd/Prestwick
	G-BIBS	Cameron P-20 balloon	Cameron Balloons Ltd
	G-BIBT	AA-5B Tiger	Fergusons (Blyth) Ltd/Newcastle
	G-BIBW	Cessna F.172N	Deltair Ltd/Liverpool
	G-BIBX	WMB.2 Windtracker balloon	I. A. Rigg
	G-BIBY	Beech F33A Bonanza	G. T. Grimward
	G-BICD	Auster 5	R. T. Parsons
	G-BICE	AT-6C Harvard IIA (41-33275)	C. M. L. Edwards
	G-BICG	Cessna F.152 II	Falcon Flying Services/Biggin Hill
	G-BICJ	Monnett Sonerai II	D. J. Marks
	G-BICM	Colt 56A balloon	Avon Advertiser Balloon Club
	G-BICN	F.8L Falco	R. J. Barber
	G-BICP	Robin DR.360	Bravo India Flying Group/Woodvale
	G-BICR	Jodel D.120A	Beehive Flying Group/White Waltham
	G-BICS	Robin R.2100A	G-BICS Group/Sibson
	G-BICT	Evans VP-1	A. S. Coombe & D. L. Tribe
	G-BICU	Cameron V-56 balloon	S. D. Bather & D. Scott
	G-BICW	PA-28-161 Warrior II	D. Gellhorn
	G-BICX	Maule M5-235C Lunar Rocket	A. T. Jeans & J. F. Clarkson/Old Sarum
	G-BICY	PA-23 Apache 160	A. M. Lynn/Sibson
	G-BIDD	Evans VP-1	G. J. McDill
	G-BIDF	Cessna F.172P	E. Alexander
	G-BIDG	Jodel 150A	D. R. Gray/Barton
	G-BIDH	Cessna 152 II	Cumbria Aero Club (G-DONA)/Carlisle
	G-BIDI	PA-28R-201 Arrow III	Ambrit Ltd
	G-BIDJ	PA-18A Super Cub 150	AB Plant (Bristol) Ltd
	G-BIDK	PA-18 Super Cub 150	R. G. Warwick
	G-BIDO	CP.301A Emeraude	A. R. Plumb
	G-BIDU	Cameron V-77 balloon	E. Eleazor
	G-BIDV	Colt 14A balloon	International Distillers & Vintners (House Trade) Ltd

Reg.	Type	Owner or Operator	Notes
G-BIDW	Sopwith 1 1/2 Strutter (replica) (A8226) ★	RAF Museum/Hendon	
G-BIDX	Jodel D.112	H. N. Nuttall & R. P. Walley	
G-BIEF	Cameron V-77 balloon	D. S. Bush	
G-BIEJ	Sikorsky S-76A	Bristow Helicopters Ltd	
G-BIEN	Jodel D.120A	R. J. Baker	
G-BIEO	Jodel D.112	Clipgate Flyers	
G-BIES	Maule M5-235C Lunar Rocker	William Proctor Farms	
G-BIET	Cameron O-77 balloon	G. M. Westley	
G-BIEY	PA-28-151 Warrior	J. A. Pothecary/Shoreham	
G-BIFA	Cessna 310R II	Booth Plant & Equipment Ltd	
G-BIFB	PA-28 Cherokee 150C	N. A. Ayub	
G-BIFH	Short SD3-30 Variant 100	Streamline Aviation (SW) Ltd	
G-BIFN	Bensen B.8M	B. Gunn	
G-BIFO	Evans VP-1	R. Broadhead	
G-BIFP	Colt 56C balloon	J. Philp	
G-BIFY	Cessna F.150L	Jureen Aviation	
G-BIFZ	Partenavia P.68C	Jet Airmotive Ltd	
G-BIGD	Cameron V-77 balloon	D. L. Clark	
G-BIGF	Thunder Ax7-77 balloon	M. D. Stever & C. A. Allen	
G-BIGJ	Cessna F.172M	Clacton Aero Club (1988) Ltd	
G-BIGK	Taylorcraft BC-12D	N. P. St. J. Ramsey	
G-BIGL	Cameron O-65 balloon	P. L. Mossman	
G-BIGM	Avenger T.200-2112 balloon	M. Murphy	
G-BIGP	Bensen B.8M	R. H. S. Cooper	
G-BIGR	Avenger T.200-2112 balloon	R. Light	
G-BIGX	Bensen B.8M	W. C. Turner	
G-BIGY	Cameron V-65 balloon	Dante Balloon Group	
G-BIGZ	Scheibe SF.25B Falke	G-BIGZ Syndicate/Saltby	
G-BIHD	Robin DR.400/160	K. B. Mainstone	
G-BIHE	Cessna FA.152	J. Easson/Edinburgh	
G-BIHF	SE-5A (replica) (F943)	K. J. Garrett/Booker	
G-BIHG	PA-28 Cherokee 140	T. M. Plewman	
G-BIHI	Cessna 172M	R. D. & S. R. Spencer	
G-BIHO	D.H.C.6 Twin Otter 310	Isles of Scilly Skybus Ltd/St. Just	
G-BIHP	Van Den Bemden gas balloon	J. J. Harris	
G-BIHT	PA-17 Vagabond	G. H. Cork	
G-BIHU	Saffrey S.200 balloon	B. L. King	
G-BIHW	Aeronca A65TAC Defender	T. J. Ingrouille	
G-BIHX	Bensen B.8M	P. P. Willmott	
G-BIHY	Isaacs Fury	P. C. Butler	
G-BIIA	Fournier RF-3	T. M. W. Webster	
G-BIIB	Cessna F.172M	Civil Service Flying Club (Biggin Hill) Ltd	
G-BIID	PA-18 Super Cub 95	875 (Westhill) Squadron ATC	
G-BIIE	Cessna F.172P	Shoreham Flight Simulator Ltd/Bournemouth	
G-BIIG	Thunder Ax6-56Z balloon	Chiltern Flyers Ltd	
G-BIIJ	Cessna F.152 II	Leicestershire Aero Club Ltd	
G-BIIK	M.S.883 Rallye 115	Chiltern Flyers Ltd	
G-BIIL	Thunder Ax6-56 balloon	G. W. Reader	
G-BIIT	PA-28-161 Warrior II	Tayside Aviation Ltd/Dundee	
G-BIIV	PA-28-181 Archer II	Stratton Motor Co Ltd	
G-BIIX	Rango NA.12 balloon	Rango Kite Co	
G-BIIZ	Great Lakes 2T-1A Sport Trainer	J. R. Lindsay	
G-BIJB	PA-18 Super Cub 150	Essex Gliding Club/North Weald	
G-BIJD	Bo 208C Junior	C. G. Stone	
G-BIJE	Piper J-3C-65 Cub	R. L. Hayward & A. G. Scott	
G-BIJS	Luton LA-4A Minor	I. J. Smith	
G-BIJU	CP-301A Emeraude	Eastern Taildraggers Flying Group (G-BHTX)	
G-BIJV	Cessna F.152 II	Falcon Flying Services/Biggin Hill	
G-BIJW	Cessna F.152 II	Falcon Flying Services/Biggin Hill	
G-BIJX	Cessna F.152 II	Falcon Flying Services/Biggin Hill	
G-BIKA	Boeing 757-236	British Airways Dover Castle	
G-BIKB	Boeing 757-236	British Airways Windsor Castle	
G-BIKC	Boeing 757-236	British Airways Edinburgh Castle	
G-BIKD	Boeing 757-236	British Airways Caernarfon Castle	
G-BIKE	PA-28R Cherokee Arrow 200	R. V. Webb Ltd/Elstree	
G-BIKF	Boeing 757-236	British Airways Carrickfergus Castle	
G-BIKG	Boeing 757-236	British Airways Stirling Castle	
G-BIKH	Boeing 757-236	British Airways Richmond Castle	
G-BIKI	Boeing 757-236	British Airways Tintagel Castle	
G-BIKJ	Boeing 757-236	British Airways Conwy Castle	

Notes	Reg.	Type	Owner or Operator
	G-BIKK	Boeing 757-236	British Airways *Eilean Donan Castle*
	G-BIKL	Boeing 757-236	British Airways *Nottingham Castle*
	G-BIKM	Boeing 757-236	British Airways *Glamis Castle*
	G-BIKN	Boeing 757-236	British Airways *Bodiam Castle*
	G-BIKO	Boeing 757-236	British Airways *Harlech Castle*
	G-BIKP	Boeing 757-236	British Airways *Enniskillen Castle*
	G-BIKR	Boeing 757-236	British Airways *Bamburgh Castle*
	G-BIKS	Boeing 757-236	British Airways *Corfe Castle*
	G-BIKT	Boeing 757-236	British Airways *Carisbrooke Castle*
	G-BIKU	Boeing 757-236	British Airways *Inveraray Castle*
	G-BIKV	Boeing 757-236	British Airways *Raglan Castle*
	G-BIKW	Boeing 757-236	British Airways *Belvoir Castle*
	G-BIKX	Boeing 757-236	British Airways *Warwick Castle*
	G-BIKY	Boeing 757-236	British Airways *Leeds Castle*
	G-BIKZ	Boeing 757-236	British Airways *Kenilworth Castle*
	G-BILA	Daletol DM.165L Viking	R. Lamplough *(stored)*
	G-BILB	WMB.2 Windtracker balloon	B. L. King
	G-BILE	Scruggs BL.2B balloon	P. D. Ridout
	G-BILF	Practavia Sprite 125	G. Harfield
	G-BILG	Scruggs BL.2B balloon	P. D. Ridout
	G-BILI	Piper J-3C-65 Cub (454467)	G-BILI Flying Group
	G-BILJ	Cessna FA.152	Shoreham Flight Simulation Ltd/Bournemouth
	G-BILK	Cessna FA.152	Exeter Flying Club Ltd
	G-BILL	PA-25 Pawnee 235	Pawnee Aviation
	G-BILR	Cessna 152	Skyviews & General Ltd
	G-BILS	Cessna 152	Skyviews & General Ltd
	G-BILU	Cessna 172RG	Full Sutton Flying Centre Ltd
	G-BILZ	Taylor JT.1 Monoplane	A. Petherbridge
	G-BIMK	Tiger T.200 Srs 1 balloon	M. K. Baron
	G-BIMM	PA-18 Super Cub 150	Clacton Aero Club (1988) Ltd
	G-BIMN	Steen Skybolt	C. R. Williamson
	G-BIMO	SNCAN Stampe SV-4C	R. A. Roberts
	G-BIMT	Cessna FA.152	Staverton Flying Services Ltd
	G-BIMU	Sikorsky S-61N	Bristow Helicopters Ltd
	G-BIMX	Rutan Vari-Eze	D. G. Crow/Biggin Hill
	G-BIMZ	Beech 76 Duchess	Barrein Engineers Ltd
	G-BINF	Saffery S.200 balloon	T. Lewis
	G-BING	Cessna F.172P	J. E. M. Patrick
	G-BINI	Scruggs BL.2C balloon	S. R. Woolfries
	G-BINL	Scruggs BL.2B balloon	P. D. Ridout
	G-BINM	Scruggs BL.2B balloon	P. D. Ridout
	G-BINO	Evans VP-1	G. Ravichadran
	G-BINR	Unicorn UE.1A balloon	Unicorn Group
	G-BINS	Unicorn UE.2A balloon	Unicorn Group
	G-BINT	Unicorn UE.1A balloon	Unicorn Group
	G-BINU	Saffery S.200 balloon	T. Lewis
	G-BINX	Scruggs BL.2B balloon	P. D. Ridout
	G-BINY	Oriental balloon	J. L. Morton
	G-BIOB	Cessna F.172P	Aerofilms Ltd/Elstree
	G-BIOC	Cessna F.150L	Seawing Flying Club/Southend
	G-BIOE	Short SD3-30 Variant 100	Gill Airways Ltd/Newcastle
	G-BIOI	Jodel DR.1051/M	H. F. Hambling
	G-BIOJ	R. Commander 112TCA	A. T. Dalby
	G-BIOK	Cessna F.152	Tayside Aviation Ltd/Dundee
	G-BIOM	Cessna F.152	Falcon Flying Services/Luton
	G-BION	Cameron V-77 balloon	Flying Doctors Balloon Syndicate
	G-BIOR	M.S.880B Rallye Club	R. L. & K. P. McLean
	G-BIOU	Jodel D.117A	Dubious Group/Booker
	G-BIOW	Slingsby T.67A	A. B. Slinger/Sherburn
	G-BIPA	AA-5B Tiger	J. Campbell/Walney Island
	G-BIPH	Scruggs BL.2B balloon	C. M. Dewsnap
	G-BIPI	Everett Blackbird Mk 1	R. Spall
	G-BIPN	Fournier RF-3	J. C. R. Rogers & I. F. Fairhead
	G-BIPO	Mudry/CAARP CAP.20LS-200	D. C. MacDonald
	G-BIPS	SOCATA Rallye 100ST	McAully Flying Group/Little Snoring
	G-BIPT	Jodel D.112	C. R. Davies
	G-BIPV	AA-5B Tiger	Solent Flight
	G-BIPW	Avenger T.200-2112 balloon	B. L. King
	G-BIPY	Bensen B.8	D. F. Hughes
	G-BIRD	Pitts S-1C Special	Pitts Artists Flying Group
	G-BIRE	Colt 56 Bottle SS balloon	K. R. Gafney
	G-BIRH	PA-18 Super Cub 135 (R-163)	I. R. F. Hammond/Lee-on-Solent

Reg.	Type	Owner or Operator	Notes
G-BIRI	C.A.S.A. 1.131E Jungmann 1000	M. G. & J. R. Jeffries	
G-BIRK	Avenger T.200-2112 balloon	D. Harland	
G-BIRL	Avenger T.200-2112 balloon	R. Light	
G-BIRM	Avenger T.200-2112 balloon	P. Higgins	
G-BIRP	Arena Mk 17 Skyship balloon	A. S. Viel	
G-BIRS	Cessna 182P	John E. Birks & Associates Ltd (G-BBBS)	
G-BIRT	Robin R.1180TD	W. D'A. Hall/Booker	
G-BIRW	M.S.505 Criquet (F+IS) ★	Museum of Flight/E. Fortune	
G-BIRY	Cameron V-77 balloon	J. J. Winter	
G-BIRZ	Zenair CH.250	A. W. F. Richards	
G-BISB	Cessna F.152 II	Sheffield Aero Club Ltd/Netherthorpe	
G-BISG	FRED Srs 3	R. A. Coombe	
G-BISH	Cameron O-42 balloon	Zebedee Balloon Service	
G-BISJ	Cessna 340A .	Billair	
G-BISK	R. Commander 112B ★	P. A. Warner	
G-BISL	Scruggs BL.2B balloon	P. D. Ridout	
G-BISM	Scruggs BL.2B balloon	P. D. Ridout	
G-BISS	Scruggs BL.2C balloon	P. D. Ridout	
G-BIST	Scruggs BL.2C balloon	P. D. Ridout	
G-BISV	Cameron O-65 balloon	Hylyne Rabbits Ltd	
G-BISW	Cameron O-65 balloon	Rango Balloon & Kite Co	
G-BISX	Colt 56A balloon	J. R. Gore	
G-BISZ	Sikorsky S-76A	Bristow Helicopters Ltd	
G-BITA	PA-18 Super Cub 150	J. & S. A. S. McCullough	
G-BITE	SOCATA TB.10 Tobago	M. A. Smith & R. J. Bristow/Fairoaks	
G-BITF	Cessna F.152 II	Tayside Aviation Ltd/Dundee	
G-BITG	Cessna F.152	T. Hayselden	
G-BITH	Cessna F.152 II	Tayside Aviation Ltd/Dundee	
G-BITK	FRED Srs 2	D. J. Wood	
G-BITM	Cessna F.172P	D. G. Crabtree/Barton	
G-BITO	Jodel D.112D	A. Dunbar/Barton	
G-BITR	Sikorsky S-76A	Bristow Helicopters Ltd	
G-BITS	Drayton B-56 balloon	M. J. Betts	
G-BITW	Short SD3-30 Variant 100	Figurepart Trading Ltd (G-EASI)	
G-BITY	FD.31T balloon	A. J. Bell	
G-BIUL	Cameron 60 SS balloon	D. C. Patrick-Brown	
G-BIUM	Cessna F.152	Sheffield Aero Club Ltd/Netherthorpe	
G-BIUP	SNCAN NC.854S	BIUP Flying Group	
G-BIUU	PA-23 Aztec 250D ★	G. Cormack/Glasgow	
G-BIUV	H.S.748 Srs 2A	Emerald Airways Ltd *City of Liverpool* (G-AYYH)/Liverpool	
G-BIUW	PA-28-161 Warrlor II	D. R. Staley	
G-BIUY	PA-28-181 Archer II	E. S. Singh	
G-BIVA	Robin R.2112	Cotswold Aero Club Ltd/Staverton	
G-BIVB	Jodel D.112	D. H. Anderson	
G-BIVC	Jodel D.112	M. J. Barmby/Cardiff	
G-BIVK	Bensen B.8	J. G. Toy	
G-BIVL	Bensen B.8	R. Gardiner	
G-BIVT	Saffery S.80 balloon	L. F. Guyot	
G-BIVV	AA-5A Cheetah	W. Dass	
G-BIVZ	D.31A Turbulent	The Tiger Club (1990) Ltd/Headcorn	
G-BIWB	Scruggs RS.5000 balloon	P. D. Ridout	
G-BIWC	Scruggs RS.5000 balloon	P. D. Ridout	
G-BIWD	Scruggs RS.5000 balloon	D. Eaves	
G-BIWF	Warren balloon	P. D. Ridout	
G-BIWG	Zelenski Mk 2 balloon	P. D. Ridout	
G-BIWJ	Unicorn UE.1A balloon	B. L. King	
G-BIWK	Cameron V-65 balloon	I. R. Williams & R. G. Bickerdicke	
G-BIWL	PA-32-301 Saratoga	Primark Enterprises Ltd	
G-BIWN	Jodel D.112	C. R. Coates	
G-BIWP	Mooney M.20J	Whiskey Papa Flying Group	
G-BIWR	Mooney M.20F	A. C. Brink	
G-BIWU	Cameron V-65 balloon	D. Stuttard & B. Skuse	
G-BIWW	AA-5 Traveler	B&K Aviation/Cranfield	
G-BIWX	AT-16 Harvard IV (FT239)	A. E. Hutton/North Weald	
G-BIWY	Westland WG.30 ★	*Instructional airframe*/Sherborne	
G-BIXA	SOCATA TB.9 Tampico	Lord de Saumarez	
G-BIXB	SOCATA TB.9 Tampico	Ablemotive Ltd	
G-BIXH	Cessna F.152	Cambridge Aero Club Ltd	
G-BIXI	Cessna 172RG Cutlass	J. F. P. Lewis/Sandown	
G-BIXL	P-51D Mustang (472216)	R. I amplough/North Weald	
G-BIXN	Boeing Stearman A.75N1	I. L. Craig-Wood & ptnrs	
G-BIXR	Cameron A-140 balloon	Skysales Ltd	

Notes	Reg.	Type	Owner or Operator
	G-BIXS	Avenger T.200-2112 balloon	M. Stuart
	G-BIXV	Bell 212	Bristow Helicopters Ltd
	G-BIXW	Colt 56B balloon	N. A. P. Bates
	G-BIXX	Pearson Srs 2 balloon	D. Pearson
	G-BIXZ	Grob G-109	V. J. R. Day
	G-BIYG	Short SD3-30 Variant 100	BAC Group Ltd
	G-BIYH	Short SD3-30 Variant 100	Gill Airways Ltd/Newcastle
	G-BIYI	Cameron V-65 balloon	Sarnia Balloon Group
	G-BIYJ	PA-18 Super Cub 95	S. Russell
	G-BIYK	Isaacs Fury	R. S. Martin/Dunkeswell
	G-BIYO	PA-31-310 Turbo Navajo	Island Aviation & Travel Ltd
	G-BIYP	PA-20 Pacer 135	R. J. Whitcombe
	G-BIYR	PA-18 Super Cub 135	Delta Foxtrot Flying Group/Dunkeswell
	G-BIYU	Fokker S.11.1 Instructor (E-15)	H. R. Smallwood & A. J. Lee/Denham
	G-BIYW	Jodel D.112	Pollard/Balaam/Bye Flying Group
	G-BIYX	PA-28 Cherokee 140	A. Gowlett/Blackpool
	G-BIYY	PA-18 Super Cub 95	A. E. & W. J. Taylor/Ingoldmells
	G-BIZF	Cessna F.172P	R. S. Bentley/Bourn
	G-BIZG	Cessna F.152	M. A. Judge
	G-BIZI	Robin DR.400/120	Headcorn Flying School Ltd
	G-BIZK	Nord 3202	A. I. Milne/Swanton Morley
	G-BIZM	Nord 3202	Magnificent Obsessions Ltd
	G-BIZN	Slingsby T.67A	G. A. Gee
	G-BIZO	PA-28R Cherokee Arrow 200	Bowlish Roofing Supplies Ltd
	G-BIZR	SOCATA TB.9 Tampico	R. M. Shears (G-BSEC)
	G-BIZT	Bensen B.8M	J. Ferguson
	G-BIZU	Thunder Ax6-56Z balloon	M. J. Loades
	G-BIZV	PA-18 Super Cub 95 (18-2001)	S. J. Pugh & R. L. Wademan
	G-BIZW	Champion 7GCBC Citabria	G. Read & Sons
	G-BIZY	Jodel D.112	Wayland Tunley & Associates/Cranfield
	G-BJAD	FRED Srs 2	C. Allison
	G-BJAE	Lavadoux Starck AS.80	D. J. & S. A. E. Phillips/Coventry
	G-BJAF	Piper J-3C-65 Cub	J. M. Mooney
	G-BJAG	PA-28-181 Archer II	K. F. Hudson & D. J. Casson/Sherburn
	G-BJAJ	AA-5B Tiger	A. H. McVicar/Prestwick
	G-BJAL	C.A.S.A. 1.131E Jungmann 1000	W. J. Perrins & E. A. C. Elliott
	G-BJAN	SA.102-5 Cavalier	J. Powlesland
	G-BJAO	Bensen B.8M	A. Gault
	G-BJAP	D.H.82A Tiger Moth (K2587)	J. A. Pothecary
	G-BJAR	Unicorn UE.3A balloon	Unicorn Group
	G-BJAS	Rango NA.9 balloon	A. Lindsay
	G-BJAV	GY-80 Horizon 160	A. J. Martlew
	G-BJAW	Cameron V-65 balloon	G. W. McCarthy
	G-BJAX	Pilatus P2-05 (U-108) ★	(stored)
	G-BJAY	Piper J-3C-65 Cub	K. L. Clarke/Ingoldmells
	G-BJBK	PA-18 Super Cub 95	M. S. Bird/Old Sarum
	G-BJBM	Monnett Sonerai II	T. C. Webber/Southend
	G-BJBO	Jodel DR.250/160	Wiltshire Flying Group
	G-BJBV	PA-28-161 Warrior II	P. A. Griffin
	G-BJBW	PA-28-161 Warrior II	Gemdemo Projects Ltd
	G-BJBX	PA-28-161 Warrior II	Haimoss Ltd
	G-BJBY	PA-28-161 Warrior II	Haimoss Ltd
	G-BJBZ	Rotorway Executive 133	P. J. D. Kerr
	G-BJCA	PA-28-161 Warrior II	D. M. & J. E. Smith
	G-BJCF	CP.1310-C3 Super Emeraude	K. M. Hodson & C. G. H. Gurney
	G-BJCI	PA-18 Super Cub 150 (modified)	The Borders (Milfield) Aero-Tour Club Ltd
	G-BJCW	PA-32R-301 Saratoga SP	G. R. Patrick & Co Ltd
	G-BJDE	Cessna F.172M	H. P. K. Ferdinand/Denham
	G-BJDF	M.S.880B Rallye 100T	W. R. Savin & ptnrs
	G-BJDI	Cessna FR.182RG	Sunningdale Aviation Services Ltd
	G-BJDK	European E.14 balloon	Aeroprint Tours
	G-BJDO	AA-5A Cheetah	J. R. Nutter & ptnrs
	G-BJDT	SOCATA TB.9 Tampico	Bignell Surgical Instruments Ltd
	G-BJDW	Cessna F.172M	J. Rae/Ipswich
	G-BJEI	PA-18 Super Cub 95	H. J. Cox
	G-BJEL	SNCAN NC.854	N. F. & S. G. Hunter
	G-BJEN	Scruggs RS.5000 balloon	N. J. Richardson
	G-BJEV	Aeronca 11AC Chief (897)	R. F. Willcox
	G-BJEX	Bo 208C Junior	G. D. H. Crawford/Thruxton
	G-BJFB	Mk 1A balloon	Aeroprint Tours
	G-BJFC	European E.8 balloon	P. D. Ridout
	G-BJFE	PA-18 Super Cub 95	J. H. Allistone

Reg.	Type	Owner or Operator	Notes
G-BJFI	Bell 47G-2A1	Helicopter Supplies & Engineering Ltd/ Bournemouth	
G-BJFL	Sikorsky S-76A	Bristow Helicopters Ltd	
G-BJFM	Jodel D.120	J. V. George & P. A. Smith/Popham	
G-BJGD	Mk IV balloon	Windsor Balloon Group	
G-BJGF	Mk 1 balloon	D. & D. Eaves	
G-BJGG	Mk 2 balloon	D. & D. Eaves	
G-BJGK	Cameron V-77 balloon	T. J. Orchard & ptnrs	
G-BJGL	Cremer balloon	G. Lowther	
G-BJGM	Unicorn UE.1A balloon	D. Eaves & P. D. Ridout	
G-BJGO	Cessna 172N	R. M. Hunt	
G-BJGX	Sikorsky S-76A	Bristow Helicopters Ltd	
G-BJGY	Cessna F.172P	Lucca Wines Ltd	
G-BJHA	Cremer balloon	G. Cope	
G-BJHB	Mooney M.20J	Zitair Flying Club Ltd/Redhill	
G-BJHK	EAA Acro Sport	D. M. Cue	
G-BJHP	Osprey 1C balloon	N. J. Richardson	
G-BJHT	Thunder Ax7-65 balloon	A. H. & L. Symonds	
G-BJHV	Voisin Replica ★	Brooklands Museum of Aviation/Weybridge	
G-BJHW	Osprey 1C balloon	N. J. Riichardson	
G-BJIA	Allport balloon	D. J. Allport	
G-BJIC	Dodo 1A balloon	P. D. Ridout	
G-BJID	Osprey 1B balloon	P. D. Ridout	
G-BJIF	Bensen B.8M	H. Redwin	
G-BJIG	Slingsby T.67A	Acebell G-BJIG Syndicate/Redhill	
G-BJIR	Cessna 550 Citation II	Gator Aviation Ltd	
G-BJIV	PA-18 Super Cub 180	Yorkshire Gliding Club (Pty) Ltd/ Sutton Bank	
G-BJJE	Dodo Mk 3 balloon	D. Eaves	
G-BJJN	Cessna F.172M	Ospreystar Ltd (stored)/Stapleford	
G-BJKB	SA.365C-3 Dauphin 2	Bond Helicopters Ltd	
G-BJKF	SOCATA TB.9 Tampico	Venue Solutions	
G-BJKW	Wills Aera II	J. K. S. Wills	
G-BJKY	Cessna F.152	Air Charter & Travel Ltd/Ronaldsway	
G-BJLB	SNCAN NC.854S	M. J. Barnaby	
G-BJLC	Monnett Sonerai IIL	P. J. Robins & R. King/Sywell	
G-BJLE	Osprey 1B balloon	I. Chadwick	
G-BJLF	Unicorn UE.1C balloon	I. Chadwick	
G-BJLG	Unicorn UE.1B balloon	I. Chadwick	
G-BJLH	PA-18 Super Cub 95 (44)	D. S. Kirkham	
G-BJLK	Short SD3-30 Variant 100	Streamline Aviation (SW) Ltd/Exeter	
G-BJLO	PA-31-310 Turbo Navajo	Superpower Engineering System	
G-BJLX	Cremer balloon	P. W. May	
G-BJLY	Cremer balloon	P. Cannon	
G-BJMG	European E.26C balloon	D. Eaves & A. P. Chown	
G-BJMI	European E.84 balloon	D. Eaves	
G-BJMJ	Bensen B.8V	J. I. Hewlett	
G-BJML	Cessna 120	D. F. Lawlor/Inverness	
G-BJMO	Taylor JT.1 Monoplane	R. C. Mark	
G-BJMR	Cessna 310R	J. McL. Robinson/Sherburn	
G-BJMW	Thunder Ax8-105 balloon	G. M. Westley	
G-BJMX	Jarre JR.3 balloon	P. D. Ridout	
G-BJMZ	European EA.8A balloon	P. D. Ridout	
G-BJNA	Arena Mk 117P balloon	P. D. Ridout	
G-BJND	Osprey Mk 1E balloon	A. Billington & D. Whitmore	
G-BJNF	Cessna F.152	Exeter Flying Club Ltd	
G-BJNG	Slingsby T.67A	Dophin Property (Management) Ltd	
G-BJNN	PA-38-112 Tomahawk	Scotia Safari Ltd/Prestwick	
G-BJNP	Rango NA.32 balloon	N. H. Ponsford	
G-BJNX	Cameron O-65 balloon	B. J. Petteford	
G-BJNY	Aeronca 11CC Super Chief	P. I. & D. M. Morgans	
G-BJNZ	PA-23 Aztec 250F	Bonus Aviation Ltd (G-FANZ) Cranfield	
G-BJOA	PA-28-181 Archer II	Channel Islands Aero Holdings (Jersey) Ltd	
G-BJOB	Jodel D.140C	T. W. M. Beck & M. J. Smith	
G-BJOE	Jodel D.120A	Forth Flying Group	
G-BJOP	BN-2B-26 Islander	Loganair Ltd/British Airways	
G-BJOT	Jodel D.117	E. Davies	
G-BJOV	Cessna F.150K	W. H. Webb & P. F. N. Burrow	
G-BJPI	Bede BD-5G	M. D. McQueen	
G-BJPV	Haigh balloon	M. J. Haigh	
G-BJRA	Osprey Mk 4B balloon	E. Osborn	

Notes	Reg.	Type	Owner or Operator
	G-BJRB	European E.254 balloon	D. Eaves
	G-BJRC	European E.84R balloon	D. Eaves
	G-BJRD	European E.84R balloon	D. Eaves
	G-BJRG	Osprey Mk 4B balloon	A. E. de Gruchy
	G-BJRH	Rango NA.36 balloon	N. H. Ponsford
	G-BJRP	Cremer balloon	M. D. Williams
	G-BJRV	Cremer balloon	M. D. Williams
	G-BJRW	Cessna U.206G	A. I. Walgate & Son Ltd
	G-BJRZ	Partenavia P.68C	Ampy Automation Digilog Ltd (G OAKP)
	G-BJSA	BN-2A-26 Islander	Police Aviation Services Ltd/Staverton
	G-BJSC	Osprey Mk 4D balloon	N. J. Richardson
	G-BJSD	Osprey Mk 4D balloon	N. J. Richardson
	G-BJSF	Osprey Mk 4B balloon	N. J. Richardson
	G-BJSG	V.S.361 Spitfire LF.IXE (ML417)	Patina Ltd/Duxford
	G-BJSI	Osprey Mk 1E balloon	N. J. Richardson
	G-BJSP	Guido 1A Srs 61 balloon	G. A. Newsome
	G-BJSS	Allport balloon	D. J. Allport
	G-BJSU	Bensen B.8M	J. D. Newlyn
	G-BJSV	PA-28-161 Warrior II	R. Gilbert & J. Cole
	G-BJSW	Thunder Ax7-65 balloon	Sandicliffe Garage Ltd
	G-BJSX	Unicorn UE-1C balloon	N. J. Richardson
	G-BJSZ	Piper J-3C-65 Cub	H. Gilbert
	G-BJTB	Cessna A.150M	Clacton Aero Club (1988) Ltd
	G-BJTK	Taylor JT.1 Monoplane	E. N. Simmons
	G-BJTO	Piper J-3C-65 Cub	K. R. Nunn
	G-BJTP	PA-18 Super Cub 95 (115302)	J. T. Parkins
	G-BJTW	European E.107 balloon	C. J. Brealey
	G-BJTY	Osprey Mk 4B balloon	A. E. de Gruchy
	G-BJUB	BVS Special 01 balloon	P. G. Wild
	G-BJUC	Robinson R-22	The Helicentre/Blackpool
	G-BJUD	Robin DR.400/180R	Lasham Gliding Soc Ltd
	G-BJUG	SOCATA TB.9 Tampico	CB Helicopters
	G-BJUI	Osprey Mk 4B balloon	B. A. de Gruchy
	G-BJUK	Short SD3-30 Variant 100	Shorts Aircraft Leasing Ltd (G-OCAS)
	G-BJUR	PA-38-112 Tomahawk	Truman Aviation Ltd/Tollerton
	G-BJUS	PA-38-112 Tomahawk	Panshanger School of Flying
	G-BJUV	Cameron V-20 balloon	Cameron Balloons Ltd
	G-BJUY	Colt Ax7-77 Golf Ball SS balloon	Lindstrand Balloons Ltd
	G-BJVC	Evans VP-2	J. J. Morrissey
	G-BJVF	Thunder Ax3 balloon	A. G. R. Calder/California
	G-BJVH	Cessna F.182Q	R. J. de Courcy Cuming/ Wellesbourne
	G-BJVJ	Cessna F.152	Cambridge Aero Club Ltd
	G-BJVK	Grob G-109	B. Kimberley/Enstone
	G-BJVM	Cessna 172N	I. C. MacLennan
	G-BJVS	CP.1310-C3 Super Emeraude	A. E. Futter/Norwich
	G-BJVT	Cessna F.152	Cambridge Aero Club Ltd
	G-BJVU	Thunder Ax6-56 Bolt SS balloon	G. V. Beckwith
	G-BJVW	Robin R.1180	Medway Flying Group Ltd/Rochester
	G-BJVX	Sikorsky S-76A	Bristow Helicopters Ltd
	G-BJWC	Saro Skeeter AOP.12 (XK 482) ★	Sloane Helicopters Ltd/Sywell
	G-BJWH	Cessna F.152	Plane Talking Ltd/Elstree
	G-BJWI	Cessna F.172P	Agricultural & General Aviation Ltd/ Bournemouth
	G-BJWJ	Cameron V-65 balloon	R. G. Turnbull & S. G. Forse
	G-BJWO	BN-2A-26 Islander	Peterborough Parachute Centre Ltd (G-BAXC)/Sibson
	G-BJWT	Wittman W.10 Tailwind	J. F. Bakewell & R. A. Shelley
	G-BJWV	Colt 17A balloon	D. T. Meyes
	G-BJWW	Cessna F.172N	Air Charter & Travel Ltd/Blackpool
	G-BJWX	PA-18 Super Cub 95	Acebell JWX Syndicate
	G-BJWY	S-55 Whirlwind HAR.21 (WV198)	Solway Aviation Museum/Carlisle
	G-BJWZ	PA-18 Super Cub 95	R. A. G. Lucas
	G-BJXA	Slingsby T.67A	Comed Aviation Ltd/Blackpool
	G-BJXB	Slingsby T.67A	A. K. Halvorsen/Barton
	G-BJXK	Fournier RF-5	G-BJXK Syndicate/Cardiff
	G-BJXP	Colt 56B balloon	S. Hodder
	G-BJXR	Auster AOP.9 (XR267)	Cotswold Aircraft Restoration Group
	G-BJXX	PA-23 Aztec 250E	V. Bojovic
	G-BJXZ	Cessna 172N	T. M. Jones
	G-BJYD	Cessna F.152 II	Cleveland Flying School Ltd/Teesside
	G-BJYG	PA-28-161 Warrior II	Browns of Stoke Ltd
	G-BJYK	Jodel D.120A	T. Fox & D. A. Thorpe

Reg.	Type	Owner or Operator	Notes
G-BJYN	PA-38-112 Tomahawk	Panshanger School of Flying Ltd (G-BJTE)	
G-BJZA	Cameron N-65 balloon	A. D. Pinner	
G-BJZB	Evans VP-2	J. A. MacLeod	
G-BJZC	Thunder Ax7-65Z balloon	Greenpeace (UK) Ltd/S. Africa	
G-BJZF	D.H.82A Tiger Moth	R. Blast	
G-BJZN	Slingsby T.67A	D. M. Upfield	
G-BJZR	Colt 42A balloon	Selfish Balloon Group	
G-BJZT	Cessna FA.152	E. Blanche/Biggin Hill	
G-BJZX	Grob G.109	Oxfordshire Sport Flying Ltd/Enstone	
G-BJZY	Bensen B.8MV	P. J. Dockerill	
G-BKAC	Cessna F.150L	Seawing Flying Club Ltd/Southend	
G-BKAE	Jodel D.120	M. P. Wakem	
G-BKAF	FRED Srs 2	L. G. Millen	
G-BKAM	Slingsby T.67M Firefly	A. J. Daley	
G-BKAO	Jodel D.112	R. Broadhead	
G-BKAR	PA-38-112 Tomahawk	D. A. Williams	
G-BKAS	PA-38-112 Tomahawk	D. A. Williams	
G-BKAY	R. Commander 114	The Rockwell Group	
G-BKAZ	Cessna 152	Skyviews & General Ltd	
G-BKBD	Thunder Ax3 balloon	G. A. McCarthy	
G-BKBF	M.S.894A Rallye Minerva 220	Earthline Ltd	
G-BKBN	SOCATA TB.10 Tobago	RFA Flying Club Ltd	
G-BKBO	Colt 17A balloon	J. Armstrong & ptnrs	
G-BKBP	Bellanca 7GCBC Scout	H. G. Jefferies & Son/Little Gransden	
G-BKBR	Cameron Chateau 84 SS balloon	Forbes Europe Ltd/France	
G-BKBS	Bensen B.8MV	Construction & Site Administration Ltd	
G-BKBV	SOCATA TB.10 Tobago	R. M. Messenger	
G-BKBW	SOCATA TB.10 Tobago	Merlin Aviation	
G-BKCB	PA-28R Cherokee Arrow 200	Bristol & Wessex Aeroplane Club Ltd	
G-BKCC	PA-28 Cherokee 180	Cowie Aviation Ltd/Staverton	
G-BKCE	Cessna F.172P II	Far North Flight Training/Wick	
G-BKCF	Rutan LongEz	I. C. Fallows	
G-BKCH	Thompson Cassutt	S. C. Thompson/Redhill	
G-BKCI	Brügger MB.2 Colibri	E. R. Newall	
G-BKCJ	Oldfield Baby Great Lakes	S. V. Roberts/Sleap	
G-BKCK	CCF Harvard IV (P5865)	E. D. & A. Haig-Thomas/North Weald	
G-BKCL	PA-30 Twin Comanche 160C	Yorkair Ltd/Leeds	
G-BKCN	Currie Wot	N. A. A. Podmore	
G-BKCR	SOCATA TB.9 Tampico	Surrey & Kent Flying Club (1982) Ltd/ Biggin Hill	
G-BKCT	Cameron V-77 balloon	Quality Products General Engineering (Wickwat) Ltd	
G-BKCV	EAA Acro Sport II	M. J. Clark	
G-BKCW	Jodel D.120A	A. Greene & G. Kerr/Dundee	
G-BKCX	Mudry CAARP CAP.10	Mahon & Associates/Booker	
G-BKCY	PA-38-112 Tomahawk II	Wellesbourne Aviation Ltd	
G-BKCZ	Jodel D.120A	M. R. Baker/Shoreham	
G-BKDC	Monnett Sonerai II	K. J. Towell	
G-BKDH	Robin DR.400/120	Thornhill Music Ltd	
G-BKDI	Robin DR.400/120	Cotswold Aero Club Ltd/Staverton	
G-BKDJ	Robin DR.400/120	M. D. Joyce & R. R. Wills	
G-BKDK	Thunder Ax7-77Z balloon	A. J. Byrne	
G-BKDP	FRED Srs 3	M. Whittaker	
G-BKDR	Pitts S.1S Special	G-BKDR Group	
G-BKDT	SE-5A (replica) (F943) ★	Yorkshire Air Museum/Elvington	
G-BKDX	Jodel DR.1050	T. G. Collins	
G-BKEK	PA-32 Cherokee Six 300	S. W. Turley	
G-BKEP	Cessna F.172M	R. Green/Glasgow	
G-BKER	SE-5A (replica) (F5447)	N. K. Geddes	
G-BKET	PA-18 Super Cub 95	H. M. MacKenzie	
G-BKEU	Taylor JT.1 Monoplane	R. J. Whybrow & J. M. Springham	
G-BKEV	Cessna F.172M	One Zero One Three Ltd	
G-BKEW	Bell 206B JetRanger 3	N. R. Foster	
G-BKEX	Rich Prototype glider	D. B. Rich	
G-BKEY	FRED Srs 3	G. S. Taylor	
G-BKEZ	PA-18 Super Cub 95	D. G. Marwick	
G-BKFA	Monnett Sonerai IIL	R. F. Bridge	
G-BKFC	Cessna F.152 II	Sulby Aerial Surveys Ltd	
G-BKFG	Thunder Ax3 balloon	P. Ray	
G-BKFI	Evans VP-1	Foxtrot India Flying Group	
G-BKFK	Isaacs Fury II	G. C. Jones	
G-BKFL	Aerosport Scamp	J. Sherwood	

Notes	Reg.	Type	Owner or Operator
	G-BKFM	QAC Quickie	F. Rothers
	G-BKFN	Bell 214ST	Bristow Helicopters Ltd
	G-BKFP	Bell 214ST	Bristow Helicopters Ltd
	G-BKFR	CP.301C Emeraude	C. R. Beard
	G-BKFW	P.56 Provost T.1 (XF597)	Sylmar Aviation & Services Ltd
	G-BKFZ	PA-28R Cherokee Arrow 200	Shacklewell Flying Group
	G-BKGA	M.S.892E Rallye 150GT	BJJ Aviation
	G-BKGB	Jodel D.120	R W. Greenwood
	G-BKGC	Maule M.6-235	Witham (Specialist) Vehicles Ltd
	G-BKGL	Beech D.18S (1164)	Classic Wings/Duxford
	G-BKGM	Beech D.18S (HB275)	A. E. Hutton/North Weald
	G-BKGR	Cameron O-65 balloon	K. Kidner & L. E. More
	G-BKGT	SOCATA Rallye 110ST	Long Marston Flying Group
	G-BKGW	Cessna F.152-II	Leicestershire Aero Club Ltd
	G-BKHA	W.S.55 Whirlwind HAR.10 (XJ763) ★	C. J. Evans
	G-BKHD	Oldfield Baby Great Lakes	P. J. Tanulak/Sleap
	G-BKHG	Piper J-3C-65 Cub (479766)	K. G. Wakefield
	G-BKHJ	Cessna 182P	Augur Films Ltd
	G-BKHL	Thunder Ax9-140 balloon	R. Carr/France
	G-BKHR	Luton LA-4 Minor	C. B. Buscombe & R. Goldsworthy
	G-BKHT	BAe 146-100	British Aerospace PLC
	G-BKHW	Stoddard-Hamilton Glasair SH.2RG	G. Fleck
	G-BKHY	Taylor JT.1 Monoplane	B. C. J. O'Neill
	G-BKHZ	Cessna F.172P	Warwickshire Flying Training Centre Ltd
	G-BKIA	SOCATA TB.10 Tobago	M. F. McGinn
	G-BKIB	SOCATA TB.9 Tampico	A. J. Baggerley & F. D. J. Simmons/ Goodwood
	G-BKIC	Cameron V-77 balloon	C. A. Butler
	G-BKIE	Short SD3-30 Variant 100	BAC Group Ltd
	G-BKIF	Fournier RF-6B	G. G. Milton
	G-BKII	Cessna F.172M	M. S. Knight/Goodwood
	G-BKIJ	Cessna F.172M	V. Speck
	G-BKIK	Cameron DG-10 airship	Airspace Outdoor Advertising Ltd
	G-BKIM	Unicorn UE.5A balloon	I. Chadwick & K. H. Turner
	G-BKIN	Alon A.2A Aircoupe	P. A. Williams & M. Quinn/Blackbushe
	G-BKIR	Jodel D.117	R. Shaw & D. M. Hardaker/Sherburn
	G-BKIS	SOCATA TB.10 Tobago	Ospreystar Ltd
	G-BKIT	SOCATA TB.9 Tampico	D. N. Garlick & ptnrs
	G-BKIU	Colt 17A balloon	Robert Pooley Ltd
	G-BKIX	Cameron V-31 balloon	G. Stevens (G-BKGJ)
	G-BKIY	Thunder Ax3 balloon	A. Hornak
	G-BKIZ	Cameron V-31 balloon	A. P. S. Cox
	G-BKJB	PA-18 Super Cub 135	Air Advertising Ltd/Cumbernauld
	G-BKJD	Bell 214ST	Bristow Helicopters Ltd
	G-BKJF	M.S.880B Rallye 100T	Journeyman Aviation Ltd
	G-BKJG	BN-2B-21 Islander	Pilatus BN Ltd/Bembridge
	G-BKJR	Hughes 269C	March Helicopters Ltd/Sywell
	G-BKJS	Jodel D.120A	S. T. & A. A. Smoothy
	G-BKJW	PA-23 Aztec 250E	Alan Williams Entertainments Ltd
	G-BKKN	Cessna 182R	R A. Marven/Elstree
	G-BKKO	Cessna 182R	B. & G. Jebson Ltd/Crosland Moor
	G-BKKR	Rand KR-2	D. Beale & S. P. Gardner
	G-BKKZ	Pitts S-1D Special	G. C. Masterton
	G-BKLC	Cameron V-56 balloon	M. A. & J. R. H. Ashworth
	G-BKLJ	Westland Scout AH.1 ★	N. R. Windley
	G-BKLO	Cessna F.172M	Stapleford Flying Club Ltd
	G-BKLP	Cessna F.172N	A. C. Roles
	G-BKMA	Mooney M.20J Srs 201	Foxtrot Whisky Aviation
	G-BKMB	Mooney M.20J Srs 201	W. A. Cook & ptnrs/Sherburn
	G-BKMD	SC.7 Skyvan Srs 3	Army Parachute Association/Netheravon
	G-BKMG	Handley Page O/400 (replica)	Paralyser Group
	G-BKMI	V.S.359 Spitfire HF.VIIIc (MT928)	Aerial Museum (North Weald) Ltd
	G-BKMK	PA-38-112 Tomahawk	D. J. Campbell/Glasgow
	G-BKMR	Thunder Ax3 balloon	B. F. G. Ribbans
	G-BKMT	PA-32R-301 Saratoga SP	Severn Valley Aviation Group
	G-BKMX	Short SD3-60 Variant 100	Loganair Ltd/British Airways
	G-BKNA	Cessna 421	Launchapart Ltd
	G-BKNB	Cameron V-42 balloon	D. N. Close
	G-BKND	Colt 56A balloon	T. A. Hains
	G-BKNI	GY-80 Horizon 160D	A. Hartigan & ptnrs/Fenland
	G-BKNL	Cameron D-96 airship	Sport Promotion SRL

Reg.	Type	Owner or Operator	Notes
G-BKNO	Monnett Sonerai IIL	M. D. Hughes	
G-BKNP	Cameron V-77 balloon	E. K. K. & C. E. Odman	
G-BKNY	Bensen B.8MPV	D. A. C. MacCormack	
G-BKNZ	CP.301A Emeraude	D. F. Micklethwait	
G-BKOA	SOCATA M.S.893E Rallye 180GT	M. & J. Grafton	
G-BKOB	Z.326 Trener Master	W. G. V. Hall	
G-BKOR	Barnes 77 balloon	Robert Pooley Ltd	
G-BKOT	Wassmer WA.81 Piranha	B. N. Rolfe	
G-BKOU	P.84 Jet Provost T.3 (XN637)	A. S. Topen/Cranfield	
G-BKOV	Jodel DR.220A	Merlin Flying Club Ltd/Hucknall	
G-BKOW	Colt 77A balloon	Hot Air Balloon Co Ltd	
G-BKPA	Hoffmann H-36 Dimona	A. Mayhew	
G-BKPB	Aerosport Scamp	E. D. Burke	
G-BKPC	Cessna A.185F	Black Knights Parachute Centre	
G-BKPD	Viking Dragonfly	E. P. Browne & G. J. Sargent	
G-BKPE	Jodel DR.250/160	J. S. & J. D. Lewer	
G-BKPK	Everett gyroplane	J. C. McHugh	
G-BKPN	Cameron N-77 balloon	R. H. Sanderson	
G-BKPS	AA-5B Tiger	Earthline Ltd	
G-BKPT	M.H.1521M Broussard (07)	R. H. Reeves/Barton	
G-BKPX	Jodel D.120A	N. H. Martin	
G-BKPY	Saab 91B/2 Safir (56321)★	Newark Air Museum Ltd	
G-BKPZ	Pitts S-1T Special	M. A. Frost	
G-BKRA	NA T-6G Texan (51-15227)	Pulsegrove Ltd/Shoreham	
G-BKRB	Cessna 172N	Saunders Caravans Ltd	
G-BKRF	PA-18 Super Cub 95	K. M. Bishop	
G-BKRG	Beechcraft C-45G	Aces High Ltd/North Weald	
G-BKRH	Brügger MB.2 Colibri	M. R. Benwell	
G-BKRI	Cameron V-77 balloon	J. R. Lowe & R. J. Fuller	
G-BKRK	SNCAN Stampe SV-4C	Strathgadie Stampe Group	
G-BKRL	Chichester-Miles Leopard	Chichester-Miles Consultants Ltd	
G-BKRN	Beechcraft D.18S ★	A. S. Topen	
G-BKRS	Cameron V-56 balloon	D. N. & L. J. Close	
G-BKRU	Ensign Crossley Racer	M. Crossley	
G-BKRV	Hovey Beta Bird	A. V. Francis	
G-BKRZ	Dragon G-77 balloon	J. R. Barber	
G-BKSB	Cessna T.310Q II	Offshore Express Ltd	
G-BKSC	Saro Skeeter AOP.12 (XN351)	R. A. L. Falconer	
G-BKSD	Colt 56A balloon	M. J. & G. C. Casson	
G-BKSE	QAC Quickie Q.2	M. D. Burns	
G-BKSH	Colt 21A balloon	J. Bartholomew & D. L. Smith	
G-BKSP	Schleicher ASK.14	J. H. Bryson/Bellarena	
G-BKSS	Jodel D.150	D. H. Wilson-Spratt/Ronaldsway	
G-BKST	Rutan Vari-Eze	R. Towle	
G-BKSX	SNCAN Stampe SV-4C	C. A. Bailey & J. A. Carr	
G-BKTA	PA-18 Super Cub 95	V. D. Long	
G-BKTH	CCF Hawker Sea Hurricane IB (Z7015)	Shuttleworth Collection/Duxford	
G-BKTM	PZL SZD-45A Ogar	Repclif Chemical Services Ltd	
G-BKTR	Cameron V-77 balloon	S. J. Hepworth	
G-BKTV	Cessna F.152	London Flight Centre Ltd/Stansted	
G-BKTY	SOCATA TB.10 Tobago	B. M. & G. M. McClelland	
G-BKTZ	Slingsby T.67M Firefly	E. Hopper (G-SFTV)	
G-BKUE	SOCATA TB.9 Tampico	W. J. Moore/Kirkbride	
G-BKUJ	Thunder Ax6-56 balloon	R. J. Bent	
G-BKUR	CP.301A Emeraude	R. Wells	
G-BKUS	Bensen B.8M	G. F. Gardener	
G-BKUU	Thunder Ax7-77-1 balloon	D. A. Kozuba-Kozubska	
G-BKUY	BAe Jetstream 3102	Jetstream Aircraft Ltd/Prestwick	
G-BKVA	SOCATA Rallye 180T	Buckminster Gliding Club Syndicate	
G-BKVB	SOCATA Rallye 110ST	Air Touring Services Ltd/Biggin Hill	
G-BKVC	SOCATA TB.9 Tampico	Air Touring Services Ltd/Biggin Hill	
G-BKVE	Rutan Vari-Eze	R. M. Smith (G-EZLT)	
G-BKVF	FRED Srs 3	A. R. Hawes	
G-BKVG	Scheibe SF.25E Super Falke	G-BKVG Ltd	
G-BKVK	Auster AOP.9 (WZ662)	J. D. Butcher	
G-BKVL	Robin DR.400/160	The Cotswold Aero Club Ltd/Staverton	
G-BKVM	PA-18 Super Cub 150 (115684)	D. G. Caffrey	
G-BKVN	PA-23 Aztec 250F	B. A. Eastwell/Shoreham	
G-BKVO	Pietenpol Air Camper	B. P. Waites	
G-BKVP	Pitts S-1D Special	P. J. Leggo	
G-BKVR	PA-28 Cherokee 140	D. P. Alexander	
G-BKVS	Bensen B.8M	K. Stephenson	

Notes	Reg.	Type	Owner or Operator
	G-BKVT	PA-23 Aztec 250E	R. E. Woolsey (G-HARV)
	G-BKVW	Airtour 56 balloon	L. D. & H. Vaughan
	G-BKVX	Airtour 56 balloon	E. G. Woolnough
	G-BKVY	Airtour 31 balloon	M. Davies
	G-BKWE	Colt 17A balloon	Hot-Air Balloon Co Ltd
	G-BKWG	PZL-104 Wilga 35A	M. A. Johnston/Tayside
	G-BKWI	Pitts S-2A	R. A. Seeley/Denham
	G-BKWR	Cameron V-65 balloon	K. J. Foster
	G-BKWW	Cameron O-77 balloon	A. M. Marten
	G-BKWY	Cessna F.152	Cambridge Aero Club
	G-BKXA	Robin R.2100	G. J. Anderson & ptnrs
	G-BKXD	SA.365N Dauphin 2	Bond Helicopters Ltd
	G-BKXF	PA-28R Cherokee Arrow 200	P. L. Brunton/Caernarfon
	G-BKXG	Cessna T.303	Wilton Construction Ltd
	G-BKXL	Cameron 70 Bottle SS balloon	Cameron Balloons Ltd/Canada
	G-BKXM	Colt 17A balloon	R. G. Turnbull
	G-BKXN	ICA IS-28M2A	T. J. Mills
	G-BKXO	Rutan LongEz	P. J. Wareham
	G-BKXP	Auster AOP.6	B. J. & W. J. Ellis
	G-BKXR	D.31A Turbulent	M. B. Hill
	G-BKXT	Cameron D-50 airship	Cameron Balloons Ltd/USA
	G-BKXX	Cameron V-65 balloon	T. Fonteyn
	G-BKYA	Boeing 737-236	British Airways Birmingham *Ariel*
	G-BKYB	Boeing 737-236	British Airways Birmingham *Portia*
	G-BKYC	Boeing 737-236	British Airways *River Wye*
	G-BKYE	Boeing 737-236	British Airways Birmingham *Hippolyta*
	G-BKYF	Boeing 737-236	British Airways Birmingham *Mistress Quickly*
	G-BKYG	Boeing 737-236	British Airways Birmingham *Prospero*
	G-BKYH	Boeing 737-236	British Airways Birmingham *Hotspur*
	G-BKYI	Boeing 737-236	British Airways *River Waveney*
	G-BKYJ	Boeing 737-236	British Airways Birmingham *Touchstone*
	G-BKYK	Boeing 737-236	British Airways *River Foyle*
	G-BKYL	Boeing 737-236	British Airways Birmingham *Titania*
	G-BKYM	Boeing 737-236	British Airways Birmingham *Moonshine*
	G-BKYN	Boeing 737-236	British Airways Birmingham *Prince Hal*
	G-BKYO	Boeing 737-236	British Airways Birmingham *Oberon*
	G-BKYP	Boeing 737-236	British Airways Manchester *River Ystwyth*
	G-BKZB	Cameron V-77 balloon	A. J. Montgomery
	G-BKZE	AS.332L Super Puma	British International Helicopters
	G-BKZF	Cameron V-56 balloon	M. Wigfall
	G-BKZG	AS.332L Super Puma	British International Helicopters
	G-BKZH	AS.332L Super Puma	British International Helicopters
	G-BKZI	Bell 206B JetRanger 2	Western Air Trading Ltd/Thruxton
	G-BKZJ	Bensen B.8MV	J. C. Birdsall
	G-BKZM	Isaacs Fury II	B. Jones
	G-BKZT	FRED Srs 2	M. G. Rusby
	G-BKZV	Bede BD-4A	G. I. J. Thomson
	G-BLAA	Fournier RF-5	A. D. Wren/Southend
	G-BLAC	Cessna FA.152	Ofteneasy Ltd
	G-BLAD	Thunder Ax7-77-1 balloon	P. J. Bishh
	G-BLAF	Stolp SA.900 V-Star	P. R. Skeels
	G-BLAG	Pitts S-1D Special	G. Ferriman
	G-BLAH	Thunder Ax7-77-1 balloon	T. Donnelly
	G-BLAI	Monnett Sonerai IIL	T. Simpson
	G-BLAM	Jodel DR.360	B. F. Baldock
	G-BLAT	Jodel 150	D. J. Dulborough & A. J. Court
	G-BLAX	Cessna FA.152	Shoreham Flight Simulation Ltd/ Bournemouth
	G-BLAY	Robin HR.100/200B	B. A. Mills
	G-BLCA	Bell 206B JetRanger 3	R.M.H. Stainless Ltd
	G-BLCF	EAA Acro Sport 2	M. J. Watkins & ptnrs
	G-BLCG	SOCATA TB.10 Tobago	Charlie Golf Flying Group (G-BHES)/ Shoreham
	G-BLCH	Colt 65D balloon	Balloon Flights Club Ltd
	G-BLCI	EAA Acro Sport	M. R. Holden
	G-BLCK	V.S.361 Spitfire F.IX (TE566)	Historic Aircraft Collection Ltd
	G-BLCM	SOCATA TB.9 Tampico	Repclif Aviation Ltd/Liverpool
	G-BLCT	Jodel DR.220 2+2	H. W. Jemmett
	G-BLCU	Scheibe SF.25B Falke	Falke Syndicate
	G-BLCW	Evans VP-1	K. D. Pearce
	G-BLCY	Thunder Ax7-65Z balloon	Thunder Balloons Ltd
	G-BLDB	Taylor JT.1 Monoplane	C. J. Bush

Reg.	Type	Owner or Operator	Notes
G-BLDC	K&S Jungster 1	A. W. Brown	
G-BLDD	WAG-Aero CUBy AcroTrainer	C. A. Laycock	
G-BLDG	PA-25 Pawnee 260C	Ouse Gliding Club Ltd/Rufforth	
G-BLDK	Robinson R-22	Lateq Aviation Ltd	
G-BLDL	Cameron 56 Truck SS balloon	Cameron Balloons Ltd	
G-BLDN	Rand KR-2	M. T. Taylor	
G-BLDP	Slingsby T.67M Firefly	Sherburn Aero Club Ltd	
G-BLEB	Colt 69A balloon	I. R. M. Jacobs	
G-BLEJ	PA-28-161 Warrior II	Eglinton Flying Club Ltd	
G-BLEP	Cameron V-65 balloon	D. Chapman	
G-BLES	Stolp SA.750 Acroduster Too	T. W. Harris	
G-BLET	Thunder Ax7-77-1 balloon	Servatruc Ltd	
G-BLEW	Cessna F.182Q	D. J. Cross	
G-BLEY	SA.365N Dauphin 2	Bond Helicopters Ltd	
G-BLEZ	SA.365N Dauphin 2	Bond Helicopters Ltd	
G-BLFI	PA-28-181 Archer II	Bonus Aviation Ltd	
G-BLFW	AA-5 Traveler	Grumman Club	
G-BLFY	Cameron V-77 balloon	A. N. F. Pertwee	
G-BLFZ	PA-31-310 Turbo Navajo C	London Executive Aviation Ltd	
G-BLGB	Short SD3-60 Variant 100	Loganair Ltd/British Airways	
G-BLGH	Robin DR.300/180R	Booker Gliding Club Ltd	
G-BLGO	Bensen B.8MV	F. Vernon	
G-BLGR	Bell 47G-4A	Lowland Advertising Ltd	
G-BLGS	SOCATA Rallye 180T	Lasham Gliding Society Ltd	
G-BLGT	PA-18 Super Cub 95	T. A. Reed/Dunkeswell	
G-BLGV	Bell 206B JetRanger 3	Part Reward Ltd	
G-BLGX	Thunder Ax7-65 balloon	The 45	
G-BLHH	Jodel DR.315	G. G. Milton	
G-BLHI	Colt 17A balloon	J. A. Folkes	
G-BLHJ	Cessna F.172P	J. Easson/Edinburgh	
G-BLHK	Colt 105A balloon	Hale Hot-Air Balloon Club	
G-BLHM	PA-18 Super Cub 95	B. N. C. Mogg	
G-BLHN	Robin HR.100/285	Tarist Ltd	
G-BLHR	GA-7 Cougar	Fotex Aviation Ltd	
G-BLHS	Bellanca 7ECA Citabria	N. J. F. Campbell	
G-BLHW	Varga 2150A Kachina	Kachina Hotel Whisky Group	
G-BLID	D.H.112 Venom FB.50 (J-1605) ★	P. G. Vallance Ltd/Charlwood	
G-BLIE	D.H.112 Venom FB.50 (J-1614)	R. J. Everett	
G-BLIG	Cameron V-65 balloon	W. Davison	
G-BLIH	PA-18 Super Cub 135	I. R. F. Hammond	
G-BLIK	Wallis WA-116/F/S	K. H. Wallis	
G-BLIP	Cameron N-77 balloon	L. A. Beardall & G. R. Hunt	
G-BLIT	Thorp T-18 CW	K. B. Hallam	
G-BLIW	P.56 Provost T.51 (177)	Provost Flying Group/Shoreham	
G-BLIX	Saro Skeeter Mk 12 (XL809)	A. P. Nowicki	
G-BLIY	M.S.892A Rallye Commodore	A. J. Brasher & K. R. Haynes	
G-BLJD	Glaser-Dirks DG.400	G. G. Hearne & M. I. Gee/Rufforth	
G-BLJF	Cameron O-65 balloon	M. D. Mitchell	
G-BLJH	Cameron N-77 balloon	Phillair	
G-BLJI	Colt 105A balloon	Tempowish Ltd	
G-BLJJ	Cessna 305 Bird Dog	P. Dawe	
G-BLJM	Beech 95-B55 Baron	Elstree Aircraft Hire Ltd	
G-BLJN	Nott-Cameron ULD-1 balloon	J. R. P. Nott	
G-BLJO	Cessna F.152	Redhill School of Flying Ltd	
G-BLJP	Cessna F.150L	C. R. & S. Hardiman	
G-BLKA	D.H.112 Venom FB.54 (WR410)	A. S. Topen	
G-BLKJ	Thunder Ax7-65 balloon	D. T. Watkins	
G-BLKK	Evans VP-1	S. R. Roberts	
G-BLKL	D.31 Turbulent	D. L. Ripley	
G-BLKM	Jodel DR.1051	T. C. Humphreys	
G-BLKP	BAe Jetstream 3102	British Aerospace (Operations) Ltd/Warton	
G-BLKY	Beech 95-58 Baron	P. R. Earp	
G-BLKZ	Pilatus P2-05 ★	Autokraft Ltd/Booker	
G-BLLA	Bensen B.8M	K. T. Donaghey	
G-BLLB	Bensen B.8M	D. H. Moss	
G-BLLD	Cameron O-77 balloon	A. Bevis	
G-BLLH	Jodel DR.220A 2+2	P. Chamberlain & D. E. Starkey	
G-BLLM	PA-23 Aztec 250E	C. & M. Thomas (G-BBNM)/Cardiff	
G-BLLN	PA-18 Super Cub 95	A. L. Hall-Carpenter	
G-BLLO	PA-18 Super Cub 95	D. G. & M. G. Margetts	
G-BLLP	Slingsby T.67B	Cleveland Flying School Ltd/Teesside	
G-BLLR	Slingsby T.67B	Trent Air Services Ltd/Cranfield	
G-BLLS	Slingsby T.67B	Western Air Training Ltd/Thruxton	

Notes	Reg.	Type	Owner or Operator
	G-BLLV	Slingsby T.67B	R. L. Brinklow
	G-BLLW	Colt 56B balloon	J. C. Stupples
	G-BLLZ	Rutan LongEz	R. S. Stoddart-Stones
	G-BLMA	Zlin 326 Trener Master	G. P. Northcott/Shoreham
	G-BLMC	Avro 698 Vulcan B.2A (XM575) ★	Aeropark/E. Midlands
	G-BLME	Robinson R-22	Lateq Aviation Ltd
	G-BLMG	Grob G.109B	Mike Golf Syndicate
	G-BLMI	PA-18 Super Cub 95	B. J. Borsberry
	G-BLMN	Rutan LongEz	G-BLMN Flying Group
	G-BLMP	PA-17 Vagabond	M. Austin/Popham
	G-BLMR	PA-18 Super Cub 150	Bidford Gliding Centre Ltd
	G-BLMT	PA-18 Super Cub 135	I. S. Runnalls
	G-BLMW	T.66 Nipper 3	S. L. Millar
	G-BLMX	Cessna FR.172H	C. J. W. Littler/Felthorpe
	G-BLMZ	Colt 105A balloon	M. D. Dickinson
	G-BLNJ	BN-2B-26 Islander	Loganair Ltd/British Airways
	G-BLNO	FRED Srs 3	L. W. Smith
	G-BLNW	BN-2B-27 Islander	Loganair Ltd/Scottish Air Ambulance Service
	G-BLOA	V.806 Viscount Freightmaster II	*withdrawn*/Southend
	G-BLOB	Colt 31A balloon	Jacques W. Soukup Enterprises Ltd
	G-BLOR	PA-30 Twin Comanche 160	R. L. C. Appleton
	G-BLOS	Cessna 185A (also flown with floats)	E. Brun
	G-BLOT	Colt Ax6-56B balloon	H. J. Anderson
	G-BLOU	Rand KR-2	D. G. Cole
	G-BLPA	Piper J-3C-65 Cub	G. A. Card & C. G. Gray
	G-BLPB	Turner TSW Hot Two Wot	J. R. Woolford
	G-BLPE	PA-18 Super Cub 95	A. Haig-Thomas
	G-BLPF	Cessna FR.172G	W. A. F. Cuninghame
	G-BLPG	J/1N Alpha (16693)	Q. J. Ball (G-AZIH)
	G-BLPH	Cessna FRA.150L	New Aerobat Group/Shoreham
	G-BLPI	Slingsby T.67B	Keepcase Ltd
	G-BLPK	Cameron V-65 balloon	A. J. & C. P. Nicholls
	G-BLPP	Cameron V-77 balloon	L. P. Purfield
	G-BLRC	PA-18 Super Cub 135	A. J. McBurnie
	G-BLRD	MBB Bo.209 Monsun 150FV	M. D. Ward
	G-BLRF	Slingsby T.67C	Bristow Helicopters Ltd/Redhill
	G-BLRG	Slingsby T.67B	R. L. Brinklow
	G-BLRH	Rutan LongEz	G. L. Tompson
	G-BLRJ	Jodel DR.1051	M. P. Hallam
	G-BLRL	CP.301C-1 Emeraude	B. C. Davis
	G-BLRM	Glaser-Dirks DG.400	D. J. Barke/Tatenhill
	G-BLRN	D.H.104 Dove 8 (WB531) ★	Pionier Hangaar Collection/Lelystad
	G-BLRW	Cameron 77 Elephant SS balloon	Forbes Europe Inc/France
	G-BLSD	D.H.112 Venom FB.55 (J-1758)	Aces High Ltd/North Weald
	G-BLSF	AA-5A Cheetah	J. P. E. Walsh (G-BGCK)
	G-BLSH	Cameron V-77 balloon	C. N. Luffingham
	G-BLSK	Colt 77A balloon	Solarmoor Ltd
	G-BLSM	H.S.125 Srs 700B	Dravidian Air Services Ltd/Heathrow
	G-BLSN	Colt AS-56 airship	D. K. Fish
	G-BLSO	Colt AS-42 airship	Huntair Ltd/Germany
	G-BLST	Cessna 421C	Cecil Aviation Ltd/Cambridge
	G-BLSU	Cameron A-210 balloon	A. C. Elson
	G-BLSX	Cameron O-105 balloon	B. J. Petteford
	G-BLTA	Thunder Ax7-77A	K. A. Schlussler
	G-BLTC	D.31 Turbulent	G. P. Smith & A. W. Burton
	G-BLTF	Robinson R-22A	Brian Seedle Helicopters/Blackpool
	G-BLTG	WAR Sea Fury (replica) (WJ237)	A. N. R. Houghton & D. H. Nourish
	G-BLTK	R. Commander 112TC	B. Rogalewski/Denham
	G-BLTM	Robin HR.200/100	B. D. Balcanquall
	G-BLTN	Thunder Ax7-65 balloon	J. A. Liddle
	G-BLTP	H.S.125 Srs 700B	Dravidian Air Services Ltd/Heathrow
	G-BLTR	Scheibe SF.25B Falke	V. Mallon/Germany
	G-BLTS	Rutan LongEz	R. W. Cutler
	G-BLTT	Slingsby T.67B	S. E. Marples
	G-BLTU	Slingsby T.67B	The Neiderhein Powered Flying Club/ Germany
	G-BLTV	Slingsby T.67B	R. L. Brinklow
	G-BLTW	Slingsby T.67B	R. L. Brinklow
	G-BLTZ	SOCATA TB.10 Tobago	Martin Ltd/Biggin Hill
	G-BLUA	Robinson R-22	J. R. Budgen
	G-BLUE	Colt Ax7-77A balloon	D. P. Busby

Reg.	Type	Owner or Operator	Notes
G-BLUI	Thunder Ax7-65 balloon	S. Johnson	
G-BLUJ	Cameron V-56 balloon	J. N. W. West	
G-BLUK	Bond Sky Dancer	J. Owen	
G-BLUL	Jodel DR.1051/M1	J. Owen	
G-BLUM	SA.365N Dauphin 2	Bond Helicopters Ltd	
G-BLUN	SA.365N Dauphin 2	Bond Helicopters Ltd	
G-BLUV	Grob G.109B	The 109 Fllying Group/North Weald	
G-BLUX	Slingsby T.67M	R. L. Brinklow	
G-BLUZ	D.H.82 Queen Bee (LF858)	B. Bayes	
G-BLVA	Airtour AH-56 balloon	A. Van Wyk	
G-BLVB	Airtour AH-56 balloon	T. C. Hinton	
G-BLVC	Airtour AH-31 balloon	Airtour Balloon Co Ltd	
G-BLVI	Slingsby T.67M	Slingsby Aviation Ltd/Kirkbymoorside	
G-BLVK	CAARP CAP-10B	E. K. Coventry/Earls Colne	
G-BLVL	PA-28-161 Warrior II	Marair (Jersey) Ltd	
G-BLVN	Cameron N-77 balloon	Servo & Electronic Sales Ltd	
G-BLVS	Cessna 150M	W. Lancs Aero Club Ltd/Woodvale	
G-BLVW	Cessna F.172H	R. & D. Holloway Ltd	
G-BLWB	Thunder Ax6-56 balloon .	J. R. Tonkin/Norwich	
G-BLWD	PA-34-200T Seneca	C.S.E. Aviation Ltd/Kidlington	
G-BLWE	Colt 90A balloon	Huntair Ltd/Germany	
G-BLWF	Robin HR.100/210	Starguide Ltd	
G-BLWH	Fournier RF-6B-100	Gloster Aero Club Ltd/Staverton	
G-BLWM	Bristol M.1C (replica) (C4994) ★	RAF Museum/Hendon	
G-BLWP	PA-38-112 Tomahawk	A. Dodd/Booker	
G-BLWT	Evans VP-1	C. J. Bellworthy	
G-BLWV	Cessna F.152	Redhill Flying Club	
G-BLWW	Taylor Mini Imp Model C	M. K. Field	
G-BLWY	Robin 2161D	A. Spencer & D. A. Rolfe	
G-BLXA	SOCATA TB.20 Trinidad	Shropshire Aero Club Ltd/Sleap	
G-BLXF	Cameron V-77 balloon	G. McFarland	
G-BLXG	Colt 21A balloon	A. Walker	
G-BLXH	Fournier RF-3	A. Rawicz-Szczerbo	
G-BLXI	CP.1310-C3 Super Emeraude	R. Howard	
G-BLXO	Jodel 150	P. R. Powell	
G-BLXP	PA-28R Cherokee Arrow 200	C. C. W. Hart	
G-BLXR	AS.332L Super Puma	Bristow Helicopters Ltd	
G-BLXS	AS.332L Super Puma	Bristow Helicopters Ltd	
G-BLXT	RAF SE-5A (B4863) ★	Museum of Army Flying/Middle Wallop	
G-BLXX	PA-23 Aztec 250F	Falcon Flying Service (G-PIED)/Biggin Hill	
G-BLXY	Cameron V-65 balloon	Gone With The Wind Ltd/Tanzania	
G-BLYD	SOCATA TB.20 Trinidad	Gourmet Trotters	
G-BLYE	SOCATA TB.10 Tobago	G. Hatton	
G-BLYK	PA-34-220T Seneca III	D. C. Bain	
G-BLYP	Robin 3000/120	Weald Air Services/Headcorn	
G-BLYT	Airtour AH-77 balloon	I. J. & B. A. Taylor	
G-BLYY	PA-28-181 Archer II	A. C. Clarke & ptnrs	
G-BLZA	Scheibe SF.25B Falke	M. J. Fogarty	
G-BLZB	Cameron N-65 balloon	D. Bareford	
G-BLZD	Robin R.1180T	Berkshire Aviation Services Ltd	
G-BLZE	Cessna F.152 II	Flairhire Ltd (G-CSSC)/Redhill	
G-BLZF	Thunder Ax7-77 balloon	H. M. Savage	
G-BLZH	Cessna F.152 II	Plane Talking Ltd/Elstree	
G-BLZM	Rutan LongEz	Zulu Mike Group/Shoreham	
G-BLZN	Bell 206B JetRanger	Helicopter Services	
G-BLZP	Cessna F.152	E. Midlands Flying School Ltd	
G-BLZR	Cameron A-140 balloon	Clipper Worldwide Trading/Venezuela	
G-BLZS	Cameron O-77 balloon	M. M. Cobbold	
G-BLZT	Short SD3-60 Variant 100	Gill Airways Ltd	
G-BMAD	Cameron V-77 balloon	M. A. Stelling	
G-BMAF	Cessna 180F	P. Channon	
G-BMAL	Sikorsky S-76A	Bond Helicopters Ltd	
G-BMAO	Taylor JT.1 Monoplane	V. A. Wordsworth	
G-BMAR	Short SD3-60 Variant 100	Loganair Ltd/British Airways (G-BLCR)	
G-BMAV	AS.350B Ecureuil	Southern Trust Co Ltd/Jersey	
G-BMAX	FRED Srs 2	D. A. Arkley	
G-BMAY	PA-18 Super Cub 135	R. W. Davies	
G-BMBB	Cessna F.150L	Dacebow Aviation	
G-BMBC	PA-31-350 Navajo Chieftain	Air Navigation & Trading Ltd/Blackpool	
G-BMBE	PA-46-310P Malibu	Barfax Distributing Co Ltd & Glasdon Group Ltd/Blackpool	
G-BMBJ	Schempp-Hirth Janus CM	Cleveland Gliding Club	

Notes	Reg.	Type	Owner or Operator
	G-BMBS	Colt 105A balloon	H. G. Davies
	G-BMBT	Thunder Ax8-90 balloon	Capital Balloon Club Ltd
	G-BMBW	Bensen B.8MR	M. E. Vahdat
	G-BMBZ	Scheibe SF.25E Super Falke	Buckminster Super Falke Syndicate
	G-BMCC	Thunder Ax7-77 balloon	H. N. Harben Ltd
	G-BMCD	Cameron V-65 balloon	M. C. Drye
	G-BMCG	Grob G.109B	Lagerholm Finnimport Ltd/Booker
	G-BMCI	Cessna F.172H	A. B. Davis/Edinburgh
	G-BMCK	Cameron O-77 balloon	D. L. Smith
	G-BMCN	Cessna F.152	Lincoln Aero Club Ltd/Sturgate
	G-BMCO	Colomban MC.15 Cri-Cri	G. P. Clarke/Enstone
	G-BMCS	PA-22 Tri-Pacer 135	Rickard Lazenby & Co. Ltd & T. A. Hodges
	G-BMCV	Cessna F.152	Leicestershire Aero Club Ltd
	G-BMCW	AS.332L Super Puma	Bristow Helicopters Ltd
	G-BMCX	AS.332L Super Puma	Bristow Helicopters Ltd
	G-BMDB	SE-5A (replica) (F235)	D. Biggs
	G-BMDC	PA-32-301 Saratoga	MacLaren Aviation/Newcastle
	G-BMDD	Slingsby T.29	A. R. Worters
	G-BMDE	Pientenpol Air Camper	P. B. Childs
	G-BMDJ	Price Ax7-77S balloon	D. A. Kozuba-Kozubska
	G-BMDK	PA-34-220T Seneca III	A1 Air Ltd
	G-BMDO	ARV Super 2	R. Lloyd
	G-BMDP	Partenavia P.64B Oscar 200	T. Gracey
	G-BMDS	Jodel D.120	J. V. Thompson
	G-BMDY	GA-7 Cougar	Eurowide Ltd/Elstree
	G-BMEA	PA-18 Super Cub 95	C. L. Towell
	G-BMEF	Cameron O-105 balloon	A. G. R. Calder/Los Angeles
	G-BMEG	SOCATA TB.10 Tobago	G. H. N. & R. V. Chamberlain
	G-BMEH	Jodel 150 Special Super Mascaret	Wm. Coupar Ltd
	G-BMEK	Mooney M.20K	Atlantic Film Investments Ltd/USA
	G-BMET	Taylor JT.1 Monoplane	M. K. A. Blyth
	G-BMEU	Isaacs Fury II	A. W. Austin
	G-BMEV	PA-32RT-300T Turbo Lance II	Arrow Aviation Ltd
	G-BMEX	Cessna A.150K	S. G. Eldred & N. A. M. Brain
	G-BMFD	PA-23 Aztec 250F	Rangemile Ltd (G-BGYY)/Coventry
	G-BMFG	Dornier Do.27A-4 (3460)	R. F. Warner
	G-BMFI	PZL SZD-45A Ogar	C. G. Wright
	G-BMFL	Rand KR-2	E. W. B. Comber & M. F. Leusby
	G-BMFN	QAC Quickie Tri-Q.200	A. H. Hartog
	G-BMFP	PA-28-161 Warrior II	Bravo-Mike-Fox-Papa Group
	G-BMFT	H.S.748 Srs 2A	Euroair Transport Ltd
	G-BMFU	Cameron N-90 balloon	J. J. Rudoni
	G-BMFY	Grob G.109B	P. J. Shearer
	G-BMFZ	Cessna F.152 II	Cornwall Flying Club Ltd/Bodmin
	G-BMGB	PA-28R Cherokee Arrow 200	Malmesbury Specialist Cars
	G-BMGC	Fairey Swordfish Mk II (W5856)	F.A.A. Museum/Yeovilton
	G-BMGG	Cessna 152 II	Falcon Flying Services/Biggin Hill
	G-BMGR	Grob G.109B	M. Clarke & D. S. Hawes
	G-BMGT	Cessna 310R	Air Service Training Ltd/Perth
	G-BMGY	Lake LA-4-200 Buccaneer	RL Estates Ltd (G-BWKS/G-BDDI)
	G-BMHA	Rutan LongEz	S. F. Elvins
	G-BMHC	Cessna U.206F	Clacton Aero Club (1988) Ltd
	G-BMHJ	Thunder Ax7-65 balloon	M. G. Robinson
	G-BMHL	Wittman W.8 Tailwind	T. G. Hoult
	G-BMHS	Cessna F.172M	Tango X-Ray Flying Group
	G-BMHT	PA-28RT-201T Turbo Arrow IV	Scalpay Ltd
	G-BMHX	Short SD3-60 Variant 100	Loganair Ltd/British Airways
	G-BMHZ	PA-28RT-201T Turbo Arrow IV	F. Kratky
	G-BMIA	Thunder Ax8-90 balloon	A. G. R. Calder/Los Angeles
	G-BMID	Jodel D.120	M. J. Ireland
	G-BMIF	AS.350B Ecureuil	Colt Car Co Ltd/Staverton
	G-BMIG	Cessna 172N	J. R. Nicholls/Conington
	G-BMIH	H.S.125 Srs 700B	Inflite Executive Charter Ltd
	G-BMIM	Rutan LongEz	R. M. Smith
	G-BMIO	Stoddard-Hamilton Glasair RG	A. H. Carrington
	G-BMIP	Jodel D.112	M. T. Kinch
	G-BMIR	Westland Wasp HAS.1 (XT788)	R. Windley
	G-BMIS	Monnett Sonerai II	B. A. Bower/Thruxton
	G-BMIV	PA-28R-201T Turbo Arrow III	Maurice Mason Ltd
	G-BMIW	PA-28-181 Archer II	Oldbus Ltd
	G-BMIY	Oldfield Baby Great Lakes	J. B. Scott (G-NOME)
	G-BMJA	PA-32R-301 Saratoga SP	J. A. Varndell

Reg.	Type	Owner or Operator	Notes
G-BMJB	Cessna 152 II	Bobbington Air Training School Ltd/ Halfpenny Green	
G-BMJC	Cessna 152 II	Cambridge Aero Club Ltd	
G-BMJD	Cessna 152 II	Donair Flying Club Ltd/E. Midlands	
G-BMJG	PA-28R Cherokee Arrow 200	D. J. D. Ritchie & ptnrs/Elstree	
G-BMJL	R. Commander 114	H. Snelson	
G-BMJM	Evans VP-1	C. A. Macleod	
G-BMJN	Cameron O-65 balloon	E. J. A. Macholc	
G-BMJO	PA-34-220T Seneca III	Petlon Polymers Ltd	
G-BMJR	Cessna T.337H	John Roberts Services Ltd (G-NOVA)	
G-BMJS	Thunder Ax7-77 balloon	Foulger Transport Ltd	
G-BMJT	Beech 76 Duchess	Mike Osborne Properties Ltd	
G-BMJX	Wallis WA-116X	K. H. Wallis	
G-BMJY	Yakovlev C18M (07)	R. J. Lamplough/North Weald	
G-BMJZ	Cameron N-90 balloon	Bristol University Hot Air Ballooning Soc	
G-BMKB	PA-18 Super Cub 135	Cubair Ltd/Redhill	
G-BMKC	Piper J-3C-65 Cub (329854)	R. J. H. Springall	
G-BMKD	Beech C90A King Air	A. E. Bristow	
G-BMKF	Jodel DR.221	L. Gilbert	
G-BMKG	PA-38-112 Tomahawk	Medallionair Ltd/Luton	
G-BMKH	Colt 105A balloon	Scotia Balloons Ltd	
G-BMKJ	Cameron V-77 balloon	R. C. Thursby	
G-BMKK	PA-28R Cherokee Arrow 200	J. H. Hutchinson	
G-BMKP	Cameron V-77 balloon	Jacques W. Soukup Enterprises Ltd	
G-BMKR	PA-28-161 Warrior II	Field Flying Group (G-BGKR)/Goodwood	
G-BMKV	Thunder Ax7-77 balloon	A. Hornak & M. J. Nadel	
G-BMKW	Cameron V-77 balloon	A. C. Garnett	
G-BMKX	Cameron 77 Elephant SS balloon	Cameron Balloons Ltd	
G-BMKY	Cameron O-65 balloon	A. R. Rich & M. E. White	
G-BMLB	Jodel D.120A	W. O. Brown	
G-BMLC	Short SD3-60 Variant 100	Loganair Ltd/British Airways	
G-BMLJ	Cameron N-77 balloon	C. J. Dunkley	
G-BMLK	Grob G.109B	Brams Syndicate	
G-BMLL	Grob G.109B	A. H. R. Stansfield	
G-BMLS	PA-28R-201 Arrow III	M. C. Thomas & D. G. Bean	
G-BMLT	Pietenpol Air Camper	W. E. R. Jenkins	
G-BMLU	Colt 90A balloon	Danish Catering Services Ltd	
G-BMLW	Cameron V-65 balloon	M. L. & L. P. Willoughby	
G-BMLX	Cessna F.150L	C. J. Freeman	
G-BMLZ	Cessna 421C	Hadagain Investments Ltd (G-OTAD/ G-BEVL)	
G-BMMC	Cessna 1310Q	Cooper Clegg Ltd	
G-BMMD	Rand KR-2	E. J. Lloyd	
G-BMMF	FRED Srs 2	J. M. Jones	
G-BMMG	Thunder Ax 7-77 balloon	G. V. Beckwith	
G-BMMI	Pazmany PL.4A	M. K. Field/Sleap	
G-BMMJ	Siren PIK-30	J. R. Greig	
G-BMMK	Cessna 182P	M. S. Knight/Goodwood	
G-BMML	PA-38-112 Tomahawk	Western Air Training Ltd/Thruxton	
G-BMMM	Cessna 152 II	Luton Flight Training Ltd	
G-BMMP	Grob G.109B	E. W. Reynolds	
G-BMMR	Dornier Do.228-200	Suckling Airways Ltd/Cambridge	
G-BMMU	Thunder Ax8-105 balloon	C. J. P. Trinder	
G-BMMV	ICA-Brasov IS-28M2A	T. Cust	
G-BMMW	Thunder Ax7-77 balloon	P. A. Georges	
G-BMMX	ICA-Brasov IS-28M2A	G-BMMX Syndicate	
G-BMMY	Thunder Ax7-77 balloon	D. A. Lawson	
G-BMNF	Beech B200 Super King Air	Bernard Matthews PLC/Norwich	
G-BMNL	PA-28R Cherokee Arrow 200	I. H. Nettleton	
G-BMNP	PA-38-112 Tomahawk	APB Leasing Ltd/Welshpool	
G-BMNT	PA-34-220T Seneca III	Channel Airways Ltd	
G-BMNV	SNCAN Stampe SV-4D	Wessex Aviation & Transport Ltd	
G-BMNW	PA-31-350 Navajo Chieftain	Crosswind Consultants	
G-BMNX	Colt 56A balloon	J. H. Dryden	
G-BMNZ	Cessna U206F	R. Loveridge	
G-BMOE	PA-28R Cherokee Arrow 200	B. J. Mason/Shoreham	
G-BMOF	Cessna U206G	Integrated Hydraulics Ltd	
G-BMOG	Thunder Ax7-77A balloon	P. J. Burn	
G-BMOH	Cameron N-77 balloon	P. J. Marshall & M. A. Clarke	
G-BMOI	Partenavia P.68R	Simmette Ltd	
G-BMOJ	Cameron V-56 balloon	S. R. Bridge	
G-BMOK	ARV Super 2	P. E. Barker	
G-BMOL	PA-23 Aztec 250D	LDL Enterprises (G-BBSR)/Elstree	

Notes	Reg.	Type	Owner or Operator
	G-BMOM	ICA-Brasov IS-28M2A	Brasov Flying Group
	G-BMOO	FRED Srs 2	N. Purllant
	G-BMOP	PA-28R-201T Turbo Arrow III	P. Murer
	G-BMOT	Bensen B.8M	R. S. W. Jones
	G-BMOV	Cameron O-105 balloon	C. Gillott
	G-DMOX	Hovey Beta Bird	A. K. Jones
	G-BMPC	PA-28-181 Archer II	C. J. & R. J. Barnes
	G-BMPD	Cameron V-65 balloon	D. E. & J. M. Hartland
	G-BMPL	Optica Industries OA.7 Optica	FLS Aerospace (Lovaux) Ltd/Bournemouth
	G-BMPP	Cameron N-77 balloon	I. B. Lumsden
	G-BMPR	PA-28R-201 Arrow III	AH Flight Services Ltd
	G-BMPS	Strojnik S-2A	G. J. Green
	G-BMPY	D.H.82A Tiger Moth	S. M. F. Eisenstein
	G-BMRA	Boeing 757-236	British Airways *Beaumaris Castle*
	G-BMRB	Boeing 757-236	British Airways *Colchester Castle*
	G-BMRC	Boeing 757-236	British Airways *Rochester Castle*
	G-BMRD	Boeing 757-236	British Airways *Bothwell Castle*
	G-BMRE	Boeing 757-236	British Airways *Killyleagh Castle*
	G-BMRF	Boeing 757-236	British Airways *Hever Castle*
	G-BMRG	Boeing 757-236	British Airways *Caerphilly Castle*
	G-BMRH	Boeing 757-236	British Airways *Norwich Castle*
	G-BMRI	Boeing 757-236	British Airways *Tonbridge Castle*
	G-BMRJ	Boeing 757-236	British Airways *Old Wardour Castle*
	G-BMSA	Stinson HW.75 Voyager	M. A. Thomas (G-BCUM)/Barton
	G-BMSB	V.S.509 Spitfire IX (MJ627)	M. S. Bayliss (G-ASOZ)
	G-BMSC	Evans VP-2	T. C. Barron
	G-BMSD	PA-28-181 Archer II	General Airline Ltd
	G-BMSE	Valentin Taifun 17E	A. J. Nurse
	G-BMSF	PA-38-112 Tomahawk	N. Bradley/Crosland Moor
	G-BMSG	Saab 32A Lansen ★	Aces High Ltd/Cranfield
	G-BMSI	Cameron N-105 balloon	Direction Air Conditioning Ltd
	G-BMSK	Hoffmann H-36 Dimona	J. MacGilvray
	G-BMSL	FRED Srs 3	A. C. Coombe
	G-BMSU	Cessna 152 II	G-BMSU Group
	G-BMTA	Cessna 152 II	Turnhouse Flying Club
	G-BMTB	Cessna 152 II	J. A. Pothecary/Shoreham
	G-BMTJ	Cessna 152 II	Creaton Aviation Services Ltd
	G-BMTL	Cessna F.152 II	Agricultural & General Aviation/ Bournemouth
	G-BMTN	Cameron O-77 balloon	Industrial Services (MH) Ltd
	G-BMTO	PA-38-112 Tomahawk	Falcon Flying Services/Biggin Hill
	G-BMTP	PA-38-112 Tomahawk	R. A. Wakefield
	G-BMTR	PA-28-161 Warrior II	London Flight Centre (Stansted) Ltd
	G-BMTS	Cessna 172N	Falcon Flying Services/Biggin Hill
	G-BMTU	Pitts S-1E Special	O. R. Howe
	G-BMTX	Cameron V-77 balloon	J. A. Langley
	G-BMUD	Cessna 182P	J. P. Edwards
	G-BMUG	Rutan LongEz	P. Richardson & J. Shanley
	G-BMUH	Bensen B.8MR	A. Shuttleworth
	G-BMUJ	Colt Drachenfisch balloon	Air 2 Air Ltd
	G-BMUK	Colt UFO balloon	Air 2 Air Ltd
	G-BMUL	Colt Kindermond balloon	Air 2 Air Ltd
	G-BMUN	Cameron 78 Harley SS balloon	Forbes Europe Inc/France
	G-BMUO	Cessna A.152	Redhill Flying Club
	G-BMUR	Cameron gas airship	Cameron Balloons Ltd
	G-BMUT	PA-34-200T Seneca II	Newcastle Aeroplane Co. Ltd
	G-BMUU	Thunder Ax7-77 balloon	G. Anorewartha
	G-BMUZ	PA-28-161 Warrior II	Newcastle-upon-Tyne Aero Club Ltd
	G-BMVA	Schiebe SF.25B Falke	C. A. Simmonds
	G-BMVB	Cessna 152	LAC (Enterprises) Ltd/Barton
	G-BMVE	PA-28RT-201 Arrow IV	F. E. Gooding/Biggin Hill
	G-BMVF	Bell 212	Bristow Helicopters Ltd
	G-BMVG	QAC Quickie Q.1	P. M. Wright
	G-BMVI	Cameron O-105 balloon	Heart of England Balloons
	G-BMVJ	Cessna 172N	Green Aviation Associates Ltd
	G-BMVL	PA-38-112 Tomahawk	Airways Aero Associations Ltd/Booker
	G-BMVM	PA-38-112 Tomahawk	Airways Aero Associations Ltd/Booker
	G-BMVO	Cameron O-77 balloon	Warners Motors (Leasing) Ltd
	G-BMVT	Thunder Ax7-77A balloon	M. L. & L. P. Willoughby
	G-BMVU	Monnet Moni	F. S. Beckett
	G-BMVV	Rutan Vari-Viggen	G. B. Roberts
	G-BMVW	Cameron O-65 balloon	S. P. Richards
	G-BMWA	Hughes 269C	R. Taylor

Reg.	Type	Owner or Operator	Notes
G-BMWE	ARV Super 2	N. R. F. McNally	
G-BMWF	ARV Super 2	N. R. Beale	
G-BMWJ	ARV Super 2	Mid-West Engines Ltd	
G-BMWM	ARV Super 2	R. Scroby	
G-BMWN	Cameron 80 SS Temple balloon	Forbes Europe Inc/France	
G-BMWP	PA-34-200T Seneca II	R. Aarons	
G-BMWR	R. Commander 112A	M. & J. Edwards	
G-BMWU	Cameron N-42 balloon	The Hot Air Balloon Co Ltd	
G-BMWV	Putzer Elster B	E. A. J. Hibbard	
G-BMWX	Robinson R-22B	Lateq Aviation Ltd	
G-BMXA	Cessna 152 II	Chamberlain Leasing	
G-BMXC	Cessna 152 II	European Flyers/Blackbushe	
G-BMXD	F.27 Friendship Mk 500	Air UK Ltd *Victor Hugo*/Norwich	
G-BMXJ	Cessna F.150L	Arrow Aircraft Group	
G-BMXL	PA-38-112 Tomahawk	Airways Aero Associatipons Ltd/Booker	
G-BMXX	Cessna 152 II	Aerohire Ltd/Halfpenny Green	
G-BMYA	Colt 56A balloon	Flying Pictures (Balloons) Ltd	
G-BMYC	SOCATA TB.10 Tobago	E. A. Grady	
G-BMYD	Beech A36 Bonanza	Seabeam Partners Ltd	
G-BMYF	Bensen B.8M	T. H. G. Russell	
G-BMYG	Cessna F.152	Rolim Ltd/Aberdeen	
G-BMYI	AA-5 Traveler	W. C. & S. C. Westran	
G-BMYJ	Cameron V-65 balloon	A. Lutz	
G-BMYN	Colt 77A balloon	J. D. Shapland & ptnrs	
G-BMYP	Fairey Gannet AEW.3 (XL502)	R. H. Cooper/Gamston	
G-BMYR	Robinson R-22	Lateq Aviation Ltd	
G-BMYS	Thunder Ax7-77Z balloon	J. E. Weidema	
G-BMYU	Jodel D.120	D. M. Griffiths	
G-BMYV	Bensen B.8M	R. G. Cotman	
G-BMYW	Hughes 269C	March Helicopters Ltd/Sywell	
G-BMZA	Air Command 503 Commander	R. W. Husband	
G-BMZB	Cameron N-77 balloon	D. C. Eager	
G-BMZC	Cessna 421C	City Air Ltd	
G-BMZD	Beech C90 King Air	Colt Transport Ltd	
G-BMZE	SOCATA TB.9 Tampico	Air Touring Services Ltd/Biggin Hill	
G-BMZF	Mikoyan Gurevich MiG-15 (1420) ★	F.A.A. Museum/Yeovilton	
G-BMZG	QAC Quickie Q.2	T. D. Edmunds	
G-BMZJ	Colt 400A balloon	G. J. Bell	
G-BMZN	Everett gyroplane	R. J. Brown	
G-BMZP	Everett gyroplane	B. C. Norris	
G-BMZS	Everett gyroplane	L. W. Cload	
G-BMZV	Cessna 172P	Shoreham Flight Simulation/Bournemouth	
G-BMZW	Bensen B.8MR	P. D. Widdicombe	
G-BMZX	Wolf W-II Boredom Fighter (146-11042)	A. R. Meakin & S. W. Watkins	
G-BNAD	Rand KR-2	P. J. Brookman	
G-BNAG	Colt 105A balloon	R. W. Batchelor	
G-BNAH	Colt Paper Bag SS balloon	Thrustell Ltd/USA	
G-BNAI	Wolf W-II Boredom Fighter (146-11083)	P. J. D. Gronow	
G-BNAJ	Cessna 152 II	Galair Ltd/Biggin Hill	
G-BNAN	Cameron V-65 balloon	A. M. Lindsay	
G-BNAO	Colt AS-105 airship	Heather Flight Ltd	
G-BNAP	Colt 240A balloon	Heather Flight Ltd	
G-BNAR	Taylor JT.1 Monoplane	C. J. Smith	
G-BNAU	Cameron V-65 balloon	J. Buckle	
G-BNAW	Cameron V-65 balloon	A. Walker	
G-BNBJ	AS.355F-1 Twin Squirrel	Coln Helicopters Ltd	
G-BNBL	Thunder Ax7-77 balloon	J. R. Henderson	
G-BNBM	Colt 90A balloon	Huntair Ltd	
G-BNBR	Cameron N-90 balloon	Airborne Promotions Ltd	
G-BNBU	Bensen B.8MV	R. Retallick	
G-BNBV	Thunder Ax7-77 balloon	J. M. Robinson	
G-BNBW	Thunder Ax7-77 balloon	I. S. & S. W. Watthews	
G-BNBY	Beech 95-B55A Baron	Richard Hannon Ltd (G-AXXR)	
G-BNBZ	LET L-200D Morava	C. A. Suckling/Redhill	
G-BNCB	Cameron V-77 balloon	Tyred & Battered Balloon Group	
G-BNCC	Thunder Ax7-77 balloon	C. J. Burnhope	
G-RNCG	QAC Quickie Q.2	T. F. Francis	
G-BNCH	Cameron V-77 balloon	Royal Engineers Balloon Club	
G-BNCJ	Cameron V-77 balloon	I. S. Bridge	

Notes	Reg.	Type	Owner or Operator
	G-BNCK	Cameron V-77 balloon	G. Randall/Germany
	G-BNCL	WG.13 Lynx HAS.2 (XX469) ★	Lancashire Fire Brigade HQ/Lancaster
	G-BNCM	Cameron N-77 balloon	S. & A. Stone Ltd
	G-BNCN	Glaser-Dirks DG.400	M. C. Costin/Husbands Bosworth
	G-BNCO	PA-38-112 Tomahawk	Cambrian Flying Club/Swansea
	G-BNCR	PA-28-161 Warrior II	Airways Aero Associations Ltd/Booker
	G-BNCS	Cessna 180	C. Elwell Transport Ltd
	G-BNCU	Thunder Ax7-77 balloon	J. A. Lister
	G-BNCV	Bensen B.8	J. M. Benton
	G-BNCW	Boeing 767-204	Britannia Airways Ltd/Luton
	G-BNCX	Hunter T.7	Lovaux Ltd *(stored)*/Bournemouth
	G-BNCY	F.27 Friendship Mk 500	Air UK Ltd *Lillie Langtry*/Norwich
	G-BNCZ	Rutan LongEz	R. M. Bainbridge/Sherburn
	G-BNDG	Wallis WA-201/R Srs1	K. H. Wallis
	G-BNDH	Colt 21A balloon	Hot-Air Balloon Co Ltd
	G-BNDN	Cameron V-77 balloon	J. A. Smith
	G-BNDO	Cessna 152 II	Simair Ltd
	G-BNDP	Brügger MB.2 Colibri	D. A. Peet
	G-BNDR	SOCATA TB.10 Tobago	A. N. Reardon/Woodvale
	G-BNDS	PA-31-350 Navajo Chieftain	Owen Air Ltd/Biggin Hill
	G-BNDT	Brügger MB.2 Colibri	Colibri Flying Group
	G-BNDV	Cameron N-77 balloon	R. E. Jones
	G-BNDW	D.H.82A Tiger Moth	N. D. Welch
	G-BNDY	Cessna 425-1	Standard Aviation Ltd/Newcastle
	G-BNED	PA-22 Tri-Pacer 135	P. Storey
	G-BNEE	PA-28R-201 Arrow III	Britannic Management (Aviation) Ltd
	G-BNEI	PA-34-200T Seneca II	A. Bucknole
	G-BNEJ	PA-38-112 Tomahawk	V. C. & S. G. Swindell
	G-BNEK	PA-38-112 Tomahawk	Pool Aviation Ltd/Welshpool
	G-BNEL	PA-28-161 Warrior II	J. A. Pothecary/Shoreham
	G-BNEN	PA-34-200T Seneca II	Warwickshire Aerocentre Ltd
	G-BNEO	Cameron V-77 balloon	J. G. O'Connell
	G-BNER	PA-34-200T Seneca II	R. I. Sharpe
	G-BNES	Cameron V-77 balloon	G. Wells
	G-BNET	Cameron O-84 balloon	J. Bennett & Son (Insurance Brokers) Ltd
	G-BNEV	Viking Dragonfly	N. W. Eyre
	G-BNEX	Cameron O-120 balloon	The Balloon Club Ltd
	G-BNFB	Short SD3-60 Variant 100	Gill Airways Ltd/Newcastle
	G-BNFG	Cameron O-77 balloon	Capital Balloon Club Ltd
	G-BNFI	Cessna 150J	T. D. Aitken
	G-BNFK	Cameron 89 Egg SS balloon	Forbes Europe Inc/France
	G-BNFL	WHE Airbuggy	Roger Savage (Photography) (G-AXXN)
	G-BNFM	Colt 21A balloon	M. E. Dworski
	G-BNFN	Cameron N-105 balloon	Air 2 Air Ltd
	G-BNFO	Cameron V-77 balloon	D. C. Patrick-Brown
	G-BNFP	Cameron O-84 balloon	A. J. & E. J. Clarke
	G-BNFR	Cessna 152 II	London Flight Centre (Stansted) Ltd
	G-BNFS	Cessna 152 II	London Flight Centre (Stansted) Ltd
	G-BNFV	Robin DR.400/120	Exeter Flying Club Ltd
	G-BNFW	H.S.125 Srs 700B	Lynton Aviation Ltd
	G-BNFY	Cameron N-77 balloon	The New Holker Estates Co Ltd
	G-BNGD	Cessna 152 II	AV Aviation Ltd
	G-BNGE	Auster AOP.6 (TW536)	R. W. W. Eastman
	G-BNGJ	Cameron V-77 balloon	Latham Timber Centres (Holdings) Ltd
	G-BNGN	Cameron V-77 balloon	A. R. & L. J. McGregor
	G-BNGO	Thunder Ax7-77 balloon	J. S. Finlan
	G-BNGP	Colt 77A balloon	Headland Services Ltd
	G-BNGR	PA-38-112 Tomahawk	Teesside Flight Centre Ltd
	G-BNGS	PA-38-112 Tomahawk	Frontline Aviation Ltd/Teesside
	G-BNGT	PA-28-181 Archer II	Berry Air/Edinburgh
	G-BNGV	ARV Super 2	N. A. Onions
	G-BNGW	ARV Super 2	Southern Gas Turbines Ltd
	G-BNGX	ARV Super 2	Southern Gas Turbines Ltd
	G-BNGY	ARV Super 2	N. R. F. McNally (G-BMWL)
	G-BNHB	ARV Super 2	Super Two Group
	G-BNHC	ARV Super 2	I. C. Whyte
	G-BNHD	ARV Super 2	Aviation (Scotland) Ltd
	G-BNHE	ARV Super 2	L. J. Joyce
	G-BNHG	PA-38-112 Tomahawk	D. A. Whitmore
	G-BNHH	Thunder Ax7-77 balloon	Gee-Tee Signs Ltd
	G-BNHI	Cameron V-77 balloon	P. J. Feltham & C. J. Nicholls
	G-BNHJ	Cessna 152 II	The Pilot Centre Ltd/Denham
	G-BNHK	Cessna 152 II	General Airline Ltd

Reg.	Type	Owner or Operator	Notes
G-BNHL	Colt 90 Beer Glass SS balloon	G. V. Beckwith	
G-BNHN	Colt Ariel Bottle SS balloon ★	British Balloon Museum/Newbury	
G-BNHO	Thunder Ax/-77 balloon	M. J. Forster	
G-BNHP	Saffrey S.330 balloon	N. H. Ponsford *Alpha II*	
G-BNHR	Cameron V-77 balloon	P. C. Waterhouse	
G-BNHT	Fournier RF-3	G-BNHT Group	
G-BNIB	Cameron A-105 balloon	A. G. E. Faulkner	
G-BNID	Cessna 152 II	Mercia Aircraft Leasing & Sales Ltd/ Coventry	
G-BNIE	Cameron O-160 balloon	D. K. Fish	
G-BNIF	Cameron O-56 balloon	D. V. Fowler	
G-BNII	Cameron N-90 balloon	Continu-Forms Holdings PLC	
G-BNIJ	SOCATA TB.10 Tobago	Flying Start Aviation	
G-BNIK	Robin HR.200/120	A. J. McNeal/Popham	
G-BNIM	PA-38-112 Tomahawk	T. S. Kemp	
G-BNIN	Cameron V-77 balloon	Cloud Nine Balloon Group	
G-BNIO	Luscombe 8A Silvaire	G. G. Pugh	
G-BNIP	Luscombe 8A Silvaire	D. R. C. Hunter & S. Maric	
G-BNIU	Cameron O-77 balloon	Nottingham Hot Air Balloon Club & Mitchell Air Power Ltd	
G-BNIV	Cessna 152 II	Aerohire Ltd/Halfpenny Green	
G-BNIW	Boeing Stearman PT-17	Lintally Ltd/E. Midlands	
G-BNIX	EMB-110P1 Bandeirante	Willowjet Ltd/Southend	
G-BNIZ	F.27 Friendship Mk.600	Channel Express (Air Services) Ltd/Bournemouth	
G-BNJA	WAG-Aero Wag-a-Bond	B. E. Maggs	
G-BNJB	Cessna 152 II	Klingair Ltd/Conington	
G-BNJC	Cessna 152 II	Stapleford Flying Club Ltd	
G-BNJD	Cessna 152 II	J. A. Pothecary/Shoreham	
G-BNJE	Cessna A.152	D. D. Delaney	
G-BNJF	PA-32RT-300 Lance II	Biggles Aviation Ltd	
G-BNJG	Cameron O-77 balloon	A. M. Figiel	
G-BNJH	Cessna 152 II	Turnhouse Flying Club	
G-BNJK	Macavia BAe 748 Turbine Tanker	Macavia International Ltd	
G-BNJM	PA-28-161 Warrior II	Teesside Flight Centre Ltd	
G-BNJO	QAC Quickie Q.2	J. D. McKay	
G-BNJR	PA-28RT-201T Turbo Arrow IV	Intelligent Micro Software Ltd	
G-BNJT	PA-28-161 Warrior II	Airways Aero Associations Ltd/Booker	
G-BNJU	Cameron 80 Bust SS balloon	Forbes Europe Inc/France	
G-BNJX	Cameron N-90 balloon	Mars UK Ltd	
G-BNKC	Cessna 152 II	Herefordshire Aero Club Ltd/Shobdon	
G-BNKD	Cessna 172N	Bristol Flying Centre Ltd	
G-BNKE	Cessna 172N	Top Cat Aviation Ltd	
G-BNKF	Colt AS-56 airship	Formtrack Ltd	
G-BNKH	PA-38-112 Tomahawk	Goodwood Terrena Ltd	
G-BNKI	Cessna 152 II	RAF Halton Aeroplane Club Ltd	
G-BNKP	Cessna 152 II	Clacton Aero Club (1988) Ltd	
G-BNKR	Cessna 152 II	Marnham Investments Ltd	
G-BNKS	Cessna 152 II	Shropshire Aero Club Ltd/Sleap	
G-BNKT	Cameron O-77 balloon	British Airways PLC	
G-BNKV	Cessna 152 II	I. C. Adams & Vectair Aviation Ltd	
G-BNKW	PA-38-112 Tomahawk	D. M. MacLean	
G-BNKX	Robinson R-22	Brian Seedle Helicopters	
G-BNLA	Boeing 747-436	British Airways *City of London*	
G-BNLB	Boeing 747-436	British Airways *City of Edinburgh*	
G-BNLC	Boeing 747-436	British Airways *City of Cardiff*	
G-BNLD	Boeing 747-436	British Airways *City of Belfast*	
G-BNLE	Boeing 747-436	British Airways *City of Newcastle*	
G-BNLF	Boeing 747-436	British Airways *City of Leeds*	
G-BNLG	Boeing 747-436	British Airways *City of Southampton*	
G-BNLH	Boeing 747-436	British Airways *City of Westminster*	
G-BNLI	Boeing 747-436	British Airways *City of Sheffield*	
G-BNLJ	Boeing 747-436	British Airways *City of Nottingham*	
G-BNLK	Boeing 747-436	British Airways *City of Bristol*	
G-BNLL	Boeing 747-436	British Airways *City of Leicester*	
G-BNLM	Boeing 747-436	British Airways *City of Durham*	
G-BNLN	Boeing 747-436	British Airways *City of Portsmouth*	
G-BNLO	Boeing 747-436	British Airways *City of Dundee*	
G-BNLP	Boeing 747 436	British Airways *City of Aberdeen*	
G-BNLR	Boeing 747-436	British Airways *City of Hull*	
G-BNLS	Boeing 747-436	British Airways *City of Chester*	
G-BNLT	Boeing 747-436	British Airways *City of Lincoln*	
G-BNLU	Boeing 747-436	British Airways *City of Bangor*	

Notes	Reg.	Type	Owner or Operator
	G-BNLV	Boeing 747-436	British Airways *City of Exeter*
	G-BNLW	Boeing 747-436	British Airways *City of Norwich*
	G-BNLX	Boeing 747-436	British Airways *City of Worcester*
	G-BNLY	Boeing 747-436	British Airways *City of Swansea*
	G-BNLZ	Boeing 747-436	British Asia Airways *City of Perth*
	G-BNMA	Cameron O-77 balloon	T. A. Hains
	G-BNMB	PA-28-151 Warrior	Britannia Airways Ltd/Luton
	G-BNMC	Cessna 152 II	M. L. Jones/Egginton
	G-BNMD	Cessna 152 II	T. M. Jones/Egginton
	G-BNME	Cessna 152 II	L. V. Atkinson
	G-BNMF	Cessna 152 II	Aerohire Ltd
	G-BNMG	Cameron O-77 balloon	Windsor Life Assurance Co Ltd
	G-BNMH	Pietenpol Air Camper	N. M. Hitchman
	G-BNMI	Colt Flying Fantasy SS balloon	Air 2 Air Ltd
	G-BNMK	Dornier Do.27A-1	G. Mackie
	G-BNML	Rand KR-2	H. C. Walker
	G-BNMO	Cessna TR.182RG	R. R. Greaves
	G-BNMP	Cessna R.182RG	P. M. Breton
	G-BNMX	Thunder Ax7-77 balloon	S. A. D. Beard
	G-BNNA	Stolp SA.300 Starduster Too	D. F. Simpson
	G-BNNB	PA-34-200 Seneca II	Shoreham Flight Simulation/Bournemouth
	G-BNNC	Cameron N-77 balloon	T. M. McCoy/Barrow
	G-BNNE	Cameron N-77 balloon	TÍhe Balloon Stable Ltd
	G-BNNF	SA.315B Alouette III Lama	PLM Dollar Group Ltd
	G-BNNG	Cessna T.337D	Somet Ltd (G-COLD)
	G-BNNI	Boeing 727-276	Sabre Airways Ltd
	G-BNNK	Boeing 737-4Q8	GB Airways Ltd
	G-BNNL	Boeing 737-4Q8	GB Airways Ltd
	G-BNNO	PA-28-161 Warrior II	W. Lancs Aero Club Ltd/Woodvale
	G-BNNR	Cessna 152	Sussex Flying Club Ltd/Shoreham
	G-BNNS	PA-28-161 Warrior II	M. J. Allen & B. E. Davies
	G-BNNT	PA-28-151 Warrior	S. T. Gilbert & D. J. Kirkwood
	G-BNNU	PA-38-112 Tomahawk	APB Leasing Ltd/Welshpool
	G-BNNX	PA-28R-201T Turbo Arrow III	P. J. Lague
	G-BNNY	PA-28-161 Warrior II	Falcon Flying Services/Biggin Hill
	G-BNNZ	PA-28-161 Warrior II	D. Heater/Fairoaks
	G-BNOA	PA-38-112 Tomahawk	I. A. Qureshi
	G-BNOB	Wittman W.8 Tailwind	M. Robson-Robinson
	G-BNOE	PA-28-161 Warrior II	Sherburn Aero Club Ltd
	G-BNOF	PA-28-161 Warrior II	BAe Flying College/Prestwick
	G-BNOG	PA-28-161 Warrior II	BAe Flying College/Prestwick
	G-BNOH	PA-28-161 Warrior II	BAe Flying College/Prestwick
	G-BNOI	PA-28-161 Warrior II	BAe Flying College/Prestwick
	G-BNOJ	PA-28-161 Warrior II	BAe (Warton) Flying Club
	G-BNOK	PA-28-161 Warrior II	BAe Flying College/Prestwick
	G-BNOL	PA-28-161 Warrior II	BAe Flying College/Prestwick
	G-BNOM	PA-28-161 Warrior II	Sherburn Aero Club Ltd
	G-BNON	PA-28-161 Warrior II	BAe Flying College/Prestwick
	G-BNOO	PA-28-161 Warrior II	BAe Flying College/Prestwick
	G-BNOP	PA-28-161 Warrior II	BAe Flying College/Prestwick
	G-BNOR	PA-28-161 Warrior II	BAe Flying College/Prestwick
	G-BNOS	PA-28-161 Warrior II	BAe Flying College/Prestwick
	G-BNOT	PA-28-161 Warrior II	BAe Flying College/Prestwick
	G-BNOU	PA-28-161 Warrior II	BAe Flying College/Prestwick
	G-BNOV	PA-28-161 Warrior II	BAe Flying College/Prestwick
	G-BNOW	PA-28-161 Warrior II	BAe Flying College/Prestwick
	G-BNOX	Cessna R.182	Char Wallahs Ltd
	G-BNOY	Colt 90A balloon	Huntair Ltd
	G-BNOZ	Cessna 152 II	Pool Aviation Ltd/Welshpool
	G-BNPD	PA-23 Aztec 250E	County Garage (Cheltenham) Ltd/ Staverton
	G-BNPE	Cameron N-77 balloon	Kent Garden Centres Ltd
	G-BNPF	Slingsby T.31M	S. Luck & ptnrs
	G-BNPH	P.66 Pembroke C.1 (WV740)	M. J. Willing/Jersey
	G-BNPI	Colt 21A balloon	Virgin Airship & Balloon Co Ltd
	G-BNPK	Cameron DP-70 airship	Cameron Balloons Ltd/USA
	G-BNPL	PA-38-112 Tomahawk	World Engines Ltd/Elstree
	G-BNPM	PA-38-112 Tomahawk	Papa Mike Aviation Ltd
	G-BNPN	PA-28-181 Archer II	Sherani Aviation/Elstree
	G-BNPO	PA-28-181 Archer II	Bonus Aviation Ltd
	G-BNPT	PA-38-112 Tomahawk II	Cormack (Aircraft Services) Ltd
	G-BNPV	Bowers Fly-Baby 1B	J. G. Day
	G-BNPY	Cessna 152 II	Traffic Management Services/Gamston

Reg.	Type	Owner or Operator	Notes
G-BNPZ	Cessna 152 II	Bristol Flying Centre Ltd	
G-BNRA	SOCATA TB.10 Tobago	W. R. M. Beesley	
G-BNRE	AB-206A JetRanger	TIndon Ltd/Little Snoring	
G-BNRG	PA-28-161 Warrior II	RAF Brize Norton Flying Club Ltd	
G-BNRH	Beech 95-E55 Baron	Nairn Flying Services Ltd/Inverness	
G-BNRI	Cessna U.206G	Target Technology Ltd	
G-BNRK	Cessna 152 II	Redhill Flying Club	
G-BNRL	Cessna 152 II	J. R. Nicholls/Sibson	
G-BNRP	PA-28-181 Archer II	Atomchoice Ltd/Goodwood	
G-BNRR	Cessna 172P	Skyhawk Group	
G-BNRU	Cameron V-77 balloon	M. A. Mueller	
G-BNRW	Colt 69A balloon	Callers Pegasus Travel Service Ltd	
G-BNRX	PA-34-200T Seneca II	R. A. & K. M. Roberts	
G-BNRY	Cessna 182Q	Reefly Ltd	
G-BNRZ	Robinson R-22B	W. Jordan Millers Ltd	
G-BNSG	PA-28R-201 Arrow III	Armada Aviation Ltd/Redhill	
G-BNSI	Cessna 152 II	Sky Leisure Aviation Ltd/Shoreham	
G-BNSL	PA-38-112 Tomahawk II	M. H. Kleiser	
G-BNSM	Cessna 152 II	Cornwall Flying Club Ltd/Bodmin	
G-BNSN	Cessna 152 II	M. K. Barnes & G. N. Olson/Bristol	
G-BNSO	Slingsby T.67M Mk II	Trent Air Services Ltd/Cranfield	
G-BNSP	Slingsby T.67M Mk II	Trent Air Services Ltd/Cranfield	
G-BNSR	Slingsby T.67M Mk II	Trent Air Services Ltd/Cranfield	
G-BNST	Cessna 172N	Traffic Management Services/Gamston	
G-BNSU	Cessna 152 II	Channel Aviation Ltd	
G-BNSV	Cessna 152 II	Channel Aviation Ltd	
G-BNSW	Cessna 152 II	One Zero One Three Ltd	
G-BNSY	PA-28-161 Warrior II	Carill Aviation Ltd/Southampton	
G-BNSZ	PA-28-161 Warrior II	Carill Aviation Ltd/Southampton	
G-BNTC	PA-28RT-201T Turbo Arrow IV	Hollingworth & Co (Midlands) Ltd	
G-BNTD	PA-28-161 Warrior II	S. S. Copsey/Ipswich	
G-BNTE	FFA AS.202/18A4 Bravo	BAe Flying College Ltd/Prestwick	
G-BNTF	FFA AS.202/18A4 Bravo	BAe Flying College Ltd/Prestwick	
G-BNTH	FFA AS.202/18A4 Bravo	BAe Flying College Ltd/Prestwick	
G-BNTI	FFA AS.202/18A4 Bravo	BAe Flying College Ltd/Prestwick	
G-BNTJ	FFA AS.202/18A4 Bravo	BAe Flying College Ltd/Prestwick	
G-BNTK	FFA AS.202/18A4 Bravo	BAe Flying College Ltd/Prestwick	
G-BNTL	FFA AS.202/18A4 Bravo	BAe Flying College Ltd/Prestwick	
G-BNTM	FFA AS.202/18A4 Bravo	BAe Flying College Ltd/Prestwick	
G-BNTN	FFA AS.202/18A4 Bravo	BAe Flying College Ltd/Prestwick	
G-BNTO	FFA AS.202/18A4 Bravo	BAe Flying College Ltd/Prestwick	
G-BNTP	Cessna 172N	Westnet Ltd	
G-BNTS	PA-28RT-201T Turbo Arrow IV	Nasaire Ltd/Liverpool	
G-BNTT	Beech 76 Duchess	L. & J. Donne	
G-BNTW	Cameron V-77 balloon	P. Goss	
G-BNTX	Short SD3-30 Variant 100	Shorts Aircraft Leasing Ltd (G-BKDN)	
G-BNTY	Short SD3-30 Variant 100	Shorts Aircraft Leasing Ltd (G-BKDO)	
G-BNTZ	Cameron N-77 balloon	Balloon Team	
G-BNUC	Cameron O-77 balloon	T. J. Bucknall	
G-BNUI	Rutan Vari-Eze	T. N. F. Skead	
G-BNUL	Cessna 152 II	M. E. & A. Dry	
G-BNUN	Beech 95-58PA Baron	British Midland Airways Ltd/E. Midlands	
G-BNUO	Beech 76 Duchess	G. A. F. Tilley	
G-BNUR	Cessna 172E	Cardiff Aeronautical Services Ltd	
G-BNUS	Cessna 152 II	Stapleford Flying Club Ltd	
G-BNUT	Cessna 152 Turbo	Stapleford Flying Club Ltd	
G-BNUV	PA-23 Aztec 250F	L. J. Martin	
G-BNUX	Hoffmann H-36 Dimona	K. H. Abel	
G-BNUY	PA-38-112 Tomahawk II	Aerohire Ltd	
G-BNUZ	Robinson R-22B	J. C. Reid	
G-BNVB	AA-5A Cheetah	W. J. Siertsema & A. M. Glazer	
G-BNVD	PA-38-112 Tomahawk	Channel Aviation Ltd	
G-BNVE	PA-28-181 Archer II	Steve Parrish Racing	
G-BNVI	ARV Super 2	Adrianair Ltd	
G-BNVT	PA-28R-201T Turbo Arrow III	Victor Tango Group	
G-BNVZ	Beech 95-B55 Baron	W. J. Forrest & P. Schon	
G-BNWA	Boeing 767-336ER	British Airways *City of Brussels*	
G-BNWB	Boeing 767-336ER	British Airways *City of Paris*	
G-BNWC	Boeing 767-336ER	British Airways *City of Frankfurt*	
G-BNWD	Boeing 767-336ER	British Airways *City of Copenhagen*	
G-BNWE	Boeing 767-336ER	British Airways *City of Lisbon*	
G-BNWF	Boeing 767-336ER	British Airways *City of Milan*	
G-BNWG	Boeing 767-336ER	British Airways *City of Strasbourg*	

Notes	Reg.	Type	Owner or Operator
	G-BNWH	Boeing 767-336ER	British Airways *City of Rome*
	G-BNWI	Boeing 767-336ER	British Airways *City of Madrid*
	G-BNWJ	Boeing 767-336ER	British Airways *City of Athens*
	G-BNWK	Boeing 767-336ER	British Airways *City of Amsterdam*
	G-BNWL	Boeing 767-336ER	British Airways *City of Luxembourg*
	G-BNWM	Boeing 767 336ER	British Airways *City of Toulouse*
	G-BNWN	Boeing 767-336ER	British Airways *William Wordsworth*
	G-BNWO	Boeing 767-336ER	British Airways *William Shakespeare*
	G-BNWP	Boeing 767-336ER	British Airways *City of Dublin*
	G-BNWR	Boeing 767-336ER	British Airways *City of Hamburg*
	G-BNWS	Boeing 767-336ER	British Airways *City of Oporto*
	G-BNWT	Boeing 767-336ER	British Airways *City of Cork*
	G-BNWU	Boeing 767-336ER	British Airways *Robert Burns*
	G-BNWV	Boeing 767-336ER	British Airways *City of Bonn*
	G-BNWW	Boeing 767-336ER	British Airways *City of Marseille*
	G-BNWX	Boeing 767-336ER	British Airways *City of Bilbao*
	G-BNWY	Boeing 767-336ER	British Airways
	G-BNWZ	Boeing 767-336ER	British Airways
	G-BNXA	BN-2A-26 Islander	Atlantic Air Transport Ltd/Coventry
	G-BNXC	Cessna 152 II	Sir W. G. Armstrong-Whitworth Flying Group/Coventry
	G-BNXD	Cessna 172N	A. Jahanfar
	G-BNXE	PA-28-161 Warrior II	Rugby Autobody Repairs/Coventry
	G-BNXI	Robin DR.400/180R	London Gliding Club Ltd/Dunstable
	G-BNXK	Nott-Cameron ULD-3 balloon	J. R. P. Nott
	G-BNXL	Glaser-Dirks DG.400	A. J. Chappell & D. A. Triplett
	G-BNXM	PA-18 Super Cub 95	G-BNXM Group
	G-BNXR	Cameron O-84 balloon	J. A. & N. J. Ballard Gray
	G-BNXT	PA-28-161 Warrior II	Falcon Flying Services/Manston
	G-BNXU	PA-28-161 Warrior II	Friendly Warrior Group
	G-BNXV	PA-38-112 Tomahawk	Falcon Flying Services/Manston
	G-BNXX	SOCATA TB.20 Trinidad	D. M. Carr
	G-BNXZ	Thunder Ax7-77 balloon	Hale Hot Air Balloon Group
	G-BNYB	PA-28-201T Turbo Dakota	Blackpool Air Centre
	G-BNYD	Bell 206B JetRanger 3	Sterling Helicopters Ltd/Norwich
	G-BNYJ	Cessna 421B	Charles Robertson (Developments) Ltd
	G-BNYK	PA-38-112 Tomahawk	APB Leasing Ltd/Welshpool
	G-BNYL	Cessna 152 II	APB Leasing Ltd/Welshpool
	G-BNYM	Cessna 172N	N. B. Lindley
	G-BNYN	Cessna 152 II	Redhill Flying Club
	G-BNYO	Beech 76 Duchess	Skyhawk Ltd
	G-BNYP	PA-28-181 Archer II	R. D. Cooper/Cranfield
	G-BNYS	Boeing 767-204ER	Britannia Airways Ltd/Luton
	G-BNYU	Faithfull Ax7-61A balloon	M. L. Faithfull
	G-BNYV	PA-38-112 Tomahawk	Channel Aviation Ltd/Guernsey
	G-BNYX	Denney Kitfox	R. W. Husband
	G-BNYY	PA-28RT-201T Turbo Arrow IV	Metafin Group Holdings
	G-BNYZ	SNCAN Stampe SV-4E	Tapestry Colour Ltd
	G-BNZB	PA-28-161 Warrior II	Falcon Flying Services/Biggin Hill
	G-BNZC	D.H.C.1 Chipmunk 22 (18671)	D. A. Horsley
	G-BNZG	PA-28RT-201T Turbo Arrow IV	Brightday Ltd
	G-BNZJ	Colt 21A balloon	N. Charbonnier
	G-BNZK	Thunder Ax7-77 balloon	T. D. Marsden
	G-BNZL	Rotorway Scorpion 133	J. R. Wraight
	G-BNZM	Cessna T.210N	A. J. M. Freeman
	G-BNZO	Rotorway Executive	M. G. Wiltshire
	G-BNZR	FRED Srs 2	R. M. Waugh
	G-BNZS	Mooney M.20K	D. G. Millington
	G-BNZV	PA-25 Pawnee 235	Northumbria Soaring Co Ltd
	G-BNZZ	PA-28-161 Warrior II	Zoom Photographic Ltd
	G-BOAA	Concorde 102	British Airways (G-N94AA)
	G-BOAB	Concorde 102	British Airways (G-N94AB)
	G-BOAC	Concorde 102	British Airways (G-N81AC)
	G-BOAD	Concorde 102	British Airways (G-N94AD)
	G-BOAE	Concorde 102	British Airways (G-N94AE)
	G-BOAF	Concorde 102	British Airways (G-N94AF/G-BFKX)
	G-BOAG	Concorde 102	British Airways (G-BFKW)
	G-BOAH	PA-28-161 Warrior II	Plane Talking Ltd/Elstree
	G-BOAI	Cessna 152 II	Galair Ltd/Biggin Hill
	G-BOAK	PA-22 Tri-Pacer 150	A. M. Noble
	G-BOAL	Cameron V-65 balloon	A. M. Lindsay
	G-BOAM	Robinson R-22B	Bristow Helicopters Ltd/Redhill

Reg.	Type	Owner or Operator	Notes
G-BOAO	Thunder Ax7-77 balloon	D. V. Fowler	
G-BOAS	Air Command 503 Commander	R. Robinson	
G-BOAU	Cameron V-77 balloon	G. T. Barstow	
G-BOBA	PA-28R-201 Arrow III	Bobbington Air Training School Ltd	
G-BOBB	Cameron O-120 balloon	J. M. Albury	
G-BOBC	BN-2T Turbine Islander	Pilatus BN Ltd (G-BJYZ)/Bembridge	
G-BOBD	Cameron O-160 balloon	A. C. K. Rawson & J. J. Rudoni	
G-BOBF	Brügger MB.2 Colibri	R. Bennett	
G-BOBG	Jodel 150	C. A. Laycock	
G-BOBH	Airtour AH-77 balloon	J. & K. Francis	
G-BOBJ	PA-38-112 Tomahawk	Air Touring Services Ltd/Biggin Hill	
G-BOBK	PA-38-112 Tomahawk	Air Touring Services Ltd/Biggin Hill	
G-BOBL	PA-38-112 Tomahawk	Salcombe Crane Hire Ltd	
G-BOBN	Cessna 310R	Edinburgh Air Charter Ltd	
G-BOBR	Cameron N-77 balloon	C. Bradley	
G-BOBS	Quickie Q.2	M. A. Hales	
G-BOBT	Stolp SA.300 Starduster Too	G-BOBT Group	
G-BOBU	Colt 90A balloon	Prescott Hot Air Balloons Ltd	
G-BOBV	Cessna F.150M	Sky Pro Ltd	
G-BOBY	Monnet Sonerai II	R. G. Hallam *(stored)*/Sleap	
G-BOBZ	PA-28-181 Archer II	Trustcomms International Ltd	
G-BOCC	PA-38-112 Tomahawk	B. Gradidge & R. A. Sparshatt-Worley	
G-BOCD	Grob G.115	Landlink PLC	
G-BOCF	Colt 77A balloon	Lindstrand Balloons Ltd	
G-BOCG	PA-34-200T Seneca II	Magenta Ltd/Kidlington	
G-BOCH	PA-32 Cherokee Six 300	J. W. Moss	
G-BOCI	Cessna 140A	D. Nieman	
G-BOCK	Sopwith Triplane (replica) (N6290)	Shuttleworth Collection/O. Warden	
G-BOCL	Slingsby T.67C	C.S.E. Aviation Ltd/Kidlington	
G-BOCM	Slingsby T.67C	C.S.E. Aviation Ltd/Kidlington	
G-BOCN	Robinson R-22B	J. Bignall	
G-BOCP	PA-34-220T Seneca III	BAe Flying College Ltd/Prestwick	
G-BOCR	PA-34-220T Seneca III	BAe Flying College Ltd/Prestwick	
G-BOCS	PA-34-220T Seneca III	BAe Flying College Ltd/Prestwick	
G-BOCT	PA-34-220T Seneca III	BAe Flying College Ltd/Prestwick	
G-BOCU	PA-34-220T Seneca III	BAe Flying College Ltd/Prestwick	
G-BOCV	PA-34-220T Seneca III	BAe Flying College Ltd/Prestwick	
G-BOCW	PA-34-220T Seneca III	BAe Flying College Ltd/Prestwick	
G-BOCX	PA-34-220T Seneca III	BAe Flying College Ltd/Prestwick	
G-BOCY	PA-34-220T Seneca III	BAe Flying College Ltd/Prestwick	
G-BODA	PA-28-161 Warrior II	C.S.E. Aviation Ltd/Kidlington	
G-BODB	PA-28-161 Warrior II	C.S.E. Aviation Ltd/Kidlington	
G-BODC	PA-28-161 Warrior II	C.S.E. Aviation Ltd/Kidlington	
G-BODD	PA-28-161 Warrior II	C.S.E. Aviation Ltd/Kidlington	
G-BODE	PA-28-161 Warrior II	C.S.E. Aviation Ltd/Kidlington	
G-BODF	PA-28-161 Warrior II	C.S.E. Aviation Ltd/Kidlington	
G-BODG	Slingsby T.31 Motor Cadet III	H. P. Vox	
G-BODH	Slingsby T.31 Motor Cadet III	H. P. Vox	
G-BODI	Stoddard-Hamilton Glasair III	Jackson Barr Ltd	
G-BODK	Rotorway Scorpion 133	J. Brannigan	
G-BODM	PA-28 Cherokee 180	W. B. Ware	
G-BODO	Cessna 152	A. R. Sarson	
G-BODP	PA-38-112 Tomahawk	D. A. Whitmore	
G-BODR	PA-28-161 Warrior II	Airways Aero Associations Ltd/Booker	
G-BODS	PA-38-112 Tomahawk	Ipswich School of Flying Ltd	
G-BODT	Jodel D.18	L. D. McPhillips	
G-BODU	Scheibe SF.25C	Monica English Memorial Trust	
G-BODX	Beech 76 Duchess	R. J. Dajczak	
G-BODY	Cessna 310R	Atlantic Air Transport Ltd/Coventry	
G-BODZ	Robinson R-22B	Langley Construction Ltd	
G-BOEC	PA-38-112 Tomahawk	R. A. Wakefield	
G-BOEE	PA-28-181 Archer II	T. B. Parmenter	
G-BOEH	Jodel DR.340	Piper Flyers Group	
G-BOEK	Cameron V-77 balloon	A. J. E. Jones	
G-BOEM	Aerotek-Pitts S-2A	Walsh Bros (Tunneling) Ltd	
G-BOEN	Cessna 172M	G-BOEN Group	
G-BOER	PA-28-161 Warrior II	M. & W. Fraser-Urquhart	
G-BOET	PA-28RT-201 Arrow IV	B. C. Chambers (G-IBEC)	
C-DOEW	Robinson R-22B	Bristow Helicopters Ltd/Redhill	
G-BOEX	Robinson R-22B	Bristow Helicopters Ltd/Redhill	
G-BOEY	Robinson R-22B	Bristow Helicopters Ltd/Redhill	
G-BOEZ	Robinson R-22B	Bristow Helicopters Ltd/Redhill	

Notes	Reg.	Type	Owner or Operator
	G-BOFC	Beech 76 Duchess	Magenta Ltd/Kidlington
	G-BOFD	Cessna U.206G	D. M. Penny
	G-BOFE	PA-34-200T Seneca II	P. R. & J. S. Covell/Ipswich
	G-BOFF	Cameron N-77 balloon	Systems-80 Double Glazing Ltd & N. M. Gabriel
	G-BOFL	Cessna 152	GEM Rewinds Ltd/Coventry
	G-BOFM	Cessna 152	GEM Rewinds Ltd/Coventry
	G-BOFO	Ultimate Aircraft 10-200	M. Werdmuller
	G-BOFW	Cessna A.150M	L. A. Mills/Little Gransden
	G-BOFX	Cessna A.150M	TDR Aviation Ltd
	G-BOFY	PA-28 Cherokee 140	Bristol & Wessex Aeroplane Club Ltd
	G-BOFZ	PA-28-161 Warrior II	R. W. Harris
	G-BOGC	Cessna 152	Skyviews & General Ltd/Leeds
	G-BOGG	Cessna 152	The Royal Artillery Aero Club Ltd/ Middle Wallop
	G-BOGI	Robin DR.400/180	A. L. M. Shepherd
	G-BOGK	ARV Super 2	D. R. Trouse
	G-BOGM	PA-28RT-201T Turbo Arrow IV	RJP Aviation
	G-BOGO	PA-32R-301T Saratoga SP	G. W. Dimmer
	G-BOGP	Cameron V-77 balloon	The Wealden Balloon Group
	G-BOGR	Colt 180A balloon	The Balloon Club of Great Britain Ltd
	G-BOGT	Colt 77A balloon	The Hot Air Balloon Co Ltd
	G-BOGV	Air Command 532 Elite	G. M. Hobman
	G-BOGW	Air Command 532 Elite	K. Ashford
	G-BOGY	Cameron V-77 balloon	C. J. Royden
	G-BOHA	PA-28-161 Warrior II	London Flight Centre (Headcorn) Ltd
	G-BOHD	Colt 77A balloon	D. B. Court
	G-BOHF	Thunder Ax8-84 balloon	B. E. Brown
	G-BOHG	Air Command 532 Elite	T. E. McDonald
	G-BOHH	Cessna 172N	Small World Aviation
	G-BOHI	Cessna 152 II	Clacton Aero Club (1988) Ltd
	G-BOHJ	Cessna 152 II	Semloh Aviation Services/Andrewsfield
	G-BOHL	Cameron A-120 balloon	J. M. Holmes
	G-BOHM	PA-28 Cherokee 180	M. J. Anthony & B. Keogh
	G-BOHO	PA-28-161 Warrior II	Egressus Flying Group
	G-BOHR	PA-28-151 Warrior	G. & J. A. Cockleton
	G-BOHS	PA-38-112 Tomahawk	Falcon Flying Services/Biggin Hill
	G-BOHT	PA-38-112 Tomahawk	Falcon Flying Services/Manston
	G-BOHU	PA-38-112 Tomahawk	Scottish Airways Flyers (Prestwick) Ltd
	G-BOHV	Wittman W.8 Tailwind	R. A. Povall
	G-BOHW	Vans RV-4	N. Woodworth
	G-BOHX	PA-44-180 Seminole	Airpart Supply Ltd/Booker
	G-BOIA	Cessna 180K	R. E. Styles & ptnrs
	G-BOIB	Wittman W.10 Tailwind	M. G. E. Hutton
	G-BOIC	PA-28R-201T Turbo Arrow III	M. J. Pearson
	G-BOID	Bellanca 7ECA Citabria	D. Mallinson
	G-BOIG	PA-28-161 Warrior II	D. Vallence-Pell/Jersey
	G-BOIH	Pitts S-1E Special	C. R. A. Scrope
	G-BOII	Cessna 172N	London Flights (Biggin Hill) Ltd
	G-BOIJ	Thunder Ax7-77 balloon	R. A. Hughes
	G-BOIK	Air Command 503 Commander	F. G. Shepherd
	G-BOIL	Cessna 172N	Upperstack Ltd
	G-BOIM	Cessna 150M	C. R. Guggenhein/Bournemouth
	G-BOIN	Bellanca 7ECA Citabria	P. D. Wheatland & J. R. Howard
	G-BOIO	Cessna 152	AV Aviation Ltd
	G-BOIP	Cessna 152	Stapleford Flying Club Ltd
	G-BOIR	Cessna 152	Shropshire Aero Club Ltd/Sleap
	G-BOIS	PA-31 Turbo Navajo	Air Care (South West) Ltd (G-AYNB)
	G-BOIT	SOCATA TB.10 Tobago	Rainsford Ltd
	G-BOIU	SOCATA TB.10 Tobago	R & B Aviation Ltd
	G-BOIV	Cessna 150M	J. B. Green
	G-BOIW	Cessna 152	London Flight Centre (Stansted) Ltd
	G-BOIX	Cessna 172N	JR Flying Ltd
	G-BOIY	Cessna 172N	London Flight Centre (Stansted) Ltd
	G-BOIZ	PA-34-200T Seneca II	Church Green Aviation Ltd
	G-BOJB	Cameron V-77 balloon	K. L. Heron & R. M. Trotter
	G-BOJD	Cameron V-77 balloon	L. H. Ellis
	G-BOJF	Air Command 532 Elite	P. J. Troy-Davies
	G-BOJH	PA-28R Cherokee Arrow 200	P. S. Kirby
	G-BOJI	PA-28RT-201 Arrow IV	Daphnes
	G-BOJK	PA-34-220T Seneca III	Redhill Flying Club (G-BRUF)
	G-BOJL	M.S.885 Super Rallye	J. A. Rees
	G-BOJM	PA-28-181 Archer II	Fernborough Ltd

Reg.	Type	Owner or Operator	Notes
G-BOJO	Colt 120A balloon	J. G. Morwood	
G-BOJR	Cessna 172P	Exeter Flying Club Ltd	
G-BOJS	Cessna 172P	I. S. H. Paul	
G-BOJU	Cameron N-77 balloon	M. A. Scholes	
G-BOJW	PA-28-161 Warrior II	G-BOJW Flying Group	
G-BOJX	PA-28-181 Archer II	Southern Air Ltd/Shoreham	
G-BOJZ	PA-28-161 Warrior II	Southern Air Ltd/Shoreham	
G-BOKA	PA-28-201T Turbo Dakota	CBG Aviation Ltd/Biggin Hill	
G-BOKB	PA-28-161 Warrior II	Southern Air Ltd/Shoreham	
G-BOKE	PA-34-200T Seneca II	Saint Associates Ltd	
G-BOKF	Air Command 532 Elite	D. Beevers	
G-BOKG	Slingsby T.31 Motor Cadet III	A. M. Witt	
G-BOKH	Whittaker MW.7	I. D. Evans	
G-BOKI	Whittaker MW.7	R. K. Willcox	
G-BOKJ	Whittaker MW.7	M. N. Gauntlett	
G-BOKL	PA-28-161 Warrior II	BAe Flying College Ltd/Prestwick	
G-BOKM	PA-28-161 Warrior II	BAe Flying College Ltd/Prestwick	
G-BOKN	PA-28-161 Warrior II	BAe Flying College Ltd/Prestwick	
G-BOKO	PA-28-161 Warrior II	BAe Flying College Ltd/Prestwick	
G-BOKP	PA-28-161 Warrior II	BAe Flying College Ltd/Prestwick	
G-BOKR	PA-28-161 Warrior II	BAe Flying College Ltd/Prestwick	
G-BOKS	PA-28-161 Warrior II	BAe Flying College Ltd/Prestwick	
G-BOKT	PA-28-161 Warrior II	BAe Flying College Ltd/Prestwick	
G-BOKU	PA-28-161 Warrior II	BAe Flying College Ltd/Prestwick	
G-BOKW	Bo 208C Junior	R. A. Farrington (G-BITT)	
G-BOKX	PA-28-161 Warrior II	W. P. J. Jackson	
G-BOKY	Cessna 152 II	London Flight Centre (Stansted) Ltd	
G-BOLB	Taylorcraft BC-12-65	G-BOLB Flying Group	
G-BOLC	Fournier RF-6B-100	W. H. Hendy	
G-BOLD	PA-38-112 Tomahawk	B. R. Pearson & B. F. Fraser-Smith/ Eaglescott	
G-BOLE	PA-38-112 Tomahawk	M. W. Kibble & E. A. Minard	
G-BOLF	PA-38-112 Tomahawk	Teesside Flight Centre Ltd	
G-BOLG	Bellanca 7KCAB Citabria	B. R. Pearson/Eaglescott	
G-BOLI	Cessna 172P	Boli Flying Club	
G-BOLJ	GA-7 Cougar	N. M. Morris	
G-BOLL	Lake LA-4 Skimmer	S. D. Foster	
G-BOLN	Colt 21A balloon	Virgin Airship & Balloon Co Ltd	
G-BOLO	Bell 206B JetRanger	Hargreaves Construction Co Ltd/ Shoreham	
G-BOLP	Colt 21A balloon	Virgin Airship & Balloon Co Ltd	
G-BOLR	Colt 21A balloon	Virgin Airship & Balloon Co Ltd	
G-BOLS	FRED Srs 2	I. F. Vaughan	
G-BOLT	R. Commander 114	R. D. Rooke/Elstree	
G-BOLU	Robin R.3000/120	Classair	
G-BOLV	Cessna 152 II	Falcon Flying Services/Biggin Hill	
G-BOLW	Cessna 152 II	JRB Aviation Ltd/Southend	
G-BOLX	Cessna 172N	D. Hill	
G-BOLY	Cessna 172N	London Flight Centre (Headcorn) Ltd	
G-BOLZ	Rand KR-2	B. Normington	
G-BOMB	Cassutt Racer IIIM	P. P. Chapman/Biggin Hill	
G-BOML	Hispano HA.1112MIL (—)	Classic Aviation Ltd/Duxford	
G-BOMN	Cessna 150F	D. G. Williams	
G-BOMO	PA-38-112 Tomahawk	Naiad Air Services	
G-BOMP	PA-28-181 Archer II	Falcon Flying Services/Manston	
G-BOMS	Cessna 172N	Aerohire Ltd/Halfpenny Green	
G-BOMT	Cessna 172N	Herefordshire Aero Club Ltd/Shobdon	
G-BOMU	PA-28-181 Archer II	RJ Aviation/Blackbushe	
G-BOMY	PA-28-161 Warrior II	Carill Aviation Ltd/Southampton	
G-BOMZ	PA-38-112 Tomahawk	BOMZ Aviation/White Waltham	
G-BONC	PA-28RT-201 Arrow IV	K. A. Hemming	
G-BOND	Sikorsky S-76A	Manchester Helicopter Centre/Barton	
G-BONE	Pilatus P2-06 (U-142)	D. C. R. Writer	
G-BONG	Enstrom F-28A	A. Lloyd-Mears	
G-BONK	Colt 180A balloon	Wye Valley Aviation Ltd	
G-BONO	Cessna 172N	M. Rowe/Sywell	
G-BONP	CFM Streak Shadow	T. J. Palmer	
G-BONR	Cessna 172N	Atlaslocal Ltd/Biggin Hill	
G-BONS	Cessna 172N	BONS Group	
G BONT	Slingsby T.67M Mk II	Slingsby Aviation Ltd/Kirkbymoorside	
G-BONU	Slingsby T.67B	R. L. Brinklow	
G-BONV	Colt 17A balloon	Bryant Group PLC	
G-BONW	Cessna 152 II	Lincoln Aero Club Ltd/Sturgate	

Notes	Reg.	Type	Owner or Operator
	G-BONY	Denney Kitfox	M. J. Walker
	G-BONZ	Beech V35B Bonanza	P. M. Coulten
	G-BOOB	Cameron N-65 balloon	C. V. Legate-Pearce
	G-BOOC	PA-18 Super Cub 150	R. R. & S. A. Marriott
	G-BOOD	Slingsby T.31M Motor Tutor	G. F. M. Garner
	G-BOOE	GA-7 Cougar	G. L. Cailes
	G-BOOF	PA-28-181 Archer II	European Flyers/Blackbushe
	G-BOOG	PA-28RT-201T Turbo Arrow IV	Simair Ltd
	G-BOOH	Jodel D.112	M. J. Hayman
	G-BOOI	Cessna 152	Stapleford Flying Club Ltd
	G-BOOL	Cessna 172N	Hockstar Ltd/Biggin Hill
	G-BOOM	Hunter T.7 (800)	R. V. Aviation Ltd/Bournemouth
	G-BOON	PA-32RT-300 Lance II	G-BOON Ltd/Luton
	G-BOOO	Brügger MB .2 Colibri	D. G. Cole
	G-BOOP	Cameron N-90 balloon	Oxford University Hot Air Balloon Club (G-BOMX)
	G-BOOU	Cameron N-77 balloon	Aqualisa Products Ltd
	G-BOOV	AS.355F-2 Twin Squirrel	Merseyside Police Authority
	G-BOOW	Aerosport Scamp	Walavia
	G-BOOX	Rutan LongEz	I. R. Thomas & I. R. Wilde
	G-BOOZ	Cameron N-77 balloon	J. E. F. Kettlety
	G-BOPA	PA-28-181 Archer II	J. E. Strutt (London) Ltd
	G-BOPB	Boeing 767-204ER	Britannia Airways Ltd *Captain Sir Ross Smith*/Luton
	G-BOPC	PA-28-161 Warrior II	Channel Aviation Ltd
	G-BOPD	Bede BD-4	S. T. Dauncey
	G-BOPG	Cessna 182Q	White Knuckle Airways Ltd/Leeds
	G-BOPH	Cessna TR.182RG	E. A. L. Sturmer
	G-BOPL	PA-28-161 Warrior II	Cambrian Flying Club/Swansea
	G-BOPM	Brooklands OA.7 Optica	FLS Aerospace (Lovaux) Ltd/Bournemouth
	G-BOPN	FLS Aerospace OA.7 Optica	FLS Aerospace (Lovaux) Ltd/Bournemouth
	G-BOPR	FLS Aerospace OA.7 Optica	FLS Aerospace (Lovaux) Ltd/Bournemouth
	G-BOPT	Grob G.115	LAC (Enterprises) Ltd/Barton
	G-BOPU	Grob G.115	LAC (Enterprises) Ltd/Barton
	G-BOPV	PA-34-200T Seneca II	Tewin Aviation
	G-BOPW	Cessna A.152	Northamptonshire School of Flying Ltd/ Sywell
	G-BOPX	Cessna A.152	Aerohire Ltd/Halfpenny Green
	G-BORA	Colt 77A balloon	Cala Homes (Southern) Ltd
	G-BORB	Cameron V-77 balloon	M. H. Wolff
	G-BORC	Colt 180A balloon	Virgin Balloon Flights Ltd
	G-BORD	Thunder Ax7-77 balloon	D. D. Owen
	G-BORE	Colt 77A balloon	Little Secret Hot-Air Balloon Group
	G-BORG	Campbell Cricket	N. G. Bailey
	G-BORH	PA-34-200T Seneca II	Airlong Charter Ltd
	G-BORI	Cessna 152 II	Staryear Ltd
	G-BORJ	Cessna 152 II	APB Leasing Ltd/Welshpool
	G-BORK	PA-28-161 Warrior II	J. A. Hilton/Coventry
	G-BORL	PA-28-161 Warrior II	Westair Flying Services Ltd/Blackpool
	G-BORM	H.S.748 Srs 2B ★	Airport Fire Service/Exeter
	G-BORN	Cameron N-77 balloon	I. Chadwick
	G-BORO	Cessna 152 II	APB Leasing Ltd/Welshpool
	G-BORR	Thunder Ax8-90 balloon	W. J. Harris
	G-BORS	PA-28-181 Archer II	Neric Ltd
	G-BORT	Colt 77A balloon	I. E. A. Joslyn/Germany
	G-BORV	Bell 206B JetRanger 3	P. V. Doman
	G-BORW	Cessna 172P	Briter Aviation Ltd/Coventry
	G-BORY	Cessna 150L	Swansea Aviation Ltd
	G-BOSB	Thunder Ax7-77 balloon	M. Gallagher
	G-BOSD	PA-34-200T Seneca II	Barnes Olson Aeroleasing Ltd
	G-BOSE	PA-28-181 Archer II	G. Fleck
	G-BOSF	Colt 69A balloon	Virgin Airship & Balloon Co Ltd
	G-BOSG	Colt 17A balloon	Virgin Airship & Balloon Co Ltd
	G-BOSJ	Nord 3400 (124)	A. I. Milne
	G-BOSM	Jodel DR.253B	M. A. Hales
	G-BOSO	Cessna A.152	Redhill Flying Club
	G-BOSP	PA-28-151 Warrior	M. E. Williams/Andrewsfield
	G-BOSR	PA-28 Cherokee 140	B. G. Bailey
	G-BOSU	PA-28 Cherokee 140	A. & R. Windley
	G-BOSV	Cameron V-77 balloon	K. H. Greenaway
	G-BOTB	Cessna 152	Stapleford Flying Club Ltd
	G-BOTD	Cameron O-105 balloon	P. J. Beglan
	G-BOTF	PA-28-151 Warrior	G-BOTF Group/Southend

Reg.	Type	Owner or Operator	Notes
G-BOTG	Cessna 152	Donington Aviation Ltd/E. Midlands	
G-BOTH	Cessna 182Q	G-BOTH Group	
G-BOTI	PA-28-151 Warrior	Falcon Flying Services/Biggin Hill	
G-BOTK	Cameron O-105 balloon	F. R. & V. L. Higgins	
G-BOTM	Bell 206B JetRanger 3	David McLean Homes Ltd	
G-BOTN	PA-28-161 Warrior II	W. Lancs Aero Club Ltd/Woodvale	
G-BOTO	Bellanca 7ECA Citabria	G-BOTO Group	
G-BOTP	Cessna 150J	R. E. Thorne	
G-BOTS	Hughes 269C	Cloghran Helicopter Club Ltd	
G-BOTU	Piper J-3C-65 Cub	T. L. Giles	
G-BOTV	PA-32RT-300 Lance II	Robin Lance Aviation Association Ltd	
G-BOTW	Cameron V-77 balloon	D. N. Malcolm	
G-BOTY	Cessna 150J	J. D. Bingham	
G-BOTZ	Bensen B.8MR	C. Jones	
G-BOUD	PA-38-112 Tomahawk	T. K. Gough	
G-BOUE	Cessna 172N	E. Alexander	
G-BOUF	Cessna 172N	Amber Valley Aviation	
G-BOUJ	Cessna 150M	J. B. Mills	
G-BOUK	PA-34-200T Seneca II	P. Sisson	
G-BOUL	PA-34-200T Seneca II	C.S.E. Aviation Ltd/Kidlington	
G-BOUM	PA-34-200T Seneca II	C.S.E. Aviation Ltd/Kidlington	
G-BOUN	Rand KR-2	W. J. Allan	
G-BOUP	PA-28-161 Warrior II	C.S.E. Aviation Ltd/Kidlington	
G-BOUR	PA-28-161 Warrior II	C.S.E. Aviation Ltd/Kidlington	
G-BOUS	PA-28RT-201 Arrow IV	Hamilton Compass Aviation Ltd	
G-BOUT	Colomban MC.12 Cri-Cri	C. K. Farley	
G-BOUV	Bensen B.8R	P. Wilkinson	
G-BOUZ	Cessna 150G	Atlantic Bridge Aviation Ltd/Lydd	
G-BOVB	PA-15 Vagabond	Oscar Flying Group/Shoreham	
G-BOVC	Everett gyroplane	J. W. Highton	
G-BOVH	PA-28-161 Warrior II	R. W. Tebby	
G-BOVK	PA-28-161 Warrior II	Hamilton Compass Aviation Ltd	
G-BOVP	Air Command 532 Elite	C. K. Park	
G-BOVR	Robinson R-22	P. J. Homan	
G-BOVS	Cessna 150M	Simair Ltd	
G-BOVT	Cessna 150M	D. H. Jacobs	
G-BOVU	Stoddard-Hamilton Glasair III	W. N. Blair-Hickman	
G-BOVV	Cameron V-77 balloon	J. P. Clifford	
G-BOVW	Colt 69A balloon	V. Hyland	
G-BOVX	Hughes 269C	Elite Helicopters Ltd	
G-BOVY	Hughes 269C	March Helicopters Ltd/Sywell	
G-BOWB	Cameron V-77 balloon	R. C. Stone	
G-BOWD	Cessna F.337G	Badgehurst Ltd (G-BLSB)	
G-BOWE	PA-34-200T Seneca II	C.S.E. Aviation Ltd/Kidlington	
G-BOWK	Cameron N-90 balloon	S. R. Bridge	
G-BOWL	Cameron V-77 balloon	P. G. & G. R. Hall	
G-BOWM	Cameron V-56 balloon	C. G. Caldecott & G. Pitt	
G-BOWN	PA-12 Super Cruiser	R. W. Bucknell	
G-BOWO	Cessna R.182	D. P. Bennett (G-BOTR)	
G-BOWP	Jodel D.120A	A. R. Gedney & ptnrs/Sibson	
G-BOWU	Cameron O-84 balloon	St Elmos Fire Syndicate	
G-BOWV	Cameron V-65 balloon	C. P. R. & S. J. Baxter	
G-BOWY	PA-28RT-201T Turbo Arrow IV	Overview Europe Ltd	
G-BOWZ	Bensen B.80V	W. M. Day	
G-BOXA	PA-28-161 Warrior II	Jersey Aero Club	
G-BOXB	PA-28-161 Warrior II	Jersey Aero Club	
G-BOXC	PA-28-161 Warrior II	Jersey Aero Club	
G-BOXG	Cameron O-77 balloon	C. M. Love	
G-BOXH	Pitts S-1S Special	D. Medrek	
G-BOXJ	Piper J-3C-65 Cub	J. L. Quick & A. J. P. Jackson/Biggin Hill	
G-BOXK	Slingsby T.67C	Slingsby Aviation Ltd/Kirkbymoorside	
G-BOXN	Robinson R-22B	Conguess Aviation Ltd	
G-BOXR	GA-7 Cougar	Technical Support Aviation Ltd	
G-BOXT	Hughes 269C	Leisure & Retail Consultants Ltd	
G-BOXU	AA-5B Tiger	J. J. Woodhouse	
G-BOXV	Pitts S-1S Special	G. R. Clark	
G-BOXW	Cassutt Racer Srs IIIM	D. I. Johnson	
G-BOXX	Robinson R-22B	J. D. Forbes-Nixon & G. E. Mendham	
G-BOXY	PA-28-181 Archer II	Sheffield Aero Club Ltd/Netherthorpe	
G-BOYB	Cessna A.152	Northamptonshire School of Flying Ltd/ Sywell	
G-BOYC	Robinson R-22B	Northern Helicopters (Leeds) Ltd	
G-BOYF	Sikorsky S-76B	Darley Stud Management Co Ltd	

Notes	Reg.	Type	Owner or Operator
	G-BOYH	PA-28-151 Warrior	Superpause Ltd/Booker
	G-BOYI	PA-28-161 Warrior II	S. J. Harris
	G-BOYL	Cessna 152 II	Aerohire Ltd/Halfpenny Green
	G-BOYM	Cameron O-84 balloon	Frontline Distribution Ltd
	G-BOYO	Cameron V-20 balloon	J. M. Willard
	G-BOYP	Cessna 172N	Guildtons Ltd
	G-BOYR	Cessna F.337G	Air-Tech (GB) Ltd
	G-BOYT	PA-38-112 Tomahawk	APB Leasing Ltd/Welshpool
	G-BOYU	Cessna A.150L	Upperstack Ltd
	G-BOYV	PA-28R-201T Turbo Arrow III	P. R. Goldsworthy
	G-BOYX	Robinson R-22B	R. Towle
	G-BOYY	Cameron A-105 balloon	Hoyers (UK) Ltd
	G-BOYZ	Laser Z.200	M. G. Jefferies
	G-BOZI	PA-28-161 Warrior II	Klingair Ltd/Conington
	G-BOZK	AS.332L Super Puma	British International Helicopters
	G-BOZM	PA-38-112 Tomahawk	S. J. Green
	G-BOZN	Cameron N-77 balloon	Calarel Developments Ltd
	G-BOZO	AA-5B Tiger	Becketts Honda Car Centre Ltd
	G-BOZP	Beech 76 Duchess	Newcastle upon Tyne Aero Club Ltd
	G-BOZR	Cessna 152 II	J. Lloyd
	G-BOZS	Pitts S-1C Special	R. J. & M. B. Trickey
	G-BOZU	Sparrow Hawk Mk II	R. V. Phillimore
	G-BOZV	CEA DR.340 Major	EH Group
	G-BOZW	Bensen B.8M	M. E. Wills
	G-BOZY	Cameron RTW-120 balloon	Oxford Promotions (UK) Ltd
	G-BOZZ	AA-5B Tiger	Solent Tiger Group/Southampton
	G-BPAA	Acro Advanced	Acro Engines & Airframes Ltd
	G-BPAB	Cessna 150M	R. C. W. Wheeler & ptnrs/Earls Colne
	G-BPAC	PA-28-161 Warror II	G. G. Pratt
	G-BPAE	Cameron V-77 balloon	I. J. Jackson
	G-BPAF	PA-28-161 Warrior II	Hendafern Ltd
	G-BPAG	Bellanca 8KCAB Decathlon	M. Stow
	G-BPAH	Colt 69A balloon	International Distillers & Vintners Ltd
	G-BPAI	Bell 47G-3B-1 (modified)	LRC Leisure Ltd
	G-BPAJ	D.H.82A Tiger Moth	P. A. Jackson (G-AOIX)
	G-BPAL	D.H.C.1 Chipmunk 22 (WG350)	M. Gardner (G-BCYE)
	G-BPAO	Air Command 503 Commander	D. J. Sagar
	G-BPAS	SOCATA TB.20 Trinidad	South East Aviation Ltd
	G-BPAU	PA-28-161 Warrior II	Lapwing Flying Group Ltd/Denham
	G-BPAV	FRED Srs 2	P. A. Valentine
	G-BPAW	Cessna 150M	A. Phillips
	G-BPAX	Cessna 150M	Barry Aviation Ltd
	G-BPAY	PA-28-181 Archer II	C. Rees
	G-BPBA	Bensen B.80MR	M. E. Green
	G-BPBB	Evans VP-2	J. S. & J. D. Penny
	G-BPBG	Cessna 152 II	Atlantic Air Transport Ltd/Coventry
	G-BPBI	Cessna 152 II	B. W. Wells & Burbage Farms Ltd
	G-BPBJ	Cessna 152 II	W. Shaw & P. G. Haines
	G-BPBK	Cessna 152 II	Burbage Farms Ltd
	G-BPBM	PA-28-161 Warrior II	Aerohire Ltd/Halfpenny Green
	G-BPBO	PA-28RT-201T Turbo Arrow IV	Music Connections Ltd
	G-BPBP	Brügger MB.2 Colibri	N. R. Osborne
	G-BPBR	PA-38-112 Tomahawk	M. A. Boocock
	G-BPBU	Cameron V-77 balloon	G-BPBU Skymaid Balloon
	G-BPBV	Cameron V-77 balloon	W. E. & L. A. Newman
	G-BPBW	Cameron O-105 balloon	R. J. Mansfield
	G-BPBY	Cameron V-77 balloon	L. Hutley (G-PBCS)
	G-BPBZ	Thunder Ax7-77 balloon	Wye Valley Aviation Ltd
	G-BPCA	BN-2B-26 Islander	Loganair Ltd/Scottish Air Ambulance Service (G-BLNX)
	G-BPCF	Piper J-3C-65 Cub	A. J. Cook
	G-BPCG	Colt AS-80 airship	N. Carbonnier
	G-BPCI	Cessna R.172K	B. E. Simpson
	G-BPCK	PA-28-161 Warrior II	W. G. Booth
	G-BPCL	SA Bulldog Srs 120/128	Isohigh Ltd/Denham
	G-BPCM	Rotorway Executive	Aircare Group
	G-BPCN	Cameron A-160 balloon	Golf Centres Balloons Ltd
	G-BPCR	Mooney M.20K	T. & R. Harris
	G-BPCV	Montgomerie-Bensen B.8MR	J. Fisher
	G-BPCX	PA-28-236 Dakota	Offshore Marine Consultants Ltd
	G-BPCY	PA-34-200T Seneca	Compton Abbas Airfield Ltd

Reg.	Type	Owner or Operator	Notes
G-BPDA	H.S.748 Srs 2A	Emerald Airways Ltd *John J. Goodall* (G-GLAS)/Liverpool	
G-BPDD	Colt 240A balloon	Heather Flight Ltd	
G-BPDE	Colt 56A balloon	J. E. Weidema	
G-BPDF	Cameron V-77 balloon	The Ballooning Business Ltd	
G-BPDG	Cameron V-77 balloon	A. & M. A. Dunning	
G-BPDJ	Christena Mini Coupe	J. J. Morrissey	
G-BPDK	Sorrell SNS-7 Hyperbipe	A. J. Cable/Barton	
G-BPDM	C.A.S.A. 1.131E Jungmann 2000 (781-32)	Spanish Acquisition/Shoreham	
G-BPDN	PA-28R-201 Arrow III	J. Hallett/Biggin Hill	
G-BPDS	PA-28-161 Warrior II	Hendafern Ltd	
G-BPDT	PA-28-161 Warrior II	Hendafern Ltd	
G-BPDU	PA-28-161 Warrior II	Sky Leisure Aviation Ltd	
G-BPDV	Pitts S-1S Special	J. Vize -	
G-BPDY	Westland-Bell 47G-3B1	Howden Helicopters/Spaldington	
G-BPEA	Boeing 757-236	British Airways	
G-BPEB	Boeing 757-236	British Airways	
G-BPEC	Boeing 757-236	British Airways	
G-BPED	Boeing 757-236	British Airways *Blair Castle*	
G-BPEE	Boeing 757-236	British Airways	
G-BPEF	Boeing 757-236	British Airways	
G-BPEI	Boeing 757-236	British Airways (G-BMRK) *Winchester Castle*	
G-BPEJ	Boeing 757-236	British Airways (G-BMRL) *Castell Dinas Bran*	
G-BPEK	Boeing 757-236	British Airways (G-BMRM) *Carew Castle*	
G-BPEL	PA-28-151 Warrior	R. W. Harris & A. J. Jahanfar	
G-BPEM	Cessna 150K	G. P. Robinson & R. G. Lindsey	
G-BPEO	Cessna 152	R. W. Harris & A. J. Jahanfar	
G-BPER	PA-38-112 Tomahawk	APB Leasing Ltd/Welshpool;	
G-BPES	PA-38-112 Tomahawk	Sherwood Flying Club Ltd/Tollerton	
G-BPEW	Robinson R-22B	Dann Antiques Ltd	
G-BPEZ	Colt 77A balloon	A. Stace	
G-BPFA	Knight GK-2 Swallow	G. Knight & D. G. Pridham	
G-BPFB	Colt 77A balloon	S. Ingram	
G-BPFC	Mooney M.20C	D. P. Tinsley	
G-BPFD	Jodel D.112	K. Manley	
G-BPFF	FF Lightning T.5 (XS452)	Ruanil Investments Ltd/Cranfield	
G-BPFF	Cameron DP-70 airship	Cameron Balloons Ltd	
G BPFG	SOCATA TB.20 Trinidad	F. T. Arnold	
G-BPFH	PA-28-161 Warrior II	M. H. Kleiser	
G-BPFI	PA-28-181 Archer II	G-BPFI Group	
G-BPFJ	Cameron 90 Can SS balloon	The Hot-Air Balloon Co Ltd	
G-BPFK	Montgomerie-Bensen B.8MR	J. W. Birkett	
G-BPFL	Davis DA-2	B. W. Griffiths	
G-BPFM	Aeronca 7AC Champion	L. A. Borrill	
G-BPFV	Boeing 767-204ER	Britannia Airways Ltd/*Bobby Moore OBE*	
G-BPFX	Colt 21A balloon	The Hot-Air Balloon Co Ltd	
G-BPFY	Consolidated PBY-6A Catalina	D. Arnold/Biggin Hill	
G-BPFZ	Cessna 152 II	C. J. Ward	
G-BPGA	Mooney M.20J	Medallionair Ltd	
G-BPGB	Cessna 150J	Magnificent Obsessions Ltd	
G-BPGC	Air Command 532 Elite	E. C. E. Brown	
G-BPGD	Cameron V-65 balloon	Gone With The Wind Ltd	
G-BPGE	Cessna U.206C	Scottish Parachute Club/Strathallan	
G-BPGF	Thunder Ax7-77 balloon	M. Schiavo	
G-BPGH	EAA Acro Sport II	G. M. Bradley	
G-BPGK	Aeronca 7AC Champion	T. M. Williams	
G-BPGL	PA-28 Cherokee 180	C. N. Ellerbrook	
G-BPGM	Cessna 152 II	J. Easson/Edinburgh	
G-BPGN	Cameron 90 Tractor SS balloon	Cameron Balloons Ltd	
G-BPGU	PA-28-181 Archer II	G. Underwood	
G-BPGV	Robinson R-22B	Polo Aviation Ltd	
G-BPGX	SOCATA TB.9 Tampico	M. Stock & M. J. Aitkin	
G-BPGY	Cessna 150H	Three Counties Aero Engineering Ltd/ Lasham	
G-BPGZ	Cessna 150G	D. F. & B. L. Sperring	
G-BPHB	PA-28-161 Warrior II	Channel Islands Aero Holdings (Jersey) Ltd	
G-BPHD	Cameron N-42 balloon	P. J. Marshall & M. A. Clarke	
G-BPHE	PA-28-161 Warrior II	Pool Aviation Ltd/Welshpool	
G-BPHG	Robin DR.400/180	K. J. & M. B. White/Redhill	

Notes	Reg.	Type	Owner or Operator
	G-BPHH	Cameron V-77 balloon	C. D. Aindow
	G-BPHI	PA-38-112 Tomahawk	S. A. Boyall
	G-BPHJ	Cameron V-77 balloon	C. W. Brown
	G-BPHK	Whittaker MW.7	R. V. Hogg
	G-BPHL	PA-28-161 Warrior II	Teesside Flight Centre Ltd
	G-BPHM	Beech A36 Bonanza	A. P. Vonk
	G-BPHO	Taylorcraft BC-12D	J. Roberts & J. K. Carr
	G-BPHP	Taylorcraft BC-12-65	D. C. Stephens
	G-BPHR	D.H.82A Tiger Moth (A-17-48)	N. Parry
	G-BPHT	Cessna 152	Bobbington Air Training School Ltd
	G-BPHU	Thunder Ax7-77 balloon	R. P. Waite
	G-BPHW	Cessna 140	J. A. Pothecary/Shoreham
	G-BPHX	Cessna 140	M. McChesney
	G-BPHZ	M.S.505 Criquet (TA+RC)	The Aircraft Restoration Co/Duxford
	G-BPID	PA-28-161 Warrior II	P. M. Ireland
	G-BPIE	Bell 206B JetRanger	Frey Aviation Ltd
	G-BPIF	Bensen-Parsons 2 seat	A. P. Barden
	G-BPIH	Rand KR-2	J. R. Rowley
	G-BPII	Denney Kitfox	J. K. Cross
	G-BPIJ	Brantly B.2B	R. B. Payne
	G-BPIK	PA-38-112 Tomahawk	Cormack (Aircraft Services) Ltd
	G-BPIL	Cessna 310B	A. L. Brown & R. A. Parsons
	G-BPIM	Cameron N‹-77 balloon	Thermalite Ltd
	G-BPIN	Glaser-Dirks DG.400	M. P. Seth-Smith & J. N. Stevenson
	G-BPIO	Cessna F.152 II	S. Harcourt
	G-BPIP	Slingsby T.31 Motor Cadet III	J. H. Beard
	G-BPIR	Scheibe SF.25E Super Falke	Coventry Gliding Club Ltd
	G-BPIU	PA-28-161 Warrior II	I. R. Jones & P. C. Rowlands
	G-BPIV	B.149 Bolingbroke Mk IVT (Z5722)	The Aircraft Restoration Co/Duxford
	G-BPIY	Cessna 152 II	Rentair Ltd
	G-BPIZ	AA-5B Tiger	D. A. Horsley
	G-BPJA	Beech 95-58 Baron	Prescott Investments Ltd
	G-BPJB	Schweizer 269C	Elborne Holdings Ltd
	G-BPJD	SOCATA Rallye 110ST	C. G. Wheeler
	G-BPJE	Cameron A-105 balloon	J. S. Eckersley
	G-BPJF	PA-38-112 Tomahawk	Air Yorkshire Ltd
	G-BPJG	PA-18 Super Cub 150	M. W. Stein
	G-BPJH	PA-18 Super Cub 95	P. J. Heron
	G-BPJL	Cessna 152 II	London Flight Centre (Headcorn) Ltd
	G-BPJN	Jodel D.18	W. J. Evans
	G-BPJO	PA-28-161 Cadet	C.S.E. Aviation Ltd/Kidlington
	G-BPJP	PA-28-161 Cadet	C.S.E. Aviation Ltd/Kidlington
	G-BPJR	PA-28-161 Cadet	C.S.E. Aviation Ltd/Kidlington
	G-BPJS	PA-28-161 Cadet	C.S.E. Aviation Ltd/Kidlington
	G-BPJU	PA-28-161 Cadet	C.S.E. Aviation Ltd/Kidlington
	G-BPJV	Taylorcraft F-21	TC Flying Group
	G-BPJW	Cessna A.150K	G. & S. A. Jones
	G-BPJZ	Cameron O-160 balloon	M. L. Gabb
	G-BPKF	Grob G.115	Soaring (Oxford) Ltd
	G-BPKI	EAA Acro Sport 1	I. C. Underwood
	G-BPKK	Denney Kitfox	R. J. Baron
	G-BPKL	Mooney M.20J	London Link Flying Ltd
	G-BPKM	PA-28-161 Warrior II	M. J. Greasby
	G-BPKO	Cessna 140	I. R. March
	G-BPKR	PA-28-151 Warrior	R. R. Harris
	G-BPLE	Cameron A-160 balloon	A. Derbyshire
	G-BPLF	Cameron V-77 balloon	C. L. Luffingham
	G-BPLG	Morane-Saulnier M.S.317	R. A. Anderson
	G-BPLH	Jodel DR.1051	M. N. King
	G-BPLI	Colt 77A balloon	Yanin International Ltd
	G-BPLM	AIA Stampe SV-4C	C. J. Jesson/Redhill
	G-BPLV	Cameron V-77 balloon	Jessops (Tailors) Ltd
	G-BPLY	Pitts S-2B Special	M. Mountstephen
	G-BPLZ	Hughes 369HS	S. G. Good
	G-BPMB	Maule M5-235C Lunar Rocket	R. A. Fleming
	G-BPMC	Air Command 503 Commander	M. A. Cheshire
	G-BPME	Cessna 152 II	London Flight Centre (Headcorn) Ltd
	G-BPMF	PA-28-151 Warrior	L. & A. Hill
	G-BPMH	Schempp-Hirth Nimbus 3DM	Southern Sailplanes/Lasham
	G-BPML	Cessna 172M	J. Birnie/Sandown
	G-BPMM	Champion 7ECA Citabria	R. G. Trute
	G-BPMO	Cessna 150M	S. L. Mills

Reg.	Type	Owner or Operator	Notes
G-BPMP	Douglas C-47A-50-DL (224211)	Air Atlantique Ltd/Coventry	
G-BPMR	PA-28-161 Warrior II	B. McIntyre	
G-BPMU	Nord 3202B	D. Fenwick (G-BIZJ)	
G-BPMV	PA-28-161 Warrior II	J. W. E. P. Donald	
G-BPMW	QAC Quickie Q.2	C. W. Tattersall (G-OICI/G-OGKN)	
G-BPMX	ARV Super 2	C. R. James	
G-BPNA	Cessna 150L	C. M. Vlieland-Boddy/Compton Abbas	
G-BPNC	Rotorway Executive	S. J. Hanson	
G-BPND	Boeing 727-2D3	Sabre Airways Ltd/Gatwick	
G-BPNF	Robinson R-22B	R. J. Chilton	
G-BPNG	Bell 206B JetRanger 3	Helisport Ltd (G-ORTC)/Biggin Hill	
G-BPNI	Robinson R-22B	S. T. Rabi	
G-BPNL	QAC Quickie Q.2	J. Catley	
G-BPNN	Montgomerie-Bensen B.8MR	M. E. Vahdat	
G-BPNO	Zlin Z.326 Trener Master	J. A. S. Bailey & S. T. Logan	
G-BPNT	BAe 146-300	Palmair Flightline/Bournemouth	
G-BPNU	Thunder Ax7-77 balloon	J. Fenton	
G-BPOA	Gloster Meteor T.7 (WF877)	Aces High Ltd/North Weald	
G-BPOB	Sopwith Camel F.1 (replica) (B2458)	Bianchi Aviation Film Services Ltd/ Booker	
G-BPOD	Stolp SA.300 Starduster Too	P. Howard & R. Boswell	
G-BPOE	Colt 77A balloon	Albatross Aviation Ltd	
G-BPOL	Pietenpol Air Camper	G. W. Postance	
G-BPOM	PA-28-161 Warrior II	Light Aircraft Leasing Ltd	
G-BPON	PA-34-200T Seneca II	London Flight Centre Air Charter Ltd	
G-BPOO	Montgomerie-Bensen B.8MR	M. E. Vahdat	
G-BPOR	Bell 206B JetRanger 3	Helicopter Training & Hire Ltd	
G-BPOS	Cessna 150M	G. Loxton	
G-BPOT	PA-28-181 Archer II	P. Fraser	
G-BPOU	Luscombe 8A Silvaire	M. J. Negus & R. Hardley	
G-BPOV	Cameron 90 Magazine SS balloon	Forbes Europe Inc/France	
G-BPOX	Enstrom 280C Shark	W. B. Steele	
G-BPOZ	Enstrom F-28A	Astral Communications Ltd	
G-BPPA	Cameron O-65 balloon	Rix Petroleum Ltd	
G-BPPD	PA-38-112 Tomahawk	AT Aviation Ltd/Cardiff	
G-BPPE	PA-38-112 Tomahawk	Norwich School of Flying	
G-BPPF	PA-38-112 Tomahawk	R. D. Preston/Wellesbourne	
G-BPPG	PA-38-112 Tomahawk	AT Aviation Ltd/Cardiff	
G-BPPI	Colt 180A balloon	A. G. E. Faulkner	
G-BPPJ	Cameron A-180 Balloon	H. R. Evans	
G-BPPK	PA-28-151 Warrior	Balgold Ltd	
G-BPPL	Enstrom F-28A	M. & P. Food Products Ltd	
G-BPPM	Beech B200 Super King Air	Gama Aviation Ltd/Fairoaks	
G-BPPN	Cessna F.182Q	GT Aviation/Bournemouth	
G-BPPO	Luscombe 8A Silvaire	I. K. Ratcliffe	
G-BPPP	Cameron V-77 balloon	Sarnia Balloon Group	
G-BPPR	Air Command 532 Elite	T. D. Inch	
G-BPPS	Mudry CAARP CAP.21	J. M. & E. M. Wicks/Earls Colne	
G-BPPU	Air Command 532 Elite	J. Hough	
G-BPPW	Schweizer 269C	Arena Aviation Ltd	
G-BPPY	Hughes 269B	N. J. Edmonds	
G-BPPZ	Taylorcraft BC-12D	Zulu Warriors Flying Group	
G-BPRA	Aeronca 11AC Chief	R. M. C. Hunter	
G-BPRC	Cameron Elephant SS balloon	Cameron Balloons Ltd	
G-BPRD	Pitts S-1C Special	S. M. Trickey	
G-BPRJ	AS.355F-1 Twin Squirrel	G. Greenall	
G-BPRL	AS.355F-1 Twin Squirrel	Yorkshire Helicopters/Leeds	
G-BPRM	Cessna F.172L	A. J. Moseley (G-AZKG)	
G-BPRN	PA-28-161 Warrior II	Air Navigation & Trading Co Ltd/Blackpool	
G-BPRO	Cessna A.150K	Armphase Ltd	
G-BPRP	Cessna 150E	L. J. Cook & K. South	
G-BPRR	Rand KR-2	M. W. Albery	
G-BPRS	Air Command 532 Elite	B. K. Snoxall	
G-BPRT	Piel CP.328	N. Reddish	
G-BPRV	PA-28-161 Warrior II	AT Aircraft Leasing Ltd/Cardiff	
G-BPRX	Aeronca 11AC Chief	R. D. Ward & J. M. Taylor	
G-BPRY	PA-28-161 Warrior II	White Wings Aviation	
G-BPSA	Luscombe 8A Silvaire	K. P. Gorman/Staverton	
G-BPSB	Air Command 532 Elite	D. K. Duckworth	
G-BPSE	NA AT-6D Harvard (483009)	Aces High Ltd/North Weald	
G-BPSH	Cameron V-77 balloon	P. G. Hossack	
G-BPSI	Thunder Ax10-160 balloon	Airborne Adventures Ltd	
G-BPSJ	Thunder Ax6-56 balloon	Capricorn Balloons Ltd	

Notes	Reg.	Type	Owner or Operator
	G-BPSK	Montgomerie-Bensen B.8M	R. J. Mann
	G-BPSL	Cessna 177	I. P. Burnett & ptnrs/White Waltham
	G-BPSO	Cameron N-90 balloon	J. Oberprieler
	G-BPSP	Cameron 90 Ship SS balloon	Forbes Europe Inc/France
	G-BPSR	Cameron V-77 balloon	K. J. A. Maxwell
	G-BPSS	Cameron A-120 balloon	Anglian Countryside Balloons
	G-BPSZ	Cameron N-180 balloon	A. Bolger
	G-BPTA	Stinson 108-2	P. S. Dudderidge
	G-BPTB	Boeing Stearman A.75N1 (442)	Aero Vintage Ltd
	G-BPTC	Taylorcraft BC-12D	R. A. Horsman
	G-BPTD	Cameron V-77 balloon	J. Lippett
	G-BPTE	PA-28-181 Archer II	London Flight Centre (Stansted) Ltd
	G-BPTF	Cessna 152	London Flight Centre (Stansted) Ltd
	G-BPTG	R. Commander 112TC	M. A. Watteau
	G-BPTH	Air Command 532 Elite	R. Wheeler
	G-BPTI	SOCATA TB.20 Trinidad	Lyndon Scaffolding Hire Ltd/Birmingham
	G-BPTL	Cessna 172N	Cleveland Flying School Ltd/Teesside
	G-BPTM	Pitts S-1T Special	RPM Aviation Ltd
	G-BPTO	Zenith CH.200-AA	B. Philips
	G-BPTP	Robinson R-22	Sarahs Lakeland Fudge
	G-BPTS	C.A.S.A. 1.131E Jungmann 2000 (E3B-153)	Aerobatic Displays Ltd/Booker
	G-BPTT	Robin DR.400/120	The Cotswold Aero Club Ltd/Staverton
	G-BPTU	Cessna 152	A. M. Alam
	G-BPTV	Bensen B.8	L. Chiappi
	G-BPTX	Cameron O-120 balloon	Skybus Ballooning
	G-BPTZ	Robinson R-22B	J. Lucketti
	G-BPUA	EAA Sport Biplane	V. Millard
	G-BPUB	Cameron V-31 balloon	M. T. Evans
	G-BPUC	QAC Quickie Q.200	S. R. Harvey
	G-BPUD	Ryan PT-22 (I-492)	R. I. Warman
	G-BPUE	Air Command 532 Elite	R. A. Fazackerley
	G-BPUF	Thunder Ax6-56Z balloon	R. C. & M. A. Trimble (G-BHRL)
	G-BPUG	Air Command 532 Elite	T. A. Holmes
	G-BPUH	Cameron A-180 balloon	Golf Centres Balloons Ltd
	G-BPUI	Air Command 532 Elite	M. A. Turner
	G-BPUJ	Cameron N-90 balloon	D. Grimshaw
	G-BPUL	PA-18 Super Cub 150	Crissair Ltd
	G-BPUM	Cessna R.182RG	R. H. Stradling
	G-BPUP	Whittaker MW-7	J. H. Beard
	G-BPUR	Piper J-3L-65 Cub	J3 Group
	G-BPUS	Rans S.9	T. A. Wright
	G-BPUU	Cessna 140	A. R. Lansdown/Swansea
	G-BPUW	Colt 90A balloon	Huntair Ltd
	G-BPUX	Cessna 150J	H. H. Goodman
	G-BPUY	Cessna 150K	M. Hewison/Luton
	G-BPVA	Cessna 172F	S. Lancashire Flyers Ltd
	G-BPVC	Cameron V-77 balloon	A. R. Noble
	G-BPVE	Bleriot IX (replica) (1197)	Bianchi Aviation Film Services Ltd/Booker
	G-BPVH	Cub Aircraft J-3C-65 Prospector	D. E. Cooper-Maguire
	G-BPVI	PA-32R-301 Saratoga SP	Market Penetration Services International Co Ltd
	G-BPVJ	Cessna 152 II	D. C. & V. R. Fieldhouse
	G-BPVK	Varga 2150A Kachina	H. W. Hall
	G-BPVM	Cameron V-77 balloon	Royal Engineers Balloon Club
	G-BPVN	PA-32R-301T Turbo Saratoga SP	Michael J. Sparshatt-Worley (Holdings) Ltd
	G-BPVO	Cassutt Racer IIIM	R. J. Adams & G. Loxton
	G-BPVU	Thunder Ax7-77 balloon	J. C. K. Robinson
	G-BPVW	C.A.S.A. 1.131E Jungmann 2000	S. A. W. Becker/Goodwood
	G-BPVX	Cassutt Racer IIIM	J. H. Tetley
	G-BPVY	Cessna 172D	R. P. Crosier
	G-BPVZ	Luscombe 8E Silvaire	W. E. Gillham & P. Ryman
	G-BPWA	PA-28-161 Warrior II	Leisure Park Management Ltd
	G-BPWC	Cameron V-77 balloon	H. B. Roberts
	G-BPWD	Cessna 120	Peregrine Flying Group
	G-BPWE	PA-28-161 Warrior II	AT Aircraft Leasing Ltd/Cardiff
	G-BPWF	PA-28 Cherokee 140 ★	(static display)/1244 Sqdn ATC/Swindon
	G-BPWG	Cessna 150M	W. R. Spicer
	G-BPWI	Bell 206B JetRanger 3	Palmer Promosport
	G-BPWK	Sportavia Fournier RF-5B	S. L. Reed
	G-BPWM	Cessna 150L	A. C. Williamson/Ipswich
	G-BPWN	Cessna 150L	City Air Charter (London) Ltd/Cranfield
	G-BPWP	Rutan LongEz	J. F. O'Hara & A. J. Voyle

Reg.	Type	Owner or Operator	Notes
G-BPWR	Cessna R.172K	A. M. Skelton	
G-BPWS	Cessna 172P	Plane Talking Ltd/Elstree	
G-BPWT	Cameron DG-19 airship	Airspace Outdoor Advertising Ltd	
G-BPWV	Colt 56A balloon	W. D. Young	
G-BPWW	Piaggio FWP.149D	G-BPWW Group	
G-BPWY	Isaacs Fury II	R. J. Knights	
G-BPWZ	PA-28-161 Warrior II	Hamilton Compass Aviation Ltd	
G-BPXA	PA-28-181 Archer II	Cherokee Flying Group/Netherthorpe	
G-BPXB	Glaser-Dirks DG.400	G. S. Griffiths	
G-BPXE	Enstrom 280C Shark	A. Healy/White Waltham	
G-BPXF	Cameron V-65 balloon	D. Pascall	
G-BPXG	Colt 42A balloon	Cooper Group Ltd	
G-BPXH	Colt 17A balloon	Sport Promotion SRL	
G-BPXJ	PA-28RT-201T Turbo Arrow IV	K. M. Hollamby/Biggin Hill	
G-BPXX	PA-34-200T Seneca II	Hockstar Ltd	
G-BPXY	Aeronca 11AC Chief	S. Hawksworth	
G-BPXZ	Cameron V-77 balloon	British School of Ballooning	
G-BPYC	Cessna 310R	Air Service Training Ltd/Perth	
G-BPYI	Cameron O-77 balloon	Fly by Night Balloon Group	
G-BPYJ	Wittman W.8 Tailwind	J. Dixon	
G-BPYK	Thunder Ax7-77 balloon	A. R. Swinnerton	
G-BPYN	Piper J-3C-65 Cub	The Aquila Group/White Waltham	
G-BPYO	PA-28-181 Archer II	Sherburn Aero Club Ltd	
G-BPYR	PA-31-310 Turbo Navajo	Multi Ltd (G-ECMA)	
G-BPYS	Cameron O-77 balloon	D. J. Goldsmith	
G-BPYT	Cameron V-77 balloon	C. M. Hodges	
G-BPYV	Cameron V-77 balloon	M. E. Weston	
G-BPYW	Air Command 532 Elite	W. V. Tatters	
G-BPYY	Cameron A-180 balloon	G. D. Fitzpatrick	
G-BPYZ	Thunder Ax7-77 balloon	J. E. Astall	
G-BPZA	Luscombe 8A Silvaire	T. P. W. Hyde	
G-BPZB	Cessna 120	C. & M. A. Grime	
G-BPZC	Luscombe 8A Silvaire	C. C. & J. M. Lovell	
G-BPZD	SNCAN NC.858S	G. Richards	
G-BPZE	Luscombe 8E Silvaire	WFG Luscombe Associates	
G-BPZßI	Christen Eagle II	S. D. Quigley	
G-BPZK	Cameron O-120 balloon	D. L. Smith	
G-BPZM	PA-28RT-201 Arrow IV	J. H. Kimber (G-ROYW/G-CRTI)	
G-BPZO	Cameron N-90 balloon	Seaward PLC	
G-BPZP	Robin DR.400/180R	Lasham Gliding Soc. Ltd	
G-BPZS	Colt 105A balloon	L. V. Mastis	
G-BPZU	Scheibe SF.25C Falke	G-BPZU Group	
G-BPZX	Cessna 152 II	Woodward & Co (Sheffield) Ltd	
G-BPZY	Pitts S-1C Special	J. S. Mitchell	
G-BPZZ	Thunder Ax8-105 balloon	Capricorn Balloons Ltd	
G-BRAA	Pitts S-1C Special	C. Davidson	
G-BRAE	Colt 69A balloon	Jentime Ltd	
G-BRAJ	Cameron V-77 balloon	H. R. Evans	
G-BRAK	Cessna 172N	C. Docketty	
G-BRAM	Mikoyan MiG-21PF (503)	Universal Aviation Group/North Weald	
G-BRAP	Thermal Aircraft 104	Thermal Aircraft	
G-BRAR	Aeronca 7AC Champion	C. D. Ward	
G-BRAV	PA-23 Aztec 250E	Planstable Enterprises Ltd (G-BBCM)	
G-BRAW	Pitts S-1 Special	P. G. Bond & P. B. Hunter	
G-BRAX	Payne Knight Twister 85B	R. Earl	
G-BRBA	PA-28-161 Warrior II	Jade Air Engineering Ltd/Shoreham	
G-BRBB	PA-28-161 Warrior II	D. P. Hughes	
G-BRBC	NA T-6G Texan	A. P. Murphy	
G-BRBD	PA-28-151 Warrior	B. E. Simpson & C. R. Hughes	
G-BRBE	PA-28-161 Warrior II	Solo Services Ltd/Shoreham	
G-BRBF	Cessna 152 II	Cumbria Aero Club/Carlisle	
G-BRBG	PA-28 Cherokee 180	Anderson MacArthur & Co	
G-BRBH	Cessna 150H	Professional Flight Management Ltd & S. J. Reeves	
G-BRBI	Cessna 172N	G-BRBI Flying Group	
G-BRBJ	Cessna 172M	I. R. March	
G-BRBK	Robin DR.400/180	R. Kemp	
G-BRBL	Robin DR.400/180	Crown Export Services	
G-BRBM	Robin DR.400/180	R. W. Davies/Headcorn	
G-BRBN	Pitts S-1S Special	D. R. Evans	
G-BRBO	Cameron V-77 balloon	N. W. B. Bews & M. B. Murby	
G-BRBP	Cessna 152	Staverton Flying Services Ltd	

Notes	Reg.	Type	Owner or Operator
	G-BRBS	Bensen B.8M	J. Simpson
	G-BRBT	Trotter Ax3-20 balloon	R. M. Trotter
	G-BRBU	Colt 17A balloon	Virgin Airship & Balloon Co Ltd
	G-BRBV	Piper J-4A Cub Coupé	M. Yeo & J. Schonburg
	G-BRBW	PA-28 Cherokee 140	Cherokee Cruiser Aircraft Group
	G-BRRX	PA-28-181 Archer II	M. J. Ireland
	G-BRBY	Robinson R-22B	BLS Aviation Ltd
	G-BRCA	Jodel D.112	G. R. Hill & R. C. Jordan
	G-BRCC	Cessna 152 II	Falcon Flying Services/Biggin Hill
	G-BRCD	Cessna A.152	D. E. Simmons/Shoreham
	G-BRCE	Pitts S-1C Special	R. O. Rogers
	G-BRCF	Montgomerie-Bensen B.8MR	J. S. Walton
	G-BRCG	Grob G.109	Oxfordshire Sportflying Ltd/Enstone
	G-BRCI	Pitts S-1C Special	G. L. Carpenter
	G-BRCJ	Cameron NS-20 balloon	Cameron Balloons Ltd
	G-BRCM	Cessna 172L	S. G. E. Plessis & D. C. C. Handley
	G-BRCO	Cameron NS-20 balloon	M. Davies
	G-BRCR	Cameron V-77 balloon	E. E. Clark
	G-BRCT	Denney Kitfox	Wessex Aviation & Transport Ltd
	G-BRCV	Aeronca 7AC Champion	J. M. Gale
	G-BRCW	Aeronca 11AC Chief	R. B. McComish
	G-BRDB	Zenair CH.701 STOL	D. L. Bowtell
	G-BRDC	Thunder Ax7-77 balloon	N. J. Morley & D. M. Levene
	G-BRDD	Avions Mudry CAP.10B	R. D. Dickson/Gamston
	G-BRDE	Thunder Ax7-77 balloon	C. C. Brash
	G-BRDF	PA-28-161 Warrior II	White Waltham Airfield Ltd
	G-BRDG	PA-28-161 Warrior II	White Waltham Airfield Ltd
	G-BRDJ	Luscombe 8A Silvaire	C. C. & J. M. Lovell
	G-BRDL	Bell 206B JetRanger 3	Clyde Helicopters Ltd
	G-BRDM	PA-28-161 Warrior II	White Waltham Airfield Ltd
	G-BRDN	M.S.880B Rallye Club	B. J. D. Peatfield
	G-BRDO	Cessna 177B	Cardinal Group
	G-BRDP	Colt Jumbo SS balloon	Virgin Airship & Balloon Co Ltd
	G-BRDT	Cameron DP-70 airship	M. M. Cobbold
	G-BRDU	Cameron DG-14 airship	Cameron Balloons Ltd
	G-BRDV	Viking Wood Products Spitfire Prototype replica (K5054)	C. Du Cros
	G-BRDW	PA-24 Comanche 180	I. P. Gibson/Switzerland
	G-BREA	Bensen B.8MR	R. Firth
	G-BREB	Piper J-3C-65 Cub	L. J. A. Cordes/Sywell
	G-BREE	Whittaker MW.7	G. Hawkins
	G-BREH	Cameron V-65 balloon	S. E. & V. D. Hurst
	G-BREK	Piper J-3C-65 Cub	C. L. H. Parr & I. Watts
	G-BREL	Cameron O-77 balloon	A. J. Moore & D. J. Green
	G-BREM	Air Command 532 Elite	T. W. Freeman
	G-BREP	PA-28RT-201 Arrow IV	P. G. McQuaid
	G-BRER	Aeronca 7AC Champion	B. & S. Medley
	G-BREU	Montgomerie-Bensen B.8	M. A. Hayward
	G-BREX	Cameron O-84 balloon	Ovolo Ltd
	G-BREY	Taylorcraft BC-12D	BREY Group
	G-BRFA	PA-31-350 Navajo Chieftain	Comed Aviation Ltd (G-BREW)
	G-BRFB	Rutan LongEz	R. A. Gardiner
	G-BRFC	P.57 Sea Prince T.1 (WP321)	Aces High Ltd/North Weald
	G-BRFE	Cameron V-77 balloon	N. J. Appleton
	G-BRFF	Colt 90A balloon	Amber Valley Aviation
	G-BRFH	Colt 90A balloon	Polydron UK Ltd
	G-BRFI	Aeronca 7DC Champion	I. J. Boyd & D. J. McCooke
	G-BRFJ	Aeronca 11AC Chief	C. M. G. Ellis
	G-BRFL	PA-38-112 Tomahawk	Teesside Flight Centre Ltd
	G-BRFM	PA-28-161 Warrior II	G. C. J. Moffatt & Co Ltd
	G-BRFN	PA-38-112 Tomahawk	Technology & Marketing Ltd
	G-BRFO	Cameron V-77 balloon	Hedge Hoppers Balloon Group
	G-BRFP	Schweizer 269C	Daedalus Aviation Ltd
	G-BRFR	Cameron N-105 balloon	Flying Pictures (Balloons) Ltd
	G-BRFS	Cameron N-90 balloon	Flying Pictures (Balloons) Ltdê
	G-BRFW	Montgomerie-Bensen B.8 Two Seat	J. M. Montgomerie
	G-BRFX	Pazmany PL.4A	D. E. Hills
	G-BRGD	Cameron O-84 balloon	J. R. H. & M. A. Ashworth
	G-BRGE	Cameron N-90 balloon	Oakfield Farm Products Ltd
	G-BRGF	Luscombe 8E Silvaire	M. H. Wood
	G-BRGG	Luscombe 8A Silvaire	M. P. & V. H. Weatherby
	G-BRGI	PA-28 Cherokee 180	Golf India Aviation Ltd

Reg.	Type	Owner or Operator	Notes
G-BRGN	BAe Jetstream 3102	Jetstream Aircraft Ltd (G-BLHC)/Prestwick	
G-BRGO	Air Command 532 Elite	D. A. Wood	
G-BRGT	PA-32 Cherokee Six 260	M. J. Smith & P. Cowley	
G-BRGW	GY-201 Minicab	R. G. White	
G-BRGX	Rotorway Executive	D. W. J. Lee	
G-BRHA	PA-32RT-300 Lance II	Lance G-BRHA Group	
G-BRHB	Boeing Stearman B.75N1	D. Calabritto	
G-BRHC	Cameron V-77 balloon	Golf Centres Balloons Ltd	
G-BRHG	Colt 90A balloon	Bath University Students Union	
G-BRHJ	PA-34-200T Seneca II	Draycott Seneca Group	
G-BRHL	Montgomerie-Bensen B.8M	A. McCredie	
G-BRHM	Bensen B.8M	H. P. Latham	
G-BRHN	Robinson R-22B	Barhale Surveying Ltd	
G-BRHO	PA-34-200 Seneca	D. A. Lewis/Luton	
G-BRHP	Aeronca O-58B Grasshopper (31923)	J. G. Townsend	
G-BRHR	PA-38-112 Tomahawk	Hamilton Compass Aviation Ltd	
G-BRHS	PA-38-112 Tomahawk	Hamilton Compass Aviation Ltd	
G-BRHT	PA-38-112 Tomahawk	Hamilton Compass Aviation Ltd	
G-BRHU	Montgomerie-Bensen B.8MR	G. L. & S. R. Moon	
G-BRHW	D.H.82A Tiger Moth	P. J. & A. J. Borsberry	
G-BRHX	Luscombe 8E Silvaire	J. Lakin	
G-BRHY	Luscombe 8E Silvaire	D. Lofts & A. R. W. Taylor/Sleap	
G-BRHZ	Stephens Akro Astro 235	N. M. Bloom & ptnrs	
G-BRIA	Cessna 310L	R. C. Pugsley	
G-BRIB	Cameron N-77 balloon	D. Stitt	
G-BRIE	Cameron N-77 balloon	Vokins Estates Ltd	
G-BRIF	Boeing 767-204ER	Britannia Airways Ltd *Horatio Nelson*	
G-BRIG	Boeing 767-204ER	Britannia Airways Ltd *Eglantyne Jebb*	
G-BRIH	Taylorcraft BC-12D	G. J. Taylor	
G-BRII	Zenair CH.600 Zodiac	A. C. Bowdrey	
G-BRIJ	Taylorcraft F-19	M. Beamand & K. E. Ballington	
G-BRIK	T.66 Nipper 3	C. W. R. Piper	
G-BRIL	Piper J-5A Cub Cruiser	P. L. Jobes	
G-BRIM	Cameron O-160 balloon	Golf Centres Balloons Ltd	
G-BRIN	SOCATA TB.20 Trinidad	Halfpenny Green Flight Centre Ltd	
G BRIO	Turner Super T-40A	D. McIntyre	
G-BRIR	Cameron V-56 balloon	I I. G. Davies & C. Dowd	
G-BRIS	Steen Skybolt	P. D. Harrison	
G-BRIV	SOCATA TB.9 Tampico Club	M. Stock & M. J. Aitkin	
G-BRIY	Taylorcraft DF-65 (42-58678)	J. A. Rollason/North Weald	
G-BRIZ	D.31 Turbulent	M. C. Hunt	
G-BRJA	Luscombe 8A Silvaire	C. W. Thirtle	
G-BRJB	Zenair CH.600 Zodiac	E. G. Brown	
G-BRJC	Cessna 120	One Twenty Group	
G-BRJK	Luscombe 8A Silvaire	C. J. L. Peat	
G-BRJL	PA-15 Vagabond	C. P. Ware & C. R. Leech	
G-BRJM	Cameron A-210 balloon	T. M. Donnelly	
G-BRJN	Pitts S-1C Special	G-BRJN Group	
G-BRJR	PA-38-112 Tomahawk	Chester Aviation Ltd	
G-BRJT	Cessna 150H	J. Eagles	
G-BRJV	PA-28-161 Cadet	Newcastle-upon-Tyne Aero Club Ltd	
G-BRJW	Bellanca 7GCBC Citabria	H. W. Weston/Staverton	
G-BRJX	Rand KR-2	J. M. Mortimer	
G-BRJY	Rand KR-2	R. E. Taylor	
G-BRKA	Luscombe 8F Silvaire	T. I. Carlin	
G-BRKC	J/1 Autocrat	J. W. Conlon	
G-BRKD	Piaggio FWP.149D	Operation Ability Ltd	
G-BRKE	Hawker Sea Hurricane XIIA (BW853)	AJD Engineering Ltd	
G-BRKH	PA-28-236 Dakota	P. A. Wright	
G-BRKJ	Stoddard-Hamilton Glasair III	R. F. E. Simard	
G-BRKL	Cameron H-34 balloon	B. J. Newman	
G-BRKN	Robinson R-22 Mariner	P. M. Webber/Greece	
G-BRKO	Oldfield Baby Great Lakes	C. Wren	
G-BRKP	Colt 31A balloon	Bavarian Balloon Co Ltd	
G-BRKR	Cessna 182R	A. R. D. Brooker	
G-BRKS	Air Command 532 Elite	G. Sandercock	
G-BRKW	Cameron V-77 balloon	T. J. Parker	
G-BRKX	Air Command 532 Elite	K. Davis	
G-BRKY	Viking Dragonfly Mk II	G. D. Price	
G-BRKZ	Air Command 532 Elite	D. C. E. Streeter	
G-BRLB	Air Command 532 Elite	F. G. Shepherd	

Notes	Reg.	Type	Owner or Operator
	G-BRLC	Thunder Ax7-77 balloon	Fuji Photo Film (UK) Ltd
	G-BRLF	Campbell Cricket (replica)	D. Wood
	G-BRLG	PA-28RT-201T Turbo Arrow IV	Specialist Welding & Metallurgical Services Ltd
	G-BRLH	Air Command 532 Elite	Childs Garages (Sherborne) Ltd
	G-BRLI	Piper J-5A Cub Cruiser	A. E. Poulson
	G-BRLJ	Evans VP-2	R. L. Jones
	G-BRLK	Air Command 532 Elite	G. L. Hunt
	G-BRLL	Cameron A-105 balloon	Adventure Flights Ltd
	G-BRLO	PA-38-112 Tomahawk	Scotia Safari Ltd/Prestwick
	G-BRLP	PA-38-112 Tomahawk	Lightstrong Ltd
	G-BRLR	Cessna 150G	D. C. Maxwell
	G-BRLS	Thunder Ax7-77 balloon	E. C. Meek
	G-BRLT	Colt 77A balloon	D. Bareford
	G-BRLU	Cameron H-24 balloon	D. K. Fish
	G-BRLV	CCF Harvard IV (93542)	B. C. Abela
	G-BRLW	Cessna 150M	Visionkind Ltd
	G-BRLX	Cameron N-77 balloon	National Power
	G-BRLY	BAe ATP	Manx Airlines Ltd
	G-BRMA	W.S.51 Dragonfly HR.5 (WG718) ★	International Helicopter Museum/ Weston-s-Mare
	G-BRMB	B.192 Belvedere HC.1 (XG452) ★	International Helicopter Museum/ Weston-s-Mare
	G-BRME	PA-28-181 Archer II	S. Edgar
	G-BRMG	V.S.384 Seafire XVII (SX336)	P. J. Woods
	G-BRMH	Bell 206B JetRanger 2	RCR Aviation Ltd (G-BBUX)
	G-BRMI	Cameron V-65 balloon	M. Davies
	G-BRMJ	PA-38-112 Tomahawk	Aerohire Ltd/Halfpenny Green
	G-BRML	PA-38-112 Tomahawk	P. H. Rogers/Coventry
	G-BRMM	Air Command 532 Elite	R. de Serville
	G-BRMN	Thunder Ax7-77 balloon	G. Restell & R. Higham
	G-BRMS	PA-28RT-201 Arrow IV	Fleetbridge Ltd
	G-BRMT	Cameron V-31 balloon	R. M. Trotter & K. L. Heron
	G-BRMU	Cameron V-77 balloon	K. J. & G. R. Ibbotson
	G-BRMV	Cameron O-77 balloon	P. D. Griffiths
	G-BRMW	Whittaker MW.7	M. R. Grunwell
	G-BRNC	Cessna 150M	D. C. Bonsall
	G-BRND	Cessna 152 II	A. C. Roles
	G-BRNE	Cessna 152 II	Aerohire Ltd/Halfpenny Green
	G-BRNJ	PA-38-112 Tomahawk	S. Eddison
	G-BRNK	Cessna 152 II	Sheffield Aero Club Ltd/Netherthorpe
	G-BRNM	Chichester-Miles Leopard	Chichester-Miles Consultants Ltd
	G-BRNN	Cessna 152 II	Sheffield Aero Club Ltd/Netherthorpe
	G-BRNP	Rotorway Executive	C. A. Laycock
	G-BRNR	Schweizer 269C	C.S.E. Aviation Ltd/Kidlington
	G-BRNT	Robin DR.400/180	M. J. Cowham
	G-BRNU	Robin DR.400/180	November Uniform Travel Syndicate Ltd/Booker
	G-BRNW	PA-28-181 Archer II	D. C. Harry/Clacton
	G-BRNW	Cameron V-77 balloon	N. Robertson & G. Smith
	G-BRNX	PA-22 Tri-Pacer 150	R. S. Tomlinson & B. Yager
	G-BRNY	Thunder Ax6-56A balloon	D. M. Williams
	G-BRNZ	PA-32 Cherokee Six 300B	IML Aviation Ltd
	G-BROB	Cameron V-77 balloon	R. W. Richardson
	G-BROE	Cameron N-65 balloon	R. H. Sanderson
	G-BROF	Air Command 532 Elite	M. J. Hoskins
	G-BROG	Cameron V-65 balloon	R. Kunert
	G-BROH	Cameron O-90 balloon	P. A. Wenlock
	G-BROI	CFM Streak Shadow Srs SA	G. W. Rowbotham
	G-BROJ	Colt 31A balloon	Virgin Airship & Balloon Co Ltd
	G-BROL	Colt AS-80 Mk II airship	Wellfarrow Ltd
	G-BROO	Luscombe 8A Silvaire	Bedwell Hey Flying Group
	G-BROP	Vans RV-4	K. E. Armstrong
	G-BROR	Piper J-3C-65 Cub	White Hart Flying Group
	G-BROX	Robinson R-22B	Zeuros Ltd
	G-BROY	Cameron V-77 balloon	T. G. S. Dixon
	G-BROZ	PA-18 Super Cub 150	P. G. Kynsey
	G-BRPE	Cessna 120	C. Briggs
	G-BRPF	Cessna 120	D. Sharp
	G-BRPG	Cessna 120	I. C. Lomax
	G-BRPH	Cessna 120	J. A. Cook
	G-BRPJ	Cameron N-90 balloon	Cloud Nine Balloon Co
	G-BRPK	PA-28 Cherokee 140	J. P. A. Gomes

Reg.	Type	Owner or Operator	Notes
G-BRPL	PA-28 Cherokee 140	Comed Aviation Ltd/Blackpool	
G-BRPM	T.66 Nipper 3	T. C. Horner	
G-BRPO	Enstrom 280C	R. Moffett	
G-BRPP	Brookland Hornet	D. E. Cox	
G-BRPR	Aeronca O-58B Grasshopper (31952)	C. S. Tolchard	
G-BRPS	Cessna 177B	N. W. Beresford	
G-BRPT	Rans S.10 Sakota	B. G. Morris	
G-BRPU	Beech 76 Duchess	Hamilton Compass Aviation Ltd	
G-BRPV	Cessna 152	GEM Rewinds Ltd/Coventry	
G-BRPX	Taylorcraft BC-12D	M. J. Brett	
G-BRPY	PA-15 Vagabond	J. P. Esson	
G-BRPZ	Luscombe 8A Silvaire	S. L. & J. P. Waring	
G-BRRA	V.S.361 Spitfire LF.IXe	Historic Aircraft Collection Ltd	
G-BRRB	Luscombe 8E Silvaire	C. G. Ferguson & D. W. Gladwin	
G-BRRD	Scheibe SF.25B Falke	M. N. Martin	
G-BRRE	Colt 69A balloon	P. Patel	
G-BRRF	Cameron O-77 balloon	Mid-Bucks Farmers Balloon Group	
G-BRRG	Glaser-Dirks DG.500M	Glider Syndicate	
G-BRRJ	PA-28RT-201T Turbo Arrow IV	M. & E. Machinery Ltd	
G-BRRK	Cessna 182Q	M. Cligman & ptnrs	
G-BRRL	PA-18 Super Cub 95	Acebell G-BRRL Syndicate/Redhill	
G-BRRM	PA-28-161 Cadet	R. H. Sellier	
G-BRRN	PA-28-161 Warrior II	C. J. & L. M. Worsley	
G-BRRO	Cameron N-77 balloon	Newbury Building Soc	
G-BRRR	Cameron V-77 balloon	L. M. Heal & A. P. Wilcox	
G-BRRS	Pitts S-1C Special	R. C. Atkinson	
G-BRRT	C.A.S.A. 1.131E Jungmann	R. A. L. Hubbard/Syerston	
G-BRRU	Colt 90A balloon	Airship Shop Ltd	
G-BRRW	Cameron O-77 balloon	D. V. Fowler	
G-BRRY	Robinson R-22B	Bristow Helicopters Ltd/Redhill	
G-BRSA	Cameron N-56 balloon	C. Wilkinson	
G-BRSC	Rans S.10 Sakota	M. A. C. Stephenson	
G-BRSD	Cameron V-77 balloon	T. J. Porter & J. E. Kelly	
G-BRSE	PA-28-161 Warrior II	Air Service Training Ltd/Perth	
G-BRSG	PA-28-161 Cadet	Holmes Rentals	
G-BRSH	C.A.S.A. 1.131E Jungmann (781-25)	J. D. Haslam	
G-BRSI	PA-28-161 Cadet	Plane Talking Ltd/Elstree	
G-BRSJ	PA-38-112 Tomahawk	Pool Aviation Ltd/Welshpool	
G-BRSK	Boeing Stearman N2S-3 (180)	Wymondham Engineering	
G-BRSL	Cameron N-56 balloon	S. Budd	
G-BRSN	Rand-Robinson KR-2	K. W. Darby	
G-BRSO	CFM Streak Shadow Srs SA	D. J. Smith	
G-BRSP	Air Command 532 Elite	D. R. G. Griffith	
G-BRSW	Luscombe 8A Silvaire	Moravian Flying Group	
G-BRSX	PA-15 Vagabond	C. Milne-Fowler	
G-BRSY	Hatz CB-1	G. A. Barrett & Son	
G-BRTA	PA-38-112 Tomahawk	R. A. Wakefield	
G-BRTB	Bell 206B JetRanger 3	Harris Technology Ltd	
G-BRTC	Cessna 150G	Thorpe Air Ltd/Goodwood	
G-BRTD	Cessna 152 II	152 Group/Goodwood	
G-BRTH	Cameron A-180 balloon	The Ballooning Business Ltd	
G-BRTJ	Cessna 150F	Jersey ATC Flying Ltd	
G-BRTK	Boeing Stearman E.75 (217786)	Eastern Stearman Ltd/North Walsham	
G-BRTL	Hughes 369E	Crewhall Ltd	
G-BRTM	PA-28-161 Warrior II	Air Service Training Ltd/Perth	
G-BRTN	Beech 95-B58 Baron	Colneway Ltd	
G-BRTP	Cessna 152	CBS Aerohire Ltd/Earls Colne	
G-BRTT	Schweizer 269C	Fairthorpe Ltd/Denham	
G-BRTV	Cameron O-77 balloon	C. Vening	
G-BRTW	Glaser-Dirks DG.400	I. J. Carruthers	
G-BRTX	PA-28-151 Warrior	Spectrum Alpha Flying Group	
G-BRTZ	Slingsby T.31 Motor Cadet III	R. R. Walters	
G-BRUA	Cessna 152 II	C. M. Vlieland-Boddy'Compton Abbas	
G-BRUB	PA-28-161 Warrior II	Flytrek Ltd/Bournemouth	
G-BRUD	PA-28-181 Archer II	Wilkins & Wilkins Special Auctions Ltd	
G-BRUE	Cameron V-77 balloon	B. J. Newman & P. L. Harrison	
G-BRUG	Luscombe 8E Silvaire	P. A. Cain & N. W. Barratt	
G-BRUH	Colt 105A balloon	D. C. Chipping	
G-BRUI	PA-44-180 Seminole	Tatenhill Aviation	
G-BRUJ	Boeing Stearman A.75N1 (16136)	M. Walker/Liverpool	
G-BRUM	Cessna A.152	Flychoice Ltd/Birmingham	

Notes	Reg.	Type	Owner or Operator
	G-BRUN	Cessna 120	O. C. Brun (G-BRDH)
	G-BRUO	Taylor JT.1 Monoplane	G. Verity
	G-BRUT	Thunder Ax8-90 balloon	Moet & Chandon (London) Ltd
	G-BRUU	EAA Biplane Model P.1	R. D. Harper
	G-BRUV	Cameron V-77 balloon	T. W. & R. F. Benbrook
	G-BRUX	PA-44-180 Seminole	Hambrair Ltd/Tollerton
	G-BRUZ	Raven Europe FS-57A balloon	R. H. Etherington
	G-BRVB	Stolp SA.300 Starduster Too	C. J. R. Flint & S. C. Lever
	G-BRVC	Cameron N-180 balloon	A. J. Street
	G-BRVE	Beech D.17S	Intrepid Aviation Co/North Weald
	G-BRVF	Colt 77A balloon	Airborne Adventures Ltd
	G-BRVG	NA SNJ-7 Texan (27)	Intrepid Aviation Co/North Weald
	G-BRVH	Smyth Model S Sidewinder	I. S. Bellamy
	G-BRVI	Robinson R-22B	Burnell Helicopters Ltd
	G-BRVJ	Slingsby T.31 Motor Cadet III	B. Outhwaite
	G-BRVK	Cameron A-210 Balloon	The Balloon Club Ltd
	G-BRVN	Thunder Ax7-77 balloon	J. T. Hughes Ltd
	G-BRVO	AS.350B Ecureuil	Malcolm Wilson (Motorsport) Ltd
	G-BRVR	Barnett J4B-2 rotorcraft	Ilkeston Contractors
	G-BRVS	Barnett J4B-2 rotorcraft	Ilkeston Contractors
	G-BRVT	Pitts S-2B Special	C. J. & M. D. Green
	G-BRVU	Colt 77A balloon	D. J. Harber
	G-BRVV	Colt 56B balloon	S. J. Hollingsworth
	G-BRVX	Cameron A-210 balloon	Bath Hot Air Balloon Club Ltd
	G-BRVY	Thunder Ax8-90 balloon	G. E. Morris
	G-BRVZ	Jodel D.117	J.G. Patton
	G-BRWA	Aeronca 7AC Champion	D. D. Smith & J. R. Edwards
	G-BRWB	NA T-6G Texan (51-14526)	Monafield Ltd
	G-BRWC	Cessna 152 II	T. Hayselden (Doncaster) Ltd
	G-BRWD	Robinson R22B	Matrix Aviation Ltd
	G-BRWF	Thunder Ax7-77	D. J. Greaves
	G-BRWH	Cameron N-77	D. J. Usher
	G-BRWO	PA-28 Cherokee 140	ML Associates
	G-BRWP	CFM Streak Shadow Srs SA	J. M. Bain
	G-BRWR	Aeronca 11AC Chief	O. T. Taylor
	G-BRWT	Scheibe SF.25C Falke	J. E. Steenson & Booker Gliding Club Ltd
	G-BRWU	Luton LA-4A Minor	R. B. Webber & P. K. Pike
	G-BRWV	Brügger MB.2 Colibri	S. J. McCollum
	G-BRWX	Cessna 172P	D. A. Abels
	G-BRWY	Cameron H-34 balloon	Cameron Balloons Ltd
	G-BRWZ	Cameron 90 Macaw SS balloon	Forbes Europe Inc/France
	G-BRXA	Cameron O-120 balloon	Gone With The Wind Ltd & R. J. Mansfield
	G-BRXB	Thunder Ax7-77 balloon	H. Peel
	G-BRXC	PA-28-161 Warrior II	Air Service Training Ltd/Perth
	G-BRXD	PA-28-181 Archer II	D. D. Stone
	G-BRXE	Taylorcraft BC-12D	W. J. Durrad
	G-BRXF	Aeronca 11AC Chief	A. B. Newman
	G-BRXG	Aeronca 7AC Champion	X-Ray Golf Flying Group
	G-BRXH	Cessna 120	J. N. Pittock & A. P. Fox
	G-BRXL	Aeronca 11AC Chief (42-78044)	P. R. A. Hammond & ptnrs
	G-BRXN	Montgomerie-Bensen B.8MR	J. C. Aitken
	G-BRXO	PA-34-200T Seneca II	Aviation Services Ltd
	G-BRXP	SNCAN Stampe SV-4C (modified)	P. G. Kavanagh & D. T. Kaberry
	G-BRXS	Howard Special T Minus	H. C. Cox
	G-BRXU	AS.332L Super Puma	Bristow Helicopters Ltd
	G-BRXV	Robinson R-22B	Pearce Enterprise Ltd
	G-BRXW	PA-24 Comanche 260	The Oak Group
	G-BRXY	Pietenpol Air Camper	P. S. Ganczakowski
	G-BRXZ	Robinson R-22B	Helisport Ltd
	G-BRYA	D.H.C.7-110 Dash Seven	Brymon Airways Ltd/British Airways *Aberdeenshire*
	G-BRYB	D.H.C.7-110 Dash Seven	Brymon Airways Ltd/British Airways *Shetland Islands*
	G-BRYC	D.H.C.7-110 Dash Seven	Brymon Airways Ltd/British Airways *Devon*
	G-BRYD	D.H.C.7-110 Dash Seven	Brymon Airways Ltd/British Airways *Cornwall*
	G-BRYG	D.H.C.8-102A Dash Eight	Brymon Airways Ltd/British Airways *Lothian*
	G-BRYH	D.H.C.8-102A Dash Eight	Brymon Airways Ltd/British Airways *Lanarkshire*

Reg.	Type	Owner or Operator	Notes
G-BRYI	D.H.C.8-311 Dash Eight	Brymon Airways Ltd/British Airways *Northumberland*	
G-BRYJ	D.H.C.8-311 Dash Eight	Brymon Airways Ltd/British Airways *Somerset*	
G-BRYN	SOCATA TB.20 Trinidad	Jones & Bradbourn (Guernsey) Ltd	
G-BRZA	Cameron O-77 balloon	L. & R. J. Mold	
G-BRZB	Cameron A-105 balloon	Headland Services Ltd	
G-BRZC	Cameron N-90 balloon	Flying Pictures (Balloons) Ltd	
G-BRZD	Hapi Cygnet S F-2A	L. G. Millen	
G-BRZE	Thunder Ax7-77 balloon	G. V. Beckwith	
G-BRZG	Enstrom F-28A	Chart Planes Inland Ltd	
G-BRZI	Cameron N-180 balloon	First Class Ballooning Ltd	
G-BRZK	Stinson 108-2	J. A. Webb & G. F. Wheeler	
G-BRZL	Pitts S-1D Special	R. T. Cardwell/Elstree	
G-BRZO	Jodel D.18	J. D. Anson	
G-BRZP	PA-28-161 Warrior II	Air Service Training Ltd/Perth	
G-BRZS	Cessna 172P	YP Flying Group/Blackpool	
G-BRZT	Cameron V-77 balloon	B. Drawbridge	
G-BRZU	Colt Flying Cheese SS balloon	N. Carbonnier	
G-BRZV	Colt Flying Apple SS balloon	Thrust Drive Ltd	
G-BRZW	Rans S.10 Sakota	D. L. Davies	
G-BRZX	Pitts S-1S Special	G-BRZX Group	
G-BRZZ	CFM Streak Shadow	P. R. Oakes	
G-BSAB	PA-46-350P Malibu Mirage	D. O. Hooper	
G-BSAI	Stoddard-Hamilton Glasair III	K. J. & P. J. Whitehead	
G-BSAJ	C.A.S.A. 1.131E Jungmann	P. G. Kynsey/Redhill	
G-BSAK	Colt 21A balloon	Northern Flights	
G-BSAR	Air Command 532 Elite	T. A. Holmes	
G-BSAS	Cameron V-65 balloon	J. R. Barber	
G-BSAT	PA-28-181 Archer II	A1 Aircraft Ltd/Biggin Hill	
G-BSAV	Thunder Ax7-77 balloon	E. A. Evans & ptnrs	
G-BSAW	PA-28-161 Warrior II	Carill Aviation Ltd/Southampton	
G-BSAX	Piper J-3C-65 Cub	Crop Aviation (UK) Ltd	
G-BSAZ	Denney Kitfox Mk 2	D. J. Richardson	
G-BSBA	PA-28-161 Warrior II	APB Leasing Ltd/Welshpool	
G-BSBG	CCF Harvard IV (20310)	A. P. St John	
G-BSBH	Short SD3-30 ★	Ulster Aviation Soc Museum *(stored)*	
G-BSBI	Cameron O-77 balloon	Calibre Motor Co Ltd	
G-BSBK	Colt 105A balloon	Zebra Ballooning Ltd	
G-BSBM	Cameron N-77 balloon	Nuclear Electric	
G-BSBN	Thunder Ax7-77 balloon	B. Pawson	
G-BSBP	Jodel D.18	R. T. Pratt	
G-BSBR	Cameron V-77 balloon	B. Bromiley	
G-BSBT	Piper J-3C-65 Cub	M. B. & L. J. Proudfoot	
G-BSBU	Firefly 8B balloon	A. R. Peart	
G-BSBV	Rans S.10 Sakota	Sportair UK Ltd	
G-BSBW	Bell 206B JetRanger 3	Leeds Central Helicopters Ltd	
G-BSBX	Montgomerie-Bensen B.8MR	B. Ibbott	
G-BSBY	Cessna 150L	Languedoc Aviation/France	
G-BSBZ	Cessna 150M	DTG Aviation	
G-BSCA	Cameron N-90 balloon	P. J. Marshall & M. A. Clarke	
G-BSCB	Air Command 532 Elite	P. H. Smith	
G-BSCC	Colt 105A balloon	A. F. Selby	
G-BSCD	Hughes 269C	Aviation Bureau	
G-BSCE	Robinson R-22B	Shaun Stevens Contractors Ltd	
G-BSCF	Thunder Ax7-77 balloon	V. P. Gardiner	
G-BSCG	Denney Kitfox Mk 2	A. C. & T. G. Pinkstone	
G-BSCH	Denney Kitfox Mk 2	Baldoon Leisure Flying Co Ltd	
G-BSCI	Colt 77A balloon	J. L. & S. Wrigglesworth	
G-BSCK	Cameron H-24 balloon	J. D. Shapland	
G-BSCL	Robinson R-22B	Sandhill Ltd	
G-BSCM	Denney Kitfox Mk 2	M. J. Wells	
G-BSCO	Thunder Ax7-77 balloon	F. J. Whalley	
G-BSCP	Cessna 152 II	Moray Flying Club (1990) Ltd/Kinloss	
G-BSCR	Cessna 172M	London Link Flying Ltd	
G-BSCS	PA-28-181 Archer II	Wing Task Ltd	
G-BSCV	PA-28-161 Warrior II	Southwood Flying Group/Southend	
G-BSCW	Taylorcraft BC-65	S. Leach	
G-BSCX	Thunder Ax8-105 balloon	Balloon Flights Club Ltd	
G-BSCY	PA-28-151 Warrior	Falcon Flying Services/Biggin Hill	
G-BSCZ	Cessna 152 II	London Flight Centre (Stansted) Ltd	
G-BSDA	Taylorcraft BC-12D	D. G. Edwards	

Notes	Reg.	Type	Owner or Operator
	G-BSDB	Pitts S-1C Special	G. Gregg
	G-BSDC	Enstrom 280FX	B. Steele
	G-BSDD	Denney Kitfox Mk 2	J. Windmill
	G-BSDG	Robin DR.400/180	B. Hodge
	G-BSDH	Robin DR.400/180	R. L. Brucciani
	G-BSDI	Corben Junior Ace Model E	J. Pearson/Eaglescott
	G-BSDJ	Piper J-4E Cub Coupé	J. Pearson/Eaglescott
	G-BSDK	Piper J-5A Cub Cruiser	S. Haughton & I. S. Hodge
	G-BSDL	SOCATA TB.10 Tobago	Delta Lima Group
	G-BSDN	PA-34-200T Seneca II	Belso Aviation Ltd
	G-BSDO	Cessna 152 II	J. Vickers
	G-BSDP	Cessna 152 II	I. S. H. Paul
	G-BSDS	Boeing Stearman E.75 (118)	E. Hopper
	G-BSDU	Bell 206B JetRanger 3	Eaglecray Ltd
	G-BSDV	Colt 31A balloon	Virgin Airship & Balloon Co Ltd
	G-BSDW	Cessna 182P	Delta Whisky Ltd
	G-BSDX	Cameron V-77 balloon	D. K. Fish
	G-BSDY	Beech 58 Baron	Astra Aviation Ltd
	G-BSDZ	Enstrom 280FX	B. Steele (G-ODSC)
	G-BSED	PA-22 Tri-Pacer 160 (modified)	M. Henderson
	G-BSEE	Rans S.9	P. M. Semler
	G-BSEF	PA-28 Cherokee 180	Prestwick Pilots Group
	G-BSEG	Ken Brock KB-2 gyroplane	H. A. Bancroft-Wilson
	G-BSEJ	Cessna 150M	Halfpenny Green Flight Centre Ltd
	G-BSEK	Robinson R-22	Lateq Aviation Ltd
	G-BSEL	Slingsby T.61G Super Falke	RAFGSA/Hullavington
	G-BSEP	Cessna 172	A. Washington & A. P. Wall
	G-BSER	PA-28 Cherokee 160	Yorkair Ltd/Leeds
	G-BSES	Denney Kitfox	M. Albert-Recht & J. J. M. Donnelly
	G-BSET	B.206 Srs 1 Basset	Beagle Basset Ltd/Shoreham
	G-BSEU	PA-28-181 Archer II	Euro Aviation 91 Ltd
	G-BSEV	Cameron O-77 balloon	UK Transplant Co-ordinators Assoc
	G-BSEW	Sikorsky S-76A	Bond Helicopters Ltd
	G-BSEX	Cameron A-180 balloon	Heart of England Balloons
	G-BSEY	Beech A36 Bonanza	K. Phillips Ltd
	G-BSEZ	Air Command 532 Elite	D. S. Robinson
	G-BSFA	Aero Designs Pulsar	S. A. Gill
	G-BSFB	C.A.S.A. 1.131E Jungmann 2000 (S5-B06)	J. A. Sykes
	G-BSFD	Piper J-3C-65 Cub	E. C. English
	G-BSFE	PA-38-112 Tomahawk II	D. J. Campbell
	G-BSFF	Robin DR.400/180R	Lasham Gliding Soc Ltd
	G-BSFJ	Thunder Ax8-105 balloon	Airborne Adventures Ltd
	G-BSFK	PA-28-161 Warrior II	Air Service Training Ltd/Perth
	G-BSFN	SE.313B Alouette II	M & P Food Products Ltd
	G-BSFP	Cessna 152 II	J. R. Nicholls
	G-BSFR	Cessna 152 II	Galair Ltd
	G-BSFS	SE.313B Alouette II	M & P Food Products Ltd
	G-BSFV	Woods Woody Pusher	M. J. Wells
	G-BSFW	PA-15 Vagabond	J. R. Kimberley
	G-BSFX	Denney Kitfox Mk 2	D. A. McFadyean
	G-BSFY	Denney Kitfox Mk 2	J. R. Howard
	G-BSGB	Gaertner Ax4 Skyranger balloon	B. Gaertner
	G-BSGC	PA-18 Super Cub 95	G. Churchill
	G-BSGD	PA-28 Cherokee 180	R. J. Cleverley
	G-BSGF	Robinson R-22B	Garingdell Aviation Ltd
	G-BSGG	Denney Kitfox Mk 2	C. G. Richardson
	G-BSGH	Airtour AH-56B balloon	G. Luck
	G-BSGJ	Monnett Sonerai II	G. A. Brady
	G-BSGK	PA-34-200T Seneca II	R. Hope & ptnrs
	G-BSGL	PA-28-161 Warrior II	Keywest Air Charter Ltd/Liverpool
	G-BSGM	Cameron V-77 balloon	A. M. Dare
	G-BSGN	PA-28-151 Warrior	J. R. Whetlor & M. Gipps/Denham
	G-BSGP	Cameron N-65 balloon	Mid-Sussex Flying School
	G-BSGR	Boeing Stearman E.75	A. G. Dunkerley
	G-BSGS	Rans S.10 Sakota	M. R. Parr
	G-BSGT	Cessna T.210N	B. J. Sharpe/Booker
	G-BSGY	Thunder Ax7-77 balloon	P. B. Kenington
	G-BSHA	PA-34-200T Seneca II	Shepherd Aviation Ltd
	G-BSHC	Colt 69A balloon	L. V. Mastis
	G-BSHD	Colt 69A balloon	Virgin Airship & Balloon Co Ltd
	G-BSHE	Cessna 152 II	J. A. Pothecary/Shoreham
	G-BSHH	Luscombe 8E Silvaire	Golf Centres Balloons Ltd

Reg.	Type	Owner or Operator	Notes
G-BSHI	Luscombe 8F Silvaire	W. H. J. Knowles	
G-BSHK	Denney Kitfox Mk 2	A. E. Cree & G. J. Cuzzocrea	
G-BSHM	Slingsby T.31 Motor Cadet III	D. Shrimpton	
G-BSHO	Cameron V-77 balloon	T. P. Barlass & D. J. Duckworth	
G-BSHP	PA-28-161 Warrior II	Air Service Training Ltd/Perth	
G-BSHR	Cessna F.172N	H. Rothwell (G-BFGE)/Blackpool	
G-BSHS	Colt 105A balloon	I. Novosad	
G-BSHT	Cameron V-77 balloon	ECM Construction Ltd	
G-BSHV	PA-18 Super Cub 135	Fen Tigers Flying Group	
G-BSHW	Hawker Tempest II (MW800)	—	
G-BSHX	Enstrom F-28A	Stephenson Aviation Ltd	
G-BSHY	EAA Acro Sport I	A. W. Hughes & R. J. Hodder	
G-BSHZ	Enstrom F-28F	Heliway Aviation	
G-BSIB	PA-28-161 Warrior II	Bobbington Air Training School Ltd	
G-BSIC	Cameron V-77 balloon	P. D. Worthy	
G-BSIF	Denney Kitfox	R. M. Kimbell & M. H. Wylde	
G-BSIG	Colt 21A balloon	E. C. & A. J. Moore	
G-BSIH	Rutan LongEz	W. S. Allen	
G-BSII	PA-34-200T Seneca II	N. H. N. Gardner	
G-BSIJ	Cameron V-77 balloon	A. S. Jones	
G-BSIK	Denney Kitfox	I. A. Davies & B. Barr	
G-BSIL	Colt 120A balloon	K. S. Hull	
G-BSIM	PA-28-181 Archer II	E. Midlands Aircraft Hire Ltd	
G-BSIN	Robinson R-22B	Actionbound Building Co Ltd	
G-BSIO	Cameron 80 Shed SS balloon	R. E. Jones	
G-BSIR	Cessna 340	Airmaster Aviation Ltd/Cardiff	
G-BSIT	Robinson R-22B	P. R. Earp	
G-BSIU	Colt 90A balloon	S. Travaglia	
G-BSIY	Schleicher ASK.14	H. F. Lamprey	
G-BSIZ	PA-28-181 Archer II	Firmdane Ltd	
G-BSJA	Cameron N-77 balloon	N. Sanders (G-SPAR)	
G-BSJB	Bensen B.8	J. W. Limbrick	
G-BSJU	Cessna 150M	A. C. Williamson	
G-BSJV	Cessna 172N	J. C. M. van Tilburg	
G-BSJW	Everett Srs 2 gyroplane	A. R. Willis	
G-BSJX	PA-28-161 Warrior II	Border Air Training Ltd/Ronaldsway	
G-BSJZ	Cessna 150J	I. S. H. Paul	
G-BSKA	Cessna 150M	Cubair Ltd/Redhill	
G-BSKC	PA-38-112 Tomahawk	J. Marioni	
G-BSKD	Cameron V-77 balloon	M. J. Gunston	
G-BSKE	Cameron O-84 balloon	The Blunt Arrows Balloon Team	
G-BSKG	Maule MX-7-180	J. R. Surbey	
G-BSKH	Cessna 421C	Widehawk Aviation Ltd/Ipswich	
G-BSKI	Thunder Ax8-90 balloon	G-BSKI Balloon Group	
G-BSKK	PA-38-112 Tomahawk	Falcon Flying Services/Biggin Hill	
G-BSKL	PA-38-112 Tomahawk	Falcon Flying Services/Biggin Hill	
G-BSKO	Maule MXT-7-180	G. B. Esslemont	
G-BSKP	V.S.379 Spitfire F.XIV (RN201)	Historic Aircraft Collection Ltd	
G-BSKR	Rand Robinson KR-2	I. L. Griffith	
G-BSKT	Maule MX-7-180	D. D. Smith	
G-BSKU	Cameron O-84 balloon	Alfred Bagnall & Sons (West) Ltd	
G-BSKW	PA-28-181 Archer II	Shropshire Aero Club Ltd	
G-BSLA	Robin DR.400/180	A. B. McCoig/Biggin Hill	
G-BSLD	PA-28RT-201 Arrow IV	E. D. Gawronek	
G-BSLE	PA-28-161 Warrior II	Air Service Training Ltd/Perth	
G-BSLG	Cameron A-180 balloon	B. J. Newman	
G-BSLH	C.A.S.A. 1.131E Jungmann 2000	P. Warden	
G-BSLI	Cameron V-77 balloon	J. D. C. & F. E. Bevan	
G-BSLJ	Denney Kitfox	A. F. Reid	
G-BSLK	PA-28-161 Warrior II	R. A. Rose	
G-BSLM	PA-28 Cherokee 160	Old Sarum Cherokee Group	
G-BSLN	Thunder Ax10-180 balloon	Albatross Aviation Ltd	
G-BSLO	Cameron A-180 balloon	Adventure Balloon Co Ltd	
G-BSLT	PA-28-161 Warrior II	P. A. Lancaster	
G-BSLU	PA-28 Cherokee 140	D. J. Budden	
G-BSLW	Bellanca 7ECA Citabria	J. A. Killerby	
G-BSLX	WAR Focke-Wulf Fw.190 (replica) (4+)	A. McLeod	
G-BSLY	Colt AS-80 GD airship	Huntair Ltd	
G-BSMB	Cessna U.206E	Army Parachute Association/Netheravon	
G-BSMD	Nord 1101 Noralpha (114)	R. J. Lamplough	
G-BSME	Bo 208C Junior	D. J. Hampson	
G-BSMF	Avro 652A Anson C.19 (TX183)	G. M. K. Fraser	

Notes	Reg.	Type	Owner or Operator
	G-BSMG	Montgomerie-Bensen B.8M	A. C. Timperley
	G-BSMH	Colt 240A balloon	Formtrack Ltd
	G-BSMJ	Piper J-3C-65 Cub	S. M. Kearney (G-BRHE)
	G-BSMK	Cameron O-84 balloon	J. C. Reavley
	G-BSML	Schweizer 269C	Handy Rise Ltd
	G-BSMM	Colt 31A balloon	D. V. Fowler
	G-BSMN	CFM Streak Shadow	K. Daniels
	G-BSMO	Denney Kitfox	G-BSMO Group
	G-BSMP	PA-34-220T Seneca III	Manor Developments Ltd
	G-BSMS	Cameron V-77 balloon	Sade Balloons Ltd
	G-BSMT	Rans S.10 Sakota	D. K. Webb
	G-BSMU	Rans S.6 Coyote II	W. D. Walker (G-MWJE)
	G-BSMV	PA-17 Vagabond (modified)	A. Cheriton
	G-BSMX	Bensen B.8MR	J. S. E. McGregor
	G-BSMZ	PA-28-161 Warrior II	Air Service Training Ltd/Perth
	G-BSND	Air Command 532 Elite	K. Brogden & W. B. Lumb
	G-BSNE	Luscombe 8E Silvaire	Aerolite Luscombe Group
	G-BSNF	Piper J-3C-65 Cub	D. A. Hammant
	G-BSNG	Cessna 172N	A. J. & P. C. MacDonald
	G-BSNI	Bensen B.8V	B. D. Gibbs
	G-BSNJ	Cameron N-90 balloon	D. P. H. Smith
	G-BSNL	Bensen B.8MR	A. C. Breane
	G-BSNN	Rans S.10 Sakota	O. & S. D. Barnard
	G-BSNO	Denney Kitfox	A. G. V. McClintock
	G-BSNP	PA-28-201T Turbo Arrow III	V. Dowd/Stapleford
	G-BSNR	BAe 146-300A	Air UK Ltd/Stansted
	G-BSNS	BAe 146-300A	Air UK Ltd/Stansted
	G-BSNT	Luscombe 8A Silvaire	G. J. Slater
	G-BSNU	Colt 105A balloon	Sun Life Assurance Soc PLC
	G-BSNV	Boeing 737-4Q8	British Airways
	G-BSNW	Boeing 737-4Q8	British Airways
	G-BSNX	PA-28-181 Archer II	Monitron International Ltd
	G-BSNY	Bensen B.8M	A. S. Deakin
	G-BSNZ	Cameron O-105 balloon	Aire Valley Balloons
	G-BSOE	Luscombe 8A Silvaire	S. B. Marsden
	G-BSOG	Cessna 172M	B. Chapman & A. R. Budden
	G-BSOI	AS.332L Super Puma	Brintel Helicopters Ltd
	G-BSOJ	Thunder Ax7-77 balloon	R. J. S. Jones
	G-BSOK	PA-28-161 Warrior II	Voyager Aviation Ltd
	G-BSOM	Glaser-Dirks DG.400	G-BSOM Group
	G-BSON	Green S.25 balloon	J. J. Green
	G-BSOO	Cessna 172F	Double Oscar Flying Group
	G-BSOR	CFM Streak Shadow Srs SA	J. P. Sorenson
	G-BSOT	PA-38-112 Tomahawk II	D. J. Campbell/Edinburgh
	G-BSOU	PA-38-112 Tomahawk II	D. J. Campbell/Prestwick
	G-BSOV	PA-38-112 Tomahawk II	A. Dodd
	G-BSOX	Luscombe 8A Silvaire	D. Gill
	G-BSOY	PA-34-220T Seneca III	BAe Flying College Ltd/Prestwick
	G-BSOZ	PA-28-161 Warrior II	Moray Flying Club Ltd/Kinloss
	G-BSPA	QAC Quickie Q.2	M. Ward
	G-BSPB	Thunder Ax8-84 balloon	Nigs Pertwee Ltd
	G-BSPC	Jodel D.140C	stored/Headcorn
	G-BSPE	Cessna F.172P	A. M. J. Clark
	G-BSPF	Cessna T.303	G-BSPF Crusader Group
	G-BSPG	PA-34-200T Seneca II	C. M. Vlieland-Boddy/Compton Abbas
	G-BSPI	PA-28-161 Warrior II	Snapfleet Ltd/Wellesbourne
	G-BSPJ	Bensen B.8	P. Soanes
	G-BSPK	Cessna 195A	Walavia
	G-BSPL	CFM Streak Shadow Srs SA	MEL (Aviation Oxygen) Ltd
	G-BSPM	PA-28-161 Warrior II	White Waltham Airfield Ltd
	G-BSPN	PA-28R-201T Turbo Arrow III	R. G. & W. Allison
	G-BSPW	Light Aero Avid Flyer C	M. J. Sewell
	G-BSPX	Lancair 320	C. H. Skelt
	G-BSPY	BN-2A Islander	Aerohire Ltd (G-AXYM)/Halfpenny Green
	G-BSPZ	PA-28-161 Warrior II	Air Service Training Ltd/Perth
	G-BSRC	Cessna 150M	R. W. Boote
	G-BSRH	Pitts S-1C Special	J. R. Groom/Biggin Hill
	G-BSRI	Lancair 235	G. Lewis
	G-BSRK	ARV Super 2	J. K. Davies
	G-BSRL	Everett Srs 2 gyroplane	R. F. E. Burley
	G-BSRP	Rotorway Executive	J. P. Dennison
	G-BSRR	Cessna 182Q	Select Management Services Ltd
	G-BSRT	Denney Kitfox Mk 2	D. E. Steade

Reg.	Type	Owner or Operator	Notes
G-BSRX	CFM Streak Shadow	R. G. M-J. Proost & F-J. Luckhurst	
G-BSRZ	Air Command 532 Elite 2-seat	A. S. G. Crabb	
G-BSSA	Luscombe 8E Silvaire	Punters Promotions Ltd/Denham	
G-BSSB	Cessna 150L	D. T. A. Rees	
G-BSSC	PA-28-161 Warrior II	Air Service Training Ltd/Perth	
G-BSSE	PA-28 Cherokee 140	Comed Aviation Ltd/Blackpool	
G-BSSF	Denney Kitfox	D. M. Orrock	
G-BSSI	Rans S.6 Coyote II	D. A. Farnworth (G-MWJA)	
G-BSSJ	FRED Srs 2	R. F. Jopling	
G-BSSK	QAC Quickie Q.2	D. G. Greatrex	
G-BSSN	Air Command 532 Elite 2-seat	R. C. Bettany	
G-BSSO	Cameron O-90 balloon	R. R. & J. E. Hatton	
G-BSSP	Robin DR.400/180R	Soaring (Oxford) Ltd	
G-BSSR	PA-28-151 Warrior	H. M. B. Lundgren	
G-BSST	Concorde 002 ★	F.A.A. Museum/Yeovilton	
G-BSSV	CFM Streak Shadow	R. W. Payne	
G-BSSW	PA-28-161 Warrior II	R. L. Hayward	
G-BSSX	PA-28-161 Warrior II	Airways Aero Associations Ltd/Booker	
G-BSSZ	Thunder Ax8-90 balloon	Capital Balloon Club Ltd	
G-BSTC	Aeronca 11AC Chief	B. Bridgman & N. J. Mortimore	
G-BSTE	AS.355F-2 Twin Squirrel	Hygrade Foods Ltd	
G-BSTH	PA-25 Pawnee 235	Scottish Gliding Union Ltd/Portmoak	
G-BSTI	Piper J-3C-65 Cub	I. Fraser & G. L. Nunn	
G-BSTJ	D.H.82A Tiger Moth (N9192)	C. A. Parker	
G-BSTK	Thunder Ax8-90 balloon	M. Williams	
G-BSTL	Rand Robinson KR-2	T. M. Scale	
G-BSTM	Cessna 172L	G-BSTM Group/Cambridge	
G-BSTO	Cessna 152 II	Plymouth School of Flying Ltd	
G-BSTP	Cessna 152 II	FR Aviation Ltd/Bournemouth	
G-BSTR	AA-5 Traveler	James Allan (Aviation & Engineering) Ltd	
G-BSTT	Rans S.6 Coyote II	D. G. Palmer	
G-BSTU	Cessna P.210N	Astec Electronic Maintenance Ltd	
G-BSTV	PA-32 Cherokee Six 300	B. C. Hudson	
G-BSTX	Luscombe 8A Silvaire	A. A. Alderdice	
G-BSTY	Thunder Ax8-90 balloon	J. W. Cato	
G-BSTZ	PA-28 Cherokee 140	Air Navigation & Trading Co Ltd/Blackpool	
G-BSUA	Rans S.6 Coyote II	A. J. Todd	
G-BSUB	Colt 77A balloon	R. R. J. Wilson & M. P. Hill	
G-BSUD	Luscombe 8A Silvaire	I. G. Harrison/Egginton	
G-BSUE	Cessna U.206G	R. A. Robinson	
G-BSUF	PA-32RT-300 Lance II	M. J. Parker	
G-BSUJ	Brügger MB.2 Colibri	M. A. Farrelly	
G-BSUK	Colt 77A balloon	K. J. Foster	
G-BSUM	Scheibe SF.27MB	M Syndicate	
G-BSUO	Scheibe SF.25C Falke	British Gliding Association Ltd	
G-BSUR	Rotorway Executive 90	Coaching for Results Ltd	
G-BSUT	Rans S.6 Coyote II	P. J. Clegg	
G-BSUU	Colt 180A balloon	British School of Ballooning	
G-BSUV	Cameron O-77 balloon	R. Moss	
G-BSUW	PA-34-200T Seneca II	TG Aviation Ltd/Manston	
G-BSUX	Carlson Sparrow II	J. Stephenson	
G-BSUZ	Denney Kitfox Mk 3	M. W. Oliver	
G-BSVA	Christen A.1 Husky	Deeside Husky Group/Aboyne	
G-BSVB	PA-28-181 Archer II	Redhill Flying Club	
G-BSVC	Cameron A-210 balloon	British School of Ballooning	
G-BSVE	Binder CP.301S Smaragd	Smaragd Flying Group	
G-BSVF	PA-28-161 Warrior II	Airways Aero Associations Ltd/Booker	
G-BSVG	PA-28-161 Warrior II	Airways Aero Associations Ltd/Booker	
G-BSVH	Piper J-3C-65 Cub	A. R. Meakin	
G-BSVI	PA-16 Clipper	Robhurst Flying Group	
G-BSVJ	Piper J-3C-65 Cub	V. S. E. Norman	
G-BSVK	Denney Kitfox Mk 2	C. M. Looney	
G-BSVM	PA-28-161 Warrior II	Falcon Flying Services/Biggin Hill	
G-BSVN	Thorp T-18	J. H. Kirkham	
G-BSVP	PA-23 Aztec 250	Time Electronics Ltd/Biggin Hill	
G-BSVR	Schweizer 269C	Martinair Ltd	
G-BSVS	Robin DR.400/100	D. McK. Chalmers	
G-BSVV	PA-38-112 Tomahawk	J. Maffia & H. Merkado	
G-BSVW	PA-38-112 Tomahawk	Falcon Flying Services/Biggin Hill	
G-BSVX	PA-38-112 Tomahawk	Languedoc Aviation Ltd/France	
G-BSVY	PA-38-112 Tomahawk	Languedoc Aviation Ltd/France	
G-BSVZ	Pietenpol Air Camper	A. F. Cashin	
G-BSWA	Luscombe 8A Silvaire	Beeswax Flying Group	

Notes	Reg.	Type	Owner or Operator
	G-BSWB	Rans S.10 Sakota	F. A. Hewitt
	G-BSWC	Boeing Stearman E.75 (112)	R. R. White
	G-BSWF	PA-16 Clipper	T. M. Storey
	G-BSWG	PA-17 Vagabond	A. Gregori
	G-BSWH	Cessna 152 II	Airspeed Aviation Ltd
	G-BSWI	Rfians S.10 Sakota	A. Gault
	G-BSWJ	Cameron O-77 balloon	T. Charlwood
	G-BSWK	Robinson R-22B	Clarity Aviation Ltd
	G-BSWM	Slingsby T.61F	L. J. McKelvie/Bellarena
	G-BSWR	BN-2B-26 Islander	Police Authority for Northern Ireland
	G-BSWV	Cameron N-77 balloon	Leicester Mercury Ltd
	G-BSWX	Cameron V-90 balloon	Cameron Balloons Ltd
	G-BSWY	Cameron N-77 balloon	Nottingham Hot Air Balloon Club
	G-BSXA	PA-28-161 Warrior II	Falcon Flying Services/Biggin Hill
	G-BSXB	PA-28-161 Warrior II	M. & Q. Associates
	G-BSXC	PA-28-161 Warrior II	L. T. Halpin/Booker
	G-BSXD	Soko P-2 Kraguj (30146)	C. J. Pearce
	G-BSXE	Bell 206B JetRanger	Textron Ltd
	G-BSXF	Cameron A-180 balloon	Gone With The Wind Ltd
	G-BSXH	Pitts S-1C Special	A. Howard
	G-BSXI	Mooney M.20E	Mooney Group
	G-BSXM	Cameron V-77 balloon	C. A. Oxby
	G-BSXN	Robinson R-22B	J. G. Gray
	G-BSXP	Air Command 532 Elite	B. J. West
	G-BSXR	Air Command 532 Elite	T. Wing
	G-BSXS	PA-28-181 Archer II	Pipe-Air Ltd
	G-BSXT	Piper J-5A Cub Cruiser	M. G. & K. J. Thompson
	G-BSXW	PA-28-161 Warrior II	Ryland Aviation Ltd/Wellesbourne
	G-BSXX	Whittaker MW.7	H. J. Stanley
	G-BSXY	Oldfield Baby Great Lakes	B. Freeman-Jones (G-JENY)
	G-BSYA	Jodel D.18	S. Harrison
	G-BSYB	Cameron N-120 balloon	M. Buono/Italy
	G-BSYC	PA-32R-300 Lance	Arrow Aviation
	G-BSYD	Cameron A-180 balloon	A. A. Brown
	G-BSYF	Luscombe 8A Silvaire	Atlantic Aviation
	G-BSYG	PA-12 Super Cruiser	S. D. Rudkin & C. W. Udale
	G-BSYH	Luscombe 8A Silvaire	N. R. Osborne
	G-BSYI	AS.355F-1 Twin Squirrel	Lynton Aviation Ltd/Denham
	G-BSYJ	Cameron N-77 balloon	Chubb Fire Ltd
	G-BSYK	PA-38-112 Tomahawk	Flychoice Ltd/Birmingham
	G-BSYL	PA-38-112 Tomahawk	Flychoice Ltd/Birmingham
	G-BSYM	PA-38-112 Tomahawk	Flychoice Ltd/Birmingham
	G-BSYO	Piper J-3C-65 Cub	C. R. Reynolds & J. D. Fuller
	G-BSYP	Bensen B.8MR	C. R. Gordon
	G-BSYU	Robin DR.400/180	P. A. Desoutter
	G-BSYV	Cessna 150M	R. D. & S. R. Spencer
	G-BSYW	Cessna 150M	J. A. F. Waller
	G-BSYY	PA-28-161 Warrior II	Air Service Training Ltd/Perth
	G-BSYZ	PA-28-161 Warrior II	Air Service Training Ltd/Perth
	G-BSZB	Stolp SA.300 Starduster Too	Cambrian Flying Club/Swansea
	G-BSZC	Beech C-45H (51 11701A)	A. A. Hodgson
	G-BSZD	Robin DR.400/180	R. Hitchman & Son & P. J. Rowland & Sons (Farmers) Ltd
	G-BSZF	Jodel DR.250/160	J. B. Randle
	G-BSZG	Stolp SA.100 Starduster	S. W. Watkins
	G-BSZH	Thunder Ax7-77 balloon	K. E. Viney & L. J. Weston
	G-BSZI	Cessna 152 II	Eglinton Flying Club Ltd
	G-BSZJ	PA-28-181 Archer II	R. D. Fuller
	G-BSZL	Colt 77A balloon	Virgin Airship & Balloon Co Ltd
	G-BSZM	Bensen B.8	J. H. H. Turner
	G-BSZN	Bucker Bu133D-1 Jungmeister	V. Lindsay
	G-BSZO	Cessna 152	A. T. Hooper & T. E. Evans/Wellesbourne
	G-BSZS	Robinson R-22B	South West Helicopters Ltd
	G-BSZT	PA-28-161 Warrior II	Astra Associates
	G-BSZU	Cessna 150F	L. A. Maynard
	G-BSZV	Cessna 150F	Midair Aviation Ltd/Bournemouth
	G-BSZW	Cessna 152	Haimoss Ltd
	G-BSZY	Cameron A-180 balloon	K. H. Benning
	G-BTAB	BAe 125 Srs 800B	Abbey Investments Co Ltd (G-BOOA)
	G-BTAD	Macair Merlin	A. T. & M. R. Dowie
	G-BTAG	Cameron O-77 balloon	H. Phethean & R. A. Shapland
	G-BTAH	Bensen B.8M	T. B. Johnson

Reg.	Type	Owner or Operator	Notes
G-BTAJ	PA-34-200T Seneca II	Ravenair Aircraft Engineering Ltd/Manchester	
G-BTAK	EAA Acro Sport II	P. G. Harrison	
G-BTAL	Cessna F.152 II	Thanet Flying Club/Manston	
G-BTAM	PA-28-181 Archer II	RJH Air Services Ltd/Fowlmere	
G-BTAN	Thunder Ax7-65Z balloon	P. M. Gaines	
G-BTAP	PA-38-112 Tomahawk	I. J. McGarrigle	
G-BTAR	PA-38-112 Tomahawk	Aerohire Ltd/Halfpenny Green	
G-BTAS	PA-38-112 Tomahawk	P. D. W. King & W. Brooks	
G-BTAT	Denney Kitfox Mk 2	M. M. Austin & D. J. Thomas	
G-BTAU	Thunder Ax7-77 balloon	S. L. G. Williams	
G-BTAV	Colt 105A balloon	D. C. Chipping	
G-BTAW	PA-28-161 Warrior II	Enpar (North) Ltd	
G-BTAX	PA-31-350 Navajo Chieftain	Jet West Ltd/Exeter	
G-BTAZ	Evans VP-2	G. S. Poulter	
G-BTBA	Robinson R-22B	Forestdale Hotels Ltd	
G-BTBB	Thunder Ax8-90 balloon	Scotia Balloons Ltd	
G-BTBC	PA-28-161 Warrior II	M. J. L. MacDonald	
G-BTBE	PA-34-200T Seneca II	–	
G-BTBF	Super Koala	E. A. Taylor (G-MWOZ)	
G-BTBG	Denney Kitfox	J. Catley	
G-BTBH	Ryan ST3KR (854)	Ryan Group	
G-BTBI	WAR P-47 Thunderbolt (replica) (85)	S. W. Ballantyne	
G-BTBJ	Cessna 195B	P. G. Palumbo	
G-BTBL	Montgomerie-Bensen B.8MR	R. de H. Dobree-Carey	
G-BTBN	Denney Kitfox Mk 2	T. M. W. & S. A. Webster	
G-BTBO	Cameron N-77 balloon	Cameron Balloons Ltd	
G-BTBP	Cameron N-90 balloon	Chianti Balloon Club	
G-BTBR	Cameron DP-80 airship	Cameron Balloons Ltd	
G-BTBS	Cameron N-180 balloon	British School of Ballooning	
G-BTBU	PA-18 Super Cub 150	Acebell Aviation Ltd & H. J. Rose	
G-BTBV	Cessna 140	A. Brinkley	
G-BTBW	Cessna 120	P. B. Cox	
G-BTBX	Piper J-3C-65 Cub	Henlow Taildraggers	
G-BTBY	PA-17 Vagabond	G. J. Smith & J. A. Clark	
G-BTCA	PA-32R-300 Lance	P. Taylor	
G-BTCB	Air Command 582 Sport	G. Scurrah	
G-BTCC	Grumman F6F-5 Hellcat (19)	Patina Ltd/Duxford	
G-BTCD	P-51D-25-NA Mustang (463221)	Patina Ltd/Duxford	
G-BTCE	Cessna 152	S. T. Gilbert	
G-BTCH	Luscombe 8E Silvaire	P. Eastwood	
G-BTCI	PA-17 Vagabond	C. F. Kennedy	
G-BTCJ	Luscombe 8C Silvaire	C. C. & J. M. Lovell	
G-BTCK	Cameron A-210 balloon	H-O-T Air Balloons	
G-BTCL	Cameron A-210 balloon	Exeter Balloons	
G-BTCM	Cameron N-90 balloon	J. D. & K. Griffiths	
G-BTCO	FRED Srs 2	I. P. Manley	
G-BTCR	Rans S.10 Sakota	S. H. Barr	
G-BTCS	Colt 90A balloon	D. N. Belton	
G-BTCT	AS.332L Super Puma	Bristow Helicopters Ltd	
G-BTCU	WSK PZL Antonov An-2T (77)	Wessex Aviation & Transport Ltd	
G-BTCW	Cameron A-180 balloon	Bristol Balloons	
G-BTCZ	Cameron 84 Chateau SS balloon	Forbes Europe Inc/France	
G-BTDA	Slingsby T.61G Falke	RAFGSA/Bicester	
G-BTDC	Denney Kitfox	D. Collinson	
G-BTDD	CFM Streak Shadow	S. J. Evans	
G-BTDE	Cessna C-165 Airmaster	G. S. Moss	
G-BTDF	Luscombe 8A Silvaire	M. Stow	
G-BTDH	P.56 Provost T.1 (WV666)	Pulsegrove Ltd/Shoreham	
G-BTDI	Robinson R-22B	R. L. Moody/Denham	
G-BTDK	Cessna 421C	RK Carbon Fibre Ltd/Manchester	
G-BTDN	Denney Kitfox	Foxy Flyers Group	
G-BTDP	TBM-3R Avenger (53319)	A. Haig-Thomas/North Weald	
G-BTDR	Aero Designs Pulsar	R. M. Hughes	
G-BTDS	Colt 77A balloon	C. P. Witter Ltd	
G-DTDT	C.A.S.A. 1.131E Jungmann 2000	T. A. Reed	
G-BTDV	PA-28-161 Warrior II	R. E. Thorne	
G-BTDW	Cessna 152 II	J. A. Blenkharn/Carlisle	
G-BTDX	PA-18 Super Cub 150	Cubair Ltd/Redhill	
G-BTDY	PA-18 Super Cub 150	Rodger Aircraft Ltd	
G-BTDZ	C.A.S.A. 1.131E Jungmann 2000	R. J. Pickin & I. M. White	
G-BTEA	Cameron N-105 balloon	Southern Balloon Group	

Notes	Reg.	Type	Owner or Operator
	G-BTEE	Cameron O-120 balloon	W. H. & J. P. Morgan
	G-BTEF	Pitts S-1 Special	Northwest Aerobatics
	G-BTEI	Everett Srs 3 gyroplane	D. G. H. Oswald
	G-BTEK	SOCATA TB.20 Trinidad	D. F. Fagan/Booker
	G-RTEL	CFM Streak Shadow	J. E. Eatwell
	G-BTEO	Cameron V-90 balloon	Cameron Balloons Ltd
	G-BTEP	Cameron DP-80 airship	Cameron Balloons Ltd
	G-BTES	Cessna 150H	Takecare Aviation Ltd/Elstree
	G-BTEU	SA.365N-2 Dauphin	Bond Helicopters Ltd
	G-BTEV	PA-38-112 Tomahawk	Cardiff Aeronautical Services Ltd
	G-BTEW	Cessna 120	D. J. Carter/Little Snoring
	G-BTEX	PA-28 Cherokee 140	McAully Flying Group Ltd/Little Snoring
	G-BTFA	Denney Kitfox Mk 2	K. R. Peek
	G-BTFB	Cameron DG-14 airship	Cameron Balloons Ltd
	G-BTFC	Cessna F.152 II	Tayside Aviation Ltd
	G-BTFD	Colt AS-105 airshiip Mk II	Media Fantasy Aviation UK Ltd
	G-BTFE	Bensen-Parsons 2-seat gyroplane	I. Brewster
	G-BTFF	Cessna T.310R II	Rajmech Ltd
	G-BTFG	Boeing Stearman A.75N1 (441)	S. J. Ellis
	G-BTFJ	PA-15 Vagabond	K. G. Day
	G-BTFK	Taylorcraft BC-12D	D. J. S. McLean
	G-BTFL	Aeronca 11AC Chief	BTFL Group
	G-BTFM	Cameron O-105 balloon	Edinburgh University Hot Air Balloon Club
	G-BTFN	Beech F33C Bonanza	Robert Hinton Design & Creative Communications Ltd
	G-BTFO	PA-28-161 Warrior II	Flyfar Ltd
	G-BTFP	PA-38-112 Tomahawk	Teesside Flight Centre Ltd
	G-BTFR	Colt AS-105 airship	Heather Flight Ltd
	G-BTFS	Cessna A.150M	Bobbington Air Training School Ltd
	G-BTFT	Beech 58 Baron	Roseberry Management Ltd
	G-BTFU	Cameron N-90 balloon	J. J. Rudoni & A. C. K. Rawson
	G-BTFV	Whittaker MW.7	S. J. Luck
	G-BTFW	Montgomerie-Bensen B.8MR	A. Mansfield
	G-BTFX	Bell 206B JetRanger 2	J. Selwyn Smith (Shepley) Ltd
	G-BTFY	Bell 206B JetRanger 2	Northern Helicopters (Leeds) Ltd
	G-BTGA	Boeing Stearman A.751N1	J. C. Lister
	G-BTGC	PA-38-112 Tomahawk	T. Hayselden
	G-BTGD	Rand-Robinson KR-2	D. W. Mullin
	G-BTGG	Rans S.10 Sakota	A. R. Cameron
	G-BTGH	Cessna 152 II	R. S. Trayhurn & P. D. Myson
	G-BTGI	Rearwin 175 Skyranger	A. H. Hunt/St Just
	G-BTGJ	Smith DSA-1 Miniplane	G. J. Knowles
	G-BTGK	PA-28-161 Warrior II	S. Dorrington
	G-BTGL	Light Aero Avid Flyer	A. F. Vizoso
	G-BTGM	Aeronca 7AC Champion	G. Gregg
	G-BTGN	Cessna 310R	Air Service Training Ltd/Perth
	G-BTGO	PA-28 Cherokee 140	Rankart Ltd
	G-BTGP	Cessna 150M	Billins Air Service Ltd
	G-BTGR	Cessna 152 II	A. J. Gomes
	G-BTGS	Stolp SA.300 Starduster Too	T. G. Solomon (G-AYMA)/Shoreham
	G-BTGT	CFM Streak Shadow	N. L. Howard (G-MWPY)
	G-BTGU	PA-34-220T Seneca III	Carill Aviation Ltd
	G-BTGV	PA-34-200T Seneca II	MS 124 Ltd
	G-BTGW	Cessna 152 II	Stapleford Flying Club Ltd
	G-BTGX	Cessna 152 II	Stapleford Flying Club Ltd
	G-BTGY	PA-28-161 Warrior II	Stapleford Flying Club Ltd
	G-BTGZ	PA-28-181 Archer II	Allzones Travel Ltd/Biggin Hill
	G-BTHA	Cessna 182P	N. J. Douglas
	G-BTHD	Yakovlev Yak-3U	Patina Ltd/Duxford
	G-BTHE	Cessna 150L	Humberside Police Flying Club
	G-BTHF	Cameron V-90 balloon	N. J. & S. J. Langley
	G-BTHH	Jodel DR.100A	H. R. Leefe
	G-BTHI	Robinson R-22B	R. Bean Commercial Vehicles
	G-BTHJ	Evans VP-2	C. J. Moseley
	G-BTHK	Thunder Ax7-77 balloon	M. J. Chandler
	G-BTHM	Thunder Ax8-105 balloon	Anglia Balloons
	G-BTHN	Murphy Renegade 912	F. A. Purvis
	G-BTHP	Thorp T.211	M. Gardner
	G-BTHR	SOCATA TB.10 Tobago	Hydrodiesel Ltd
	G-BTHU	Light Aero Avid Flyer	M. Morris
	G-BTHW	Beech F33C Bonanza	Robin Lance Aviation Associates Ltd
	G-BTHX	Colt 105A balloon	R. Ollier
	G-BTHY	Bell 206B JetRanger 3	J. W. Sandle

Reg.	Type	Owner or Operator	Notes
G-BTHZ	Cameron V-56 balloon	C. N. Marshall	
G-BTIA	BAe 146-200QC	British Aerospace PLC (G-PRIN)/Woodford	
G-BTIC	PA-22 Tri-Pacer 150	T. Richards & G. C. Winters	
G-BTID	PA-28-161 Warrior II	Plymouth School of Flying Ltd	
G-BTIE	SOCATA TB.10 Tobago	India Echo Group	
G-BTIF	Denney Kitfox Mk 3	C. R. Thompson	
G-BTIG	Montgomerie-Bensen B.8MR	P. Crawley	
G-BTIH	PA-28-151 Warrior	MPM Aviation	
G-BTII	AA-5B Tiger	B. D. Greenwood	
G-BTIJ	Luscombe 8E Silvaire	S. J. Hornsby	
G-BTIK	Cessna 152 II	B. R. Pearson/Eaglescott	
G-BTIL	PA-38-112 Tomahawk	B. R. Pearson/Eaglescott	
G-BTIM	PA-28-161 Cadet	Mid-Sussex Timber Co Ltd	
G-BTIN	Cessna 150C	Cormack (Aircraft Services) Ltd	
G-BTIO	SNCAN Stampe SV-4C	L. J. & A. A. Rice	
G-BTIP	Denney Kitfox Mk 3	P. A. Hardy	
G-BTIR	Denney Kitfox Mk 2	M. Stevenson	
G-BTIS	AS.355F-1 Twin Squirrel	Walsh Aviation (G-TALI)	
G-BTIU	M.S.892A Rallye Commodore 150	W. H. Cole	
G-BTIV	PA-28-161 Warrior II	Warrior Group/Eaglescott	
G-BTIX	Cameron V-77 balloon	S. A. Simington	
G-BTIZ	Cameron A-105 balloon	A. G. E. Faulkner	
G-BTJA	Luscombe 8E Silvaire	M. W. & L. M. Rudkin	
G-BTJB	Luscombe 8E Silvaire	M. Loxton	
G-BTJC	Luscombe 8F Silvaire	S. C. & M. Goddard	
G-BTJD	Thunder Ax8-90 balloon	T. C. Restell	
G-BTJE	Hiller UH-12E4	T. J. Clark	
G-BTJF	Thunder Ax10-180 balloon	Airborne Adventures Ltd	
G-BTJH	Cameron O-77 balloon	H. Stringer	
G-BTJJ	PA-38-112 Tomahawk	Deltair Ltd/Liverpool	
G-BTJK	PA-38-112 Tomahawk	Western Air Training Ltd/Thruxton	
G-BTJL	PA-38-112 Tomahawk	W. C. Cowie	
G-BTJN	Montgomerie-Bensen B.8MR	A. Hamilton	
G-BTJO	Thunder Ax9-140 balloon	Abbey Plant Co Ltd	
G-BTJS	Montgomerie-Bensen B.8MR	T. C. & P. K. Jackson	
G-BTJU	Cameron V-90 balloon	C. W. Jones (Floorings) Ltd	
G-BTJV	PZL SZD-50-3 Puchacz	Kent Gliding Club Ltd/Challock	
G-BTJX	Rans S.10 Sakota	M. Goacher	
G-BTKA	Piper J-5A Cub Cruiser	S. J. Rudkin	
G-BTKB	Renegade Spirit 912	G. S. Blundell	
G-BTKD	Denney Kitfox Mk 4	J. F. White	
G-BTKG	Light Aero Avid Flyer	D. S. Posner	
G-BTKI	NA T-6G Texan	P. S. & S. M. Warner	
G-BTKL	MBB Bo 105DB-4	Veritair Ltd/Halfpenny Green	
G-BTKN	Cameron O-120 balloon	The Ballooning Business Ltd	
G-BTKP	CFM Streak Shadow	G. D. Martin	
G-BTKS	Rans S.10 Sakota	J. R. I. Rolfe & ptnrs	
G-BTKT	PA-28-161 Warrior II	Eastern Executive Air Charter Ltd	
G-BTKU	Cameron A-105 balloon	S. Bedir	
G-BTKV	PA-22 Tri-Pacer 160	M. Hanna	
G-BTKW	Cameron O-105 balloon	P. Spellward	
G-BTKX	PA-28-181 Archer II	Symtec Computers Ltd	
G-BTKY	PA-28-181 Archer II	Primark Enterprises Ltd	
G-BTKZ	Cameron V-77 balloon	S. P. Richards	
G-BTLA	Sikorsky S-76B	Falcon of Friendship Ltd	
G-BTLB	Wassmer WA.52 Europa	M. D. O'Brien/Shoreham	
G-BTLC	SA.365N2 Dauphin 2	Bond Helicopters Ltd	
G-BTLE	PA-31-350 Navajo Chieftain	Boal Air Services (UK) Ltd	
G-BTLG	PA-28R Cherokee Arrow 200	A. P. Reilly	
G-BTLM	PA-22 Tri-Pacer 160	F & H (Aircraft) Ltd	
G-BTLP	AA-1C Lynx	Partlease Ltd	
G-BTMA	Cessna 172N	East of England Flying Group Ltd	
G-BTMF	Taylorcraft BC-12D	C. M. Churchill/Cambridge	
G-BTMH	Colt 90A balloon	Douwe Egberts UK Ltd	
G-BTMJ	Maule MX-7-180	C. M. McGill	
G-BTMK	Cessna R.172K XP	S. P. & A. C. Barker	
G-BTML	Cameron 90 Rupert Bear SS balloon	Flying Pictures (Balloons) Ltd	
G-BTMM	Cameron N-105 balloon	M. F. Glue	
G-BTMN	Thunder Ax9-120 S2 balloon	Canterbury Balloons	
G-BTMO	Colt 69A balloon	Thunder & Colt	
G-BTMP	Everett Srs 2 gyroplane	P. W. McLaughlin	

Notes	Reg.	Type	Owner or Operator
	G-BTMR	Cessna 172M	Cumbria Aero Club/Carlisle
	G-BTMS	Light Aero Avid Flyer	M. J. Schyns
	G-BTMT	Denney Kitfox	Skulk Flying Group
	G-BTMV	Everett Srs 2 gyroplane	L. Armes
	G BTMW	Zenair CI I.701 STOL	L. Lewls
	G-BTMX	Denney Kitfox Mk 3	C. D. Weiswall
	G-BTMY	Cameron 80 Train SS balloon	Cameron Balloons Ltd
	G-BTMZ	PA-38-112 Tomahawk	T. Drew
	G-BTNA	Robinson R-22B	MG Group Ltd
	G-BTNB	Robinson R-22B	Davron Aviation
	G-BTNC	AS.365N-2 Dauphin 2	Bond Helicopters Ltd
	G-BTND	PA-38-112 Tomahawk	S. P. Warsop
	G-BTNE	PA-28-161 Warrior II	A. T. Hooper & T. E. Evans/Wellesbourne
	G-BTNH	PA-28-161 Warrior II	Cardiff Aeronautical Services Ltd
	G-BTNJ	Cameron V-90 balloon	P. L. Harrison & B. J. Newman
	G-BTNL	Thunder Ax10-180 balloon	Adventure Balloon Co Ltd
	G-BTNO	Aeronca 7AC Champion	November Oscar Group/Netherthorpe
	G-BTNP	Light Aero Avid Flyer Commuter	N. Evans
	G-BTNR	Denney Kitfox Mk 3	J. W. G. Ellis
	G-BTNS	PZL-104 Wilga 80	R. W. Husband
	G-BTNT	PA-28-151 Warrior	Britannia Airways Ltd/Luton
	G-BTNU	BAe 146-300	British Aerospace (G-BSLS)
	G-BTNV	PA-28-161 Warrior II	D. K. Oakeley & A. M. Dawson
	G-BTNW	Rans S.6-ESA Coyote II	A. F. Stafford
	G-BTNX	Colt 105A balloon	Gone With The Wind Ltd
	G-BTNZ	AS.332L-1 Super Puma	British International Helicopters
	G-BTOA	Mong Sport MS-2	G. Gilding
	G-BTOC	Robinson R-??B	Heli Air Ltd
	G-BTOD	PA-38-112 Tomahawk	V. F. & J. A. Shirley
	G-BTOG	D.H.82A Tiger Moth	P. T. Szluha
	G-BTOI	Cameron N-77 balloon	The Nestle Co Ltd
	G-BTOJ	Mooney M.10 Cadet	D. W. Vernon
	G-BTOL	Denney Kitfox Mk 3	C. R. Phillips
	G-BTON	PA-28 Cherokee 140	W. A. & K. C. Ryan
	G-BTOO	Pitts S-1C Special	G. H. Matthews
	G-BTOP	Cameron V-77 balloon	J. J. Winter
	G-BTOR	Lancair 320	R. W. Fairless
	G-BTOS	Cessna 140	J. L. Kaiser
	G-BTOT	PA-15 Vagabond	D. Harker
	G-BTOU	Cameron O-120 balloon	R. St. J. Gillespie
	G-BTOW	SOCATA Rallye 180GT	Cambridge University Gliding Trust Ltd
	G-BTOZ	Thunder Ax9-120 S2 balloon	H. G. Davies
	G-BTPA	BAe ATP	British Airways *Strathallan*/Glasgow
	G-BTPB	Cameron N-105 balloon	Test Valley Balloon Group
	G-BTPC	BAe ATP	British Airways *Strathblane*/Glasgow
	G-BTPD	BAe ATP	British Airways *Strathconon*/Glasgow
	G-BTPE	BAe ATP	British Airways *Strathdon*/Glasgow
	G-BTPF	BAe ATP	British Airways *Strathearn*/Glasgow
	G-BTPG	BAe ATP	British Airways *Strathfillan*/Glasgow
	G-BTPH	BAe ATP	British Airways *Strathnaver*/Glasgow
	G-BTPJ	BAe ATP	British Airways *Strathpeffer*/Glasgow
	G-BTPK	BAe ATP	British Airways/Glasgow
	G-BTPL	BAe ATP	British Airways/Glasgow
	G-BTPM	BAe ATP	British Airways/Glasgow
	G-BTPN	BAe ATP	British Airways/Glasgow
	G-BTPO	BAe ATP	British Airways/Glasgow
	G-BTPT	Cameron N-77 balloon	Derbyshire Building Soc
	G-BTPV	Colt 90A balloon	Virgin Airship & Balloon Co Ltd
	G-BTPX	Thunder Ax8-90 balloon	J. L. Guy
	G-BTPZ	Isaacs Fury II	M. A. Farrelly
	G-BTRB	Colt Mickey Mouse SS balloon	Benedikt Haggeney GmbH
	G-BTRC	Light Aero Avid Speedwing	B. Williams
	G-BTRE	Cessna F.172H	Hero Aviation/Stapleford
	G-BTRF	Aero Designs Pulsar	C. Smith
	G-BTRG	Aeronca 65C Super Chief	H. J. Cox
	G-BTRH	Aeronca 7AC Champion	D. W. Leach
	G-BTRI	Aeronca 11CC Super Chief	H. J. Cox
	G-BTRK	PA-28-161 Warrior II	Stapleford Flying Club Ltd
	G-BTRL	Cameron N-105 balloon	J. Lippett
	G-BTRN	Thunder Ax9-120 S2 balloon	Solar Communications Ltd
	G-BTRO	Thunder Ax8-90 balloon	Capital Balloon Club Ltd
	G-BTRP	Hughes 369E	P. C. Shann
	G-BTRR	Thunder Ax7-77 balloon	S. M. Roberts

Reg.	Type	Owner or Operator	Notes
G-BTRS	PA-28-161 Warrior II	Tyberry Aviation	
G-BTRT	PA-28R Cherokee Arrow 200-II	C. E. Yates	
G-BTRU	Robin DR.400/180	R. & M. Engineering Ltd	
G-BTRW	Slingsby T.61F Venture T.2	B. Kerby & G. Grainer	
G-BTRX	Cameron V-77 balloon	R. P. Jones & N. P.Hemsley	
G-BTRY	PA-28-161 Warrior II	Air Service Training Ltd/Perth	
G-BTRZ	Jodel D.18	R. M. Johnson & R. Collin	
G-BTSA	Cessna 150K	M. E. Bartlett	
G-BTSB	Corben Baby Ace D	D. G. Kelly	
G-BTSC	Evans VP-2	T. Blakeney	
G-BTSD	Midget Mustang	R. Fitzpatrick	
G-BTSE	—	—	
G-BTSI	BAe 125-1000	Shell Aircraft Ltd/Heathrow	
G-BTSJ	PA-28-161 Warrior II	Plymouth School of Flying Ltd	
G-BTSK	Beech F33C Bonanza	Jetwing Ltd/White Waltham	
G-BTSL	Cameron 70 Glass SS balloon	M. R. Humphrey & J. R .Clifton	
G-BTSM	Cessna 180A	C. Couston	
G-BTSN	Cessna 150G	N. A. Bilton/Norwich	
G-BTSP	Piper J-3C-65 Cub	J. A. Walshe & A. Corcoran	
G-BTSR	Aeronca 11AC Chief	P. A. Wensak	
G-BTST	Bensen B.9	V. Scott	
G-BTSU	Bensen B.8MR	B. T. Goggin	
G-BTSV	Denney Kitfox Mk 3	D. J. Sharland	
G-BTSW	Colt AS-80 Mk II airship	Huntair Ltd	
G-BTSX	Thunder Ax7-77 balloon	C. Moris-Gallimore	
G-BTSY	EE Lightning F.6 (XR724)	Lightning Association	
G-BTSZ	Cessna 177A	K. D. Harvey	
G-BTTA	Hawker Sea Fury FB.10 (243)	Classic Aviation Ltd/Duxford	
G-BTTB	Cameron V-90 balloon	Royal Engineers Balloon Club	
G-BTTD	Montgomerie-Bensen B.8MR	P. A. Howell	
G-BTTE	Cessna 150L	A. Watson	
G-BTTH	Beech F33C Bonanza	Bonanza Flying Group	
G-BTTI	Thunder Ax8-90 balloon	Capital Balloon Club Ltd	
G-BTTJ	Thunder Ax9-120 S2 balloon	G. D. & L. Fitzpatrick	
G-BTTK	Thunder Ax8-105 balloon	Tempowish Ltd	
G-BTTL	Cameron V-90 balloon	A. J. Baird	
G-BTTO	BAe ATP	Trident Aviation Leasing Services Ltd (G-OEDE)	
G-BTTP	BAe 146-300	Air UK Ltd/Stansted	
G-BTTR	Aerotek Pitts S-2A Special	Ebork Ltd	
G-BTTS	Colt 77A balloon	Rutland Balloon Club	
G-BTTV	Schweizer 269C	Helisport Ltd/Biggin Hill	
G-BTTW	Thunder Ax7-77 balloon	J. Kenny	
G-BTTY	Denney Kitfox Mk 2	K. J. Fleming	
G-BTTZ	Slingsby T.61F Venture T.2	I. R. F. Hammond	
G-BTUA	Slingsby T.61F Venture T.2	M. W. Olliver	
G-BTUB	Yakovlev C.11	M. G. & J. R. Jefferies	
G-BTUC	EMB-312 Tucano	Short Bros PLC/Belfast City	
G-BTUD	CFM Image	D. G. Cook (G-MWPV)	
G-BTUG	SOCATA Rallye 180T	Herefordshire Gliding Club Ltd/Shobdon	
G-BTUH	Cameron N-65 balloon	B. J. Godding	
G-BTUJ	Thunder Ax9-120 balloon	Humbug Balloon Group	
G-BTUK	Aerotek Pitts S-2A Special	Wickenby Aviation Ltd	
G-BTUL	Aerotek Pitts S-2A Special	C & S Aviation	
G-BTUM	Piper J-3C-65 Cub	G-BTUM Syndicate	
G-BTUN	Colt Flying Drinks Can SS balloon	BIAS UK Ltd	
G-BTUR	PA-18 Super Cub 95 (modified)	L-18 Syndicate	
G-BTUS	Whittaker MW.7	J. F. Bakewell	
G-BTUU	Cameron O-120 balloon	J. L. Guy	
G-BTUV	Aeronca A65TAC Defender	J. T. Ingrouille	
G-BTUW	PA-28-151 Warrior	F. Lennon	
G-BTUX	AS.365N-2 Dauphin 2	Bond Helicopters Ltd/Aberdeen	
G-BTUZ	American General AG-5B Tiger	Grocontinental Ltd/Tilstock	
G-BTVA	Thunder Ax7-77 balloon	C. E. Wood	
G-BTVB	Everett Srs 3 gyroplane	J. Pumford	
G-BTVC	Denney Kitfox Mk 2	P. Mitchell	
G-BTVE	Hawker Demon 1 (K8203)	Demon Displays Ltd	
G-BTVF	Hotorway Executive 90	E. P. Sadler	
G-BTVG	Cessna 140	V. C. Gover	
G-BTVH	Colt 77A balloon	D. N. & L. J. Close (G-ZADT/G-ZBCA)	
G-BTVR	PA-28 Cherokee 140	West of Scotland Flying Club Ltd	
G-BTVU	Robinson R-22B	A. Cortellini	
G-BTVV	Cessna FA.337G	B. Maddock	

Notes	Reg.	Type	Owner or Operator
	G-BTVW	Cessna 152 II	A. T. Hooper & T. E. Evans/Wellesbourne
	G-BTVX	Cessna 152 II	A. T. Hooper & T. E. Evans/Wellesbourne
	G-BTWB	Denney Kitfox Mk 3	J. E. Tootell (G-BTTM)
	G-BTWC	Slingsby T.61F Venture T.2	RAFGSA/Bicester
	G-BTWD	Slingsby T.61F Venture T.2	York Gliding Centre/Rufforth
	G-BTWE	Slingsby T.61F Venture T.2	RAFGSA/Bicester
	G-BTWF	D.H.C.1 Chipmunk 22	J. A. & V. G. Sims
	G-BTWI	EAA Acro Sport I	Detail Offers Ltd
	G-BTWJ	Cameron V-77 balloon	S. J. & J. A. Bellamy
	G-BTWK	Colt 210A balloon	Virgin Airship & Balloon Co Ltd
	G-BTWL	WAG-Aero Acro Sport Trainer	R. N. R. Bellamy/St Just
	G-BTWM	Cameron V-77 balloon	D. I. Gray-Fisk
	G-BTWN	Maule MXT-7-180	C. T. Rolls
	G-BTWP	Robinson R-22B	Sloane Helicopters Ltd/Sywell
	G-BTWR	Bell P-63A-7-BE Kingcobra (269097)	Patina Ltd/Duxford
	G-BTWS	Thunder Ax7-77 balloon	Bavarian Balloon Co Ltd
	G-BTWU	PA-22 Tri-Pacer 135	Prestige Air (Engineers) Ltd
	G-BTWV	Cameron O-90 balloon	Bodkin House Hotel
	G-BTWW	AB-206B JetRanger 2	PLM Dollar Group Ltd
	G-BTWX	SOCATA TB.9 Tampico	Nordic Property & Investments Ltd
	G-BTWY	Aero Designs Pulsar	J. J. Pridal
	G-BTWZ	Rans S.10 Sakota	D. G. Hey
	G-BTXB	Colt 77A balloon	Shellgas South West Area
	G-BTXC	Team Minimax	D. B. Almey (G-MWFC)
	G-BTXD	Rans S.6-ESA Coyote II	M. Isterling
	G-BTXF	Cameron V-90 balloon	Gone With The Wind Ltd
	G-BTXH	Colt AS-56 airship	Huntair Ltd
	G-BTXI	Noorduyn AT-16 Harvard IIB (FE695)	Patina Ltd/Duxford
	G-BTXM	Colt 21A balloon	Virgin Airship & Balloon Co Ltd
	G-BTXO	BAe 146-100	Trident Aviation Leasing Services Ltd
	G-BTXR	Cassutt Racer	S. N. Lester
	G-BTXS	Cameron O-120 balloon	Southern Balloon Group
	G-BTXT	Maule MXT-7-180	R. G. Humphries
	G-BTXV	Cameron A-210 balloon	The Ballooning Business Ltd
	G-BTXW	Cameron V-77 balloon	P. C. Waterhouse
	G-BTXX	Bellanca 8KCAB Decathlon	Sherwood Flying Club Ltd/Tollerton
	G-BTXZ	Zenair CH.250	B. F. Arnall
	G-BTYC	Cessna 150L	JJ Aviation
	G-BTYD	Cameron N-90 balloon	S. J. Colin
	G-BTYE	Cameron A-180 balloon	K. J. A. Maxwell & D. S. Messmer
	G-BTYF	Thunder Ax10-180 S2 balloon	P. Glydon
	G-BTYH	Pottier P.80S	R. Pickett
	G-BTYI	PA-28-181 Archer II	T. E. Westley
	G-BTYK	Cessna 310R	E. H. J. Moody
	G-BTYT	Cessna 152 II	M. J. Green
	G-BTYW	Cessna 120	P. J. Singleton & C. J. Archer
	G-BTYX	Cessna 140	G-BTYX Group
	G-BTYY	Curtiss Robin C-2	R. R. L. Windus
	G-BTYZ	Colt 210A balloon	T. M. Donnelly
	G-BTZA	Beech F33A Bonanza	G-BTZA Group/Edinburgh
	G-BTZB	Yakovlev Yak-50 (69)	J. S. Allison
	G-BTZD	Yakovlev Yak-1	Historic Aircraft Collection Ltd/Audley End
	G-BTZE	LET Yakovlev C.11	Bianchi Aviation Film Services Ltd/Booker
	G-BTZL	Oldfield Baby Lakes	J. M. Roach
	G-BTZN	BAe 146-300	British World Airlines Ltd/Stansted
	G-BTZO	SOCATA TB.20 Trinidad	Hydrodiesel Ltd
	G-BTZP	SOCATA TB.9 Tampico	Newcastle-upon-Tyne Aero Club Ltd
	G-BTZR	Colt 77B balloon	P. J. Fell
	G-BTZS	Colt 77A balloon	P. T. R. Ollivers
	G-BTZU	Cameron Concept SS balloon	Gone With The Wind Ltd
	G-BTZV	Cameron V-77 balloon	A. W. Sumner
	G-BTZX	Piper J-3C-65 Cub	D. A. Woodhams & J. T. Coulthard
	G-BTZY	Colt 56A balloon	T. M. Donnelly
	G-BTZZ	CFM Streak Shadow	D. R. StenneWtt
	G-BUAA	Corben Baby Ace D	B. F. Hill
	G-BUAB	Aeronca 11AC Chief	J. Reed
	G-BUAC	Slingsby T.31 Motor Cadet III	D. A. Wilson
	G-BUAF	Cameron N-77 balloon	S. J. Colin
	G-BUAG	Jodel D.18	A. L. Silcox
	G-BUAI	Everett Srs 3 gyroplane	P. Stanlake

Reg.	Type	Owner or Operator	Notes
G-BUAJ	Cameron N-90 balloon	J. R. & S. J. Huggins	
G-BUAK	Thunder Ax8-105 S2 balloon	G. D. & L. Fitzpatrick	
G-BUAM	Cameron V-77 balloon	Broadland Balloons Ltd	
G-BUAN	Cessna 172N	Bell Aviation	
G-BUAO	Luscombe 8A Silvaire	G. H. Matthews	
G-BUAR	V.S.358 Seafire LF.IIIc (PP972)	Wizzard Investments Ltd	
G-BUAT	Thunder Ax9-120 balloon	J. Fenton	
G-BUAU	Cameron A-180 balloon	Out Of This World Balloons	
G-BUAV	Cameron O-105 balloon	K. D. Johnson	
G-BUAW	Pitts S-1C Special	E. J. Hedges	
G-BUAX	Rans S.10 Sakota	J. W. Topham	
G-BUAY	Cameron A-210 balloon	Virgin Balloon Flights Ltd	
G-BUBA	PA-18 Super Cub 150 (modified)	B. Jackson	
G-BUBB	Light Aero Avid Flyer	D. Hookins	
G-BUBC	QAC Quickie Tri-Q.200	D. J. Clarke	
G-BUBL	Thunder Ax8-105 balloon	Moet & Chandon (London) Ltd	
G-BUBN	BN-2B-26 Islander	Isles of Scilly Skybus Ltd/St Just	
G-BUBO	BN-2B-26 Islander	Pilatus BN Ltd/Bembridge	
G-BUBR	Cameron A-250 balloon	Bath Hot-Air Balloon Club	
G-BUBS	Lindstrand LBL-77B balloon	B. J. Bower	
G-BUBT	Stoddard-Hamilton Glasair IIRGS	M. D. Evans	
G-BUBU	PA-34-220T Seneca III	Brinor (Holdings) Ltd/Ipswich	
G-BUBW	Robinson R-22B	Forth Helicopters/Edinburgh	
G-BUBY	Thunder Ax8-105 S2 balloon	T. M. Donnelly	
G-BUCA	Cessna A.150K	M. K. Shaw	
G-BUCB	Cameron H-34 balloon	Flying Pictures (Balloons) Ltd	
G-BUCC	C.A.S.A. 1.131E Jungmann 2000 (BU+CC)	R. A. Roberts (G-BUEM)/Shoreham	
G-BUCG	Schleicher ASW.20L (modified)	W. B. Andrews	
G-BUCH	Stinson V-77 Reliant	Pullmerit Ltd	
G-BUCI	Auster AOP.9 (XP242)	Historic Aircraft Flight Reserve Collection/ Middle Wallop	
G-BUCJ	D.H.C.2 Beaver 1 (XP772)	Historic Aircraft Flight Reserve Collection/ Middle Wallop	
G-BUCK	C.A.S.A. 1.131E Jungmann 1000 (BU+CK)	Jungmann Flying Group/White Waltham	
G-BUCM	Hawker Sea Fury FB.11 (VX653)	Patina Ltd/Duxford	
G-BUCO	Pietenpol Air Camper	A. James	
G-BUCS	Cessna 150F	A. Bucknole	
G-BUCT	Cessna 150L	A. Bucknole	
G-BUDA	Slingsby T.61F Venture T.2	RAF Germany Gliding Association	
G-BUDB	Slingsby T.61F Venture T.2	RAF Germany Gliding Association	
G-BUDC	Slingsby T.61F Venture T.2	D. Collinson	
G-BUDE	PA-22 Tri-Pacer 135 (tailwheel)	B. A. Bower/Thruxton	
G-BUDF	Rand-Robinson KR-2	J. B. McNab	
G-BUDH	Light Aero Avid Flyer	D. Cowen	
G-BUDI	Aero Designs Pulsar	R. W. L. Oliver	
G-BUDK	Thunder Ax7-77 balloon	W. Evans	
G-BUDL	Auster 3	M. Pocock	
G-BUDM	Colt Flying Hand SS balloon	BIAS (UK) Ltd	
G-BUDN	Cameron 90 Shoe SS balloon	L. Mastis	
G-BUDO	PZL-110 Koliber 150	A. S. Vine	
G-BUDR	Denney Kitfox Mk 3	N. J. P. Mayled	
G-BUDS	Rand-Robinson KR-2	D. W. Munday	
G-BUDT	Slingsby T.61F Venture T.2	G-BUDT Group	
G-BUDU	Cameron V-77 balloon	T. M. G. Amery	
G-BUDV	Cameron A-210 balloon	Balloonair SA	
G-BUDW	Brügger MB.2 Colibri	J. M. Hoblyn	
G-BUEA	Aérospatiale ATR-42-300	CityFlyer Express Ltd/British Airways	
G-BUEB	Aérospatiale ATR-42-300	CityFlyer Express Ltd/British Airways	
G-BUEC	Vans RV-6	D. W. Richardson & R. D. Harper	
G-BUED	Slingsby T.61F Venture T.2	SE Kent Civil Service Flying Club	
G-BUEE	Cameron A-210 balloon	Bristol Balloons	
G-BUEF	Cessna 152	Three Counties Aero Engineering Ltd/ Lasham	
G-BUEG	Cessna 152	Plymouth School of Flying Ltd	
G-BUEI	Thunder Ax8-105 balloon	Anglia Balloons	
G-BUEJ	Colt 77B balloon	P. M. Taylor	
G-BUEK	Slingsby T.61F Venture T.2	P. B. Duhig & W. Retzler	
G-BUEL	Colt Bottle 11 SS balloon	Jentime Ltd	
G-BUEN	VPM M.14 Scout	W. M. Day	
G-BUEO	Maule MX-7-180	K. & S. C. Knight	
G-BUEP	Maule MX-7-180	G. M. Bunn	

Notes	Reg.	Type	Owner or Operator
	G-BUES	Cameron N-77 balloon	Bath City Council – Parks Section
	G-BUET	Colt Flying Drinks Can SS balloon	Flying Pictures (Balloons) Ltd
	G-BUEU	Colt 21A balloon	Flying Pictures (Balloons) Ltd
	G-BUEV	Cameron O-77 balloon	Council for Positively Belfast
	G-BUEW	Rans S.6 Coyote II	D. J. O'Gorman (G-MWYF)
	G-BUEX	Schweizer 269C	Vic Lamb Aviation Ltd (G-HFLR)
	G-BUEZ	Hunter F.6A (XF375)	Old Flying Machine Co Ltd/Duxford
	G-BUFA	Cameron R-77 gas balloon	Noble Adventures Ltd
	G-BUFC	Cameron R-77 gas balloon	Noble Adventures Ltd
	G-BUFE	Cameron R-77 gas balloon	Noble Adventures Ltd
	G-BUFG	Slingsby T.61F Venture T.2	T. W. Eagles
	G-BUFH	PA-28-161 Warrior II	The Tiger Leisure Group
	G-BUFJ	Cameron V-90 balloon	Whitbread Hop Farm
	G-BUFL	BAe Jetstream 3101	Jetstream Aircraft Ltd/Prestwick
	G-BUFK	Cassutt Racer IIIM	D. I. H. Johnstone & W. T. Barnard
	G-BUFM	BAe Jetstream 3102	Air Swift Ltd (G-LAKH)/Stansted
	G-BUFN	Slingsby T.61F Venture T.2	BUFN Group
	G-BUFO	Cameron 70 UFO SS balloon	Virgin Airship & Balloon Co Ltd
	G-BUFP	Slingsby T.61F Venture T.2	Venture Group
	G-BUFR	Slingsby T.61F Venture T.2	R. F. Warren & P. A. Hazell
	G-BUFT	Cameron O-120 balloon	Prime Time Balloons Ltd
	G-BUFU	Colt 105A balloon	Basemore Ltd
	G-BUFV	Light Aero Avid Flyer	S. C. Ord
	G-BUFX	Cameron N-90 balloon	Kerridge Computer Co Ltd
	G-BUFY	PA-28-161 Warrior II	Bickertons Aerodromes Ltd
	G-BUGB	Stolp SA.750 Acroduster Too	D. Burnham
	G-BUGC	Jurca MJ.5 Sirocco	A. Burani (G-BWDJ)
	G-BUGD	Cameron V-77 balloon	Cameron Balloons Ltd
	G-BUGE	Bellanca 7GCAA Cltabria	Welsh Dragon Aviation Ltd
	G-BUGF	Cameron A-210 balloon	Adventure Ballooning
	G-BUGG	Cessna 150F	C. P. J. Taylor & D. M. Forshaw
	G-BUGH	Rans S.10 Sakota	D. T. Smith
	G-BUGI	Evans VP-2	R. G. Boyes
	G-BUGJ	Robin DR.400/180	Alfred Graham Ltd
	G-BUGL	Slnigsby T.61F Venture T.2	VMG Group
	G-BUGM	CFM Streak Shadow	The Shadow Group
	G-BUGN	Colt 210A balloon	Balloon Club of GB Ltd
	G-BUGO	Colt 56B balloon	D. W. & P. Allum
	G-BUGP	Cameron V-77 balloon	G. J. & R. Plant
	G-BUGS	Cameron V-77 balloon	A Load of Hot Air
	G-BUGT	Slingsby T.61F Venture T.2	J. F. R. Jones
	G-BUGV	Slingsby T.61F Venture T.2	The Gliding Centre/Edgehill
	G-BUGW	Slingsby T.61F Venture T.2	Rankart Ltd
	G-BUGX	M.S.880B Rallye Club	The Rallye Group
	G-BUGY	Cameron V-65 balloon	Dante Balloon Group
	G-BUGZ	Slingsby T.61F Venture T.2	Dishforth Flying Club
	G-BUHA	Slingsby T.61F Venture T.2	A. W. Swales
	G-BUHB	BAe 146-300	Eurowings/Germany
	G-BUHC	BAe 146-300	Air UK Ltd (G-BTMI)/Stansted
	G-BUHJ	Boeing 737-4Q8	British Airways/Gatwick
	G-BUHK	Boeing 737-4Q8	British Airways/Gatwick
	G-BUHL	Boeing 737-4S3	GB Airways Ltd/Gatwick
	G-BUHM	Cameron V-77 balloon	L. A. Watts
	G-BUHO	Cessna 140	CAW Corporation Ltd
	G-BUHP	Flyair 1100 balloon	R. White
	G-BUHR	Slingsby T.61F Venture T.2	Lleweni Parc Ltd
	G-BUHS	Stoddard-Hamilton Glasair SH-TD-1	S. J. Marsh
	G-BUHT	Cameron A-210 balloon	British School of Ballooning
	G-BUHU	Cameron N-105 balloon	Flying Pictures (Balloons) Ltd
	G-BUHX	Robinson R-22B	Seiont Construction
	G-BUHY	Cameron A-210 balloon	Adventure Balloon Co Ltd
	G-BUHZ	Cessna 120	C. P. & C. J. Wilkes
	G-BUIB	MBB Bo 105DBS/4	Bond Helicopters Ltd (G-BDYZ)
	G-BUIC	Denney Kitfox Mk 2	C. R. Northrop & B. M. Chilvers
	G-BUIE	Cameron N-90 balloon	Flying Pictures (Balloons) Ltd
	G-BUIF	PA-28-161 Warrior II	Newcastle-upon-Tyne Aero Club Ltd
	G-BUIG	Campbell Cricket (replica)	T. A. Holmes
	G-BUIH	Slingsby T.61F Venture T.2	Yorkshire Gliding Club (Pty) Ltd
	G-BUII	Cameron A-210 balloon	Aire Valley Balloons
	G-BUIJ	PA-28-161 Warrior II	Tradecliff Ltd
	G-BUIK	PA-28-161 Warrior II	I. H. Webb
	G-BUIL	CFM Streak Shadow	P. N. Bevan & L. M. Poor

Reg.	Type	Owner or Operator	Notes
G-BUIN	Thunder Ax7-77 balloon	Free Flight Aerostat Group	
G-BUIP	Denney Kitfox Mk 2	Avcomm Developments Ltd	
G-BUIR	Light Aero Avid Speedwing Mk 4	K. N. Pollard	
G-BUIU	Cameron V-90 balloon	Prescott Hot Air Balloons Ltd	
G-BUIW	Robinson R-22B	Findon Air Services/Shoreham	
G-BUIZ	Cameron N-90 balloon	Virgin Airship & Balloon Co Ltd	
G-BUJA	Slingsby T.61F Venture T.2	RAFGSA/Bicester	
G-BUJB	Slingsby T.61F Venture T.2	Falke Syndicate	
G-BUJE	Cessna 177B	FG93 Group	
G-BUJG	AS.350B-2 Ecureuil	R. J. & E. M. Frost (G-HEAR)	
G-BUJH	Colt 77B balloon	A. D. Watt & ptnrs	
G-BUJI	Slingsby T.61F Venture T.2	R. A. Boddy	
G-BUJJ	Light Aero Avid Flyer	A. C. Debrett	
G-BUJK	Montgomerie-Bensen B.8MR	J. M. Montgomerie	
G-BUJL	Aero Designs Pulsar	J. J. Lynch	
G-BUJM	Cessna 120	De Cadenet Engineering Ltd/Bickmarsh	
G-BUJN	Cessna 172N	De Cadenet Engineering Ltd/Coventry	
G-BUJO	PA-28-161 Warrior II	Rainsford Ltd	
G-BUJP	PA-28-161 Warrior II	De Cadenet Engineering Ltd/Coventry	
G-BUJR	Cameron A-180 balloon	W. I. Hooker & C. Parker	
G-BUJT	BAe Jetstream 3100	British Aerospace PLC/Prestwick	
G-BUJU	Cessna 150H	S. J. N. Robbie	
G-BUJV	Light Aero Avid Speedwing Mk 4	C. Thomas	
G-BUJW	Thunder Ax8-90 S2 balloon	R. T. Fagan	
G-BUJX	Slingsby T.61F Venture T.2	R. J. Chichester-Constable	
G-BUJY	D.H.82A Tiger Moth	Aero Vintage Ltd	
G-BUJZ	Rotorwÿay Executive 90	T. W. Aisthorpe & R. J. D. Crick	
G-BUKA	Fairchild SA227AC Metro III	Air Corbière Ltd/Coventry	
G-BUKB	Rans S.10 Sakota	M. K. Blatch & M. P. Lee	
G-BUKC	Cameron A-180 balloon	Cloud Nine Balloon Co	
G-BUKE	Boeing Stearman A.75N1	R. G. Rance (G-BRIP)	
G-BUKF	Denney Kitfox Mk 4	M. R. Crosland	
G-BUKG	Robinson R-22B	Heliair Ltd/Wellesbourne	
G-BUKH	D.31 Turbulent	J. S. Smith	
G-BUKI	Thunder Ax7-77 balloon	Adventures Aloft	
G-BUKK	Bucker Bu133C Jungmeister (U-80)	E. J. F. McEntee/White Waltham	
G-BUKN	PA-15 Vagabond	M. A. & A. M. Watts	
G-BUKO	Cessna 120	N. G. Abbott	
G-BUKP	Denney Kitfox Mk 2	T. D. Reid	
G-BUKR	M.S.880B Rallye Club 100T	G-BUKR Flying Group	
G-BUKS	Colt 77B balloon	R. & M. Bairstow	
G-BUKT	Luscombe 8A Silvaire	M. G. Talbot & J. N. Willshaw	
G-BUKU	Luscombe 8E Silvaire	F. G. Miskelly	
G-BUKX	PA-28-161 Warrior II	LNP Ltd	
G-BUKY	CCF Harvard IVM (52-8543)	P. R. Monk & A. H. Soper	
G-BUKZ	Evans VP-2	P. R. Farnell	
G-BULB	Thunder Ax7-77 balloon	Shiltons of Rothbury	
G-BULC	Light Aero Avid Flyer Mk 4	A. G. Batchelor	
G-BULD	Cameron N-105 balloon	S. J. Boxall	
G-BULE	Price TPB.2 balloon	A. G. R. Calder	
G-BULF	Colt 77A balloon	M. V. Farrant	
G-BULG	Vans RV-4	J. R. Ware	
G-BULH	Cessna 172N	B. R. Gaunt	
G-BULJ	CFM Steak Shadow	C. C. Brown	
G-BULK	Thunder Ax9-120 S2 balloon	Lindsay Marketing Associates	
G-BULL	SA Bulldog 120/128	J. D. Richardson	
G-BULM	Aero Designs Pulsar	J. Webb	
G-BULN	Colt 210A balloon	H. G. Davies	
G-BULO	Luscombe 8A Silvaire	G-BULO Flying Group/Andrewsfield	
G-BULP	Thunder Ax9-120 S2 balloon	Prescott Hot Air Balloons Ltd	
G-BULR	PA-28 Cherokee 140	R. & W. Wale (General Woodworks) Ltd	
G-BULT	Campbell Cricket	A. T. Pocklington	
G-BULW	Rans S.10 Sakota	V. G. Gale	
G-BULY	Light Aero Avid Flyer	D. R. Piercy	
G-BULZ	Denney Kitfox Mk 2	T. G. F. Trenchard	
G-BUMP	PA-28-181 Archer II	M. Dunlop	
G-BUNB	Slingsby T.61F Venture T.2	RAFGSA Cranwell Gliding Club	
C-BUNC	PZL-104 Wilga 35	Paravia Group	
G-BUND	PA-28RT-201T Turbo Arrow IV	Jenrick Ltd & A. Somerville	
G-BUNE	Colt Flying Drinks Can SS balloon	Pepsi Cola Overseas Ltd	
G-BUNF	Colt Flying Drinks Can SS balloon	Pepsi Cola Overseas Ltd	
G-BUNG	Cameron N-77 balloon	The Balloon Squad	

Notes	Reg.	Type	Owner or Operator
	G-BUNH	PA-28RT-201T Turbo Arrow IV	QA Communications Ltd
	G-BUNI	Cameron 90 Bunny SS balloon	Virgin Airship & Balloon Co Ltd
	G-BUNJ	Squarecraft SA.102-5 Cavalier	J. A. Smith
	G-BUNM	Denney Kitfox Mk 3	P. J. Carter
	G-BUNN	Whittaker MW.6-S Fat Boy Flyer	M. R. Grunwell
	G BUNO	Lancair 320	J. Softley
	G-BUNS	Cessna F.150K	R. W. H. Cole
	G-BUNV	Thunder Ax7-77 balloon	P. J. Waller
	G-BUNX	Cameron V-77 balloon	J. H. Bailey
	G-BUNZ	Thunder Ax10-180 S2 balloon	T. M. Donnelly
	G-BUOA	Whittaker MW.6-S Fat Boy Flyer	D. A. Izod
	G-BUOB	CFM Streak Shadow	A. M. Simmons
	G-BUOC	Cameron A-210 balloon	G. N. & K. A. Connolly
	G-BUOD	SE-5A (replica)	M. D. Waldron
	G-BUOE	Cameron V-90 balloon	Dusters & Co
	G-BUOF	D.62B Condor	K. Jones
	G-BUOI	PA-20 Pacer	A. Phillips
	G-BUOJ	Cessna 172N	Falcon Flying Services/Biggin Hill
	G-BUOK	Rans S.6-ESA Coyote II	M. Morris
	G-BUOL	Denney Kitfox Mk 3	J. G. D. Barbour
	G-BUON	Light Aero Avid Aerobat	I. A. J. Lappin
	G-BUOO	QAC Quickie Tri-Q.200	P. Crossman
	G-BUOP	Skycycle D.2 airship	G. E. Dorrington
	G-BUOR	C.A.S.A. 1.131E Jungmann 2000	M. J. Aherne
	G-BUOS	V.S.394 Spitfire FR.XVIII	A. J. Reynard & Park Avenue Investments Ltd
	G-BUOT	Colt 77A balloon	Thunder & Colt
	G-BUOW	Aero Designs Pulsar XP	RAE Bedford Flying Club
	G-BUOX	Cameron V-77 balloon	R. M. Pursey & C. M. Richardson
	G-BUOZ	Thunder Ax10-180 balloon	Ashleader Ltd
	G-BUPA	Rutan LongEz	G. J. Banfield
	G-BUPB	Stolp SA.300 Starduster Too	Summit Aviation Ltd/Shoreham
	G-BUPC	Rollason Beta B.2	C. A. Rolph
	G-BUPF	Bensen B.8R	G. M. Hobman
	G-BUPG	Cessna 180K	T. P. A. Norman
	G-BUPH	Colt 25A balloon	Wellfarrow Ltd
	G-BUPI	Cameron V-77 balloon	S. A. Masey (G-BOUC)
	G-BUPJ	Fournier RF-4D	M. R. Shelton
	G-BUPM	VPM M.16 Tandem Trainer	J. G. Erskine
	G-BUPN	PA-46-350P Malibu	K. Fletcher/Coventry
	G-BUPO	Zlin Z.526F Trener Master	P. J. Behr & F. Mendelssohn/France
	G-BUPP	Cameron V-42 balloon	T. M. Gilchrist
	G-BUPR	Jodel D.18	R. W. Burrows
	G-BUPS	Aérospatiale ATR-42-300	Titan Airways Ltd/Stansted
	G-BUPT	Cameron O-105 balloon	Chiltern Balloons
	G-BUPU	Thunder Ax7-77 balloon	R. C. Barkworth & D. G. Maguire
	G-BUPV	Great Lakes 2T-1A	R. J. Fray
	G-BUPW	Denney Kitfox Mk 3	D. Sweet
	G-BURA	Thunder Ax8-105 S2 balloon	Airship Shop Ltd
	G-BURD	Cessna F.172N	L. M. Bateman & Co Ltd/Halfpenny Green
	G-BURE	Jodel D.9	L. J. Kingsford
	G-BURF	Rand-Robinson KR-2	P. J. H. Moorhouse & B. L. Hewart
	G-BURG	Colt 77A balloon	S. J. Humphreys
	G-BURH	Cessna 150E	BURH Flying Group
	G-BURI	Enstrom F-28C	F. B. Holben
	G-BURK	Luscombe 8A Silvaire	M. Stow
	G-BURL	Colt 105A balloon	Scotia Balloons Ltd
	G-BURM	EE Canberra TT.18 (WJ680)	Mitchell Aircraft Ltd/North Weald
	G-BURN	Cameron O-120 balloon	I. Bentley
	G-BURP	Rotorway Executive 90	A. G. A. Edwards
	G-BURR	Auster AOP.9	R. P. D. Folkes
	G-BURS	Sikorsky S-76A	Lynton Aviation Ltd (G-OHTL)
	G-BURT	PA-28-161 Warrior II	I. P. Stockwell
	G-BURV	BAe 125 Srs 800B	Raytheon Corporate Jets Inc
	G-BURW	Light Aero Avid Speedwing	A. Charlton
	G-BURY	Cessna 152 II	M. L. Grunnill
	G-BURZ	Hawker Nimrod II (K3661)	Historic Aircraft Collection Ltd
	G-BUSB	Airbus A.320-111	British Airways *Island of Jersey*
	G-BUSC	Airbus A.320-111	British Airways
	G-BUSD	Airbus A.320-111	British Airways *Island of Mull*
	G-BUSE	Airbus A.320-111	British Airways *Isles of Scilly*
	G-BUSF	Airbus A.320-111	British Airways *Isle of Anglesey*
	G-BUSG	Airbus A.320-211	British Airways *Isle of Wight*

Reg.	Type	Owner or Operator	Notes
G-BUSH	Airbus A.320-211	British Airways *Isle of Jura*	
G-BUSI	Airbus A.320-211	British Airways *Isle of Anglesey*	
G-BUSJ	Airbus A.320-211	British Airways *Isle of Sark*	
G-BUSK	Airbus A.320-211	British Airways *Island of Guernsey*	
G-BUSN	Rotorway Executive 90	B. Seymour	
G-BUSR	Aero Designs Pulsar	S. S. Bateman & R. A. Watts	
G-BUSS	Cameron 90 Bus SS balloon	L. V. Mastis	
G-BUST	Lancair IV	C. C. Butt	
G-BUSV	Colt 105A balloon	M. N. J. Kirby	
G-BUSW	R. Commander 114	Costello Automotive Ltd/Biggin Hill	
G-BUSY	Thunder Ax6-56A balloon	M. E. Hooker	
G-BUSZ	Light Aero Avid Speedwing Mk 4	G. N. S. Farrant	
G-BUTA	C.A.S.A. 1.131E Jungmann 2000	K. D. Dunkerley	
G-BUTB	CFM Streak Shadow	F. A. H. Ashmead	
G-BUTC	Cyclone AX3/582	Cyclone Hovercraft Ltd (G-MYHO)	
G-BUTD	Vans RV-6	N. W. Beadle	
G-BUTE	Anderson EA-1 Kingfisher	T. Crawford (G-BRCK)	
G-BUTF	Aeronca 11AC Chief	N. J. Mortimore	
G-BUTG	Zenair CH.601HD	J. M. Scott	
G-BUTH	CEA DR.220 2+2	A. R. Norman	
G-BUTJ	Cameron O-77 balloon	A. J. A. Bubb	
G-BUTK	Murphy Rebel	D. Webb	
G-BUTL	PA-24 Comanche 250	D. Buttle (G-ARLB)/Blackbushe	
G-BUTM	Rans S.6-116 Coyote II	M. Rudd	
G-BUTN	MBB Bo 105DBS/4	Bond Helicopters Ltd (G-AZTI)	
G-BUTO	Pitts S-1 Special	J. M. Alexander	
G-BUTP	Bede BD-5G	Heather Flight Ltd	
G-BUTT	Cessna FA.150K	C. R. Guggenheim (G-AXSJ)	
G-BUTU	OA.7 Optica Srs 300	FLS Aerospace (Lovaux) Ltd/Bournemouth	
G-BUTV	OA.7 Optica Srs 300	FLS Aerospace (Lovaux) Ltd/Bournemouth	
G-BUTX	C.A.S.A. 1.133C Jungmeister	A. J. E. Smith & D. T. Kaberry	
G-BUTY	Brügger MB.2 Colibri	R. M. Lawday	
G-BUTZ	PA-28 Cherokee 180C	A. J. & J. M. Davis (G-DARL)	
G-BUUA	Slingsby T.67M Mk II	Hunting Aircraft Ltd/Topcliffe	
G-BUUB	Slingsby T.67M Mk II	Hunting Aircraft Ltd/Topcliffe	
G-BUUC	Slingsby T.67M Mk II	Hunting Aircraft Ltd/Topcliffe	
G-BUUD	Slingsby T.67M Mk II	Hunting Aircraft Ltd/Topcliffe	
G-BUUE	Slingsby T.67M Mk II	Hunting Aircraft Ltd/Topcliffe	
G-BUUF	Slingsby T.67M Mk II	Hunting Aircraft Ltd/Topcliffe	
G-BUUG	Slingsby T.67M Mk II	Hunting Aircraft Ltd/Topcliffc	
G-BUUI	Slingsby T.67M Mk II	Hunting Aircraft Ltd/Topcliffe	
G-BUUJ	Slingsby T.67M Mk II	Hunting Aircraft Ltd/Topcliffe	
G-BUUK	Slingsby T.67M Mk II	Hunting Aircraft Ltd/Topcliffe	
G-BUUL	Slingsby T.67M Mk II	Hunting Aircraft Ltd/Topcliffe	
G-BUUM	PA-28RT-201 Arrow IV	Bluebird Flying Group	
G-BUUN	Lindstrand LBL-105A balloon	Flying Pictures (Balloons) Ltd	
G-BUUO	Cameron N-90 balloon	Bryan Brois Ltd	
G-BUUP	BAe ATP	Manx Airlines Ltd	
G-BUUS	Skyraider gyroplane	Sycamore Aviation Ltd	
G-BUUT	Interavia 70TA	Aero Vintage Ltd	
G-BUUU	Cameron 77 Bottle SS balloon	United Distillers UK Ltd	
G-BUUV	Lindstrand LBL-77A balloon	Virgin Airship & Balloon Co Ltd	
G-BUUX	PA-28 Cherokee 180D	Aero Group 78/Netherthorpe	
G-BUVA	PA-22 Tri-Pacer 135	Oaksey VA Group	
G-BUVB	Colt 77A balloon	T. L. Regan	
G-BUVE	Colt 77B balloon	M. P. & M. Nicholson	
G-BUVF	D.H.C.2 Beaver 1	DSG (Guernsey) Ltd	
G-BUVG	Cameron N-56 balloon	Cameron Balloons Ltd	
G-BUVH	Cameron Dragon SS balloon	Cameron Balloons Ltd	
G-BUVI	Colt 210A balloon	R. S. Hunjan	
G-BUVK	Cameron A-210 balloon	British School of Ballooning	
G-BUVL	Fisher Super Koala	A. D. Malcolm	
G-BUVM	CEA DR.250/160	G. G. Milton	
G-BUVN	C.A.S.A. 1.131E Jungmann	DSG (Guernsey) Ltd	
G-BUVO	Cessna F.182P	BUVO Group (G-WTFA)/Southend	
G-BUVP	C.A.S.A. 1.131E Jungmann	DSG (Guernsey) Ltd	
G-BUVR	Christen A.1 Husky	L. L. Bowman	
G-BUVS	Colt 77A balloon	Supergas Ltd	
G-BUVT	Colt 77A balloon	Supergas Ltd	
G-BUVW	Cameron N-90 balloon	Bristol Balloon Fiestas Ltd	
G-BUVX	CFM Streak Shadow	G. K. R. Linney	
G-BUVZ	Thunder Ax10-180 S2 balloon	Lakeside Lodge Balloon Rides (Cambridgeshire) Ltd	

Notes	Reg.	Type	Owner or Operator
	G-BUWA	V.S.349 Spitfire Vc (AR614)	Classic Aviation Ltd/Duxford
	G-BUWE	SE-5A (replica) (C9533)	D. Biggs
	G-BUWF	Cameron N-105 balloon	R. E. Jones
	G-BUWH	Parsons 2-seat gyroplane	R. V. Brunskill
	G-BUWI	Lindstrand LBL-77A balloon	Capital Balloon Club Ltd
	G-BUWJ	Pitts S-1C Special	D. I. Cooke
	G-BUWK	Rans S.6-116 Coyote II	R. Warriner
	G-BUWL	Piper J-4A Cub Coupé	V. F. Kemp
	G-BUWM	BAe ATP	Jetstream Aircraft Ltd/Prestwick
	G-BUWN	Lindstrand LBL-180A balloon	Lindstrand Balloons Ltd
	G-BUWO	Lindstrand LBL-240A balloon	Lindstrand Balloons Ltd
	G-BUWP	BAe ATP	British Airways
	G-BUWR	CFM Streak Shadow	T. Harvey
	G-BUWS	Denney Kitfox Mk 2	J. E. Brewis
	G-BUWT	Rand-Robinson KR-2	C. M. Coombe
	G-BUWU	Cameron V-77 balloon	M. J. Newman
	G-BUWV	CFM Streak Shadow	J. Morris
	G-BUWW	Cameron O-105 balloon	M. T. Evans
	G-BUWY	Cameron V-77 balloon	C. Dunseath
	G-BUWZ	Robin HR.200/120B	A. Cox
	G-BUXA	Colt 210A balloon	R. S. Hunjan
	G-BUXB	Sikorsky S-76A	Air Hanson Ltd
	G-BUXC	CFM Streak Shadow	J. Hosier
	G-BUXD	Maule MXT-7-160	A. R. Binnington
	G-BUXE	Cameron A-250 balloon	B. J. Petteford
	G-BUXG	Glaser-Dirks DG.400	J. J. Mason
	G-BUXI	Steen Skybolt	M. Frankland
	G-BUXJ	Slingsby T.61F Venture T.2	XIX Crawley Flying Club
	G-BUXK	Pietenpol Air Camper	G. R. G. Smith
	G-BUXL	Taylor JT.1 Monoplane	M. W. Elliott
	G-BUXM	QAC Quickie Q.2	A. J. Ross & D. Ramwell
	G-BUXN	Beech C23 Sundowner	Private Pilots Syndicate
	G-BUXO	Pober P-9 Pixie	P-9 Flying Group
	G-BUXP	Falcon XPS	J. C. & B. E. Greenslade
	G-BUXR	Cameron A-250 balloon	Celebration Balloon Flights
	G-BUXS	MBB Bo 105DBS/4	Bond Helicopters Ltd (G-PASA/G-BGWP)
	G-BUXT	Dornier Do.228-202K	Suckling Airways Ltd/Cambridge
	G-BUXU	Beech D.17S	S. J. Ellis
	G-BUXV	PA-22 Tri-Pacer 160 (tailwheel)	Bogavia Two
	G-BUXW	Thunder Ax8-90 S2 balloon	C. W. Brown
	G-BUXX	PA-17 Vagabond	R. H. Hunt
	G-BUXY	PA-25 Pawnee 235	Bath, Wilts & North Dorset Gliding Club Ltd
	G-BUXZ	Yakovlev Yak-3U	Old Flying Machine Co/Duxford
	G-BUYA	Lindstrand LBL-77A balloon	Lindstrand Balloons Ltd
	G-BUYB	Aero Designs Pulsar	A. P. Fenn
	G-BUYC	Cameron 80 Concept balloon	P. J. Dorward
	G-BUYD	Thunder Ax8-90 balloon	Anglia Balloons
	G-BUYE	Aeronca 7AC Champion	R. Mazey
	G-BUYF	Falcon XP	J. C. Greenslade
	G-BUYG	Colt 12 Flying Bottle SS balloon	United Distillers PLC
	G-BUYH	Cameron A-210 balloon	Newbury Ballooning Co & Land Securities Properties Ltd
	G-BUYI	Thunder Ax7-77 balloon	Chelmsford Management Ltd
	G-BUYJ	Lindstrand LBL-105A balloon	D. Briggs
	G-BUYK	Denney Kitfox Mk 4	R. D. L. Mayes
	G-BUYL	RAF 2000 gyroplane	Newtownair Gyroplanes Ltd
	G-BUYM	Thunder Ax8-105 balloon	Scotair Balloons
	G-BUYN	Cameron O-84 balloon	J. T. L. Challenger
	G-BUYO	Colt 77A balloon	J. Deans
	G-BUYR	Mooney M.20C	C. R. Weldon
	G-BUYS	Robin DR.400/180	F. A. Spear
	G-BUYT	Ken Brock KB-2 gyroplane	J. E. Harris
	G-BUYU	Bowers Fly-Baby 1A	J. A. Nugent
	G-BUYY	PA-28 Cherokee 180	Global Trading Aviation Services Ltd
	G-BUZA	Denney Kitfox Mk 3	R. Hill
	G-BUZB	Aero Designs Pulsar XP	M. J. Whatley
	G-BUZC	Everett Srs 3A gyroplane	M. P. L'Hermette
	G-BUZD	AS.332L Super Puma	Brintel Helicopters Ltd
	G-BUZE	Light Aero Avid Speedwing	N. L. E. & R. A. Dupee
	G-BUZF	Colt 77B balloon	I. J. Jackson
	G-BUZG	Zenair CH.601HD	N. C. White
	G-BUZH	Aero Designs Star-Lite SL-1	R. J. W. Wood

Reg.	Type	Owner or Operator	Notes
G-BUZI	AS.355F-1 Twin Squirrel	B. C. Seedle Helicopters/Blackpool	
G-BUZJ	Lindstrand LBL-105A balloon	Flying Pictures (Balloons) Ltd	
G-BUZK	Cameron V-77 balloon	J. T. Wilkinson & E. Evans	
G-BUZL	VPM M.16 Tandem Trainer	Roger Savage (Photography)	
G-BUZM	Light Aero Avid Flyer Mk 3	R. McLuckie & O. G. Jones	
G-BUZN	Cessna 172H	H. Jones	
G-BUZO	Pietenpol Air Camper	D. A. Jones	
G-BUZR	Lindstrand LBL-77A balloon	Lindstrand Balloons Ltd	
G-BUZS	Colt Flying Pig SS balloon	Banco Bilbao Vizcaya	
G-BUZT	Kölh Twinstar Mk 3	A. C. Goadby	
G-BUZV	Ken Brock KB-2 gyroplane	K. Hughes	
G-BUZY	Cameron A-250 balloon	P. J. D. Kerr	
G-BUZZ	AB-206B JetRanger 2	Markoss Aviation Ltd	
G-BVAA	Light Aero Avid Aerobat Mk 4	R. W. Brown	
G-BVAB	Zenair CH.601HDS	A. R. Bender	
G-BVAC	Zenair CH.601HD	A. G. Cozens	
G-BVAF	Piper J-3C-65 Cub	N. M. Hitchman	
G-BVAG	Lindstrand LBL-90A balloon	T. Moult & ptnrs	
G-BVAH	Denney Kitfox Mk 3	V. A. Hutchinson	
G-BVAI	PZL-110 Koliber 150	N. J. & R. F. Morgan	
G-BVAJ	Rotorway Executive 90	Rotorbuild Helicopters Ltd	
G-BVAM	Evans VP-1	R. F. Selby	
G-BVAN	M.S.892E Rallye 150	C. J. Freeman & A. G. E. Camisa	
G-BVAO	Colt 25A balloon	J. M. Frazer	
G-BVAP	Thunder Ax10-180 S2 balloon	British School of Ballooning	
G-BVAT	Murphy Renegade 912	B. J. Towers	
G-BVAU	Cameron A-210 balloon	Broadland Balloons Ltd	
G-BVAW	Staaken Z-1 Flitzer (D-692)	D. J. Evans & L. R. Williams	
G-BVAX	Colt 77A balloon	Vax Appliances Ltd	
G-BVAY	Rutan Vari-Eze	D. A. Young	
G-BVAZ	Montgomerie-Bensen B.8MR	R. Patrick	
G-BVBD	Sikorsky S-52-3	J. Windmill	
G-BVBE	P.84 Jet Provost T.3A (XN461)	R. E. Todd	
G-BVBF	PA-28-151 Warrior	R. K. Spence	
G-BVBG	PA-32R Cherokee Lance 300	R. K. Spence	
G-BVBI	D.H.114 Heron 2	Gloster Aviation Services Ltd/Staverton	
G-BVBJ	Colt Flying Jar 1 SS balloon	Flying Pictures (Balloons) Ltd	
G-BVBK	Colt Flying Jar 2 SS balloon	Flying Pictures (Balloons) Ltd	
G-BVBL	PA-38-112 Tomahawk	Aerohire Ltd/Halfpenny Green	
G-BVBM	Lindstrand LBL-180A balloon	A. M. Rocliffe & S. R. Wong	
G-BVBN	Cameron A-210 balloon	Heart of England Balloons	
G-BVBO	Sikorsky S-52-3	Ilkeston Contractors	
G-BVBP	Avro 683 Lancaster X	Aces High Ltd/North Weald	
G-BVBR	Light Aero Avid Speedwing	H. R. Rowley	
G-BVBS	Cameron N-77 balloon	Marley Building Materials Ltd	
G-BVBT	D.H.C.1 Chipmunk T.10 (WK511)	T. J. Manna/Cranfield	
G-BVBU	Cameron V-77 balloon	Cameron Balloons Ltd	
G-BVBV	Light Aero Avid Flyer	D. A. Jarvis	
G-BVBX	Cameron N-90M balloon	Virgin Airship & Balloon Co Ltd	
G-BVCA	Cameron N-105 balloon	Flying Pictures (Balloons) Ltd	
G-BVCB	Rans S.10 Sakota	M. D. T. Barley	
G-BVCC	Monnett Sonerai 2LT	J. Eggleston	
G-BVCF	Lindstrand Flying M SS balloon	International Balloons Ltd	
G-BVCG	Vans RV-6	G. J. Newby & E. M. Farquharson	
G-BVCI	Robinson R-22B	Ocean Shields Ltd	
G-BVCJ	Agusta A.109A-II	Castle Air Charters Ltd (G-CLRL/G-EJCB)	
G-BVCK	Lindstrand LBL-105A balloon	International Balloons Ltd	
G-BVCL	Rans S.6-116 Coyote II	S. L. Roobottom & C. S. Simmons	
G-BVCM	Cessna 525 Citation/Jet	Kwik Fit PLC/Edinburgh	
G-BVCN	Colt 56A balloon	N. R. Mason	
G-BVCO	FRED Srs 2	I. W. Bremner	
G-BVCP	Metisse	C. W. R. Piper	
G-BVCS	Aeronca 7BCM Champion	P. C. Isbell	
G-BVCT	Denney Kitfox Mk 4	A. F. Reid	
G-BVCV	Fairchild PT-19A Cornell	R. J. Fox	
G-BVCX	Sikorsky S-76A	Brintel Helicopters Ltd	
G-BVCY	Cameron H-24 balloon	Bryant Group PLC	
G-BVCZ	Colt 240A balloon	Schemedraw Ltd	
G-BVDA	Lindstrand LBL-240A balloon	International Balloons Ltd	
G-BVDB	Thunder Ax7-77 balloon	M. J. Smith	
G-BVDC	Vans RV-3	D. Calabritto	
G-BVDD	Colt 69A balloon	R. M. Cambridge & D. Harrison-Morris	

Notes	Reg.	Type	Owner or Operator
	G-BVDE	Taylor JT.1 Monoplane	C. R. J. Norman
	G-BVDF	Cameron 115 Doll SS balloon	Cameron Balloons Ltd
	G-BVDH	PA-28RT-201 Arrow IV	P. Heffron
	G-BVDI	Vans RV-4	J. P. Leigh
	G-BVDJ	Campbell Cricket (replica)	S. Jennings
	G-BVDM	Cameron C-60 balloon	G. W. G. C. Sudlow
	G-BVDN	PA-34-220T Seneca III	J. N. Sennett (G-IGHA/G-IPUT)
	G-BVDO	Lindstrand LBL-105A balloon	J. Burlinson
	G-BVDP	Sequoia F.8L Falco	T. G. Painter
	G-BVDR	Cameron O-77 balloon	T. Duggan
	G-BVDS	Lindstrand LBL-69A balloon	I. Ollerenshaw
	G-BVDT	CFM Streak Shadow	H. J. Bennet
	G-BVDW	Thunder Ax8-90 balloon	R. P. Jones
	G-BVDY	Cameron 60 Concept balloon	K. A. & G. N. Connolly
	G-BVDZ	Taylorcraft BC-12D	P. N. W. England
	G-BVEA	Mosler Motors N.3 Pup	N. Lynch (G-MWEA)
	G-BVEB	PA-32R-301 Saratoga HP	B. J. Strickland
	G-BVEC	Aérospatiale ATR-42-300	CityFlyer Express Ltd/British Airways
	G-BVED	Aérospatiale ATR-42-300	CityFlyer Express Ltd/British Airways
	G-BVEE	—	—
	G-BVEF	Aérospatiale ATR-42-300	CityFlyer Express Ltd/British Airways
	G-BVEG	P.84 Jet Provost T.3A (XN629)	Transair (UK) Ltd/North Weald
	G-BVEH	Jodel D.112	D. J. Rees
	G-BVEI	Colt 90A balloon	Thunder & Colt
	G-BVEJ	Cameron V-90 balloon	J. D. A. Snields & A. R. Craze
	G-BVEK	Cameron 80 Concept balloon	J. G. Andrews
	G-BVEL	Evans VP-1 Srs 2	M. J. & S. J. Quinn
	G-BVEN	Cameron 80 Concept balloon	Aire Valley Balloons
	G-BVEO	BAe ATP	Jetstream Aircraft Ltd/Prestwick
	G-BVEP	Luscombe 8A Silvaire	Mid-West Aviation Ltd
	G-BVER	D.H.C.2 Beaver 1 (XV268)	A. F. Allan (G-BTDM)
	G-BVES	Cessna 340A	Welsh Dragon Aviation Ltd/Cardiff
	G-BVEU	Cameron O-105 balloon	H. C. Wright
	G-BVEV	PA-34-200 Seneca	Executive Aviation Services
	G-BVEW	Lindstrand LBL-150A balloon	P. A. & N. J. Foot
	G-BVEX	Lindstrand LBL-105A balloon	Lindstrand Balloons Ltd
	G-BVEY	Denney Kitfox Mk 4	Penny Hydraulics Ltd
	G-BVEZ	P.84 Jet Provost T.3A	Magnificent Obsessions Ltd
	G-BVFA	Rans S.10 Sakota	D. Parkinson & D. Allam
	G-BVFB	Cameron N-31 balloon	Bath City Council
	G-BVFF	Cameron V-77 balloon	R. G. Barry
	G-BVFK	BN-2T Turbine Islander	Pilatus BN Ltd/Bembridge
	G-BVFL	Lindstrand LBL-21A balloon	International Balloons Ltd
	G-BVFM	Rans S.6-ESA Coyote II	P. G. Walton
	G-BVFN	Pitts S-1 Special	I. McKenzie
	G-BVFO	Light Aero Avid Speedwing	P. Chisman
	G-BVFP	Cameron V-90 balloon	C. Duppa-Miller
	G-BVFR	CFM Streak Shadow	M. G. B. Stebbing
	G-BVFS	Slingsby T.31M Cadet	V. M. Crabb
	G-BVFT	Maule M5-235C	R. T. Love
	G-BVFU	Cameron 105 Sphere SS balloon	Lascar Investments Ltd
	G-BVFW	Nanchang CJ-6A (1532008)	Elmair Ltd
	G-BVFX	Nanchang CJ-6A	Elmair Ltd
	G-BVFY	Colt 210A balloon	Scotair Balloons
	G-BVFZ	Maule M5-180C	C. N. White
	G-BVGA	Bell 206B JetRanger 3	Findon Air Services/Shoreham
	G-BVGB	Thunder Ax8-105 S2 balloon	Flying Pictures (Balloons) Ltd
	G-BVGC	Cessna 411A	Taylor Aircraft Services Ltd (G-AVEK)
	G-BVGD	Aerotechnik L-13 SEH Vivat	Oxfordshire Sport Flying Ltd/Enstone
	G-BVGE	W.S.55 Whirlwind HAR.10 (XJ729)	Austen Associates Partnership
	G-BVGF	Shaw Europa	A. Graham & G. G. Beal
	G-BVGG	Lindstrand LBL-69A balloon	Lindstrand Balloons Ltd
	G-BVGH	Hunter T.7 (XL573)	B. J. Pover
	G-BVGI	Pereira Osprey II	B. Weare
	G-BVGJ	Cameron C-80 balloon	D. T. Watkins
	G-BVGK	Lindstrand LBL Flying Newspaper SS balloon	International Balloons Ltd
	G-BVGL	Sikorsky S-76A	Bond Helicopters Ltd
	G-BVGM	Sikorsky S-76A	Bond Helicopters Ltd
	G-BVGO	Denney Kitfox Mk 4-1200	Willow Motors
	G-BVGP	Bücker Bü133C Jungmeister	R. H. Reeves
	G-BVGR	RAF BE-2e (A1325)	Aero Vintage Ltd

Reg.	Type	Owner or Operator	Notes
G-BVGS	Robinson R-22B	Independent Car Auctions (UK) Ltd	
G-BVGT	Auster J/1 (modified)	L. A. Groves	
G-BVGV	Colt 21A balloon	Red Bull Trading GmbH	
G-BVGW	Luscombe 8A Silvaire	L. A. Groves	
G-BVGX	Thunder Ax8-90 S2 balloon	G-BVGX Group	
G-BVGY	Luscombe 8E Silvaire	T. Groves	
G-BVGZ	Fokker Dr.1 (replica)	Museum of Army Flying/Middle Wallop	
G-BVHC	Grob G.115D-2	Short Bros PLC/Plymouth	
G-BVHD	Grob G.115D-2	Short Bros PLC/Plymouth	
G-BVHE	Grob G.115D-2	Short Bros PLC/Plymouth	
G-BVHF	Grob G.115D-2	Short Bros PLC/Plymouth	
G-BVHG	Grob G.115D-2	Short Bros PLC/Plymouth	
G-BVHI	Rans S.10 Sakota	P. D. Rowley	
G-BVHJ	Cameron A-180 balloon	Southern Flight Company Ltd	
G-BVHK	Cameron V-77 balloon	G. Rich	
G-BVHL	Nicollier HN.700 Menestrel II	I. H. R. Walker	
G-BVHM	PA-38-112 Tomahawk	A. J. Gomes (G-DCAN)	
G-BVHN	Lindstrand LBL G144 balloon	Lindstrand Balloons Ltd	
G-BVHO	Cameron V-90 balloon	R. S. Mohr	
G-BVHP	Colt 42A balloon	Huntair Ltd	
G-BVHR	Cameron V-90 balloon	D. C. Boxall	
G-BVHS	Murphy Rebel	J. Brown & ptnrs	
G-BVHT	Light Aero Avid Speedwing Mk 4	R. S. Holt	
G-BVHU	Colt 13 Flying Bottle SS balloon	BIAS International Ltd	
G-BVHV	Cameron N-105 balloon	Flying Pictures (Balloons) Ltd	
G-BVHX	BN-2T-4R Defender 4000	Pilatus BN Ltd/Bembridge	
G-BVHY	BN-2T-4R Defender 4000	Pilatus BN Ltd/Bembridge	
G-BVIA	Rand-Robinson KR-2	K. Atkinson	
G-BVIC	EE Canberra B.6 (XH568)	Classic Aviation Projects Ltd	
G-BVID	Lindstrand Lozenge SS balloon	Respatex International Ltd	
G-BVIE	PA-18 Super Cub 95 (modified)	R. W. Sage (G-CLIK)	
G-BVIF	Montgomerie-Bensen B.8MR	R. M. & D. Mann	
G-BVIG	Cameron A-250 balloon	Balloon Flights International Ltd	
G-BVIH	PA-28-161 Warrior II	Ocean Developments Ltd (G-GFCE/ G-BNJP)	
G-BVIK	Maule MXT-7-180	Iberian Investments Ltd	
G-BVIL	Maule MXT-7-180	Aeromarine Ltd	
G-BVIM	Cameron V-77 balloon	The Ballooning Business Ltd	
G-BVIN	Rans S.6-ESA Coyote II	K. J. Vincent	
G-BVIO	Colt Flying Drinks Can SS balloon	Flying Pictures (Balloons) Ltd	
G-BVIR	Lindstrand LBL-69A balloon	A. G. E. Faulkner	
G-BVIS	Brügger MB.2 Colibri	M. J. Sharp	
G-BVIT	Campbell Cricket	A. N. Nisbet	
G-BVIV	Light Aero Avid Aerobat	J. & V. Hobday	
G-BVIW	PA-18 Super Cub 150	Rodger Aircraft Ltd	
G-BVIX	Lindstrand LBL-180A balloon	Humbug Balloon Group	
G-BVIY	Cameron A-105 balloon	J. L. M. Van Hoesel	
G-BVIZ	Shaw Europa	T. J. Punter & P. G. Jeffers	
G-BVJA	Fokker 100	British Midland Airways Ltd/E. Midlands	
G-BVJB	Fokker 100	British Midland Airways Ltd/E. Midlands	
G-BVJC	Fokker 100	British Midland Airways Ltd/E. Midlands	
G-BVJD	Fokker 100	British Midland Airways Ltd/E. Midlands	
G-BVJE	AS.350B-1 Ecureuil	I. S. & G. Steel Stockholders Ltd	
G-BVJF	Montgomerie-Bensen B.8MR	D. M. F. Harvey	
G-BVJG	Cyclone AX3/K	T. D. Reid (G-MYOP)	
G-BVJH	Aero Designs Pulsar	J. A. C. Tweedle	
G-BVJJ	Cameron DP-90 airship	Cameron Balloons Ltd	
G-BVJK	Glaser-Dirks DG.400	B. A. Eastwell	
G-BVJL	Colt 240A balloon	Anglian Countryside Balloons	
G-BVJM	VPM M.16 Tandem Trainer	D. Nash	
G-BVJN	Shaw Europa	N. Adam	
G-BVJO	Cameron R-77 balloon	Bondbaste Ltd	
G-BVJP	Aérospatiale ATR-42-300	Gill Airways Ltd/Newcastle	
G-BVJS	Colt Piggy Bank SS balloon	Iduna-Bausparkasse AG	
G-BVJT	Cessna F.406	Nor Leasing	
G-BVJU	Evans VP-1	B. A. Schlussler	
G-BVJV	Airbus A.320-231	Airworld Aviation Ltd/Gatwick	
G-BVJW	Airbus A.320-231	Airworld Aviation Ltd *Mallorca*/Gatwick	
G-BVJX	Marquart MA.5 Charger	M. L. Martin	
G-BVJY	H.S.125 Srs 700B	Aviamost Ltd	
G-BVJZ	PA-28-161 Warrior II	A. R. Fowkes	
G-BVKA	Boeing 737-59D	British Midland Airways Ltd/E. Midlands	

Notes	Reg.	Type	Owner or Operator
	G-BVKB	Boeing 737-59D	British Midland Airways Ltd/E. Midlands
	G-BVKC	Boeing 737-59D	British Midland Airways Ltd/E. Midlands
	G-BVKD	Boeing 737-59D	British Midland Airways Ltd/E. Midlands
	G-BVKE	Team Minimax 88	A. M. Pepper
	G-BVKF	Shaw Europa	T. R. Sinclair
	G-BVKG	Colt Flying Hot Dog SS balloon	Longbreak Ltd
	G-BVKH	Thunder Ax8-90 balloon	R. G. Gruzelier
	G-BVKJ	Bensen B.8	J. Bagnall
	G-BVKK	Slingsby T.61F Venture T.2	The Gliding Centre/Edgehill
	G-BVKL	Cameron A-180 balloon	W. I. & C. Hooker
	G-BVKM	Rutan Vari-Eze	P. R. Fabish
	G-BVKP	Sikorsky S-76A	Bristow Helicopters Ltd
	G-BVKR	Sikorsky S-76A	Bristow Helicopters Ltd
	G-BVKU	Slingsby T.61F Venture T.2	R. W. Curtis
	G-BVKV	Cameron N-90 balloon	Pringle of Scotland Ltd
	G-BVKW	Lindstrand LBL-240A balloon	Bridges Van Hire Ltd
	G-BVKX	Colt 14A balloon	H. C. J. Williams
	G-BVKY	Colt 69A balloon	Thunder & Colt
	G-BVKZ	Thunder Ax9-120 balloon	D. J. Head
	G-BVLA	Lancair 320	A. R. Welstead
	G-BVLB	Cameron 77 Can SS balloon	Cameron Balloons Ltd
	G-BVLC	Cameron N-42 balloon	Cameron Balloons Ltd
	G-BVLD	Campbell Cricket (replica)	C. Berry
	G-BVLE	McCandless M.4 gyroplœane	H. Walls
	G-BVLF	Starstreak Shadow SS-D	B. R. Johnson
	G-BVLG	AS.355F-1 Twin Squirrel	Lynton Aviation Ltd
	G-BVLH	Shaw Europa	D. Barraclough
	G-BVLI	Cameron V-77 balloon	Autographics Ltd
	G-BVLK	Rearwin 8125 Cloudster	M. C. Hiscock
	G-BVLL	Lindstrand LBL-210A balloon	A. G. E. Faulkner
	G-BVLM	D.H.115 Vampire T.55 (209)	R. J. Verrall/Bournemouth
	G-BVLN	Aero Designs Pulsar XP	D. A. Campbell
	G-BVLP	PA-38-112 Tomahawk	D. A. Whitmore
	G-BVLR	Vans RV-4	RV4 Group
	G-BVLS	Thunder Ax8-90 S2 balloon	J. R. Henderson
	G-BVLT	Bellanca 7GCBC Citabria	Rodger Aircraft Ltd
	G-BVLU	D.31 Turbulent	C. D. Bancroft
	G-BVLV	Shaw Europa	Euro 39 Group
	G-BVLW	Light Aero Avid Flyer Mk 4	D. M. Johnstone
	G-BVLX	Slingsby T.61F Venture T.2	RAFGSA/Bicester
	G-BVLY	Robinson R-22B	Fowlers Leasing Ltd
	G-BVLZ	Lindstrand LBL-120A balloon	Balloon Flights Club Ltd
	G-BVMA	Beech 200 Super King Air	Manhattan Air Ltd (G-VPLC)/Bournemouth
	G-BVMB	Hunter T.7 (XL613)	Hunter Aviation Ltd
	G-BVMC	Robinson R-44 Astro	E. Wooton
	G-BVMD	Luscombe 8E Silvaire	G. M. Scott
	G-BVMF	Cameron V-77 balloon	P. A. Meecham
	G-BVMG	Bensen B.80V	D. Moffat
	G-BVMH	WAG-Aero Sport Trainer (39624)	D. M. Jagger
	G-BVMI	PA-18 Super Cub 150	T. P. & M. M. Spurge
	G-BVMJ	Cameron 90 Eagle SS balloon	Classic Event/Berlin
	G-BVML	Lindstrand LBL-210A balloon	Ballooning Adventures Ltd
	G-BVMM	Robin HR.200/100	M. G. Owne
	G-BVMN	Ken Brock KB-2 gyroplane	S. McCullagh
	G-BVMO	R. Commander 685	Flightpath Ltd
	G-BVMR	Cameron V-90 balloon	I. R. Comley
	G-BVMU	Yakovlev Yak-52	J. E. & A. Ashby
	G-BVMV	Lindstrand LBL-150A balloon	International Balloons Ltd
	G-BVMW	Lindstrand LBL-77A balloon	International Balloons Ltd
	G-BVMX	Short SD3-60 Variant 100	Gill Airways Ltd (G-BPFS/G-REGN/G-OCIA)
	G-BVMY	Short SD3.60 Variant 100	Loganair Ltd/British Airways (G-OEEC/G-BPKY)
	G-BVMZ	Robin HR.100/210	Chiltern Handbags (London) Ltd
	G-BVNA	Cuby II	P. Scott (G-MYMA)
	G-BVNG	D.H.60G-III Moth Major (EC-ADE)	J. A. Pothecary/Shoreham
	G-BVNH	Agusta A.109C	Brecqhou Development Ltd (G-LAXO)
	G-BVNI	Taylor JT-2 Titch	T. V. Adamson
	G-BVNL	R. Commander 114	W. J. Hemmings & ptnrs
	G-BVNM	Boeing 737-4S3	British Airways (G-BPKA)
	G-BVNN	Boeing 737-4S3	British Airways (G-BPKB)
	G-BVNO	Boeing 737-4S3	British Airways (G-BPKE)
	G-BVNR	Cameron N-105 balloon	Novogas SpA

Reg.	Type	Owner or Operator	Notes
G-BVNS	PA-28-181 Archer II	GT Aviation/Bournemouth	
G-BVNT	Thunder Ax9-120 S2 balloon	C. E. & J. Wood	
G-BVNU	FLS Aerospace Sprint Club	FLS Aerospace (Lovaux) Ltd	
G-BVNV	Colt 210A balloon	Atlas Industry Ltd	
G-BVNX	Sikorsky S-76A	British International Helicopters	
G-BVNY	Rans S.7 Courier	Sportair UK Ltd	
G-BVOA	PA-28-181 Archer II	Millen Aviation Services	
G-BVOB	F.27 Friendship Mk 500	Air UK Ltd/Stansted	
G-BVOC	Cameron V-90 balloon	S. Masey	
G BVOD	Montgomerie-Parsons 2-seat gyroplane	J. M. Montgomerle	
G-BVOG	Cameron RN-9 balloon	Cameron Balloons Ltd	
G-BVOH	Campbell Cricket (replica)	B. F. Pearson	
G-BVOI	Rans S.6-116 Coyote II	A. P. Bacon	
G-BVOJ	Lindstrand LBL-31A balloon	Flying Pictures (Balloons) Ltd	
G-BVOK	Yakovlev Yak-52	D. J. Gilmour/North Weald	
G-BVOL	Douglas C-47A (KG391)	Airborne Initiative Promotions Ltd	
G-BVOM	F.27 Friendship Mk 500	Air UK Ltd/Stansted	
G-BVON	Lindstrand LBL-105A balloon	International Balloons Ltd	
G-BVOO	Lindstrand LBL-105A balloon	International Balloons Ltd	
G-BVOP	Cameron N-90 balloon	Cambury Ltd	
G-BVOR	CFM Streak Shadow	J. A. Lord	
G-BVOS	Shaw Europa	Durham Europa Group	
G-BVOT	Glaser-Dirks DG.800A	W. R. McNair	
G-BVOU	H.S.748 Srs 2A	Emerald Airways Ltd/Liverpool	
G-BVOV	H.S.748 Srs 2A	Emerald Airways Ltd/Liverpool	
G-BVOW	Shaw Europa	Europa Syndicate	
G-BVOX	Taylorcraft F-22	Cubair Ltd/Redhill	
G-BVOY	Rotorway Executive 90	E. Drinkwater	
G-BVOZ	Colt 56A balloon	British School of Ballooning	
G-BVPA	Thunder Ax8-105 S2 balloon	Firefly Balloon Promotions	
G-BVPB	Robinson R-44 Astro	Chantler Timber	
G-BVPD	C.A.S.A. 1.131E Jungmann	M. C. Garland	
G-BVPF	Lindstrand LBL-69A balloon	International Balloons Ltd	
G-BVPG	Lindstrand LBL-180A balloon	International Balloons Ltd	
G-BVPH	Bensen-Parsons 2-seat gyroplane	I. A. Leedham	
G-BVPI	Evans VP-1	C. M. Gibson	
G-BVPK	Cameron O-90 balloon	Mobil Oil Co Ltd	
G-BVPL	Zenalr CH.601HD	D. Harker	
G-BVPM	Evans VP-2 Coupé	P. Marigold	
G-BVPN	Piper J-3C-65 Cub	R. W. Sage (G-TAFY)	
G-BVPO	D.H.100 Vampire FB.6	R. J. Verrall/Bournemouth	
G-BVPP	Folland Gnat T.1	T. J. Manna/Cranfield	
G-BVPR	Robinson R-22B	Datum Enterprises Ltd (G-KNIT)	
G-BVPS	Jodel D.112	P. J. Sharp	
G-BVPT	Dornier Do.228-202K	Suckling Airways Ltd/Cambridge	
G-BVPU	Cameron A-140 balloon	Cameron Balloons Ltd	
G-BVPV	Lindstrand LBL-77B balloon	A. R. Greensides	
G-BVPW	Rans S.6-116 Coyote II	J. G. Beesley	
G-BVPX	Lovegrove Tyro Gyro Mk II	P. C. Lovegrove	
G-BVPY	CFM Streak Shadow	R. J. Mitchell	
G-BVPZ	Lindstrand LBL-210A balloon	International Balloons Ltd	
G-BVRA	Shaw Europa	E. J. J. & S. M. Pels	
G-BVRC	Bell 206B JetRanger 3	Heli Venture (UK) Ltd (G-BSJC)	
G-BVRD	VPM M.16 Tandem Trainer	Whisky Mike (Aviation) Ltd	
G-BVRE	Vans RV-6A	J. J. Martin	
G-BVRH	Taylorcraft BL-65	Ebork Ltd	
G-BVRI	Thunder Ax6-56 balloon	Voyager Balloons	
G-BVRK	Rans S.6-ESA Coyote II	J. Secular (G-MYPK)	
G-BVRL	Lindstrand LBL-21A balloon	M. J. Green	
G-BVRM	Cameron A-210 balloon	Virgin Balloon Flights Ltd	
G-BVRN	F.27 Friendship Mk 500	Air UK Ltd/Stansted	
G-BVRP	Lindstrand LBL-90A balloon	Lindstrand Balloons Ltd	
G-BVRR	Lindstrand LBL-77A balloon	I. Ollerenshaw	
G-BVRS	Beech B90 King Air	Cook Aviation Services Ltd (G-KJET/G-AXFE)	
G-BVRT	EMB-110P1 Bandeirante	Knight Air Ltd (G-I ATC)	
G-BVRU	Lindstrand LBL-105A balloon	Flying Pictures (Balloons) Ltd	
G-BVRV	Vans RV-4	A. Troughton	
G-BVRY	Cyclone AX3/582	J. Toone	
G-BVRZ	PA-18 Super Cub 95	A. J. Clarry	
G-BVSA	BAe 146-300	British Aerospace PLC	

Notes	Reg.	Type	Owner or Operator
	G-BVSB	Team Minimax	C. Nice
	G-BVSC	Bell 206B JetRanger 3	RCR Aviation Ltd/Thruxton
	G-BVSD	SE.3130 Alouette II (V-54)	R. E. Dagless
	G-BVSF	Aero Designs Pulsar	S. N. & R. J. Freestone
	G-BVSJ	BN-2B-26 Islander	Pilatus BN Ltd/Bembridge
	G-BVSK	BN-2T Turbine Islander	Pilatus BN Ltd/Bembridge
	G-BVSL	BN-2T Turbine Islander	Pilatus BN Ltd/Bembridge
	G-BVSM	RAF 2000 gyroplane	K. Quigley
	G-BVSN	Light Aero Avid Speedwing	D. J. & C. Park
	G-BVSO	Cameron A-120 balloon	Heavens Above
	G-BVSP	P.84 Jet Provost T.3A	Special Scope (JP) Group
	G-BVSR	Colt 210A balloon	Eagle Security Ltd
	G-BVSS	Jodel D.150	A. P. Burns
	G-BVST	Jodel D.150	A. Shipp
	G-BVSV	Cameron C-80 balloon	Cameron Balloons Ltd
	G-BVSW	Cameron C-80 balloon	Cameron Balloons Ltd
	G-BVSX	Team Minimax 91	G. N. Smith
	G-BVSY	Thunder Ax9-120 balloon	Candytwist Balloons
	G-BVSZ	Pitts S-1E (S) Special	R. C. F. Bailey
	G-BVTA	Tri Kis	P. J. Webb
	G-BVTC	P.84 Jet Provost T.5A	Global Aviation Ltd
	G-BVTD	CFM Streak Shadow	M. Walton
	G-BVTE	Fokker 70	British Midland Airways Ltd/E. Midlands
	G-BVTF	Fokker 70	British Midland Airways Ltd/E. Midlands
	G-BVTG	Fokker 70	British Midland Airways Ltd/E. Midlands
	G-BVTH	Fokker 70	British Midland Airways Ltd/E. Midlands
	G-BVTJ	Aérospatiale ATR-72-202	CityFlyer Express Ltd/British Airways
	G-BVTK	Aérospatiale ATR-72-202	CityFlyer Express Ltd/British Airways
	G-BVTL	Colt 31A balloon	A. Lindsay
	G-BVTM	Cessna F.152 II	RAF Halton Aeroplane Club (G-WACS)
	G-BVTN	Cameron N-90 balloon	Cameron Balloons Ltd
	G-BVTO	PA-28-151 Warrior	Falcon Flying Services (G-SEWL)/ Biggin Hill
	G-BVTU	Lindstrand LBL-105A balloon	International Balloons Ltd
	G-BVTV	Rotorway Executive 90	Southern Helicopters Ltd
	G-BVTW	Aero Designs Pulsar	J. D. Webb
	G-BVTX	D. H. C.1 Chipmunk T.10 (WP809)	Airspares UK
	G-BVTY	Dornier Do.228-202K	Dornier Luftfahrt GmbH
	G-BVTZ	Dornier Do.228-202K	Suckling Airways (Luton) Ltd
	G-BVUA	Cameron O-105 balloon	D. C. Eager
	G-BVUB	Cessna U.206G	Caledonian Seaplanes Ltd
	G-BVUC	Colt 56A balloon	Thunder & Colt
	G-BVUD	Cameron A-250 balloon	British School of Ballooning
	G-BVUE	Cameron C-80 balloon	British School of Ballooning
	G-BVUF	Thunder Ax10-180 S2 balloon	A. J. Nunns
	G-BVUG	Betts TB.1	T. A. Betts
	G-BVUH	Thunder Ax6-65B balloon	N. C. A. Crawley
	G-BVUI	Lindstrand LBL-25A balloon	Lindstrand Balloons Ltd
	G-BVUJ	Ken Brock KB-2 gyroplane	R. J. Hutchinson
	G-BVUK	Cameron V-77 balloon	H. G. Griffiths & W. A. Steel
	G-BVUL	PA-34-200T Seneca II	Air Transport Services Ltd
	G-BVUM	Rans S.6-116 Coyote II	G. L. Donaldson
	G-BVUN	Vans RV-4	I. G. & M. Glenn
	G-BVUO	Cameron R-150 balloon	Bombaste Ltd
	G-BVUP	Schleicher ASW-24E	E. & C. F. Sprecht
	G-BVUT	Evans VP-1 Srs 2	P. J. Weston
	G-BVUU	Cameron C-80 balloon	T. M. C. McCoy
	G-BVUV	Shaw Europa	A. P. Marks
	G-BVUW	BAe 146-100	British Aerospace PLC
	G-BVUZ	Cessna 120	N. O. Anderson
	G-BVVA	Yakovlev Yak-52	T. W. Freeman
	G-BVVB	Carlson Sparrow Mk II	L. M. McCullen
	G-BVVC	Hunter F.6A (XF516)	P. Hellier
	G-BVVE	Jodel D.112	P. M. Standen & A. J. Roxburgh
	G-BVVF	Nanchang CJ-6A	Yak China Ltd
	G-BVVG	Nanchang CJ-6A	Yak China Ltd
	G-BVVH	Shaw Europa	T. G. Hoult
	G-BVVI	Hawker Audax I	Aero Vintage Ltd
	G-BVVJ	Cameron N-77 balloon	Cameron Balloons Ltd
	G-BVVK	D.H.C.6 Twin Otter 310	Loganair Ltd/British Airways
	G-BVVL	EAA Acro Sport II	D. Park
	G-BVVM	Zenair CH.601HD	J. G. Small

Reg.	Type	Owner or Operator	Notes
G-BVVN	Brügger MB.2 Colibri	N. F. Andrews	
G-BVVO	Yakovlev Yak-50	J. M. Roach	
G-BVVP	Shaw Europa	J. S. Melville	
G-BVVR	Stits SA-3A Playboy	A. D. Pearce	
G-BVVS	Vans RV-4	E. C. English	
G-BVVT	Colt 240A balloon	R. W. Keron	
G-BVVV	Bell 206L-1 LongRanger 2	RCR Aviation Ltd	
G-BVVW	Yakovlev Yak-52	David Young Cars	
G-BVVX	Yakovlev Yak-18A	J. M. & E. M. Wicks	
G-BVVY	Air Command 532 Elite	T. A. Holmes (G-CORK)	
G-BVVZ	Corby CJ-1 Starlet	A. E. Morris	
G-BVWA	M. S. 880B Rallye Club	A. P. Evans	
G-BVWB	Thunder Ax8-90 S2 balloon	S. C. Clayton	
G-BVWC	EE Canberra B.6 (WK163)	Classic Aviation Projects Ltd	
G-BVWE	Cameron C-80 balloon	Mid-Bucks Farmers Balloon Group	
G-BVWF	P.84 Jet Provost T.5 (XS230)	Transair (UK) Ltd	
G-BVWH	Cameron N-90 Bulb SS balloon	Virgin Airship & Balloon Co Ltd	
G-BVWI	Cameron 65 Bulb SS balloon	Virgin Airship & Balloon Co Ltd	
G-BVWK	Air & Space 18A gyroplane	Whisky Mike (Aviation) Ltd	
G-BVWL	Air & Space 18A gyroplane	Whisky Mike (Aviation) Ltd	
G-BVWM	Shaw Europa	Europa Syndicate	
G-BVWN	Hunter T.7 (XL600)	E. Stead	
G-BVWO	Lindstrand LBL-90A balloon	International Balloons Ltd	
G-BVWP	D.H.C.1 Chipmunk 22 (WP856)	T. W. M. Beck	
G-BVWR	Bell 206B JetRanger 2	Ford Helicopters Ltd	
G-BVWW	Lindstrand LBL-90A balloon	R. B. Naylor	
G-BVWX	VPM M.16 Tandem Trainer	M. L. Smith	
G-BVWY	Porterfield CP.65	B. Morris	
G-BVWZ	PA-32-301 Saratoga	R. Howton/Biggin Hill	
G-BVXA	Cameron N-105 balloon	R. E. Jones	
G-BVXB	Cameron V-77 balloon	L. A. Lawton	
G-BVXC	EE Canberra B.6 (WT333)	Classic Aviation Projects Ltd	
G-BVXD	Cameron O-84 balloon	N. J. Langley	
G-BVXE	Steen Skybolt	T. J. Reeve (G-LISA)	
G-BVXF	Cameron O-120 balloon	Gone With The Wind Ltd	
G-BVXG	Lindstrand LBL-90A balloon	G. C. Elson	
G-BVXH	Lindstrand LBL-77A balloon	International Balloons Ltd	
G-BVXI	Klemm KL.35	J. J. van Egmond/Netherlands	
G-BVXJ	C.A.S.A. 1.133 Jungmeister	J. D. Haslam	
G-BVXK	Yakovlev Yak-52	E. Gavazzi	
G-BVXM	AS.350B Ecureuil	The Berkeley Leisure Group Ltd	
G-BVXP	Cameron N-105 balloon	P. M. Gaines	
G-BVXR	D.H.104 Devon C.2	M. Whale & M. W. A. Lunn	
G-BVXS	Taylorcraft BC-12D	J. M. Allison	
G-BVXU	Zenair CH.601HD	P. J. Roy	
G-BVXV	—	—	
G-BVXW	SC.7 Skyvan Srs 3a Variant 100	Hunting Aviation Ltd/Kidlington	
G-BVXX	BN-2B-26 Islander	Pilatus BN Ltd/Bembridge	
G-BVXY	BN-2B-26 Islander	Pilatus BN Ltd/Bembridge	
G-BVXZ	Lindstrand LBL-210A balloon	Aerial Promotions Ltd	
G-BVYA	Airbus A.320-231	Caledonian Airways Ltd/Loch Katrine	
G-BVYB	Airbus A.320-231	Caledonian Airways Ltd/Loch Hourn	
G-BVYC	Airbus A.320-231	Caledonian Airways Ltd/Loch Tay	
G-BVYD	BN-2B-26 Islander	Pilatus BN Ltd/Bembridge	
G-BVYE	BN-2B-26 Islander	Pilatus BN Ltd/Bembridge	
G-BVYF	PA-31-350 Navajo Chieftain	Cube Air Finance Ltd (G-SAVE)	
G-BVYG	CEA DR.300/120	London Gliding Club (Pty) Ltd/Dunstable	
G-BVYJ	Cameron 90 SS balloon	Chubb Fire Ltd	
G-BVYK	Team Minimax	S. B. Churchill	
G-BVYL	Colt 56A balloon	Old St. Andrews Ltd	
G-BVYM	CEA DR. 300/140	London Gliding Club (Pty) Ltd/Dunstable	
G-BVYN	Agusta-Bell 412	RCR Aviation Ltd	
G-BVYO	Robin R.2160	Mistral Aviation Ltd	
G-BVYP	PA-25 Pawnee 235	Bidford Glidng Centre Ltd	
G-BVYR	Cameron A-250 balloon	Voyager Balloons	
G-BVYT	QAC Quickie Q.2	N. A. Evans	
G-BVYU	Cameron A-120 balloon	B. J. Petteford	
G-BVYX	Light Aero Avid Speedwing Mk 4	G. J. Keen	
G-BVYY	Pietenpol Air Camper	J. H. Orchard	
G-BVYZ	Stemme S.10V	L. Gubbay & S. Sagar	
G-BVZA	Lindstrand LBL-77A balloon	International Balloons Ltd	
G-BVZB	Lindstrand LBL-31A balloon	International Balloons Ltd	
G-BVZD	Tri Kis	R. T. Clegg	

Notes	Reg.	Type	Owner or Operator
	G-BVZE	Boeing 737-59D	British Midland Airways Ltd/E. Midlands
	G-BVZF	Boeing 737-59D	British Midland Airways Ltd/E. Midlands
	G-BVZG	Boeing 737-5Q8	British Midland Airways Ltd/E. Midlands
	G-BVZH	Boeing 737-5Q8	British Midland Airways Ltd/E. Midlands
	G-BVZI	Boeing 737-5Q8	British Midland Airways Ltd/E. Midlands
	G-BVZJ	Rand-Robinson KR-2	J. P. McConnell-Wood
	G-BVZM	Cessna 210M	Zone Travel Ltd
	G-BVZN	Cameron C-80 balloon	Sky Fly Balloons
	G-BVZO	Rans S.6-116 Coyote II	P. Atkinson
	G-BVZP	Rotorway Executive 90	P. D. Logan
	G-BVZR	Zenair CH.601HD	J. D. White
	G-BVZS	H.S.748 Andover CC.2	Arch Aviation Ltd
	G-BVZT	Lindstrand LBL-90A balloon	Pork Farms Bowyers
	G-BVZU	Airbus A.320-231	Airworld Aviation Ltd/Gatwick
	G-BVZV	Rans S.6-116 Coyote II	J. Fothergill
	G-BVZW	F.27 Friendship Mk 500	Channel Express (Air Services) Ltd/Bournemouth
	G-BVZX	Cameron H-34 balloon	Chianti Balloon Club
	G-BVZY	Mooney M.20R	Flemming Frandsen Aircraft Sales Ltd
	G-BVZZ	D.H.C.1 Chipmunk 22	Portsmouth Naval Gliding Club
	G-BWAA	Cameron N-133 balloon	Brunel Ford
	G-BWAB	Jodel D.14	W. A. Braim
	G-BWAC	Waco YKS-7	D. N. & C. E. Peters
	G-BWAD	RAF 2000 gyroplane	J. R. Legge
	G-BWAE	RAF 2000 gyroplane	B. J. Crockett
	G-BWAF	Hunter F.6A	R. V. Aviation Ltd/Bournemouth
	G-BWAG	Cameron O-120 balloon	M. F. Glue
	G-BWAH	Montgomerie-Bensen B.8MR	S. J. O. Tinn
	G-BWAI	CFM Streak Shadow	J. M. Heath
	G-BWAJ	Cameron V-77 balloon	R. S. & S. H. Ham
	G-BWAK	Robinson R-22B	Sloane Helicopters Ltd/Sywell
	G-BWAM	Cameron C-60 balloon	C. Schabus GmbH & Co KEG
	G-BWAN	Cameron N-77 balloon	Air 2 Air Ltd
	G-BWAO	Cameron C-80 balloon	Air 2 Air Ltd
	G-BWAP	FRED Srs 3	R. J. Smyth
	G-BWAR	Denney Kitfox Mk 3	C. E. Brookes
	G-BWAT	Pietenpol Air Camper	D. R. Waters
	G-BWAU	Cameron V-90 balloon	K. M. & A. M. F. Hall
	G-BWAV	Schweizer 269C	Leisure & Retail Consultants Ltd
	G-BWAW	Lindstrand LBL-77A balloon	D. Bareford
	G-BWAZ	AS.350B-2 Ecureuil	Bellini Aviation (1993) Ltd
	G-BWBA	Cameron V-65 balloon	Dante Balloon Group
	G-BWBB	Lindstrand LBL-14A balloon	International Balloons Ltd
	G-BWBC	Cameron N-90AS balloon	Radio/Tele FFH GmbH & Co
	G-BWBD	Lindstrand LBL-90A balloon	International Balloons Ltd
	G-BWBE	Colt Flying Ice Cream Cone SS balloon	Benedikt Haggeney GmbH
	G-BWBF	Colt Flying Ice Cream Cone SS balloon	Benedikt Haggeney GbmH
	G-BWBG	Cvjetkovic CA-65 Skyfly	T. White & M. C. Fawkes
	G-BWBH	Colt Fork Lift Truck SS balloon	Jungheinrich AG
	G-BWBI	Taylorcraft F-22A	Tri Society
	G-BWBJ	Colt 21A balloon	U. Schneider
	G-BWBK	Lindstrand LBL-77B balloon	International Balloons Ltd
	G-BWBL	Lindstrand LBL-90A balloon	International Balloons Ltd
	G-BWBM	Lindstrand LBL-90A balloon	International Balloons Ltd
	G-BWBN	Cameron V-90 balloon	The Small School at Red House Ltd
	G-BWBO	Lindstrand LBL-77A balloon	Lindstrand Balloons Ltd
	G-BWBP	Bell 212	Bristow Helicopters Ltd
	G-BWBR	Cameron A-180 balloon	Virgin Balloon Flights Ltd
	G-BWBS	P.84 Jet Provost T.5A	Downbird UK
	G-BWBT	Lindstrand LBL-90A balloon	British Telecommunications PLC
	G-BWBV	Colt Piggy Bank SS balloon	Iduna-Bausparkasse AG
	G-BWBW	Cameron A-180 balloon	Virgin Balloon Flights Ltd
	G-BWBY	Schleicher ASH.26E	F. B. Jeynes
	G-BWBZ	ARV Super 2	J. N. C. Shields
	G-BWCA	CFM Streak Shadow	R. Thompson
	G-BWCC	Van Den Bemden Gas balloon	Piccard Balloon Group
	G-BWCD	Cameron A-120 balloon	Canterbury Balloons (G-OCBC)
	G-BWCE	Campbell Cricket	M. K. Hoban
	G-BWCG	Lindstrand LBL-42A balloon	International Balloons Ltd
	G-BWCH	Lindstrand LBL-9S balloon	International Balloons Ltd

Reg.	Type	Owner or Operator	Notes
G-BWCI	Light Aero Avid Hauler Mk 4	A. K. Voase	
G-BWCJ	Lindstrand LBL-14M balloon	International Balloons Ltd	
G-BWCK	Everett Srs 2 gyroplane	A. C. S. M. Hart	
G-BWCL	Lindstrand LBL-180A balloon	Lindstrand Balloons Ltd	
G-BWCM	Lindstrand LBL-77A balloon	International Balloons Ltd	
G-BWCN	Dornier Do.28D-2	Target Skysports	
G-BWCO	Dornier Do.28D-2	Sidetarget Ltd	
G-BWCP	Airbus A.320-212	Leisure International Airways Ltd	
G-BWCR	H.S.125 Srs 700B	Raytheon Corporate Jets Inc	
G-BWCS	P.84 Jet Provost T.5	Downbird UK	
G-BWCT	Tipsy T.66 Nipper 1	J. S. Hemmings & C. R. Steer	
G-BWCU	Bell 206L-1 LongRanger	Aeromega Ltd	
G-BWCV	Shaw Europa	M. P. Chetwynd-Talbot	
G-BWCW	Barnett J4B rotorcraft	S. H. Kirkby	
G-BWCX	Lindstrand LBL-90A balloon	Virgin Airship & Balloon Co Ltd	
G-BWCY	Murphy Rebel	A. Konieczek	
G-BWCZ	Mini-500	D. Nieman	
G-BWDA	Aerospatiale ATR-72-202	Gill Airways Ltd/Newcastle	
G-BWDB	Aerospatiale ATR-72-202	Gill Airways Ltd/Newcastle	
G-BWDE	PA-31P Pressurised Navajo	Norvic Aero Engines Ltd (G-HWKN)	
G-BWDF	PZL-104 Wilga 35A	Shivair Ltd	
G-BWDG	Lindstrand LBL-240A balloon	International Balloons Ltd	
G-BWDH	Cameron N-105 balloon	Bridges Van Hire Ltd	
G-BWDI	Cessna 340	Planstable Enterprises Ltd	
G-BWDK	Lindstrand LBL-60A balloon	Lindstrand Balloons Ltd	
G-BWDL	Cameron 80 Concept balloon	Pegasus Ballooning Ltd	
G-BWDM	Lindstrand LBL-120A balloon	G. D. & L. Fitzpatrick	
G-BWDN	CFM Streak Shadow SA	White Rabbit Ltd	
G-BWDO	Sikorsky S-76B	Air Hanson Ltd	
G-BWDP	Shaw Europa	J.y S. J. Valentine	
G-BWDR	P.84 Jet Provost T.3A	Global Aviation Ltd	
G-BWDS	P.84 Jet Provost T.3A	Global Aviation Ltd	
G-BWDT	PA-34-220T Seneca II	A. C. Morgan (G-BKHS)/Biggin Hill	
G-BWDU	Cameron V-90 balloon	Bath & West Security	
G-BWDV	Schweizer 269C	C.S.E Aviation Ltd/Kidlington	
G-BWDX	Shaw Europa	J. B. Crane	
G-BWDY	Sky 65-24 balloon	Sky Balloons Ltd	
G-BWDZ	Sky 105-24 balloon	G. Andrewartha	
G-BWEA	Lindstrand LBL-120A balloon	S. R. Seager	
G BWEB	P.04 Jet Provost T.5A	J. S. Everett	
G-BWEC	Cassutt-Colson Variant	N. R. Thomason & M. P. J. Hill	
G-BWED	Thunder Ax7-77 balloon	J. Tod	
G-BWEE	Cameron V-42 balloon	Aeromantics Ltd	
G-BWEF	SNCAN Stampe SV-4C	Acebell BWEF Syndicate (G-BOVL)	
G-BWEG	Shaw Europa	Wessex Europa Group	
G-BWEH	HOAC Katana DV.20	MWE (Mid-West Engines) Ltd	
G-BWEI	Cessna 172N	A. P. Dyer	
G-BWEL	Sky 200-24 balloon	Sky Balloons Ltd	
G-BWEM	V.S.358 Seafire L.III	C. J. Warrillow	
G-BWEN	Macair Merlin GT	B. W. Davies	
G-BWEO	Lindstrand AM400 balloon	Lindstrand Balloons Ltd	
G-BWEP	Lindstrand AM2200 balloon	Lindstrand Balloons Ltd	
G-BWER	Lindstrand AM400 balloon	Lindstrand Balloons Ltd	
G-BWET	PA-28-161 Warrior II	Taylor Aircraft Services Ltd	
G-BWEU	Cessna F.152 II	Sky Pro Ltd	
G-BWEV	Cessna 152 II	Haimoss Ltd	
G-BWEW	Cameron N-105 balloon	Flying Pictures (Balloons) Ltd	
G-BWEX	Dornier Do.228-202K	Suckling Airways (Luton) Ltd	
G-BWEY	Bensen B.8	F. G. Shepherd	
G-BWEZ	Piper J-3C-65 Cub	J. G. McTaggart	
G-BWFB	D.H.104 Devon C.2	ASB Colton Aviation Ltd	
G-BWFD	HOAC Katana DV.20	Mid-West Engines Ltd	
G-BWFE	HOAC Katana DV.20	Mid-West Engines Ltd	
G-BWFG	Robin HR.200/120B	Mistral Aviation Ltd	
G-BWFH	Shaw Europa	R. W. Baylie & B. L. Wratten	
G-BWFI	HOAC Katana DV.20	Mid-West Engines Ltd	
G-BWFJ	Evans VP-1	P. A. West	
G-BWFK	Lindstrand LBL-77A balloon	Virgin Airship & Balloon Co. Ltd	
G-BWFL	Cessna 500 Citation	Crown Investment Holdings Ltd	
G-BWFM	Yakovlev Yak-50	Classic Aviation Ltd/Duxford	
G-BWFN	Hapi Cygnet SF-2A	T. Crawford	
G-BWFO	Colomban MC.15 Cri-Cri	O. G. Jones	
G-BWFP	Yakovlev Yak-52	M. C. Lee	

Notes	Reg.	Type	Owner or Operator
	G-BWFR	Hunter F.58	The Old Flying Machine Co. Ltd/Duxford
	G-BWFS	Hunter F.58	The Old Flying Machine Co. Ltd/Duxford
	G-BWFT	Hunter T.8M	B. J. Pover & B. R. Pearson
	G-BWFU	Yakovlev C.11	M. Rusche
	G-BWFV	HOAC Katana DV.20	Mid-West Engines Ltd
	G-BWFW	HOAC Katana DV.20	Mid-West Engines Ltd
	G-BWFX	Shaw Europa	A. D. Stewart
	G-BWFY	AS.350B-1 Ecureuil	P. Pilkington & K. M. Armitage
	G-BWFZ	Murphy Rebel	I. E. Spencer (G-SAVS)
	G-BWGA	Lindstrand LBL-105A balloon	Air 2 Air Ltd
	G-BWGB	Hawker 800XP	Raytheon Corporate Jets Inc
	G-BWGC	Hawker 800XP	Raytheon Corporate Jets Inc
	G-BWGF	P.84 Jet Provost T.5A	Global Aviation Ltd
	G-BWGG	MH.1521C-1 Broussard	R. H. Reeves
	G-BWGH	Shaw Europa	J. H. Frizell
	G-BWGI	VPM M.16 Tandem Trainer	Whisky Mike (Aviation) Ltd
	G-BWGJ	Chilton DW.1A	T. J. Harrison
	G-BWGK	Hunter GA.11	B. J. Pover & B. J. Pearson
	G-BWGL	Hunter T.8C	B. J. Pover & B. J. Pearson
	G-BWGM	Hunter T.8C	B. J. Pover & B. J. Pearson
	G-BWGN	Hunter T.8C	B. J. Pover & B. J. Pearson
	G-BWGO	Slingsby T.67M-200	R. Gray
	G-BWGP	Cameron C-80 balloon	P. J. & C. M. Gentle
	G-BWGR	TB-25N Mitchell (151632)	Aces High Ltd/North Weald
	G-BWGS	P.84 Jet Provost T.5A	J. S. Everett
	G-BWGT	P.84 Jet Provost T.4	Global Aviation Ltd
	G-BWGU	Cessna 150F	W. Davies
	G-BWGX	Cameron N-42 balloon	Newbury Building Soc.
	G-BWGY	HOAC Katana DV.20	Mid-West Engines Ltd
	G-BWGZ	HOAC Katana DV.20	Mid-West Engines Ltd
	G-BWHA	Hawker Hurricane IIB	Historic Flying Ltd/Audley End
	G-BWHB	Cameron O-65 balloon	G. Aimo
	G-BWHC	Cameron N-77 balloon	Travelsphere Ltd
	G-BWHD	Lindstrand LBL-31 balloon	Army Air Corps Balloon Club
	G-BWHF	PA-31-325 Navajo	Gulnare Ltd/Welshpool
	G-BWHG	Cameron N-65 balloon	Coffee Nannini SRL
	G-BWHH	PA-18 Super Cub 135	J. W. Macleod
	G-BWHI	D.H.C.1 Chipmunk 22A	J. Romain/Duxford
	G-BWHJ	Starstreak Shadow SA-II	N. Irwin
	G-BWHK	Rans S.6-116 Coyote II	N. D. White
	G-BWHM	Sky 140-24 balloon	Sky Balloons Ltd
	G-BWHN	AS.332L Super Puma	Brintel Helicopters Ltd
	G-BWHP	C.A.S.A. 1.131E Jungmann	J. F. Hopkins
	G-BWHR	Tipsy T.66 Nipper Srs 1	L. R. Marnef
	G-BWHS	RAF 2000 gyroplane	V. G. Freke
	G-BWHT	Everett Campbell Cricket	B. B. Woodman
	G-BWHU	Westland Scout AH.1	N. J. F. Boston
	G-BWHV	Denney Kitfox Mk 2	A. C. Dove
	G-BWHW	Cameron A-180 balloon	Societe Bombard SARL
	G-BWHX	Mil Mi-8	Orbit Resources Ltd
	G-BWHY	Robinson R-22	Helicentre Ltd/Blackpool
	G-BWHZ	Mil Mi-8	Orbit Resources Ltd
	G-BWIA	Rans S.10 Sakota	P. A. Beck
	G-BWIB	SA Bulldog Srs 120/122	L. Bax
	G-BWID	D.31 Turbulent	A. M. Turney
	G-BWIE	Hunter T.7A	Lansen Ltd/Bruntingthorpe
	G-BWIF	Robinson R-44 Astro	Sloane Helicopters Ltd/Sywell
	G-BWII	Cessna 150G	J. D. G. Hicks
	G-BWIJ	Shaw Europa	R. Lloyd
	G-BWIK	D.H.82A Tiger Moth	G. H. Fullbrook & B. J. Ellis
	G-BWIL	Rans S.10 Sakota	J. C. Longmore (G-WIEN)
	G-BWIM	Sikorsky S-76A (modified)	Bristow Helicopters Ltd
	G-BWIN	Douglas DC-10-30	Laker Airways/Caledonian Airways
	G-BWIO	HOAC Katana DV.20	HOAC Flugzeugwerk Wiener Neustadt GmbH
	G-BWIP	Cameron N-90 balloon	Noble Adventures Ltd
	G-BWIR	Dornier Do.328-100	Suckling Airways (Luton) Ltd
	G-BWIS	Mooney M.20M	Flemming Frandsen Aircraft Sales Ltd
	G-BWIT	QAC Quickie 1	D. E. Johnson & ptnrs
	G-BWIU	Hunter F.58	Historic Flying Ltd/Duxford
	G-BWIV	Shaw Europa	J. R. Lockwood-Goose
	G-BWIW	Sky 180-24 balloon	G. D. & L. Fitzpatrick
	G-BWIX	Sky 120-24 balloon	J. M. Percival

Reg.	Type	Owner or Operator	Notes
G-BWIY	Lindstrand LBL-105A balloon	Lindstrand Balloons Ltd	
G-BWIZ	QAC Quickie Tri-Q	B. J. Cain	
G-BWJA	—	—	
G-BWJB	Thunder Ax8-105 balloon	Justerini & Brooks Ltd	
G-BWJC	Cameron N-65 balloon	Cameron Balloons Ltd	
G-BWJD	Cameron R-200 balloon	Bondbaste Ltd	
G-BWJE	Sky 105-24 balloon	Sky Balloons Ltd	
G-BWJF	BAe Jetstream 4107	Trident Turboprop (Australia) Pty Ltd	
G-BWJG	Mooney M.20J	Samic Ltd	
G-BWJH	Shaw Europa	A. R. R. & J. A. S. T. Hood	
G-BWJI	Cameron V-90 balloon	Calarel Developments Ltd	
G-BWJJ	Cameron N-105 balloon	Cameron Balloons Ltd	
G-BWJK	Rotorway Executive 152	N. Kirk (G-OKIT)	
G-BWJL	Cameron N-120 balloon	Cameron Balloons Ltd	
G-BWJM	Bristol M1C *(replica)*	Shuttleworth Collection/O. Warden	
G-BWJN	Montgomerie-Bensen B.8	M. G. Mee	
G-BWJO	BN-2T Turbine Islander	Pilatus BN Ltd/Bembridge	
G-BWJP	Cessna 172C	Midair Aviation Ltd/Bournemouth	
G-BWJR	Sky 120-24 balloon	B. Brogan	
G-BWJS	Colt 120A balloon	Cameron Balloons Ltd	
G-BWJT	Yakovlev Yak-50	Badsaddle Stables Ltd	
G-BWJU	D.H.C.1 Chipmunk 22 (WK639)	Bolsover Consultancy Ltd	
G-BWJV	—	—	
G-BWJW	Westland Scout Ah.1	Austen Associates Partnership	
G-BWJX	H.S.125 Srs 700B	Raytheon Corporate Jets Inc	
G-BWJY	D.H.C.1 Chipmunk 22 (WG469)	K. J. Thompson	
G-BWJZ	D.H.C.1 Chipmunk 22 (WK638)	J. Zemlik	
G-BWKA	Hunter F.58	R.V. Aviation Ltd/Bournemouth	
G-BWKB	Hunter F.58	R.V. Aviation Ltd/Bournemouth	
G-BWKC	Hunter F.58	R.V. Aviation Ltd/Bournemouth	
G-BWKD	Cameron O-120 balloon	K.E. Viney	
G-BWKE	Cameron AS-105GD airship	Gefe-Flug GmbH/Germany	
G-BWKF	Cameron N-105 balloon	R. M. M. Botti/Italy	
G-BWKG	Shaw Europa	T. C. Jackson	
G-BWKH	—	—	
G-BWKI	—	—	
G-BWKJ	Rans S.7 Courier	J. P. Kovacs	
G-BWKK	Auster A.O.P.9 (XP279)	R. W. Fairless & D. R. White	
G-BWKL	H.S.125 Srs 700B	Kernekod Exports Ltd	
G-BWKM	MBB BK-117C-1	McAlpine Helicopters Ltd/Kidlington	
G-BWKN	Airbus A.320-212	Leisure International Airways Ltd	
G-BWKO	Airbus A.320-212	Leisure International Airways Ltd	
G-BWKP	Sky 105-24 balloon	Sky Balloons Ltd	
G-BWKR	Sky 90-24 balloon	B. Drawbridge	
G-BWKT	Stephens Akro Laser	P. D. Begley	
G-BWKU	Cameron A-250 balloon	British School of Ballooning	
G-BWKV	Cameron V-77 balloon	Poppies (UK) Ltd	
G-BWKW	Thunder Ax8-90 balloon	Venice Simplon Orient Express Ltd	
G-BWKX	Cameron A-250 balloon	Hot Airlines	
G-BWKY	Avro RJ85	British Aerospace (Operations) Ltd	
G-BWKZ	Lindstrand LBL-77A balloon	Lambert Smith Hampton Group Ltd	
G-BWLA	Lindstrand LBL-77A balloon	Virgin Airship & Balloon Co Ltd	
G-BWLB	Lindstrand Dreher Bottle SS balloon	International Balloons Ltd	
G-BWLC	Hughes 369E	Ford Helicopters Ltd	
G-BWLD	Cameron O-120 balloon	D. Pedri	
G-BWLE	Bell 212	Bristow Helicopters Ltd/Redhill	
G-BWLF	Cessna 404	Nor Leasing (G-BNXS)	
G-BWLG	BAe 146-200QC	Trident Aviation Leasing Service (G-PRCS)	
G-BWLH	Lindstrand LBL HS-100 airship	International Balloons Ltd	
G-BWLI	AS.350B-2 Ecureuil	TWR Group Ltd (G-IINA)/Kidlington	
G-BWLJ	Taylorcraft DCO-65	C. Evans	
G-BWLK	Lindstrand LBL-69A balloon	International Balloons Ltd	
G-BWLL	Murphy Rebel	F. W. Parker	
G-BWLM	Sky 65-24 balloon	Dachstein Tauern Balloons KG	
G-BWLN	Cameron O-84 balloon	Reggiana Riduttori SRL	
G-BWLO	Bell 206A JetRanger	RCR Aviation Ltd	
G-BWLP	—	—	
G-BWLR	MH.1521M Broussard	Chicory Crops Ltd	
G-BWLS	—	—	
G-BWLT	—	—	
G-BWLU	Sky 90-24 balloon	Sky Balloons Ltd	
G-BWLV	—		

Notes	Reg.	Type	Owner or Operator
	G-BWLW	Light Aero Avid Speedwing Mk4	P. C. Creswick
	G-BWLX	Westland Scout AH.1	R. E. Dagless
	G-BWLY	Rotorway Executive 90	P. W. & I. P. Bewley
	G-BWLZ	Wombat gyroplane	J. M. Shippen
	G-DWMA	Colt 105A balloon	Bristol & West Motor Auction Ltd
	G-BWMB	Jodel D.119	C. Hughes
	G-BWMC	Cessna 182P	Actra Associates
	G-BWMD	—	—
	G-BWME	—	—
	G-BWMF	Gloster Meteor T.7	Meteor Flight (Yatesbury)
	G-BWMG	—	—
	G-BWMH	—	—
	G-BWMI	PA-28RT-201T Turbo Arrow IV	Taylor Aircraft Services Ltd
	G-BWMJ	—	—
	G-BWMK	—	—
	G-BWML	—	—
	G-BWMM	—	—
	G-BWMN	—	—
	G-BWMO	—	—
	G-BWMP	—	—
	G-BWMS	—	—
	G-BWMT	—	—
	G-BWMU	—	—
	G-BWMV	—	—
	G-BWMX	—	—
	G-BWMY	—	—
	G-BWNA	AS.350B Ecureuil	RCR Aviation Ltd (G-BFNC)/Thruxton
	G-BWNX	Thunder Ax10-180 S2 balloon	Gone With The Wind Ltd (G-OWBC)
	G-BWOC	PA-31-350 Navajo Chieftain	BWOC Ltd
	G-BWON	Shaw Europa	G. T. Birks
	G-BWOW	Cameron N-105 balloon	S. J. Colin
	G-BWRR	Cessna 182Q	W. Rennie-Roberts
	G-BWSI	K&S SA.102.5 Cavalier	B. W. Shaw
	G-BWTL	Aerospatiale ATR-72-202	CityFlyer Express/British Airways
	G-BWTM	Aerospatiale ATR-72-202	CityFlyer Express/British Airways
	G-BWVE	Bell 206B JetRanger	Willow Vale Electronics Ltd (G-BOSX)
	G-BWWJ	Hughes 269C	Dave Nieman Models Ltd (G-BMYZ)
	G-BWWW	BAe Jetstream 3102	British Aerospace PLC/Warton

G-ABNT, Civilian C.A.C.1 Coupe.

G-AMTM, J/1 Autocrat.

G-BTZN, BAe 146-300.

G-PFBT V.806 Viscount.

G-YAKS, Yakovlev Yak-52.

Out-of-Sequence Registrations

Notes	Reg.	Type	Owner or Operator
	G-BXAX	Cameron N-77 balloon	Flying Pictures Balloons Ltd
	G-BXEG	Aerospatiale ATR-42-300	CityFlyer Express Ltd/British Airways
	G-BXPS	PA-23 Aztec 250C	N. H. Bailey (G-AYLY)
	G-BXUK	Robinson R-44 Astro	Heli Air Ltd
	G-BXVI	V.S.361 Spitfire F.XVI (RW386)	D. Arnold
	G-BYAA	Boeing 767-204ER	Britannia Airways Ltd *Sir Matt Busby CBE*
	G-BYAB	Boeing 767-204ER	Britannia Airways Ltd *Brian Johnston CBE MC*
	G-BYAC	Boeing 757-204	Britannia Airways Ltd
	G-BYAD	Boeing 757-204	Britannia Airways Ltd
	G-BYAE	Boeing 757-204	Britannia Airways Ltd
	G-BYAF	Boeing 757-204	Britannia Airways Ltd
	G-BYAG	Boeing 757-204	Britannia Airways Ltd
	G-BYAH	Boeing 757-204	Britannia Airways Ltd
	G-BYAI	Boeing 757-204	Britannia Airways Ltd
	G-BYAJ	Boeing 757-204	Britannia Airways Ltd
	G-BYAK	Boeing 757-28A	Britannia Airways Ltd
	G-BYAL	Boeing 757-28A	Britannia Airways Ltd
	G-BYAM	Boeing 757-2T7	Britannia Airways Ltd (G-DRJC)
	G-BYAN	Boeing 757-204	Britannia Airways Ltd
	G-BYAO	Boeing 757-204	Britannia Airways Ltd
	G-BYAP	Boeing 757-204	Britannia Airways Ltd
	G-BYAR	Boeing 757-204	Britannia Airways Ltd
	G-BYAS	Boeing 757-204	Britannia Airways Ltd
	G-BYAT	Boeing 757-204	Britannia Airways Ltd
	G-BYAU	Boeing 757-204	Britannia Airways Ltd
	G-BYAW	Boeing 757-204	Britannia Airways Ltd *Eric Morecombe OBE*
	G-BYEE	Mooney M.20K	H. W. Robertson
	G-BYIJ	C.A.S.A. 1.131E Jungmann 2000	K. B. Palmer
	G-BYLL	F.8L Falco	N. J. Langrick/Sherburn
	G-BYLS	Bede BD-4	G. H. Bayliss
	G-BYNG	Cessna T.303	J. M. E. Byng (G-PTWB)
	G-BYRE	Rans S.10 Sakota	R. J. & M. B. Trickey
	G-BYSE	AB-206B JetRanger 2	Bewise Ltd (G-BFND)
	G-BYSL	Cameron O-56 balloon	S. S. M. Askey
	G-BYTE	Robinson R-22B	Capital Helicopters Ltd
	G-BZBH	Thunder Ax6-65 balloon	R. B. & G. Clarke
	G-BZKK	Cameron V-56 balloon	P. J. Green & C. Bosley *Gemini II*
	G-CAFZ	PA-31-350 Navajo Chieftain	London Flight Centre (Stansted) Ltd (G-BPPT)
	G-CALL	PA-23 Aztec 250F	Woodgate Aviation (IOM) Ltd
	G-CALV	PA-39 Twin Comanche 160 C/R	M. & V. Rahmani (G-AZFO)
	G-CAMM	Hawker Cygnet (replica)	D. M. Cashmore
	G-CARS	Pitts S-2A Special (replica) (BAPC134) ★	Toyota Ltd
	G-CAXF	Cameron O-77 balloon	R. D. & S. J. Sarjeant
	G-CAYN	Dornier Do.228-201	Cayenne Ltd (G-MLNR)
	G-CBAC	Short SD3-60 Variant 200	BAC Leasing Ltd (G-BLYH)
	G-CBAL	PA-28-161 Warrior II	Britannia Airways Ltd
	G-CBEA	BAe Jetstream 3102-01	European Airways Ltd
	G-CBIL	Cessna 182K	K. A. Clarke/Newcastle
	G-CBJB	Sikorsky S-76A	Bond Helicopters Ltd
	G-CBKT	Cameron O-77 balloon	Caledonian Airways Ltd
	G-CBOR	Cessna F.172N	P. Seville
	G-CBRA	AS.365N-2 Dauphin 2	Lattice Ltd
	G-CBVF	Cameron A-210 balloon	Virgin Balloon Flights Ltd
	G-CCAR	Cameron N-77 balloon	The Colt Car Co Ltd
	G-CCAT	AA-5A Cheetah	Plane Talking Ltd (G-OAJH/G-KILT/ G-BJFA)/Elstree
	G-CCCC	Cessna 172H	K. E. Wilson
	G-CCCP	Yakovlev Yak-52	R. J. N. Howarth
	G-CCDI	Cameron N-77 balloon	Charles Church Developments PLC
	G-CCLY	Bell 206B JetRanger 3	Ciceley Ltd (G-TILT/G-BRJO)
	G-CCOL	AA-5A Cheetah	Lowlog Ltd (G-BIVU)
	G-CCON	Beech F33C Bonanza	P. J. Withinshaw
	G-CCOZ	Monnett Sonerai II	P. R. Cozens

Reg.	Type	Owner or Operator	Notes
G-CCUB	Piper J-3C-65 Cub	Cormack (Aircraft Services) Ltd	
G-CDBS	MBB Bo 105DBS	Bond Helicopters Ltd/Aberdeen	
G-CDEE	Pitts S-2B Special	G. C. Dodds & R. W. Davies	
G-CDET	Culver LCA Cadet	H. B. Fox/Booker	
G-CDGA	Taylor JT.1 Monoplane	R. M. Larimore	
G-CDON	PA-28-161 Warrior II	East Midlands Flying Club PLC	
G-CDRU	C.A.S.A. 1.131E Jungmann 2000	P. Cunniff/White Waltham	
G-CEAL	Short SD3-60 Variant 100	Community Express Airlines Ltd (G-BPXO)	
G-CEAS	HPR-7 Herald 214	Channel Express (Air Services) Ltd (G-BEBB)/Bournemouth	
G-CEGA	PA-34-200T Seneca II	Mercia Aviation/Wellesbourne	
G-CEJA	Cameron V-77 balloon	N. L. Jaques (G-BTOF)	
G-CERT	Mooney M.20K	Fairline Boats PLC/Conington	
G-CEXB	F.27 Friendship Mk 500	Channel Express (Air Services) Ltd/ Bournemouth	
G-CEXP	HPR-7 Herald 209	Channel Express (Air Services) Ltd (G-BFRJ)/Bournemouth	
G-CEXS	L.188C Electra	Channel Express (Air Services) Ltd/ Bournemouth	
G-CFBI	Colt 56A balloon	G. A. Fisher	
G-CFLT	AS.355F-1 Twin Squirrel	Osten Airfinance Ltd (G-BNBI)	
G-CFLY	Cessna 172F	I. Hughes & B. T. Williams	
G-CGCG	Robinson R-22B	J .M. Henderson	
G-CGHM	PA-28 Cherokee 140	M. J. Flynn	
G-CGOD	Cameron N-77 balloon	Abbey Plant Co Ltd	
G-CHAA	Cameron O-90 balloon	The Balloon Club Ltd	
G-CHAL	Robinson R-22B	Plane Talking Ltd/Elstree	
G-CHAM	Cameron 90 Pot SS balloon	Nestlé UK Ltd	
G-CHAR	Grob G.109B	RAFGSA/Bicester	
G-CHAS	PA-28-181 Archer II	C. H. Elliott	
G-CHAV	Shaw Europa	Chavenage Flying Group	
G-CHEM	PA-34-200T Seneca II	Channel Islands Air Charter Ltd	
G-CHES	BN-2A-26 Islander	The Cheshire Constabulary (G-PASY/ G-BPCB/G-BEXA/G-MALI/G-DIVE)	
G-CHIK	Cessna F.152	Stapleford Flying Club Ltd (G-BHAZ)	
G-CHIL	Robinson R-22HP	Lateq Aviation Ltd	
G-CHIP	PA-28-181 Archer II	C. M. Hough/Fairoaks	
G-CHIS	Robinson R-22B	Bradmore Helicopter Leasing	
G-CHKL	Cameron 120 Kookaburra SS balloon	Eagle Ltd	
G-CHI A	AS.355F-1 Twin Squirrel	Clyde Helicopters Ltd	
G-CHLT	Stemme S.10	F. C. Y. Cheung/Hong Kong	
G-CHMP	Bellanca 7ACA Champ	I. J. Langley	
G-CHNL	F.27 Friendship Mk 600	Channel Express (Air Services) Ltd/Bournemouth	
G-CHNX	L.188AF Electra	Channel Express (Air Services) Ltd/ Bournemouth	
G-CHOK	Cameron V-77 balloon	A. J. Moore	
G-CHOP	Westland-Bell 47G-3B1	Wessex Air Contracts Ltd	
G-CHRP	Colt Flying Book SS balloon	Chronicle Communications Ltd	
G-CHRR	Colt Flying Book SS balloon	Chronicle Communications Ltd	
G-CHTA	AA-5A Cheetah	Rapid Spin Ltd (G-BFRC)/Biggin Hill	
G-CHUB	Colt N-51 balloon	Chubb Fire Security Ltd	
G-CHUK	Cameron O-77 balloon	L. C. Taylor	
G-CHYL	Robinson R-22B	Pentech	
G-CIAS	BN-2B-21 Islander	Channel Island Air Search Ltd (G-BKJM)	
G-CICI	Cameron R-15 balloon	Ballooning Endeavours Ltd	
G-CIII	Oldfield Baby Lakes	G. Cooper	
G-CIPI	AJEP Wittman W.8 Tailwind	M. H. D. Soltau (G-AYDU)	
G-CITY	PA-31-350 Navajo Chieftain	Woodgate Aviation (IOM) Ltd	
G-CIVA	Boeing 747-436	British Airways *City of St. Davids*	
G-CIVB	Boeing 747-436	British Airways *City of Lichfield*	
G-CIVC	Boeing 747-436	British Airways *City of St. Andrews*	
G-CIVD	Boeing 747-436	British Airways *City of Coventry*	
G-CIVE	Boeing 747-436	British Airways *City of Sunderland*	
G-CIVF	Boeing 747-436	British Airways *City of St Albans*	
G-CIVG	Boeing 747-436	British Airways *City of Wells*	
G-CIVH	Boeing 747-436	British Airways	
G-CIVI	Boeing 747-436	British Airways	
G CJBC	PA-28 Cherokee 180	J. B. Cave/Halfpenny Green	
G-CJCI	Pilatus P2-06 (CC+43)	Pilatus P2 Flying Group	
G-CJIM	Taylor JT.1 Monoplane	J. Crawford	
G-CJUD	Denney Kitfox Mk 3	C. W. Judge	

Notes	Reg.	Type	Owner or Operator
	G-CKCK	Enstrom 280FX	Southern Air Ltd/Shoreham
	G-CKEN	Wombat autogyro	K. H. Durran
	G-CLAC	PA-28-161 Warrior II	Clacton Light Aviation Co
	G-CLAS	Short SD3-60 Variant 100	BAC Express Ltd (G-BLED)
	G-CLEA	PA-28-161 Warrior II	Creative Logistics Enterprises & Aviation Ltd & R. J. Harrison
	G-CLEM	Bo 208A2 Junior	A. W. Webster (G-ASWE)
	G-CLIC	Cameron A-105 balloon	Matrix Computer Maintenance Ltd
	G-CLIP	AS.355N Twin Squirrel	Quantel Ltd/Biggin Hill
	G-CLOS	PA-34-200 Seneca II	Greenclose Aviation Services Ltd/ Bournemouth
	G-CLUB	Cessna FRA.150M	Osprey Flying Club/Cranfield
	G-CLUE	PA-34-200T Seneca II	Bristol Office Machines Ltd
	G-CLUX	Cessna F.172N	J. & K. Aviation/Liverpool
	G-CLYV	Robinson R-22B	C. A. Ecroyd
	G-CMDR	R. Commander 114	J. N. Scott & G. C. Bishop
	G-CMGC	PA-25 Pawnee 235	Midland Gliding Club Ltd (G-BFEX)/ Long Mynd
	G-COCO	Cessna F.172M	P. C. Sheard & R. C. Larder
	G-COIN	Bell 206B JetRanger 2	C. Sarno
	G-COKE	Cameron O-65 balloon	M. C. Bradley
	G-COLA	Beech F33C Bonanza	John Bradley & Barry Ltd and J. A. Kelman (G-BUAZ)
	G-COLL	Enstrom 280C-UK-2 Shark	SG Aviation Services Ltd
	G-COLR	Colt 69A balloon	British School of Ballooning
	G-COMB	PA-30 Twin Comanche 160B	J. T. Bateson (G-AVBL)/Ronaldsway
	G-COMM	PA-23 Aztec 250C	C. J. Neale (G-AZMG)
	G-COMP	Cameron N-90 balloon	Computacenter Ltd
	G-CONB	Robin DR.400/180	Winchcombe Farm (G-BUPX)
	G-CONC	Cameron N-90 balloon	British Airways
	G-COOK	Cameron N-77 balloon	IAZ (International) Ltd
	G-COOP	Cameron N-31 balloon	Rango Balloon & Kite Co
	G-COOT	Taylor Coot A	P. M. Napp
	G-COPS	Piper J-3C-65 Cub	R. W. Sproat & C. E. Simpson
	G-COPY	AA-5A Cheetah	Emberden Ltd (G-BIEU)/Biggin Hill
	G-CORC	Bell 206B JetRanger 2	Air Corcoran Ltd (G-CJHI/G-BBFB)
	G-CORD	Slingsby T.66 Nipper 3	B. A. Wright & K. E. Wilson (G-AVTB)
	G-COSY	Lindstrand LBL-56A balloon	Eastern Electricity PLC
	G-COTT	Cameron 60 Cottage SS balloon	Nottingham Hot-Air Balloon Club
	G-COUP	Ercoupe 415C	S. M. Gerrard
	G-COUR	AB-206B JetRanger	Speed Helicopters Ltd (G-FSDG/ G-ROOT/G-JETR/G-BKBR)
	G-COWS	ARV Super 2	T. C. Harrold (G-BONB)
	G-COZI	Rutan Cozy III	D. G. Machin
	G-CPCD	CEA DR.221	P. G. Bumpus & R. Thwaites
	G-CPCH	PA-28-151 Warrior	P. C. Hancock (G-BRGJ)
	G-CPEL	Boeing 757-236	British Airways (G-BRJE) *Walmer Castle*
	G-CPFC	Cessna F.152	Falcon Flying Services/Biggin Hill
	G-CPLI	Robinson R-22B	Thurston Helicopters (Engineering) Ltd
	G-CPOL	AS.355F-1 Twin Squirrel	Thames Valley Police Authority
	G-CPTM	PA-28-151 Warrior	T. J. Mackay & C. M. Pollett (G-BTOE)
	G-CPTS	AB-206B JetRanger 2	A. R. B. Aspinall
	G-CRAK	Cameron N-77 balloon	Mobile Windscreens Ltd
	G-CRAN	Robin R.1180T	Gould Group
	G-CRAY	Robinson R-22B	W. H. Grimshaw
	G-CRES	Denney Kitfox Mk 3	J. Smith
	G-CRIC	Colomban MC.15 Cri-Cri	A. B. Cameron
	G-CRIL	R. Commander 112B	Rockwell Aviation Group/Cardiff
	G-CRIS	Taylor JT.1 Monoplane	C. R. Steer
	G-CRML	Cessna 414A	Fairport Ltd
	G-CROL	Maule MXT-7-180	D. C. Croll & ptnrs
	G-CRPH	Airbus A.320-231	Airtours International Airways Ltd
	G-CRUS	Cessna T.303	B. A. Groves
	G-CRUZ	Cessna T.303	Bank Farm Ltd
	G-CRZY	Thunder Ax8-105 balloon	R. Carr (G-BDLP)/France
	G-CSBM	Cessna F.150M	T. W. & S. J. Eagles
	G-CSCS	Cessna F.172N	Conegate Ltd
	G-CSFC	Cessna 150L	Shropshire Aero Club Ltd/Sleap
	G-CSFT	PA-23 Aztec 250D	Aces High Ltd (G-AYKU)/North Weald
	G-CSNA	Cessna 421C	William Loughran Ltd
	G-CSVS	Boeing 757-236	Airtours International Airways Ltd (G-IEAC)

Reg.	Type	Owner or Operator	Notes
G-CSZB	V.807B Viscount	British World Airlines Ltd (G-AOXU)	
G-CTCL	SOCATA TB.10 Tobago	Merryfield Leasing Ltd (G-BSIV)	
G-CTEK	Bell 206B JetRanger	Lateq Aviation Ltd/Booker	
G-CTKL	Noorduyn AT-16 Harvard IIB (54137)	Key Audio Systems Ltd	
G-CTOY	Denney Kitfox Mk 3	G. S. Cass	
G-CTPW	Bell 206B JetRanger 3	C. T. Wheatley	
G-CTRN	Enstrom F-28C-UK	Manchester Helicopter Centre/Barton	
G-CTWW	PA-34-200T Seneca II	Control Techniques Drives Ltd (G-ROYZ/G-GALE)	
G-CUBB	PA-18 Super Cub 180	Bidford Gliding Centre Ltd	
G-CUBI	PA-18 Super Cub 135 (51-15673)	T. Watson	
G-CUBY	Piper J-3C-65 Cub	C. A. Bloom (G-BTZW)	
G-CURE	Colt 77A balloon	Flying Pictures (Balloons) Ltd	
G-CWAG	Sequoia F. 8L Falco	C. C. Wagner	
G-CWBM	Currie Wot	B. V. Mayo (G-BTVP)	
G-CWIZ	AS.350B Ecureuil	HFI Engineering (G-DJEM/G-ZBAC/ G-SEBI/G-BMCU)	
G-CWOT	Currie Wot	T. E. G. Buckett	
G-CXCX	Cameron N-90 balloon	Cathay Pacific Airways (London) Ltd	
G-CYGI	Hapi Cygnet SF-2A	B. Brown	
G-CYLS	Cessna T.303	Gledhill Water Storage Ltd (G-BKXI)/Blackpool	
G-CYMA	GA-7 Cougar	Cyma Petroleum Ltd (G-BKOM)/Elstree	
G-CZAR	Cessna 560 Citation V	Stadium City Ltd	
G-CZCZ	Avions Mudry CAP.10B	P. R. Moorhead	
G-DAAH	PA-28RT-201T Turbo Arrow IV	R. Peplow/Halfpenny Green	
G-DAAL	Avro 748 Srs 1	Emerald Airways Ltd (G-BEKG/G-VAJK)/ Liverpool	
G-DAAM	Robinson R-22B	A. A. Macaskill	
G-DACA	P.57 Sea Prince T.1 ★	P. G. Vallance Ltd/Charlwood	
G-DACC	Cessna 401B	Niglon Ltd (G-AYOU)/Birmingham	
G-DADS	Hughes 369HS	Executive Aviation Services Ltd	
G-DADY	Lindstrand LBL-77A balloon	International Balloons Ltd	
G-DAFT	AS.355F-2 Twin Squirrel	Powersense Ltd (G-BNNN)/Hayes	
G-DAFY	Beech 58 Baron	Ortac Air Ltd/Guernsey	
G-DAJB	Boeing 757-2T7	Monarch Airlines Ltd/Luton	
G-DAJC	Boeing 767-31KER	Airtours International Airways Ltd	
G-DAKK	Douglas C-47A	South Coast Airways/Bournemouth	
G-DAKS	Douglas C-47A (TS423)	Aces High Ltd/North Weald	
G-DAMY	Shaw Europa	Hart Aviation Ltd	
G-DAND	SOCATA TB.10 Tobago	Whitemoor Engineering Co Ltd	
G-DANI	Cessna 500 Citation	Assigntravel Ltd (G-BFAR)	
G-DANS	AS.355F-2 Twin Squirrel	Frewton Ltd (G-BTNM)	
G-DAPH	Cessna 180K	M. R. L. Astor	
G-DARA	PA-34-220T Seneca III	Pinta Investments Ltd	
G-DARR	Cessna 421C	Channon Asset Management Ltd (G-BNEZ)	
G-DASH	R. Commander 112A	Josef D. J. Jons & Co Ltd (G-BDAJ)	
G-DASI	Short SD3-60	Gill Airways Ltd (G-BKKW)/Newcastle	
G-DASU	Cameron V-77 balloon	D. & L. S. Litchfield	
G-DAVE	Jodel D.112	D. A. Porter/Sturgate	
G-DAYS	Shaw Europa	A. Hall & ptnrs	
G-DAYY	Lindstrand Fruit Bottle SS balloon	International Balloons Ltd	
G-DBAF	BAC One-Eleven 201AC	Trygon Ltd (G-ASJG) *(stored)*/Southend	
G-DBAL	H.S.125 Srs 3B	Osprey Aviation Ltd (G-BSAA)	
G-DCCC	BAe 125 Srs 800B	Raytheon Corporate Jets Inc	
G-DCCH	MBB Bo 105D	Devon & Cornwall Police Authority	
G-DCCI	BAe 125-1000B	Consolidated Contractors International (UK) Ltd (G-BUPL)	
G-DCEA	PA-34-200T Seneca II	M. J. Greasby/Booker	
G-DCFR	Cessna 550 Citation II	Chauffair (CI) Ltd (G-WYLX/G-JETD)	
G-DCIO	Douglas DC-10-30	British Airways *Epping Forest*/Gatwick	
G-DCKK	Cessna F.172N	M. Manston	
G-DCSW	PA-32R-301 Saratoga SP	A. W. Kendrick	
G-DCXL	Jodel D.140C	X-Ray Lima Group	
G-DDAY	PA-28R-201T Turbo Arrow III	G-DDAY Group (G-BPDO)	
G-DDCD	D.H.104 Dove 8	C. Daniel (G-ARUM)/Biggin Hill	
G-DDMV	NA T-6G Texan (41)	E. A. Morgan	
G-DEBB	Beech 35-B33 Debonair	Spitfire Aviation Ltd/Bournemouth	

Notes	Reg.	Type	Owner or Operator
	G-DEJL	Robinson R-22B	D. E. J. Lomas
	G-DELI	Thunder Ax7-77 balloon	Heather Flight Ltd
	G-DELL	Robinson R-22B	Delta Helicopters Ltd/Luton
	G-DELS	Robin DR.400/180	W. D. Nightingale
	G-DELT	Robinson R-22B	D. P. Fiske
	G-DEMH	Cessna F.172M (modified)	M. Hammond (G-BFLO)
	G-DENA	Cessna F.150G	Aviators Flight Centre (G-AVFO)/Southend
	G-DENB	Cessna F.150G	Aviators Flight Centre (G-ATZZ)/Southend
	G-DENC	Cessna F.150G	Aviators Flight Centre (G-AVAP)/Southend
	G-DENI	PA-32 Cherokee Six 300	Aviators Flight Centre (G-BAIA)/Southend
	G-DENS	Binder CP.301S Smaragd	J. K. Davies
	G-DENW	PA-44-180 Seminole	D. A. Woodhams
	G-DERB	Robinson R-22B	Derbyshire Helicopters (G-BPYH)
	G-DERV	Cameron Truck SS balloon	J. M. Percival
	G-DESI	Aero Designs Pulsar XP	D. F. Gaughan
	G-DESS	Mooney M.20J	W. E. Newnes
	G-DEVS	PA-28 Cherokee 180	180 Group (G-BGVJ)
	G-DEXP	ARV Super 2	J. P. Jenkins
	G-DEXY	Beech E90 King Air	Tornado Ltd
	G-DFLT	Cessna F.406 Caravan II	Direct Flight Ltd/Norwich
	G-DFLY	PA-38-112 Tomahawk	G. K. Snape
	G-DFVA	Cessna R.172K	R. A. Plowright
	G-DGDG	Glaser-Dirks DG.400/17	DG400 Flying Group/Lasham
	G-DGLD	HPR-7 Herald 214	Channel Express Group (Air Services) Ltd (G-BAVX)/Bournemouth
	G-DGWW	Rand-Robinson KR-2	W. Wilson/Liverpool
	G-DHAV	D.H.115 Vampire T.11	de Havilland Aviation Ltd
	G-DHCB	D.H.C.2 Beaver 1	Seaflite Ltd (G-BTDL)
	G-DHCI	D.H.C.1 Chipmunk 22	Felthorpe Flying Group Ltd (G-BBSE)
	G-DHLB	Cameron N-90 balloon	DHL International (UK) Ltd
	G-DHLI	Colt 90 World SS balloon	Virgin Airship & Balloon Co Ltd
	G-DHLZ	Colt 31A balloon	Virgin Airship & Balloon Co Ltd
	G-DHTM	D.H.82A Tiger Moth (replica)	E. G. Waite-Roberts
	G-DHVV	D.H.115 Vampire T.55 (U-1214)	Lindsay Wood Promotions Ltd
	G-DHWW	D.H.115 Vampire T.55 (XG775)	Lindsay Wood Promotions Ltd
	G-DHXX	D.H.100 Vampire FB.6 (LZ551/G)	Lindsay Wood Promotions Ltd
	G-DHYY	D.H.115 Vampire T.11	Lindsay Wood Promotions Ltd
	G-DHZZ	D.H.115 Vampire T.55 (U-1230)	Lindsay Wood Promotions Ltd
	G-DIAL	Cameron N-90 balloon	A. J. Street
	G-DIAT	PA-28 Cherokee 140	RAF Benevolent Fund's IAT/Bristol & Wessex Aeroplane Club (G-BCGK)/Lulsgate
	G-DICK	Thunder Ax6-56Z balloon	R. D. Sargeant
	G-DIET	Lindstrand Drinks Can SS balloon	International Balloons Ltd
	G-DIME	R. Commander 114	B. J. Ratcliffe & H. B. Richardson
	G-DINA	AA-5B Tiger	MRM of Fenton
	G-DING	Colt 77A balloon	G. J. Bell
	G-DINT	B.156 Beaufighter IF	T. E. Moore
	G-DIPI	Cameron Tub SS balloon	Virgin Airship & Balloon Co Ltd
	G-DIPS	Taylor JT.1 Monoplane	B. J. Halls
	G-DIRE	Robinson R-22B	Techspan Aviation Ltd
	G-DIRK	Glaser-Dirks DG.400	D. McK. Chalmers
	G-DIRT	Thunder Ax7-77Z balloon	R. J. Ngbaronye
	G-DISC	Cessna U.206A	C. M. J. Parton (G-BGWR)
	G-DISK	PA-24 Comanche 250	A. Johnston (G-APZG)
	G-DISO	Jodel 150	P. F. Craven & J. H. Shearer
	G-DIVA	Cessna R.172K XPII	M. Gardner
	G-DIWY	PA-32 Cherokee Six 300	Industrial Foam Systems Ltd
	G-DIZO	Jodel D.120A	D. Aldersea (G-EMKM)
	G-DIZY	PA-28R-201T Turbo Arrow III	Medway Arrow Group
	G-DJHB	Beech A23-19 Musketeer	Nayland Aiglet Group (G-AZZE)
	G-DJIM	MHCA-1	J. Crawford
	G-DJJA	PA-28-181 Archer II	Choice Aircraft/Fowlmere
	G-DJLW	H.S.125 Srs 3B/RA	Source Ltd (G-AVVB)
	G-DJNH	Denney Kitfox Mk 3	D. J. N. Hall
	G-DKDP	Grob G.109	D. W. & J. E. Page
	G-DKGF	Viking Dragonfly	P. C. Dowbor
	G-DLCB	Shaw Europa	D. J. Lockett
	G-DLDL	Robinson R-22B	A. J. Wagstaff
	G-DLOM	SOCATA TB.20 Trinidad	J. N. A. Adderley/Guernsey
	G-DLTA	Slingsby T.67M Firefly	Firefly Aerial Promotions Ltd (G-SFTX)
	G-DMCA	Douglas DC-10-30	Monarch Airlines Ltd/Luton

Reg.	Type	Owner or Operator	Notes
G-DMCS	PA-28R Cherokee Arrow 200-II	D. L. Johns & F. K. Parker (G-CPAC)	
G-DNCS	PA-28R-201T Turbo Arrow III	BRT Arrow Ltd/Barton	
G-DNLB	MBB Bo 105DBS/4	Bond Helicopters Ltd (G-BCDH/G-BTBD/G-BUDP)	
G-DNLD	Cameron 97 Donald SS balloon	The Walt Disney Co Ltd	
G-DNVT	G.1159C Gulfstream IV	Shell Aircraft Ltd/Heathrow	
G-DOCA	Boeing 737-436	British Airways *River Ballinderry*	
G-DOCB	Boeing 737-436	British Airways *River Bush*	
G-DOCC	Boeing 737-436	British Airways *River Affric*	
G-DOCD	Boeing 737-436	British Airways *River Aire*	
G-DOCE	Boeing 737-436	British Airways *River Alness*	
G-DOCF	Boeing 737-436	British Airways *River Beauly*	
G-DOCG	Boeing 737-436	British Airways *River Blackwater*	
G-DOCH	Boeing 737-436	British Airways *River Brue*	
G-DOCI	Boeing 737-436	British Airways *River Carron*	
G-DOCJ	Boeing 737-436	British Airways *River Glass*	
G-DOCK	Boeing 737-436	British Airways *River Lochay*	
G-DOCL	Boeing 737-436	British Airways *River Lune*	
G-DOCM	Boeing 737-436	British Airways *River Meon*	
G-DOCN	Boeing 737-436	British Airways *River Ottery*	
G-DOCO	Boeing 737-436	British Airways *River Parett*	
G-DOCP	Boeing 737-436	British Airways *River Swift*	
G-DOCR	Boeing 737-436	British Airways *River Tavy*	
G-DOCS	Boeing 737-436	British Airways *River Teifi*	
G-DOCT	Boeing 737-436	British Airways *River Tene*	
G-DOCU	Boeing 737-436	British Airways *River Teviot*	
G-DOCV	Boeing 737-436	British Airways *River Thurso*	
G-DOCW	Boeing 737-436	British Airways *River Till*	
G-DOCX	Boeing 737-436	British Airways *River Tirry*	
G-DOCZ	Boeing 737-436	British Airways (G-BVBZ) *River Wharfe*	
G-DODD	Cessna F.172P-II	K. Watts/Elstree	
G-DODI	PA-46-350P Malibu	Sunseeker Sales (UK) Ltd	
G-DOFY	Bell 206B JetRanger 3	Cinnamond Ltd	
G-DOGS	Cessna R.182RG	P. Bennett & J. R. Shawe	
G-DOLY	Cessna T.303	R. M. Jones (G-BJZK)	
G-DONI	AA-5B Tiger	D. M. Maclean (G-BLLT)	
G-DONS	PA-28RT-201T Turbo Arrow IV	D. J. Murphy	
G-DONZ	Shaw Europa	D. J. Smith & D. McNicholl	
G-DOOR	M.S.893E Rallye 180GT	Lynair Flying Group	
G-DOOZ	AS.355F-2 Twin Squirrel	Lynton Aviation Ltd (G-BNSX)	
G-DORB	Bell 206B JetRanger 3	Dorb Crest Homes Ltd	
G-DOVE	Cessna 182Q	P. J. Contracting	
G-DOWN	Colt 31A balloon	M. Williams	
G-DPPS	AS.355N Twin Squirrel	Dyfed-Powys Police Authority	
G-DRAC	Cameron Dracula Skull SS balloon	Shiplake Investments Ltd	
G-DRAG	Cessna 152 (tailwheel)	L. M. Maynard & D. C. Scouller (G-REME/G-BRNF)	
G-DRAI	Robinson R-22B	J. M. Hawkes	
G-DRAR	Hughes 369E	Readmans Ltd	
G-DRAW	Colt 77A balloon	Readers Digest Association Ltd	
G-DRAY	Taylor JT.1 Monoplane	L. J. Dray	
G-DRBG	Cessna 172M	M. R. & K. E. Slack (G-MUIL)	
G-DRGN	Cameron N-105 balloon	W. I. Hooker & C. Parker	
G-DRNT	Sikorsky S-76A	Bond Helicopters Ltd/Aberdeen	
G-DROP	Cessna U.206C	Peterborough Parachute Centre Ltd (G-UKNO/G-BAMN)/Sibson	
G-DRSV	CEA DR.315 (modified)	R. S. Voice	
G-DRYI	Cameron N-77 balloon	J. Barbour & Sons Ltd	
G-DRYS	Cameron N-90 balloon	J. Barbour & Sons Ltd	
G-DRZF	CEA DR.360	C. A. Parker/Sywell	
G-DSGC	PA-25 Pawnee 235C	Devon & Somerset Gliding Club Ltd	
G-DSID	PA-34-220T Seneca III	D. Sidoli & Sons (Shrewsbury) Ltd	
G-DTCP	PA-32R Cherokee Lance 300	Campbell Aviation Ltd (G-TEEM)	
G-DUCH	Beech 76 Duchess	C. D. Weiswall	
G-DUDS	C.A.S.A. 1.131E Jungmann 2000	D. H. Pattison	
G-DUET	Wood Duet	C. Wood	
G-DUNN	Zenair CH.250	A. Dunn	
G-DURO	Shaw Europa	R. Swinden	
G-DURX	Thunder 77A balloon	V. Trimble	
G-DUST	Stolp SA.300 Starduster Too	J. V. George	
G-DUVL	Cessna F.172N	A. J. Simpson/Denham	
G-DVBF	Lindstrand LBL-210A balloon	Virgin Balloon Flights Ltd	

Notes	Reg.	Type	Owner or Operator
	G-DVON	D.H.104 Devon C.2 (VP955)	C. L. Thatcher
	G-DWIA	Chilton D.W.1A	D. Elliott
	G-DWIB	Chilton D.W.1B (replica)	J. Jennings
	G-DWPH	Ultramagic M-77	Ultramagic UK
	G-DXRG	Cameron 105 Agfa SS balloon	Cameron Balloons Ltd
	G DYNE	Cessna 411	Commair Aviation Ltd/E. Midlands
	G-DYOU	PA-38-112 Tomahawk	Airways Aero Associations Ltd/Booker
	G-DZEL	Shaw Europa	R. J. W. Wood
	G-EAGL	Cessna 421C	Moseley Group (PSV) Ltd & Clowes Estates Ltd/E. Midlands
	G-EBJI	Hawker Cygnet (replica)	C. J. Essex
	G-ECAV	Beech 200 Super King Air	GEC Avionics Ltd/Rochester
	G-ECBH	Cessna F.150K	Air Fenland Ltd
	G-ECDX	D.H.71 Tiger Moth (replica)	M. D. Souch
	G-ECGC	Cessna F.172N-II	Leicestershire Aero Club Ltd
	G-ECGO	Bo 208C Junior	M. F. R. B. Collett
	G-ECHO	Enstrom 280C-UK-2 Shark	ALP Electrical (Maidenhead) Ltd (G-LONS/G-BDIB)/Booker
	G-ECJM	PA-28R-201T Turbo Arrow III	Regishire Ltd (G-FESL/G-BNRN)
	G-ECKE	Avro 504K (replica) (D8781)	N. Wright & C. M. Kettlewell
	G-ECOS	AS.355F-1 Twin Squirrel	Pace Micro Technology Ltd (G-DOLR/G-BPVB)
	G-ECOX	Grega GN.1 Air Camper	H. C. Cox
	G-EDEN	SOCATA TB.10 Tobago	N. G. Pistol & ptnrs
	G-EDGE	Jodel 150	A. D. Edge
	G-EDIE	Robinson R-44	Serve Offer Ltd
	G-EDNA	PA-38-112 Tomahawk	D. J. Clucas
	G-EDOT	Cessna T.337D	R. M. & J. A. Nicol (G-BJIY)
	G-EDRY	Cessna T.303	Pat Eddery Ltd
	G-EEAC	PA-31 Turbo Navajo	E. Alexander (G-SKKA/G-FOAL/ G-RMAE/G-BAEG)
	G-EEGL	Christen Eagle II	A. J. Wilson
	G-EENY	GA-7 Cougar	Plane Talking Ltd/Elstree
	G-EEUP	SNCAN Stampe SV-4C	A. M. Wajih
	G-EEVS	Agusta A.109A-II	Castle Air Charters Ltd (G-OTSL)
	G-EEZE	Rutan LongEz	A. J. Nurse
	G-EFRY	Light Aero Avid Aerobat	J. J. Donely
	G-EFSM	Slingsby T.67M-260	Slingsby Aviation Ltd (G-BPLK)
	G-EFTE	Bolkow Bo 207	N. J. Heaton
	G-EGAP	Sequoia F.8L Falco	E. G. A. Prance
	G-EGEE	Cessna 310Q	D. J. Pursey & H. Kloosterboer (G-AZVY)
	G-EGEL	Christen Eagle II	D. J. Daly
	G-EGGG	Lindstrand Humpty SS balloon	International Balloons Ltd
	G-EGGS	Robin DR.400/180	R. Foot
	G-EGHB	Ercoupe 415D	J. H. Spanton
	G-EGHH	Hunter F.58	Jet Heritage Charitable Foundation Ltd/Bournemouth
	G-EGJA	SOCATA TB.20 Trinidad	D. A. Williamson/Alderney
	G-EGLD	PA-28-161 Cadet	J. Appleton/Denham
	G-EGLE	Christen Eagle II	R. L. Mitcham & ptnrs
	G-EGLT	Cessna 310R	Tilling Associates Ltd (G-BHTV)
	G-EGUL	Christen Eagle II	P. N. Davis (G-FRYS)
	G-EGVL	Cameron A-250 balloon	The Balloon Club Ltd
	G-EHAP	Sportavia-Pützer RF.7	R. G. Boyes
	G-EHBJ	C.A.S.A. 1.131E Jungmann 2000	Mangreen Holdings Ltd
	G-EHIL	Westland-Agusta EH.101 (ZH647)	Westland Helicopters Ltd/Yeovil
	G-EHMM	Robin DR.400/180R	Booker Gliding Club Ltd
	G-EIBM	Robinson R-22B	Trustees of Bernard Hunter (G-BUCL)
	G-EIIR	Cameron N-77 balloon	D. V. Howard
	G-EIKY	Shaw Europa	J. D. Milbank
	G-EIWT	Cessna FR.182RG	P. P. D. Howard-Johnston/Edinburgh
	G-EJGO	Z.226HE Trener	N. J. Radford
	G-EJOC	AS.350B Ecureuil	Elmsdale (UK) Ltd (G-GEDS/G-HMAN/ G-SKIM/G-BIVP)
	G-ELBC	PA-34-200 Seneca II	Stapleford Flying Club Ltd (G-BANS)
	G-ELDG	Douglas DC-9-32	British Midland Airways Ltd The Orloff Diamond/E. Midlands
	G-ELDH	Douglas DC-9-32	British Midland Airways Ltd The Hastings Diamond/E. Midlands
	G-ELDI	Douglas DC-9-32	British Midland Airways Ltd The Regent Diamond/E. Midlands
	G-ELEC	Westland WG.30 Srs 200	Westland Helicopters Ltd (G-BKNV)/Yeovil

Reg.	Type	Owner or Operator	Notes
G-ELFI	Robinson R-22B	Tiger Helicopters	
G-ELIZ	Denney Kitfox Mk 2	A. J. Ellis	
G-ELKA	Christen Eagle II	Activity Aviation Ltd & D. Aitken	
G-ELMH	NA AT-6D Harvard III	M. Hammond	
G-ELRA	BAe 125-1000	Raytheon Corporate Jets Inc	
G-EMAK	PA-28R-201 Arrow III	D. & G. Rathbone	
G-EMAU	AS.355N Twin Squirrel	E. Midlands Air Support Unit	
G-EMAZ	PA-28-181 Archer II	E. J. Stanley	
G-EMER	PA-34-200 Seneca II	Haimoss Ltd & R. P. Thomas	
G-EMIN	Shaw Europa	Gemini Group	
G-EMJA	C.A.S.A. 1.131E Jungmann 2000	P. J. Brand	
G-EMMA	Cessna F.182Q	Watkiss Group Aviation	
G-EMMS	PA-38-112 Tomahawk	Ravenair/Manchester	
G-EMMY	Rutan Vari-Eze	M. J. Tooze	
G-EMNI	Speedtwin Mk 2	A. J. Clarry	
G-EMSI	Shaw Europa	P. W. L. Thomas	
G-EMSY	D.H.82A Tiger Moth	B. E. Micklewright (G-ASPZ)	
G-ENCE	Partenavia P.68B	P. Davies (G-OROY/G-BFSU)	
G-ENIE	Tipsy T.66 Nipper 3	E. J. Clarke	
G-ENII	Cessna F.172M	J. Howley	
G-ENNA	PA-28-161 Warrior II	G-ENNA Group	
G-ENNY	Cameron V-77 balloon	B. G. Jones	
G-ENOA	Cessna F.172F	M. K. Acors (G-ASZW)	
G-ENRI	Lindstrand LBL-105A balloon	P. G. Hall	
G-ENRY	Cameron N-105 balloon	P. G. & G. R. Hall	
G-ENSI	Beech F33A Bonanza	Special Analysis & Simulation Technology Ltd	
G-ENTT	Cessna F.152 II	Southern Flight Training Ltd (G-BHHI)	
G-ENTW	Cessna F.152 II	Southern Flight Training Ltd (G-BFLK)	
G-ENUS	Cameron N-90 balloon	Wye Valley Aviation Ltd	
G-EOFF	Taylor JT.2 Titch	G. H. Wylde	
G-EORG	PA-38-112 Tomahawk	Airways Aero Association/Booker	
G-EPDI	Cameron N-77 balloon	R. Moss	
G-EPED	PA-31-350 Navajo Chieftain	Pedley Furniture International Ltd (G-BMCJ)	
G-EPOX	Aero Designs Pulsar XP	K. F. Farey	
G-ERCO	Ercoupe 415D	J. H. Stanton	
G-ERDS	D.H.82A Tiger Moth	W. A. Gerdes	
G-ERIC	R. Commander 112TC	P. P. Patterson/Newcastle	
G-ERIK	Cameron N-77 balloon	T. M. Donnelly	
G-ERIX	Boeing Stearman A75N-1	P. P. Stanitzeck/Munich	
G-ERMO	ARV Super 2	P. R. Booth (G-BMWK)	
G-ERMS	Thunder Ax3 balloon	B. R. & M. Boyle	
G-ERNI	PA-28-181 Archer II	E. L. Collins (G-OSSY)	
G-EROS	Cameron H-34 balloon	Evening Standard Co Ltd	
G-ERRY	AA-5B Tiger	Herefordshire Aero Club Ltd (G-BFMJ)	
G-ERTY	D.H.82A Tiger Moth	C. Schumacher	
G-ESKY	PA-23 Aztec 250	Keen Leasing Ltd (G-BBNN)	
G-ESSX	PA-28-161 Warrior II	Courtenay Enterprises (G-BHYY)/ Biggin Hill	
G-ESTE	AA-5A Cheetah	Biblio International Ltd (G-GHNC)	
G-ETBY	PA-32 Cherokee Six 260	Yarnhaven Ltd (G-AWCY)	
G-ETCD	Colt 77A balloon	Philips Electronics Ltd	
G-ETDA	PA-28-161 Warrior II	T. Griffiths	
G-ETDB	PA-38-112 Tomahawk	R. A. Wakefield	
G-ETDC	Cessna 172P	Osprey Air Services Ltd	
G-ETFT	Colt Financial Times SS balloon	Financial Times Ltd (G-BSGZ)	
G-ETIN	Robinson R-22B	I. & E. Whitmore	
G-ETOM	BAe 125 Srs 800B	Broadstone Estate Ltd (G-BVFC/ G-TPHK/G-FDSL)	
G-EURA	Agusta-Bell 47J-2	E. W. Schnedlitz (G-ASNV)	
G-EVAN	Taylor JT.2 Titch	E. Evans	
G-EVER	Robinson R-22B	Technology Sales Training Ltd	
G-EVET	Cameron 80 Concept balloon	K. J. Foster	
G-EVNT	Lindstrand LBL-180A balloon	Redmalt Ltd	
G-EWAN	Prostar PT-2C	C. G. Shaw	
G-EWEL	Sikorsky S-76A	Chase Montagu Ltd	
G-EWFN	SOCATA TB-20 Trinidad	Trinidad Ltd (G-BRTY)	
G-EWIZ	Pitts S-2E Special	R. H. Jago	
G-EXEC	PA-34-200 Seneca	Sky Air Travel Ltd	
G-EXEX	Cessna 404	Atlantic Air Transport Ltd/Coventry	
G-EXIT	M.S.893E Rallye 180GT	K. J. Reynolds/Rochester	
G-EXLR	BAe 125-1000B	Raytheon Corporate Jets Inc	

Notes	Reg.	Type	Owner or Operator
	G-EXPR	Colt 90A balloon	Cellular Mann Ltd
	G-EXTR	Extra EA.260	D. M. Britten
	G-EYAS	Denney Kitfox Mk 2	E. J. Young
	G-EYCO	Robin DR.400/180	L. M. Gould
	G-EYES	Cessna 402C	Air Corbière Ltd (G-BLCE)/Coventry
	G-EYRE	Bell 206L-1 LongRanger	Hideroute Ltd (G-STVI)
	G-EZOS	Rutan Vari-Eze	O. Smith/Teesside
	G-FABB	Cameron V-77 balloon	P. Trumper
	G-FABM	Beech 95-B55 Baron	F. B. Miles (G-JOND/G-BMVC)
	G-FABS	Thunder Ax9-120 S2 balloon	Fabulous Flights Balloon Co
	G-FAGN	Robinson R-22B	C. R. Weldon
	G-FAIR	SOCATA TB.10 Tobago	Sally Marine Ltd/Guernsey
	G-FALC	Aeromere F.8L Falco	P. W. Hunter (G-AROT)/Elstree
	G-FAMY	Maule M5-180C	R. J. & K. C. Grimstead
	G-FANC	Fairchild 24R-46 Argus III	A. T. Fines
	G-FANG	AA-5A Cheetah	W. Perry
	G-FANL	Cessna FR.172K XP-II	J. Woodhouse & Co
	G-FARM	SOCATA Rallye 235GT	Bristol Cars Ltd
	G-FARO	Aero Designs Star-Lite SL.1	M. K. Faro
	G-FARR	Jodel 150	G. H. Farr
	G-FAST	Cessna 337G	Seillans Land Investigations Ltd
	G-FAYE	Cessna F.150M	Cheshire Air Training Services Ltd/Liverpool
	G-FBIX	D.H.100 Vampire FB.9 (WL505)	D. G. Jones
	G-FBMW	Cameron N-90 balloon	Bayrische Motorenwerke
	G-FBWH	PA-28R Cherokee Arrow 180	F. A. Short
	G-FCSP	Robin DR.400/180	FCS Photochemicals
	G-FDAV	SA.341G Gazelle 1	Federal Aviation Ltd (G-RIFA/G-ORGE/G-BBHU)
	G-FEBE	Cessna 340A	C. Dugard Ltd & E. C. Dugard
	G-FEFE	Scheibe SF.25B Falke	A. M. Thomson
	G-FELT	Cameron N-77 balloon	Allan Industries Ltd
	G-FFBR	Thunder Ax8-105 balloon	Fuji Photo Film (UK) Ltd
	G-FFEN	Cessna F.150M	Suffolk Aero Club Ltd/Ipswich
	G-FFHI	AS.355F-1 Twin Squirrel	Ford Farm Helicopters (G-GWHH/G-BKUL)
	G-FFOR	Cessna 310R II	Air Service Training Ltd (G-BMGF)/Perth
	G-FFRA	Dassault Falcon 20DC	FR Aviation Ltd/Bournemouth
	G-FFRB	Dassault Falcon 20DC	FR Aviation Ltd/Bournemouth
	G-FFRI	AS.355F-1 Twin Squirrel	Ford Farm Racing (G-GLOW/G-PAPA/G-CNET/G-MCAH)
	G-FFTI	SOCATA TB.20 Trinidad	Romsure Ltd
	G-FFTN	Bell 206B JetRanger 3	Kensington Aviation Ltd
	G-FFWD	Cessna 310R	Keef & Co Ltd (G-TVKE/G-EURO)
	G-FGID	FG-1D Corsair (88297)	Patina Ltd/Duxford
	G-FHAS	Scheibe SF.25E Super Falke	Burn Gliding Club Ltd
	G-FIAT	PA-28 Cherokee 140	RAF Benevolent Fund's IAT/Bristol & Wessex Aeroplane Club (G-BBYW)/Lulsgate
	G-FIBS	AS.350B Ecureuil	Irvine Aviation Ltd/Denham
	G-FIFE	Cessna FA.152	Tayside Aviation Ltd (G-BFYN)/Dundee
	G-FIFI	SOCATA TB.20 Trinidad	OLM Aviation Ltd (G-BMWS)
	G-FIGA	Cessna 152	Aerohire Ltd/Halfpenny Green
	G-FIGB	Cessna 152	Aerohire Ltd/Halfpenny Green
	G-FIJR	L.188PF Electra	Hunting Cargo Airlines Ltd/E. Midlands
	G-FIJV	L.188CF Electra	Hunting Cargo Airlines Ltd/E. Midlands
	G-FILE	PA-34-200T Seneca	S. D. Cole
	G-FILO	Robin DR.400/180	Baron G. van der Elst
	G-FINA	Cessna F.150L	D. Norris (G-BIFT)
	G-FINN	Cameron 90 Reindeer SS balloon	Forbes Europe Inc/France
	G-FINS	AB-206B JetRanger 3	Brian Seedle Helicopters (G-FSCL)
	G-FISH	Cessna 310R-II	Warner Group
	G-FISK	Pazmany PL-4A	K. S. Woodard
	G-FISS	Robinson R-22B	B. G. & D. Bushell
	G-FITZ	Cessna 335	Solving Systems Ltd (G-RIND)
	G-FIZU	L.188C Electra	Hunting Cargo Airlines Ltd/E. Midlands
	G-FIZZ	PA-28-161 Warrior II	Arrow Air Centre Ltd/Shipdham
	G-FJMS	Partenavia P.68B	F. J. M. Sanders (G-SVHA)
	G-FLAK	Beech 95-E55 Baron	J. K. Horne
	G-FLAV	PA-28-161 Warrior II	The Crew Flying Group/Tollerton
	G-FLCA	Fleet Model 80 Canuck	E. C. Taylor
	G-FLCO	Sequoia F.8L Falco	J. B. Mowforth

Reg.	Type	Owner or Operator	Notes
G-FLEN	PA-28-161 Warrior II	Winchfield Enterprises Ltd	
G-FLII	GA-7 Cougar	Plane Talking Ltd (G-GRAC)/Elstree	
G-FLIK	Pitts S-1S Special	R. P. Millinship/Leicester	
G-FLIP	Cessna FA.152	J. R. Nicholls (G-BOES)/Sibson	
G-FLOX	Shaw Europa	DPT Group	
G-FLPI	R. Commander 112A	L. Freeman & Son/Newcastle	
G-FLSI	FLS Aerospace Sprint 160	FLS Aerospace (Lovaux) Ltd/Bournemouth	
G-FLTI	Beech F90 King Air	Flightline Ltd/Southend	
G-FLTY	EMB-110P1 Bandeirante	Flightline Ltd (G-ZUSS/G-REGA)/ Southend	
G-FLTZ	Beech 58 Baron	Stesco Ltd (G-PSVS)	
G-FLUF	Lindstrand Bunny SS balloon	Lindstrand Balloons Ltd	
G-FLUG	Gyroflug SC.01B-160 Speed Canard	B. Houghton	
G-FLYA	Mooney M.20J	Flya Aviation Ltd	
G-FLYI	PA-34-200 Seneca	BLS Aviation Ltd (G-BHVO)/Elstree	
G-FLYR	AB-206B JetRanger 2	Kwik Fit Euro Ltd (G-BAKT)	
G-FLYT	Shaw Europa	D. W. Adams	
G-FLYV	Slingsby T.67M-200	Firefly Aerial Promotions Ltd	
G-FMAM	PA-28-151 Warrior	Essex Radio PLC (G-BBXV)/Southend	
G-FMSG	Cessna FA.150K	G. Owen (G-POTS/G-AYUY)/Gamston	
G-FNLD	Cessna 172N	Papa Hotel Flying Group	
G-FNLY	Cessna F.172M	Plane Talking Ltd (G-WACX/G-BAEX)/ Elstree	
G-FOGG	Cameron N-90 balloon	J. P. E. Money-Kyrle	
G-FOLD	Light Aero Avid Speedwing	S. R. Winder	
G-FOLY	Aerotek Pitts S-2A Modified	A. A. Laing	
G-FOOD	Beech B200 Super King Air	Specbridge Ltd/Gamston	
G-FOPP	Lancair 320	Airsport (UK) Ltd	
G-FORC	SNCAN Stampe SV-4C	I. A. Marsh/Elstree	
G-FORD	SNCAN Stampe SV-4B	P. Meeson & R. A. J. Spurrell/ White Waltham	
G-FORM	Lindstrand Newspaper SS balloon	International Balloons Ltd	
G-FOTO	PA-E23 Aztec 250F	Aerofilms Ltd (G-BJDH/G-BDXV)	
G-FOWL	Colt 90A balloon	Chesterfield Cold Storage Ltd	
G-FOXA	PA-28-161 Cadet	Leicestershire Aero Club Ltd	
G-FOXC	Denney Kitfox Mk 3	Junipa Sales (Aviation) Ltd	
G-FOXD	Denney Kitfox	M. Hanley	
G-FOXE	Denney Kitfox Mk 2	K. M. Pinkard	
G-FOXG	Denney Kitfox Mk 2	Kitfox Group	
G-FOXI	Denney Kitfox	B. Johns	
G-FOXM	Bell 206B JetRanger 2	Tyringham Charter & Group Services (G-STAK/G-BNIS)	
G-FOXS	Denney Kitfox Mk 2	S. P. Watkins & C. C. Rea	
G-FOXX	Denney Kitfox	R. O. F. Harper	
G-FOXZ	Denney Kitfox	M. Smalley & ptnrs	
G-FPCL	GA-7 Cougar	Eurowide Ltd	
G-FRAD	Dassault Falcon 20E	FR Aviation Ltd (G-BCYF)/Bournemouth	
G-FRAE	Dassault Falcon 20E	FR Aviation Ltd/Bournemouth	
G-FRAF	Dassault Falcon 20E	FR Aviation Ltd/Bournemouth	
G-FRAG	PA-32 Cherokee Six 300E	G-FRAG Group	
G-FRAH	Dassault Falcon 20DC	FR Aviation Ltd/Bournemouth	
G-FRAI	Dassault Falcon 20E	FR Aviation Ltd/Bournemouth	
G-FRAJ	Dassault Falcon 20E	FR Aviation Ltd/Bournemouth	
G-FRAK	Dassault Falcon 20DC	FR Aviation Ltd/Bournemouth	
G-FRAL	Dassault Falcon 20DC	FR Aviation Ltd/Bournemouth	
G-FRAM	Dassault Falcon 20DC	FR Aviation Ltd/Bournemouth	
G-FRAN	Piper J-3C-90 Cub (480321)	Essex L-4 Group (G-BIXY)	
G-FRAO	Dassault Falcon 20DC	FR Aviation Ltd/Bournemouth	
G-FRAP	Dassault Falcon 20DC	FR Aviation Ltd/Bournemouth	
G-FRAR	Dassault Falcon 20DC	FR Aviation Ltd/Bournemouth	
G-FRAS	Dassault Falcon 20C	FR Aviation Ltd/Bournemouth	
G-FRAT	Dassault Falcon 20C	FR Aviation Ltd/Bournemouth	
G-FRAU	Dassault Falcon 20C	FR Aviation Ltd/Bournemouth	
G-FRAW	Dassault Falcon 20ECM	FR Aviation Ltd/Bournemouth	
G-FRAX	Cessna 441	FR Aviation Ltd (G-BMTZ)/Bournemouth	
G-FRAY	Cassutt IIIM (modified)	C. I. Fray	
G-FRAZ	Cessna 441	FR Aviation Ltd/Bournemouth	
G-FRBY	Beech E55 Baron	FR Finances Ltd	
G-FRCE	H.S. Gnat T.1	Butane Buzzard Aviation Ltd/Cranfield	
G-FREE	Pitts S-2A Special	Pegasus Flying Group/Fairoaks	

Notes	Reg.	Type	Owner or Operator
	G-FRJB	Britten Sheriff SA-1 ★	Aeropark/E. Midlands
	G-FRST	PA-44-180T Turbo Seminole	WAM (GB) Ltd
	G-FSDT	Hughes 269A	R. E. Dagless
	G-FSII	Gregory Free Spirit Mk II balloon	M. J. Gregory & R. P. Hallam
	G-FSIX	EE Lightning F.6	Downderry Construction Group Ltd
	G-FSPL	PA-32R Cherokee Lance 300	J. D. I. Richardson & Goodridge (UK) Ltd
	G-FTAX	Cessna 421C	CRV Leasing (G-BFFM)
	G-FTFT	Colt Financial Times SS balloon	Financial Times Ltd
	G-FTIL	Robin DR.400/180R	Niederrhein Powered Flying Club
	G-FTIM	Robin DR.400/100	W. C. Cowie
	G-FTIN	Robin DR.400/100	G. D. Clark & M. J. D. Theobold
	G-FTWO	AS.355F-2 Twin Squirrel	McAlpine Helicopters Ltd (G-OJOR/
			G-BMUS)/Hayes
	G-FUEL	Robin DR.400/180	R. Darch/Compton Abbas
	G-FUGA	Fouga CM.170R Magister	Royalair Services Ltd (G-BSCT)
	G-FULL	PA-28R Cherokee Arrow 200-II	Arrow Flight Services Ltd
			(G-HWAY/G-JULI)/Shoreham
	G-FUND	Thunder Ax7-65Z balloon	Soft Sell Ltd
	G-FUNN	Plumb BGP-1	J. D. Anson
	G-FUSI	Robinson R-22B	F. M. Usher-Smith
	G-FUZY	Cameron N-77 balloon	Allan Industries Ltd
	G-FUZZ	PA-18 Super Cub 95	G. W. Cline
	G-FVBF	Lindstrand LBL-210A balloon	Virgin Balloon Flights Ltd
	G-FWPW	PA-28-236 Dakota	P. A. & F. C. Winters
	G-FWRP	Cessna 421C	Aerienne Ltd/Southampton
	G-FXII	V.S.366 Spitfire F.XII (EN224)	P. R. Arnold
	G-FXIV	V.S.379 Spitfire FR.XIV (MV370)	R. Lamplough
	G-FZZI	Cameron H-34 balloon	Virgin Airship & Balloon Co Ltd
	G-FZZY	Colt 69A balloon	Hot-Air Balloon Co Ltd
	G-FZZZ	Colt 56A balloon	Hot-Air Balloon Co Ltd
	G-GABD	GA-7 Cougar	Scotia Safari Ltd/Prestwick
	G-GACA	P.57 Sea Prince T.1 ★	P. G. Vallance Ltd/Charlwood
	G-GAGA	AA-5B Tiger	Kadala Aviation Ltd (G-BGPG)/Elstree
	G-GAII	Hunter GA.11 (XE685)	B. J. Pover
	G-GAJB	AA-5B Tiger	G. A. J. Bowles (G-BHZN)
	G-GALA	PA-28 Cherokee 180E	E. Alexander (G-AYAP)
	G-GAMA	Beech 95-58 Baron	Gama Aviation Ltd (G-BBSD)/Fairoaks
	G-GAME	Cessna T.303	Twinflite Aviation Ltd
	G-GANE	Sequoia F.8L Falco	S. J. Gane
	G-GANJ	Fournier RF-6B-100	Soaring Equipment Ltd/Coventry
	G-GASC	Hughes 369HS	Crewhall Ltd (G-WELD/G-FROG)
	G-GASP	PA-28-181 Archer II	G-GASP Flying Group
	G-GASS	Thunder Ax7-77 balloon	Servowarm Balloon Syndicate
	G-GATI	Beech 200 Super King Air	Branderman Ltd (G-ONEA)
	G-GAUL	Cessna 550 Citation II	Chauffair Ltd
	G-GAWA	Cessna 140	R. A. Page (G-BRSM)/Coventry
	G-GAYL	Learjet 35A	Northern Executive Aviation Ltd (G-ZING)/
			Manchester
	G-GAZA	SA.341G Gazelle 1	Stratton Motor Co (Norfolk) Ltd
			(G-RALE/G-SFTG)
	G-GAZI	SA.341G Gazelle 1	Stratton Motor Co (Norfolk) Ltd & UCC
			International Group Ltd (G-BKLU)
	G-GAZZ	SA.341G Gazelle 1	Stratton Motor Co (Norfolk) Ltd & UCC
			International Group Ltd
	G-GBAO	Robin R.1180TD	J. Kay-Movat
	G-GBLR	Cessna F.150L	Blue Max Flying Group
	G-GBSL	Beech 76 Duchess	M. H. Cundsy (G-BGVG)
	G-GBTA	Boeing 737-436	British Airways (G-BVHA)
			County of Middlesex
	G-GBUE	Robin DR.400/120A	G-GBUE Group (G-BPXD)
	G-GCAA	PA-28R Cherokee Arrow 200	Southern Air Ltd/Shoreham
	G-GCAB	PA-30 Twin Comanche 180	Southern Air Ltd/Shoreham
	G-GCAT	PA-28 Cherokee 140B	H. Skelton (G-BFRH)
	G-GCCL	Beech 76 Duchess	A. J. & S. B. Duckworth
	G-GCJL	BAe Jetstream 4100	Jetstream Aircraft Ltd/Prestwick
	G-GCKI	Mooney M.20K	A. L. Burton & A. J. Daly
	G-GCNZ	Cessna 150M	Firecrest Aviation Ltd/Elstree
	G-GDAM	PA-18 Super Cub 135	A. D. Martin
	G-GDAY	Robinson R-22B	C. J. H. & P. A. J. Richardson
	G-GDEZ	BAe 125-1000B	Frewton Ltd
	G-GDOG	PA-28R Cherokee Arrow 200-II	S. J. Rogers (G-BDXW)/Blackbushe
	G-GEAR	Cessna FR.182Q	Deeperton Ltd

Reg.	Type	Owner or Operator	Notes
G-GEEE	Hughes 369HS	B. P. Stein (G-BDOY)	
G-GEEP	Robin R.1180T	Organic Concentrates Ltd/Booker	
G-GEES	Cameron N-77 balloon	N. A. Carr	
G-GEEZ	Cameron N-77 balloon	Charnwood Forest Turf Accountants Ltd	
G-GEMS	Thunder Ax8-90 S2 balloon	Alexander The Jewellers Ltd (G-BUNP)	
G-GENN	GA-7 Cougar	Chalrey Ltd (G-BNAB/G-BGYP)	
G-GEOF	Pereira Osprey 2	G. Crossley	
G-GEUP	Cameron N-77 balloon	D. P. & B. O. Turner	
G-GFAB	Cameron N-105 balloon	The Andrew Brownsword Collection Ltd	
G-GFCA	PA-28-161 Cadet	A. M. Norman	
G-GFCB	PA-28-161 Cadet	S. F. Tebby & Sons	
G-GFCC	PA-28-161 Cadet	C. P. Scamp/Staverton	
G-GFCD	PA-34-220T Seneca III	Stonehurst Aviation Ltd (G-KIDS)	
G-GFCF	PA-28-161 Cadet	Aerohire Ltd (G-RHBH)	
G-GFKY	Zenair CH.250	K. Jarman & KM Services Ltd	
G-GFLY	Cessna F.150L	W. Lancs Aero Club Ltd/Woodvale	
G-GFRY	Bell 206L-3 LongRanger	Turbine Helicopters Ltd	
G-GGGG	Thunder Ax7-77A balloon	T. A. Gilmour	
G-GGLE	PA-22 Colt 108 (tailwheel)	J. R. Colthurst	
G-GGOW	Colt 77A balloon	City of Glasgow District Council	
G-GHCL	Bell 206B JetRanger 2	Grampian Helicopter Charter Ltd (G-SHVV)	
G-GHIA	Cameron N-120 balloon	J. R. & S. M. Christopher	
G-GHIN	Thunder Ax7-77 balloon	N. T. Parry	
G-GHRW	PA-28RT-201 Arrow IV	Leavesden Flight Centre Ltd (G-ONAB/ G-BHAK)	
G-GHSI	PA-44-180T Turbo Seminole	M. G. Roberts	
G-GHZM	Robinson R-22B	Grampian Helicopter Charter Ltd (G-FENI)	
G-GIGI	M.S.893A Rallye Commodore	J. R. Scarborough (G-AYVX)	
G-GIRO	Schweizer 269C	D. E. McDowell	
G-GJCD	Robinson R-22B	J. C. Lane	
G-GJET	Learjet 35A	Gama Aviation Ltd (G-CJET/G-SEBE/ G-ZIPS/G-ZONE)	
G-GJKK	Mooney M.20K	Davey & Shaw	
G-GLAD	G.37 Gladiator II	Patina Ltd/Duxford	
G-GLAW	Cameron N-90 balloon	George Law Ltd	
G-GLED	Cessna 150M	Firecrest Aviation Ltd/Booker	
G-GLUE	Cameron N-65 balloon	L. J. M. Muir & G. D. Hallett	
G-CLUG	PA-31-350 Navajo Chieftain	Champagne-Air Ltd (G-BLOE/G-NITE)	
G-GMAX	SNCAN Stampe SV-4C	Glidegold Ltd (G-BXNW)	
G-GMPA	AS.355F-2 Twin Squirrel	Greater Manchester Police Authority (G-BPOI)	
G-GMSI	SOCATA TB.9 Tampico	D. Ormrod	
G-GNAT	H.S. Gnat T.1 (XS101)	Ruanil Investments Ltd/Cranfield	
G-GNSY	HPR-7 Herald 209	Channel Express (Air Services) Ltd (G-BFRK)/Bournemouth	
G-GNTA	SAAB SF.340A	Business Air Ltd/Aberdeen	
G-GNTB	SAAB SF.340A	Business Air Ltd/Aberdeen	
G-GNTC	SAAB SF.340A	Business Air Ltd/Aberdeen	
G-GNTD	SAAB SF.340A	Business Air Ltd/Aberdeen	
G-GNTE	SAAB SF.340A	Business Air Ltd/Aberdeen	
G-GNTF	SAAB SF.340A	Business Air Ltd/Aberdeen	
G-GNTG	SAAB SF.340A	Business Air Ltd/Aberdeen	
G-GNTZ	BAe 146-200	Business Air Ltd/Frankfurt	
G-GOBT	Colt 77A balloon	British Telecom PLC	
G-GOCC	AA-5A Cheetah	Lowlog Ltd (G-BPIX)/Elstree	
G-GOCX	Cameron N-90 balloon	Cathay Pacific Airways Ltd	
G-GOGW	Cameron N-90 balloon	Great Western Trains Ltd	
G-GOLD	Thunder Ax6-56A balloon	Joseph Terry & Sons Ltd	
G-GOLF	SOCATA TB.10 Tobago	E. H. Scamell & ptnrs	
G-GOMM	PA-32R Cherokee Lance 300	D. A. Shipley	
G-GONE	D.H.112 Venom FB.50	J. E. Davies	
G-GOOD	SOCATA TB-20 Trinidad	Skyforce Charters Ltd	
G-GOOS	Cessna F.182Q	P. J. Clegg	
G-GORE	CFM Streak Shadow	D. N. & E. M. Gore	
G-GOSS	Jodel DR.221	D. Folens	
G-GOZO	Cessna R.182	Transmatic Fyllan Ltd (G-BJZO)/Cranfield	
G-GPMW	PA-28RT-201T Turbo Arrow IV	M. Worrall & ptnrs	
G-GPST	Phillips ST.1 Speedtwin	P. J. C. Phillips	
G-GRAM	PA-31-350 Navajo Chieftain	Newquay Air Ltd (G-BRHF)	
G-GRAY	Cessna 172N	Truman Aviation Ltd/Tollerton	
G-GREG	Jodel DR.220 2+2	J. T. Wilson	
G-GREN	Cessna T.310R	D. Hughes & P. Appleyard/Leeds	

Notes	Reg.	Type	Owner or Operator
	G-GRID	AS.355F-1 Twin Squirrel	National Grid Co PLC
	G-GRIF	R. Commander 112TCA	M. J. Chilton (G-BHXC)
	G-GROW	Cameron N-77 balloon	Derbyshire Building Society
	G-GSFC	Robinson R-22B	Weller Helicopters Ltd/Redhill
	G-GSML	Enstrom 280C-UK	Southern Air Ltd (G-BNNV)
	G-GTAX	PA-31-350 Navajo Chieftain	Hadagain Investments Ltd (G-OIAS)
	G-GTHM	PA-38-112 Tomahawk	Truman Aviation Ltd/Tollerton
	G-GTPL	Mooney M.20K	W. R. Emberton/Spain
	G-GUCK	Beech C23 Sundowner 180	G-GUCK Group (G-BPYG)
	G-GULF	Lindstrand LBL-105A balloon	Virgin Balloon Flights Ltd
	G-GULL	Petrel Amphibian	Amphibians UK Ltd
	G-GUNN	Cessna F.172H	J. G. Gunn (G-AWGC)
	G-GUNS	Cameron V-77 balloon	Royal School of Artillery Hot Air Balloon Club
	G-GURL	Cameron A-210 balloon	British School of Ballooning
	G-GUSS	PA-28-151 Warrior	A. M. R. Dudley (G-BJRY)
	G-GUYI	PA-28-181 Archer II	B. Butler
	G-GUYS	PA-34-200T Seneca	G. B. Faulkner (G-BMWT)
	G-GVBF	Lindstrand LBL-180A balloon	Virgin Balloon Flights Ltd
	G-GWEN	Cessna F.172M	R. E. Youngsworth (G-GBLP)
	G-GWIL	AS.350B Ecureuil	Talan Ltd
	G-GWIZ	Colt Clown SS balloon	Oxford Promotions (UK) Ltd
	G-GWYN	Cessna F.172M	Gwyn Aviation
	G-GYAV	Cessna 172N	Southport & Merseyside Aero Club (1979) Ltd/Liverpool
	G-GYMM	PA-28R Cherokee Arrow 200	D. J. Warner & J. B. A. Ainsworth (G-AYWW)
	G-GYRO	Campbell Cricket	J. W. Pavitt
	G-GZDO	Cessna 172N	Cambridge Hall Aviation
	G-HAEC	CAC-18 Mustang 23 (A68-192)	Classic Aviation Ltd/Duxford
	G-HAHA	PA-18 Super Cub 150	D. J. Hockings (G-BSWE)
	G-HAIG	Rutan LongEz	R. Carey & D. W. Parfrey
	G-HAJJ	Glaser-Dirks DG.400	P. W. Endean
	G-HALC	PA-28R Cherokee Arrow 200	Halcyon Aviation Ltd
	G-HALL	PA-22 Tri-Pacer 160	F. P. Hall (G-ARAH)
	G-HALO	Elisport CH-7 Angel	Taylor Woodhouse Ltd
	G-HALP	SOCATA TB.10 Tobago	D. H. Halpern (G-BITD)/Elstree
	G-HAMA	Beech 200 Super King Air	Gama Aviation Ltd/Fairoaks
	G-HAMI	Fuji FA.200-180	S. A. R. Rose & K. G. Cameron (G-OISF/G-BAPT)
	G-HAMP	Bellanca 7ACA Champ	R. J. Grimstead
	G-HANS	Robin DR.400 2+2	Headcorn Flying School Ltd
	G-HAPR	B.171 Sycamore HR.14 (XG547) ★	International Helicopter Museum/Weston-s-Mare
	G-HARE	Cameron N-77 balloon	M. A. Pratt & N. I. Cakebread
	G-HARF	G.1159C Gulfstream 4	Fayair (Jersey) 1984 Ltd
	G-HARH	Sikorsky S-76B	Fayair (Jersey) 1984 Ltd
	G-HART	Cessna 152	Atlantic Air Transport Ltd/Coventry
	G-HARY	Alon A-2 Aircoupe	Northumbria Horse Riding Holidays (G-ATWP)
	G-HATZ	Hatz CB-1	J. Pearson
	G-HAUG	Sikorsky S-76B	Norbrook Laboratories Ltd (G-HPLC)
	G-HAUL	Westland WG.30 Srs 300 ★	International Helicopter Museum/Weston-super-Mare
	G-HAZE	Thunder Ax8-90 balloon	T. G. Church
	G-HBMW	Robinson R-22	Howarth Helicopter Services Ltd (G-BOFA)
	G-HBUG	Cameron N-90 balloon	Thorn EMI Computeraid (G-BRCN)
	G-HCSL	PA-34-220T Seneca III	Hollowbrook Computer Services Ltd
	G-HCTL	PA-31-350 Navajo Chieftain	Field Aircraft Services (Heathrow) Ltd (G-BGOY)
	G-HDBD	H.S.748 Srs 2B	British Aerospace PLC/Woodford
	G-HDEW	PA-32R-301 Saratoga SP	Lord Howard de Walden (G-BRGZ)
	G-HDOG	Colt Flying Hot Dog SS balloon	Longbreak Ltd
	G-HEAD	Colt 56 Flying Head SS balloon	Lindstrand Balloons Ltd
	G-HELE	Bell 206B JetRanger 3	B. E. E. Smith (G-OJFR)
	G-HELN	PA-18 Super Cub 95	J. J. Anziani (G-BKDG)/Booker
	G-HELP	Colt 17A balloon	Virgin Airship & Balloon Co Ltd
	G-HELV	D.H.115 Vampire T.55 (U-1215)	Hunter Wing Ltd/Bournemouth
	G-HEMS	SA.365N Dauphin 2	Express Newspapers PLC/Denham
	G-HENS	Cameron N-65 balloon	Harrells Dairies Ltd
	G-HENY	Cameron V-77 balloon	R. S. D'Alton

Reg.	Type	Owner or Operator	Notes
G-HERA	Robinson R-22B	T. Pexton	
G-HERB	PA-28R-201 Arrow III	J. E. Shepherd	
G-HERO	PA-32RT-300 Lance II	Air Alize Communication (G-BOGN)/ Stapleford	
G-HERS	Jodel D.18	A. Usherwood	
G-HEVY	Boeing 707-324C	HeavyLift Cargo Airlines Ltd/Stansted	
G-HEWI	Piper J-3C-90 Cub	Denham Grasshopper Group (G-BLEN)	
G-HEWS	Hughes 369D ★	*Spares' use*/Sywell	
G-HEYY	Cameron 77 Bear SS balloon	Hot-Air Balloon Co Ltd George	
G-HFBM	Curtiss Robin C-2	D. M. Forshaw	
G-HFCA	Cessna A.150L	Horizon Flying Club Ltd/Ipswich	
G-HFCB	Cessna F.150L	Horizon Flying Club Ltd (G-AZVR)/Ipswich	
G-HFCI	Cessna F.150L	Horizon Flying Club Ltd/Ipswich	
G-HFCL	Cessna F.152	Horizon Flying Club Ltd (G-BGLR)/Ipswich	
G-HFCT	Cessna F.152	Stapleford Flying Club Ltd	
G-HFIX	V.S.361 Spitfire HF.IXe (MJ730)	D. W. Pennell (G-BLAS)	
G-HFLA	Schweizer 269C	Sterling Helicopters Ltd/Norwich	
G-HFTG	PA-23 Aztec 250E	Hawkair (G-BSOB/G-BCJR)	
G-HGAS	Cameron N-77 balloon	Handygas Ltd	
G-HGPI	SOCATA TB.20 Trinidad	M. J. Jackson/Bournemouth	
G-HHUN	Hunter F.4 (XE677)	Hunter Wing Ltd/Bournemouth	
G-HIBM	Cameron N-145 balloon	IBM UK Ltd	
G-HIEL	Robinson R-22B	Hields Aviation	
G-HIHI	PA-32R-301 Saratoga SP	Longslow Dairy Ltd	
G-HIII	Extra EA.300	Firebird Aerobatics Ltd/Booker	
G-HIIL	Shaw Europa	G. S. Hill	
G-HILS	Cessna F.172H	Lowdon Aviation Group (G-AWCH)	
G-HILT	SOCATA TB.10 Tobago	B. A. Groves	
G-HINT	Cameron N-90 balloon	Hinton Garage Bath Ltd	
G-HIPE	Sorrell SNS-7 Hiperbipe	T. A. S. Rayner	
G-HIPO	Robinson R-22B	Hippo Helicopters Ltd (G-BTGB)	
G-HIRE	GA-7 Cougar	London Aerial Tours Ltd (G-BGSZ)/ Biggin Hill	
G-HISS	Aerotek Pitts S-2A Special	L. V. Adams & J. Maffia (G-BLVU)	
G-HIVA	Cessna 337A	High Voltage Applications Ltd (G-BAES)	
G-HIVE	Cessna F.150M	M. P. Lynn (G-BCXT)/Sibson	
G-HJCB	BAe 125-1000B	J. C. Bamford Excavators Ltd (G-BUUY)	
G-HJSS	AIA Stampe SV-4C (modified)	H. J. Smith (G-AZNF)	
G HLEN	AS.350B Ecureuil	N. Edmonds (G-LOLY)	
G-HLFT	SC.5 Belfast 2	HeavyLift Cargo Airlines Ltd/Stansted	
G-HLIX	Cameron 80 Oil Can SS balloon	Hot-Air Balloon Co Ltd	
G-HMBB	MBB BK-117B-1C	McAlpine Helicopters Ltd	
G-HMES	PA-28-161 Warrior II	Cleveland Flying School Ltd/Teesside	
G-HMJB	PA-34-220T Seneca III	Firfax Systems Ltd	
G-HMPH	Bell 206B JetRanger 2	Mightycraft Ltd (G-BBUY)	
G-HMPT	AB-206B JetRanger 2	Kensington Aviation Ltd	
G-HNRY	Cessna 650 Citation VI	Quantel Ltd/Biggin Hill	
G-HNTR	Hunter T.7 (XL572) ★	Hunter Wing Ltd/Bournemouth	
G-HOBO	Denney Kitfox Mk 4	W. M. Hodgkins & C. A. Boswell	
G-HOCK	PA-28 Cherokee 180	Arabact Ltd (G-AVSH)	
G-HOFC	Shaw Europa	J. W. Lang	
G-HOFM	Cameron N-56 balloon	Hot-Air Balloon Co Ltd	
G-HOHO	Colt Santa Claus SS balloon	Oxford Promotions (UK) Ltd	
G-HOLY	ST.10 Diplomate	Sussex Spraying Services Ltd/Shoreham	
G-HOME	Colt 77A balloon	Anglia Balloon School Tardis	
G-HONE	Hunter F.58	Aeromech International Resources Ltd	
G-HONG	Slingsby T.67M-200	Hunting Aviation Ltd	
G-HONK	Cameron O-105 balloon	T. F. W. Dixon & Son Ltd	
G-HOOV	Cameron N-56 balloon	H. R. Evans	
G-HOPE	Beech F33A Bonanza	Hurn Aviation Ltd	
G-HOPI	Cameron N-42 balloon	Cameron Balloons Ltd	
G-HOPS	Thunder Ax8-90 balloon	A. C. & B. Munn	
G-HOPY	Vans RV-6A	R. C. Hopkinson	
G-HORN	Cameron V-77 balloon	S. Herd	
G-HORS	Cameron Horse SS balloon	Cameron Balloons Ltd	
G-HOST	Cameron N-77 balloon	D. Grimshaw	
G-HOTI	Colt 77A balloon	R. Ollier	
G-HOTT	Cameron O-120 balloon	D. L. Smith	
G-HOTZ	Colt 77B balloon	C. J. & S. M. Davies	
G-HOUS	Colt 31A balloon	Anglia Balloons Ltd	
G-HOWE	Thunder Ax7-77 balloon	M. F. Howe	
G-HPAA	BN-2B-26 Islander	Hampshire Police Authority (Air Support Unit) (G-BSWP)	

Notes	Reg.	Type	Owner or Operator
	G-HRAY	AB-206B JetRanger 3	Hecray Co Ltd (G-VANG/G-BIZA)
	G-HRHI	B.206 Srs 1 Basset (XS770)	Universal Salvage (Holdings) Ltd
	G-HRIO	Robin HR.100/120	D. Peters
	G-HRIS	Cessna P210N	Birmingham Aerocentre Ltd
	G-HRLK	SAAB 91D/2 Safir	Sylmar Aviation & Services Ltd (G-BRZY)
	G-HHLM	Brügger MB.2 Colibri	S. J. Perkins & D. Dobson
	G-HROI	R. Commander 112A	Bravo Whisky Flying Ltd
	G-HRON	D.H.114 Heron 2 (XR442)	M. E. R. Coghlan (G-AORH)
	G-HRVD	CCF Harvard IV	M. Slater (G-BSBC)
	G-HRVY	Enstrom 280C	Sky Enterprises Ltd (G-DUGY/G-BEEL)
	G-HRZN	Colt 77A balloon	A. J. Spindler
	G-HSAA	Hughes 369HS	Heliwork Services Ltd/Thruxton
	G-HSDW	Bell 206B JetRanger	Winfield Shoe Co Ltd
	G-HSHS	Colt 105A balloon	H. & S. Aviation Ltd
	G-HSOO	Hughes 369HE	Helisport Ltd (G-BFYJ)/Redhill
	G-HTAX	PA-31-350 Navajo Chieftain	Hadagain Inve\stments Ltd
	G-HTPS	SA. 341G Gazelle 1	J. Malcolm (G-BRNI)
	G-HTWO	Hunter F.58	Aeromech International Resources Ltd
	G-HUBB	Partenavia P.68B	G-HUBB Ltd
	G-HUCH	Cameron 80 Carrots SS balloon	L. V. Mastis (G-BYPS)
	G-HUEY	Bell UH-1H	Butane Buzzard Aviation Corporation Ltd
	G-HUFF	Cessna 182P	A. E. G. Cousins
	G-HUGO	Colt 240A balloon	Adventure Ballooning
	G-HULL	Cessna F.150M	A. D. McLeod
	G-HUMF	Robinson R-22B	Plane Talking Ltd/Elstree
	G-HURI	CCF Hawker Hurricane XIIA (Z7381)	Patina Ltd/Duxford
	G-HURN	Robinson R-22B	Coventry Helicopter Centre Ltd
	G-HURR	Hawker Hurricane XIIB (BE417)	Autokraft Ltd
	G-HURY	Hawker Hurricane IV (KZ321)	Patina Ltd/Duxford
	G-HUTT	Denney Kitfox Mk 2	D. Watt
	G-HVDM	V.S.361 Spitfire F.IX (MK732)	DSG (Guernsey) Ltd/Holland
	G-HVIP	Hunter T.68	Golden Europe Jet De Luxe Club Ltd/Bournemouth
	G-HVRD	PA-31-350 Navajo Chieftain	London Flight Centre (Stansted) Ltd (G-BEZU)
	G-HVRS	Robinson R-22B	Northern Helicopters (Leeds) Ltd
	G-HWKR	Colt 90A balloon	P. A. Henderson
	G-HYLT	PA-32R-301 Saratoga SP	Pump & Plant Services
	G-IABC	Tri Kis	A. & B. Caple/Biggin Hill
	G-IAFT	Cessna 152	Marnham Investments Ltd
	G-IAMP	Cameron H-34 balloon	Air 2 Air Ltd
	G-IBBS	Shaw Europa	R. H. Gibbs
	G-IBED	Robinson R-22A	P. D. Spinks (G-BMHN)
	G-IBET	Cameron 70 Can SS balloon	M. R. Humphrey & J. R. Clifton
	G-IBFW	PA-28R-201 Arrow III	J. B. Roberts
	G-IBRO	Cessna F.152 II	E. Midlands Aircraft Hire Ltd
	G-ICAB	Robinson R-44 Astro	J. R. Clark Ltd
	G-ICCL	Robinson R-22B	Thorneygrove Ltd (G-ORZZ)
	G-ICES	Thunder Ax6-56 balloon	British Balloon Museum & Library Ltd
	G-ICEY	Lindstrand LBL-77A balloon	Iceland Frozen Foods PLC
	G-ICFR	BAe 125 Srs 800A	Chauffair (CI) Ltd (G-BUCR)/ Farnborough
	G-ICKY	Lindstrand LBL-77A balloon	R. R. Green & ptnrs
	G-ICOM	Cessna F.172M	T. J. & P. S. Nicholson (G-BFXI)
	G-ICSG	AS.355F-1 Twin Squirrel	Industrial Control Services PLC (G-PAMI/G-BUSA)
	G-IDDI	Cameron N-77 balloon	Allen & Harris Ltd
	G-IDDY	D.H.C.1 Super Chipmunk	P. G. Kavanagh & D. T. Kaberry (G-BBMS)
	G-IDEA	AA-5A Cheetah	Lowlog Ltd (G-BGNO)
	G-IDUP	Enstrom 280C Shark	Stephenson Marine Ltd (G-BRZF)
	G-IDWR	Hughes 369HS	Ryburn Air Ltd (G-AXEJ)
	G-IECL	H.S.125 Srs 700B	Inflite Executive Charter Ltd/Stansted
	G-IEJH	Jodel D.150A	E. J. Horsfall (G-BPAM)
	G-IEYE	Robin DR. 400/180	J. S. Haslam
	G-IFIT	PA-31-350 Navajo Chieftain	Dart Group PLC (G-NABI/ G-MARG)/Bournemouth
	G-IFLI	AA-5A Cheetah	ABC Aviation Ltd
	G-IFLP	PA-34-200T Seneca II	Golf-Sala Ltd/Coventry
	G-IFOX	Robinson R-22B	Brillant PR
	G-IFTB	Beech 200C Super King Air	Albion Aviation Management Ltd

Reg.	Type	Owner or Operator	Notes
G-IFTC	H.S.125 Srs F3B/RA	Albion Aviation Management Ltd (G-OPOL/G-BXPU/G-IBIS/G-AXPU)	
G-IGEL	Cameron N-90 balloon	Computacenter Ltd	
G-IGLA	Colt 240A balloon	Heart of England Balloons	
G-IGLE	Cameron V-90 balloon	A. A. Laing	
G-IHSA	Robinson R-22B	R. J. Everett	
G-IHSB	Robinson R-22B	Polar Save Aviation Ltd	
G-IIAC	Aeronca 11AC Chief	J. N. W. Moss & ptnrs (G-BTPY)	
G-IIAN	Aero Designs Pulsar	I. G. Harrison	
G-IIIG	Boeing Stearman A.75N1	Aerosuperbatics Ltd (G-BSDR)/Rendcomb	
G-IIII	Aerotek Pitts S-2B Special	B. K. Lecomber	
G-IIIL	Pitts S-1T Special	Skylark Aerobatics	
G-IIIR	Pitts S-1 Special	R. O. Rogers	
G-IIIT	Aerotek Pitts S-2A Special	Aerobatic Displays Ltd	
G-IIIX	Pitts S-1S Special	L. C. Seeger (G-LBAT/G-UCCI/G-BIYN)	
G-IINA	AS.350B-2 Ecureuil	Endeavour Aviation Ltd	
G-IIRB	Bell 206B JetRanger 3	Robard Consultants Ltd	
G-IIRG	Stoddard-Hamilton Glasair IIRGS	D. S. Watson	
G-IITI	Extra EA.300	Aerobatic Displays Ltd/Booker	
G-IIXX	Parsons 2-seat gyroplane	J. K. Padden	
G-IJAC	Light Aero Avid Speedwing Mk 4	I. J. A. Charlton	
G-IJJB	Beech B200 Super King Air	JJB Sports Ltd (G-BMVY)	
G-IJOE	PA-28RT-201T Turbo Arrow IV	R. P. Wilson	
G-IJRC	Robinson R-22B	J. R. Clark Ltd (G-BTJP)	
G-IJYS	BAe Jetstream 3102	Jackie Stewart (G-BTZT)	
G-IKBP	PA-28-161 Warrior II	Hendafern Ltd/Shoreham	
G-IKIS	Cessna 210M	A. C. Davison	
G-ILEE	Colt 56A balloon	Lindsay Marketing Associates	
G-ILES	Cameron O-90 balloon	G. N. Lantos	
G-ILLE	Boeing Stearman A.75L3 (379)	J. Griffin	
G-ILLY	PA-28-181 Archer II	A. G. & K. M. Spiers	
G-ILSE	Corby CJ-1 Starlet	S. Stride	
G-ILTS	PA-32 Cherokee Six 300	P. G. Teasdale (G-CVOK)	
G-ILYS	Robinson R-22B	BJ Aviation/Welshpool	
G-IMAG	Colt 77A balloon	Flying Pictures (Balloons) Ltd	
G-IMAN	Colt 31A balloon	Benedikt Haggeney GmbH	
G-IMBY	Pietenpol Air Camper	P. F. Bockh	
G-IMLI	Cessna 310Q	P. D. Carne (G-AZYK)	
G-IMPW	PA-32R-301 Saratoga SP	C. M. Juggins	
G-IMPX	R. Commander 112B	T. L. & S. Hull	
G-IMPY	Light Aero Avid Flyer C	T. R. C. Griffin	
G-INAV	Aviation Composites Mercury	Europa Aviation Ltd	
G-INCA	Glaser-Dirks DG.400	H. W. Ober	
G-INCH	Montgomerie-Bensen B.8MR	I. H. C. Branson (G-BRES)	
G-INDC	Cessna T.303	Howarth Timber (Aircharters) Ltd	
G-INDE	PA-44-180 Seminole	Le Patron Holdings Ltd (G-BHNM)	
G-INDY	Robinson R-44 Astro	Reynard Racing Cars Ltd	
G-INGA	Thunder Ax8-84 balloon	M. L. J. Ritchie	
G-INGB	Robinson R-22B	Ashton Helicopters Ltd	
G-INNI	Jodel D.112	R. G. Andrews	
G-INNS	Robinson R-44 Astro	Everards Brewery Ltd	
G-INNY	SE-5A (replica) (F5459)	R. M. Ordish/Old Sarum	
G-INOW	Monnett Moni	T. W. Clark	
G-INTC	Robinson R-22B	Intec Project Engineering Ltd	
G-INTL	Short SD3-60 Variant 100	Interline Ltd	
G-INVU	AB-206B JetRanger 2	Catto Aviation Ltd (G-XXII/G-GGCC/ G-BEHG)	
G-IOOI	Robin DR.400/160	N. B. Mason & S. J. O'Rourke	
G-IOSI	Jodel DR.1051	A. Burbidge & R. Slater	
G-IPSI	Grob G.109B	G-IPSI Ltd (G-BMLO)	
G-IPSY	Rutan Vari-Eze	R. A. Fairclough/Biggin Hill	
G-IPUP	B.121 Pup 2	Plane Talking Ltd/Elstree	
G-IRIS	AA-5B Tiger	A. H. McVicar (G-BIXU)	
G-IRLS	Cessna FR.172J	R. C. Chapman	
G-IRLY	Colt 90A balloon	S. A. Burnett & L. P. Purfield	
G-IRPC	Cessna 182Q	R. P. Carminke (G-BSKM)	
G-ISCA	PA-28RT-201 Arrow IV	D. J. & P. Pay	
G-ISDN	Boeing Stearman A.75N1	D. R. L. Jones	
G-ISEE	BAe 146-200	British Aerospace PLC	
G-ISEH	Cessna 182R	SEH (Holdings) Ltd (G-BIWS)/Ipswich	
G-ISFC	PA-31-310 Turbo Navajo B	SFC (Air Taxis) Ltd (G-BNEF)/ Stapleford	

Notes	Reg.	Type	Owner or Operator
	G-ISIS	D.H.82A Tiger Moth	D. R. & M. Wood (G-AODR)
	G-ISKY	Bell 206B JetRanger 3	RJS Aviation Ltd (G-PSCI/G-BOKD)
	G-ISLE	Short SD3-60	Loganair Ltd/British Airways (G-BLEG)
	G-ISMO	Robinson R-22B	LGH Aviation Ltd/Bournemouth
	G-ISTT	Thunder Ax8-84 balloon	RAF Halton Hot Air Balloon Club
	G-ITAL	Cameron N-77 balloon	P. Leith-Smith
	G-ITII	Aerotech Pitts S-2A Special	Aerobatic Displays Ltd
	G-ITTU	PA-23 Aztec 250E	D. Byrne & M. Cummings (G-BCSW)
	G-IVAC	Airtour AH-77B balloon	R. B. Webb
	G-IVAN	Shaw TwinEze	I. Shaw
	G-IVAR	Yakovlev Yak-50	I. G. Anderson
	G-IVEL	Fournier RF-4D	V. S. E. Norman (G-AVNY)
	G-IVIV	Robinson R-44 Astro	Simlot Ltd
	G-IVOR	Aeronca 11AC Chief	South Western Aeronca Group/Plymouth
	G-IWON	Cameron V-90 balloon	D. P. P. Jenkinson (G-BTCV)
	G-IYAK	Yakovlev C-11	E. K. Coventry/Earls Colne
	G-IZEL	SA.341G Gazelle 1	Fairview Securities (Investments) Ltd (G-BBHW)
	G-IZMO	Thunder Ax8-90 balloon	Landrell Fabric Engineering Ltd
	G-JACT	Partenavia P.68C	JCT 600 Ltd (G-NVIA)/Leeds
	G-JAKE	D.H.C.1 Chipmunk 22	J. M. W. Henstock (G-BBMY)/Netherthorpe
	G-JAKI	Mooney M.20R	A. D. Russell
	G-JALC	Boeing 757-225	Airtours International Airways Ltd
	G-JAMP	PA-28-151 Warrior	ANP Ltd (G-BRJU)/White Waltham
	G-JANA	PA-28-181 Archer II	Croaker Aviation/Stapleford
	G-JANB	Colt Flying Bottle SS balloon	Justerini & Brooks Ltd
	G-JANI	Robinson R-44 Astro	Heli Air Ltd
	G-JANK	PA-E23 Aztec 250C	M. R. Keen (G-ATCY)/Liverpool
	G-JANM	Airbus A.320-212	Airtours International Airways Ltd (G-KMAM)
	G-JANN	PA-34-220T Seneca III	TEL (IOM) Ltd
	G-JANS	Cessna FR.172J	I. G. Aizlewood/Luton
	G-JANT	PA-28-181 Archer II	Janair Aviation Ltd
	G-JARA	Robinson R-22B	J. A. R. Allwright
	G-JASE	PA-28-161 Warrior II	Ipswich School of Flying Ltd
	G-JASP	PA-23 Turbo Aztec 250E	Landsurcon (Air Survey) Ltd/Staverton
	G-JAWZ	Pitts S-1S Special	S. Howes
	G-JAYI	J/1 Autocrat	Bravo Aviation Ltd
	G-JAZZ	AA-5A Cheetah	Jazz Club
	G-JBAC	EMB-110P1 Bandeirante	Knight Air Ltd/BAC Leasing (G-BGYV)
	G-JBDH	Robin DR.400/180	D. Hoolahan/Biggin Hill
	G-JBET	Beech F33A Bonanza	J. Bett/Glasgow
	G-JBJB	Colt 69A balloon	Justerini & Brooks Ltd
	G-JBPR	Wittman W.10 Tailwind	P. A. Rose & J. P. Broadhurst
	G-JBWI	Robinson R-22B	N. J. Wagstaff Leasing
	G-JCAS	PA-28-181 Archer II	Charlie Alpha Ltd
	G-JCFR	Cessna 550 Citation II	Chauffair Ltd (G-JETC)/Gatwick
	G-JCGR	Cessna T.207	Ingenieur Gesellschaft fur Interfaces GmbH
	G-JCJC	Colt Flying Jeans SS balloon	J. C. Balloon Co Ltd
	G-JCUB	PA-18 Super Cub 135	Piper Cub Consortium Ltd/Jersey
	G-JDEE	SOCATA TB.20 Trinidad	Melville Associates Ltd (G-BKLA)
	G-JDEL	Jodel 150	K. F. & R. Richardson (G-JDLI)
	G-JDFW	Airbus A.320-212	Airtours International Airways Ltd (G-SCSR)
	G-JDIX	Mooney M.20B	ADH Ltd (G-ARTB)
	G-JDTI	Cessna 421C	Eastfield Air Ltd/Sturgate
	G-JEAD	F.27 Friendship Mk 500	Jersey European Airways Ltd
	G-JEAE	F.27 Friendship Mk 500	Jersey European Airways Ltd
	G-JEAG	F.27 Friendship Mk 500	Jersey European Airways Ltd
	G-JEAH	F.27 Friendship Mk 500	Jersey European Airways Ltd
	G-JEAI	F.27 Friendship Mk 500	Jersey European Airways Ltd
	G-JEAJ	BAe 146-200	Jersey European Airways Ltd (G-OLCA) Pride of Guernsey
	G-JEAK	BAe 146-200	Jersey European Airways Ltd (G-OLCB)
	G-JEAL	BAe 146-300	Jersey European Airways Ltd (G-BTXN) Pride of Belfast
	G-JEAM	BAe 146-300	Jersey European Airways Ltd (G-BTJT) Pride of Jersey
	G-JEAN	Cessna 500 Citation	Foster Associates Ltd

Reg.	Type	Owner or Operator	Notes
G-JEAO	BAe 146-100	Jersey European Airways Ltd (G-UKPC/ G-BKXZ)	
G-JEAP	F.27 Friendship Mk 500	Jersey European Airways Ltd	
G-JEAR	BAe 146-200	Jersey European Airways Ltd (G-HWPB/G-BSRU/G-OSKI)	
G-JEAS	BAe 146-200	Jersey European Airways Ltd (G-OLHB/G-BSRV/G-OSUN)	
G-JEET	Cessna FA.152	Luton Flight Training (G-BHMF)	
G-JEFF	PA-38-112 Tomahawk	R. J. Alford	
G-JENA	Mooney M.20K	P. Leverkuehn/Biggin Hill	
G-JENI	Cessna R.182	R. A. Bentley	
G-JENN	AA-5B Tiger	Plane Talking Ltd/Elstree	
G-JERS	Robinson R-22B	Ravenheat Manufacturing Ltd	
G-JESS	PA-28R-201T Turbo Arrow III	N. E. & M. A. Beddgood (G-REIS)	
G-JETA	Cessna 500 Citation II	IDS Aircraft Ltd/Heathrow	
G-JETH	Hawker Sea Hawk FGA.6 (XE489) ★	P. G. Vallance Ltd/Charlwood	
G-JETI	BAe 125 Srs 800B	Alkharafi Aviation Ltd	
G-JETJ	Cessna 550 Citation II	Keelex 187 Ltd (G-EJET/G-DJBE)	
G-JETM	Gloster Meteor T.7 (VZ638) ★	P. G. Vallance Ltd/Charlwood	
G-JETN	Learjet 35A	Heathrow Jet Charter Ltd (G-JJSG)	
G-JETP	P.84 Jet Provost T.52A (T.4)	Shadow Valley Investments Ltd	
G-JETX	Bell 206B JetRanger 3	Tripgate Ltd	
G-JFOX	Denney Kitfox Mk 2	J. Fox (G-LANG)	
G-JFWI	Cessna F.172N	Staryear Ltd	
G-JGAL	Beech E90 King Air	Vaux (Aviation) Ltd/Newcastle	
G-JGMN	C.A.S.A. 1.131E Jungmann 2000	P. D. Scandrett/Staverton	
G-JHAS	Schweizer 269C	Eastman Securities Ltd	
G-JHEW	Robinson R-22B	Burbage Farms Ltd	
G-JIII	Stolp SA.300 Starduster Too	VTIO Co/Cumbernauld	
G-JILL	R. Commander 112TCA	MLP Aviation Ltd	
G-JIMB	B.121 Pup 1	BLS Aviation Ltd (G-AWWF)/Elstree	
G-JJAN	PA-28-181 Archer II	Redhill Flying Club	
G-JLEE	AB-206B JetRanger 3	Lee Aviation Ltd (G-JOKE/G-CSKY/ G-TALY)	
G-JLHS	Beech A36 Bonanza	I. G. Meredith	
G-JLMW	Cameron V-77 balloon	J. L. McK. Watkins	
G-JLRW	Beech 76 Duchess	Moorfield Developments Ltd/Elstree	
G-JLXI	BAe Jetstream 61	Jetstream Aircraft Ltd/Prestwick	
G-JMAC	BAe Jetstream 4100	British Aerospace PLC (G-JAMD/G JXLI)	
G-JMAT	Schweizer 269C	John Matchett Ltd	
G-JMDI	Schweizer 269C	Dunstan Hall Ltd (G-FLAT)	
G-JMTS	Robin DR.400/180	J. R. Whiting	
G-JMTT	PA-28R-201T Turbo Arrow III	E. W. Passmore (G-BMHM)	
G-JNNB	Colt 90A balloon	Justerini & Brooks Ltd	
G-JODL	Jodel DR.1050/M	M. J. Barton	
G-JODY	Bell 206B JetRanger 3	Bellini Aviation (1993) Ltd	
G-JOEY	BN-2A Mk III-2 Trislander	Aurigny Air Services (G-BDGG)/Guernsey	
G-JOIN	Cameron V-65 balloon	Derbyshire Building Society	
G-JOJO	Cameron A-210 balloon	Worcester Balloons	
G-JOLY	Cessna 120	J. D. Tarrant & B. V. Meade	
G-JONE	Cessna 172M	A. Pierce	
G-JONH	Robinson R-22B	Scotia Helicopters Ltd	
G-JONI	Cessna FA.152	Barmoor Aviation (G-BFTU)	
G-JONO	Colt 77A balloon	The Sandcliffe Motor Group	
G-JONZ	Cessna 172P	Truman Aviation Ltd/Tollerton	
G-JOON	Cessna 182D	J. Maffia	
G-JOSH	Cameron N-105 balloon	GT Flying Clubs Ltd	
G-JOYS	Beech 58 Baron	Dunmhor Transport Ltd	
G-JOYT	PA-28-181 Archer II	S. W. TaylorN (G-BOVO)/Redhill	
G-JPAD	Robinson R-44 Astro	Selby Farms Ltd	
G-JPOT	PA-32R-301 Saratoga SP	Motec Moulding Ltd (G-BIYM)	
G-JPRO	P.84 Jet Provost T.5A	Ruddington Aviation Ltd	
G-JPVA	P.84 Jet Provost T.5A (XW289)	T. J. Manna (G-BVXT)/Cranfield	
G-JSCL	Rans S.10 Sakota	D. L. Davies	
G-JSON	Cameron N-105 balloon	J. Bennett & Son (Insurance Brokers) Ltd	
G-JSPC	BN-2T Turbine Islander	Rhine Army Parachute Association (G-BUBG)	
G-JSSD	SA. Jetstream 3001	Jetstream Aircraft Ltd (G-AXJZ)/Prestwick	
G-JTCA	PA-23 Aztec 250E	J. D. Tighe (G-BBCU)/Sturgate	
G-JTWO	Piper J-2 Cub	A. T. Hooper & C. C. Silk (G-BPZR)	
G-JTYE	Aeronca 7AC Champion	J. Tye	
G-JUDE	CEA DR.400/180	R. G. Carrell	

Notes	Reg.	Type	Owner or Operator
	G-JUDI	AT-6D Harvard III (FX301)	A. A. Hodgson
	G-JUDY	AA-5A Cheetah	Plane Talking Ltd/Elstree
	G-JUIN	Cessna 303	M. J. Newman/Denham
	G-JULU	Cameron V-90 balloon	Datacentre Ltd
	G-JUNG	C.A.S.A. 1.131E Jungmann 1000 (E3R-143)	K. H. Wilson
	G-JURE	SOCATA TB.10 Tobago	J. & C. A. Ure
	G-JURG	R. Commander 114A	P. J. Taylor
	G-JVBF	Lindstrand LBL-210A balloon	Virgin Balloon Flights Ltd
	G-JVMD	Cessna 172N	Brandon Aviation (G-BNTV)
	G-JWBB	Jodel DR.1050	D. J. Durell (G-LAKI)
	G-JWDG	AA-5A Cheetah	Plane Talking Ltd (G-OCML/G-JAVA)
	G-JWDS	Cessna F.150G	C. R. & S. A. Hardiman (G-AVNB)
	G-JWFT	Robinson R-22B	Tukair Aircraft Charter
	G-JWIV	Jodel DR.1051	C. M. Fitton
	G-KAFE	Cameron N-65 balloon	D. M. Williams
	G-KAIR	PA-28-181 Archer II	Academy Lithoplates Ltd
	G-KAMM	Hawker Hurricane XIIA	M. Hammond
	G-KARA	Brugger MB.2 Colibri	C. L. Hill
	G-KARI	Fuji FA.200-160	I. Mansfield & F. M. Fiore (G-BBRE)
	G-KART	PA-28-161 Warrior II	Newcastle-upon-Tyne Aero Club Ltd
	G-KARY	Fuji FA.200-180AO	C. J. Zetter (G-BEYP)
	G-KATA	HOAC Katana DV.20	Aeromarine Ltd
	G-KATE	Westland WG.30 Srs 100	(stored)/Penzance
	G-KATS	PA-28 Cherokee 140	P. S. Scott (G-BIRC)
	G-KATT	Cessna 152 II	Aerohire Ltd (G-BMTK)/Halfpenny Green
	G-KAUR	Colt 315A balloon	R. S. Hunjan
	G-KAWA	Denney Kitfox	T. W. Maton
	G-KAXF	Hunter F.6A	T. J. Manna
	G-KAXL	Westland Scout AH.1	T. J. Manna
	G-KBKB	Thunder Ax8-90 S2 balloon	G. Boulden
	G-KBPI	PA-28-161 Warrior II	Goodwood Aerodrome & Motor Circuit Ltd (G-BFSZ)
	G-KCIG	Sportavia RF-5B	Exeter Sperber Syndicate
	G-KDET	PA-28-161 Cadet	Rapidspin Ltd/Biggin Hill
	G-KDFF	Scheibe SF.25E Super Falke	K. & S. C. A. Dudley
	G-KDIX	Jodel D.9 Bebe	D. J. Wells
	G-KDLN	Zlin Z.37A-2 Cmelak	J. Richardsz
	G-KEAB	Beech 65-B80 Queen Air ★	Instructional airframe (G-BSSL/ G-BFEP)/Shoreham
	G-KEAC	Beech 65-A80 Queen Air	G-KEAC Flying Group (G-REXY/G-AVNG)
	G-KEEN	Stolp SA.300 Starduster Too	Holland Aerobatics Ltd
	G-KELL	Vans RV-6	J. D. Kelsall
	G-KEMC	Grob G.109	Eye-Fly
	G-KENB	Air Command 503 Commander	K. Brogden
	G-KENI	Rotorway Executive	A. J. Wheatley
	G-KENM	Luscombe 8A Silvaire	J. R. Malpass
	G-KERY	PA-28 Cherokee 180	Seawing Flying Club Ltd (G-ATWO)/ Southend
	G-KEST	Steen Skybolt	S. Thursfield & K. E. Eld
	G-KEVN	Robinson R-22B	K. P. Gallen (G-BONX)
	G-KEYB	Cameron O-84 balloon	B. P. Key
	G-KEYS	PA-23 Aztec 250F	T. M. Tuke & W. T. McCarter/Eglinton
	G-KEYY	Cameron N-77 balloon	R. Astill & ptnrs (G-BORZ)
	G-KFOX	Denney Kitfox	C. H. T. Trace
	G-KFZI	KFZ-1 Tigerfalck	L. R. Williams
	G-KHRE	M.S.893E Rallye 150SV	J. L. Clarke
	G-KILY	Robinson R-22A	Lateq Aviation Ltd/Booker
	G-KIMB	Robin DR.340/1Q40	R. M. Kimbell
	G-KINE	AA-5A Cheetah	Walsh Aviation
	G-KINK	Cessna 340	Hulbert of Dudley (Holdings) Ltd (G-PLEV)
	G-KIRK	Piper J-3C-65 Cub	M. J. Kirk
	G-KISS	Rand KR-2	E. A. Rooney
	G-KITE	PA-28-181 Archer II	CAVOK Aviation
	G-KITF	Denney Kitfox	Junipa Sales (Aviation) Ltd
	G-KITI	Pitts S-2E Special	B. R. Cornes
	G-KITS	Shaw Europa	Europa Aviation Ltd
	G-KITY	Denney Kitfox Mk 2	Kitfox KFM Group
	G-KIWI	Cessna 404 Titan	Aviation Beauport Ltd (G-BHNI)
	G-KKDL	SOCATA TB.20 Trinidad	Egerton Hospital Equipment Ltd (G-BSHU)

Reg.	Type	Owner or Operator	Notes
G-KKES	SOCATA TB.20 Trinidad	Kestrel Aviation International Ltd (G-BTLH)/Biggin Hill	
G-KLAY	Enstrom 280C Shark	I. G. Shrigley (G-BGZD)	
G-KLEE	Bell 206B JetRanger 3	Taylor-Ryan Aviation (G-SIZL/G-BOSW)	
G-KLIK	Air Command 532 Elite	Roger Savage (Photography)	
G-KNAP	PA-28-161 Warrior II	Newland Aeroleasing Ltd (G-BIUX)	
G-KNOB	Lindstrand LBL-180A balloon	Wye Valley Aviation Ltd	
G-KNOW	PA-32 Cherokee Six 300	P. J. Fydelor	
G-KODA	Cameron O-77 balloon	United Photofinishers Ltd	
G-KOLB	Kölb Twinstar Mk 3	P. A. Akines	
G-KOLI	PZL-110 Koliber 150	D. Sadler	
G-KONG	Slingsby T.67M-200	Hunting Aviation Ltd	
G-KOOL	D.H.104 Devon C.2 ★	E. Surrey Technical College/nr Redhill	
G-KOTA	PA-28-236 Dakota	JF Packaging	
G-KRAY	Robinson R-22HP	Direct Helicopters (Southend) Ltd (G-BOBO)	
G-KRII	Rand KR-2	M. R. Cleveley	
G-KRIS	Maule M5-235C Lunar Rocket	M. G. Pickering	
G-KSIR	Stoddard-Hamilton Glasair IIRGS	R. Cayzer	
G-KSVB	PA-24 Comanche 260	J. R. Pettit (G-ENIU/G-AVJU)	
G-KTEE	Cameron V-77 balloon	D. C. & N. P. Bull	
G-KUTU	Quickie Q.2	R. Nash & J. Parkinson	
G-KWAX	Cessna 182E Skylane	J. E. & V. T. Brewis	
G-KWIK	Partenavia P.68B	Phlight Avia Ltd	
G-KWIP	Shaw Europa	D. Elliott	
G-KWKI	QAC Quickie Q.200	B. M. Jackson	
G-KYAK	Yakovlev C.11	Patina Ltd/Duxford	
G-LABS	Shaw Europa	C. T. H. Pattinson	
G-LACA	PA-28-161 Warrior II	LAC (Enterprises) Ltd/Barton	
G-LACB	PA-28-161 Warrior II	LAC (Enterprises) Ltd/Barton	
G-LACR	Denney Kitfox	C. M. Rose	
G-LADE	PA-32 Cherokee Six 300E	Telefax 2000 Ltd	
G-LADI	PA-30 Twin Comanche 160	E. C. Clark (G-ASOO)/Biggin Hill	
G-LADS	R. Commander 114	D. F. Soul	
G-LAGR	Cameron N-90 balloon	Bass & Tennent Sales Ltd	
G-LAIN	Robinson R-22B	R&R Developments Ltd	
G-LAIR	Stoddard-Hamilton Glasair IIS	D. L. Swallow	
G-LAKE	Lake LA-250 Renegade	Stanford Ltd	
G-LAMM	Shaw Europa	S. A Lamb	
G-LAMS	Cessna F.152 II	Rentalr Ltd	
G-LANC	Avro 683 Lancaster X (KB889) ★	Imperial War Museum/Duxford	
G-LAND	Robinson R-22B	Heli-Point Hire	
G-LANE	Cessna F.172N	G. C. Bantin	
G-LAPN	Light Aero Avid Aerobat	R. M. & A. P. Shorter	
G-LARA	Robin DR.400/180	K. D. & C. A. Brackwell	
G-LARE	PA-39 Twin Comanche C/R	Glareways (Neasden) Ltd	
G-LARK	Helton Lark 95	J. Fox	
G-LASR	Stoddard-Hamilton Glasair II	P. Taylor	
G-LASS	Rutan Vari-Eze	S. Roberts/Liverpool	
G-LATK	Robinson R-44	Ardern Consultancy Ltd (G-BVMK)	
G-LAXY	Everett Srs 3 gyroplane	G. D. Western	
G-LAZA	Lazer Z.200	M. Hammond	
G-LAZR	Cameron O-77 balloon	Laser Civil Engineering Ltd	
G-LAZY	Lindstrand Armchair SS balloon	The Air Chair Co. Ltd	
G-LBCS	Colt 31A balloon	Virgin Airship & Balloon Co Ltd	
G-LBLB	Lindstrand LBL-105A balloon	Lindstrand Balloons Ltd	
G-LBLI	Lindstrand LBL-105A balloon	Lindstrand Balloons Ltd	
G-LBLZ	Lindstrand LBL-105A balloon	Lindstrand Balloons Ltd	
G-LBMM	PA-28-161 Warrior II	S. C. May	
G-LBNK	Cameron N-105 balloon	Virgin Airship & Balloon Co. Ltd	
G-LBRC	PA-28RT-201 Arrow IV	D. J. V. Morgan	
G-LCGL	CLA.7 Swift (replica)	J. M. Greenland	
G-LCOK	Colt 69A balloon	Hot-Air Balloon Co Ltd (G-BLWI)	
G-LCON	AS.355N Twin Squirrel	Lancashire Constabulary/Warton	
G-LCRC	Boeing 757-23A	Airtours International Airways Ltd (G-IEAB)	
G-LDYS	Colt 56A balloon	P. Glydon & J. Coote	
G-LEAM	PA-28-236 Dakota	South Yorkshire Caravans Ltd (G-BHLS)	
G-LEAP	BN-2T Turbine Islander	Army Parachute Association (G-BLND)/ Netheravon	
G-LEAR	Learjet 35A	Northern Executive Aviation Ltd/ Manchester	
G-LEAU	Cameron N-31 balloon	P. L. Mossman	

Notes	Reg.	Type	Owner or Operator
	G-LECA	AS.355F-1 Twin Squirrel	S. W. Electricity Board (G-BNBK)/Bristol
	G-LEDN	Short SD3-30 Variant 100	Streamline Aviation (SW) Ltd (G-BIOF)/Exeter
	G-LEED	Denney Kitfox Mk 2	G. T. Leedham
	G-LEES	Glaser-Dirks DG.400	G-LEES Group
	G-LEEZ	Bell 206L-1 LongRanger 2	Pennine Helicopters Ltd (G-BPCT)
	G-LEGO	Cameron O-77 balloon	C. H. Pearce Construction PLC
	G-LEGS	Short SD3-60	Loganair Ltd/British Airways (G-BLEF)
	G-LEIC	Cessna FA.152	Leicestershire Aero Club Ltd
	G-LEND	Cameron N-77 balloon	Southern Flight Co Ltd
	G-LENI	AS.355F-1 Twin Squirrel	Mala Services (South West) Ltd (G-ZFDB/G-BLEV)
	G-LENN	Cameron V-56 balloon	Anglia Balloon School Ltd
	G-LENS	Thunder Ax7-77Z balloon	Big Yellow Balloon Group
	G-LEOS	Robin DR.400/120	P. G. Newens
	G-LEPF	Fairchild 24R-46A Argus III	J. M. Greenland
	G-LESJ	Denney Kitfox Mk 3	L. A. James
	G-LEVI	Aeronca 7AC Champion	G-LEVI Group
	G-LEXI	Cameron N-77 balloon	Sedgemoor 500 Balloon Group
	G-LEZE	Rutan LongEz	K. G. M. Loyal & ptnrs
	G-LFBA	MBB BK-117C-1C	McAlpine Helicopters Ltd/Kidlington
	G-LFIX	V.S.509 Spitfire T.IX (ML407)	C. S. Grace
	G-LFSA	PA-38-112 Tomahawk	Liverpool Flying School Ltd (G-BSFC)
	G-LFSB	PA-38-112 Tomahawk	Liverpool Flying School Ltd (G-BLYC)
	G-LFSC	PA-28 Cherokee 140	Liverpool Flying School Ltd (G-BGTR)
	G-LFSI	PA-28 Cherokee 140	Soko hAviation Ltd (G-AYKV)/Liverpool
	G-LFVB	V.S.349 Spitfire LF.Vb (EP120)	Patina Ltd/Duxford
	G-LIAN	Robinson R-22B	Cotwell Air Services/Booker
	G-LIBB	Cameron V-77 balloon	R. R. McCormick & R. J. Mercer
	G-LIBS	Hughes 369HS	A. Harvey & R. White
	G-LICK	Cessna 172N	Dacebow Aviation (G-BNTR)
	G-LIDA	Hoffmann HK-36R Super Dimona	W. D. Inglis
	G-LIDE	PA-31-350 Navajo Chieftain	Keen Leasing Ltd
	G-LIFE	Thunder Ax6-56Z balloon	D. F. Maine
	G-LILI	Cessna 425	Ortac Air Ltd (G-YOTT/G-NORC/G-BICL)
	G-LILY	Bell 206B JetRanger 3	T. S. Brown (G-NTBI)
	G-LIMA	R. Commander 114	Tricolore Aeroclub Ltd
	G-LINC	Hughes 369HS	Hawkair Ltd
	G-LINE	AS.355N Twin Squirrel	National Grid Co PLC
	G-LIOA	Lockheed 10A Electra ★ (NC5171N)	Science Museum/Wroughton
	G-LION	PA-18 Super Cub 135 (R-167)	C. Moore
	G-LIOT	Cameron O-77 balloon	D. Eliot
	G-LIPE	Robinson R-22B	Sloane Helicopters FLtd & Westleigh Construction Ltd (G-BTXJ)
	G-LIPP	BN-2T Turbine Islander	Rhine Army Parachute Association (G-BKJG)
	G-LITE	R. Commander 112A	J. Males
	G-LITZ	Pitts S-1E Special	J. A. Hughes/Leicester
	G-LIVH	Piper J-3C-65 Cub (332038)	M. D. Cowburn
	G-LIZA	Cessna 340A	J. H. Fry & J. C. Merkens (G-BMDM)
	G-LIZI	PA-28 Cherokee 160	R. J. Walker & J. R. Lawson (G-ARRP)
	G-LIZY	Westland Lysander III (V9673) ★	G. A. Warner/Duxford
	G-LIZZ	PA-E23 Aztec 250E	C. R. Cox & T. D. Nathan (G-BBWM)
	G-LLYD	Cameron N-31 balloon	Virgin Airship & Balloon Co Ltd
	G-LNYS	Cessna F.177RG	J. W. Clarke (G-BDCM)
	G-LOAF	Schempp-Hirth Janus CM	G. W. Kirton
	G-LOAN	Cameron N-77 balloon	Newbury Building Soc
	G-LOBO	Cameron O-120 balloon	Solo Aerostatics
	G-LOCH	Piper J-3C-90 Cub	J. M. Greenland
	G-LOFA	L.188CF Electra	Air Atlantique Ltd/Coventry
	G-LOFB	L.188CF Electra	Air Atlantique Ltd/Coventry
	G-LOFC	L.188CF Electra	Air Atlantique Ltd/Coventry
	G-LOFM	Maule MX-7-180A	Atlantic Air Transport Ltd/Coventry
	G-LOFT	Cessna 500 Citation	Atlantic Air Transport Ltd/Coventry
	G-LOGS	Robinson R-22B	M. Chantler & ptnrs
	G-LOKO	Cameron 105 Loco SS balloon	Cameron Balloons Ltd
	G-LOLL	Cameron V-77 balloon	Test Valley Balloon Group
	G-LOLO	Robinson R-22B	McMurdo International Ltd (G-NIKI)
	G-LONG	Bell 206L LongRanger	Walsh Aviation
	G-LOOP	Pitts S-1C Special	G. M. Roberts & K. E. Wells
	G-LOOT	EMB-110P1 Bandeirante	*stored* (G-BNOC)/Southend
	G-LORD	PA-34-200T Seneca II	Aerohire Ltd/Halfpenny Green

Reg.	Type	Owner or Operator	Notes
G-LORI	H.S.125 Srs 403B	Re-Enforce Trading Co Ltd (G-AYOJ)	
G-LORT	Light Aero Avid Speedwing 4	G. E. Laucht	
G-LORY	Thunder Ax4-31Z balloon	A. J. Moore	
G-LOSM	Gloster Meteor NF.11 (WM167)	Hunter Wing Ltd/Bournemouth	
G-LOSS	Cameron N-77 balloon	D. K. Fish	
G-LOST	Denney Kitfox Mk 3	H. Balfour-Paul	
G-LOTI	Bleriot XI (replica) ★	Brooklands Museum Trust Ltd	
G-LOTO	BN-2A-26 Islander	Scottish Parachute Club (Islander) Ltd (G-BDWG)	
G-LOUI	Extra EA.300	L. C. A. Knapp (G-OHER)	
G-LOWA	Colt 77A balloon	K. D. Pierce	
G-LOWE	Monnett Sonerai I	J. L. Kinch	
G-LOYA	Cessna FR.172J	T. R. Scorer (G-BLVT)	
G-LOYD	SA.341G Gazelle 1	Apollo Manufacturing (Derby) Ltd (G-SFTC)	
G-LRBW	Lindstrand HS-110 balloon	International Balloons Ltd	
G-LSFI	AA-5A Cheetah	T. G. Dughan (G-BGSK)	
G-LSHI	Colt 77A balloon	Lambert Smith Hampton Ltd	
G-LSMI	Cessna F.152	Falcon Flying Services/Biggin Hill	
G-LTEK	Bell 206B JetRanger 2	Lateq Aviation Ltd (G-BMIB)/Booker	
G-LTFC	PA-28 Cherokee 140B	London Transport Flying Club Ltd (G-AXTI)/Fairoaks	
G-LTNG	EE Lightning T.5 (XS451)	Lightning Flying Club	
G-LUAR	SOCATA TB.10 Tobago	M. E. Muldoon	
G-LUBE	Cameron N-77 balloon	A. C. K. Rawson	
G-LUCA	Thunder Ax7-77Z balloon	R. De-Leyser	
G-LUCE	Cameron A-210 balloon	Aerial Promotions Ltd	
G-LUCK	Cessna F.150M	Aviators Ltd	
G-LUED	Aero Designs Pulsar	R. & H. D. Blamires	
G-LUFT	Pützer Elster C	Bath Stone Co Ltd (G-BOPY)	
G-LUKE	Rutan LongEz	S. G. Busby	
G-LULU	Grob G.109	A. P. Bowden	
G-LUNA	PA-32RT-300T Turbo Lance II	D. N. Brown & R. J. H. Creese	
G-LUSC	Luscombe 8E Silvaire	M. Fowler	
G-LUSI	Luscombe 8E Silvaire	J. P. Hunt & D. M. Robinson	
G-LUST	Luscombe 8E Silvaire	M. Griffiths	
G-LUXE	BAe 146-300	British Aerospace PLC (G-SSSH)	
G-LYDA	Hoffman H-36 Dimona	R. G. Trute	
G-LYND	PA-25 Pawnee 235	Glyndwr Soaring Group (G-BSFZ/ G-ASFZ)/Lleweni Parc	
G-LYNE	P-51D-20-NA Mustang (44-72028)	E. N. Robinson & M. C. B. Anderson	
G-LYNX	Westland WG.13 Lynx (ZB500) ★	International Helicopter Museum/ Weston-s-Mare	
G-LYTE	Thunder Ax7-77 balloon	G. M. Bulmer	
G-MAAC	Advanced Airship Corporation	Advanced Airship Corporation Ltd ANR-1	
G-MABI	Cessna F.150L	Shobdon Aircraft Maintenance (G-BGOJ)	
G-MACH	SIAI-Marchetti SF.260	Cheyne Motors Ltd/Popham	
G-MACK	PA-28R Cherokee Arrow 200-II	Haimoss Ltd	
G-MADD	Robinson R-22B	Great Excitement Ltd (G-MEAT)	
G-MAFE	Dornier Do.228-202K	FR Aviation Ltd (G-OALF/G-MLDO)/ Bournemouth	
G-MAFF	BN-2T Turbine Islander	FR Aviation Ltd (G-BJEO)/Bournemouth	
G-MAFI	Dornier Do.228-200	FR Aviation Ltd/Bournemouth	
G-MAGC	Cameron Grand Illusion SS balloon	L. V. Mastis	
G-MAGG	Pitts S-1SE Special	C. A. Boardman	
G-MAGY	AS.350B Ecureuil	McAlpine Helicopters Ltd (G-BIYC)/Kidlington	
G-MAIR	PA-34-200T Seneca II	Barnes Olson Aeroleasing Ltd	
G-MAJA	BAe Jetstream 4102	Manx Airlines Ltd/British Midland	
G-MAJB	BAe Jetstream 4102	Manx Airlines Ltd/British Airways (G-BVKT)	
G-MAJC	BAe Jetstream 4102	Manx Airlines Ltd/British Airways (G-LOGJ)	
G-MAJD	BAe Jetstream 4102	Manx Airlines Ltd/British Airways (G-WAWR)	
G-MAJE	BAe Jetstream 4102	Manx Airlines Ltd/British Airways (G-LOGK)	
G-MAJF	BAe Jetstream 4102	Manx Airlines Ltd/British Airways (G-WAWL)	

Notes	Reg.	Type	Owner or Operator
	G-MAJG	BAe Jetstream 4102	Manx Airlines Ltd/British Airways (G-LOGL)
	G-MAJH	BAe Jetstream 4102	Manx Airlines Ltd/British Airways (G-WAYR)
	G-MAJI	BAe Jetstream 4102	Manx Airlines Ltd/British Airways (G-WAND)
	G-MAJJ	BAe Jetstream 4102	Manx Airlines Ltd/British Airways (G-WAFT)
	G-MAJK	BAe Jetstream 4102	Manx Airlines Ltd/British Airways
	G-MAJL	BAe Jetstream 4102	Manx Airlines Ltd/British Airways
	G-MAJM	BAe Jetstream 4102	Manx Airlines Ltd/British Airways
	G-MAJS	Airbus A.300-605R	Monarch Airlines Ltd/Luton
	G-MALA	PA-28-181 Archer II	M. & D. Aviation (G-BIIU)
	G-MALC	AA-5 Traveler	B. P. Hogan (G-BCPM)
	G-MALK	Cessna F.172N	J. Easson/Edinburgh
	G-MALS	Mooney M.20K-231	G-MALS Group/White Waltham
	G-MALT	Colt Flying Hop SS balloon	P. J. Stapley
	G-MAMC	Rotorway Executive 90	J. R. Carmichael
	G-MAMO	Cameron V-77 balloon	The Marble Mosaic Co Ltd
	G-MANA	BAe ATP	Manx Airlines Ltd (G-LOGH)
	G-MANB	BAe ATP	Manx Airlines Ltd (G-LOGG/G-JATP)
	G-MANC	BAe ATP	Manx Airlines Ltd (G-LOGF)
	G-MAND	PA-28-161 Warrior II	Halfpenny Green Flight Centre Ltd (G-BRKT)
	G-MANE	BAe ATP	Manx Airlines Ltd/British Airways (G-LOGB)
	G-MANF	BAe ATP	Manx Airlines Ltd/British Airways (G-LOGA)
	G-MANG	BAe ATP	Manx Airlines Ltd/British Airways (G-LOGD/G-OLCD)
	G-MANH	BAe ATP	Manx Airlines Ltd/British Airways (G-LOGC/G-OLCC)
	G-MANI	Cameron V-90 balloon	M. P. G. Papworth
	G-MANJ	BAe ATP	Manx Airlines Ltd (G-LOGE/G-BMYL)
	G-MANL	BAe ATP	British Midland Airways Ltd (G-ERIN/ G-BMYK)
	G-MANM	BAe ATP	Manx Airlines Ltd (G-OATP/G-BZWW)
	G-MANN	SA.341G Gazelle 1	First City Air PLC (G-BKLW)
	G-MANS	BAe 146-200	Manx Airlines Ltd (G-CHSR)
	G-MANX	FRED Srs 2	S. Styles
	G-MAPR	Beech A36 Bonanza	Openair Ltd
	G-MARE	Schweizer 269C	The Earl of Caledon
	G-MASC	Jodel 150A	K. F. & R. Richardson
	G-MASH	Westland-Bell 47G-4A	Defence Products Ltd (G-AXKU)
	G-MASS	Cessna 152	MK Aero Support Ltd (G-BSHN)
	G-MATE	Moravan Zlin Z.50LX	D. T. Karberry
	G-MATS	Colt GA-42 airship	Lindstrand Balloons Ltd
	G-MATT	Robin R.2160	Entrepren-Air Ltd (G-BKRC)
	G-MATZ	PA-28 Cherokee 140	Midland Air Training School (G-BASI)
	G-MAUD	BAe ATP	British Midland Airways Ltd (G-BMYM)
	G-MAUK	Colt 77A balloon	B. Meeson
	G-MAVE	Shaw Europa	D. A. & A. D. Field
	G-MAVI	Robinson R-22B	Yorkshire Helicopter Centre Ltd/Doncaster
	G-MAWL	Maule M4-210C Rocket	D. Group
	G-MAXI	PA-34-200T Seneca II	G. C. Rogers
	G-MAYO	PA-28-161 Warrior II	Jermyk Engineering/Fairoaks
	G-MAZY	D.H.82A Tiger Moth	Newark Air Museum
	G-MCAR	PA-32 Cherokee Six 300D	Miller Aerial Spraying Ltd (G-LADA/ G-AYWK)/Wickenby
	G-MCEA	Boeing 757-225	Airtours International Airways Ltd
	G-MCKE	Boeing 757-28A	Monarch Airlines Ltd/Luton
	G-MCMS	Aero Designs Pulsar	M. C. Manning
	G-MCOX	Fuji FA.200-180AO	W. Surrey Engineering (Shepperton) Ltd
	G-MCPI	Bell 206B JetRanger 3	D. A. C. Pipe (G-ONTB)
	G-MDAC	PA-28-181 Archer II	B. R. McKay/Bournemouth
	G-MDEW	Lindstrand Drinks Can SS balloon	Lindstrand Balloons Ltd
	G-MDKD	Robinson R-22B	D. K. Duckworth
	G-MDTV	Cameron N-105 balloon	Ideas Factory
	G-MEAH	PA-28R Cherokee Arrow 200-II	Stapleford Flying Club Ltd (G-BSNM)
	G-MEAN	Agusta A.109A	Castle Air Charters Ltd (G-BRYL/G-ROPE/ G-OAMH)
	G-MEDA	Airbus A.320-231	British Mediterranean Airways Ltd

Reg.	Type	Owner or Operator	Notes
G-MEGA	PA-28R-201T Turbo Arrow III	Travelworth Ltd	
G-MELD	AA-5A Cheetah	Meld Ltd (G-BHCB)/Blackbushe	
G-MELT	Cessna F.172H	Vectair Aviation Ltd (G-AWTI)	
G-MELV	SOCATA Rallye 235E	Wallis & Sons Ltd (G-BIND)	
G-MEME	PA-28R-201 Arrow III	Henry J. Clare Ltd	
G-MEOW	CFM Streak Shadow	S. D. Hicks	
G-MERC	Colt 56A balloon	A. F. & C. D. Selby	
G-MERE	Lindstrand LBL-77A balloon	G. T. Restell	
G-MERF	Grob G.115A	W. Murphy (G-EGVV)	
G-MERI	PA-28-181 Archer II	Scotia Safari Ltd/Glasgow	
G-MERL	PA-28RT-201 Arrow IV	M. Giles	
G-META	Bell 222	The Metropolitan Police/Lippitts Hill	
G-METB	Bell 222	The Metropolitan Police/Lippitts Hill	
G-METC	Bell 222	The Metropolitan Police (G-JAMC)/ Lippitts Hill	
G-METD	AS.355N Twin Squirrel	The Metropolitan Police (G-BUJF)/ Lippitts Hill	
G-METE	Gloster Meteor F.8 (VZ467)	Classic Jets Ltd	
G-MEUP	Cameron A-120 balloon	N. J. Tovey	
G-MEYO	Enstrom 280FX	R. J. Howard	
G-MFHL	Robinson R-22B	MFH Ltd	
G-MFLI	Cameron V-90 balloon	J. M. Percival	
G-MFMF	Bell 206B JetRanger 3	S.W. Electricity Board (G-BJNJ)/Bristol	
G-MFMM	Scheibe SF.25C Falke	S. Lancs Falke Syndicate/Liverpool	
G-MHBD	Cameron O-105 balloon	K. Hull	
G-MHCA	Enstrom F-28C-UK	Trimcares Ltd (G-SHWW/G-SMUJ/ G-BHTF)	
G-MHCB	Enstrom 280C	Manchester Helicopter Centre	
G-MICH	Robinson R-22B	A. P. Codling (G-BNKY)	
G-MICK	Cessna F.172N	G-MICK Flying Group	
G-MICY	Everett Srs 1 gyroplane	D. M. Hughes	
G-MICZ	PA-46-310P Malibu	Mitchell Instruments Ltd	
G-MIDG	Midget Mustang	C. E. Bellhouse	
G-MIFF	Robin DR.400/180	G. E. Bickerton	
G-MIII	Extra EA.300/L	Firebird Aerobatics Ltd	
G-MIKE	Brookland Hornet	M. H. J. Goldring	
G-MIKY	Cameron 90 Mickey SS balloon	The Walt Disney Co Ltd	
G-MILE	Cameron N-77 balloon	Miles Air Ltd	
G-MILI	Bell 206B JetRanger 3	Southern Air Ltd/Shoreham	
G-MIMA	BAc 146-200	Manx Airlines Ltd (G-CNMF)	
G-MIND	Cessna 404	Atlantic Air Transport Ltd (G-SKKC/G-OHUB)/Coventry	
G-MINI	Currie Wot	D. Collinson	
G-MINS	Nicollier HN.700 Menestrel II	R. Fenion	
G-MINT	Pitts S-1S Special	T. G. Sanderson/Tollerton	
G-MINX	Bell 47G-4A	R. F. Warner (G-FOOR)	
G-MISH	Cessna 182R	M. Konstantinovic (G-RFAB/G-BIXT)	
G-MISS	Taylor JT.2 Titch	A. Brennan	
G-MIST	Cessna T.210K	J. Summers (G-AYGM)	
G-MITS	Cameron N-77 balloon	Colt Car Co Ltd	
G-MITZ	Cameron N-77 balloon	Colt Car Co Ltd	
G-MKAK	Colt 77A balloon	Virgin Airship & Balloon Co Ltd	
G-MKVB	V.S.349 Spitfire LF.VB (BM597)	Historic Aircraft Collection Ltd	
G-MKVI	D.H. Vampire FB.6 (VZ304)	T. C. Topen/Bruntingthorpe	
G-MKXI	V.S.365 Spitfire PR.XI (PL965)	C. P. B. Horsley	
G-MLAS	Cessna 182E ★	Parachute jump trainer/St Merryn	
G-MLFF	PA-23 Aztec 250E	Brands Hatch Circuit Ltd (G-WEBB/ G-BJBU)	
G-MLGL	Colt 21A balloon	Colt Balloons Ltd	
G-MLWI	Thunder Ax7-77 balloon	M. L. & L. P. Willoughby	
G-MOAC	Beech F33A Bonanza	Chalkfarm Productions Ltd	
G-MOAK	Schempp-Hirth Nimbus 3DM	P. W. Lever/Portmoak	
G-MOBI	AS.355F-1 Twin Squirrel	M. J. O'Brien (G-MUFF/G-CORR)	
G-MOET	Partenavia P.68B	Phlight Avia Ltd (G-HPVC)/Coventry	
G-MOFF	Cameron O-77 balloon	D. M. Moffat	
G-MOFZ	Cameron O-90 balloon	D. M. Moffat	
G-MOGI	AA-5A Cheetah	TL Aviation Ltd (G-BFMU)	
G-MOGY	Robinson R-22B	Hireheli Ltd/Booker	
G-MOKE	Cameron V-77 balloon	D. D. Owen	
G-MOLE	Taylor JT.2 Titch	S. R. Mowle	
G-MOLI	Cameron A-250 balloon	J. J. Rudoni	
G-MOLL	PA-32-301T Turbo Saratoga	K. Morrissey	
G-MOLY	PA-23 Apache 160	R. R. & M. T. Thorogood (G-APFV)/St Just	

Notes	Reg.	Type	Owner or Operator
	G-MONB	Boeing 757-2T7	Monarch Airlines Ltd/Luton
	G-MONC	Boeing 757-2T7	Monarch Airlines Ltd/Luton
	G-MOND	Boeing 757-2T7	Monarch Airlines Ltd/Luton
	G-MONE	Boeing 757-2T7	Monarch Airlines Ltd/Luton
	G-MONG	Boeing 737-3Y0	Monarch Airlines Ltd/Luton
	G-MONI	Monnett Moni	B. S. Carpenter/Booker
	G-MONJ	Boeing 757-2T7	Monarch Airlines Ltd/Luton
	G-MONK	Boeing 757-2T7	Monarch Airlines Ltd/Luton
	G-MONR	Airbus A.300-605R	Monarch Airlines Ltd/Luton
	G-MONS	Airbus A.300-605R	Monarch Airlines Ltd/Luton
	G-MONV	Boeing 737-33A	Monarch Airlines Ltd/Luton
	G-MONW	Airbus A.320-212	Monarch Airlines Ltd/Luton
	G-MONX	Airbus A.320-212	Monarch Airlines Ltd/Luton
	G-MONY	Airbus A.320-212	Monarch Airlines Ltd/Canada 3000 (C-GVNY)
	G-MONZ	Airbus A.320-212	Monarch Airlines Ltd/Luton
	G-MOON	Mooney M.20K	M. A. Eccles
	G-MOOR	SOCATA TB.10 Tobago	J. R. Smith & ptnrs (G-MILK)
	G-MOOS	P.56 Provost T.1 (XF690)	T. J. Manna (G-BGKA)/Cranfield
	G-MORE	Schleicher ASH.26E	B. H. Owen
	G-MOSS	Beech D55 Baron	A. W. Moss & Son (Civil & Railway Engineering Ltd (G-AWAD)
	G-MOTH	D.H.82A Tiger Moth (K2567)	M. C. Russell
	G-MOTO	PA-24 Comanche 160	C. C. Letchford & A. J. Redknapp (G-EDHE/G-ASFH)
	G-MOTT	Light Aero Avid Speedwing	J. B. Ott
	G-MOUL	Maule M6-235	E. L. Klinge
	G-MOUR	H.S. Gnat T.1 (XR991)	D. J. Gilmour
	G-MOUS	Cameron 90 Mickey SS balloon	The Walt Disney Co Ltd
	G-MOVE	PA-60-601P Aerostar	A. Cazaz & A. Gillen
	G-MOVI	PA-32R-301 Saratoga SP	Rentair (G-MARI)
	G-MOZZ	Avions Mudry CAP.10B	M. B. Smith/Booker
	G-MPBH	Cessna FA.152	Metropolitan Police Flying Club (G-FLIC/ G-BILV)/Biggin Hill
	G-MPCD	Airbus A.320-212	Monarch Airlines Ltd/Canada 3000 (C-FTDU)
	G-MPWH	Rotorway Executive	Neric Ltd
	G-MPWI	Robin HR.100/210	Propwash Investments Ltd/Cardiff
	G-MPWT	PA-34-220T Seneca III	Neric Ltd
	G-MRCI	Sequoia F.8L Falco	M. R. Clark
	G-MRKT	Lindstrand LBL-90A balloon	Marketplace Public Relations (London) Ltd
	G-MRPP	PA-34-220T Seneca III	Dagless Ltd
	G-MRSN	Robinson R-22B	Northern Helicopters (Leeds) Ltd
	G-MRST	PA-28 RT-201 Arrow IV	Winchfield Enterprises Ltd
	G-MRTC	Cessna 550 Citation II	Terry Coleman (UK) Ltd (G-SSOZ)
	G-MRTI	Cameron 110 Eagle SS balloon	Eagle Airways Ltd
	G-MRTY	Cameron N-77 balloon	R. A. & P. G. Vale
	G-MSAL	MS.733 Alcyon (143)	D. R. C. Bell/Booker
	G-MSDJ	AS.350B-1 Ecureuil	Denis Ferranti Hoverknights Ltd (G-BPOH)
	G-MSES	Cessna 150L	Airtime Aviation Services/Bournemouth
	G-MSFC	PA-38-112 Tomahawk	Sherwood Flying Club Ltd/Tollerton
	G-MSOO	Mini-500	R. H. Ryan
	G-MSTC	AA-5A Cheetah	Mid-Sussex Timber Co Ltd (G-BIJT)
	G-MUIR	Cameron V-65 balloon	L. C. M. Muir
	G-MULL	Douglas DC-10-30	British Airways *New Forest*/Gatwick
	G-MUMS	PA-28-161 Warrior II	A. J. Wood
	G-MUNI	Mooney M.20J	Sequoia Aviation Ltd
	G-MURY	Robinson R-44 Astro	Simlot Ltd
	G-MUSO	Rutan LongEz	M. Moran
	G-MUST	CA-18 Mustang 22	Fairoaks Aviation Services Ltd
	G-MUTE	Colt 31A balloon	Redmalt Ltd
	G-MUZO	Shaw Europa	J. T. Grant
	G-MXIX	V.S.390 Spitfire PR.XIX	E. C. English
	G-MXVI	V.S.361 Spitfire LF.XVIe (TE184)	Myrick Aviation Services Ltd
	G-NAAS	AS.355F-1 Twin Squirrel	Northumbria Ambulance Service NHS Trust (G-BPRG/G-NWPA)
	G-NACA	Norman NAC.2 Freelance 180	NDN Aircraft Ltd/Sandown
	G-NACI	Norman NAC.1 Srs 100	I. J. Blackwood
	G-NACL	Norman NAC.6 Fieldmaster	EPA Aircraft Co Ltd (G-BNEG)
	G-NACM	Norman NAC.6 Fieldmaster	EPA Aircraft Co Ltd
	G-NACN	Norman NAC.6 Fieldmaster	EPA Aircraft Co Ltd
	G-NACO	Norman NAC.6 Fieldmaster	EPA Aircraft Co Ltd

Reg.	Type	Owner or Operator	Notes
G-NACP	Norman NAC.6 Fieldmaster	EPA Aircraft Co Ltd	
G-NANA	VPM M.16 Tandem Trainer	J. W. P. Lewis	
G-NASA	Lockheed T-33A-5-LO (91007)	A. S. Topen (G-TJET)	
G-NASH	AA-5A Cheetah	F. P. Lund	
G-NATT	R. Commander 114A	Northgleam Ltd	
G-NATX	Cameron O-65 balloon	A. G. E. Faulkner	
G-NATY	H. S. Gnat T.1 (XR537)	F. C. Hackett-Jones	
G-NAVO	PA-31-325 Navajo C/R	Exxtor Aircraft Trading (CI) Ltd (G-BMPV)	
G-NBDD	Robin DR.400/180	J. N. Binks	
G-NBSI	Cameron N-77 balloon	Nottingham Hot-Air Balloon Club	
G-NCUB	Piper J-3C-65 Cub	N. Thomson (G-BGXV)/Norwich	
G-NDGC	Grob G.109	R. G. Trute	
G-NDNI	NDN.1 Firecracker	N. W. G. Marsh	
G-NDOL	Shaw Europa	G. K. Brunwin	
G-NDRW	Colt AS-80 Mk II airship	Huntair Ltd	
G-NEAL	PA-32 Cherokee Six 260	VSD Group (G-BFPY)	
G-NEAT	Shaw Europa	M. Burton	
G-NEEL	Rotorway Executive 90	P. N. Haigh	
G-NEGS	Thunder Ax7-77 balloon	R. Holden	
G-NEIL	Thunder Ax3 balloon	Islington Motors (Trowbridge) Ltd	
G-NEPB	Cameron N-77 balloon	The Post Office	
G-NERC	PA-31-350 Navajo Chieftain	Natural Environment Research Council (G-BBXX)	
G-NERI	PA-28-181 Archier II	Moulin Ltd (G-BMKO)	
G-NESU	BN-2B-20 Islander	Pilatus BN Ltd (G-BTVN)/Bembridge	
G-NETY	PA-18 Super Cub 150	N. B. Mason	
G-NEVS	Aero Designs Pulsar XP	N. Warrener	
G-NEWR	PA-31-350 Navajo Chieftain	Eastern Air Executive Ltd/Sturgate	
G-NEWS	Bell 206B JetRanger 3	David Reed Homes Ltd	
G-NEWT	Beech 35 Bonanza	J. A. West (G-APVW)	
G-NEXT	AS.355F-1 Twin Squirrel	Bristow Helicopters Ltd (G-WDKR/ G-OMAV)	
G-NFLC	H.P.137 Jetstream Mk1	Cranfield University (G-AXUI)	
G-NGBI	AA-5B Tiger	Flightline Ltd (G-JAKK/G-BHWI)/Southend	
G-NGRM	Spezio DAL.1	C. D. O'Malley	
G-NHRH	PA-28 Cherokee 140	H. Dodd	
G-NHVH	Maule M5-235C Lunar Rocket	Commercial Go-Karts Ltd/Exeter	
G-NICH	Robinson R-22B	Panair Ltd	
G-NICO	Robinson R-22B	H. J. Pessall	
G-NIGE	Luscombe 8E Silvaire	G. J. Richardson (G-BSHG)	
G-NIGL	Shaw Europa	N. M. Graham	
G-NIGS	Thunder Ax7-65 balloon	A. N. F. Pertwee	
G-NIKE	PA-28-181 Archer II	Key Properties Ltd/White Waltham	
G-NINA	PA-28-161 Warrior II	A. G. Bailey (G-BEUC)	
G-NINE	Murphy Renegade 912	R. F. Bond	
G-NIOS	PA-32R-301 Saratoga SP	E. L. Sasso de Terza	
G-NISR	R. Commander 690A	Z. I. Bilbeisi	
G-NITA	PA-28 Cherokee 180	Dove Naish & Ptnrs (G-AVVG)	
G-NIUK	Douglas DC-10-30	Caledonian Airways Ltd *Loch Loyal*	
G-NJAG	Cessna 207	G. H. Nolan Ltd	
G-NJML	PA-34-220T Seneca III	Oxford Management Ltd	
G-NJSH	Robinson R-22B	T. F. Hawes	
G-NLEE	Cessna 182Q	J. S. Lee (G-TLTD)	
G-NNAC	PA-18 Super Cub 135	P. A. Wilde	
G-NOBI	Spezio HES-1 Tuholer Sport	R. Wheeler	
G-NOCK	Cessna FR.182RG II	D. J. Morris & R. A. D. Wilson	
G-NODE	AA-5B Tiger	Abraxas Aviation Ltd/Elstree	
G-NODY	American General AG-5B Tiger	Curd & Green Ltd/Elstree	
G-NOIR	Bell 222	Arlington Securities PLC (G-OJLC/ G-OSEB/G-BNDA)	
G-NONI	AA-5 Traveler	P. Nutley (G-BBDA)	
G-NORD	SNCAN NC.854	W. J. McCollum	
G-NOTR	McD Douglas MD-520N Notar	Air Hanson	
G-NOTT	Nott ULD-2 balloon	J. R. P. Nott	
G-NOVO	Colt AS-56 airship	Astec Communications Ltd	
G-NPNP	Cameron N-105 balloon	Air 2 Air Ltd (G-BURX)	
G-NPWR	Cameron RX-100 balloon	Nuclear Electric PLC	
G-NRDC	NDN.6 Fieldmaster	EPA Aircraft Co Ltd	
G-NROY	PA-32RT-300 Lance II	Roys Motor Co (G-LYNN/G-BGNY)	
G-NSGI	Cessna 421C	Northern Scaffold Group PLC	
G-NSTG	Cessna F.150F	N. S. T. Griffin (G-ATNI)/Blackpool	
G-NTEE	Robinson R-44	Springfield Helicopters Ltd	
G-NTOO	SA.365N-2 Dauphin 2	Bond Helicopters Ltd	

Notes	Reg.	Type	Owner or Operator
	G-NTWO	SA.365N-2 Dauphin 2	Bond Helicopters Ltd
	G-NUTZ	AS.355F-1 Twin Squirrel	Cotfast Ltd (G-BLRI)
	G-NVBF	Lindstrand LBL-210A balloon	Virgin Balloon Flights Ltd
	G-NWAC	PA-31-310 Turbo Navajo	North West Air Charters Ltd (G-BDUJ)
	G-NWNW	Cameron V-90 balloon	Royal Mail
	G-NWPI	AS.355F-2 Twin Squirrel	North Wales Police Authority
	G-NWPR	Cameron N-77 balloon	Post Office N.W. Postal Board
	G-NYTE	Cessna F.337G	Photoair (G-BATH)
	G-NZGL	Cameron O-105 balloon	P. G. & P. M. Vale
	G-NZSS	Boeing Stearman N2S-5 (27)	Ace Aviation Ltd
	G-OAAA	PA-28-161 Warrior II	Shoreham Flight Simulation/Bournemouth
	G-OAAC	Airtour AH-77B balloon	Army Air Corps
	G-OAAL	PA-38-112 Tomahawk	Hebridean Air Services Ltd
	G-OAAS	Short SD3-60 Variant 100	Aurigny Air Services Ltd (G-BLIL)/Guernsey
	G-OABC	Colt 69A balloon	P. A. C. Stuart-Kregor
	G-OABG	Hughes 369E	A. B. Gee of Ripley Ltd
	G-OACE	Valentin Taifun 17E	J. E. Dallison
	G-OACG	PA-34-200T Seneca II	ACG Building Contractors Ltd (G-BUNR)
	G-OADY	Beech 76 Duchess	Citation Leasing Ltd
	G-OAFC	Airtour 56AH balloon	P. J. Donnellan & L. A. Watts
	G-OAFT	Cessna 152 II	Bobbington Air Training School Ltd (G-BNKM)/Halfpenny Green
	G-OAFY	SA.341G Gazelle 1	P. A. G. Seers (G-SFTH/G-BLAP)
	G-OAHC	Beech F33C Bonanza	Clacton Aero Club (1988) Ltd (G-BTTF)
	G-OAHF	Boeing 757-27B	Britannia Airways Ltd/Luton
	G-OAJS	PA-39 Twin Comanche 160 C/R	Go-AJS Ltd (G-BCIO)
	G-OAKI	BAe Jetstream 3102	Air Kilroe Ltd/Manchester
	G-OAKJ	BAe Jetstream 3202	Air Kilroe Ltd (G-BOTJ)/Manchester
	G-OALA	Airbus A.320-231	All Leisure Airlines Ltd/Gatwick
	G-OALD	SOCATA TB.20 Trinidad	Gold Aviation/Biggin Hill
	G-OAMG	Bell 206B JetRanger 3	Alan Mann Helicopters Ltd/Fairoaks
	G-OAMP	Cessna F.177RG	Ampy Automation Digilog Ltd (G-AYPF)
	G-OAMY	Cessna 152 II	Warwickshire Flying Training Centre Ltd/ Birmingham
	G-OANC	PA-28-161 Warrior II	Millwood Ltd(G-BFAD)
	G-OANI	PA-28-161 Warrior II	J. A. Caliva
	G-OAPR	Brantly B.2B	Helicopter International Magazine/ Weston-s-Mare
	G-OAPW	Glaser-Dirks DG.400	S. W. Brown & D. T. S. Walsh
	G-OARG	Cameron C-80 balloon	G. & R. Madelin
	G-OART	PA-23 Aztec 250D	Levenmere Ltd (G-AXKD)
	G-OARV	ARV Super 2	P. R. Snowden
	G-OASH	Robinson R-22B	J. C. Lane
	G-OASP	AS.355F-1 Twin Squirrel	Avon & Somerset Constabulary & Gloucestershire Constabulary
	G-OATS	PA-38-112 Tomahawk	Truman Aviation Ltd/Tollerton
	G-OATV	Cameron V-77 balloon	W. G. Andrews
	G-OAUS	Sikorsky S-76A	Darley Stud Management Co Ltd
	G-OAVX	Beech 200 Super King Air	ATS Vulcan Ltd (G-IBCA/G-BMCA)
	G-OBAA	Beech B200 Super King Air	BAA PLC
	G-OBAL	Mooney M.20J	Britannia Airways Ltd/Luton
	G-OBAN	Jodel D.140B	S. R. Cameron (G-ATSU)
	G-OBAT	Cessna F.152 II	M. & M. Entwistle (G-OENT)
	G-OBBC	Colt 90A balloon	R. A. & M. A. Riley
	G-OBEA	BAe Jetstream 3102-01	Community Express Airlines Ltd
	G-OBEL	Cessna 500 Citation	Ferron Trading Ltd (G-BOGA)
	G-OBEN	Cessna 152 II	Astra Associates (G-NALI/G-BHVM)
	G-OBEY	PA-23 Aztec 250C	Creaton Aircraft Services (G-BAAJ)
	G-OBHD	Short SD3-60 Variant 100	Jersey European Airways Ltd (G-BNDK)
	G-OBHX	Cessna F.172H	BHX Flying Group (G-AWMU)
	G-OBIL	Robinson R-22B	PAC Helicopters
	G-OBJH	Colt 77A balloon	Eurogas & Corralgas
	G-OBLC	Beech 76 Duchess	Tatenhill Aviation
	G-OBLK	Short SD3-60 Variant 100	Jersey European Airways Ltd (G-BNDI)
	G-OBLN	D.H.115 Vampire T.11	de Havilland Aviation Ltd
	G-OBMD	Boeing 737-33A	British Midland Airways Ltd/E. Midlands
	G-OBMF	Boeing 737-4Y0	British Midland Airways Ltd/E. Midlands
	G-OBMG	Boeing 737-4Y0	British Midland Airways Ltd/E. Midlands
	G-OBMH	Boeing 737-33A	British Midland Airways Ltd/E. Midlands
	G-OBMJ	Boeing 737-33A	British Midland Airways Ltd/E. Midlands
	G-OBMK	Boeing 737-4S3	British Midland Airways Ltd/E. Midlands

Reg.	Type	Owner or Operator	Notes
G-OBML	Boeing 737-3Q8	British Midland Airways Ltd (G-KKUH)/ E. Midlands	
G-OBMM	Boeing 737-4Y0	British Midland Airways Ltd/E. Midlands	
G-OBMN	Boeing 737-46B	British Midland Airways Ltd (G-BOPJ)/ E. Midlands	
G-OBMO	Boeing 737-4Q8	British Midland Airways Ltd/E. Midlands	
G-OBMP	Boeing 737-3Q8	British Midland Airways Ltd/E. Midlands	
G-OBMS	Cessna F.172N	D. Beverley & W. F. van Schoten	
G-OBMW	AA-5 Traveler	Fretcourt Ltd (G-BDFV)	
G-OBMX	Boeing 737-59D	British Midland Airways Ltd/E. Midlands	
G-OBMY	Boeing 737-59D	British Midland Airways Ltd/E. Midlands	
G-OBMZ	Boeing 737-53A	British Midland Airways Ltd/E. Midlands	
G-OBNF	Cessna 310K	Fadmoor Flying Group	
G-OBOH	Short SD3-60	Jersey European Airways Ltd (G-BNDJ)	
G-OBOY	Aviat Pitts S-2B Special	G. L. Carpenter	
G-OBRU	Bell 206B JetRanger 2	Clyde Helicopters Ltd (G-GOBP/G-BOUY)	
G-OBRY	Cameron N-180 balloon	Bryant Group PLC	
G-OBSF	AA-5A Cheetah	Lowlog Ltd (G-ODSF/G-BEUW)	
G-OBSV	Partenavia P.68B Observer	Porton Holdings Ltd	
G-OBTS	Cameron C-80 balloon	Bedford Tyre Service (Chichester) Ltd	
G-OBUD	Colt 69A balloon	Hot-Air Balloon Co Ltd	
G-OBUY	Colt 69A balloon	Virgin Airship & Balloon Co Ltd	
G-OBWA	BAC One-Eleven 518FG	British World Airlines Ltd (G-BDAT/ G-AYOR)/Stansted	
G-OBWB	BAC One-Eleven 518FG	British World Airlines Ltd (G-BDAS/ G-AXMH)/Stansted	
G-OBWC	BAC One-Eleven 520FN	British World Airlines Ltd (G-BEKA)/ Stansted	
G-OBWD	BAC One-Eleven 518FG	British World Airlines Ltd (G-BDAE/ G-AXMI)/Stansted	
G-OBWE	BAC One-Eleven 531FS	British World Airlines Ltd (G-BJYM)/ Stansted	
G-OBYA	Boeing 767-304ER	Britannia Airways Ltd/Luton	
G-OBYB	Boeing 767-304ER	Britannia Airways Ltd/Luton	
G-OBYC	Boeing 767-304ER	Britannia Airways Ltd/Luton	
G-OBYD	Boeing 767-304ER	Britannia Airways Ltd/Luton	
G-OBYT	AB-206A JetRanger	Specialist Computer Holdings Ltd (G-BNRC)	
G-OCAA	H.S. 125 Srs 700B	MAGEC Aviation Ltd (G-BHLF)/Luton	
G-OCAD	Sequoia F.8L Falco	Falco Flying Group	
G-OCAM	AA-5A Cheetah	Plane Talking Ltd (G-BLHO)/Elstree	
G-OCAR	Colt 77A balloon	Ridgeway Balloon Group	
G-OCAT	Eiri PIK-20E	P. D. Turner/Rufforth	
G-OCAZ	AA-5B Tiger	Caslon Ltd (G-OMED/G-BERL)	
G-OCBB	Bell 206B JetRanger 2	Helispeed Ltd (G-BASE)	
G-OCCA	PA-32R-301 Saratoga SP	Plane Talking Ltd (G-BRIX)/Elstree	
G-OCCI	BAe 125 Srs 800B	Consolidated Contractors International (UK) Ltd	
G-OCDB	Cessna 550 Citation II	Paycourt Ltd (G-ELOT)	
G-OCDS	Aviamilano F.8L Falco II	W. W. Churchill (G-VEGL)	
G-OCEA	Short SD3-60 Variant 100	Community Express Airlines Ltd (G-BRMX)	
G-OCFR	Learjet 35A	Chauffair (CI) Ltd (G-VIPS/G-SOVN/ G-PJET)	
G-OCGJ	Robinson R-22B	Pyramid Aviation Ltd/Halfpenny Green	
G-OCJK	Schweizer 269C	Bradford Independent Helicopters	
G-OCJS	Cameron V-90 balloon	C. J. Sandell	
G-OCND	Cameron O-77 balloon	D. P. H. Smith & Dalby	
G-OCOP	Bell 206LT LongRanger	Veritair Ltd	
G-OCPC	Cessna FA.152	Westward Airways (Lands End) Ltd/St Just	
G-OCPI	Cessna 500 Citation	Cooling Power Industries Ltd & Stadium City Ltd (G-OXEC)	
G-OCPL	AA-5A Cheetah	BLS Aviation Ltd (G-RCPW/G-BERM)	
G-OCPS	Colt 120A balloon	CPS Fuels Ltd	
G-OCRI	Colomban MC.15 Cri-Cri	M. J. J. Dunning	
G-OCSI	EMB-110P2 Bandeirante	Willowjet Ltd (G-BHJZ)	
G-OCST	AB-206B JetRanger	Fieldgrove Trading	
G-OCSZ	EMB-110P1 Bandeirante	Willowjet Ltd (G-DORK)	
G-OCTA	BN-2A Mk III-2 Trislander	Aurigny Air Services Ltd (G-BCXW)	
G-OCTI	PA-32 Cherokee Six 260	J. K. Sharkey (G-BGZX)/Elstree	
G-OCTU	PA-28-161 Cadet	Plane Talking Ltd/Denham	
G-OCUB	Piper J-3C-90 Cub	C. A. Foss & P. A. Brook/Shoreham	
G-OCWT	AS.350B-2 Ecureuil	Carter Wind Turbines (Aviation) Ltd	

Notes	Reg.	Type	Owner or Operator
	G-ODAD	Colt 77A balloon	K. Meehan
	G-ODAM	AA-5A Cheetah	Stop & Go Ltd (G-FOUX)
	G-ODDY	Lindstrand LBL-105A balloon	V. Hyland
	G-ODEL	Falconar F-11-3	G. F. Brummell
	G-ODEN	PA-28-161 Cadet	J. Appleton/Denham
	G-ODER	Cameron O-77 balloon	W. H. Morgan
	G-ODHL	Cameron N-77 balloon	DHL International (UK) Ltd
	G-ODIG	Bell 206B JetRanger 2	H. McCaig (G-NEEP)
	G-ODIL	Bell 206B JetRanger	Yorkshire Helicopter Centre Ltd
	G-ODIN	Avions Mudry CAP.10B	D. Davis
	G-ODIS	Cameron Cabin SS balloon	Cameron Balloons Ltd
	G-ODIY	Colt 69A balloon	P. Glydon
	G-ODJH	Mooney M.20C	D. J. Hockings (G-BMLH)/Biggin Hill
	G-ODLY	Cessna 310J	R. J. Huband (G-TUBY/G-ASZZ)
	G-ODMC	AS.350B-1 Ecureuil	D. M. Coombs (G-BPVF)/Denham
	G-ODNP	Cessna 310R	Bostonair Ltd/Humberside
	G-ODTW	Shaw Europa	D. T. Walters
	G-OEAB	EMB-110P2 Bandeirante	Knight Air Ltd (G-BKWB/G-CHEV)/Leeds
	G-OEAC	Mooney M.20J	N. R. Capon/Elstree
	G-OEBA	Robin DR.400/140B	EB Aviation (G-JMHB)
	G-OECH	AA-5A Cheetah	Plane Talking Ltd (G-BKBE)/Elstree
	G-OEDA	BAe Jetstream 3102	Jetstream Aircraft Ltd (G-LOGV/G-BSZK)
	G-OEDB	PA-38-112 Tomahawk	Air Delta Bravo Ltd (G-BGGJ)/Elstree
	G-OEDF	BAe ATP	Trident Aviation Leasing Services Ltd (G-BUKJ)
	G-OEDG	BAe Jetstream 3102	Jetstream Aircraft Ltd (G-GLAM/G-IBLX)
	G-OEDH	BAe ATP	Trident Aviation Leasing Services Ltd (G-BTUE)
	G-OEDI	BAe ATP	Trident Aviation Leasing Services Ltd (G-BTNI/G-SLAM)
	G-OEDJ	BAe ATP	— (G-BUUR)
	G-OEDK	BAe ATP	—
	G-OEDL	BAe Jetstream 3116	Jetstream Aircraft Ltd (G-OAKK/G-BSIW)
	G-OEDP	Cameron N-77 balloon	M. J. Betts
	G-OEGG	Cameron 65 Egg SS balloon	Virgin Airship & Balloon Co Ltd
	G-OERS	Cessna 172N	E. R. Stevens (G-SSRS)
	G-OEXC	Airbus A.320-212	Excalibur Airways Ltd/E. Midlands
	G-OEYE	Rans S.10 Sakota	P. Thompson
	G-OEZY	Shaw Europa	A. W. Wakefield
	G-OFBJ	Thunder Ax7-77 balloon	N. D. Hicks
	G-OFCM	Cessna F17 2L	F. C. M. Aviation Ltd (G-AZUN)/Guernsey
	G-OFER	PA-18 Super Cub 150	M. S. W. Meagher
	G-OFHJ	Cessna 441	Tilling Associates Ltd (G-HSON)
	G-OFHL	AS.350B Ecureuil	Ford Helicopters Ltd (G-BLSP)
	G-OFIT	SOCATA TB.10 Tobago	G. S.M. Brain (G-BRIU)
	G-OFIZ	Cameron 80 Can SS balloon	Virgin Airship & Balloon Co Ltd
	G-OFJC	Eiri PIK-20E	M. J. Aldridge
	G-OFJS	Robinson R-22B	Classic Air Travel (G-BNXJ)
	G-OFLG	SOCATA TB.10 Tobago	Studley Pool Management Ltd (G-JMWT)
	G-OFLI	Colt 105A balloon	Virgin Airship & Balloon Co Ltd
	G-OFLT	EMB-110P1 Bandeirante	Flightline Ltd (G-MOBL/G-BGCS)/Southend
	G-OFLY	Cessna 210M	A. P. Mothew/Stapleford
	G-OFOR	Thunder Ax3 balloon	T. J. Ellenreider & ptnrs
	G-OFOX	Denney Kitfox	P. R. Skeels
	G-OFRB	Everett gyroplane	Roger Savage (Photography)
	G-OFRT	L.188C Electra	Channel Express (Air Services) Ltd/Bournemouth
	G-OFRY	Cessna 152 II	Devon School of Flying (G-BPHS)/Dunkeswell
	G-OFTI	PA-28 Cherokee 140	I. Chaplin (G-BRKU)
	G-OGAN	Shaw Europa	G-OGAN Group
	G-OGAR	PZL SZD-45A Ogar	N. C. Grayson
	G-OGAS	Westland WG.30 Srs 100	(stored) (G-BKNW)/Penzance
	G-OGAT	Beech 200 Super King Air	Branderman Ltd
	G-OGAV	Lindstrand LBL-240A balloon	Out Of This World
	G-OGAZ	SA.341G Gazelle 1	M. Wood Haulage (G-OCJR/G-BRGS)
	G-OGCA	PA-28-161 Warrior II	Aerohire Ltd/Halfpenny Green
	G-OGEE	Pitts S-2B Special	R. G. Gee
	G-OGEM	PA-28-181 Archer II	GEM Rewinds Ltd
	G-OGET	PA-39 Twin Comanche 160 C/R	P. G. Kitchingman (G-AYXY)
	G-OGGS	Thunder Ax8-84 balloon	G. Gamble & Sons (Quorn) Ltd
	G-OGIL	Short SD3-30 ★	N.E. Aircraft Museum (G-BITV)/Usworth

Reg.	Type	Owner or Operator	Notes
G-OGJS	Puffer Cozy	G. J. Stamper	
G-OGOA	AS.350B Ecureuil	Lomas Helicopters Ltd (G-PLMD/G-NIAL)	
G-OGOB	Schweizer 269C	Kingfisher Helicopters Ltd (G-GLEE/ G-BRUW)	
G-OGOC	Robinson R-22B	Avonline Group Ltd (G-HODG)	
G-OGTS	Air Command 532 Elite	GTS Engineering (Coventry) Ltd	
G-OHCP	AS.355F-1 Twin Squirrel	Cabair Helicopters Ltd (G-BTVS/ G-STVE/G-TOFF/G-BKJX)	
G-OHDC	Colt Agfa Film Cassette SS balloon	Flying Pictures (Balloons) Ltd	
G-OHEA	H.S.125 Srs 3B/RA	B. L. Schroder (G-AVRG)	
G-OHHL	Robinson R-22B	Helicopter Training & Hire Ltd	
G-OHIG	EMB-110P1 Bandeirante	Willowjet Ltd (G-OPPP)	
G-OHMS	AS.355F-1 Twin Squirrel	S.W. Electricity PLC	
G-OHOG	PA-28 Cherokee 140	C. R. Guggenheim (G-AVFY)	
G-OHOP	PA-31 Turbo Navajo	Channel Islands Air Charter Ltd (G-BEYY)	
G-OIBM	R. Commander 114	GT Aviation (G-BLVZ)/Bournemouth	
G-OIBO	PA-28 Cherokee 180	Britannia Airways Ltd (G-AVAZ)	
G-OICE	Cessna 525 Citationjet	Iceland Frozen Foods PLC	
G-OICV	Robinson R-22B	ICV Ltd (G-BPWH)	
G-OIDW	Cessna F.150G	I. D. Wakeling	
G-OIEA	PA-31P Pressurised Navajo	Skyrock Aviation Ltd (G-BBTW)/Cyprus	
G-OIFM	Cameron 90 Dude SS balloon	Air 2 Air Ltd	
G-OIGS	Enstrom F-28C	M. Thompson (G-BGSN)	
G-OILA	Aérospatiale ATR-72-210	British World Airlines Ltd/Aberdeen	
G-OILB	Aérospatiale ATR-72-210	British World Airlines Ltd/Aberdeen	
G-OILX	AS.355F-1 Twin Squirrel	Firstearl Ltd (G-RMGN/G-BMCY)	
G-OIMC	Cessna 152 II	E. Midlands Flying School Ltd	
G-OING	AA-5A Cheetah ★	Abraxas Aviation Ltd (G-BFPD)/Denham	
G-OINK	Piper J-3C-65 Cub	A. R. Harding (G-BILD/G-KERK)	
G-OIOI	EH Industries EH.101	Westland Helicopters Ltd/Yeovil	
G-OISO	Cessna FRA.150L	Les Oiseaux (G-BBJW)	
G-OITA	Boeing 767-33A	Alitalia	
G-OITB	Boeing 767-33A	Alitalia	
G-OITC	Boeing 767-33A	Alitalia	
G-OITF	Boeing 767-33AER	Alitalia	
G-OITN	AS.355F-1 Twin Squirrel	Independent Television News Ltd	
G-OJAC	Mooney M.20J	Hornet Engineering Ltd	
G-OJAE	Hughes 269C	J. A. & C. M. Wilson	
G-OJAV	BN-2A Mk III-2 Trislander	Willowjet Ltd (G-BDOS)	
G-OJBM	Cameron N-90 balloon	JBM Communications Ltd	
G-OJCB	AB-206B JetRanger 2	Yorkshire Helicopter Centre Ltd	
G-OJCM	Rotorway Executive 90	J. C. Mead & G. Wilson	
G-OJCW	PA-32RT-300 Lance II	CW Group	
G-OJDC	Thunder Ax7-77 balloon	J. Crosby	
G-OJEN	Cameron V-77 balloon	Jensport Ltd	
G-OJET	BAe 146-100	ATC Lasham Ltd (G-BRJS/G-OBAF/ G-SCHH)	
G-OJFC	Beech A36 Bonanza	J. Cross	
G-OJHB	Colt Flying Ice Cream Cone SS balloon	Benedikt Haggeney GmbH	
G-OJIM	PA-28R-201T Turbo Arrow III	Motomecca Spares Ltd	
G-OJJB	Mooney M.20K	Fly Over Ltd	
G-OJMR	Airbus A.300-605R	Monarch Airlines Ltd/Luton	
G-OJNB	Linsdstrand LBL-21A balloon	Justerini & Brooks Ltd	
G-OJON	Taylor JT.2 Titch	J. H. Fell	
G-OJSY	Short SD3-60	BAC Express Ltd (G-BKKT)	
G-OJTA	Stemme S-10V	OJT Associates	
G-OJVH	Cessna F.150H	Yorkshire Light Aircraft Ltd (G-AWJZ)/ Leeds	
G-OJVI	Robinson R-22B	Defence Products Ltd (G-OJVJ)	
G-OJWS	PA-28-161 Warrior II	L. E. Guernieri	
G-OKAG	PA-28R Cherokee Arrow 180	N. F. & B. R. Green/Stapleford	
G-OKAY	Pitts S-1E Special	J. S. Mortimore & R. J. Allan	
G-OKBT	Colt 25A Mk II balloon	British Telecommunications PLC	
G-OKCC	Cameron N-90 balloon	D. J. Head	
G-OKED	Cessna 150L	Haimoss Ltd	
G-OKEN	PA-28R-201T Turbo Arrow III	W. B. Bateson/Blackpool	
G-OKES	Robinson R-44 Astro	Kestrel Aviation International Ltd	
G-OKEY	Robinson R-22B	Key Properties Ltd/Booker	
G-OKIS	Tri Kis	B. W. Davies	
G-OKLE	Sikorsky S-76B	KLM ERA Helicopters BV	
G-OKMA	Tri R-Kis	K. Miller	
G-OKPW	Tri Kis	K. P. Wordsworth	

Notes	Reg.	Type	Owner or Operator
	G-OKYA	Cameron V-77 balloon	Army Balloon Club
	G-OKYM	PA-28 Cherokee 140	D. Hotham (G-AVLS)
	G-OLAH	Short SD3-60 Variant 100	Gill Airways Ltd (G-BPCO/G-RMSS/ G-BKKU)
	G-OLAU	Robinson R-22B	MPW Aviation Ltd
	G-OLAW	Lindstrand LBL-25A balloon	George Law Plant
	G-OLDE	Cessna 421C	Richard Nash Cars Ltd (G-BBSV)
	G-OLDN	Bell 206L LongRanger	Gulfstream Air Services (UK) Ltd (G-TBCA/G-BFAL)
	G-OLDV	Colt 90A balloon	Virgin Airship & Balloon Co Ltd
	G-OLDY	Luton LA-5 Major	M. P. & A. P. Sargent
	G-OLEE	Cessna F.152	Aerohire Ltd/Halfpenny Green
	G-OLFC	PA-38-112 Tomahawk	M. W. Glencross (G-BGZG)
	G-OLFT	R. Commander 114	B. C. Richens (G-WJMN)/Redhill
	G-OLIZ	Robinson R-22B	P & I Data Services Ltd
	G-OLLE	Cameron O-84 balloon	N. A. Robertson
	G-OLLI	Cameron O-31 SS balloon	N. A. Robertson
	G-OLLY	PA-31-350 Navajo Chieftain	Barnes Olsen Aeroleasing Ltd (G-BCES)
	G-OLMA	Partenavia P.68B	C. M. Evans (G-BGBT)
	G-OLOW	Robinson R-44 Astro	Rotaspot Ltd
	G-OLPG	Colt 77A balloon	Eurogas & Corralgas
	G-OLRT	Robinson R-22B	Benbom Bros (Exploitation) Ltd
	G-OLSC	Cessna 182A	Factultra (G-ATNU)
	G-OLVR	FRED Srs 2	A. R. Oliver
	G-OMAC	Cessna FR.172E	R. Knox & R. Conway
	G-OMAF	Dornier Do.228-200	FR Aviation Ltd/Bournemouth
	G-OMAP	R. Commander 685	Cooper Aerial Surveys Ltd/Sandtoft
	G-OMAR	PA-34-220T Seneca III	Redhill Flying Club
	G-OMAT	PA-28 Cherokee 140	Midland Air Training School (G-JIMY/ G-AYUG)/Coventry
	G-OMAX	Brantly B.2B	P. D. Benmax (G-AVJN)
	G-OMDH	Hughes 369E	Stilgate Ltd/Booker
	G-OMEC	AB-206B JetRanger 3	Kallas Ltd (G-OBLD)
	G-OMGD	H.S.125 Srs 700B	MAGEC Aviation Ltd/Luton
	G-OMGE	BAe 125 Srs 800B	GEC Marconi Ltd (G-BTMG)/Luton
	G-OMGG	BAe 125 Srs 800B	MAGEC Aviation Ltd/Luton
	G-OMHC	PA-28RT-201 Arrow IV	Tattenhill Aviation
	G-OMIG	Aero-Vodochody MiG-15UTI (6247)	Classic Aviation Ltd/Duxford
	G-OMJB	Bell 206B JetRanger 2	Coventry Helicopter Centre Ltd
	G-OMJT	Rutan LongEz	M. J. Timmons
	G-OMKF	Aero Designs Pulsar	M. K. Faro
	G-OMMG	Robinson R-22B	BLS Aviation Ltd (G-BPYX)/Elstree
	G-OMMM	Colt 90A balloon	3M Health Care Ltd
	G-OMNI	PA-28R Cherokee Arrow 200D	R. J. Fray (G-BAWA)
	G-OMOG	AA-5A Cheetah	Popham Flight (G-BHWR)
	G-OMRB	Cameron V-77 balloon	M. R. Bayne
	G-OMRG	Hoffmann H-36 Dimona	M. R. Grimwood (G-BLHG)
	G-OMXS	Lindstrand LBL-105A balloon	Virgin Airship & Balloon Co Ltd
	G-ONAF	Naval Aircraft Factory N3N-3	P. M. H. Threadway
	G-ONAV	PA-31-310 Turbo Navajo C	Panther Aviation Ltd (G-IGAR)
	G-ONCL	Colt 77A balloon	N. C. Lindsay
	G-ONHH	Forney F-1A Aircoupe	H. Dodd (G-ARHA)
	G-ONKA	Aeronca K	N. J. R. Minchin
	G-ONOW	Bell 206A JetRanger 2	J. Luckett (G-AYMX)
	G-ONZO	Cameron N-77 balloon	G. Burrows & Nationwide Retail Systems Ltd
	G-OOAA	Airbus A.320-231	Air 2000 Ltd/Manchester
	G-OOAB	Airbus A.320-231	Air 2000 Ltd/Manchester
	G-OOAC	Airbus A.320-231	Air 2000 Ltd/Manchester
	G-OOAD	Airbus A.320-231	Air 2000 Ltd/Manchester
	G-OODE	SNCAN Stampe SV-4C (G)	Chocks Away Ltd (G-AZNN)
	G-OODI	Pitts S-1D Special	I. R. B. Frank (G-BBBU)
	G-OODW	PA-28-181 Archer II	Goodwood Terrena Ltd
	G-OOER	Lindstrand LBL-25A balloon	Airborne Adventures Ltd
	G-OOGA	GA-7 Cougar	Plane Talking Ltd/Elstree
	G-OOGI	GA-7 Cougar	Plane Talking Ltd (G-PLAS/G-BGHL)
	G-OOJB	Cessna 421C	Ferron Trading Ltd (G-BKSO)
	G-OOLE	Cessna 172M	P. S. Eccersley (G-BOSI)
	G-OOLI	Robinson R-22B	Wyatt Air Partnership (G-DMCD)/Redhill
	G-OONE	Mooney M.20J	N. A. Folley
	G-OONI	Thunder Ax7-77 balloon	Fivedata Ltd
	G-OONS	AB-206B JetRanger 3	Helicopter Training & Hire Ltd (G-LIND)

Reg.	Type	Owner or Operator	Notes
G-OONY	PA-28-161 Warrior II	D. A. Field & P. B. Jenkins	
G-OOOA	Boeing 757-28A	Air 2000/Canada 3000 (C-FOOA)	
G-OOOB	Boeing 757-28A	Air 2000/Canada 3000 (C-FOOB)	
G-OOOC	Boeing 757-28A	Air 2000/Canada 3000 (C-FXOC)	
G-OOOD	Boeing 757-28A	Air 2000/Canada 3000 (C-FXOD)	
G-OOOG	Boeing 757-23A	Air 2000/Canada 3000 (C-FOOG)	
G-OOOI	Boeing 757-23A	Air 2000 Ltd/Manchester	
G-OOOJ	Boeing 757-23A	Air 2000 Ltd/Manchester	
G-OOOM	Boeing 757-225	Air 2000 Ltd/Manchester	
G-OOOO	Mooney M.20J	Pergola Ltd	
G-OOOS	Boeing 757-236	Air 2000 Ltd (G-BRJD)/Manchester	
G-OOOT	Boeing 757-236	Air 2000 Ltd (G-BRJJ)/Manchester	
G-OOOU	Boeing 757-2Y0	Air 2000 Ltd/Manchester	
G-OOOV	Boeing 757-225	Air 2000 Ltd/Manchester	
G-OOOW	Boeing 757-225	Air 2000 Ltd/Manchester	
G-OOOX	Boeing 757-2Y0	Air 2000 Ltd/Manchester	
G-OOPS	AB-206A JetRanger	Feature Forward Ltd (G-BNRD)	
G-OOSE	Rutan Vari-Eze	J. A. Towers	
G-OOSY	D.H.82A Tiger Moth	M. Goosey	
G-OOTC	PA-28R-201T Turbo Arrow III	T. J. Caton (G-CLIV)	
G-OOUT	Colt Flying Shuttlecock SS balloon	Shiplake Investments Ltd	
G-OOXP	Aero Designs Pulsar XP	T. D. Baker	
G-OPAG	PA-34-200 Seneca II	A. H. Lavender (G-BNGB)/Biggin Hill	
G-OPAL	Robinson R-22B	Pebblestar Ltd	
G-OPAM	Cessna F.152	PJC Leasing Ltd (G-BFZS)/Stapleford	
G-OPAS	V.806 Viscount	British World Airlines Ltd (G-AOYN)	
G-OPAT	Beech 76 Duchess	Ray Holt (Land Drainage) Ltd/(G-BHAO)	
G-OPBH	Aero Designs Pulsar	P. B. Hutchinson	
G-OPDS	Denney Kitfox Mk 4	P. D. Sparling	
G-OPFC	BAe 125-1000	Raytheon Corporate Jets Inc	
G-OPFE	V.808C Viscount	British World Airlines Ltd (G-BBDK)	
G-OPFI	V.802 Viscount	British World Airlines Ltd (G-BLNB/ G-AOHV)/Southend	
G-OPIB	EE Lightning F.6	Downderry Construction Group Ltd	
G-OPIC	Cessna FRA.150L	Air Survey (G-BGNZ)	
G-OPIK	Eiri PIK-20E	A. J. McWilliam/Newtownards	
G-OPIT	CFM Streak Shadow Srs SA	W. M. Kilner	
G-OPJC	Cessna 152 II	PJC Leasing Ltd/Stapleford	
G-OPJD	PA-28RT-201T Turbo Arrow IV	F. T. Ahmed	
G-OPJK	Shaw Europa	P. J. Kember	
G-OPKF	Cameron 90 Bowler SS balloon	Flying Pictures (Balloons) Ltd	
G-OPLB	Cessna 340A II	Ridgewood Ltd (G-FCHJ/G-BJLS)	
G-OPLC	D.H.104 Dove 8	W. G. T. Pritchard & I. Darcy-Bean (G-BLRB)	
G-OPME	PA-23 Aztec 250D	P. M. Evans (G-ODIR/G-AZGB)/Jersey	
G-OPMT	Lindstrand LBL-105A balloon	Pace Micro Technology Ltd	
G-OPPL	AA-5A Cheetah	London School of Flying Ltd (G-BGNN)/ Elstree	
G-OPPS	Mudry CAP.231	Bianchi Aviation Film Services Ltd/Booker	
G-OPRA	PA-31 Turbo Navajo	Lakeland Airways (G-VICK/G-AWED)	
G-OPSF	PA-38-112 Tomahawk	Panshanger School of Flying (G-BGZI)	
G-OPST	Cessna 182R	Lota Ltd/Shoreham	
G-OPUP	B.121 Pup 2	P. W. Hunter (G-AXEU)	
G-OPWH	Dassault Falcon 900B	Aviation Partnershp/Kidlington	
G-OPWK	AA-5A Cheetah	A. H. McVicar (G-OAEL)/Prestwick	
G-OPWS	Mooney M.20K	A. C. Clarke	
G-ORAF	CFM Streak Shadow	G. A. & S. M. Taylor	
G-ORAR	PA-28-181 Archer III	South Yorkshire Air Services Ltd	
G-ORAY	Cessna F.182Q II	G. A. Barrett (G-BHDN)	
G-ORBY	Sukhoi Su-26MX	N. J. Wakefield & ptnrs/White Waltham	
G-ORCL	Cessna 421C	G. W. Squire	
G-ORDN	PA-31R Cherokee Arrow 200-II	M. T. Coppen (G-BAJT)	
G-ORDO	PA-30 Twin Comanche B	A. C. & A. M. Gordon	
G-ORED	BN-2T Turbine Islander	The Red Devils (G-BJYW)/Farnborough	
G-OREG	BN-2A MkIII-1 Trislander	M. G. Roberts	
G-OREY	Cameron O-90 balloon	P. McCallum	
G-ORFC	Jurca MJ.5 Sirocco	D. J. Phillips	
G-ORFE	Cameron 76 Golf SS balloon	British School of Ballooning	
G-ORFI	Aérospatiale ATR-42-300	Gill Airways Ltd/Newcastle	
G-ORIG	Glaser-Dirks DG.800	I. Godfrey	
G-ORIX	ARV K1 Super 2	P. M. Harrison (G-BUXH/G-BNVK)	
G-ORJB	Cessna 500 Citation	L'Equipe Air Ltd (G-OKSP)	
G-ORJW	Laverda F.8L Falco Srs 4	W. R. M. Sutton	

Notes	Reg.	Type	Owner or Operator
	G-ORMB	Robinson R-22B	R. M. Bailey
	G-OROB	Robinson R-22B	Corniche Helicopters (G-TBFC)
	G-OROD	PA-18 Super Cub 150	R. J. O. Walker
	G-ORON	Cameron 77A balloon	A. M. Rocliffe
	G-OROZ	AS.350B-2 Ecureuil	Flightpaths Ltd
	G-ORPR	Cameron O-77 balloon	Outright PR Ltd
	G-ORSP	Beech A36 Bonanza	Select Plant Hire Co Ltd
	G-ORTM	Glaser-Dirks DG.400	J. P. C. Fuchs
	G-ORTW	Lindstrand AM-25000 balloon	Lindstrand Balloons Ltd
	G-ORVB	McCulloch J-2	R. V. Bowles (G-BLGI/G-BKKL)
	G-ORVR	Partenavia P.68B	Ravenair (G-BFBD)
	G-OSAB	Enstrom 280FX	Goadby Air Services Ltd
	G-OSAL	Cessna 421C	Pace Micro Technology Ltd
	G-OSCB	Colt 90A balloon	J. Willis
	G-OSCC	PA-32 Cherokee Six 300	Plant Aviation Ltd (G-BGFD)/Elstree
	G-OSCH	Cessna 421C	Sureflight Aviation Ltd (G-SALI)
	G-OSDI	Beech 95-58 Baron	K. L. Hawes (G-BHFY)
	G-OSEA	BN-2B-26 Islander	W. T. Johnson & Sons (Huddersfield) Ltd (G-BKOL)
	G-OSEE	Robinson R-22B	J. P. Dennison
	G-OSFC	Cessna F.152	Stapleford Flying Club Ltd (G-BIVJ)
	G-OSFT	PA-31-310 Turbo Navajo C	Wishbone Air BVBA (G-MDAS/G-BCJZ)
	G-OSII	Cessna 172N	A. J. Gomes (G-BIVY)
	G-OSIS	Pitts S-1S Special	M. C. Boddington & I. M. Castle
	G-OSIX	PA-32 Cherokee Six 260	Strata Surveys Ltd (G-AZMO)
	G-OSKP	Enstrom 480	Southern Air Ltd/Shoreham
	G-OSKY	Cessna 172M	D. T. & S. H. Gilliam
	G-OSLO	Schweizer 269C	Hanover Aviation Leasing Ltd
	G-OSMT	Shaw Europa	S. M. Thomas
	G-OSNB	Cessna 550 Citation II	Scottish & Newcastle Breweries PLC (G-JFRS)
	G-OSND	Cessna FRA.150M	Brinkley Light Aircraft Services (G-BDOU)
	G-OSOO	Hughes 369E	Tyrone Fabrication Ltd
	G-OSOW	PA-28 Cherokee 140	Go-Hog Flying Ltd (G-AVWH)/ Bournemouth
	G-OSPS	PA-18 Super Cub 95	J. W. Macleod
	G-OSST	Colt 77A balloon	British Airways PLC
	G-OSTC	AA-5A Cheetah	C. B. Dew
	G-OSTU	AA-5A Cheetah	Plane Talking Ltd (G-BGCL)/Elstree
	G-OSUP	Lindstrand LBL-90A balloon	British Airways Balloon Club
	G-OSUS	Mooney M.20K	J. B. King
	G-OSVO	Cameron 30 Hopper Servo SS balloon	Servo & Electronic Sales Ltd
	G-OSWA	Enstrom F-28C-UK-2	S. Atherton (G-BZZZ/G-BBBZ)
	G-OTAF	Aero L-39ZO Albatros	A. J. E. Smith & R. J. Lamplough
	G-OTAL	ARV Super 2	N. R. Beale (G-BNGZ)
	G-OTAM	Cessna 172M	T. W. Woods
	G-OTBY	PA-32 Cherokee Six 300	GOTBY Ltd
	G-OTCH	CFM Streak Shadow	H. E. Gotch
	G-OTEL	Thunder Ax8-90 balloon	Scotia Balloons Ltd
	G-OTHE	Enstrom 280C-UK Shark	The Engineering Co Ltd (G-OPJT/ G-BKCO)
	G-OTHL	Robinson R-22B	TWS Helicopters Ltd (G-DSGN)
	G-OTIM	Bensen B.8MV	T. J. Deane
	G-OTNT	Cameron Cider Bottle SS balloon	A. J. Round
	G-OTOE	Aeronca 7AC Champion	J. M. Gale (G-BRWW)
	G-OTOW	Cessna 175BX	C. P. & C. J. Wilkes
	G-OTRG	Cessna TR.182RG	Thermodata Components
	G-OTSB	BN-2A Mk III-2 Trislander	Aurigny Air Services Ltd (G-BDTO)
	G-OTSW	Pitts S-1E Special	R. A. Bowes (G-BLHE)
	G-OTTI	Cameron 34 Otti SS balloon	Cameron Balloons Ltd
	G-OTTO	Cameron 82 Katalog SS balloon	Cameron Balloons Ltd
	G-OTUG	PA-18 Super Cub 150	B. Walker & Co (Dursley) Ltd
	G-OTUP	Lindstrand LBL-180A balloon	Airborne Adventures Ltd
	G-OTVS	BN-2T Turbine Islander	Headcorn Parachute Club Ltd (G-BPBN/ G-BCMY) (stored)
	G-OTWO	Rutan Defiant	D. G. Foreman
	G-OTYJ	PA-28-161 Cadet	Holmes Rentals (G-OLSF)
	G-OULD	Gould Mk I balloon	C. A. Gould
	G-OURO	Shaw Europa	D. Dufton
	G-OUSA	Colt 105A balloon	Continental Airlines Inc
	G-OUVI	Cameron O-105 balloon	Bristol University Hot Air Ballooning Soc
	G-OUZO	Airbus A.320-212	All Leisure Airlines Ltd

Reg.	Type	Owner or Operator	Notes
G-OVAA	Colt Jumbo SS balloon	Virgin Airship & Balloon Co Ltd	
G-OVAX	Colt AS-80 Mk II airship	Vax Appliances Ltd	
G-OVBF	Cameron A-250 balloon	Virgin Balloon Flights Ltd	
G-OVFM	Cessna 120	Commair Group	
G-OVFR	Cessna F.172N	Western Air Training Ltd	
G-OVID	Light Aero Avid Flyer	Drefach Ltd	
G-OVMC	Cessna F.152 II	Staverton Flying Services Ltd	
G-OVNE	Cessna 401A	M. A. Billings/Ipswich	
G-OVNR	Robinson R-22B	Heli-Fun Ltd	
G-OVVB	Beech A36 Bonanza	Air Hanson Aircraft Sales Ltd	
G-OWAC	Cessna F.152	Barnes Olson Aeroleasing Ltd (G-BHEB)	
G-OWAK	Cessna F.152	Falcon Flying Services (G-BHEA)/ Biggin Hill	
G-OWAR	PA-28-161 Warrior II	Bickertons Aerodromes Ltd	
G-OWAZ	Pitts S-1C Special	P. E. S. Latham (G-BRPI)	
G-OWBC	Thunder Ax10-180 S2 balloon	Windermere Balloon Co	
G-OWCG	Bell 222	Winchester Commodities Group Ltd (G-VERT/G-JLBZ/G-BNDB)	
G-OWEL	Colt 105A balloon	S. R. Seager	
G-OWEN	K & S Jungster	R. C. Owen	
G-OWET	Thurston TSC-1A2 Teal	D. Nieman	
G-OWGC	Slingsby T.61F Venture T.2	Wolds Gliding Club Ltd	
G-OWIN	BN-2A-8 Islander	UK Parachute Services Ltd (G-AYXE)	
G-OWIZ	Luscombe 8A Silvaire	J. Wilson & J. V. George	
G-OWLC	PA-31 Turbo Navajo	Top Nosh Ltd (G-AYFZ)	
G-OWOW	Cessna 152 II	Falcon Flying Services (G-BMSZ)/ Biggin Hill	
G-OWVA	PA-28 Cherokee 140	Woodvale Aviation Co Ltd	
G-OWWF	Colt 2500A balloon	Virgin Atlantic Airways Ltd	
G-OWWW	Shaw Europa	J. F. & W. R. C. Williams-Wynne	
G-OWYN	Aviamilano F.14 Nibbio	J. R. Wynn	
G-OXBY	Cameron N-90 balloon	C. A. Oxby	
G-OXLI	BAe Jetstream 4100	British Aerospace PLC/Prestwick	
G-OXRG	Colt Film Can SS balloon	Flying Pictures (Balloons) Ltd	
G-OXTC	PA-23 Aztec 250D	Falcon Flying Services (G-AZOD)/ Biggin Hill	
G-OXVI	V.S.361 Spitfire LF.XVIe (TD248)	E. K. Coventry/Earls Colne	
G-OYAK	Yakovlev C-11 (27)	E. K. Coventry/Earls Colne	
G-OZAR	Enstrom 480	Heliway Aviation (G-BWFF)	
G-OZBA	Airbus A.320-212	Monarch Airlines Ltd (G-MALE)/Luton	
G-OZBB	Airbus A.320-212	Monarch Airlines Ltd-/Luton	
G-OZEE	Light Aero Avid Speedwing Mk 4	S. C. Goozee	
G-OZLN	Zlin Z.242L	I. E. Humphries	
G-OZOI	Cessna R.182	J. R. G. & F. L. G. Fleming (G-ROBK)	
G-OZRH	BAe 146-200	Flightline Ltd/Gatwick	
G-OZUP	Colt 77A balloon	Yanin International Ltd	
G-PACE	Robin R.1180T	Millicron Instruments Ltd/Coventry	
G-PACL	Robinson R-22B	D. K. Griffiths	
G-PADI	Cameron V-77 balloon	T. R. Duffell	
G-PAIZ	PA-12 Super Cruiser	B. R. Pearson/Eaglescott	
G-PALS	Enstrom 280C-UK-2 Shark	G. Firbank	
G-PAMS	PA-60 Aerostar 601P	E. G. Rigby (G-GAIR)	
G-PAPU	Beech 58PA Baron	Jetmore Ltd (G-NIPU)	
G-PARA	Cessna 207	Activity Aviation Ltd	
G-PARI	Cessna 172RG Cutlass	Applied Signs Ltd	
G-PARR	Cameron 90 Bottle SS balloon	Virgin Airship & Balloon Co Ltd	
G-PASC	MBB Bo 105DBS/4	Police Aviation Services Ltd (G-BNPS)	
G-PASD	MBB Bo 105DBS/4	Police Aviation Services Ltd (G-BNRS)	
G-PASE	AS.355F-1 Twin Squirrel	Police Aviation Services Ltd	
G-PASF	AS.355F-1 Twin Squirrel	Police Aviation Services Ltd (G-SCHU)	
G-PASG	MBB Bo 105DBS/4	Police Aviation Services Ltd (G-MHSL)	
G-PASU	BN-2T Turbine Islander	Police Aviation Services Ltd (G-BJYY)	
G-PASV	BN-2B-21 Islander	Police Aviation Services Ltd (G-BKJH)	
G-PASX	MBB Bo 105DBS/4	Police Aviation Services Ltd	
G-PATS	Shaw Europa	N. Surman	
G-PATY	Colt Flying Sausage balloon	Colt Balloons Ltd	
G-PAWL	PA-28 Cherokee 140	M. Y. Choudhury (G-AWEU)	
G-PAWS	AA-5A Cheetah	M. Entwistle	
G-PAXX	PA-20 Pacer 135	D. W. & M. R. Grace	
G-PAZY	Pazmany PL.4A	C. R. Nash (G-BLAJ)	
G-PBBT	Cameron N-56 balloon	Test Valley Balloon Club	
G-PBES	Robinson R-22B	P. B. Ellis (G-EXOR/G-CMCM)	

Notes	Reg.	Type	Owner or Operator
	G-PCAF	Pietenpol Air Camper	C. C. & F. M. Barley
	G-PCDP	Zlin Z.526F Trener Master	Zlin Group
	G-PCOR	Bell 206B JetRanger 3	Crest Engineering Ltd (G-BRMF)/ Biggin Hill
	G-PCUB	PA-18 Super Cub 135	M. J. Wilson/Redhill
	G-PDHJ	Cessna T.182R	P. G. Vallance Ltd
	G-PDOC	PA-44-180 Seminole	Medicare (G-PVAF)
	G-PDON	WMB.2 Windtracker balloon	P. J. Donnellan
	G-PDSI	Cessna 172N	DA Flying Group
	G-PEAK	AB-206B JetRanger 2	Peak Air Charter (G-BLJE)
	G-PEAL	Aerotek Pitts S-2A	Plymouth Executive Aviation Ltd
	G-PEAT	Cessna 421B	Euroflight Ltd (G-BBIJ)
	G-PEGG	Colt 90A balloon	Michael Pegg Partnership Ltd
	G-PEGI	PA-34-200T Seneca II	Tayflite Ltd
	G-PEKT	SOCATA TB.20 Trinidad	Gamebore Cartridge Co. Ltd
	G-PELE	Cameron 80 Pele SS balloon	Cameron Balloons Ltd
	G-PENN	AA-5B Tiger	L. F. Banks
	G-PENY	Sopwith LC-1T Triplane (5492)	J. S. Penny
	G-PERR	Cameron 60 Bottle SS balloon ★	British Balloon Museum/Newbury
	G-PERS	Colt Soapbox SS balloon	G. V. Beckwith
	G-PEST	Hawker Tempest II	Autokraft Ltd
	G-PETR	PA-28 Cherokee 140	Kirkland Ltd (G-BCJL)
	G-PFAA	EAA Biplane Model P	E. W. B. Comber
	G-PFAB	Colomban MC.15 Cri-Cri	P. Fabish
	G-PFAC	FRED Srs 2	G. R. Yates
	G-PFAD	Wittman W.8 Tailwind	M. R. Stamp
	G-PFAF	FRED Srs 2	M. S. Perkins
	G-PFAG	Evans VP-1	P. A. Evans
	G-PFAH	Evans VP-1	J. A. Scott
	G-PFAI	Clutton EC.2 Easy Too	G. W. Cartledge
	G-PFAL	FRED Srs 2	J. McD. Robinson/Bann Foot
	G-PFAO	Evans VP-1	P. W. Price
	G-PFAP	Currie Wot/SE-5A (C1904)	J. H. Seed
	G-PFAR	Isaacs Fury II (K2059)	C. J. Repik
	G-PFAT	Monnett Sonerai II	H. B. Carter
	G-PFAU	Rand KR-2	D. E. Peace
	G-PFAW	Evans VP-1	R. F. Shingler
	G-PFAY	EAA Biplane	A. K. Lang & A. L. Young
	G-PFBT	V.806 Viscount	British World Airways Ltd (G-AOYP)/ Southend
	G-PFML	Robinson R-44	D. A. Walker & Co
	G-PHIL	Brookland Hornet	A. J. Philpotts
	G-PHON	Cameron Phone SS balloon	Redmalt Ltd (G-BTEY)
	G-PHSI	Colt 90A balloon	P. H. Strickland & Simpson (Piccadilly) Ltd
	G-PHTG	SOCATA TB.10 Tobago	A. R. Murray
	G-PIAF	Thunder Ax7-65 balloon	L. Battersley
	G-PICT	Colt 180A balloon	G. M. & D. C. Houston
	G-PIDS	Boeing 757-225	Airtours International Airways Ltd
	G-PIEL	CP.301A Emeraude	P. R. Thorne (G-BARY)
	G-PIES	Thunder Ax7-77Z balloon	Pork Farms Ltd
	G-PIET	Pietenpol Air Camper	N. D. Marshall
	G-PIGS	SOCATA Rallye 150ST	Boonhill Flying Group (G-BDWB)
	G-PIGY	SC.7 Skyvan Srs 3A Variant 100	Hunting Aviaton Ltd
	G-PIIX	Cessna P.210N	D. E. Glass (G-KATH)
	G-PIKE	Robinson R-22 Mariner	Sloane Helicopters Ltd/Sywell
	G-PIKK	PA-28 Cherokee 140	L. P. & I. Keegan (G-AVLA)
	G-PILE	Rotorway Executive 90	J. B. Russell
	G-PINE	Thunder Ax8-90 balloon	J. A. Pine
	G-PING	AA-5A Cheetah	Garrick Aviation (G-OCWC/G-WULL)
	G-PINT	Cameron 65 Barrel SS balloon	D. K. Fish
	G-PINX	Lindstrand Pink Panther SS balloon	Virgin Airship & Balloon Co Ltd
	G-PIPA	PA-28-181 Archer III	N. J. & P. D. Fuller
	G-PIPS	Vans RV-4	C. J. Marsh
	G-PITS	Pitts S-2AE Special	The Eitlean Group
	G-PITZ	Pitts S-2A Special	A. K. Halvorsen
	G-PIXS	Cessna 336	Atlantic Bridge Aviation Ltd/Biggin Hill
	G-PJMD	Hughes 369D	Sylner Aviation Ltd (G-BMJV)
	G-PJRT	BAe Jetstream 4100	British Aerospace PLC/Prestwick
	G-PKPK	Schweizer 269C	G. B. Parsons
	G-PLAN	Cessna F.150L	G-PLAN Flying Group
	G-PLAX	AS.355F-1 Twin Squirrel	Dollar Air Services Ltd (G-BPMT)
	G-PLAY	Robin R.2100A	Cotswold Aero Club Ltd/Staverton

Reg.	Type	Owner or Operator	Notes
G-PLEE	Cessna 182Q	W. J. & M. Barnes	
G-PLGI	H.S.125 Srs 700B	Polygram Record Operations Ltd (G-BFXT)	
G-PLIV	Pazmany PL.4	B. P. North	
G-PLMB	AS.350B Ecureuil	PLM Dollar Group Ltd (G-BMMB)	
G-PLMC	AS.350B Ecureuil	PLM Dollar Group Ltd (G-BKUM)	
G-PLMF	AS.350B-1 Ecureuil	PLM Helicopters Ltd	
G-PLMH	AS.350B-2 Ecureuil	PLM Dollar Group Ltd	
G-PLMI	SA.365C-1 Dauphin	PLM Helicopters Ltd	
G-PLOW	Hughes 269B	Sulby Aerial Surveys Ltd (G-AVUM)	
G-PLUG	Colt 105A balloon	Eastern Electricity PLC	
G-PLUS	PA-34-200T Seneca II	C. G. Strasser/Jersey	
G-PLXI	BAe ATP/Jetstream 61	Jetstream Aircraft Ltd (G-MATP)/Prestwick	
G-PLYD	SOCATA TB.20 Trinidad	Bath Stone Co. Ltd	
G-PMAM	Cameron V-65 balloon	P. A. Meecham	
G-POAH	Sikorsky S-76B	P&O Aviation Ltd	
G-POLY	Cameron N-77 balloon	Empty Wallets Balloon Group	
G-POND	Oldfield Baby Lakes	M. Beamand	
G-PONY	Colt 31A balloon	Ace Balloons (Bath) Ltd	
G-POOH	Piper J-3C-65 Cub	P. & H. Robinson	
G-POOL	ARV Super 2	Falstaff Finance Ltd (G-BNHA)	
G-POPA	Beech A36 Bonanza	R. G. Jones	
G-POPE	Eiri PIK-20E-1	C. J. Hadley	
G-POPI	SOCATA TB.10 Tobago	I. S. Hacon & C. J. Earle (G-BKEN)	
G-POPP	Colt 105A balloon	Flying Pictures (Balloons) Ltd	
G-POPS	PA-34-220T Seneca III	Alpine Ltd	
G-PORK	AA-5B Tiger	J. W. & B. A. Flint (G-BFHS)	
G-PORT	Bell 206B JetRanger 3	Image Computer System Ltd	
G-POSH	Colt 56A balloon	B. K. Rippon (G-BMPT)	
G-POWL	Cessna 182R	Hillhouse Estates Ltd	
G-PPLH	Robinson R-22B	Henderson Financial Management Ltd	
G-PPLI	Pazmany PL.1	G. Anderson	
G-PPPP	Denney Kitfox Mk 3	W. J. Dale	
G-PRAG	Brügger MB.2 Colibri	Colibri Flying Group	
G-PRIM	PA-38-112 Tomahawk	Braddock Ltd	
G-PRIT	Cameron N-90 balloon	N. Duppa-Miller	
G-PRNT	Cameron V-90 balloon	GS Print (West Midlands) Ltd	
G-PROD	AS.350B-2 Ecureuil	Prodrive Ltd	
G-PROP	AA-5A Cheetah	Photonic Science Ld (G-BHKU)	
G-PROV	P.84 Jet Provost T.52A (T.4)	Bushfire Investments Ltd	
G-PRTT	Cameron N-31 balloon	J. M. Albury	
G-PRUE	Cameron O-84 balloon	Lalondes Residential Ltd	
G-PRXI	V.S.365 Spitfire PR.XI (PL983)	Old Flying Machine Co/Duxford	
G-PSON	Colt Cylinder One SS balloon	M. E. White	
G-PTER	Beech C90 King Air	Moseley Group (PSV) Ltd (G-BIEE)	
G-PTRE	SOCATA TB.20 Trinidad	Trantshore Ltd (G-BNKU)	
G-PTWO	Pilatus P2-05 (U-110)	C. M. Lee	
G-PUBS	Colt 56 Glass SS balloon	The Balloonatics	
G-PUFF	Thunder Ax7-77A balloon	Intervarsity Balloon Club	
G-PUMA	AS.332L Super Puma	Bond Helicopters Ltd	
G-PUMB	AS.332L Super Puma	Bond Helicopters Ltd	
G-PUMD	AS.332L Super Puma	Bond Helicopters Ltd	
G-PUME	AS.332L Super Puma	Bond Helicopters Ltd	
G-PUMG	AS.332L Super Puma	Bond Helicopters Ltd	
G-PUMH	AS.332L Super Puma	Bond Helicopters Ltd	
G-PUMI	AS.332L Super Puma	Bond Helicopters Ltd	
G-PUMJ	AS.332L Super Puma	Bond Helicopters Ltd (G-BLZJ)	
G-PUMK	AS.332L Super Puma	Bond Helicopters Ltd	
G-PUML	AS.332L Super Puma	Bond Helicopters Ltd	
G-PUNK	Thunder Ax8-105 balloon	G. E. Harris	
G-PUPP	B.121 Pup 2	P. A. Teichman (G-BASD)/Elstree	
G-PURE	Cameron 70 Can SS balloon	The Hot-Air Balloon Co Ltd	
G-PURR	AA-5A Cheetah	Plane Talking Ltd (G-BJDN)	
G-PURS	Rotorway Executive	J. E. Houseman	
G-PUSH	Rutan LongEz	E. G. Peterson	
G-PUSI	Cessna T.303	W. R. Swinburn Ltd	
G-PUSS	Cameron N-77 balloon	Bristol Balloons	
G-PUTT	Cameron 76 Golf SS balloon	Lakeside Lodge Golf Centre	
G-PYLN	Cameron Pylon SS balloon	Air 2 Air Ltd (G-BUSO)	
G-PYOB	SA.341G Gazelle 1	Rigley Corporation Ltd (G-WELA/G-SFTD/G-RIFC)	
G-PYRO	Cameron N-65 balloon	D. E. Wells	

Notes	Reg.	Type	Owner or Operator
	G-PZAZ	PA-31-350 Navajo Chieftain	ML Associates (G-VTAX/G-UTAX)
	G-RAAD	Mooney M.20L	As-Al Ltd
	G-RAAR	BAe 125 Srs 800B	Osprey Executive Aviation Ltd/Southend
	G-RACH	Robinson R-22B	Heli Air Ltd
	G-RACO	PA-28R Cherokee Arrow 200-II	Graco Group Ltd
	G-RAEM	Rutan LongEz	G. F. H. Singleton
	G-RAFA	Grob G.115	RAF College Flying Club Ltd/Cranwell
	G-RAFB	Grob G.115	RAF College Flying Club Ltd/Cranwell
	G-RAFC	Robin R.2112	Group Alpha
	G-RAFE	Thunder Ax7-77 balloon	N. A. & J. K. Fishlock
	G-RAFF	Learjet 35A	Graff Aviation Ltd/Heathrow
	G-RAFG	Slingsby T.67C	BBC Club/Denham
	G-RAFI	P.84 Jet Provost T.4	R. M. Muir
	G-RAFT	Rutan LongEz	H. C. Mackinnon
	G-RAFW	Mooney M.20E	S. L. Monksfield (G-ATHW)
	G-RAGG	Maule M5-235C Lunar Rocket	P. Ragg
	G-RAGS	Pietenpol Air Camper	R. F. Billington
	G-RAHL	Beech 400A Beechjet	Air Hanson Aircraft Sales Ltd
	G-RAID	AD-4NA Skyraider (126922)	Patina Ltd/Duxford
	G-RAIL	Colt 105A balloon	Ballooning World Ltd
	G-RAIN	Maule M5-235C Lunar Rocket	D. S. McKay & J. A. Rayment/ Hinton-in-the-Hedges
	G-RAMI	Bell 206B JetRanger 3	Northern Helicopters (Leeds) Ltd
	G-RAMM	Hughes 369HM	R. A. Kingson
	G-RAMP	Piper J-3C-65 Cub	K. N. Whittall
	G-RAMS	PA-32R-301 Saratoga SP	Air Tobago Ltd/Netherthorpe
	G-RAMY	Bell 206B JetRanger	R & M International Engineering Ltd
	G-RANA	Cameron 82 Cheese SS balloon	Consorizio per la Tutela del Formaggio
	G-RAND	Rand KR-2	R. L. Wharmby
	G-RANS	Rans S.10 Sakota	J. D. Weller
	G-RANZ	Rans S-10 Sakota	B. A. Phillips
	G-RAPA	BN-2T-4R Defender 4000	Pilatus BN Ltd (G-BJBH)/Bembridge
	G-RAPE	Colt 300A balloon	Adventure Balloon Co Ltd
	G-RAPH	Cameron O-77 balloon	P. H. Jenkins
	G-RAPP	Cameron H-34 balloon	Cameron Balloons Ltd
	G-RARE	Thunder Ax5-42 SS balloon	International Distillers & Vintners Ltd
	G-RASC	Evans VP-2	K. A. Stewart & G. Oldfield
	G-RATE	AA-5A Cheetah	Holmes Rentals (G-BIFF)
	G-RATZ	Shaw Europa	R. Muller
	G-RAVI	Colt 300A balloon	R. S. Hunjan
	G-RAVL	H.P.137 Jetstream Srs 200	Cranfield Institute of Technology (G-AWVK)
	G-RAYA	Denney Kitfox Mk 4	A. K. Ray
	G-RAYS	Zenair CH.250	B. O. & F. A. Smith
	G-RBBB	Shaw Europa	W. M. Goodburn & I. H. MacLeod
	G-RBOS	Colt AS-105 airship ★	Science Museum/Wroughton
	G-RBOW	Thunder Ax-7-65 balloon	P. G. & S. D. Viney
	G-RBUT	Hughes 369HS	R. C. Button
	G-RCDI	H.S.125 Srs 700B	Aravco Ltd (G-BJDJ)/Heathrow
	G-RCED	R. Commander 114	Echo Delta Ltd
	G-RCEJ	BAe 125 Srs 800B	Aravco Ltd (G-GEIL)/Farnborough
	G-RCMC	Murphy Renegade 912	R. C. M. Collisson
	G-RCMF	Cameron V-77 balloon	Mouldform Ltd
	G-RDCI	R. Commander 112A	A. C. Hendriksen (G-BFWG)
	G-RDON	WMB.2 Windtracker balloon	P. J. Donnellan (G-BICH)
	G-REAH	PA-32R-301 Saratoga SP	T. & S. Y. Reah (G-CELL)/Elstree
	G-REAP	Pitts S-1S Special	R. Dixon
	G-REAS	Vans RV-6A	D. W. Reast
	G-REAT	GA-7 Cougar	Plane Talking Ltd/Elstree
	G-REBI	Colt 90A balloon	Capricorn Balloons Ltd (G-BOYD)
	G-REBL	Hughes 269B	M. I. Edwards
	G-RECK	PA-28 Cherokee 140B	R. J. Grantham & D. Boatswain (G-AXJW)
	G-RECO	Jurca MJ-5L Sirocco	J. D. Tseliki
	G-REDB	Cessna 310Q	Leisure Park Management Ltd (G-BBIC)
	G-REDX	Experimental Aviation Berkut	G. V. Waters
	G-REEK	AA-5A Cheetah	J. R. & S. Nutter
	G-REEN	Cessna 340	E. & M. Green (G-AZYR)/Guernsey
	G-REES	Jodel D.140C	W. H. Greenwood
	G-REGS	Thunder Ax7-77 balloon	M. E. Gregory
	G-REID	Rotorway Scorpion 133	G. F. Burridge & S. B. Evans (G-BGAW)
	G-RENE	Murphy Renegade 912	J. A. Cuthbertson
	G-RENO	SOCATA TB.10 Tobago	Lamond Ltd

Reg.	Type	Owner or Operator	Notes
G-RENT	Robinson R-22B	Rentatruck Self Drive Ltd	
G-REPM	PA-38-112 Tomahawk	Nultree Ltd	
G-REST	Beech P35 Bonanza	C. R. Taylor (G-ASFJ)	
G-RETA	C.A.S.A. 1.131 Jungmann 2000	R. I. Warman (G-BGZC)	
G-REXS	PA-28-181 Archer II	Exeter Flying Club Ltd	
G-REZE	Rutan Vari-Eze	S. D. Brown & S. P. Evans	
G-RFIL	Colt 77A balloon	The Aerial Display Co Ltd	
G-RFIO	Aeromot AMT--200 Super Ximango	G. McLean & R. B. Beck	
G-RFSB	Sportavia RF-5B	S. W. Brown	
G-RGER	Bell 206B JetRanger 3	T. D. T. Waring	
G-RGUS	Fairchild 24R-46A Argus 3 (44-83185)	R. C. Handgraff	
G-RHHT	PA-32RT-300 Lance II	R. W. Struth & ptnrs	
G-RHYS	Rotorway Executive 90	B. Williams	
G-RICC	AS.350B-2 Ecureuil	McAlpine Helicopters Ltd & Gabriel Enterprises Ltd (G-BTXA)	
G-RICH	Cessna F.152	Cloudshire Ltd/Wellesbourne	
G-RICK	Beech 95-B55 Baron	James Jack (Invergordon) Ltd (G-BAAG)	
G-RIDE	Stephens Akro	R. Mitchell/Coventry	
G-RIDS	Lancair 235	R. Y. Kendal	
G-RIFB	Hughes 269C	R. F. Rhodes & J. C. McHugh	
G-RIGB	Thunder Ax7-77 balloon	Antrum & Andrews Ltd	
G-RIGS	PA-60 Aerostar 601P	Techno Engineering	
G-RILY	Monnett Sonerai II	R. Wheeler	
G-RINO	Thunder Ax7-77 balloon	D. J. Head	
G-RINT	CFM Streak Shadow	D. Grint	
G-RISE	Cameron V-77 balloon	D. L. Smith	
G-RIST	Cessna 310R-II	Air Service Training Ltd (G-DATS)/Perth	
G-RIVT	Vans RV-6	N. Reddish	
G-RIZE	Cameron O-90 balloon	S. F. Burden/Netherlands	
G-RIZI	Cameron N-90 balloon	R. Wiles	
G-RJAH	Boeing Stearman A.75N1	R. J. Horne	
G-RJGR	Boeing 757-225	Airtours International Airways Ltd	
G-RJMI	AA-5A Cheetah	Garrick Aviation	
G-RJMS	PA-28R-201 Arrow III	M. G. Hill	
G-RJWW	Maule M5-235C Lunar Rocket	Paw Flying Services Ltd (G-BRWG)	
G-RLFI	Cessna FA.152	Tayside Aviation Ltd (G-DFTS)/Dundee	
G-RLMC	Cessna 421C	R. D. Lygo	
G-RMCI	Short SD3-60 Variant 100	Gill Airways Ltd (G-BLPU)	
G-RMUG	Cameron 90 Mug SS balloon	Nestle UK Ltd	
G-RNAS	D.H.104 Sea Devon C.20 (XK896)	D. W. Hermiston-Hooper/Staverton	
G-RNIE	Cameron 70 Ball SS balloon	Virgin Airship & Balloon Co Ltd	
G-RNLI	V.S.236 Walrus I	R. E. Melton	
G-RNRM	Cessna A.185F	RN & R. Marines Sport Parachute Association/Dunkeswell	
G-ROAR	Cessna 401	Special Scope Ltd (G-BZFL/G-AWSF)	
G-ROBB	Grob G.109B	A. P. Mayne	
G-ROBD	Shaw Europa	R. D. Davies	
G-ROBI	Grob G.109B	A. W. McGarrigle/Cardiff	
G-ROBN	Robin R.1180T	J. G. Beaumont	
G-ROBT	Hawker Hurricane I	R. A. Roberts	
G-ROBY	Colt 17A balloon	Virgin Airship & Balloon Co Ltd	
G-ROCH	Cessna T.303	R. S. Bentley	
G-ROCK	Thunder Ax7-77 balloon	The Long Rake Spar Co Ltd	
G-ROCR	Schweizer 269C	Leisure & Retail Consultants Ltd	
G-RODD	Cessna 310R II	R. J. Herbert Engineering Ltd (G-TEDD/G-MADI)	
G-RODI	Isaacs Fury (K3731)	M. R. Baker/Shoreham	
G-RODS	A-Bell 206B JetRanger 2	Nunkeeling Ltd (G-NOEL/G-BCWN)	
G-ROGG	Robinson R-22B	Catto Aviation Ltd	
G-ROGY	Cameron 60 Concept balloon	A. A. Laing	
G-ROLA	PA-34-200T Seneca	Mala Services Ltd	
G-ROLF	PA-32R-301 Saratoga SP	P. F. Larkins	
G-ROLL	Pitts S-2A Special	Aerial & Aerobatic Services	
G-ROLO	Robinson R-22B	Plane Talking Ltd/Elstree	
G-ROMA	Hughes 369HS	Helicopters (Northern) Ltd (G-ROPI/G-ONPP)/Blackpool	
G-RONA	Shaw Europa	C. M. Noakes	
G-RONC	Aeronca 11AC Chief	I. A. Scott (G-BULV)	
G-RONG	PA-28R Cherokee Arrow 200-II	W. R. Griffiths	
G-RONI	Cameron V-77 balloon	R. E. Simpson	
G-RONS	Robin DR.400/180	R. & K. Baker	

Notes	Reg.	Type	Owner or Operator
	G-RONW	FRED Srs 2	K. Atkinson
	G-ROOK	Cessna F.172P	Crop Aviation (UK) Ltd
	G-ROPA	Shaw Europa	R. G. Gray
	G-RORI	Folland Gnat T.1	R. C. McCarthy
	G-RORO	Cessna 337B	C. Keane (G-AVIX)
	G-RORY	Piaggio FWP.149D	R. McCarthy (G TOWN)/Booker
	G-ROSE	Evans VP-1	W. K. Rose
	G-ROSI	Thunder Ax7-77 balloon	J. E. Rose
	G-ROSS	Practavia Pilot Sprite	F. M. T. Ross
	G-ROSY	Robinson R-22B	Aquaprint Ltd
	G-ROTI	Luscombe 8A Silvaire	A. L. Chapman & ptnrs
	G-ROTO	Rotorway Executive 90	S. R. Porter
	G-ROTR	Brantly B.2B	GP Services
	G-ROTS	CFM Streak Shadow Srs SA	P. White
	G-ROUP	Cessna F.172M	Stapleford Flying Club Ltd (G-BDPH)
	G-ROUS	PA-34-200T Seneca II	C.S.E. Aviation Ltd/Kidlington
	G-ROUT	Robinson R-22B	Hooley Bridge Helicopter Services
	G-ROVE	PA-18 Super Cub 135	Caledonian Seaplanes Ltd/Cumbernauld
	G-ROWE	Cessna F.182P	D. Rowe
	G-ROWL	AA-5B Tiger	Aviation Simulation/Biggin Hill
	G-ROWN	Beech 200 Super King Air	Holiday Chemical Holdings Ltd (G-BHLC)
	G-ROWS	PA-28-151 Warrior	Mustarrow Ltd
	G-ROZY	Cameron R.36 balloon	Jacques W. Soukup Enterprises Ltd
	G-RPEZ	Rutan LongEz	B. A. Fairston & D. Richardson
	G-RRRR	Privateer Motor Glider	R. F. Selby
	G-RRSG	Thunder Ax7-77 balloon	M. T. Stevens
	G-RSFT	PA-28-181 Warrior II	SFT Aviation Ltd (G-WARI)/Bournemouth
	G-RSKR	PA-28-161 Warrior II	Southern Air Ltd (G-BOJY)/Shoreham
	G-RSMA	Bell 206B JetRanger 3	Gama Leasing Ltd (G-SHZZ/G-BNUW)
	G-RSSF	Denney Kitfox Mk 2	R. W. Somerville
	G-RSWW	Robinson R-22B	Woodstock Enterprises
	G-RTBI	Thunder Ax6-56 balloon	Norwich & District Balloon Club
	G-RUBB	AA-5B Tiger	R. Bessant
	G-RUBI	Thunder Ax7-77 balloon	Warren & Johnson
	G-RUBY	PA-28RT-201T Turbo Arrow IV	Arrow Aircraft Group (G-BROU)
	G-RUDD	Cameron V-65 balloon	N. A. Apsey
	G-RUDI	QAC Quickie Q.2	R. Brandenberger
	G-RUGB	Cameron 89 Egg SS balloon	K. L. Watson
	G-RUIA	Cessna F.172M	F. Daly
	G-RUMN	AA-1A Trainer	D. A. Whitmore & A. Ward
	G-RUMP	Robinson R-22B	Sloane Helicopters Ltd/Sywell
	G-RUNT	Cassutt Racer IIIM	The Cassutt Flying Group
	G-RUSO	Robinson R-22B	N. P. Graham
	G-RUSS	Cessna 172N	Leisure Lease/Southend
	G-RVEE	Vans RV-6	J. C. A. Wheeler
	G-RVIT	Vans RV-6	P. J. Shotbolt
	G-RVVI	Vans RV-6	J. E. Alsford & J. N. Parr
	G-RWHC	Cameron A-180 balloon	Hourds Ltd
	G-RWIN	Rearwin 175	G. Kay
	G-RWSS	Denney Kitfox Mk 2	R. W. Somerville
	G-RWWW	W.S.55 Whirlwind HCC.12 (XR486)	Whirlwind Helicopters Ltd/Redhill
	G-RXUK	Lindstrand LBL-105A balloon	Flying Pictures (Balloons) Ltd
	G-SAAB	R. Commander 112TC	SAAB Group (G-BEFS)
	G-SAAM	Cessna T.182R	H. C. Danby & M. D. Harvey (G-TAGL)
	G-SABA	PA-28R-201T Turbo Arrow III	C. Geravelis (G-BFEN)
	G-SABR	NA F-86A Sabre (8178)	Golden Apple Operations Ltd/Bournemouth
	G-SACB	Cessna F.152 II	Sky Pro Ltd (G-BFRB)
	G-SACD	Cessna F.172H	Northbrook College of Design & Technology (G-AVCD)/Shoreham
	G-SACE	Cessna F.150L	Arrow Aircraft Ltd (G-AZLK)
	G-SACF	Cessna 152 II	T. M. & M. L. Jones
	G-SACI	PA-28-161 Warrior II	PJC (Leasing) Ltd
	G-SACO	PA-28-161 Warrior II	The Barn Gallery
	G-SACR	PA-28-161 Cadet	Sherburn Aero Club Ltd
	G-SACS	PA-28-161 Cadet	Sherburn Aero Club Ltd
	G-SACT	PA-28-161 Cadet	Sherburn Aero Club Ltd
	G-SACU	PA-28-161 Cadet	Sherburn Aero Club Ltd
	G-SACZ	PA-28-161 Warrior II	J. C. Macartney & ptnrs
	G-SADE	Cessna F.150L	N. E. Sams (G-AZJW)

Reg.	Type	Owner or Operator	Notes
G-SAFE	Cameron N-77 balloon	P. J. Waller	
G-SAFR	SAAB 91D Safir	B. Johansson	
G-SAGA	Grob G.109B	G-GROB Ltd/Booker	
G-SAGE	Luscombe 8A Silvaire	S. J. Sage (G-AKTL)	
G-SAHI	Trago Mills SAH-1	Lovaux Ltd/Bournemouth	
G-SAIR	Cessna 421C	Air Support Aviation Services Ltd (G-OBCA)	
G-SALA	PA-32 Cherokee Six 300E	Stonebold Ltd	
G-SALL	Cessna F.150L (Tailwheel)	D. D. Smith	
G-SAMG	Grob G.109B	RAFGSA/Bicester	
G-SAMM	Cessna 340A	M. R. Cross	
G-SAMY	Shaw Europa	N. Starling	
G-SAMZ	Cessna 150D	N. E. Sams (G-ASSO)/Cranfield	
G-SANB	Beech E90 King Air	Maynard & Harris Holdings Ltd (G-BGNU)	
G-SAND	Schweizer 269C	Aerocroft Ltd	
G-SARA	PA-28-181 Archer II	L. C. MacKnight	
G-SARH	PA-28-161 Warrior II	Sussex Flying Club Ltd/Shoreham	
G-SARK	BAC.167 Strikemaster	Sark International Airways Ltd	
G-SARO	Saro Skeeter Mk 12 (XL812)	F. F. Chamberlain	
G-SASU	AS.355F-1 Twin Squirrel	Aeromega Ltd (G-BSSM/G-BMTC/ G-BKUK)	
G-SATI	Cameron 105 Sphere SS balloon	Cameron Balloons Ltd	
G-SATL	Cameron 105 Sphere SS balloon	Cameron Balloons Lt†d	
G-SAUF	Colt 90A balloon	K. H. Medau	
G-SBAS	Beech B200 Super King Air	Bond Helicopters Ltd (G-BJJV)/Aberdeen	
G-SBEA	Boeing 737-204ADV	Sabre Airways (G-BFVB)	
G-SBEB	Boeing 737-204ADV	Sabre Airways (G-BAZH)	
G-SBLT	Steen Skybolt	M. A. McCallum & H. Lees	
G-SBUS	BN-2A-26 Islander	Isles of Scilly Skybus Ltd (G-BMMH)/ St Just	
G-SCAN	Vinten-Wallis WA-116/100	K. H. Wallis	
G-SCAT	Cessna F.150F	Abraxas Aviation Ltd (G-ATRN)	
G-SCFO	Cameron O-77 balloon	M. K. Grigson	
G-SCLX	FLS Aerospace Sprint 160	FLS Aerospace (Lovaux) Ltd (G-PLYM)/ Bournemouth	
G-SCPL	PA-28 Cherokee 140	R. D. Coombes (G-BPVL)/Staverton	
G-SCTA	Westland Scout AH.1	H. Butcher Technology Realisation Ltd	
G-SCTT	HPR-7 Herald 210	Channel Express (Air Services) Ltd (G-ASPJ)/Bournemouth	
G-SCUB	PA-18 Super Cub 135 (542447)	N. D. Needham Farms	
G-SDEV	D.H.104 Sea Devon C.20 (XK895)	P. C. Gill & W.C Gentle	
G-SDLW	Cameron O-105 balloon	P. J. Smart	
G-SEAB	Republic RC-3 Seabee	B. A. Farries	
G-SEAI	Cessna U.206G	Aerofloat Ltd	
G SEAT	Colt 42 balloon	Virgin Airship & Balloon Co Ltd	
G-SEED	Piper J-3C-65 Cub	J. H. Seed	
G-SEEK	Cessna T.210N	Verikeen Ltd	
G-SEGA	Cameron 90 Sonic SS balloon	Virgin Airship & Balloon Co Ltd	
G-SEGO	Robinson R-22B	G. Seago	
G-SEJW	PA-28-161 Warrior II	Truman Aviation Ltd/Tollerton	
G-SELL	Robin DR.400/180	L. S. Thorne	
G-SEND	Colt 90A balloon	Redmalt Ltd	
G-SENX	PA-34-200T Seneca II	Senair Charter Ltd (G-DARE/G-WOTS/ G-SEVL)	
G-SEPB	AS.355N Twin Squirrel	Metropolitan Police (G-AVSE)	
G-SEPC	AS.355N Twin Squirrel	McAlpine Helicopters Ltd (G-BWGV)/ Kidlington	
G-SEPT	Cameron N-105 balloon	Deproco UK Ltd	
G-SERA	Enstrom F-28A-UK	W. R. Pitcher (G-BAHU)	
G-SERL	SOCATA TB.10 Tobago	R. J. & G. Searle (G-LANA)/Rochester	
G-SETA	AS.355F-1 Twin Squirrel	McAlpine Helicopters Ltd (G-NEAS/ G-CMMM/G-BNBJ)	
G-SEVA	SE-5A (replica) (F141)	I. D. Gregory	
G-SEVE	Cessna 172N	M. Connolly	
G-SEXI	Cessna 172M	Trade Orders Ltd	
G-SEXY	AA-1 Yankee	I. C. Kenyon (G-AYLM)	
G-SFHR	PA-23 Aztec 250F	Comed Aviation Ltd (G-BHSO)	
G-SFOX	Rotorway Executive 90	Magpie Computer Services Ltd (G-BUAH)	
G-SFPA	Cessna F.406	Scottish Fisheries Protection Agency	
G-SFPB	Cessna F.406	Scottish Fisheries Protection Agency	
G-SFRY	Thunder Ax7-77 balloon	R. J. Fry	
G-SFTZ	Slingsby T.67M Firefly	Mega Yield Ltd	
G-SGAS	Colt 77A balloon	Avongas Ltd	

Notes	Reg.	Type	Owner or Operator
	G-SHAA	Enstrom 280-UK	Ribble Aviation Ltd
	G-SHAW	PA-30 Twin Comanche 160B	E. R. Meredith & M. D. Faiers
	G-SHCC	AB-206B JetRanger 2	Yorkshire Helicopter Centre Ltd
	G-SHEA	BAe 125 Srs 800B	Shell Aircraft Ltd (G-BUWC)/Heathrow
	G-SHEB	BAe 125 Srs 800B	Shell Aircraft Ltd (G-BUWD)/Heathrow
	G-SHEC	BAe 125-1000B	Shell Aircraft Ltd (G-SCCC)
	G-SHED	PA-28-181 Archer II	P. T. Crouch & R. M. Gingell (G-BRAU)
	G-SHEL	Cameron O-56 balloon	The Shell Company of Hong Kong Ltd
	G-SHFL	Cameron N-77 balloon	M. C. Bradley/Hong Kong
	G-SHGG	Enstrom 280C Shark	Edwards Aviation Ltd
	G-SHIM	CFM Streak Shadow	E. S. Shimmin
	G-SHIP	PA-23 Aztec 250F H	Midland Air Museum/Coventry
	G-SHIV	GA-7 Cougar	Westley Aviation Services
	G-SHNN	Enstrom 280C	CJ Services
	G-SHOO	Hughes TH-55A	Starline Helicopters Ltd
	G-SHOP	H.S. 125 Srs F400B	Frewton Ltd (G-BTUF)
	G-SHOT	Cameron V-77 balloon	E. C. Moore
	G-SHOW	M.S.733 Alycon	Vintage Aircraft Team/Cranfield
	G-SHPP	Hughes TH-55A	R. P. Bateman & A. C. Braithwaite
	G-SHRL	Jodel D.18	K. Fern
	G-SHRR	AB-206B JetRanger 2	Frank Owen Commercial Vehicle Spares (G-FSDA/G-AWJW)
	G-SHUG	PA-28R-201T Turbo Arrow III	N. E. Rennie
	G-SHUU	Enstrom 280C-UK-2 Shark	D. Ellis (G-OMCP/G-KENY/G-BJFG)
	G-SIAL	Hunter F.58	Sark International Airways Ltd
	G-SIAN	Cameron V-77 balloon	S. M. Jones
	G-SIGN	PA-39 Twin Comanche 160 C/R	M. P. Bolshaw & P. Karl/Elstree
	G-SIIB	Pitts S-2B Special	M. Davies (G-BUVY)
	G-SIII	Extra EA.300	Firebird Aerobatics Ltd/Booker
	G-SIMI	Cameron A-315 balloon	R. S. Hunjan
	G-SING	Beech B60 Duke	P. W. Huntley
	G-SION	PA-38-112 Tomahawk II	Naiad Air Services
	G-SIPA	SIPA 903	T. J. McRae (G-BGBM)
	G-SITE	AS.355F-1 Twin Squirrel	Bridge Street Nominees Ltd (G-BPHC)
	G-SIVA	MDH Hughes 369E	C. J. Siva-Jothy (G-TBIX)/Redhill
	G-SIXC	Douglas DC-6A	Atlantic Air Transport Ltd/Coventry
	G-SIXX	Colt 77A balloon	G. E. Harris & S. C. Kinsey
	G-SIZE	Lindstrand LBL-310A balloon	Adventure Balloon Co Ltd
	G-SJAB	PA-39 Twin Comanche 160 C/R	Foyle Flyers Ltd
	G-SJGM	Cessna 182R	S. J. G. Mole/Halfpenny Green
	G-SJMC	Boeing 767-31KER	Airtours International Airways Ltd
	G-SKAN	Cessna F.172M	R. Mitchell & J. D. Walton (G-BFKT)
	G-SKIL	Cameron N-77 balloon	M. C. & W. A. Swift
	G-SKIP	Cameron N-77 balloon	Skipton Building Soc
	G-SKIS	Tri Kis	M. Martin
	G-SKKB	PA-31 Turbo Navajo	Rentair Ltd (G-BBDS)
	G-SKSA	Airship Industries SKS.500	Airship Industries Ltd/Cardington
	G-SKSG	Airship Industries SKS.600/03	Interport Marine Agencies Ltd
	G-SKYD	Pitts S-2B Special	Skydancer Aviation Ltd
	G-SKYE	Cessna TU.206G	RAF Sport Parachute Association
	G-SKYH	Cessna 172N	Elgor Hire Purchase & Credit Ltd/ Southend
	G-SKYI	Air Command 532 Elite	P. J. Troy-Davies
	G-SKYM	Cessna F.337E	Bencray Ltd (G-AYHW) *(stored)*/Blackpool
	G-SKYP	Cameron A-120 balloon	Esthwaite Holidays Ltd
	G-SKYR	Cameron A-180 balloon	PSH Skypower Ltd
	G-SKYS	Cameron O-84 balloon	J. R. Christopher
	G-SKYY	Cameron A-250 balloon	PSH Skypower Ltd
	G-SKYZ	PA-34-200T Seneca II	Park Aeroleasing Ltd
	G-SLAC	Cameron N-77 balloon	The Scottish Life Assurance Co
	G-SLCI	Thunder Ax8-90 balloon	S. L. Cuhat
	G-SLEA	Mudry/CAARP CAP.10B	P. D. Southerington/Sturgate
	G-SLII	Cameron O-90 balloon	R. B. & A. M. Harris
	G-SLIM	Colt 56A balloon	Hot-Air Balloon Co Ltd
	G-SLYN	PA-28-161 Warrior II	G. E. Layton
	G-SMAF	Sikorsky S-76A	Fayair (Jersey) 1984 Ltd
	G-SMAX	Cameron O-105 balloon	Cameron Balloons Ltd
	G-SMIG	Cameron O-65 balloon	Hong Kong Balloon & Airship Club
	G-SMIT	Messerschmitt Bf.109G-6	Fairoaks Aviation Services Ltd
	G-SMJJ	Cessna 414A	Gull Air Ltd/Guernsey
	G-SMTC	Colt Flying Hut SS balloon	Shiplake Investments Ltd
	G-SMTH	PA-28 Cherokee 140	D. M. Banner (G-AYJS)/Liverpool
	G-SNAP	Cameron V-77 balloon	C. J. S. Limon
	G-SNAX	Colt 69A balloon	Derwent Valley Foods Ltd

Reg.	Type	Owner or Operator	Notes
G-SNAZ	Enstrom F-28F	Thornhill Music Ltd (G-BRCP)	
G-SNDY	Piper J-3C-65 Cub	R. R. K. Mayall	
G-SNOW	Cameron V-77 balloon	M. J. Snow	
G-SOAR	Eiri PIK-20E	F. W. Fay	
G-SOFA	Cameron N-65 balloon	GT Flying Club Ltd	
G-SOFT	Thunder Ax7-77 balloon	A. J. Bowen	
G-SOKO	Soko P-2 Kraguj (30149)	Soko Aviation (G-BRXK)/Liverpool	
G-SOLA	Aero Designs Star-Lite SL.1	J. P. Lethaby	
G-SOLD	Robinson R-22A	Travel Management Ltd	
G-SOLO	Pitts S-2S Special	Landitfast Ltd	
G-SONA	SOCATA TB.10 Tobago	J. Greenwood (G-BIBI)	
G-SONY	Aero Commander 200D	General Airline Ltd (G-BGPS)	
G-SOOC	Hughes 369HS	Colour Library Books (G-BRRX)	
G-SOOE	Hughes 369E	Feabrex Steel Fabrication Ltd	
G-SOOK	Sukhoi Su-26M	S. Jones	
G-SOOM	Glaser-Dirks DG.500M	Glaser-Dirks UK	
G-SOOR	AB-206A JetRanger	Weathershield Aviation Ltd (G-FMAL/ G-RIAN/G-BHSG	
G-SOOS	Colt 21A balloon	P. J. Stapley	
G-SOOT	PA-28 Cherokee 180	Thornton Browne Ltd (G-AVNM)/Exeter	
G-SORT	Cameron N-90 balloon	The Post Office	
G-SOUL	Cessna 310R	Atlantic Air Transport Ltd/Coventry	
G-SOUP	Cameron C-80 balloon	M. G. Barlow	
G-SPAM	Light Aero Avid Aerobat	R. W. Fair	
G-SPEE	Robinson R-22B	Speed Helicopters Ltd (G-BPJC)	
G-SPEY	AB-206B JetRanger 3	Castle Air Charters Ltd (G-BIGO)	
G-SPIN	Pitts S-2A Special	R. P. Grace & P. L. Goldberg	
G-SPIT	V.S.379 Spitfire FR.XIV (MV293)	Patina Ltd (G-BGHB)/Duxford	
G-SPOG	Jodel DR.1050	A. C. Frost (G-AXVS)	
G-SPOL	MBB Bo 105CBS/4	Clyde Helicopters Ltd	
G-SROE	Westland Scout AH.1	Bolenda Engineering Ltd	
G-SRVO	Cameron N-90 balloon	Servo & Electronic Sales Ltd	
G-SSBS	Colting Ax77 balloon	K. J. & M. E. Gregory	
G-SSFC	PA-34-200 Seneca II	SFC (Air Taxis) Ltd (G-BBXG)/ Stapleford	
G-SSFT	PA-28-161 Warrior II	SFT Aviation Ltd (G-BHIL)/Bournemouth	
G-SSGS	Shaw Europa	SGS Partnership	
G-SSIX	Rans S.6-116 Coyote II	J. V. Squires	
G-SSKY	BN-2B-26 Islander	Isles of Scilly Skybus Ltd (G-BSWT)	
G-SSSC	Sikorsky S-76C	Bond Helicopters Ltd/Aberdeen	
G-SSSD	Sikorsky S-76C	Bond Helicopters Ltd/Aberdeen	
G-SSSE	Sikorsky S-76C	Bond Helicopters Ltd/Aberdeen	
G-SSTI	Cameron N-105 balloon	British Airways	
G-SSWV	Sportavia Fournier RF-5B	Skylark Flying Group	
G-STAG	Cameron O-65 balloon	The New Holker Estates Co Ltd	
G-STAT	Cessna U.206F	SMK Engineers Ltd	
G-STAV	Cameron O-84 balloon	Nestle UK Ltd	
G-STEF	Hughes 369HS	Source Ltd (G-BKTK)/Thruxton	
G-STEN	Stemme S.10	W. A. H. Kahn	
G-STEP	Schweizer 269C	Geraint Hill Car Sales Ltd	
G-STER	Bell 206B JetRanger 3	Albany Helicopters Ltd	
G-STEV	Jodel DR.221	S. W. Talbot/Long Marston	
G-STMI	Robinson R-22B	D. K. Frampton	
G-STMM	Robinson R-44 Astro	St Merryn Meat Ltd	
G-STMP	SNCAN Stampe SV-4A	W. R. Partridge	
G-STOX	Bell 206B JetRanger 2	Catto Aviation Ltd (G-BNIR)	
G-STOY	Robinson R-22B	Tickstop Ltd	
G-STRK	CFM Streak Shadow Srs SA	E. J. Hadley	
G-STRM	Cameron N-90 balloon	Royal Mail Streamline	
G-STUA	Aerotek Pitts S-2A Special (modified)	Aero-Balance Aviation/White Waltham	
G-STUB	Christen Pitts S-2B Special	R. N. Goode & T. L. P. Delaney	
G-STVN	HPR-7 Herald 210	Channel Express (Air Services) Ltd/ Bournemouth	
G-STWO	ARV Super 2	G. E. Morris	
G-STYL	Pitts S-1S Special	A. Stanford	
G-SUEE	Airbus A.320-231	Airtours International Airways Ltd (G-IEAG)	
G-SUFC	H.S.125 Srs 600B	Chase Montagu Ltd (G-BETV)	
G-SUIT	Cessna 210N	Edinburgh Air Centre Ltd	
G-SUKI	PA-38-112 Tomahawk	Western Air Training Ltd (G-BPNV)	
G-SULY	Monnett Moni	M. J. Sullivan	
G-SUMT	Robinson R-22B	Frankham Bros Ltd (G-BUKD)	

Notes	Reg.	Type	Owner or Operator
	G-SUPA	PA-18 Super Cub 150	Crop Aviation (UK) Ltd
	G-SURG	PA-30 Twin Comanche 160B	A. R. Taylor (G-VIST/G-AVHZ)
	G-SURV	BN-2T-4R Defender 4000	Pilatus BN Ltd (G-BVHZ)
	G-SUSI	Cameron V-77 baloon	H. S. & C. J. Dryden
	G-SUSY	P-51D-25-NA Mustang (472773)	P. J. Morgan
	G-SUZI	Beech 95-B55 Baron	Bebecar (UK) Ltd (G-BAXR)
	G-SUZN	PA-28-161 Warrior II	The St. George Flying Club/Teesside
	G-SUZY	Taylor JT.1 Monoplane	D. I. Law
	G-SVBF	Cameron A-180 balloon	Virgin Balloon Flights Ltd
	G-SVIV	SNCAN Stampe SV-4C	A. J. Clarry & S. F. Bancroft
	G-SVJM	AS.355F-1 Twin Squirrel	Plane Talking Ltd (G-BOPS)/Elstree
	G-SVLB	H.S.125 Srs 700B	Solvalub Trading Ltd (G-BNBO)
	G-SWAC	BAe Jetstream 3102	Serib Wings SRL (G-BRUK)
	G-SWAD	BAe Jetstream 3102	Jetstream Aircraft Ltd (G-LOGP/G-BPZJ)
	G-SWEB	Cameron N-90 balloon	Air 2 Air Ltd
	G-SWET	Cessna 500 Citation	Michael Car Centres Ltd
	G-SWFT	Beech 200 Super King Air	Air Swift Ltd (G-SIBE/G-MCEO/G-BILY)
	G-SWIF	V.S.541 Swift F.7	Jet Heritage Ltd/Bournemouth
	G-SWIM	Taylor Coot Amphibian (modified)	R. J. Hopkins
	G-SWIS	D.H.100 Vampire FB.6 (J-1149)	Hunter Wing Ltd/Bournemouth
	G-SWIV	Lindstrand LBL-240A balloon	Airborne Adventures Ltd
	G-SWOT	Currie Super Wot (C3011)	J. D. Haslam/Breighton
	G-SWPR	Cameron N-56 balloon	A. Brown
	G-SWSH	Mini-500	Aerial Enterprises Ltd
	G-SWUN	Pitts S-1M Special (modified)	T. G. Lloyd (G-BSXH)
	G-SYCO	Shaw Europa	J. W. E. de Frayssinet
	G-SYFW	Focke-Wulf Fw.190 replica (2+1)	M. R. Parr
	G-TACK	Grob G.109B	Oval (275) Ltd/Bristol
	G-TAFF	C.A.S.A. 1.131E Jungmann	A. Horsfall (G-BFNE)
	G-TAFI	Bücker Bu133 Jungmeister	R. J. Lamplough
	G-TAGS	PA-28-161 Warrior II	Air Service Training Ltd/Perth
	G-TAIL	Cessna 150J	Tailwind Flying Group
	G-TAIR	PA-34-200T Seneca II	Branksome Dene Garage/Bournemouth
	G-TAMY	Cessna 421B	Malcolm Enamellers (Midlands) Ltd
	G-TANI	GA-7 Cougar	S. Spier (G-VJAI/G-OCAB/G-BICF)/Elstree
	G-TANK	Cameron N-90 balloon	Hoyers (UK) Ltd
	G-TAPE	PA-23 Aztec 250D	D. J. Hare (G-AWVW)
	G-TART	PA-28-236 Dakota	C. A. Herbert
	G-TARV	ARV Super 2	B. & P. B. Childs
	G-TASK	Cessna 404	Bravo Aviation Ltd
	G-TATE	Cameron A-180 balloon	Freetime (UK) Ltd
	G-TATT	GY-20 Minicab	L. Tattershall
	G-TAXI	PA-23 Aztec 250E	Yorkair Ltd/Leeds
	G-TAYI	Grob G.115	Soaring (Oxford) Ltd (G-DODO)
	G-TAYS	Cessna F.152 II	Tayside Aviation Ltd (G-LFCA)/Dundee
	G-TBAG	Murphy Renegade II	M. R. Tetley
	G-TBIO	SOCATA TB.10 Tobago	R. A. Perrot
	G-TBXX	SOCATA TB.20 Trinidad	D. A. Phillips & Co
	G-TBZO	SOCATA TB.20 Trinidad	D. L. Clarke & M. J. M. Hopper/Shoreham
	G-TCAN	Colt 69A balloon	H. C. J. Williams
	G-TCMP	Robinson R-22B	M. S. Wilford
	G-TCTC	PA-28RT-201 Arrow IV	Terry Coleman (UK) Ltd
	G-TCUB	Piper J-3C-65 Cub	C. Kirk
	G-TDFS	IMCO Callair A.9	Dollarhigh Ltd (G-AVZA)
	G-TEAL	Thurston TSC-1A1 Teal	K. Heeley/Crosland Moor
	G-TECC	Aeronca 7AC Champion	T. E. C. Cushing/Little Snoring
	G-TECH	R. Commander 114	P. A. Reed (G-BEDH)/Denham
	G-TECK	Cameron V-77 balloon	G. M. N. Spencer
	G-TEDF	Cameron N-90 balloon	Fort Vale Engineering Ltd
	G-TEDS	SOCATA TB.10 Tobago	E. W. Lyon (G-BHCO)
	G-TEDY	Evans VP-1	N. K. Marston (G-BHGN)
	G-TEFC	PA-28 Cherokee 140	A. R. Knight
	G-TELY	Agusta A.109A-II	Castle Air Charters Ltd
	G-TEMP	PA-28 Cherokee 180	BEV Piper Group (G-AYBK)/Andrewsfield
	G-TEMT	Hawker Tempest II	Autokraft Ltd
	G-TENT	J/1N Alpha	R. Callaway-Lewis (G-AKJU)
	G-TERY	PA-28-181 Archer II	T. Barlow (G-BOXZ)/Barton
	G-TESS	Quickie Q.2	D. Evans
	G-TEST	PA-34-200 Seneca	Stapleford Flying Club Ltd (G-BLCD)
	G-TEWS	PA-28 Cherokee 140	M. J. & M. J. Tew (G-KEAN/G-AWTM)
	G-TFCI	Cessna FA.152	Tayside Aviation Ltd/Dundee
	G-TFOX	Denney Kitfox Mk 2	F. A. Roberts

Reg.	Type	Owner or Operator	Notes
G-TFRB	Air Command 532 Elite	F. R. Blennerhassett	
G-TFUN	Valentin Taifun 17E	NW Taifun Group	
G-TGAS	Cameron O-160 balloon	G. A. Fisher	
G-TGER	AA-5B Tiger	Plane Talking Ltd (G-BFZP)/Elstree	
G-THCL	Cessna 550 Citation II	Tower House Consultants Ltd	
G-THEA	Boeing Stearman E.75	L. M. Walton	
G-THLS	MBB Bo 105DBS/4	Bond Helicopters Ltd (G-BCXO)	
G-THOM	Thunder Ax6-56 balloon	T. H. Wilson	
G-THOR	Thunder Ax8-105 balloon	N. C. Faithfull/Holland	
G-THOS	Thunder Ax7-77 balloon	M. J. Wilson-Whitaker & S. Walwin	
G-THSL	PA-28R-201 Arrow III	D. M. Markscheffe	
G-TICK	Cameron V-77 balloon	T. J. Tickler	
G-TIDS	Jodel 150	J. B. Dovey/Ipswich	
G-TIGA	D.H.82A Tiger Moth	D. E. Leatherland (G-AOEG)	
G-TIGB	AS.332L Super Puma	Bristow Helicopters Ltd (G-BJXC)	
G-TIGC	AS.332L Super Puma	Bristow Helicopters Ltd (G-BJYH)	
G-TIGE	AS.332L Super Puma	Bristow Heliocpters Ltd (G-BJYJ)	
G-TIGF	AS.332L Super Puma	Bristow Helicopters Ltd	
G-TIGG	AS.332L Super Puma	Bristow Helicopters Ltd	
G-TIGI	AS.332L Super Puma	Bristow Helicopters Ltd	
G-TIGL	AS.332L Super Puma	Bristow Helicopters Ltd	
G-TIGM	AS.332L Super Puma	Bristow Helicopters Ltd	
G-TIGO	AS.332L Super Puma	Bristow Helicopters Ltd	
G-TIGP	AS.332L Super Puma	Bristow Helicopters Ltd	
G-TIGR	AS.332L Super Puma	Bristow Helicopters Ltd	
G-TIGS	AS.332L Super Puma	Bristow Helicopters Ltd	
G-TIGT	AS.332L Super Puma	Bristow Helicopters Ltd	
G-TIGU	AS.332L Super Puma	Bristow Helicopters Ltd	
G-TIGV	AS.332L Super Puma	Bristow Helicopters Ltd	
G-TIGW	AS.332L Super Puma	Bristow Helicopters Ltd	
G-TIGZ	AS.332L Super Puma	British International Helicopters	
G-TIII	Aerotek Pitts S-2A	J. E. R. Seeger (G-BGSE)	
G-TILE	Robinson R-22B	Tile Aviation Ltd	
G-TILL	Robinson R-22B	P. A. Till	
G-TIMB	Rutan Vari-Eze	T. M. Bailey (G-BKXJ)	
G-TIME	Ted Smith Aerostar 601P	Business Aircraft Rental Service Ltd	
G-TIMJ	Rand KR-2	N. Seaton	
G-TIMK	PA-28-181 Archer II	T. Baker	
G-TIMM	Folland Gnat T.1 (XM693)	T. J. Manna/Cranfield	
G-TIMP	Aeronca 7BCM Champion	T. E. Phillips	
G-TIMS	Falconar F-12A	T. Sheridan	
G-TIMW	PA-28 Cherokee 140C	W. H. Sanders (G-AXSH)	
G-TINA	SOCATA TB.10 Tobago	A. Lister	
G-TINS	Cameron N-90 balloon	Bass & Tennent Sales Ltd	
G-TINY	Z.526F Trener Master	Air V8 Ltd	
G-TIPS	Tipsy T.66 Nipper Srs 5	R. F. L. Cuypers	
G-TJAY	PA-22 Tri-Pacer 135	D. D. Saint	
G-TJHI	Cessna 500 Citation	Trustair Ltd (G-CCCL/G-BEIZ)/Blackpool	
G-TJPM	BAe 146-300QT	TNT Express Worldwide (UK) Ltd (G-BRGK)	
G-TKIS	Tri Kis	T. J. Bone	
G-TKPZ	Cessna 310R	Ace Aviation Consultancy & Edinburgh Air Charter Ltd (G-BRAH)	
G-TLME	Robinson R-44 Astro	TJB Associates Ltd	
G-TLOL	Cessna 421C	Littlewoods Organisation Ltd/Liverpool	
G-TMKI	P.56 Provost T.1	T. J. Manna/Cranfield	
G-TMMC	AS.355F-1 Twin Squirrel	The Colt Car Co Ltd (G-JLCO)	
G-TNTA	BAe 146-200QT	TNT Express Worldwide Ltd	
G-TNTB	BAe 146-200QT	TNT Express Worldwide Ltd	
G-TNTE	BAe 146-300QT	TNT Express Worldwide Ltd (G-BRPW)	
G-TNTG	BAe 146-300QT	TNT European Airlines Ltd (G-BSUY)	
G-TNTK	BAe 146-300QT	TNT European Airlines Ltd (G-BSXL)	
G-TNTL	BAe 146-300QT	TNT European Airlines Ltd (G-BSGI)	
G-TNTM	BAe 146-300QT	TNT European Airlines Ltd (G-BSLZ)	
G-TNTN	Thunder Ax6-56 balloon	D. P. & A. Dickinson	
G-TNTR	BAe 146-300QT	TNT Express Worldwide (UK) Ltd (G-BRGM)	
G-TOAD	Jodel D.140B	Mothballs Ltd	
G-TOAK	SOCATA TB.20 Trinidad	R. Chown	
G-TOBA	SOCATA TB.10 Tobago	E. Downing	
G-TOBE	PA-28R Cherokee Arrow 200	J. Bradley & Barry Ltd (G-BNRO)	
G-TOBI	Cessna F.172K	G. Hall (G-AYVB)	
G-TODD	ICA IS-28M2A	C. I. Roberts & C. D. King	

Notes	Reg.	Type	Owner or Operator
	G-TODE	Ruschmeyer R.90-230RG	Tode Ltd
	G-TOFT	Colt 90A balloon	C. S. Perceval
	G-TOMG	P.84 Jet Provost T.4	Gosh That's Aviation Ltd/North Weald
	G-TOMI	H.S.125 Srs 600B	Falcon Jet Centre Ltd(G-BBEP/G-BJOY)/
			Heathrow
	G-TOMK	PA-23 Aztec 250F	Liverpool Flying School Ltd (G-BFEC)
	G-TOMS	PA-38-112 Tomahawk	R. J. Alford
	G-TONE	Pazmany PL.4	J. A. Walmsley
	G-TOOL	Thunder Ax8-105 balloon	W. J. Honey
	G-TOPS	AS.355F-1 Twin Squirrel	Sterling Helicopters (G-BPRH)
	G-TORE	P.84 Jet Provost T.3A (XM405)	Butane Buzzard Aviation Ltd/Cranfield
	G-TOTO	Cessna F.177RG	C. R. & J. Cox (G-OADE/G-AZKH)
	G-TOUR	Robin R.2112	Barnes Martin Ltd
	G-TOWS	PA-25 Pawnee 260	Lasham Gliding Soc Ltd
	G-TOYS	Enstrom 280C-UK-2 Shark	Stephenson Aviation Ltd (G-BISE)
	G-TRAK	Optica Industries OA.7 Optica	FLS Aerospace (Lovaux) Ltd
			(G-BLFC)/Bournemouth
	G-TRAN	Beech 76 Duchess	Transair (UK) Ltd (G-NIFR)/Fairoaks
	G-TRAV	Cameron A-210 balloon	Bakers World Travel Ltd
	G-TREE	Bell 206B JetRanger 3	LGH Aviation Ltd
	G-TREK	Jodel D.18	R. H. Mole/Leicester
	G-TREN	Boeing 737-4S3	GB Airways Ltd (G-BRKG)/Gatwick
	G-TRIB	Lindstrand HS-110 balloon	International Balloons Ltd
	G-TRIC	D.H.C.1 Chipmunk 22A (18013)	D. M. Barnett (G-AOSZ)
	G-TRIM	Monnett Moni	J. E. Bennell
	G-TRIN	SOCATA TB.20 Trinidad	Isnet Ltd
	G-TRIO	Cessna 172M	Plane Talking Ltd (G-BNXY)/Elstree
	G-TRIP	PA-32R-301 Saratoga SP	C. P. Lockyer (G-HOSK)
	G-TRIX	V.S.509 Spitfire T.IX (PV202)	R. A. Roberts
	G-TROP	Cessna 310R	Southern Air Ltd/Shoreham
	G-TRUC	Cassutt Speed One	J. A. H. Chadwick
	G-TRUE	MDH Hughes 369E	Horizon Helicopter Hire
	G-TRUK	Stoddard-Hamilton Glasair RG	M. P. Jackson
	G-TRUX	Colt 77A balloon	Highway Truck Rental Ltd
	G-TSAM	BAe 125 Srs 800B	British Aerospace PLC/Warton
	G-TSAR	Beech 58 Baron	Czar Aviation Ltd
	G-TSFT	PA-28-161 Warrior II	SFT Aviation Ltd (G-BLDJ)/Bournemouth
	G-TSGJ	PA-28-181 Archer II	Golf Juliet Flying Club
	G-TSIX	AT-6C Harvard IIA (111836)	J. Zemlik/Breighton
	G-TSMI	R. Commander 114	J. J. J. C. Herbaux
	G-TTAM	Taylor JT.2 Titch	C. H. Morris
	G-TTEL	PA-E23 Aztec 250D	Target Technology Electronics Ltd
			(G-BBXE)
	G-TTHC	Robinson R-22B	North West Auto Engineering
	G-TUBS	Beech 65-80 Queen Air	A. H. Bowers (G-ASKM)
	G-TUDR	Cameron V-77 balloon	Jacques W. Soukup Enterprises Ltd
	G-TUGG	PA-18 Super Cub 150	Ulster Gliding Club Ltd/Bellarena
	G-TUKE	Robin DR.400/160	Tukair/Headcorn
	G-TURB	D.31 Turbulent	A. Ryan-Fecitt
	G-TURK	Cameron 80 Sultan SS balloon	Forbes Europe Inc/France
	G-TURN	Steen Skybolt	M. Hammond
	G-TVIJ	CCF Harvard IV (T-6J) (28521)	R. W. Davies (G-BSBE)
	G-TVMM	Cessna 310Q	TVMM Aviation (G-CETA/G-BBIM)
	G-TVPA	AS.355F-1 Twin Squirrel	Thames Valley Police Authority (G-BPRI)
	G-TVSI	Campbell Cricket	C. Smith (G-AYHH)
	G-TVTV	Cameron 90 TV SS balloon	Ckameron Balloons Ltd
	G-TWEL	PA-28-181 Archer II	Universal Salvage (Holdings) Ltd
	G-TWEY	Colt 69A balloon	British Telecom Thameswey
	G-TWIN	PA-44-180 Seminole	Bonus Aviation Ltd/Cranfield
	G-TWIZ	R. Commander 114	B. C. Cox & K. E. Kirkland
	G-TWTD	Hawker Sea Hurricane IB	Hawker Restorations Ltd
		(AE977)	
	G-TYGA	AA-5B Tiger	Hovemere Ltd (G-BHNZ)/Biggin Hill
	G-TYRE	Cessna F.172M	Staverton Flying Services Ltd
	G-UAPA	Robin DR.400/140B	Aeromarine Ltd
	G-UAPO	Ruschmeyer R.90-230RG	Iberian Investments Ltd
	G-UBAC	Short SD3-60 Variant 100	BAC Leasing Ltd (G-BMLD)
	G-UBBE	Cameron Clown SS balloon	Cameron Balloons Ltd
	G-UDAY	Robinson R-22B	Elmar Plant Hire Ltd
	G-UEST	Bell 206B JetRanger 2	Leisure & Retail Consultants Ltd
			(G-RYOB/G-BLWU)

Reg.	Type	Owner or Operator	Notes
G-UFLY	Cessna F.150H	Westair Flying Services Ltd (G-AVVY)/Blackpool	
G-UIDA	Aero Designs Star-Lite SL.1	I. J. Widger (G-BRKK)	
G-UIDE	Jodel D.120	S. T. Gilbert/Popham	
G-UILD	Grob G.109B	Runnymede Consultants Ltd	
G-UILE	Lancair 320	R. J. Martin	
G-UKAC	BAe 146-300	Air UK Ltd/Stansted	
G-UKAG	BAe 146-300	Air UK Ltd/Stansted	
G-UKFA	Fokker 100	Air UK Ltd/Stansted	
G-UKFB	Fokker 100	Air UK Ltd/Stansted	
G-UKFC	Fokker 100	Air UK Ltd/Stansted	
G-UKFD	Fokker 100	Air UK Ltd/Stansted	
G-UKFE	Fokker 100	Air UK Ltd/Stansted	
G-UKFF	Fokker 100	Air UK Ltd/Stansted	
G-UKFG	Fokker 100	Air UK Ltd/Stansted	
G-UKFH	Fokker 100	Air UK Ltd/Stansted	
G-UKFI	Fokker 100	Air UK Ltd/Stansted	
G-UKFJ	Fokker 100	Air UK Ltd/Stansted	
G-UKHP	BAe 146-300	Air UK Ltd/Stansted	
G-UKID	BAe 146-300	Air UK Ltd/Stansted	
G-UKJF	BAe 146-100	Air UK Ltd/Stansted	
G-UKLC	Boeing 737-42C	K.L.M.	
G-UKLD	Boeing 737-42C	K.L.M.	
G-UKLF	Boeing 737-42C	K.L.M.	
G-UKLG	Boeing 737-42C	K.L.M.	
G-UKLH	Boeing 767-39HER	Leisure International Airways Ltd *Caribbean Star*	
G-UKLI	Boeing 767-39HER	Leisure International Airways Ltd *Atlantic Star*	
G-UKLM	Sikorsky S-76B	KLM ERA Helicopters BV/Norwich	
G-UKLU	Sikorsky S-76B	KLM ERA Helicopters BV/Norwich	
G-UKRB	Colt 105A balloon	Virgin Airship & Balloon Co Ltd	
G-UKRC	BAe 146-300	Air UK Ltd (G-BSMR)/Stansted	
G-UKSC	BAe 146-300	Air UK Ltd/Stansted	
G-UKTA	Fokker 50	Air UK Ltd *City of Norwich*/Stansted	
G-UKTB	Fokker 50	Air UK Ltd *City of Aberdeen*/Stansted	
G-UKTC	Fokker 50	Air UK Ltd *City of Bradford*/Stansted	
G-UKTD	Fokker 50	Air UK Ltd *City of Leeds*/Stansted	
G-UKTE	Fokker 50	Air UK Ltd *City of Hull*/Stansted	
G-UKTF	Fokker 50	Air UK Ltd *City of York*/Stansted	
G-UKTG	Fokker 50	Air UK Ltd/*City of Durham*/Stansted	
G-UKTH	Fokker 50	Air UK Ltd/*City of Amsterdam*/Stansted	
G-UKTI	Fokker 50	Air UK Ltd/*City of Stavanger*/Stansted	
G-ULAB	Robinson R-22B	Bradmore Helicopter Leasing	
G-ULIA	Cameron V-77 balloon	J. & R. Bayly	
G-ULPS	Everett Srs 1 gyroplane	The Aziz Corporation Ltd (G-BMNY)	
G-UMBO	Thunder Ax7-77A balloon	Virgin Airship & Balloon Co Ltd	
G-UMMI	PA-31-310 Turbo Navajo	Everts Balloon Co Ltd (G-BGSO)	
G-UNDY	Cessna 340	Morris Cohen (Underwear) Ltd (G-BBNR)	
G-UNIK	AB-206B JetRanger 2	RCR Aviation Ltd (G-TPPH/G-BCYP)	
G-UNIP	Cameron Oil Container SS balloon	Flying Pictures (Balloons) Ltd	
G-UNIT	Partenavia P.68B	Phlight Aviation Ltd (G-BCNT)/Coventry	
G-UNRL	Lindstrand LBL-21A balloon	Virgin Balloon & Airship Co. Ltd	
G-UORO	Shaw Europa	D. Dufton	
G-UPCC	Robinson R-22B	Deltair Ltd (G-MUSS)/Liverpool	
G-UPDN	Cameron V-65 balloon	R. J. O. Evans	
G-UPHL	Cameron 80 Concept SS balloon	Uphill Motor Co Ltd	
G-UPMW	Robinson R-22B	Catto Helicopters	
G-UPPP	Colt 77A balloon	M. Williams	
G-UPPY	Cameron DP-80 airship	Jacques W. Soukup Enterprises Ltd	
G-UPUP	Cameron V-77 balloon	S. F. Burden	
G-UROP	Beech 95-B55 Baron	Pooler International Ltd/Sleap	
G-URRR	Air Command 582 Sport	L. Armes	
G-USAM	Cameron Uncle Sam SS balloon	Jacques W. Soukup Enterprises Ltd	
G-USGB	Colt 105A balloon	Virgin Airship & Balloon Co. Ltd	
G-USIL	Thunder Ax7-77 balloon	Capital Balloon Club Ltd	
G-USMC	Cameron 90 Chestie SS balloon	Jacques W. Soukup Enterprises Ltd	
G-USSR	Cameron 90 Doll SS balloon	Jacques W. Soukup Enterprises Ltd	
G-USSY	PA-28-181 Archer II	Western Air Training Ltd/Thruxton	
G-USTI	Cameron H-34 balloon	Allen & Harris Ltd	
G-USTV	Messerschmitt Bf.109G-2 (6)	Imperial War Museum/Duxford	
G-USTY	FRED Srs 2	K. Jones	

Notes	Reg.	Type	Owner or Operator
	G-UTSI	Rand KR-2	K. B. Gutridge
	G-UTSY	PA-28R-201 Arrow III	D. G. Perry/Stapleford
	G-UTZY	SA.341G Gazelle 1	MW Helicopters Ltd (G-BKLV)
	G-UZEL	SA.341G Gazelle 1	S. E. Hobbs (UK) Ltd (G-BRNH)
	G-UZLE	Colt 77A balloon	Flying Pictures (Balloons) Ltd
	G-VAEL	Airbus A.340-311	Virgin Atlantic Airways Ltd *Maiden Toulouse*
	G-VAGA	PA-15 Vagabond	D. A. Crompton
	G-VAJT	M.S.894E Rallye 220GT	R. W. B. Rolfe
	G-VANS	Vans RV-4	T. R. Grief
	G-VANZ	Vans RV-6A	S. J. Baxter
	G-VARG	Varga 2150A Kachina	B. F. Hill
	G-VAUN	Cessna 340	H. E. Peacock
	G-VBUS	Airbus A.340-311	Virgin Atlantic Airways Ltd *Lady in Red*
	G-VCJH	Robinson R-22B	Great Northern Helicopters Ltd
	G-VCSI	Rotorway Executive	Qual-Rect Ltd
	G-VDIR	Cessna T.310R	Thornhill Music Ltd
	G-VEGA	Slingsby T.65A Vega (BGA2729)	C. H. Griffiths
	G-VELA	SIAI-Marchetti S.205-22R	D. P. & P. A. Dawson
	G-VENI	D.H.112 Venom FB.50 (WE402)	Lindsay Wood Promotions Ltd/Bournemouth
	G-VERA	GY-201 Minicab	D. K. Shipton
	G-VETS	Enstrom 280C-UK	Southern Air Ltd (G-FSDC/G-BKTG)
	G-VFAB	Boeing 747-4Q8	Virgin Atlantic Airways Ltd *Lady Penelope*
	G-VFLY	Airbus A.340-311	Virgin Atlantic Airways Ltd *Dragon Lady*
	G-VGIN	Boeing 747-243B	Virgin Atlantic Airways Ltd *Scarlet Lady*
	G-VHFA	PA-23 Aztec 250	Martini Airport Services (G-BZFE/G-AZFE)
	G-VHOT	Boeing 747-4Q8	Virgin Atlantic Airways Ltd *Tubular Belle*
	G-VIBA	Cameron DP-80 airship	Jacques W. Soukup Enterprises Ltd
	G-VICC	PA-28-161 Warrior II	Design Publications Ltd (G-JFHL)
	G-VICE	Hughes 369E	Nunkeeling Ltd
	G-VICI	D.H.112 Venom FB.50	Lindsay Wood Promotions Ltd/Bournemouth
	G-VICM	Beech F33C Bonanza	Charles W. Michie Ltd
	G-VIDI	D.H.112 Venom FB.50 (WE275)	Lindsay Wood Promotions Ltd/Bournemouth
	G-VIEW	Vinten-Wallis WA-116/100	K. H. Wallis
	G-VIIA	Boeing 777-236	British Airways
	G-VIIB	Boeing 777-236	British Airways
	G-VIIC	Boeing 777-236	British Airways
	G-VIID	Boeing 777-236	British Airways
	G-VIIE	Boeing 777-236	British Airways
	G-VIKE	Bellanca 1730A Viking	Peter Dolan & Co Ltd
	G-VIKY	Cameron A-120 balloon	D. W. Pennell
	G-VIPI	BAe 125 Srs 800B	Yeates of Leicester Ltd
	G-VIPP	PA-31-350 Navajo Chieftain	Capital Trading Aviation Ltd (G-OGRV/G-BMPX)
	G-VIRG	Boeing 747-287B	Virgin Atlantic Airways Ltd *Maiden Voyager*
	G-VITE	Robin R.1180T	G-VITE Flying Group
	G-VIVA	Thunder Ax7-65 balloon	G. C. Ludlow
	G-VIXN	D.H.110 Sea Vixen FAW.2 (XS587) ★	P. G. Vallance Ltd/Charlwood
	G-VIZZ	Sportavia RS.180 Sportsman	Exeter Fournier Group
	G-VJCB	Agusta A.109A-II	J. C. Bamford Excavators Ltd (G-BOUA)
	G-VJET	Avro 698 Vulcan B.2 (XL426)	Vulcan Restoration Trust/Southend
	G-VJFK	Boeing 747-238B	Virgin Atlantic Airways Ltd *Boston Belle*
	G-VJIM	Colt 77 Jumbo Jim SS balloon	L. V. Mastis
	G-VLAD	Yakovlev Yak-50	W. J. J. Kamper
	G-VLAX	Boeing 747-238B	Virgin Atlantic Airways Ltd *California Girl*
	G-VLCN	Avro 698 Vulcan B.2	C. Walton Ltd/Bruntingthorpe
	G-VMAX	Mooney M.20K	Glidegold Ltd
	G-VMDE	Cessna P.210N	Royton Express Deliveries (Welwyn) Ltd
	G-VMIA	Boeing 747-123	Virgin Atlantic Airways Ltd (G-HIHO) *Spirit of Sir Freddie*
	G-VMJM	SOCATA TB.10 Tobago	J. H. Michaels (G-BTOK)/Denham
	G-VMPR	D.H.115 Vampire T.11	J. N. Kerr & J. Jones
	G-VNOM	D.H.112 Venom FB.50	A. S. Topen
	G-VOAR	PA-28-181 Archer III	Aeronaval Ltd
	G-VODA	Cameron N-77 balloon	Racal Telecom PLC
	G-VOID	PA-28RT-201 Arrow IV	Newbus Aviation Ltd
	G-VOLT	Cameron N-77 balloon	National Power

Reg.	Type	Owner or Operator	Notes
G-VOYG	Boeing 747-283B	Virgin Atlantic Airways Ltd (G-BMGS) *Shady Lady*	
G-VPII	Evans VP-2	V. D. J. Hitchings (G-EDIF)	
G-VPSJ	Shaw Europa	J. D. Bean	
G-VRVI	Cameron O-90 balloon	Cooling Services Ltd	
G-VSBC	Beech B200 Super King Air	Vickers Shipbuilding & Engineering Ltd/Walney Island	
G-VSKY	Airbus A.340-311	Virgin Atlantic Airways Ltd *China Girl*	
G-VSOP	Cameron 60 Bottle SS balloon	J. R. Parkington & Co Ltd	
G-VTII	D.H.115 Vampire T.11 (WZ507)	J. Turnbull & ptnrs/Cranfield	
G-VTOL	H.S. Harrier T.52 ★	Brooklands Museum of Aviation/ Weybridge	
G-VULC	Avro 698 Vulcan B.2A (XM655) ★	Radarmoor Ltd/Wellesbourne	
G-VVBK	PA-34-200T Seneca II	Computaplane Ltd (G-BSBS/G-BDRI)	
G-VVIP	Cessna 421C	Capital Trading Aviation Ltd (G-BMWB)	
G-VYGR	Colt 120A balloon	The Ballooning Experience Ltd	
G-WAAC	Cameron N-56 balloon	N. P. Hemsley	
G-WACA	Cessna F.152 II	Wycombe Air Centre Ltd	
G-WACB	Cessna F.152 II	Wycombe Air Centre Ltd	
G-WACE	Cessna F.152 II	Wycombe Air Centre Ltd	
G-WACF	Cessna 152 II	Wycombe Air Centre Ltd	
G-WACG	Cessna F.152 II	Wycombe Air Centre Ltd	
G-WACH	Cessna FA.152 II	Wycombe Air Centre Ltd	
G-WACI	Beech 76 Duchess	Wycombe Air Centre Ltd	
G-WACJ	Beech 76 Duchess	Wycombe Air Centre Ltd	
G-WACK	Short SD3-60 Variant 100	Loganair Ltd/British Airways (G-BMAJ)	
G-WACL	Cessna F.172N	Wycombe Air Centre Ltd (G-BHGG)	
G-WACO	Waco UPF-7	RGV (Aircraft Services) & Co/Staverton	
G-WACP	PA-28 Cherokee 180	Wycombe Air Centre Ltd (G-BBPP)	
G-WACR	PA-28 Cherokee 180	Wycombe Air Centre Ltd (G-BCZF)	
G-WACT	Cessna F.152 II	Plymouth School of Flying Ltd (G-BKFT)	
G-WACU	Cessna FA.152	Wycombe Air Centre Ltd (G-BJZU)	
G-WACW	Cessna 172P	Wycombe Air Centre Ltd	
G-WACY	Cessna F.172P	Wycombe Air Centre Ltd	
G-WACZ	Cessna F.172M	Wycombe Air Centre Ltd (G-BCUK)	
G-WAFC	Cessna F.150M	Willowair Flying Club Ltd (G-BDFI)	
G-WAGI	Robinson R-22B	J. Wagstaff	
G-WAIR	PA-32-301 Saratoga	Thorne Aviation	
G-WAIT	Cameron V-77 balloon	C. P. Brown	
G-WALS	Cessna A.152	Redhill Flying Club	
G-WALT	Cameron Flying Castle SS balloon	Cameron Balloons Ltd	
G-WARD	Taylor JT.1 Monoplane	R. P. J. Hunter	
G-WARE	PA-28-161 Warrior II	W. J. Ware	
G-WARK	Schweizer 269C	J. & J. Havakin	
G-WARP	Cessna 182F	L. Rawson (G-ASHB)	
G-WARR	PA-28-161 Warrior II	T. J. & G. M. Laundy	
G-WASH	Noble 120 balloon	Noble Adventures Ltd	
G-WASP	Brantly B.2B	W. C. Evans & M. L. Morris (G-ASXE)	
G-WATH	Colt 77A balloon	Ballooning Adventures Ltd	
G-WATS	PA-34-220T Seneca III	G-WATS Aviation Ltd (G-BOVJ)	
G-WATT	Cameron Cooling Tower SS balloon	National Power	
G-WATZ	PA-28-151 Warrior	Air Nova/Liverpool	
G-WAVE	Grob G.109B	M. L. Murdoch/Cranfield	
G-WAZZ	Pitts S-1S Special	T. A. Shears (G-BRRP)/White Waltham	
G-WBAT	Wombat gyroplane	C. D. Julian (G-BSID)	
G-WBMG	Cameron N Ele-90 SS balloon	WBMG Environmental Communications (G-BUYV)	
G-WBPR	BAe 125 Srs 800B	Trusthouse Forte PLC/Heathrow	
G-WBTS	Falconar F-11	W. C. Brown (G-BDPL)	
G-WCAT	Colt Flying Mitt SS balloon	Interline Develoments Ltd	
G-WCEI	M.S.894E Rallye 220GT	R. A. L. Lucas (G-BAOC)	
G-WDEB	Thunder Ax-7-77 balloon	W. de Bock	
G-WEAC	BN-2A Mk III-2 Trislander	Keen Leasing Ltd (G-BEFP)	
G-WEEZ	Mooney M.20J	Weyland Ltd	
G-WELI	Cameron N-77 balloon	M. A. Shannon	
G-WELL	Beech E90 King Air	CEGA Aviation Ltd/Goodwood	
G-WELS	Cameron N-65 balloon	K. J. Vickery	
G-WEND	PA-28RT-201 Arrow IV	Chingford Magnetic Signs	
G-WERY	SOCATA TB.20 Trinidad	WERY Flying Group/Sherburn	
G-WEST	Agusta A.109A	Westland Helicopters Ltd/Yeovil	
G-WESX	CFM Streak Shadow	D. J. Sagar	

Notes	Reg.	Type	Owner or Operator
	G-WETI	Cameron N-31 balloon	C. A. Butter & J. J. T. Cooke
	G-WFFW	PA-28-161 Warrior II	N. F. Duke
	G-WFRD	Bell 206L-4 LongRanger	Wickford Development Co Ltd
	G-WGAL	Bell 206B JetRanger 3	Watkiss Group Aviation Ltd (G-OICS)
	G-WGCL	Aero Commander 685	Cooper Aeiral Surveys Ltd/Sandtoft
	G-WGCS	PA-18 Super Cub 95	S. C. Thompson
	G-WGSC	Pilatus PC-6/B2-H4 Turbo Porter	D. M. Ponny
	G-WHAT	Colt 77A balloon	C. Wolstenholme
	G-WHFO	Colt 10 Bottle SS balloon	Virgin Airship & Balloon Co Ltd (G-BUCN)
	G-WHIM	Colt 77A balloon	D. L. Morgan
	G-WHIR	Montgomerie-Bensen B.8MR	A. P. Barden (G-BROT)
	G-WHIZ	Pitts S-1 Special	K. M. McLeod
	G-WHOG	CFM Streak Shadow	B. R. Cannell
	G-WILD	Pitts S-1T Special	S. W. Knox
	G-WILY	Rutan LongEz	B. Wronski & W. S. Allen
	G-WIMP	Colt 56A balloon	C. Wolstenholme Wimp
	G-WINE	Thunder Ax7-77Z balloon	R. Brooker
	G-WINK	AA-5B Tiger	B. St J. Cooke
	G-WINS	PA-32 Cherokee Six 300	Cheyenne Ltd
	G-WIRE	AS.355F-1 Twin Squirrel	National Grid Co PLC (G-CEGB/G-BLJL)
	G-WIRL	Robinson R-22B	C. A. Rosenberg
	G-WISH	Lindstrand LBL Cake SS balloon	Oxford Promotions (UK) Ltd
	G-WIZA	Robinson R-22B	Burman Aviation Ltd (G-PERL)/Cranfield
	G-WIZD	Lindstrand LBL-180A balloon	T. H. Wilson
	G-WIZO	PA-34-220T Seneca III	Focusfar Ltd
	G-WIZZ	AB-206B JetRanger 2	Lateq Aviation Ltd/Booker
	G-WLLY	Bell 206A JetRanger	J. W. F. Ashworth (G-RODY/G-ROGR/ G-AXMM)
	G-WMAA	MBB Bo 105DBS/4	Bond Helicopters Ltd (G-PASB/G-BDMC)
	G-WMCC	BAe Jetstream 3102	Maersk Air/British Airways (G-TALL)/ Birmingham
	G-WMPA	AS.355F-2 Twin Squirrel	W. Midlands Police Authority/Birmingham
	G-WMTM	AA-5B Tiger	T. & W. E. Menham/Biggin Hill
	G-WOLF	PA-28 Cherokee 140	N. B. Savage
	G-WOOD	Beech 95-B55A Baron	T. D. Broadhurst (G-AYID)/Sleap
	G-WOOL	Colt 77A balloon	A. P. Woolhouse
	G-WORK	Thunder Ax10-180 S2 balloon	T. J. Bucknall}
	G-WOTG	BN-2T Turbine Islander	RAF Sport Parachute Association (G-BJYT)
	G-WOZA	PA-32RT-300 Lance II	O. C. Kruppa (G-BYBB)/Germany
	G-WRCF	Beech 200 Super King Air	Air Foyle Executive Ltd/Luton
	G-WREN	Pitts S-2A Special	Northamptonshire School of Flying Ltd/Sywell
	G-WRFM	Enstrom 280C-UK Shark	Skywalker Enterprises (G-CTSI/ G-BKIO)/Shoreham
	G-WRIT	Thunder Ax7-77A balloon	G. Pusey
	G-WSEC	Enstrom F-28C	M. J. Easy (G-BONF)
	G-WSFT	PA-23 Aztec 250F	SFT Aviation Ltd (G-BTHS)/Bournemouth
	G-WSKY	Enstrom 280C-UK-2 Shark	GTS Engineering (Coventry) Ltd (G-BEEK)
	G-WULF	WAR Focke-Wulf Fw.190 (08)	P. C. Logsdon
	G-WVBF	Lindstrand LBL-210A balloon	Virgin Balloon Flights Ltd
	G-WWAS	PA-34-220T Seneca III	A. Smith (G-BPPB)
	G-WWII	V.S.379 Spitfire XIV (SM832)	Patina Ltd/Duxford
	G-WWWG	Shaw Europa	C. F. Williams-Wynne
	G-WYCH	Cameron 90 Witch SS balloon	Jacques W. Soukup Enterprises Ltd
	G-WYMP	Cessna F.150J	L. Scattergood & R. Hall (G-BAGW)
	G-WYNN	Rand KR-2	W. Thomas
	G-WYNS	Aero Designs Pulsar XP	H. E. Perkins
	G-WYNT	Cameron N-56 balloon	Jacques W. Soukup Enterprises Ltd
	G-WYPA	MBB Bo 105DBS/4	W. Yorkshire Police Authority
	G-WYZZ	Air Command 532 Elite	C. H. Gem (G-BPAK)
	G-WZZZ	Colt AS-56 airship	Lindstrand Balloons Ltd
	G-XALP	Schweizer 269C	R. F. Jones
	G-XANT	Cameron N-105 balloon	Flying Pictures (Balloons) Ltd
	G-XARV	ARV Super 2	P. R. Snowden (G-OPIG/G-BMSJ)
	G-XCEL	AS.355F-1 Twin Squirrel	Tri-Ventures Group Ltd (G-HBAC/G-HJET)
	G-XCUB	PA-18 Super Cub 150	M. C. Barraclough
	G-XIIX	Robinson R-22B	J. Hayward
	G-XLXL	Robin DR.400/160	Reinsurance Flying Group (G-BAUD)
	G-XPOL	AS.355F-1 Twin Squirrel	Aeromega Ltd (G-BPRF)
	G-XPXP	Aero Designs Pulsar XP	B. J. Edwards
	G-XRAY	Rand KR-2	R. S. Smith

Reg.	Type	Owner or Operator	Notes
G-XRMC	BAe 125 Srs 800B	RMC Group Services Ltd	
G-XSFT	PA-23 Aztec 250F	SFT Aviation Ltd (G-CPPC/G-BGBH)/ Bournemouth	
G-XSKY	Cameron N-77 balloon	Ballooning World Ltd	
G-XTRA	Extra EA.230	Firebird Aerobatics Ltd/Booker	
G-XVIE	V.S.361 Spitfire LF.XVIe (TB252)	Historic Flying Ltd	
G-XXIV	AB-206B JetRanger 3	Hampton Printing (Bristol) Ltd	
G-XXVI	Sukhoi Su-26M	A. N. Onn & T. R. G. Barnaby	
G-YAKA	Yakovlev Yak-50	J. Griffen	
G-YAKI	Yakovlev Yak-52	Yak One Ltd/White Waltham	
G-YAKL	Yakovlev Yak-50	Bar-Belle Aviation	
G-YAKS	Yakovlev Yak-52	Two Bees Associates Ltd	
G-YANK	PA-28-181 Archer II	G-YANK Flying Group	
G-YAWW	PA-28RT-201T Turbo Arrow IV	Barton Aviation Ltd	
G-YBAA	Cessna FR.172J	H. Norman	
G-YEAR	Mini-500	D. J. Waddington	
G-YELL	Murphy Rebel	A. D. Keen	
G-YEOM	PA-31-350 Navajo Chieftain	Foster Yeoman Ltd/Exeter	
G-YEWS	Rotorway Executive 152	D. G. Pollard	
G-YIII	Cessna F.150L	Skyviews & General Ltd/Sherburn	
G-YJBM	Airbus A.320-231	Airtours International Airways Ltd (G-IEAF)	
G-YKSZ	Yakovlev Yak-52	J. N. & C. J. Carter	
G-YMBO	Robinson R-22M Mariner	Coax Connectors Ltd	
G-YMYM	Lindstrand LBL Ice Cream SS balloon	Lindstrand Balloons Ltd	
G-YNOT	D.62B Condor	T. Littlefair (G-AYFH)	
G-YOGI	Robin DR.400/140B	R. M. & A. M. Gosling (G-BDME)	
G-YORK	Cessna F.172M	P. J. Smith	
G-YPSY	Andreasson BA-4B	C. W. N. Huke & A-L. N. M. Cox	
G-YRAT	VPM M.16 Tandem Trainer	A. J. Unwin	
G-YRIL	Luscombe 8E Silvaire	C. Potter	
G-YROI	Air Command Commander 532	W. B. Lumb	
G-YROS	Montgomerie-Bensen B.8M	C. Tuxworth	
G-YROY	Montgomerie-Bensen B.8MR	R. D. Armishaw	
G-YSFT	PA-23 Aztec 250F	SFT Aviation Ltd (G-BEJT)/Bournemouth	
G-YSKY	PA-31-350 Navajo Chieftain	Hawkair	
G-YTWO	Cessna F.172M	Sherburn Aero Club Ltd	
G-YUGO	H.S.125 Srs 1B/R-522	RCR Aviation Ltd (G-ATWH)	
G-YULL	PA-28 Cherokee 180E	Lansdowne Chemical Co (G-BFAJ)/ Kidlington	
G-YUMM	Cameron N-90 balloon	Wunderbar Ltd	
G-YUPI	Cameron N-90 balloon	H. C. Wright	
G-YURO	Shaw Europa	Europa Aviation Ltd	
G-YVET	Cameron V-90 balloon	K. J. Foster	
G-ZACH	Robin DR.400/100	A. P. Wellings/Sandown (G-FTIO)	
G-ZAIR	Zenair CH 601HD	C. B. Shaw	
G-ZAND	Robinson R-22B	Sloane Helicopters Ltd/Sywell	
G-ZAPC	Short SD3-30 Variant 100	Titan Airways Ltd (G-RNMO/G-BFZW)	
G-ZAPD	Short SD3-60 Variant 100	Titan Airways Ltd (G-OLGW/ G-BOFK)/Stansted	
G-ZAPG	Short SD3-60 Variant 100	Titan Airways Ltd (G-CPTL/ G-BOFI)/Stansted	
G-ZAPI	Cessna 500 Citation	Titan Airways Ltd (G-BHTT)/Stansted	
G-ZAP	BAe 146-200QC	Titan Airways Ltd (G-BTIA/G-PRIN)/ Stansted	
G-ZARA	Nord 3400	D. E. Bain & ptnrs	
G-ZARI	AA-5B Tiger	C. A. Ringrose (G-BHVY)	
G-ZAZA	PA-18 Super Cub 95	Airbourne Taxi Services Ltd	
G-ZBRA	Thunder Ax10-160 balloon	Zebra Ballooning Ltd	
G-ZEBO	Thunder Ax8-105 S2 balloon	E. Herndon	
G-ZEBR	Colt 210A balloon	Zebra Ballooning Ltd	
G-ZEIN	Slingsby T.67M-260	R.V. Aviation Ltd/Bournemouth	
G-ZEPI	Colt GA-42 gas airship	Lindstrand Balloons Ltd (G-ISPY/G-BPRB)	
G-ZERO	AA-5B Tiger	G-ZERO Syndicate	
G-ZGBE	Beech 95-58PA Baron	GB Express Ltd (G-BNKL)/Bournemouth	
G-ZIGG	Robinson R-22B	Uriah Woodhead & Son Ltd	
G-ZIGI	Robin DR.400/180	Golf India Flying Group	
G-ZIPI	Robin DR.400/180	Stahl Engineering Co Ltd/Headcorn	
G-ZIPY	Wittman W.8 Tailwind	M. J. Butler	
G-ZLIN	Z.526 Trener Master	N. J. Arthur	
G-ZLYN	Z.526F Trener	Air V8 Ltd	

Notes	Reg.	Type	Owner or Operator
	G-ZOOL	Cessna FRA.152	Falcon Flying Services (G-BGXZ)/ Biggin Hill
	G-ZORO	Shaw Europa	N. T. Read
	G-ZSFT	PA-23 Aztec 250	SFT Aviation Ltd (G-SALT/G-BGTH)/ Bournemouth
	G-ZSOL	Zlin Z.50L	T. W. Cassells
	G-ZULU	PA-28-161 Warrior II	S. F. Tebby & Son
	G-ZUMP	Cameron N-77 balloon	Allen & Harris Ltd
	G-ZUMY	Task Silhouette	P. J. Wells
	G-ZZIP	Mooney M.20J	D. A. H. Dixon
	G-ZZZA	Boeing 777-236	British Airways
	G-ZZZB	Boeing 777-236	British Airways
	G-ZZZC	Boeing 777-236	British Airways *Sir Charles Edward Kingsford-Smith*
	G-ZZZD	Boeing 777-236	British Airways *Wilbur/Orville Wright*
	G-ZZZE	Boeing 777-236	British Airways

Military to Civil Cross-Reference

Serial carried	Civil identity	Serial carried	Civil identity
07 (Fr AF)	G-BKPT	18393 (RCAF)	G-BCYK
3 (Luftwaffe)	G-BAYV	18671 (671 RCAF)	G-BNZC
5 (Croatian AF)	G-BEDB	20310 (310 RCAF)	G-BSBG
6 (Luftwaffe)	G-USTV	20385 (385 RCAF)	G-BGPB
19 (USN)	G-BTCC	28521 (TA-521 USAF)	G-TVIJ
23 (USAAC)	N49272	30146 (Yugoslav Army)	G-BSXD
26 (US)	G-BAVO	30149 (Yugoslav Army)	G-SOKO
27 (USN)	G-BRVG	31923 (USAAC)	G-BRHP
27 (CIS)	G-OYAK	31952 (USAAC)	G-BRPR
27 (USAAC)	G-AGYY	34037 (USAAF)	N9115Z
27 (USAAC)	G-NZSS	39624 (D-39 USAAF)	G-BVMH
28 (USAAC)	N8162G	53319 (319/RB USN)	G-BTDP
41/BA (USN)	G-DDMV	54137 (69 USN)	G-CTKL
44 (K-33 USAAF)	G-BJLH	56321 (U-AB RNorAF)	G-BKPY
45 (Aeronavale)	G-BHFG	80425 (USN)	N7235C
69 (CIS)	G-BTZB	86711 (USN)	N4845V
75	G-AFDX	88297 (29 USN)	G-FGID
77 (Soviet AF)	G-BTCU	88439 (USN)	N55JP
85 (USAAF)	G-BTBI	91007 (USAF)	G-NASA
112 (USAAC)	G-BSWC	93542 (LTA-542 USAF)	G-BRLV
114 (Luftwaffe)	G-BSMD	111836 (JZ-6 USN)	G-TSIX
118 (USAAC)	G-BSDS	115042 (TA-042 USAF)	G-BGHU
120 (Fr AF)	G-AZGC	115302 (TP USAAF)	G-BJTP
143 (Fr AF)	G-MSAL	115684 (D-C USAAF)	G-BKVM
152/17	G-ATJM	121714	NX700HL
157 (Fr AF)	G-AVEB	121752 (USN)	N800H
168	G-BFDE	124485 (DF-A USAAF)	G-BEDF
177 (Irish AC)	G-BLIW	126922 (JS/937 USN)	G-RAID
180 (USN)	G-BRSK	151632 (USAAF)	G-BWGR
208 (USN)	N75664	1532008 (08 China AAF)	G-BVFW
209 (RJordanAF	G-BVLM	18-2001 (USAAF)	G-BIZV
243 (Iraq A F)	G-BTTA	217786 (USAAF)	G-BRTK
320 (USAAC)	G-BPMD	219993	N139DP
379 (USAAC)	G-ILLE	224211 (M2-Z USAF)	G-BPMP
385 (RCAF)	G-BGPB	226671 (MX-X USAAF)	N47DD
390 (USAAC)	G-BTRJ	231983 (USAAF)	F-BDRS
422-15	G-AVJO	236800 (A-44 USAAF)	G-BHPK
441 (USN)	G-BTFG	269097 (USAF)	G-BTWR
442 (USN)	G-BPTB	314887 (USAAF)	G-AJPI
503 (Hungarian AF)	G-BRAM	315509 (W7 USAAF)	G-BHUB
781-25 (Span AF)	G-BRSH	329405 (A-23 USAAF)	G-BCOB
781-32 (Span AF)	G-BPDM	329417 (USAAF)	G-BDHK
800 (RJordan AF)	G-BOOM	329471 (F-44 USAAF)	G-BGXA
854 (USAAC)	G-BTBH	329601 (D-44 USAAF)	G-AXHR
855 (USAAC)	N56421	329854 (R-44 USAAF)	G-BMKC
897 (USN)	G-BJEV	329934 (B-72 USAAF)	G-BCPH
1164 (USAAC)	G-BKGL	330485 (C-44 USAAF)	G-AJES
1197	G-BPVE	332038 (A-24 USAAF)	G-LIVH
1411 (US Coast Guard)	N444M	40-1766	N50755
1420 (Polish AF)	G-BMZF	408133 (B-44 USAAF)	G-BDCD
2345	G-ATVP	413573 (B6-K USAF)	N6526D
2807 (VE-103 USN)	G-BHTH	454467 (J-44 USAAF)	G-BILI
3066	G-AETA	454537 (J-04 USAAF)	G-BFDL
3398 (FrAF)	G-BFYO	461748	G-BHDK
3460	G-BMFG	463221 (G4-S USAAF)	G-BTCD
4253/18	G-BFPL	472216 (AJ-L USAAF)	G-BIXL
5492	G-PENY	472773 (AJ-C USAF)	G-SUSY
5894	G-BFVH	473877	N167F
6247 (Polish AF)	G-OMIG	474008 (VF-R USAF)	N51RR
7198/18	G-AANJ	474425 (OC-G USAF)	N11T
7797 (USAAF)	G-BGFAF	479744 (M-49 USAAF)	G-BGPD
8178 (FU-178 USAF)	G-SABR	479766 (D-63 USAAF)	G-BKHG
8449M	G-ASWJ	480015 (M-44 USAAF)	G-AKIB
14863 (USAAF)	G-BGOR	480133 (B-44 USAAF)	G-BDCD
16136 (205 USN)	G-BRUJ	480321 (H-44 USAAF)	G-FRAN
16693 (693 RCAF)	G-BLPG	480480 (E-44 USAAF)	G-BECN
18013 (RCAF)	G-TRIC	480636 (A-58 USAAÚF)	G-AXHP

Serial carried	Civil identity	Serial carried	Civil identity
480752 (E-39 USAAF)	G-BCXJ	K3661	G-BURZ
483009 (USAF)	G-BPSE	K3731	G-RODI
41-33275 (CE USAAC)	G-BICE	K4235 (KX-H)	G-AHMJ
42-58678 (IY USAAC)	G-BRIY	K5054	G-BRDV
42-78044 (USAAC)	G-BRXL	K5414 (XV)	G-AENP
44-30861	N9089Z	K8203	G-BTVE
44-79609 (PR USAAF)	G-BHXY	L2301	G-AIZG
44-80594 (USAAF)	G-BEDJ	N1854	G-AIBE
44-83184	G-RGUS	N2308 (HP-B)	G-AMRK
45-49192	N47DD	N4877 (VX-F)	G-AMDA
51-1371 (VF-S USAAF)	NL1051S	N5182	G-APUP
542447	G-SCUB	N5195	G-ABOX
542474 (R-184)	G-PCUB	N6181	G-EBKY
51 11701A (AF258 USAF)	G-BSZC	N6290	G-BOCK
51-14526 (USAF)	G-BRWB	N6452	G-BIAU
51-15227 (USN)	G-BKRA	N6466	G-ANKZ
51-15673 (USAF)	G-CUBI	N6797	G-ANEH
52-8543	G-BUKY	N6847	G-APAL
54-21261 (USAF)	N33VC	N6848	G-BALX
607327 (09-L USAAF)	G-ARAO	N6965 (FL-J)	G-AJTW
A16-199 (SF-R RAAF)	G-BEOX	N6985	G-AHMN
A-17-48 (RAAF)	G-BPHR	N9191	G-ALND
A68-192 (RAAF)	G-HAEC	N9192 (RCO-N)	G-BSTJ
A-806 (Swiss AF)	G-BTLL	N9389	G-ANJA
A1325	G-BVGR	P5865 (LE-W)	G-BKCK
A8226	G-BIDW	P6382	G-AJRS
B1807	G-EAVX	R-163 (RNethAF)	G-BIRH
B2458	G-BPOB	R-167 (RNethAF)	G-LION
B4863 (G)	G-BLXT	R1914	G-AHUJ
B6401	G-AWYY	S1287	G-BEYB
B7270	G-BFCZ	S1579	G-BBVO
C1904 (Z)	G-PFAP	T5424	G-AJOA
C3011 (S)	G-SWOT	T5493	G-ANEF
C4994	G-BLWM	T5672	G-ALRI
C9533	G-BUWE	T5854	G-ANKK
D5397/17	G-BFXL	T5879	G-AXBW
D7889	G-AANM	T6099	G-AOGR
D8084	G-ACAA	T6313	G-AHVU
D8096 (D)	G-AEPH	T6818 (44)	G-ANKT
D8781	G-ECKE	T6991	G-ANOR
E-15 (RNethAF)	G-BIYU	T7230	G-AFVE
E3B-143 (Span AF)	G-JUNG	T7281	G-ARTL
E3B-153 (781-75 Span AF)	G-BPTS	T7404 (04)	G-ANMV
E449	G-EBJE	T7471	G-AJHU
EM-01 (Spanish AF)	G-AAOR	T7842	G-AMTF
F141 (G)	G-SEVA	T7909	G-ANON
F235 (B)	G-BMDB	T9707	G-AKKR
F904	G-EBIA	U-80 (Swiss AF)	G-BUKK
F938	G-EBIC	U-0247 (Class B identity)	G-AGOY
F943	G-BIHF	U-108 (Swiss AF)	G-BJAX
F943	G-BKDT	U-110 (Swiss AF)	G-PTWO
F5447 (N)	G-BKER	U-142 (Swiss AF)	G-BONE
F5459 (Y)	G-INNY	U-1214	G-DHVV
F8010	G-BDWJ	U-1215 (215)	G-HELV
F8614	G-AWAU	U-1230 (Swiss AF)	G-DHZZ
G-48-1 (Class B)	G-ALSX	V-54 (Swiss AF)	G-BVSD
H5199	G-ADEV	V1075	G-AKPF
— (I-492 USAAC)	G-BPUD	V3388	G-AHTW
J-1149 (Swiss AF)	G-SWIS	V9281 (RU-M)	G-BCWL
J-1605 (Swiss AF)	G-BLID	V9441 (AR-A)	G-AZWT
J-1614 (Swiss AF)	G-BLIE	V9673 (MA-J)	G-LIZY
J-1758 (Swiss AF)	G-BLSD	W5856 (A2A)	G-BMGC
J7326	G-EBQP	W9385 (YG-L)	G-ADND
J9941 (57)	G-ABMR	Z5722	G-BPIV
K1786	G-AFTA	Z7015 (7-L)	G-BKTH
K2050	G-ASCM	Z7197	G-AKZN
K2059	G-PFAR	Z7381 (XR-T)	G-HURI
K2075	G-BEER	AE977	G-TWTD
K2567	G-MOTH	AP506	G-ACWM
K2572	G-AOZH	AP507 (KX-P)	G-ACWP
K2587	G-BJAP	AR213 (PR-D)	G-AIST
K3215	G-AHSA	AR501 (NN-D)	G-AWII

MILITARY/CIVIL CROSS REFERENCE

Serial carried	Civil identity	Serial carried	Civil identity
AR614	G-BUWA	RH377	G-ALAH
BB807	G-ADWO	RL962	G-AHED
BE417 (AE-K)	G-HURR	RM221	G-ANXR
BM597 (PR-O)	G-MKVB	RN201	G-BKSP
BW853	G-BRKE	RN218 (N)	G-BBJI
DE208	G-AGYU	RR299 (HT-E)	G-ASKH
DE623	G-ANFI	RT486	G-AJGJ
DE970	G-AOBJ	RT520	G-ALYB
DE992	G-AXXV	RW386	G-BXVI
DF128 (RCO-U)	G-AOJJ	SM832 (YB-A)	G-WWII
DF155	G-ANFV	SX336	G-BRMG
DF198	G-BBRB	TA634 (8K-K)	G-AWJV
DE470	G-ANMY	TA719	G-ASKC
DG590	G-ADMW	TB252 (GW-H)	G-XVIE
DK431	G-ASTL	TD248 (D)	G-OXVI
DR613	G-AFJB	TE184	G-MXVI
EM720	G-AXAN	TE566 (DU-A)	G-BLCK
EM903	G-APBI	TJ569	G-AKOW
EN224	G-FXII	TJ672	G-ANIJ
EP120 (AE-A)	G-LFVB	TJ704	G-ASCD
FB226 (MT-A)	G-BDWM	TS423	G-DAKS
FE695	G-BTXI	TS798	G-AGNV
FE992 (K-T)	G-BDAM	TW439	G-ANRP
FH153	G-BBHK	TW467 (ROD-F)	G-ANIE
FR870 (GA-S)	N1009N	TW511	G-APAF
FR886	G-BDMS	TW517	G-BDFX
FT239	G-BIWX	TW536 (TS-V)	G-BNGE
FT391	G-AZBN	TW591	G-ARIH
FX301 (FD-NQ)	G-JUDI	TW641	G-ATDN
HB275	G-BKGM	TX183	G-BSMF
HB751	G-BCBL	VF512 (PF-M)	G-ARRX
HH982	G-AHXE	VF516	G-ASMZ
HM580	G-ACUU	VF526	G-ARXU
KB889 (NA-I)	G-LANC	VF548	G-ASEG
KG391 (AG)	G-BVOL	VL348	G-AVVO
KL161 (VO-B)	N88972	VL349	G-AWSA
KZ321	G-HURY	VM360	G-APHV
LB294	G-AHWJ	VP955	G-DVON
LB375	G-AHGW	VR192	G-APIT
LF858	G-BLUZ	VR249 (FA-EY)	G-APIY
LZ551/G	G-DHXX	VR259	G-APJB
LZ766	G-ALCK	VS356	G-AOLU
MD497	G-ANLW	VS610 (K-L)	G-AOKL
MH434 (MN-B)	G-ASJV	VS623	G-AOKZ
MJ627 (9G-P)	G-BMSB	VX118	G-ASNB
MJ730 (GN-?)	G-HFIX	VX147	G-AVIL
MK732 (OU-U)	G-HVDM	VX653	G-BUCM
ML407 (OU-V)	G-LFIX	VX926	G-ASKJ
ML417 (2I-T)	G-BJSG	VZ304 (A-T)	G-MKVI
MP425	G-AITB	VZ467	G-METE
MT-11 (RBelg AF)	G-BRFU	VZ638	G-JETM
MT438	G-AREI	VZ728	G-AGOS
MT928 (ZX-M)	G-BKMI	WA576	G-ALSS
MV293 (OI-C)	G-SPIT	WA577	G-ALST
MV370 (EB-Q)	G-FXIV	WB531	G-BLRN
MW800 (HF-V)	G-BSHW	WB571 (34)	G-AOSF
NJ695	G-AJXV	WB585 (RCU-X)	G-AOSY
NJ703	G-AKPI	WB588 (D)	G-AOTD
NJ719	G-ANFU	WB660	G-ARMB
NL750	G-AOBH	WB702	G-AOFE
NM181	G-AZGZ	WB703	G-ARMC
NP181	G-AOAR	WB763 (14)	G-BBMR
NP184	G-ANYP	WD286 (J)	G-BBND
NP303	G-ANZJ	WD292	G-BCRX
NX611 (YF-C)	G-ASXX	WD305	G-ARGG
NZ5648	NX55JP	WD363 (5)	G-BCIH
PL965	G-MKVI	WD379 (K)	G-APLO
PL983	G-PRXI	WD388	G-BDIC
PP972 (6M-D)	G-BUAR	WD413	G-BFIR
PV202 (VZ-M)	G-TRIX	WE275	G-VIDI
RG333	G-AIEK	WE402	G-VENI
RG333	G-AKEZ	WE569	G-ASAJ

Serial carried	Civil identity	Serial carried	Civil identity
WF877	G-BPOA	XL426	G-VJET
WG307	G-BCYJ	XL502	G-BMYP
WG316	G-BCAH	XL572	G-HNTR
WG348	G-BBMV	XL573	G-BVGH
WG350	G-BPAL	XL600	G-BVWN
WG422 (16)	G-BFAX	XL613	G-BVMB
WG472	G-AOTY	XL809	G-BLIX
WG718	G-BRMA	XL812	G-SARO
WJ237 (113/O)	G-BLTG	XL954	N4232C
WJ358	G-ARYD	XM405 (42)	G-TORE
WJ680 (C-T)	G-BURM	XM553	G-AWSV
WJ945	G-BEDV	XM575	G-BLMC
WK163	G-BVWC	XM655	G-VULC
WK511 (RN)	G-BVBT	XM685 (513/PO)	G-AYZJ
WK522	G-BCOU	XM693	G-TIMM
WK611	G-ARWB	XM819	G-APXW
WK622	G-BCZH	XN351	G-BKSC
WK628	G-BBMW	XN435	G-BGBU
WL505	G-FBIX	XN437	G-AXWA
WL626	G-BHDD	XN441	G-BGKT
WM167	G-LOSM	XN461	G-BVBE
WP321 (750/CU)	G-BRFC	XN629	G-BVEG
WP788	G-BCHL	XN637	G-BKOU
WP790	G-BBNC	XP254	G-ASCC
WP800 (2)	G-BCXN	XP279	G-BWKK
WP808	G-BDEU	XP282	G-BGTC
WP809 (778)	G-BVTX	XP355	G-BEBC
WP835	G-BDCB	XR240	G-BDFH
WP843 (F)	G-BDBP	XR241	G-AXRR
WP856 (904 RN)	G-BVWP	XR267	G-BJXR
WP857 (24)	G-BDRJ	XR442	G-HRON
WP903	G-BCGC	XR486	G-RWWW
WP971	G-ATHD	XR537	G-NATY
WP977	G-BHRD	XR724	G-BTSY
WR410 (N)	G-BLKA	XR944	G-ATTB
WT333	G-BVXC	XR991	G-MOUR
WT933	G-ALSW	XS101	G-GNAT
WV198	G-BJWY	XS230	G-BVWF
WV493 (A-P)	G-BDYG	XS451	G-LTNG
WV666 (O-D)	G-BTDH	XS452 (BT)	G-BPFE
WV686	G-BLFT	XS587 (252/V)	G-VIXN
WV740	G-BNPH	XS770	G-HRHI
WV783	G-ALSP	XT788 (442)	G-BMIR
WZ507	G-VTII	XV268	G-BVER
WZ662	G-BKVK	XW289	G-JPVA
WZ711	G-AVHT	XW635	G-AWSW
WZ868 (H CUAS)	G-ARMF	XW784	G-BBRN
WZ876	G-BBWN	XX469	G-BNCL
XE489	G-JETH	ZA647	G-EHIL
XE677	G-HHUN	2+1 (Luftwaffe)	G-SYFW
XE685	G-GAII	4+ (Luftwaffe)	G-BSLX
XF375	G-BUEZ	6+ (Luftwaffe)	G-USTV
XF516	G-BVVC	07 (Russian AF)	G-BMJY
XF597 (AH)	G-BKFW	08+ (Luftwaffe)	G-WULF
XF690	G-MOOS	14+ (Luftwaffe)	G-BBII
XF785	G-ALBN	F+IS (Luftwaffe)	G-BIRW
XF836 (J-G)	G-AWRY	BU+CC (Luftwaffe)	G-BUCC
XF877 (JX)	G-AWVF	BU+CK (Luftwaffe)	G-BUCK
XG452	G-BRMB	CC+43 (Luftwaffe)	G-CJCI
XG496	G-ANDX	LG+01 (Luftwaffe)	G-AYSJ
XG547	G-HAPR	LG+03 (Luftwaffe)	G-AEZX
XG775	G-DHWW	NJ+C11 (Luftwaffe)	G-ATBG
XH568	G-BVIC	RF+16 (Luftwaffe)	G-PTWO
XJ389	G-AJJP	S5-B06 (Luftwaffe)	G-BSFB
XJ729	G-BVGE	TA+RC (Luftwaffe)	G-BPHZ
XJ763	G-BKHA	6J+PR (Luftwaffe)	G-AWHB
XK416	G-AYUA	7A+WN (Luftwaffe)	G-AZMH
XK417	G-AVXY	97+04 (Luftwaffe)	G-APVF
XK482	G-BJWC	— (Luftwaffe)	G-BOML
XK895 (19/CU)	G-SDEV	— (HL-67/8 USAAF)	G-AKAZ
XK896	G-RNAS	146-11042 (7)	G-BMZX
XK940	G-AYXT	146-11083 (5)	G-BNAI

Toy Balloons

Notes	Reg.	Type	Owner or Operator
	G-FYAN	Williams	M. D. Williams
	G-FYAO	Williams	M. D. Williams
	G-FYAU	Williams MK 2	M. D. Williams
	G-FYAV	Osprey Mk 4E2	C. D. Egan & C. Stiles
	G-FYAZ	Osprey Mk 4D2	M. A. Roblett
	G-FYBP	European E.84PW	D. Eaves
	G-FYBR	Osprey Mk 4G2	A. J. Pugh
	G-FYBU	Portswood Mk XVI	M. A. Roblett
	G-FYBX	Portswood Mk XVI	I. Chadwick
	G-FYCC	Osprey Mk 4G2	A. Russell
	G-FYCL	Osprey Mk 4G	P. J. Rogers
	G-FYCV	Osprey Mk 4D	M. Thomson
	G-FYCZ	Osprey Mk 4D2	P. Middleton
	G-FYDC	European EDH-1	D. Eaves & H. Goddard
	G-FYDF	Osprey Mk 4D	K. A. Jones
	G-FYDI	Williams Westwind Two	M. D. Williams
	G-FYDN	European 8C	P. D. Ridout
	G-FYDO	Osprey Mk 4D	N. L. Scallan
	G-FYDP	Williams Westwind Three	M. D. Williams
	G-FYDS	Osprey Mk 4D	N. L. Scallan
	G-FYDW	Osprey Mk 4B	R. A. Balfre
	G-FYEB	Rango Rega	N. H. Ponsford
	G-FYEI	Portswood Mk XVI	A. Russell
	G-FYEJ	Rango NA.24	N. H. Ponsford
	G-FYEK	Unicorn UE.1C	D. & D. Eaves
	G-FYEL	European E.84Z	D. Eaves
	G-FYEO	Eagle Mk 1	M. E. Scallon
	G-FYEV	Osprey Mk 1C	M. E. Scallen
	G-FYEZ	Firefly Mk 1	M. E. & N. L. Scallan
	G-FYFA	European E.84LD	D. Goddard & D. Eaves
	G-FYFG	European E.84DE	D. Eaves
	G-FYFH	European E.84DS	D. Eaves
	G-FYFI	European E.84DS	M. Stelling
	G-FYFJ	Williams Westland 2	M. D. Williams
	G FYFN	Osprey Saturn 2	J. & M. Woods
	G-FYFT	Rango NA-32BC	Rango Kite & Balloon Co
	G-FYFV	Saffrey Grand Edinburgh	I. G. & G. M. McIntosh
	G-FYFW	Rango NA-55	Rango Kite & Balloon Co
	G-FYFY	Rango NA-55RC	A. M. Lindsay
	G-FYGA	Rango NA-50RC	Rango Kite & Balloon Co
	G-FYGB	Rango NA-105RC	Rango Kite & Balloon Co
	G-FYGC	Rango NA-42B	L. J. Wardle
	G-FYGI	Rango NA-55RC	Advertair Ltd
	G-FYGJ	Airspeed 300	N. Wells
	G-FYGK	Rango NA-42POC	Rango Balloon & Kite Co
	G-FYGL	Glowball	J. J. Noble

Microlights

Reg.	Type	Notes	Reg.	Type	Notes
G-MBAA	Hiway Skytrike Mk 2		G-MBHA	Trident Trike	
G-MBAB	Hovey Whing-Ding II		G-MBHE	American Aerolights Eagle	
G-MBAD	Weedhopper JC-24A		G-MBHH	Flexiform Sealander	
G-MBAF	R. J. Swift 3			Skytrike	
G-MBAL	Hiway Demon		G-MBHK	Flexiform Skytrike	
G-MBAN	American Aerolights Eagle		G-MBHP	American Aerolights	
G-MBAR	Skycraft Scout			Eagle II	
G-MBAS	Typhoon Tripacer 250		G-MBHT	Chargus T.250	
G-MBAU	Hiway Skytrike		G-MBHX	Pterodactyl Ptraveller	
G-MBAW	Pterodactyl Ptraveller		G-MBHZ	Pterodactyl Ptraveller	
G-MBAZ	Rotec Rally 2B		G-MBIA	Flexiform Sealander	
G-MBBB	Skycraft Scout 2			Skytrike	
G-MBBG	Weedhopper JC-24B		G-MBIO	American Aerolights Eagle	
G-MBBM	Eipper Quicksilver MX			Z Drive	
G-MBBT	Ultrasports Tripacer 330		G-MBIT	Hiway Demon Skytrike	
G-MBBY	Flexiform Sealander		G-MBIU	Hiway Super Scorpion	
G-MBCA	Chargus Cyclone T.250		G-MBIV	Flexiform Skytrike	
G-MBCI	Hiway Skytrike		G-MBIW	Hiway Demon Tri-Flyer	
G-MBCJ	Mainair Sports Tri-Flyer			Skytrike	
G-MBCK	Eipper Quicksilver MX		G-MBIY	Ultra Sports	
G-MBCL	Hiway Demon Triflyer		G-MBIZ	Mainair Tri-Flyer	
G-MBCM	Hiway Demon 175		G-MBJA	Eurowing Goldwing	
G-MBCO	Flexiform Sealander		G-MBJD	American Aerolights Eagle	
	Buggy		G-MBJE	Airwave Nimrod	
G-MBCU	American Aerolights Eagle		G-MBJF	Hiway Skytrike Mk II	
G-MBCX	Airwave Nimrod 165		G-MBJG	Airwave Nimrod	
G-MBCZ	Chargus Skytrike 160		G-MBJI	Southern Aerosports	
G-MBDD	Skyhook Skytrike			Scorpion	
G-MBDE	Flexiform Skytrike		G-MBJK	American Aerolights Eagle	
G-MBDF	Rotec Rally 2B		G-MBJL	Airwave Nimrod	
G-MBDG	Eurowing Goldwing		G-MBJM	Striplin Lone Ranger	
G-MBDH	Hiway Demon Triflyer		G-MBJN	Electraflyer Eagle	
G-MBDI	Flexiform Sealander		G-MBJO	Birdman Cherokee	
G-MBDJ	Flexiform Sealander		G-MBJP	Hiway Skytrike	
	Triflyer		G-MBJR	American Aerolights Eagle	
G-MBDM	Southdown Sigma Trike		G-MBJT	Hiway Skytrike II	
G-MBDU	Chargus Titan 38		G-MBJU	American Eagle 215B	
G-MBDZ	Eipper Quicksilver MX		G-MBJZ	Eurowing Catto CP.16	
G-MBEA	Hornet Nimrod		G-MBKC	Southdown Lightning	
G-MBED	Chargus Titan 38		G-MBKS	Hiway Skytrike 160	
G-MBEG	Eipper Quicksilver MX		G-MBKT	Mitchell Wing B.10	
G-MBEJ	Electraflyer Eagle		G-MBKU	Hiway Demon Skytrike	
G-MBEN	Eipper Quicksilver MX		G-MBKW	Pterodactyl Ptraveller	
G-MBEP	American Aerolights Eagle		G-MBKY	American Aerolight Eagle	
G-MBES	Skyhook Cutlass		G-MBKZ	Hiway Skytrike	
G-MBET	MEA Mistral Trainer		*G-MBLA	Flexiform Skytrike	
G-MBEU	Hiway Demon T.250		G-MBLB	Eipper Quicksilver MX	
G-MBEV	Chargus Titan 38		G-MBLF	Hiway Demon 195 Tri	
G-MBFA	Hiway Skytrike 250			Pacer	
G-MBFE	American Aerolights Eagle		G-MBLJ	Eipper Quicksilver MX	
G-MBFF	Southern Aerosports		G-MBLK	Southdown Puma	
	Scorpion		G-MBLM	Hiway Skytrike	
G-MBFK	Hiway Demon		G-MBLN	Pterodactyl Ptraveller	
G-MBFM	Hiway Hang Glider		G-MBLO	Sealander Skytrike	
G-MBFU	Ultrasports Tripacer		G-MBLR	Ultrasports Tripacer	
G-MBFX	Hiway Skytrike 250		G-MBLU	Southdown Lightning	
G-MBFY	Mirage II			L.195	
G-MBFZ	M. S. S. Goldwing		G-MBLV	Ultrasports Hybrid	
G-MBGA	Solar Wings Typhoon		G-MBLY	Flexiform Sealander Trike	
G-MBGB	American Aerolights Eagle		G-MBLZ	Southern Aerosports	
G-MBGF	Twamley Trike			Scorpion	
G-MBGJ	Hiway Skytrike Mk 2		G-MBME	American Aerolights	
G-MBGK	Electra Flyer Eagle			Eagle Z Drive	
G-MBGP	Solar Wings Typhoon		G-MBMG	Rotec Rally 2B	
	Skytrike		G-MBMJ	Mainair Tri-Flyer	
G-MBGS	Rotec Rally 2B		G-MBMO	Hiway Skytrike 160	
G-MBGX	Southdown Lightning				
G-MBGY	Hiway Demon Skytrike				

Reg.	Type	Notes	Reg.	Type	Notes
G-MBMR	Ultrasports Tripacer Typhoon		G-MBUK	Mainair 330 Tri Pacer	
G-MBMS	Hornet		G-MBUO	Southern Aerosports Scorpion	
G-MBMT	Mainair Tri-Flyer		G-MBUP	Hiway Skytrike	
G-MBMU	Eurowing Goldwing		G-MBUZ	Wheeler Scout Mk II	
G-MBMW	Solar Wings Typhoon		G-MBVA	Volmer Jensen VJ-23E	
G-MBMZ	Sealander Tripacer		G-MBVC	American Aerolights Eagle	
G-MBNA	American Aerolights Eagle		G-MBVK	Ultraflight Mirage II	
G-MBNG	Hiway Demon Skytrike		G-MBVL	Southern Aerosports Scorpion	
G-MBNH	Southern Airsports Scorpion		G-MBVS	Hiway Skytrike	
G-MBNJ	Eipper Quicksilver MX		G-MBVV	Hiway Skytrike	
G-MBNK	American Aerolights Eagle		G-MBVW	Skyhook TR.2	
G-MBNN	Southern Microlight Gazelle P.160N		G-MBWA	American Aerolights Eagle	
G-MBNT	American Aerolights Eagle		G-MBWB	Hiway Skytrike	
G-MBNY	Steer Terror Fledge II		G-MBWE	American Aerolights Eagle	
G-MBOA	Flexiform Hilander		G-MBWF	Mainair Triflyer Striker	
G-MBOD	American Aerolights Eagle		G-MBWG	Huntair Pathfinder	
G-MBOE	Solar Wing Typhoon Trike		G-MBWH	Designability Duet I	
G-MBOF	Pakes Jackdaw		G-MBWL	Huntair Pathfinder	
G-MBOH	Microlight Engineering Mistral		G-MBWP	Ultrasports Trike	
			G-MBWT	Huntair Pathfinder	
G-MBOK	Dunstable Microlight		G-MBWW	Southern Aerosports Scorpion	
G-MBOM	Hiway Hilander				
G-MBON	Eurowing Goldwing Canard		G-MBWX	Southern Aerosports Scorpion	
G-MBOR	Chotia 460B Weedhopper		G-MBWY	American Aerolights Eagle	
G-MBOT	Hiway 250 Skytrike		G-MBXE	Hiway Skytrike	
G-MBOU	Wheeler Scout		G-MBXJ	Hiway Demon Skytrike	
G-MBOX	American Aerolights Eagle		G-MBXK	Ultrasports Puma	
G-MBPA	Weedhopper Srs 2		G-MBXO	Sheffield Trident	
G-MBPD	American Aerolights Eagle		G-MBXR	Hiway Skytrike 150	
G-MBPG	Hunt Skytrike		G-MBXT	Eipper Quicksilver MX2	
G-MBPJ	Moto-Delta		G-MBXW	Hiway Skytrike	
G-MBPM	Eurowing Goldwing		G-MBXX	Ultraflight Mirage II	
G-MBPN	American Aerolights Eagle		G-MBYD	American Aerolights Eagle	
G-MBPO	Volnik Arrow		G-MBYH	Maxair Hummer	
G-MBPI I	Hiway Demon		G-MBYI	Ultraflight Lazair	
G-MBPW	Weedhopper		G-MBYK	Huntair Pathfinder Mk 1	
G-MBPX	Eurowing Goldwing		G-MBYL	Huntair Pathfinder 330	
G-MBPY	Ultrasports Tripacer 330		G-MBYM	Eipper Quicksilver MX	
G-MBRB	Electraflyer Eagle 1		G-MBYO	American Aerolights Eagle	
G-MBRD	American Aerolights Eagle		G-MBYR	American Aerolights Eagle	
G-MBRE	Wheeler Scout		G-MBYS	Ultraflight Mirage II	
G-MBRH	Ultraflight Mirage Mk II		G-MBYT	Ultraflight Mirage II	
G-MBRM	Hiway Demon		G-MBYX	American Aerolights Eagle	
G-MBRS	American Aerolights Eagle		G-MBYY	Southern Aerosports Scorpion	
G-MBRV	Eurowing Goldwing				
G-MBSA	Ultraflight Mirage II		G-MBZB	Hiway Skytrike	
G-MBSD	Southdown Puma DS		G-MBZF	American Aerolights Eagle	
G-MBSF	Ultraflight Mirage II		G-MBZG	Twinflight Scorpion 2 seat	
G-MBSG	Ultraflight Mirage II		G-MBZH	Eurowing Goldwing	
G-MBSN	American Aerolights Eagle		G-MBZL	Weedhopper	
G-MBSS	Ultrasports Puma 2		G-MBZM	UAS Storm Buggy	
G-MBST	Mainair Gemini Sprint		G-MBZN	Ultrasports Puma	
G-MBSX	Ultraflight Mirage II		G-MBZP	Skyhook TR2	
G-MBTA	UAS Storm Buggy 5 Mk 2		G-MBZV	American Aerolights Eagle	
G-MBTB	Davies Tri-Flyer S		G-MBZZ	Southern Aerosports Scorpion	
G-MBTC	Weedhopper JC-24B				
G-MBTE	Hiway Demon		G-MGAG	Aviasud Mistral	
G-MBTF	Mainair Tri-Flyer Skytrike		G-MGGT	CFM Streak Shadow SAM	
G-MBTG	Mainair Gemini		G-MGOD	Medway Raven	
G-MBTH	Whittaker MW.4		G-MGOM	Medway Hybred 44XLR	
G-MBTI	Hovey Whing Ding		G-MGOO	Renegade Spirit UK Ltd	
G-MBTJ	Solar Wings Microlight		G-MGPD	Cycl Pegasus XL-R	
G-MBTO	Mainair Tri-Flyer 250		G-MGRW	Cyclone AX3/503	
G-MBTW	Raven Vector 600		G-MGUY	CFM Shadow Srs BD	
G-MBUA	Hiway Demon		G-MGWH	Thruster T.300	
G-MBUB	Horne Sigma Skytrike		G-MJAA	Ultrasports Tripacer	
G-MBUC	Huntair Pathfinder		G-MJAB	Ultrasports Skytrike	
G-MBUH	Hiway Skytrike		G-MJAD	Eipper Quicksilver MX	
G-MBUI	Wheeler Scout Mk I				

Reg.	Type	Notes	Reg.	Type	Notes
G-MJAE	American Aerolights Eagle		G-MJGV	Eipper Quicksilver MX2	
G-MJAF	Ultrasports Puma 440		G-MJGW	Solar Wings TrikeB	
G-MJAG	Skyhook TR1		G-MJHC	Ultrasports Tripacer 330	
G-MJAH	American Aerolights Eagle		G-MJHF	Skyhook Sailwing Trike	
G-MJAI	American Aerolights Eagle		G-MJHK	Hiway Demon 195	
G-MJAJ	Eurowing Goldwing		G-MJHM	Ultrasports Trike	
G-MJAL	Wheeler Scout 3		G-MJHN	American Aerolights Eagle	
G-MJAM	Eipper Quicklsilver MX		G-MJHR	Southdown Lightning	
G-MJAN	Hiway Skytrike		G-MJHU	Eipper Quicksilver MX	
G-MJAP	Hiway 160		G-MJHV	Hiway Demon 250	
G-MJAZ	Aerodyne Vector 610		G-MJHW	Ultrasports Puma 1	
G-MJBI	Eipper Quicksilver MX		G-MJHX	Eipper Quicksilver MX	
G-MJBK	Swallow AeroPlane Swallow B		G-MJHZ	Southdown Sailwings	
			G-MJIA	Flexiform Striker	
G-MJBL	American Aerolights Eagle		G-MJIB	Hornet 250	
G-MJBS	Ultralight Stormbuggy		G-MJIC	Ultrasports Puma 330	
G-MJBV	American Aerolights Eagle		G-MJIE	Hornet 330	
G-MJBX	Pterodactyl Ptraveller		G-MJIF	Mainair Triflyer	
G-MJBZ	Huntair Pathfinder		G-MJIJ	Ultrasports Tripacer 250	
G-MJCB	Hornet 330		G-MJIK	Southdown Sailwings Lightning	
G-MJCD	Sigma Tetley Skytrike				
G-MJCE	Ultrasports Tripacer		G-MJIN	Hiway Skytrike	
G-MJCI	Kruchek Firefly 440		G-MJIO	American Aerolights Eagle	
G-MJCJ	Hiway Spectrum		G-MJIR	Eipper Quicksilver MX	
G-MJCK	Southern Aerosports Scorpion		G-MJIZ	Southdown Lightning	
			G-MJJA	Huntair Pathfinder	
G-MJCL	Eipper Quicksilver MX		G-MJJB	Eipper Quicksilver MX	
G-MJCN	S.M.C. Flyer Mk 1		G-MJJF	Solar Wings Typhoon	
G-MJCU	Tarjani		G-MJJJ	Moyes Knight	
G-MJCW	Hiway Super Scorpion		G-MJJK	Eipper Quicksilver MX2	
G-MJCX	American Aerolights Eagle		G-MJJM	Birdman Cherokee Mk 1	
G-MJCZ	Southern Aerosports Scorpion 2		G-MJJN	Ultrasports Puma	
			G-MJJO	Flexiform Skytrike Dual	
G-MJDA	Hornet Trike Executive		G-MJJV	Wheeler Scoutá	
G-MJDE	Huntair Pathfinder		G-MJJX	Hiway Skytrike	
G-MJDG	Hornet Supertrike		G-MJJY	Tirith Firefly	
G-MJDH	Huntair Pathfinder		G-MJKB	Striplin Skyranger	
G-MJDJ	Hiway Skytrike Demon		G-MJKE	Mainair Triflyer 330	
G-MJDK	American Aerolights Eagle		G-MJKF	Hiway Demon	
G-MJDO	Southdown Puma 440		G-MJKG	John Ivor Skytrike	
G-MJDP	Eurowing Goldwing		G-MJKH	Eipper Quicksilver MX II	
G-MJDR	Hiway Demon Skytrike		G-MJKI	Eipper Quicksilver MX	
G-MJDU	Eipper Quicksilver àMX2		G-MJKJ	Eipper Quicksilver MX	
G-MJDW	Eipper Quicksilver MX		G-MJKO	Goldmarque 250 Skytrike	
G-MJEE	Mainair Triflyer Trike		G-MJKS	Mainair Triflyer	
G-MJEF	Gryphon 180		G-MJKV	Hornet	
G-MJEG	Eurowing Goldwing		G-MJKX	Ultralight Skyrider Phantom	
G-MJEH	Rotec Rally 2B		G-MJLA	Ultrasports Puma 2	
G-MJEJ	American Aerolights Eagle		G-MJLB	Ultrasports Puma 2	
G-MJEL	GMD-01 Trike		G-MJLH	American Aerolights Eagle 2	
G-MJEO	American Aerolights Eagle				
G-MJER	Flexiform Striker		G-MJLI	Hiway Demon Skytrike	
G-MJET	Stratos Prototype 3 Axis 1		G-MJLL	Hiway Demon Skytrike	
G-MJEX	Eipper Quicksilver MX		G-MJLR	Skyhook SK-1	
G-MJEY	Southdown Lightning		G-MJLS	Rotec Rally 2B	
G-MJFB	Flexiform Striker		G-MJLT	American Aerolights Eagle	
G-MJFD	Ultrasports Tripacer		G-MJLU	Skyhook	
G-MJFH	Eipper Quicksilver MX		G-MJLY	American Aerolights Eagle	
G-MJFI	Flexiform Striker		G-MJMA	Hiway Demon	
G-MJFJ	Hiway Skytrike 250		G-MJME	Ultrasports Tripacer Mega II	
G-MJFK	Flexiform Skytrike Dual				
G-MJFM	Huntair Pathfinder		G-MJMM	Chargus Vortex	
G-MJFO	Eipper Quicksilver MX		G-MJMP	Eipper Quicksilver MX	
G-MJFP	American Aerolights Eagle		G-MJMR	Solar Wings Typhoon	
G-MJFS	American Aerolights Eagle		G-MJMS	Hiway Skytrike	
G-MJFV	Ultrasports Tripacer		G-MJMT	Hiway Demon Skytrike	
G-MJFX	Skyhook TR-1		G-MJMW	Eipper Quicksilver MX2	
G-MJGE	Eipper Quicksilver MX		G-MJMX	Ultrasports Tripacer	
G-MJGG	Skyhook TR-1		G-MJNB	Hiway Skytrike	
G-MJGI	Eipper Quicksilver MX		G-MJNE	Hornet Supreme Dual Trike	
G-MJGN	Greenslade Monotrike				
G-MJGO	Barnes Avon Skytrike		G-MJNH	Skyhook Cutlass Trike	
G-MJGT	Skyhook Cutlass Trike				

Reg.	Type	Notes	Reg.	Type	Notes
G-MJNK	Hiway Skytrike		G-MJTM	Aerostructure Pipistrelle 2B	
G-MJNL	American Aerolights Eagle		G-MJTN	Eipper Quicksilver MX	
G-MJNM	American Aerolights Double Eagle		G-MJTO	Jordan Duet Srs 1	
G-MJNN	Ultraflight Mirage II		G-MJTP	Flexiform Striker	
G-MJNO	American Aerolights Double Eagle		G-MJTR	Southdown Puma DS Mk 1	
			G-MJTW	Eurowing Trike	
G-MJNR	Ultralight Solar Buggy		G-MJTX	Skyrider Phantom	
G-MJNS	Swallow AeroPlane Swallow B		G-MJTY	Huntair Pathfinder	
			G-MJTZ	Skyrider Airsports Phantom	
G-MJNT	Hiway Skytrike				
G-MJNU	Skyhook Cutlass		G-MJUC	MBA Tiger Cub 440	
G-MJNV	Eipper Quicksilver MX		G-MJUE	Southdown Lightning II	
G-MJNY	Skyhook Sabre Trike		G-MJUH	MBA Tiger Cub 440	
G-MJOC	Huntair Pathfinder		G-MJUI	Flexiform Striker	
G-MJOD	Rotec Rally 2B		G-MJUJ	Eipper Quicksilver Mk II	
G-MJOE	Eurowing Goldwing		G-MJUL	Southdown Puma Sprint	
G-MJOG	American Aerolights Eagle		G-MJUM	Flexiform Striker	
G-MJOI	Hiway Demon		G-MJUR	Skyrider Airsports Phantom	
G-MJOJ	Flexiform Skytrike				
G-MJOL	Skyhook Cutlass		G-MJUS	MBA Tiger Cub 440	
G-MJOM	Southdown Puma 40F		G-MJUT	Eurowing Goldwing	
G-MJOR	Solair Phoenix		G-MJUU	Eurowing Goldwing	
G-MJOS	Southdown Lightning 170		G-MJUV	Huntair Pathfinder 1	
G-MJOU	Hiway Demon 175		G-MJUW	MBA Tiger Cub 440	
G-MJOW	Eipper Quicksilver MX		G-MJUX	Skyrider Airsports Phantom	
G-MJPA	Rotec Rally 2B				
G-MJPC	American Aerolights Double Eagle		G-MJUZ	Dragon Srs 150	
			G-MJVA	Skyrider Airsports Phantom	
G-MJPD	Hiway Demon Skytrike				
G-MJPE	Hiway Demon Skytrike		G-MJVE	Hybred Skytrike	
G-MJPG	American Aerolights Eagle 430R		G-MJVF	CFM Shadow	
			G-MJVG	Hiway Skytrike	
G-MJPI	Flexiform Striker		G-MJVJ	Flexiform Striker Dual	
G-MJPK	Hiway Vulcan		G-MJVL	Flexiform Striker	
G-MJPO	Eurowing Goldwing		G-MJVM	Dragon 150	
G-MJPT	Dragon		G-MJVN	Ultrasports Puma 440	
G-MJPU	Solar Wings Typhoon		G-MJVP	Eipper Quicksilver MX II	
G-MJPV	Fipper Quicksilver MX		G-MJVR	Flexiforn Striker	
G-MJRD	Hiway Super Scorpion		G-MJVI	Eipper Quicksilver MX	
G-MJRE	Hiway Demon		G-MJVU	Eipper Quicksilver MX II	
G-MJRG	Ultrasports Puma		G-MJVV	Hornet Supreme Dual	
G-MJRI	American Aerolights Eagle		G-MJVW	Airwave Nimrod	
G-MJRK	Flexiform Striker		G-MJVX	Skyrider Phantom	
G-MJRL	Eurowing Goldwing		G-MJVY	Dragon Srs 150	
G-MJRN	Flexiform Striker		G-MJVZ	Hiway Demon Tripacer	
G-MJRO	Eurowing Goldwing		G-MJWB	Eurowing Goldwing	
G-MJRP	Mainair Triflyer 330		G-MJWD	Solar Wings Typhoon XL	
G-MJRR	Striplin Skyranger Srs 1		G-MJWF	Tiger Cub 440	
G-MJRS	Eurowing Goldwing		G-MJWG	MBA Tiger Cub	
G-MJRT	Southdown Lightning DS		G-MJWI	Flexiform Striker	
G-MJRU	MBA Tiger Cub 440		G-MJWJ	MBA Tiger Cub 440	
G-MJRX	Ultrasports Puma II		G-MJWK	Huntair Pathfinder	
G-MJSA	Mainair 2-Seat Trike		G-MJWN	Flexiform Striker	
G-MJSE	Skyrider Airsports Phantom		G-MJWR	MBA Tiger Cub 440	
			G-MJWS	Eurowing Goldwing	
G-MJSF	Skyrider Airsports Phantom		G-MJWU	Maxair Hummer TX	
			G-MJWV	Southdown Puma MS	
G-MJSL	Dragon 200		G-MJWW	MBA Super Tiger Cub 440	
G-MJSO	Hiway Skytrike		G-MJWZ	Ultrasports Panther XL	
G-MJSP	MBA Super Tiger Cub 440		G-MJXA	Flexiform Striker	
G-MJSS	American Aerolights Eagle		G-MJXB	Eurowing Goldwing	
G-MJST	Pterodactyl Ptraveler		G-MJXD	MBA Tiger Cub 440	
G-MJSV	MBA Tiger Cub		G-MJXE	Hiway Demon	
G-MJSY	Eurowing Goldwing		G-MJXF	MBA Tiger Cub 440	
G-MJSZ	DH Wasp		G-MJXJ	MBA Tiger Cub 440	
G-MJTC	Solar Wings Typhoon		G-MJXM	Hiway Skytrike	
G-MJTD	Gardner T-M Scout		G-MJXR	Huntair Pathfinder II	
G-MJTE	Skyrider Airsports Phantom		G-MJXS	Huntair Pathfinder II	
			G-MJXT	Phoenix Falcon 1	
G-MJTF	Gryphon Wing		G-MJXV	Flexiform Striker	
G-MJTL	Aerostructure Pipistrelle 2B		G-MJXX	Flexiform Striker Dual	
			G-MJXY	Hiway Demon Skytrike	

Reg.	Type	Notes	Reg.	Type	Notes
G-MJYA	Huntair Pathfinder		G-MMCY	Flexiform Striker	
G-MJYC	Ultrasports Panther XL Dual 440		G-MMCZ	Flexiform Striker	
			G-MMDC	Eipper Quicksilver MXII	
G-MJYD	MBA Tiger Cub 440		G-MMDE	Solar Wings Typhoon	
G-MJYF	Mainair Gemini Flash		G-MMDF	Southdown Lightning II	
G-MJYG	Skyhook Orion Canard		G-MMDJ	Solar Wings Typhoon	
G-MJYM	Southdown Puma Sprint		G-MMDK	Flexiform Striker	
G-‹MJYP	Mainair Triflyer 440		G-MMDN	Flexiform Striker	
G-MJYR	Catto CP.16		G-MMDO	Southdown Sprint	
G-MJYS	Southdown Puma Sprint		G-MMDP	Southdown Sprint	
G-MJYT	Southdown Puma Sprint		G-MMDR	Huntair Pathfinder II	
G-MJYV	Mainair Triflyer 2 Seat		G-MMDS	Ultrasports Panther XLS	
G-MJYW	Wasp Gryphon III		G-MMDU	MBA Tiger Cub 440	
G-MJYX	Mainair Triflyer		G-MMDV	Ultrasports Panther	
G-MJYY	Hiway Demon		G-MMDW	Pterodactyl Pfledgling	
G-MJZA	MBA Tiger Cub		G-MMDX	Solar Wings Typhoon	
G-MJZB	Flexiform Striker Dual		G-MMDZ	Flexiform Dual Strike	
G-MJZC	MBA Tiger Cub 440		G-MMEE	American Aerolights Eagle	
G-MJZD	Mainair Gemini Flash		G-MMEF	Hiway Super Scorpion	
G-MJZH	Southdown Lightning 195		G-MMEG	Eipper Quicksilver MX	
G-MJZJ	Hiway Cutlass Skytrike		G-MMEI	Hiway Demon	
G-MJZK	Southdown Puma Sprint 440		G-MMEJ	Flexiform Striker	
			G-MMEK	Solar Wings Typhoon XL2	
G-MJZL	Eipper Quicksilver MX II		G-MMEL	Solar Wings Typhoon XL2	
G-MJZO	Flexiform Striker		G-MMEN	Solar Wings Typhoon XL2	
G-MJZP	MBA Tiger Cub 440		G-MMEP	MBA Tiger Cub 440	
G-MJZT	Flexiform Striker		G-MMES	Southdown Puma Sprint	
G-MJZU	Flexiform Striker		G-MMET	Skyhook Sabre TR-1 Mk II	
G-MJZW	Eipper Quicksilver MX II		G-MMEW	MBA Tiger Cub 440	
G-MJZX	Maxair Hummer TX		G-MMEX	Solar Wings Sprint	
G-MMAC	Dragon Srs 150		G-MMEY	MBA Tiger Cub 440	
G-MMAE	Dragon Srs 150		G-MMEZ	Southdown Puma Sprint	
G-MMAG	MBA Tiger Cub 440		G-MMFC	Flexiform Striker	
G-MMAH	Eipper Quicksilver MX II		G-MMFD	Flexiform Striker	
G-MMAI	Dragon Srs 150		G-MMFE	Flexiform Striker	
G-MMAJ	Mainair Tri-Flyer 440		G-MMFG	Flexiform Striker	
G-MMAK	MBA Tiger Cub 440		G-MMFI	Flexiform Striker	
G-MMAL	Flexiform Striker Dual		G-MMFK	Flexiform Striker	
G-MMAM	MBA Tiger Cub 440		G-MMFL	Flexiform Striker	
G-MMAN	Flexiform Striker		G-MMFM	Piranha Srs 200	
G-MMAO	Southdown Puma Sprint		G-MMFN	MBA Tiger Cub 440	
G-MMAP	Hummer TX		G-MMFS	MBA Tiger Cub 440	
G-MMAR	Southdown Puma Sprint		G-MMFT	MBA Tiger Cub 440	
G-MMAT	Southdown Puma Sprint		G-MMFV	Tri-Flyer 440	
G-MMAU	Flexiform Rapier		G-MMFY	Flexiform Dual Striker	
G-MMAW	Mainair Rapier		G-MMFZ	AES Sky Ranger	
G-MMAX	Flexiform Striker		G-MMGA	Bass Gosling	
G-MMAZ	Southdown Puma Sprint		G-MMGB	Southdown Puma Sprint	
G-MMBD	Spectrum 330		G-MMGC	Southdown Puma Sprint	
G-MMBE	MBA Tiger Cub 440		G-MMGD	Southdown Puma Sprint	
G-MMBH	MBA Super Tiger Cub 440		G-MMGE	Hiway Super Scorpion	
G-MMBJ	Solar Wings Typhoon		G-MMGF	MBA Tiger Cub 440	
G-MMBL	Southdown Puma		G-MMGL	MBA Tiger Cub 440	
G-MMBN	Eurowing Goldwing		G-MMGN	Southdown Puma Sprint	
G-MMBS	Flexiform Striker		G-MMGP	Southdown Puma Sprint	
G-MMBT	MBA Tiger Cub 440		G-MMGS	Solar Wings Panther Dual	
G-MMBU	Eipper Quicksilver MX II		G-MMGT	Solar Wings Typhoon	
G-MMBV	Huntair Pathfinder		G-MMGU	Flexiform Sealander	
G-MMBX	MBA Tiger Cub 440		G-MMGX	Southdown Puma	
G-MMBY	Solar Wings Panther XL		G-MMHB	Skyhook TR-1 Pixie	
G-MMBZ	Solar Wings Typhoon P		G-MMHE	Southdown Puma Sprint	
G-MMCD	Southdown Lightning DS		G-MMHF	Southdown Puma Sprint	
G-MMCE	MBA Tiger Cub 440		G-MMHK	Hiway Super Scorpion	
G-MMCF	Solar Wings Panther 330		G-MMHL	Hiway Super Scorpion	
G-MMCG	Eipper Quicksilver MX I		G-MMHM	Goldmarque Gyr	
G-MMCI	Southdown Puma Sprint		G-MMHN	MBA Tiger Cub 440	
G-MMCJ	Flexiform Striker		G-MMHP	Hiway Demon	
G-MMCM	Southdown Puma Sprint		G-MMHR	Southdown Puma Sprint	
G-MMCO	Southdown Sprint		G-MMHS	SMD Viper	
G-MMCS	Southdown Puma Sprint		G-MMHT	Flexiform Viper	
G-MMCV	Solar Wings Typhoon III		G-MMHX	Hornet Invader 440	
G-MMCW	Southdown Puma Sprint		G-MMHY	Hornet Invader 440	
G-MMCX	MBA Super Tiger Cub 440		G-MMHZ	Solar Wings Typhoon XL	

Reg.	Type	Notes	Reg.	Type	Notes
G-MMIB	MEA Mistral		G-MMND	Eipper Quicksilver MX II-Q2	
G-MMIC	Luscombe Vitality		G-MMNF	Hornet	
G-MMIE	MBA Tiger Cub 440		G-MMNG	Solar Wings Typhoon XL	
G-MMIF	Wasp Gryphon		G-MMNN	Buzzard	
G-MMIH	MBA Tiger Cub 440		G-MMNS	Mitchell U-2 Super Wing	
G-MMII	Southdown Puma Sprint 440		G-MMNT	Flexiform Striker	
			G-MMNW	Mainair Tri-Flyer 330	
G-MMIJ	Ultrasports Tripacer		G-MMNX	Solar Wings Panther XL	
G-MMIL	Eipper Quicksilver MX II		G-MMOB	Southdown Sprint	
G-MMIM	MBA Tiger Cub 440		G-MMOD	MBA Tiger Cub 440	
G-MMIR	Mainair Tri-Flyer 440		G-MMOF	MBA Tiger Cub 440	
G-MMIV	Southdown Puma Sprint		G-MMOH	Solar Wings Typhoon XL	
G-MMIW	Southdown Puma Sprint		G-MMOI	MBA Tiger Cub 440	
G-MMIY	Eurowing Goldwing		G-MMOK	Solar Wings Panther XL	
G-MMJD	Southdown Puma Sprint		G-MMOL	Skycraft Scout R3	
G-MMJE	Southdown Puma Sprint		G-MMOO	Southdown Storm	
G-MMJF	Ultrasports Panther Dual 440		G-MMOW	Mainair Gemini Flash	
			G-MMOX	Mainair Gemini Flash	
G-MMJG	Mainair Tri-Flyer 440		G-MMOY	Mainair Gemini Sprint	
G-MMJJ	Solar Wings Typhoon		G-MMPG	Southdown Puma	
G-MMJM	Southdown Puma Sprint		G-MMPH	Southdown Puma Sprint	
G-MMJN	Eipper Quicksilver MX II		G-MMPI	Pterodactyl Ptraveller	
G-MMJT	Southdown Puma Sprint		G-MMPJ	Mainair Tri-Flyer 440	
G-MMJU	Hiway Demon		G-MMPL	Flexiform Dual Striker	
G-MMJV	MBA Tiger Cub 440		G-MMPN	Chargus T250	
G-MMJW	Southdown Puma Sprint		G-MMPO	Mainair Gemini Flash	
G-MMJX	Teman Mono-Fly		G-MMPT	SMD Gazelle	
G-MMJY	MBA Tiger Cub 440		G-MMPU	Ultrasports Tripacer 250	
G-MMJZ	Skyhook Pixie		G-MMPW	Airwave Nimrod	
G-MMKA	Ultrasports Panther Dual		G-MMPX	Ultrasports Panther Dual 440	
G-MMKC	Southdown Puma Sprint				
G-MMKD	Southdown Puma Sprint		G-MMPZ	Teman Mono-Fly	
G-MMKE	Birdman Chinook WT-11		G-MMRA	Mainair Tri-Flyer 250	
G-MMKG	Solar Wings Typhoon XL		G-MMRD	Skyhook Cutlass CD	
G-MMKH	Solar Wings Typhoon XL		G-MMRF	MBA Tiger Cub 440	
G-MMKI	Ultrasports Panther 330		G-MMRH	Hiway Demon	
G-MMKJ	Ultrasports Panther 330		G-MMRJ	Solar Wings Panther XL	
G-MMKK	Mainair Flash		G-MMRK	Ultrasports Panther XL	
G-MMKL	Mainair Flash		G-MMRL	Solar Wings Panther XL	
G-MMKM	Flexiform Dual Striker		G-MMHN	Southdown Puma Sprint	
G-MMKP	MBA Tiger Cub 440		G-MMRO	Mainair Gemini 440	
G-MMKR	Southdown Lightning DS		G-MMRP	Mainair Gemini	
G-MMKU	Southdown Puma Sprint		G-MMRT	Southdown Puma Sprint	
G-MMKV	Southdown Puma Sprint		G-MMRU	Tirith Firebird FB-2	
G-MMKW	Solar Wings Storm		G-MMRV	MBA Tiger Cub 440	
G-MMKZ	Ultrasports Puma 440		G-MMRW	Flexiform Dual Striker	
G-MMLB	MBA Tiger Cub 440		G-MMRX	Willmot J.W.1	
G-MMLE	Eurowing Goldwing SP		G-MMRY	Chargus T.250	
G-MMLF	MBA Tiger Cub 440		G-MMRZ	Ultrasports Panther Dual 440	
G-MMLH	Hiway Demon				
G-MMLK	MBA Tiger Cub 440		G-MMSA	Ultrasports Panther XL	
G-MMLM	MBA Tiger Cub 440		G-MMSC	Mainair Gemini	
G-MMLO	Skyhook Pixie		G-MMSE	Eipper Quicksilver MX	
G-MMLP	Southdown Sprint		G-MMSG	Solar Wings Panther XL-S	
G-MMLV	Southdown Puma 330		G-MMSH	Solar Wings Panther XL	
G-MMLX	Ultrasports Panther		G-MMSM	Mainair Gemini Flash	
G-MMMB	Mainair Tri-Flyer		G-MMSN	Mainair Gemini	
G-MMMD	Flexiform Dual Striker		G-MMSO	Mainair Tri-Flyer 440	
G-MMMG	Eipper Quicksilver MXL		G-MMSP	Mainair Gemini Flash	
G-MMMH	Hadland Willow		G-MMSR	MBA Tiger Cub 440	
G-MMMI	Southdown Lightning		G-MMSS	Solar Wings Panther 330	
G-MMMJ	Southdown Sprint		G-MMST	Southdown Puma Sprint	
G-MMMK	Hornet Invader		G-MMSV	Southdown Puma Sprint	
G-MMML	Dragon 150		G-MMSW	MBA Tiger Cub 440	
G-MMMN	Ultrasports Panther Dual 440		G-MMSZ	Medway Half Pint	
			G-MMTA	Ultrasports Panther XL	
G-MMMP	Flexiform Dual Striker		G-MMTC	Ultrasports Panther Dual	
G-MMMR	Flexiform Striker		G-MMTD	Mainair Tri-Flyer 330	
G-MMMS	MBA Tiger Cub 440		G-MMTG	Mainair Gemini	
G-MMMW	Flexiform Striker		G-MMTH	Southdown Puma Sprint	
G-MMNA	Eipper Quicksilver MX II		G-MMTI	Southdown Puma Sprint	
G-MMNB	Eipper Quicksilver MX		G-MMTJ	Southdown Puma Sprint	
G-MMNC	Eipper Quicksilver MX		G-MMTK	Medway Hybred	

Reg.	Type	Notes	Reg.	Type	Notes
G-MMTL	Mainair Gemini		G-MMXT	Mainair Gemini Flash	
G-MMTM	Mainair Tri-Flyer 440		G-MMXU	Mainair Gemini Flash	
G-MMTO	Mainair Tri-Flyer		G-MMXV	Mainair Gemini Flash	
G-MMTR	Ultrasports Panther		G-MMXW	Mainair Gemini	
G-MMTS	Solar Wings Panther XL		G-MMXX	Mainair Gemini	
G-MMTT	Solar Wings Panther XL		G-MMYA	Solar Wings Pegasus XL	
G-MMTV	American Aerolights Eagle		G-MMYB	Solar Wings Pegasus XL	
G-MMTX	Mainair Gemini 440		G-MMYD	CFM Shadow Srs B	
G-MMTY	Fisher FP.202U		G-MMYF	Southdown Puma Sprint	
G-MMTZ	Eurowing Goldwing		G-MMYI	Southdown Puma Sprint	
G-MMUA	Southdown Puma Sprint		G-MMYJ	Southdown Puma Sprint	
G-MMUC	Mainair Gemini 440		G-MMYK	Southdown Puma Sprint	
G-MMUE	Mainair Gemini Flash		G-MMYL	Cyclone 70	
G-MMUG	Mainair Tri-Flyer		G-MMYN	Ultrasports Panther XL	
G-MMUH	Mainair Tri-Flyer		G-MMYO	Southdown Puma Sprint	
G-MMUJ	Southdown Puma Sprint 440		G-MMYR	Eipper Quicksilver MXII	
			G-MMYS	Southdown Puma Sprint	
G-MMUK	Mainair Tri-Flyer		G-MMYT	Southdown Puma Sprint	
G-MMUL	Ward Elf E.47		G-MMYU	Southdown Puma Sprint	
G-MMUN	Ultrasports Panther Dual XL		G-MMYV	Webb Trike	
			G-MMYY	Southdown Puma Sprint	
G-MMUO	Mainair Gemini Flash		G-MMYZ	Southdown Puma Sprint	
G-MMUP	Airwave Nimrod 140		G-MMZA	Mainair Gemini Flash	
G-MMUS	Mainair Gemini		G-MMZB	Mainair Gemini Flash	
G-MMUU	ParaPlane PM-1		G-MMZC	Mainair Gemini Flash	
G-MMUV	Southdown Puma Sprint		G-MMZE	Mainair Gemini Flash	
G-MMUW	Mainair Gemini Flash		G-MMZF	Mainair Gemini Flash	
G-MMUX	Mainair Gemini		G-MMZG	Ultrasports Panther XL-S	
G-MMVA	Southdown Puma Sprint		G-MMZI	Medway 130SX	
G-MMVC	Ultrasports Panther XL		G-MMZJ	Mainair Gemini Flash	
G-MMVG	MBA Tiger Cub 440		G-MMZK	Mainair Gemini Flash	
G-MMVH	Southdown Raven		G-MMZL	Mainair Gemini Flash	
G-MMVI	Southdown Puma Sprint		G-MMZM	Mainair Gemini Flash	
G-MMVJ	Southdown Puma Sprint		G-MMZN	Mainair Gemini Flash	
G-MMVL	Ultrasports Panther XL-S		G-MMZO	Microflight Spectrum	
G-MMVM	Whiteley Orion 1		G-MMZP	Ultrasports Panther XL	
G-MMVN	Solar Wings Typhoon		G-MMZR	Southdown Puma Sprint	
G-MMVO	Southdown Puma Sprint		G-MMZS	Eipper Quicksilver MX1	
G-MMVP	Mainair Gemini Flash		G-MMZU	Southdown Puma DS	
G-MMVR	Hiway Skytrike 1		G-MMZV	Mainair Gemini Flash	
G-MMVS	Skyhook Pixie		G-MMZW	Southdown Puma Sprint	
G-MMVX	Southdown Puma Sprint		G-MMZX	Southdown Puma Sprint	
G-MMVZ	Southdown Puma Sprint		G-MMZY	Ultrasports Tripacer 330	
G-MMWA	Mainair Gemini Flash		G-MMZZ	Maxair Hummer	
G-MMWB	Huntair Pathfinder II		G-MNAA	Striplin Sky Ranger	
G-MMWC	Eipper Quicksilver MXII		G-MNAD	Mainair Gemini Flash	
G-MMWF	Hiway Skytrike 250		G-MNAE	Mainair Gemini Flash	
G-MMWG	Greenslade Mono-Trike		G-MNAF	Solar Wings Panther XL	
G-MMWH	Southdown Puma Sprint 440		G-MNAH	Solar Wings Panther XL	
			G-MNAI	Ultrasports Panther XL-S	
G-MMWI	Southdown Lightning		G-MNAK	Solar Wings Panther XL-S	
G-MMWJ	Pterodactyl Ptraveler		G-MNAL	MBA Tiger Cub 440	
G-MMWL	Eurowing Goldwing		G-MNAM	Solar Wings Panther XL-S	
G-MMWN	Ultrasports Tripacer		G-MNAN	Solar Wings Panther XL-S	
G-MMWO	Ultrasports Panther XL		G-MNAO	Solar Wings Panther XL-S	
G-MMWS	Mainair Tri-Flyer		G-MNAT	Solar Wings Pegasus XL-R	
G-MMWT	CFM Shadow		G-MNAU	Solar Wings Pegasus XL-R	
G-MMWX	Southdown Puma Sprint		G-MNAV	Southdown Puma Sprint	
G-MMWZ	Southdown Puma Sprint		G-MNAW	Solar Wings Pegasus XL-R	
G-MMXC	Mainair Gemini Flash		G-MNAX	Solar Wings Pegasus XL-R	
G-MMXD	Mainair Gemini Flash		G-MNAY	Ultrasports Panther XL-S	
G-MMXE	Mainair Gemini Flash		G-MNAZ	Solar Wings Pegasus XL-R	
G-MMXG	Mainair Gemini Flash		G-MNBA	Solar Wings Pegasus XL-R	
G-MMXH	Mainair Gemini Flash		G-MNBB	Solar Wings Pegasus XL-R	
G-MMXI	Horizon Prototype		G-MNBC	Solar Wings Pegasus XL-R	
G-MMXJ	Mainair Gemini Flash		G-MNBD	Mainair Gemini Flash	
G-MMXK	Mainair Gemini Flash		G-MNBE	Southdown Puma Sprint	
G-MMXL	Mainair Gemini Flash		G-MNBF	Mainair Gemini Flash	
G-MMXM	Mainair Gemini Flash		G-MNBG	Mainair Gemini Flash	
G-MMXN	Southdown Puma Sprint		G-MNBH	Southdown Puma Sprint	
G-MMXO	Southdown Puma Sprint		G-MNBI	Ultrasports Panther XL	
G-MMXP	Southdown Puma Sprint		G-MNBJ	Skyhook Pixie	
G-MMXR	Southdown Puma DSfi		G-MNBM	Southdown Puma Sprint	

Reg.	Type	Notes	Reg.	Type	Notes
G-MNBN	Mainair Gemini Flash		G-MNFR	Wright Tri-Flyer	
G-MNBP	Mainair Gemini Flash		G-MNFV	Ultrasports Trike	
G-MNBR	Mainair Gemini Flash		G-MNFW	Medway Hybred 44XL	
G-MNBS	Mainair Gemini Flash		G-MNFX	Southdown Puma Sprint	
G-MNBT	Mainair Gemini Flash		G-MNFY	Hornet 250	
G-MNBU	Mainair Gemini Flash		G-MNFZ	Southdown Puma Sprint	
G-MNBV	Mainair Gemini Flash		G-MNGA	Aerial Arts Chaser 110SX	
G-MNBW	Mainair Gemini Flash		G-MNGB	Mainair Gemini Flash	
G-MNCA	Hiway Demon 175		G-MNGD	Quest Air Services	
G-MNCF	Mainair Gemini Flash		G-MNGF	Solar Wings Pegasus	
G-MNCG	Mainair Gemini Flash		G-MNGG	Solar Wings Pegasus XL-R	
G-MNCH	Lancashire Micro Trike 330		G-MNGH	Skyhook Pixie	
G-MNCI	Southdown Puma Sprint		G-MNGJ	Skyhook Zipper	
G-MNCJ	Mainair Gemini Flash		G-MNGK	Mainair Gemini Flash	
G-MNCK	Southdown Puma Sprint		G-MNGL	Mainair Gemini Flash	
G-MNCL	Southdown Puma Sprint		G-MNGM	Mainair Gemini Flash	
G-MNCM	CFM Shadow Srs B		G-MNGN	Mainair Gemini Flash	
G-MNCO	Eipper Quicksilver MXII		G-MNGO	Solar Wings Storm	
G-MNCP	Southdown Puma Sprint		G-MNGR	Southdown Puma Sprint	
G-MNCR	Flexiform Striker		G-MNGS	Southdown Puma 330	
G-MNCS	Skyrider Airsports Phantom		G-MNGT	Mainair Gemini Flash	
G-MNCU	Medway Hybred		G-MNGU	Mainair Gemini Flash	
G-MNCV	Medway Typhoon XL		G-MNGW	Mainair Gemini Flash	
G-MNCW	Hornet Dual Trainer		G-MNGX	Southdown Puma Sprint	
G-MNCX	Mainair Gemini Flash		G-MNGZ	Mainair Gemini Flash	
G-MNCZ	Solar Wings Pegasus XL		G-MNHB	Solar Wings Pegasus XL-R	
G-MNDA	Thruster TST		G-MNHC	Solar Wings Pegasus XL-R	
G-MNDB	Southdown Puma Sprint		G-MNHD	Solar Wings Pegasus XL-R	
G-MNDC	Mainair Gemini Flash		G-MNHE	Solar Wings Pegasus XL-R	
G-MNDD	Mainair Scorcher Solo		G-MNHF	Solar Wings Pegasus XL-R	
G-MNDE	Medway Half Pint		G-MNHH	Solar Wings Panther XL-S	
G-MNDF	Mainair Gemini Flash		G-MNHI	Solar Wings Pegasus XL-R	
G-MNDG	Southdown Puma Sprint		G-MNHJ	Solar Wings Pegasus XL-R	
G-MNDH	Hiway Skytrike		G-MNHK	Solar Wings Pegasus XL-R	
G-MNDI	MBA Tiger Cub 440		G-MNHL	Solar Wings Pegasus XL-R	
G-MNDM	Mainair Gemini Flash		G-MNHM	Solar Wings Pegasus XL-R	
G-MNDO	Mainair Flash		G-MNHN	Solar Wings Pegasus XL-R	
G-MNDP	Southdown Puma Sprint		G-MNHP	Solar Wings Pegasus XL-R	
G-MNDU	Midland Sirocco 377GB		G-MNHR	Solar Wings Pegasus XL-R	
G-MNDV	Midland Sirocco 377GB		G-MNHS	Solar Wings Pegasus XL-R	
G-MNDW	Midland Sirocco 377GB		G-MNHT	Solar Wings Pegasus XL-R	
G-MNDY	Southdown Puma Sprint		G-MNHU	Solar Wings Pegasus XL-R	
G-MNDZ	Southdown Puma Sprint		G-MNHV	Solar Wings Pegasus XL-R	
G-MNEF	Mainair Gemini Flash		G-MNHX	Solar Wings Typhoon S4	
G-MNEG	Mainair Gemini Flash		G-MNHZ	Mainair Gemini Flash	
G-MNEH	Mainair Gemini Flash		G-MNIA	Mainair Gemini Flash	
G-MNEI	Medway Hybred 440		G-MNID	Mainair Gemini Flash	
G-MNEK	Medway Half Pint		G-MNIE	Mainair Gemini Flash	
G-MNEL	Medway Half Pint		G-MNIF	Mainair Gemini Flash	
G-MNEM	Solar Wings Pegasus Dual		G-MNIG	Mainair Gemini Flash	
G-MNEN	Southdown Puma Sprint		G-MNIH	Mainair Gemini Flash	
G-MNEO	Southdown Raven		G-MNII	Mainair Gemini Flash	
G-MNEP	Aerostructure Pipstrelle P.2B		G-MNIL	Southdown Puma Sprint	
			G-MNIM	Maxair Hummer	
G-MNER	CFM Shadow Srs B		G-MNIO	Mainair Gemini Flash	
G-MNET	Mainair Gemini Flash		G-MNIP	Mainair Gemini Flash	
G-MNEV	Mainair Gemini Flash		G-MNIS	CFM Shadow Srs B	
G-MNEX	Mainair Gemini Flash		G-MNIT	Aerial Arts 130SX	
G-MNEY	Mainair Gemini Flash		G-MNIU	Solar Wings Pegasus Photon	
G-MNEZ	Skyhook TR1 Mk 2				
G-MNFA	Solar Wings Typhoon		G-MNIV	Solar Wings Typhoon	
G-MNFB	Southdown Puma Sprint		G-MNIW	Airwave Nimrod 165	
G-MNFE	Mainair Gemini Flash		G-MNIX	Mainair Gemini Flash	
G-MNFF	Mainair Gemini Flash		G-MNIY	Skyhook Pixie Zipper	
G-MNFG	Southdown Puma Sprint		G-MNIZ	Mainair Gemini Flash	
G-MNFH	Mainair Gemini Flash		G-MNJA	Southdown Lightning	
G-MNFI	Medway Half Pint		G-MNJB	Southdown Raven	
G-MNFJ	Mainair Gemini Flash		G-MNJC	MBA Tiger Cub 440	
G-MNFK	Mainair Gemini Flash		G-MNJD	Southdown Puma Sprint	
G-MNFL	AMF Chevvron		G-MNJF	Dragon 150	
G-MNFM	Mainair Gemini Flash		G-MNJG	Mainair Tri-Flyer	
G-MNFN	Mainair Gemini Flash		G-MNJH	SW Pegasus Flash	
G-MNFP	Mainair Gemini Flash		G-MNJI	SW Pegasus Flash	

Reg.	Type	Notes	Reg.	Type	Notes
G-MNJJ	SW Pegasus Flash		G-MNMV	Mainair Gemini Flash	
G-MNJK	SW Pegasus Flash		G-MNMW	Aerotech MW.6 Merlin	
G-MNJL	SW Pegasus Flash		G-MNMY	Cyclone 70	
G-MNJM	SW Pegasus Flash		G-MNNA	Southdown Raven	
G-MNJN	SW Pegasus Flash		G-MNNB	Southdown Raven	
G-MNJO	SW Pegasus Flash		G-MNNC	Southdown Raven	
G-MNJP	SW Pegasus Flash		G-MNND	SW Pegasus Flash	
G-MNJR	SW Pegasus Flash		G-MNNE	Mainair Gemini Flash	
G-MNJS	Southdown Puma Sprint		G-MNNF	Mainair Gemini Flash	
G-MNJT	Southdown Raven		G-MNNG	Solar Wings Photon	
G-MNJU	Mainair Gemini Flash		G-MNNI	Mainair Gemini Flash	
G-MNJV	Medway Half Pint		G-MNNJ	Mainair Gemini Flash	
G-MNJW	Mitchell Wing B10		G-MNNK	Mainair Gemini Flash	
G-MNJX	Medway Hybred 44XL		G-MNNL	Mainair Gemini Flash	
G-MNKB	SW Pegasus Photon		G-MNNM	Mainair Scorcher Solo	
G-MNKC	SW Pegasus Photon		G-MNNN	Southdown Raven	
G-MNKD	SW Pegasus Photon		G-MNNO	Southdown Raven	
G-MNKE	SW Pegasus Photon		G-MNNP	Mainair Gemini Flash	
G-MNKG	SW Pegasus Photon		G-MNNR	Mainair Gemini Flash	
G-MNKH	SW Pegasus Photon		G-MNNS	Eurowing Goldwing	
G-MNKI	SW Pegasus Photon		G-MNNT	Medway Hybred 44XLR	
G-MNKJ	SW Pegasus Photon		G-MNNU	Mainair Gemini Flash	
G-MNKK	SW Pegasus Photon		G-MNNV	Mainair Gemini Flash	
G-MNKL	Mainair Gemini Flash		G-MNNY	SW Pegasus Flash	
G-MNKM	MBA Tiger Cub 440		G-MNNZ	SW Pegasus Flash	
G-MNKN	Skycraft Scout Mk III		G-MNPA	SW Pegasus Flash	
G-MNKO	SW Pegasus Flash		G-MNPB	SW Pegasus Flash	
G-MNKP	SW Pegasus Flash		G-MNPC	Mainair Gemini Flash	
G-MNKR	SW Pegasus Flash		G-MNPF	Mainair Gemini Flash	
G-MNKS	SW Pegasus Flash		G-MNPG	Mainair Gemini Flash	
G-MNKT	Solar Wings Typhoon S4		G-MNPH	Flexiform Dual Striker	
G-MNKU	Southdown Puma Sprint		G-MNPI	Southdown Pipistrelle 2C	
G-MNKV	SW Pegasus Flash		G-MNPL	Ultrasports Panther 330	
G-MNKW	SW Pegasus Flash		G-MNPV	Mainair Scorcher Solo	
G-MNKX	SW Pegasus Flash		G-MNPW	AMF Chevvron	
G-MNKY	Southdown Raven		G-MNPX	Mainair Gemini Flash	
G-MNKZ	Southdown Raven		G-MNPY	Mainair Scorcher Solo	
G-MNLB	Southdown Raven X		G-MNPZ	Mainair Scorcher Solo	
G-MNLC	Southdown Raven		G-MNRA	CFM Shadow Srs B	
G-MNLE	Southdown Raven X		G-MNRD	Ultraflight Lazair	
G-MNLH	Romain Cobra Biplane		G-MNRE	Mainair Scorcher Solo	
G-MNLI	Mainair Gemini Flash		G-MNRF	Mainair Scorcher Solo	
G-MNLK	Southdown Raven		G-MNRG	Mainair Scorcher Solo	
G-MNLL	Southdown Raven		G-MNRI	Hornet Dual Trainer	
G-MNLM	Southdown Raven		G-MNRJ	Hornet Dual Trainer	
G-MNLN	Southdown Raven		G-MNRK	Hornet Dual Trainer	
G-MNLO	Southdown Raven		G-MNRL	Hornet Dual Trainer	
G-MNLP	Southdown Raven		G-MNRM	Hornet Dual Trainer	
G-MNLS	Southdown Raven		G-MNRN	Hornet Dual Trainer	
G-MNLT	Southdown Raven		G-MNRP	Southdown Raven	
G-MNLU	Southdown Raven		G-MNRR	Southdown Raven X	
G-MNLV	Southdown Raven		G-MNRS	Southdown Raven	
G-MNLW	Medway Half Pint		G-MNRT	Midland Ultralights Sirocco	
G-MNLX	Mainair Gemini Flash		G-MNRW	Mainair Gemini Flash II	
G-MNLY	Mainair Gemini Flash		G-MNRX	Mainair Gemini Flash II	
G-MNLZ	Southdown Raven		G-MNRY	Mainair Gemini Flash	
G-MNMA	SW Pegasus Flash		G-MNRZ	Mainair Scorcher Solo	
G-MNMC	Southdown Puma MS		G-MNSA	Mainair Gemini Flash	
G-MNMD	Southdown Raven		G-MNSB	Southdown Puma Sprint	
G-MNME	Hiway Skytrike		G-MNSE	Mainair Gemini Flash	
G-MNMG	Mainair Gemini Flash		G-MNSF	Hornet Dual Trainer	
G-MNMH	Mainair Gemini Flash		G-MNSH	SW Pegasus Flash II	
G-MNMI	Mainair Gemini Flash		G-MNSI	Mainair Gemini Flash	
G-MNMJ	Mainair Gemini Flash		G-MNSJ	Mainair Gemini Flash	
G-MNMK	Solar Wings Pegasus XL-R		G-MNSL	Southdown Raven X	
G-MNML	Southdown Puma Sprint		G-MNSM	Hornet Demon	
G-MNMM	Aerotech MW.5 Sorcerer		G-MNSN	SW Pegasus Flash II	
G-MNMN	Medway Hybred 44XLR		G-MNSP	Aerial Arts 130SX	
G-MNMO	Mainair Gemini Flash		G-MNSR	Mainair Gemini Flash	
G-MNMR	Solar Wings Typhoon 180		G-MNSS	American Aerolights Eagle	
G-MNMS	Wheeler Scout		G-MNSV	CFM Shadown Srs B	
G-MNMT	Southdown Raven		G-MNSW	Southdown Raven X	
G-MNMU	Southdown Raven		G-MNSX	Southdown Raven X	

Reg.	Type	Notes	Reg.	Type	Notes
G-MNSY	Southdown Raven X		G-MNWK	CFM Shadow Srs B	
G-MNTB	Solar Wings Typhoon S4		G-MNWL	Aerial Arts 130SX	
G-MNTC	Southdown Raven X		G-MNWN	Mainair Gemini Flash II	
G-MNTD	Aerial Arts Chaser 110SX		G-MNWO	Mainair Gemini Flash II	
G-MNTE	Southdown Raven X		G-MNWP	SW Pegasus Flash II	
G-MNTF	Southdown Raven X		G-MNWR	Medway Hybred 44LR	
G-MNTG	Southdown Raven X		G-MNWT	Southdown Raven	
G-MNTH	Mainair Gemini Flash		G-MNWU	SW Pegasus Flash II	
G-MNTI	Mainair Gemini Flash		G-MNWV	SW Pegasus Flash II	
G-MNTK	CFM Shadow Srs B		G-MNWW	Solar Wings Pegasus XL-R	
G-MNTM	Southdown Raven X		G-MNWX	Solar Wings Pegasus XL-R	
G-MNTN	Southdown Raven X		G-MNWY	CFM Shadow Srs B	
G-MNTO	Southdown Raven X		G-MNWZ	Mainair Gemini Flash II	
G-MNTP	CFM Shadow Srs B		G-MNXA	Southdown Raven X	
G-MNTS	Mainair Gemini Flash II		G-MNXB	Solar Wings Photon	
G-MNTT	Medway Half Pint		G-MNXC	Aerial Arts 110SX	
G-MNTU	Mainair Gemini Flash II		G-MNXD	Southdown Raven	
G-MNTV	Mainair Gemini Flash II		G-MNXE	Southdown Raven X	
G-MNTW	Mainair Gemini Flash II		G-MNXF	Southdown Raven	
G-MNTX	Mainair Gemini Flash II		G-MNXG	Southdown Raven X	
G-MNTY	Southdown Raven X		G-MNXI	Southdown Raven X	
G-MNTZ	Mainair Gemini Flash II		G-MNXM	Medway Hybred 44XLR	
G-MNUA	Mainair Gemini Flash II		G-MNXN	Medway Hybred 44XLR	
G-MNUB	Mainair Gemini Flash II		G-MNXO	Medway Hybred 44XLR	
G-MNUC	SW Pegasus Flash II		G-MNXR	Mainair Gemini Flash II	
G-MNUD	SW Pegasus Flash II		G-MNXS	Mainair Gemini Flash II	
G-MNUE	SW Pegasus Flash II		G-MNXT	Mainair Gemini Flash II	
G-MNUF	Mainair Gemini Flash II		G-MNXU	Mainair Gemini Flash II	
G-MNUG	Mainair Gemini Flash II		G-MNXX	CFM Shadow Srs BD	
G-MNUH	Southdown Raven X		G-MNXY	Whittaker MW.5 Sorcerer	
G-MNUI	Skyhook Cutlass Dual		G-MNXZ	Whittaker MW.5 Sorcerer	
G-MNUJ	SW Pegasus Photon		G-MNYA	SW Pegasus Flash II	
G-MNUM	Southdown Puma Sprint		G-MNYB	Solar Wings Pegasus XL-R	
G-MNUO	Mainair Gemini Flash II		G-MNYC	Solar Wings Pegasus XL-R	
G-MNUP	Mainair Gemini Flash II		G-MNYD	Aerial Arts 110SX Chaser	
G-MNUR	Mainair Gemini Flash II		G-MNYE	Aerial Arts 110SX Chaser	
G-MNUS	Mainair Gemini Flash II		G-MNYF	Aerial Arts 110SX Chaser	
G-MNUT	Southdown Raven X		G-MNYG	Southdown Raven	
G-MNUU	Southdown Raven X		G-MNYH	Southdown Puma Sprint	
G-MNUV	Southdown Raven X		G-MNYI	Southdown Raven X	
G-MNUW	Southdown Raven X		G-MNYJ	Mainair Gemini Flash II	
G-MNUX	Solar Wings Pegasus XL-R		G-MNYK	Mainair Gemini Flash II	
G-MNUY	Mainair Gemini Flash II		G-MNYL	Southdown Raven X	
G-MNVA	Solar Wings Pegasus XL-R		G-MNYM	Southdown Raven X	
G-MNVB	Solar Wings Pegasus XL-R		G-MNYO	Southdown Raven X	
G-MNVC	Solar Wings Pegasus XL-R		G-MNYP	Southdown Raven X	
G-MNVE	Solar Wings Pegasus XL-R		G-MNYS	Southdown Raven X	
G-MNVF	SW Pegasus Flash II		G-MNYT	Solar Wings Pegasus XL-R	
G-MNVG	SW Pegasus Flash II		G-MNYU	Solar Wings Pegasus XL-R	
G-MNVH	SW Pegasus Flash II		G-MNYV	Solar Wings Pegasus XL-R	
G-MNVI	CFM Shadow Srs B		G-MNYW	Solar Wings Pegasus XL-R	
G-MNVJ	CFM Shadow Srs B		G-MNYX	Solar Wings Pegasus XL-R	
G-MNVK	CFM Shadow Srs B		G-MNYZ	SW Pegasus Flash	
G-MNVL	Medway Half Pint		G-MNZA	SW Pegasus Flash II	
G-MNVM	Southdown Raven X		G-MNZB	Mainair Gemini Flash II	
G-MNVN	Southdown Raven X		G-MNZC	Mainair Gemini Flash II	
G-MNVO	Hovey Whing-Ding II		G-MNZD	Mainair Gemini Flash II	
G-MNVP	Southdown Raven X		G-MNZE	Mainair Gemini Flash II	
G-MNVR	Mainair Gemini Flash II		G-MNZF	Mainair Gemini Flash II	
G-MNVS	Mainair Gemini Flash II		G-MNZG	Aerial Arts 110SX	
G-MNVT	Mainair Gemini Flash II		G-MNZI	Prone Power Typhoon 2	
G-MNVU	Mainair Gemini Flash II		G-MNZJ	CFM Shadow Srs BD	
G-MNVV	Mainair Gemini Flash II		G-MNZK	Solar Wings Pegasus XL-R	
G-MNVW	Mainair Gemini Flash II		G-MNZL	Solar Wings Pegasus XL-R	
G-MNVZ	SW Pegasus Photon		G-MNZM	Solar Wings Pegasus XL-R	
G-MNWA	Southdown Raven X		G-MNZN	SW Pegasus Flash II	
G-MNWB	Thruster TST		G-MNZO	SW Pegasus Flash II	
G-MNWC	Mainair Gemini Flash II		G-MNZP	CFM Shadow Srs B	
G-MNWD	Mainair Gemini Flash		G-MNZR	CFM Shadow Srs BD	
G-MNWF	Southdown Raven X		G-MNZS	Aerial Arts 130SX	
G-MNWG	Southdown Raven X		G-MNZU	Eurowing Goldwing	
G-MNWI	Mainair Gemini Flash II		G-MNZV	Southdown Raven X	
G-MNWJ	Mainair Gemini Flash II		G-MNZW	Southdown Raven X	

Reg.	Type	Notes	Reg.	Type	Notes
G-MNZX	Southdown Raven X		G-MTDD	Aerial Arts Chaser 110SX	
G-MNZY	Striker Tri-Flyer 330		G-MTDE	American Aerolights 110SX	
G-MNZZ	CFM Shadow Srs B		G-MTDF	Mainair Gemini Flash II	
G-MTAA	Solar Wings Pegasus XL-R		G-MTDG	Solar Wings Pegasus XL-R	
G-MTAB	Mainair Gemini Flash II		G-MTDH	Solar Wings Pegasus XL-R	
G-MTAC	Mainair Gemini Flash II		G-MTDI	Solar Wings Pegasus XL-R	
G-MTAD	Mainair Gemini Skyflash		G-MTDJ	Medway Hybred 44XL	
G-MTAE	Mainair Gemini Flash II		G-MTDK	Aerotech MW.5 Sorcerer	
G-MTAF	Mainair Gemini Flash II		G-MTDL	Solar Wings Pegasus XL-R	
G-MTAG	Mainair Gemini Flash II		G-MTDM	Mainair Gemini Flash II	
G-MTAH	Mainair Gemini Flash II		G-MTDN	Ultraflight Lazair IIIE	
G-MTAI	Solar Wings Pegasus XL-R		G-MTDO	Eipper Quicksilver MXII	
G-MTAJ	Solar Wings Pegasus XL-R		G-MTDP	Solar Wings Pegasus XL-R	
G-MTAK	Solar Wings Pegasus XL-R		G-MTDR	Mainair Gemini Flash II	
G-MTAL	Solar Wings Photon		G-MTDS	Solar Wings Photon	
G-MTAM	SW Pegasus Flash		G-MTDT	Solar Wings Pegasus XL-R	
G-MTAO	Solar Wings Pegasus XL-R		G-MTDU	CFM Shadow Srs BD	
G-MTAP	Southdown Raven X		G-MTDV	Solar Wings Pegasus XL-R	
G-MTAR	Mainair Gemini Flash II		G-MTDW	Mainair Gemini Flash II	
G-MTAS	Whittaker MW.5 Sorcerer		G-MTDX	CFM Shadow Srs BD	
G-MTAT	Solar Wings Pegasus XL-R		G-MTDY	Mainair Gemini Flash II	
G-MTAV	Solar Wings Pegasus XL-R		G-MTDZ	Eipper Quicksilver MXII	
G-MTAW	Solar Wings Pegasus XL-R		G-MTEA	Solar Wings Pegasus XL-R	
G-MTAX	Solar Wings Pegasus XL-R		G-MTEB	Solar Wings Pegasus XL-R	
G-MTAY	Solar Wings Pegasus XL-R		G-MTEC	Solar Wings Pegasus XL-R	
G-MTAZ	Solar Wings Pegasus XL-R		G-MTED	Solar Wings Pegasus XL-R	
G-MTBA	Solar Wings Pegasus XL-R		G-MTEE	Solar Wings Pegasus XL-R	
G-MTBB	Southdown Raven X		G-MTEF	Solar Wings Pegasus XL-R	
G-MTBC	Mainair Gemini Flash II		G-MTEG	Mainair Gemini Flash II	
G-MTBD	Mainair Gemini Flash II		G-MTEH	Mainair Gemini Flash II	
G-MTBE	CFM Shadow Srs BD		G-MTEJ	Mainair Gemini Flash II	
G-MTBF	Mirage Mk II		G-MTEK	Mainair Gemini Flash II	
G-MTBG	Mainair Gemini Flash II		G-MTEL	Mainair Gemini Flash II	
G-MTBH	Mainair Gemini Flash II		G-MTEM	Mainair Gemini Flash II	
G-MTBJ	Mainair Gemini Flash II		G-MTEN	Mainair Gemini Flash II	
G-MTBK	Southdown Raven X		G-MTEO	Midland Ultralight Sirocco 337	
G-MTBL	Solar Wings Pegasus XL-R		G-MTER	Solar Wings Pegasus XL-R	
G-MTBN	Southdown Raven X		G-MTES	Solar Wings Pegasus XL-R	
G-MTBO	Southdown Raven X		G-MTET	Solar Wings Pegasus XL-R	
G-MTBP	Aerotech MW.5 Sorcerer		G-MTEU	Solar Wings Pegasus XL-R	
G-MTBR	Aerotech MW.5 Sorcerer		G-MTEV	Solar Wings Pegasus XL-R	
G-MTBS	Aerotech MW.5 Sorcerer		G-MTEW	Solar Wings Pegasus XL-R	
G-MTBT	Aerotech MW.5 Sorcerer		G-MTEX	Solar Wings Pegasus XL-R	
G-MTBV	Solar Wings Pegasus XL-R		G-MTEY	Mainair Gemini Flash II	
G-MTBW	Mainair Gemini Flash II		G-MTFA	Solar Wings Pegasus XL-R	
G-MTBX	Mainair Gemini Flash II		G-MTFB	Solar Wings Pegasus XL-R	
G-MTBY	Mainair Gemini Flash II		G-MTFC	Medway Hybred 44XLR	
G-MTBZ	Southdown Raven X		G-MTFE	Solar Wings Pegasus XL-R	
G-MTCA	CFM Shadow Srs B		G-MTFF	Mainair Gemini Flash II	
G-MTCB	Snowbird Mk III		G-MTFG	AMF Chevvron 232	
G-MTCC	Mainair Gemini Flash II		G-MTFH	Aerotech MW.5B Sorcerer	
G-MTCD	Southdown Raven X		G-MTFI	Mainair Gemini Flash II	
G-MTCE	Mainair Gemini Flash II		G-MTFJ	Mainair Gemini Flash II	
G-MTCG	Solar Wings Pegasus XL-R		G-MTFL	AMF Lazair IIIE	
G-MTCH	Solar Wings Pegasus XL-R		G-MTFM	Solar Wings Pegasus XL-R	
G-MTCJ	Aerial Arts Avenger		G-MTFN	Aerotech MW.5 Sorcerer	
G-MTCK	SW Pegasus Flash		G-MTFO	Solar Wings Pegasus XL-R	
G-MTCL	Southdown Raven X		G-MTFP	Solar Wings Pegasus XL-R	
G-MTCM	Southdown Raven X		G-MTFR	Solar Wings Pegasus XL-R	
G-MTCN	Solar Wings Pegasus XL-R		G-MTFS	Solar Wings Pegasus XL-R	
G-MTCO	Solar Wings Pegasus XL-R		G-MTFT	Solar Wings Pegasus XL-R	
G-MTCP	Aerial Arts Chaser 110SX		G-MTFU	CFM Shadow Series BD	
G-MTCR	Solar Wings Pegasus XL-R		G-MTFX	Mainair Gemini Flash	
G-MTCT	CFM Shadow Srs BD		G-MTFZ	CFM Shadow Srs BD	
G-MTCU	Mainair Gemini Flash II		G-MTGA	Mainair Gemini Flash	
G-MTCV	Microflight Spectrum		G-MTGB	Thruster TST Mk 1	
G-MTCW	Mainair Gemini Flash		G-MTGC	Thruster TST Mk 1	
G-MTCX	Solar Wings Pegasus XL-R		G-MTGD	Thruster TST Mk 1	
G-MTCZ	Ultrasports Tripacer 250		G-MTGE	Thruster TST Mk 1	
G-MTDA	Hornet Dual Trainer		G-MTGF	Thruster TST Mk 1	
G-MTDB	Owen Pola Mk 1		G-MTGH	Mainair Gemini Flash IIA	
G-MTDC	Owen Pola Mk 1		G-MTGJ	Solar Wings Pegasus XL-R	

Reg.	Type	Notes	Reg.	Type	Notes
G-MTGK	Solar Wings Pegasus XL-R		G-MTJT	Mainair Gemini Flash IIA	
G-MTGL	Solar Wings Pegasus XL-R		G-MTJV	Mainair Gemini Flash IIA	
G-MTGM	Solar Wings Pegasus XL-R		G-MTJW	Mainair Gemini Flash IIA	
G-MTGO	Mainair Gemini Flash		G-MTJX	Hornet Dual Trainer	
G-MTGP	Thruster TST Mk 1		G-MTJY	Mainair Gemini Flash IIA	
G-MTGR	Thruster TST Mk 1		G-MTJZ	Mainair Gemini Flash IIA	
G-MTGS	Thruster TST Mk 1		G-MTKA	Thruster TST Mk 1	
G-MTGT	Thruster TST Mk 1		G-MTKB	Thruster TST Mk 1	
G-MTGU	Thruster TST Mk 1		G-MTKD	Thruster TST Mk 1	
G-MTGV	CFM Shadow Srs BD		G-MTKE	Thruster TST Mk 1	
G-MTGX	Hornet Dual Trainer		G-MTKG	Solar Wings Pegasus XL-R	
G-MTGY	Southdown Lightning		G-MTKH	Solar Wings Pegasus XL-R	
G-MTHB	Aerotech MW.5B Sorcerer		G-MTKI	Solar Wings Pegasus XL-R	
G-MTHC	Raven X		G-MTKJ	Solar Wings Pegasus XL-R	
G-MTHD	Hiway Demon 195		G-MTKK	Solar Wings Pegasus XL-R	
G-MTHG	Solar Wings Pegasus XL-R		G-MTKM	Gardner T-M Scout S.2	
G-MTHH	Solar Wings Pegasus XL-R		G-MTKN	Mainair Gemini Flash IIA	
G-MTHI	Solar Wings Pegasus XL-R		G-MTKO	Mainair Gemini Flash IIA	
G-MTHJ	Solar Wings Pegasus XL-R		G-MTKP	Solar Wings Pegasus XL-R	
G-MTHK	Solar Wings Pegasus XL-R		G-MTKR	CFM Shadow Srs BD	
G-MTHM	Solar Wings Pegasus XL-R		G-MTKS	CFM Shadow Srs BD	
G-MTHN	Solar Wings Pegasus XL-R		G-MTKU	CFM Shadow Srs BD	
G-MTHO	Solar Wings Pegasus XL-R		G-MTKV	Mainair Gemini Flash	
G-MTHS	CFM Shadow Srs BD		G-MTKW	Mainair Gemini Flash IIA	
G-MTHT	CFM Shadow Srs BD		G-MTKX	Mainair Gemini Flash IIA	
G-MTHU	Hornet Dual Trainer		G-MTKY	Mainair Gemini Flash IIA	
G-MTHV	CFM Shadow Srs BD		G-MTKZ	Mainair Gemini Flash IIA	
G-MTHW	Mainair Gemini Flash II		G-MTLA	Mainair Gemini Flash IIA	
G-MTHX	Mainair Gemini Flash IIA		G-MTLB	Mainair Gemini Flash IIA	
G-MTHY	Mainair Gemini Flash IIA		G-MTLC	Mainair Gemini Flash IIA	
G-MTHZ	Mainair Gemini Flash IIA		G-MTLD	Mainair Gemini Flash IIA	
G-MTIA	Mainair Gemini Flash IIA		G-MTLE	See main Register	
G-MTIB	Mainair Gemini Flash IIA		G-MTLG	Solar Wings Pegasus XL-R	
G-MTIC	Mainair Gemini Flash IIA		G-MTLH	Solar Wings Pegasus XL-R	
G-MTID	Southdown Raven X		G-MTLI	Solar Wings Pegasus XL-R	
G-MTIE	Solar Wings Pegasus XL-R		G-MTLJ	Solar Wings Pegasus XL-R	
G-MTIF	Solar Wings Pegasus XL-R		G-MTLK	Raven X	
G-MTIG	Solar Wings Pegasus XL-R		G-MTLL	Mainair Gemini Flash IIA	
G-MTIH	Solar Wings Pegasus XL-R		G-MTLM	Thruster TST Mk 1	
G-MTII	Solar Wings Pegasus XL-R		G-MTLN	Thruster TST Mk 1	
G-MTIJ	Solar Wings Pegasus XL-R		G-MTLO	Thruster TST Mk 1	
G-MTIK	Southdown Raven X		G-MTLP	Thruster TST Mk 1	
G-MTIL	Mainair Gemini Flash IIA		G-MTLR	Thruster TST Mk 1	
G-MTIM	Mainair Gemini Flash IIA		G-MTLS	Solar Wings Pegasus XL-R	
G-MTIN	Mainair Gemini Flash IIA		G-MTLT	Solar Wings Pegasus XL-R	
G-MTIO	Solar Wings Pegasus XL-R		G-MTLU	Solar Wings Pegasus XL-R	
G-MTIP	Solar Wings Pegasus XL-R		G-MTLV	Solar Wings Pegasus XL-R	
G-MTIR	Solar Wings Pegasus XL-R		G-MTLW	Solar Wings Pegasus XL-R	
G-MTIS	Solar Wings Pegasus XL-R		G-MTLX	Medway Hybred 44XLR	
G-MTIT	Solar Wings Pegasus XL-R		G-MTLY	Solar Wings Pegasus XL-R	
G-MTIU	Solar Wings Pegasus XL-R		G-MTLZ	Whittaker MW.5 Sorceror	
G-MTIV	Solar Wings Pegasus XL-R		G-MTMA	Mainair Gemini Flash IIA	
G-MTIW	Solar Wings Pegasus XL-R		G-MTMB	Mainair Gemini Flash IIA	
G-MTIX	Solar Wings Pegasus XL-R		G-MTMC	Mainair Gemini Flash IIA	
G-MTIY	Solar Wings Pegasus XL-R		G-MTMD	Whittaker MW.6 Merlin	
G-MTIZ	Solar Wings Pegasus XL-R		G-MTME	Solar Wings Pegasus XL-R	
G-MTJA	Mainair Gemini Flash IIA		G-MTMF	Solar Wings Pegasus XL-R	
G-MTJB	Mainair Gemini Flash IIA		G-MTMG	Solar Wings Pegasus XL-R	
G-MTJC	Mainair Gemini Flash IIA		G-MTMH	Solar Wings Pegasus XL-R	
G-MTJD	Mainair Gemini Flash IIA		G-MTMI	Solar Wings Pegasus XL-R	
G-MTJE	Mainair Gemini Flash IIA		G-MTMJ	Maxair Hummer	
G-MTJF	Mainair Gemini Flash IIA		G-MTMK	Raven X	
G-MTJG	Medway Hybred 44XLR		G-MTML	Mainair Gemini Flash IIA	
G-MTJH	SW Pegasus Flash		G-MTMM	CFM Shadow Srs BD	
G-MTJI	Raven X		G-MTMO	Raven X	
G-MTJK	Mainair Gemini Flash IIA		G-MTMP	Hornet Dual Trainer/Raven	
G-MTJL	Mainair Gemini Flash IIA		G-MTMR	Hornet Dual Trainer/Raven	
G-MTJM	Mainair Gemini Flash IIA		G-MTMT	Mainair Gemini Flash IIA	
G-MTJN	Midland Ultralights Sirocco 377GB		G-MTMU	Mainair Gemini Flash IIA	
			G-MTMV	Mainair Gemini Flash IIA	
G-MTJP	Medway Hybred 44XLR		G-MTMW	Mainair Gemini Flash IIA	
G-MTJR	Solar Wings Pegasus XL-R		G-MTMX	CFM Shadow Srs BD	
G-MTJS	Solar Wings Pegasus XL-Q		G-MTMY	CFM Shadow Srs BD	

Reg.	Type	Notes	Reg.	Type	Notes
G-MTMZ	CFM Shadow Srs BD		G-MTRA	Mainair Gemini Flash IIA	
G-MTNB	Raven X		G-MTRB	Mainair Gemini Flash IIA	
G-MTNC	Mainair Gemini Flash IIA		G-MTRC	Midlands Ultralights	
G-MTND	Medway Hybred 44XLR			Sirocco 377GB	
G-MTNE	Medway Hybred 44XLR		G-MTRD	Midlands Ultralights	
G-MTNF	Medway Hybred 44XLR			Sirocco 377GB	
G-MTNG	Mainair Gemini Flash IIA		G-MTRE	Whittaker MW.6 Merlin	
G-MTNH	Mainair Gemini Flash IIA		G-MTRF	Mainair Gemini Flash IIA	
G-MTNI	Mainair Gemini Flash IIA		G-MTRG	Mainair Gemini Flash IIA	
G-MTNJ	Mainair Gemini Flash IIA		G-MTRJ	AMF Chevvron 232	
G-MTNK	Weedhopper JC-24B		G-MTRK	Hornet Dual Trainer	
G-MTNL	Mainair Gemini Flash IIA		G-MTRL	Hornet Dual Trainer	
G-MTNM	Mainair Gemini Flash IIA		G-MTRM	Solar Wings Pegasus XL-R	
G-MTNO	Solar Wings Pegasus XL-Q		G-MTRN	Solar Wings Pegasus XL-R	
G-MTNP	Solar Wings Pegasus XL-Q		G-MTRO	Solar Wings Pegasus XL-R	
G-MTNR	Thruster TST Mk 1		G-MTRP	Solar Wings Pegasus XL-R	
G-MTNS	Thruster TST Mk 1		G-MTRR	Solar Wings Pegasus XL-R	
G-MTNT	Thruster TST Mk 1		G-MTRS	Solar Wings Pegasus XL-R	
G-MTNU	Thruster TST Mk 1		G-MTRT	Raven X	
G-MTNV	Thruster TST Mk 1		G-MTRU	Solar Wings Pegasus XL-Q	
G-MTNW	Thruster TST Mk 1		G-MTRV	Solar Wings Pegasus XL-Q	
G-MTNX	Mainair Gemini Flash II		G-MTRW	Raven X	
G-MTNY	Mainair Gemini Flash IIA		G-MTRX	Whittaker MW.5 Sorceror	
G-MTNZ	Solar Wings Pegasus XL-Q		G-MTRY	Noble Hardman Snowbird	
G-MTOA	Solar Wings Pegasus XL-R			Mk IV	
G-MTOB	Solar Wings Pegasus XL-R		G-MTRZ	Mainair Gemini Flash IIA	
G-MTOC	Solar Wings Pegasus XL-R		G-MTSB	Mainair Gemini Flash IIA	
G-MTOD	Solar Wings Pegasus XL-R		G-MTSC	Mainair Gemini Flash IIA	
G-MTOE	Solar Wings Pegasus XL-R		G-MTSD	Raven X	
G-MTOF	Solar Wings Pegasus XL-R		G-MTSG	CFM Shadow Srs BD	
G-MTOG	Solar Wings Pegasus XL-R		G-MTSH	Thruster TST Mk 1	
G-MTOH	Solar Wings Pegasus XL-R		G-MTSI	Thruster TST Mk 1	
G-MTOI	Solar Wings Pegasus XL-R		G-MTSJ	Thruster TST Mk 1	
G-MTOJ	Solar Wings Pegasus XL-R		G-MTSK	Thruster TST Mk 1	
G-MTOK	Solar Wings Pegasus XL-R		G-MTSL	Thruster TST Mk 1	
G-MTOL	Solar Wings Pegasus XL-R		G-MTSM	Thruster TST Mk 1	
G-MTOM	Solar Wings Pegasus XL-R		G-MTSN	Solar Wings Pegasus XL-R	
G-MTON	Solar Wings Pegasus XL-R		G-MTSO	Solar Wings Pegasus XL-R	
G-MTOO	Solar Wings Pegasus XL-R		G-MTSP	Solar Wings Pegasus XL-R	
G-MTOP	Solar Wings Pegasus XL-R		G-MTSR	Solar Wings Pegasus XL-R	
G-MTOR	Solar Wings Pegasus XL-R		G-MTSS	Solar Wings Pegasus XL-R	
G-MTOS	Solar Wings Pegasus XL-R		G-MTST	Thruster TST Mk 1	
G-MTOT	Solar Wings Pegasus XL-R		G-MTSU	Solar Wings Pegasus XL-R	
G-MTOU	Solar Wings Pegasus XL-R		G-MTSV	Solar Wings Pegasus XL-R	
G-MTOV	Solar Wings Pegasus XL-R		G-MTSX	Solar Wings Pegasus XL-R	
G-MTOW	Solar Wings Pegasus XL-R		G-MTSY	Solar Wings Pegasus XL-R	
G-MTOX	Solar Wings Pegasus XL-R		G-MTSZ	Solar Wings Pegasus XL-R	
G-MTOY	Solar Wings Pegasus XL-R		G-MTTA	Solar Wings Pegasus XL-R	
G-MTOZ	Solar Wings Pegasus XL-R		G-MTTB	Solar Wings Pegasus XL-R	
G-MTPA	Mainair Gemini Flash IIA		G-MTTC	Solar Wings Pegasus XL-R	
G-MTPB	Mainair Gemini Flash IIA		G-MTTD	Solar Wings Pegasus XL-R	
G-MTPC	Raven X		G-MTTE	Solar Wings Pegasus XL-R	
G-MTPE	Solar Wings Pegasus XL-R		G-MTTF	Aerotech MW.6 Merlin	
G-MTPF	Solar Wings Pegasus XL-R		G-MTTH	CFM Shadow Srs BD	
G-MTPG	Solar Wings Pegasus XL-R		G-MTTI	Mainair Gemini Flash IIA	
G-MTPH	Solar Wings Pegasus XL-R		G-MTTK	Southdown Lightning DS	
G-MTPI	Solar Wings Pegasus XL-R		G-MTTL	Hiway Sky-Trike	
G-MTPJ	Solar Wings Pegasus XL-R		G-MTTM	Mainair Gemini Flash IIA	
G-MTPK	Solar Wings Pegasus XL-R		G-MTTN	Ultralight Flight Phantom	
G-MTPL	Solar Wings Pegasus XL-R		G-MTTO	Mainair Gemini Flash IIA	
G-MTPM	Solar Wings Pegasus XL-R		G-MTTP	Mainair Gemini Flash IIA	
G-MTPN	Solar Wings Pegasus XL-Q		G-MTTR	Mainair Gemini Flash IIA	
G-MTPO	Solar Wings Pegasus XL-Q		G-MTTS	Mainair Gemini Flash IIA	
G-MTPP	Solar Wings Pegasus XL-R		G-MTTU	Solar Wings Pegasus XL-R	
G-MTPR	Solar Wings Pegasus XL-R		G-MTTW	Mainair Gemini Flash IIA	
G-MTPS	Solar Wings Pegasus XL-Q		G-MTTX	Solar Wings Pegasus XL-Q	
G-MTPT	Thruster TST Mk 1		G-MTTY	Solar Wings Pegasus XL-Q	
G-MTPU	Thruster TST Mk 1		G-MTTZ	Solar Wings Pegasus XL-Q	
G-MTPV	Thruster TST Mk 1		G-MTUA	Solar Wings Pegasus XL-R	
G-MTPW	Thruster TST Mk 1		G-MTUB	Thruster TST Mk 1	
G-MTPX	Thruster TST Mk 1		G-MTUC	Thruster TST Mk 1	
G-MTPY	Thruster TST Mk 1		G-MTUD	Thruster TST Mk 1	
G-MTPZ	Solar Wings Pegasus XL-R		G-MTUE	Thruster TST Mk 1	

Reg.	Type	Notes	Reg.	Type	Notes
G-MTUF	Thruster TST Mk 1		G-MTXT	MBA Tiger Cub 440	
G-MTUG	Thruster TST Mk 1		G-MTXU	Noble Hardman Snowbird	
G-MTUH	Solar Wings Pegasus XL-R			Mk IV	
G-MTUI	Solar Wings Pegasus XL-R		G-MTXW	Noble Hardman Snowbird	
G-MTUJ	Solar Wings Pegasus XL-R			Mk IV	
G-MTUK	Solar Wings Pegasus XL-R		G-MTXY	Hornet Dual Trainer	
G-MTUL	Solar Wings Pegasus XL-R		G-MTXZ	Mainair Gemini Flash IIA	
G-MTUN	Solar Wings Pegasus XL-Q		G-MTYA	Solar Wings Pegasus XL-Q	
G-MTUP	Solar Wings Pegasus XL-Q		G-MTYC	Solar Wings Pegasus XL-Q	
G-MTUR	Solar Wings Pegasus XL-Q		G-MTYD	Solar Wings Pegasus XL-Q	
G-MTUS	Solar Wings Pegasus XL-Q		G-MTYE	Solar Wings Pegasus XL-Q	
G-MTUT	Solar Wings Pegasus XL-Q		G-MTYF	Solar Wings Pegasus XL-Q	
G-MTUU	Mainair Gemini Flash IIA		G-MTYG	Solar Wings Pegasus XL-Q	
G-MTUV	Mainair Gemini Flash IIA		G-MTYH	Solar Wings Pegasus XL-Q	
G-MTUX	Medway Hybred 44XLR		G-MTYI	Solar Wings Pegasus XL-Q	
G-MTUY	Solar Wings Pegasus XL-Q		G-MTYL	Solar Wings Pegasus XL-Q	
G-MTVA	Solar Wings Pegasus XL-R		G-MTYM	Solar Wings Pegasus XL-Q	
G-MTVB	Solar Wings Pegasus XL-R		G-MTYN	Solar Wings Pegasus XL-Q	
G-MTVC	Solar Wings Pegasus XL-R		G-MTYO	Solar Wings Pegasus XL-Q	
G-MTVE	Solar Wings Pegasus XL-R		G-MTYP	Solar Wings Pegasus XL-Q	
G-MTVF	Solar Wings Pegasus XL-R		G-MTYR	Solar Wings Pegasus XL-Q	
G-MTVG	Mainair Gemini Flash IIA		G-MTYS	Solar Wings Pegasus XL-Q	
G-MTVH	Mainair Gemini Flash IIA		G-MTYT	Solar Wings Pegasus XL-Q	
G-MTVI	Mainair Gemini Flash IIA		G-MTYU	Solar Wings Pegasus XL-Q	
G-MTVJ	Mainair Gemini Flash IIA		G-MTYV	Raven X	
G-MTVK	Solar Wings Pegasus XL-R		G-MTYW	Raven X	
G-MTVL	Solar Wings Pegasus XL-R		G-MTYX	Raven X	
G-MTVM	Solar Wings Pegasus XL-R		G-MTYY	Solar Wings Pegasus XL-R	
G-MTVN	Solar Wings Pegasus XL-R		G-MTZA	Thruster TST Mk 1	
G-MTVO	Solar Wings Pegasus XL-R		G-MTZB	Thruster TST Mk 1	
G-MTVP	Thruster TST Mk 1		G-MTZC	Thruster TST Mk 1	
G-MTVR	Thruster TST Mk 1		G-MTZD	Thruster TST Mk 1	
G-MTVS	Thruster TST Mk 1		G-MTZE	Thruster TST Mk 1	
G-MTVT	Thruster TST Mk 1		G-MTZF	Thruster TST Mk 1	
G-MTVV	Thruster TST Mk 1		G-MTZG	Mainair Gemini Flash IIA	
G-MTVX	Solar Wings Pegasus XL-Q		G-MTZH	Mainair Gemini Flash IIA	
G-MTVY	Solar Wings Pegasus XL-Q		G-MTZI	Solar Wings Pegasus XL-R	
G-MTVZ	Powerchute Raider		G-MTZJ	Solar Wings Pegasus XL-R	
G-MTWA	Solar Wings Pegasus XL-R		G-MTZK	Solar Wings Pegasus XL-R	
G-MTWB	Solar Wings Pegasus XL-R		G-MTZL	Mainair Gemini Flash IIA	
G-MTWD	Solar Wings Pegasus XL-R		G-MTZK	Solar Wings Pegasus XL-R	
G-MTWE	Solar Wings Pegasus XL-R		G-MTZM	Mainair Gemini Flash IIA	
G-MTWF	Mainair Gemini Flash IIA		G-MTZN	Mainair Gemini Flash IIA	
G-MTWG	Mainair Gemini Flash IIA		G-MTZO	Mainair Gemini Flash IIA	
G-MTWH	CFM Shadow Srs BD		G-MTZP	Solar Wings Pegasus XL-Q	
G-MTWK	CFM Shadow Srs BD		G-MTZR	Solar Wings Pegasus XL-Q	
G-MTWL	CFM Shadow Srs BD		G-MTZS	Solar Wings Pegasus XL-Q	
G-MTWM	CFM Shadow Srs BD		G-MTZT	Solar Wings Pegasus XL-Q	
G-MTWN	CFM Shadow Srs BD		G-MTZV	Mainair Gemini Flash IIA	
G-MTWP	CFM Shadow Srs BD		G-MTZW	Mainair Gemini Flash IIA	
G-MTWR	Mainair Gemini Flash IIA		G-MTZX	Mainair Gemini Flash IIA	
G-MTWS	Mainair Gemini Flash IIA		G-MTZY	Mainair Gemini Flash IIA	
G-MTWW	Solar Wings Typhoon		G-MTZZ	Mainair Gemini Flash IIA	
G-MTWX	Mainair Gemini Flash IIA		G-MVAA	Mainair Gemini Flash IIA	
G-MTWY	Thruster TST Mk 1		G-MVAB	Mainair Gemini Flash IIA	
G-MTWZ	Thruster TST Mk 1		G-MVAC	CFM Shadow Srs BD	
G-MTXA	Thruster TST Mk 1		G-MVAD	Mainair Gemini Flash IIA	
G-MTXB	Thruster TST Mk 1		G-MVAF	Southdown Puma Sprint	
G-MTXC	Thruster TST Mk 1		G-MVAG	Thruster TST Mk 1	
G-MTXD	Thruster TST Mk 1		G-MVAH	Thruster TST Mk 1	
G-MTXE	Hornet Dual Trainer		G-MVAI	Thruster TST Mk 1	
G-MTXG	Solar Wings Pegasus XL-Q		G-MVAJ	Thruster TST Mk 1	
G-MTXH	Solar Wings Pegasus XL-Q		G-MVAK	Thruster TST Mk 1	
G-MTXI	Solar Wings Pegasus XL-Q		G-MVAL	Thruster TST Mk 1	
G-MTXJ	Solar Wings Pegasus XL-Q		G-MVAM	CFM Shadow Srs BD	
G-MTXK	Solar Wings Pegasus XL-Q		G-MVAN	CFM Shadow Srs BD	
G-MTXL	Noble Hardman Snowbird		G-MVAO	Mainair Gemini Flash IIA	
	Mk IV		G-MVAP	Mainair Gemini Flash IIA	
G-MTXM	Mainair Gemini Flash IIA		G-MVAR	Solar Wings Pegasus XL-R	
G-MTXO	Whittaker MW.6		G-MVAS	Solar Wings Pegasus XL-R	
G-MTXP	Mainair Gemini Flash IIA		G-MVAT	Solar Wings Pegasus XL-R	
G-MTXR	CFM Shadow Srs BD		G-MVAU	Solar Wings Pegasus XL-R	
G-MTXS	Mainair Gemini Flash IIA		G-MVAV	Solar Wings Pegasus XL-R	

Reg.	Type	Notes	Reg.	Type	Notes
G-MVAW	Solar Wings Pegasus XL-Q		G-MVEA	Solar Wings Pegasus XL-R	
G-MVAX	Solar Wings Pegasus XL-Q		G-MVEB	Solar Wings Pegasus XL-R	
G-MVAY	Solar Wings Pegasus XL-Q		G-MVEC	Solar Wings Pegasus XL-R	
G-MVAZ	Solar Wings Pegasus XL-Q		G-MVED	Solar Wings Pegasus XL-R	
G-MVBA	Solar Wings Pegasus XL-Q		G-MVEE	Medway Hybred 44XLR	
G-MVBB	CFM Shadow Srs BD		G-MVEF	Solar Wings Pegasus XL-R	
G-MVBC	Aerial Arts Tri-Flyer 130SX		G-MVEG	Solar Wings Pegasus XL-R	
G-MVBD	Mainair Gemini Flash IIA		G-MVEI	CFM Shadow Srs BD	
G-MVBE	Mainair Scorcher		G-MVEJ	Mainair Gemini Flash IIA	
G-MVBF	Mainair Gemini Flash IIA		G-MVEK	Mainair Gemini Flash IIA	
G-MVBG	Mainair Gemini Flash IIA		G-MVEL	Mainair Gemini Flash IIA	
G-MVBH	Mainair Gemini Flash IIA		G-MVEN	CFM Shadow Srs BD	
G-MVBI	Mainair Gemini Flash IIA		G-MVEO	Mainair Gemini Flash IIA	
G-MVBJ	Solar Wings Pegasus XL-R		G-MVEP	Mainair Gemini Flash IIA	
G-MVBK	Mainair Gemini Flash IIA		G-MVER	Mainair Gemini Flash IIA	
G-MVBL	Mainair Gemini Flash IIA		G-MVES	Mainair Gemini Flash IIA	
G-MVBM	Mainair Gemini Flash IIA		G-MVET	Mainair Gemini Flash IIA	
G-MVBN	Mainair Gemini Flash IIA		G-MVEV	Mainair Gemini Flash IIA	
G-MVBO	Mainair Gemini Flash IIA		G-MVEW	Mainair Gemini Flash IIA	
G-MVBP	Thruster TST Mk 1		G-MVEX	Solar Wings Pegasus XL-Q	
G-MVBR	Thruster TST Mk 1		G-MVEY	Solar Wings Pegasus XL-Q	
G-MVBS	Thruster TST Mk 1		G-MVEZ	Solar Wings Pegasus XL-Q	
G-MVBT	Thruster TST Mk 1		G-MVFA	Solar Wings Pegasus XL-Q	
G-MVBU	Thruster TST Mk 1		G-MVFB	Solar Wings Pegasus XL-Q	
G-MVBY	Solar Wings Pegasus XL-R		G-MVFC	Solar Wings Pegasus XL-Q	
G-MVBZ	Solar Wings Pegasus XL-R		G-MVFD	Solar Wings Pegasus XL-Q	
G-MVCA	Solar Wings Pegasus XL-R		G-MVFE	Solar Wings Pegasus XL-Q	
G-MVCB	Solar Wings Pegasus XL-R		G-MVFF	Solar Wings Pegasus XL-Q	
G-MVCC	CFM Shadow Srs BD		G-MVFG	Solar Wings Pegasus XL-Q	
G-MVCD	Medway Hybred 44XLR		G-MVFH	CFM Shadow Srs BD	
G-MVCE	Mainair Gemini Flash IIA		G-MVFJ	Thruster TST Mk 1	
G-MVCF	Mainair Gemini Flash IIA		G-MVFK	Thruster TST Mk 1	
G-MVCH	Noble Hardman Snowbird Mk IV		G-MVFL	Thruster TST Mk 1	
			G-MVFM	Thruster TST Mk 1	
G-MVCI	Noble Hardman Snowbird Mk IV		G-MVFN	Thruster TST Mk 1	
			G-MVFO	Thruster TST Mk 1	
G-MVCJ	Noble Hardman Snowbird Mk IV		G-MVFP	Solar Wings Pegasus XL-R	
			G-MVFR	Solar Wings Pegasus XL-R	
G-MVCL	Solar Wings Pegasus XL-Q		G-MVFS	Solar Wings Pegasus XL-R	
G-MVCM	Solar Wings Pegasus XL-Q		G-MVFT	Solar Wings Pegasus XL-R	
G-MVCN	Solar Wings Pegasus XL-Q		G-MVFU	Solar Wings Pegasus XL-R	
G-MVCO	Solar Wings Pegasus XL-Q		G-MVFV	Solar Wings Pegasus XL-R	
G-MVCP	Solar Wings Pegasus XL-Q		G-MVFW	Solar Wings Pegasus XL-R	
G-MVCR	Solar Wings Pegasus XL-Q		G-MVFX	Solar Wings Pegasus XL-R	
G-MVCS	Solar Wings Pegasus XL-Q		G-MVFY	Solar Wings Pegasus XL-R	
G-MVCT	Solar Wings Pegasus XL-Q		G-MVFZ	Solar Wings Pegasus XL-R	
G-MVCV	Solar Wings Pegasus XL-Q		G-MVGA	Aerial Arts Chaser S	
G-MVCW	CFM Shadow Srs BD		G-MVGB	Medway Hybred 44XLR	
G-MVCY	Mainair Gemini Flash IIA		G-MVGC	AMF Chevvron 232	
G-MVCZ	Mainair Gemini Flash IIA		G-MVGD	AMF Chevvron 232	
G-MVDA	Mainair Gemini Flash IIA		G-MVGE	AMF Chevvron 232	
G-MVDB	Medway Hybred 44XLR		G-MVGF	Aerial Arts Chaser S	
G-MVDC	Medway Hybred 44XLR		G-MVGG	Aerial Arts Chaser S	
G-MVDD	Thruster TST Mk 1		G-MVGH	Aerial Arts Chaser S	
G-MVDE	Thruster TST Mk 1		G-MVGI	Aerial Arts Chaser S	
G-MVDF	Thruster TST Mk 1		G-MVGJ	Aerial Arts Chaser S	
G-MVDG	Thruster TST Mk 1		G-MVGK	Aerial Arts Chaser S	
G-MVDH	Thruster TST Mk 1		G-MVGL	Medway Hybred 44XLR	
G-MVDJ	Medway Hybred 44XLR		G-MVGM	Mainair Gemini Flash IIA	
G-MVDK	Aerial Arts Chaser S		G-MVGN	Solar Wings Pegasus XL-R	
G-MVDL	Aerial Arts Chaser S		G-MVGO	Solar Wings Pegasus XL-R	
G-MVDM	Aerial Arts Chaser S		G-MVGR	Solar Wings Pegasus XL-R	
G-MVDN	Aerial Arts Chaser S		G-MVGS	Solar Wings Pegasus XL-R	
G-MVDO	Aerial Arts Chaser S		G-MVGT	Solar Wings Pegasus XL-Q	
G-MVDP	Aerial Arts Chaser S		G-MVGU	Solar Wings Pegasus XL-Q	
G-MVDR	Aerial Arts Chaser S		G-MVGV	Solar Wings Pegasus XL-Q	
G-MVDT	Mainair Gemini Flash IIA		G-MVGW	Solar Wings Pegasus XL-Q	
G-MVDU	Solar Wings Pegasus XL-R		G-MVGX	Solar Wings Pegasus XL-Q	
G-MVDV	Solar Wings Pegasus XL-R		G-MVGY	Medway Hybred 44XL	
G-MVDW	Solar Wings Pegasus XL-R		G-MVGZ	Ultraflight Lazair IIIE	
G-MVDX	Solar Wings Pegasus XL-R		G-MVHA	Aerial Arts Chaser S	
G-MVDY	Solar Wings Pegasus XL-R		G-MVHB	Powerchute Raider	
G-MVDZ	Solar Wings Pegasus XL-R		G-MVHC	Powerchute Raider	

Reg.	Type	Notes	Reg.	Type	Notes
G-MVHD	CFM Shadow Srs BD		G-MVKB	Medway Hybred 44XLR	
G-MVHE	Mainair Gemini Flash IIA		G-MVKC	Mainair Gemini Flash IIA	
G-MVHF	Mainair Gemini Flash IIA		G-MVKE	Solar Wings Pegasus XL-R	
G-MVHG	Mainair Gemini Flash IIA		G-MVKF	Solar Wings Pegasus XL-R	
G-MVHH	Mainair Gemini Flash IIA		G-MVKG	Solar Wings Pegasus XL-R	
G-MVHI	Thruster TST Mk 1		G-M¨VKH	Solar Wings Pegasus XL-R	
G-MVHJ	Thruster TST Mk 1		G-MVKI	Solar Wings Pegasus XL-R	
G-MVHK	Thruster TST Mk 1		G-MVKJ	Solar Wings Pegasus XL-R	
G-MVHL	Thruster TST Mk 1		G-MVKK	Solar Wings Pegasus XL-R	
G-MVHM	Whittaker MW.5 Sorcerer		G-MVKL	Solar Wings Pegasus XL-R	
G-MVHN	Aerial Arts Chaser S		G-MVKM	Solar Wings Pegasus XL-R	
G-MVHO	Solar Wings Pegasus XL-Q		G-MVKN	Solar Wings Pegasus XL-Q	
G-MVHP	Solar Wings Pegasus XL-Q		G-MVKO	Solar Wings Pegasus XL-Q	
G-MVHR	Solar Wings Pegasus XL-Q		G-MVKP	Solar Wings Pegasus XL-Q	
G-MVHS	Solar Wings Pegasus XL-Q		G-MVKR	Solar Wings Pegasus XL-Q	
G-MVHT	Solar Wings Pegasus XL-Q		G-MVKS	Solar Wings Pegasus XL-Q	
G-MVHU	Solar Wings Pegasus XL-Q		G-MVKT	Solar Wings Pegasus XL-Q	
G-MVHV	Solar Wings Pegasus XL-Q		G-MVKU	Solar Wings Pegasus XL-Q	
G-MVHW	Solar Wings Pegasus XL-Q		G-MVKV	Solar Wings Pegasus XL-Q	
G-MVHX	Solar Wings Pegasus XL-Q		G-MVKW	Solar Wings Pegasus XL-Q	
G-MVHY	Solar Wings Pegasus XL-Q		G-MVKX	Solar Wings Pegasus XL-Q	
G-MVHZ	Hornet Dual Trainer		G-MVKY	Aerial Arts Chaser S	
G-MVIA	Solar Wings Pegasus XL-R		G-MVKZ	Aerial Arts Chaser S	
G-MVIB	Mainair Gemini Flash IIA		G-MVLA	Aerial Arts Chaser S	
G-MVIC	Mainair Gemini Flash IIA		G-MVLB	Aerial Arts Chaser S	
G-MVID	Aerial Arts Chaser S		G-MVLC	Aerial Arts Chaser S	
G-MVIE	Aerial Arts Chaser S		G-MVLD	Aerial Arts Chaser S	
G-MVIF	Medway Hybred 44XLR		G-MVLE	Aerial Arts Chaser S	
G-MVIG	CFM Shadow Srs B		G-MVLF	Aerial Arts Chaser S	
G-MVIH	Mainair Gemini Flash IIA		G-MVLG	Aerial Arts Chaser S	
G-MVIL	Noble Hardman Snowbird Mk IV		G-MVLH	Aerial Arts Chaser S	
			G-MVLJ	CFM Shadow Srs B	
G-MVIM	Noble Hardman Snowbird Mk IV		G-MVLL	Mainair Gemini Flash IIA	
			G-MVLP	CFM Shadow Srs BD	
G-MVIN	Noble Hardman Snowbird Mk IV		G-MVLR	Mainair Gemini Flash IIA	
			G-MVLS	Aerial Arts Chaser S	
G-MVIO	Noble Hardman Snowbird Mk IV		G-MVLT	Aerial Arts Chaser S	
			G-MVLU	Aerial Arts Chaser S	
G-MVIP	AMF Chevvron 232		G MVLW	Aerial Arts Chaser S	
G-MVIR	Thruster TST Mk 1		G-MVLX	Solar Wings Pegasus XL-Q	
G-MVIS	Thruster TST Mk 1		G-MVLY	Solar Wings Pegasus XL-Q	
G-MVIU	Thruster TST Mk 1		G-MVMA	Solar Wings Pegasus XL-Q	
G-MVIV	Thruster TST Mk 1		G-MVMB	Solar Wings Pegasus XL-Q	
G-MVIW	Thruster TST Mk 1		G-MVMC	Solar Wings Pegasus XL-Q	
G-MVIX	Mainair Gemini Flash IIA		G-MVMD	Powerchute Raider	
G-MVIY	Mainair Gemini Flash IIA		G-MVME	Thruster TST Mk 1	
G-MVIZ	Mainair Gemini Flash IIA		G-MVMG	Thruster TST Mk 1	
G-MVJA	Mainair Gemini Flash IIA		G-MVMI	Thruster TST Mk 1	
G-MVJB	Mainair Gemini Flash IIA		G-MVMK	Medway Hybred 44XLR	
G-MVJC	Mainair Gemini Flash IIA		G-MVML	Aerial Arts Chaser S	
G-MVJD	Solar Wings Pegasus XL-R		G-MVMM	Aerial Arts Chaser S	
G-MVJE	Mainair Gemini Flash IIA		G-MVMN	Mainair Gemini Flash IIA	
G-MVJF	Aerial Arts Chaser S		G-MVMO	Mainair Gemini Flash IIA	
G-MVJG	Aerial Arts Chaser S		G-MVMR	Mainair Gemini Flash IIA	
G-MVJH	Aerial Arts Chaser S		G-MVMT	Mainair Gemini Flash IIA	
G-MVJI	Aerial Arts Chaser S		G-MVMU	Mainair Gemini Flash IIA	
G-MVJJ	Aerial Arts Chaser S		G-MVMV	Aerotech MW.5 (K) Sorcerer	
G-MVJK	Aerial Arts Chaser S				
G-MVJL	Mainair Gemini Flash IIA		G-MVMW	Mainair Gemini Flash IIA	
G-MVJM	Microflight Spectrum		G-MVMX	Mainair Gemini Flash IIA	
G-MVJN	Solar Wings Pegasus XL-Q		G-MVMY	Mainair Gemini Flash IIA	
G-MVJO	Solar Wings Pegasus XL-Q		G-MVMZ	Mainair Gemini Flash IIA	
G-MVJP	Solar Wings Pegasus XL-Q		G-MVNA	Powerchute Raider	
G-MVJR	Solar Wings Pegasus XL-Q		G-MVNB	Powerchute Raider	
G-MVJS	Solar Wings Pegasus XL-Q		G-MVNC	Powerchute Raider	
G-MVJT	Solar Wings Pegasus XL-Q		G-MVND	Powerchute Raider	
G-MVJU	Solar Wings Pegasus XL-Q		G-MVNE	Powerchute Raider	
G-MVJV	Solar Wings Pegasus XL-Q		G-MVNF	Powerchute Raider	
G-MVJW	Solar Wings Pegasus XL-Q		G-MVNI	Powerchute Raider	
G-MVJX	Solar Wings Pegasus XL-Q		G-MVNJ	Powerchute Raider	
G-MVJZ	Birdman Cherokee		G-MVNK	Powerchute Raider	
G-MVKA	Medway Hybred 44XLR		G-MVNL	Powerchute Raider	

Reg.	Type	Notes	Reg.	Type	Notes
G-MVNM	Mainair Gemini Flash IIA		G-MVRG	Aerial Arts Chaser S	
G-MVNN	Whittaker MW.5 (K) Sorcerer		G-MVRH	Solar Wings Pegasus XL-Q	
G-MVNO	Aerotech MW.5 (K) Sorcerer		G-MVRI	Solar Wings Pegasus XL-Q	
			G-MVRJ	Solar Wings Pegasus XL-Q	
			G-MVRK	Solar Wings Pegasus XL-Q	
G-MVNP	Aerotech MW.5 (K) Sorcerer		G-MVRL	Aerial Arts Chaser S	
			G-MVRM	Mainair Gemini Flash IIA	
G-MVNR	Aerotech MW.5 (K) Sorcerer		G-MVRN	Rans S.4 Coyote	
			G-MVRO	CFM Shadow Srs BD	
G-MVNS	Aerotech MW.5 (K) Sorcerer		G-MVRP	CFM Shadow Srs BD	
			G-MVRR	CFM Shadow Srs BD	
G-MVNT	Whittaker MW.5 (K) Sorcerer		G-MVRT	CFM Shadow Srs BD	
			G-MVRU	Solar Wings Pegasus XL-Q	
G-MVNU	Aerotech MW.5 Sorcerer		G-MVRV	Powerchute Kestrel	
G-MVNV	Aerotech MW.5 Sorcerer		G-MVRW	Solar Wings Pegasus XL-Q	
G-MVNW	Mainair Gemini Flash IIA		G-MVRX	Solar Wings Pegasus XL-Q	
G-MVNX	Mainair Gemini Flash IIA		G-MVRY	Medway Hybred 44XLR	
G-MVNY	Mainair Gemini Flash IIA		G-MVRZ	Medway Hybred 44XLR	
G-MVNZ	Mainair Gemini Flash IIA		G-MVSA	Solar Wings Pegasus XL-Q	
G-MVOA	Aerial Arts Alligator		G-MVSB	Solar Wings Pegasus XL-Q	
G-MVOB	Mainair Gemini Flash IIA		G-MVSC	Solar Wings Pegasus XL-Q	
G-MVOD	Aerial Arts Chaser 110SX		G-MVSD	Solar Wings Pegasus XL-Q	
G-MVOE	Solar Wings Pegasus XL-R		G-MVSE	Solar Wings Pegasus XL-Q	
G-MVOF	Mainair Gemini Flash IIA		G-MVSG	Aerial Arts Chaser S	
G-MVOH	CFM Shadow Srs B		G-MVSI	Medway Hybred 44XLR	
G-MVOI	Noble Hardman Snowbird Mk IV		G-MVSJ	Aviasud Mistral 532	
			G-MVSK	Aerial Arts Chaser S	
G-MVOJ	Noble Hardman Snowbird Mk IV		G-MVSL	Aerial Arts Chaser S	
			G-MVSM	Midland Ultralights Sirocco	
G-MVOK	Noble Hardman Snowbird Mk IV		G-MVSN	Mainair Gemini Flash IIA	
			G-MVSO	Mainair Gemini Flash IIA	
G-MVOL	Noble Hardman Snowbird Mk IV		G-MVSP	Mainair Gemini Flash IIA	
			G-MVSR	Medway Hybred 44XLR	
G-MVON	Mainair Gemini Flash IIA		G-MVSS	Hornet RS-ZA	
G-MVOO	AMF Chevvron 232		G-MVST	Mainair Gemini Flash IIA	
G-MVOP	Aerial Arts Chaser S		G-MVSU	Microflight Spectrum	
G-MVOR	Mainair Gemini Flash IIA		G-MVSV	Mainair Gemini Flash IIA	
G-MVOS	Southdown Raven		G-MVSW	Solar Wings Pegasus XL-Q	
G-MVOT	Thruster TST Mk 1		G-MVSX	Solar Wings Pegasus XL-Q	
G-MVOU	Thruster TST Mk 1		G-MVSY	Solar Wings Pegasus XL-Q	
G-MVOV	Thruster TST Mk 1		G-MVSZ	Solar Wings Pegasus XL-Q	
G-MVOW	Thruster TST Mk 1		G-MVTA	Solar Wings Pegasus XL-Q	
G-MVOX	Thruster TST Mk 1		G-MVTC	Mainair Gemini Flash IIA	
G-MVOY	Thruster TST Mk 1		G-MVTD	Whittaker MW.6 Merlin	
G-MVPA	Mainair Gemini Flash IIA		G-MVTE	Whittaker MW.6 Merlin	
G-MVPB	Mainair Gemini Flash IIA		G-MVTF	Aerial Arts Chaser S	
G-MVPC	Mainair Gemini Flash IIA		G-MVTG	Solar Wings Pegasus XL-Q	
G-MVPD	Mainair Gemini Flash IIA		G-MVTI	Solar Wings Pegasus XL-Q	
G-MVPE	Mainair Gemini Flash IIA		G-MVTJ	Solar Wings Pegasus XL-Q	
G-MVPF	Medway Hybred 44XLR		G-MVTK	Solar Wings Pegasus XL-Q	
G-MVPG	Medway Hybred 44XLR		G-MVTL	Aerial Arts Chaser S	
G-MVPH	Whittaker MW.6 Merlin		G-MVTM	Aerial Arts Chaser S	
G-MVPI	Mainair Gemini Flash IIA		G-MVUA	Mainair Gemini Flash IIA	
G-MVPJ	Rans S.5		G-MVUB	Thruster T.300	
G-MVPK	CFM Shadow Srs B		G-MVUC	Medway Hybred 44XLR	
G-MVPL	Medway Hybred 44XLR		G-MVUD	Medway Hybred 44XLR	
G-MVPM	Whittaker MW.6 Merlin		G-MVUE	Solar Wings Pegasus XL-Q	
G-MVPN	Whittaker MW.6 Merlin		G-MVUF	Solar Wings Pegasus XL-Q	
G-MVPO	Whittaker MW.6 Merlin		G-MVUG	Solar Wings Pegasus XL-Q	
G-MVPR	Solar Wings Pegasus XL-Q		G-MVUH	Solar Wings Pegasus XL-Q	
G-MVPS	Solar Wings Pegasus XL-Q		G-MVUI	Solar Wings Pegasus XL-Q	
G-MVPT	Solar Wings Pegasus XL-Q		G-MVUJ	Solar Wings Pegasus XL-Q	
G-MVPU	Solar Wings Pegasus XL-Q		G-MVUK	Solar Wings Pegasus XL-Q	
G-MVPW	Solar Wings Pegasus XL-R		G-MVUL	Solar Wings Pegasus XL-Q	
G-MVPX	Solar Wings Pegasus XL-Q		G-MVUM	Solar Wings Pegasus XL-Q	
G-MVPY	Solar Wings Pegasus XL-Q		G-MVUN	Solar Wings Pegasus XL-Q	
G-MVPZ	Rans S.5		G-MVUO	AMF Chevvron 232	
G-MVRA	Mainair Gemini Flash IIA		G-MVUP	Aviasud Mistral	
G-MVRB	Mainair Gemini Flash IIA		G-MVUR	Hornet ZA	
G-MVRC	Mainair Gemini Flash IIA		G-MVUS	Aerial Arts Chaser S	
G-MVRD	Mainair Gemini Flash IIA		G-MVUT	Aerial Arts Chaser S	
G-MVRE	CFM Shadow Srs BD		G-MVUU	Hornet R-ZA	
G-MVRF	Rotec Rally 2B		G-MVVF	Medway Hybred 44XLR	

MICROLIGHTS

G-MVVG – G-MWCF

Reg.	Type	Notes	Reg.	Type	Notes
G-MVVG	Medway Hybred 44XLR		G-MVYV	Noble Hardman Snowbird Mk IV	
G-MVVH	Medway Hybred 44XLR		G-MVYW	Noble Hardman Snowbird Mk IV	
G-MVVI	Medway Hybred 44XLR				
G-MVVJ	Medway Hybred 44XLR		G-MVYX	Noble Hardman Snowbird Mk IV	
G-MVVK	Solar Wings Pegasus XL-R				
G-MVVM	Solar Wings Pegasus XL-R		G-MVYY	Aerial Arts Chaser S508	
G-MVVN	Solar Wings Pegasus XL-Q		G-MVYZ	CFM Shadow Srs BD	
G-MVVP	Solar Wings Pegasus XL-Q		G-MVZA	Thruster T.300	
G-MVVR	Medway Hybred 44XLR		G-MVZB	Thruster T.300	
G-MVVT	CFM Shadow Srs BD		G-MVZC	Thruster T.300	
G-MVVU	Aerial Arts Chaser S		G-MVZD	Thruster T.300	
G-MVVV	AMF Chevvron 232		G-MVZE	Thruster T.300	
G-MVVW	Aerial Arts Chaser S		G-MVZF	Thruster T.300	
G-MVVZ	Powerchute Raider		G-MVZG	Thruster T.300	
G-MVWA	Powerchute Raider		G-MVZH	Thruster T.300	
G-MVWB	Powerchute Raider		G-MVZI	Thruster T.300	
G-MVWD	Powerchute Raider		G-MVZJ	Solar Wings Pegasus XL-Q	
G-MVWE	Powerchute Raider		G-MVZK	Challenger II	
G-MVWF	Powerchute Raider		G-MVZL	Solar Wings Pegasus XL-Q	
G-MVWH	Powerchute Raider		G-MVZM	Aerial Arts Chaser S	
G-MVWN	Thruster T.300		G-MVZN	Aerial Arts Chaser S	
G-MVWO	Thruster T.300		G-MVZO	Medway Hybred 44XLR	
G-MVWP	Thruster T.300		G-MVZP	Renegade Spirit UK	
G-MVWR	Thruster T.300		G-MVZR	Aviasud Mistral	
G-MVWS	Thruster T.300		G-MVZS	Mainair Gemini Flash IIA	
G-MVWU	Medway Hybred 44XLR		G-MVZT	Solar Wings Pegasus XL-Q	
G-MVWV	Medway Hybred 44XLR		G-MVZU	Solar Wings Pegasus XL-Q	
G-MVWW	Aviasud Mistral 532		G-MVZV	Solar Wings Pegasus XL-Q	
G-MVWX	Microflight Spectrum		G-MVZW	Hornet R-ZA	
G-MVWZ	Aviasud Mistral		G-MVZX	Renegade Spirit UK	
G-MVXA	Whittaker MW.6 Merlin		G-MVZY	Aerial Arts Chaser S	
G-MVXB	Mainair Gemini Flash IIA		G-MVZZ	AMF Chevvron 232	
G-MVXC	Mainair Gemini Flash IIA		G-MWAB	Mainair Gemini Flash IIA	
G-MVXD	Medway Hybred 44XLR		G-MWAC	Solar Wings Pegasus XL-Q	
G-MVXE	Medway Hybred 44XLR		G-MWAD	Solar Wings Pegasus XL-Q	
G-MVXF	Weedhopper JC-31A		G-MWAE	CFM Shadow Srs BD	
G-MVXG	Aerial Arts Chaser S		G-MWAF	Solar Wings Pegasus XL-R	
G-MVXH	Microflight Spectrum		G-MWAG	Solar Wings Pegasus Xl -R	
G-MVXI	Medway Hybred 44XLR		G-MWAH	Hornet RS-ZA	
G-MVXJ	Medway Hybred 44XLR		G-MWAI	Solar Wings Pegasus XL-R	
G-MVXK	Medway Hybred 44XLR		G-MWAJ	Renegade Spirit UK	
G-MVXL	Thruster TST Mk 1		G-MWAL	Solar Wings Pegasus XL-Q	
G-MVXM	Medway Hybred 44XLR		G-MWAM	Thruster T.300	
G-MVXN	Aviasud Mistral		G-MWAN	Thruster T.300	
G-MVXP	Aerial Arts Chaser S		G-MWAO	Thruster T.300	
G-MVXR	Mainair Gemini Flash IIA		G-MWAP	Thruster T.300	
G-MVXS	Mainair Gemini Flash IIA		G-MWAR	Thruster T.300	
G-MVXT	Mainair Gemini Flash IIA		G-MWAS	Thruster T.300	
G-MVXU	Aviasud Mistral		G-MWAT	Solar Wings Pegasus XL-Q	
G-MVXV	Aviasud Mistral		G-MWAU	Mainair Gemini Flash IIA	
G-MVXW	Rans S.4 Coyote		G-MWAV	Solar Wings Pegasus XL-R	
G-MVXX	AMF Chevvron 232		G-MWAW	Whittaker MW.6 Merlin	
G-MVXZ	Minimax		G-MWBH	Hornet RS-ZA	
G-MVYA	Aerial Arts Chaser S		G-MWBI	Medway Hybred 44XLR	
G-MVYB	Solar Wings Pegasus XL-Q		G-MWBJ	Medway Sprint	
G-MVYC	Solar Wings Pegasus XL-Q		G-MWBK	Solar Wings Pegasus XL-Q	
G-MVYD	Solar Wings Pegasus XL-Q		G-MWBL	Solar Wings Pegasus XL-Q	
G-MVYE	Thruster TST Mk 1		G-MWBM	Hornet RS-ZA	
G-MVYG	Hornet R-ZA		G-MWBN	Hornet RS-ZA	
G-MVYH	Hornet R-ZA		G-MWBO	Rans S.4 Coyote	
G-MVYI	Hornet R-ZA		G-MWBP	Hornet RS-ZA	
G-MVYJ	Hornet R-ZA		G-MWBR	Hornet RS-ZA	
G-MVYK	Hornet R-ZA		G-MWBS	Hornet RS-ZA	
G-MVYM	Hornet R-ZA		G-MWBU	Hornet RS-ZA	
G-MVYN	Hornet R-ZA		G-MWBW	Hornet RS-ZA	
G-MVYO	Hornet R-ZA		G-MWBX	Hornet RS-ZA	
G-MVYP	Medway Hybred 44XLR		G-MWBY	Hornet RS-ZA	
G-MVYH	Medway Hybred 44XLR		G-MWBZ	Hornet RS-ZA	
G-MVYS	Mainair Gemini Flash IIA		G-MWCA	Hornet RS-ZA	
G-MVYT	Noble Hardman Snowbird Mk IV		G-MWCB	Solar Wings Pegasus XL-Q	
			G-MWCE	Mainair Gemini Flash IIA	
G-MVYU	Noble Hardman Snowbird Mk IV		G-MWCF	Solar Wings Pegasus XL-R	

Reg.	Type	Notes	Reg.	Type	Notes
G-MWCG	Microflight Spectrum		G-MWGC	Medway Hybred 44XLR	
G-MWCH	Rans S.6 Coyote		G-MWGD	Medway Hybred 44XLR	
G-MWCI	Powerchute Kestrel		G-MWGE	Medway Hybred 44XLR	
G-MWCJ	Powerchute Kestrel		G-MWGF	Renegade Spirit UK	
G-MWCK	Powerchute Kestrel		G-MWGG	Mainair Gemini Flash IIA	
G-MWCL	Powerchute Kestrel		G-MWGI	Whittaker MW.5 (K)	
G-MWCM	Powerchute Kestrel			Sorcerer	
G-MWCN	Powerchute Kestrel		G-MWGJ	Whittaker MW.5 (K)	
G-MWCO	Powerchute Kestrel			Sorcerer	
G-MWCP	Powerchute Kestrel		G-MWGK	Whittaker MW.5 (K)	
G-MWCR	Southdown Puma Sprint			Sorcerer	
G-MWCS	Powerchute Kestrel		G-MWGL	Solar Wings Pegasus XL-Q	
G-MWCU	Solar Wings Pegasus XL-R		G-MWGM	Solar Wings Pegasus XL-Q	
G-MWCV	Solar Wings Pegasus XL-Q		G-MWGN	Rans S.4 Coyote	
G-MWCW	Mainair Gemini Flash IIA		G-MWGO	Aerial Arts Chaser 110SX	
G-MWCX	Medway Hybred 44XLR		G-MWGR	Solar Wings Pegasus XL-Q	
G-MWCY	Medway Hybred 44XLR		G-MWGT	Powerchute Kestrel	
G-MWCZ	Medway Hybred 44XLR		G-MWGU	Powerchute Kestrel	
G-MWDB	CFM Shadow Srs BD		G-MWGV	Powerchute Kestrel	
G-MWDC	Solar Wings Pegasus XL-R		G-MWGW	Powerchute Kestrel	
G-MWDD	Solar Wings Pegasus XL-Q		G-MWGY	Powerchute Kestrel	
G-MWDE	Hornet RS-ZA		G-MWGZ	Powerchute Kestrel	
G-MWDF	Hornet RS-ZA		G-MWHC	Solar Wings Pegasus XL-Q	
G-MWDG	Hornet RS-ZA		G-MWHD	Microflight Spectrum	
G-MWDH	Hornet RS-ZA		G-MWHE	Microflight Spectrum	
G-MWDI	Hornet RS-ZA		G-MWHF	Solar Wings Pegasus XL-Q	
G-MWDJ	Mainair Gemini Flash IIA		G-MWHG	Solar Wings Pegasus XL-Q	
G-MWDK	Solar Wings Pegasus XL-R		G-MWHH	Team Minimax	
G-MWDL	Solar Wings Pegasus XL-R		G-MWHI	Mainair Gemini Flash IIA	
G-MWDM	Renegade Spirit UK		G-MWHJ	Solar Wings Pegasus XL-Q	
G-MWDN	CFM Shadow Srs BD		G-MWHK	Renegade Spirit UK	
G-MWDP	Thruster TST Mk 1		G-MWHL	Solar Wings Pegasus XL-Q	
G-MWDS	Thruster T.300		G-MWHM	Whittaker MW.6 Merlin	
G-MWDZ	Eipper Quicksilver MXL II		G-MWHO	Mainair Gemini	
G-MWEE	Solar Wings Pegasus XL-Q			Flash IIA	
G-MWEF	Solar Wings Pegasus XL-Q		G-MWHP	Rans S.6-ESD Coyote	
G-MWEG	Solar Wings Pegasus XL-Q		G-MWHR	Mainair Gemini Flash IIA	
G-MWEH	Solar Wings Pegasus XL-Q		G-MWHS	AMF Chevvron 232	
G-MWEI	Mainair Gemini Flash IIA		G-MWHT	SW Pegasus Quasar	
G-MWEK	Whittaker MW.5 Sorcerer		G-MWHU	SW Pegasus Quasar	
G-MWEL	Mainair Gemini Flash IIA		G-MWHV	SW Pegasus Quasar	
G-MWEM	Medway Hybred 44XLR		G-MWHW	Solar Wings Pegasus XL-Q	
G-MWEN	CFM Shadow Srs BD		G-MWHX	Solar Wings Pegasus XL-Q	
G-MWEO	Whittaker MW.5 Sorcerer		G-MWHY	Mainair Gemini Flash IIA	
G-MWEP	Rans S.4 Coyote		G-MWHZ	Trion J-1	
G-MWER	Solar Wings Pegasus XL-Q		G-MWIA	Mainair Gemini Flash IIA	
G-MWES	Rans S.4 Coyote		G-MWIB	Aviasud Mistral	
G-MWET	Hornet RS-ZA		G-MWIC	Whittaker MW.5 Sorcerer	
G-MWEU	Hornet RS-ZA		G-MWID	Solar Wings Pegasus XL-Q	
G-MWEV	Hornet RS-ZA		G-MWIE	Solar Wings Pegasus XL-Q	
G-MWEZ	CFM Shadow Srs CD		G-MWIF	Rans S.6-ESD Coyote II	
G-MWFA	Solar Wings Pegasus XL-R		G-MWIG	Mainair Gemini Flash IIA	
G-MWFB	CFM Shadow Srs BD		G-MWIH	Mainair Gemini Flash IIA	
G-MWFD	Team Minimax		G-MWIJ	Medway Hybred 44XLR	
G-MWFE	Robin 330/Lightning 195		G-MWIK	Medway Hybred 44XLR	
G-MWFF	Rans S.4 Coyote		G-MWIL	Medway Hybred 44XLR	
G-MWFG	Powerchute Kestrel		G-MWIM	SW Pegasus Quasar	
G-MWFH	Powerchute Kestrel		G-MWIN	Mainair Gemini Flash IIA	
G-MWFI	Powerchute Kestrel		G-MWIO	Rans S.4 Coyote	
G-MWFK	Powerchute Kestrel		G-MWIP	Whittaker MW.6 Merlin	
G-MWFL	Powerchute Kestrel		G-MWIR	Solar Wings Pegasus XL-Q	
G-MWFN	Powerchute Kestrel		G-MWIS	Solar Wings Pegasus XL-Q	
G-MWFO	Solar Wings Pegasus XL-R		G-MWIT	Solar Wings Pegasus XL-Q	
G-MWFP	Solar Wings Pegasus XL-R		G-MWIU	Solar Wings Pegasus XL-Q	
G-MWFS	Solar Wings Pegasus XL-Q		G-MWIV	Mainair Gemini Flash IIA	
G-MWFT	MBA Tiger Cub 440		G-MWIW	SW Pegasus Quasar	
G-MWFU	Quad City Challenger II UK		G-MWIX	SW Pegasus Quasar	
G-MWFV	Quad City Challenger II UK		G-MWIY	SW Pegasus Quasar	
G-MWFW	Rans S.4 Coyote		G-MWIZ	CFM Shadow Srs BD	
G-MWFX	Quad City Challenger II UK		G-MWJD	SW Pegasus Quasar	
G-MWFY	Quad City Challenger II UK		G-MWJF	CFM Shadow Srs BD	
G-MWFZ	Quad City Challenger II UK		G-MWJG	Solar Wings Pegasus XL-R	
G-MWGA	Rans S.5 Coyote		G-MWJH	SW Pegasus Quasar	

Reg.	Type	Notes	Reg.	Type	Notes
G-MWJI	SW Pegasus Quasar		G-MWMZ	Solar Wings Pegasus XL-Q	
G-MWJJ	SW Pegasus Quasar		G-MWNA	Solar Wings Pegasus XL-Q	
G-MWJK	SW Pegasus Quasar		G-MWNB	Solar Wings Pegasus XL-Q	
G-MWJL	AMF Chevvron 232		G-MWNC	Solar Wings Pegasus XL-Q	
G-MWJM	AMF Chevvron 232		G-MWND	Tiger Cub Developments	
G-MWJN	Solar Wings Pegasus XL-Q			RL.5A	
G-MWJO	Solar Wings Pegasus XL-Q		G-MWNE	Mainair Gemini Flash IIA	
G-MWJP	Medway Hybred 44XLR		G-MWNF	Renegade Spirit UK	
G-MWJR	Medway Hybred 44XLR		G-MWNG	Solar Wings Pegasus XL-Q	
G-MWJS	SW Pegasus Quasar		G-MWNK	SW Pegasus Quasar	
G-MWJT	SW Pegasus Quasar		G-MWNL	SW Pegasus Quasar	
G-MWJU	SW Pegasus Quasar		G-MWNM	SW Pegasus Quasar	
G-MWJV	SW Pegasus Quasar		G-MWNN	SW Pegasus Quasar	
G-MWJW	Whittaker MW.5 Sorcerer		G-MWNO	AMF Chevvron 232	
G-MWJX	Medway Puma Sprint		G-MWNP	AMF Chevvron 232	
G-MWJY	Mainair Gemini Flash IIA		G-MWNR	Renegade Spirit UK	
G-MWJZ	CFM Shadow Srs CD		G-MWNS	Mainair Gemini Flash IIA	
G-MWKA	Renegade Spirit UK		G-MWNT	Mainair Gemini Flash IIA	
G-MWKE	Hornet R-ZA		G-MWNU	Mainair Gemini Flash IIA	
G-MWKO	Solar Wings Pegasus XL-Q		G-MWNV	Powerchute Kestrel	
G-MWKP	Solar Wings Pegasus XL-Q		G-MWNW	Powerchute Kestrel	
G-MWKW	Microflight Spectrum		G-MWNX	Powerchute Kestrel	
G-MWKX	Microflight Spectrum		G-MWNY	Powerchute Kestrel	
G-MWKY	Solar Wings Pegasus XL-Q		G-MWNZ	Powerchute Kestrel	
G-MWKZ	Solar Wings Pegasus XL-Q		G-MWOB	Powerchute Kestrel	
G-MWLA	Rans S.4 Coyote		G-MWOC	Powerchute Kestrel	
G-MWLB	Medway Hybred 44XLR		G-MWOD	Powerchute Kestrel	
G-MWLC	Medway Hybred 44XLR		G-MWOE	Powerchute Kestrel	
G-MWLD	CFM Shadow Srs BD		G-MWOF	Microflight Spectrum	
G-MWLE	Solar Wings Pegasus XL-R		G-MWOH	Solar Wings Pegasus XL-R	
G-MWLF	Solar Wings Pegasus XL-R		G-MWOI	Solar Wings Pegasus XL-R	
G-MWLG	Solar Wings Pegasus XL-R		G-MWOJ	Mainair Gemini Flash IIA	
G-MWLH	Solar Wings Pegasus XL-R		G-MWOK	Mainair Gemini Flash IIA	
G-MWLI	SW Pegasus Quasar		G-MWOL	Mainair Gemini Flash IIA	
G-MWLJ	SW Pegasus Quasar		G-MWOM	SW Pegasus Quasar TC	
G-MWLK	SW Pegasus Quasar		G-MWON	CFM Shadow Srs CD	
G-MWLL	Solar Wings Pegasus XL-Q		G-MWOO	Renegade Spirit UK	
G-MWLM	Solar Wings Pegasus XL-Q		G-MWOP	SW Pegasus Quasar	
G-MWLN	Whittaker MW.6-S Fatboy		G-MWOR	Solar Wings Pegasus XL-Q	
	Flyer		G-MWOS	Cosmos Chronos	
G-MWLO	Whittaker MW.6 Merlin		G-MWOT	Icarus Covert Insertion &	
G-MWLP	Mainair Gemini Flash IIA			Recovery Vehicle	
G-MWLR	Mainair Gemini Flash IIA		G-MWOU	Medway Hybred 44XLR	
G-MWLS	Medway Hybred 44XLR		G-MWOV	Whittaker MW.6 Merlin	
G-MWLT	Mainair Gemini Flash IIA		G-MWOW	CFM Shadow Srs B	
G-MWLU	Solar Wings Pegasus XL-R		G-MWOX	Solar Wings Pegasus XL-Q	
G-MWLW	Team Minimax		G-MWOY	Solar Wings Pegasus XL-Q	
G-MWLX	Mainair Gemini Flash IIA		G-MWPA	Mainair Gemini Flash IIA	
G-MWLY	Rans S.4 Coyote		G-MWPB	Mainair Gemini Flash IIA	
G-MWLZ	Rans S.4 Coyote		G-MWPC	Mainair Gemini Flash IIA	
G-MWMA	Powerchute Kestrel		G-MWPD	Mainair Gemini Flash IIA	
G-MWMB	Powerchute Kestrel		G-MWPE	Solar Wings Pegasus XL-Q	
G-MWMC	Powerchute Kestrel		G-MWPF	Mainair Gemini Flash IIA	
G-MWMD	Powerchute Kestrel		G-MWPG	Microflight Spectrum	
G-MWMF	Powerchute Kestrel		G-MWPH	Microflight Spectrum	
G-MWMG	Powerchute Kestrel		G-MWPI	Microflight Spectrum	
G-MWMH	Powerchute Kestrel		G-MWPJ	Solar Wings Pegasus XL-Q	
G-MWMI	SW Pegasus Quasar		G-MWPK	Solar Wings Pegasus XL-Q	
G-MWMJ	SW Pegasus Quasar		G-MWPL	MBA Tiger Cub 440	
G-MWMK	SW Pegasus Quasar		G-MWPN	CFM Shadow Srs CD	
G-MWML	SW Pegasus Quasar		G-MWPO	Mainair Gemini Flash IIA	
G-MWMM	Mainair Gemini Flash IIA		G-MWPP	CFM Streak Shadow	
G-MWMN	Solar Wings Pegasus XL-Q			(G-BTEM)	
G-MWMO	Solar Wings Pegasus XL-Q		G-MWPR	Whittaker MW.6 Merlin	
G-MWMP	Solar Wings Pegasus XL-Q		G-MWPS	Renegade Spirit UK	
G-MWMR	Solar Wings Pegasus XL-R		G-MWPU	SW Pegasus Quasar TC	
G-MWMS	Mainair Gemini Flash		G-MWPX	Solar Wings Pegasus XL-R	
G-MWMT	Mainair Gemini Flash IIA		G-MWPZ	Renegade Spirit UK	
G-MWMU	CFM Shadow Srs CD		G-MWRA	Mainair Gemini Flash IIA	
G-MWMV	Solar Wings Pegasus XL-R		G-MWRB	Mainair Gemini Flash IIA	
G-MWMW	Renegade Spirit UK		G-MWRC	Mainair Gemini Flash IIA	
G-MWMX	Mainair Gemini Flash IIA		G-MWRD	Mainair Gemini Flash IIA	
G-MWMY	Mainair Gemini Flash IIA		G-MWRE	Mainair Gemini Flash IIA	

Reg.	Type	Notes	Reg.	Type	Notes
G-MWRF	Mainair Gemini Flash IIA		G-MWUF	Solar Wings Pegasus XL-R	
G-MWRG	Mainair Gemini Flash IIA		G-MWUG	Solar Wings Pegasus XL-R	
G-MWRH	Mainair Gemini Flash IIA		G-MWUH	Renegade Spirit UK	
G-MWRI	Mainair Gemini Flash IIA		G-MWUI	AMF Chevvron 232C	
G-MWRJ	Mainair Gemini Flash IIA		G-MWUJ	Medway Hybred 44XLR	
G-MWRK	Rans S.6 Coyote II		G-MWUK	Rans S.6-ESD Coyote II	
G-MWRL	CFM Shadow Srs CD		G-MWUL	Rans S.6-ESD Coyote II	
G-MWRM	Medway Hybred 44XLR		G-MWUO	Solar Wings Pegasus XL-Q	
G-MWRN	Solar Wings Pegasus XL-R		G-MWUP	Solar Wings Pegasus XL-R	
G-MWRO	Solar Wings Pegasus XL-R		G-MWUR	Solar Wings Pegasus XL-R	
G-MWRP	Solar Wings Pegasus XL-R		G-MWUS	Solar Wings Pegasus XL-R	
G-MWRR	Mainair Gemini Flash IIA		G-MWUT	Solar Wings Pegasus XL-R	
G-MWRS	Ultravia Super Pelican		G-MWUU	Solar Wings Pegasus XL-R	
G-MWRT	Solar Wings Pegasus XL-R		G-MWUV	Solar Wings Pegasus XL-R	
G-MWRU	Solar Wings Pegasus XL-R		G-MWUW	Solar Wings Pegasus XL-R	
G-MWRV	Solar Wings Pegasus XL-R		G-MWUX	Solar Wings Pegasus XL-Q	
G-MWRW	Solar Wings Pegasus XL-Q		G-MWUY	Solar Wings Pegasus XL-Q	
G-MWRX	Solar Wings Pegasus XL-Q		G-MWUZ	Solar Wings Pegasus XL-Q	
G-MWRY	CFM Shadow Srs CD		G-MWVA	Solar Wings Pegasus XL-Q	
G-MWRZ	AMF Chevvron 232		G-MWVB	Solar Wings Pegasus XL-R	
G-MWSA	Team Minimax		G-MWVE	Solar Wings Pegasus XL-R	
G-MWSB	Mainair Gemini Flash IIA		G-MWVF	Solar Wings Pegasus XL-R	
G-MWSC	Rans S.6-ESD Coyote II		G-MWVG	CFM Shadow Srs CD	
G-MWSD	Solar Wings Pegasus XL-Q		G-MWVH	CFM Shadow Srs CD	
G-MWSE	Solar Wings Pegasus XL-R		G-MWVI	Whittaker MW.6 Merlin	
G-MWSF	Solar Wings Pegasus XL-R		G-MWVJ	Mainair Mercury	
G-MWSG	Solar Wings Pegasus XL-R		G-MWVK	Mainair Mercury	
G-MWSH	SW Pegasus Quasar TC		G-MWVL	Rans S.6-ESD Coyote II	
G-MWSI	SW Pegasus Quasar TC		G-MWVM	SW Pegasus Quasar II	
G-MWSJ	Solar Wings Pegasus XL-Q		G-MWVN	Mainair Gemini Flash IIA	
G-MWSK	Solar Wings Pegasus XL-Q		G-MWVO	Mainair Gemini Flash IIA	
G-MWSL	Mainair Gemini Flash IIA		G-MWVP	Renegade Spirit UK	
G-MWSM	Mainair Gemini Flash IIA		G-MWVS	Mainair Gemini Flash IIA	
G-MWSN	SW Pegasus Quasar TC		G-MWVT	Mainair Gemini Flash IIA	
G-MWSO	Solar Wings Pegasus XL-R		G-MWVU	Medway Hybred 44XLR	
G-MWSP	Solar Wings Pegasus XL-R		G-MWVW	Mainair Gemini Flash IIA	
G-MWSR	Solar Wings Pegasus XL-R		G-MWVX	Quad City Challenger II UK	
G-MWSS	Medway Hybred 44XLR		G-MWVY	Mainair Gemini Flash IIA	
G-MWST	Medway Hybred 44XLR		G-MWVZ	Mainair Gemini Flash IIA	
G-MWSU	Medway Hybred 44XLR		G-MWWA	SW Pegasus Quasar II	
G-MWSV	SW Pegasus Quasar TC		G-MWWB	Mainair Gemini Flash IIA	
G-MWSW	Whittaker MW.6 Merlin		G-MWWC	Mainair Gemini Flash IIA	
G-MWSX	Whittaker MW.5 Sorcerer		G-MWWD	Mainair Gemini Flash IIA	
G-MWSY	Whittaker MW.5 Sorcerer		G-MWWE	Team Minimax	
G-MWSZ	CFM Shadow Srs CD		G-MWWF	Kolb Twinstar Mk 3	
G-MWTA	Solar Wings Pegasus XL-Q		G-MWWG	Solar Wings Pegasus XL-Q	
G-MWTB	Solar Wings Pegasus XL-Q		G-MWWH	Solar Wings Pegasus XL-Q	
G-MWTC	Solar Wings Pegasus XL-Q		G-MWWI	Mainair Gemini Flash IIA	
G-MWTD	Microflight Spectrum		G-MWWJ	Mainair Gemini Flash IIA	
G-MWTE	Microflight Spectrum		G-MWWK	Mainair Gemini Flash IIA	
G-MWTF	Mainair Gemini		G-MWWL	Rans S.6-ESD Coyote II	
G-MWTG	Mainair Gemini Flash IIA		G-MWWM	Kolb Twinstar Mk 2	
G-MWTH	Mainair Gemini Flash IIA		G-MWWN	Mainair Gemini Flash IIA	
G-MWTI	Solar Wings Pegasus XL-Q		G-MWWO	Solar Wings Pegasus XL-R	
G-MWTJ	CFM Shadow Srs CD		G-MWWP	Rans S.4 Coyote	
G-MWTK	Solar Wings Pegasus XL-R		G-MWVR	Mainair Gemini Flash IIA	
G-MWTL	Solar Wings Pegasus XL-R		G-MWWR	Microflight Spectrum	
G-MWTM	Solar Wings Pegasus XL-R		G-MWWS	Thruster T.300	
G-MWTN	CFM Shadow Srs CD		G-MWWT	Thruster Super T.300	
G-MWTO	Mainair Gemini Flash IIA		G-MWWU	Air Creation Fun 18 GTBI	
G-MWTP	CFM Shadow Srs CD		G-MWWV	Solar Wings Pegasus XL-Q	
G-MWTR	Mainair Gemini Flash IIA		G-MWWW	Whittaker MW.6-S Fatboy	
G-MWTS	Whittaker MW.6-S Fatboy Flyer			Flyer	
			G-MWWX	Microflight Spectrum	
G-MWTT	Rans S.6-ESD Coyote II		G-MWWY	Microflight Spectrum	
G-MWTU	Solar Wings Pegasus XL-R		G-MWWZ	Cyclone Chaser S	
G-MWTX	Medway Hybred 44XLR		G-MWXA	Mainair Gemini Flash IIA	
G-MWTY	Mainair Gemini Flash IIA		G-MWXB	Mainair Gemini Flash IIA	
G-MWTZ	Mainair Gemini Flash IIA		G-MWXC	Mainair Gemini Flash IIA	
G-MWUA	CFM Shadow Srs CD		G-MWXD	Mainair Gemini Flash IIA	
G-MWUB	Solar Wings Pegasus XL-R		G-MWXE	Flexiform Skytrike	
G-MWUC	Solar Wings Pegasus XL-R		G-MWXF	Mainair Mercury	
G-MWUD	Solar Wings Pegasus XL-R		G-MWXG	SW Pegasus Quasar IITC	

Reg.	Type	Notes	Reg.	Type	Notes
G-MWXH	SW Pegasus Quasar IITC		G-MYAM	Renegade Spirit UK	
G-MWXI	SW Pegasus Quasar IITC		G-MYAN	Whittaker MW.5 (K)	
G-MWXJ	Mainair Mercury			Sorcerer	
G-MWXK	Mainair Mercury		G-MYAO	Mainair Gemini Flash IIA	
G-MWXL	Mainair Gemini Flash IIA		G-MYAP	Thruster T.300	
G-MWXN	Mainair Gemini Flash IIA		G-MYAR	Thruster T.300	
G-MWXO	Mainair Gemini Flash IIA		G-MYAS	Mainair Gemini Flash IIA	
G-MWXP	Solar Wings Pegasus XL-Q		G-MYAT	Team Minimax	
G-MWXR	Solar Wings Pegasus XL-Q		G-MYAV	Mainair Mercury	
G-MWXS	Mainair Gemini Flash IIA		G-MYAW	Team Minimax	
G-MWXU	Mainair Gemini Flash IIA		G-MYAY	Microflight Spectrum	
G-MWXV	Mainair Gemini Flash IIA		G-MYAZ	Renegade Spirit UK	
G-MWXW	Cyclone Chaser S		G-MYBA	Rans S.6-ESD Coyote II	
G-MWXX	Cyclone Chaser S 447		G-MYBB	Maxair Drifter	
G-MWXY	Cyclone Chaser S 447		G-MYBC	CFM Shadow Srs CD	
G-MWXZ	Cyclone Chaser S 508		G-MYBD	SW Pegasus Quaser IITC	
G-MWYA	Mainair Gemini Flash IIA		G-MYBE	SW Pegasus Quaser IITC	
G-MWYB	Solar Wings Pegasus XL-Q		G-MYBF	Solar Wings Pegasus XL-Q	
G-MWYC	Solar Wings Pegasus XL-Q		G-MYBG	Solar Wings Pegasus XL-Q	
G-MWYD	CFM Shadow Srs C		G-MYBH	Quicksilver GT500	
G-MWYE	Rans S.6-ESD Coyote II		G-MYBI	Rans S.6-ESD Coyote II	
G-MWYF	Rans S.6 Coyote II		G-MYBJ	Mainair Gemini Flash IIA	
G-MWYG	Mainair Gemini Flash IIA		G-MYBK	SW Pegasus Quasar IITC	
G-MWYH	Mainair Gemini Flash IIA		G-MYBL	CFM Shadow Srs C	
G-MWYI	SW Pegasus Quasar II		G-MYBM	Team Minimax	
G-MWYJ	SW Pegasus Quasar IITC		G-MYBN	Hiway Demon 175	
G-MWYL	Mainair Gemini Flash IIA		G-MYBO	Solar Wings Pegasus XL-R	
G-MWYM	Cyclone Chaser S 1000		G-MYBP	Solar Wings Pegasus XL-R	
G-MWYN	Rans S.6-ESD Coyote II		G-MYBR	Solar Wings Pegasus XL-Q	
G-MWYS	CGS Hawk 1 Arrow		G-MYBS	Solar Wings Pegasus XL-Q	
G-MWYT	Mainair Gemini Flash IIA		G-MYBT	SW Pegasus Quasar IITC	
G-MWYU	Solar Wings Pegasus XL-Q		G-MYBU	Cyclone Chaser S447	
G-MWYV	Mainair Gemini Flash IIA		G-MYBV	Solar Wings Pegasus XL-Q	
G-MWYX	Mainair Gemini Flash IIA		G-MYBW	Solar Wings Pegasus XL-Q	
G-MWYY	Mainair Gemini Flash IIA		G-MYBX	Solar Wings Pegasus XL-Q	
G-MWYZ	Solar Wings Pegasus XL-Q		G-MYBY	Solar Wings Pegasus XL-Q	
G-MWZA	Mainair Mercury		G-MYBZ	Solar Wings Pegasus XL-Q	
G-MWZB	AMF Chevvron 2-32C		G-MYCA	Whittaker MW.6 Merlin	
G-MWZC	Mainair Gemini Flash IIA		G-MYCB	Cyclone Chaser S 447	
G-MWZD	SW Pegasus Quasar IITC		G-MYCD	CFM Shadow Srs CD	
G-MWZE	SW Pegasus Quasar IITC		G-MYCE	SW Pegasus Quasar IITC	
G-MWZF	SW Pegasus Quasar IITC		G-MYCF	SW Pegasus Quasar IITC	
G-MWZG	Mainair Gemini Flash IIA		G-MYCJ	Mainair Mercury	
G-MWZH	Solar Wings Pegasus XL-R		G-MYCK	Mainair Gemini Flash IIA	
G-MWZI	Solar Wings Pegasus XL-R		G-MYCL	Mainair Mercury	
G-MWZJ	Solar Wings Pegasus XL-R		G-MYCM	CFM Shadow Srs CD	
G-MWZK	Solar Wings Pegasus XL-R		G-MYCN	Mainair Mercury	
G-MWZL	Mainair Gemini Flash IIA		G-MYCO	Whittaker MW.6 Merlin	
G-MWZM	Team Minimax 91		G-MYCP	Whittaker MW.6 Merlin	
G-MWZN	Mainair Gemini Flash IIA		G-MYCR	Mainair Gemini Flash IIA	
G-MWZO	SW Pegasus Quasar IITC		G-MYCS	Mainair Gemini Flash IIA	
G-MWZP	SW Pegasus Quasar IITC		G-MYCT	Team Minimax	
G-MWZR	SW Pegasus Quasar IITC		G-MYCV	Mainair Mercury	
G-MWZS	SW Pegasus Quasar IITC		G-MYCW	Powerchute Kestrel	
G-MWZT	Solar Wings Pegasus XL-R		G-MYCX	Powerchute Kestrel	
G-MWZU	Solar Wings Pegasus XL-R		G-MYCY	Powerchute Kestrel	
G-MWZV	Solar Wings Pegasus XL-R		G-MYCZ	Powerchute Kestrel	
G-MWZW	Solar Wings Pegasus XL-R		G-MYDA	Powerchute Kestrel	
G-MWZX	Solar Wings Pegasus XL-R		G-MYDB	Powerchute Kestrel	
G-MWZY	Solar Wings Pegasus XL-R		G-MYDC	Mainair Mercury	
G-MWZZ	Solar Wings Pegasus XL-R		G-MYDD	CFM Shadow Srs CD	
G-MYAA	CFM Shadow Srs CD		G-MYDE	CFM Shadow Srs CD	
G-MYAB	Solar Wings Pegasus XL-R		G-MYDF	Team Minimax	
G-MYAC	Solar Wings Pegasus XL-Q		G-MYDG	Solar Wings Pegasus XL-R	
G-MYAD	Solar Wings Pegasus XL-Q		G-MYDI	Solar Wings Pegasus XL-R	
G-MYAE	Solar Wings Pegasus XL-Q		G-MYDJ	Solar Wings Pegasus XL-R	
G-MYAF	Solar Wings Pegasus XL-Q		G-MYDK	Rans S.6-ESD Coyote II	
G-MYAG	Quad City Challenger II		G-MYDL	Whittaker MW.5 (K)	
G-MYAH	Whittaker MW.5 Sorcerer			Sorcerer	
G-MYAI	Mainair Mercury		G-MYDM	Whittaker MW.6-S Fatboy	
G-MYAJ	Rans S.6-ESD Coyote II			Flyer	
G-MYAK	SW Pegasus Quasar IITC		G-MYDN	Quad City Challenger II	
G-MYAL	Rotec Rally 2B		G-MYDO	Rans S.5 Coyote	

Reg.	Type	Notes	Reg.	Type	Notes
G-MYDP	Kolb Twinstar Mk 3		G-MYHG	Cyclone AX/503	
G-MYDR	Thruster Tn.300		G-MYHH	Cyclone AX/503	
G-MYDS	Quad City Challenger II		G-MYHI	Rans S.6-ESD Coyote II	
G-MYDT	Thruster T.300		G-MYHJ	Cyclone AX3/503	
G-MYDU	Thruster T.300		G-MYHK	Rans S.6-ESD Coyote II	
G-MYDV	Thruster T.300		G-MYHL	Mainair Gemini Flash IIA	
G-MYDW	Whittaker MW.6 Merlin		G-MYHM	Cyclone AX3/503	
G-MYDX	Rans S.6-ESD Coyote II		G-MYHN	Mainair Gemini Flash IIA	
G-MYDZ	Mignet HM.1000 Balerit		G-MYHP	Rans S.6-ESD Coyote II	
G-MYEA	Solar Wings Pegasus XL-Q		G-MYHR	Cyclone AX3/503	
G-MYEC	Solar Wings Pegasus XL-Q		G-MYHS	Powerchute Kestrel	
G-MYED	Solar Wings Pegasus XL-R		G-MYHX	Mainair Gemini Flash IIA	
G-MYEE	Thruster TST Mk 1		G-MYIA	Quad City Challenger II	
G-MYEF	–		G-MYIE	Whittaker MW.6 Merlin	
G-MYEG	Solar Wings Pegasus XL-R		G-MYIF	CFM Shadow Srs CD	
G-MYEH	Solar Wings Pegasus XL-R		G-MYIG	Renegade Spirit	
G-MYEI	Cyclone Chaser S447		G-MYIH	Mainair Gemini Flash IIA	
G-MYEJ	Cyclone Chaser S447		G-MYII	Team Minimax	
G-MYEK	SW Pegasus Quasar IITC		G-MYIJ	Cyclone AX3/503	
G-MYEL	SW Pegasus Quasar IITC		G-MYIK	Kolb Twinstar Mk 3	
G-MYEM	SW Pegasus Quasar IITC		G-MYIL	Cyclone Chaser S 508	
G-MYEN	SW Pegasus Quasar IITC		G-MYIM	SW Pegasus Quasar IITC	
G-MYEO	SW Pegasus Quasar IITC		G-MYIN	SW Pegasus Quasar IITC	
G-MYEP	CFM Shadow Srs CD		G-MYIO	SW Pegasus Quasar IITC	
G-MYER	Cyclone AX3/503		G-MYIP	CFM Shadow Srs CD	
G-MYES	Rans S.6-ESD Coyote II		G-MYIR	Rans S.6-ESD Coyote II	
G-MYET	Whittaker MW.6 Merlin		G-MYIS	Rans S.6-ESD Coyote II	
G-MYEU	Mainair Gemini Flash IIA		G-MYIT	Cyclone Chaser S 508	
G-MYEV	Whittaker MW.6 Merlin		G-MYIU	Cyclone AX3/503	
G-MYEX	Powerchute Kestrel		G-MYIV	Mainair Gemini Flash IIA	
G-MYFA	Powerchute Kestrel		G-MYIW	Mainair Mercury	
G-MYFE	Rans S.6-ESD Coyote II		G-MYIX	Quad City Challenger II	
G-MYFF	–		G-MYIY	Mainair Gemini Flash IIA	
G-MYFG	Hunt Avon Skytrike		G-MYIZ	Team Minimax 2	
G-MYFH	Quad City Challenger II		G-MYJA	—	
G-MYFI	Cyclone AX3/503		G-MYJB	Mainair Gemini Flash IIA	
G-MYFJ	SW Pegasus Quasar IITC		G-MYJC	Mainair Gemini Flash IIA	
G-MYFK	SW Pegasus Quasar IITC		G-MYJD	Rans S.6-ESD Coyote II	
G-MYFL	SW Pegasus Quasar IITC		G-MYJE	CFM Shadow Srs CD	
G-MYFM	Renegade Spirit UK		G-MYJF	Thruster T.300	
G-MYFN	Rans S.5 Coyote		G-MYJG	Thruster Super T.300	
G-MYFO	Cyclone Chaser S		G-MYJH	Thruster Super T.300	
G-MYFP	Mainair Gemini Flash IIA		G-MYJJ	SW Pegasus Quasar IITC	
G-MYFR	Mainair Gemini Flash IIA		G-MYJK	SW Pegasus Quasar IITC	
G-MYFS	Solar Wings Pegasus XL-R		G-MYJL	Rans S.6-ESD Coyote II	
G-MYFT	Mainair Scorcher		G-MYJM	Mainair Gemini Flash IIA	
G-MYFU	Mainair Gemini Flash IIA		G-MYJN	Mainair Mercury	
G-MYFV	Cyclone AX3/503		G-MYJO	Cyclone Chaser S 508	
G-MYFW	Cyclone AX3/503		G-MYJP	Renegade Spirit UK	
G-MYFX	Solar Wings Pegasus XL-Q		G-MYJR	Mainair Mercury	
G-MYFY	Cyclone AX3/503		G-MYJS	SW Pegasus Quasar IITC	
G-MYFZ	Cyclone AX3/503		G-MYJT	SW Pegasus Quasar IITC	
G-MYGD	Cyclone AX3/503		G-MYJU	SW Pegasus Quasar IITC	
G-MYGE	Whittaker MW.6 Merlin		G-MYJW	Cyclone Chaser S 508	
G-MYGF	Team Minimax		G-MYJX	Whittaker MW.8	
G-MYGG	Mainair Mercury		G-MYJY	Rans S.6-ESD Coyote II	
G-MYGH	Rans S.6-ESD Coyote II		G-MYJZ	Whittaker MW.5D Sorcerer	
G-MYGI	Cyclone Chaser S447		G-MYKA	Cyclone AX3/503	
G-MYGJ	Mainair Mercury		G-MYKB	Kölb Twinstar Mk 3	
G-MYGK	Cyclone Chaser S508		G-MYKC	Mainair Gemini Flash IIA	
G-MYGL	Team Minimax		G-MYKD	Cyclone Chaser S 447	
G-MYGM	Quad City Challenger II		G-MYKE	CFM Shadow Srs BD	
G-MYGN	AMF Chevvron 240		G-MYKF	Cyclone AX3/503	
G-MYGO	CFM Shadow Srs CD		G-MYKG	Mainair Gemini Flash IIA	
G-MYGP	Rans S.6-ESD Coyote II		G-MYKH	Mainair Gemini Flash IIA	
G-MYGR	Rans S.6-ESD Coyote II		G-MYKI	Mainair Mercury	
G-MYGS	Whittaker MW.5 (K) Sorcerer		G-MYKJ	Team Minimax	
			G-MYKK	—	
G-MYGT	Solar Wings Pegasus XL-R		G-MYKL	Medway Raven	
G-MYGU	Solar Wings Pegasus XL-R		G-MYKM	Medway Raven	
G-MYGV	Solar Wings Pegasus XL-R		G-MYKN	Rans S.6-ESD Coyote II	
G-MYGZ	Mainair Gemini Flash IIA		G-MYKO	Whittaker MW.6-S Fat Boy Flyer	
G-MYHF	Mainair Gemini Flash IIA				

Reg.	Type	Notes	Reg.	Type	Notes
G-MYKP	SW Pegasus Quasar IITC		G-MYNO	SW Pegasus Quantum 15	
G-MYKR	SW Pegasus Quasar IITC		G-MYNP	SW Pegasus Quantum 15	
G-MYKS	SW Pegasus Quasar IITC		G-MYNR	SW Pegasus Quantum 15	
G-MYKT	Cyclone AX3/503		G-MYNS	SW Pegasus Quantum 15	
G-MYKU	Medway Raven		G-MYNT	SW Pegasus Quantum 15	
G-MYKV	Mainair Gemini Flash IIA		G-MYNU	SW Pegasus Quantum 15	
G-MYKW	Mainair Mercury		G-MYNV	SW Pegasus Quantum 15	
G-MYKX	Mainair Mercury		G-MYNW	Cyclone Chaser S 447	
G-MYKY	Mainair Mercury		G-MYNX	CFM Streak Shadow	
G-MYKZ	Team Minimax (G-BVAV)			Srs S-A1	
G-MYLA	Rans S.6-ESD Coyote II		G-MYNY	Kölb Twinstar Mk 3	
G-MYLB	Team Minimax		G-MYNZ	SW Pegasus Quantum 15	
G-MYLC	SW Pegasus Quantum 15		G-MYOA	Rans S.6-ESD Coyote II	
G-MYLD	Rans S.6-ESD Coyote II		G-MYOB	Mainair Mercury	
G-MYLE	SW Pegasus Quantum 15		G-MYOC	—	
G-MYLF	Rans S.6-ESD Coyote II		G-MYOD	SW Pegasus Quasar IITC	
G-MYLG	Mainair Gemini Flash IIA		G-MYOE	SW Pegasus Quantum 15	
G-MYLH	SW Pegasus Quantum 15		G-MYOF	Mainair Mercury	
G-MYLI	SW Pegasus Quantum 15		G-MYOG	Kölb Twinstar Mk 3	
G-MYLJ	Cyclone Chaser S 447		G-MYOH	CFM Shadow Srs CD	
G-MYLK	SW Pegasus Quantum 15		G-MYOI	Rans S.6-ESD Coyote II	
G-MYLL	SW Pegasus Quantum 15		G-MYOL	Air Creation Fun 18S	
G-MYLM	SW Pegasus Quasar IITC			GTBIS	
G-MYLN	Kölb Twinstar Mk 3		G-MYOM	Mainair Gemini Flash IIA	
G-MYLO	Rans S.6-ESD Coyote II		G-MYON	CFM Shadow Srs CD	
G-MYLP	Kölb Twinstar Mk 3		G-MYOO	Kölb Twinstar Mk 3	
	(G-BVCR)		G-MYOR	Kölb Twinstar Mk 3	
G-MYLR	Mainair Gemini Flash IIA		G-MYOT	Rans S.6-ESD Coyote II	
G-MYLS	Mainair Mercury		G-MYOU	SW Pegasus Quantum 15	
G-MYLT	Mainair Blade		G-MYOV	Mainair Mercury	
G-MYLU	Experience/Hunt Wing		G-MYOW	Mainair Gemini Flash IIA	
G-MYLV	CFM Shadow Srs CD		G-MYOX	Mainair Mercury	
G-MYLW	Rans S.6-ESD Coyote II		G-MYOY	Cyclone AX3/503	
G-MYLX	Medway Raven		G-MYOZ	Quad City Challenger II UK	
G-MYLY	Medway Raven		G-MYPA	Rans S.6-ESD Coyote II	
G-MYLZ	SW Pegasus Quantum 15		G-MYPB	Cyclone Chaser S 447	
G-MYMB	SW Pegasus Quantum 15		G-MYPC	Kölb Twinstar Mk 3	
G-MYMC	SW Pegasus Quantum 15		G-MYPD	Mainair Mercury	
G-MYMD	SW Pegasus Quantum 15		G-MYPE	Mainair Gemini Flash IIA	
G-MYME	Cyclone AX3/503		G-MYPF	SW Pegasus Quasar IITC	
G-MYMF	Cyclone AX3/503		G-MYPG	SW Pegasus XL-Q	
G-MYMG	Team Minimax		G-MYPH	SW Pegasus Quantum 15	
G-MYMH	Rans S.6-ESD Coyote II		G-MYPI	SW Pegasus Quantum 15	
G-MYMI	Kölb Twinstar Mk 3		G-MYPJ	Rans S.6-ESD Coyote II	
G-MYMJ	Medway Raven		G-MYPK	Rans S.6-ESD Coyote II	
G-MYMK	Mainair Gemini Flash IIA		G-MYPL	CFM Shadow Srs CD	
G-MYML	Mainair Mercury		G-MYPM	Cyclone AX3/503	
G-MYMM	Ultraflight Fun 18S		G-MYPN	SW Pegasus Quantum 15	
G-MYMN	Whittaker MW.6 Merlin		G-MYPO	Hunt Wing/Experience	
G-MYMO	Mainair Gemini Flash IIA		G-MYPP	Whittaker MW.6-S Fatboy	
G-MYMP	Rans S.6-ESD Coyote II			Flyer	
	(G-CHAZ)		G-MYPR	Cyclone AX3/503	
G-MYMR	Rans S.6-ESD Coyote II		G-MYPS	Whittaker MW.6 Merlin	
G-MYMS	Rans S.6-ESD Coyote II		G-MYPT	CFM Shadow Srs CD	
G-MYMT	Mainair Mercury		G-MYPU	Microchute UQ	
G-MYMU	Kölb Twinstar Mk 3		G-MYPV	Mainair Mercury	
G-MYMV	Mainair Gemini Flash IIA		G-MYPW	Mainair Gemini Flash IIA	
G-MYMW	Cyclone AX3/503		G-MYPX	SW Pegasus Quantum 15	
G-MYMX	SW Pegasus Quantum 15		G-MYPY	SW Pegasus Quantum 15	
G-MYMY	Cyclone Chaser S 508		G-MYPZ	Quad City Challenger II	
G-MYMZ	Cyclone AX3/503		G-MYRA	Kölb Twinstar Mk 3	
G-MYNA	CFM Shadow Srs BD		G-MYRB	Whittaker MW.5 Sorcerer	
G-MYNB	SW Pegasus Quantum 15		G-MYRC	Mainair Blade	
G-MYNC	Mainair Mercury		G-MYRD	Mainair Blade	
G-MYND	Mainair Gemini Flash IIA		G-MYRE	Cyclone Chaser S	
G-MYNE	Rans S.6-ESD Coyote II		G-MYRF	SW Pegasus Quantum 15	
G-MYNF	Mainair Mercury		G-MYRG	Team Minimax	
G-MYNH	Rans S.6-ESD Coyote II		G-MYRH	Quad City Challenger II	
G-MYNI	Team Minimax		G-MYRI	Medway 44XLH	
G-MYNJ	Mainair Mercury		G-MYRJ	Quad City Challenger II	
G-MYNK	SW Pegasus Quantum 15		G-MYRK	Renegade Spirit UK	
G-MYNL	SW Pegasus Quantum 15		G-MYRL	Team Minimax	
G-MYNN	SW Pegasus Quantum 15		G-MYRM	SW Pegasus Quantum 15	

Reg.	Type	Notes	Reg.	Type	Notes
G-MYRN	SW Pegasus Quantum 15		G-MYUM	Mainair Blade	
G-MYRO	Cyclone AX3/503		G-MYUN	Mainair Blade	
G-MYRP	Letov LK-2M Sluka		G-MYUO	Cycl Pegasus Quantum 15	
G-MYRR	Letov LK-2M Sluka		G-MYUP	Letov LK-2M Sluka	
G-MYRS	SW Pegasus Quantum 15		G-MYUR	Hunt Wing	
G-MYRT	SW Pegasus Quantum 15		G MYUS	CFM Shadow Srs CD	
G-MYRU	Cyclone AX3/503		G-MYUT	Hunt Wing	
G-MYRV	Cyclone AX3/503		G-MYUU	Cycl Pegasus Quantum 15	
G-MYRW	Mainair Mercury		G-MYUV	Cycl Pegasus Quantum 15	
G-MYRX	Mainair Gemini Flash IIA		G-MYUW	Mainair Mercury	
G-MYRY	SW Pegasus Quantum 15		G-MYUY	Microchute UQ	
G-MYRZ	SW Pegasus Quantum 15		G-MYUZ	Rans S.6-ESD Coyote II	
G-MYSA	Cyclone Chaser S 508		G-MYVA	Kolb Twinstar Mk 3	
G-MYSB	SW Pegasus Quantum 15		G-MYVB	Mainair Blade	
G-MYSC	SW Pegasus Quantum 15		G-MYVC	Cycl Pegasus Quantum 15	
G-MYSD	Quad City Challenger II		G-MYVD	—	
G-MYSF	Robinson Powered		G-MYVE	Mainair Blade	
	Paraglider		G-MYVF	Cycl Pegasus Quantum 15	
G-MYSG	Mainair Mercury		G-MYVG	Letov LK-2M Sluka	
G-MYSH	Mainair Blade		G-MYVH	Mainair Mercury	
G-MYSI	HM14/93		G-MYVI	Air Creation Fun 18S	
G-MYSJ	Mainair Gemini Flash IIA			GTBIS	
G-MYSK	Team Minimax		G-MYVJ	Cycl Pegasus Quantum 15	
G-MYSL	Aviasud Mistral		G-MYVK	Cycl Pegasus Quantum 15	
G-MYSM	CFM Shadow Srs CD		G-MYVL	Mainair Mercury	
G-MYSN	Whittaker MW.6 Merlin		G-MYVM	Cycl Pegasus Quantum 15	
G-MYSO	Cyclone AX3/503		G-MYVN	Cyclone AX3/503	
G-MYSP	Rans S.6-ESD Coyote II		G-MYVO	—	
G-MYSR	SW Pegasus Quatum 15		G-MYVP	Rans S.6-ESD Coyote II	
G-MYST	Aviasud Mistral		G-MYVR	Cycl Pegasus Quantum 15	
G-MYSU	Rans S.6-ESD Coyote II		G-MYVS	Mainair Mercury	
G-MYSV	Aerial Arts Chaser		G-MYVT	Letov LK-2M Sluka	
G-MYSW	SW Pegasus Quantum 15		G-MYVU	Medway Raven	
G-MYSX	SW Pegasus Quantum 15		G-MYVV	Medway Hybred 44XLR	
G-MYSY	SW Pegasus Quantum 15		G-MYVW	Medway Raven	
G-MYSZ	Mainair Mercury		G-MYVX	Medway Hybred 44XLR	
G-MYTA	Team Minimax		G-MYVY	Mainair Blade	
G-MYTB	Mainair Mercury		G-MYVZ	Maianir Blade	
G-MYTC	SW Pegasus XL-Q		G-MYWA	Mainair Mercury	
G-MYTD	Mainair Blade		G-MVWB	Corniche/Scorpion	
G-MYTE	Rans S.6-ESD Coyote II		G-MYWC	Hunt Wing	
G-MYTG	Mainair Blade		G-MYWD	Thruster T.600	
G-MYTH	CFM Shadow Srs CD		G-MYWE	Thruster T.600	
G-MYTI	Cycl Pegasus Quantum 15		G-MYWF	CFM Shadow Srs CD	
G-MYTJ	SW Pegasus Quantum 15		G-MYWG	Clycl Pegasus Quantum 15	
G-MYTK	Mainair Mercury		G-MYWH	Hunt Wing/Experience	
G-MYTL	Mainair Blade		G-MYWI	Cycl Pegasus Quantum 15	
G-MYTM	Cyclone AX3/503		G-MYWJ	Cycl Pegasus Quantum 15	
G-MYTN	SW Pegasus Quantum 15		G-MYWK	Cycl Pegasus Quantum 15	
G-MYTO	Quad City Challenger II		G-MYWL	Cycl Pegasus Quantum 15	
G-MYTP	Arrowflight Hawk II		G-MYWM	CFM Shadow Srs CD	
G-MYTR	Cycl Pegasus Quantum 15		G-MYWN	Cyclone Chaser S 508	
G-MYTS	Hunt Avon Trike		G-MYWO	Cycl Pegasus Quantum 15	
G-MYTT	Quad City Challenger II		G-MYWP	Kolb Twinstar Mk 3	
G-MYTU	Mainair Blade		G-MYWR	Cycl Pegasus Quantum 15	
G-MYTV	Hunt Avon Skytrike		G-MYWS	Cyclone Chaser S 447	
G-MYTW	Mainair Blade		G-MYWT	Cycl Pegasus Quantum 15	
G-MYTX	Mainair Mercury		G-MYWU	Cycl Pegasus Quantum 15	
G-MYTY	CFM Streak Shadow Srs M		G-MYWV	Rans S.4 Coyote	
G-MYTZ	Air Creation Fun 18S		G-MYWW	Cycl Pegasus Quantum 15	
	GTBIS		G-MYWX	Cycl Pegasus Quantum 15	
G-MYUA	Air' Creation Fun 18S		G-MYWY	Mainair Blade	
	GTBIS		G-MYWZ	Thruster TST Mk 1	
G-MYUB	Mainair Mercury		G-MYXA	Team Minimax 91	
G-MYUC	Mainair Blade		G-MYXB	Rans S.6-ESD Coyote II	
G-MYUD	Mainair Mercury		G-MYXC	Quad City Challenger II	
G-MYUE	Mainair Mercury		G-MYXD	Cycl Pegasus Quasar IITC	
G-MYUF	Renegade Spirit		G-MYXE	Cycl Pegasus Quantum 15	
G-MYUG	Hunt Avon Skytrike		G-MYXF	Air Creation Fun GT503	
G-MYUH	SW Pegasus XL-Q		G-MYXG	Rans S.6-ESD Coyote II	
G-MYUJ	Maverick		G-MYXH	Cyclone AX3/503	
G-MYUK	Mainair Mercury		G-MYXI	Aries 1	
G-MYUL	Quad City Challenger II		G-MYXJ	Mainair Blade	

Reg.	Type	Notes	Reg.	Type	Notes
G-MYXK	Quad City Challenger II		G-MYZO	—	
G-MYXL	Mignet HM.1000 Balerit		G-MYZP	—	
G-MYXM	Mainair Blade		G-MYZR	—	
G-MYXN	Mainair Blade		G-MYZS	—	
G-MYXO	Letov LK-2M Sluka		G-MYZT	—	
G-MYXP	Rans S.6-ESD Coyote II		G-MYZU	—	
G-MYXR	Renegade Spirit UK		G-MYZV	—	
G-MYXS	Kölb Twinstar Mk 3		G-MYZW	—	
G-MYXT	Cycl Pegasus Quantum 15		G-MYZX	—	
G-MYXU	Thruster T.300		G-MYZY	—	
G-MYXV	Quad City Challenger II		G-MYZZ	—	
G-MYXW	Cycl Pegasus Quantum 15		G-MZAA	Mainair Blade	
G-MYXX	Cycl Pegasus Quantum 15		G-MZAB	Mainair Blade	
G-MYXY	CFM Shadow Srs CD		G-MZAC	Quad City Challenger II	
G-MYXZ	Cycl Pegasus Quantum 15		G-MZAD	Mainair Blade 912	
G-MYYA	Mainair Blade		G-MZAE	Mainair Blade	
G-MYYB	Cycl Pegasus Quantum 15		G-MZAF	Mainair Blade	
G-MYYC	Cycl Pegasus Quantum 15		G-MZAG	Mainair Blade	
G-MYYD	Cyclone Chaser S 447		G-MZAH	Rans S.6-ESD Coyote II	
G-MYYE	Hunt Wing		G-MZAI	Mainair Blade	
G-MYYF	Quad City Challenger II		G-MZAJ	Mainair Blade	
G-MYYG	Mainair Blade		G-MZAK	Mainair Mercury	
G-MYYH	Mainair Blade		G-MZAL	—	
G-MYYI	Cycl Pegasus Quantum 15		G-MZAM	Mainair Blade	
G-MYYJ	Hunt Wing		G-MZAN	—	
G-MYYK	Cycl Pegasus Quantum 15		G-MZAO	—	
G-MYYL	Cyclone AX3/503		G-MZAP	Mainair Blade	
G-MYYM	Microchute Motor 27		G-MZAR	—	
G-MYYN	Cycl Pegasus Quantum 15		G-MZAS	Mainair Blade	
G-MYYO	Medway Raven X		G-MZAT	Mainair Blade	
G-MYYP	AMF Chevvron 2-45CS		G-MZAU	Mainair Blade	
G-MYYR	Team Minimax 91		G-MZAV	—	
G-MYYS	Team Minimax		G-MZAW	—	
G-MYYT	Hunt Wing		G-MZAX	—	
G-MYYU	Mainair Mercury		G-MZAY	—	
G-MYYV	Rans S.6-ESD Coyote IIXL		G-MZAZ	Mainair Blade	
G-MYYW	Mainair Blade		G-MZBC	Cycl Pegasus Quantum 15	
G-MYYX	Cycl Pegasus Quantum 15		G-MZCP	SW Pegasus XL-Q	
G-MYYY	—		G-MZCS	Team Minimax	
G-MYYZ	Medway Raven X		G-MZDP	AMF Chevvron 232	
G-MYZA	Whittaker MW.6 Merlin		G-MZIP	Renegade Spirit UK	
G-MYZB	Cycl Pegasus Quantum 15		G-MZIZ	Renegade Spirit UK	
G-MYZC	Cyclone AX3/503			(G-MWGP)	
G-MYZD	Cycl Pegasus Quantum 15		G-MZKJ	Mainair Blade	
G-MYZE	Team Minimax		G-MZKW	Quad City Challenger II	
G-MYZF	Cyclone AX3/503		G-MZMA	SW Pegasus Quasar IITC	
G-MYZG	Cyclone AX3/503		G-MZOO	Renegade Spirit UK	
G-MYZH	Chargus Titan 38		G-MZPD	Cycl Pegasus Quantum 15	
G-MYZI	RL-5A LW Sherwood		G-MZPJ	Team Minimax	
	Ranger		G-MZPW	Cycl Pegasus Quasar IITC	
G-MYZJ	Cycl Pegasus Quantum 15		G-MZRS	CFM Shadow Srs CD	
G-MYZK	—		G-MZSM	Mainair Blade	
G-MYZL	—		G-MZZY	Mainair Blade 912	
G-MYZM	—		G-MZZZ	Whittaker MW.6-S Fatboy	
G-MYZN	Whittaker MW.6-S Fatboy			Flyer	
	Flyer				

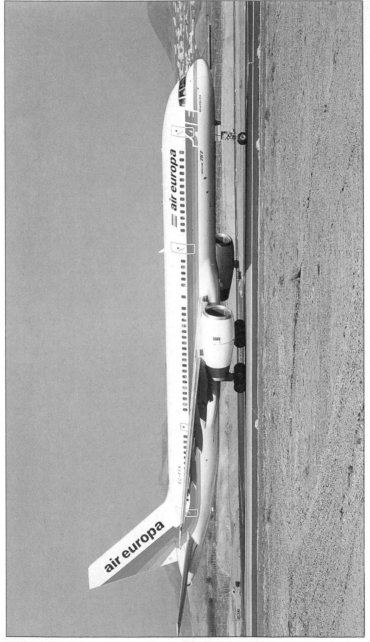

EC-FFK, Boeing 757-236.

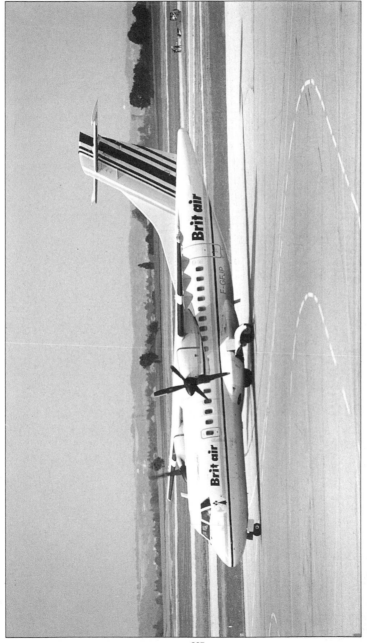

F-GFJP, Aéospatiale ATR-42-300.

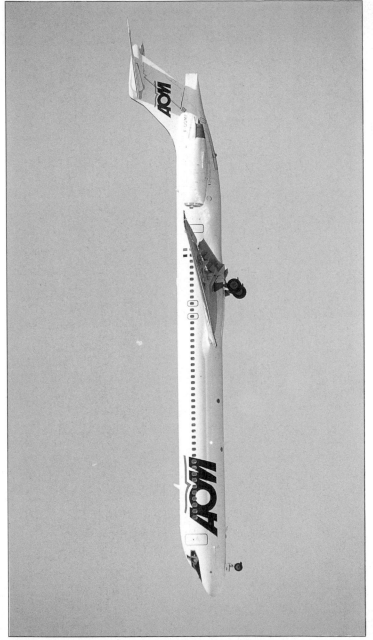

F-GGMF, McD Douglas MD-83.

N19072, Douglas DC-10-30.

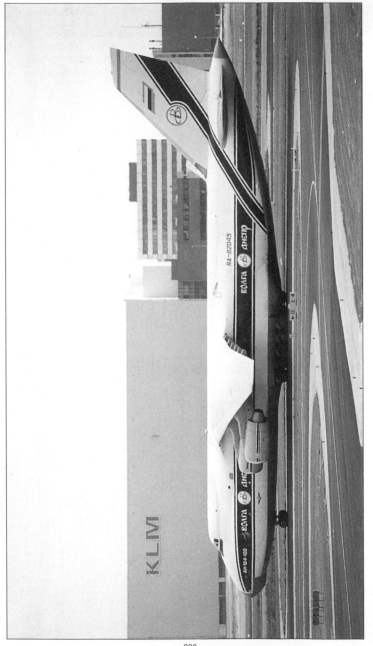

RA 82045, An-124 (VDA/HLA).

Overseas Airliner Registrations

(Aircraft included in this section are those most likely to be seen at UK and major European airports on scheduled or charter services.)

Reg.	Type	Owner or Operator	Notes

A4O (Oman)

A4O-GH	Boeing 767-3P6ER (603)	Gulf Air	
A4O-GI	Boeing 767-3P6ER (604)	Gulf Air	
A4O-GJ	Boeing 767-3P6ER (605)	Gulf Air	
A4O-GK	Boeing 767-3P6ER (606)	Gulf Air *Al Buraimi*	
A4O-GL	Boeing 767-3P6ER (607)	Gulf Air *Musandam*	
A4O-GM	Boeing 767-3P6ER (608)	Gulf Air	
A4O-GN	Boeing 767-3P6ER (609)	Gulf Air *Alryyan*	
A4O-GO	Boeing 767-3P6ER (610)	Gulf Air	
A4O-GP	Boeing 767-3P6ER (611)	Gulf Air	
A4O-GR	Boeing 767-3P6ER (612)	Gulf Air	
A4O-GS	Boeing 767-3P6ER (613)	Gulf Air *Al Ain*	
A4O-GT	Boeing 767-3P6ER (614)	Gulf Air	
A4O-GU	Boeing 767-3P6ER (615)	Gulf Air	
A4O-GV	Boeing 767-3P6ER (616)	Gulf Air *Doha*	
A4O-GW	Boeing 767-3P6ER (617)	Gulf Air	
A4O-GX	Boeing 767-3P6ER (618)	Gulf Air	
A4O-GY	Boeing 767-3P6ER (619)	Gulf Air	
A4O-GZ	Boeing 767-3P6ER (620)	Gulf Air	
A4O-LA	Airbus A.340-312	Gulf Air *Dhofar*	
A4O-LB	Airbus A.340-312	Gulf Air *Al Fateh*	
A4O-LC	Airbus A.340-312	Gulf Air *Doha*	
A4O-LD	Airbus A.340-312	Gulf Air	
A4O-LE	Airbus A.340-312	Gulf Air/EgyptAir	
A4O-LF	Airbus A.340-312	Gulf Air	
A4O-SO	Boeing 747SP-27	Oman Royal Flight	
A4O-SP	Boeing 747SP-27	Oman Government	
A4O-TA	L.1011-385 TriStar 200 (105)	Gulf Air	
A4O-TB	L.1011-385 TriStar 200 (106)	Gulf Air	
A4O-TT	L.1011-385 TriStar 200 (107)	Gulf Air	
A4O-TV	L.1011-385 TriStar 200 (108)	Gulf Air	
A4O-TZ	L.1011-385 TriStar 200 (104)	Gulf Air	

A6 (United Arab Emirates)

A6-EKA	Airbus A.310-304	Emirate Airlines	
A6-EKB	Airbus A.310-304	Emirate Airlines	
A6-EKC	Airbus A.300-605R	Emirate Airlines	
A6-EKD	Airbus A.300-605R	Emirate Airlines	
A6-EKE	Airbus A.300-605R	Emirate Airlines	
A6-EKF	Airbus A.300-605R	Emirate Airlines	
A6-EKG	Airbus A.310-308	Emirate Airlines	
A6-EKH	Airbus A.310-308	Emirate Airlines	
A6-EKI	Airbus A.310-308	Emirate Airlines	
A6-EKJ	Airbus A.310-308	Emirate Airlines	
A6-EKK	Airbus A.310-308	Emirate Airlines	
A6-EKL	Airbus A.310-308	Emirate Airlines	
A6-EKM	Airbus A.300-605R	Emirate Airlines	
A6-EKN	Airbus A.310-308	Emirate Airlines	
A6-EKO	Airbus A.300-605R	Emirate Airlines	
A6-EKP	Airbus A.310-308	Emirate Airlines	
A6-HRM	Boeing 707-3L6C	UAE Government	

A7 (Qatar)

A7-AAA	Boeing 707-3P1C	Qatar Government	
A7-AAC	Boeing 707-336C	Qatar Government	
A7-ABK	Boeing 747SR-81	Qatar Airways	
A7-ABL	Boeing 747SR-81	Qatar Airways	

Reg.	Type	Owner or Operator
A7-	L.1011-385 TriStar 1	Qatar Airways
A7-	L.1011-385 TriStar 1	Qatar Airways
A7-	L.1011-385 TriStar 1	Qatar Airways
A7-HHK	Airbus A.340-211	Qatar Government

AP (Pakistan)

AP-AXG	Boeing 707-340C	Pakistan International Airlines
AP-AYV	Boeing 747-282B	Pakistan International Airlines
AP-AYW	Boeing 747-282B	Pakistan International Airlines
AP-BAK	Boeing 747-240B (SCD)	Pakistan International Airlines
AP-BAT	Boeing 747-240B (SCD)	Pakistan International Airlines
AP-BBK	Boeing 707-323C	Pakistan International Airlines
AP-BCL	Boeing 747-217B	Pakistan International Airlines
AP-BCM	Boeing 747-217B	Pakistan International Airlines
AP-BCN	Boeing 747-217B	Pakistan International Airlines
AP-BCO	Boeing 747-217B	Pakistan International Airlines
AP-BDZ	Airbus A.310-308	Pakistan International Airlines
AP-BEB	Airbus A.310-308	Pakistan International Airlines
AP-BEC	Airbus A.310-308	Pakistan International Airlines
AP-BEG	Airbus A.310-308	Pakistan International Airlines
AP-BEQ	Airbus A.310-308	Pakistan International Airlines
AP-BEU	Airbus A.310-308	Pakistan International Airlines

B (China/Taiwan)

B-150	McD Douglas MD-11	China Airlines
B-151	McD Douglas MD-11	China Airlines
B-152	McD Douglas MD-11	China Airlines
B-153	McD Douglas MD-11	China Airlines
B-160	Boeing 747-209F (SCD)	China Airlines
B-161	Boeing 747-409	China Airlines
B-162	Boeing 747-409	China Airlines
B-163	Boeing 747-409	China Airlines
B-164	Boeing 747-409	China Airlines
B-1862	Boeing 747SP-09	China Airlines
B-1864	Boeing 747-209B (SCD)	China Airlines
B-1866	Boeing 747-209B	China Airlines
B-1880	Boeing 747SP-09	China Airlines
B-1886	Boeing 747-209B	China Airlines
B-1888	Boeing 747-209B	China Airlines
B-1894	Boeing 747-209F (SCD)	China Airlines
B-2438	Boeing 747SP-J6	Air China
B-2442	Boeing 747SP-J6	Air China
B-2443	Boeing 747-4J6	Air China
B-2445	Boeing 747-4J6	Air China
B-2446	Boeing 747-2J6B (SCD)	Air China
B-2447	Boeing 747-4J6	Air China
B-2448	Boeing 747-2J6B (SCD)	Air China
B-2450	Boeing 747-2J6B (SCD)	Air China
B-2452	Boeing 747SP-J6	Air China
B-2454	Boeing 747SP-27	Air China
B-2456	Boeing 747-4J6 (SCD)	Air China
B-2458	Boeing 747-4J6 (SCD)	Air China
B-2460	Boeing 747-4J6 (SCD)	Air China
B-2462	Boeing 747-2J6F (SCD)	Air China
B-2464	Boeing 747-4J6	Air China
B-2466	Boeing 747-4J6	Air China
B-16401	Boeing 747-45E	EVA Airways
B-16402	Boeing 747-45E	EVA Airways
B-16461	Boeing 747-45E (SCD)	EVA Airways
B-16462	Boeing 747-45E (SCD)	EVA Airways
B-16463	Boeing 747-45E (SCD)	EVA Airways
B-16465	Boeing 747-45E (SCD)	EVA Airways

Note: China Airlines also operates N4508H and N4522V, both Boeing 747SP-09s.
EVA Airways operates Boeing 747-45Es which retain the US registrations
N403EV, N405EV, N406EV, N407EV, N408EV and N409EV.

C9 (Mozambique)

Note: LAM operates Boeing 767-2B1ER EI-CEM and ZS-SRA on lease.

C-F and C-G (Canada)

Reg.	Type	Owner or Operator
C-FBCA	Boeing 747-475 (884)	Canadian Airlines International *Grant McConachie*
C-FBEF	Boeing 767-233ER (617)	Air Canada
C-FBEG	Boeing 767-233ER (618)	Air Canada
C-FBEM	Boeing 767-233ER (619)	Air Canada
C-FCAB	Boeing 767-375ER (631)	Canadian Airlines International
C-FCAE	Boeing 767-375ER (632)	Canadian Airlines International
C-FCAF	Boeing 767-375ER (633)	Canadian Airlines International
C-FCAG	Boeing 767-375ER (634)	Canadian Airlines International
C-FCAJ	Boeing 767-375ER (635)	Canadian Airlines International
C-FCAU	Boeing 767-375ER (636)	Canadian Airlines International
C-FCRA	Boeing 747-475 (882)	Canadian Airlines International *T. Russ Baker*
C-FCRD	Douglas DC-10-30	Canadian Airlines International
C-FCRE	Douglas DC-10-30	Canadian Airlines International
C-FGHZ	Boeing 747-4F6	Canadian Airlines International
C-FMWP	Boeing 767-333ER (631)	Air Canada
C-FMWQ	Boeing 767-333ER (632)	Air Canada
C-FMWU	Boeing 767-333ER (633)	Air Canada
C-FMWV	Boeing 767-333ER (634)	Air Canada
C-FMWY	Boeing 767-333ER (635)	Air Canada
C-FMXC	Boeing 767-333ER (636)	Air Canada
C-FOCA	Boeing 767-375ER (640)	Canadian Airlines International
C-FOOA	Boeing 757-28A	Canada 3000/Air 2000 (G-OOOA)
C-FOOB	Boeing 757-28A	Canada 3000/Air 2000 (G-OOOB)
C-FOOE	Boeing 757-28A	Canada 3000 Airlines
C-FOOG	Boeing 757-23A	Canada 3000/Air 2000 (G-OOOG)
C-FPCA	Boeing 767-375ER (637)	Canadian Airlines International
C-FTCA	Boeing 767-375ER (638)	Canadian Airlines International
C-FTNA	L.1011-385 TriStar 150 (501)	Air Transat
C-FTND	L.1011-385 TriStar 150 (549)	Air Transat
C-FTNC	L.1011-385 TriStar 150 (503)	Air Transat
C-FTNH	L.1011-385 TriStar 150 (508)	Air Transat
C-FTNI	L.1011-385 TriStar 100	Royal Airlines
C-FTNK	L.1011-385 TriStar 100	Royal Airlines
C-FTNP	Airbus A.340-313 (982)	Air Canada
C-FTNQ	Airbus A.340-313 (981)	Air Canada
C-FTOC	Boeing 747-133 (303)	Air Canada
C-FTOD	Boeing 747-133 (304)	Air Canada
C-FTOE	Boeing 747-133 (305)	Air Canada
C-FVNM	Boeing 767-209ER (621)	Air Canada
C-FWCR	L.1011-385 TriStar 1	Air Transat
C-FXCA	Boeing 767-375ER (639)	Canadian Airlines International
C-FXOC	Boeing 757-28A	Canada 3000/Air 2000 (G-OOOC)
C-FXOF	Boeing 757-28A	Canada 3000 Airlines
C-FXOK	Boeing 757-23A	Canada 3000 Airlines
C-FXOO	Boeing 757-28A	Canada 3000 Airlines
C-GAGA	Boeing 747-233B (SCD) (306)	Air Canada
C-GAGB	Boeing 747-233B (SCD) (307)	Air Canada
C-GAGC	Boeing 747-238B (SCD) (308)	Air Canada
C-GAGL	Boeing 747-433 (SCD) (341)	Air Canada
C-GAGM	Boeing 747-433 (SCD) (342)	Air Canada
C-GAGN	Boeing 747-433 (SCD) (343)	Air Canada
C-GAUY	Boeing 767-233ER (609)	Air Canada
C-GAVA	Boeing 767-233ER (610)	Air Canada
C-GAVC	Boeing 767-233ER (611)	Air Canada
C-GAVF	Boeing 767-233ER (612)	Air Canada
C-GCIH	Boeing 747-212B	Air Club International
C-GCIT	Airbus A.310-324	Air Club International
C-GCIV	Airbus A.310-324	Air Club International
C-GCPC	Douglas DC-10-30 (901)	Canadian Airlines International
C-GCPD	Douglas DC-10-30 (902)	Canadian Airlines International
C-GCPE	Douglas DC-10-30ER (903)	Canadian Airlines International
C-GCPF	Douglas DC-10-30ER (904)	Canadian Airlines International
C-GCPG	Douglas DC-10-30ER (905)	Canadian Airlines International

Notes	Reg.	Type	Owner or Operator
	C-GCPH	Douglas DC-10-30ER (906)	Canadian Airlines International
	C-GCPI	Douglas DC-10-30ER (907)	Canadian Airlines International
	C-GCPJ	Douglas DC-10-30 (908)	Canadian Airlines International
	C-GDSP	Boeing 767-233ER (613)	Air Canada
	C-GDSS	Boeing 767-233ER (614)	Air Canada
	C-GDSU	Boeing 767-233ER (615)	Air Canada
	C-GDSY	Boeing 767-233ER (616)	Air Canada
	C-GLCA	Boeing 767-375ER (641)	Canadian Airlines International
	C-GMWW	Boeing 747-475 (881)	Canadian Airlines International *Maxwell W. Ward*
	C-GNXA	Boeing 747-230B	—
	C-GNXH	Boeing 747-129 (SCD) (413)	—
	C-GTSE	Boeing 757-23A	Air Transat
	C-GTSF	Boeing 757-23A	Air Transat
	C-GTSJ	Boeing 757-236	Air Transat
	C-GTSN	Boeing 757-28A	Air Transat
	C-GTSZ	L.1011-385 TriStar 100 (548)	Air Transat

Note: Airline fleet number carried on aircraft is shown in parenthesis.

CN (Morocco)

	CN-RGA	Boeing 747-428	Royal Air Maroc
	CN-RME	Boeing 747-2B6B (SCD)	Royal Air Maroc
	CN-RMF	Boeing 737-4B6	Royal Air Maroc
	CN-RMG	Boeing 737-4B6	Royal Air Maroc
	CN-RMI	Boeing 737-2B6	Royal Air Maroc *El Ayounne*
	CN-RMJ	Boeing 737-2B6	Royal Air Maroc *Oujda*
	CN-RMK	Boeing 737-2B6	Royal Air Maroc *Smara*
	CN-RML	Boeing 737-2B6	Royal Air Maroc
	CN-RMM	Boeing 737-2B6C	Royal Air Maroc
	CN-RMN	Boeing 737-2B6C	Royal Air Maroc
	CN-RMO	Boeing 727-2B6	Royal Air Maroc
	CN-RMP	Boeing 727-2B6	Royal Air Maroc
	CN-RMQ	Boeing 727-2B6	Royal Air Maroc
	CN-RMR	Boeing 727-2B6	Royal Air Maroc
	CN-RMT	Boeing 757-2B6	Royal Air Maroc
	CN-RMU	Boeing 737-53A	Royal Air Maroc
	CN-RMV	Boeing 737-5B6	Royal Air Maroc
	CN-RMW	Boeing 737-5B6	Royal Air Maroc
	CN-RMX	Boeing 737-4B6	Royal Air Maroc
	CN-RMY	Boeing 737-5B6	Royal Air Maroc
	CN-RMZ	Boeing 757-2B6	Royal Air Maroc
	CN-RNA	Boeing 737-4B6	Royal Air Maroc
	CN-RNB	Boeing 737-5B6	Royal Air Maroc
	CN-RNC	Boeing 737-4B6	Royal Air Maroc
	CN-RND	Boeing 737-4B6	Royal Air Maroc
	CN-RNF	Boeing 737-4B6	Royal Air Maroc
	CN-RNG	Boeing 737-5B6	Royal Air Maroc

CS (Portugal)

	CS-TEA	L.1011-385 TriStar 500	B.W.I.A.
	CS-TEB	L.1011-385 TriStar 500	TAP — Air Portugal *Infante D. Henrique*
	CS-TEC	L.1011-385 TriStar 500	TAP — Air Portugal *Gago Coutinho*
	CS-TED	L.1011-385 TriStar 500	TAP — Air Portugal *Bartolomeu de Gusmao*
	CS-TEE	L.1011-385 TriStar 500	TAP — Air Portugal *St Antonio de Lisboa*
	CS-TEF	L.1011-385 TriStar 500	Air-India (to V2-LEJ)
	CS-TEG	L.1011-385 TriStar 500	Air-India (to V2-LEK)
	CS-TEH	Airbus A.310-304	TAP — Air Portugal *Bartolomeu Dias*
	CS-TEI	Airbus A.310-304	TAP — Air Portugal *Fernao de Magalhaes*
	CS-TEJ	Airbus A.310-304	TAP — Air Portugal *Pedro Nunes*
	CS-TEM	Boeing 737-282	TAP — Air Portugal *Setubal*
	CS-TEN	Boeing 737-282	TAP — Air Portugal *Braga*
	CS-TEO	Boeing 737-282	TAP — Air Portugal *Evora*
	CS-TEP	Boeing 737-282	TAP — Air Portugal *Porto*
	CS-TEQ	Boeing 737-282C	TAP — Air Portugal *Vila Real*
	CS-TER	Boeing 737-230	TAP — Air Portugal *Aveiro*
	CS-TES	Boeing 737-230	TAP — Air Portugal *Viana do Castelo*

Reg.	Type	Owner or Operator	Notes
CS-TEV	Boeing 737-230	TAP — Air Portugal	
CS-TEW	Airbus A.310-304	TAP — Air Portugal *Vasco da Gama*	
CS-TEX	Airbus A.310-304	TAP — Air Portugal *Joao XXI*	
CS-TGP	Boeing 737-3Q8	SATA Air Acores	
CS-TIB	Boeing 737-382	TAP — Air Portugal *Acores*	
CS-TIC	Boeing 737-382	TAP — Air Portugal *Algarve*	
CS-TID	Boeing 737-382	TAP — Air Portugal *Alto Minho*	
CS-TIE	Boeing 737-382	TAP — Air Portugal *Costa Azul*	
CS-TIF	Boeing 737-3K9	TAP — Air Portugal *Costa Verde*	
CS-TIG	Boeing 737-3K9	TAP — Air Portugal	
CS-TIH	Boeing 737-3K9	TAP — Air Portugal	
CS-TIK	Boeing 737-382	TAP — Air Portugal *Costa do Estoril*	
CS-TIL	Boeing 737-382	TAP — Air Portugal *Lisboa*	
CS-TIN	Boeing 737-33A	TAP — Air Portugal	
CS-TIO	Boeing 737-33A	TAP — Air Portugal	
CS-TNA	Airbus A.320-211	TAP — Air Portugal *Grao Vasco*	
CS-TNB	Airbus A.320-211	TAP — Air Portugal *Gil Vicente*	
CS-TNC	Airbus A.320-211	TAP — Air Portugal *Pero da Covilha*	
CS-TND	Airbus A.320-211	TAP — Air Portugal *Garcia de Orta*	
CS-TNE	Airbus A.320-211	TAP — Air Portugal *Sa de Miranda*	
CS-TNF	Airbus A.320-211	TAP — Air Portugal *Fernao Lopes*	
CS-TOA	Airbus A.340-312	TAP — Air Portugal *Ferrei Mendes Pinto*	
CS-TOB	Airbus A.340-312	TAP — Air Portugal	
CS-TOC	Airbus A.340-312	TAP — Air Portugal *Wenceslau de Moraes*	
CS-TOD	Airbus A.340-312	TAP — Air Portugal *D. Francisco de Almeida*	
CS-TPA	Fokker 100	Portugalia *Albatroz*	
CS-TPB	Fokker 100	Portugalia *Pelicano*	
CS-TPC	Fokker 100	Portugalia	
CS-TPD	Fokker 100	Portugalia *Condor*	
CS-TPE	Fokker 100	Portugalia *Gaviao*	
CS-TPF	Fokker 100	Portugalia	

CU (Cuba)

CU-T1208	Ilyushin IL-62M	Cubana *Capt Wifredo Perez*	
CU-T1209	Ilyushin IL-62M	Cubana	
CU-T1215	Ilyushin IL-62M	Cubana	
CU-T1216	Ilyushin IL-62M	Cubana	
CU-T1217	Ilyushin IL-62M	Cubana	
CU-T1218	Ilyushin IL-62M	Cubana	
CU-T1225	Ilyushin IL-62M	Cubana	
CU-T1252	Ilyushin IL-62M	Cubana	
CU-T1259	Ilyushin IL-62M	Cubana	
CU-T1280	Ilyushin IL-62M	Cubana	
CU-T1282	Ilyushin IL-62M	Cubana	
CU-T1283	Ilyushin IL-62M	Cubana	

Note: AOM French Airlines operate European flights for Cubana using DC-10-30s
F-GTDF and F-GTDH

D2 (Angola)

D2-TOJ	Boeing 707-349C	TAAG Angola Airlines	
D2-TOK	Boeing 707-324C	Angola Air Charter	
D2-TOL	Boeing 707-347C	Angola Air Charter	
D2-TON	Boeing 707-324C	Angola Air Charter	
D2-TOP	Boeing 707-382B	TAAG Angola Airlines	
D2-TOR	Boeing 707-351C	Angola Air Charter	
D2-TPR	Boeing 707-3J6B	TAAG Angola Airlines	

D (Germany)

D-ABAB	Boeing 737-4K5	Air Berlin	
D-ABAC	Boeing 737-4Y0	Air Berlin	
D-ABAD	Boeing 737-4Y0	Air Berlin	
D-ABAE	Boeing 737-46J	Air Berlin	
D-ABAF	Boeing 737-4Y0	Air Berlin	

Notes	Reg.	Type	Owner or Operator
	D-ABAG	Boeing 737-46J	Air Berlin
	D-ABAH	Boeing 737-46J	Air Berlin
	D-ABAI	Boeing 737-46J	Air Berlin
	D-AB	Boeing 737-46J	Air Berlin
	D-AB	Boeing 737-46J	Air Berlin
	D-ABEA	Boeing 737-330	Lufthansa *Saarbrücken*
	D-ABEB	Boeing 737-330	Lufthansa *Xanten*
	D-ABEC	Boeing 737-330	Lufthansa *Karlsrühe*
	D-ABED	Boeing 737-330	Lufthansa *Hagen*
	D-ABEE	Boeing 737-330	Lufthansa *Ulm*
	D-ABEF	Boeing 737-330	Lufthansa *Weiden i.d. Opf*
	D-ABEH	Boeing 737-330	Lufthansa *Bad Kissingen*
	D-ABEI	Boeing 737-330	Lufthansa *Bamberg*
	D-ABEK	Boeing 737-330	Lufthansa *Wuppertal*
	D-ABEL	Boeing 737-330	Lufthansa *Pforzheim*
	D-ABEM	Boeing 737-330	Lufthansa *Eberswalde*
	D-ABEN	Boeing 737-330	Lufthansa *Neubrandenburg*
	D-ABEO	Boeing 737-330	Lufthansa *Plauen*
	D-ABEP	Boeing 737-330	Lufthansa *Naumburg (Saale)*
	D-ABER	Boeing 737-330	Lufthansa *Merseburg*
	D-ABES	Boeing 737-330	Lufthansa *Koethen/Anhalt*
	D-ABET	Boeing 737-330	Lufthansa *Gelsenkirchen*
	D-ABEU	Boeing 737-330	Lufthansa *Goslar*
	D-ABEW	Boeing 737-330	Lufthansa *Detmold*
	D-ABFA	Boeing 737-230	Lufthansa *Regensburg*
	D-ABFB	Boeing 737-230	Lufthansa *Flensburg*
	D-ABFC	Boeing 737-230	Lufthansa *Würzburg*
	D-ABFP	Boeing 737-230	Lufthansa *Offenbach*
	D-ABFR	Boeing 737-230	Lufthansa *Solingen*
	D-ABFU	Boeing 737-230	Lufthansa *Mülheim a.d.Ruhr*
	D-ABFX	Boeing 737-230	Lufthansa *Tübingen*
	D-ABHC	Boeing 737-230	Lufthansa *Friedrichshafen*
	D-ABHF	Boeing 737-230	Lufthansa *Heilbronn*
	D-ABHH	Boeing 737-230	Lufthansa *Marburg*
	D-ABHM	Boeing 737-230	Lufthansa *Landshut*
	D-ABHN	Boeing 737-230	Lufthansa *Trier*
	D-ABIA	Boeing 737-530	Lufthansa *Greifswald*
	D-ABIB	Boeing 737-530	Lufthansa *Esslingen*
	D-ABIC	Boeing 737-530	Lufthansa *Krefeld*
	D-ABID	Boeing 737-530	Lufthansa *Aachen*
	D-ABIE	Boeing 737-530	Lufthansa *Hildesheim*
	D-ABIF	Boeing 737-530	Lufthansa *Landau*
	D-ABIH	Boeing 737-530	Lufthansa *Bruchsal*
	D-ABII	Boeing 737-530	Lufthansa *Lörrach*
	D-ABIK	Boeing 737-530	Lufthansa *Rastatt*
	D-ABIL	Boeing 737-530	Lufthansa *Memmingen*
	D-ABIM	Boeing 737-530	Lufthansa *Salzgitter*
	D-ABIN	Boeing 737-530	Lufthansa *Langenhagen*
	D-ABIO	Boeing 737-530	Lufthansa *Wesel*
	D-ABIP	Boeing 737-530	Lufthansa *Oberhausen*
	D-ABIR	Boeing 737-530	Lufthansa *Anklam*
	D-ABIS	Boeing 737-530	Lufthansa *Rendsburg*
	D-ABIT	Boeing 737-530	Lufthansa *Neumünster*
	D-ABIU	Boeing 737-530	Lufthansa *Limburg a.d. Lahn*
	D-ABIW	Boeing 737-530	Lufthansa *Bad Nauheim*
	D-ABIX	Boeing 737-530	Lufthansa *Iserlohn*
	D-ABIY	Boeing 737-530	Lufthansa *Lingen*
	D-ABIZ	Boeing 737-530	Lufthansa *Kirchheim unter Teck*
	D-ABJA	Boeing 737-530	Lufthansa *Bad Segeberg*
	D-ABJB	Boeing 737-530	Lufthansa *Rheine*
	D-ABJC	Boeing 737-530	Lufthansa *Erding*
	D-ABJD	Boeing 737-530	Lufthansa *Freising*
	D-ABJE	Boeing 737-530	Lufthansa *Ingelheim am Rhein*
	D-ABJF	Boeing 737-530	Lufthansa *Aalen*
	D-ABJH	Boeing 737-530	Lufthansa *Heppenheim/Bergstr*
	D-ABJI	Boeing 737-530	Lufthansa *Sieburg*
	D-ABKA	Boeing 737-430	Lufthansa *Heide*
	D-ABKB	Boeing 737-430	Lufthansa *Tegernsee*
	D-ABKC	Boeing 737-430	Lufthansa *Straubing*
	D-ABKD	Boeing 737-430	Lufthansa *Helmstedt*
	D-ABKF	Boeing 737-430	Lufthansa *Hameln*
	D-ABKK	Boeing 737-430	Lufthansa *Weimar*
	D-ABMA	Boeing 737-230	Lufthansa *Idar-Oberstein*
	D-ABMB	Boeing 737-230	Lufthansa *Ingolstadt*

Reg.	Type	Owner or Operator	Notes
D-ABMC	Boeing 737-230	Lufthansa *Norderstedt*	
D-ABMD	Boeing 737-230	Lufthansa *Paderborn*	
D-ABME	Boeing 737-230	Lufthansa *Schweinfurt*	
D-ABMF	Boeing 737-230	Lufthansa *Verden*	
D-ABNA	Boeing 757-230	Condor Flugdienst	
D-ABNB	Boeing 757-230	Condor Flugdienst	
D-ABNC	Boeing 757-230	Condor Flugdienst	
D-ABND	Boeing 757-230	Condor Flugdienst	
D-ABNE	Boeing 757-230	Condor Flugdienst	
D-ABNF	Boeing 757-230	Condor Flugdienst	
D-ABNH	Boeing 757-230	Condor Flugdienst	
D-ABNI	Boeing 757-230	Condor Flugdienst	
D-ABNK	Boeing 757-230	Condor Flugdienst	
D-ABNL	Boeing 757-230	Condor Flugdienst	
D-ABNM	Boeing 757-230	Condor Flugdienst	
D-ABNN	Boeing 757-230	Condor Flugdienst	
D-ABNO	Boeing 757-230	Condor Flugdienst	
D-ABNP	Boeing 757-230	Condor Flugdienst	
D-ABNR	Boeing 757-230	Condor Flugdienst	
D-ABNS	Boeing 757-230	Condor Flugdienst	
D-ABNT	Boeing 757-230	Condor Flugdienst	
D-ABNX	Boeing 757-230	Condor Flugdienst	
D-ABTA	Boeing 747-430 (SCD)	Lufthansa *Sachsen*	
D-ABTB	Boeing 747-430 (SCD)	Lufthansa *Brandenburg*	
D-ABTC	Boeing 747-430 (SCD)	Lufthansa *Mecklenburg-Verpommern*	
D-ABTD	Boeing 747-430 (SCD)	Lufthansa/Condor Flugdienst *Hamburg*	
D-ABTE	Boeing 747-430 (SCD)	Lufthansa *Sachsen-Anhalt*	
D-ABTF	Boeing 747-430 (SCD)	Lufthansa *Thüringen*	
D-ABTH	Boeing 747-430 (SCD)	Lufthansa *Duisburg*	
D-ABUA	Boeing 767-330ER	Condor Flugdienst	
D-ABUB	Boeing 767-330ER	Condor Flugdienst	
D-ABUC	Boeing 767-330ER	Condor Flugdienst/Lufthansa	
D-ABUD	Boeing 767-330ER	Condor Flugdienst	
D-ABUE	Boeing 767-330ER	Condor Flugdienst	
D-ABUF	Boeing 767-330ER	Condor Flugdienst	
D-ABUH	Boeing 767-330ER	Condor Flugdienst	
D-ABUI	Boeing 767-330ER	Condor Flugdienst	
D-ABVA	Boeing 747-430	Lufthansa *Berlin*	
D-ABVB	Boeing 747-430	Lufthansa *Bonn*	
D-ABVC	Boeing 747-430	Lufthansa *Baden-Württemberg*	
D-ABVD	Boeing 747-430	Lufthansa *Bochum*	
D-ABVE	Boeing 747-430	Lufthansa *Potsdam*	
D-ABVF	Boeing 747-430	Lufthansa *Frankfurt am Main*	
D-ABVH	Boeing 747-430	Lufthansa *Düsseldorf*	
D-ABVK	Boeing 747-430	Lufthansa *Hannover*	
D-ABVL	Boeing 747-430	Lufthansa *Muenchen*	
D-ABVN	Boeing 747-430	Lufthansa *Dortmund*	
D-ABVO	Boeing 747-430	Lufthansa	
D-ABWA	Boeing 737-330	Germania	
D-ABWB	Boeing 737-330	Germania	
D-ABWC	Boeing 737-330QC	Lufthansa	
D-ABWD	Boeing 737-330QC	Lufthansa *Westerland/Sylt*	
D-ABWE	Boeing 737-330QC	Lufthansa *Goerlitz*	
D-ABWF	Boeing 737-330QC	Lufthansa *Ruedesheim am Rhein*	
D-ABWH	Boeing 737-330QC	Lufthansa *Rothenburg*	
D-ABWS	Boeing 737-3S3F	Lufthansa Cargo	
D-ABXA	Boeing 737-330QC	Lufthansa *Giessen*	
D-ABXB	Boeing 737-330QC	Lufthansa *Passau*	
D-ABXC	Boeing 737-330QC	Lufthansa *Delmenhorst*	
D-ABXD	Boeing 737-330	Lufthansa *Siegen*	
D-ABXE	Boeing 737-330	Lufthansa *Hamm*	
D-ABXF	Boeing 737-330	Lufthansa *Minden*	
D-ABXH	Boeing 737-330	Lufthansa *Cuxhaven*	
D-ABXI	Boeing 737-330	Lufthansa *Berchtesgaden*	
D-ABXK	Boeing 737-330	Lufthansa *Ludwigsburg*	
D-ABXL	Boeing 737-330	Lufthansa *Neuss*	
D-ABXM	Boeing 737-330	Lufthansa *Herford*	
D-ABXN	Boeing 737-330	Lufthansa *Böblingen*	
D-ADXO	Boeing 737-330	Lufthansa *Schwäbisch-Gmünd*	
D-ABXP	Boeing 737-330	Lufthansa *Fulda*	
D-ABXR	Boeing 737-330	Lufthansa *Celle*	
D-ABXS	Boeing 737-330	Lufthansa *Sindelfingen*	
D-ABXT	Boeing 737-330	Lufthansa *Reutlingen*	
D-ABXU	Boeing 737-330	Lufthansa *Seeheim-Jugenheim*	

Notes	Reg.	Type	Owner or Operator
	D-ABXW	Boeing 737-330	Lufthansa *Hanau*
	D-ABXX	Boeing 737-330	Lufthansa *Bad Homburg v.d. Höhe*
	D-ABXY	Boeing 737-330	Lufthansa *Hof*
	D-ABXZ	Boeing 737-330	Lufthansa *Bad Mergentheim*
	D-ABYL	Boeing 747-230B (SCD)	Lufthansa *Saarland*
	D-ABYM	Boeing 747-230B (SCD)	Lufthansa *Schleswig Holstein*
	D-ABYO	Boeing 747-230F (SCD)	Lufthansa Cargo *America*
	D-ABYP	Boeing 747-230B	Lufthansa *Niedersachen*
	D-ABYQ	Boeing 747-230B	Lufthansa *Bremen*
	D-ABYR	Boeing 747-230B (SCD)	Lufthansa *Nordrhein-Westfalen*
	D-ABYT	Boeing 747-230F (SCD)	Lufthansa Cargo
	D-ABYU	Boeing 747-230F (SCD)	Lufthansa Cargo *Asia*
	D-ABYW	Boeing 747-230F (SCD)	Lufthansa Cargo
	D-ABYX	Boeing 747-230B (SCD)	Lufthansa *Köln*
	D-ABYY	Boeing 747-230F (SCD)	Lufthansa Cargo
	D-ABYZ	Boeing 747-230F (SCD)	Lufthansa Cargo
	D-ABZA	Boeing 747-230F (SCD)	Lufthansa Cargo *Düsseldorf*
	D-ABZB	Boeing 747-230F (SCD)	Lufthansa Cargo *Europa*
	D-ABZC	Boeing 747-230F (SCD)	Lufthansa Cargo
	D-ABZD	Boeing 747-230B	Lufthansa *Kiel*
	D-ABZE	Boeing 747-230B (SCD)	Lufthansa *Stuttgart*
	D-ABZF	Boeing 747-230F (SCD)	Lufthansa Cargo *Africa*
	D-ABZH	Boeing 747-230B	Lufthansa *Bonn*
	D-ABZI	Boeing 747-230F (SCD)	Lufthansa Cargo *Australia*
	D-ACFA	BAe 146-200	Eurowings
	D-ACLA	Canadair Regional Jet 100ER	Lufthansa CityLine
	D-ACLB	Canadair Regional Jet 100ER	Lufthansa CityLine
	D-ACLC	Canadair Regional Jet 100ER	Lufthansa CityLine
	D-ACLD	Canadair Regional Jet 100ER	Lufthansa CityLine
	D-ACLE	Canadair Regional Jet 100ER	Lufthansa CityLine
	D-ACLF	Canadair Regional Jet 100ER	Lufthansa CityLine
	D-ACLG	Canadair Regional Jet 100ER	Lufthansa CityLine
	D-ACLH	Canadair Regional Jet 100ER	Lufthansa CityLine
	D-ACLI	Canadair Regional Jet 100ER	Lufthansa CityLine
	D-ACLJ	Canadair Regional Jet 100ER	Lufthansa CityLine
	D-ACLK	Canadair Regional Jet 100ER	Lufthansa CityLine
	D-ACLL	Canadair Regional Jet 100ER	Lufthansa CityLine
	D-ACLM	Canadair Regional Jet 100ER	Lufthansa CityLine
	D-ACLN	Canadair Regional Jet 100ER	Lufthansa CityLine
	D-ACLO	Canadair Regional Jet 100ER	Lufthansa CityLine
	D-ACLP	Canadair Regional Jet 100ER	Lufthansa CityLine
	D-ACLQ	Canadair Regional Jet 100ER	Lufthansa CityLine
	D-ACLR	Canadair Regional Jet 100ER	Lufthansa CityLine
	D-ACLS	Canadair Regional Jet 100ER	Lufthansa CityLine
	D-ACLT	Canadair Regional Jet 100ER	Lufthansa CityLine
	D-ACLU	Canadair Regional Jet 100ER	Lufthansa CityLine
	D-ACLV	Canadair Regional Jet 100ER	Lufthansa CityLine
	D-ACLW	Canadair Regional Jet 100ER	Lufthansa CityLine
	D-ACLX	Canadair Regional Jet 100ER	Lufthansa CityLine
	D-ADBA	Boeing 737-3L9	Deutsche BA
	D-ADBB	Boeing 737-3L9	Deutsche BA
	D-ADBC	Boeing 737-3L9	Deutsche BA
	D-ADBD	Boeing 737-3L9	Deutsche BA
	D-ADBE	Boeing 737-3L9	Deutsche BA
	D-ADBF	Boeing 737-3L9	Deutsche BA
	D-ADBG	Boeing 737-3L9	Deutsche BA
	D-ADBH	Boeing 737-3L9	Deutsche BA
	D-ADEI	BAe 146-200QT	Eurowings/TNT Express Europe
	D-ADEP	F.27 Friendship Mk 600	WDL
	D-ADFA	Fokker 100	Deutsche BA
	D-ADFB	Fokker 100	Deutsche BA
	D-ADFC	Fokker 100	Deutsche BA
	D-ADFD	Fokker 100	Deutsche BA
	D-ADFE	Fokker 100	Deutsche BA
	D-ADFO	Douglas DC-10-30	Lufthansa
	D-ADJO	Douglas DC-10-30	Condor Flugdienst
	D-ADLO	Douglas DC-10-30	Condor Flugdienst
	D-ADOP	F.27 Friendship Mk 600	WDL
	D-ADPO	Douglas DC-10-30	Condor Flugdienst
	D-ADQO	Douglas DC-10-30	Condor Flugdienst
	D-ADSA	SAAB 2000	Deutsche BA
	D-ADSB	SAAB 2000	Deutsche BA
	D-ADSC	SAAB 2000	Deutsche BA
	D-ADSD	SAAB 2000	Deutsche BA

Reg.	Type	Owner or Operator	Notes
D-ADSE	SAAB 2000	Deutsche BA	
D-ADSO	Douglas DC-10-30	Condor Flugdienst	
D-ADUA	Douglas DC-8-73AF	Lufthansa Cargo	
D-ADUC	Douglas DC-8-73AF	Lufthansa Cargo	
D-ADUE	Douglas DC-8-73AF	Lufthansa Cargo	
D-ADUI	Douglas DC-8-73AF	Lufthansa Cargo	
D-ADUO	Douglas DC-8-73AF	Lufthansa Cargo	
D-AELC	F.27 Friendship Mk 600	WDL	
D-AELD	F.27 Friendship Mk 600	WDL	
D-AELE	F.27 Friendship Mk 600	WDL	
D-AELF	F.27 Friendship Mk 600	WDL	
D-AELG	F.27 Friendship Mk 600	WDL	
D-AELH	F.27 Friendship Mk 600	WDL	
D-AELI	F.27 Friendship Mk 600	WDL	
D-AELJ	F.27 Friendship Mk 600	WDL	
D-AELK	F.27 Friendship Mk 600	WDL	
D-AELL	F.27 Friendship Mk 200	WDL	
D-AERB	McD Douglas MD-11	LTU	
D-AERF	Airbus A.330-322	LTU	
D-AERG	Airbus A.330-322	LTU	
D-AERH	Airbus A.330-322	LTU	
D-AERJ	Airbus A.330-322	LTU	
D-AERK	Airbus A.330-322	LTU	
D-AERL	L.1011-385 TriStar 500	LTU	
D-AERT	L.1011-385 TriStar 500	LTU	
D-AERW	McD Douglas MD-11	LTU	
D-AERX	McD Douglas MD-11	LTU	
D-AERZ	McD Douglas MD-11	LTU	
D-AEWG	Aérospatiale ATR-72-212	Eurowings	
D-AEWH	Aérospatiale ATR-72-212	Eurowings	
D-AEWI	Aérospatiale ATR-72-212	Eurowings	
D-AEWK	Aérospatiale ATR-72-212	Eurowings	
D-AEWL	Aérospatiale ATR-72-212	Eurowings	
D-	Aérospatiale ATR-72-212	Eurowings	
D-	Aérospatiale ATR-72-212	Eurowings	
D-AFFE	Fokker 50	Lufthansa CityLine	
D-AFFF	Fokker 50	Lufthansa CityLine	
D-AFFG	Fokker 50	Lufthansa CityLine	
D-AFFH	Fokker 50	Lufthansa CityLine	
D-AFFI	Fokker 50	Lufthansa CityLine	
D-AFFJ	Fokker 50	Lufthansa CityLine	
D-AFFK	Fokker 50	Lufthansa CityLine	
D-AFFL	Fokker 50	Lufthansa CityLine	
D-AFKK	Fokker 50	Lufthansa CityLine	
D-AFKL	Fokker 50	Lufthansa CityLine	
D-AFKM	Fokker 50	Lufthansa CityLine	
D-AFKN	Fokker 50	Lufthansa CityLine	
D-AFKO	Fokker 50	Lufthansa CityLine	
D-AFKP	Fokker 50	Lufthansa CityLine	
D-AFKU	Fokker 50	Lufthansa CityLine	
D-AGEA	Boeing 737-35B	Germania	
D-AGEB	Boeing 737-35B	Germania	
D-AGEC	Boeing 737-35B	Germania/Condor Flugdienst	
D-AGED	Boeing 737-35B	Germania/Condor Flugdienst	
D-AGEE	Boeing 737-35B	Germania	
D-AGEF	Boeing 737-35B	Germania	
D-AGEG	Boeing 737-35B	Germania	
D-AGEH	Boeing 737-3L9	Germania	
D-AGEI	Boeing 737-3L9	Germania	
D-AGEJ	Boeing 737-3L9	Germania	
D-AGWB	McD Douglas MD-83	Aero Lloyd	
D-AGWC	McD Douglas MD-83	Aero Lloyd	
D-AHLA	Airbus A.310-304	Hapag-Lloyd	
D-AHLB	Airbus A.310-304	Hapag-Lloyd	
D-AHLC	Airbus A.310-308	Hapag-Lloyd	
D-AHLD	Boeing 737-5K5	Hapag-Lloyd	
D-AHLE	Boeing 737-5K5	Hapag-Lloyd	
D-AHLF	Boeing 737-5K5	Hapag-Lloyd	
D-AHLG	Boeing 737-4K5	Hapag-Lloyd	
D-AHLI	Boeing 737-5K5	Hapag-Lloyd	
D-AHLJ	Boeing 737-4K5	Hapag-Lloyd	
D-AHLK	Boeing 737-4K5	Hapag-Lloyd	
D-AHLL	Boeing 737-4K5	Hapag-Lloyd	
D-AHLM	Boeing 737-4K5	Hapag-Lloyd	

Notes	Reg.	Type	Owner or Operator
	D-AHLN	Boeing 737-5K5	Hapag-Lloyd
	D-AHLO	Boeing 737-4K5	Hapag-Lloyd
	D-AHLP	Boeing 737-4K5	Hapag-Lloyd
	D-AHLQ	Boeing 737-4K5	Hapag-Lloyd
	D-AHLR	Boeing 737-4K5	Hapag-Lloyd
	D-AHLS	Boeing 737-4K5	Hapag-Lloyd
	D-AHLT	Boeing 737-4K5	Hapag-Lloyd
	D-AHLU	Boeing 737-4K5	Hapag-Lloyd
	D-AHLV	Airbus A.310-204	Hapag-Lloyd
	D-AHLW	Airbus A.310-204	Hapag-Lloyd
	D-AHLX	Airbus A.310-204	Hapag-Lloyd
	D-AHLZ	Airbus A.310-204	Hapag-Lloyd
	D-AHOI	BAe 146-300	Hamburg Airlines
	D-AIAH	Airbus A.300-603	Lufthansa *Lindau/Bodensee*
	D-AIAI	Airbus A.300-603	Lufthansa *Erbach/Odenwald*
	D-AIAK	Airbus A.300-603	Lufthansa *Kronberg/Taunus*
	D-AIAL	Airbus A.300-603	Lufthansa *Stade*
	D-AIAM	Airbus A.300-603	Lufthansa *Rosenheim*
	D-AIAN	Airbus A.300-603	Lufthansa *Nördlingen*
	D-AIAP	Airbus A.300-603	Lufthansa *Donauwörth*
	D-AIAR	Airbus A.300-603	Lufthansa *Bingen am Rhein*
	D-AIAS	Airbus A.300-603	Lufthansa *Monchengladbach*
	D-AIAT	Airbus A.300-603	Lufthansa *Bottrop*
	D-AIAU	Airbus A.300-603	Lufthansa *Bocholt*
	D-AI	Airbus A.300-603	Lufthansa
	D-AIBA	Airbus A.340-211	Lufthansa *Neurnberg*
	D-AIBC	Airbus A.340-211	Lufthansa *Leverkusen*
	D-AIBD	Airbus A.340-211	Lufthansa *Essen*
	D-AIBE	Airbus A.340-211	Lufthansa *Stuttgart*
	D-AIBF	Airbus A.340-211	Lufthansa *Luebeck*
	D-AIBH	Airbus A.340-211	Lufthansa *Bremerhaven*
	D-AIDC	Airbus A.310-304	Lufthansa *Neustadt a.d. Weinstrasse*
	D-AIDD	Airbus A.310-304	Lufthansa *Emden*
	D-AIDE	Airbus A.310-304	Lufthansa *Speyer*
	D-AIDF	Airbus A.310-304	Lufthansa *Aschaffenburg*
	D-AIDH	Airbus A.310-304	Lufthansa *Wetzlar*
	D-AIDI	Airbus A.310-304	Lufthansa *Fellbach*
	D-AIDK	Airbus A.310-304	Lufthansa *Donaueschingen*
	D-AIDL	Airbus A.310-304	Lufthansa *Obersdorf*
	D-AIDM	Airbus A.310-304	Lufthansa *Chemnitz*
	D-AIDN	Airbus A.310-304	Lufthansa *Gütersloh*
	D-AIGA	Airbus A.340-311	Lufthansa *Oldenburg*
	D-AIGB	Airbus A.340-311	Lufthansa *Recklinghausen*
	D-AIGC	Airbus A.340-311	Lufthansa *Wilhelmshaven*
	D-AIGD	Airbus A.340-311	Lufthansa
	D-AIGF	Airbus A.340-311	Lufthansa
	D-AIGH	Airbus A.340-311	Lufthansa
	D-AIGI	Airbus A.340-311	Lufthansa
	D-AIGK	Airbus A.340-311	Lufthansa
	D-AI	Airbus A.340-313	Lufthansa
	D-AILA	Airbus A.319-100	Lufthansa
	D-AILB	Airbus A.319-100	Lufthansa
	D-AILC	Airbus A.319-100	Lufthansa
	D-AILD	Airbus A.319-100	Lufthansa
	D-AILE	Airbus A.319-100	Lufthansa
	D-AILF	Airbus A.319-100	Lufthansa
	D-AILH	Airbus A.319-100	Lufthansa
	D-AIPA	Airbus A.320-211	Lufthansa *Buxtehude*
	D-AIPB	Airbus A.320-211	Lufthansa *Heidelberg*
	D-AIPC	Airbus A.320-211	Lufthansa *Braunschweig*
	D-AIPD	Airbus A.320-211	Lufthansa *Freiburg*
	D-AIPE	Airbus A.320-211	Lufthansa *Kassel*
	D-AIPF	Airbus A.320-211	Lufthansa *Leipzig*
	D-AIPH	Airbus A.320-211	Lufthansa *Münster*
	D-AIPK	Airbus A.320-211	Lufthansa *Wiesbaden*
	D-AIPL	Airbus A.320-211	Lufthansa *Ludwigshafen am Rhein*
	D-AIPM	Airbus A.320-211	Lufthansa *Troisdorf*
	D-AIPP	Airbus A.320-211	Lufthansa *Starnberg*
	D-AIPR	Airbus A.320-211	Lufthansa *Kaufbeuren*
	D-AIPS	Airbus A.320-211	Lufthansa *Augsburg*
	D-AIPT	Airbus A.320-211	Lufthansa *Cottbus*
	D-AIPU	Airbus A.320-211	Lufthansa *Dresden*
	D-AIPW	Airbus A.320-211	Lufthansa *Schwerin*
	D-AIPX	Airbus A.320-211	Lufthansa *Mannheim*

Reg.	Type	Owner or Operator	Notes
D-AIPY	Airbus A.320-211	Lufthansa *Magdeburg*	
D-AIPZ	Airbus A.320-211	Lufthansa *Erfurt*	
D-AIQA	Airbus A.320-211	Lufthansa *Mainz*	
D-AIQB	Airbus A.320-211	Lufthansa *Bielefeld*	
D-AIQC	Airbus A.320-211	Lufthansa *Zwickau*	
D-AIQD	Airbus A.320-211	Lufthansa *Jena*	
D-AIQE	Airbus A.320-211	Lufthansa *Gera*	
D-AIQF	Airbus A.320-211	Lufthansa *Halle a.d. Saale*	
D-AIQH	Airbus A.320-211	Lufthansa *Dessau*	
D-AIQK	Airbus A.320-211	Lufthansa *Rostock*	
D-AIQL	Airbus A.320-211	Lufthansa *Stralsund*	
D-AIQM	Airbus A.320-211	Lufthansa *Nordenham*	
D-AIQN	Airbus A.320-211	Lufthansa *Laupheim*	
D-AIQP	Airbus A.320-211	Lufthansa *Suhl*	
D-AIQR	Airbus A.320-211	Lufthansa *Lahr/Schwarzwald*	
D-AIQS	Airbus A.320-211	Lufthansa *Eisenach*	
D-AIRA	Airbus A.321-131	Lufthansa *Finkenwerder*	
D-AIRB	Airbus A.321-131	Lufthansa *Baden-Baden*	
D-AIRC	Airbus A.321-131	Lufthansa *Erlangen*	
D-AIRD	Airbus A.321-131	Lufthansa *Coburg*	
D-AIRE	Airbus A.321-131	Lufthansa *Osnabrueck*	
D-AIRF	Airbus A.321-131	Lufthansa *Kempen*	
D-AIRH	Airbus A.321-131	Lufthansa *Garmisch-Partenkirchen*	
D-AIRK	Airbus A.321-131	Lufthansa *Freudenstadt/Schwarzwald*	
D-AIRL	Airbus A.321-131	Lufthansa *Kulmbach*	
D-AIRM	Airbus A.321-131	Lufthansa *Darmstadt*	
D-AIRN	Airbus A.321-131	Lufthansa	
D-AIRO	Airbus A.321-131	Lufthansa	
D-AIRP	Airbus A.321-131	Lufthansa	
D-AIRR	Airbus A.321-131	Lufthansa	
D-AIRS	Airbus A.321-131	Lufthansa	
D-AIRT	Airbus A.321-131	Lufthansa	
D-AIRU	Airbus A.321-131	Lufthansa	
D-AIRW	Airbus A.321-131	Lufthansa	
D-AIRX	Airbus A.321-131	Lufthansa	
D-AIRY	Airbus A.321-131	Lufthansa	
D-AISY	F.27 Friendship Mk 600	Ratioflug	
D-AJET	BAe 146-200	Eurowings	
D-ALAA	Airbus A.320-232	Aero Lloyd	
D-ALAD	Airbus A.320-232	Aero Lloyd	
D-ALAC	Airbus A.320-232	Aero Lloyd	
D-ALLD	McD Douglas MD-83	Aero Lloyd	
D-ALLE	McD Douglas MD-83	Aero Lloyd	
D-ALLF	McD Douglas MD-83	Aero Lloyd	
D-ALLG	McD Douglas MD-87	Aero Lloyd	
D-ALLH	McD Douglas MD-87	Aero Lloyd	
D-ALLJ	McD Douglas MD-87	Aero Lloyd	
D-ALLK	McD Douglas MD-83	Aero Lloyd *Oberursel Taunus*	
D-ALLL	McD Douglas MD-83	Aero Lloyd	
D-ALLM	McD Douglas MD-83	Aero Lloyd	
D-ALLN	McD Douglas MD-83	Aero Lloyd	
D-ALLO	McD Douglas MD-83	Aero Lloyd	
D-ALLP	McD Douglas MD-83	Aero Lloyd *Kassel*	
D-ALLQ	McD Douglas MD-83	Aero Lloyd	
D-ALLR	McD Douglas MD-83	Aero Lloyd	
D-ALLS	McD Douglas MD-82	Aero Lloyd	
D-ALLT	McD Douglas MD-82	Aero Lloyd	
D-ALLU	McD Douglas MD-83	Aero Lloyd	
D-ALLW	McD Douglas MD-83	Aero Lloyd	
D-ALOA	BAe 146-200	Hamburg Airlines	
D-AMUI	Boeing 757-2G5	LTU-Sud	
D-AMUJ	Boeing 767-3G5ER	LTU-Sud	
D-AMUK	Boeing 757-225	LTU-Sud	
D-AMUM	Boeing 757-2G5	LTU-Sud	
D-AMUN	Boeing 767-3G5ER	LTU-Sud	
D-AMUP	Boeing 767-33AER	LTU-Sud	
D-AMUQ	Boeing 757-2G5	LTU-Sud	
D-AMUR	Boeing 767-3G5ER	LTU-Sud	
D-AMUS	Boeing 767-3G5ER	LTU-Sud	
D-AMUU	Boeing 757-225	LTU-Sud	
D-AMUV	Boeing 757-2G5	LTU-Sud	
D-AMUW	Boeing 757-2G5	LTU-Sud	
D-AMUX	Boeing 757-2G5	LTU-Sud	

Notes	Reg.	Type	Owner or Operator
	D-AMUY	Boeing 757-2G5	LTU-Sud
	D-AMUZ	Boeing 757-2G5	LTU-Sud
	D-ANFA	Aérospatiale ATR-72-202	Eurowings
	D-ANFB	Aérospatiale ATR-72-202	Eurowings
	D-ANFC	Aérospatiale ATR-72-202	Eurowings
	D-ANFD	Aérospatiale ATR-72-202	Eurowings
	D-ANFE	Aérospatiale ATR-72-202	Eurowings
	D-ANFF	Aérospatiale ATR-72-202	Eurowings
	D-ANTJ	BAe 146-200QT	Eurowings/TNT Express Europe
	D-APOM	Airbus A.310-304	Hapag-Lloyd
	D-APON	Airbus A.310-304	Royal Nepal Airlines
	D-AQUI	Junkers Ju.52/3m	Lufthansa *Traditionsflug*
	D-AVRA	Avro RJ85	Lufthansa CityLine
	D-AVRB	Avro RJ85	Lufthansa CityLine
	D-AVRC	Avro RJ85	Lufthansa CityLine
	D-AVRD	Avro RJ85	Lufthansa CityLine
	D-AVRE	Avro RJ85	Lufthansa CityLine
	D-AVRF	Avro RJ85	Lufthansa CityLine
	D-AVRG	Avro RJ85	Lufthansa CityLine
	D-AVRH	Avro RJ85	Lufthansa CityLine
	D-AVRI	Avro RJ85	Lufthansa CityLine
	D-AVR	Avro RJ85	Lufthansa CityLine
	D-AVR	Avro RJ85	Lufthansa CityLine
	D-AVR	Avro RJ85	Lufthansa CityLine
	D-AVR	Avro RJ85	Lufthansa CityLine
	D-AVR	Avro RJ85	Lufthansa CityLine
	D-AVRO	Avro RJ85	Lufthansa CityLine
	D-AZUR	BAe 146-200	Hamburg Airlines
	D-BAAA	Aérospatiale ATR-42-300	Eurowings
	D-BACH	D.H.C.8-311 Dash Eight	Augsburg Airways
	D-BAGB	D.H.C.8-103 Dash Eight	Augsburg Airways
	D-BAKA	F.27 Friendship Mk 100	WDL
	D-BAKB	F.27 Friendship Mk 600	WDL
	D-BAKC	F.27 Friendship Mk 600	WDL
	D-BAKD	F.27 Friendship Mk 600	WDL
	D-BAKE	F.27 Friendship Mk 200	WDL
	D-BAKI	F.27 Friendship Mk 100	WDL
	D-BAKO	F.27 Friendship Mk 100	WDL
	D-BBBB	Aérospatiale ATR-42-300	Eurowings
	D-BCCC	Aérospatiale ATR-42-300	Eurowings
	D-BCRM	Aérospatiale ATR-42-300	Eurowings
	D-BCRN	Aérospatiale ATR-42-300	Eurowings
	D-BCRO	Aérospatiale ATR-42-300QC	Eurowings
	D-BCRP	Aérospatiale ATR-42-300QC	Eurowings
	D-BCRQ	Aérospatiale ATR-42-300	Eurowings
	D-BCRR	Aérospatiale ATR-42-300	Eurowings
	D-BCRS	Aérospatiale ATR-42-300	Eurowings
	D-BCRT	Aérospatiale ATR-42-300	Eurowings
	D-BDDD	Aérospatiale ATR-42-300	Eurowings
	D-BEEE	Aérospatiale ATR-42-300	Eurowings
	D-BELT	D.H.C.8-311 Dash Eight	Contactair/Lufthansa CityLine
	D-BEYT	D.H.C.8-311 Dash Eight	Contactair/Lufthansa CityLine
	D-BFFF	Aérospatiale ATR-42-300	Eurowings
	D-BGGG	Aérospatiale ATR-42-300	Eurowings
	D-BHHH	Aérospatiale ATR-42-300	Eurowings
	D-BIER	D.H.C.8-102 Dash Eight	Augsburg Airways
	D-BIRT	D.H.C.8-103 Dash Eight	Augsburg Airways
	D-BJJJ	Aérospatiale ATR-42-300	Eurowings
	D-BKIM	D.H.C.8-311 Dash Eight	Contactair/Lufthansa CityLine
	D-BKIR	D.H.C.8-311 Dash Eight	Contactair/Lufthansa CityLine
	D-BKIS	D.H.C.8-311 Dash Eight	Contactair/Lufthansa CityLine
	D-BOBA	D.H.C.8-311 Dash Eight	Hamburg Airlines
	D-BOBL	D.H.C.8-102 Dash Eight	Hamburg Airlines
	D-BOBO	D.H.C.8-102 Dash Eight	Hamburg Airlines
	D-BOBU	D.H.C.8-311 Dash Eight	Hamburg Airlines
	D-BOBY	D.H.C.8-102 Dash Eight	Hamburg Airlines
	D-CABE	Swearingen SA227AC Metro III	Saxonia Airlines
	D-CDIB	SAAB SF.340A	Deutsche BA
	D-CDIC	SAAB SF.340A	Deutsche BA
	D-CDID	SAAB SF.340A	Deutsche BA
	D-CDIE	SAAB SF.340A	Deutsche BA
	D-CDIF	SAAB SF.340A	Deutsche BA
	D-CDIZ	Dornier Do.228-201	Deutsche BA
	D-CMIC	Dornier Do.228-202K	Ratioflug

Reg.	Type	Owner or Operator	Notes
D-COLC	Swearingen SA227AC Metro III	OLT/Roland Air	
D-COLT	Swearingen SA226AC Metro III	OLT/Roland Air	
D-ICRJ	Swearingen SA226TC Metro II	OLT/Roland Air	
D-ICRL	Swearingen SA226TC Metro II	OLT/Roland Air	
D-IHCW	Swearingen SA226TC Metro II	OLT/Roland Air	

EC (Spain)

EC-BIH	Douglas DC-9-32	Aviaco *Roncesvalles*
EC-BIK	Douglas DC-9-32	Aviaco *Castillo de Guanapay*
EC-BIM	Douglas DC-9-32	Iberia *Ciudad de Santander*
EC-BIP	Douglas DC-9-32	Aviaco *Castillo de Monteagudo*
EC-BIR	Douglas DC-9-32	Binter Canarias
EC-BIS	Douglas DC-9-32	Iberia *Ciudad de Alicante*
EC-BIT	Douglas DC-9-32	Iberia *Ciudad de San Sebastian*
EC-BQV	Douglas DC-9-32	Iberia *Ciudad de Ibiza*
EC-BQY	Douglas DC-9-32	Aviaco *Mar Menor*
EC-BQZ	Douglas DC-9-32	Binter Canarias
EC-BYE	Douglas DC-9-32	Aviaco *Cala Galdana*
EC-BYF	Douglas DC-9-32	Aviaco *Hernan Cortes*
EC-BYI	Douglas DC-9-32	Aviaco *Pedro de Valdivia*
EC-BYJ	Douglas DC-9-32	Aviaco
EC-CAI	Boeing 727-256	Iberia *Castilla la Nueva*
EC-CAJ	Boeing 727-256	Iberia *Cataluna*
EC-CBA	Boeing 727-256	Iberia *Vascongadas*
EC-CBF	Boeing 727-256	Iberia *Gran Canaria*
EC-CBM	Boeing 727-256	Iberia *Castilla La Vieja*
EC-CBO	Douglas DC-10-30	Iberia *Costa del Sol*
EC-CBP	Douglas DC-10-30	Iberia *Costa Dorada*
EC-CEZ	Douglas DC-10-30	Iberia *Costa del Azahar*
EC-CFA	Boeing 727-256	Iberia *Jerez Xeres Sherry*
EC-CFB	Boeing 727-256	Iberia *Rioja*
EC-CFC	Boeing 727-256	Iberia *Tarragona*
EC-CFD	Boeing 727-256	Iberia *Montilla-Moriles*
EC-CFE	Boeing 727-256	Iberia *Penedes*
EC-CFF	Boeing 727-256	Iberia *Valdepenas*
EC-CFG	Boeing 727-256	Iberia *La Mancha*
EC-CFH	Boeing 727-256	Iberia *Priorato*
EC-CFI	Doeing 727-256	Iberia *Carinena*
EC-CFK	Boeing 727-256	Iberia *Rivero*
EC-CGN	Douglas DC-9-32	Aviaco *Martin Alonso Pinzon*
EC-CGO	Douglas DC-9-32	Aviaco *Pedro Alonso Nino*
EC-CGP	Douglas DC-9-32	Aviaco *Juan Sebastian Elcano*
EC-CGQ	Douglas DC-9-32	Aviaco *Alonso de Ojeda*
EC-CGR	Douglas DC-9-32	Aviaco *Francisco de Orellana*
EC-CID	Boeing 727-256	Iberia *Malaga*
EC-CIE	Boeing 727-256	Iberia *Esparragosa*
EC-CLB	Douglas DC-10-30	Iberia *Costa Blanca*
EC-CLD	Douglas DC-9-32	Aviaco *Hernando de Soto*
EC-CSJ	Douglas DC-10-30	Iberia *Costa de la Luz*
EC-CTR	Douglas DC-9-34CF	Iberia *Hernan Cortes*
EC-CTS	Douglas DC-9-34CF	Aviaco *Francisco de Pizarro*
EC-CTT	Douglas DC-9-34CF	Iberia *Pedro de Valladolid*
EC-CTU	Douglas DC-9-34CF	Aviaco *Pedro de Alvarado*
EC-DCC	Boeing 727-256	Iberia *Albarino*
EC-DCD	Boeing 727-256	Iberia *Chacoli*
EC-DCE	Boeing 727-256	Iberia *Mentrida*
EC-DDV	Boeing 727-256	Iberia *Acueducto de Segovia*
EC-DDX	Boeing 727-256	Iberia *Monasterio de Poblet*
EC-DDY	Boeing 727-256	Iberia *Cuevas de Altamira*
EC-DDZ	Boeing 727-256	Iberia *Murallas de Avila*
EC-DEA	Douglas DC-10-30	Iberia *Rias Gallegas*
EC-DGB	Douglas DC-9-34	Iberia *Castillo de Javier*
EC-DGC	Douglas DC-9-34	Aviaco *Castillo de Sotomayor*
EC-DGD	Douglas DC-9-34	Aviaco *Castillo de Arcos*
EC-DGE	Douglas DC-9-34	Aviaco *Castillo de Bellver*
EC-DHZ	Douglas DC-10-30	Iberia *Costas Canarias*
EC-DIA	Boeing 747-256B	Iberia *Tirso de Molina*
EC-DIB	Boeing 747-256B	Iberia *Cervantes*
EC-DLC	Boeing 747-256B (SCD)	Iberia *Francisco de Quevedo*
EC-DLD	Boeing 747-256B (SCD)	Iberia *Lupe de Vega*
EC-DLE	Airbus A.300B4-120	Iberia *Donana*

Notes	Reg.	Type	Owner or Operator
	EC-DLF	Airbus A.300B4-120	Iberia *Canadas del Teide*
	EC-DLG	Airbus A.300B4-120	Iberia *Las Tablas de Daimiel*
	EC-DLH	Airbus A.300B4-120	Iberia *Aigues Tortes*
	EC-DNP	Boeing 747-256B	Iberia *Juan Ramon Jimenez*
	EC-DNQ	Airbus A.300B4-120	Iberia *Islas Cies*
	EC-DNR	Airbus A.300B4-120	Iberia *Ordesa*
	EC-EEK	Boeing 747-256B (SCD)	Iberia *Garcia Lorca*
	EC-EFX	Boeing 757-2G5	LTE International Airways *Bluebird I*
	EC-EGH	Boeing 757-2G5	LTE International Airways *Bluebird II*
	EC-EIG	McD Douglas MD-83	Spanair *Sunlight*
	EC-ELT	BAe 146-200QT	Pan Air Lineas Aéreas/TNT
	EC-ELY	Boeing 737-3K9	Viva Air
	EC-EMD	Douglas DC-8-62F	Cargosur
	EC-EMX	Douglas DC-8-62F	Cargosur
	EC-ENQ	Boeing 757-2G5	LTE International Airways *Bluebird III*
	EC-EON	Airbus A.300B4-203	Iberia *Penalara*
	EC-EOO	Airbus A.300B4-203	Iberia *Covadouga*
	EC-EPA	BAe 146-200QT	Pan Air Lineas Aéreas/TNT
	EC-ETB	Boeing 737-4Y0	Futura International Airways
	EC-EUC	McD Douglas MD-87	Iberia *Ciudad de Burgos*
	EC-EUD	McD Douglas MD-87	Iberia *Ciudad de Toledo*
	EC-EUE	McD Douglas MD-87	Iberia *Ciudad de Sevilla*
	EC-EUL	McD Douglas MD-87	Iberia *Ciudad de Cadiz*
	EC-EVB	McD Douglas MD-87	Iberia *Arrecife de Lanzarote*
	EC-EVE	Boeing 737-4Y0	Futura International Airways
	EC-EXF	McD Douglas MD-87	Iberia *Ciudad de Pamplona*
	EC-EXG	McD Douglas MD-87	Iberia *Ciudad de Almeria*
	EC-EXM	McD Douglas MD-87	Iberia *Ciudad de Zaragoza*
	EC-EXN	McD Douglas MD-87	Iberia *Ciudad de Badajoz*
	EC-EXR	McD Douglas MD-87	Iberia *Ciudad de Oviedo*
	EC-EXT	McD Douglas MD-87	Iberia *Ciudad de Albacete*
	EC-EXY	Boeing 737-4Y0	Futura International Airways
	EC-EYB	McD Douglas MD-87	Iberia *Ciudad de Onis*
	EC-EYX	McD Douglas MD-87	Iberia *Ciudad de Caceres*
	EC-EYY	McD Douglas MD-87	Iberia *Ciudad de Barcelona*
	EC-EYZ	McD Douglas MD-87	Iberia *Ciudad de Las Palmas*
	EC-EZA	McD Douglas MD-87	Iberia *Ciudad de Segovia*
	EC-EZS	McD Douglas MD-87	Iberia *Ciudad de Mahon*
	EC-FAS	Airbus A.320-211	Iberia *Sierra de Cazorla*
	EC-FBQ	Airbus A.320-211	Iberia *Montseny*
	EC-FBR	Airbus A.320-211	Iberia *Sierra de Segura*
	EC-FBS	Airbus A.320-211	Iberia *Timanfaya*
	EC-FCB	Airbus A.320-211	Iberia *Montana de Covadonga*
	EC-FCU	Boeing 767-3Y0ER	Spanair *Baleares*
	EC-FDA	Airbus A.320-211	Iberia *Lagunas de Ruidera*
	EC-FDB	Airbus A.320-211	Iberia *Lago de Sanabria*
	EC-FEE	Boeing 757-236	Air Europa *Catalunya*
	EC-FEF	Boeing 757-236	Air Europa
	EC-FEO	Airbus A.320-211	Iberia *Delta del Ebro*
	EC-FER	Boeing 737-3Q8	Viva Air/Monarch (G-BWJA)
	EC-FEY	McD Douglas MD-87	Iberia *Ciudad de Jaen*
	EC-FEZ	McD Douglas MD-87	Iberia *Ciudad de Malaga*
	EC-FFA	McD Douglas MD-87	Iberia *Ciudad de Avila*
	EC-FFH	McD Douglas MD-8fl7	Iberia *Ciudad de Logrono*
	EC-FFI	McD Douglas MD-87	Iberia *Ciudad de Cuenca*
	EC-FFK	Boeing 757-236	Air Europa *Galicia*
	EC-FFN	Boeing 737-36E	Viva Air
	EC-FFY	BAe 146-300	Pan Air Lineas Aéreas/TNT
	EC-FGH	Airbus A.320-211	Iberia *Caldera de Taburiente*
	EC-FGM	McD Douglas MD-88	Aviaco *Torre de Hercules*
	EC-FGR	Airbus A.320-211	Iberia *Dehesa de Moncayo*
	EC-FGU	Airbus A.320-211	Iberia *Sierra Espuna*
	EC-FGV	Airbus A.320-211	Iberia *Monfrague*
	EC-FHA	Boeing 767-3Y0ER	Spanair *Canarias*
	EC-FHD	McD Douglas MD-87	Iberia *Ciudad de Leon*
	EC-FHG	McD Douglas MD-88	Aviaco *La Almudiana*
	EC-FHK	McD Douglas MD-87	Iberia *Ciudad de Tarragona*
	EC-FHR	Boeing 737-36E	Viva Air
	EC-FIA	Airbus A.320-211	Iberia *Isla de la Cartuja*
	EC-FIC	Airbus A.320-211	Iberia *Sierra de Grazalema*
	EC-FIG	McD Douglas MD-88	Aviaco *Penon de Ifach*
	EC-FIH	McD Douglas MD-88	Aviaco *Albaicin*
	EC-FIX	McD Douglas MD-83	Centennial Airlines
	EC-FJE	McD Douglas MD-88	Aviaco *Gibralfaro*

Reg.	Type	Owner or Operator	Notes
EC-FJR	Boeing 737-3Y0	Air Europa	
EC-FJZ	Boeing 737-3Y0	Air Europa	
EC-FKD	Airbus A.320-211	Iberia *Monte Alhoya*	
EC-FKH	Airbus A.320-211	Iberia *Canon del Río Lobos*	
EC-FKI	Boeing 737-375	Air Europa *Virgen de la Vega*	
EC-FKJ	Boeing 737-3Y0	Air Europa	
EC-FLD	Boeing 737-4Y0	Futura International Airways	
EC-FLF	Boeing 737-36E	Viva Air	
EC-FLG	Boeing 737-36E	Viva Air	
EC-FLK	McD Douglas MD-88	Aviaco *Palacio de la Magdalena*	
EC-FLN	McD Douglas MD-88	Aviaco *Puerta de Tierra*	
EC-FLP	Airbus A.320-211	Iberia *Torcal de Antequera*	
EC-FLQ	Airbus A.320-211	Iberia *Dunas de Liencres*	
EC-FML	Airbus A.320-211	Iberia *Hayedo de Tejera Negra*	
EC-FMN	Airbus A.320-211	Iberia *Cadi Moixeno*	
EC-FND	McD Douglas MD-88	Aviaco *Playa de la Concha*	
EC-FNR	Airbus A.320-211	Iberia *Monte el Valle*	
EC-FOF	McD Douglas MD-88	Aviaco *Cesar Manrique Lanzarote*	
EC-FOG	McD Douglas MD-88	Aviaco *La Giralda*	
EC-FOZ	McD Douglas MD-88	Aviaco *Montjuic*	
EC-FPD	McD Douglas MD-88	Aviaco *Lagos de Coradonga*	
EC-FPJ	McD Douglas MD-88	Aviaco *Rio de Vigo*	
EC-FQY	Airbus A.320-211	Iberia *Jaan Miro*	
EC-FSY	McD Douglas MD-83	Spanair *Sunrise*	
EC-FSZ	McD Douglas MD-83	Centennial Airlines	
EC-FTL	Boeing 757-236	Air Europa *Castilla y Leon*	
EC-FTR	Boeing 757-256	Iberia *Sierra de Guadarrama*	
EC-FTS	McD Douglas MD-83	Spanair *Sunbird*	
EC-FTT	McD Douglas MD-83	Spanair *Sunray*	
EC-FTU	McD Douglas MD-83	Spanair *Sunshine*	
EC-FUT	Boeing 737-3Q8	Air Europa	
EC-FVA	Douglas DC-8-71F	Cargosur	
EC-FVB	McD Douglas MD-83	Oasis International Airlines	
EC-FVC	McD Douglas MD-83	Oasis International Airlines	
EC-FVJ	Boeing 737-3Y0	Air Europa	
EC-FVR	McD Douglas MD-83	Spanair *Sundance*	
EC-FVV	McD Douglas MD-83	Centennial Airlines	
EC-FVX	McD Douglas MD-83	Oasis International Airlines	
EC-FVY	BAe 146-200QT	Pan Air Lineas Aéreas/TNT	
EC-FXA	McD Douglas MD-83	Spanair *Sundance*	
EC-FXB	Airbus A.310-324	Oasis International Airlines	
EC-FXC	Boeing 737-3Q8	Air Europa	
EC-FXI	McD Douglas MD-82	Spanair *Sunseeker*	
EC-FXP	Boeing 737-4Q8	Air Europa *Villanueva del Conde*	
EC-FXQ	Boeing 737-4Q8	Air Europa *Salamanca*	
EC-FXU	Boeing 757-256	Iberia *Xacobeo 93*	
EC-FXV	Boeing 757-256	Iberia *Argentina*	
EC-FXX	McD Douglas MD-87	Oasis International Airlines	
EC-FXY	McD Douglas MD-83	Spanair *Sunbeam*	
EC-FYF	Boeing 737-3Y0	Air Europa *Canarias*	
EC-FYJ	Boeing 757-256	Iberia	
EC-FYK	Boeing 757-256	Iberia	
EC-FYL	Boeing 757-256	Iberia	
EC-FYM	Boeing 757-256	Iberia	
EC-FYN	Boeing 757-256	Iberia	
EC-FZC	McD Douglas MD-83	Spanair *Sunflower*	
EC-FZE	BAe 146-200QT	Pan Air Lineas Aéreas/TNT	
EC-FZQ	McD Douglas MD-83	Centennial Airlines	
EC-FZT	Boeing 737-4Y0	Futura International Airways	
EC-FZZ	Boeing 737-4Y0	Air Europa *Baleares*	
EC-GAG	Boeing 747-256B	Iberia	
EC-GAT	McD Douglas MD-83	Spanair	
EC-GAZ	Boeing 737-4Y0	Air Europa	
EC-GBA	McD Douglas MD-83	Spanair *Sungod*	
EC-GBN	Boeing 737-4Y0	Air Europa	
EC-GBU	Boeing 737-36E	Viva Air	
EC-GBV	McD Douglas MD-83	Centennial Airlines	
EC-GBX	Boeing 757-236	Air Europa	
EC-BGY	McD Douglas MD-83	Oasis International Airlines	
EC-GCA	Boeing 757-236	Air Europa	
EC-GCB	Boeing 757-236	Air Europa	
EC-GCI	Boeing 727-256	Iberia *Murcia*	
EC-GCJ	Boeing 727-256	Iberia *Galicia*	
EC-GCK	Boeing 727-256	Iberia *Asturias*	

Notes	Reg.	Type	Owner or Operator
	EC-GCL	Boeing 727-256	Iberia *Andalucia*
	EC-GCM	Boeing 727-256	Iberia *Tenerife*
	EC-GCV	McD Douglas MD-82	Spanair
	EC-GCY	Douglas DC-8-62F	Canarias Cargo
	EC-GEE	Douglas DC-8-62F	Canarias Cargo
	EC-	BAe 146-200QT	Pan Air Lineas Aéreas/TNT
	EC-	McD Douglas MD-83	Centennial Airlines

EI (Republic of Ireland)

Including complete current Irish Civil Register

EI-ABI	D.H.84 Dragon	Aer Lingus Teo *Iolar* (EI-AFK)
EI-ADV	PA-12 Super Cruiser	R. E. Levis
EI-AFE	Piper J3C-65 Cub	J. Conlon
EI-AFF	B.A. Swallow 2	J. J. Sullivan & ptnrs
EI-AFN	B.A. Swallow 2 ★	J. McCarthy
EI-AGB	Miles M.38 Messenger 4 ★	J. McLoughlin
EI-AGD	Taylorcraft Plus D ★	B. & K. O'Sullivan
EI-AGJ	J/1 Autocrat	W. G. Rafter
EI-AHA	D.H.82A Tiger Moth ★	J. H. Maher
EI-AHI	D.H.82A Tiger Moth	High Fidelity Flyers
EI-AHR	D.H.C.1 Chipmunk 22 ★	C. Lane
EI-AKM	Piper J-3C-65 Cub	Setanta Flying Group
EI-ALH	Taylorcraft Plus D	N. Reilly
EI-ALP	Avro 643 Cadet	J. C. O'Loughlin
EI-ALU	Avro 631 Cadet	M. P. Cahill *(stored)*
EI-AMK	J/1 Autocrat	Irish Aero Club
EI-ANT	Champion 7ECA Citabria	S. Donohoe
EI-ANY	PA-18 Super Cub 95	Bogavia Group
EI-AOB	PA-28 Cherokee 140	J. Surdival & ptnrs
EI-AOK	Cessna F.172G	R. J. Cloughley & N. J. Simpson
EI-AOP	D.H.82A Tiger Moth ★	Institute of Technology/Dublin
EI-AOS	Cessna 310B	Joyce Aviation Ltd
EI-APF	Cessna F.150F	L. O. Kennedy
EI-APS	Schleicher ASK.14	SLG Group
EI-ARH	Currie Wot/S.E.5 Replica	L. Garrison
EI-ARM	Currie Wot/S.E.5 Replica	L. Garrison
EI-ARW	Jodel D.R.1050	P. Walsh & P. Ryan
EI-AST	Cessna F.150H	Liberty Flying Group
EI-ATJ	B.121 Pup 1	L. O'Leary
EI-ATK	PA-28 Cherokee 140	Mayo Flying Club Ltd
EI-ATS	M.S.880B Rallye Club	ATS Group
EI-AUE	M.S.880B Rallye Club	Kilkenny Flying Club Ltd
EI-AUG	M.S.894 Rallye Minerva 220	K. O'Leary
EI-AUJ	M.S.880B Rallye Club	Ormond Flying Club Ltd
EI-AUM	J/1 Autocrat	J. G. Rafter
EI-AUO	Cessna FA.150K Aerobat	Kerry Aero Club
EI-AUS	J/5F Aiglet Trainer	T. Stephens & T. Lennon
EI-AUT	Forney F-1A Aircoupe	Joyce Aviation Ltd
EI-AUV	PA-23 Aztec 250C	Shannon Executive Aviation
EI-AUY	Morane-Saulnier M.S.502	G. Warner/Duxford
EI-AVB	Aeronca 7AC Champion	T. Brett
EI-AVC	Cessna F.337F	Christy Keane (Saggart) Ltd
EI-AVM	Cessna F.150L	P. Kearney
EI-AWE	Cessna F.150M	Third Flight Group
EI-AWH	Cessna 210J	Rathcode Flying Club Ltd
EI-AWP	D.H.82A Tiger Moth	O. Bruton
EI-AWR	Malmo MFI-9 Junior	M. R. Nesbitt & S. Duignan
EI-AWU	M.S.880B Rallye Club	Longford Aviation Ltd
EI-AYA	M.S.880B Rallye Club	Limerick Flying Club Ltd
EI-AYB	GY-80 Horizon 180	Westwing Flying Group
EI-AYD	AA-5 Traveler	P. Howick & ptnrs
EI-AYF	Cessna FRA.150L	Garda Flying Club
EI-AYI	M.S.880B Rallye Club	J. McNamara
EI-AYK	Cessna F.172M	S. T. Scully
EI-AYN	BN-2A Islander	Gallway Aviation Services Ltd
EI-AYO	Douglas DC-3A ★	Science Museum, Wroughton
EI-AYR	Schleicher ASK-16	Kilkenny Airport Ltd
EI-AYS	PA-22 Colt 108	M. F. Skelly
EI-AYV	M.S.892A Rallye Commodore 150	P. Murtagh
EI-AYY	Evans VP-1	M. Donoghue

Reg.	Type	Owner or Operator	Notes
EI-BAF	Thunder Ax6-56 balloon	W. G. Woollett	
EI-BAJ	SNCAN Stampe SV-4C	Dublin Tiger Group	
EI-BAO	Cessna F.172G	O. Bruton	
EI-BAR	Thunder Ax8-105 balloon	J. Burke & V. Hourihane	
EI-BAS	Cessna F.172M	Falcon Aviation Ltd	
EI-BAT	Cessna F.150M	Donegal Aero Club Ltd	
EI-BAV	PA-22 Colt 108	J. Davy	
EI-BBC	PA-28 Cherokee 180C	Piper Aero Club Ltd	
EI-BBD	Evans VP-1	Volksplane Group	
EI-BBE	Champion 7FC Tri-Traveler (tailwheel)	P. Forde & D. Connaire	
EI-BBG	M.S.880B Rallye Club	Weston Ltd	
EI-BBI	M.S.892 Rallye Commodore	Kilkenny Airport Ltd	
EI-BBJ	M.S.880B Rallye Club	Weston Ltd	
EI-BBM	Cameron O-65 balloon	Dublin Ballooning Club	
EI-BBN	Cessna F.150M	Sligo N.W. Aero Club	
EI-BBO	M.S.893E Rallye 180GT	J. G. Lacey & ptnrs	
EI-BBV	Piper J-3C-65 Cub	F. Cronin	
EI-BCE	BN-2A-26 Islander	Galway Aviation Services Ltd	
EI-BCF	Bensen B.8M	T. A. Brennan	
EI-BCH	M.S.892A Rallye Commodore 150	The Condor Group	
EI-BCJ	F.8L Falco 1 Srs 3	D. Kelly	
EI-BCK	Cessna F.172K	H. Caulfield	
EI-BCL	Cessna 182P	F. Doherty	
EI-BCM	Piper J-3C-65 Cub	Kilmoon Flying Group	
EI-BCN	Piper J-3C-65 Cub	Snowflake Flying Group	
EI-BCO	Piper J-3C-65 Cub	J. Molloy	
EI-BCP	D.628 Condor	A. Delaney	
EI-BCS	M.S.880B Rallye Club	Organic Fruit & Vegetables of Ireland Ltd	
EI-BCU	M.S.880B Rallye Club	Weston Ltd	
EI-BCW	M.S.880B Rallye Club	Kilkenny Flying Club	
EI-BDH	M.S.880B Rallye Club	Munster Wings Ltd	
EI-BDK	M.S.880B Rallye Club	Limerick Flying Club Ltd	
EI-BDL	Evans VP-2	M. Blake	
EI-BDM	PA-23 Aztec 250D ★	Industrial Training School	
EI-BDP	Cessna 182P	S. Bruton	
EI-BDR	PA-28 Cherokee 180	Cherokee Group	
EI-BEA	M.S.880B Rallye 100ST	Weston Ltd	
EI-BED	Boeing 747-130	Aerlinte Eireann Teo St Kieran	
EI-BEN	Piper J-3C-65 Cub	J. J. Sullivan	
EI BEO	Cessna 310Q	Iona National Airways Ltd	
EI-BEP	M.S.892A Rallye Commodore 150	H. Lynch & J. O'Leary	
EI-BEY	Naval N3N-3 ★	Huntley & Huntley Ltd	
EI-BFF	Beech A.23 Musketeer	E. Hopkins	
EI-BFH	Bell 212	Irish Helicopters Ltd	
EI-BFI	M.S.880B Rallye 100ST	J. O'Neill	
EI-BFM	M.S.893E Rallye 235GT	FM Group	
EI-BFO	Piper J-3C-90 Cub	D. Gordon	
EI-BFP	M.S.800B Rallye 100ST	Weston Ltd	
EI-BFR	M.S.880B Rallye 100ST	J. Power	
EI-BFV	M.S.880B Rallye 100T	Ormond Flying Club	
EI-BGA	SOCATA Rallye 100ST	J. J. Frew	
EI-BGB	M.S.880B Rallye Club	Limerick Flying Club Ltd	
EI-BGD	M.S.880B Rallye Club	N. Kavanagh	
EI-BGG	M.S.892E Rallye 150GT	M. J. Hanlon	
EI-BGH	Cessna F.172N	Golf Hotel Group	
EI-BGJ	Cessna F.152	Hibernian Flying Club	
EI-BGT	Colt 77A balloon	K. Haugh	
EI-BGU	M.S.880B Rallye Club	M. F. Neary	
EI-BHB	M.S.887 Rallye 125	Hotel Bravo Flying Club	
EI-BHC	Cessna F.177RG	P. V. Maguire	
EI-BHF	M.S.892A Rallye Commodore 150	B. Mullen	
EI-BHI	Bell 206B JetRanger 2	J. Mansfield	
EI-BHK	M.S.880B Rallye Club	J. Lawlor & B. Lyons	
EI-BHL	Beech E90 King Air	Stewart Singlam Fabrics Ltd	
EI-BHM	Cessna F.337E H	Dublin Institute of Technology	
EI-BHN	M.S.893A Rallye Commodore 180	T. Garvan	
EI-BHO	Sikorsky S-61N	Irish Helicopters Ltd	
EI-BHP	M.S.893A Rallye Commodore 180	Spanish Point Flying Club	
EI-BHT	Beech 77 Skipper	Waterford Aero Club	
EI-BHV	Champion 7EC Traveler	Condor Group	
EI-BHW	Cessna F.150F	R. Sharpe	
EI-BHY	SOCATA Rallye 150ST	D. Killian	
EI-BIB	Cessna F.152	Galway Flying Club	

Notes	Reg.	Type	Owner or Operator
	EI-BIC	Cessna F.172N	Oriel Flying Group Ltd
	EI-BID	PA-18 Super Cub 95	D. MacCarthy
	EI-BIF	SOCATA Rallye 235E	Empire Enterprises Ltd
	EI-BIG	Zlin 526	P. von Lonkhuyzen
	EI-BIJ	AB-206B JetRanger 2	Medavia Properties Ltd
	EI-BIK	PA-18 Super Cub 180	Dublin Gliding Club
	EI-BIM	M.S.880B Rallye Club	D. Millar
	EI-BIO	Piper J-3C-65 Cub	Monasterevin Flying Club
	EI-BIR	Cessna F.172M	B. Harrison & ptnrs
	EI-BIS	Robin R.1180TD	Robin Aiglon Group
	EI-BIT	M.S.887 Rallye 125	Spanish Point Flying Club
	EI-BIU	Robin R.2112A	Wicklow Flying Group
	EI-BIV	Bellanca 8KCAB Citabria	Aerocrats Flying Group
	EI-BIW	M.S.880B Rallye Club	E. J. Barr
	EI-BJA	Cessna FRA.150L	Blackwater Flying Group
	EI-BJC	Aeronca 7AC Champion	E. Griffin
	EI-BJG	Robin R.1180	N. Hanley
	EI-BJJ	Aeronca 15AC Sedan	A. A. Alderdice & S. H. Boyd
	EI-BJK	M.S.880B Rallye 110ST	Jordan Larkin Flying Group
	EI-BJM	Cessna A.152	Leinster Aero Club
	EI-BJO	Cessna R.172K	P. Hogan & G. Ryder
	EI-BJS	AA-5B Tiger	P. Morrisey
	EI-BJT	PA-38-112 Tomahawk	O. Bruton
	EI-BKC	Aeronca 115AC Sedan	J. Lynch
	EI-BKF	Cessna F.172H	M. & M. C. Veale
	EI-BKK	Taylor JT.1 Monoplane	Waterford Aero Club
	EI-BKN	M.S.880B Rallye 100ST	Weston Ltd
	EI-BKS	Eipper Quicksilver	Irish Microlight Ltd
	EI-BKT	AB-206B JetRanger 3	Irish Helicopters Ltd
	EI-BKU	M.S.892A Rallye Commodore 150	Limerick Flying Club Ltd
	EI-BLB	SNCAN Stampe SV-4C	J. E. Hutchinson & R. A. Stafford
	EI-BLD	Bolkow Bo 105C	Irish Helicopters Ltd
	EI-BLE	Eipper Microlight	R. P. St George-Smith
	EI-BLG	AB-206B JetRanger 3	Monarch Property Services Ltd
	EI-BLN	Eipper Quicksilver MX	O. J. Conway & B. Daffy
	EI-BLO	Catto CP.16	R. W. Hall
	EI-BLU	Evans VP-1	S. Pallister
	EI-BLW	PA-23 Aztec 250C	— (stored)
	EI-BLY	Sikorsky S-61N	Irish Helicopters Ltd
	EI-BMA	M.S.880B Rallye Club	W. Rankin & M. Kelleher
	EI-BMB	M.S.880B Rallye 100T	Clyde Court Development Ltd
	EI-BMC	Hiway Demon Skytrike	S. Pallister
	EI-BMF	Laverda F.8L Falco	M. Slazenger & H. McCann
	EI-BMH	M.S.880B Rallye Club	N. J. Bracken
	EI-BMI	SOCATA TB.9 Tampico	Ashford Flying Group
	EI-BMJ	M.S.880B Rallye 100T	Weston Ltd
	EI-BML	PA-23 Aztec 250	Bruton Aircraft Engineering Ltd
	EI-BMM	Cessna F.152 II	E. Hopkins
	EI-BMN	Cessna F.152 II	Iona National Airways Ltd
	EI-BMO	Robin R.2160	L. Gavin & ptnrs
	EI-BMU	Monnet Sonerai II	P. Forde & D. Connaire
	EI-BMV	AA-5 Traveler	E. Tierney & K. Harold
	EI-BMW	Vulcan Air Trike	L. Maddock
	EI-BNA	Douglas DC-8-63CF	Aer Turas Teo
	EI-BNB	Lake LA-4-200 Buccaneer	O. J. Irwin
	EI-BND	Conroy CL-44-0	Buffalo Airways
	EI-BNF	Goldwing Canard	T. Morelli
	EI-BNG	M.S.892A Rallye Commodore 150	Shannon Executive Aviation
	EI-BNH	Hiway Skytrike	M. Martin
	EI-BNJ	ELvans VP-2	G. A. Cashman
	EI-BNK	Cessna U.206F	Irish Parachute Club Ltd
	EI-BNL	Rand KR-2	K. Hayes
	EI-BNP	Rotorway 133	R. L. Renfroe
	EI-BNT	Cvjetkovic CA-65	B. Tobin & P. G. Ryan
	EI-BNU	M.S.880B Rallye Club	P. A. Doyle
	EI-BOA	Pterodactyl Ptraveller	A. Murphy
	EI-BOE	SOCATA TB.10 Tobago	P. Byron & ptnrs
	EI-BOH	Eipper Quicksilver	J. Leech
	EI-BOR	Bell 222	Westair Ltd
	EI-BOV	Rand KR-2	G. O'Hara & G. Callan
	EI-BOX	Duet	K. Riccius
	EI-BPB	PA-28R Cherokee Arrow 200	Rathcoole Flying Club
	EI-BPE	Viking Dragonfly	G. Bracken
	EI-BPJ	Cessna 182A	Falcon Parachute Club Ltd

Reg.	Type	Owner or Operator	Notes
EI-BPL	Cessna F.172K	Phoenix Flying	
EI-BPO	Southdown Sailwings	A. Channing	
EI-BPP	Quicksilver MX	J. A. Smith	
EI-BPT	Skyhook Sabre	T. McGrath	
EI-BPU	Hiway Demon	A. Channing	
EI-BRH	Mainair Gemini Flash	J. Deeney	
EI-BRK	Flexiform Trike	L. Maddock	
EI-BRS	Cessna P.172D	D. & M. Hillery	
EI-BRT	Flexwing M17727	M. J. McCrystal	
EI-BRU	Evans VP-1	R. Smith & T. Coughlan	
EI-BRV	Hiway Demon	M. Garvey & C. Tully	
EI-BRW	Ultralight Deltabird	A. & E. Aerosports	
EI-BRX	Cessna FRA.150L	Trim Flying Club Ltd	
EI-BSB	Jodel D.112	W. Kennedy	
EI-BSC	Cessna F.172N	S. Phelan	
EI-BSD	Enstrom F-28A	Clark Aviation	
EI-BSF	H.S.748 Srs 1 ★	Ryanair cabin trainer/Dublin	
EI-BSG	Bensen B.80	J. Todd	
EI-BSK	SOCATA TB.9 Tampico	Weston Ltd	
EI-BSL	PA-34-220T Seneca	E. L. Symons	
EI-BSN	Cameron O-65 balloon	W. Woollett	
EI-BSO	PA-28 Cherokee 140B	D. Rooney	
EI-BSQ	Thundercolt Ax6-56Z balloon	D. Hooper	
EI-BST	Bell 206B JetRanger	Celtic Helicopters Ltd	
EI-BSU	Champion 7KCAB	R. Bentley	
EI-BSV	SOCATA TB.20 Trinidad	J. Condron	
EI-BSW	Solar Wings Pegasus XL-R	E. Fitzgerald	
EI-BSX	Piper J-3C-65 Cub	J. & T. O'Dwyer	
EI-BTN	L.1101-385 TriStar 1	Air Tara Ltd (leased to Air America)	
EI-BTS	Boeing 747-283B (SCD)	Air Tara Ltd (leased to Philippine A/L)	
EI-BTX	McD Douglas MD-82	Air Tara Ltd (leased to AeroMexico)	
EI-BTY	McD Douglas MD-82	Air Tara Ltd	
EI-BUA	Cessna 172M	Skyhawks Flying Club	
EI-BUC	Jodel D.9 Bebe	D. Lyons	
EI-BUF	Cessna 210N	210 Group	
EI-BUG	SOCATA ST.10 Diplomate	J. Cooke	
EI-BUH	Lake LA.4-200 Buccaneer	Derg Aviation (Group) Ltd	
EI-BUJ	M.S.892A Rallye Commodore 150	T. Cunniffe	
EI-BUL	MW-5 Sorcerer	J. Conlon	
EI-BUN	Beech 76 Duchess	The 172 Flying Group Ltd	
EI-BUO	Quickkit Glass S.005E	C. Lavery & C. Donaldson	
EI-BUR	PA-38-112 Tomahawk	Westair Aviation Ltd	
EI-BUS	PA-38-112 Tomahawk	Westair Aviation Ltd	
EI-BUT	M.S.893A Commodore 180	T. Keating	
EI-BUU	Solar Wings Pegasus XL-R	R. L. T. Hudson	
EI-BUV	Cessna 172RG	J. J. Spollen	
EI-BUW	Noble Hardman Snowbird IIIA	T.I.F.C. & I.S. Ltd	
EI-BUX	Agusta A.109A	Orring Ltd	
EI-BUZ	Robinson R-22	Leoni Aviation Ltd	
EI-BVB	Whittaker MW.6 Merlin	R. England	
EI-BVC	Cameron N-65 balloon	E. Shepherd	
EI-BVF	Cessna F.172N	First Phantom Group	
EI-BVJ	AMF Chevvron 232	W. T. King & S. G. Dunäne	
EI-BVK	PA-38-112 Tomahawk	Pegasus Flying Group Ltd	
EI-BVN	Bell 206B Jet Ranger 3	Helicopter Hire (Ireland) Ltd	
EI-BVQ	Cameron Can SS balloon	T. McCormack	
EI-BVS	Cessna 172RG	P. Bruno	
EI-BVT	Evans VP-2	J. J. Sullivan	
EI-BVY	Zenith 200AA-RW	J. Matthews & ptnrs	
EI-BWD	McD Douglas MD-83	Air Tara Ltd (leased to TWA)	
EI-BWF	Boeing 747-283B	Air Tara Ltd	
EI-BWH	Partenavia P.68C	K. Buckley	
EI-BXA	Boeing 737-448	Aer Lingus Teo St Conleth	
EI-BXB	Boeing 737-448	Aer Lingus Teo St Gall	
EI-BXC	Boeing 737-448	Aer Lingus Teo St Brendan	
EI-BXD	Boeing 737-448	Aer Lingus Teo St Colman	
EI-BXI	Boeing 737-448	Aer Lingus Teo St Finnian	
EI-BXK	Boeing 737-448	Aer Lingus Teo St Caimin	
EI-BXL	Polaris F1B-OK350	M. McKeon	
EI-BXM	Boeing 737-2T4	Air Tara Ltd	
EI-BXN	Boeing 737-448	Aer Lingus Teo	
EI-BXO	Fouga CM.170 Magister	G. W. Connolly	
EI-BXP	PA-23 Aztec 250E	Galway Aviation Services Ltd	
EI-BXT	D.62B Condor	J. Sweeney	

Notes	Reg.	Type	Owner or Operator
	EI-BXU	PA-28-161 Warrior II	W. T. King
	EI-BXX	AB-206B JetRanger	Westair Aviation Ltd
	EI-BYA	Thruster TST Mk 1	E. Fagan
	EI-BYD	Cessna 150J	Kestrel Flying Group
	EI-BYE	PA-31-350 Navajo Chieftain	EI-Air Exports Ltd
	EI-BYF	Cessna 150M	Twentieth Air Training Group
	EI-BYG	SOCATA TB.9 Tampico	Weston Ltd
	EI-BYH	Cessna 340A	Claddagh Air Carriers
	EI-BYI	Colt 77A balloon	J. Keena
	EI-BYJ	Bell 206B JetRanger	Celtic Helicopters Ltd
	EI-BYK	PA-23 Aztec 250E	M. F. Hilary
	EI-BYL	Zenith CH.250	A. Corcoran & J. Martin
	EI-BYO	Aérospatiale ATR-42-300	GPA Group Ltd (leased to Brit Air)
	EI-BYR	Bell 206L-3 LongRanger 3	Ven Air Ltd
	EI-BYS	Robinson R-22B	G. V. Maloney
	EI-BYV	Hughes 369D	Irish Helicopters Ltd
	EI-BYX	Champion 7GCAA	P. J. Gallagher
	EI-BYY	Piper J-3C-85 Cub	A. J. Haines
	EI-BYZ	PA-44-180 Seminole	O. Bruton
	EI-BZA	Boeing 747-283B	Air Tara Ltd (leased to Philippine A/L)
	EI-BZB	Airbus A.300C4	GPA Group Ltd (leased to Philippine A/L)
	EI-BZE	Boeing 737-3Y0	GPA Group Ltd (leased to Philippine A/L)
	EI-BZF	Boeing 737-3Y0	Pergola Ltd (leased to Philippine A/L)
	EI-BZH	Boeing 737-3Y0	Dormacken Ltd (leased to Philippine A/L)
	EI-BZI	Boeing 737-3Y0	GPA Group Ltd (leased to Philippine A/L)
	EI-BZJ	Boeing 737-3Y0	Pergola Ltd (leased to Philippine A/L)
	EI-BZK	Boeing 737-3Y0	GPA Group Ltd (leased to Philippine A/L)
	EI-BZL	Boeing 737-3Y0	Dormacken Ltd (leased to Philippine A/L)
	EI-BZM	Boeing 737-3Y0	Dormacken Ltd (leased to Philippine A/L)
	EI-BZN	Boeing 737-3Y0	GPA Group Ltd (leased to Philippine A/L)
	EI-CAA	Cessna FR.172J	A. Ross
	EI-CAC	Grob G.115	European College of Aeronautics
	EI-CAD	Grob G.115	Exchequer Leasing Ltd
	EI-CAE	Grob G.115	D. Kehoe
	EI-CAL	Boeing 767-3Y0ER	Aer Lingus Teo (leased to S.A.S.)
	EI-CAM	Boeing 767-3Y0ER	Aer Lingus Teo (leased to TWA)
	EI-CAN	Aerotech MW.5 Sorcerer	V. Vaughan
	EI-CAO	Cameron O-84 balloon	K. Haugh
	EI-CAP	Cessna R.182RG	Skyline Flight Management Ltd
	EI-CAU	AMF Chevvron 232	H. Sydner
	EI-CAW	Bell 206B JetRanger	Celtic Helicopters Ltd
	EI-CAX	Cessna P.210N	J. J. Dunne
	EI-CAY	Mooney M.20C	Ranger Flights Ltd
	EI-CBB	Douglas DC-9-15	GPA Finance Ltd (stored)
	EI-CBC	Aérospatiale ATR-72-201	Air Tara Ltd (leased to American Eagle)
	EI-CBD	Aérospatiale ATR-72-201	Air Tara Ltd (leased to American Eagle)
	EI-CBF	Aérospatiale ATR-42-300	Air Tara Ltd (leased to Trans World Express)
	EI-CBG	Douglas DC-9-51	GPA Finance Ltd (leased to Hawaiian)
	EI-CBH	Douglas DC-9-51	GPA Finance Ltd (leased to Hawaiian)
	EI-CBI	Douglas DC-9-51	Air Tara Ltd (leased to Hawaiian)
	EI-CBJ	D.H.C. 8-102 Dash Eight	GPA Group Ltd (leased in Alaska)
	EI-CBK	Aérospatiale ATR-42-300	Air Tara Ltd
	EI-CBR	McD Douglas MD-83	Irish Aerospace Ltd (leased to Avianca)
	EI-CBS	McD Douglas MD-83	Dormacken Ltd (leased to Avianca)
	EI-CBU	McD Douglas MD-87	Air Tara Ltd (leased to AeroMexico)
	EI-CBY	McD Douglas MD-83	Dormacken Ltd (leased to Avianca)
	EI-CBZ	McD Douglas MD-83	Dormacken Ltd (leased to Avianca)
	EI-CCA	Beech 19A Musketeer	P. F. McCooke
	EI-CCB	PA-44-180 Seminole	S. Bruton
	EI-CCC	McD Douglas MD-83	Air Tara Ltd (leased to Avianca)
	EI-CCD	Grob G.115A	M.O.D. Aviation Ltd
	EI-CCE	McD Douglas MD-83	Dormacken Ltd (leased to Avianca)
	EI-CCF	Aeronca 11AC Chief	O. Bruton
	EI-CCH	Piper J-3C-65 Cub	M. Slattery
	EI-CCJ	Cessna 152	Irish Aero Club
	EI-CCK	Cessna 152	Irish Aero Club
	EI-CCM	Cessna 152	Irish Aero Club
	EI-CCN	Grob G.115A	European College of Aeronautics
	EI-CCO	PA-44-180 Seminole	S. Bruton
	EI-CCQ	Slingsby T.61F Venture T.2	Kerry Aero Club Ltd
	EI-CCT	Robinson R-22B	Air Investments Ltd
	EI-CCV	Cessna R.172K-XP	Kerry Aero Club
	EI-CCY	AA-1B Trainer	N. & C. Whisler

Reg.	Type	Owner or Operator	Notes
EI-CDA	Boeing 737-548	Aer Lingus Teo *St Columba*	
EI-CDB	Boeing 737-548	Aer Lingus Teo *St Albert*	
EI-CDC	Boeing 737-548	Aer Lingus Teo *St Munchin*	
EI-CDD	Boeing 737-548	Aer Lingus Teo *St Macartan*	
EI-CDF	Boeing 737-548	Aer Lingus Teo *St Cronan*	
EI-CDG	Boeing 737-548	Aer Lingus Teo *St Moling*	
EI-CDH	Boeing 737-548	Aer Lingus Teo *St Ronan*	
EI-CDI	McD Douglas MD-11	GPA Group Ltd *(leased to Garuda)*	
EI-CDJ	McD Douglas MD-11	GPA Group Ltd *(leased to Garuda)*	
EI-CDK	McD Douglas MD-11	GPA Group Ltd *(leased to Garuda)*	
EI-CDL	McD Douglas MD-11	GPA Group Ltd *(leased to Garuda)*	
EI-CDM	McD Douglas MD-11	GPA Group Ltd *(leased to Garuda)*	
EI-CDN	McD Douglas MD-11	GPA Group Ltd *(leased to Garuda)*	
EI-CDP	Cessna 182L	O. Bruton	
EI-CDQ	SA.300 Starduster Too	A. O'Rourke	
EI-CDS	Boeing 737-548	Aer Lingus Teo *St Malachy*	
EI-CDV	Cessna 150F	Blue Heron Aircraft Services Ltd	
EI-CDW	Robinson R-22B	Rathcoole Flying Club Ltd	
EI-CDX	Cessna 210K	Falcon Aviation Ltd	
EI-CDY	McD Douglas MD-83	Dormacken Ltd *(leased to Avianca)*	
EI-CEB	Airbus A.300B4	Pergola Ltd *(leased to Philippine A/L)*	
EI-CEC	PA-31-350 Navajo Chieftain	Aer Atlantic	
EI-CEG	M.S.893A Rallye 180GT	M. Farrelly	
EI-CEK	McD Douglas MD-83	Irish Aerospace Ltd	
EI-CEL	Rans S.6 Coyote	D. O'Gorman	
EI-CEN	Thruster T.300	P. J. Murphy	
EI-CEO	Boeing 747-259B (SCD)	GPA Group Ltd *(leased to Airstar)*	
EI-CEP	McD Douglas MD-83	Dormacken Ltd *(leased to Avianca)*	
EI-CEQ	McD Douglas MD-83	Dormacken Ltd *(leased to Avianca)*	
EI-CER	McD Douglas MD-83	Irish Aerospace Ltd *(leased to Avianca)*	
EI-CES	Taylorcraft BC-65	N. O'Brien	
EI-CET	L.188CF Electra	Hunting Cargo Airlines (Ireland) Ltd	
EI-CEX	Lake LA-4-200	Derg Developments Ltd	
EI-CEY	Boeing 757-2Y0	Pergola Ltd *(leased to Avianca)*	
EI-CEZ	Boeing 757-2Y0	GPA Group Ltd *(leased to Avianca)*	
EI-CFE	Robinson R-22B	Windsor Motors Ltd	
EI-CFF	PA-12 Super Cruiser	J. O'Dwyer & J. Molloy	
EI-CFG	CP.301B Emeraude	Southlink Ltd	
EI-CFH	PA-12 Super Cruiser	G. Treacy	
EI-CFI	PA-34-200T Seneca II	Mockfield Construction	
EI CFK	Varga 2150A Kachina	W. M. Patterson	
EI-CFL	Airbus A.300B4	Air Tara Ltd	
EI-CFM	Cessna 172P	M. P. Cahill	
EI-CFN	Cessna 172P	L. Kane	
EI-CFO	Piper J-3C-65 Cub	D. O'Connor & ptnrs	
EI-CFP	Cessna 172P	S. Bruton	
EI-CFV	M.S.880B Rallye Club	Kilkenny Flying Club	
EI-CFX	Robinson R-22B	Glenwood Transport	
EI-CFY	Cessna 172N	K. A. O'Conner	
EI-CFZ	McD Douglas MD-83	Air Tara Ltd *(leased to Avianca)*	
EI-CGB	Team Minimax	M. Garvey	
EI-CGC	Stinson 108-3	S. Bruton	
EI-CGD	Cessna 172M	W. Phelan & M. Casey	
EI-CGE	Hiway Demon	T. E. Carr	
EI-CGF	Luton LA-5 Major	F. Doyle & J. Duggan	
EI-CGG	Ercoupe 415C	Irish Ercoupe Group	
EI-CGH	Cessna 210N	J. J. Spollen	
EI-CGI	McD Douglas MD-83	Irish Aerospace Ltd *(leased to Air Liberte Tunisia)*	
EI-CGJ	Solar Wings Pegasus XL-R	P. Heraty	
EI-CGK	Robinson R-22B	Skyfare Ltd	
EI-CGM	Solar Wings Pegasus XL-R	Microflight Ltd	
EI-CGN	Solar Wings Pegasus XL-R	M. Ffrench	
EI-CGO	Douglas DC-8-63AF	Aer Turas Teo	
EI-CGP	PA-28 Cherokee 140C	A. Barlow	
EI-CGQ	AS.350B Ecureuil	Caulstown Air Ltd	
EI-CGT	Cessna 152 II	Eitleann Property Ltd	
EI-CGU	Robinson R-22HP	Santail Ltd	
EI-CGV	Piper J-5A Cub Cruiser	J5 Group	
EI-CGW	Powerchute Kestrel	C. Kiernan	
EI-CHF	PA-44-180 Seminole	A. Barlow	
EI-CHH	Boeing 737-317	GPA Group *(leased to Frontier A/L)*	
EI-CHI	Mooney M.20C	—	
EI-CHJ	Cessna FR.172K	O. Bruton	

Notes	Reg.	Type	Owner or Operator
	EI-CHK	Piper J-3C-65 Cub	N. Higgins
	EI-CHL	Bell 206L-3 Long Ranger 3	Celtic Helicopters Ltd
	EI-CHM	Cessna 150M	K. A. O'Connor
	EI-CHN	M.S.880B Rallye Club	P. & O. Furlong
	EI-CHP	D.H.C.8-103 Dash Eight	GPA Propjet Ltd *(leased USAir Express)*
	EI-CHR	CFM Shadow Srs BD	J. Smith
	EI-CHS	Cessna 172M	Kerry Aero Club Ltd
	EI-CHT	Solar Wings Pegasus XL-R	G. W. Maher
	EI-CHV	Agusta A.109A	Celtic Helicopters Ltd
	EI-CHW	L.188CF Electra	Hunting Cargo Airlines (Ireland) Ltd
	EI-CHX	L.188CF Electra	Hunting Cargo Airlines (Ireland) Ltd
	EI-CHY	—	—
	EI-CHZ	L.188CF Electra	Hunting Cargo Airlines (Ireland) Ltd
	EI-CIA	M.S.880B Rallye Club	M. Maher
	EI-CIF	PA-28 Cherokee 180C	E. Tierney & K. A. Harold
	EI-CIG	PA-18 Super Cub 150	K. A. O'Connor
	EI-CIH	Ercoupe 415CD	J. G. Lacey
	EI-CII	—	—
	EI-CIJ	Cessna 340	Airlink Airways Ltd
	EI-CIK	Mooney M.20C	A. & P. Aviation Ltd
	EI-CIM	Light Aero Avid Speedwing Mk IV	P. Swan
	EI-CIN	Cessna 150K	F. McGovern
	EI-CIO	Bell 206L-3 LongRanger	Sean Quinn Properties Ltd
	EI-CIQ	Aérospatiale ATR-42-300	GPA Finance Ltd *(leased to Brit Air)*
	EI-CIR	Cessna 551 Citation II	Air Group Finance Ltd
	EI-CIV	PA-28 Cherokee 140	G. Cashman & E. Callanan
	EI-CIW	McD Douglas MD-83	Carotene Ltd *(leased to TWA)*
	EI-CIY	Boeing 767-330ER	Air Europe SpA
	EI-CIZ	Steen Skybolt	J. Keane
	EI-CJA	Boeing 767-35HER	Air Europe SpA
	EI-CJB	Boeing 767-35HER	Air Europe SpA
	EI-CJC	Boeing 737-204ADV	Ryanair Ltd
	EI-CJD	Boeing 737-204ADV	Ryanair Ltd
	EI-CJE	Boeing 737-204ADV	Ryanair Ltd
	EI-CJF	Boeing 737-204ADV	Ryanair Ltd
	EI-CJG	Boeing 737-204ADV	Ryanair Ltd
	EI-CJH	Boeing 737-204ADV	Ryanair Ltd
	EI-CJI	Boeing 737-2E7ADV	Ryanair Ltd
	EI-CJK	Airbus A.300B4-103	TransLift Airways Ltd
	EI-CJL	—	—
	EI-CJM	Bell 206B JetRanger	A. McConnell
	EI-CJO	Hoffmann H.36 Dimona	O. Masters
	EI-CJR	SNCAN Stampe SV-4A	C. Scully & P. Ryan
	EI-CJS	Jodel D.120A	L. Maddock
	EI-CJT	Slingsby Motor Cadet III	J. Tarrant
	EI-CJV	Moskito 2	M. Peril & ptnrs
	EI-CJW	Boeing 737-2P6	Dormacken Ltd *(leased to Air Tran)*
	EI-CJX	Boeing 757-2Y0	Dormacken Ltd *(leased to Transaero)*
	EI-CJY	Boeing 757-2Y0	Dormacken Ltd *(leased to Transaero)*
	EI-CJZ	Whittaker MW.6 Merlin	M. McCarthy
	EI-CKA	Jodel DR.400/180R	D. & B. Lodge
	EI-CKD	Boeing 767-3Y0ER	GPA Group Ltd *(leased to Aeroflot)*
	EI-CKE	Boeing 767-3Y0ER	GPA Group Ltd *(leased to Aeroflot)*
	EI-CKF	Hunt Wing	G. A. Murphy
	EI-CKG	Avon Hunt Weightlift	B. Kelly
	EI-CKH	PA-18 Super Cub 95	G. Brady & C. Keenan
	EI-CKI	Thruster TST Mk 1	S. Pallister
	EI-CKJ	Cameron N-77 balloon	F. Meldon
	EI-CKK	Boeing 737-2P6	Dormacken Ltd *(leased to Air South)*
	EI-CKL	Boeing 737-2P6	Dormacken Ltd *(leased to Air South)*
	EI-CKN	Whittaker MW.6-S Fatboy Flyer	B. Audoire
	EI-CKO	Hornet Dual Trainer	—
	EI-CKP	Boeing 737-2K2	Ryanair Ltd
	EI-CKQ	Boeing 737-2K2	Ryanair Ltd
	EI-CKR	Boeing 737-2K2	Ryanair Ltd
	EI-CKS	Boeing 737-2T5	Ryanair Ltd
	EI-CKT	Mainair Gemini Flash	C. Burke
	EI-CKU	Solar Wings Pegasus SLR	M. O'Regan
	EI-CKV	Boeing 737-3Y0	Wedgeling Ltd *(leased to America West)*
	EI-CKW	Boeing 737-2P6	Dormacken Ltd *(leased to Air South)*
	EI-CKX	Jodel D.112	J. Greene
	EI-CKY	Cessna F.406	Irish Air Tours Ltd
	EI-CKZ	Jodel D.18	J. O'Brien
	EI-CLA	HOAC Katana DV.20	Weston Ltd

Reg.	Type	Owner or Operator	Notes
EI-CLB	Aerospatiale ATR-72-212	Tarquin Ltd *(leased to Avianova)*	
EI-CLC	Aerospatiale ATR-72-212	Tarquin Ltd *(leased to Avianova)*	
EI-CLD	Aerospatiale ATR-72-212	Tarquin Ltd *(leased to Avianova)*	
EI-CLE	Quad City Challenger II	M. Tormey	
EI-CLF	FH.227E Friendship	Ireland Airways	
EI-CLG	BAe 146-300	Aer Lingus Commuter *St Finbarr*	
EI-CLH	BAe 146-300	Aer Lingus Commuter *St Aoife*	
EI-CLI	BAe 146-300	Aer Lingus Commuter *St Eithne*	
EI-CLJ	BAe 146-300	Aer Lingus Commuter	
EI-CLK	Boeing 737-2P6	Dormacken Ltd	
EI-CLL	Whittaker MW.6-S Fat Boy Flyer	S. Curtin	
EI-CLM	Boeing 757-28A	ILFC Ireland Ltd *(leased to Transaero)*	
EI-CLN	Boeing 737-2C9	Airlease (103) Ltd *(leased to Transaero)*	
EI-CLO	Boeing 737-2C9	Airlease (103) Ltd *(leased to Transaero)*	
EI-CLP	Boeing 757-2Y0	Kolding Ltd *(leased to Venus Airlines)*	
EI-CLQ	Cessna F.172N	A. H. Soper	
EI-CLR	Boeing 767-3Y0ER	Air Tara Ltd *(leased to Air Europe Spa)*	
EI-CLS	Boeing 767-352ER	ILFC (Ireland) Ltd *(leased to Air Europe Spa)*	
EI-CLT	Bell 206B JetRanger	Mistwood Ltd	
EI-CLU	Boeing 757-28A	ILFC (Ireland) Ltd *(leased to Air Europe Spa)*	
EI-CLV	Boeing 757-28A	ILFC (Ireland) Ltd *(leased to Transaero)*	
EI-CLW	Boeing 737-3Y0	GPA Finance Ltd *(leased to Air One)*	
EI-CLX	Cessna 310Q	Cork Aviation Centre	
EI-CLZ	Boeing 737-3Y0	GPA Finance Ltd *(leased to Air One)*	
EI-CMB	PA-28 Cherokee 140	Kestrel Flying Group Ltd	
EI-CMC	—	—	
EI-CMD	Boeing 767-324ER	GECAS	
EI-CME	Boeing 767-324ER	GECAS	
EI-CMF	CFM Streak Shadow	O. Williams	
EI-CMG	Short SD3-60 Variant 100	Irish Air Tours	
EI-CMH	Boeing 767-324ER	GECAS	
EI-CMI	Robinson R-22B	Toriamos Ltd	
EI-CMJ	Aérospatiale ATR-72-212	Tarquin Ltd *(leased to Avianova)*	
EI-CMK	Goldwing ST	M. Garigan	
EI-CML	—	—	
EI-CMM	McD Douglas MD-83	GECA *(leased to Eurofly)*	
EI-CMN	—	—	
EI-CMO	—	—	
EI-CMP	—	—	
EI-CRI	Beech 350 Super King Air	Westair Aviation Ltd	
EI-CRK	Airbus A.330-301	Aer Lingus Teo *St Brigid*	
EI-CTY	BAe 146-200	CityJet	
EI-CUB	Piper J-3C-65 Cub	Galway Flying Club	
EI-DLA	Douglas DC-10-30	Dormacken Ltd	
EI-DMI	PA-31-325 Turbo Navajo C	Dawn Meats	
EI-DUB	Airbus A.330-301	Aer Lingus Teo *St Patrick*	
EI-EDR	PA-28R Cherokee Arrow 200	Victor Mike Flying Group Ltd	
EI-EEC	PA-23 Aztec 250	Westair Ltd	
EI-EIO	PA-34-200T Seneca II	K. A. O'Connor	
EI-ETC	Aeronca 15AC Sedan	H. Moreau	
EI-EWW	Boeing 727-243	Hunting Cargo Airlines/TNT	
EI-EXP	Short SD3-30 Variant 100	Ireland Airways	
EI-FKA	Fokker 50	Aer Lingus Commuter *St Fintan*	
EI-FKB	Fokker 50	Aer Lingus Commuter *St Fergal*	
EI-FKC	Fokker 50	Aer Lingus Commuter *St Fidelma*	
EI-FKD	Fokker 50	Aer Lingus Commuter *St Flannan*	
EI-FKE	Fokker 50	Aer Lingus Commuter *St Pappin*	
EI-FKF	Fokker 50	Aer Lingus Commuter *St Ultan*	
EI-FKG	—	Aer Lingus Commuter	
EI-FKH	—	Aer Lingus Commuter	
EI-FLY	SOCATA TB.9 Tampico	Hotel Bravo Flying Group Ltd	
EI-GER	Maule MX7-180A	P. Costigan	
EI-GFC	SOCATA TB.9 Tampico	Galway Flying Club Ltd	
EI-HCA	Boeing 727-225F	Hunting Cargo Airlines (Ireland) Ltd	
EI-HCB	Boeing 727-223F	Hunting Cargo Airlines (Ireland) Ltd	
EI-HCC	Boeing 727-223F	Hunting Cargo Airlines (Ireland) Ltd	
EI-HCD	Boeing 727-223F	Hunting Cargo Airlines (Ireland) Ltd	
EI-IICI	Boeing 727-225F	Hunting Cargo Airlines (Ireland) Ltd/TNT	
EI-HCS	Grob G.109B	H. Sydner	
EI-HER	Bell 206B JetRanger 3	Irish Helicopters Ltd	
EI-JET	BAe 146-200	CityJet	
EI-JFK	Airbus A.330-301	Aer Lingus *Colmcille*	

Notes	Reg.	Type	Owner or Operator
	EI-JTC	PA-31-350 Navajo Chieftain	T. Brennan
	EI-JWM	Robinson R-22B	Jair Aviation Co Ltd
	EI-LCH	Boeing 727-281	Hunting Cargo Airlines (Ireland) Ltd
	EI-LRS	Hughes 269C	Lynch Roofing Systems Ltd
	EI-POD	Cessna 177B	Trim Flying Club Ltd
	EI-SHN	Airbus A.330-301	Aer Lingus Teo *St Flannan*
	EI-SKY	Boeing 727-281	Hunting Cargo Airlines (Ireland) Ltd/TNT
	EI-SXT	Canadair CL.600 Challenger	Sextant Ireland Ltd
	EI-TCK	Cessna 421A	T. C. Killeen
	EI-TKI	Robinson R-22B	Hydraulic Services Ltd
	EI-TLE	Airbus A.320-231	TransLift Airways Ltd
	EI-TLF	Airbus A.320-231	TransLift Airways Ltd
	EI-TLG	Airbus A.320-231	TransLift Airways Ltd
	EI-TLI	Airbus A.320-231	TransLift Airways Ltd
	EI-TLJ	Airbus A.320-231	TransLift Airways Ltd
	EI-TNT	Boeing 727-281	TNT Express Worldwide Ltd
	EI-UFO	PA-22 Tri-Pacer 150	W. Treacy
	EI-WAC	PA-23 Aztec 250E	Westair Aviation Ltd
	EI-WCC	Robinson R-22B	Westair Aviation Ltd
	EI-WDC	H.S.125 Srs 3B	Westair Aviation Ltd
	EI-XMA	Robinson R-22B	Westair Aviation Ltd
	EI-XMC	Robinson R-22B	McAuliffe Photographic Laboratories

Notes	Reg.	Type	Notes	Reg.	Type

EK (Armenia)

The following are operated by Armenian Airlines with the registrations prefixed by EK.

Reg.	Type		Reg.	Type
65044	Tu-134A		85196	Tu-154B
65072	Tu-134A		85200	Tu-154B
65650	Tu-134A		85210	Tu-154B
65731	Tu-134A-3		85279	Tu-154B-1
65822	Tu-134A		85403	Tu-154B-2
65831	Tu-134A3		85442	Tu-154B-2
65848	Tu-134A-3		85536	Tu-154B-2
65884	Tu-134A		85566	Tu-154B-2
65975	Tu-134A3		86117	IL-86
85162	Tu-154B		86118	IL-86
85166	Tu-154B			

Notes	Reg.	Type	Owner or Operator

EL (Liberia)

Reg.	Type	Owner or Operator
EL-AJO	Douglas DC-8-55F	Liberia World Airlines
EL-AJQ	Douglas DC-8-54F	Liberia World Airlines
EL-AKK	Boeing 707-323B	Liberia World Airlines
EL-JNS	Boeing 707-323C	Skyair Cargo
EL-ZGS	Boeing 707-309C	Jet Cargo Liberia

EP (Iran)

Reg.	Type	Owner or Operator
EP-IAA	Boeing 747SP-86	Iran Air *Kurdistan*
EP-IAB	Boeing 747SP-86	Iran Air
EP-IAC	Boeing 747SP-86	Iran Air *Fars*
EP-IAD	Boeing 747SP-86	Iran Air
EP-IAG	Boeing 747-286B (SCD)	Iran Air *Azarabadegan*
EP-IAH	Boeing 747-286B (SCD)	Iran Air *Khuzestan*
EP-IAM	Boeing 747-186B	Iran Air
EP-IBA	Airbus A.300-605R	Iran Air
EP-IBB	Airbus A.300-605R	Iran Air
EP-ICA	Boeing 747-2J9F	Iran Air
EP-ICC	Boeing 747-2J9F	Iran Air

Reg.	Type	Notes	Reg.	Type	Notes

ER (Moldova)

The following are operated by Air Moldova with the registrations prefixed by ER.

Reg.	Type		Reg.	Type
65036	Tu-134A		85044	Tu-154B
65050	Tu-134A		85090	Tu-154B
65051	Tu-134A-3		85285	Tu-154A-1
65071	Tu-134A-3		85324	Tu-154B-2
65094	Tu-134A-3		85332	Tu-154B-2
65140	Tu-134A-3		85384	Tu-154B-2
65707	Tu-134A-3		85405	Tu-154B-2
65741	Tu-134A		85409	Tu-154B-2
65791	Tu-134A-3		85565	Tu-154B-2
65897	Tu-134A			

Reg.	Type	Owner or Operator	Notes

ES (Estonia)

Reg.	Type	Owner or Operator
ES-ABC	Boeing 737-5Q8	Estonian Air
ES-ABD	Boeing 737-5Q8	Estonian Air
ES-LTP	Tupolev Tu-154M	ELK Estonian Aviation
ES-LTR	Tupolev Tu-154M	Estonian Aviation

ET (Ethiopia)

Reg.	Type	Owner or Operator
ET-AIE	Boeing 767-260ER	Ethiopian Airlines
ET-AIF	Boeing 767-260ER	Ethiopian Airlines
ET-AIV	Boeing 707-327C	Ethiopian Airlines
ET-AIZ	Boeing 767-260ER	Ethiopian Airlines
ET-AJS	Boeing 757-260PF	Ethiopian Airlines
ET-AJX	Boeing 757-260	Ethiopian Airlines
ET-AKC	Boeing 757-260	Ethiopian Airlines
ET-AKE	Boeing 757-260	Ethiopian Airlines
ET-AKF	Boeing 757-260	Ethiopian Airlines

Reg.	Type	Notes	Reg.	Type	Notes

EW (Belarus)

The following are operated by Belavia with the registrations prefixed by EW.

Reg.	Type		Reg.	Type
65049	Tu-134A		85372	Tu-154B-2
65082	Tu-134A		85411	Tu-154B-2
65085	Tu-134A		85419	Tu-154B-2
65106	Tu-134A		85465	Tu-154B-2
65108	Tu-134A		85509	Tu-154B-2
65133	Tu-134A-3		85538	Tu-154B-2
65145	Tu-134A		85545	Tu-154B-2
65149	Tu-134A		85580	Tu-154B-2
65664	Tu-134A		85581	Tu-154B-2
65676	Tu-134A		85582	Tu-154B-2
65754	Tu-134A		85583	Tu-154B-2
65772	Tu-134A		85591	Tu-154B-2
65803	Tu-134A		85593	Tu-154B-2
65821	Tu-134A		85703	Tu-154M
65832	Tu-134A		85706	Tu-154M
65861	Tu-134A-3		85748	Tu-154M
65892	Tu-134A		86062	IL-86
65957	Tu-134A		The following are operated by
65974	Tu-134A		Belair:
85059	Tu-154B		65565	Tu-134A-1
85260	Tu-154B-1		65605	Tu-134A
85331	Tu-154B-3		76836	IL-76TD
85339	Tu-154B-2		76837	IL-76TD
85352	Tu-154B-2			

Notes	Reg.	Type	Notes	Reg.	Type

EX (Kyrgyzstan)

The following are operated by Kyrgyzstan Airlines with the registrations prefixed by EX.

Reg.	Type	Reg.	Type
65111	Tu-134A-3	85259	Tu-154B-1
65119	Tu-134A-3	85294	Tu-154B-1
65125	Tu-134A-3	85313	Tu-154B-2
65778	Tu-134A-3	85369	Tu-154B-2
65779	Tu-134A-3	85444	Tu-154B-2
65789	Tu-134A-3	85491	Tu-154B-2
76815	IL-76TD	85497	Tu-154B-2
85021	Tu-154B-1	85519	Tu-154B-2
85252	Tu-154B-1	85590	Tu-154B-2
85257	Tu-154B-1	85718	Tu-154M

EY (Tajikistan)

The following are operated by Tajik Air with the registrations prefixed by EY.

Reg.	Type	Reg.	Type
65763	Tu-134A-3	85406	Tu-154B-2
65788	Tu-134A-3	85440	Tu-154B-2
65820	Tu-134A-3	85466	Tu-154B-2
65835	Tu-134A-3	85469	Tu-154B-2
65875	Tu-134A-3	85475	Tu-154B-2
65876	Tu-134A-3	85487	Tu-154B-2
65895	Tu-134A-3	85511	Tu-154B-2
85247	Tu-154B-1	85691	Tu-154M
85251	Tu-154B-1	85692	Tu-154M
85281	Tu-154B-1	85717	Tu-154M
85385	Tu-154B-2		

EZ (Turkmenistan)

Turkmenistan Airlines operates the following with the registrations prefixed by EZ.

Reg.	Type	Reg.	Type
A001	Boeing 737-341	85246	Tu-154B-1
A002	Boeing 737-332	85250	Tu-154B-1
A003	Boeing 737-332	85345	Tu-154B-2
A010	Boeing 757-23A	85383	Tu-154B-2
F421	IL-76TD	85394	Tu-154B-2
F422	IL-76TD	85410	Tu-154B-2
F424	IL-76TD	85492	Tu-154B-2
F426	IL-76TD	85507	Tu-154B-2
F427	IL-76TD	85532	Tu-154B-2
F428	IL-76TD	85549	Tu-154B-2
85241	Tu-154B-1	85560	Tu-154B-2

Notes	Reg.	Type	Owner or Operator

F (France)

Reg.	Type	Owner or Operator
F-BGNR	V.708 Viscount ★	Air Service Training Ltd/Perth
F-BMKS	S.E.210 Caravelle 10B	Air Toulouse International
F-BPPA	Aero Spacelines Super Guppy-201	Airbus Inter Transport Airbus *Skylink 2*
F-BPUA	F.27 Friendship Mk 500	Air France
F-BPUC	F.27 Friendship Mk 500	Air France
F-BPUD	F.27 Friendship Mk 500	Air France
F-BPUE	F.27 Friendship Mk 500	Air France
F-BPUF	F.27 Friendship Mk 500	Air France
F-BPUG	F.27 Friendship Mk 500	Air France
F-BPUH	F.27 Friendship Mk 500	Air France
F-BPUJ	F.27 Friendship Mk 500	Air France
F-BPUK	F.27 Friendship Mk 500	Air France
F-BPUL	F.27 Friendship Mk 500	Air France
F-BPVB	Boeing 747-128	Air France
F-BPVE	Boeing 747-128 ★	British Aviation Heritage/Bruntingthorpe
F-BPVF	Boeing 747-128	Air France
F-BPVG	Boeing 747-128	Corsair
F-BPVH	Boeing 747-128	Air France
F-BPVJ	Boeing 747-128	Air France
F-BPVM	Boeing 747-128	Air France
F-BPVP	Boeing 747-128	Air France

Reg.	Type	Owner or Operator	Notes
F-BPVR	Boeing 747-228F (SCD)	Air France	
F-BPVS	Boeing 747-228B (SCD)	Air France	
F-BPVT	Boeing 747-228B (SCD)	Air France	
F-BPVU	Boeing 747-228B (SCD)	Air France	
F-BPVV	Boeing 747-228F (SCD)	Air France	
F-BPVX	Boeing 747-228B (SCD)	Air France	
F-BPVY	Boeing 747-228B	Air France	
F-BPVZ	Boeing 747-228F (SCD)	Air France	
F-BSUN	F.27 Friendship Mk 500	Air France	
F-BSUO	F.27 Friendship Mk 500	Air France	
F-BTDD	Douglas DC-10-30	AOM French Airlines	
F-BTDE	Douglas DC-10-30	AOM French Airlines	
F-BTDG	Boeing 747-2B3B (SCD)	Air France	
F-BTDH	Boeing 747-2B3B (SCD)	Air France	
F-BTGV	Aero Spacelines Super Guppy-201	Airbus Inter Transport Airbus *Skylink 1*	
F-BTSC	Concorde 101	Air France	
F-BTSD	Concorde 101	Air France	
F-BUAF	Airbus A.300B2	Air Inter Europe	
F-BUAG	Airbus A.300B2	Air Inter Europe	
F-BUAH	Airbus A.300B2	Air Inter Europe	
F-BUAI	Airbus A.300B2	Air Inter Europe	
F-BUAJ	Airbus A.300B2	Air Inter Europe	
F-BUAK	Airbus A.300B2	Air Inter Europe	
F-BUAL	Airbus A.300B4	Air Inter Europe	
F-BUAN	Airbus A.300B2	Air Inter Europe	
F-BUAO	Airbus A.300B2	Air Inter Europe	
F-BUAP	Airbus A.300B2	Air Inter Europe	
F-BUAQ	Airbus A.300B4	Air Inter Europe	
F-BUTI	F.28 Fellowship 1000	T.A.T. European	
F-BVFA	Concorde 101	Air France	
F-BVFB	Concorde 101	Air France	
F-BVFC	Concorde 101	Air France	
F-BVFF	Concorde 101	Air France	
F-BVGA	Airbus A.300B2	Air France	
F-BVGB	Airbus A.300B2	Air France	
F-BVGC	Airbus A.300B2	Air France	
F-BVGD	Airbus A.300B2	Air Inter Europe	
F-BVGE	Airbus A.300B2	Air Inter Europe	
F-BVGF	Airbus A.300B2	Air Inter Europe	
F-BVGG	Airbus A.300B4	Air France	
F-BVGH	Airbus A.300B4	Air France	
F-BVGI	Airbus A.300B4	Air Charter	
F-BVGJ	Airbus A.300B4	Air France	
F-BVGL	Airbus A.300B4	Air France	
F-BVGM	Airbus A.300B4	Air France	
F-BVGN	Airbus A.300B4	Air France	
F-BVGO	Airbus A.300B4	Air France	
F-BVGT	Airbus A.300B4	Air Charter	
F-BVJL	Beech 99A	T.A.T. European	
F-GATS	EMB-110P2 Bandeirante	—	
F-GBBR	F.28 Fellowship 1000	T.A.T. European/Delta Air Transport	
F-GBBS	F.28 Fellowship 1000	T.A.T. European/Delta Air Transport	
F-GBBT	F.28 Fellowship 1000	T.A.T. European/Air Littoral	
F-GBBX	F.28 Fellowship 1000	T.A.T. European/Air Littoral	
F-GBEA	Airbus A.300B2	Air Inter Europe	
F-GBGA	EMB-110P2 Bandeirante	Aigle Azur	
F-GBLE	EMB-110P2 Bandeirante	Air Atlantique	
F-GBME	EMB-110P2 Bandeirante	Air Atlantique	
F-GBOX	Boeing 747-2B3F (SCD)	Air France Cargo	
F-GBRM	EMB-110P2 Bandeirante	Air Atlantique	
F-GBRQ	FH.227B Friendship	T.A.T. European	
F-GBRU	F.27J Friendship	T.A.T. European	
F-GBRV	F.27J Friendship	ACE Transvalair	
F-GBYA	Boeing 737-228	Air France	
F-GBYB	Boeing 737-228	Air France	
F-GBYC	Boeing 737-228	Air France	
F-GBYD	Boeing 737-228	Air France	
F-GBYE	Boeing 737-228	Air France	
F-GBYF	Boeing 737-228	Air France	
F-GBYG	Boeing 737-228	Air France	
F-GBYH	Boeing 737-228	Air France	
F-GBYI	Boeing 737-228	Air France	
F-GBYJ	Boeing 737-228	Air France	
F-GBYK	Boeing 737-228	Air France	

Notes	Reg.	Type	Owner or Operator
	F-GBYL	Boeing 737-228	Air France
	F-GBYM	Boeing 737-228	Air France
	F-GBYN	Boeing 737-228	Air France
	F-GBYO	Boeing 737-228	Air France
	F-GBYP	Boeing 737-228	Air France
	F-GBYQ	Boeing 737-228	Air France
	F-GCBA	Boeing 747-228B	Air France
	F-GCBB	Boeing 747-228B (SCD)	Air France/SABENA
	F-GCBD	Boeing 747-228B (SCD)	Air France
	F-GCBE	Boeing 747-228F (SCD)	Air France
	F-GCBF	Boeing 747-228B (SCD)	Air France
	F-GCBG	Boeing 747-228F (SCD)	Air France Cargo
	F-GCBH	Boeing 747-228F (SCD)	Air France Cargo
	F-GCBI	Boeing 747-228B (SCD)	Air France
	F-GCBJ	Boeing 747-228B (SCD)	Air France
	F-GCBK	Boeing 747-228F (SCD)	Air France Cargo
	F-GCBL	Boeing 747-228F (SCD)	Air France Cargo
	F-GCBM	Boeing 747-228F	Air France Cargo
	F-GCFC	FH.227B Friendship	T.A.T. European
	F-GCGQ	Boeing 727-227	EAS Europe Airlines
	F-GCJL	Boeing 737-222	Euralair International/Air Charter
	F-GCJO	FH.227B Friendship	ACE Transvalair
	F-GCLA	EMB-110P1 Bandeirante	Aigle Azur
	F-GCLL	Boeing 737-222	Air Liberte
	F-GCLM	FH.227B Friendship	ACE Transvalair
	F-GCLO	FH.227B Friendship	ACE Transvalair
	F-GCPT	FH.227B Friendship	T.A.T. European
	F-GCPU	FH.227B Friendship	T.A.T. European
	F-GCPX	FH.227B Friendship	T.A.T. European
	F-GCPY	FH.227B Friendship	T.A.T. European
	F-GCSL	Boeing 737-222	Air Liberte
	F-GCVL	S.E.210 Caravelle 12	Air Provence International
	F-GCVM	S.E.210 Caravelle 12	Air Provence International
	F-GDAQ	L.100-30 Hercules	Jet Fret
	F-GDFC	F.28 Fellowship 4000	T.A.T. European
	F-GDFD	F.28 Fellowship 4000	T.A.T. European
	F-GDJK	Douglas DC-10-30	Air Martinique
	F-GDJM	Douglas DC-8-62CF	Cargo Lion
	F-GDPP	Douglas DC-3C	France DC-3/L'Envolée Air Inter
	F-GDSG	UTA Super Guppy	Airbus Inter Transport Airbus Skylink 3
	F-GDSK	F.28 Fellowship 4000	T.A.T. European
	F-GDUS	F.28 Fellowship 2000	T.A.T. European
	F-GDUT	F.28 Fellowship 2000	T.A.T. European
	F-GDUU	F.28 Fellowship 2000	T.A.T. European/British Airways
	F-GDUV	F.28 Fellowship 2000	T.A.T. European
	F-GDUY	F.28 Fellowship 4000	T.A.T. European
	F-GDUZ	F.28 Fellowship 4000	T.A.T. European
	F-GDXL	Aérospatiale ATR-42-300	Brit Air/Air France
	F-GDXT	Fairchild F.27J (SCD)	ACE Transvalair
	F-GEAI	UTA Super Guppy	Airbus Inter Transport Airbus Skylink 4
	F-GECK	F.28 Fellowship 1000	T.A.T. European
	F-GEDR	EMB-110P1 Bandeirante	Air Toulouse International
	F-GEGD	Aérospatiale ATR-42-300	Air Littoral
	F-GEGE	Aérospatiale ATR-42-300	Air Littoral
	F-GEGF	Aérospatiale ATR-42-300	Air Littoral
	F-GELG	SAAB SF.340A	Brit Air/Air France
	F-GELP	S.E.210 Caravelle	Air Toulouse International
	F-GEMA	Airbus A.310-203	Air France
	F-GEMB	Airbus A.310-203	Air France
	F-GEMC	Airbus A.310-203	Air France
	F-GEMD	Airbus A.310-203	Air France
	F-GEME	Airbus A.310-203	Air France
	F-GEMG	Airbus A.310-203	Air France
	F-GEMN	Airbus A.310-304	Air France
	F-GEMO	Airbus A.310-304	Air France
	F-GEMP	Airbus A.310-304	Air France
	F-GEMQ	Airbus A.310-304	Air France
	F-GEQJ	Aérospatiale ATR-42-300	Regional Airlines
	F-GESB	EMB-110P1 Bandeirante	Air Toulouse International
	F-GETA	Boeing 747-3B3 (SCD)	Air France
	F-GETB	Boeing 747-3B3 (SCD)	Air France
	F-GEXA	Boeing 747-4B3	Air France
	F-GEXB	Boeing 747-4B3	Air France
	F-GEXI	Boeing 737-2L9	EAS Europe Airlines

Reg.	Type	Owner or Operator	Notes
F-GEXJ	Boeing 737-2Q8	EAS Europe Airlines	
F-GFBZ	SAAB SF.340A	Brit Air	
F-GFEN	EMB-120 Brasilia	Air Littoral	
F-GFEO	EMB-120 Brasilia	Air Littoral	
F-GFEP	EMB-120 Brasilia	Air Littoral	
F-GFEQ	EMB-120 Brasilia	Air Littoral	
F-GFER	EMB-120 Brasilia	Air Littoral	
F-GFES	Aérospatiale ATR-42-300	Air Littoral	
F-GFIN	EMB-120 Brasilia	Air Littoral	
F-GFJP	Aérospatiale ATR-42-300	Brit Air/Air France	
F-GFKA	Airbus A.320-111	Air France *Ville de Paris*	
F-GFKB	Airbus A.320-111	Air France *Ville de Rome*	
F-GFKD	Airbus A.320-111	Air France *Ville de Londres*	
F-GFKE	Airbus A.320-111	Air France *Ville de Bonn*	
F-GFKF	Airbus A.320-111	Air France *Ville de Madrid*	
F-GFKG	Airbus A.320-111	Air France *Ville d'Amsterdam*	
F-GFKH	Airbus A.320-211	Air France *Ville de Bruxelles*	
F-GFKI	Airbus A.320-211	Air France *Ville de Lisbonne*	
F-GFKJ	Airbus A.320-211	Air France *Ville de Copenhague*	
F-GFKK	Airbus A.320-211	Air France *Ville d'Athenes*	
F-GFKL	Airbus A.320-211	Air France *Ville de Dublin*	
F-GFKM	Airbus A.320-211	Air France *Ville de Luxembourg*	
F-GFKN	Airbus A.320-211	Air France	
F-GFKO	Airbus A.320-211	Air France	
F-GFKP	Airbus A.320-211	Air France *Ville de Nice*	
F-GFKQ	Airbus A.320-111	Air France *Ville de Berlin*	
F-GFKR	Airbus A.320-211	Air France *Ville de Marseille*	
F-GFKS	Airbus A.320-211	Air France	
F-GFKT	Airbus A.320-211	Air France	
F-GFKU	Airbus A.320-211	Air France	
F-GFKV	Airbus A.320-211	Air France *Ville de Bordeaux*	
F-GFKX	Airbus A.320-211	Air Charter *Ville de Francfurt*	
F-GFKY	Airbus A.320-211	Air France *Ville de Toulouse*	
F-GFKZ	Airbus A.320-211	Air France *Ville de Turin*	
F-GFLV	Boeing 737-2K5	Air France	
F-GFLX	Boeing 737-2K5	Air France	
F-GFPR	Swearingen SA226AT Merlin IVA	Regional Airlines	
F-GFUA	Boeing 737-33A	Air France	
F-GFUD	Boeing 737-33A	Air France	
F-GFUG	Boelng 737-4D3	Corsair	
F-GFUH	Boeing 737-4B3	Corsair	
F-GFUJ	Boeing 737-33A	Air France	
F-GFVI	Boeing 737-230C	L'Aéropostale	
F-GFYL	Boeing 737-2A9C	Euralair International/Air Charter	
F-GFYN	Aérospatiale ATR-42-300	Air Littoral	
F-GFZB	McD Douglas MD-83	Air Liberte	
F-GGBV	SAAB SF.340A	Aigle Azur	
F-GGEA	Airbus A.320-111	Air Inter Europe	
F-GGEB	Airbus A.320-111	Air Inter Europe	
F-GGEC	Airbus A.320-111	Air Inter Europe	
F-GGEE	Airbus A.320-111	Air Inter Europe	
F-GGEF	Airbus A.320-111	Air Inter Europe	
F-GGEG	Airbus A.320-111	Air Inter Europe	
F-GGFI	Boeing 737-210C	T.A.T. European	
F-GGFJ	Boeing 737-248C	T.A.T. European	
F-GGGR	Boeing 727-2H3	Belair *Villa Squeville*	
F-GGLK	Aérospatiale ATR-42-300	T.A.T. European	
F-GGLR	Aérospatiale ATR-42-300	Brit Air/Air France	
F-GGMA	McD Douglas MD-83	AOM French Airlines	
F-GGMB	McD Douglas MD-83	AOM French Airlines	
F-GGMD	McD Douglas MD-83	AOM French Airlines	
F-GGME	McD Douglas MD-83	AOM French Airlines	
F-GGMF	McD Douglas MD-83	AOM French Airlines	
F-GGPA	Boeing 737-242C	T.A.T. European	
F-GGPB	Boeing 737-204C	T.A.T. European	
F-GGPC	Boeing 737-204C	T.A.T. European	
F-GGVP	Boeing 737-2K2C	L'Aéropostale	
F-GGVQ	Boeing 737-2K2C	L'Aéropostale	
F-GHDB	SAAB SF.340A	Brit Air/Air France	
F-GHEB	McD Douglas MD-83	Air Liberte	
F-GHEC	McD Douglas MD-83	Air Liberte	
F-GHED	McD Douglas MD-83	Air Liberte	
F-GHEF	Airbus A.300-622R	Air Liberte	
F-GHEG	Airbus A.300-622R	Air Liberte	

Notes	Reg.	Type	Owner or Operator
	F-GHEI	McD Douglas MD-83	Air Liberte
	F-GHEJ	Airbus A.310-324	Air Liberte
	F-GHEK	McD Douglas MD-83	Air Liberte
	F-GHEX	EMB-120RT Brasilia	Flandre Air/T.A.T. European
	F-GHEY	EMB-120RT Brasilia	Flandre Air/T.A.T. European
	F-GHGD	Boeing 767-27EER	Air France/Balkan
	F-GHGE	Boeing 767-27EER	Air France/Balkan *Preslav*
	F-GHGF	Boeing 767-3Q8ER	Air France
	F-GHGG	Boeing 767-3Q8ER	Air France
	F-GHGH	Boeing 767-37EER	Air France
	F-GHGI	Boeing 767-328ER	Air France
	F-GHGJ	Boeing 767-328ER	Air France
	F-GHGK	Boeing 767-328ER	Air France
	F-GHHO	McD Douglas MD-83	Air Liberte
	F-GHHP	McD Douglas MD-83	Air Liberte
	F-GHIA	EMB-120RT Brasilia	Air Littoral
	F-GHIB	EMB-120RT Brasilia	Air Littoral
	F-GHJE	Aérospatiale ATR-42-300	Brit Air
	F-GHMI	SAAB SF.340A	Brit Air/Air France
	F-GHMJ	SAAB SF.340A	Brit Air
	F-GHMK	SAAB SF.340A	Brit Air
	F-GHMU	S.E.210 Caravelle 10B3	Air Toulouse International
	F-GHOI	Douglas DC-10-30	AOM French Airlines
	F-GHOL	Boeing 737-53C	Euralair International/Air France
	F-GHPI	Aérospatiale ATR-42-300	Brit Air
	F-GHPK	Aérospatiale ATR-42-300	Brit Air
	F-GHPS	Aérospatiale ATR-42-300	Brit Air/Air France
	F-GHPU	Aérospatiale ATR-72-101	Brit Air
	F-GHPV	Aérospatiale ATR-72-101	Brit Air
	F-GHPX	Aérospatiale ATR-42-300	Brit Air/Air France
	F-GHPY	Aérospatiale ATR-42-300	Brit Air/Air France
	F-GHPZ	Aérospatiale ATR-42-300	Brit Air/Air France
	F-GHQA	Airbus A.320-211	Air Inter Europe
	F-GHQB	Airbus A.320-211	Air Inter Europe
	F-GHQC	Airbus A.320-211	Air Inter Europe
	F-GHQD	Airbus A.320-211	Air Inter Europe
	F-GHQE	Airbus A.320-211	Air Inter Europe
	F-GHQF	Airbus A.320-211	Air Inter Europe
	F-GHQG	Airbus A.320-211	Air Inter Europe
	F-GHQH	Airbus A.320-211	Air Inter Europe
	F-GHQI	Airbus A.320-211	Air Inter Europe
	F-GHQJ	Airbus A.320-211	Air Inter Europe
	F-GHQK	Airbus A.320-211	Air Inter Europe
	F-GHQL	Airbus A.320-211	Air Inter Europe
	F-GHQM	Airbus A.320-211	Air Inter Europe
	F-GHQO	Airbus A.320-211	Air Inter Europe
	F-GHQP	Airbus A.320-211	Air Inter Europe
	F-GHQQ	Airbus A.320-211	Air Inter Europe
	F-GHQR	Airbus A.320-211	Air Inter Europe
	F-GHUL	Boeing 737-53C	Euralair International/Air France
	F-GHVA	Swearingen SA227AC Metro III	Regional Airlines
	F-GHVG	Swearingen SA227AC Metro III	Regional Airlines
	F-GHVM	Boeing 737-33A	Air France
	F-GHVN	Boeing 737-33A	Air France
	F-GHVO	Boeing 737-33A	Air France
	F-GHVS	SAAB SF.340B	Regional Airlineµs
	F-GHVT	SAAB SF.340B	Regional Airlines
	F-GHVU	SAAB SF.340B	Regional Airlines
	F-GHXK	Boeing 737-2A1	Corsair
	F-GHXL	Boeing 737-2S3	Air Toulouse International
	F-GHXM	Boeing 737-53A	—
	F-GIAH	F.28 Fellowship 1000	T.A.T. European
	F-GIAI	F.28 Fellowship 1000	T.A.T. European
	F-GIAZ	Douglas DC-3C	Dakota Air Legend
	F-GIGO	Aérospatiale ATR-72-201	Air Littoral
	F-GIIA	Aérospatiale ATR-42-300	Air Atlantique
	F-GIJS	Airbus A.300B4	Air Inter Europe
	F-GILN	Swearingen SA227AC Metro III	Regional Airlines
	F-GIMH	F.28 Fellowship 1000	T.A.T. European
	F-GIMJ	Boeing 747-121	Corsair
	F-GINL	Boeing 737-53C	Euralair International/Air France
	F-GIOA	Fokker 100	T.A.T. European/British Airways
	F-GIOG	Fokker 100	Compagnie Corse Mediterranee

Reg.	Type	Owner or Operator	Notes
F-GIOH	Fokker 100	T.A.T. European	
F-GIOI	Fokker 100	T.A.T. European/British Airways	
F-GIOJ	Fokker 100	T.A.T. European/British Airways	
F-GIOK	Fokker 100	T.A.T. European	
F-GIOV	Fokker 100	T.A.T. European	
F-GIOX	Fokker 100	T.A.T. European	
F-GIRC	Aérospatiale ATR-42-300	T.A.T. European	
F-GISA	Boeing 747-428 (SCD)	Air France	
F-GISB	Boeing 747-428 (SCD)	Air France	
F-GISC	Boeing 747-428 (SCD)	Air France	
F-GISD	Boeing 747-428 (SCD)	Air France	
F-GISE	Boeing 747-428 (SCD)	Air France	
F-GITA	Boeing 747-428	Air France	
F-GITB	Boeing 747-428	Air France	
F-GITC	Boeing 747-428	Air France	
F-GITD	Boeing 747-428	Air France	
F-GITE	Boeing 747-428	Air France	
F-GITF	Boeing 747-428	Air France	
F-GITH	Boeing 747-428	Air France	
F-GIUB	Boeing 747-428F (SCD)	Air France Cargo	
F-GIVG	Aérospatiale ATR-42-300	Regional Airlines	
F-GIXA	Boeing 737-2K2C	L'Aéropostale	
F-GIXB	Boeing 737-33AQC	L'Aéropostale	
F-GIXC	Boeing 737-38BQC	L'Aéropostale	
F-GIXD	Boeing 737-33AQC	L'Aéropostale	
F-GIXE	Boeing 737-3B3QC	L'Aéropostale	
F-GIXF	Boeing 737-3B3QC	L'Aéropostale	
F-GIXG	Boeing 737-382QC	L'Aéropostale	
F-GIXH	Boeing 737-3S3QC	L'Aéropostale	
F-GIXI	Boeing 737-348QC	L'Aéropostale	
F-GIXJ	Boeing 737-3Y0QC	L'Aéropostale	
F-GIXK	Boeing 737-33AQC	L'Aéropostale	
F-GIXL	Boeing 737-348QC	L'Aéropostale	
F-GJAK	EMB-120RT Brasilia	Air Littoral	
F-GJDL	Boeing 737-210C	Air Charter/Euralair International	
F-GJEG	Beech 1900-1	T.A.T. European	
F-GJNA	Boeing 737-528	Air France	
F-GJNB	Boeing 737-528	Air France	
F-GJNC	Boeing 737-528	Air France	
F-GJND	Boeing 737-528	Air France	
F-GJNE	Boeing 737-528	Air France	
F-GJNF	Boeing 737-528	Air France	
F-GJNG	Boeing 737-528	Air France	
F-GJNH	Boeing 737-528	Air France	
F-GJNI	Boeing 737-528	Air France	
F-GJNJ	Boeing 737-528	Air France	
F-GJNK	Boeing 737-528	Air France	
F-GJNM	Boeing 737-528	Air France	
F-GJNN	Boeing 737-528	Air France	
F-GJNO	Boeing 737-528	Air France	
F-GJVA	Airbus A.320-211	Air Inter Europe	
F-GJVB	Airbus A.320-211	Air Inter Europe	
F-GJVC	Airbus A.320-211	Air Inter Europe	
F-GJVD	Airbus A.320-211	Air Inter Europe	
F-GJVE	Airbus A.320-211	Air Inter Europe	
F-GJVF	Airbus A.320-211	Air Inter Europe	
F-GJVG	Airbus A.320-211	Air Inter Europe	
F-GJVV	Airbus A.320-211	Air Inter Europe	
F-GJVX	Airbus A.320-211	Air Inter Europe	
F-GJVY	Airbus A.320-211	Air Inter Europe	
F-GJVZ	Airbus A.320-211	Air Inter Europe	
F-GKDY	Boeing 727-225F	L'Aéropostale	
F-GKDZ	Boeing 727-225F	L'Aéropostale	
F-GKLJ	Boeing 747-121	Corsair	
F-GKLX	Fokker 100	Air Littoral/Air Inter Europe	
F-GKLY	Fokker 100	Air Littoral/Air Inter Europe	
F-GKMY	Douglas DC-10-30	AOM French Airlines	
F-GKNA	Aérospatiale ATR-42-300	T.A.T. European	
F-GKNB	Aérospatiale ATR-42-300	T.A.T. European	
F-GKNC	Aérospatiale ATR-42-300	T.A.T. European	
F-GKND	Aérospatiale ATR-42-300	T.A.T. European	
F-GKNE	Aérospatiale ATR-42-300	T.A.T. European	
F-GKNF	Aérospatiale ATR-42-300	T.A.T. European	

Notes	Reg.	Type	Owner or Operator
	F-GKNG	Aérospatiale ATR-42-300	T.A.T. European
	F-GKNH	Aérospatiale ATR-42-300	Brit Air
	F-GKOA	Aérospatiale ATR-72-202	T.A.T. European
	F-GKOB	Aérospatiale ATR-72-202	T.A.T. European
	F-GKOC	Aérospatiale ATR-72-202	T.A.T. European
	F-GKOD	Aérospatiale ATR-72-202	T.A.T. European
	F-GKPC	Aérospatiale ATR-72-102	Compagnie Corse Mediterranée
	F-GKPD	Aéropsatiale ATR-72-102	Compagnie Corse Mediterranée
	F-GKPE	Aérospatiale ATR-72-102	Compagnie Corse Mediterranée
	F-GKPF	Aérospatiale ATR-72-102	Compagnie Corse Mediterranée
	F-GKPH	Aérospatiale ATR-72-202	Compagnie Corse Mediterranée
	F-GKST	Beech 1900-1	Proteus Air System
	F-GKTA	Boeing 737-3M8	EAS Europe Airlines/TEA Europe
	F-GKTB	Boeing 737-3M8	EAS Europe Airlines/TEA Europe
	F-GKTD	Airbus A.310-304	Sudan Airways
	F-GKXA	Airbus A.320-211	Air France *Ville de Nantes*
	F-GLGE	Airbus A.320-211	Air France/Air Charter
	F-GLGM	Airbus A.320-211	Air France
	F-GLGN	Airbus A.320-211	Air France
	F-GLIB	Aérospatiale ATR-42-310	Air Inter Europe
	F-GLIR	Fokker 100	Air Littoral/Air Inter Europe
	F-GLIS	Fokker 70	Air Littoral
	F-GLIT	Fokker 70	Air Littoral
	F-GLIU	Fokker 70	Air Littoral
	F-GLIV	Fokker 70	Air Littoral
	F-GLIX	Fokker 70	Air Littoral
	F-GLIY	Canadair Regional Jet 100ER	Air Littoral
	F-GLIZ	Canadair Regional Jet 100ER	Air Littoral
	F-GLMX	Douglas DC-10-30	AOM French Airlines
	F-GLNA	Boeing 747-206B	Corsair
	F-GLNI	BAe 146-200	Air Jet
	F-GLPJ	Beech 1900C-1	Flandre Air
	F-GLXF	Boeing 737-219	Air Toulouse International
	F-GLXG	Boeing 737-2M8	Air Toulouse International
	F-GLXH	Boeing 737-2D6	Air Toulouse International
	F-GLZA	Airbus A.340-311	Air France
	F-GLZB	Airbus A.340-311	Air France
	F-GLZC	Airbus A.340-311	Air France
	F-GLZD	Airbus A.340-211	Air France
	F-GLZE	Airbus A.340-211	Air France
	F-GLZF	Airbus A.340-211	Air France
	F-GLZG	Airbus A.340-311	Air France
	F-GLZH	Airbus A.340-311	Air France
	F-GLZI	Airbus A.340-311	Air France
	F-GMDA	Airbus A.330-301	Air Inter Europe
	F-GMDB	Airbus A.330-301	Air Inter Europe
	F-GMDC	Airbus A.330-301	Air Inter Europe
	F-GMDD	Airbus A.330-301	Air Inter Europe
	F-GMJD	Boeing 737-2K5	Aigle Azur
	F-GMPG	Fokker 100	Compagnie Corse Mediterranée
	F-GMPP	McD Douglas MD-83	—
	F-GMVB	SAAB 2000	Regional Airlines
	F-GMVC	SAAB 2000	Regional Airlines
	F-GMVD	SAAB 2000	Regional Airlines
	F-GMVH	BAe Jetstream 3206	Regional Airlines
	F-GMVI	BAe Jetstream 3206	Regional Airlines
	F-GMVJ	BAe Jetstream 3206	Regional Airlines
	F-GMVK	BAe Jetstream 3206	Regional Airlines
	F-GMVL	BAe Jetstream 3206	Regional Airlines
	F-GMVM	BAe Jetstream 3206	Regional Airlines
	F-GMVN	BAe Jetstream 3206	Regional Airlines
	F-GMVO	BAe Jetstream 3206	Regional Airlines
	F-GMVP	BAe Jetstream 3206	Regional Airlines
	F-GMVQ	SAAB SF.340B	Regional Airlines
	F-GMVV	SAAB SF.340B	Regional Airlines
	F-GMVX	SAAB SF.340B	Regional Airlines
	F-GMVY	SAAB SF.340B	Regional Airlines
	F-GMVZ	SAAB SF.340B	Regional Airlines
	F-GMZA	Airbus A.321-111	Air Inter Europe
	F-GMZB	Airbus A.321-111	Air Inter Europe
	F-GMZC	Airbus A.321-111	Air Inter Europe
	F-GMZD	Airbus A.321-111	Air Inter Europe
	F-GMZE	Airbus A.321-111	Air Inter Europe

Reg.	Type	Owner or Operator	Notes
F-GMZF	Airbus A.321-111	Air Inter Europe	
F-GMZG	Airbus A.321-111	Air Inter Europe	
F-GNDC	Douglas DC-10-30	AOM French Airlines	
F-GNEM	Douglas DC-10-30	AOM French Airlines	
F-GNIB	Airbus A.340-211	Air France	
F-GNIC	Airbus A.340-211	Air France	
F-GNID	Airbus A.340-311	Air France	
F-GNIE	Airbus A.340-311	Air France	
F-GNME	Canadair Regional Jet 100ER	Air Littoral/Air France	
F-GNMN	Canadair Regional Jet 100ER	Air Littoral/Air France	
F-GNZB	F.28 Fellowship 1000	T.A.T European/Delta Air Transport	
F-GOMA	BAe 146-200QC	Air Jet	
F-GPAN	Boeing 747-2B3F (SCD)	Air France Cargo	
F-GPDJ	Airbus A.310-221	Air Liberte	
F-GPJM	Boeing 747-206B	Corsair	
F-GPMA	Airbus A.319-100	Air Inter Europe	
F-GPMB	Airbus A.319-100	Air Inter Europe	
F-GPMC	Airbus A.319-100	Air Inter Europe	
F-GPMD	Airbus A.319-100	Air Inter Europe	
F-GPME	Airbus A.319-100	Air Inter Europe	
F-GPMF	Airbus A.319-100	Air Inter Europe	
F-GPMG	Airbus A.319-100	Air Inter Europe	
F-GPMH	Airbus A.319-100	Air Inter Europe	
F-GPMI	Airbus A.319-100	Air Inter Europe	
F-GPVD	Douglas DC-10-30	Air Liberte	
F-GPVE	Douglas DC-10-30	Air Liberte	
F-GPXA	Fokker 100	Air Inter Europe	
F-GPXB	Fokker 100	Air Inter Europe	
F-GPXC	Fokker 100	Air Inter Europe	
F-GPXD	Fokker 100	Air Inter Europe	
F-GPXE	Fokker 100	Air Inter Europe	
F-GRJA	Canadair Regional Jet 100ER	Brit Air	
F-GRJB	Canadair Regional Jet 100ER	Brit Air	
F-GRJC	Canadair Regional Jet 100ER	Brit Air	
F-GRJD	Canadair Regional Jet 100ER	Brit Air	
F-GRJE	Canadair Regional Jet 100ER	Brit Air	
F-GRJF	Canadair Regional Jet 100ER	Brit Air	
F-GRMC	McD Douglas MD-83	AOM French Airlines	
F-GRMG	McD Douglas MD-83	AOM French Airlines	
F-GRMH	McD Douglas MD-83	AOM French Airlines	
F-GRSA	Boeing 737-33A	Star Europe	
F-GSTA	Airbus A.300-608ST	Airbus Inter Transport	
F-GSTB	Airbus A.300-608ST	Airbus Inter Transport	
F-GSUN	Boeing 747-312	Corsair	
F-GTDF	Douglas DC-10-30	AOM French Airlines	
F-GTDG	Douglas DC-10-30	AOM French Airlines	
F-GTDH	Douglas DC-10-30	AOM French Airlines	
F-ODJG	Boeing 747-2Q2B	Air Gabon	
F-ODLX	Douglas DC-10-30	AOM French Airlines *Diamant*	
F-ODLY	Douglas DC-10-30	AOM French Airlines *Turquoise*	
F-ODLZ	Douglas DC-10-30	AOM French Airlines *Saphir*	
F-ODSV	Airbus A.310-304	Alyemda	
F-ODVF	Airbus A.310-304	Royal Jordanian *Princess Raiyah*	
F-ODVG	Airbus A.310-304	Royal Jordanian *Prince Faisal*	
F-ODVH	Airbus A.310-304	Royal Jordanian *Prince Hamzeh*	
F-ODVI	Airbus A.310-304	Royal Jordanian *Princess Haya*	
F-OGQN	Airbus A.310-304	Sudan Airways *Khartoum*	
F-OGQQ	Airbus A.310-308	Aeroflot *Tchaikovsky*	
F-OGQR	Airbus A.310-308	Aeroflot *Rachmaninov*	
F-OGQT	Airbus A.310-308	Aeroflot *Moussorgksy*	
F-OGQU	Airbus A.310-308	Aeroflot *Skriabin*	
F-OGQY	Airbus A.310-324	Uzbekistan Airways	
F-OGQZ	Airbus A.310-324	Uzbekistan Airways	
F-OGSY	Boeing 737-348	L'Aéropostale	
F-OGYA	Airbus A.320-211	Royal Jordanian *Cairo*	
F-OGYB	Airbus A.320-211	Royal Jordanian *Baghdad*	
F-OGYM	Airbus A.310-324	Aeroflot	
F-OGY	Airbus A.310-324	Aeroflot	
F-OHCS	Boeing 737-348	L'Aéropostale	
F-OHLH	Airbus A.310-304	Middle East Airlines	
F-OHLI	Airbus A.310-304	Middle East Airlines	
F-OLGA	Fokker 100	Palair Macedonia	
F-OLGB	Fokker 100	Palair Macedonia	

HA (Hungary)

Reg.	Type	Owner or Operator
HA-LBI	Tupolev Tu-134A-3	Malev
HA-LBK	Tupolev Tu-134A-3	Malev
HA-LBN	Tupolev Tu-134A-3	Malev
HA-LBO	Tupolev Tu-134A-3	Malev
HA-LBR	Tupolev Tu-134A-3	Malev
HA-LCA	Tupolev Tu-154B-2	Malev Cargo
HA-LCE	Tupolev Tu-154B-2	Malev
HA-LCG	Tupolev Tu-154B-2	Malev
HA-LCH	Tupolev Tu-154B-2	Malev
HA-LCM	Tupolev Tu-154B-2	Malev
HA-LCN	Tupolev Tu-154B-2	Malev
HA-LCO	Tupolev Tu-154B-2	Malev
HA-LCP	Tupolev Tu-154B-2	Malev
HA-LCR	Tupolev Tu-154B-2	Malev
HA-LCU	Tupolev Tu-154B-2	Malev
HA-LCV	Tupolev Tu-154B-2	Malev
HA-LEA	Boeing 737-2QB	Malev
HA-LEB	Boeing 737-2M8	Malev
HA-LEC	Boeing 737-2T5	Malev
HA-LED	Boeing 737-3Y0	Malev
HA-LEF	Boeing 737-3Y0	Malev
HA-LEG	Boeing 737-3Y0	Malev *Szent Istvan-Sanctus Stephanus*
HA-LEI	Boeing 737-2T4	Malev
HA-LEJ	Boeing 737-3Q8	Malev
HA-LEK	Boeing 737-2K9	Malev
HA-LEM	Boeing 737-2T4	Malev
HA-LEN	Boeing 737-4Y0	Malev
HA-LEO	Boeing 737-4Y0	Malev
HA-LHA	Boeing 767-27GER	Malev
HA-LHB	Boeing 767-27GER	Malev
HA-LMA	Fokke 70	Malev
HA-LMB	Fokke 70	Malev
HA-LMC	Fokke 70	Malev
HA-LMD	Fokke 70	Malev

HB (Switzerland)

Reg.	Type	Owner or Operator
HB-AEE	Dornier Do.328-100	Air Engiadina
HB-AEF	Dornier Do.328-100	Air Engiadina
HB-AEG	Dornier Do.328-100	Air Engiadina
HB-AEH	Dornier Do.328-100	Air Engiadina
HB-AHB	SAAB SF.340A	Crossair
HB-AKA	SAAB SF.340B	Crossair
HB-AKB	SAAB SF.340B	Crossair
HB-AKC	SAAB SF.340B	Crossair
HB-AKD	SAAB SF.340B	Crossair
HB-AKE	SAAB SF.340B	Crossair
HB-AKF	SAAB SF.340B	Crossair
HB-AKG	SAAB SF.340B	Crossair
HB-AKH	SAAB SF.340B	Crossair
HB-AKI	SAAB SF.340B	Crossair
HB-AKK	SAAB SF.340B	Crossair
HB-AKL	SAAB SF.340B	Crossair
HB-AKM	SAAB SF.340B	Crossair
HB-AKN	SAAB SF.340B	Crossair
HB-AKO	SAAB SF.340B	Crossair
HB-AKP	SAAB SF.340B	Crossair
HB-IBF	Douglas DC-8-63	ASA Air Starline
HB-ICJ	S.E. 210 Caravelle 10B3	Aero Jet
HB-IEE	Boeing 757-23A	Petrolair
HB-IEH	Boeing 737-2V6	Petrolair
HB-IGC	Boeing 747-357 (SCD)	Swissair *Bern*
HB-IGD	Boeing 747-357 (SCD)	Swissair *Basel*
HB-IGE	Boeing 747-357	Swissair *Genéve*
HB-IGF	Boeing 747-357	Swissair *Zürich*
HB-IGG	Boeing 747-357 (SCD)	Swissair *Ticino*
HB-IIA	Boeing 737-3M8	TEA Switzerland *City of Akureyri*
HB-IIB	Boeing 737-3M8	TEA Switzerland *Isle of Avalon*
HB-IIC	Boeing 737-3M8	TEA Switzerland *Emmental*

Reg.	Type	Owner or Operator	Notes
HB-IID	Boeing 737-3Y0	TEA Switzerland *City of Hanoi*	
HB-IIE	Boeing 737-3Q8	TEA Switzerland *Isle of Kos*	
HB-IJA	Airbus A.320-214	Swissair *Opfikon*	
HB-IJB	Airbus A.320-214	Swissair	
HB-IJC	Airbus A.320-214	Swissair	
HB-IJD	Airbus A.320-214	Swissair	
HB-IJE	Airbus A.320-214	Swissair *Solothurn*	
HB-IJF	Airbus A.320-214	Swissair *Bellevue*	
HB-IJG	Airbus A.320-214	Swissair	
HB-IJH	Airbus A.320-214	Swissair	
HB-IJI	Airbus A.320-214	Swissair	
HB-IJJ	Airbus A.320-214	Swissair	
HB-IJK	Airbus A.320-214	Swissair	
HB-IJL	Airbus A.320-214	Swissair	
HB-IJM	Airbus A.320-214	Swissair	
HB-IJN	Airbus A.320-214	Swissair	
HB-IJO	Airbus A.320-214	Swissair	
HB-IJP	Airbus A.320-214	Swissair	
HB-INA	McD Douglas MD-81	Swissair *Höri*	
HB-INB	McD Douglas MD-81	Swissair	
HB-INF	McD Douglas MD-81	Swissair *Steinmaur*	
HB-INM	McD Douglas MD-81	Swissair *Lausanne*	
HB-INN	McD Douglas MD-81	Swissair *Bülach*	
HB-INO	McD Douglas MD-81	Swissair *Bellinzona*	
HB-INP	McD Douglas MD-81	Swissair *Oberglatt*	
HB-INR	McD Douglas MD-81	Crossair	
HB-INS	McD Douglas MD-81	Swissair *Meyrin*	
HB-INT	McD Douglas MD-81	Swissair *Grand-Saconnex*	
HB-INU	McD Douglas MD-81	Swissair *Vernier*	
HB-INV	McD Douglas MD-82	Crossair *Dubendorf*	
HB-INW	McD Douglas MD-82	Crossair	
HB-INX	McD Douglas MD-81	Swissair *Wallisellen*	
HB-INY	McD Douglas MD-81	Swissair *Bassersdorf*	
HB-INZ	McD Douglas MD-81	Crossair *Regensdorf*	
HB-IOA	Airbus A.321-111	Swissair *Lausanne*	
HB-IOB	Airbus A.321-111	Swissair *Aargau*	
HB-IOC	Airbus A.321-111	Swissair *Neu chatel*	
HB-IOD	Airbus A.321-111	Swissair *Kloten*	
HB-IOE	Airbus A.321-111	Swissair	
HB-IOF	Airbus A.321-111	Swissair	
HB-IPF	Airbus A.310-322	Swissair *Glarus*	
HB-IPG	Airbus A.310-322	Swissair *Zug*	
HB-IPH	Airbus A.310-322	Swissair *Appenzell i. Rh*	
HB-IPI	Airbus A.310-322	Swissair *Luzern*	
HB-IPK	Airbus A.310-322	Swissair	
HB-IPL	Airbus A.310-325	Swissair	
HB-IPM	Airbus A.310-325	Swissair	
HB-IPN	Airbus A.310-325	Swissair	
HB-IPV	Airbus A.319-111	Swissair	
HB-IPW	Airbus A.319-111	Swissair	
HB-IPX	Airbus A.319-111	Swissair	
HB-IPY	Airbus A.319-111	Swissair	
HB-IPZ	Airbus A.319-111	Swissair	
HB-ISB	Douglas DC-3C	Classic Air	
HB-ISC	Douglas DC-3C	Classic Air	
HB-ISX	McD Douglas MD-81	Crossair *Binningen*	
HB-ISZ	McD Douglas MD-83	Crossair	
HB-IUG	McD Douglas MD-81	Crossair *Illnau-Effretikon*	
HB-IUH	McD Douglas MD-81	Crossair *Wangen-Bruttisellen*	
HB-IVC	Fokker 100	Swissair *Chur*	
HB-IVD	Fokker 100	Swissair *Dietlikon*	
HB-IVE	Fokker 100	Swissair *Baden*	
HB-IVF	Fokker 100	Swissair *Sion*	
HB-IVG	Fokker 100	Swissair *Genthod*	
HB-IVH	Fokker 100	Swissair *Stadel*	
HB-IVI	Fokker 100	Swissair *Bellevue*	
HB-IVK	Fokker 100	Swissair *Hochfelden*	
HB-IWA	McD Douglas MD-11	Swissair *Obwalden*	
HB-IWB	McD Douglas MD-11	Swissair *Graubünden*	
HB-IWC	McD Douglas MD-11	Swissair *Schaffhausen*	
HB-IWD	McD Douglas MD-11	Swissair *Thurgau*	
HB-IWE	McD Douglas MD-11	Swissair *Nidwalden*	
HB-IWF	McD Douglas MD-11	Swissair *Vaud*	
HB-IWG	McD Douglas MD-11	Swissair *Asia Valais/Wallis*	

Notes	Reg.	Type	Owner or Operator
	HB-IWH	McD Douglas MD-11	Swissair *St Gallen*
	HB-IWI	McD Douglas MD-11	Swissair *Uri*
	HB-IWK	McD Douglas MD-11	Swissair *Fribourg*
	HB-IWL	McD Douglas MD-11	Swissair *Appenzell a.Rh*
	HB-IWM	McD Douglas MD-11	Swissair *Jura*
	HB-IWN	McD Douglas MD-11	Swissair *Basel-Land*
	HB-IWO	McD Douglas MD-11	Swissair
	HB-IXF	Avro RJ85	Crossair
	HB-IXG	Avro RJ85	Crossair
	HB-IXH	Avro RJ85	Crossair
	HB-IXK	Avro RJ85	Crossair
	HB-IXO	Avro RJ100	Crossair
	HB-IXP	Avro RJ100	Crossair
	HB-IXQ	Avro RJ100	Crossair
	HB-IXR	Avro RJ100	Crossair
	HB-IXS	Avro RJ100	Crossair
	HB-IXT	Avro RJ100	Crossair
	HB-IXU	Avro RJ100	Crossair
	HB-IXV	Avro RJ100	Crossair
	HB-IXW	Avro RJ100	Crossair
	HB-IXX	Avro RJ100	Crossair
	HB-IXZ	BAe 146-300	Crossair
	HB-	Avro RJ85	Crossair
	HB-	Avro RJ85	Crossair
	HB-IZA	SAAB 2000	Crossair
	HB-IZB	SAAB 2000	Crossair
	HB-IZC	SAAB 2000	Crossair
	HB-IZD	SAAB 2000	Crossair
	HB-IZE	SAAB 2000	Crossair
	HB-IZF	SAAB 2000	Crossair
	HB-IZG	SAAB 2000	Crossair
	HB-IZH	SAAB 2000	Crossair
	HB-IZI	SAAB 2000	Crossair
	HB-IZK	SAAB 2000	Crossair
	HB-IZL	SAAB 2000	Crossair
	HB-IZM	SAAB 2000	Crossair
	HB-IZN	SAAB 2000	Crossair
	HB-IZO	SAAB 2000	Crossair
	HB-IZP	SAAB 2000	Crossair
	HB-IZQ	SAAB 2000	Crossair
	HB-IZR	SAAB 2000	Crossair
	HB-IZS	SAAB 2000	Crossair
	HB-IZT	SAAB 2000	Crossair
	HB-IZU	SAAB 2000	Crossair

HK (Colombia)

Note: Avianca operates a Boeing 747-259B (SCD) registered EI-CEO.

HL (Korea)

	HL7315	Douglas DC-10-30	Korean Air
	HL7316	Douglas DC-10-30	Korean Air
	HL7317	Douglas DC-10-30	Korean Air
	HL7371	McD Douglas MD-11	Korean Air
	HL7372	McD Douglas MD-11	Korean Air
	HL7373	McD Douglas MD-11	Korean Air
	HL7374	McD Douglas MD-11	Korean Air
	HL7375	McD Douglas MD-11	Korean Air
	HL7401	Boeing 747-249F	Korean Air Cargo
	HL7441	Boeing 747-230F	Korean Air Cargo
	HL7443	Boeing 747-2B5B	Korean Air
	HL7451	Boeing 747-2B5F (SCD)	Korean Air Cargo
	HL7452	Boeing 747-2B5F (SCD)	Korean Air Cargo
	HL7453	Boeing 747-212B	Korean Air
	HL7454	Boeing 747-2B5B (SCD)	Korean Air Cargo
	HL7458	Boeing 747-2B5F (SCD)	Korean Air Cargo
	HL7459	Boeing 747-2B5F (SCD)	Korean Air Cargo
	HL7463	Boeing 747-2B5B	Korean Air
	HL7464	Boeing 747-2B5B	Korean Air
	HL7468	Boeing 747-3B5	Korean Air

Reg.	Type	Owner or Operator	Notes
HL7469	Boeing 747-3B5	Korean Air	
HL7470	Boeing 747-3B5 (SCD)	Korean Air	
HL7471	Boeing 747-273C	Korean Air Cargo	
HL7474	Boeing 747-2S4F (SCD)	Korean Air Cargo	
HL7475	Boeing 747-2B5F (SCD)	Korean Air Cargo	
HL7476	Boeing 747-2B5F (SCD)	Korean Air Cargo	
HL7477	Boeing 747-4B5	Korean Air	
HL7478	Boeing 747-4B5	Korean Air	
HL7479	Boeing 747-4B5	Korean Air	
HL7480	Boeing 747-4B5 (SCD)	Korean Air	
HL7481	Boeing 747-4B5	Korean Air	
HL7482	Boeing 747-4B5	Korean Air	
HL7483	Boeing 747-4B5	Korean Air	
HL7484	Boeing 747-4B5	Korean Air	
HL7485	Boeing 747-4B5	Korean Air	
HL7486	Boeing 747-4B5	Korean Air	
HL7487	Boeing 747-4B5	Korean Air	
HL7488	Boeing 747-4B5	Korean Air	
HL7489	Boeing 747-4B5	Korean Air	
HL7490	Boeing 747-4B5	Korean Air	
HL7491	Boeing 747-4B5	Korean Air	
HL7492	Boeing 747-4B5	Korean Air	
HL7493	Boeing 747-4B5	Korean Air	
HL7494	Boeing 747-4B5	Korean Air	
HL7495	Boeing 747-4B5	Korean Air	
HL7496	Boeing 747-4B5	Korean Air	

Note: Korean Air Cargo also operates the 747-249F 9V-SQV.

HS (Thailand)

HS-TGA	Boeing 747-2D7B	Thai Airways International *Visuthakasatriya*
HS-TGB	Boeing 747-2D7B	Thai Airways International *Sirisobhakya*
HS-TGC	Boeing 747-2D7B	Thai Airways International *Dararasmi*
HS-TGD	Boeing 747-3D7	Thai Airways International *Suchada*
HS-TGE	Boeing 747-3D7	Thai Airways International *Chutamat*
HS-TGF	Boeing 747-2D7B	Thai Airways International *Phimara*
HS-TGG	Boeing 747-2D7B	Thai Airways International *Sriwanna*
HS-TGH	Boeing 747-4D7	Thai Airways International *Chaiprakarn*
HS-TGJ	Boeing 747-4D7	Thai Airways International *Hariphunchai*
HS-TGK	Boeing 747-4D7	Thai Airways International *Alongkorn*
HS-TGL	Boeing 747-4D7	Thai Airways International
HS-TGM	Boeing 747-4D7	Thai Airways International *Chao Phraya*
HS-TGN	Boeing 747-4D7	Thai Airways International *Simongkhon*
HS-TGO	Boeing 747-4D7	Thai Airways International *Bowonrangsi*
HS-TGP	Boeing 747-4D7	Thai Airways International *Thepprasit*
HS-TGR	Boeing 747-4D7	Thai Airways International *Siriwatthana*
HS-TGS	Boeing 747-2D7B	Thai Airways International *Chainarai*
HS-TMA	Douglas DC-10-30ER	Thai Airways International *Kwanmuang*
HS-TMB	Douglas DC-10-30ER	Thai Airways International *Thepalai*
HS-TMC	Douglas DC-10-30ER	Thai Airways International *Sri Ubon*
HS-TMD	McD Douglas MD-11	Thai Airways International *Phra Nakhon*
HS-TME	McD Douglas MD-11	Thai Airways International
HS-TMF	McD Douglas MD-11	Thai Airways International *Phichit*
HS-TMG	McD Douglas MD-11	Thai Airways International

HZ (Saudi Arabia)

HZ-AHA	L.1011-385 TriStar 200	Saudia — Saudi Arabian Airlines
HZ-AHB	L.1011-385 TriStar 200	Saudia — Saudi Arabian Airlines
HZ-AHC	L.1011-385 TriStar 200	Saudia — Saudi Arabian Airlines
HZ-AHD	L.1011-385 TriStar 200	Saudia — Saudi Arabian Airlines
HZ-AHE	L.1011-385 TriStar 200	Saudia — Saudi Arabian Airlines
HZ-AHF	L.1011-385 TriStar 200	Saudia — Saudi Arabian Airlines
HZ-AHG	L.1011-385 TriStar 200	Saudia — Saudi Arabian Airlines
HZ-AHH	L.1011-385 TriStar 200	Saudia — Saudi Arabian Airlines
HZ-AHI	L.1011-385 TriStar 200	Saudia — Saudi Arabian Airlines
HZ-AHJ	L.1011-385 TriStar 200	Saudia — Saudi Arabian Airlines
HZ-AHL	L.1011-385 TriStar 200	Saudia — Saudi Arabian Airlines
HZ-AHM	L.1011-385 TriStar 200	Saudia — Saudi Arabian Airlines

Notes	Reg.	Type	Owner or Operator
	HZ-AHN	L.1011-385 TriStar 200	Saudia — Saudi Arabian Airlines
	HZ-AHO	L.1011-385 TriStar 200	Saudia — Saudi Arabian Airlines
	HZ-AHP	L.1011-385 TriStar 200	Saudia — Saudi Arabian Airlines
	HZ-AHQ	L.1011-385 TriStar 200	Saudia — Saudi Arabian Airlines
	HZ-AHR	L.1011-385 TriStar 200	Saudia — Saudi Arabian Airlines
	HZ-AIA	Boeing 747-168B	Saudia — Saudi Arabian Airlines
	HZ-AIB	Boeing 747-168B	Saudia — Saudi Arabian Airlines
	HZ-AIC	Boeing 747-168B	Saudia — Saudi Arabian Airlines
	HZ-AID	Boeing 747-168B	Saudia — Saudi Arabian Airlines
	HZ-AIE	Boeing 747-168B	Saudia — Saudi Arabian Airlines
	HZ-AIF	Boeing 747SP-68	Saudia — Saudi Arabian Airlines
	HZ-AIG	Boeing 747-168B	Saudia — Saudi Arabian Airlines
	HZ-AIH	Boeing 747-168B	Saudia — Saudi Arabian Airlines
	HZ-AII	Boeing 747-168B	Saudia — Saudi Arabian Airlines
	HZ-AIJ	Boeing 747SP-68	Saudi Royal Flight
	HZ-AIK	Boeing 747-368	Saudia — Saudi Arabian Airlines
	HZ-AIL	Boeing 747-368	Saudia — Saudi Arabian Airlines
	HZ-AIM	Boeing 747-368	Saudia — Saudi Arabian Airlines
	HZ-AIN	Boeing 747-368	Saudia — Saudi Arabian Airlines
	HZ-AIO	Boeing 747-368	Saudia — Saudi Arabian Airlines
	HZ-AIP	Boeing 747-368	Saudia — Saudi Arabian Airlines
	HZ-AIQ	Boeing 747-368	Saudia — Saudi Arabian Airlines
	HZ-AIR	Boeing 747-368	Saudia — Saudi Arabian Airlines
	HZ-AIS	Boeing 747-368	Saudia — Saudi Arabian Airlines
	HZ-AIT	Boeing 747-368	Saudia — Saudi Arabian Airlines
	HZ-AIU	Boeing 747-268F (SCD)	Saudia — Saudi Arabian Airlines
	HZ-AJA	Airbus A.300-620	Saudia — Saudi Arabian Airlines
	HZ-AJB	Airbus A.300-620	Saudia — Saudi Arabian Airlines
	HZ-AJC	Airbus A.300-620	Saudia — Saudi Arabian Airlines
	HZ-AJD	Airbus A.300-620	Saudia — Saudi Arabian Airlines
	HZ-AJE	Airbus A.300-620	Saudia — Saudi Arabian Airlines
	HZ-AJF	Airbus A.300-620	Saudia — Saudi Arabian Airlines
	HZ-AJG	Airbus A.300-620	Saudia — Saudi Arabian Airlines
	HZ-AJH	Airbus A.300-620	Saudia — Saudi Arabian Airlines
	HZ-AJI	Airbus A.300-620	Saudia — Saudi Arabian Airlines
	HZ-AJJ	Airbus A.300-620	Saudia — Saudi Arabian Airlines
	HZ-AJK	Airbus A.300-620	Saudia — Saudi Arabian Airlines
	HZ-HM6	L.1011-385 TriStar 500	Saudi Royal Flight

Note: Saudia also operates other aircraft on lease.

I (Italy)

	I-BIXA	Airbus A.321-112	Alitalia *Piazza di Duomo*
	I-BIXB	Airbus A.321-112	Alitalia
	I-BIXC	Airbus A.321-112	Alitalia
	I-BIXD	Airbus A.321-112	Alitalia *Piazza Pretorio Palermo*
	I-BIXE	Airbus A.321-112	Alitalia *Piazza di Spagna*
	I-BIXF	Airbus A.321-112	Alitalia
	I-BIXG	Airbus A.321-112	Alitalia
	I-BIXI	Airbus A.321-112	Alitalia *Piazza an Marco*
	I-BIXL	Airbus A.321-112	Alitalia
	I-BIXM	Airbus A.321-112	Alitalia
	I-BIXN	Airbus A.321-112	Alitalia
	I-BIXO	Airbus A.321-112	Alitalia *Piazza Piebiscito*
	I-BIXP	Airbus A.321-112	Alitalia
	I-BIXQ	Airbus A.321-112	Alitalia
	I-BIXR	Airbus A.321-112	Alitalia
	I-BIXS	Airbus A.321-112	Alitalia
	I-BIXU	Airbus A.321-112	Alitalia *Piazza Della Signoria*
	I-BUSB	Airbus A.300B4-203	Alitalia *Tiziano*
	I-BUSC	Airbus A.300B4-203	Alitalia *Botticelli*
	I-BUSD	Airbus A.300B4-203	Alitalia *Caravaggio*
	I-BUSF	Airbus A.300B4-203	Alitalia *Tintoretto*
	I-BUSG	Airbus A.300B4-203	Alitalia *Canaletto*
	I-BUSH	Airbus A.300B4-203	Alitalia *Mantegna*
	I-BUSJ	Airbus A.300B4-203	Alitalia *Tiepolo*
	I-BUSL	Airbus A.300B4-203	Alitalia *Pinturicchio*
	I-BUSM	Airbus A.300B2-203	Alitalia *Raffaello*
	I-BUSN	Airbus A.300B2-203	Alitalia *Giotto*
	I-BUSP	Airbus A.300B4-103	Alitalia *Masaccio*
	I-BUSQ	Airbus A.300B4-103	Alitalia *Michelangelo*
	I-BUSR	Airbus A.300B4-103	Alitalia *Cimabue*

Reg.	Type	Owner or Operator	Notes
I-BUST	Airbus A.300B4-103	Alitalia *Piero della Francesca*	
I-DACM	McD Douglas MD-82	Alitalia *La Spezia*	
I-DACN	McD Douglas MD-82	Alitalia *Rieti*	
I-DACP	McD Douglas MD-82	Alitalia *Padova*	
I-DACQ	McD Douglas MD-82	Alitalia *Taranto*	
I-DACR	McD Douglas MD-82	Alitalia *Carrara*	
I-DACS	McD Douglas MD-82	Alitalia *Maratea*	
I-DACT	McD Douglas MD-82	Alitalia *Valtellina*	
I-DACU	McD Douglas MD-82	Alitalia *Fabriano*	
I-DACV	McD Douglas MD-82	Alitalia *Riccione*	
I-DACW	McD Douglas MD-82	Alitalia *Vieste*	
I-DACX	McD Douglas MD-82	Alitalia *Piacenza*	
I-DACY	McD Douglas MD-82	Alitalia *Novara*	
I-DACZ	McD Douglas MD-82	Alitalia *Castelfidardo*	
I-DAND	McD Douglas MD-82	Alitalia *Bolzano*	
I-DANF	McD Douglas MD-82	Alitalia *Vicenza*	
I-DANG	McD Douglas MD-82	Alitalia *Benevento*	
I-DANH	McD Douglas MD-82	Alitalia *Messina*	
I-DANL	McD Douglas MD-82	Alitalia *Cosenza*	
I-DANM	McD Douglas MD-82	Alitalia *Vicenza*	
I-DANP	McD Douglas MD-82	Alitalia *Fabriano*	
I-DANQ	McD Douglas MD-82	Alitalia *Lecce*	
I-DANR	McD Douglas MD-82	Alitalia *Matera*	
I-DANU	McD Douglas MD-82	Alitalia *Trapani*	
I-DANV	McD Douglas MD-82	Alitalia *Forte dei Marmi*	
I-DANW	McD Douglas MD-82	Alitalia	
I-DATA	McD Douglas MD-82	Alitalia *Gubbio*	
I-DATB	McD Douglas MD-82	Alitalia *Bergamo*	
I-DATC	McD Douglas MD-82	Alitalia *Foggia*	
I-DATD	McD Douglas MD-82	Alitalia *Savona*	
I-DATE	McD Douglas MD-82	Alitalia *Grosseto*	
I-DATF	McD Douglas MD-82	Alitalia *Vittorio Veneto*	
I-DATG	McD Douglas MD-82	Alitalia *Arezzo*	
I-DATH	McD Douglas MD-82	Alitalia *Pescara*	
I-DATI	McD Douglas MD-82	Alitalia *Siracusa*	
I-DATJ	McD Douglas MD-82	Alitalia *Lunigiana*	
I-DATK	McD Douglas MD-82	Alitalia *Ravenna*	
I-DATL	McD Douglas MD-82	Alitalia	
I-DAIM	McD Douglas MD-82	Alitalia	
I-DATN	McD Douglas MD-82	Alitalia	
I-DATO	McD Douglas MD-82	Alitalia *Reggio Emilia*	
I-DATP	McD Douglas MD-82	Alitalia	
I-DATQ	McD Douglas MD-82	Alitalia	
I-DATR	McD Douglas MD-82	Alitalia *Livorno*	
I-DATS	McD Douglas MD-82	Alitalia	
I-DATU	McD Douglas MD-82	Alitalia *Verona*	
I-DAVA	McD Douglas MD-82	Alitalia *Cuneo*	
I-DAVB	McD Douglas MD-82	Alitalia *Ferrara*	
I-DAVC	McD Douglas MD-82	Alitalia *Lucca*	
I-DAVD	McD Douglas MD-82	Alitalia *Mantova*	
I-DAVF	McD Douglas MD-82	Alitalia *Oristano*	
I-DAVG	McD Douglas MD-82	Alitalia *Pesaro*	
I-DAVH	McD Douglas MD-82	Alitalia *Salerno*	
I-DAVI	McD Douglas MD-82	Alitalia *Assisi*	
I-DAVJ	McD Douglas MD-82	Alitalia *Parma*	
I-DAVK	McD Douglas MD-82	Alitalia *Pompei*	
I-DAVL	McD Douglas MD-82	Alitalia *Reggio Calabria*	
I-DAVM	McD Douglas MD-82	Alitalia *Caserta*	
I-DAVN	McD Douglas MD-82	Alitalia *Volterra*	
I-DAVP	McD Douglas MD-82	Alitalia *Gorizia*	
I-DAVR	McD Douglas MD-82	Alitalia *Pisa*	
I-DAVS	McD Douglas MD-82	Alitalia *Catania*	
I-DAVT	McD Douglas MD-82	Alitalia *Como*	
I-DAVU	McD Douglas MD-82	Alitalia *Udine*	
I-DAVV	McD Douglas MD-82	Alitalia *Pavia*	
I-DAVW	McD Douglas MD-82	Alitalia *Camerino*	
I-DAVX	McD Douglas MD-82	Alitalia *Asti*	
I-DAVZ	McD Douglas MD-82	Alitalia *Brescia*	
I-DAWA	McD Douglas MD-82	Alitalia *Roma*	
I-DAWB	McD Douglas MD-82	Alitalia *Cagliari*	
I-DAWC	McD Douglas MD-82	Alitalia *Campobasso*	
I-DAWD	McD Douglas MD-82	Alitalia *Catanzaro*	
I-DAWE	McD Douglas MD-82	Alitalia *Milano*	
I-DAWF	McD Douglas MD-82	Alitalia *Firenze*	
I-DAWG	McD Douglas MD-82	Alitalia *L'Aquila*	

Notes	Reg.	Type	Owner or Operator
	I-DAWH	McD Douglas MD-82	Alitalia *Palermo*
	I-DAWI	McD Douglas MD-82	Alitalia *Ancona*
	I-DAWJ	McD Douglas MD-82	Alitalia *Genova*
	I-DAWL	McD Douglas MD-82	Alitalia *Perugia*
	I-DAWM	McD Douglas MD-82	Alitalia *Potenza*
	I-DAWO	McD Douglas MD-82	Alitalia *Bari*
	I-DAWP	McD Douglas MD-82	Alitalia *Torino*
	I-DAWQ	McD Douglas MD-82	Alitalia *Trieste*
	I-DAWR	McD Douglas MD-82	Alitalia *Venezia*
	I-DAWS	McD Douglas MD-82	Alitalia *Aosta*
	I-DAWT	McD Douglas MD-82	Alitalia *Napoli*
	I-DAWU	McD Douglas MD-82	Alitalia *Bologna*
	I-DAWV	McD Douglas MD-82	Alitalia *Trento*
	I-DAWW	McD Douglas MD-82	Alitalia *Riace*
	I-DAWY	McD Douglas MD-82	Alitalia *Agrigento*
	I-DAWZ	McD Douglas MD-82	Alitalia *Avellino*
	I-DEMC	Boeing 747-243B (SCD)	Alitalia *Taormina*
	I-DEMF	Boeing 747-243B (SCD)	Alitalia *Portofino*
	I-DEMG	Boeing 747-243B	Alitalia *Cervinia*
	I-DEML	Boeing 747-243B	Alitalia *Sorrento*
	I-DEMN	Boeing 747-243B	Alitalia *Portocervo*
	I-DEMP	Boeing 747-243B	Alitalia *Capri*
	I-DEMR	Boeing 747-243F (SCD)	Alitalia *Titano*
	I-DEMS	Boeing 747-243B	Alitalia *Monte Argentario*
	I-DEMT	Boeing 747-243B (SCD)	Alitalia *Monte Catini*
	I-DEMV	Boeing 747-243B	Alitalia *Sestriere*
	I-DEMY	Boeing 747-230B	Alitalia *Asolo*
	I-DIBI	Douglas DC-9-32	Alitalia *Isola del Giglioa*
	I-DIBU	Douglas DC-9-32	Alitalia *Isola di Pantelleria*
	I-DIKM	Douglas DC-9-32	Alitalia *Positano*
	I-DIKP	Douglas DC-9-32	Alitalia *Isola di Marettimo*
	I-DIKR	Douglas DC-9-32	Alitalia *Piemonte*
	I-DIZE	Douglas DC-9-32	Alitalia *Isola della Meloria*
	I-DUPA	McD Douglas MD-11C	Alitalia *Gioacchino Rossini*
	I DUPB	McD Douglas MD-11	Alitalia *Pietro Mascagni*
	I-DUPC	McD Douglas MD-11	Alitalia *V. Bellini*
	I-DUPD	McD Douglas MD-11	Alitalia *G. Donizetti*
	I-DUPE	McD Douglas MD-11C	Alitalia *Giuseppe Verdi*
	I-DUPI	McD Douglas MD-11C	Alitalia *Gioacomo Puccini*
	I-DUPO	McD Douglas MD-11C	Alitalia *Nicolo Paganini*
	I-DUPU	McD Douglas MD-11C	Alitalia *Antonio Vivaldi*
	I-FLRA	BAe 146-200	Meridiana
	I-FLRE	BAe 146-200	Meridiana
	I-FLRI	BAe 146-200	Meridiana
	I-FLRO	BAe 146-200	Meridiana
	I-FLYY	Douglas DC-9-51	Eurofly
	I-FLYZ	Douglas DC-9-51	Eurofly
	I-JETA	Boeing 737-229	Air One
	I-REJA	Fokker 70	Avianova
	I-REJB	Fokker 70	Avianova
	I-REJE	Fokker 70	Avianova
	I-REJI	Fokker 70	Avianova
	I-RE	Fokker 70	Avianova
	I-RE	Fokker 70	Avianova
	I-RE	Fokker 70	Avianova
	I-RE	Fokker 70	Avianova
	I-RIFH	Douglas DC-9-32	Alitalia *Isola di Ponza*
	I-RIFJ	Douglas DC-9-32	Alitalia *Isola della Capraiafl*
	I-RIFM	Douglas DC-9-32	Alitalia *Marche*
	I-RIFP	Douglas DC-9-32	Alitalia *Veneto*
	I-RIFS	Douglas DC-9-32	Alitalia *Basilicata*
	I-RIFT	Douglas DC-9-32	Alitalia *Friuli Venezia Giulia*
	I-RIFU	Douglas DC-9-32	Alitalia *Valle d'Aosta*
	I-RIFV	Douglas DC-9-32	Alitalia *Lazio*
	I-RIFW	Douglas DC-9-32	Alitalia *Lombardia*
	I-SMEA	Douglas DC-9-51	Meridiana
	I-SMEE	Douglas DC-9-51	Meridiana
	I-SMEI	Douglas DC-9-51	Meridiana
	I-SMEJ	Douglas DC-9-51	Meridiana
	I-SMEL	McD Douglas MD-82	Meridiana
	I-SMEM	McD Douglas MD-82	Meridiana
	I-SMEO	Douglas DC-9-51	Meridiana

Reg.	Type	Owner or Operator	Notes
I-SMEP	McD Douglas MD-82	Meridiana	
I-SMER	McD Douglas MD-82	Meridiana	
I-SMES	McD Douglas MD-82	Meridiana	
I-SMET	McD Douglas MD-82	Meridiana	
I-SMEU	Douglas DC-9-51	Meridiana	
I-SMEV	McD Douglas MD-82	Meridiana	
I-TEAA	Boeing 737-3M8	TEA Italia	
I-TEAE	Boeing 737-3M8	TEA Italia	
I-TEAI	Boeing 737-3M8	TEA Italia	
I-TNTC	BAe146-200QT	Mistral Air/TNT	

Note: Meridiana also operates an MD-82 which retains the registration PH-SEZ. Air
Europe SpA operates Boeing 767s registered EI-CIY, EI-CJA, EI-CJB, EI-CLR and
EI-CLS plus Boeing 757 EI-CLU. Alitalia employs four 767s registered G-OITA,
G-OITB, G-OITC and G-OITF.

JA (Japan)

JA8071	Boeing 747-446	Japan Airlines	
JA8072	Boeing 747-446	Japan Airlines	
JA8073	Boeing 747-446	Japan Airlines	
JA8074	Boeing 747-446	Japan Airlines	
JA8075	Boeing 747-446	Japan Airlines	
JA8076	Boeing 747-446	Japan Airlines	
JA8077	Boeing 747-446	Japan Airlines	
JA8078	Boeing 747-446	Japan Airlines	
JA8079	Boeing 747-446	Japan Airlines	
JA8080	Boeing 747-446	Japan Airlines	
JA8081	Boeing 747-446	Japan Airlines	
JA8082	Boeing 747-446	Japan Airlines	
JA8085	Boeing 747-446	Japan Airlines	
JA8086	Boeing 747-446	Japan Airlines	
JA8087	Boeing 747-446	Japan Airlines	
JA8088	Boeing 747-446	Japan Airlines	
JA8089	Boeing 747-446	Japan Airlines	
JA8094	Boeing 747-481	All Nippon Airways	
JA8095	Boeing 747-481	All Nippon Airways	
JA8096	Boeing 747-481	All Nippon Airways	
JA8097	Boeing 747-481	All Nippon Airways	
JA8098	Boeing 747-481	All Nippon Airways	
JA8104	Boeing 747-246B	Japan Airlines	
JA8105	Boeing 747-246B	Japan Airlines	
JA8108	Boeing 747-246B	Japan Airlines	
JA8113	Boeing 747-246B	Japan Airlines	
JA8115	Boeing 747-146A	Japan Airlines	
JA8122	Boeing 747-246B	Japan Airlines	
JA8123	Boeing 747-246F (SCD)	Japan Airlines	
JA8125	Boeing 747-246B	Japan Airlines	
JA8130	Boeing 747-246B	Japan Airlines	
JA8131	Boeing 747-246B	Japan Airlines	
JA8132	Boeing 747-246F	Japan Airlines	
JA8140	Boeing 747-246B	Japan Airlines	
JA8141	Boeing 747-246B	Japan Airlines	
JA8154	Boeing 747-246B	Japan Airlines	
JA8160	Boeing 747-221F (SCD)	Japan Airlines	
JA8161	Boeing 747-246B	Japan Airlines	
JA8162	Boeing 747-246B	Japan Airlines	
JA8163	Boeing 747-346	Japan Airlines	
JA8165	Boeing 747-221F (SCD)	Japan Airlines	
JA8166	Boeing 747-346	Japan Airlines	
JA8169	Boeing 747-246B	Japan Airlines	
JA8171	Boeing 747-246F (SCD)	Japan Airlines	
JA8173	Boeing 747-346	Japan Airlines	
JA8174	Boeing 747-281B	All Nippon Airways	
JA8175	Boeing 747-281B	All Nippon Airways	
JA8177	Boeing 747-346	Japan Airlines	
JA8178	Boeing 747-346	Japan Airlines	
JA8179	Boeing 747-346	Japan Airlines	
JA8180	Boeing 747-246F (SCD)	Japan Airlines	
JA8181	Boeing 747-281B	All Nippon Airways	
JA8182	Boeing 747-281B	All Nippon Airways	

Notes	Reg.	Type	Owner or Operator
	JA8185	Boeing 747-346	Japan Airlines
	JA8190	Boeing 747-281B	All Nippon Airways
	JA8192	Boeing 747-2D3B	All Nippon Airways
	JA8193	Boeing 747-212F (SCD)	Japan Airlines
	JA8901	Boeing 747-446	Japan Airlines
	JA8902	Boeing 747-446	Japan Airlines
	JA8906	Boeing 747-446	Japan Airlines
	JA8909	Boeing 747-446	Japan Airlines
	JA8910	Boeing 747-446	Japan Airlines
	JA8911	Boeing 747-446	Japan Airlines
	JA8913	Boeing 747-446	Japan Airlines
	JA8914	Boeing 747-446	Japan Airlines
	JA8915	Boeing 747-446	Japan Airlines
	JA8916	Boeing 747-446	Japan Airlines
	JA8917	Boeing 747-446	Japan Airlines
	JA8918	Boeing 747-446	Japan Airlines
	JA8919	Boeing 747-446	Japan Airlines
	JA8920	Boeing 747-446	Japan Airlines
	JA8958	Boeing 747-481	All Nippon Airways
	JA8962	Boeing 747-481	All Nippon Airways

Note: Japan Airlines also operates a Boeing 747-246F which retains its US registration N211JL and two 747-346s N212JL and NZ213JL.

JY (Jordan)

	JY-AGA	L.1011-385 TriStar 500	Royal Jordanian *Amman*
	JY-AGB	L.1011-385 TriStar 500	Royal Jordanian *Princess Alia*
	JY-AGC	L.1011-385 TriStar 500	Royal Jordanian *Princess Zein*
	JY-AGD	L.1011-385 TriStar 500	Royal Jordanian *Prince Ali*
	JY-AGE	L.1011-385 TriStar 500	Royal Jordanian *Princess Aysha*
	JY-AJK	Boeing 707-384C	Royal Jordanian Cargo
	JY-AJL	Boeing 707-324C	Royal Jordanian Cargo
	JY-AJM	Boeing 707-365C	Royal Jordanian Cargo
	JY-AJN	Boeing 707-3J6C	Royal Jordanian Cargo
	JY-AJO	Boeing 707-3J6C	Royal Jordanian Cargo
	JY-HKJ	L.1011-385 TriStar 500	Jordan Government

Note: Royal Jordanian also operates four A.310-304s registered F-ODVF, F-ODVG, F-ODVH and F-ODVI. Similarly two A.320-211s retain the registrations F-OGYA and F-OGYB.

LN (Norway)

	LN-BRA	Boeing 737-405	Braathens SAFE *Eirik Blodoeks*
	LN-BRB	Boeing 737-405	Braathens SAFE *Inge Bardson*
	LN-BRC	Boeing 737-505	Braathens SAFE
	LN-BRD	Boeing 737-505	Braathens SAFE
	LN-BRE	Boeing 737-405	Braathens SAFE
	LN-BRF	Boeing 737-505	Braathens SAFE
	LN-BRG	Boeing 737-505	Braathens SAFE
	LN-BRH	Boeing 737-505	Braathens SAFE
	LN-BRI	Boeing 737-405	Braathens SAFE *Harald Harfagre*
	LN-BRJ	Boeing 737-505	Braathens SAFE
	LN-BRK	Boeing 737-505	Braathens SAFE
	LN-BRM	Boeing 737-505	Braathens SAFE
	LN-BRN	Boeing 737-505	Braathens SAFE
	LN-BRO	Boeing 737-505	Braathens SAFE
	LN-BRP	Boeing 737-405	Braathens SAFE *Harold Hardrade*
	LN-BRQ	Boeing 737-405	Braathens SAFE
	LN-BRR	Boeing 737-505	Braathens SAFE
	LN-BRS	Boeing 737-505	Braathens SAFE
	LN-BRT	Boeing 737-505	Braathens SAFE
	LN-BRU	Boeing 737-505	Braathens SAFE *Eirik Magnusson*
	LN-BRV	Boeing 737-505	Braathens SAFE
	LN-BRX	Boeing 737-505	Braathens SAFE
	LN-BUB	Boeing 737-4Q8	Braathens SAFE *Magnus den Gode*
	LN-BUC	Boeing 737-505	Braathens SAFE
	LN-FOG	L.188AF Electra	Fred Olsen Airtransport/DHL
	LN-FOH	L.188AF Electra	Fred Olsen Airtransport/DHL
	LN-FOI	L.188CF Electra	Fred Olsen Airtransport

Reg.	Type	Owner or Operator	Notes
LN-FOL	L.188AF Electra	Fred Olsen Airtransport/DHL	
LN-FON	L.188PF Electra	Fred Olsen Airtransport/DHL	
LN-FOO	L.188AF Electra	Fred Olsen Airtransport/DHL	
LN-KOC	EMB-120RT Brasilia	Wideroe Norskair	
LN-KOD	EMB-120RT Brasilia	Wideroe Norskair	
LN-KOE	EMB-120RT Brasilia	Wideroe Norskair	
LN-RCD	Boeing 767-383ER	Scandinavian Airlines System (S.A.S.) *Glyda Viking*	
LN-RCE	Boeing 767-383ER	S.A.S. *Aase Viking*	
LN-RCG	Boeing 767-383ER	S.A.S. *Yrsa Viking*	
LN-RCH	Boeing 767-383ER	S.A.S. *Ingegerd Viking*	
LN-RCI	Boeing 767-383ER	S.A.S. *Helga Viking*	
LN-RCK	Boeing 767-383ER	S.A.S. *Tor Viking*	
LN-RCL	Boeing 767-383ER	S.A.S. *Sven Viking*	
LN-RLA	Douglas DC-9-41	S.A.S. *Are Viking*	
LN-RLE	McD Douglas MD-82	S.A.S. *Vegard Viking*	
LN-RLF	McD Douglas MD-82	S.A.S. *Finn Viking*	
LN-RLG	McD Douglas MD-82	S.A.S.	
LN-RLH	Douglas DC-9-41	S.A.S. *Einar Viking*	
LN-RLN	Douglas DC-9-41	S.A.S. *Halldor Viking*	
LN-RLP	Douglas DC-9-41	S.A.S. *Froste Viking*	
LN-RLR	McD Douglas MD-82	S.A.S. *Vegard Viking*	
LN-RLS	Douglas DC-9-41	S.A.S. *Asmund Viking*	
LN-RLT	Douglas DC-9-41	S.A.S. *Audun Viking*	
LN-RLX	Douglas DC-9-41	S.A.S. *Sote Viking*	
LN-RLZ	Douglas DC-9-41	S.A.S. *Bodvar Viking*	
LN-RMA	McD Douglas MD-81	S.A.S. *Hasting Viking*	
LN-RMD	McD Douglas MD-82	S.A.S. *Fenge Viking*	
LN-RMF	McD Douglas MD-83	S.A.S. *Torgny Viking*	
LN-RMG	McD Douglas MD-87	S.A.S. *Snorre Viking*	
LN-RMH	McD Douglas MD-87	S.A.S. *Solmund Viking*	
LN-RMJ	McD Douglas MD-81	S.A.S. *Rand Viking*	
LN-RMK	McD Douglas MD-87	S.A.S. *Ragnhild Viking*	
LN-RML	McD Douglas MD-81	S.A.S. *Aud Viking*	
LN-RMM	McD Douglas MD-81	S.A.S. *Blenda Viking*	
LN-RMN	McD Douglas MD-82	S.A.S. *Ivar Viking*	
LN-RMO	McD Douglas MD-81	S.A.S. *Bergljot Viking*	
LN-RMP	McD Douglas MD-87	S.A.S. *Reidun Viking*	
LN-RMR	McD Douglas MD-81	S.A.S. *Olav Viking*	
LN-RMS	McD Douglas MD-81	S.A.S. *Nial Viking*	
LN-RMT	McD Douglas MD-81	S.A.S. *Jarl Viking*	
LN-RMU	McD Douglas MD-87	S.A.S. *Grim Viking*	
LN-RMX	McD Douglas MD-87	S.A.S. *Vidar Viking*	
LN-RMY	McD Douglas MD-87	S.A.S. *Ingolf Viking*	
LN-RNB	Fokker 50	S.A.S. *Commuter Brae Viking*	
LN-RNC	Fokker 50	S.A.S. *Commuter Elvink Viking*	
LN-RND	Fokker 50	S.A.S. *Commuter Inge Viking*	
LN-RNE	Fokker 50	S.A.S. *Commuter Ebbe Viking*	
LN-RNF	Fokker 50	S.A.S. *Commuter Leif Viking*	
LN-RNG	Fokker 50	S.A.S. *Commuter Gudrid Viking*	
LN-RNH	Fokker 50	S.A.S. *Commuter Harald Viking*	
LN-WND	Douglas DC-3C	Dakota Norway	

LV (Argentina)

LV-MLO	Boeing 747-287B	Aerolineas Argentinas	
LV-MLP	Boeing 747-287B	Aerolineas Argentinas	
LV-MLR	Boeing 747-287B	Aerolineas Argentinas	
LV-OEP	Boeing 747-287B	Aerolineas Argentinas	
LV-OOZ	Boeing 747-287B	Aerolineas Argentinas	
LV-OPA	Boeing 747-287B	Aerolineas Argentinas	

LX (Luxembourg)

LX-ACO	Boeing 747SP-44	Corsair	
LX-ACV	Boeing 747-271C (SCD)	Cargolux *City of Echternach*	
LX-BCV	Boeing 747-271C (SCD)	Cargolux	
LX-DCV	Boeing 747-228F (SCD)	Cargolux/El Al	
LX-ECV	Boeing 747-271C (SCD)	Cargolux	
LX-FCV	Boeing 747-4R7F (SCD)	Cargolux *City of Luxembourg*	

Notes	Reg.	Type	Owner or Operator
	LX-GCV	Boeing 747-4R7F (SCD)	Cargolux City of Esch/Alzette
	LX-ICV	Boeing 747-428F (SCD)	Cargolux
	LX-LGB	Fokker 50	Luxair
	LX-LGC	Fokker 50	Luxair Prince Guillaume
	LX-LGD	Fokker 50	Luxair Prince Felix
	LX-LGE	Fokker 50	Luxair Prince Louis
	LX-LGF	Boeing 737-4C9	Sobelair
	LX-LGG	Boeing 737-4C9	Luxair Chateau de Bourscheid
	LX-LGK	EMB-120ER Brasilia	Luxair
	LX-LGL	EMB-120ER Brasilia	Luxair
	LX-LGM	EMB-120ER Brasilia	Luxair
	LX-LGO	Boeing 737-5C9	Luxair Chateau de Clervaux
	LX-LGP	Boeing 737-5C9	Luxair Chateau de Bourglinster
	LX-LGR	Boeing 737-528	Luxair
	LX-LGS	Boeing 737-528	Luxair
	LX-SKS	EMB-110P1 Bandeirante	Sky Service

LY (Lithuania)

	LY-AAM	Yakovlev Yak-42	Lithuanian Airlines
	LY-AAN	Yakovlev Yak-42	Lithuanian Airlines
	LY-AAO	Yakovlev Yak-42	Lithuanian Airlines
	LY-AAP	Yakovlev Yak-42	Lithuanian Airlines
	LY-AAQ	Yakovlev Yak-42	Lithuanian Airlines
	LY-AAR	Yakovlev Yak-42	Lithuanian Airlines
	LY-AAS	Yakovlev Yak-42D	Lithuanian Airlines
	LY-AAT	Yakovlev Yak-42	Lithuanian Airlines
	LY-AAU	Yakovlev Yak-42D	Lithuanian Airlines
	LY-AAV	Yakovlev Yak-42D	Lithuanian Airlines
	LY-AAW	Yakovlev Yak-42D	Lithuanian Airlines
	LY-AAX	Yakovlev Yak-42D	Lithuanian Airlines
	LY-ABB	Tupolev Tu-134A	Lithuanian Airlines
	LY-ABC	Tupolev Tu-134A	Lithuanian Airlines
	LY-ABD	Tupolev Tu-134A	Lithuanian Airlines
	LY-ABE	Tupolev Tu-134A-3	Lithuanian Airlines
	LY-ABF	Tupolev Tu-134A-3	Lithuanian Airlines
	LY-ABG	Tupolev Tu-134A-3	Lithuanian Airlines
	LY-ABH	Tupolev Tu-134A-3	Lithuanian Airlines
	LY-ABI	Tupolev Tu-134A	Lithuanian Airlines
	LY-BSD	Boeing 737-2T4	Lithuanian Airlines Steponas Darius
	LY-BSG	Boeing 737-2T4	Lithuanian Airlines
	LY-GPA	Boeing 737-2Q8	Lithuanian Airlines

LZ (Bulgaria)

	LZ-ABB	Airbus A.320-231	Balkan Bulgarian Airlines Rila
	LZ-ABC	Airbus A.320-231	Balkan Bulgarian Airlines Rhodope
	LZ-ABD	Airbus A.320-231	Balkan Bulgarian Airlines Pirin
	LZ-AZC	Ilyushin IL-18V	Air Zory
	LZ-AZR	Ilyushin IL-18D	Air Zory
	LZ-AZZ	Ilyushin IL-18D (F)	Air Zory
	LZ-BAC	Antonov An-12	Balkan Bulgarian Airlines/HeavyLift
	LZ-BAE	Antonov An-12	Balkan Bulgarian Airlines/HeavyLift
	LZ-BAF	Antonov An-12	Balkan Bulgarian Airlines
	LZ-BEH	Ilyushin IL-18V	Bajlkan Bulgarian Airlines
	LZ-BEI	Ilyushin IL-18V	Balkan Bulgarian Airlines
	LZ-BEU	Ilyushin IL-18V	Balkan Bulgarian Airlines
	LZ-BOA	Boeing 737-53A	Balkan Bulgarian Airlines City of Sofia
	LZ-BOB	Boeing 737-53A	Balkan Bulgarian Airlines City of Plovdiv
	LZ-BOC	Boeing 737-53A	Balkan Bulgarian Airlines City of Varna
	LZ-BTA	Tupolev Tu-154B	Balkan Bulgarian Airlines
	LZ-BTC	Tupolev Tu-154B	Balkan Bulgarian Airlines
	LZ-BTE	Tupolev Tu-154B	Balkan Bulgarian Airlines
	LZ-BTF	Tupolev Tu-154B	Balkan Bulgarian Airlines
	LZ-BTG	Tupolev Tu-154B	Balkan Bulgarian Airlines
	LZ-BTH	Tupolev Tu-154M	Balkan Bulgarian Airlines
	LZ-BTI	Tupolev Tu-154M	Balkan Bulgarian Airlines
	LZ-BTJ	Tupolev Tu-154B-1	Palair Macedonian
	LZ-BTK	Tupolev Tu-154B	Balkan Bulgarian Airlines
	LZ-BTL	Tupolev Tu-154B	Balkan Bulgarian Airlines

Reg.	Type	Owner or Operator	Notes
LZ-BTM	Tupolev Tu-154B	Balkan Bulgarian Airlines	
LZ-BTN	Tupolev Tu-154M	Balkan Bulgarian Airlines	
LZ-BTO	Tupolev Tu-154B-1	Balkan Bulgarian Airlines	
LZ-BTP	Tupolev Tu-154B-1	Balkan Bulgarian Airlines	
LZ-BTQ	Tupolev Tu-154M	Balkan Bulgarian Airlines	
LZ-BTR	Tupolev Tu-154B-2	Balkan Bulgarian Airlines	
LZ-BTS	Tupolev Tu-154B-2	Balkan Bulgarian Airlines	
LZ-BTT	Tupolev Tu-154B-2	Balkan Bulgarian Airlines	
LZ-BTU	Tupolev Tu-154B-2	Balkan Bulgarian Airlines	
LZ-BTV	Tupolev Tu-154B-2	Balkan Bulgarian Airlines	
LZ-BTW	Tupolev Tu-154M	Balkan Bulgarian Airlines	
LZ-BTX	Tupolev Tu-154M	Balkan Bulgarian Airlines	
LZ-BTY	Tupolev Tu-154M	Balkan Bulgarian Airlines	
LZ-BTZ	Tupolev Tu-154M	Balkan Bulgarian Airlines	
LZ-MIG	Tupolev Tu-154M	Air VIA Bulgarian Airways	
LZ-MIK	Tupolev Tu-154M	Air VIA Bulgarian Airways	
LZ-MIL	Tupolev Tu-154M	Air VIA Bulgarian Airways	
LZ-MIR	Tupolev Tu-154M	Air VIA Bulgarian Airways	
LZ-MIS	Tupolev Tu-154M	Air VIA Bulgarian Airways	
LZ-SFA	Antonov An-12B	Air Sofia	
LZ-SFG	Antonov An-12	Air Sofia	
LZ-SFK	Antonov An-12	Air Sofia	
LZ-SFL	Antonov An-12	Air Sofia	
LZ-SFM	Antonov An-12	Air Sofia	
LZ-TUG	Tupolev Tu-134A-3	Balkan Bulgarian Airlines	
LZ-TUK	Tupolev Tu-134A	Balkan Bulgarian Airlines	
LZ-TUM	Tupolev Tu-134A-3	Balkan Bulgarian Airlines	
LZ-TUS	Tupolev Tu-134A	Balkan Bulgarian Airlines	
LZ-TUT	Tupulev Tu-134A-3	Balkan Bulgarian Airlines	
LZ-TUU	Tupolev Tu-134A-3	Balkan Bulgarian Airlines	
LZ-TUV	Tupolev Tu-134A-3	Balkan Bulgarian Airlines	
LZ-TUZ	Tupolev Tu-134A-3	Balkan Bulgarian Airlines	

Note: Balkan also operates two Boeing 767-27EERs F-GHGD and F-GHGE on lease from Air France.

N (USA)

N14AZ	Boeing 707-336C	Seagreen Air Transport	
N18AZ	Boeing 707-351C	Seagreen Air Transport	
N21AZ	Boeing 707-351C	Seagreen Air Transport	
N24UA	Douglas DC-8-61F	American International Airways	
N29AZ	Boeing 707-323C	Seagreen Air Transport	
N102CK	L.1011-385 TriStar 200	American International Airways	
N103CK	L.1011-385 TriStar 200	American International Airways	
N104CK	L.1011-385 TriStar 200	American International Airways	
N105CK	L.1011-385 TriStar 200	American International Airways	
N106CK	L.1011-385 TriStar 200	American International Airways	
N105UA	Boeing 747-451	United Airlines	
N106UA	Boeing 747-451	United Airlines	
N107WA	Douglas DC-10-30CF	World Airways/Federal Express	
N114FE	Boeing 727-24C	Federal Express	
N115FE	Boeing 727-116C	Federal Express	
N116KB	Boeing 747-312	Singapore Airlines	
N117FE	Boeing 727-25C	Federal Express	
N117KC	Boeing 747-312	Singapore Airlines	
N117WA	Douglas DC-10-30	World Airways	
N121KG	Boeing 747-312	Singapore Airlines	
N122KH	Boeing 747-312	Singapore Airlines	
N123KJ	Boeing 747-312	Singapore Airlines	
N124KK	Boeing 747-312	Singapore Airlines	
N125KL	Boeing 747-312	Singapore Airlines	
N133JC	Douglas DC-10-40	Northwest Airlines	
N133TW	Boeing 747-156	Trans World Airlines	
N134TW	Boeing 747-156	Trans World Airlines	
N137AA	Douglas DC-10-30	American Airlines	
N140AA	Douglas DC-10-30	American Airlines *(stored)*	
N140UA	Boeing 747SP-21	United Airlines	
N141AA	Douglas DC-10-30	American Airlines	
N141UA	Boeing 747SP-21	United Airlines	
N141US	Douglas DC-10-40	Northwest Airlines	
N142UA	Boeing 747SP-21	United Airlines	

Notes	Reg.	Type	Owner or Operator
	N143AA	Douglas DC-10-30	American Airlines
	N143FE	Boeing 727-21C	Federal Express
	N143UA	Boeing 747SP-21	United Airlines
	N144AA	Douglas DC-10-30	American Airlines
	N144FE	Boeing 727-21C	Federal Express
	N144JC	Douglas DC-10-40	Northwest Airlines
	N144UA	Boeing 747SP-21	United Airlines
	N145SP	Boeing 707-323B	Seagreen Air Transport
	N145UA	Boeing 747SP-21	United Airlines
	N145US	Douglas DC-10-40	Northwest Airlines
	N146UA	Boeing 747SP-21	United Airlines
	N146US	Douglas DC-10-40	Northwest Airlines
	N147UA	Boeing 747SP-21	United Airlines
	N147US	Douglas DC-10-40	Northwest Airlines
	N148UA	Boeing 747SP-21	United Airlines
	N148US	Douglas DC-10-40	Northwest Airlines
	N149US	Douglas DC-10-40	Northwest Airlines
	N150US	Douglas DC-10-40	Northwest Airlines
	N151UA	Boeing 747-222B	United Airlines
	N151US	Douglas DC-10-40	Northwest Airlines
	N152UA	Boeing 747-222B	United Airlines
	N152US	Douglas DC-10-40	Northwest Airlines
	N153UA	Boeing 747-123	United Airlines
	N153US	Douglas DC-10-40	Northwest Airlines
	N154US	Douglas DC-10-40	Northwest Airlines
	N155UA	Boeing 747-123	United Airlines
	N155US	Douglas DC-10-40	Northwest Airlines
	N156UA	Boeing 747-123	United Airlines
	N156US	Douglas DC-10-40	Northwest Airlines
	N157UA	Boeing 747-123	United Airlines
	N157US	Douglas DC-10-40	Northwest Airlines
	N158UA	Boeing 747-238B	United Airlines
	N158US	Douglas DC-10-40	Northwest Airlines
	N159UA	Boeing 747-238B	United Airlines
	N159US	Douglas DC-10-40	Northwest Airlines
	N160UA	Boeing 747-238B	United Airlines
	N160US	Douglas DC-10-40	Northwest Airlines
	N161UA	Boeing 747-238B	United Airlines
	N161US	Douglas DC-10-40	Northwest Airlines
	N162US	Douglas DC-10-40	Northwest Airlines
	N163AA	Douglas DC-10-30	American Airlines
	N163UA	Boeing 747-238B	United Airlines
	N164AA	Douglas DC-10-30	American Airlines
	N164UA	Boeing 747-238B	United Airlines
	N165UA	Boeing 747-238B	United Airlines
	N166AA	Douglas DC-10-10ER	American Airlines
	N171DN	Boeing 767-332ER	Delta Air Lines
	N171UA	Boeing 747-422	United Airlines *Spirit of Seattle II*
	N172DN	Boeing 767-332ER	Delta Air Lines
	N172UA	Boeing 747-422	United Airlines
	N173DN	Boeing 767-332ER	Delta Air Lines
	N173UA	Boeing 747-422	United Airlines
	N174DN	Boeing 767-332ER	Delta Air Lines
	N174UA	Boeing 747-422	United Airlines
	N175DN	Boeing 767-332ER	Delta Air Lines
	N175UA	Boeing 747-422	United Airlines
	N176DN	Boeing 767-332ER	Delta Air Lines
	N176UA	Boeing 747-422	United Airlines
	N177DN	Boeing 767-332ER	Delta Air Lines
	N177UA	Boeing 747-422	United Airlines
	N178DN	Boeing 767-332ER	Delta Air Lines
	N178UA	Boeing 747-422	United Airlines
	N179DN	Boeing 767-332ER	Delta Air Lines
	N179UA	Boeing 747-422	United Airlines
	N180DN	Boeing 767-332ER	Delta Air Lines
	N180UA	Boeing 747-422	United Airlines
	N181AT	L.1011-385 TriStar 100	American Trans Air
	N181DN	Boeing 767-332ER	Delta Air Lines
	N181UA	Boeing 747-422	United Airlines
	N182DN	Boeing 767´-332ER	Delta Air Lines
	N182UA	Boeing 747-422	United Airlines
	N183AT	L.1011-385 TriStar 1	American Trans Air
	N183DN	Boeing 767-332ER	Delta Air Lines
	N183UA	Boeing 747-422	United Airlines

Reg.	Type	Owner or Operator	Notes
N184DN	Boeing 767-332ER	Delta Air Lines	
N184UA	Boeing 747-422	United Airlines	
N185AT	L.1011-385 TriStar 50	American Trans Air	
N185DN	Boeing 767-332ER	Delta Air Lines	
N185UA	Boeing 747-422	United Airlines	
N186AT	L.1011-385 TriStar 50	American Trans Air	
N186DN	Boeing 767-332ER	Delta Air Lines	
N186UA	Boeing 747-422	United Airlines	
N187AT	L.1011-385 TriStar 50	American Trans Air	
N187DN	Boeing 767-332ER	Delta Air Lines	
N187UA	Boeing 747-422	United Airlines	
N188AT	L.1011-385 TriStar 50	American Trans Air	
N188DN	Boeing 767-332ER	Delta Air Lines	
N188UA	Boeing 747-422	United Airlines	
N189AT	L.1011-385 TriStar 50	American Trans Air	
N189DN	Boeing 767-332ER	Delta Air Lines	
N189UA	Boeing 747-422	United Airlines	
N190AT	L.1011-385 TriStar 50	American Trans Air	
N190DN	Boeing 767-332ER	Delta Air Lines	
N190UA	Boeing 747-422	United Airlines	
N191AT	L.1011-385 TriStar 50	American Trans Air	
N191DN	Boeing 767-332ER	Delta Air Lines	
N191UA	Boeing 747-422	United Airlines	
N192AT	L.1011-385 TriStar 50	American Trans Air	
N192UA	Boeing 747-422	United Airlines	
N193AT	L.1011-385 TriStar 50	American Trans Air	
N193UA	Boeing 747-422	United Airlines	
N194AT	L.1011-385 TriStar 100	American Trans Air	
N194UA	Boeing 747-422	United Airlines	
N195AT	L.1011-385 TriStar 150	American Trans Air	
N195UA	Boeing 747-422	United Airlines	
N196AT	L.1011-385 TriStar 50	American Trans Air	
N197AT	L.1011-385 TriStar 50	American Trans Air	
N202AE	Boeing 747-2B4B (SCD)	Middle East Airlines	
N202PH	Boeing 747-121	Tower Air	
N203AE	Boeing 747-2B4B (SCD)	Middle East Airlines	
N204AE	Boeing 747-2B4B (SCD)	Middle East Airlines	
N207AE	Boeing 747-211B	Philippine Airlines	
N208AE	Boeing 747-211B	Philippine Airlines	
N211JL	Boeing 747-246F	Japan Airlines	
N211NW	Douglas DC-10-30	Northwest Airlines	
N212JL	Boeing 747-346	Japan Airlines	
N213JL	Boeing 747-346	Japan Airlines	
N220NW	Douglas DC-10-30	Northwest Airlines	
N221NW	Douglas DC-10-30	Northwest Airlines	
N223NW	Douglas DC-10-30	Northwest Airlines	
N224NW	Douglas DC-10-30	Northwest Airlines	
N225NW	Douglas DC-10-30	Northwest Airlines	
N226NW	Douglas DC-10-30	Northwest Airlines	
N227NW	Douglas DC-10-30	Northwest Airlines	
N228NW	Douglas DC-10-30	Northwest Airlines	
N271WA	McD Douglas MD-11	World Airways	
N272WA	McD Douglas MD-11	World Airways	
N273WA	McD Douglas MD-11	World Airways	
N274WA	McD Douglas MD-11F	World Airways	
N275WA	McD Douglas MD-11CF	World Airways	
N276WA	McD Douglas MD-11CF	World Airways	
N277WA	McD Douglas MD-11	World Airways	
N280WA	McD Douglas MD-11	World Airways/Ghana Airways	
N301FE	Douglas DC-10-30AF	Federal Express	
N301UP	Boeing 767-34AFER	United Parcel Service	
N302FE	Douglas DC-10-30AF	Federal Express	
N302UP	Boeing 767-34AFER	United Parcel Service	
N303EA	L.1011-385 TriStar 1	Rich International Airways	
N303FE	Douglas DC-10-30AF	Federal Express	
N303UP	Boeing 767-34AFER	United Parcel Service	
N303TW	Boeing 747-257B	—	
N304EA	L.1011-385 TriStar 1	Rich International Airways	
N304FE	Douglas DC-10-30AF	Federal Express	
N304UP	Boeing 767-34AFER	United Parcel Service	
N305FE	Douglas DC-10-30AF	Federal Express *John David*	
N305TW	Boeing 747-284B	Trans World Airlines	
N305UP	Boeing 767-34AFER	United Parcel Service	
N306FE	Douglas DC-10-30AF	Federal Express *John Peter Jr*	

Notes	Reg.	Type	Owner or Operator
	N306UP	Boeing 767-34AFER	United Parcel Service
	N307FE	Douglas DC-10-30AF	Federal Express *Erin Lee*
	N307UP	Boeing 767-34AFER	United Parcel Service
	N308FE	Douglas DC-10-30AF	Federal Express *Ann*
	N308UP	Boeing 767-34AFER	United Parcel Service
	N309FE	Douglas DC-10-30AF	Federal Express *Stacey*
	N300UP	Boeing 767-34AFER	United Parcel Service
	N310FE	Douglas DC-10-30AF	Federal Express *John Shelby*
	N310UP	Boeing 767-34AFER	United Parcel Service
	N311FE	Douglas DC-10-30AF	Federal Express *Abe*
	N312AA	Boeing 767-223ER	American Airlines
	N312FE	Douglas DC-10-30AF	Federal Express *Angela*
	N313AA	Boeing 767-223ER	American Airlines
	N313EA	L.1011-385 TriStar 1	Rich International Airways
	N313FE	Douglas DC-10-30AF	Federal Express *Brandon Parks*
	N314FE	Douglas DC-10-30AF	Federal Express *Caitlin-Ann*
	N315AA	Boeing 767-223ER	American Airlines
	N315FE	Douglas DC-10-30AF	Federal Express *Kevin*
	N316AA	Boeing 767-223ER	American Airlines
	N316FE	Douglas DC-10-30AF	Federal Express *Brandon*
	N317AA	Boeing 767-223ER	American Airlines
	N317FE	Douglas DC-10-30CF	Federal Express
	N318FE	Douglas DC-10-30CF	Federal Express
	N319AA	Boeing 767-223ER	American Airlines
	N319EA	L.1011 TriStar 1	Rich International Airways
	N319FE	Douglas DC-10-30CF	Federal Express
	N320AA	Boeing 767-223ER	American Airlines
	N320FE	Douglas DC-10-30CF	Federal Express
	N321AA	Boeing 767-223ER	American Airlines
	N321FE	Douglas DC-10-30CF	Federal Express
	N322AA	Boeing 767-223ER	American Airlines
	N322FE	Douglas DC-10-30CF	Federal Express *King Frank*
	N323AA	Boeing 767-223ER	American Airlines
	N324AA	Boeing 767-223ER	American Airlines
	N325AA	Boeing 767-223ER	American Airlines
	N327AA	Boeing 767-223ER	American Airlines
	N328AA	Boeing 767-223ER	American Airlines
	N329AA	Boeing 767-223ER	American Airlines
	N330AA	Boeing 767-223ER	American Airlines
	N332AA	Boeing 767-223ER	American Airlines
	N334AA	Boeing 767-223ER	American Airlines
	N335AA	Boeing 767-223ER	American Airlines
	N336AA	Boeing 767-223ER	American Airlines
	N338AA	Boeing 767-223ER	American Airlines
	N339AA	Boeing 767-223ER	American Airlines
	N341AA	Boeing 767-323ER	American Airlines
	N341HA	L.188F Electra	Channel Express (Air Services) Ltd
	N343HA	L.188AF Electra	Channel Express (Air Services) Ltd
	N344HA	L.188AF Electra	Channel Express (Air Services) Ltd
	N345JW	Douglas DC-8-63AF	Arrow Air
	N351AA	Boeing 767-323ER	American Airlines
	N352AA	Boeing 767-323ER	American Airlines
	N353AA	Boeing 767-323ER	American Airlines
	N354AA	Boeing 767-323ER	American Airlines
	N355AA	Boeing 767-323ER	American Airlines
	N356Q	L.188F Electra	Hunting Cargo Airlines Ltd
	N357AA	Boeing 767-323ER	American Airlines
	N358AA	Boeing 767-323ER	American Airlines
	N359AA	Boeing 767-323ER	American Airlines
	N360AA	Boeing 767-323ER	American Airlines
	N360Q	L.188F Electra	Hunting Cargo Airlines Ltd
	N361AA	Boeing 767-323ER	American Airlines
	N362AA	Boeing 767-323ER	American Airlines
	N363AA	Boeing 767-323ER	American Airlines
	N366AA	Boeing 767-323ER	American Airlines
	N368AA	Boeing 767-323ER	American Airlines
	N369AA	Boeing 767-323ER	American Airlines
	N370AA	Boeing 767-323ER	American Airlines
	N371AA	Boeing 767-323ER	American Airlines
	N372AA	Boeing 767-323ER	American Airlines
	N373AA	Boeing 767-323ER	American Airlines
	N374AA	Boeing 767-323ER	American Airlines
	N376AN	Boeing 767-323ER	American Airlines
	N377AN	Boeing 767-323ER	American Airlines

Reg.	Type	Owner or Operator	Notes
N378AN	Boeing 767-323ER	American Airlines	
N379AA	Boeing 767-323ER	American Airlines	
N380AN	Boeing 767-323ER	American Airlines	
N381AN	Boeing 767-323ER	American Airlines	
N382AN	Boeing 767-323ER	American Airlines	
N383AN	Boeing 767-323ER	American Airlines	
N384AA	Boeing 767-323ER	American Airlines	
N385AM	Boeing 767-323ER	American Airlines	
N386AA	Boeing 767-323ER	American Airlines	
N387AM	Boeing 767-323ER	American Airlines	
N388AA	Boeing 767-323ER	American Airlines	
N389AA	Boeing 767-323ER	American Airlines	
N390AA	Boeing 767-323ER	American Airlines	
N391AA	Boeing 767-323ER	American Airlines	
N403EV	Boeing 747-45E	EVA Airways	
N405EV	Boeing 747-45E	EVA Airways	
N406EV	Boeing 747-45E	EVA Airways	
N407EV	Boeing 747-45E	EVA Airways	
N408EV	Boeing 747-45E	EVA Airways	
N409EV	Boeing 747-45E	EVA Airways	
N417DG	Douglas DC-10-30	Aeromexico Ciudad de Mexico	
N441J	Douglas DC-8-63CF	Arrow Air	
N470EV	Boeing 747-273C	Evergreen International Airlines	
N471EV	Boeing 747-273C	Evergreen International Airlines	
N472EV	Boeing 747-131	Evergreen International Airlines	
N473EV	Boeing 747-121F (SCD)	Evergreen International Airlines	
N474EV	Boeing 747-121	Evergreen International Airlines	
N479EV	Boeing 747-132 (SCD)	Evergreen International Airlines	
N481EV	Boeing 747-132 (SCD)	Evergreen International Airlines	
N482EV	Boeing 747-212B (SCD)	Evergreen International Airlines	
N485EV	Boeing 747-212B (SCD)	Evergreen International Airlines	
N512AT	Boeing 757-225	American Trans Air	
N514AT	Boeing 757-23N	American Trans Air	
N515AT	Boeing 757-23N	American Trans Air	
N516AT	Boeing 757-23N	American Trans Air	
N522SJ	L.100-20 Hercules	Southern Air Transport	
N524MD	Douglas DC-10-30	Aeroflot	
N601EV	Boeing 767-3T7ER	EVA Airways	
N601FE	McD Douglas MD-11F	Federal Express Christy	
N601TW	Boeing 767-231ER	Trans World Airlines	
N601US	Boeing 747-151	Northwest Airlines	
N602AA	Boeing 747SP-31	American Airlines	
N602EV	Boeing 767-3T7ER	EVA Airways	
N602FE	McDouglas MD-11F	Federal Express Malcolm Baldrige	
N602FF	Boeing 747-124	Tower Air	
N602TW	Boeing 767-231ER	Trans World Airlines	
N602UA	Boeing 767-222ER	United Airlines	
N603FE	McD Douglas MD-11F	Federal Express Elizabeth	
N603FF	Boeing 747-130	Tower Air Suzie	
N603TW	Boeing 767-231ER	Trans World Airlines	
N603US	Boeing 747-151	Northwest Airlines	
N604FE	McD Douglas MD-11F	Federal Express Hollis	
N604FF	Boeing 747-121	Tower Air	
N605FE	McD Douglas MD-11F	Federal Express April Star	
N605FF	Boeing 747-136	Tower Air	
N605TW	Boesing 767-231ER	Trans World Airlines	
N605UA	Boeing 767-222ER	United Airlines	
N606FE	McD Douglas MD-11F	Federal Express Louis III	
N606FF	Boeing 747-136	Tower Air	
N606TW	Boeing 767-231ER	Trans World Airlines	
N606UA	Boeing 767-222ER	United Airlines City of Chicago	
N607FE	McD Douglas MD-11F	Federal Express Dana Elena	
N607PE	Boeing 747-238B (022)	Tower Air	
N607TW	Boeing 767-231ER	Trans World Airlines	
N607UA	Boeing 767-222ER	United Airlines City of Denver	
N608FE	McD Douglas MD-11F	Federal Express Scott	
N608FF	Boeing 747-131	Tower Air	
N608TW	Boeing 767-231ER	Trans World Airlines	
N608UA	Boeing 767-222ER	United Airlines	
N608US	Boeing 747-151	Northwest Airlines	
N609FE	McD Douglas MD-11F	Federal Express	
N609FF	Boeing 747-121	Tower Air	
N609TW	Boeing 767-231ER	Trans World Airlines	
N609UA	Boeing 767-222ER	United Airlines	

Notes	Reg.	Type	Owner or Operator
	N610FE	McD Douglas MD-11F	Federal Express
	N610FF	Boeing 747-282B	Tower Air
	N610TW	Boeing 767-231ER	Trans World Airlines
	N610UA	Boeing 767-222ER	United Airlines
	N611FE	McD Douglas MD-11F	Federal Express
	N611FF	Boeing 747-282B	Tower Air
	N611UA	Boeing 767-222ER	United Airlines
	N611US	Boeing 747-251B	Northwest Airlines
	N612FE	McD Douglas MD-11F	Federal Express
	N612US	Boeing 747-251B	Northwest Airlines
	N613US	Boeing 747-251B	Northwest Airlines
	N614FE	McD Douglas MD-11F	Federal Express
	N614FF	Boeing 747-238B	Tower Air
	N614US	Boeing 747-251B	Northwest Airlines
	N615FF	Boeing 747-121F	Tower Air Cargo
	N615US	Boeing 747-251B	Northwest Airlines
	N616FE	McD Douglas MD-11F	Federal Express
	N616FF	Boeing 747-212B	Tower Air
	N616US	Boeing 747-251F (SCD)	Northwest Airlines
	N617FE	McD Douglas MD-11F	Federal Express
	N617FF	Boeing 747-121F	Tower Air Cargo
	N617US	Boeing 747-251F (SCD)	Northwest Airlines
	N618FF	Boeing 747-243B	Tower Air
	N618US	Boeing 747-251F (SCD)	Northwest Airlines
	N619US	Boeing 747-251F (SCD)	Northwest Airlines
	N620FE	Boeing 747-133	Federal Express
	N622US	Boeing 747-251B	Northwest Airlines
	N623US	Boeing 747-251B	Northwest Airlines
	N624US	Boeing 747-251B	Northwest Airlines
	N625US	Boeing 747-251B	Northwest Airlines
	N626US	Boeing 747-251B	Northwest Airlines
	N627US	Boeing 747-251B	Northwest Airlines
	N628US	Boeing 747-251B	Northwest Airlines
	N629US	Boeing 747-251F (SCD)	Northwest Airlines
	N630SJ	Boeing 747-124	Polar Air Cargo
	N630US	Boeing 747-2J9F	Northwest Airlines
	N631US	Boeing 747-251B	Northwest Airlines
	N632US	Boeing 747-251B	Northwest Airlines
	N633US	Boeing 747-227B	Northwest Airlines
	N634US	Boeing 747-227B	Northwest Airlines
	N635US	Boeing 747-227B	Northwest Airlines
	N636FE	Boeing 747-245F (SCD)	Federal Express
	N636US	Boeing 747-251B	Northwest Airlines
	N637US	Boeing 747-251B	Northwest Airlines
	N638FE	Boeing 747-245F (SCD)	Federal Express
	N638US	Boeing 747-251B	Northwest Airlines
	N639FE	Boeing 747-2R7F (SCD)	Federal Express
	N639US	Boeing 747-251F (SCD)	Northwest Airlines
	N640FE	Boeing 747-245F (SCD)	Federal Express
	N640US	Boeing 747-251F (SCD)	Northwest Airlines
	N641FE	Boeing 747-245F (SCD)	Federal Express
	N641UA	Boeing 767-322ER	United Airlines
	N642UA	Boeing 767-322ER	United Airlines
	N643UA	Boeing 767-322ER	United Airlines
	N644UA	Boeing 767-322ER	United Airlines
	N645UA	Boeing 767-322ER	United Airlines
	N646UA	Boeing 767-322ER	United Airlines
	N647UA	Boeing 767-322ER	United Airlines
	N648UA	Boeing 767-322ER	United Airlines
	N649UA	Boeing 767-322ER	United Airlines
	N650TW	Boeing 767-205ER	Trans World Airlines
	N650UA	Boeing 767-322ER	United Airlines
	N651TW	Boeing 767-205ER	Trans World Airlines
	N651UA	Boeing 767-322ER	United Airlines
	N652UA	Boeing 767-322ER	United Airlines
	N653UA	Boeing 767-322ER	United Airlines
	N653US	Boeing 767-2B7ER	USAir/British Airways
	N654UA	Boeing 767-322ER	United Airlines
	N654US	Boeing 767-2B7ER	USAir/British Airways
	N655UA	Boeing 767-322ER	United Airlines
	N655US	Boeing 767-2B7ER	USAir/British Airways
	N656UA	Boeing 767-322ER	United Airlines
	N657UA	Boeing 767-322ER	United Airlines
	N658UA	Boeing 767-322ER	United Airlines

Reg.	Type	Owner or Operator	Notes
N659UA	Boeing 767-322ER	United Airlines	
N660UA	Boeing 767-322ER	United Airlines	
N661AV	Douglas DC-8-63AF	Arrow Air	
N661UA	Boeing 767-322ER	United Airlines	
N661US	Boeing 747-451	Northwest Airlines	
N662UA	Boeing 767-322ER	United Airlines	
N662US	Boeing 747-451	Northwest Airlines	
N663UA	Boeing 767-322ER	United Airlines	
N663US	Boeing 747-451	Northwest Airlines	
N664US	Boeing 747-451	Northwest Airlines	
N665US	Boeing 747-451	Northwest Airlines	
N666US	Boeing 747-451	Northwest Airlines	
N667US	Boeing 747-451	Northwest Airlines	
N668US	Boeing 747-451	Northwest Airlines	
N669US	Boeing 747-451	Northwest Airlines	
N671UP	Boeing 747-123F (SCD)	United Parcel Service	
N672UP	Boeing 747-123F (SCD)	United Parcel Service	
N672US	Boeing 747-451	Northwest Airlines	
N673UP	Boeing 747-123F (SCD)	United Parcel Service	
N674UP	Boeing 747-123F (SCD)	United Parcel Service	
N675UP	Boeing 747-123F (SCD)	United Parcel Service	
N676UP	Boeing 747-123F (SCD)	United Parcel Service	
N677UP	Boeing 747-123F (SCD)	United Parcel Service	
N681UP	Boeing 747-121F (SCD)	United Parcel Service	
N682UP	Boeing 747-121F (SCD)	United Parcel Service	
N683UP	Boeing 747-121F (SCD)	United Parcel Service	
N687AA	Boeing 757-223ET	American Airlines	
N688AA	Boeing 757-223ET	American Airlines	
N689AA	Boeing 757-223ET	American Airlines	
N690AA	Boeing 757-223ET	American Airlines	
N691AA	Boeing 757-223ET	American Airlines	
N692AA	Boeing 757-223ET	American Airlines	
N701CK	Boeing 747-146F (SCD)	American International Airways	
N702CK	Boeing 747-146F (SCD)	American International Airways	
N703CK	Boeing 747-146F (SCD)	American International Airways	
N704CK	Boeing 747-146F (SCD)	American International Airways	
N706CK	Boeing 747-238B	American International Airways	
N707CK	Boeing 747-269B (SCD)	American International Airways	
N708CK	Boeing 747-269B (SCD)	American International Airways	
N724DA	L.1011-385 TriStar 200	Delta Air Lines	
N735PL	Douglas DC-8-62AF	Air Transport International	
N735SJ	Boeing 747-121F (SCD)	Polar Air Cargo	
N736DY	L.1011-385 TriStar 250	Delta Air Lines	
N737D	L.1011-385 TriStar 250	Delta Air Lines	
N740DA	L.1011-385 TriStar 250	Delta Air Lines	
N740SJ	Boeing 747-246F	Southern Air Transport	
N741DA	L.1011-385 TriStar 250	Delta Air Lines	
N741PR	Boeing 747-2F6B	Philippine Airlines	
N741SJ	Boeing 747-246B	Southern Air Transport	
N742PR	Boeing 747-2F6B	Philippine Airlines	
N742SJ	Boeing 747-249F (SCD)	Southern Air Transport	
N743PR	Boeing 747-2F6B	Philippine Airlines	
N744PR	Boeing 747-2F6B	Philippine Airlines	
N750AT	Boeing 757-212	American Trans Air	
N751AT	Boeing 757-212	American Trans Air	
N751DA	L.1011-385 TriStar 500	Delta Air Lines	
N752AT	Boeing 757-212	American Trans Air	
N752DA	L.1011-385 TriStar 500	Delta Air Lines	
N753DA	L.1011-385 TriStar 500	Delta Air Lines	
N754AT	Boeing 757-2Q8	American Trans Air	
N754DL	L.1011-385 TriStar 500	Delta Air Lines	
N755AT	Boeing 757-2Q8	American Trans Air	
N755DL	L.1011-385 TriStar 500	Delta Air Lines	
N756AT	Boeing 757-2Q8	American Trans Air	
N756DR	L.1011-385 TriStar 500	Delta Air Lines	
N757AT	Boeing 757-212	American Trans Air	
N759DA	L.1011-385 TriStar 500	Delta Air Lines	
N760DH	L.1011-385 TriStar 500	Delta Air Lines	
N761DA	L.1011-385 TriStar 500	Delta Air Lines	
N762DA	L.1011-385 TriStar 500	Delta Air Lines	
N763DL	L.1011-385 TriStar 500	Delta Air Lines	
N764BE	L.1011-385 TriStar 50	Rich International Airways	
N764DA	L.1011-385 TriStar 500	Delta Air Lines	
N765DA	L.1011-385 TriStar 500	Delta Air Lines	

Notes	Reg.	Type	Owner or Operator
	N766BE	L.1011-385 TriStar 50	Rich International Airways
	N766DA	L.1011-385 TriStar 500	Delta Air Lines
	N766UA	Boeing 777-222	United Airlines
	N767DA	L.1011-385 TriStar 500	Delta Air Lines
	N767UA	Boeing 777-222	United Airlines
	N768DL	L.1011-385 TriStar 500	Delta Air Lines
	N768UA	Boeing 777-222	United Airlines
	N769DL	L.1011-385 TriStar 500	Delta Air Lines
	N769UA	Boeing 777-222	United Airlines
	N770UA	Boeing 777-222	United Airlines
	N771UA	Boeing 777-222	United Airlines
	N772CA	Douglas DC-8-62	Rich International Airways
	N772UA	Boeing 777-222	United Airlines
	N773UA	Boeing 777-222	United Airlines
	N774UA	Boeing 777-222	United Airlines
	N775UA	Boeing 777-222	United Airlines
	N776UA	Boeing 777-222	United Airlines
	N777UA	Boeing 777-222	United Airlines
	N778UA	Boeing 777-222	United Airlines
	N784AL	Douglas DC-8-63CF	Arrow Air
	N791AL	Douglas DC-8-62AF	Arrow Air
	N791FT	Douglas DC-8-73AF	Emery Worldwide
	N792FT	Douglas DC-8-73AF	Emery Worldwide
	N795FT	Douglas DC-8-73AF	Emery Worldwide
	N796AL	Douglas DC-8-63AF	Emery Worldwide
	N796FT	Douglas DC-8-73AF	Emery Worldwide
	N797AL	Douglas DC-8-63AF	Emery Worldwide
	N801CK	Douglas DC-8-55F	American International Airways
	N801DE	McD Douglas MD-11	Delta Air Lines
	N801DH	Douglas DC-8-73AF	DHL Airlines
	N801UP	Douglas DC-8-73AF	United Parcel Service
	N802BN	Douglas DC-8-62AF	Arrow Air
	N802CK	Douglas DC-8-54F	American International Airways
	N802DE	McD Douglas MD-11	Delta Air Lines
	N802DH	Douglas DC-8-73AF	DHL Airlines
	N802UP	Douglas DC-8-73AF	United Parcel Service
	N803DE	McD Douglas MD-11	Delta Air Lines
	N803DH	Douglas DC-8-73AF	DHL Airlines
	N803UP	Douglas DC-8-63AF	United Parcel Service
	N804CK	Douglas DC-8-51F	American International Airways
	N804DE	McD Douglas MD-11	Delta Air Lines
	N804DH	Douglas DC-8-73AF	DHL Airlines
	N804UP	Douglas DC-8-51	United Parcel Service
	N805CK	Douglas DC-8-51F	American International Airways
	N805DE	McD Douglas MD-11	Delta Air Lines
	N805DH	Douglas DC-8-73AF	DHL Airlines
	N805UP	Douglas DC-8-73CF	United Parcel Service
	N806CK	Douglas DC-8-54F	American International Airways
	N806DE	McD Douglas MD-11	Delta Air Lines
	N806UP	Douglas DC-8-73AF	United Parcel Service
	N807CK	Douglas DC-8-55F	American International Airways
	N807DE	McD Douglas MD-11	Delta Air Lines
	N807UP	Douglas DC-8-73AF	United Parcel Service
	N808CK	Douglas DC-8-55F	American International Airways
	N808DE	McD Douglas MD-11	Delta Air Lines
	N808UP	Douglas DC-8-73AF	United Parcel Service
	N809CK	Douglas DC-8-73AF	American International Airways
	N809DE	McD Douglas MD-11	Delta Air Lines
	N809UP	Douglas DC-8-73AF	United Parcel Service
	N810CK	Douglas DC-8-52F	American International Airways
	N810DE	McD Douglas MD-11	Delta Air Lines
	N810UP	Douglas DC-8-71AF	United Parcel Service
	N811CK	Douglas DC-8-63AF	American International Airways
	N811DE	McD Douglas MD-11	Delta Air Lines
	N811UP	Douglas DC-8-73AF	United Parcel Service
	N812CK	Douglas DC-8-61AF	American International Airways
	N812DE	McD Douglas MD-11	Delta Air Lines
	N812UP	Douglas DC-8-73AF	United Parcel Service
	N813CK	Douglas DC-8-61AF	American International Airways
	N813DE	McD Douglas MD-11	Delta Air Lines
	N813UP	Douglas DC-8-73AF	United Parcel Service
	N814DE	McD Douglas MD-11	Delta Air Lines
	N814UP	Douglas DC-8-73AF	United Parcel Service

Reg.	Type	Owner or Operator	Notes
N815CK	Douglas DC-8-61F	American International Airways	
N815DE	McD Douglas MD-11	Delta Air Lines	
N815EV	Douglas DC-8-73CF	Evergreen International Airlines	
N816CK	Douglas DC-8-61F	American International Airways	
N817CK	Douglas DC-8-61F	American International Airways	
N817EV	Douglas DC-8-62AF	Evergreen International Airlines	
N818UP	Douglas DC-8-73AF	United Parcel Service	
N819UP	Douglas DC-8-73AF	United Parcel Service	
N820BX	Douglas DC-8-71AF	Burlington Express	
N821BX	Douglas DC-8-71AF	Burlington Express	
N822BX	Douglas DC-8-71AF	Burlington Express	
N824BX	Douglas DC-8-71AF	Burlington Express	
N831FT	Boeing 747-121F (SCD)	Polar Air Cargo	
N832FT	Boeing 747-121F (SCD)	Polar Air Cargo	
N836UP	Douglas DC-8-73AF	United Parcel Service	
N840SJ	Boeing 747-246F (SCD)	Southern Air Transport	
N840UP	Douglas DC-8-73AF	United Parcel Service	
N845FT	Boeing 747-122	Polar Air Cargo	
N850FT	Boeing 747-122	Polar Air Cargo	
N851UP	Douglas DC-8-73AF	United Parcel Service	
N852FT	Boeing 747-122	Polar Air Cargo	
N852UP	Douglas DC-8-73AF	United Parcel Service	
N859FT	Boeing 747-123	Polar Air Cargo	
N863BX	Boeing 707-321C	Burlington Express	
N865F	Douglas DC-8-63AF	Emery Worldwide	
N866UP	Douglas DC-8-73AF	United Parcel Service	
N867BX	Douglas DC-8-63AF	Burlington Express	
N867UP	Douglas DC-8-73AF	United Parcel Service	
N868BX	Douglas DC-8-63AF	Burlington Express	
N868UP	Douglas DC-8-73AF	United Parcel Service	
N869BX	Douglas DC-8-63AF	Burlington Express	
N870BX	Doulgas DC-8-63AF	Burlington Express	
N870SJ	Douglas DC-8-71AF	Southern Air Transport	
N870TV	Douglas DC-8-73AF	Emery Worldwide	
N872SJ	Douglas DC-8-71AF	Southern Air Transport	
N873SJ	Douglas DC-8-73AF	Southern Air Transport	
N874SJ	Douglas DC-8-73AF	Southern Air Transport	
N874UP	Douglas DC-8-73AF	United Parcel Service	
N875SJ	Douglas DC-8-71AF	Southern Air Transport	
N880UP	Douglas DC-8-73AF	United Parcel Service	
N894UP	Douglas DC-8-73AF	United Parcel Service	
N901SJ	L.100-30 Hercules	Southern Air Transport	
N905SJ	L.100-30 Hercules	Southern Air Transport	
N906R	Douglas DC-8-63CF	Air Transport International	
N906SJ	L.100-30 Hercules	Southern Air Transport	
N907SJ	L.100-30 Hercules	Southern Air Transport	
N908SJ	L.100-30 Hercules	Southern Air Transport	
N909SJ	L.100-30 Hercules	Southern Air Transport	
N910SJ	L.100-30 Hercules	Southern Air Transport	
N912SJ	L.100-30 Hercules	Southern Air Transport	
N916SJ	L.100-30 Hercules	Southern Air Transport	
N918SJ	L.100-30 Hercules	Southern Air Transport	
N919SJ	L.100-30 Hercules	Southern Air Transport	
N920SJ	L.100-30 Hercules	Southern Air Transport	
N921R	Douglas DC-8-63AF	Emery Worldwide	
N921SJ	L.100-30 Hercules	Southern Air Transport	
N923SJ	L.100-30 Hercules	Southern Air Transport	
N929R	Douglas DC-8-63AF	Emery Worldwide	
N950R	Douglas DC-8-63AF	Emery Worldwide	
N951R	Douglas DC-8-63AF	Emery Worldwide	
N952R	Douglas DC-8-63AF	Emery Worldwide	
N957R	Douglas DC-8-63AF	Emery Worldwide	
N959R	Douglas DC-8-63AF	Emery Worldwide	
N961R	Douglas DC-8-73AF	Emery Worldwide	
N964R	Douglas DC-8-63AF	Emery Worldwide	
N990CF	Douglas DC-8-62AF	Emery Worldwide	
N993CF	Douglas DC-8-62AF	Emery Worldwide	
N994CF	Douglas DC-8-62AF	Emery Worldwide	
N995CF	Douglas DC-8-62AF	Emery Worldwide	
N996CF	Douglas DC-8-62AF	Emery Worldwide	
N997CF	Douglas DC-8-62AF	Emery Worldwide	
N998CF	Douglas DC-8-62AF	Emery Worldwide	
N1738D	L.1011-385 TriStar 250	Delta Air Lines	

Notes	Reg.	Type	Owner or Operator
	N1739D	L.1011-385 TriStar 250	Delta Air Lines
	N1750B	McD Douglas MD-11 (1AA)	American Airlines
	N1751A	McD Douglas MD-11 (1AB)	American Airlines
	N1752K	McD Douglas MD-11 (1AC)	American Airlines
	N1753	McD Douglas MD-11 (1AD)	American Airlines
	N1754	McD Douglas MD-11 (1AE)	American Airlines
	N1755	McD Douglas MD-11 (1AΓ)	American Airlines
	N1756	McD Douglas MD-11 (1AG)	American Airlines
	N1757A	McD Douglas MD-11 (1AH)	American Airlines
	N1758B	McD Douglas MD-11 (1AJ)	American Airlines
	N1759	McD Douglas MD-11 (1AK)	American Airlines
	N1760A	McD Douglas MD-11 (1AM)	American Airlines
	N1761R	McD Douglas MD-11 (1AN)	American Airlines
	N1762B	McD Douglas MD-11 (1AP)	American Airlines
	N1763	McD Douglas MD-11 (1AR)	American Airlines
	N1764B	McD Douglas MD-11 (1AS)	American Airlines
	N1765B	McD Douglas MD-11 (1AT)	American Airlines
	N1766A	McD Douglas MD-11 (1AU)	American Airlines
	N1767A	McD Douglas MD-11 (1AV)	American Airlines
	N1768D	McD Douglas MD-11 (1AL)	American Airlines
	N1803	Douglas DC-8-62AF	Arrow Air
	N1804	Douglas DC-8-62AF	Arrow Air
	N1805	Douglas DC-8-62	Rich International Airways
	N1808E	Douglas DC-8-62AF	Arrow Air
	N2674U	Douglas DC-8-73AF	Emery Worldwide
	N3140D	L.1011-385 TriStar 500 (598)	B.W.I.A. *Sunjet St. Lucia*
	N4508H	Boeing 747SP-09	China Airlines
	N4522V	Boeing 747SP-09	China Airlines
	N4703U	Boeing 747-122F	Polar Air Cargo
	N4714U	Boeing 747-122	United Airlines
	N4716U	Boeing 747-122	United Airlines
	N4717U	Boeing 747-122	United Airlines *Edward E. Carlson*
	N4718U	Boeing 747-122	United Airlines *Thomas F. Gleed*
	N4719U	Boeing 747-122	United Airlines *Friendship Japan*
	N4720U	Boeing 747-122	United Airlines
	N4723U	Boeing 747-122	United Airlines *William A. Patterson*
	N4724U	Boeing 747-122	United Airlines
	N4727U	Boeing 747-122	United Airlines *Robert E. Johnson*
	N4728U	Boeing 747-122	United Airlines *Gardner Cowles*
	N4729U	Boeing 747-122	United Airlines
	N4732U	Boeing 747-122	United Airlines
	N4735U	Boeing 747-122	United Airlines
	N4935C	Douglas DC-8-63	Rich International Airways
	N7036T	L.1011-385 TriStar 100	Trans World Airlines
	N7375A	Boeing 767-323ER	American Airlines
	N8076U	Douglas DC-8-71AF	Emery Worldwide
	N8084U	Douglas DC-8-71AF	Emery Worldwide
	N8085U	Douglas DC-8-71AF	Emery Worldwide
	N8086U	Douglas DC-8-71AF	Emery Worldwide
	N8087U	Douglas DC-8-71AF	Emery Worldwide
	N8089U	Douglas DC-8-71AF	Southern Air Transport
	N8097U	Douglas DC-8-71AF	Southern Air Transport
	N8228P	Douglas DC-10-30	Aeromexico *Castillo de Chapultepec*
	N8875Z	Boeing 727-225	Delta Air Lines
	N8879Z	Boeing 727-225	Delta Air Lines
	N8889Z	Boeing 727-225	Delta Air Lines
	N8890Z	Boeing 727-225	Delta Air Lines
	N8891Z	Boeing 727-225	Delta Air Lines
	N8968U	Douglas DC-8-62AF	Arrow Air
	N12061	Douglas DC-10-30	Continental Airlines *Richard M. Adams*
	N12064	Douglas DC-10-30	Continental Airlines
	N12114	Boeing 757-224	Continental Airlines
	N13066	Douglas DC-10-30	Continental Airlines
	N13067	Douglas DC-10-30	Continental Airlines
	N13110	Boeing 757-224	Continental Airlines
	N14062	Douglas DC-10-30	Continental Airlines
	N14063	Douglas DC-10-30	Continental Airlines
	N14115	Boeing 757-224	Continental Airlines
	N15069	Douglas DC-10-30ER	Continental Airlines
	N17010	Boeing 747-143	Continental Airlines
	N17011	Boeing 747-143	Continental Airlines
	N17025	Boeing 747-238B	Continental Airlines
	N17104	Boeing 757-224	Continental Airlines

Reg.	Type	Owner or Operator	Notes
N17105	Boeing 757-224	Continental Airlines	
N19072	Douglas DC-10-30	Continental Airlines	
N31019	L.1011-385 TriStar 50	Trans World Airlines	
N31023	L.1011-385 TriStar 50	Trans World Airlines	
N31029	L.1011-385 TriStar 100	Trans World Airlines	
N31030	L.1011-385 TriStar 100	Trans World Airlines	
N31031	L.1011-385 TriStar 100	Trans World Airlines	
N33021	Boeing 747-243B	Continental Airlines	
N33103	Boeing 757-224	Continental Airlines	
N39356	Boeing 767-323ER	American Airlines	
N39364	Boeing 767-323ER	American Airlines	
N39365	Boeing 767-323ER	American Airlines	
N39367	Boeing 767-323ER	American Airlines	
N41068	Douglas DC-10-30	Continental Airlines	
N42086	Douglas DC-8-62AF	Arrow Air	
N53110	Boeing 747-131	Trans World Airlines	
N53116	Boeing 747-131	Trans World Airlines	
N54325	Boeing 727-231	Trans World Airlines	
N68060	Douglas DC-10-30	Continental Airlines *Robert F. Six*	
N68065	Douglas DC-10-30	Continental Airlines *Robert P. Gallaway*	
N76073	Douglas DC-10-30	Continental Airlines	
N78019	Boeing 747-230B	Continental Airlines	
N81027	L.1011-385 TriStar 50	Trans World Airlines *(stored)*	
N83071	Douglas DC-10-30ER	Continental Airlines	
N87070	Douglas DC-10-30ER	Continental Airlines	
N93104	Boeing 747-131	Trans World Airlines	
N93105	Boeing 747-131	Trans World Airlines	
N93107	Boeing 747-131	Trans World Airlines	
N93108	Boeing 747-131	Trans World Airlines	
N93109	Boeing 747-131	Trans World Airlines	
N93117	Boeing 747-131	Trans World Airlines *(stored)*	
N93119	Boeing 747-131	Trans World Airlines	

OD (Lebanon)

OD-AFD	Boeing 707-3B4C	Middle East Airlines
OD-AFE	Boeing 707-3B4C	Middle East Airlines
OD-AGD	Boeing 707-323C	TMA of Lebanon
OD-AGO	Boeing 707-321C	TMA of Lebanon
OD-AGP	Boeing 707-321C	TMA of Lebanon
OD-AGS	Boeing 707-331C	TMA of Lebanon
OD-AGU	Boeing 707-347C	Middle East Airlines
OD-AGV	Boeing 707-347C	Middle East Airlines
OD-AGX	Boeing 707-327C	TMA of Lebanon
OD-AGY	Boeing 707-327C	TMA of Lebanon
OD-AHC	Boeing 707-323C	Middle East Airlines
OD-AHD	Boeing 707-323C	Middle East Airlines
OD-AHE	Boeing 707-323C	Middle East Airlines
OD-AHF	Boeing 707-323B	Middle East Airlines

Note: MEA also uses the 747s N202AE, N203AE and N204AE when not on lease, two Airbus A.310s leased from KLM as PH-AGE and PH-AGF and two A.310-304s registered F-OHLH and F-OHLI.

OE (Austria)

OE-ILF	Boeing 737-3Z9	Lauda Air *Bob Marley*
OE-ILG	Boeing 737-3Z9	Lauda Air *John Lennon*
OE-LAA	Airbus A.310-324	Austrian Airlines *New York*
OE-LAB	Airbus A.310-324	Austrian Airlines *Tokyo*
OE-LAC	Airbus A.310-324	Austrian Airlines *Paris*
OE-LAD	Airbus A.310-325	Austrian Airlines *Chicago*
OE-LAG	Airbus A.340-212	Austrian Airlines *Europe*
OE-LAH	Airbus A.340-212	Austrian Airlines *Asia*
OF-I AS	Boeing 767-33AER	Lauda Air *Ayrton Senna*
OE-LAT	Boeing 767-31AER	Lauda Air
OE-LAU	Boeing 767-3Z9ER	Lauda Air *Johann Strauss*
OE-LAW	Boeing 767-3Z9ER	Lauda Air *Franz Schubert*
OE-LAX	Boeing 767-3Z9ER	Lauda Air *James Dean*

Notes	Reg.	Type	Owner or Operator
	OE-LBA	Airbus A.321-111	Austrian Airlines
	OE-LBB	Airbus A.321-111	Austrian Airlines
	OE-LBC	Airbus A.321-111	Austrian Airlines
	OE-LBD	Airbus A.321-111	Austrian Airlines
	OE-LBE	Airbus A.321-111	Austrian Airlines
	OE-LBF	Airbus A.321-111	Austrian Airlines
	OE-LDP	McD Douglas MD-81	Austrian Airlines *Niederösterreich*
	OE-LDR	McD Douglas MD-81	Austrian Airlines *Wien*
	OE-LDS	McD Douglas MD-81	Austrian Airlines *Burgenland*
	OE-LDT	McD Douglas MD-81	Austrian Airlines *Kärnten*
	OE-LDU	McD Douglas MD-81	Austrian Airlines *Steiermark*
	OE-LDV	McD Douglas MD-81	Austrian Airlines *Oberösterreich*
	OE-LDW	McD Douglas MD-81	Austrian Airlines *Salzburg*
	OE-LDX	McD Douglas MD-82	Austrian Airlines *Tirol*
	OE-LDY	McD Douglas MD-82	Austrian Airlines *Vorarlberg*
	OE-LDZ	McD Douglas MD-82	Austrian Airlines *Graz*
	OE-LEC	D.H.C.8-311 Dash Eight	Tyrolean Airways
	OE-LFA	Fokker 50	Tyrolean Airways *Schwechat*
	OE-LFD	Fokker 50	Tyrolean Airways *Woethersee*
	OE-LFE	Fokker 50	Tyrolean Airways
	OE-LFF	Fokker 50	Tyrolean Airways *Karpfenberg*
	OE-LFG	Fokker 70	Tyrolean Airways *Stadt Innsbruck*
	OE-LFH	Fokker 70	Tyrolean Airways *Stadt Salzburg*
	OE-LFK	Fokker 70	Tyrolean Airways *Stadt Wien*
	OE-LFO	Fokker 70	Austrian Airlines *Wiener Naustadt*
	OE-LFP	Fokker 70	Austrian Airlines
	OE-LFQ	Fokker 70	Austrian Airlines
	OE-LFR	Fokker 70	Austrian Airlines
	OE-LLE	D.H.C.8-106 Dash Eight	Tyrolean Airways *Seefeld*
	OE-LLF	D.H.C.8-106 Dash Eight	Tyrolean Airways *Stadt Kufstein*
	OE-LLG	D.H.C.8-106 Dash Eight	Tyrolean Airways
	OE-LLH	D.H.C.8-106 Dash Eight	Tyrolean Airways *Stadt Kitzbühel*
	OE-LLK	D.H.C.8-106 Dash Eight	Tyrolean Airways *Stadt Salzburg*
	OE-LLL	D.H.C.8-106 Dash Eight	Tyrolean Airways *Stadt Graz*
	OE-LLM	D.H.C.8-103 Dash Eight	Tyrolean Airways *Stadt Klagenfurt*
	OE-LLU	D.H.C.7-102 Dash Seven	Tyrolean Airways *Stadt Wien*
	OE-LLV	D.H.C.8-314 Dash Eight	Tyrolean Airways *Land Tirol*
	OE-LLW	D.H.C.8-314 Dash Eight	Tyrolean Airways *Land Steiermark*
	OE-LLX	D.H.C.8-314 Dash Eight	Tyrolean Airways *Land Salzburg*
	OE-LLY	D.H.C.8-314 Dash Eight	Tyrolean Airways
	OE-LLZ	D.H.C.8-314 Dash Eight	Tyrolean Airways
	OE-LMA	McD Douglas MD-82	Austrian Airlines *Linz*
	OE-LMB	McD Douglas MD-82	Austrian Airlines *Eisenstadt*
	OE-LMC	McD Douglas MD-82	Austrian Airlines *Baden*
	OE-LMD	McD Douglas MD-83	Austrian Airlines *Villach*
	OE-LME	McD Douglas MD-83	Austrian Airlines *Krems*
	OE-LMK	McD Douglas MD-87	Austrian Airlines *St Pölten*
	OE-LML	McD Douglas MD-87	Austrian Airlines *Salzburg*
	OE-LMM	McD Douglas MD-87	Austrian Airlines *Innsbruck*
	OE-LMN	McD Douglas MD-87	Austrian Airlines *Klagenfurt*
	OE-LMO	McD Douglas MD-87	Austrian Airlines *Bregenz*
	OE-LNH	Boeing 737-4Z9	Lauda Air *Elvis Presley*
	OE-LNI	Boeing 737-4Z9	Lauda Air *Janise Joplin*
	OE-LNK	Boeing 737-4Z9	Lauda Air
	OE-LRA	Canadair Regional Jet 100ER	Lauda Air
	OE-LRB	Canadair Regional Jet 100ER	Lauda Air
	OE-LRD	Canadair Regional Jet 100ER	Lauda Air
	OE-LRE	Canadair Regional Jet 100ER	Lauda Air
	OE-LRF	Canadair Regional Jet 100ER	Lauda Air
	OE-LRG	Canadair Regional Jet 100ER	Lauda Air
	OE-LTA	D.H.C.8-314 Dash Eight	Tyrolean Airways *Stadt Linz*
	OE-LTB	D.H.C.8-314 Dash Eight	Tyrolean Airways *Stadt Graz*
	OE-LTC	D.H.C.8-314 Dash Eight	Tyrolean Airways
	OE-LTD	D.H.C.8-314 Dash Eight	Tyrolean Airways *Oberosterreich*

OH (Finland)

	OH-LAA	Airbus A.300B4-203	Finnair
	OH-LAB	Airbus A.300B4-203	Finnair
	OH-LGA	McD Douglas MD-11	Finnair
	OH-LGB	McD Douglas MD-11	Finnair
	OH-LGC	McD Douglas MD-11	Finnair

Reg.	Type	Owner or Operator	Notes
OH-LGD	McD Douglas MD-11	Finnair	
OH-LHA	Douglas DC-10-30ER	Finnair	
OH-LMA	McD Douglas MD-87	Finnair	
OH-LMB	McD Douglas MD-87	Finnair	
OH-LMC	McD Douglas MD-87	Finnair	
OH-LMG	McD Douglas MD-83	Finnair	
OH-LMH	McD Douglas MD-82	Finnair	
OH-LMN	McD Douglas MD-82	Finnair	
OH-LMO	McD Douglas MD-82	Finnair	
OH-LMP	McD Douglas MD-82	Finnair	
OH-LMR	McD Douglas MD-83	Finnair	
OH-LMS	McD Douglas MD-83	Finnair	
OH-LMT	McD Douglas MD-82	Finnair	
OH-LMU	McD Douglas MD-83	Finnair	
OH-LMV	McD Douglas MD-83	Finnair	
OH-LMW	McD Douglas MD-82	Finnair	
OH-LMX	McD Douglas MD-82	Finnair	
OH-LMY	McD Douglas MD-82	Finnair	
OH-LMZ	McD Douglas MD-82	Finnair	
OH-LPA	McD Douglas MD-82	Finnair	
OH-LPB	McD Douglas MD-83	Finnair	
OH-LPC	McD Douglas MD-83	Finnair	
OH-LYN	Douglas DC-9-51	Finnair	
OH-LYO	Douglas DC-9-51	Finnair	
OH-LYP	Douglas DC-9-51	Finnair	
OH-LYR	Douglas DC-9-51	Finnair	
OH-LYS	Douglas DC-9-51	Finnair	
OH-LYT	Douglas DC-9-51	Finnair	
OH-LYU	Douglas DC-9-51	Finnair	
OH-LYV	Douglas DC-9-51	Finnair	
OH-LYW	Douglas DC-9-51	Finnair	
OH-LYX	Douglas DC-9-51	Finnair	
OH-LYY	Douglas DC-9-51	Finnair	
OH-LYZ	Douglas DC-9-51	Finnair	

Note: Finnair also operates a DC-10-30ER which retains its US registration N345HC.

OK (Czech Republic)

OK-BYV	Ilyushin IL-62M	Georgia Air Prague	
OK-FBF	Ilyushin IL-62	Georgia Air Prague	
OK-GBH	Ilyushin IL-62	Georgia Air Prague	
OK-HFL	Tupolev Tu-134A	Ceskoslovenske Aerolinie (CSA)	
OK-HFM	Tupolev Tu-134A	CSA	
OK-IFN	Tupolev Tu-134A	CSA	
OK-JGY	Boeing 727-230	Air Terrex	
OK-TCD	Tupolev Tu-154M	CSA *Trencianske Teplic*	
OK-TGX	Boeing 727-51	European Air Charter	
OK-UCE	Tupolev Tu-154M	CSA *Marianske Lazne*	
OK-UCF	Tupolev Tu-154M	CSA *Smokovec*	
OK-VCG	Tupolev Tu-154M	CSA *Luhacovice*	
OK-WAA	Airbus A.310-304	CSA *Praha*	
OK-WAB	Airbus A.310-304	CSA *Bratislava*	
OK-WGF	Boeing 737-4Y0	CSA *Jihlava*	
OK-WGG	Boeing 737-4Y0	CSA *Liberec*	
OK-XGA	Boeing 737-55S	CSA *Pizen*	
OK-XGB	Boeing 737-55S	CSA *Olomouc*	
OK-XGC	Boeing 737-55S	CSA *Ceske Budejovice*	
OK-XGD	Boeing 737-55S	CSA *Poprad*	
OK-XGE	Boeing 737-55S	CSA *Kosice*	

OM (Slovakia)

OM-GAT	Tupolev Tu-134A-3	Air Transport Europe	
OM-CHD	Boeing 727-230	Air Slovakia	
OM-UFB	Boeing 707-321B	Slovtrans Air	
OM-UGT	SAAB SF.340B	Tatra Air	
OM-UGU	SAAB SF.340B	Tatra Air	

OO (Belgium)

Reg.	Type	Owner or Operator
OO-CAH	Boeing 727-2X3	Constellation International Airways
OO-DHC	Convair Cv.580	European Air Transport (DHL)
OO-DHD	Convair Cv.580	European Air Transport (DHL)
OO-DHE	Convair Cv.580	European Air Transport (DHI)
OO-DHF	Convair Cv.580	European Air Transport (DHL)
OO-DHH	Convair Cv.580	European Air Transport (DHL)
OO-DHI	Convair Cv.580	European Air Transport (DHL)
OO-DHJ	Convair Cv.580	European Air Transport (DHL)
OO-DHM	Boeing 727-31F	European Air Transport (DHL)
OO-DHN	Boeing 727-31F	European Air Transport (DHL)
OO-DHO	Boeing 727-31F	European Air Transport (DHL)
OO-DHP	Boeing 727-35F	European Air Transport (DHL)
OO-DHQ	Boeing 727-35F	European Air Transport (DHL)
OO-DHR	Boeing 727-23F	European Air Transport (DHL)
OO-DHS	Boeing 727-223F	European Air Transport (DHL)
OO-DHT	Boeing 727-223F	European Air Transport (DHL)
OO-DHU	Boeing 727-223F	European Air Transport (DHL)
OO-DHV	Boeing 727-223F	European Air Transport (DHL)
OO-DHW	Boeing 727-223F	European Air Transport (DHL)
OO-DHX	Boeing 727-223F	European Air Transport (DHL)
OO-DJA	F.28 Fellowship 3000	Delta Air Transport
OO-DJB	F.28 Fellowship 4000	Delta Air Transport
OO-DJC	BAe 146-200	Delta Air Transport/SABENA
OO-DJE	BAe 146-200	Delta Air Transport/SABENA
OO-DJF	BAe 146-200	Delta Air Transport/SABENA
OO-DJG	BAe 146-200	Delta Air Transport/SABENA
OO-DJH	BAe 146-200	Delta Air Transport/SABENA
OO-DJJ	BAe 146-200	Delta Air Transport/SABENA
OO-DJK	Avro RJ85	Delta Air Transport/SABENA
OO-DJL	Avro RJ85	Delta Air Transport/SABENA
OO-DJN	Avro RJ85	Delta Air Transport/SABENA
OO-DJO	Avro RJ85	Delta Air Transport/SABENA
OO-DJP	Avro RJ85	Delta Air Transport/SABENA
OO-D	Avro RJ85	Delta Air Transport/SABENA
OO-D	Avro RJ85	Delta Air Transport/SABENA
OO-D	Avro RJ85	Delta Air Transport/SABENA
OO-D	Avro RJ85	Delta Air Transport/SABENA
OO-D	Avro RJ85	Delta Air Transport/SABENA
OO-D	Avro RJ85	Delta Air Transport/SABENA
OO-D	Avro RJ85	Delta Air Transport/SABENA
OO-DTF	EMB-120ER Brasilia	Delta Air Transport
OO-DTG	EMB-120ER Brasilia	Delta Air Transport
OO-DTH	EMB-120ER Brasilia	Delta Air Transport
OO-DTI	EMB-120ER Brasilia	Delta Air Transport
OO-DTJ	EMB-120RT Brasilia	Delta Air Transport
OO-DTK	EMB-120ER Brasilia	Delta Air Transport
OO-DTL	EMB-120ER Brasilia	Delta Air Transport
OO-DTN	EMB-120ER Brasilia	Delta Air Transport
OO-DTO	EMB-120ER Brasilia	Delta Air Transport
OO-EDA	BAe Jetstream 3102	Euro Direct Belgium Airlines
OO-FEL	F.27 Friendship Mk 500	Sky Freighters
OO-HUB	Convair Cv.580	European Air Transport (DHL)
OO-ILI	Boeing 757-23A	Air Belgium
OO-ILJ	Boeing 737-46B	Air Belgium
OO-ING	Airbus A.300B4-103	—
OO-JOT	Douglas DC-10-30	ChallengAir
OO-LLS	Boeing 727-2X3	Constellation International Airways
OO-LRM	Douglas DC-10-30	ChallengAir/Corsair
OO-LTJ	Boeing 737-3M8	EBA EuroBelgian Airlines
OO-LTL	Boeing 737-3M8	EBA EuroBelgian Airlines
OO-LTM	Boeing 737-3M8	EBA EuroBelgian Airlines
OO-LTP	Boeing 737-33A	EBA EuroBelgian Airlines
OO-LTQ	Boeing 737-436	EBA EuroBelgian Airlines
OO-LTS	Boeing 737-436	EBA EuroBelgian Airlines
OO-LTU	Boeing 737-33A	EBA EuroBelgian Airlines
OO-LTV	Boeing 737-3Y0	EBA EuroBelgian Airlines
OO-LTW	Boeing 737-33A	EBA EuroBelgian Airlines
OO-LTY	Boeing 737-3Q8	EBA EuroBelgian Airlines
OO-MJE	BAe 146-200	Delta Air Transport
OO-MTD	EMB-120RT Brasilia	Delta Air Transport
OO-PHN	Douglas DC-10-30	Skyjet

Reg.	Type	Owner or Operator	Notes
OO-SBJ	Boeing 737-46B	Sobelair *Juliette*	
OO-SBM	Boeing 737-429	Sobelair	
OO-SBN	Boeing 737-4Y0	EBA EuroBelgian Airlines	
OO-SBQ	Boeing 737-229	Sobelair	
OO-SBT	Boeing 737-229	Sobelair	
OO-SBY	Boeing 767-33AER	Sobelair	
OO-SBZ	Boeing 737-329	Sobelair	
OO-SCA	Airbus A.310-222	SABENA	
OO-SCB	Airbus A.310-222	SABENA	
OO-SCC	Airbus A.310-322	SABENA	
OO-SCI	Airbus A.310-222	Air Malta	
OO-SDA	Boeing 737-229	SABENA	
OO-SDD	Boeing 737-229	SABENA	
OO-SDE	Boeing 737-229	SABENA	
OO-SDF	Boeing 737-229	SABENA	
OO-SDG	Boeing 737-229	SABENA	
OO-SDJ	Boeing 737-229C	SABENA	
OO-SDK	Boeing 737-229C	SABENA	
OO-SDL	Boeing 737-229	SABENA	
OO-SDM	Boeing 737-229	SABENA	
OO-SDN	Boeing 737-229	SABENA	
OO-SDO	Boeing 737-229	SABENA	
OO-SDP	Boeing 737-229C	SABENA	
OO-SDR	Boeing 737-229C	SABENA	
OO-SDV	Boeing 737-329	SABENA	
OO-SDW	Boeing 737-329	SABENA	
OO-SDX	Boeing 737-329	SABENA	
OO-SDY	Boeing 737-329	SABENA	
OO-SGC	Boeing 747-329 (SCD)	SABENA	
OO-SGD	Boeing 747-329 (SCD)	SABENA	
OO-SLG	Douglas DC-10-30	SABENA	
OO-SLH	Douglas DC-10-30	Sobelair	
OO-SYA	Boeing 737-329	SABENA	
OO-SYB	Boeing 737-329	SABENA	
OO-SYC	Boeing 737-429	SABENA	
OO-SYD	Boeing 737-429	SABENA	
OO-SYE	Boeing 737-529	SABENA	
OO-SYF	Boeing 737-429	SABENA	
OO-SYG	Boeing 737-529	SABENA	
OO-SYH	Boeing 737-529	SABENA	
OO-SYI	Boeing 737-529	SABENA	
OO-SYJ	Boeing 737-529	SABENA	
OO-SYK	Boeing 737-529	SABENA	
OO-VDO	Boeing 737-4Y0	Chartair *Ville de Charleroi*	
OO-VLE	Fokker 50	V.L.M.	
OO-VLM	Fokker 50	V.L.M.	
OO-VLN	Fokker 50	V.L.M. *Royal Antwerp F.C.*	

Note: SABENA also operates Dash Eights PH-SDI, PH-SDJ, PH-SDM, PH-SDN, PH-SDO, PH-SDP, PH-SDR and PH-SDS on lease from Schreiner Airways and the Boeing 747-228B F-GCBB on lease from Air France. Delta Air Transport operates the F-28 F-GBBS in SABENA livery.

OY (Denmark)

OY-APA	Boeing 737-5L9	Maersk Air	
OY-APB	Boeing 737-5L9	Maersk Air	
OY-ASY	EMB-110P1 Bandeirante	Muk Air	
OY-AUO	Swearingen SA226TC Metro II	Jetair	
OY-BHT	EMB-110P2 Bandeirante	Muk Air	
OY-BJT	Swearingen SA226TC Metro II	Jetair	
OY-BNM	EMB-110P2 Bandeirante	Muk Air	
OY-BPB	Douglas DC-3C	Flyvende MuseumsFly	
OY-BPL	Swearingen SA227AC Metro III	Metro Airways	
OY-CCL	F.27 Friendship Mk 600	Alkair	
OY-CHA	Swearingen SA226AT Merlin IV	Jetair	
OY-CIB	Aérospatiale ATR-42-300	Cimber Air	
OY-CIC	Aérospatiale ATR 42 300	Cimber Air	
OY-CID	Aérospatiale ATR-42-300	Cimber Air	
OY-CIE	Aérospatiale ATR-42-300	Cimber Air	
OY-CIF	Aérospatiale ATR-42-300	Cimber Air	
OY-CIG	Aérospatiale ATR-42-300	Cimber Air	

Notes	Reg.	Type	Owner or Operator
	OY-CIH	Aérospatiale ATR-42-300	Cimber Air
	OY-CLB	BAe Jetstream 3102	Newair of Denmark
	OY-CLC	BAe Jetstream 3102	Newair of Denmark
	OY-CNA	Airbus A.300B4-120	Premiair
	OY-CND	Airbus A.320-231	Premiair
	OY-CNE	Airbus A.320-231	Premiair
	OY-CNF	Airbus A.320-231	Premiair
	OY-CNG	Airbus A.320-231	Premiair
	OY-CNH	Airbus A.320-231	Premiair
	OY-CNI	Airbus A.320-231	Premiair
	OY-CNK	Airbus A.300B4-120	Premiair
	OY-CNL	Airbus A.300B4-120	Premiair
	OY-CNT	Douglas DC-10-10	Premiair
	OY-CNU	Douglas DC-10-10	Premiair
	OY-CNY	Douglas DC-10-10	Premiair
	OY-CRR	H.P. 137 Jetstream 1	Newair of Denmark *(stored)*
	OY-CRT	H.P. 137 Jetstream 1	Newair of Denmark *(stored)*
	OY-EDA	BAe Jetstream 3103	Sun-Air
	OY-EDB	BAe Jetstream 3103	Sun-Air
	OY-JEO	Swearingen SA226TC Metro II	Jetair
	OY-JER	Swearingen SA226TC Metro II	Jetair
	OY-KAE	Fokker 50	S.A.S. Commuter *Hans Viking*
	OY-KAF	Fokker 50	S.A.S. Commuter *SigvatV Viking*
	OY-KAG	Fokker 50	S.A.S. Commuter *Odensis Viking*
	OY-KAH	Fokker 50	S.A.S. Commuter *Bjorn Viking*
	OY-KAI	Fokker 50	S.A.S. Commuter *Skjold VIking*
	OY-KAK	Fokker 50	S.A.S. Commuter *Turid Viking*
	OY-KDH	Boeing 767-383ER	S.A.S. *Thyra Viking*
	OY-KDL	Boeing 767-383ER	S.A.S. *Tjodhild Viking*
	OY-KDM	Boeing 767-383ER	S.A.S. *Ingva Viking1*
	OY-KDN	Boeing 767-383ER	S.A.S. *Ulf Viking*
	OY-KDO	Boeing 767-383ER	S.A.S. *Svea Viking*
	OY-KGD	Douglas DC-9-21	S.A.S. *Ubbe Viking*
	OY-KGF	Douglas DC-9-21	S.A.S. *Rolf Viking*
	OY-KGL	Douglas DC-9-41	S.A.S. *Angantyr Viking*
	OY-KGM	Douglas DC-9-41	S.A.S. *Arnfinn Viking*
	OY-KGN	Douglas DC-9-41	S.A.S. *Gram Viking*
	OY-KGO	Douglas DC-9-41	S.A.S. *Holte Viking*
	OY-KGP	Douglas DC-9-41	S.A.S. *Torbern Viking*
	OY-KGR	Douglas DC-9-41	S.A.S. *Holger Viking*
	OY-KGS	Douglas DC-9-41	S.A.S. *Hall Viking*
	OY-KGT	McD Douglas MD-82	
	OY-KGY	McD Douglas MD-81	S.A.S. *Rollo Viking*
	OY-KGZ	McD Douglas MD-81	S.A.S. *Hagbard Viking*
	OY-KHC	McD Douglas MD-81	S.A.S. *Faste Viking*
	OY-KHF	McD Douglas MD-87	S.A.S. *Ragnar Viking*
	OY-KHG	McD Douglas MD-81	S.A.S. *Alle Viking*
	OY-KHI	McD Douglas MD-87	S.A.S. *Torkel Viking*
	OY-KHK	McD Douglas MD-81	S.A.S. *Roald Viking*
	OY-KHL	McD Douglas MD-81	S.A.S. *Knud Viking*
	OY-KHM	McD Douglas MD-81	S.A.S. *Mette Viking*
	OY-KHN	McD Douglas MD-81	S.A.S. *Dan Viking*
	OY-KHP	McD Douglas MD-81	S.A.S. *Arild Viking*
	OY-KHR	McD Douglas MD-81	S.A.S. *Torkild Viking*
	OY-KHT	McD Douglas MD-82	S.A.S. *Gorm Viking*
	OY-KHU	McD Douglas MD-87	S.A.S. *Ravn Viking*
	OY-KHW	McD Douglas MD-87	S.A.S. *Ingemund Viking*
	OY-KIA	Douglas DC-9-21	S.A.S. *Guttorm Viking*
	OY-KID	Douglas DC-9-21	S.A.S. *Rane Viking*
	OY-KIE	Douglas DC-9-21	S.A.S. *Skate Viking*
	OY-KIF	Douglas DC-9-21	S.A.S. *Svipdag Viking*
	OY-KIG	McD Douglas MD-81	S.A.S.
	OY-KIH	McD Douglas MD-81	S.A.S.
	OY-KII	McD Douglas MD-81	S.A.S.
	OY-MAC	Boeing 737-5L9	Maersk Air
	OY-MAD	Boeing 737-5L9	Maersk Air
	OY-MAE	Boeing 737-5L9	Maersk Air
	OY-MAP	Boeing 737-3L9	Maersk Air
	OY-MAR	Boeing 737-3L9	Maersk Air
	OY-MAS	Boeing 737-3L9	Maersk Air
	OY-MAT	Boeing 737-3L9	Maersk Air
	OY-MAU	Boeing 737-3L9	Maersk Air

Reg.	Type	Owner or Operator	Notes
OY-MBM	Fokker 50	Maersk Air	
OY-MMA	Short SD3-60 Variant 100	Muk Air	
OY-MMG	Fokker 50	Maersk Air	
OY-MMH	Fokker 50	Maersk Air	
OY-MMI	Fokker 50	Maersk Air	
OY-MMJ	Fokker 50	Maersk Air	
OY-MMS	Fokker 50	Maersk Air	
OY-MMT	Fokker 50	Maersk Air	
OY-MMU	Fokker 50	Maersk Air	
OY-MMV	Fokker 50	Maersk Air	
OY-MUA	EMB-110P1 Bandeirante	Muk Air	
OY-MUB	Short SD3-30	Muk Air	
OY-MUE	BAe Jetstream 3100	Muk Air	
OY-MUF	F.27 Friendship	Newair of Denmark	
OY-SAU	Boeing 727-2J4	Sterling European Airlines	
OY-SBH	Boeing 727-2B7	Sterling European Airlines	
OY-SBI	Boeing 727-270	Sterling European Airlines	
OY-SBN	Boeing 727-2B7	Sterling European Airlines	
OY-SBO	Boeing 727-2K3	Sterling European Airlines	
OY-SCC	Boeing 727-212	Sterling European Airlines	
OY-SRB	F.27 Friendship Mk 600	Alkair	
OY-SRD	F.27 Friendship Mk 500	Starair	
OY-SVF	BAe Jetstream 3102	Sun-Air	
OY-SVJ	BAe Jetstream 3102	Sun-Air	
OY-SVK	BAe Jetstream 3102	Sun-Air	
OY-SVO	BAe Jetstream 3102	Sun-Air	
OY-SVR	BAe Jetstream 3103	Sun-Air	
OY-SVS	BAe Jetstream 4100	Sun-Air	
OY-SVW	BAe Jetstream 4100	Sun-Air	
OY-SVY	BAe Jetstream 3102	Sun-Air	
OY-SVZ	BAe Jetstream 3102	Sun-Air	
OY-UPJ	Boeing 727-22C	Starair/UPS	
OY-UPS	Boeing 727-31C	Starair/UPS	
OY-UPT	Boeing 727-22C	Starair/UPS	

P4 (Aruba)

P4-TBN	Boeing 707-3L6B	Jade Air	

PH (Netherlands)

PH-AGE	Airbus A.310-203	Middle East Airlines	
PH-AGF	Airbus A.310-203	Middle East Airlines	
PH-AGG	Airbus A.310-203	Koninklijke Luchtvaart Maatschappij (K.L.M.) Vincent van Gogh	
PH-AGH	Airbus A.310-203	K.L.M. Pieter de Hoogh	
PH-AGI	Airbus A.310-203	K.L.M. Jan Toorop	
PH-AGK	Airbus A.310-203	K.L.M. Johannes Vermeer	
PH-AHE	Boeing 757-27B	Air Holland	
PH-AHI	Boeing 757-27B	Air Holland	
PH-BDA	Boeing 737-306	K.L.M. Willem Barentsz	
PH-BDB	Boeing 737-306	K.L.M. Olivier van Noort	
PH-BDC	Boeing 737-306	K.L.M. Cornelis De Houteman	
PH-BDD	Boeing 737-306	K.L.M. Anthony van Diemen	
PH-BDE	Boeing 737-306	K.L.M. Abel J. Tasman	
PH-BDG	Boeing 737-306	K.L.M. Michiel A. de Ruyter	
PH-BDH	Boeing 737-306	K.L.M. Petrus Plancius	
PH-BDI	Boeing 737-306	K.L.M. Maarten H. Tromp	
PH-BDK	Boeing 737-306	K.L.M. Jan H. van Linschoten	
PH-BDL	Boeing 737-306	K.L.M. Piet Heyn	
PH-BDN	Boeing 737-306	K.L.M. Willem van Ruysbroeck	
PH-BDO	Boeing 737-306	K.L.M. Jacob van Heemskerck	
PH-BDP	Boeing 737-306	K.L.M. Jacob Roggeveen	
PH-BDR	Boeing 737-406	K.L.M. Willem C. Schouten	
PH-BDS	Boeing 737-406	K.L.M. Jorris van Spilbergen	
PH-BDT	Boeing 737-406	K.L.M. Gerrit de Veer	
PH-BDU	Boeing 737-406	K.L.M. Marco Polo	
PH-BDW	Boeing 737-406	K.L.M. Leifur Eiriksson	
PH-BDY	Boeing 737-406	K.L.M. Vasco da Gama	

Notes	Reg.	Type	Owner or Operator
	PH-BDZ	Boeing 737-406	K.L.M. *Christophorus Columbus*
	PH-BFA	Boeing 747-406	K.L.M. *City of Atlanta*
	PH-BFB	Boeing 747-406	K.L.M. *City of Bangkok*
	PH-BFC	Boeing 747-406 (SCD)	K.L.M. Asia *City of Calgary*
	PH-BFD	Boeing 747-406 (SCD)	K.L.M. Asia *City of Dubai*
	PH-BFE	Boeing 747-406 (SCD)	K.L.M. *City of Melbourne*
	PH-BFF	Boeing 747-406 (SCD)	K.L.M. *City of Freetown*
	PH-BFG	Boeing 747-406	K.L.M. *City of Guayaquil*
	PH-BFH	Boeing 747-406 (SCD)	K.L.M. *City of Hong Kong*
	PH-BFI	Boeing 747-406 (SCD)	K.L.M. *City of Jakarta*
	PH-BFK	Boeing 747-406 (SCD)	K.L.M. *City of Karachi*
	PH-BFL	Boeing 747-406	K.L.M. *City of Lima*
	PH-BFM	Boeing 747-406 (SCD)	K.L.M. Asia *City of Mexico*
	PH-BFN	Boeing 747-406	K.L.M. *City of Nairobi*
	PH-BFO	Boeing 747-406 (SCD)	K.L.M. *City of Orlando*
	PH-BFP	Boeing 747-406 (SCD)	K.L.M. *City of Paramaribo*
	PH-BFR	Boeing 747-406 (SCD)	K.L.M. *City of Rio de Janiero*
	PH-BTA	Boeing 737-406	K.L.M. *Fernao de Magalhaes*
	PH-BTB	Boeing 737-406	K.L.M. *Henry Hudson*
	PH-BTC	Boeing 737-406	K.L.M. *David Livingstone*
	PH-BTD	Boeing 737-306	K.L.M. *James Cook*
	PH-BTE	Boeing 737-306	K.L.M. *Roald Amundsen*
	PH-BTF	Boeing 737-406	K.L.M. *Alexander von Humboldt*
	PH-BTG	Boeing 737-406	K.L.M.
	PH-BUH	Boeing 747-306 (SCD)	K.L.M. *Dr Albert Plesman*
	PH-BUI	Boeing 747-306 (SCD)	K.L.M. *Wilbur Wright*
	PH-BUK	Boeing 747-306 (SCD)	K.L.M. *Louis Blériot*
	PH-BUL	Boeing 747-306 (SCD)	K.L.M. *Charles A. Lindbergh*
	PH-BUM	Boeing 747-306 (SCD)	K.L.M. *Charles E. Kingsford-Smith*
	PH-BUN	Boeing 747-306 (SCD)	K.L.M. *Anthony H. G. Fokker*
	PH-BUO	Boeing 747-306	K.L.M. *Missouri*
	PH-BUP	Boeing 747-306	K.L.M. *The Ganges*
	PH-BUR	Boeing 747-306	K.L.M. *The Indus*
	PH-BUT	Boeing 747-306	K.L.M. *Admiral Richard E. Byrd*
	PH-BUU	Boeing 747-306 (3CD)	K.L.M. *Sir Frank Whittle*
	PH-BUV	Boeing 747-306 (SCD)	K.L.M. *Sir Geoffrey de Havilland*
	PH-BUW	Boeing 747-306 (SCD)	K.L.M. *Leonardo da Vinci*
	PH-BZA	Boeing 767-306ER	K.L.M. *Blue Bridge*
	PH-BZB	Boeing 767-306ER	K.L.M. *Brooklyn Bridge*
	PH-BZC	Boeing 767-306ER	K.L.M. *Pont Neuf*
	PH-BZD	Boeing 767-306ER	K.L.M. *Rialto Brug*
	PH-BZE	Boeing 767-306ER	K.L.M. *Sydney Harbour Bridge*
	PH-BZF	Boeing 767-306ER	K.L.M. *Golden Gate*
	PH-BZG	Boeing 767-306ER	K.L.M. *Tower Bridge*
	PH-BZH	Boeing 767-306ER	K.L.M.
	PH-BZI	Boeing 767-306ER	K.L.M.
	PH-BZK	Boeing 767-306ER	K.L.M.
	PH-CHB	F.28 Fellowship 4000	K.L.M. CityHopper *Birmingham*
	PH-CHD	F.28 Fellowship 4000	K.L.M. CityHopper *Maastricht*
	PH-CHF	F.28 Fellowship 4000	K.L.M. CityHopper *Guernsey*
	PH-CHN	F.28 Fellowship 4000	K.L.M. CityHopper *Belfast*
	PH-DDA	Douglas DC-3	Dutch Dakota Association
	PH-DDZ	Douglas DC-3	Dutch Dakota Association
	PH-DTB	Douglas DC-10-30	K.L.M. *Ludwig van Beethoven*
	PH-DTC	Douglas DC-10-30	K.L.M. *Frédéric François Chopin*
	PH-DTL	Douglas DC-10-30	African Safari Airways
	PH-FWD	Cessna F.406 Caravan II	Twente Airlines
	PH-FWF	Cessna F.406 Caravan II	Twente Airlines
	PH-FWG	Cessna F.406 Caravan II	Twente Airlines
	PH-FWH	Cessna F.406 Caravan II	Twente Airlines
	PH-HVF	Boeing 737-3K2	Transavia *Johan Cruijff*
	PH-HVG	Boeing 737-3K2	Transavia *Wubbo Ockels*
	PH-HVJ	Boeing 737-3K2	Transavia *Nelli Cooman*
	PH-HVK	Boeing 737-3K2	Transavia
	PH-HVM	Boeing 737-3K2	Transavia
	PH-HVN	Boeing 737-3K2	Transavia
	PH-HVT	Boeing 737-3K2	Transavia
	PH-HVV	Boeing 737-3K2	Transavia
	PH-KCA	McD Douglas MD-11	K.L.M. *Amy Johnson*
	PH-KCB	McD Douglas MD-11	K.L.M. *Maria Montessori*
	PH-KCC	McD Douglas MD-11	K.L.M. *Marie Curie*
	PH-KCD	McD Douglas MD-11	K.L.M. *Florence Nightingale*
	PH-KCE	McD Douglas MD-11	K.L.M. *Audrey Hepburn*
	PH-KCF	McD Douglas MD-11	K.L.M. *Annie Romein*

Reg.	Type	Owner or Operator	Notes
PH-KCG	McD Douglas MD-11	K.L.M. *Maria Callas*	
PH-KCH	McD Douglas MD-11	K.L.M. *Anna Pavlova*	
PH-KCK	McD Douglas MD-11	K.L.M. *Marie Servaes*	
PH-KFG	F.27 Friendship Mk 200	F.27 Friendship Flight Association	
PH-KJA	BAe Jetstream 3108	BASE Regional Airlines	
PH-KJB	BAe Jetstream 3108	BASE Regional Airlines	
PH-KJG	BAe Jetstream 3108	BASE Regional Airlines	
PH-KLC	Fokker 100	K.L.M. *Jan Hendrik Oort*	
PH-KLD	Fokker 100	K.L.M. *Jan Adriaensz Leeghwater*	
PH-KLE	Fokker 100	K.L.M. *Geradus Johannis Vossius*	
PH-KLG	Fokker 100	K.L.M. *Johannes Blaeu*	
PH-KLH	Fokker 100	K.L.M. *Christiaan Huygens*	
PH-KLI	Fokker 100	K.L.M. *Antonie van Leeuwenhoek*	
PH-KSB	SAAB SF.340B	K.L.M. CityHopper *Bristol*	
PH-KSC	SAAB SF.340B	K.L.M. CityHopper *Cardiff*	
PH-KSD	SAAB SF.340B	K.L.M. CityHopper *Neurenberg*	
PH-KSE	SAAB SF.340B	K.L.M. CityHopper *Southampton*	
PH-KSF	SAAB SF.340B	K.L.M. CityHopper *Basel*	
PH-KSG	SAAB SF.340B	K.L.M. CityHopper *Mulhouse*	
PH-KSI	SAAB SF.340B	K.L.M. CityHopper *Eindhoven*	
PH-KSK	SAAB SF.340B	K.L.M. CityHopper *Rotterdam*	
PH-KSL	SAAB SF.340B	K.L.M. CityHopper *Luxembourg*	
PH-KSM	SAAB SF.340B	K.L.M. CityHopper *Malmoe*	
PH-KVA	Fokker 50	K.L.M. CityHopper *Bremen*	
PH-KVB	Fokker 50	K.L.M. CityHopper *Brussels*	
PH-KVC	Fokker 50	K.L.M. CityHopper *Stavanger*	
PH-KVD	Fokker 50	K.L.M. CityHopper *Dusseldorf*	
PH-KVE	Fokker 50	K.L.M. CityHopper *Amsterdam*	
PH-KVF	Fokker 50	K.L.M. CityHopper *Paris/Paris*	
PH-KVG	Fokker 50	K.L.M. CityHopper *Stuttgart*	
PH-KVH	Fokker 50	K.L.M. CityHopper *Hannover*	
PH-KVI	Fokker 50	K.L.M. CityHopper *Bordeaux*	
PH-KVK	Fokker 50	K.L.M. CityHopper *London*	
PH-KZA	Fokker 70	K.L.M. CityHopper	
PH-KZB	Fokker 70	K.L.M. CityHopper	
PH-KZC	Fokker 70	K.L.M. CityHopper	
PH-KZD	Fokker 70	K.L.M. CityHopper	
PH-MCE	Boeing 747-21AC (SCD)	Martinair *Prins van Oranje*	
PH-MCF	Boeing 747-21AC (SCD)	Martinair *Prins Claus*	
PH-MCG	Boeing 767-31AER	Martinair *Prins Johan Friso*	
PH-MCH	Boeing 767-31AER	Martinair *Prins Constantijn*	
PH-MCI	Boeing 767-31AER	Martinair *Prins Pieter-Christiaan*	
PH-MCL	Boeing 767-31AER	Martinair *Koningin Beatrix*	
PH-MCM	Boeing 767-31AER	Martinair *Prins Floris*	
PH-MCN	Boeing 747-228F	Martinair *Prins Bernhard*	
PH-MCP	McD Douglas MD-11CF	Martinair	
PH-MCR	McD Douglas MD-11CF	Martinair	
PH-MCS	McD Douglas MD-11CF	Martinair	
PH-MCT	McD Douglas MD-11CF	Martinair	
PH-MCU	McD Douglas MD-11CF	Martinair	
PH-MCV	Boeing 767-31AER	Martinair	
PH-NVF	F.27 Friendship Mk100	Fokker Friendship Association	
PH-OZA	Boeing 737-3L9	Air Holland	
PH-OZB	Boeing 737-3Y0	Air Holland	
PH-RAZ	Swearingen SA226TC Metro II	Rijnmond Air Services	
PH-SDI	D.H.C.8-311A Dash Eight	Schreiner Airways/SABENA	
PH-SDJ	D.H.C.8-311A Dash Eight	Schreiner Airways/SABENA	
PH-SDM	D.H.C.8-311 Dash Eight	Schreiner Airways/SABENA	
PH-SDN	D.H.C.8-311 Dash Eight	Schreiner Airways/SABENA	
PH-SDP	D.H.C.8-311 Dash Eight	Schreiner Airways/SABENA	
PH-SDR	D.H.C.8-311 Dash Eight	Schreiner Airways/SABENA	
PH-SDS	D.H.C.8-311 Dash Eight	Schreiner Airways/SABENA	
PH-SEZ	McD Douglas MD-82	Meridiana	
PH-TKA	Boeing 757-2K2ER	Transavia	
PH-TKB	Boeing 757-2K2ER	Transavia	
PH-TKC	Boeing 757-2K2ER	Transavia	
PH-TKD	Boeing 757-2K2ER	Transavia	
PH-TSU	Boeing 737-3Y0	Transavia	
PH-TSW	Boeing 737-3L9	Transavia	
PH-TSX	Boeing 737-3K2	Transavia	
PH-TSY	Boeing 737-3K2	Transavia	
PH-TSZ	Boeing 737-3K2	Transavia	
PH-XLA	EMB-120RT Brasilia	Air Exel Commuter	
PH-XLB	EMB-120RT Brasilia	Air Exel Commuter	

Notes　　*Reg.*　　*Type*　　　　　　　　*Owner or Operator*

PK (Indonesia)

	Reg.	Type	Owner or Operator
	PK-GIG	McD Douglas MD-11	Garuda Indonesian Airways
	PK-GII	McD Douglas MD-11	Garuda Indonesian Airways
	PK-GIJ	McD Douglas MD-11	Garuda Indonesian Airways
	PK-	McD Douglas MD-11	Garuda Indonesian Airways
	PK-	McD Douglas MD-11	Garuda Indonesian Airways
	PK-	McD Douglas MD-11	Garuda Indonesian Airways
	PK-GSA	Boeing 747-2U3B	Garuda Indonesian Airways
	PK-GSB	Boeing 747-2U3B	Garuda Indonesian Airways
	PK-GSC	Boeing 747-2U3B	Garuda Indonesian Airways
	PK-GSD	Boeing 747-2U3B	Garuda Indonesian Airways
	PK-GSE	Boeing 747-2U3B	Garuda Indonesian Airways
	PK-GSF	Boeing 747-2U3B	Garuda Indonesian Airways

Note: MD-11s EI-CDI, EI-CDJ and EI-CDK are also operated by Garuda.

PP (Brazil)

	Reg.	Type	Owner or Operator
	PP-VMA	Douglas DC-10-30	VARIG
	PP-VMB	Douglas DC-10-30	VARIG
	PP-VMD	Douglas DC-10-30	VARIG
	PP-VMQ	Douglas DC-10-30	VARIG
	PP-VMT	Douglas DC-10-30F	VARIG Cargo
	PP-VMU	Douglas DC-10-30F	VARIG Cargo
	PP-VMV	Douglas DC-10-30	VARIG
	PP-VMW	Douglas DC-10-30	VARIG
	PP-VMX	Douglas DC-10-30	VARIG
	PP-VMY	Douglas DC-10-30	VARIG
	PP-VNN	Boeing 767-241ER	VARIG
	PP VNO	Boeing 767-241ER	VARIG
	PP-VNP	Boeing 767-241ER	VARIG
	PP-VNQ	Boeing 767-241ER	VARIG
	PP-VNR	Boeing 767-241ER	VARIG
	PP-VNS	Boeing 767-241ER	VARIG
	PP-VOA	Boeing 747-341	VARIG
	PP-VOB	Boeing 747-341	VARIG
	PP-VOC	Boeing 747-341	VARIG
	PP-VOI	Boeing 767-341ER	VARIG
	PP-VOJ	Boeing 767-341ER	VARIG
	PP-VOK	Boeing 767-341ER	VARIG
	PP-VOL	Boeing 767-341ER	VARIG
	PP-VOP	McD Douglas MD-11	VARIG
	PP-VOQ	McD Douglas MD-11	VARIG
	PP-VPJ	McD Douglas MD-11	VARIG
	PP-VPK	McD Douglas MD-11	VARIG
	PP-VPL	McD Douglas MD-11	VARIG
	PP-VPM	McD Douglas MD-11	VARIG

Notes　　*Reg.*　　*Type*　　　　　　*Notes*　　*Reg.*　　*Type*

RA (Russia)

Although many of the aircraft previously operated by Aeroflot have been transferred to one of the numerous new CIS carriers, in a large number of cases the livery and visible titles remain unchanged at present. Those known to be used by Russia International/ Aeroflot are shown with the code AFL in parenthesis after the type. Other identifies used are AIS (AIS Airlines), HLA (HeavyLift), LSV (Alak Airlines), MSC (Moscow Airways), ORT (Orient Avia), TRJ (AJT Air), TSO (Transaero), TYM (Tyumen Airlines), UPA (Air Foyle), URA (Uralinteravia), VDA (Volga Dnepr) and VKO (Vnukovo Airlines).

Reg.	Type		Reg.	Type
65017	Tu-134A-3 (TYM)		65141	Tu-134A
65020	Tu-134A		65550	Tu-134A
65024	Tu-134A		65552	Tu-134A-3 (AFL)
65035	Tu-134A		65559	Tu-134A-3 (AFL)
65054	Tu-134A		65566	Tu-134A (AFL)
65064	Tu-134A		65567	Tu-134A (AFL)
65074	Tu-134A-3 (AFL)		65568	Tu-134A (AFL)
65087	Tu-134A		65607	Tu-134A (URA)
65139	Tu-134A		65614	Tu-134A (AFL)

Reg.	Type	Notes	Reg.	Type	Notes
65620	Tu-134A		76482	IL-76TD (AFL)	
65644	Tu-134		76484	IL-76TD	
65646	Tu-134A		76485	IL-76TD	
65647	Tu-134A		76486	IL-76TD	
65655	Tu-134A		76487	IL-76TD	
65656	Tu-134A		76488	IL-76TD (AFL)	
65658	Tu-134A		76489	IL-76TD	
65659	Tu-134A		76491	IL-76TD	
65660	Tu-134A		76493	IL-76TD	
65661	Tu-134A		76494	IL-76TD	
65665	Tu-134A		76496	IL-76TD	
65666	Tu-134A		76497	IL-76TD	
65667	Tu-134A		76498	IL-76TD (MSC)	
65669	Tu-134A		76499	IL-76TD	
65680	Tu-134A-3		76506	IL-76T (URA)	
65681	Tu-134A		76509	IL-76T (URA)	
65697	Tu-134A (AFL)		76519	IL-76T (AFL)	
65703	Tu-134A		76522	IL-76TD	
65717	Tu-134A-3 (AFL)		76750	IL-76TD (AFL)	
65739	Tu-134A		76751	IL-76TD (AFL)	
65758	Tu-134A		76752	IL-76TD	
65769	Tu-134A-3 (AFL)		76754	IL-76TD	
65770	Tu-134A-3 (AFL)		76756	IL-76TD	
65771	Tu-134A		76757	IL-76TD	
65781	Tu-134A-3 (AFL)		76758	IL-76TD	
65783	Tu-134A-3 (AFL)		76761	IL-76TD	
65784	Tu-134A-3 (AFL)		76764	IL-76TD	
65785	Tu-134A-3 (AFL)		76777	IL-76TD	
65794	Tu-134A		76780	IL-76TD	
65796	Tu-134A		76781	IL-76TD	
65801	Tu-134A		76784	IL-76TD	
65855	Tu-134A-3 (AIS)		76785	IL-76TD (AFL)	
65863	Tu-134A		76786	IL-76TD	
65864	Tu-134A		76787	IL-76TD	
65894	Tu-134A		76788	IL-76TD	
65904	Tu-134A-3		76789	IL-76TD	
65905	Tu-134A-3		76792	IL-76TD	
65911	Tu-134A-3		76795	IL-76TD (AFL)	
65912	Tu-134A-3		76796	IL-76TD (LSV)	
65016	Tu-134A		76800	IL-76TD (AFL)	
65919	Tu-134A (AFL)		76801	IL-76TD	
65921	Tu-134A-3 (AFL)		76806	IL-76TD	
65923	Tu-134A		76812	IL-76TD	
65926	Tu-134A		76814	IL-76TD (LSV)	
65935	Tu-134A		76832	IL-76TD	
65939	Tu-134A		76834	IL-76TD	
65955	Tu-134A		76835	IL-76TD	
65956	Tu-134A		76838	IL-76TD (AFL)	
65960	Tu-134A (TYM)		76839	IL-76TD	
65965	Tu-134A				
65976	Tu-134A		82007	An-124	
65978	Tu-134A-3 (AFL)		82008	An-124	
			82009	An-124	
76352	IL-76TD (URA)		82033	An-124	
76386	IL-76TD (URA)		82042	An-124 (VDA/HLA)	
76401	IL-76TD (HLA)		82043	An-124 (VDA/HLA)	
76436	IL-76TD		82044	An-124 (VDA/HLA)	
76450	IL-76TD		82045	An-124 (VDA/HLA)	
76454	IL-76TD		82046	An-124 (VDA/HLA)	
76460	IL-76TD (AFL)		82047	An-124 (VDA/HLA)	
76466	IL-76TD				
76467	IL-76TD (AFL)		85001	Tu-154	
76468	IL-76TD (AFL)		85002	Tu-154	
76469	IL-76TD (AFL)		85004	Tu-154	
76470	IL-76TD (AFL)		85005	Tu-154	
76471	IL-76TD		85006	Tu-154	
76472	IL-76TD		85007	Tu-154	
76473	IL-76TD (AFL)		85008	Tu-154	
76474	IL-76TD (AFL)		85009	Tu-154	
76475	IL-76TD		85012	Tu-154	
76476	IL-76TD (AFL)		85013	Tu-154	
76477	IL-76TD (AFL)		85014	Tu-154	
76478	IL-76TD (AFL)		85015	Tu-154	
76479	IL-76TD (AFL)		85016	Tu-154	

RA

Notes	Reg.	Type	Notes	Reg.	Type
	85018	Tu-154 (AFL)		85145	Tu-154B
	85019	Tu-154S (TSO)		85146	Tu-154B
	85024	Tu-154		85149	Tu-154B
	85025	Tu-154		85150	Tu-154B
	85028	Tu-154B (VKO)		85151	Tu-154B
	85031	Tu-154		85153	Tu-154B
	85033	Tu-154B (VKO)		85155	Tu-154B
	85034	Tu-154		85156	Tu-154B-1 (VKO)
	85037	Tu-154		85160	Tu-154B
	85040	Tu-154		85165	Tu-154B
	85041	Tu-154		85167	Tu-154B
	85042	Tu-154		85171	Tu-154B
	85043	Tu-154		85172	Tu-154B
	85049	Tu-154		85173	Tu-154B
	85051	Tu-154		85174	Tu-154B
	85052	Tu-154		85176	Tu-154B
	85055	Tu-154		85178	Tu-154B (AFL)
	85056	Tu-154		85180	Tu-154B
	85057	Tu-154 (VKO)		85181	Tu-154B
	85060	Tu-154A		85182	Tu-154B-1 (VKO)
	85061	Tu-154A		85183	Tu-154B
	85062	Tu-154C (AFL)		85184	Tu-154B
	85064	Tu-154A		85185	Tu-154B
	85065	Tu-154A		85186	Tu-154B
	85069	Tu-154A		85187	Tu-154B
	85070	Tu-154A		85190	Tu-154B (AFL)
	85071	Tu-154A		85191	Tu-154B
	85072	Tu-154A		85193	Tu-154B
	85074	Tu-154A		85195	Tu-154B
	85075	Tu-154B (AIS)		85201	Tu-154B
	85078	Tu-154A		85202	Tu-154B
	85079	Tu-154A		85204	Tu-154B
	85080	Tu-154A		85205	Tu-154B
	05001	Tu-154C (AFL)		85206	Tu-154B (AFL)
	85082	Tu-154A (AFL)		85207	Tu-154B
	85083	Tu-154A		85210	Tu-154B
	85084	Tu-154S (VKO)		85212	Tu-154B
	85085	Tu-154A		85213	Tu-154B
	85086	Tu-154A		85215	Tu-154B-1 (VKO)
	85087	Tu-154A		85216	Tu-154B
	85088	Tu-154A		85217	Tu-154B
	85089	Tu-154A		85219	Tu-154B
	85091	Tu-154A		85220	Tu-154B (AFL)
	85092	Tu-154B-1		85223	Tu-154B
	85094	Tu-154B-1		85226	Tu-154B
	85096	Tu-154B-2		85228	Tu-154B
	85098	Tu-154A		85229	Tu-154B-1
	85099	Tu-154B (VKO)		85233	Tu-154B-1
	85100	Tu-154A		85235	Tu-154B-1
	85101	Tu-154A		85236	Tu-154B-1
	85105	Tu-154A		85237	Tu-154B-1
	85106	Tu-154B-2 (AFL)		85238	Tu-154B-1
	85107	Tu-154A		85242	Tu-154B-1
	85108	Tu-154A		85244	Tu-154B-1 (AFL)
	85109	Tu-154B-1		85247	Tu-154B-1
	85110	Tu-154A		85253	Tu-154B-1
	85112	Tu-154A		85255	Tu-154B-1 (TYM)
	85114	Tu-154A		85256	Tu-154B-1
	85115	Tu-154A (AFL)		85261	Tu-154B-1
	85117	Tu-154A		85263	Tu-154B-1
	85119	Tu-154A		85264	Tu-154B-1
	85123	Tu-154B		85265	Tu-154B-1
	85124	Tu-154B		85266	Tu-154B-1
	85129	Tu-154B		85267	Tu-154B-1
	85130	Tu-154B		85270	Tu-154B-1
	85131	Tu-154B		85273	Tu-154B-1
	85134	Tu-154B		85275	Tu-154B-1
	85135	Tu-154B		85277	Tu-154B-1
	85138	Tu-154B		85279	Tu-154B-1
	85139	Tu-154B		85280	Tu-154B-1
	85140	Tu-154B (VKO)		85283	Tu-154B-1
	85141	Tu-154B		85284	Tu-154B-1
	85142	Tu-154B		85287	Tu-154B-1
	85143	Tu-154B		85289	Tu-154B-1

Reg.	Type	Notes	Reg.	Type	Notes
85291	Tu-154B-1		85427	Tu-154B-2 (TYM)	
85292	Tu-154B-2		85429	Tu-154B-2	
85293	Tu-154B-1		85432	Tu-154B-2	
85296	Tu-154B-1		85434	Tu-154B-2 (TYM)	
85298	Tu-154B-1		85435	Tu-154B-2	
85299	Tu-154B-2 (VKO)		85436	Tu-154B-2 (AFL)	
85300	Tu-154B-2		85437	Tu-154B-2	
85301	Tu-154B-2 (VKO)		85439	Tu-154B-2	
85302	Tu-154B-2		85441	Tu-154B-2	
85303	Tu-154B-2		85443	Tu-154B-2	
85304	Tu-154B-2 (VKO)		85446	Tu-154B-2	
85305	Tu-154B-2		85448	Tu-154B-2	
85306	Tu-154B-2		85450	Tu-154B-2 (TYM)	
85307	Tu-154B-2		85451	Tu-154B-2 (TYM)	
85308	Tu-154B-2		85452	Tu-154B-2	
85309	Tu-154B-2		85453	Tu-154B-2	
85310	Tu-154B-2		85454	Tu-154B-2	
85312	Tu-154B-2 (TYM)		85456	Tu-154B-2	
85314	Tu-154B-2 (TYM)		85457	Tu-154B-2	
85315	Tu-154B-2		85458	Tu-154B-2	
85318	Tu-154B-2		85461	Tu-154B-2	
85319	Tu-154B-2		85462	Tu-154B-2 (AFL)	
85323	Tu-154B-2		85463	Tu-154B-2	
85328	Tu-154B-2		85467	Tu-154B-2	
85330	Tu-154B-2		85468	Tu-154B-2	
85333	Tu-154B-2		85470	Tu-154B-2	
85334	Tu-154B-2		85471	Tu-154B-2	
85335	Tu-154B-2 (TYM)		85472	Tu-154B-2	
85336	Tu-154B-2		85476	Tu-154B-2	
85337	Tu-154B-2		85477	Tu-154B-2	
85340	Tu-154B-2		85481	Tu-154B-2 (TYM)	
85341	Tu-154B-2		85485	Tu-154B-2	
85343	Tu-154B-2		85486	Tu-154B-2	
85346	Tu-154B-2		85489	Tu-154B-2	
85347	Tu-154B-2		85494	Tu-154B-2	
85348	Tu-154B-2		85495	Tu-154B-2 (AFL)	
85349	Tu-154B-2		85498	Tu-154B-2 (TYM)	
85351	Tu-154B-2		85500	Tu-154B-2	
85353	Tu-154B-2		85501	Tu-154B-2	
85354	Tu 154B-2		85502	Tu-154B-2 (TYM)	
85357	Tu-154B-2		85503	Tu-154B-2	
85358	Tu-154B-2		85504	Tu-154B-2	
85360	Tu-154B-2		85505	Tu-154B-2	
85361	Tu-154B-2 (TYM)		85506	Tu-154B-2	
85363	Tu-154B-2 (AFL)		85508	Tu-154B-2	
85364	Tu-154B-2		85510	Tu-154B-2	
85365	Tu-154B-2		85512	Tu-154B-2	
85366	Tu-154B-2 (TYM)		85514	Tu-154B-2 (AFL)	
85367	Tu-154B-2		85520	Tu-154B-2	
85371	Tu-154B-2		85522	Tu-154B-2 (TYM)	
85373	Tu-154B-2 (AFL)		85523	Tu-154B-2 (MSC)	
85374	Tu-154B-2		85525	Tu-154C-2	
85375	Tu-154B-2		85526	Tu-154B-2	
85376	Tu-154B-2		85527	Tu-154B-2	
85377	Tu-154B-2		85529	Tu-154B-2	
85378	Tu-154B-2 (TYM)		85530	Tu-154B-2	
85380	Tu-154B-2		85534	Tu-154B-2	
85381	Tu-154B-2		85540	Tu-154B-2 (AFL)	
85386	Tu-154B-2		85550	Tu-154B-2 (TYM)	
85388	Tu-154B-2		85551	Tu-154B-2	
85389	Tu-154B-2		85552	Tu-154B-2	
85390	Tu-154B-2		85553	Tu-154B-2	
85392	Tu-154B-2 (AFL)		85554	Tu-154B-2	
85400	Tu-154B-2		85555	Tu-154B-2	
85402	Tu-154B-2		85557	Tu-154B-2	
85404	Tu-154B-2		85559	Tu-154B-2	
85406	Tu-154B-2		85562	Tu-154B-2	
85412	Tu-154B-2		85563	Tu-154B-2	
85414	Tu-154B-2		85564	Tu-154B-2 (AFL)	
85417	Tu-154B-2		85566	Tu-154B-2	
85418	Tu-154B-2		85567	Tu-154B-2	
85421	Tu-154B-2		85568	Tu-154B-2 (AFL)	
85425	Tu-154B-2		85570	Tu-154B-2 (AFL)	
85426	Tu-154B-2		85571	Tu-154B-2	

Notes	Reg.	Type	Notes	Reg.	Type
	85572	Tu-154B-2		85665	Tu-154M (AFL)
	85573	Tu-154B-2		85666	Tu-154M
	85574	Tu-154B-2		85667	Tu-154M
	85577	Tu-154B-2		85668	Tu-154M (AFL)
	85579	Tu-154B-2		85669	Tu-154M (AFL)
	85584	Tu-154B-2 (AFL)		85670	Tu-154M (AFL)
	85585	Tu-154B-2		85671	Tu-154M (AFL)
	85586	Tu-154B-2		85672	Tu-154M
	85587	Tu-154B-2		85675	Tu-154M
	85588	Tu-154B-2		85676	Tu-154M
	85592	Tu-154B-2 (AFL)		85677	Tu-154M
	85594	Tu-154B-2		85678	Tu-154M
	85595	Tu-154B-2 (AFL)		85679	Tu-154M
	85596	Tu-154B-2		85680	Tu-154M
	85597	Tu-154B-2		85681	Tu-154M (MSV)
	85601	Tu-154B-2		85682	Tu-154M
	85602	Tu-154B-2		85683	Tu-154M
	85603	Tu-154B-2		85684	Tu-154M
	85604	Tu-154B-2		85686	Tu-154M
	85605	Tu-154B-2		85687	Tu-154M
	85606	Tu-154B-2		85688	Tu-154M
	85607	Tu-154B-2		85689	Tu-154M (AFL)
	85609	Tu-154M		85690	Tu-154M
	85610	Tu-154M (VKO)		85693	Tu-154M
	85611	Tu-154M (VKO)		85694	Tu-154M
	85612	Tu-154M		85695	Tu-154M
	85613	Tu-154M		85697	Tu-154M
	85614	Tu-154M		85698	Tu-154M
	85615	TU-154M		85699	Tu-154M
	85616	Tu-154M		85702	Tu-154M
	85617	Tu-154M		85704	Tu-154M (TRJ)
	85618	Tu-154M (VKO)		85708	Tu-154M
	85619	Tu-154M (VKO)		85710	Tu-154M (AFL)
	85021	Tu-154M (VKO)		85712	Tu-154M (LSV)
	85622	Tu-154M (VKO)		85713	Tu-154M (LSV)
	85623	Tu-154M (VKO)		85714	Tu-154M (LSV)
	85624	Tu-154M (VKO)		85722	Tu-154M
	85625	Tu-154M (AFL)		85723	Tu-154M
	85626	Tu-154M (AFL)		85724	Tu-154M
	85627	Tu-154M		85728	Tu-154M (AFL)
	85628	Tu-154M (VKO)		85731	Tu-154M
	85629	Tu-154M (AFL)		85736	Tu-154M (VKO)
	85630	Tu-154M (AFL)		85743	Tu-154M (VKO)
	85631	Tu-154M (AFL)		85745	Tu-154M (VKO)
	85632	Tu-154M (VKO)		85750	Tu-154M
	85633	Tu-154M (VKO)		85751	Tu-154M
	85634	Tu-154M (AFL)		85752	Tu-154M (AFL)
	85635	Tu-154M (VKO)		85755	Tu-154M (AFL)
	85636	Tu-154M		85758	Tu-154M (AFL)
	85637	Tu-154M (AFL)		85767	Tu-154M (AFL)
	85638	Tu-154M (AFL)		85768	Tu-154M (AFL)
	85639	Tu-154M (AFL)		85769	Tu-154M (AFL)
	85640	Tu-154M (AFL)		85770	Tu-154M (AFL)
	85641	Tu-154M (AFL)		85779	Tu-154M (TRJ)
	85642	Tu-154M (AFL)		85783	Tu-154M (AFL)
	85644	Tu-154M (AFL)		85785	Tu-154M (AFL)
	85645	Tu-154M		85786	Tu-154M (AFL)
	85646	Tu-154M (AFL)		85790	Tu-154M (AFL)
	85647	Tu-154M (AFL)		85792	Tu-154M (AFL)
	85648	Tu-154M (AFL)		85793	Tu-154M (AFL)
	85649	Tu-154M (AFL)		85810	Tu-154M (AFL)
	85650	Tu-154M (AFL)		85811	Tu-154M (AFL)
	85651	Tu-154M			
	85652	Tu-154M		86003	IL-86
	85653	Tu-154M		86004	IL-86 (TRJ)
	85654	Tu-154M		86005	IL-86 (VKO)
	85655	Tu-154M		86006	IL-86 (VKO)
	85657	Tu-154M		86007	IL-86 (VKO)
	85658	Tu-154M		86008	IL-86 (VKO)
	85659	Tu-154M		86009	IL-86 (VKO)
	85660	Tu-154M		86010	IL-86 (VKO)
	85661	Tu-154M (AFL)		86011	IL-86 (VKO)
	85662	Tu-154M (AFL)		86013	IL-86 (VKO)
	85663	Tu-154M (AFL)		86014	IL-86 (VKO)

Reg.	Type	Notes	Reg.	Type	Notes
86015	IL-86 (AFL)		86460	IL-62	
86017	IL-86 (VKO)		86461	IL-62	
86018	IL-86 (VKO)		86462	IL-62M	
86050	IL-86		86463	IL-62M	
86051	IL-86		86464	IL-62M	
86054	IL-86 (AFL)		86465	IL-62M	
86055	IL-86 (VKO)		86466	IL-62MK	
86058	IL-86 (AFL)		86467	IL-62M (AFL)	
86059	IL-86 (AFL)		86468	IL-62MK	
86060	IL-86		86469	IL-62M	
86061	IL-86		86471	IL-62M	
86062	IL-86		86472	IL-62M	
86063	IL-86		86473	IL-62M	
86065	IL-86 (AFL)		86474	IL-62M (AFL)	
86066	IL-86 (AFL)		86475	IL-62M	
86067	IL-86 (AFL)		86476	IL-62M	
86070	IL-86		86477	IL-62M (AFL)	
86073	IL-86		86478	IL-62M (AFL)	
86074	IL-86 (AFL)		86479	IL-62M	
86075	IL-86 (AFL)		86480	IL-62M	
86076	IL-86		86481	IL-62M	
86078	IL-86		86482	IL-62M	
86079	IL-86 (AFL)		86483	IL-62M (AFL)	
86080	IL-86 (AFL)		86484	IL-62M	
86081	IL-86 (VKO)		86485	IL-62M (AFL)	
86082	IL-86 (VKO)		86486	IL-62M	
86084	IL-86 (AFL)		86487	IL-62M	
86085	IL-86 (VKO)		86488	IL-62M (AFL)	
86087	IL-86 (AFL)		86489	IL-62M (AFL)	
86088	IL-86 (AFL)		86490	IL-62M	
86089	IL-86 (VKO)		86491	IL-62M	
86091	IL-86 (VKO)		86492	IL-62M (AFL)	
86092	IL-86		86493	IL-62M	
86093	IL-86		86494	IL-62M	
86094	IL-86		86495	IL-62M	
86095	IL-86 (AFL)		86496	IL-62M	
86096	IL-86 (AFL)		86497	IL-62M (AFL)	
86097	IL-86 (VKO)		86498	IL-62M	
86102	IL-86		86499	IL-62M	
86103	IL-86 (AFL)		86500	IL-62M	
86104	IL-86 (VKO)		86501	IL-62M	
86105	IL-86		86502	IL-62M (AFL)	
86106	IL-86		86503	IL-62M	
86107	IL-86		86504	IL-62M	
86108	IL-86		86505	IL-62M	
86109	IL-86		86506	IL-62M (AFL)	
86110	IL-86 (AFL)		86507	IL-62M (AFL)	
86111	IL-86 (VKO)		86508	IL-62M	
86112	IL-86		86509	IL-62M	
86113	IL-86 (AFL)		86510	IL-62M (AFL)	
86114	IL-86		86511	IL-62M	
86115	IL-86 (AFL)		86512	IL-62M (AFL)	
86120	IL-86 (AFL)		86514	IL-62M (AFL)	
86121	IL-86		86515	IL-62M (MSC)	
86122	IL-86		86516	IL-62M	
86123	IL-86 (TSO)		86517	IL-62MK (AFL)	
86124	IL-86 (AFL)		86518	IL-62M (AFL)	
86126	IL-62MK (ORT)		86519	IL-62M	
86136	IL-86 (MSC)		86520	IL-62MK (AFL)	
86138	IL-86 (MSC)		86521	IL-62M	
86140	IL-86 (TRJ)		86522	IL-62M (AFL)	
86146	IL-86		86523	IL-62M (AFL)	
86147	IL-86		86524	IL-62M (AFL)	
86148	IL-86		86527	IL-62MK	
86149	IL-86		86528	IL-62MK	
86450	IL-62		86530	IL-62MK	
86451	IL-62		86531	IL-62M (AFL)	
86452	IL-62M		86532	IL-62MK (AFL)	
86453	IL-62M		86533	IL-62M (AFL)	
86454	IL-62M		86534	IL-62M (AFL)	
86455	IL-62M		86536	IL-62M	
86457	IL-62M		86537	IL-62M	
86458	IL-62M		86538	IL-62M	
86459	IL-62M		86539	IL-62MK	

Notes	Reg.	Type	Notes	Reg.	Type
	86540	IL-62M		86672	IL-62
	86554	IL-62M		86673	IL-62M
	86555	IL-62M		86674	IL-62
	86558	IL-62M (AFL)		86675	IL-62
	86560	IL-62M		86680	IL-62
	86562	IL-62M (AFL)		86681	IL-62
	86563	IL-62M		86682	IL-62
	86564	IL-62M (AFL)		86683	IL-62
	86565	IL-62M (AFL)		86684	IL-62
	86566	IL-62M (AFL)		86685	IL-62
	86567	IL-62M (ORT)		86686	IL-62
	86568	IL-62M (ORT)		86687	IL-62
	86590	IL-62M (ORT)		86689	IL-62
	86605	IL-62		86690	IL-62
	86606	IL-62		86691	IL-62
	86608	IL-62		86692	IL-62M
	86611	IL-62		86693	IL-62M
	86612	IL-62		86695	IL-62
	86614	IL-62		86696	IL-62
	86615	IL-62		86697	IL-62
	86616	IL-62		86698	IL-62
	86617	IL-62		86699	IL-62
	86618	IL-62M		86700	IL-62M
	86619	IL-62M		86701	IL-62M
	86620	IL-62M		86702	IL-62M
	86621	IL-62M		86703	IL-62M
	86622	IL-62M		86705	IL-62M
	86623	IL-62M		86706	IL-62M
	86624	IL-62M		86707	IL-62M
	86627	IL-76M (URA)		86708	IL-62MK
	86649	IL-62		86709	IL-62MK
	86650	IL-62		86710	IL-62MK
	86652	IL-62		86711	IL-62M
	86653	IL-62		86712	IL-62M
	86654	IL-62		86715	IL-76M (AFL)
	86655	IL-62		86720	IL-76M (URA)
	86656	IL-62M		86747	IL-76M (URA)
	86657	IL-62		86896	IL-76MD (AFL)
	86661	IL-62			
	86662	IL-62		96005	IL-96-300 (AFL)
	86663	IL-62		96007	IL-96-300 (AFL)
	86664	IL-62		96008	IL-96-300 (AFL)
	86665	IL-62		96010	IL-96-300 (AFL)
	86666	IL-62		96011	IL-96-300 (AFL)
	86668	IL-62			
	86669	IL-62			

Note: Aeroflot also operates Airbus A.310s registered F-OGQQ, F-OGQR, F-OQGT, F-OGQU, F-OGYM and F-OGYN, Boeing 767s which remain EI-CKD, EI-CKE and the DC-10.30 N524MD. Transaero operates Boeing 757s EI-CJX, EI-CJY and EI-CLM.

Notes	Reg.	Type	Owner or Operator

RP (Philippines)

RP-C5745	Boeing 747-212B	Philippine Airlines
RP-C5746	Boeing 747-212B	Philippine Airlines
RP-C5751	Boeing 747-4F6	Philippine Airlines
RP-C5752	Boeing 747-4F6	Philippine Airlines

Note: Philippine Airlines operates four Boeing 747-2F6Bs which retain their U.S. identities N741PR, N742PR, N743PR and N744PR, two 747-283Bs registered EI-BTS and EI-BZA and two 747-211Bs registered N207AE and N208AE.

S2 (Bangladesh)

S2-ACO	Douglas DC-10-30	Bangladesh Biman *The City of Hazrat-Shah Makhdoom (R.A.)*
S2-ACP	Douglas DC-10-30	Bangladesh Biman *The City of Dhaka*
S2-ACQ	Douglas DC-10-30	Bangladesh Biman *The City of Hazrat-Shah Jalal (R.A.)*

Reg.	Type	Owner or Operator	Notes
S2-ACR	Douglas DC-10-30	Bangladesh Biman *The New Era*	
S2-ADB	Douglas DC-10-30	Bangladesh Biman	
S2-	Airbus A.310-324	Bangladesh Biman	
S2-	Airbus A.310-324	Bangladesh Biman	

S5 (Slovenia)

S5-AAA	Airbus A.320-231	Adria Airways/Cretan Airlines	
S5-AAB	Airbus A.320-231	Adria Airways	
S5-AAC	Airbus A.320-231	Adria Airways	
S5-ABA	McD Douglas MD-82	Adria Airways	
S5-ABB	McD Douglas MD-82	Adria Airways	
S5-ABF	Douglas DC-9-32	Adria Airways	
S5-ABH	Douglas DC-9-32	Adria Airways	

S7 (Seychelles)

S7-AAS	Boeing 767-2Q8ER	Air Seychelles *Isle of Aldabra*	
S7-AAX	Boeing 757-28A	Air Seychelles *Aride*	

SE (Sweden)

SE-CFP	Douglas DC-3	Flygande Veteraner *Fridtjof Viking*	
SE-DAR	Douglas DC-9-41	S.A.S. *Agnar Viking*	
SE-DAS	Douglas DC-9-41	S.A.S. *Garder Viking*	
SE-DAU	Douglas DC-9-41	S.A.S. *Hadding Viking*	
SE-DAW	Douglas DC-9-41	S.A.S. *Gotrik Viking*	
SE-DAX	Douglas DC-9-41	S.A.S. *Helsing Viking*	
SE-DBM	Douglas DC-9-41	S.A.S. *Ossur Viking*	
SE-DBO	Douglas DC-9-21	S.A.S. *Siger Viking*	
SE-DDP	Douglas DC-9-41	S.A.S. *Brun Viking*	
SE-DDR	Douglas DC-9-41	S.A.S. *Atle Viking*	
SE-DDS	Douglas DC-9-41	S.A.S. *Alrik Viking*	
SE-DDT	Douglas DC-9-41	S.A.S. *Amund Viking*	
SE-DFR	McD Douglas MD-81	S.A.S. *Ingjald Viking*	
SE-DFS	McD Douglas MD-82	S.A.S. *Gaut Viking*	
SE-DFT	McD Douglas MD-82	S.A.S. *Assur Viking*	
SE-DFY	McD Douglas MD-81	S.A.S. *Ottar Viking*	
SE-DGA	F.28 Fellowship 1000	S.A.S. *Alf Viking*	
SE-DGB	F.28 Fellowship 1000	S.A.S. *Brage Viking*	
SE-DGC	F.28 Fellowship 1000	S.A.S. *Dag Viking*	
SE-DGE	F.28 Fellowship 4000	S.A.S. *Erik Viking*	
SE-DGF	F.28 Fellowship 4000	S.A.S. *Egil Viking*	
SE-DGG	F.28 Fellowship 4000	S.A.S. *Gunnhild Viking*	
SE-DGH	F.28 Fellowship 4000	S.A.S. *Hjalmar Viking*	
SE-DGI	F.28 Fellowship 4000	S.A.S. *Ingeborg Viking*	
SE-DGK	F.28 Fellowship 4000	S.A.S. *Knut Viking*	
SE-DGL	F.28 Fellowship 4000	S.A.S. *Loke Viking*	
SE-DGM	F.28 Fellowship 4000	S.A.S. *Hild Viking*	
SE-DGN	F.28 Fellowship 4000	S.A.S. *Gunnar Viking*	
SE-DGO	F.28 Fellowship 4000	S.A.S. *Odd Viking*	
SE-DGP	F.28 Fellowship 4000	S.A.S. *Steinar Viking*	
SE-DGR	F.28 Fellowship 4000	S.A.S. *Randver Viking*	
SE-DGS	F.28 Fellowship 4000	S.A.S. *Sigrun Viking*	
SE-DGT	F.28 Fellowship 4000	S.A.S. *Tola Viking*	
SE-DGU	F.28 Fellowship 4000	S.A.S. *Ulfljot Viking*	
SE-DGX	F.28 Fellowship 4000	S.A.S. *Vemund Viking*	
SE-DHC	McD Douglas MD-83	Transwede *Carl von Linne*	
SE-DHG	McD Douglas MD-87	Transwede	
SE-DHI	McD Douglas MD-87	Transwede	
SE-DHN	McD Douglas MD-83	Transwede *Nobel*	
SE-DHS	Douglas DC-10-10	Premiair *Baloo*	
SE-DIA	McD Douglas MD-81	S.A.S. *Ulvrik Viking*	
SE-DIB	McD Douglas MD-87	S.A.S. *Varin Viking*	
SE-DIC	McD Douglas MD-87	S.A.S. *Grane Viking*	
SE-DIF	McD Douglas MD-87	S.A.S. *Hjorulv Viking*	
SE-DIH	McD Douglas MD-87	S.A.S. *Slagfinn Viking*	

Reg.	Type	Owner or Operator
SE-DII	McD Douglas MD-81	S.A.S. *Sigtrygg Viking*
SE-DIK	McD Douglas MD-82	S.A.S. *Stenkil Viking*
SE-DIL	McD Douglas MD-81	S.A.S. *Tord Viking*
SE-DIN	McD Douglas MD-81	S.A.S. *Eskil Viking*
SE-DIP	McD Douglas MD-87	S.A.S. *Jarl Viking*
SE-DIR	McD Douglas MD-81	S.A.S. *Nora Viking*
SE-DIS	McD Douglas MD-81	S.A.S. *Sigmund Viking*
SE-DIU	McD Douglas MD-87	S.A.S. *Torsten Viking*
SE-DIX	McD Douglas MD-81	S.A.S. *Adils Viking*
SE-DIY	McD Douglas MD-81	S.A.S. *Albin Viking*
SE-DIZ	McD Douglas MD-82	S.A.S. *Sigyn Viking*
SE-DLC	Douglas DC-9-41	Nordic East *City of Stockholm*
SE-DLS	McD Douglas MD-83	Transwede *Piraten*
SE-DLU	McD Douglas MD-83	Transwede *Norrsken*
SE-DMA	McD Douglas MD-87	S.A.S. *Lage Viking*
SE-DMB	McD Douglas MD-81	S.A.S. *Bjarne Viking*
SE-DMD	McD Douglas MD-81	S.A.S. *Holmfrid Viking*
SE-DME	McD Douglas MD-81	S.A.S. *Kristen Viking*
SE-DMY	McD Douglas MD-81	S.A.S.
SE-DMZ	McD Douglas MD-81	S.A.S.
SE-DOC	Boeing 767-383ER	S.A.S. *Gudrun Viking*
SE-DPA	Boeing 737-33AQC	Falcon Aviation
SE-DPB	Boeing 737-33AQC	Falcon Aviation
SE-DPC	Boeing 737-33AQC	Falcon Aviation
SE-DPH	McD Douglas MD-83	S.A.S.
SE-DPI	McD Douglas MD-83	S.A.S. *Erik Viking*
SE-DPM	L.1011-385 TriStar 50	Air Ops
SE-DPN	Boeing 737-3G7	—
SE-DPP	L.1011-385 TriStar 50	Air Ops
SE-DPS	McD Douglas MD-83	Nordic Air *Sunset of Stockholm*
SE-DPV	L.1011-385 TriStar 1	Air Ops
SE-DPX	L.1011-385 TriStar 50	Air Ops
SE-DRA	BAc 146-200	Malmö Aviation
SE-DRB	BAe 146-200A	Malmö Aviation
SE-DRC	BAe 146-200A	Malmö Aviation
SE-DRD	BAe 146-200	Malmö Aviation
SE-DRE	BAe 146-200A	Malmö Aviation
SE-DRF	BAe 146-200A	Malmö Aviation
SE-DRG	BAe 146-200A	Malmö Aviation
SE-DRH	BAe 146-100	Malmö Aviation
SE-DRI	BAe 146-200A	Malmö Aviation
SE-DSB	L.1011-385 TriStar 1	Air Ops
SE-DSC	L.1011-385 TriStar 50	Air Ops
SE-DSD	L.1011-385 TriStar 100	Air Ops
SE-DSF	Airbus A.300B4-203	Air Ops
SE-DSH	Airbus A.300B4-203	Air Ops
SE-DSK	Boeing 757-236	Sunways
SE-DSL	Boeing 757-236	Sunways
SE-DTB	Boeing 737-4Y0	Nordic East
SE-DTC	L.1011-385 TriStar 1	Nordic East
SE-DTD	L.1011-385 TriStar 1	Nordic East
SE-DUC	Fokker 100	Transwede *Cornelis*
SE-DUD	Fokker 100	Transwede *Tyst*
SE-DUE	Fokker 100	Transwede *Emil*
SE-DUH	Fokker 100	Transwede
SE-DUI	Fokker 100	Transwede
SE-DUK	Boeing 757-236	Transwede
SE-KGA	FH.227B Friendship	—
SE-KGB	FH.227B Friendship	—
SE-KZD	F.27 Friendship Mk 100	Air Nordic
SE-KZE	F.27 Friendship Mk 100	Air Nordic
SE-KZF	F.27 Friendship Mk 100	Air Nordic
SE-KZG	F.27 Friendship Mk 100	Air Nordic
SE-KZH	F.27 Friendship Mk 100	Air Nordic
SE-LFA	Fokker 50	S.A.S. Commuter *Jorund Viking*
SE-LFB	Fokker 50	S.A.S. Commuter *Sture Viking*
SE-LFC	Fokker 50	S.A.S. Commuter *Ylva Viking*
SE-LFK	Fokker 50	S.A.S. Commuter *Alvar Viking*
SE-LFN	Fokker 50	S.A.S. Commuter *Edmund Viking*
SE-LFO	Fokker 50	S.A.S. Commuter *Folke Viking*
SE-LFP	Fokker 50	S.A.S. Commuter *Ingemar Viking*
SE-LFR	Fokker 50	S.A.S. Commuter *Vagn Viking*
SE-LFS	Fokker 50	S.A.S. Commuter *Vigge Viking*

SP (Poland)

SP-LCC	Tupolev Tu-154M	Polskie Linie Lotnicze (LOT)
SP-LCD	Tupolev Tu-154M	LOT
SP-LCE	Tupolev Tu-154M	LOT
SP-LCF	Tupolev Tu-154M	LOT
SP-LCL	Tupolev Tu-154M	LOT
SP-LCM	Tupolev Tu-154M	LOT
SP-LCN	Tupolev Tu-154M	LOT
SP-LCO	Tupolev Tu-154M	LOT
SP-LKA	Boeing 737-55D	LOT
SP-LKB	Boeing 737-55D	LOT
SP-LKC	Boeing 737-55D	LOT
SP-LKD	Boeing 737-55D	LOT
SP-LKE	Boeing 737-55D	LOT
SP-LKF	Boeing 737-55D	LOT
SP-LLA	Boeing 737-45D	LOT
SP-LLB	Boeing 737-45D	LOT
SP-LLC	Boeing 737-45D	LOT
SP-LLD	Boeing 737-45D	LOT
SP-LLE	Boeing 737-45D	LOT
SP-LOA	Boeing 767-25DER	LOT *Gneizao*
SP-LOB	Boeing 767-25DER	LOT *Kracow*
SP-LPA	Boeing 767-35DER	LOT *Warszawa*

ST (Sudan)

ST-AFA	Boeing 707-3J8C	Sudan Airways
ST-AFB	Boeing 707-3J8C	Sudan Airways
ST-AIX	Boeing 707-369C	Sudan Airways
ST-AKW	Boeing 707-330C	Azza Transport
ST-AMF	Boeing 707-321C	Transarabian Air Transport
ST-ANP	Boeing 707-351C	Transarabian Air Transport

Note: Sudan Airways also operates the A.300-622 F-ODTK and A.310-304s F-OGQN *Khartoum* and F-GKTD.

SU (Egypt)

SU-BCB	Airbus A.300B4-203	EgyptAir *Osiris*
SU-BCC	Airbus A.300B4-203	EgyptAir *Nout*
SU-BDG	Airbus A.300B4-203	EgyptAir *Aton*
SU-DAA	Boeing 707-351C	ZAS Airline of Egypt
SU-DAC	Boeing 707-336C	Memphis Air
SU-DAR	Airbus A.300B4-203	ZAS Airline of Egypt
SU-DAS	Airbus A.300B4-203	ZAS Airline of Egypt
SU-GAH	Boeing 767-266ER	EgyptAir *Nefertiti*
SU-GAI	Boeing 767-266ER	EgyptAir *Nefertari*
SU-GAJ	Boeing 767-266ER	EgyptAir *Tiye*
SU-GAL	Boeing 747-366 (SCD)	EgyptAir *Hatshepsut*
SU-GAM	Boeing 747-366 (SCD)	EgyptAir *Cleopatra*
SU-GAO	Boeing 767-366ER	EgyptAir *Ramses II*
SU-GAP	Boeing 767-366ER	EgyptAir *Thutmosis III*
SU-GAR	Airbus A.300-622R	EgyptAir *Zoser*
SU-GAS	Airbus A.300-622R	EgyptAir *Cheops*
SU-GAT	Airbus A.300-622R	EgyptAir *Chephren*
SU-GAU	Airbus A.300-622R	EgyptAir *Mycerinus*
SU-GAV	Airbus A.300-622R	EgyptAir *Menes*
SU-GAW	Airbus A.300-622R	EgyptAir *Ahmuse*
SU-GAX	Airbus A.300-622R	EgyptAir *Tut-Ankh-Amun*
SU-GAY	Airbus A.300-622R	EgyptAir *Seti I*
SU-GAZ	Airbus A.300-622R	EgyptAir
SU-GBA	Airbus A.320-231	EgyptAir *Aswan*
SU-GBB	Airbus A.320-231	EgyptAir *Luxor*
SU-GBC	Airbus A.320-231	EgyptAir *Hurghada*
SU-GBD	Airbus A.320-231	EgyptAir *Taba*
SU-GBE	Airbus A.320-231	EgyptAir *El Alamein*
SU-GBF	Airbus A.320-231	EgyptAir *Sharm El Sheikh*

Notes	Reg.	Type	Owner or Operator
	SU-GBG	Airbus A.320-231	EgyptAir *Saint Catherine*
	SU-	Airbus A.340-211	EygptAir
	SU-	Airbus A.340-211	EygptAir
	SU-	Airbus A.340-211	EygptAir
	SU-RAA	Airbus A.320-231	Shorouk Air
	SU-RAB	Airbus A.320-231	Shorouk Air

Note: EgyptAir operates the A.340-312 A4O-LE on lease from Gulf Air.

SX (Greece)

SX-BAQ	McD Douglas MD-83	Venus Airlines
SX-BAY	Airbus A.300B4-203	Apollo Airlines
SX-BAZ	Airbus A.300B4-203	Apollo Airlines *City of Thessaloniki*
SX-BBW	McD Douglas MD-82	Venus Airlines
SX-BBZ	Boeing 757-236	Venus Airlines
SX-BCA	Boeing 737-284	Olympic Airways *Apollo*
SX-BCB	Boeing 737-284	Olympic Airways *Hermes*
SX-BCC	Boeing 737-284	Olympic Airways *Hercules*
SX-BCD	Boeing 737-284	Olympic Airways *Hephaestus*
SX-BCE	Boeing 737-284	Olympic Airways *Dionysus*
SX-BCF	Boeing 737-284	Olympic Airways *Poseidon*
SX-BCG	Boeing 737-284	Olympic Airways *Phoebus*
SX-BCH	Boeing 737-284	Olympic Airways *Triton*
SX-BCI	Boeing 737-284	Olympic Airways *Proteus*
SX-BCK	Boeing 737-284	Olympic Airways *Nereus*
SX-BCL	Boeing 737-284	Olympic Airways *Isle of Thassos*
SX-BEB	Airbus A.300B4-103	Olympic Airways *Odysseus*
SX-BED	Airbus A.300B4-103	Olympic Airways *Telemachus*
SX-BEE	Airbus A.300B4-103	Olympic Airways *Nestor*
SX-BEF	Airbus A.300B4-103	Olympic Airways *Ajax*
SX-BEG	Airbus A.300B4 103	Olympic Airways *Diomedes*
SX-BEH	Airbus A.300B4-103	Olympic Airways *Pileus*
SX-BEI	Airbus A.300B4-103	Olympic Airways *Neoptolemos*
SX-BEK	Airbus A.300-605R	Olympic Airways *Macedonia*
SX-BEL	Airbus A.300-605R	Olympic Airways *Athena*
SX-BEM	Airbus A.300-605R	Olympic Airways
SX-BEN	Airbus A.300-605R	Olympic Airways
SX-BFI	Airbus A.300B4-203	Apollo Airlines
SX-BKA	Boeing 737-484	Olympic Airways *Vergina*
SX-BKB	Boeing 737-484	Olympic Airways *Olynthos*
SX-BKC	Boeing 737-484	Olympic Airways *Philipoli*
SX-BKD	Boeing 737-484	Olympic Airways *Amphipoli*
SX-BKE	Boeing 737-484	Olympic Airways *Stagira*
SX-BKF	Boeing 737-484	Olympic Airways *Dion*
SX-BKG	Boeing 737-484	Olympic Airways
SX-CBA	Boeing 727-284	Olympic Airways *Mount Olympus*
SX-CBB	Boeing 727-284	Olympic Airways *Mount Pindos*
SX-CBC	Boeing 727-284	Olympic Airways *Mount Parnassus*
SX-CBD	Boeing 727-284	Olympic Airways *Mount Helicon*
SX-CBE	Boeing 727-284	Olympic Airways *Mount Athos*
SX-CBF	Boeing 727-284	Olympic Airways *Mount Taygetus*
SX-CBG	Boeing 727-230	Olympic Airways *Mount Menalon*
SX-CBH	Boeing 727-230	Olympic Airways *Mount Vermio*
SX-CBI	Boeing 727-230	Greek Government (VIP)
SX-OAB	Boeing 747-284B	Olympic Airways *Olympic Eagle*
SX-OAC	Boeing 747-212B	Olympic Airways *Olympic Spirit*
SX-OAD	Boeing 747-212B	Olympic Airways *Olympic Flame*
SX-OAE	Boeing 747-212B	Olympic Airways *Olympic Peace*

TC (Turkey)

TC-ACA	Boeing 737-4Y0	Istanbul Airlines
TC-ACI	Tupolev Tu-154M	Active Air
TC-ACT	Tupolev Tu-154M	Active Air
TC-ACV	Tupolev Tu-154M	Active Air
TC-AFA	Boeing 737-4Q8	Pegasus Airlines
TC-AFB	Boeing 727-228	Istanbul Airlines
TC-AFC	Boeing 727-228	Istanbul Airlines

Reg.	Type	Owner or Operator	Notes
TC-AFK	Boeing 737-4Y0	Pegasus Airlines	
TC-AFM	Boeing 737-4Q8	Pegasus Airlines	
TC-AFN	Boeing 727-230	Istanbul Airlines	
TC-AFO	Boeing 727-230	Istanbul Airlines	
TC-AFP	Boeing 727-230	Istanbul Airlines	
TC-AFR	Boeing 727-230	Istanbul Airlines	
TC-AFT	Boeing 727-230	Istanbul Airlines	
TC-AFV	Boeing 727-230F	Istanbul Cargo	
TC-AFZ	Boeing 737-4Y0	Pegasus Airlines	
TC-AGA	Boeing 737-4Y0	Istanbul Airlines	
TC-AHA	Boeing 757-236	Istanbul Airlines	
TC-AJA	Boeing 757-236	Istanbul Airlines	
TC-ALC	Boeing 737-248	Albatros Airline *Can*	
TC-ALK	Boeing 727-230	Air Alfa *Sena*	
TC-ALM	Boeing 727-230	Air Alfa	
TC-ALN	Airbus A.300B4-103	Air Alfa	
TC-ALP	Airbus A.300B4-203	Air Alfa *Egress*	
TC-ALR	Airbus A.300B4-203	Air Alfa *Mert*	
TC-ALT	Boeing 737-248	Kibris Turkish Airlines	
TC-ALY	Yakovlev Yak-42	Albatros Airline	
TC-APA	Boeing 737-4S3	Istanbul Airlines	
TC-AVA	Boeing 737-4S3	Istanbul Airlines	
TC-AYA	Boeing 737-4Y0	Istanbul Airlines	
TC-AZA	Boeing 737-4Y0	Istanbul Airlines	
TC-BIR	Boeing 737-3M8	Birgenair	
TC-GEN	Boeing 757-225	Birgenair *(Destroyed 2/96)*	
TC-INA	McD Douglas MD-83	Sunway	
TC-INB	McD Douglas MD-83	Sunway	
TC-INC	McD Douglas MD-83	Sunway	
TC-JBF	Boeing 727-2F2	Turkish Airlines *Adana*	
TC-JBG	Boeing 727-2F2	Kibris Turkish Airlines *Yavruvatan*	
TC-JBJ	Boeing 727-2F2	Kibris Turkish Airlines *Besparmak*	
TC-JBM	Boeing 727-2F2	Turkish Airlines *Menderas*	
TC-JCA	Boeing 727-2F2F	Turkish Airlines Cargo *Edime*	
TC-JCB	Boeing 727-2F2	Turkish Airlines *Kars*	
TC-JCD	Boeing 727-2F2F	Turkish Airlines Cargo *Sinop*	
TC-JCE	Boeing 727-2F2	Turkish Airlines *Hatay*	
TC-JCK	Boeing 727-243	Turkish Airlines *Erciyes*	
TC-JCL	Airbus A.310-203	Turkish Airlines *Seyhan*	
TC-JCM	Airbus A.310-203	Turkish Airlines *Ceyhan*	
TC-JCN	Airbus A.310-203	Turkish Airlines *Dicle*	
TC-JCO	Airbus A.310-203	Turkish Airlines *Firat*	
TC-JCR	Airbus A.310-203	Turkish Airlines *Kizilirmak*	
TC-JCS	Airbus A.310-203	Turkish Airlines *Yesilirmak*	
TC-JCU	Airbus A.310-203	Turkish Airlines *Sakarya*	
TC-JCV	Airbus A.310-304	Turkish Airlines *Aras*	
TC-JCY	Airbus A.310-304	Turkish Airlines *Coruh*	
TC-JCZ	Airbus A.310-304	Turkish Airlines *Ergene*	
TC-JDA	Airbus A.310-304	Turkish Airlines *Aksu*	
TC-JDB	Airbus A.310-304ET	Turkish Airlines *Goksu*	
TC-JDC	Airbus A.310-304ET	Turkish Airlines *Meric*	
TC-JDD	Airbus A.310-304ET	Turkish Airlines *Dalaman*	
TC-JDE	Boeing 737-4Y0	Turkish Airlines *Kemer*	
TC-JDF	Boeing 737-4Y0	Turkish Airlines *Ayvalik*	
TC-JDG	Boeing 737-4Y0	Turkish Airlines *Marmaris*	
TC-JDH	Boeing 737-4Y0	Turkish Airlines *Amasra*	
TC-JDI	Boeing 737-4Q8	Turkish Airlines *Urgup*	
TC-JDJ	Airbus A.340-311	Turkish Airlines *Istanbul*	
TC-JDK	Airbus A.340-311	Turkish Airlines *Isparta*	
TC-JDL	Airbus A.340-311	Turkish Airlines *Ankara*	
TC-JDT	Boeing 737-4Y0	Turkish Airlines *Istanbul*	
TC-JDU	Boeing 737-5Y0	Turkish Airlines *Trabzon*	
TC-JDV	Boeing 737-5Y0	Turkish Airlines *Bursa*	
TC-JDY	Boeing 737-4Y0	Turkish Airlines *Ankara*	
TC-JDZ	Boeing 737-4Y0	Turkish Airlines *Izmir*	
TC-JEA	Boeing 737-42J	Turkish Airlines *Kusadasi*	
TC-JEC	Boeing 727-228	Kibris Turkish Airlines *Yesilada*	
TC-JED	Boeing 737-4Q8	Turkish Airlines *Bodrum*	
TC-JEE	Boeing 737-4Q8	Turkish Airlines *Cesme*	
TC-JEF	Boeing 737-4Q8	Turkish Airlines *Goereme*	
TC-JEG	Boeing 737-4Q8	Turkish Airlines	
TC-JEH	Boeing 737-4Q8	Turkish Airlines	

Notes	Reg.	Type	Owner or Operator
	TC-JEI	Boeing 737-4Q8	Turkish Airlines *Artvin*
	TC-JEJ	Boeing 737-4Q8	Turkish Airlines
	TC-JEK	Boeing 737-4Q8	Turkish Airlines
	TC-JEL	Boeing 737-4Q8	Turkish Airlines *Eskisehir*
	TC-JEM	Boeing 737-4Q8	Turkish Airlines *Malatya*
	TC-JEN	Boeing 737-4Q8	Turkish Airlines *Gelibolu*
	TC-JEO	Boeing 737-4Q8	Turkish Airlines *Anadolu*
	TC-JEP	Boeing 737-4Q8	Turkish Airlines *Trakya*
	TC-JER	Boeing 737-4Y0	Turkish Airlines *Mugla*
	TC-JET	Boeing 737-4Y0	Turkish Airlines *Canakkale*
	TC-JEU	Boeing 737-4Y0	Turkish Airlines *Kayseri*
	TC-JEV	Boeing 737-4Y0	Turkish Airlines *Efes*
	TC-JEY	Boeing 737-4Y0	Turkish Airlines *Side*
	TC-JEZ	Boeing 737-4Y0	Turkish Airlines *Bergama*
	TC-JYK	Airbus A.310-203	Kibris Turkish Airlines *Erenkoy*
	TC-ONA	Airbus A.320-211	Onur Air *Birtug*
	TC-ONB	Airbus A.320-211	Onur Air *Nazar*
	TC-ONC	Airbus A.320-211	Onur Air *Bosphorus*
	TC-OND	Airbus A.320-211	Onur Air *Yeditepe*
	TC-ONE	Airbus A.320-212	Onur Air *Marmara*
	TC-ONF	Airbus A.320-231	Onur Air *Nurce*
	TC-ONG	Airbus A.320-231	Onur Air
	TC-RAA	Airbus A.300B4-2C	Holiday Airlines
	TC-RAB	Airbus A.300B2-101	Holiday Airlines
	TC-RAC	Boeing 727-230	Holiday Airlines *Igdis*
	TC-RAD	Tupolev Tu-154M	Holiday Airlines
	TC-RUT	Boeing 727-230	TUR European Airways
	TC-SUN	Boeing 737-3Y0	Sun Express
	TC-SUP	Boeing 737-3Y0	Sun Express
	TC-SUR	Boeing 737-3Y0	Sun Express
	TC-SUS	Boeing 737-430	Sun Express
	TC-SUT	Boeing 737-4Y0	Sun Express
	TC-TKA	Airbus A.300B4-203	Onur Air
	TC-TKB	Airbus A.300B4-203	Onur Air

TF (Iceland)

	TF-ABF	Boeing 737-230C	Air Atlanta Iceland
	TF-ABK	Boeing 737-3Y0	Air Atlanta Iceland/AviaReps
	TF-ABL	L.1011-385 TriStar1	Air Atlanta Iceland
	TF-ABP	L.1011-385 TriStar1	Air Atlanta Iceland
	TF-ABX	Boeing 737-230C	Air Atlanta Iceland
	TF-FIA	Boeing 737-408	Icelandair *Aldis*
	TF-FIB	Boeing 737-408	Icelandair *Eydis*
	TF-FIC	Boeing 737-408	Icelandair *Vedis*
	TF-FID	Boeing 737-408	Icelandair *Heiddis*
	TF-FIE	Boeing 737-4S3	Icelandair
	TF-FIH	Boeing 757-208	Icelandair *Hafdis*
	TF-FII	Boeing 757-208	Icelandair *Fanndis*
	TF-FIJ	Boeing 757-208	Icelandair *Svandis*
	TF-	Boeing 757-200	Icelandair
	TF-FIR	Fokker 50	Icelandair *Asdis*
	TF-FIS	Fokker 50	Icelandair *Sigdis*
	TF-FIT	Fokker 50	Icelandair *Freydis*
	TF-FIU	Fokker 50	Icelandair *Valdis*

TJ (Cameroon)

	TJ-CAB	Boeing 747-2H7B (SCD)	Cameroon Airlines *Mont Cameroun*

TR (Gabon)

Note: Air Gabon operates Boeing 747-2Q2B F-ODJG for which the registration TR-LXK
has been reserved.

Reg.	Type	Owner or Operator	Notes

TS (Tunisia)

Reg.	Type	Owner or Operator
TS-IMA	Airbus A.300B4-203	Tunis-Air *Amilcar*
TS-IMB	Airbus A.320-211	Tunis-Air *Fahrat Hached*
TS-IMC	Airbus A.320-211	Tunis-Air *7 Novembre*
TS-IMD	Airbus A.320-211	Tunis-Air *Khereddine*
TS-IME	Airbus A.320-211	Tunis-Air *Tabarka*
TS-IMF	Airbus A.320-211	Tunis-Air *Jerba*
TS-IMG	Airbus A.320-211	Tunis-Air *Abou el Kacem Chebbi*
TS-IMH	Airbus A.320-211	Tunis-Air *Ali Belhaouane*
TS-IMI	Airbus A.320-211	Tunis-Air
TS-IOC	Boeing 737-2H3	Tunis-Air *Salammbo*
TS-IOD	Boeing 737-2H3C	Tunis-Air *Bulla Regia*
TS-IOE	Boeing 737-2H3	Tunis-Air *Zarzis*
TS-IOF	Boeing 737-2H3	Tunis-Air *Sousse*
TS-IOG	Boeing 737-5H3	Tunis-Air *Sfax*
TS-IOH	Boeing 737-5H3	Tunis-Air *Hammamet*
TS-IOI	Boeing 737-5H3	Tunis-Air
TS-IOJ	Boeing 737-5H3	Tunis-Air *Mahida*
TS-JHQ	Boeing 727-2H3	Tunis-Air *Tozeur-Nefta*
TS-JHR	Boeing 727-2H3	Tunis-Air *Bizerte*
TS-JHS	Boeing 727-2H3	Tunis-Air *Kairouan*
TS-JHT	Boeing 727-2H3	Tunis-Air *Sidi Bousaid*
TS-JHU	Boeing 727-2H3	Tunis-Air *Hannibal*
TS-JHW	Boeing 727-2H3	Tunis-Air *Ibn Khaldoun*

TU (Ivory Coast)

Reg.	Type	Owner or Operator
TU-TAC	Airbus A.310-304	Air Afrique
TU-TAD	Airbus A.310-304	Air Afrique
TU-TAE	Airbus A.310-304	Air Afrique
TU-TAF	Airbus A.310-304	Air Afrique
TU-TAG	Airbus A.310-304	Air Afrique
TU-TAH	Airbus A.300-605R	Air Afrique
TU-TAI	Alrbus A.300-605R	Air Afrique
TU-TAL	Douglas DC-10-30	Air Afrique *Libreville*
TU-TAO	Airbus A.300B4-203	Air Afrique *Nouackchott*
TU-TAR	Airbus A.310-304	Air Afrique
TU-TAS	Airbus A.300B4-203	Air Afrique *Bangui*
TU-TAT	Airbus A.300B4-203	Air Afrique
TU-TAU	Airbus A.310-304	Air Afrique

Reg.	Type	Notes	Reg.	Type	Notes

UK (Uzbekistan)

The following are operated by Uzbekistan Airways with registrations prefixed by UK.

Reg.	Type	Reg.	Type
76351	IL-76TD	85286	Tu-154B-1
76352	IL-76TD	85322	Tu-154B-2
76353	IL-76TD	85344	Tu-154B-2
76358	IL-76TD	85356	Tu-154B-2
76359	IL-76TD	85370	Tu-154B-2
76447	IL-76TD	85397	Tu-154B-2
76448	IL-76TD	85398	Tu-154B-2
76449	IL-76TD	85401	Tu-154B-2
76782	IL-76TD	85416	Tu-154B-2
76793	IL-76TD	85423	Tu-154B-2
76794	IL-76TD	85433	Tu-154B-2
76805	IL-76TD	85438	Tu-154B-2
76811	IL-76TD	85449	Tu-154B-2
76813	IL-76TD	85575	Tu-154B-2
76824	IL-76TD	85578	Tu-154B-2
85050	Tu-154B	85600	Tu-154B-2
85189	Tu-154B	85711	Tu-154M
85245	Tu-154B-1	85764	Tu-154M
85248	Tu-154B-1	85776	Tu-154M
85249	Tu-154B-1	86012	IL-86
85272	Tu-154B-1	86016	IL-86

Notes	Reg.	Type	Notes	Reg.	Type
	86052	IL-86		86575	IL-62M
	86053	IL-86		86576	IL-62M
	86056	IL-86		86577	IL-62M
	86057	IL-86		86578	IL-62M
	86064	IL-86		86610	IL-62M
	86072	IL-86		86659	IL-62M
	86083	IL-86		86704	IL-62M
	86090	IL-86		86932	IL-62M
	86569	IL-62M		86933	IL-62M
	86573	IL-62M		86934	IL-62M
	86574	IL-62M			

Note: Uzbekistan Airways also operates two Airbus A.310-324s registered F-OGQY and F-OGQZ.

UN (Kazakhstan)

The following are operated by Kazakhstan Airlines with registrations prefixed by UN.

Reg.	Type	Reg.	Type
001	Boeing 747SP-31	85231	Tu-154B-1
002	Boeing 757-2M8	85240	Tu-154B-1
65115	Tu-134A-3	85271	Tu-154B-1
65121	Tu-134A-3	85276	Tu-154B-1
65130	Tu-134A-3	85290	Tu-154B-1
65138	Tu-134A	85387	Tu-154B-2
65147	Tu-134A-3	85396	Tu-154B-2
65551	Tu-134A-3	85431	Tu-154B-2
65767	Tu-134A-3	85455	Tu-154B-2
65776	Tu-134A	85464	Tu-154B-2
65787	Tu-134A	85478	Tu-154B-2
65900	Tu-134A-3	85521	Tu-154B-2
76371	IL-76TD	85537	Tu-154B-2
76374	IL-76TD	85589	Tu-154B-2
76435	IL-76TD	85719	Tu-154M
76810	IL-76TD	85781	Tu-154M
85066	Tu-154B	86068	IL-86
85076	Tu-154B-1	86069	IL-86
85111	Tu-154B	86071	IL-86
85113	Tu-154B	86077	IL-86
85151	Tu-154B-1	86086	IL-86
85221	Tu-154B	86101	IL-86
85230	Tu-154B-1	86116	IL-86

Notes	Reg.	Type	Owner or Operator

UR (Ukraine)

Reg.	Type	Owner or Operator
UR-BFA	Boeing 737-2L9	Air Ukraine
UR-	Boeing 737-4Y0	Ukraine International
UR-GAC	Boeing 737-247	Ukraine International
UR-GAE	Boeing 737-3Y0	Ukraine International

The following are prefixed with UR. Airline codes BSL – BSL Airlines, KHO – Khors Air, UKC – Air Ukraine Cargo, UKR – Air Ukraine, UPA – Air Foyle

Notes	Reg.	Type	Notes	Reg.	Type
	65048	Tu-134A-3 (UKR)		65752	Tu-134A-3 (UKR)
	65073	Tu-134A (UKR)		65757	Tu-134A-3 (UKR)
	65076	Tu-134A-3 (UKR)		65761	Tu-134A (UKR)
	65077	Tu-134A (UKR)		65764	Tu-134A-3 (UKR)
	65089	Tu-134A (UKR)		65765	Tu-134A (UKR)
	65093	Tu-134A-3 (UKR)		65773	Tu-134A-3 (UKR)
	65107	Tu-134A (UKR)		65782	Tu-134A (UKR)
	65109	Tu-134A (UKR)		65790	Tu-134A-3 (UKR)
	65114	Tu-134A-3 (UKR)		65826	Tu-134A-3 (UKR)
	65134	Tu-134A-3 (UKR)		65841	Tu-134A (UKR)
	65135	Tu-134A-3 (UKR)		65852	Tu-134A (UKR)
	65556	Tu-134A-3 (UKR)		65864	Tu-134A (UKR)
	65718	Tu-134A-3 (UKR)		65877	Tu-134A-3 (UKR)
	65746	Tu-134A (UKR)		65888	Tu-134A-3 (UKR)

Reg.	Type	Notes	Reg.	Type	Notes
76395	IL-76MD (KHO)		85288	Tu-154B-1 (UKR)	
76396	IL-76MD (KHO)		85316	Tu-154B-2 (UKR)	
76397	IL-76MD (KHO)		85350	Tu-154B-2 (UKR)	
76398	IL-76MD (KHO)		85362	Tu-154B-2 (UKR)	
76399	IL-76MD (KHO)		85368	Tu-154B-2 (UKR)	
76555	IL-76MD (UKC)		85379	Tu-154B-2 (UKR)	
76705	IL-76MD (UKC)		85395	Tu-154B-2 (UKR)	
76721	IL-76MD (BSL)		85399	Tu-154B-2 (UKR)	
76730	IL-76MD (BSL)		85407	Tu-154B-2 (UKR)	
76742	IL-76MD (BSL)		85424	Tu-154B-2 (UKR)	
76744	IL-76MD (BSL)		85445	Tu-154B-2 (UKR)	
76759	IL-76MD (BSL)		85460	Tu-154B-2 (UKR)	
76760	IL-76MD (BSL)		85476	Tu-154B-2 (UKR)	
78755	IL-76MD (KHO/UPA)		85482	Tu-154B-2 (UKR)	
78775	IL-76MD (KHO)		85490	Tu-154B-2 (UKR)	
82008	An-124 (UPA)		85499	Tu-154B-2 (UKR)	
82027	An-124 (UPA)		85513	Tu-154B-2 (UKR)	
82029	An-124 (UPA)		85526	Tu-154B-2 (UKR)	
82066	An-124 (UPA)		85535	Tu-154B-2 (UKR)	
85068	Tu-154B (UKR)		85561	Tu-154B-2 (BSL)	
85116	Tu-154B-1 (UKR)		85700	Tu-154M (UKR)	
85118	Tu-154B (UKR)		85701	Tu-154M (UKR)	
85132	Tu-154B (UKR)		85707	Tu-154M (UKR)	
85137	Tu-154B (UKR)		86132	IL-62M (UKR)	
85148	Tu-154B (UKR)		86133	IL-62M (UKR)	
85152	Tu-154B (UKR)		86134	IL-62M (UKR)	
85154	Tu-154B (UKR)		86135	IL-62M (UKR)	
85179	Tu-154B-1 (UKR)		86580	IL-62M (UKR)	
85218	Tu-154B (UKR)		86581	IL-62M (UKR)	
85232	Tu-154B-1 (UKR)		86582	IL-62M (UKR)	
85269	Tu-154B-1 (UKR)				

Reg.	Type	Owner or Operator	Notes

V2 (Antigua)

V2-LEC	Airbus A.310-324	Air-India
V2-LED	Airbus A.310-324	Air-India
V2-LEH	Douglas DC-10-30	Skyjet

Note: Seagreen Air Transport operates Boeing 707s registered N14AZ, N18AZ, N21AZ, N29AZ and N145SP.

V5 (Namibia)

| V5-SPF | Boeing 747SP-44 | Air Namibia |

V8 (Brunei)

V8-BKH	Airbus A.340-211	Royal Brunei Airlines (VIP)
V8-DPD	Airbus A.310-304	Brunei Royal Flight
V8-PJB	Airbus A.340-212	Brunei Government
V8-RBA	Boeing 757-2M6	Royal Brunei Airlines
V8-RBB	Boeing 757-2M6	Royal Brunei Airlines
V8-RBE	Boeing 767-33AER	Royal Brunei Airlines
V8-RBF	Boeing 767-33AER	Royal Brunei Airlines
V8-RBG	Boeing 767-33AER	Royal Brunei Airlines
V8-RBH	Boeing 767-33AER	Royal Brunei Airlines
V8-RBJ	Boeing 767-33AER	Royal Brunei Airlines
V8-RBK	Boeing 767-33AER	Royal Brunei Airlines
V8-RBL	Boeing 767-33AER	Royal Brunei Airlines

VH (Australia)

VH-EBQ	Boeing 747-238B	QANTAS Airways *City of Bunbury*
VH-EBR	Boeing 747-238B	QANTAS Airways *City of Mt Gambier*
VH-EBS	Boeing 747-238B	QANTAS Airways *City of Broken Hill*

Notes	Reg.	Type	Owner or Operator
	VH-EBT	Boeing 747-338	QANTAS Airways *City of Wagga Wagga*
	VH-EBU	Boeing 747-338	QANTAS Airways *City of Warrnambool*
	VH-EBV	Boeing 747-338	QANTAS Airways *Geraldton*
	VH-EBW	Boeing 747-338	QANTAS Airways *City of Tamworth*
	VH-EBX	Boeing 747-338	QANTAS Airways *City of Wodonga*
	VH-EBY	Boeing 747-338	QANTAS Airways *City of Mildura*
	VH-OJA	Boeing 747-438	QANTAS Airways *City of Canberra*
	VH-OJB	Boeing 747-438	QANTAS Airways *City of Sydney*
	VH-OJC	Boeing 747-438	QANTAS Airways *City of Melbourne*
	VH-OJD	Boeing 747-438	QANTAS Airways *City of Brisbane*
	VH-OJE	Boeing 747-438	QANTAS Airways *City of Adelaide*
	VH-OJF	Boeing 747-438	QANTAS Airways *City of Perth*
	VH-OJG	Boeing 747-438	QANTAS Airways *City of Hobart*
	VH-OJH	Boeing 747-438	QANTAS Airways *City of Darwin*
	VH-OJI	Boeing 747-438	QANTAS Airways *Longreach*
	VH-OJJ	Boeing 747-438	QANTAS Airways *Winton*
	VH-OJK	Boeing 747-438	QANTAS Airways *City of Newcastle*
	VH-OJL	Boeing 747-438	QANTAS Airways *City of Ballaarat*
	VH-OJM	Boeing 747-438	QANTAS Airways *City of Gosford*
	VH-OJN	Boeing 747-438	QANTAS Airways *City of Dubbo*
	VH-OJO	Boeing 747-438	QANTAS Airways *City of Toowoomba*
	VH-OJP	Boeing 747-438	QANTAS Airways *City of Albury*
	VH-OJQ	Boeing 747-438	QANTAS Airways *City of Mandurah*
	VH-OJR	Boeing 747-438	QANTAS Airways *City of Bathurst*

VR-H (Hong Kong)

VR-HIA	Boeing 747-267B	Cathay Pacific Airways
VR-HIB	Boeing 747-267B	Cathay Pacific Airways
VR-HIC	Boeing 747-267B	Cathay Pacific Airways
VR-HID	Boeing 747-267B	Cathay Pacific Airways
VR-HIE	Boeing 747-267B	Cathay Pacific Airways
VR-HIF	Boeing 747-267B	Cathay Pacific Airways
VR-HIH	Boeing 747-267F (SCD)	Cathay Pacific Cargo
VR-HII	Boeing 747-367	Cathay Pacific Airways
VR-HIJ	Boeing 747-367	Cathay Pacific Airways
VR-HIK	Boeing 747-367	Cathay Pacific Airways
VR-HKG	Boeing 747-267B	Cathay Pacific Airways
VR-HKM	Boeing 747-132F (SCD)	Air Hong Kong
VR-HKN	Boeing 747-132F (SCD)	Air Hong Kong
VR-HKO	Boeing 747-249F (SCD)	Air Hong Kong
VR-HOL	Boeing 747-367	Cathay Pacific Airways
VR-HOM	Boeing 747-367	Cathay Pacific Airways
VR-HON	Boeing 747-367	Cathay Pacific Airways
VR-HOO	Boeing 747-467	Cathay Pacific Airways
VR-HOP	Boeing 747-467	Cathay Pacific Airways
VR-HOR	Boeing 747-467	Cathay Pacific Airways
VR-HOS	Boeing 747-467	Cathay Pacific Airways
VR-HOT	Boeing 747-467	Cathay Pacific Airways
VR-HOU	Boeing 747-467	Cathay Pacific Airways
VR-HOV	Boeing 747-467	Cathay Pacific Airways
VR-HOW	Boeing 747-467	Cathay Pacific Airways
VR-HOX	Boeing 747-467	Cathay Pacific Airways
VR-HOY	Boeing 747-467	Cathay Pacific Airways
VR-HOZ	Boeing 747-467	Cathay Pacific Airways
VR-HUA	Boeing 747-467	Cathay Pacific Airways
VR-HUB	Boeing 747-467	Cathay Pacific Airways
VR-HUD	Boeing 747-467	Cathay Pacific Airways
VR-HUE	Boeing 747-467	Cathay Pacific Airways
VR-HUF	Boeing 747-467	Cat hay Pacific Airways
VR-HUG	Boeing 747-467	Cathay Pacific Airways
VR-HUH	Boeing 747-467F	Cathay Pacific Airways
VR-HUI	Boeing 747-467	Cathay Pacific Airways
VR-HUJ	Boeing 747-467	Cathay Pacific Airways
VR-HUK	Boeing 747-467F	Cathay Pacific Airways
VR-HVX	Boeing 747-267F (SCD)	Cathay Pacific Airways
VR-HVY	Boeing 747-236F (SCD)	Cathay Pacific Airways *Hong Kong Jumbo*
VR-HVZ	Boeing 747-267F (SCD)	Cathay Pacific Airways

VT (India)

VT-EBE	Boeing 747-237B	Air-India *Shahjehan*
VT-EBN	Boeing 747-237B	Air-India *Rajendra Chola*
VT-EDU	Boeing 747-237B	Air-India *Akbar*
VT-EFJ	Boeing 747-237B	Air-India *Chandragupta*
VT-EFU	Boeing 747-237B	Air-India *Krishna Deva Raya*
VT-EGA	Boeing 747-237B	Air-India *Samudra Gupta*
VT-EGB	Boeing 747-237B	Air-India *Mahendra Varman*
VT-EGC	Boeing 747-237B	Air-India *Harsha Vardhana*
VT-EJG	Airbus A.310-304	Air-India *Vamuna*
VT-EJH	Airbus A.310-304	Air-India *Tista*
VT-EJI	Airbus A.310-304	Air-India *Saraswati*
VT-EJJ	Airbus A.310-304	Air-India *Beas*
VT-EJK	Airbus A.310-304	Air-India *Gomti*
VT-EJL	Airbus A.310-304	Air-India *Sabarmati*
VT-ENQ	Boeing 747-212B	Air-India *Himalaya*
VT-EPW	Boeing 747-337 (SCD)	Air-India *Shivaji*
VT-EPX	Boeing 747-337 (SCD)	Air-India *Narasimha Varman*
VT-EQS	Airbus A.310-304	Air-India *Krishna*
VT-EQT	Airbus A.310-304	Air-India *Narmada*
VT-ESM	Boeing 747-437	Air-India *Konark*
VT-ESN	Boeing 747-437	Air-India *Tanjore*
VT-ESO	Boeing 747-437	Air-India *Khajuraho*
VT-ESP	Boeing 747-437	Air-India *Ashoka*
VT-EVA	Boeing 747-437	Air-India

Note: Airbus A310-324s V2-LEC and V2-LED now operate some of the 747s' routes. Air-India Cargo operates Douglas DC-8s and Boeing 747s on lease from various airlines.

XA (Mexico)

Note: Aeromexico operates DC-10-30 N8228P *Castillo de Chapultepec.*

YA (Afghanistan)

YA-FAX	Boeing 727-228	Ariana Afghan Airlines
YA-FAY	Boeing 727-228	Ariana Afghan Airlines
YA-FAZ	Boeing 727-228	Ariana Afghan Airlines

YI (Iraq)

YI-AGE	Boeing 707-370C	Iraqi Airways
YI-AGF	Boeing 707-370C	Iraqi Airways
YI-AGG	Boeing 707-370C	Iraqi Airways
YI-AGK	Boeing 727-270	Iraqi Airways *Ninevah*
YI-AGL	Boeing 727-270	Iraqi Airways *Basrah*
YI-AGM	Boeing 727-270	Iraqi Airways *Al Habbania*
YI-AGN	Boeing 747-270C (SCD)	Iraqi Airways *Tigris*
YI-AGO	Boeing 747-270C (SCD)	Iraqi Airways *Euphrates*
YI-AGP	Boeing 747-270C (SCD)	Iraqi Airways *Shat-al-Arab*
YI-AGQ	Boeing 727-270	Iraqi Airways *Ataameem*
YI-AGR	Boeing 727-270	Iraqi Airways *Babylon*
YI-AGS	Boeing 727-270	Iraqi Airways
YI-AKQ	Ilyushin IL-76M	Iraqi Airways
YI-AKT	Ilyushin IL-76M	Iraqi Airways
YI-AKU	Ilyushin IL-76M	Iraqi Airways
YI-AKV	Ilyushin IL-76M	Iraqi Airways
YI-AKW	Ilyushin IL-76M	Iraqi Airways
YI-ALR	Ilyushin IL-76MD	Iraqi Airways
YI-ALT	Ilyushin IL-76MD	Iraqi Airways
YI-ALU	Ilyushin IL-76MD	Iraqi Airways
YI-ALV	Ilyushin IL-76MD	Iraqi Airways
YI-ALW	Ilyushin IL-76MD	Iraqi Airways
YI-ALX	Ilyushin IL-76MD	Iraqi Airways
YI-ANB	Ilyushin IL-76MD	Iraqi Airways

Notes	Reg.	Type	Owner or Operator
	YI-ANC	Ilyushin IL-76MD	Iraqi Airways
	YI-AND	Ilyushin IL-76MD	Iraqi Airways
	YI-ANE	Ilyushin IL-76MD	Iraqi Airways
	YI-ANF	Ilyushin IL-76MD	Iraqi Airways
	YI-ANG	Ilyushin IL-76MD	Iraqi Airways
	YI-ANH	Ilyushin IL-76MD	Iraqi Airways
	YI-ANI	Ilyushin IL-76MD	Iraqi Airways

YK (Syria)

YK-AGA	Boeing 727-294		Syrian Arab Airlines *October 6*
YK-AGB	Boeing 727-294		Syrian Arab Airlines *Damascus*
YK-AGC	Boeing 727-294		Syrian Arab Airlines *Palmyra*
YG-AGD	Boeing 727-269		Syrian Arab Airlines
YK-AGE	Boeing 727-269		Syrian Arab Airlines
YK-AGF	Boeing 727-269		Syrian Arab Airlines
YK-AHA	Boeing 747SP-94		Syrian Arab Airlines *16 Novembre*
YK-AHB	Boeing 747SP-94		Syrian Arab Airlines *Arab Solidarity*
YK-AIA	Tupolev Tu-154M		Syrian Arab Airlines
YK-AIB	Tupolev Tu-154M		Syrian Arab Airlines
YK-AIC	Tupolev Tu-154M		Syrian Arab Airlines
YK-ATA	Ilyushin IL-76M		Syrian Arab Airlines
YK-ATB	Ilyushin IL-76M		Syrian Arab Airlines
YK-ATC	Ilyushin IL-76M		Syrian Arab Airlines
YK-ATD	Ilyushin IL-76M		Syrian Arab Airlines
YK-AYA	Tupolev Tu-134B-3		Syrian Arab Airlines
YK-AYB	Tupolev Tu-134B-3		Syrian Arab Airlines
YK-AYC	Tupolev Tu-134B-3		Syrian Arab Airlines
YK-AYD	Tupolev Tu-134B-3		Syrian Arab Airlines
YK-AYE	Tupolev Tu-134B-3		Syrian Arab Airlines
YK-AYF	Tupolev Tu-134B-3		Syrian Arab Airlinoo

YL (Latvia)

YL-BAA	Boeing 737-236		Transaero
YL-BAB	Boeing 737-236		Transaero
YL-BAC	Boeing 737-236		Transaero
YL-	Avro RJ70		AirBaltic
YL-	Avro RJ70		AirBaltic
YL-	Avro RJ70		AirBaltic
YL-LAI	Tupolev Tu-154M		BEL Baltic Express Line
YL-LBB	Tupolev Tu-134B-3		Lat Charter
YL-LBF	Tupolev Tu-134B-3		Lat Charter
YL-LBH	Tupolev Tu-134B-3		Lat Charter
YL-RAA	Antonov An-26		RAF-Avia
YL-RAB	Antonov An-26		RAF-Avia
YL-RAC	Antonov An-26		RAF-Avia

YR (Romania)

YR-ABA	Boeing 707-3K1C		Tarom
YR-ABC	Boeing 707-3K1C		Tarom
YR-BCI	BAC One-Eleven 525FT		Tarom
YR-BCJ	BAC One-Eleven 525FT		Tarom
YR-BCK	BAC One-Eleven 525FT		Tarom
YR-BCL	BAC One-Eleven 525FT		Tarom
YR-BCM	BAC One-Eleven 525FT		Tarom
YR-BCN	BAC One-Eleven 525FT		Tarom
YR-BCO	BAC One Eleven 525FT		Tarom
YR-BGA	Boeing 737-38J		Tarom *Alba Iulia*
YR-BGB	Boeing 737-38J		Tarom *Bucuresti*
YR-BGC	Boeing 737-38J		Tarom *Constanta*
YR-BGD	Boeing 737-38J		Tarom *Deva*
YR-BGE	Boeing 737-38J		Tarom *Timisoara*
YR-BRB	RomBac One-Eleven 561RC		Tarom
YR-BRC	RomBac One-Eleven 561RC		Tarom
YR-IMF	Ilyushin IL-18V		Tarom
YR-IMG	Ilyushin IL-18V		Tarom

Reg.	Type	Owner or Operator	Notes
YR-IMJ	Ilyushin IL-18D	Tarom	
YR-IML	Ilyushin IL-18D	Tarom	
YR-IRC	Ilyushin IL-62	Tarom	
YR-IRD	Ilyushin IL-62M	Tarom	
YR-IRE	Ilyushin IL-62M	Tarom	
YR-JBA	BAC One-Eleven 528FL	Jaro International	
YR-JBB	BAC One-Eleven 528FL	Jaro International	
YR-LCA	Airbus A.310-325	Tarom *Transilvania*	
YR-LCB	Airbus A.310-325	Tarom *Moldova*	
YR-TPB	Tupolev Tu-154B	Tarom	
YR-TPD	Tupolev Tu-154B	Tarom	
YR-TPE	Tupolev Tu-154B-1	Tarom	
YR-TPF	Tupolev Tu-154B-1	Tarom	
YR-TPG	Tupolev Tu-154B-1	Tarom	
YR-TPI	Tupolev Tu-154B-2	Tarom	
YR-TPK	Tupolev Tu-154B-2	Tarom	
YR-TPL	Tupolev Tu-154B-2	Tarom	

YU (Yugoslavia)

YU-AHN	Douglas DC-9-32	Jugoslovenski Aerotransport (JAT)	
YU-AHU	Douglas DC-9-32	JAT	
YU-AHV	Douglas DC-9-32	JAT	
YU-AJH	Douglas DC-9-32	JAT	
YU-AJI	Douglas DC-9-32	JAT	
YU-AJJ	Douglas DC-9-32	JAT	
YU-AJK	Douglas DC-9-32	JAT	
YU-AJL	Douglas DC-9-32	JAT	
YU-AJM	Douglas DC-9-32	JAT	
YU-AKB	Boeing 727-2H9	JAT	
YU-AKD	Boeing 727-2L8	Aviogenex *Split*	
YU-AKE	Boeing 727-2H9	JAT	
YU-AKF	Boeing 727-2H9	JAT	
YU-AKG	Boeing 727-2H9	JAT	
YU-AKH	Boeing 727-2L8	Aviogenex *Dubrovnik*	
YU-AKI	Boeing 727-2H9	JAT	
YU-AKJ	Boeing 727-2H9	JAT	
YU-AKM	Boeing 727-243	Aviogenex *Pula*	
YU-AMB	Douglas DC-10-30	JAT *Edvard Rusijan*	
YU-AND	Boeing 737-3H9	JAT	
YU-ANF	Boeing 737-3H9	JAT	
YU-ANI	Boeing 737-3H9	JAT	
YU-ANK	Boeing 737-3H9	JAT	
YU-ANP	Boeing 737-2K3	Aviogenex *Zadar*	
YU-ANU	Boeing 737-2K3	Aviogenex *Tivat*	
YU-ANV	Boeing 737-3H9	JAT	
YU-AOF	Boeing 737-2K5	Aviogenex	
YU-AOG	Boeing 737-2K5	Aviogenex	

Note: Both JAT and Aviogenex were affected by the war in Yugoslavia with aircraft grounded or leased out. Operations restarted in late 1994.

YV (Venezuela)

YV-134C	Douglas DC-10-30	VIASA	
YV-135C	Douglas DC-10-30	VIASA	
YV-136C	Douglas DC-10-30	VIASA	
YV-137C	Douglas DC-10-30	VIASA	
YV-138C	Douglas DC-10-30	VIASA	
YV-139C	Douglas DC-10-30	VIASA	

Z3 (Macedonia)

Note: Palair Macedonia operates Fokker 100s F-OLGA and F-OLGB plus Tu-154B-1 LZ-BTJ.

Notes	Reg.	Type	Owner or Operator

Z (Zimbabwe)

Z-WKS	Boeing 707-330B	Air Zimbabwe
Z-WKU	Boeing 707-330B	Air Zimbabwe
Z WMJ	Douglas DC-8-55F	Affretair *Captain Jack Malloch*
Z-WPE	Boeing 767-2N0ER	Air Zimbabwe *Victoria Falls*
Z-WPF	Boeing 767-2N0ER	Air Zimbabwe *Chimanimani*
Z-WSB	Douglas DC-8-55F	Affretair

ZK (New Zealand)

ZK-NBS	Boeing 747-419	Air New Zealand *Mataatua*
ZK-NBT	Boeing 747-419	Air New Zealand
ZK-NBU	Boeing 747-419	Air New Zealand
ZK-NBV	Boeing 747-419	Air New Zealand
ZK-NZV	Boeing 747-219B	Air New Zealand *Aotea*
ZK-NZW	Boeing 747-219B	Air New Zealand *Tainui*
ZK-NZX	Boeing 747-219B	Air New Zealand *Takitimu*
ZK-NZY	Boeing 747-219B	Air New Zealand *Te Arawa*
ZK-NZZ	Boeing 747-219B	Air New Zealand *Tokomaru*
ZK-SUH	Boeing 747-475	Air New Zealand
ZK-SUI	Boeing 747-441	Air New Zealand

ZP (Paraguay)

ZP-CCE	Boeing 707-321B	Lineas Aéreas Paraguayas
ZP-CCG	Boeing 707-321B	Lineas Aéreas Paraguayas
ZP-CCH	Douglas DC-8-63	Lineas Aéreas Paraguayas

ZS (South Africa)

ZS-SAC	Boeing 747-312	South African Airways *Shosholoza*
ZS-SAJ	Boeing 747-312	South African Airways
ZS-SAL	Boeing 747-244B	South African Airways *Tafelberg*
ZS-SAM	Boeing 747-244B	South African Airways *Drakensberg*
ZS-SAN	Boeing 747-244B	South African Airways *Lebombo*
ZS-SAO	Boeing 747-244B	South African Airways *Magaliesberg*
ZS-SAP	Boeing 747-244B	South African Airways *Swartberg*
ZS-SAR	Boeing 747-244F (SCD)	South African Airways *Waterberg*
ZS-SAT	Boeing 747-344	South African Airways *Johannesburg*
ZS-SAU	Boeing 747-344	South African Airways *Cape Town*
ZS-SAV	Boeing 747-444	South African Airways *Durban*
ZS-SAW	Boeing 747-444	South African Airways *Bloemfontein*
ZS-SAX	Boeing 747-444	South African Airways
ZS-SAY	Boeing 747-444	South African Airways *Vulindlela*
ZS-SAZ	Boeing 747-312	South African Airways
ZS-SPA	Boeing 747SP-44	Alliance Air
ZS-SPB	Boeing 747SP-44	South African Airways
ZS-SPC	Boeing 747SP-44	South African Airways
ZS-SPE	Boeing 747SP-44	South African Airways *Hantarn*

3B (Mauritius)

3B-NAK	Boeing 767-23BER	Air Mauritius *City of Curepipe*
3B-NAL	Boeing 767-23BER	Air Mauritius *City of Port Louis*
3B-NAQ	Boeing 747SP-27	Air Mauritius *Chateau Banares*
3B-NAT	Airbus A.340-312	Air Mauritius *Paille-en-Queue*
3B-NAU	Airbus A.340-312	Air Mauritius
3B-NAV	Airbus A.340-312	Air Mauritius
3B-NAY	Airbus A.340-312	Air Mauritius

Reg.   *Type*   *Owner or Operator*   *Notes*

3D (Swaziland)

3D-ADV	Douglas DC-8-54F	African International Airways
3D-AFR	Douglas DC-8-54F	African International Airways
3D-AFX	Douglas DC-8-54F	African International Airways

Reg.   *Type*   *Notes*   *Reg.*   *Type*   *Notes*

4K (Azerbaijan)

The following are operated by Azerbaijan Airlines with the registrations prefixed by 4K.

AZ1	Boeing 727-235		85177	Tu-154B-1
AZ2	Boeing 727-235		85192	Tu-154B-1
AZ3	Boeing 707-341C		85199	Tu-154B-1
AZ4	Boeing 707-399C		85211	Tu-154B-1
65702	Tu-134B-3		85214	Tu-154B-1
65705	Tu-134B-3		85274	Tu-154B-1
65708	Tu-134B-3		85329	Tu-154B-2
65709	Tu-134B-3		85364	Tu-154B-2
65710	Tu-134B-3		85391	Tu-154B-2
65711	Tu-134B-3		85548	Tu-154B-2
65713	Tu-134B-3		85698	Tu-154M
65714	Tu-134B-3		85729	Tu-154M
85147	Tu-154B-1		85734	Tu-154M
85158	Tu-154B-1			

4L (Georgia)

4L-AAA	Boeing 737-375	Orbi Georgian Airways

The following are operated by Orbi with the registrations prefixed by 4L.

65750	Tu-134A-3		85188	Tu-154B
65774	Tu-134A-3		85197	Tu-154B
65798	Tu-134A-3		85198	Tu-154B
65808	Tu-134A		85203	Tu-154B
65810	Tu-134A-3		85359	Tu-154B-2
65857	Tu-134A-3		85430	Tu-154B-2
65865	Tu-134A-3		85496	Tu-154B-2
85168	Tu-154B		85518	Tu-154B-2
85170	Tu-154B-1			

Reg.   *Type*   *Owner or Operator*   *Notes*

4R (Sri Lanka)

4R-ADA	Airbus A.340-311	Air Lanka
4R-ADB	Airbus A.340-311	Air Lanka
4R-ADC	Airbus A.340-311	Air Lanka
4R-ULA	L.1011-385 TriStar 500	Air Lanka *City of Jayewardenepura*
4R-ULB	L.1011-385 TriStar 500	Air Lanka *City of Kandy*
4R-ULC	L.1011-385 TriStar 100	Air Lanka *City of Anuradhapura*
4R-ULE	L.1011-385 TriStar 500	Air Lanka *City of Ratnapura*

4X (Israel)

4X-ABN	Boeing 737-258	El Al/Arkia
4X-ABO	Boeing 737-258	El Al/Arkia
4X-AXA	Boeing 747-258B	El Al
4X-AXB	Boeing 747-258B	El Al
4X-AXC	Boeing 747-258B	El Al
4X-AXD	Boeing 747-258C	El Al
4X-AXF	Boeing 747-258C	El Al
4X-AXH	Boeing 747-258B (SCD)	El Al
4X-AXK	Boeing 747-245F (SCD)	El Al Cargo

Notes	Reg.	Type	Owner or Operator
	4X-AXL	Boeing 747-245F (SCD)	El Al Cargo
	4X-AXQ	Boeing 747-238B	El Al
	4X-AXZ	Boeing 747-124F (SCD)	El Al Cargo
	4X-BAF	Boeing 737-281	Arkia
	4X-EAA	Boeing 767-258	El Al
	4X-EAB	Boeing 767-258	FI Al
	4X-EAC	Boeing 767-258ER	El Al
	4X-EAD	Boeing 767-258ER	El Al
	4X-EBL	Boeing 757-258	El Al/Arkia
	4X-EBM	Boeing 757-258	El Al/Arkia
	4X-EBR	Boeing 757-258	El Al/Arkia
	4X-EBS	Boeing 757-258	El Al
	4X-EBT	Boeing 757-258	El Al
	4X-EBU	Boeing 757-258	El 6Al
	4X-EBV	Boeing 757-258	El Al
	4X-ELA	Boeing 747-458	El Al
	4X-ELB	Boeing 747-458	El Al
	4X-ELC	Boeing 747-458	El Al

5A (Libya)

	5A-DAI	Boeing 727-224	Libyan Arab Airlines
	5A-DAK	Boeing 707-3L5C	Libyan Arab Airlines
	5A-DIB	Boeing 727-2L5	Libyan Arab Airlines
	5A-DIC	Boeing 727-2L5	Libyan Arab Airlines
	5A-DID	Boeing 727-2L5	Libyan Arab Airlines
	5A-DIE	Boeing 727-2L5	Libyan Arab Airlines
	5A-DIF	Boeing 727-2L5	Libyan Arab Airlines
	5A-DIG	Boeing 727-2L5	Libyan Arab Airlines
	5A-DIH	Boeing 727-2L5	Libyan Arab Airlines
	5A-DII	Boeing 727-2L5	Libyan Arab Airlines
	5A-DJU	Boeing 707-351C	Libyan Arab Airlines

Note: Services to the UK suspended. Libyan Arab's two A.310-203 are operated as
7T-VJE and 7T-VJF with Royal Jordanian.

5B (Cyprus)

	5B-DAQ	Airbus A.310-203	Cyprus Airways *Soli*
	5B-DAR	Airbus A.310-203	Cyprus Airways *Aepia*
	5B-DAS	Airbus A.310-203	Cyprus Airways *Salamis*
	5B-DAT	Airbus A.320-231	Cyprus Airways *Praxandros*
	5B-DAU	Airbus A.320-231	Cyprus Airways *Evelthon*
	5B-DAV	Airbus A.320-231	Cyprus Airways *Kinyras*
	5B-DAW	Airbus A.320-231	Cyprus Airways *Agapinor*
	5B-DAX	Airbus A.310-204	Cyprus Airways *Engomi*
	5B-DAZ	Boeing 707-328C	Avistar
	5B-DBA	Airbus A.320-231	Cyprus Airways *Evagoras*
	5B-DBB	Airbus A.320-231	Eurocypria Airways *Akamas*
	5B-DBC	Airbus A.320-231	Eurocypria Airways *Tefkros*
	5B-DBD	Airbus A.320-231	Eurocypria Airways *Onosilos*

5N (Nigeria)

	5N-ANN	Douglas DC-10-30	Nigeria Airways *Yunkari*
	5N-AOQ	Boeing 707-355C	Okada Air
	5N-ARQ	Boeing 707-338C	DAS Air Cargo
	5N-ATY	Douglas DC-8-55F	Liberia World Airlines
	5N-AUE	Airbus A.310-222	Nigeria Airways *River Yobe*
	5N-AUF	Airbus A.310-222	Nigeria Airways *River Ethiope*
	5N-AUG	Airbus A.310-222	Nigeria Airways *Lekki Peninsula*
	5N-AUH	Airbus A.310-222	Nigeria Airways *Rima River*
	5N-BBD	Boeing 707-338C	ADC Airlines
	5N-BBF	Boeing 727-231	ADC Airlines
	5N-BBG	Boeing 727-231	ADC Airlines
	5N-EDO	Boeing 747-146	Okada Air *Lady Cherry*
	5N-MKA	Douglas DC-8-55F	MK Airlines
	5N-MKC	Douglas DC-8-55F	MK Airlines

Reg.	Type	Owner or Operator	Notes
5N-MKE	Douglas DC-8-55F	MK Airlines	
5N-MKF	Douglas DC-8-55F	MK Airlines	
5N-MXX	Boeing 707-323C	Merchant Express	
5N-TKE	Boeing 727-82	Triax Airlines	
5N-TTK	Boeing 727-264	Triax Airlines	

5R (Madagascar)

5R-MFT	Boeing 747-2B2B (SCD)	Air Madagascar *Tolom Piavotana*	

5X (Uganda)

5X-JEF	Boeing 707-379C	DAS Air Cargo	
5X-JET	Boeing 707-351C	DAS Air Cargo	
5X-JOE	Douglas DC-10-30	DAS Air Cargo	
5X-JON	Boeing 707-369C	DAS Air Cargo *Spirit of John*	
5X-UCF	L.100-30 Hercules	Uganda Air Cargo *The Silver Lady*	

5Y (Kenya)

5Y-AXI	Boeing 707-330B	African Airlines International	
5Y-AXM	Boeing 707-330B	African Airlines International	
5Y-BEL	Airbus A.310-304	Kenya Airways *Nyayo Star*	
5Y-BEN	Airbus A.310-304	Kenya Airways *Harambee Star*	
5Y-BFT	Airbus A.310-304	Kenya Airways *Uhuru Star*	
5Y-SIM	Boeing 707-336C	Simba Air Cargo	

Note: ASA African Safari Airways operates a DC-10-30 which carries the registration PH-DTL.

6Y (Jamaica)

6Y-	Airbus A.310-300	Air Jamaica	

7O (Yemen)

7O-ACV	Boeing 727-2N8	Yemenia	
7O-ACW	Boeing 727-2N8	Yemenia	
7O-ACX	Boeing 727-2N8	Yemenia	
7O-ACY	Boeing 727-2N8	Yemenia	
7O-ADA	Boeing 727-2N8	Yemenia	
7O-ADF	Iluyshin IL-76TD	Yemenia	

Note: Alyemda operates the Airbus A.310-304 F-ODSV.

7T (Algeria)

7T-VEA	Boeing 727-2D6	Air Algerie *Tassili*	
7T-VEB	Boeing 727-2D6	Air Algerie *Hoggar*	
7T-VED	Boeing 737-2D6C	Air Algerie *Atlas Saharien*	
7T-VEF	Boeing 737-2D6	Air Algerie *Saoura*	
7T-VEG	Boeing 737-2D6	Air Algerie *Monts des Ouleds Neils*	
7T-VEH	Boeing 727-2D6	Air Algerie *Lalla Khadidja*	
7T-VEI	Boeing 727-2D6	Air Algerie *Djebel Amour*	
7T-VEJ	Boeing 737-2D6	Air Algerie *Chrea*	
7T-VEK	Boeing 737-2D6	Air Algerie *Edough*	
7T-VFL	Boeing 737-2D6	Air Algerie *Akfadou*	
7T-VEM	Boeing 727-2D6	Air Algerie *Mont du Ksall*	
7T-VEN	Boeing 737-2D6	Air Algerie *La Soummam*	
7T-VEO	Boeing 737-2D6	Air Algerie *La Titteri*	
7T-VEP	Boeing 727-2D6	Air Algerie *Mont du Tessala*	
7T-VEQ	Boeing 737-2D6	Air Algerie *Le Zaccar*	

Notes	Reg.	Type	Owner or Operator
	7T-VER	Boeing 737-2D6	Air Algerie *Le Souf*
	7T-VES	Boeing 737-2D6C	Air Algerie *Le Tadmaït*
	7T-VET	Boeing 727-2D6	Air Algerie *Georges du Rhumel*
	7T-VEU	Boeing 727-2D6	Air Algerie *Djurdjura*
	7T-VEV	Boeing 727-2D6	Air Algerie
	7T-VEW	Boeing 727-2D6	Air Algerie
	7T-VEX	Boeing 727-2D6	Air Algerie *Djemila*
	7T-VEY	Boeing 737-2D6	Air Algerie *Rhoufi*
	7T-VEZ	Boeing 737-2T4	Air Algerie *Monts du Daia*
	7T-VJA	Boeing 737-2T4	Air Algerie *Monts des Babors*
	7T-VJB	Boeing 737-2T4	Air Algerie *Monts des Bibons*
	7T-VJC	Airbus A.310-203	Air Algerie
	7T-VJD	Airbus A.310-203	Air Algerie
	7T-VJE	Airbus A.310-203	Air Algerie/Royal Jordanian
	7T-VJF	Airbus A.310-203	Air Algerie/Royal Jordanian
	7T-VJG	Boeing 767-3D6	Air Algerie
	7T-VJH	Boeing 767-3D6	Air Algerie
	7T-VJI	Boeing 767-3D6	Air Algerie

9A (Croatia)

	9A-CTA	Boeing 737-230	Croatia Airlines
	9A-CTB	Boeing 737-230	Croatia Airlines
	9A-CTC	Boeing 737-230	Croatia Airlines
	9A-CTD	Boeing 737-230	Croatia Airlines
	9A-CTE	Boeing 737-230	Croatia Airlines

9G (Ghana)

	9G-ADM	Boeing 707-321C	GM Airlines
	9G-ADS	Boeing 707-323C	Occidental Airlines
	9G-ANA	Douglas DC-10-30	Ghana Airways
	9G-EBK	Boeing 707-321C	Alpine Air
	9G-MKD	Douglas DC-8-55F	MK Airlines

Note: Ghana Airways also operates MD-11 N280WA on lease.

9H (Malta)

	9H-ABE	Boeing 737-2Y5	Air Malta *Alof de Wignacourt*
	9H-ABF	Boeing 737-2Y5	Air Malta *Manuel Pinto*
	9H-ABG	Boeing 737-2Y5	Air Malta *Jean de Lavalette*
	9H-ABP	Airbus A.320-211	Air Malta *Nicholas de Cottoner*
	9H-ABQ	Airbus A.320-211	Air Malta *Hughes Loubenx de Verdelle*
	9H-ABR	Boeing 737-3Y5	Air Malta *Juan de Homedes*
	9H-ABS	Boeing 737-3Y5	Air Malta *Antoines de Paule*
	9H-ABT	Boeing 737-3Y5	Air Malta *Ferdinand von Hompesch*
	9H-ACM	Avro RJ70	Air Malta
	9H-ACN	Avro RJ70	Air Malta
	9H-ACO	Avro RJ70	Air Malta
	9H-ACP	Avro RJ70	Air Malta *Pieta*

Note: Air Malta also operates Airbus A.310-222 OO-SCI on lease.

9J (Zambia)

	9J-AFT	Boeing 707-347C	Impala Air Cargo *City of Lusaka*

9K (Kuwait)

	9K-ADB	Boeing 747-269B (SCD)	Kuwait Airways *Al-Jaberiya*
	9K-ADD	Boeing 747-269B (SCD)	Kuwait Airways *Al-Salmiya*
	9K-ADE	Boeing 747-469 (SCD)	Kuwait Airways *Al-Jabariya*
	9K-ADF	Boeing 747-469 (SCD)	Kuwait Airways *Al-Grain*
	9K-ADG	Boeing 747-469 (SCD)	Kuwait Airways *Garouh*

Reg.	Type	Owner or Operator	Notes
9K-ALA	Airbus A.310-308	Kuwait Airways *Al-Jahra*	
9K-ALB	Airbus A.310-308	Kuwait Airways *Gharnada*	
9K-ALC	Airbus A.310-308	Kuwait Airways *Kadhma*	
9K-ALD	Airbus A.310-308	Kuwait Government	
9K-AMA	Airbus A.300-605R	Kuwait Airways *Failaka*	
9K-AMB	Airbus A.300-605R	Kuwait Airways *Burghan*	
9K-AMC	Airbus A.300-605R	Kuwait Airways *Wafra*	
9K-AMD	Airbus A.300-605R	Kuwait Airways Wara	
9K-AME	Airbus A.300-605R	Kuwait Airways *Al-Rawdhatain*	
9K-ANA	Airbus A.340-313	Kuwait Airways *Warba*	
9K-ANB	Airbus A.340-313	Kuwait Airways *Al-Sabahiya*	
9K-ANC	Airbus A.340-313	Kuwait Airways *Al-Mobarakia*	
9K-AND	Airbus A.340-313	Kuwait Airways *Al-Riggah*	

9M (Malaysia)

9M-MHL	Boeing 747-4H6 (SCD)	Malaysian Airline System *Kuala Lumpur*
9M-MHM	Boeing 747-4H6 (SCD)	Malaysian Airline System *Penang*
9M-MHN	Boeing 747-4H6	Malaysian Airline System *Malacca*
9M-MHO	Boeing 747-4H6	Malaysian Airline System *Alor Setar*
9M-MPA	Boeing 747-4H6	Malaysian Airline System *Ipoh*
9M-MPB	Boeing 747-4H6	Malaysian Airline System *Shah Alam*
9M-MPC	Boeing 747-4H6	Malaysian Airline System *Kuantan*
9M-MPD	Boeing 747-4H6	Malaysian Airline System *Serembam*
9M-MPE	Boeing 747-4H6	Malaysian Airline System
9M-MPF	Boeing 747-4H6	Malaysian Airline System *Kota Bharu*
9M-MPG	Boeing 747-4H6	Malaysian Airline System
9M-MPH	Boeing 747-4H6	Malaysian Airline System *Langkawi*

9N (Nepal)

9N-ACA	Boeing 757-2F8	Royal Nepal Airlines
9N-ACB	Boeing 757-2F8C	Royal Nepal Airlines *Gandaki*

Note: Royal Nepal also operates Airbus A.310-304 registered D-APON.

9Q (Zaïre)

9Q-CBW	Boeing 707-329C	Scibe Airlift Zaïre
9Q-CJT	Boeing 707-123B	Transair Cargo
9Q-CKB	Boeing 707-323C	Express Cargo
9Q-CKK	Boeing 707-366C	Express Cargo
9Q-CLI	Douglas DC-10-30	Air Zaïre *Mont Ngaliema*
9Q-CLV	Douglas DC-8-54F	Air Zaïre Cargo
9Q-CMD	Boeing 707-441	Blue Airlines
9Q-CRA	Boeing 707-366C	New ACS
9Q-CSB	Boeing 707-373C	Skydec Cargo
9Q-CSZ	Boeing 707-323C	Shabair
9Q-CTJ	Boeing 707-123B	New ACS
9Q-CVG	Boeing 707-358C	Transair Cargo

9V (Singapore)

9V-SFA	Boeing 747-412F (SCD)	Singapore Airlines
9V-SFB	Boeing 747-412F (SCD)	Singapore Airlines
9V-SFC	Boeing 747-412F (SCD)	Singapore Airlines
9V-SFD	Boeing 747-412F (SCD)	Singapore Airlines
9V-SKA	Boeing 747-312	Singapore Airlines
9V-SKD	Boeing 747-312	Singapore Airlines
9V-SKM	Boeing 747-312 (SCD)	Singapore Airlines
9V-SKN	Boeing 747-312 (SCD)	Singapore Airlines
9V-SKP	Doeing 747-312 (SCD)	Singapore Airlines
9V-SKQ	Boeing 747-212F (SCD)	Singapore Airlines
9V-SMA	Boeing 747-412	Singapore Airlines
9V-SMB	Boeing 747-412	Singapore Airlines
9V-SMC	Boeing 747-412	Singapore Airlines

Notes	Reg.	Type	Owner or Operator
	9V-SMD	Boeing 747-412	Singapore Airlines
	9V-SME	Boeing 747-412	Singapore Airlines
	9V-SMF	Boeing 747-412	Singapore Airlines
	9V-SMG	Boeing 747-412	Singapore Airlines
	9V-SMH	Boeing 747-412	Singapore Airlines
	9V-SMI	Boeing 747-412	Singapore Airlines
	9V-SMJ	Boeing 747-412	Singapore Airlines
	9V-SMK	Boeing 747-412	Singapore Airlines
	9V-SML	Boeing 747-412	Singapore Airlines
	9V-SMM	Boeing 747-412	Singapore Airlines
	9V-SMN	Boeing 747-412	Singapore Airlines
	9V-SMO	Boeing 747-412	Singapore Airlines
	9V-SMP	Boeing 747-412	Singapore Airlines
	9V-SMQ	Boeing 747-412	Singapore Airlines
	9V-SMR	Boeing 747-412	Singapore Airlines
	9V-SMS	Boeing 747-412	Singapore Airlines
	9V-SMT	Boeing 747-412	Singapore Airlines
	9V-SMU	Boeing 747-412	Singapore Airlines
	9V-SMV	Boeing 747-412	Singapore Airlines
	9V-SMW	Boeing 747-412	Singapore Airlines
	9V-SMY	Boeing 747-412	Singapore Airlines
	9V-SMZ	Boeing 747-412	Singapore Airlines
	9V-SPA	Boeing 747-412	Singapore Airlines
	9V-SPB	Boeing 747-412	Singapore Airlines
	9V-SPC	Boeing 747-412	Singapore Airlines
	9V-SPD	Boeing 747-412	Singapore Airlines
	9V-SPE	Boeing 747-412	Singapore Airlines
	9V-SPF	Boeing 747-412	Singapore Airlines
	9V-SPG	Boeing 747-412	Singapore Airlines
	9V-SPH	Boeing 747-412	Singapore Airlines
	9V-SQQ	Boeing 747-212B	Singapore Airlines
	9V-SQS	Boeing 747-212B	Singapore Airlines
	9V-SQT	Boeing 747-245F (SCD)	Singapore Airlines
	9V-SQU	Boeing 747-245F (SCD)	Singapore Airlines

Note: Singapore Airlines also operates Boeing 747-312 N116KB, N117KC, N121KG, N122KH, N123KJ, N124KK and N125KL.

9XR (Rwanda)

	9XR-JA	Boeing 707-328C	Air Rwanda

9Y (Trinidad and Tobago)

	9Y-TGJ	L.1011-385 TriStar 500 (595)	B.W.I.A. *Sunjet Trinidad*
	9Y-TGN	L.1011-385 TriStar 500 (596)	B.W.I.A. *Sunjet Barbados*
	9Y-THA	L.1011-385 TriStar 500 (597)	B.W.I.A. *Sunjet Antigua*
	9Y-	Airbus A.340-300	B.W.I.A.
	9Y-	Airbus A.340-300	B.W.I.A
	9Y-	Airbus A.340-300	B.W.I.A.

Note: B.W.I.A. also operates a TriStar 500 which retains the registration N3140D (598) and named *Sunjet St Lucia*. Similarly CS-TEA is leased from Air Portugal.

Aircraft included in this section are those based in the UK but which retain their non-British identities.

Reg.	Type	Owner or Operator	Notes
A40-AB	V.1103 VC10 ★	Brooklands Museum (G-ASIX)	
C-FCFD	B.170 Freighter 31M	British Airways Employees	
CF-EQS	Boeing-Stearman PT-17 ★	Imperial War Museum/Duxford	
CF-KCG	Grumman TBM-3E Avenger AS.3★	Imperial War Museum/Duxford	
D-692	Staaken Z-1 Flitzer	D. J. Evans & L. R. Williams (G-BVAW)	
D-HMQV	Bolkow Bo 102 ★	International Helicopter Museum (IHM)/ Weston-s-Mare	
D-IFSB	D.H.104 Dove 6 ★	Mosquito Aircraft Museum	
F-BDRS	Boeing B-17G (231983) ★	Imperial War Museum/Duxford	
F-BMCY	Potez 840 ★	Sumburgh Fire Service	
HA-MEP	Antonov An-2	AeroSuperBatics Ltd	
LY-AFA	Yakovlev Yak-52	Termikas Co Ltd	
LY-AFB	Yakovlev Yak-52	Termikas Co Ltd	
LY-AKQ	Yakovlev Yak-52	—	
LY-AKW	Yakovlev Yak-52	A. Harris	
LY-AKX	Yakovlev Yak-52	—	
LY-ALG	Yakovlev Yak-52	Warwick Aero Services Ltd	
LY-ALN	Yakovlev Yak-52	G. G. L. James	
LY-ALO	Yakovlev Yak-52	Sky Associates (UK) Ltd	
LY-ALS	Yakovlev Yak-52	M. Jefferies	
LY-ALT	Yakovlev Yak-52	Titan Airways Ltd/Stansted	
LY-ALU	Yakovlev Yak-52	M. Jefferies	
LY-ALY	Yakovlev Yak-52	M. Jefferies	
LY-AMI	Yakovlev Yak-18T	—	
LY-AMP	Yakovlev Yak-52	—	
LY-AMS	Yakovlev Yak-52	—	
LY-AMU	Yakovlev Yak-52	G. Sharpe	
LY-AMV	Yakovlev Yak-52	—	
LY-ANH	Yakovlev Yak-52	K. Hare	
LY-ANI	Yakovlev Yak-52	—	
N2FU	Learjet 35A	Motor Racing Development Corpn	
N11T	P-51D Mustang (474425)	Dutch Historic Aircraft Co	
N12FU	Dassault Falcon 20C	Motor Racing Development Corpn	
N18E	Boeing 247D ★	Science Museum/Wroughton	
N18JC	H.295 Super Courier	Atlantic Bridge Aviation	
N18V	Beech D.17S Traveler (DR628)	R. Lamplough	
N27TS	Cessna 501 Citation	Eagle SP 147 Inc	
N33VC	Lockheed T-33A (54-21261)	Old Flying Machine Co/Duxford	
N36SF	Hawker Sea Fury FB.10 (361)	J. Bradshaw/Benson	
N43SV	Boeing Stearman E.75N-1	V. S. E. Norman	
N47DD	Republic P-47D Thunderbolt (45-49192) ★	Imperial War Museum/Duxford	
N47DD	Republic P-47D Thunderbolt (226671)	The Fighter Collection/Duxford	
N51RR	P-51D Mustang (474008)	D. Gilmour/North Weald	
N55JP	FG-1D Corsair (NZ5648)	Old Flying Machine Co/Duxford	
N71AF	R. Commander 680W	Metropolitan Aviation	
N121C	Cessna 550 Citation II	Digital Equipment Corpn	
N133N	Cessna 500 Citation	Eastwind Inc	
N139DP	Bell P-39Q-5-BE Airacobra (219993)	The Fighter Collection/Duxford	
N167F	P-51D Mustang (473877)	RLS 51 Ltd/Duxford	
N200CX	Cessna 550 Citation II	Heron 550 Inc	
N260QB	Pitts S-2S Special	D. Baker	
N300GX	G.1159A Gulfstream 3	Glaxo PLC	
N339BB	Sikorsky S-76A	Air Hanson Ltd/Blackbushe	
N444M	Grumman G.44 Widgeon (1411)	M. Dunkerley/Biggin Hill	
N500LN	Howard 500	D. Baker	
N707KS	Boeing 707-321B	Kalair Corpn/Stansted	
N707TJ	Boeing Stearman A.75N1	V. S. E. Norman (Crunchie)/Rendcomb	
N736GX	Cessna R.172K (tailwheel)	Mission Aviation Fellowship/Headcorn	
N800H	F8F-2 Bearcat (121752)	The Fighter Collection/Duxford	
N809P	Dassault Falcon 20C	FR Aviation Ltd	
N999PJ	M.S.760 Paris 2	Aces High Ltd/North Weald	

Notes	Reg.	Type	Owner or Operator
	N1009N	P-40N Kittyhawk (FR870)	B. J. Grey/Duxford
	N1344	Ryan PT-22	H. Mitchell
	N1447Q	Cessna 150L	US Embassy Flying Club/Denham
	N2929W	PA-28-151 Warrior	R. Lobell
	N3145X	P-38J Lightning (67543)	Fighter Collection/Duxford
	N3922B	Boeing Stearman E.75N1	P. Hoffman/Swanton Morley
	N3929B	Boeing Stearman E.75N1	Eastern Stearman Ltd
	N4232C	P.66 Pembroke (XL954)	(stored)/Tatenhill
	N4575C	G.21C Goose	Blue Arrow Challenge Ltd
	N4596N	Boeing Stearman PT-13D	N. Mason & D. Gilmour/North Weald
	N4712V	Boeing Stearman PT-13D	Wessex Aviation & Transport Ltd
	N4727V	Spad S.VII (S4523)	Imperial War Museum/Duxford
	N4806E	Douglas A-26C Invader ★	R. & R. Cadman/Southend
	N4845V	FM-2 Wildcat	Fighter Collection/Duxford
	N5057V	Boeing Stearman PT-13D	V. S. E. Norman/Rendcomb
	N5237V	Boeing B-17G (483868) ★	RAF Museum/Hendon
	N5824H	PA-38-112 Tomahawk	Lakenheath Aero Club
	N6268	Travel Air Model 2000 (626/18)	Personal Plane Services Ltd
	N6526D	P-51D Mustang (413573) ★	RAF Museum/Henlow
	N6690Z	PA-25 Pawnee 235	Marchington Gliding Club/Tatenhill
	N7253C	F7F-3 Tigercat (80425)	The Fighter Collection/Duxford
	N7614C	B-25J Mitchell	Imperial War Museum/Duxford
	N7777G	L.749A Constellation ★	Science Museum (G-CONI)/Wroughton
	N8162G	Boeing Stearman PT-17	Eastern Stearman Ltd
	N9050T	Douglas C-47A (sections only) ★	Dakota's American Bistro/Fleet
	N9089Z	TB-25J Mitchell (44-30861) ★	Aces High Ltd (G-BKXW)/North Weald
	N9115Z	TB-25N Mitchell (34037) ★	RAF Museum/Hendon
	N9606H	Fairchild M.62A Cornell ★	Rebel Air Museum/Earls Colne
	N26634	PA-24 Comanche 250	P. Biggs (G-BFKR)
	N33600	Cessna L-19A Bird Dog (111989) ★	Museum of Army Flying/Middle Wallop
	N43069	PA-28-161 Warrior II	D. Wards
	N49272	Fairchild PT-23 (23)	H. Mitchell
	N50755	Boeing Stearman PT-27 (40-1766)	Eastern Stearman Ltd
	N53091	Boeing Stearman A.75N1	Eastern Stearman Ltd
	N54426	Boeing Stearman A.75N1	R. Simpson
	N54922	Boeing Stearman N2S-4	V. S. E. Norman (Crunchie)
	N56421	Ryan PT-22 (855)	PT Flight/Cosford
	N58566	BT-13 Valiant	PT Flight/Cosford
	N67867	G.44 Widgeon	M. Hales
	N75664	Boeing Stearman E.75N1 (208)	—
	N88972	B-25D-30-ND Mitchell (KL161)	Fighter Collection/Duxford
	N91342	PA-28-112 Tomahawk	Lakenheath Aero Club
	N91437	PA-38-112 Tomahawk	Lakenheath Aero Club
	N91457	PA-38-112 Tomahawk	Lakenheath Aero Club
	N91590	PA-38-112 Tomahawk	Lakenheath Aero Club
	N96240	Beech D.18S	Visionair Ltd (G-AYAH) (derelict)/Rochester
	N99153	T-28C Trojan ★	Norfolk & Suffolk Aviation Museum/Flixton
	NC663Y	Waco RNF	P. & J. Baker
	NC5171N	Lockheed 10A Electra ★	Science Museum (G-LIOA)/Wroughton
	NC15214	Waco UKC-S	P. H. McConnell/White Waltham
	NC16403	Cessna C.34 Airmaster	Sylmar Aviation (G-BSEB)
	NC18028	Beech D.17S	P. H. McConnell
	NX700HL	F8F-2B Bearcat (121714)	B. J. S. Grey/Duxford
	OM-UIN	Antonov An-2	Avia Special/White Waltham
	RA-01325	Yakovlev Yak-52	Bar Belle Aviation
	RA-01378	Yakovlev Yak-52	T. Evans
	RA-02166	Sukhoi Su-26	N. Lamb
	RA-7604	Sukhoi Su-29	R. N. Goode/White Waltham
	RA-44480	Yakovlev Yak-18T	R. N. Goode/White Waltham
	RA-44481	Yakovlev Yak-18T	R. N. Goode/White Waltham
	RA-44483	Yakovlev Yak-18T	R. N. Goode/White Waltham
	RA-44500	Yakovlev Yak-55M	B. MacMillan
	RA-44501	Yakovlev Yak-52	G. Fulbrook
	UR-67477	LET L-410UVP	—
	VH-BRC	S.24 Sandringham ★	Southampton Hall of Aviation
	VH-SNB	D.H.84 Dragon ★	Museum of Flight/E. Fortune
	VH-UTH	GAL Monospar ST-12 ★	Newark Air Museum (stored)
	VR-BEP	WS.55 Whirlwind 3 ★	East Midlands Aeropark (G-BAMH)
	VR-BET	WS.55 Whirlwind 3 ★	IHM (G-ANJV)/Weston-s-Mare
	VR-BEU	WS.55 Whirlwind 3 ★	IHM (G-ATKV)/Weston-s-Mare
	VR-BKC	Boeing 727-1H2	USAL Inc

Reg.	Type	Owner or Operator	Notes
VR-BKG	Dassault Falcon 50	Sioux Co Ltd/Luton	
VR-BKQ	Agusta A.109A-II	USAL Ltd/Fairoaks	
VR-BKY	H.S.125 Srs F.3B	Corporate Jet Services Inc	
VR-BMF	Dassault Falcon 50	Glaxo (Bermuda) Ltd/Heathrow	
VR-BMZ	Gulfstream Commander 690D	Marlborough Fine Art (London) Ltd	
VR-BNB	H.S.125 Srs 700A	Speedflight Ltd/Guernsey	
VR-BNZ	G.1159A Gulfstream 3	Dennis Vanguard International Ltd	
VR-BOO	McD Douglas MD-87	Ford Motor Co Ltd/Stansted	
VR-BOP	McD Douglas MD-87	Ford Motor Co Ltd/Stansted	
VR-BOR	Boeing 707-351B	Al Wisar Trading Ltd	
VR-BPS	Consolidated PBY-5A Catalina	Plane Sailing Ltd (G-BLSC)/Duxford	
VR-BUB	Cessna 500 CItation	Starway Co Ltd	
VR-BUL	Cessna 560 Citation V	Fegotila Ltd/Staverton	
VR-BVI	H.S.125 Srs F400A	Group 4 Ltd/Staverton	
VR-CBQ	Boeing 727-212	Aravco Ltd	
VR-CBW	G.1159C Gulfstream 4	Rolls-Royce PLC	
VR-CCK	Agusta A.109A-II	Tarmac PLC/E. Midlands	
VR-CCO	Agusta A.109A	Aerospace Finance Ltd/Fairoaks	
VR-CCQ	Dassault Falcon 50	Frank Williams Racing/Kidlington	
VR-CCS	BAC One-Eleven 401AK	AMC Aviation	
VR-CCT	Beech C90-1 King Air	Corgi Investments Ltd	
VR-CEB	Cessna 500 Citation	Goldfeder Jet Inc	
VR-CEZ	Dassault Falcon 50	IIR Aviation	
VR-CIC	Canadair CL.601 Challenger	TGC Aviation Ltd	
VR-CIT	Cessna 550 Citation II	TAG Aviation	
VR-CMF	G.1159C Gulfstream 4	Aravco Ltd/Heathrow	
VR-CMM	Boeing 727-30	MME Farms Maintenance	
VR-CYM	G.1159C Gulfstream 4	Jet Fly Corporation/Heathrow	
5N-ABW	Westland Widgeon 2 ★	IHM (G-AOZE)/Weston-s-Mare	

Radio Frequencies

The frequencies used by the larger airfields/airports are listed below. Abbreviations used: TWR — Tower, APP — Approach, A/G — Air-ground advisory. It is possible for changes to be made from time to time with the frequencies allocated which are all quoted in Megahertz (MHz).

Airfield	TWR	APP	A/G	Airfield	TWR	APP	A/G
Aberdeen	118.1	120.4		Ipswich			118.325
Alderney	125.35			Jersey	119.45	120.3	
Andrewsfield			130.55	Kidlington	118.875	125.325	
Audley End			122.35	Land's End	130.7		
Barton			122.7	Leeds Bradford	120.3	123.75	
Barrow			123.2	Leicester	122.125		
Belfast Intl	118.3	120.0		Liverpool	118.1	119.85	
Belfast City	130.75	130.85		London City	118.075	132.7	
Bembridge			123.25	Luton	132.55	129.55	
Biggin Hill	134.8	129.4		Lydd	120.7		
Birmingham	118.3	118.05		Manchester	118.625	119.4	
Blackbushe			122.3	Manston	119.27	129.45	
Blackpool	118.4	135.95		Netherthorpe			123.275
Bodmin			122.7	Newcastle	119.7	124.375	
Booker			126.55	Newquay	123.4	125.55	
Bourn			129.8	North Denes	123.4		
Bournemouth	125.6	119.625		North Weald			123.525
Bristol/Filton	132.35	122.72		Norwich	124.25	119.35	
Bristol/Lulsgate	133.85	120.6		Old Warden			123.05
Cambridge	122.2	123.6		Perth	119.8	122.3	
Cardiff Wales	125.0	125.85		Plymouth	122.6	133.55	
Carlisle		123.6		Popham			129.8
Compton Abbas			122.7	Prestwick	118.15	120.55	
Conington			129.725	Redhill	120.275		
Coventry	124.8	119.25		Rochester			122.25
Cranfield	123.2	122.85		Ronaldsway	118.9	120.85	
Denham			130.725	Sandown			123.5
Dundee	122.9			Sandtoft			130.425
Dunkeswell			123.475	Scilly Isles			123.15
Dunsfold	124.325	135.17		Seething			122.6
Duxford			122.075	Sherburn			122.6
East Midlands	124.0	119.65		Shipdham			119.55
Edinburgh	118.7	121.2		Shobdon			123.5
Elstree			122.4	Shoreham	125.4	123.15	
Exeter	119.8	128.15		Sibson			122.3
Fairoaks			123.425	Sleap			122.45
Felthorpe			123.5	Southampton	118.2	131.0	
Fenland			122.925	Southend	127.725	128.95	
Gamston			130.475	Stansted	123.8	125.55	
Gatwick	124.225	126.825		Stapleford			122.8
Glasgow	118.8	119.1		Sumburgh	118.25	123.15	
Gloucester/Staverton	122.9	125.65		Swansea	119.7		
Goodwood	120.65	122.45		Swanton Morley			123.5
Guernsey	119.95	128.65		Sywell			122.7
Halfpenny Green			123.0	Teesside	119.8	118.85	
Haverfordwest			122.2	Thruxton			130.45
Hawarden	124.95	123.35		Tollerton			122.8
Headcorn			122.0	Wellesbourne			124.02
Heathrow	118.7	119.725		White Waltham			122.6
	118.5	134.975		Wick	119.7		
Hethel			122.35	Wickenby			122.45
Hucknall			130.8	Woodford	126.925	130.75	
Humberside	118.55	124.675		Woodvale	119.75	121.0	
Ingoldmells			130.45	Yeovil	125.4	130.8	
Inverness	122.6						

Airline Flight Codes

Three-letter flight codes are now in general use. Those listed below identify both UK and overseas carriers appearing in the book.

AAF	Aigle Azur	F	BZH	Brit Air	F	IST	Istanbul A/L	TC
AAG	Air Atlantique	G	CCA	Air China	B	ITF	Air Inter	F
AAL	American A/L	N	CDN	Canadian A/L Intl	C	JAL	Japan A/L	JA
AAN	Oasis	EC	CFE	City Flyer	G	JAT	JAT	YU
ABB	Air Belgium	OO	CFG	Condor	D	JEA	Jersey European A/W	G
ABD	Atlanta Icelandic	TF	CKT	Caledonian	G	KAC	Kuwait A/W	9K
ABK	Albatros A/L	TC	CLH	Lufthansa CityLine	D	KAL	Korean Air	HL
ABR	Hunting	G	CLX	Cargolux	LX	KAR	Kar-Air	OH
ACA	Air Canada	C	CMM	Canada 3000 A/L	C	KIS	Contactair	D
ACF	Air Charter Intl	F	CNA	Centennial	EC	KLM	KLM	PH
ADR	Adria A/W	S5	COA	Continental A/L	N	KQA	Kenya A/W	5Y
AEA	Air Europa	EC	CPA	Cathay Pacific	VR-H	KYV	Kibris Turkish	TC
AEF	Aero Lloyd	D	CRL	Corse Air	F	LAA	Libyan Arab A/L	5A
AEL	Air Europe Spa	I	CRX	Crossair	HB	LAJ	British Meditrn	G
AFG	Ariana	YA	CSA	Czech A/L	OK	LAZ	Bulgarian A/L	LZ
AFL	Aeroflot	RA	CTN	Croatia A/L	9A	LDA	Lauda Air	OE
AFM	Affretair	Z	CUB	Cubana	CU	LEI	Air UK Leisure	G
AFR	Air France	F	CYP	Cyprus A/W	5B	LFA	Air Alfa	TC
AGX	Aviogenex	YU	DAH	Air Algerie	7T	LGL	Luxair	LX
AHK	Air Hong Kong	VR-H	DAL	Delta A/L	N	LIB	Air Liberte	F
AHR	Air Holland	PH	DAN	Maersk Air	OY	LIT	Air Littoral	F
AIC	Air-India	VT	DAT	Delta Air Transport	OO	LKA	Alkair	OY
AIH	Airtours (European)	G	DLH	Lufthansa	D	LOG	Loganair	G
AIJ	Air Jet	F	DQI	Cimber Air	OY	LOT	Polish A/L (LOT)	SP
AKD	Akdeniz A/L	TC	DYA	Alyemda	7O	LTE	LTE	EC
AKV	Active Air	TC	EAF	European A/Ch	G	LTS	LTU Sud	D
ALK	Air Lanka	4R	EAW	European A/W	G	LTU	LTU	D
ALT	All Leisure	G	EBA	EuroBelgian A/L	OO	MAH	Malev	HA
AMC	Air Malta	9H	EIA	Evergreen Intl	N	MAS	Malaysian A/L	9M
AMM	Air 2000	G	EIN	Aer Lingus	EI	MAU	Air Mauritius	3B
AMT	American Trans Air	N	ELY	El Al	4X	MEA	Middle East A/L	OD
ANA	All Nippon A/W	JA	ERL	Euralair	F	MNX	Manx A/L	G
ANZ	Air New Zealand	ZK	ETH	Ethiopian A/L	ET	MON	Monarch A/L	G
AOM	AOM French A/L	F	EWW	Emery	N	MOR	Morefly	LN
APW	Arrow Air	N	EXC	Excalibur	G	MPH	Martinair	PH
ARG	Argentine A/W	LV	EXS	Channel Express	G	MSK	Maersk Air Ltd	G
ATT	Aer Turas	EI	EZY	easyJet	G	MSR	Egyptair	SU
AUA	Austrian A/L	OE	FDX	Federal Express	N	NAW	Newair	OY
AUI	Ukraine Intl	UR	FIN	Finnair	OH	NEX	Northern Executive	G
AUR	Aurigny A/S	G	FLT	Flightline	G	NGA	Nigeria A/W	5N
AVA	Avianca	HK	FOB	Ford	G	NWA	Northwest A/L	N
AWC	Titan A/W	G	FOF	Fred Olsen	LN	OAL	Olympic A/L	SX
AWD	Airworld	G	FRO	European A/L	OO	OHY	Onur Air	TC
AYC	Aviaco	EC	FUA	Futura	EC	PAL	Philippine A/L	RP
AZA	Alitalia	I	GBL	GB Airways	G	PGA	Portugalia	CS
AZR	Air Zaire	9Q	GFA	Gulf Air	A40	PGT	Pegasus	TC
AZW	Air Zimbabwe	Z	GHA	Ghana A/W	9G	PIA	Pakistan Intl	AP
AZX	Air Bristol	G	GIA	Garuda	PK	PIE	Air South West	G
BAG	Deutsche BA	D	GIL	Gill A/W	G	QFA	Qantas	VH
BAL	Britannia A/L	G	GMI	Germania	D	QSC	African Safaris	5Y
BAW	British Airways	G	GNT	Business Air	G	RAM	Royal Air Maroc	CN
BBC	Bangladesh Biman	S2	HAS	Hamburg A/L	D	RBA	Royal Brunei	V8
BCS	European A/T	OO	HLA	HeavyLift	G	RIA	Rich Intl	N
BCY	CityJet	EI	HLD	Holiday A/L	TC	RJA	Royal Jordanian	JY
BER	Air Berlin	N	HLF	Hapag-Lloyd	D	RNA	Royal Nepal A/L	9N
BHY	Birgenair	TC	IAW	Iraqi A/W	YI	ROT	Tarom	YR
BIA	Baltic Intl	YL	IBE	Iberia	EC	RPX	BAC Express A/L	G
BIH	British Intl Heli	G	ICE	Icelandair	TF	RWD	Air Rwanda	9XR
BMA	British Midland	G	INS	Instone A/L	G	RYR	Ryanair	EI
BRA	Braathens	LN	IRA	Iran Air	EP	SAA	South African A/W	ZS
BRU	Belavia	EW	IRT	Augsburg A/W	D	SAB	Sabena	OO
BWA	BWIA	9Y	IOS	Skybus	G	SAS	SAS	SE OY LN
BWL	British World	G	ISS	Meridiana	I	SAY	Suckling A/W	G

AIRLINE FLIGHT CODES

SEY	Air Seychelles	S7	THA	Thai A/W Intl	HS	ULE	Leisure Intl	G
SIA	Singapore A/L	9V	THY	Turkish A/L	TC	UNI	Community Expr	G
SJM	Southern AT	N	TIH	Airtours (US)	G	UPA	Air Foyle	G
SLR	Sobelair	OO	TLA	TransLift	EI	UPS	United Parcels	N
SPP	Spanair	EC	TLE	Air Toulouse	F	USA	USAir	N
3UD	Sudan A/W	ST	TMA	Trans Mediterranean	OD	UYC	Cameroon A/L	TJ
SUT	Sultan Air	TC	TOW	Tower Air	N	UZB	Uzbekistan A/W	UK
SVA	Saudia	HZ	TRA	Transavia	PH	VIA	Viasa	YV
SWE	Swedair	SE	TSC	Air Transat	C	VIR	Virgin Atlantic	G
SWR	Swissair	HB	TSW	TEA Switzerland	HB	VIV	Viva Air	EC
SWW	Sunways	TC	TWA	TWA	N	VKG	Premiair	OY
SWY	Sunways A/L	SE	TWE	Transwede	SE	VLM	VLM	OO
SXS	Sun Express	TC	TYR	Tyrolean	OE	VRG	Varig	PP
SYR	Syrian Arab	YK	UAE	Emirates A/L	A6	WDL	WDL	D
TAP	Air Portugal	CS	UAL	United A/L	N	WOA	World A/W	N
TAR	Tunis Air	TS	UGA	Uganda A/L	5X	ZAC	Zambia A/W	9J
TAT	TAT	F	UKA	Air UK	G	ZAS	ZAS A/L of Egypt	SU
TCT	TUR European	TC	UKR	Air Ukraine	UR			

FLIGHTDECK

MANCHESTERS' PREMIER AVIATION STORE

☑ Scanning Receivers ☑ Books & Videos

☑ A/C Spotting Software ☑ Accessories

☑ Binoculars & Scopes ☑ Airliner T Shirts

☑ Helpful Advice ☑ Display Models

☑ Maps & Charts ☑ Shortwave Sets

*For illustrated catalogue send £1.00 to: Dept CAM96
192 Wilmslow Road, Heald Green, Cheadle, Ches. SK8 3BH
Open: 9.30am - 5.30pm Mon to Sat. Note: Closed Wednesdays
Tel: 0161-499 9350 Fax: 0161-499 9349. 3 miles from Airport*

British Aircraft Preservation Council Register

The British Aircraft Preservation Council was formed in 1967 to co-ordinate the works of all bodies involved in the preservation, restoration and display of historical aircraft. Membership covers the whole spectrum of national, Service, commercial and voluntary groups, and meetings are held regularly at the bases of member organisations. The Council is able to provide a means of communication, helping to resolve any misunderstandings or duplication of effort. Every effort is taken to encourage the raising of standards of both organisation and technical capacity amongst the member groups to the benfit of everyone interested in aviation. To assist historians, the B.A.P.C. register has been set up and provides an identity for those aircraft which do not qualify for a Service serial or inclusion in the UK Civil Register.

Aircraft on the current B.A.P.C. Register are as follows:

Reg.	Type	Owner or Operator	Notes
6	Roe Triplane Type IV (replica)	Manchester Museum of Science & Industry	
7	Southampton University MPA	Southampton Hall of Aviation	
8	Dixon ornithopter	The Shuttleworth Collection	
9	Humber Monoplane (replica)	Midland Air Museum/Coventry	
10	Hafner R.II Revoplane	Museum of Army Flying/Middle Wallop	
12	Mignet HM.14	Museum of Flight/E. Fortune	
13	Mignet HM.14	Brimpex Metal Treatments	
14	Addyman standard training glider	N. H. Ponsford	
15	Addyman standard training glider	The Aeroplane Collection	
16	Addyman ultra-light aircraft	N. H. Ponsford	
17	Woodhams Sprite	The Aeroplane Collection	
18	Killick MP Gyroplane	N. H. Ponsford	
20	Lee-Richards annular biplane (replica)	Newark Air Musem	
21	Thruxton Jackaroo	M. J. Brett	
22	Mignet HM.14 (G-AEOF)	Aviodome/Schiphol	
25	Nyborg TGN-III glider	Midland Air Museum	
27	Mignet HM.14	M. J. Abbey	
28	Wright Flyer (replica)	Corn Exchange/Leeds	
29	Mignet HM.14 (replica) (G-ADRY)	Brooklands Museum of Aviation/ Weybridge	
32	Crossley Tom Thumb	Midland Air Museum	
33	DFS.108-49 Grunau Baby IIb	Russavia Collection	
34	DFS.108-49 Grunau Baby IIb	D. Elsdon	
35	EoN primary glider	Russavia Collection	
36	Fieseler Fi.103 (V-1) (replica)	Kent Battle of Britain Museum/Hawkinge	
37	Blake Bluetit	The Shuttleworth Collection	
38	Bristol Scout replica (A1742)	Stored/Wroughton	
40	Bristol Boxkite (replica)	Bristol City Museum	
41	B.E.2C (replica) (6232)	Historical Aircraft Museum/RAF St Athan	
42	Avro 504 (replica) (H1968)	Historical Aircraft Museum/RAF St Athan	
43	Mignet HM.14	Lincolnshire Aviation Museum	
44	Miles Magister (L6906)	Museum of Berkshire Aviation (G-AKKY)/ Woodley	
45	Pilcher Hawk (replica)	Stanford Hall Museum	
46	Mignet HM.14	Alan McKechnie Racing Ltd	
47	Watkins Monoplane	Historical Aircraft Museum/RAF St Athan	
48	Pilcher Hawk (replica)	Glasgow Museum of Transport	
49	Pilcher Hawk	Royal Scottish Museum/Edinburgh	
50	Roe Triplane Type 1	Science Museum/S. Kensington	
51	Vickers Vimy IV	Science Museum/S. Kensington	
52	Lilienthal glider	Science Museum Store/Hayes	
53	Wright Flyer (replica)	Science Museum/S. Kensington	
54	JAP-Harding monoplane	Science Museum/S. Kensington	
55	Levavasseur Antoinette VII	Science Museum/S. Kensington	
56	Fokker E.III (210/16)	Science Museum/S. Kensington	
57	Pilcher Hawk (replica)	Science Museum/S. Kensington	
58	Yokosuka MXY7 Ohka II (15-1585)	F.A.A. Museum/Yeovilton	
59	Sopwith Camel (replica) (D3419)	Historical Aircraft Museum/RAF St Athan	
60	Murray M.1 helicopter	The Aeroplane Collection Ltd	
61	Stewart man-powered ornithopter	Lincolnshire Aviation Museum	
62	Cody Biplane (304)	Science Museum/S. Kensington	
63	Hurricane (replica) (L1592)	Kent Battle of Britain Museum/Hawkinge	
64	Hurricane (replica) (P3059)	Kent Battle of Britain Museum/Hawkinge	

Notes	Reg.	Type	Owner or Operator
	65	Spitfire (replica) (N3289)	Kent Battle of Britain Museum/Hawkinge
	66	Bf 109 (replica) (1480)	Kent Battle of Britain Museum/Hawkinge
	67	Bf 109 (replica) (14)	Kent Battle of Britain Museum/Hawkinge
	68	Hurricane (replica) (H3426)	Midland Air Museum
	69	Spitfire (replica) (N3313)	Kent Battle of Britain Museum/Hawkinge
	70	Auster AOP.5 (TJ398)	Museum of Flight/E. Fortune
	71	Spitfire (replica) (P8140)	Norfolk & Suffolk Aviation Museum
	72	Hurricane (replica) (V7767)	N. Weald Aircraft Restoration Flight
	73	Hurricane (replica)	—
	74	Bf 109 (replica) (6357/6)	Kent Battle of Britain Museum/Hawkinge
	75	Mignet HM.14 (G-AEFG)	N. H. Ponsford
	76	Mignet HM.14 (G-AFFI)	Yorkshire Air Museum/Elvington
	77	Mignet HM.14 (replica) (G-ADRG)	Stratford Aircraft Collection
	79	Fiat G.46-4 (MM53211)	British Air Reserve/Lympne
	80	Airspeed Horsa (KJ351)	Museum of Army Flying/Middle Wallop
	81	Hawkridge Dagling	Russavia Collection
	82	Hawker Hind (Afghan)	RAF Museum/Hendon
	83	Kawasaki Ki-100-1b	Aerospace Museum/Cosford
	84	Nakajima Ki-46 (Dinah III)	Historical Aircraft Museum/RAF St Athan
	85	Weir W-2 autogyro	Museum of Flight/E. Fortune
	86	de Havilland Tiger Moth (replica)	Yorkshire Aircraft Preservation Soc
	87	Bristol Babe (replica) (G-EASQ)	Bomber County Museum/Hemswell
	88	Fokker Dr 1 (replica) (102/18)	F.A.A. Museum/Yeovilton
	89	Cayley glider (replica)	Manchester Museum of Science & Industry
	90	Colditz Cock (replica)	Imperial War Museum/Duxford
	91	Fieseler Fi 103 (V.1)	Lashenden Air Warfare Museum
	92	Fieseler Fi 103 (V.1)	Historical Aircraft Museum/RAF St Athan
	93	Fieseler Fi 103 (V.1)	Imperial War Museum/Duxford
	94	Fieseler Fi 103 (V.1)	Aerospace Museum/Cosford
	95	Gizmer autogyro	F. Fewsdale
	96	Brown helicopter	NE Aircraft Museum
	97	Luton L.A.4A Minor	NE Aircraft Museum
	98	Yokosuka MXY7 Ohka II	Manchester Museum of Science & Industry
	99	Yokosuka MXY7 Ohka II	Aerospace Museum/Cosford
	100	Clarke glider	RAF Museum/Hendon
	101	Mignet HM.14	Lincolnshire Aviation Museum
	103	Pilcher glider (replica)	Personal Plane Services Ltd
	105	Blériot XI (replica)	Aviodome/Schiphol
	106	Blériot XI	RAF Museum/Hendon
	107	Blériot XXVII	RAF Museum/Hendon
	108	Fairey Swordfish IV (HS503)	Cosford Aerospace Museum
	109	Slingsby Kirby Cadet TX.1	RAF Museum/Henlow store
	110	Fokker D.VII replica (static) (5125)—	
	111	Sopwith Triplane replica (static) (N5492)	F.A.A. Museum/Yeovilton
	112	D.H.2 replica (static) (5964)	Museum of Army Flying/Middle Wallop
	113	S.E.5A replica (static) (B4863)	—
	114	Vickers Type 60 Viking (static) (G-EBED)	Brooklands Museum of Aviation/Weybridge
	115	Mignet HM.14	Essex Aviation Group/Andrewsfield
	116	Santos-Dumont Demoiselle (replica)	Cornwall Aero Park/Helston
	117	B.E.2C (replica)	N. Weald Aircraft Restoration Flight
	118	Albatros D.V (replica) (C19/18)	S. Yorks Aviation Soc/Firbeck
	119	Bensen B.7	NE Aircraft Museum
	120	Mignet HM.14 (G-AEJZ)	Bomber County Museum/Hemswell
	121	Mignet HM.14 (G-AEKR)	S. Yorks Aviation Soc/Firbeck
	122	Avro 504 (replica)	British Broadcasting Corp
	123	Vickers FB.5 Gunbus (replica)	A. Topen (stored)/Cranfield
	124	Lilienthal Glider Type XI (replica)	Science Museum/S. Kensington
	125	Clay Cherub (G-BDGP)	B. R. Clay
	126	D.31 Turbulent (static)	Midland Air Museum store
	127	Halton Jupiter MPA	The Shuttleworth Collection
	128	Watkinson Cyclogyroplane Mk IV	IHM/Weston-s-Mare
	129	Blackburn 1911 Monoplane (replica)	Cornwall Aero Park/Helston store
	130	Blackburn 1912 Monoplane (replica)	Cornwall Aero Park/Helston store
	131	Pilcher Hawk (replica)	C. Paton
	132	Blériot XI (G-BLXI)	Musée de L'Automobile/France
	133	Fokker Dr 1 (replica) (425/17)	Newark Air Museum
	134	Pitts S-2A static (G-CARS)	Toyota Ltd/Sywell

Reg.	Type	Owner or Operator	Notes
135	Bristol M.1C (replica) (C4912)	—	
136	Deperdussin Seaplane (replica)	Reno/Nevada	
137	Sopwith Baby Floatplane (replica) (8151)	—	
138	Hansa Brandenburg W.29 Floatplane (replica) (2292)	—	
139	Fokker Dr 1 (replica) 150/17	—	
142	SE-5A (replica) (F5459)	Cornwall Aero Park/Helston	
143	Paxton MPA	R. A. Paxton/Staverton	
144	Weybridge Mercury MPA	Cranwell Gliding Club	
145	Oliver MPA	D. Oliver (stored)/Warton	
146	Pedal Aeronauts Toucan MPA	The Shuttleworth Collection	
147	Bensen B.7	Norfolk & Suffolk Aviation Museum	
148	Hawker Fury II (replica) (K7271)	Aerospace Museum/Cosford	
149	Short S.27 (replica)	F.A.A. Museum (stored)/Yeovilton	
150	SEPECAT Jaguar GR.1 (replica) (XX725) -	RAF Exhibition Flight	
151	SEPECAT Jaguar GR.1 (replica) (XZ363)	RAF Exhibition Flight	
152	BAe Hawk T.1 (replica) (XX263)	RAF Exhibition Flight	
153	Westland WG.33	IHM/Weston-s-Mare	
154	D.31 Turbulent	Lincolnshire Aviation Museum	
155	Panavia Tornado GR.1 (replica) (ZA446)	RAF Exhibition Flight	
157	Waco CG-4A	Pennine Aviation Museum	
158	Fieseler Fi 103 (V.1)	Defence Ordnance Disposal School/ Chattenden	
159	Yokosuka MXY7 Ohka II	Defence Ordnance Disposal School/ Chattenden	
160	Chargus 108 hang glider	Museum of Flight/E. Fortune	
161	Stewart Ornithopter Coppelia	Bomber County Museum	
162	Goodhart Newbury Manflier MPA	Science Museum/Wroughton	
163	AFEE 10/42 Rotabuggy (replica)	Museum of Army Flying/Middle Wallop	
164	Wight Quadruplane Type 1 (replica)	Wessex Aviation Soc/Wimborne	
165	Bristol F.2b (E2466)	RAF Museum/London	
167	S.E.5A replica	Newark Air Museum	
168	D.H.60G Moth (static replica) (G-AAAH)	Hilton Hotel/Gatwick	
169	SEPECAT Jaguar GR.1 (static replica) (XX110)	No 1 S. of T.T. RAF Halton	
170	Pilcher Hawk (replica)	A. Gourlay/Strathallan	
171	BAe Hawk T.1 (replica) (XX297)	RAF Exhibition Flight/Abingdon	
172	Chargus Midas Super 8 hang glider	Science Museum/Wroughton	
173	Birdman Promotions Grasshopper	Science Museum/Wroughton	
174	Bensen B.7	Science Museum/Wroughton	
175	Volmer VJ-23 Swingwing	Manchester Museum of Science & Industry	
176	SE-5A (replica) (A4850)	S. Yorks Aviation Soc/Firbeck	
177	Avro 504K (replica) (G-AACA)	Brooklands Museum of Aviation/ Weybridge	
178	Avro 504K (replica) (E373)	Bygone Times Antique Warehouse/ Eccleston, Lancs	
179	Sopwith Pup (replica) (A7317)	Midland Air Museum/Coventry	
181	RAF B.E.2b (replica) (687)	RAF Museum/Hendon	
182	Wood Ornithopter	Manchester Museum of Science & Industry	
183	Zurowski ZP.1	Newark Air Museum	
184	Spitfire IX (replica) (EN398)	Aces High Ltd/North Weald	
185	Waco CG-4A (243809)	Museum of Army Flying/Middle Wallop	
186	D.H.82B Queen Bee (K3584)	Mosquito Aircraft Museum	
187	Roe Type 1 biplane (replica)	Brooklands Museum of Aviation/ Weybridge	
188	McBroom Cobra 88	Science Museum/Wroughton	
189	Blériot XI (replica)	—	
190	Spitfire (replica) (EN398)	Macclesfield Historical Aviation Soc	
191	BAe Harrier GR.5 (replica) (ZD472)	RAF Exhibition Flight	
192	Weedhopper JC-24	The Aeroplane Collection	
193	Hovey WD-11 Whing Ding	The Aeroplane Collection	
194	Santos Dumont Demoiselle (replica)	Brooklands Museum of Aviation/ Weybridge	
195	Moonraker 77 hang glider	Museum of Flight/E. Fortune	

Notes	Reg.	Type	Owner or Operator
	196	Sigma 2M hang glider	Museum of Flight/E. Fortune
	197	Cirrus III hang glider	Museum of Flight/E. Fortune
	198	Fieseler Fi.103 (V-1)	Imperial War Museum/Lambeth
	199	Fieseler Fi.103 (V-1)	Science Museum/S. Kensington
	200	Bensen B.7	K. Fern Collection/Stoke
	201	Mignet HM.14	Caernarfon Air Museum
	202	Spitfire V (replica) (MW467)	Maes Artro Craft Centre
	203	Chrislea LC.1 Airguard (G-AFIN)	The Aeroplane Collection
	204	McBroom hang glider	The Aeroplane Collection
	205	Hurricane (replica) (BE421)	RAF Museum/Hendon
	206	Spitfire (replica) (MH486)	RAF Museum/Hendon
	207	Austin Whippet (replica) (K.158)	NE Aircraft Museum
	208	SE-5A (replica) (D2700)	Prince's Mead Shopping Precinct/ Farnborough
	209	Spitfire IX (replica) (MJ751)	Museum of D-Day Aviation/Shoreham
	210	Avro 504J (replica) (C4451)	Southampton Hall of Aviation
	211	Mignet HM.14 (replica) (G-ADVU)	Burns Garage/Congleton
	212	Bensen B.8	IHM/Weston-s-Mare
	213	Vertigo MPA	IHM/Weston-s-Mare
	214	Spitfire prototype (replica) (K5054)	The Spitfire Soc
	215	Airwave hang-glider	Southampton Hall of Aviation
	216	D.H.88 Comet (replica) (G-ACSS)	Trout Lake Air Force
	217	Spitfire (replica) (N9926)	RAF Museum/Bentley Priory
	218	Hurricane (replica) (P3386)	RAF Museum/Bentley Priory
	219	Hurricane (replica) (L1710)	RAF Memorial Chapel/Biggin Hill
	220	Spitfire (replica) (N3194)	RAF Memorial Chapel/Biggin Hill
	221	Spitfire (replica) (MH777)	RAF Museum/Northolt
	222	Spitfire (replica) (BR600)	RAF Museum/Uxbridge
	223	Hurricane (replica) (V7467)	RAF Museum/Coltishall
	224	Spitfire V (replica)	Ambassador Hotel/Norwich
	225	Spitfire (replica) (P8448)	RAF Museum/Swanton Morley
	226	Spitfire (replica) (EN343)	RAF Museum/Benson
	227	Spitfire (replica) (L1070)	RAF Museum/Turnhouse
	228	Olympus hang-glider	NE Aircraft Museum/Usworth
	229	Spitfire (replica) (MJ832)	RAF Museum/Digby
	230	Spitfire (replica) (AA908)	Eden Camp/Malton
	231	Mignet HM.14	South Copeland Aviation Group
	232	AS.58 Horsa I/II	Mosquito Aircraft Museum
	233	Broburn Wanderlust sailplane	Museum of Berkshire Aviation/Woodley
	234	Vickers FB.5 Gunbus (replica)	Macclesfield Historical Aviation Soc
	235	Fieseler Fi.103 (V-1) (replica)	Eden Camp Wartime Museum
	236	Hurricane (replica) (P2793)	Eden Camp Wartime Museum
	237	Fieseler Fi.103 (V-1)	RAF Museum/Cardington
	238	Waxflatter ornithopter	Personal Plane Services Ltd
	239	Fokker D.VIII 5/8 scale replica	Norfolk & Suffolk Aviation Museum

Note: Registrations/Serials carried are mostly false identities. MPA = Man Powered Aircraft, IHM = International Helicopter Museum.

Future Allocations Log (In-Sequence)

The grid provides the facility to record future in-sequence registrations as they are issued or seen. To trace a particular code, refer to the left hand column which contains the three letters following the G prefix. The final letter can be found by reading across the columns headed A to Z. For example, the box for G-BWSD is located five rows down (BWS) and then four across to the D column.

G-	A	B	C	D	E	F	G	H	I	J	K	L	M	N	O	P	R	S	T	U	V	W	X	Y	Z
BWN																									
BWO																									
BWP																									
BWR																									
BWS																									
BWT																									
BWU																									
BWV																									
BWW																									
BWX																									
BWY																									
BWZ																									
BXA																									
BXR																									
BXC																									
BXD																									
BXE																									
BXF																									
BXG																									
BXH																									
BXI																									
BXJ																									
BXK																									
BXL																									
BXM																									
BXN																									
BXO																									
BXP																									
BXR																									
BXS																									
BXT																									
BXU																									
BXV																									
BXW																									
BXX	A	B	C	D	E	F	G	H	I	J	K	L	M	N	O	P	R	S	T	U	V	W	X	Y	Z

Credit: *Wal Gandy*

Future Allocations Log (Out-of-Sequence)

This grid can be used to record out-of-sequence registrations as they are issued or seen. The first column is provided for the ranges prefixed with G-B, ie from G-BWxx to G-BZxx. The remaining columns cover the sequences from G-Cxxx to G-Zxxx and in this case it is necessary to insert the last three letters in the appropriate section.

G-B	G-C	G-E	G-G	G-J	G-L	G-N	G-O	G-P	G-S	G-U
										G-V
	G-D	G-F	G-H		G-M	G-O				
				G-K						
										G-W
								G-R		
									G-T	
										G-X
G-C	G-E	G-G	G-I	G-L	G-N					
										G-Y
										G-Z